W9-DGX-966

BRIDGING ENGLISH

THIRD EDITION

JOSEPH O'BEIRNE MILNER

Wake Forest University

LUCY FLOYD MORCOCK MILNER

Salem College
North Carolina Governor's School

Merrill
Prentice Hall

Upper Saddle River, New Jersey
Columbus, Ohio

Library of Congress Cataloging-in-Publication Data

Milner, Joseph O'Beirne
  Bridging English/Joseph O'Beirne Milner, Lucy Floyd Morcock Milner.—3rd ed.
    p. cm.
  Includes bibliographical references (p.) and index.
  ISBN 0-13-045306-4 (pbk.)
   1. English language—Study and teaching (Secondary) I. Milner, Lucy Floyd Morcock,
II. Title.

LB1631 .M455 2003
428'.0071'2   2002019577

Vice President and Publisher: Jeffery W. Johnston
Editor: Linda Ashe Montgomery
Editorial Assistant: Evelyn Olson
Production Editor: Sheryl Glicker Langner
Design Coordinator: Diane Ernsberger
Text Designer: Rebecca Bobb
Photo Coordinator: Sandy Schaefer
Cover Designer: Ali Mohrman
Cover art: Christy Terry
Production Manager: Laura Messerly
Director of Marketing: Ann Castel Davis
Marketing Manager: Krista Groshong
Marketing Coordinator: Tyra Cooper

This book was set by in Garamond Book by Carlisle Communications, Ltd. It was printed and bound by Courier Kendallville, Inc. The cover was printed by Phoenix Color Corp.

Photo Credits: p. 1 by Mark Siler; pp. 74, 232, 287, 353 by Cary Clifford; pp. 13, 264 by Scott Cunningham/Merrill; p. 46 by Rhoda Sidney/PH College; pp. 98, 150 by Holly Tackett; p. 189 by Ken Karp/Prentice Hall; pp. 243, 398 by Anne Vega/Merrill; pp. 315, 424 by Anthony Magnacca/Merrill.

Pearson Education Ltd.
Pearson Education Australia Pty. Limited
Pearson Education Singapore Pte. Ltd.
Pearson Education North Asia Ltd.
Pearson Education Canada, Ltd.
Pearson Educación de Mexico, S.A. de C. V.
Pearson Education—Japan
Pearson Education Malaysia Pte. Ltd.
Pearson Education, *Upper Saddle River, New Jersey*

Copyright © 2003, 1999, 1993 by Pearson Education, Inc., Upper Saddle River, New Jersey 07458. All rights reserved. Printed in the United States of America. This publication is protected by Copyright and permission should be obtained from the publisher prior to any prohibited reproduction, storage in a retrieval system, or transmission in any form or by any means, electronic, mechanical, photocopying, recording, or likewise. For information regarding permission(s), write to: Rights and Permissions Department.

10 9 8 7 6 5 4
ISBN: 0-13-045306-4

Ellsworth

for

Jonathan O'Beirne Milner

Benjamin Southwood Milner

Peter Cooper Milner

Preface

We wrote the first edition of *Bridging English* (1993) because we could not find a balanced, comprehensive English methods textbook whose theory was rigorous and whose practice was accessible and pertinent. We revised the first edition (1999) to strengthen its comprehensiveness, theoretical soundness, and practical usefulness. Reviewers and users report that both texts effectively moved readers from theories of learning, language, and literacy to classroom realities in today's schools. One colleague and his class call our text *BE* because, as he explains, it captures what his students need to know and be in order to confidently enter secondary English classrooms and actively engage the students waiting there. Its readers appear also drawn to its student-centered, constructivist, developmental, inquiry based, and reflective perspective. Many colleagues report that this is one textbook their students do not sell back because they regard it not simply as a general introduction to English education, but as a reference and resource with which to begin their professional libraries. Many teachers tell us that it occupies an honored spot on their desks always ready for use.

We have revised the second edition of our text, as we did the first, for two primary reasons: 1) to address new developments in the field of English education, and 2) to clarify, expand, and vivify many of our original ideas. In this thorough revision, we have tried to retain and strengthen what has proven most valuable while we demonstrate and animate both the old and new ideas and methods. In clearer, crisper prose, each of its now fifteen chapters presents conceptual frameworks, a multitude of tested teaching activities, and invitations to the reader to reflect on both.

STRENGTHS OF THE FIRST AND SECOND EDITIONS

In the first two editions of *Bridging English,* we attempted to bridge many different shores: of self (as the reader prepares to move from the role of student to that of teacher), of instructional theories, of methods, of texts, of cultural expectations of English classrooms. With a consciousness of the quandaries of prospective teachers, we challenged readers to make personal connections between their previous experiences as students and their future expectations as teachers. Two textual features particularly—Invitations to Reflection and Teaching Activities—engaged readers and invited them to reflect, to test, and to plan. Readers tell us that the texts' breadth and balance "brought it all together"—an understanding and grasp of literature, language, and learning. We have retained many of the valued aspects of the first two editions such as:

- the interplay of learning, language, and literary theory with best teaching practice
- the numerous sequences of instruction, teaching activities, and concrete examples of teachable texts that range from literary classics to works by minority and young adult writers, from print to non-print
- a balanced view of the debated pedagogical issues in the English Education field: grammar and writing instruction, cooperative learning, reader response based approaches to literature, multicultural literature, technology in the classroom, authentic assessment, and critical and cultural literacy
- the treatment of numerous vital, but sometimes overlooked subjects such as the history of the English language, ten schools of literary criticism, the canon wars' debate, oral language, poetry, nonfiction, media, and evaluation
- an authorial voice that filters and interprets its information and ideas through decades of teaching at the secondary and college levels

CHANGES IN THE THIRD EDITION

Like its predecessors, the third edition of *Bridging English* grows from our ongoing experience, observations, and reflections on English classrooms. It represents our course notes passed on to our younger colleagues. We feel again a little like E. B. White, who explained of his writing that he just wanted to keep the minutes of his own meeting. In these intervening years, our meeting has continued and has entertained many provocative developments in our field and in ourselves. With these changes in mind we update, amend, and enlarge this third edition. Because we pay attention to new currents in this student generation, in the field itself, and in schooling in our society, our revisions include the following:

- In our largest reorganization, we move the chapter on organization to the front of the book and divide the chapter on oral language and scripted drama into two.
- We present additional graphic organizers and clearer chapter subdivisions to provide better visual and verbal maps of approaches, sequences, and methods of instruction.
- We sharpen our focus and expand our treatment of many crucial issues.

- Approaches to Teaching Grammar
- Learning with Technology
- Multi-lingual Students
- National Language Arts Standards
- High Stakes Testing
- We add current and important research in the field to seminal and still relevant early research studies.
- We enlarge the Appendices and include new titles in its lists of texts.
- To the insights of many veteran teachers included in the first and second editions, we add those of young teachers who have read these editions and currently teach.
- We include more concrete, authentic classroom situations and problems in our Invitations to Reflection.
- We have tightened our exposition, demonstrated more and explained less, and reduced redundancies.

As we have incorporated these changes, we have tried again to avoid the decision made by an Austrian film company that wanted to remake Richard Rodgers and Oscar Hammerstein's 1965 classic, *The Sound of Music*. The Austrians knew that the original was too long and that they had to work within boundaries, so they decided to leave out the music. In our revisions, we have tried to trim old ideas in order to make way for new ones without leaving out the music.

NOTE TO ENGLISH EDUCATORS

This edition of *Bridging English,* like the first two, is designed for English methods courses that vary from state to state, from school to school, and from teacher to teacher. The chapters are self-sufficient and independent of one another and can be shifted around with no loss of coherence or momentum. Indeed in our own methods courses, each of us progresses through the text differently. After sampling many of you, our readers, we have organized this text, as many of you do your courses, to begin with Chapter 1, Envisioning English, and then to move to Organizing Instruction, Chapter 2. We then build on these organizing constructs (including a completely rewritten section on Learning with Technology) as we present Teaching Activities throughout the subsequent chapters.

In those states and locales where literature-based instruction is paramount, we hope again that you can interface chapters on drama, prose, and poetry with those sections of the writing and evaluation chapters focused on literature. In our examples of teaching prose fiction, we have tried to select either widely read novels or short stories that are often anthologized and are therefore either known or easily available to the reader. In our examples of classroom practice, we again name the teachers whose ideas we include. Some of you have wanted us to distinguish the seminal thinkers in the field from the able practitioners in the classroom. Our repeated citing of our original sources will hopefully identify them, but to omit the names of classroom teachers would diminish our grateful acknowledgment of both those who have contributed to the solid building of our field and those who continue to explore, test, and renew it by their persistent action.

ACKNOWLEDGMENTS

Our third edition has benefited from the critiques and suggestions of reviewers who became valuable, if interior, counselors, critics, and supporters throughout this revision process: Sam D. Gill, University of North Carolina at Wilmington; Janet Busboom, Mercer University; Carolyn Moran, Tennessee State University; Marlene Deringer, Otterbein College; Richard Shaw, North Dakota State University; and Catherine Lucas, San Francisco State University. We also surveyed all of those identified by our publisher as users. We have been guided by the insight and good judgment of all of these colleagues as we have read and pondered their ideas.

We continue to be indebted to other college and university English educators and middle and secondary teachers whose ideas and practices enlarge and strengthen our individual efforts and resolves. You will find many of their names within this textbook. Three abiding friends and gifted teachers, Becky Brown, Nancy Doda, and Julia Neenan, continuously enrich their students' lives, our lives, and so this book. Each embodies with unique intelligence and grace the finest ideals of a teacher: understanding that is scholarly, practical, and moral; a coherent pedagogical position that is clearheaded and creative; an insight into and compassion for students that keep them steadfast despite inevitable disappointments and frustrations; and a dedication to the common good of the young and of the community of those who teach them.

We are also grateful for what we have learned from teaching and observing our students. A number of them—undergraduate and masters students—contributed substantially to our revision process with their detailed critique of the first editions and their classroom demonstrations of its best ideas. Throughout this third edition, we scatter the creative teaching ideas of Stella Beale, Mary Beth Braker, Meg Davis, Mindi Fry, Shelley Hale, Melissa McCabe, Anna Milner, Cameron Morris, Emily Orser, Julie Pederson, Jill Snyder, and others. They make us confident that this text is grounded in classroom actualities and reflective practice.

We are deeply indebted to the staff of the Education Department at Wake Forest University whose able skills and willing spirits helped move our manuscript through various awkward stages and into readable shape. We owe a special debt to Robin Hawkins, the department's administrative assistant, who deftly and serenely organized the work of student assistants and who knew long before we did how to make personal computers produce words and tables. We are again particularly grateful for the conscientious, intelligent, and cheerful labors of Karen Doub, who undertook reference checking and compiling, and Kathryn Jacinto, who undertook permission correspondence. The surrounding support of other staff and colleagues once again greatly humanized the environment in which we labored.

At Merrill/Prentice Hall, our debts begin with our editor, Linda Montgomery, who initiated this third edition and launched it with energy, intelligence, and vision. Dawn Potter, a poet, teacher, and musician, brought unparalleled experience to her discerning and gracious copyediting. She has become our model for this essential role in the production of a book. After shaping our prose, she would often offer her own reflections on the art of teaching and we have included some of those quiet, astute insights. Like our second edition, our third has profited from the work of Lois Oster, who has carefully indexed these pages and thereby greatly enhanced readers' access to them.

Our deepest gratitude goes once again to our production editor, Sheryl Langner, whose equanimity, perseverance, and discriminating judgment have made this third edition better in every way. She adds to her deep knowledge, a generous humanity and even-tempered wit that represent the best imaginable virtues in one whose labors must constantly accommodate the diverse sensibilities and cranky timing of authors and production schedules. She possesses the perfect blend of active intelligence, quiet grace, and steady firmness. Again, we cannot imagine completing a book without her.

Finally, we are grateful to our three sons for all kinds of help, but mostly we are just grateful they are our sons. In the years between our first and second editions, each chose to become a high school teacher and entered his own classroom in widely different circumstances and locales: ESL and social studies classrooms in the inner city schools of Houston, Texas; physics and geometry classrooms of rural King and Queen County, Virginia; and economics and politics classrooms of Winston-Salem, North Carolina. Each experienced all of the challenges of beginning a teaching career, all of the occasions of uncertainty, enthusiasm, bewilderment, hope, self-doubt, and joy. Since then two have changed the scope of their teaching by entering divinity schools and preparing for ministry. One of their wives, our former student, has become a high school English teacher, however, and stories of classroom life—the surprising achievements, the perplexing disappointments, and the persistent questions—still occupy us in numerous family talks. Through the teaching experiences of our son Jonathan and our daughter-in-law Anna, we continue to sharpen our empathy for and our dedication to all those who take up this essential work of teaching. We once again dedicate this book to our children and through them to beginning teachers everywhere.

Contents

Note: Every effort has been made to provide accurate and current Internet information in this book. However, the Internet and information posted on it are constantly changing, so it is inevitable that some of the Internet addresses listed in this textbook will change.

1

Envisioning English

⌒ *There is no intellectual activity*
more American than
quarreling about what
education means, especially
within the context of school.
Americans rely on their
schools, even more than on
their courts, to express their
vision of who they are.

Neil Postman ⌒

*B*laise Pascal observed in the seventeenth century that "The last thing one knows when writing a book is what to put first." Most authors arrive at their subjects through years of experience, knowledge, and reflection. The larger and more complicated the subject, the more difficult the point of entry. English education is such a rich and various field that we could begin at any number of places:

- adolescent students
- secondary schools
- learning theory and research
- the study of language
- the study of literature
- the study of writing
- crucial issues in English education
- the profession of teaching

Each of these subjects makes sense as a starting point in a text about teaching English. We delay each, however, until we have first queried you, the reader. We will alternate statement with query. By the end of this first chapter, you should understand why we consider the reader to be the most logical beginning.

INITIAL DEFINITIONS

In 1916 an educator asked, "Well, then, what is secondary English?" The formal existence of our discipline was only several decades old and its national organization, the National Council of Teachers of English (NCTE), was only five years old. The answer in 1916, however, was "Nobody knows. But opinions are now being codified all over the land. . . . The chaotic mass is crystallizing" (Ward, 1916, p. 178). Fifty years later the definition had not yet satisfactorily crystallized. John Dixon (1967, p. 1) called English teaching "a quicksilver among metals—mobile, living and elusive." Of interest to us initially is what teaching high school English means for you, the prospective teacher at the threshold of your own English classroom. Something has drawn you to this doorway. We imagine it was your student experiences in other English classrooms, experiences that were positive on some level; otherwise, you would not be about to enter this profession. Through the first of a series of Invitations to Reflection, we ask you to recall memories of former classrooms and connect them with teaching expectations for your own.

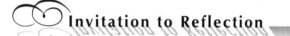

Invitation to Reflection 1-1

1. Recall *one positive memory* of an English class.
2. Your best memories arise from which years of schooling (elementary, middle, secondary, or college)?
3. Recall a *cluster of positive memories* about your past English schooling. What language activities predominate in these memories? Reading? Talking? Listening? Writing?
4. Do you recall an especially positive encounter with print or nonprint texts? Which one? With writing? Talking? Listening?
5. Do you have memories of certain English teachers whom you would like to imitate as a teacher? Who were they, and what did they do that inspired you?
6. What memories do you have of unpleasant classroom events that you hope to avoid in your teaching?
7. Which of the following best describes the center of your interest in becoming a teacher? (Rank order them if you wish.)
   - adolescent students
   - print literature
   - nonprint literature
   - language (writing)
   - language (speaking)
   - the act of teaching
   - the life of schools
   - other (explain)
8. At this moment how would you answer anyone who asked you, Why do you want to become an English teacher?

Your visitable past is our starting point and your seeable teaching future our destination. At present, your own experience with other teachers and learners probably provides your main source of ideas about teaching. You will draw on that experience as you encounter the theories and practices of other models of teaching. This book will serve partly to introduce you to some of these new ways to reflect on your past experience and imagine your future actions. As a first step in that introduction, we invite you to join a central and persistent debate among English teachers: What is English?

Invitation to Reflection 1-2

As a first approach to defining English, consider three descriptors of the discipline of English education:

- communication arts
- language arts
- English

The differences among them may seem innocuous enough, but each represents a very different understanding of the task we set for ourselves. Answer the following questions.

1. Which descriptive term is the most comprehensive? The least?
2. What does the term *communication arts* suggest to you that *language arts* does not? What powers of communication can you imagine outside of speaking, listening, reading, and writing? How important is the study of language to a communication arts curriculum? What is the role of literature in it? Is literature more than a vehicle for teaching other skills?
3. Why might the term *language arts* be used at the elementary and middle school levels but not in high school? What term is most common to the high school curricula?
4. Does the term *English* embrace literature *and* language in your mind? How, then, does it differ from *language arts*?
5. Which of the three terms best describes the subject you aim to teach?

A BRIEF HISTORY

In this text we will follow current practice and refer to our discipline as *English;* but disagreements persist about how English is conceived as a discipline, how it is organized, and how it is taught. The debate over terminology embodies a central tension that has been a part of our profession from its beginning. Some of this tension can be understood by looking at the history of the profession. As with families, we profit from knowing where we came from, who our ancestors were, what hopes they formed, what forces influenced their decisions, what habits of mind they developed, and what experiences of living they passed on to us. Knowing the origins of our profession helps us find our bearings.

The teaching of reading and writing began in the United States with this country's founding. The earliest settlers, with their vision of an informed citizenry free and competent enough to be self-governing, believed in teaching American children the rudiments of how to read and write. Learning occurred in homes or colonial "dame" schools organized by neighbors and taught by a designated community member. Even when communities had built school buildings, hired teachers, and purchased primers and grammar books, English instruction at all levels more resembled today's elementary school language skills development than our contemporary high school language and literature study.

English as taught in today's schools is a young discipline that arose only toward the end of the nineteenth century. Many different surveyors with differing interests and aims tried to establish its boundaries. Public and private school teachers and administrators, college professors, politicians, and the public—all were involved in drawing its limits. In the 1890s, a Committee of Ten attempted to clarify the purpose of high school English, to reconcile and balance the different strands that then were being taught under the umbrella of English—grammar, philology, rhetoric, literature—and to unify the field into a common focus. Their published *Report* (1894), often regarded as the charter of high school English, stated:

> The main objects of the teaching of English in schools seem to be two: (1) to enable the pupil to understand the expressed thoughts of others and to give expression to thoughts of his own; and (2) to cultivate a taste for reading, to give the pupil some acquaintance with good literature, and to furnish him with the means of extending that acquaintance. (as quoted in Nelms, 2000, p. 50)

More than one hundred years later, for all the committee's efforts to focus English teaching toward a uniform standard, its compromises still haunt the profession. Nelms (2000, p. 51) and others have pointed out that from the first what could have been two disciplines—communication and literature—were joined as one. "The utilitarian stood side by side with the belletristic: the need for practical competence with the aspiration for social grace; what would become known as the language arts (reading, listening, writing, speaking) with the literary canon." Nelms enumerates the consequence of this original work: Over a century there were "genuine but faltering efforts to maintain the precarious balance assumed in [the committee's] simple statement of goals. Literature has usually emerged the master, at least with older, college-bound students; communication skills the handmaiden—with all the inequity those gender-laden

terms imply." Applebee (1994, p. 49) describes the situation this way: "The English language arts have a long-standing predisposition to come unglued—to separate into the myriad individual studies from which they were assembled." Questions of definition have been persistent and vexing even with the founding of the National Council of Teachers of English in 1911. Three years after NCTE was founded, speech teachers broke away to establish speech as a separate subject in high school.

Each of the four subsequent decades saw an attempt to reconcile secondary English as "academic preparation for college for the few" or as "practical preparation for life for the many." Despite these decades of theorizing, research, and practice, at mid-twentieth century, Congress considered the English curriculum of its public schools a failed tradition. In 1962 the expanded National Defense Education Act's research and demonstration centers (dubbed Project English) determined to reform the field. In the summer of 1966, NCTE, the Modern Language Association (MLA), and the British National Association of Teachers of English (NATE) sponsored a groundbreaking invitational seminar at Dartmouth College (now known as the Dartmouth Seminar) to consider common problems in the discipline and to define English, both the subject and the way in which it should be taught. But posing the question itself caused trouble. Some wanted to ask, "What is the subject matter of English?" Others thought that *what English is as an academic body of knowledge* was subordinate to *how English functions* as a part of the lives of students and teachers. The proper question for them became "What do we want students and teachers to do?" Speculate on your own answers.

⬤ Invitation to Reflection 1–3

1. Do you think the question "What is English?" can be answered in the same way as these questions: What is algebra? What is physics? What is American history? Are these questions interchangeable?

2. Which of the following do you think is appropriate content for a high school course in English?
   - language study (grammar)
   - language skills
   - writing
   - speaking
   - listening
   - reading
   - viewing
   - print literature
   - nonprint literature (film, music)
   - communication skills
   - students' own lives
   - social/cultural context of students' lives
   - other (explain)

3. If you don't define English in terms of content, how would you define what you think should actually happen in English classrooms? What would you want students to be doing?

4. Language arts or English is basic to elementary and middle school education as well as a requirement of all four years of most high schools. Do you think it is prominent in the curriculum because of its specialized content? Is it prominent because of its unique function of connecting different kinds of learning and experience? What could be other reasons for its prominence?

5. Do you think of teaching as the transmission of knowledge from teacher to student? If so, what is important to transmit? The great humanist tradition of literature? Functional skills of reading, writing, talking, listening, and viewing? Personal understanding and enlightenment? Moral values? Other? (If so, what?)

Had those Dartmouth conferees scrutinized the English curricula of the 1950s and 1960s high schools we attended as students, they would have seen classrooms divided at midyear into the primary content halves of English study: language and literature. In each semester, the teachers focused on distinct bodies of knowledge, but their general teaching strategies were similar in both. Teachers passed to the students their superior understanding of literature or language through lectures, whole-class discussions, drills, written exercises, quizzes, and occasional writing assignments. The literature read were texts that were considered classics of the western world, and the language taught was traditional rules of grammar. Once teachers had "covered" the subject, they tested students to see how well they had "learned" it. The galvanizing center of the classroom was the teacher. Teachers determined content and agenda; and they guided, monitored, and evaluated student achievement. With conscientious industry, knowledge, conviction, and vision, they passed on the cultural heritage and the requisite language skills to read, write, and talk about it. Our teachers stood within a long-established educational tradition. You have probably experienced at least one such classroom in your schooling. What you will become is built on that legacy.

The late 1960s and early 1970s following the Dartmouth Seminar were a time of new orientations; of new visions, energy, and idealism; and of experimentation with the teaching of language, literature, and composition. Shadiow (2000, p. 68) describes the forces at work on English teachers in the 1960s, 1970s, and 1980s: "We became teachers about the same time that transformational grammar opted for a place in the curriculum; and a review of NCTE annual convention programs reminds us that we sought to implement Moffett's student-centered curriculum, Michigan's APEX elective system, Rosenblatt's reader-response theory, Hillock's schema for measuring growth in writing, and the Bay Area Writing Project's process priorities in composition—to name a few."

These forces will be described elsewhere in this book and by the end, these and other seminal English educators will feel like your ancestors indeed. For now, in sum, these classrooms struggled to be student-centered, personal response-focused, process-oriented, imagination-based, and culturally sensitive. Not surprisingly, a counterreaction arose in opposition to them. The critics were part of a general conservative, back-to-the-basics movement in the culture at large. Suhor (1977, pp. 81–82) summarizes their tendency to make blanket judgments, to use "research" data selectively (or ignore it altogether), to raise indignant questions, and to offer simplistic solutions with buzz words such as "grammar," "phonics," and "basics." Donelson (2000, p. 45) tells a personal anecdote that describes the force of the reaction to the shifts in the teaching of English in the late 1960s and 1970s. During a public debate, someone pointed a finger at him and began to chide him for contributing to the destruction of the Golden Age, the Camelot, of high school English:

> We had destroyed the dream and the English curricula by dropping the teaching of grammar, by refusing to hold the line on good usage (her example was the distinction between *shall* and *will*), by having students write in journals instead of having them write formal essays, by ignoring classics we had once made students love in favor of second-rate and near-pornographic modern material, and (her last point was almost shouted in triumph) by becoming liberal and politically correct and introducing multicultural things, all second or third rate.

While Suhor regretted that "conservative rhetoric lacked articulateness (in the sense of 'complexity,' not 'illiteracy')," he chided the profession for its own inability to articulate its case, the case for the new English (as quoted by Tchudi [2000], p. 38).

CORE BELIEFS

We begin to articulate our case for English at the beginning of this new century by asking you to think again about your experience as a young learner. We believe that it is hard to define English apart from the ways in which it is taught in the classroom. We value definitions of English that match classroom actualities. The physical arrangements betray the teacher's assumptions; selection of instructional strategies and methods, materials, and texts expose the teacher's values and goals. The images and principles (implicit and explicit) of your former high school classrooms influence your image of your own future classroom. Figure 1–1 is our visual aid.

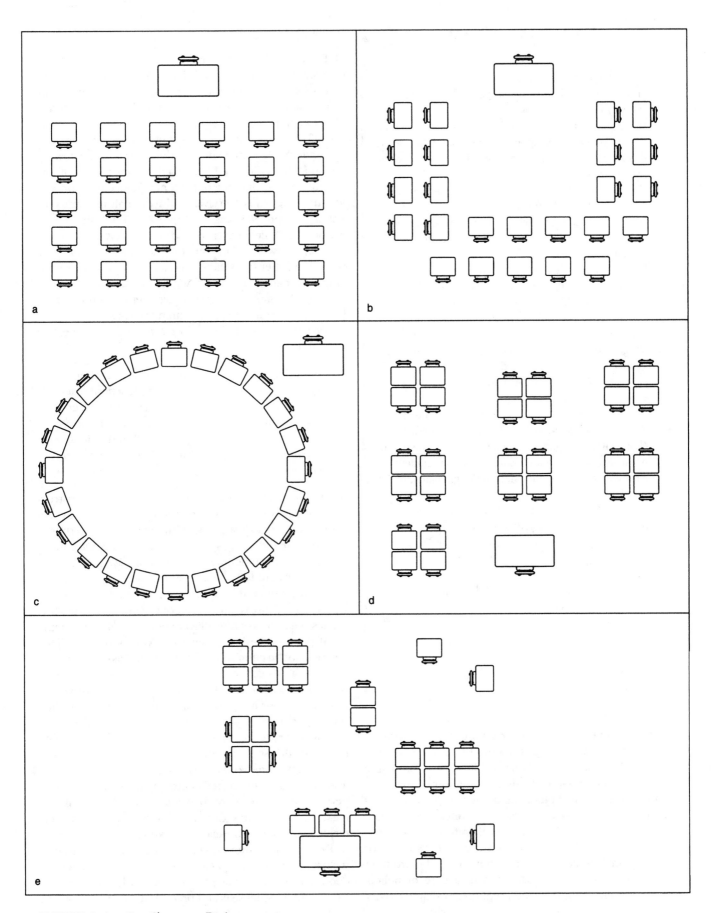

FIGURE 1–1   Five Classroom Designs

Invitation to Reflection 1-4

1. Visualize yourself as a teacher in your own English classroom. Which of the five classroom arrangements shown in Figure 1–1 do you envision?

2. Is the arrangement you chose the one that is most common in your own experience with school? What does this arrangement imply about the relationship between teacher and students?

3. Who is most intellectually and physically active, the teacher or the student? Are they equally engaged?

4. Which configuration would make you most comfortable as a teacher? Which would you have preferred as a student?

5. In your imagined classroom, do you see yourself characteristically sitting, standing at a podium or desk, or walking about the room? If you see yourself sitting, are you at a teacher's desk, on an elevated chair, or at a student desk?

6. Imagine that you want an alternative classroom design. Which would be your second choice of physical arrangement? Would those changes dictate changes in your teaching method?

7. What precisely do you see you and your students doing in this classroom? Would your class design change if the assignment were, say, Native American narratives, loyalty in friendship, or slang in student writing? How would the physical design match the lesson design?

8. Place each of the arrangements in Figure 1–1 on a continuum from the most student–centered (students are active and often are independent agents and subjects of their own learning) to the most teacher–centered (the students receive knowledge from the teacher).

9. Who or what would you place at the center of your planning and practice?
   • teacher
   • student
   • subject
   • process

If you went directly to your own classroom without passing through an "English methods" course and text, you could link those formative images to available teacher resources—the steady proliferation of state and school district curriculum standards and guidelines, inservice training workshops and institutes, professional meetings, and periodic and book literature—and generate enough teaching ideas to construct a year's worth of lesson plans. Effective teachers, though, need more than busy classes; they need basic tenets, a core of beliefs about learning, language, and literature, to shape activity into engaging, purposive, and effective learning.

Bridging English

McEwan (1992, p. 102) believes that a confusing "multitude of institutional and cultural demands" are placed on the English teacher. Where there is no clear vision of the nature of the subject, the English classroom "becomes a storage closet of stray topics, a place to teach anything that does not fall clearly within the orbit of other areas of the school curriculum." He names a few of those areas of the curriculum that have "invaded" the English classroom without careful scrutiny or deliberate intent: "moral education, critical thinking skills, 'survival skills,' journalism, library research, and public speaking" (pp. 102–103). With no guiding principles, English teaching can become what McEwan calls "a patchwork" of instructional activities—a crazy quilt pieced together from the used materials of other projects without a pattern or design. While such a piece might be attractive hanging in a craft shop, it does not represent the best pattern from which to fashion learning.

We have envisioned *Bridging English* as a bridge over several dimensions:

you as student	to	you as teacher
college/university study	to	high school teaching
educational theory	to	classroom practice
positions within the field	to	opposed positions within the field
eclectic methods of of instruction	to	integrated principles of instruction

The first three bridges have been easier to construct than the last two. With the next-to-the-last one, we have set about trying to do justice to multiple positions and thus to bridge their differences with understanding. Of course, we realize that sometimes two positions are mutually exclusive. It is hard to believe in student-centered, constructivist education and be content to lecture for a class period about the use of dialect in Zora Neale Hurston's short stories, regardless of how clever your examples and graphics. If process writing is central to your writing project, you will not be comfortable selecting and assigning topics for an out-of-class essay to which you give grades A through F two weeks later, no matter how extensive and perceptive your marginal comments to students on their returned papers. If you believe in broadening the selection of literary texts, you will not teach only the novels and poems of British males, no matter how enthusiastic you are about William Wordsworth, Charles Dickens, and W. H. Auden. If you are interested in inviting students to respond personally and feelingly to written works, you will not make traditional New Critical questions of form the centerpiece of your whole-class discussions.

Despite such competing and irreconcilable positions, we have tried to present each fairly so that the reader can choose from the diverse perspectives within our field. Because others—theorists and practitioners with whom we both sympathize and differ—provide an essential context for our work, we attempt to present their ideas with as much sympathy and fair-mindedness as we hope they bring to ours. We want again to leave room for readers to move around in this text and get their own bearings; however, we recognize that the decisions we make about how to run our own classrooms originate in foundational ideas about learning, language, and literature.[1] We now address that final span from disparate ideas to integrated principles of instruction.

Importance of Core Beliefs

Bridging English will be little more than a catalog of teaching activities if it does not help you develop what philosopher R. S. Peters calls a "conceptual scheme." Such a scheme raises knowledge beyond "a collection of disjointed facts" and enables us to "understand the 'reason why' of things." We call these "core beliefs," foundational concepts that drive what we do in our classrooms. We have heard them called "anchoring ideas," "basic axioms," or "operating principles." Geneticists call them their "central dogma." Whatever the term, these beliefs are central to who you will be, what you will do, and how you will regard your students. They will anchor your planning and teaching of a lesson, a unit, or a course with a logic and purposiveness that would be missing without them. Your teaching practice and your students' learning will be stronger, more focused, and more coherent with such a grounding.

We know of no other college or university courses that require students to absorb a subject, formulate a position on that subject, and then perform effectively (and publicly!) in it to the extent that preteaching courses do. In these courses, something more is required than standard academic performance: attending class, reading texts, writing papers, and completing exams. Prospective English teachers usually enter methods courses with a mixture of personal history and expectations and some field experiences; they encounter new points of view and work to synthesize them with their prior knowledge; they leave to teach one hundred or more adolescents each day. While premedicine, prelaw, preministry, and even prebusiness courses are usually followed by years of professional training and apprenticeship before novices enter actively into their professions, English methods stu-

dents take their final exams in methods one week and often begin student teaching the next. We want this text to help prepare you for this work, both its theory and its practice. When you step into a classroom as a teacher, you are entering deep waters, but they are not uncharted. Each of the following chapters focuses on a key aspect of English instruction and addresses the core beliefs that undergird that aspect. Consider now a cluster of first principles that are foundational to our teaching lives. These should guide and steady all that you undertake as a teacher.

Traditional Principles of Learning

We define our principles first by enumerating a cluster of ideas about the ways in which students (and teachers) most effectively learn that operated in the schools that we knew as students, that our children attended several decades later, and that many children experience today. Four beliefs about learning and teaching are at the heart of traditional schooling:

1. Learning involves a process of acquiring discrete pieces of information and certain observable skills.
2. The teacher's first responsibility is to transfer his or her knowledge to students; the students' primary responsibility is to receive and store that knowledge.
3. Learning can be measured by tests of the students' mastery of knowledge and skills.
4. The interactions between the teacher and the students are the primary focus of this process—from the teacher's organizing and sequencing the subject content, the teacher's clear and unambiguous explanation and illustration of that content and modeling of those skills, to the teacher's assessing students' ability to reproduce the specified knowledge and skills on paper-and-pencil tests or through other observable demonstrations.

Clearly, the teacher's role is at center stage in this traditional educational drama; students have essential but supporting parts. This conception of education dominates the views of many school superintendents, school boards, principals, teachers, and students today. It influences the critiques of education that flow from family dining tables, editors' boardrooms, and politicians' podiums. In the modern era, challenges to it have been heard from the time of Jean Jacques Rousseau (1712-1778) in France and John Dewey (1859-1952) in the United States, through the reforming decades of the 1960s and 1970s, and even into the more politically conservative decades of the 1980s and 1990s, with their countercalls back to tradition. Yet despite these constant and robust challenges, the traditional model persists in the daily rounds of schools everywhere, where teachers direct whole-class instruction to students who sit and listen, receive and absorb; administrators judge the success of

---

[1]As you may discover in your own teaching, sometimes we find ourselves incapable of acting on our beliefs, we yield to the resistance of earlier training and of former habits, or we are coerced by particularly adverse circumstances into a strategy that we don't wholeheartedly endorse. In other words, our teaching is as active, constructivist, process-oriented, and recursive as we suggest your students' learning be, and as prone to stray sometimes from our better judgments and our most conscientious resolves. We do, however, attempt to guide and evaluate our own practice from a coherent position about learning, language, and literature that grows from the traditional principles of learning that we first knew but that now embraces alternatives to that tradition.

classrooms by their silence; and the public evaluates schools by how well their students perform on nationally normed standardized tests. These forces are never more insistent at present than in the local, state, and national initiatives that tie what is taught to local, state, and national standards and what is learned to standardized assessment. Because this traditional view is so pervasive and tenacious, all prospective and experienced teachers need to have a clear and distinct alternative in mind before attempting to resist or to jettison this model.

Alternative Beliefs About Learning, Learners, and Teaching

Three educators who have worked on school renewal projects for almost two decades have summarized an alternative set of underlying assumptions and principles about how students best learn in the main teaching fields: reading, writing, mathematics, science, and social studies. We present their summary as a useful glossary of concepts that you will encounter throughout this text and that we consider to be essential guides for teaching (Figure 1–2). We do not normally teach by lists of terms. We will apply these terms throughout this text, a perpetual "showing," not "telling," but we wanted you to review the vocabulary as we begin. We briefly describe how they would influence learning, learners, and teaching.

Student-Centered, Active, Constructivist Learning. Zemelman, Daniels, and Hyde's ideas offer counterpoints to the traditionalist views. At the heart of the difference is a conception of learning as an active process of constructing meaning by taking in new information, connecting it to prior understandings, and then testing the new knowledge by applying it. Learning is not waiting for the revelation but making it, not uncovering knowledge but creating it. Learning is active and productive, not passive and receptive. Whereas "good students" were traditionally defined as quiet and docile, their alternative counterparts are characterized as engaged and questioning. Center stage is no longer held by the teacher alone but by the teacher and students in consort choosing the most fruitful and responsible paths to learning.

Our observations and those of others (cognitive and developmental psychologists among them) convince us that learning is not a lockstep process that all students begin and conclude together, some sprinting ahead, some keeping up, and others falling behind or faltering. Far from being a neat or linear act of taking in and absorbing information or ideas, learning is messy and roundabout. Learning arises individually out of a particular learner's natural capacities, interests, and experiences and keeps stride with that person's developmental readiness. Strategies, activities, and texts should therefore be grounded in the actualities of the student's personal history and experience.

FIGURE 1–2

Zemelman, Daniels, and Hyde's underlying principles, assumptions, and theories of best practices

Source: Reprinted by permission of Steven Zemelman, Harvey Daniels, and Arthur Hyde. *Best Practice: New Standards for Teaching and Learning in America's Schools,* pp. 7–8 (Heinemann, A division of Reed Elsevier, Inc., Portsmouth, NH. 1993).

Child-centered. The best starting point for schooling is kids' real interests; all across the curriculum, investigating students' own questions should always take precedence over studying arbitrarily and distantly selected "content."

Experiential. Active, hands-on, concrete experience is the most powerful and natural form of learning. Students should be immersed in the most direct possible experience of the content of every subject.

Reflective. Balancing the immersion in direct experience must be opportunities for learners to look back, to reflect, to debrief, to abstract from their experiences what they have felt and thought and learned.

Authentic. Real, rich, complex ideas and materials are at the heart of the curriculum. Lessons or textbooks which water down, control, or over-simplify content ultimately disempower students.

Holistic. Children learn best when they encounter whole, real ideas, events, and materials in purposeful contexts, and not by studying sub parts isolated from actual use.

Social. Learning is always socially constructed and often interactional; teachers need to create classroom interactions which "scaffold" learning.

Collaborative. Cooperative learning activities tap the social power of learning better than competitive and individualistic approaches.

Democratic. The classroom is a model community; students learn what they live as citizens of the school.

Cognitive. The most powerful learning for children comes from developing true understanding of concepts and higher-order thinking associated with various fields of inquiry and self-monitoring of their thinking.

Developmental. Children grow through a series of definable but not rigid stages, and schooling should fit its activities to the developmental level of students.

Constructivist. Children do not just receive content; in a very real sense, they recreate and re-invent every cognitive system they encounter, including language, literacy, and mathematics.

Psycholinguistic. The process of young children's natural oral language acquisition provides our best model of complex human learning and, once learned, language itself becomes the primary tool for more learning, whatever the subject matter.

Challenging. Students learn best when faced with genuine challenges, choices and responsibility in their own learning.

Learners. Soviet psychologist Lev Vygotsky (1978) describes the dynamics of such learning. A child has a point, an "actual developmental level," at which he or she understands concepts and completes tasks without assistance from a more knowledgeable person. This same child also has a point, a "level of potential development," at which he or she can complete more complex tasks with the assistance of teachers or more expert peers. Between these two points lies the ground on which most school learning should take place. Vygotsky calls this the "zone of proximal development," and it is here that more knowing others (teachers and/or expert peers) can influence and coach the student to move past what he or she presently knows and can do and move toward new learning that the student absorbs and calls upon without assistance. We often call the work a teacher sets up to enable a student to move into, within, and through this zone of proximal development *enabling structures.* Others call this work *scaffolding,* because just as carpenters use a scaffold to build a wall that will one day stand on its own, so teachers must develop supports for student learning that will eventually fall away and allow the learning to stand without assistance.

Teachers. The role of teacher changes with these alternative beliefs about learning. Rather than presenters, interpreters, regulators, and judges, teachers define themselves as facilitators, coaches, and fellow learners. Whereas traditional teachers more often aim instruction toward finished products and measure student achievement by them, their counterparts value the process as well as the products it produces. These teachers ask students not only to choose, sequence, and monitor their own learning but also to participate in its evaluation. If learning is seen as a personal, dynamic, recursive act, it cannot be effectively encouraged nor fairly measured by periodic performance on tests and papers. Howard Gardner (1983) has articulated and validated what many have observed: Individuals express their intelligence with far greater diversity than that which is possible using only the verbal and logical modes commonly valued and assessed in schools. Teachers must provide a range of opportunities for response so that students can construct their meanings and enlarge their strengths. Even in English classrooms devoted to using language logically and persuasively, the neglected intelligences (musical, spatial, kinesthetic, interpersonal, and intrapersonal) deserve recognition and expression. Being free to participate, these intelligences will enter the students' progress toward unfolding awareness and meaning.

Subject Matter. One of our field's seminal thinkers, James Moffett (1968), developed a simple matrix, shown in Figure 1–3, that included all that an English teacher should teach. He called it "the universe of discourse" because it covers all four of the basic language arts—speak-

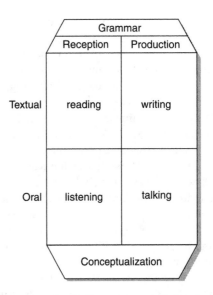

FIGURE 1–3 James Moffett's universe of discourse

Source: This figure is based on the ideas in James Moffett's 1968 *Teaching the Universe of Discourse,* and Moffett & Wagner's 1976 *Student-Centered Language Arts and Reading, K–13,* Boston: Houghton Mifflin.

ing, listening, reading and writing—the central work of the English classroom. We simplify Moffett's matrix as an overview of the basic structure of the content of English teaching. We begin with a partitioned square.

The matrix's first (lower) level contains the world of oral language. This is the primary, fundamental way in which human beings use language. Many linguists and philosophers believe that the discovery of language is what made us human. The second level is written, textual language. Most cultures now use writing. Each of the two levels of discourse is important in its own way, but each has its distinct characteristics. The matrix is divisible laterally as well, left and right. The left side represents reception of language; the right side represents the production of language.

When we refer to reception of oral language at the lower left level, we are dealing with *listening;* when we refer to oral production on the bottom right, we are dealing with *talking.* When we refer to reception of textual language at the upper left level, we are dealing with *reading;* when we refer to production of textual language on the upper right, we are dealing with *writing.* The relationships between these are reciprocal and dynamic. Not one should be passive. It is that simple, that universal.

In addition to this simple division, Moffett believes that the base or foundation of this universe of discourse is not grammar or rules of usage but conceptualization or thinking. That base supports each partition, yet this base is often neglected or stripped from the curriculum of schools. The results are, according to Moffett and Wagner (1976, p. 17), that "[w]holeness and purposeful order are lost." Classrooms that respect and build on the base of thinking and conceptualization invite students into active, participatory learning that integrates speaking, listening, reading, and writing around issues that matter. In today's world, such a classroom now necessarily includes what many call the fifth language art, viewing.

Children and cultures move in a progression from thinking to talking and listening and finally to reading and writing. Moffett and Wagner (1976) describe, however, a different state of affairs that is true of many schools even a quarter century later. "Despite our innovations [language arts] is still not four way. It is heavily biased against the productive activities of speaking and writing, against oral comprehension and composition, and against nonliterature. Not only does it favor receptive activities—in particular, reading and literature—but it fills the curriculum with information about language that cannot be justified in teaching speaking, listening, reading, and writing" (p. 17).

Grammar, at the top of the universe of discourse, is not unimportant. It is the language about language but not a language itself. Moffett says that teachers who do not *do* language but talk and teach endlessly *about* grammar are merely piling "words on words" rather than using "words on world." He wants teachers to have students *do* language rather than *talk* about it. Moffett and Wagner summarize the consequences of such a shift. "You need not fear you have no subject and try to manufacture one by making kids read about writing and write about reading. Words on words strengthen nothing but doubts, because they merely shadow what you're trying to teach, which is words on world. The special province of the language teacher, and therefore the main definition of language arts, is communication consciousness" (p. 23).

The economist John Maynard Keynes makes the point in another field: "Practical men, who believe themselves to be quite exempt from any intellectual influences, are usually the slaves of some defunct economist." We need an organizing center around which we can gather and through which, whether through agreement or dissent, we can deepen and refine our thinking and so our teaching. Moffett's ideas have been our organizing center since we entered the profession, as we have wrestled to enact them, revise them, and extend them in our classrooms. Indeed, Moffett's matrix is not merely the universe of discourse but also the universe of our text. Our work unfolds chapter by chapter from language itself to its basic oral reception and production (listening and talking) and then to its textual level of reception (reading) and production (writing). Surrounding these chapters are the essential generic acts of teaching: organizing instruction, planning lessons, evaluating learning, and entering the profession.

Student-Centered Mnemonics

We present two near-acronyms that our students find to be useful reminders of these core beliefs of learning,

learners, and teachers. They, too, come from Moffett and Wagner, and their implications will grow gradually clearer as you progress through this book. Test them now against what you have just read for coherence and clarity. If you are like our students, you can easily remember the three I's and the three pronouns when you feel suddenly adrift.

Individualization, Interaction, Integration. For decades the three R's (*R*eading, w*R*iting, and a*R*ithmetic) were regarded as the backbone of learning for the young. Moffett and Wagner (1976, 1992) suggest three essential I's as hallmarks of an effective language-learning program, their equivalent of the three R's: *I*ndividualization, *I*nteraction, and *I*ntegration. All three must be present in a classroom if students are to experience the full range and power of language.

Individualization: If learning language is personal, the process will vary from individual to individual. Teachers not only must acknowledge student differences of timing, interest, style, knowledge, and attitude but also must set up structures that accommodate and encourage those differences. Teachers must give students practice in making their own choices of sequence, material, and activity. Classrooms should be organized so that individual differences can be honored and student uniqueness can be manifest.

Interaction: As students increase their sense and confidence of self, they often expand their desire to communicate. Interaction exploits that desire; it invites flexibility of classroom structure whereby students in pairs or small or large groups can join together in the varied and continuous social use of language. Students need many opportunities to talk, listen, and write to each other.

Integration: Finally, language learning must not be separated from other subjects or fields of knowledge but must be integral to them. Language teachers need to promote authentic communication about issues active in their students' experience, whether from their homes, communities, other subjects, or other arts.

I-You-It. Moffett and Wagner (1976) envision another learning progression that begins with the individual and moves to the public: I-You-It.

I: Intellectual growth originates with personal experience. The child properly operates out of the egocentric center of the self.

You: Growth and maturity lead the child to reach out to others and begin to understand their perspectives.

It: As growth continues, the growing child can embrace more distant, less immediately personal experience and knowledge.

Effective instruction imitates that organic process by starting with the personal and slowly moving toward the public, by originating in experiential, personal centers of the self and moving toward more general, communal understandings and applications.

∞ INDIVIDUAL DECISIONS

How are you to decide which of these beliefs deserves your acceptance and which will guide your teaching choices? One way to address these differences and arrive at reasoned conclusions is to look at a history of the profession. Several good resources are available for this purpose (Applebee, 1974; Hook, 1979; Graff, 1987; Gerlach and Monseau, 1991; special editions of the *English Journal*). Another way is to appeal to the systematic theory of learning, language, and literature. Another is to observe in classrooms and to talk with experienced teachers. Another is to read about or conduct research. Yet another is to reflect on one's own experience. To which of those five sources would you most readily turn in attempting to decide what you should teach in English classes? This text will touch on history, theory, practice, and research, but these are significant only to the extent that you exercise your own reflection on them. You stand at an intersection between these vital resources of the field and your own experience as a student and now as a prospective teacher.

Grossman's study at Stanford (1990) of six beginning English teachers demonstrates the advantage of careful reflection on our purposes in teaching. Grossman found that the students who entered the profession without much consideration of what they were doing as teachers of English continued to transmit literary history, to engage largely in textual explication, and to assign their students language exercises that focused on correctness. Those who studied pedagogy and human development in their preparation for teaching taught quite differently. They aimed their students toward an active transaction with texts, gave them a sense of the connection between writing and reading and their daily lives, and engaged them in an exploration of language that centered on the variety of actual usage. Dixon (1967, p. 27) captures that place of decision for all teachers, a vital place where the individual teacher asks, "How will I teach my students?" "We come here to the border country between scholarship and the intuitive understandings of observant and sympathetic teachers. Ideally the one kind of evidence should feed the other."

∞ Invitation to Reflection 1–5

Most English teachers at some point in their careers will teach William Shakespeare's plays and poetry. Read Sonnet 116, "Let Me Not to the Marriage of True Minds," and then turn to Appendix A for a series of possible literature lessons involving it. Using the ideas in Chapter 1, please reflect on how the poem might be effectively taught to high school students.

Let Me Not to the Marriage of True Minds

Let me not to the marriage of true minds
Admit impediments. Love is not love
Which alters when it alteration finds.
Or bends with the remover to remove:
O, no! it is an ever-fixéd mark,
That looks on tempests and is never shaken;
It is the star to every wandering bark,
Whose worth's unknown, although his height be taken.
Love's not Time's fool, though rosy lips and cheeks
Within his bending sickle's compass come;
Love alters not with his brief hours and weeks,
But bears it out ever to the edge of doom.
　　If this be error, and upon me proved,
　　I never writ, nor no man ever loved.

William Shakespeare

1. Which of the teaching ideas or lessons of Appendix A were typical of your English classes in high school? College?
2. Which are you more likely to find in a traditional classroom?
3. Which are you more likely to find in a student-centered class governed by the alternative principles of Figure 1–2?
4. Borrow or revise any of these ideas and/or create your own to sequence a lesson that moves from Moffett and Wagner's *I-You-It.* Do your ideas include each of the three *I's*? (You should specify the age and ability of the students.)
5. Can you visualize any of these teaching ideas in your own English classroom? Do they interest you enough to join that class as a student?

∞ CONCLUSION

Bridging English invites you over the threshold into many English classrooms. They are furnished differently, inhabited with a spectrum of individual teachers, visited by a multitude of different learners, and outfitted with a variety of desks, textbooks, paperbacks, magazines, dictionaries, file cabinets, overhead projectors, posters, and personal computers. No one of them represents the one right room for you. We open these rooms so that you can gather ideas for designing your own. Yet just as a house requires a sure foundation for its strength and durability, your teaching requires foundational beliefs. We do not expect you to construct such a foundation instantaneously but only to begin that work, layering by idea, by practice, and by reflection. You have time to build and to furnish; in fact, good teachers never stop.

You began this book with a visit to your past. In these first pages you have been invited to envision your future as a teacher and, ideally, you will continue to re-vision your classroom throughout your teaching life. Blaise Pascal was right about the difficulty of knowing what to put first in a book. If you understand now why we focus our beginning on you, the reader, however, you have begun to grasp what is central to our core beliefs. As in our classrooms, we try to put students at the center, so here we put you, the reader, first. We will continue to ask you to be an actor in this book, not simply its audience.

2

Organizing Instruction

Organization is nothing but getting things into connection with one another, so that they work easily, flexibly, and fully.

John Dewey

*M*cLuhan has made us aware that the medium is the message. Our organization of physical space and time in English classrooms reflects basic assumptions about our students, ourselves as teachers, and the learning enterprise that joins us. The various classroom configurations that we considered in Figure 1–1 correspond with four fundamental ways in which classrooms and the learning there are organized. Many general methods courses cover similar material, but we find that these approaches and models hold a different light when illuminated by our discipline of English instruction. So before we turn to the content of most English classrooms—language and literature—we briefly outline the four most basic organizational patterns for teaching: lecture, whole-class discussion, group work, and individual work. Each of these four has an educational history, an established practice, and a logic of its own. Each makes a legitimate claim for our consideration. We encourage you to enter our general definitions and concrete elaborations of the four with openness to their substantial possibilities for learning.

Often, teachers select one of these and never shift to another. You might find one that is most congenial to you, that you regard as most effective with your students, and that you may favor in your choices of instruction. As with reading choices, though, your classroom organization may well change over the trajectory of your career. Skilled teachers have more than one option in their repertoire and move fluidly between them. In the hands of able teachers, each strategy can be energizing for student learning. You should be open to the potential for each and for choosing different strategies to meet different needs. Variables that will influence your decision of instructional strategy include the following:

- developmental level of students
- dynamics of the group of students in your class
- nature of the subject to be taught
- nature of the work you hope students will accomplish
- strategies used in preceding and following lessons
- physical possibilities and limitations of your classroom
- resources of your school and community
- time of the school and calendar year

Invitation to Reflection 2–1

We asked variations of these questions in Chapter 1, concerning the following organizational patterns:

lecture	group work
whole-class discussion	individual work

1. Which of the four organizational patterns comes to mind first when you think of an English classroom?
2. Which of the four was most common in your own middle school or high school English class? In college?
3. Think back to three of your favorite teachers. Which did they use?
4. Look at Figure 1–1. Which arrangement resembles that of those favorite teachers? Did the room setup suggest anything about the teachers' approaches to learning and teaching?
5. Who does most of the talking in each? Which allows for the most collaboration between students? In which are students most independent in their work?
6. Choose a different organizational pattern for each of the following scenarios:
   - an introductory lesson on the Holocaust (average ninth-grade students)
   - a lesson on an individual poem (average tenth-grade students) in a genre unit on poetry
   - an introductory lesson on the theme of satire and society (a heterogeneous group of eleventh graders)
   - a concluding lesson on persuasive writing the day before students turn in their papers (twelfth-grade AP Language students)
7. Consider how you might combine several strategies and desk arrangements within one class period on any of these subjects.

We now elaborate each strategy and describe its unique claims so that you can entertain the possibilities of each and avoid the trap of using only one.

↷ LECTURE

In his definitive study of schooling in America, John Goodlad (1984, p. 121) found that the dominant organizational pattern in high school classrooms was that of "a teacher standing or sitting in front of a class imparting knowledge to a group of students. Explaining and lecturing constituted the most frequent teaching activities." The teacher was central to "determining the activities, as well as the tone, of the classroom" (p. 123). The students "generally engage[d] in a rather narrow range of classroom activities— listening to teachers, writing answers to questions, and taking tests and quizzes" (p. 124). Goodlad's study found that large percentages of the students surveyed "appeared to be passively content with classroom life. In general, they felt positive about both peers and teachers" (p. 124). Indeed, students are socialized to this classroom organization by the end of the early elementary grades; and teachers, "on the whole . . . at all levels did not know how to vary their instructional procedures, did not want to, or had some kind of difficulty doing so" (pp. 121–123). Almost a decade later, Applebee (1993) found that the technique that had a "heavy emphasis" in high school literature classes was "whole-class discussion of texts read by all students" (p. 136).

Our own observations of North Carolina high schools are that whole-class discussions dominate English classrooms, but these are often disguised lectures punctuated by occasional questions. Teachers command center stage, their agendas and answers prevail, and their speaking time dominates the discourse. Many colleges and universities still refer to teachers as lecturers. Figure 1–1a shows the typical physical arrangement. The teacher is at the front and center of the classroom; the students face the front, backs to each other, in orderly rows. If the teacher moves, the movement is primarily up front around the desk, lectern, or overhead projector. This approach is based on the notion that knowledge flows from a knowledgeable teacher to less-knowledgeable students. Paulo Freire's (1970) analogy of teachers filling meek "receptacles" contains within it the visual image of a teacher raised above the students to facilitate ease of pouring.

Four Types of Lecture

If the transmission of knowledge is of primary importance and if lecturing is an efficient way for learners to master new knowledge, it makes sense for the class to be so arranged. We believe that Freire's banking model for passing on knowledge is neither primary nor efficient.

That, however, is not the only kind of lecture; and some kinds fall within our bias toward more active, student-centered, constructivist classrooms. We schematize four types in Table 2–1 that differ according to structure, duration (timing), intent, and student role. The likeness between these types is only that each is a form of teacher-talk. Their differences are more pronounced than their similarities. They progress from a prepared lecture that dominates an entire period to teacher-talk in response to questions students ask that lasts until those questions are answered satisfactorily. Students also move progressively from being silent receivers to being more active questioners. The center of knowledge shifts from the teacher as knower to the student as generator of knowledge.

We have had teachers who could detail the differences between the English Romantic poets and their predecessors, outline the social and historical changes between the two, enumerate divergent styles and themes, illustrate those differences with textual references, finish, and gracefully summarize the hour's lesson just as the bell rang. The grimmest foreshadowing of such a *total lecture* is the appearance on a lectern of sheets of paper yellowed at the edges. On the other hand, the *partial lecture* and the *kernel lecture* both acknowledge a legendary benchmark of public speakers and preachers for how long an interested audience can attend: twenty minutes. Many feel that the attention spans of today's adolescents,

raised as they are with television's and computers' staccato movement and nano pulses, are even more limited. These briefer lectures respect those limits. Finally, we have witnessed such energetic, able authorities as James Britton and Buckminster Fuller build their presentations around student or audience questions in stunning *interactive lectures.* They remain the center of knowledge, but students are engaged in prompting and shaping their presentations through audience questions. We have seen educational reformer John Holt rise to give a lecture and say simply: "I don't give talks anymore. I'll be happy to answer any questions." A more student-centered use of the form invites students themselves to become centers of knowledge about a particular subject and then to answer questions posed by fellow classmates. Such an assignment uses an interactive lecture but establishes a new center of knowledge, the student.

Four Rhetorical Strategies

Teachers who choose lectures as the appropriate vehicle for a given lesson still have other decisions to make. We mention three *rhetorical strategies.* The Greek origin of the word *rhetoric, rhetor* (orator), reminds us of the ancients' lively interest in the art of speaking and writing effectively and persuasively. If teachers choose to lecture, they should do so with clarity and intention, knowing

TABLE 2–1   Four lecture types

Lecture Type	Structure	Timing	Intent	Student Role	Example
Total	Organized, structured (usually prewritten) talk that covers a prescribed body of knowledge	Entire class period	To cover content of lesson	To receive, transcribe, and remember	The differences between the English Romantic poets and their predecessors
Partial	Preorganized presentation of small discrete portions of knowledge	A limited part of a period; could occur more than once after students have responded	To prime students to apply the concepts presented	To apply and illustrate	Four central qualities of the Romantic poets, which students illustrate in a rereading of several poems
Kernel	Shorter, more pithy and contentious presentation; tries to go to the core of the lesson; can resemble a feisty polemic	Can occur at any time as a prompt or stimulant for a lesson	To generate response and to challenge	To rebut and defend; stake a pro or con position	The Romantics were caught in a losing battle against the change from a rural, agrarian culture to an urban, industrial society in the early nineteenth century. Their poetry has little to say to us today.
Interactive	Presentation of knowledge that originates in asking students questions or answering theirs	Can last an entire period or some portion; sometimes impromptu	To engage students and to convey knowledge	To listen actively and to interact	Responses to student questions about four poems

they have at their disposal all of the rhetorical methods described since the time of Aristotle. Whatever the scope of lecture, teachers can appeal to reason (argument) and/or emotion (persuasion) with *analysis, definition and classification, comparison and contrast,* and *illustration.* We mention here four general organizing principles that make students more engaged and content more memorable. One of the sad but frequent complaints of teachers is "I told them this material more than once, and they just don't listen." These strategies promise to make the teacher's point more memorable.

> *Analysis:* This organization takes a subject and divides it into its constituent parts to create an understanding of that subject.
> *Definition and classification:* This organization does not break down the general into its component parts but sets forth a subject by examining it sequentially item by item.
> *Comparison and contrast:* This organization articulates contending positions. Sometimes it works to show how both opposing positions are persuasive. It invites students to understand ambiguity and see situations as often too complex for an either/or resolution. It can also invite students to support or attack the opposed positions.
> *Illustration:* This organization presents its subject essentially through example or illustration. Given our field of literature and language, we have a blessedly rich store of vivid illustration.

A traditional total lecture is associated with the thorough coverage of a subject and is often organized by *analysis* or *definition and classification.* But these principles could also be used in the kind of minilessons suggested by Calkins (1986) and Atwell (1987, 1998) for a writing workshop. If, for instance, problems have arisen about what students should do with their completed work, the teacher might break down the necessary steps that a writer must take to be published. *Comparison and contrast* can quickly energize classroom talk that moves the conversation further along and presents, like written texts, new ideas or information to which students can respond and on which they can work. For instance, to initiate small-group discussions of texts, we present three contending responses to a short story and ask students to choose which they find most persuasive. Or, in talking with students about Robert Frost's "Mending Wall," we might present Montgomery's (1962) view that the poem could as easily be praising walls and recognizing the need for separation as criticizing walls and artificial boundaries. Two teachers, René Matthews and Robin Chandler (1998), introduce Toni Morrison's *Beloved* with the *illustration* of the real-life slave Margaret Garner. In January 1856, this mother joined a group of other slaves who were crossing the frozen Ohio River to escape Kentucky plantations. When U.S. marshalls caught them in Cincin-

nati and prepared to return them to Kentucky under the 1850 Fugitive Slave Act, Margaret attempted to kill her children to prevent their reenslavement. After students are invited to respond to Margaret Garner's story, they are challenged to research other slave narratives and to listen for their echoes in Morrison's novel.

The only lectures with which we are comfortable in our own classrooms are those that are brief, present new concepts or knowledge, and immediately invite students to test or apply these new ideas. On those rare occasions we also like to have visuals or manipulatives to hook students' interest, participation, and understanding.

Lecture's Critics

Despite the lecture's predominance in classrooms for decades, critics have attacked the lecture strategy on theoretical and practical grounds. Dixon (1967, p. 34) writes of the "agreed concern" of the Dartmouth Conference to substitute the "round table" for the "disappearing dais." Howard Gardner (Birk, 1996, p. 7) believes that the lecture favors students with linguistic intelligence. They are best suited to "translate" or "convert" the lecturer's words into understanding, while others with different intelligences and learning styles suffer. Pragmatists and researchers worry that even those who can comprehend and absorb the content of a lecture will rapidly lose what they hear. Constructivists believe that the lecture removes the locus for meaning making from the student. Even if lecturers attempt to connect their content with student knowledge and experience, few students can inwardly make their own connections. Lectures are far removed from what reformers value in an active, experiential, inductive, hands-on learning environment.

Often criticism focuses on the worst practices of lecture, usually those of the total lecture. We have found little research about the amount of time devoted to lecture in U.S. high school classrooms at present and no research that acknowledges a variety of lecture types. We are wary of teacher self-report. In fact, as lecturing has become suspect—even vilified—many teachers say that they do not lecture (in a local university, only 25 percent said that they lecture), while students report that lecture is the predominant classroom activity (in that same university, students reported that 75 percent of their teachers lecture). In speaking about effective schools and direct instruction, Synge (2000) says that those teachers who use lecture are often ineffectual in how they present it. We do know of teacher talk that is effective, however, and want to say a word in its defense.

Lecture's Best Exemplars

A legendary American lecturer is philosopher and psychologist William James (1842–1910), whom generations of Harvard students characterized as brilliantly spellbinding in the classroom. He employed the full range of vivid and animated expression, energetic and unconventional gesture, and spontaneous and idiosyncratic blackboard use; but he seems to be remembered most for the originality of his responses to student questions and challenges. Barzun's (1983) description of his daily use of students' responses to "bring forth a new perception, a new formulation" (p. 278) makes us assume that he used at least interactive lecture in portions of his classes. James, writing for teachers, calls for "the kind of teaching that respects freedom and compulsion, individuality and the claims of common reason and common action" (p. 280). His own classroom reflected his encouragement of spontaneity and his willingness to encounter and engage his students, even though he began with lecture. In fact, he defined an uneducated person as "one who is nonplused by all but the most habitual situations," whereas the educated person is one who can "extricate himself from circumstances in which he never was placed before" (p. 282). James himself, even when he described his annual September "trepidation" of returning to the classroom with his mind a "blank" (p. 277), opened himself to the novel and unexpected from his students. This is not the picture that critics present of a wooden lecturer. Granted, many regard James as a genius, with a rare intellectual vitality, a comprehensive grasp of his subject, and an intuitive sense of the students before him; but those hallmarks of the gifted lecturer can be embodied in people who are not geniuses.

Closer at hand, a Wake Forest University colleague of ours, Edwin Wilson, is almost universally mentioned by his former students as their most outstanding university teacher. He relies in the classroom almost totally on lecture (and outside of the classroom, although he is also the provost, he schedules one-hour private interviews with each of his students). Former students often recount hearing the echoes of his speech in describing the English Romantics years later. His example alone would require us to be generous about the educational possibilities of lecture, although we think he communicates human spirit as much as literary knowledge. And every school has distinguished lecturers. History teacher John Giles at our sons' former high school grows so animated in his occasional lectures that he leaps onto his desk to emphasize points. We borrow a familiar logical argument from William James: "If you wish to upset the law that all crows are black, . . . it is enough if you prove one single crow to be white." Our own white crow is Edwin Wilson.

Thus, the image of the student as passive container simply waiting to be filled by the teacher is not always fair to the dynamics between the two. Lecturers and lectures vary. Your selection of the type and the timing deserves careful deliberation. We recommend that you make careful choices so that you can throw out the bathwater and save the baby.

Invitation to Reflection 2-2

1. Which is the most common form of lecture that you have experienced as a student?
   total   kernel
   partial   interactive
2. Name a lecturer whom you consider to be excellent. What qualities distinguish that person's style? Would you characterize that lecturer's characteristic approach as total, partial, kernel, or interactive? Which of the four rhetorical strategies we mentioned did he or she typically employ: analysis, definition and classification, comparison and contrast, or illustration?
3. Have you ever known a teacher to take a strong position on a subject in order to prompt your response? If so, what was the effect on you?
4. Timpson and Tobin (1982) speak of lecturing as a kind of performance whose success can be enhanced by several behaviors. Read their tips and check those that your experience would confirm.
   - moving around the room rather than remaining rooted
   - modulating and varying voice
   - using cuing devices to focus attention (key terms on the blackboard, gestures, pictures, charts)
   - pausing for reflective silence and emphasis

WHOLE-CLASS DISCUSSION

Figure 1–1a, 1–1b, and 1–1c are common arrangements for whole-class discussion. The aim of these discussions is to focus students on a common subject and involve them more actively in their own learning. The classroom in Figure 1–1c mirrors whole-class discussion at its most democratic. The teacher claims no head or center position. All are actively involved, sharing equally in the process of exploring and learning. In most English classrooms, however, the teacher's role is not that of the other learners. The teacher most often selects the text or idea under consideration and prompts, guides, and shapes the conversation. Our students recently praised a master teacher for her ability to let students stray from the topic under discussion with brief personal ramblings and then to reel them back into the focal point. In discussions, because teachers' roles are neither that of the purveyor of knowledge nor that of equal participant with the students, they walk a tightrope. Too much leaning toward one side or the other can create a mishap.

Sometimes discussions only masquerade as democratic process but are, in fact, just a different seating arrangement for a lecture. Teachers may pose questions, but the answers sought and expected are predetermined. In a respected general methods text, Grambs and Carr (1991, p. 92) state what a discussion is not:

- Discussion is *not* recitation.
- Discussion is *not* just talking by people who know little and care less about the subject being discussed.
- Discussion is *not* a debate in which different factions try to win.
- Discussion is *not* a chance for two or three students to show off their verbal acrobatics.
- Discussion is *not* a bull session, where individuals exchange prejudices or feelings.

A keen, young observer of classrooms, Benjamin Milner, adds, with feeling,

- Discussion is *not* a discursive sharing of personal and rambling anecdotes.

Discussion is an instructional approach based on assumptions about the importance of a social context for learning. Socrates modeled education as vigorous, active dialogue between novices and more-knowing others. Rousseau projected an ideal model of one child and one adult in face-to-face work. William James demonstrated dynamic dialogue within a whole classroom of students. Vygotsky (1978) and Bruner (1986) tested the hypothesis that education grows from the social interactions of a learner with others, not in isolation: We help each other construct meaning. Martin (1983, p. 6) captures the impulse and drive of this social interaction at its best:

As individuals we have to assimilate our experiences and build them into our continuing picture of the world; as social beings we need to legitimize the world picture we are continuously constructing and maintaining. So we hold out to others—in talk—our observations, discoveries, reflections, opinions, attitudes and values; and the responses we receive in the course of these conversations profoundly affect both the world picture we are creating and our view of ourselves.

Invitation to Reflection 2–3

As you walk into any high school, you see clusters of students engaged in talk, gathering outside the building before the school day begins, assembled around lockers and in corridors between classes, in cafeterias at lunch, and at school events after hours. As you pass those students, you hear them talking together with energy. Imagine that scene and consider what assumptions you make about their talk.

1. Would you assume that they are involved in a "discussion"?
2. What is the difference in their informal talks together outside of class and what you normally mean by a discussion in class?

These students disperse into different classes and in one English class, a teacher makes the following assignment: "Read the short story 'I Stand Here Ironing' by Tillie Olsen, and be prepared to discuss it in class tomorrow." Consider your assumptions about tomorrow's whole-class "discussion." Base this imagined class on one you have recently observed or one you experienced as a high school student.

3. What would you expect it to be like? A disguised lecture on the story? An active exchange of ideas with the teacher and students exploring the story together?
4. Who would have the greater share of classroom talk, students or the teacher?
5. Would students move beyond the boundaries of the teacher's questions to explore new ground on their own? Would students be allowed to introduce their speculative questions or observations outside of a response to the teacher's questions?
6. Would students direct their responses to each other, or would they dispatch them through the teacher?
7. Would the teacher's questions be aimed at leading students to a single reading or interpretation of the story?
8. What would be the arrangement of desks? Does the arrangement influence the discussion dynamics?
9. In your just-imagined class discussion, did you think in terms of an ideal or what you have actually experienced or observed? Did the ideal and the real differ?

Dimensions of Whole-Class Discussion

Martin explained why we converse with others in any setting. Classroom talk shares these motives but differs from the informal conversations that we engage in everywhere else. Noden and Moss (1994, p. 504) identify several "possible student responses" that able teachers associate with classroom discussion: "(a) an aesthetic response, (b) a rhetorical response, (c) a metacognitive response, and (d) a shared inquiry response." In their article "Perceiving Discussion as Eskimos Perceive Snow," they argue that just as Alaskan Eskimos profit from forty-two names for what the non-Eskimo calls snow, so teachers profit from a nuanced awareness of the possible dynamics of discussion. The teacher "denies a number of rich avenues for understanding" if discussion implies only the common recitative answering of questions about texts. We present four essential dimensions of whole-class discussion to open our consideration of the inner workings of this classroom staple. Discussion can, of course, occur in small groups or between pairs. For the sake of clarity, we focus in this section on the dynamics of a whole class engaged in discussion.

Turn-Taking Discussions. Whole-class discussions often resemble this simple pattern: Teacher asks, students answer, the floor returns to the teacher (who can choose how long to keep it), and the cycle begins again. Beach and Marshall (1991) explain that a three-part sequence of this turn taking—teacher question, student response, teacher evaluation—is the most frequently observed pattern in classrooms. Cazden (1988, p. 29) calls this pattern IRE: The teacher *I*nitiates the questions, the students *Re*spond, and the teacher *E*valuates. This sequence encourages serial questioning in which a teacher queries one student and receives a response and then goes to the next and repeats the exercise to all those who are willing or forced. Seldom do students respond to each other's answers or pose questions themselves to other students. They struggle to find the one acceptable answer and then wait for the teacher to validate it and pose the next question. If they do interact with their peers, they often go through the teacher as a dispatcher of turns. Students' raising their hands and the teacher's recognizing the person who next holds the floor typify these arrangements.

The last part of this three-part sequence, teacher evaluation, is the part missing in normal conversation. In classrooms it might be a "Very interesting, Angela," or a simple murmured "Hmmmmm" and a head shake, but most teachers feel that some immediate feedback is necessary. (On many teacher evaluation instruments, instructional feedback is one of the principal items.) This last move returns the floor to the teacher, who is then "positioned to ask another question—either following up on the student's response … or turning to a slightly different agenda" (Beach & Marshall, p. 54).

Pseudoquestions. Beach and Marshall (1991) also note the presence in many classrooms of questions posed for which the questioner already has an answer in mind. These pseudoquestions create a different dynamic from that of ordinary conversations in which questions are normally asked in order to obtain information. Their effect is profound. They establish the teacher as the more-knowing one, with privileged knowledge and a privileged classroom position, and the students as seekers after the teacher's insights. The teacher is the fielder of questions; the students are the answerers. In such a setting, students rarely initiate their own speculative questions. They might ask for information or clarification, but seldom do they enter the interpretive enterprise. In this context, we might better understand the common scenario of the student's prosaic question following the teacher's passionate reading of a poem: "Will this be on the test?" Clearly, the student is a spectator of the teacher's performance and asks one of the few subject-related questions available to him or her.

Schaffer (1989, p. 40) describes a breakthrough insight she gained about discussions: "If there are certain points we want students to know … we should tell them. We should not use it as a discussion item, because the point is not really open for discussion."

Student Responses. We have mentioned how taking turns and pseudoquestions foster assumptions about the role of students as merely cogs within the wheel that is turned by the teacher. Something more subtle also develops. Language and literature students, in inverse proportion to their regard for the teacher's superior knowledge and response, devalue their own. Rather than growing through discussion to expand, enrich, and qualify their original responses, they substitute or replace their earlier insights with those of the teacher. Furthermore, they dismiss other students' remarks as ignorant and naïve, comments to be endured until the teacher produces the valid response. These assumptions undermine students' discovery of how to integrate new learning with old, to build on the ground of their own and others' knowledge and understanding, and, in sum, to construct a strategy for developing their own knowledge. It is a model of appropriation, not of learning.

Furthermore, Marshall (2000), in looking into sixty classrooms across the United States, observed a social hindrance to student responses. He noted that students do not want to ask even the simplest questions or volunteer any answers that would make them seem to be the teacher's stooges.

Teacher Assumptions. In their role as leaders of class discussions, teachers can easily deceive themselves about the true nature of class dynamics, especially if those discussions are lively, with several students engaged in strong and active answers. At that moment, a teacher is so busy fielding questions, doing justice to responses, asking follow-up questions, evaluating responses, and connecting them to what was said earlier, that he or she assumes or hopes that the numerous other students are as engaged. The reality may be significantly different. Especially when able talkers take responsibility, the passivity of those less able increases. So many high school students are masters of the polite appearance of listening that the teacher, deceived, forges on.

Reform of Discussion

The usual protocols of whole-class discussion leave the teacher in clear control of the classroom. To relinquish that control is anxiety-producing for most teachers, but especially for young teachers who have few alternative teacher models, who struggle to define and claim their own roles as teachers, and who might be evaluated by administrators who mistakenly equate silent classes with good classes. We must lay a careful foundation gradually and, brick by brick, build toward alternative patterns. Certain principles and skills require time to develop. Too many teachers turn away from alternative arrangements because their one or two experiments meet with failure. Discussions happen within the total ethos of the individual classroom, of the classroom in the school, of the school in the community, and of the community in the national norms of what teaching and learning mean. Traditional habits do not change easily.

Classroom Research. Smagorinsky and Fly (1994) suggest general changes that teachers can make in their conduct of whole-class discussions. These suggestions originate in their interest in small-group work, why it sometimes produces authentic explorations and other times stiff, unproductive work—a kind of fill-in-the-blank approach to the subject. They examined the classroom talk of tenth-grade students in two settings: a teacher-led discussion and a small-group discussion of two coming-of-age stories. They concluded that what happened in the whole-class setting was essential to students' development of the ability "to talk on their own" (p. 55). The quality of small-group talk—its shape or style, not solely its content—was based on the quality of whole-class discussion. Small-group work was "an extension of the continuum of discussions enacted during the school year" (p. 58). Four discussion-leading techniques facilitated, first, whole-class interactions and then small-group interactions:

1. Prompting students to generate a contextual framework to guide interpretation
2. Prompting students to elaborate their responses
3. Building on student contributions to generate questions
4. Making the process of analysis explicit (p. 55)

These are important techniques for beginning teachers to try. In the first technique, when teachers prompted students to create their own strategies, students developed an independent framework for interpreting literature or analyzing writing. The teacher's modeling an interpretive strategy did not result in students' being able to apply the technique on their own. In the researchers' transcription of a class discussion of one of the stories, the teacher prods students to develop a "conceptual context through which to interpret the literary character's experience" (p. 56). These conceptual strategies are not presented as abstract principles but are embodied or expressed implicitly in the questions posed to students.

Second, Smagorinsky and Fly recommend that teachers resist the temptation to elaborate on students' responses for them, rather than prompting students' own elaboration. Teachers should relinquish their explanatory talk to students' exploratory attempts at understanding, even when those are fumbling. Third, teachers also need to generate questions from the flow of conversation, not from a preconceived list. Nystrand and Gamoran (1991) call this kind of question posing *uptake*. When students' comments generate a follow-up question or a request for expansion of an answer, students learn not only to elaborate on responses and defend their views but also to take themselves more seriously, to probe more deeply into their responses, and to cultivate a way to push themselves to greater insight. Nystrand and Gamoran's insights remind us of the admonition to water a plant deeply so it will send down strong roots. Finally, Smagorinsky and Fly found that discussions grew richer and more productive when teachers called attention to common strategies for reading literature or writing effectively. They recommend that teachers build on students' interpretive activity by prodding them to wonder aloud, search for evidence, make generalizations, and check them with subsequent reading. These are not the fancy acrobatics of New Critical scholars but the necessary work of competent and interested readers made explicit.

Classroom Practice. Schaffer (1989, pp. 40–42) uses student-written questions as the basis for her discussions. Three of her seven postulates for teachers in assigning and "fielding" these questions reiterate and extend the ideas of Smagorinsky and Fly.

- Our discussion questions must be important to our students.
- We must allow enough "wait time" for reflection before we call on students to speak.[1]
- The students who speak the least may need this sort of activity the most.

Probst (1988b, p. 35) poses both questions and a strategy for using them that encourage a "loose and flexible" pattern of discussion that still drives toward the reader's personal engagement with the text. He suggests that teachers select questions from the list shown in Table 2–2 that are suitable for their students, the time available, and the text being read. These should be reworded, written on small pages of a booklet (if not bound, then stapled or clipped together), and given to small groups of students to prompt and guide their discussion. (He omits the "focus" column in his booklets.) A young teacher, Mary Beth Braker, has explained to us that she keeps a copy of these reader response questions "taped to my podium, my desk, and my lesson plan book. These questions serve as a constant reminder to me of what I want my classroom question and discussion sessions to do— to bond my young adult readers to a text personally and intimately; to guide them in using the skills they already possess—first reactions, associations, visual images—to connect with a literary text. My most successful moments in the classroom have involved adaptations of these questions."

---

[1]Research studies show that when a teacher pauses after a question to wait for student response, the students give better answers (Rowe, 1974; Tobin, 1987). Yet Tobin also found that teachers typically wait only one second for student response before they start talking. (Other estimates are even lower.)

TABLE 2–2
Probst's reader response
questions for literature
discussions

Focus	Questions
First reaction	What is your first reaction or response to the text? Describe or explain it briefly.
Feelings	What feelings did the text awaken in you? What emotions did you feel as you read the text?
Perceptions	What did you see happening in the text? Paraphrase it—retell the major events briefly.
Visual images	What image was called to mind by the text? Describe it briefly.
Associations	What memory does the text call to mind—of people, places, events, sights, smells, or even of something more ambiguous, perhaps feelings or attitudes?
Thoughts, ideas	What idea or thought was suggested by the text? Explain it briefly.
Selection of textual elements	Upon what, in the text, did you focus most intently as you read—what word, phrase, image, idea?
Judgments of importance	What is the most important word in the text? What is the most important phrase in the text? What is the most important aspect of the text?
Identification of problems	What is the most difficult word in the text? What is there in the text or in your reading that you have the most trouble understanding?
Author	What sort of person do you imagine the author of this text to be?
Patterns of response	How did you respond to the text—emotionally or intellectually? Did you feel involved with the text or distant from it?
Other readings	How did your reading of the text differ from that of your discussion partner (or the others in your group)? In what ways were they similar?
Evolution of your reading	How did your understanding of the text or your feelings about it change as you talked?
Evaluations	Do you think the text is a good one? Why or why not?
Literary associations	Does this text call to mind any other literary work (poem, play, film, story—any genre)? If it does, what is the work and what is the connection you see between the two?
Writing	If you were to be asked to write about your reading of this text, upon what would you focus? Would you write about some association or memory, some aspect of the text itself, about the author, or about some other matter?
Other readers	What did you observe about your discussion partner (or the others in your group) as the talk progressed?

Source: Robert E. Probst, "Dialogue with a Text," *English Journal,* January, 1988, pp. 35–36, National Council of Teachers of English. Reprinted by permission.

Dixon (1967, pp. 34–35) describes more generally a teacher's role in facilitating and extending a discussion: "Here a teacher can help by noticing and reinforcing potential change in the level or direction of the discussion, summing up an attitude perhaps, making an issue quite explicit, or calling for an instance when generalizing seems to have lost touch with reality. Learning to do so, without disturbing the tentative informal exploration that good talk becomes, is a matter of awareness and tact" and, we add, experience. These techniques are examples of the broader strategy, mentioned in Chapter 1, called *scaffolding:* a temporary structure of learning techniques or strategies that support and strengthen a growing

learner and that can be gradually withdrawn as students become more proficient and, finally, independent.

Four experienced English teachers memorably describe the traditional teacher-controlled approach to whole-class discussions, their growing dissatisfaction with it, their desire to reach more students, and their development of an alternative. In 1994, the *English Journal* posed this question for its readers: "What has been the most significant change in your approach to teaching since 1987?" The answers of Robert Perrin (1994) and David Noskin (1994) testify to how one can move away from teachers' turn-taking discussions to student-initiated conversations.

Perrin (1994, p. 89) describes his established ritual for discussion: "Start with five-by-seven index cards; write ten to fifteen questions, carefully crafted and sequentially ordered; conduct class by asking the questions in order." This pattern worked for most students, but Perrin realized that the questions were too *me* centered." "Students felt little responsibility for their own learning; instead, they knew I would lead them through the essays, poems, plays, or novels—highlighting what *I* thought was important." Perrin changed his routine by asking students to write down two questions about the assigned text on three-by-five cards, "any questions, so long as the questions were 'real' and related, at least in some way, to the reading." He fought back guilt—his preparation was rereading the text. He struggled with anxiety—what if students didn't write questions or the written questions were "odd"? In fact, though, his students were excited, and his discussions became invigorating. "*They* determined what we talked about; *they* found out what they wanted to know; *they* were responsible for directing their learning." As Probst (2000) has observed, "students' instincts will take them to the essential stuff."

Like Perrin, Noskin (1994, p. 89) once thought he understood the ingredients for an "ordered, involved, informative, and well-paced" discussion: "involving the majority of students, asking for a balance of lower and higher level questions, and providing sufficient wait time for students to generate answers." Today he describes those discussions differently, as "rehearsed, passive, unintellectual, and mechanical." Rather than effective discussions, he now describes them as "pseudodiscussion[s]" in which he controlled "the intellectual climate through a series of teacher-generated questions, in which all communication was channeled through me." This new understanding, which he calls the most significant change in his teaching, requires new arrangements.

> First, the students must take ownership of the discussion. This can be accomplished by appointing discussion leaders, having students come to class ready to share one question, commenting and sharing significant passages from the previous night's reading, or asking students to share their ideas with one or two others and then choosing one of those ideas to bring to the entire class. I also realize that my role has to be that of a *facilitator*. I might begin by asking a student to share a puzzlement or reaction to a piece of literature. Other times, I might use a favorite passage or idea, but the discussion must quickly become theirs. I can encourage, clarify, mediate, and participate as long as I do not dominate. Finally, I have learned that an effective discussion is more aptly perceived as a conversation. (Noskin 1994, p. 89)

He acknowledges the need for setting guidelines for behavior as the year begins that establish "a semblance of order and genuine mutual respect" and encourage "an open and nonthreatening exchange of ideas." Now in Noskin's classes, when students express ideas, other students respond directly to them. "In the past, my stu-

dents were responding to me. Now they are talking to one another."

Teachers Matthews and Chandler (1998, p. 88) changed both their curriculum and their approach to it in order to engage more of their racially diverse high school juniors in active learning from literature and each other. Their homework assignment was to create reader-response pages in their journals and respond each night to the assigned readings of Morrison's *Beloved*. They were to note page numbers read and mark a column for class discussion notes, a column for their reactions, and another for their classmates' response to them (answering questions or making comments). Each night students responded in the top-left quadrant. The class began with students writing reactions to each other as the teachers checked the journal homework. Then the teachers simply opened the floor for questions. They explained that they "did not plan climactic conclusions for these discussions. We simply listened to our students and tried to show them the connections in what they were saying and reading from day to day."

Questions

Like Noskin and Perrin, as beginning teachers, we once regarded the central act of preparation each night to be writing out and sequencing questions for the next day's discussion. Even when our classroom organization embraced other approaches, we couldn't feel completely comfortable about going into class without an outline of some essential questions. The margins of every novel, short story and most poems that we read, remain littered with questions. This habit has its benefits: a ready means of response to texts and an encapsulation of personal wonders about them. It joins our private acts of reading with the public sharing of perplexities and pleasures. We continue to think that question writing is solemn work. Aristotle ("Metaphysics II") wrote, "Those who wish to succeed must ask the right preliminary questions." Nash and Shiman (1974, p. 38) observed that "questioning is perhaps the central skill in the teaching-learning experience." Bruner (1983, p. 191), reflecting on his lifetime of teaching, writes, "I had no question in my mind (nor do I now) that teaching is a form of dialogue, an extension of dialogue. Dialogue is organized around questions." Dewey (1933, p. 266) was equally unequivocal about the importance of questions: "What's in a question, you ask? Everything. It is the way of evoking stimulating response or stultifying inquiry. It is, in essence, the very core of teaching." Neil Postman (1988, p. 26) notes that "all the knowledge we ever have is a result of questions . . . since questions are the most important intellectual tool we have, is it not incredible that the art and science of question-asking is not systematically taught?" Yes. Questions differ, and not any question will do.

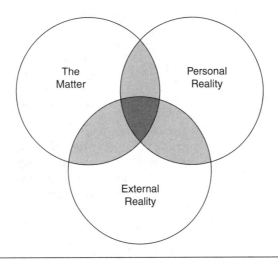

WHITE QUESTIONS

> *The Matter:* What does Huck say when he decides not to turn Jim in to the authorities?
> *Personal Reality:* When would you support a friend when everyone else thought he or she was wrong?
> *External Reality:* What was the responsibility of persons finding runaway slaves?

SHADED QUESTIONS

> *The Matter/Personal Reality:* In what situations might someone be less than willing to take the consequences for his or her actions?
> *Personal Reality/External Reality:* Given the social and political circumstances, to what extent would you have done as Huck did?
> *The Matter/External Reality:* What were the issues during that time which caused both Huck's and Jim's actions to be viewed as wrong?

DENSE QUESTIONS

> *The Matter/Personal Reality/External Reality:* When is it right to go against the social and/or political structures of the time as Huck did when he refused to turn Jim in to the authorities?

Source: From L. Christenbury and P. P. Kelly, *Questioning: A Path to Critical Thinking,* 1983, p. 16, National Council of Teachers of English. Reprinted with permission.

FIGURE 2-1   Christenbury and Kelly's questioning circle

The Questioning Circle. Handbooks have been written about question posing. We scatter such advice throughout this book. Leila Christenbury and Patricia Kelly (1983), frustrated by the traditional questioning hierarchies (e.g., those of Bloom, Sanders, Taba, and Herber), developed an approach to questioning that is not linear, invariant, and hierarchical: one lower-level question progressing to a slightly more challenging question, and all moving toward the most sophisticated, penetrating question of all. These older hierarchies "imply a linear or sequential theory of learning, a theory that we reject" (p. 5). Christenbury and Kelly's alternative model for developing questions works at the intersection of three circles: the matter, personal reality, and external reality (Figure 2-1). Christenbury and Kelly, teachers, scholars, and researchers themselves, explain: "While each circle represents a different domain of cognition, the circles overlap—as does knowledge—and are not ordered" (p. 13). They define these three circles when used in the study of literature as follows:

The Matter: The subject under discussion, the text

Personal Reality: The individual reader's experience, knowledge, feelings, and values that are brought to the reading of the text

External Reality: The "world" and other literature; "the experience, history, and concepts of other peoples and cultures"

Questions surrounding literary texts, for instance, can address each of the three separate circles (white) as well as the intersections of two circles (gray, or shaded) and the converging point (black, or dense) of all three. Christenbury and Kelly consider the dense point to contain the "central, most important questions . . . whose answers provide the deepest consideration of the issue" (p. 14).

They propose that teachers write questions from each of the areas—white, gray, and black—but they prescribe no order for asking them. The teacher draws on those components as the right timing presents itself during discussion. The order is flexible. Unlike hierarchical taxonomies, the central question might initiate discussion or arise in the middle or, more traditionally, at the last. The questioning circle suggests a way for teachers to integrate the text, personal response, and the wider context of both. Thus, the discussion "builds on a variety of perspectives" (p. 17). Figure 2-1 also contains questions that Christenbury and Kelly wrote to illustrate each of the three areas. They probe one single significant incident in *The Adventures of Huckleberry Finn.*

As examples of dense questions, we pose the following questions (matter/personal reality/external reality) that might be raised in a discussion of Mark Twain's use of language in *The Adventures of Huckleberry Finn:*

- What is your reaction as either a minority or majority reader to Mark Twain's references to African Americans in his novel?
- Does Twain's implicit criticism of nineteenth-century racial prejudice and practice mitigate his use of such language?
- Should his novel be banned from public school curricula because of its language?

Opening Questions. The first question posed to open a discussion can set the stage for all that follows. Many fine starting points will be suggested in other chapters. We here mention a few for classes engaged in literature study because it is in such discussions that many of us have the strongest pull toward traditional close textual reading. Once you have begun close analysis of texts, breaking off is hard to do.

Many questioning hierarchies recommend beginning with lower-level questions and moving toward the culminating higher-order ones. Christenbury and Kelly (1983, p. 17) explain the disadvantage of this sequence: "If a teacher using a hierarchical schema carefully orchestrates the questions from lower order to higher order and then springs the 'big question,' the effect on students is often not a positive one. To answer the 'big question,' the class needs to repeat the ground already covered; to many students this hardly seems worth the effort." They suggest a reversal: starting with the most significant questions, those at which the matter, personal reality, and external reality intersect. These questions can arise at any time in a discussion—a radical enough suggestion. Alternating dense with white or shaded questions causes, as they explain, "the complex and central dense questions to be answered with added perception, knowledge and understanding" (p. 14). Starting with the dense question and keeping it as the discussion's focus can also stir student interest, generate questions from the shaded and white areas, keep the conversation moving around a central rivet, and at the end account for the most important responses to a subject that would have evolved had separate questions been posed—riveting!

Another broad approach to opening questions takes as its starting point one particular and significant question about a subject. For instance, if the class has completed Shakespeare's *Julius Caesar,* the one question might be any of the following:

- What makes Brutus ready for a conspiracy?
- How do political altruism and personal gain vie as motive forces in the play?
- What weaknesses and strengths of the common people are presented?

McKeown and Beck (1999, p. 26) suggest a way to develop such questions: "Teachers must identify places in the text that are key to building an understanding of the focus and then develop questions that initiate a discussion of these ideas. Questions that focus on the authors' ideas work better than questions that elicit facts and details. Talk that focuses on literature information is flat and static." Ferrara (1981, p. 69) liked to open his Great Books discussions with global queries such as the following questions about Machiavelli's *The Prince:*

- If you were Lorenzo and you read this book, what would you do about it? Would you take on Machiavelli as an advisor? Why or why not?

Here are other strong summary questions:

- In Faulkner's "A Rose for Emily," what in Emily's past helps explain why she might rather cohabit with a corpse than continue occasionally seeing a live man?
- Why does Hamlet fail to act?
- Who was the most unrealistic member of the family in Williams's *The Glass Menagerie?*
- Was Sethe wrong to attempt to kill all her children and to actually kill one of them in *Beloved?* Should she be convicted for murder?

Two other kinds of these comprehensive questions focus on the title and on the nagging questions that readers often take away from a text's conclusion. Thus, we might ask the following questions:

- How does Joyce Carol Oates's short story title "Where Are You Going, Where Have You Been?" sum up Connie's tragedy?
- What is the rich paradox in Richard Wright's title *Native Son?*
- Was Sammy's quitting the A&P a foolish or a noble gesture in John Updike's "A & P"?

The teacher's task becomes to listen, to think, and then to encourage, react, and build on student responses (uptake), not to plan for or try to remember the next question in a sequence and certainly not to try to account for all the details of the text. If students consider the big questions, try out hypotheses, add support for their positions, and select telling details of the text or the ideas under study, teachers often find that the essence of a text has been discussed and what has been aired will be memorable.

Sometimes an honest admission of perplexity initiates productive discussions. A teacher can simply tell the class that the text or the writing dilemma is a mystery or is confusing and that he or she needs students' help in figuring it out. When the classroom enterprise is focused on inquiry and exploration and when trust and respect between teacher and students have built over time, such vulnerability can unleash strong efforts from students.

Speculative Questions. These broad initial questions should initiate a speculative process that continues during class. In this inquiring classroom, teachers and students ideally ask questions of each other as they fashion new understandings together. The reality of schools is often quite different. Twenty years ago, Goodlad (1984) observed that only 1 percent of the high school teachers' questions solicited more than the most superficial thought from students. Although effective teachers will use a variety of questions, the speculative, divergent ones should predominate. For instance, in teaching Frost's "Mending Wall," teacher Emily Orser (2001, personal communication) explored the ideas of walls in the poem and then asked her students to consider the first line ("Something there is that doesn't love a wall") and the last line ("'Good fences make good neighbors.'"). Are the walls being mended (artificially reconstructed), or are they themselves mending (caring and joining together)? Do we wall out each other needlessly, or do walls help establish needed boundaries?

As Postman and Weingartner (1969, p. 34) memorably state, teachers who effectively create inquiry-based classrooms "emphatically [do] not view questions as a means of seducing students into parroting the text or syllabus; rather, [they see] questions as instruments to open engaged minds to unsuspected possibilities." Postman and Weingartner suggest what is central to the effectiveness of these able teachers: "Generally, each of [their] lessons poses a problem for students" (p. 36). In his revised *How to Read a Book,* Mortimer Adler (1972) proposes another benchmark for how to arrive at this deeper range of questions in literature study. He believes readers should never say, "I disagree," until they can say, "I understand." Such understanding requires a deeper level of thoughtful speculation and inference, not a more superficial quick response (pp. 142–143).

Responses

The questions teachers ask and the classroom structures and practices they establish are essential to promoting engaged participation of all students. If active inquiry animates a class, the progressing conversation itself validates appropriate and correct responses. If teachers do respond verbally and directly to individual students, these responses should be as genuine as the questions. Of course as class leaders, teachers must sometimes negoti-

ate wrong or ineffective responses. An unequivocal reaction to wrong responses can motivate students, provide a gauge for how they are doing and a "blueprint" for how they can improve, and facilitate student self-evaluation (Good & Brophy, 2000; Beach & Marshall, 1991). But the response should be measured. Research demonstrates that ridicule, humiliation, and punishment for incorrect responses create an environment that undermines confident and effective learning (Probst, 1988a; Borich, 1992). They discourage risk taking and speculating, hallmarks of active, student-centered, constructivist classrooms.

Nancy Rost Goulden (1998) suggests an additional step: expect, and teach your students to expect, that every student will speak every day about the lesson. She bravely frames a first rule for "a fully participatory classroom: the teacher will not depend exclusively on volunteers in class discussion" (p. 92). She suggests several steps to shift the pattern "from minority participation to universal participation" (p. 93). One is a technique she calls "go-rounds"—the "first cousin to old-fashioned recitation" (p. 92). In answer to a question or prompt, all students individually must prepare a brief response, make jotted notes, and respond with an oral answer if the teacher calls on them. Not all responses are actually spoken, but as other questions are posed, the teacher can tap those who did not speak earlier. Not all questions would be followed by this deliberate "wait time," but enough to give students a chance to collect their thoughts and compose an initial response. The principle is not to punish or motivate through embarrassment, but to shift class discussion patterns from the activity of highly motivated, assertive volunteers to the activity of all. Even if all students are not given a chance to speak, each will have entertained an answer to the question at hand.

An image from early Jewish community life captures our ideal for discussion in English classes, whether with a whole class or a small group. Midrash was a way of interpreting Jewish texts in which a group inquired, speculated, puzzled over, and teased out meaning. Often the participants filled gaps in the text. Always they examined words and debated their import. Bill Moyers (1997) calls midrash "an assault on silence." Elie Wiesel, Primo Levi, and other survivors have written of the famous midrash in Auschwitz in which God was put on trial. We value the image for the process it recalls and for the seriousness, openness, and expectation of those engaged in it.

 **Invitation to Reflection** **2-4**

James Marshall and his colleagues (1999, p. 383) undertook a modest ethnographic study of how one university English department teaches literature to its undergraduates. They talked to the faculty members and studied their syllabi and writing assignments. What they discovered is relevant to your envisioning discussion in your school classrooms because the university is your most recent experience, it often provides a normative script for high school literature teaching, and it is "so powerful, so taken for granted, so seldom questioned or even acknowledged . . . pointing it out is like reminding people that they tend to breathe fairly regularly." We present the "script" for talking in the classroom that Marshall discovered and then ask you several questions about it.

> *Talking.* In leading classroom discussion, faculty members told us that they wanted to be in control. As one of our colleagues said, "Obviously, I have an agenda. I mean, when I read a story I normally think, 'This is important, and this and this,' so I certainly come in with my agenda. If I don't make it known to my students right away, it might come out in group discussion. But I selected these stories for certain purposes." Or, as another put it, "I try to think about the one main thing that must be said as far as I'm concerned in this class, and whether it is a question or just some main point. That seems really crucial to me." Faculty members, in other words, usually scripted classroom discussions ahead of time. Sometimes there were unlooked-for and much welcomed observations, questions, or insights that pulled those discussions one or even two levels deeper. But the norm—and the norm is what we were trying to describe—was to think of the discussion as anchored in a reading the teacher had already constructed through a series of "main things" that had to be covered. (pp. 383–384)

1. Do you recognize this script?
2. Do you think it is the best script for college classes? High school classes? Middle school classes?
3. Do you believe that it is appropriate for you as a high school literature teacher to select texts, develop interpretations, and determine emphases that you believe are crucial for your students' learning?
4. Name any essential revisions you would make in the script above for high school or middle school literature teaching. Imagine a way both to be true to your sense of purpose and also engage students in inquiring and constructing meaning of their own.

∽ GROUP WORK

A group-centered approach to learning is like the discussion approach in many ways: The teacher is not the sole provider of knowledge, students actively participate in their learning, and learning revolves around genuine inquiry and evolves out of interaction. But group-centered work is defined by a crucial difference: The teacher sets students on a more independent course so that group discoveries are made without the direct intervention of the teacher. Teachers provide a structure and assistance for learning, but their roles change. Students have a greater share of the classroom's talk space and more individual responsibility for the learning experience. More than whole-class or even individual approaches, the group approach allows students to generate ideas, use language (listening and talking especially), learn from each other, teach each other, and recognize that their thoughts and experiences are valuable and essential to new learning.

Collaborative Learning

Group work can be structured so that individual group members work independently toward a group goal. The members may meet, but they interact minimally and work individually. More typically, however, group work is structured so that the individual group members work together cooperatively to achieve a common purpose. This collaboration is integral to the group structure we value most. It is an approach to learning based on carefully formulated and researched assumptions.

Vygotsky, Bruner, and others believe that individuals do not construct knowledge in a vacuum. Learning occurs in a social context; it is not an individual act. Barnes, Britton, and Torbe's (1990) studies of talking to learn show the powerful advances that are made because of authentic talk that emerges when students learn together. In such a context, they can try out half-formed ideas, wrestle with new information, and make tentative suggestions as they help each other move toward deepening understanding. James Britton (1986, p. 120) calls this constructing of shared meaning "leap frogging." Parker and Goodkin (1987, p. 38) explain that if there is "no social interaction with others who offer us an expanded range of alternative viewpoints, no new viewpoints to incorporate into our thinking, [there can be] no intellectual development." Vygotsky (1978, p. 88) is more succinct: "Human learning presupposes a specific social nature and a process by which children grow into the intellectual life of those around them." Collaborative learning encourages genuine conversation that flows naturally from one to the other.

Collaborative learning takes students seriously and asks that they take each other seriously and direct their talking and listening to each other. It acknowledges that if all talking must be funneled through the teacher in a classroom of twenty to thirty other learners, individual talking time is necessarily limited. Group collaboration allows for frequent opportunities to use language. The teacher's removal from a central place becomes like uncorking a bottle. Students' interactions and responses to each other flow more freely and confidently. Proponents of collaborative learning believe that we should engage students in "conversation at as many points in both the writing and the reading process as possible" (Bruffe, 1984, p. 642).

Teachers must resist the notion that small-group work is not real teaching, that it is a teacher's holiday. Invariably, when our student teachers learn that we will be visiting them on a day they have scheduled group work, they request that we come when they are "really teaching." The teacher's preparation for small groups is significant (just as facilitating it is). Generally, teachers must be carefully organized; ready to tolerate talk, confusion, and surprises; energized for authentic conversation; and, mainly, willing to step down from the controlling center of the classroom.

Earlier in this chapter we discussed Smagorinsky and Fly's (1994) insights about ways in which the discourse of whole-class discussions can positively influence the work of small groups. But will those acts be enough to change the level of discourse if it is habitually less serious, focused, and purposeful in other areas of school life? If teachers are not directly involved, how can they be sure that the group discourse moves beyond the discursive conversations that are typical of the time between classes and after school hours?

They must recognize that "the art of conversing is at once a profound social and cognitive activity, based on real respect, not etiquette" (Moffett & Wagner, 1992, p. 80). We consider conversation to be an art of hearing as well as talking. We must listen to others' descriptions of reality as we hope they listen to ours. In classrooms, teachers can listen attentively and respond actively and spontaneously; they can validate the serious responses of others; they can make connections between old and new knowledge. They can nudge students toward habits of questioning, self-disclosure, sensitivity, and tact. This is not to say that the work of groups is always earnest and intense. Part of the importance of the group is that it brings natural language to the classroom. With the young, this brings humor and wit as well as serious inquiry. Use the range.

Practical Decisions About Group Work

The structure of a group can take a number of shapes, but two common ones for the English classroom focus on a task or project or on inquiry or exploration. These provide defined starting points—group goals, organization, and process—for incorporating collaborative learning into your classroom. After we delineate these two group structures, we discuss five essential group features and, finally, common group dynamics.

Task or Project.
In a task or project design, the teacher, alone or in consultation with students, assigns specific work or activities to the members of the group. The group functions like a team or committee, with common goals and individual responsibilities. Group completion of the assigned task depends first on the solitary work of individuals and then on the collaborative work of combining these isolated pieces into a whole. For example, as a prereading activity for John Steinbeck's *The Grapes of Wrath* or Karen Hesse's *Out of the Dust,* a teacher might ask groups to create a collage (visual, recorded, or oral) of the

1930s Depression images that each member gathers. The assignment establishes the structure of individual data gathering and collaborative design and presentation. The steps introduce students to group work and build on a process that many have experienced in student clubs and civic and religious groups.

Inquiry or Exploration.
The inquiry or exploration group is less structured. The teacher gives a group of students a more general goal, a finite amount of time for achieving it, and much flexibility about the process of doing so. Whether students are discussing explicit questions or the most general, they are working together to arrive at the most satisfying conclusions they can. In English classes, this type of group is often used to explore texts, both professional authors' and those of fellow students. In our chapters on language, literature, and writing, we frequently suggest small-group inquiry. One important message in the assignment is that students do not have to depend on their teacher for a response to the material.

The inquiry method of learning asks students to look at the facts of language and life around them in order to frame generalizations. It is grounded in a foundation of questioning. It involves students in the scientific method: raising questions, posing a problem, generating hypotheses, testing those hypotheses, and drawing conclusions. It encourages students to question genuinely, to observe openly, and to explore areas of inquiry confidently. It can initiate lifelong inquiry. Freire (1970, pp. 75–77) reminds us again that students must learn not only to read "the word" but also to read the "world."

Five Group Features.
Just as you select your wardrobe with a consideration of the occasion for which you are dressing, so your choices about group work must fit the learning occasion. Groups, whatever their purpose and design, have five important features that teachers must consider carefully in composing them: size, stability, selection, roles, and self-consciousness.

Size. The sizes of groups should vary to accommodate the task that they are to undertake.

> *Large groups* (five or six students): These groups are appropriate when students work on sizable projects in class over long periods of time.
> *Small groups* (three or four students): These groups are useful when more intimate matters are primary.

Johnson (1990) recommends that no collaborative learning group have more than four students. He observes, in fact, that the great mistake in traditional classrooms is to make groups too big. Book and Galvin (1975) place the ideal group size at five students. Sometimes you need the variety of perspectives that five members afford; at other times students need the security and confidence that a small group of two or three provides.

Stability. English teachers who consistently use groups usually vary their composition. Change vitalizes group interaction and strengthens one group advantage: Students come to know each other more personally. Change also discourages cliques or dysfunctional groups. If the group composition remains constant for a long period of time, however, real depth of personal sharing and communal exploration can develop.

Selection. Placing students in groups can be done by the teacher, the students, or random chance.

- *Teacher assignment:* At times, teachers choose to constitute groups with a range of varying ability levels or cognitive styles or to distribute other variables evenly (such as a mix of male and female students). At other times, homogenous grouping might be desirable. Some teachers knowingly form groups to separate friends or to contain potential troublemakers.
- *Arbitrary assignment:* Random features such as birth month or height can be used to determine groups. (The sense of fate is often more pleasing to students than our decisions or even the students' own preferences.)
- *Self-assignment:* Individual students might privately record their preferred topic or task or even select two other students with whom to work. Another variation of self-assignment is to give individual students time before entering a group to begin or complete individual tasks as an entrance requirement.

Roles. As we have implied, one of the great hazards for students who are inexperienced with groups is aimlessness. Group work can seem indistinguishable from lunch chat. A strategy that encourages active involvement of all members of a group is to assign specific responsibilities to each member. Common roles are that of leader or group facilitator, researcher, recorder, writer, reporter, compromiser, or standard setter. Oran, DeMarrais, and Lewis (2001, pp. 28–29) describe innovative roles for group members of Literature Circles: word keeper, illustrator, historian, geographer, character analyst, questioner. Another assignment of roles is not by talk but by content responsibilities. Each student is responsible for a particular bit of information that is necessary to accomplish the group goal. Whatever the designated role, each has specific duties and responsibilities and should complement each other. Students profit from the opportunity to take on a wide spectrum of functions or offices.

Most groups need a leader or facilitator to keep the group on task, to help it be both cohesive and productive. The designated leader can be teacher-appointed or group-selected. (You can practice a subtle form of leadership designation by putting a set of questions or directions in front of a student whom you hope will take on

that role.) The leader can rotate or remain fixed until the completion of the work. We value democratic leadership and observe that group members are more responsive, involved, and satisfied when they feel that they have influence on group decisions.

Self-Consciousness. Some teachers work deliberately to introduce and orient students to the collaborative skills necessary for group effectiveness: how decisions are made, how typical group roles function, how to move discussion and decision making along, the educational problems and pitfalls of the group process, and the potential advantages of the process. Some teachers feel that this self-consciousness paralyzes groups and compromises their success. Others feel that it makes students more motivated, more directed, and more confident in their work. It helps the group maintain its status as educative and helps prevent it from slipping into chat. It diminishes negative communication behaviors such as being inattentive, rambling from topic, leaving decisions and work to only one or two members, excluding some members, and blaming others. We find that some evaluation of group process is important for student accountability and our planning. If students do not have this metacognitive view of the process, the evaluation itself alerts them. Figure 2–2 is an example of such a form.

Group Dynamics. Even if the classroom climate is well prepared and specific group assignments are well developed, the groups still may not be ready to work productively. In their work with small groups in writing workshops, Brooke, Mirtz, and Evans (1994, pp. 37–38) found predictable challenges for students in those groups: (1) questions of handling "established patterns of interaction (and literacy) they bring with them . . . especially their established ways of managing public and private discourse; (2) the problem of diversity and individual differences, of the fact that other people (in the group, in the class) seem to be operating in ways that make little sense or directly challenge the ways in which they act; and (3) the problem of educational context," how this experience relates to previous school experiences or how it makes sense in this classroom at this moment. They refer to group theorists (Tuckman, 1965; Rothwell, 1992) who claim that all groups must move through stages in which the group members negotiate among themselves how they will function. Even though their task is assigned by someone outside, the group itself must sort out group dynamics. Brooke et al. (1994, p. 51) name three stages of this sorting:

- *Storming:* The storming stage is characterized by clashes of individual agendas, as the group struggles to work out for itself a set of regular procedures and roles for its members.

Team Name _____

Your Name _____

Your Group's Responsibility _____

Directions: Rate your own group work by circling one of the numbers in the scale (from 1 to 5) that best measures your response to the questions stated at the left. Answer Question 10 on a separate sheet.

Criterion	Very Ineffective	Somewhat Ineffective	Not Sure	Somewhat Effective	Very Effective
1. How would you rate the effectiveness of your group?	1	2	3	4	5
2. How effective was the assignment in getting you interested in the subject and in guiding your work?	1	2	3	4	5
3. How effectively did your group work together by the conclusion of your assignment?	1	2	3	4	5
4. How well did all the group members participate?	1	2	3	4	5
5. How well did democracy work in your group? Did the members take equal responsibility for the group's work?	1	2	3	4	5
6. How effective was the group in considering the ideas that you contributed?	1	2	3	4	5
7. How effective was the leader in encouraging everyone to talk and work together?	1	2	3	4	5
8. How effective were you in encouraging others to speak or to become involved?	1	2	3	4	5
9. How effective was the group's attitude toward the work?	1	2	3	4	5
10. What did you learn from this experience? Could you have accomplished the same results in whole-class or individual work?					

FIGURE 2–2   Small-group evaluation form

Norming: The norming stage occurs as the group moves out of storming and into the establishment of standard procedures and roles.

Performing: The performing stage occurs once the norms have been established and the group falls into a pattern of performing according to the procedures and roles it has created.

No schema can represent the idiosyncrasies and complexities of individual group processes, but Brooke et al. advise anticipating these stages as a possible progression.

Five Group Designs.

Implementation of task or inquiry group work includes the following five designs: *jigsaw, fishbowl, think-pair-share, buzz,* and *simulation.*

Jigsaw.   In this strategy the teacher assigns students a task in an original home group (Forrestal, 1990). Once the task is complete in that group, individual discussants move to a different sharing group so that each new group (some-

times called an interchange group) has someone to report the learning achieved in the home groups. The great strength of this process is that each group member is responsible for transmitting the learning of its home group. Figure 2-3 is the jigsaw assignment that teacher Julia Neenan (1992, personal communication) created for tenth graders studying Sophocles' *Antigone.* As you can see, she is explicit about her expectations. She had discovered that students need to be able to give clear and distinct answers to a direct question: "What am I expected to know by the end?" Because a student's peers are held accountable for what the group learns, students must understand and teach well to their second group. Neenan said that her students were so energized that she could have left the room and her absence would never have been noticed. She felt that her students learned in a period and a half what by another strategy would have taken three days.

Fishbowl.   In a fishbowl group, four or five discussants talk together about a specific topic while seated in the

FIGURE 2–3 Neenan's jig-saw questions about *Antigone*

You are responsible for the following from the collaborative learning activity on *Antigone:*

1. You should be able to argue that Antigone is the tragic hero of the play, understanding what tragic hero means according to Aristotle.
2. You should be able to argue that Creon is the tragic hero.
3. You should understand Aristotle's concept of tragedy and be able to apply it to the play and contemporary drama.
4. You should be able to list the five types of conflicts, to define them, and to apply them to the play and other dramas. You should be able to say which is most important in this play.
5. You should be able to identify, understand, and discuss the significance of selected metaphors and mythological references in the play.
6. You should understand the role of Teiresias in the play and be able to explain how the scene in which he appears suggests important facts about the Greek's religious beliefs. You should also be able to explain the symbolism behind some of his specific characteristics—e.g., that he is blind.

center of a ring that is formed by the rest of their class-mates sitting outside the inner circle, listening. Granted, the small-group discussion is public, yet it still shares the qualities of a more private conversation. After the discussants have concluded their talk, the listeners can respond in discussion with the whole class or in small groups. Teacher Jonathan Milner used this strategy often with his average ninth graders who had mixed English language proficiencies. The students within the inner circle liked being on center stage. Their talk became more authentic and directed to classmates, not to the teacher. He reports that the listeners were often bursting to talk and would ply the discussants with questions or rebuttals when time was called. His English As a Second Language (ESL) students liked listening without the worry of their being required to talk.

Think-Pair-Share. The think-pair-share group begins work when the teacher poses a provocative question, perhaps one of Christenbury and Kelly's dense questions. For a limited amount of time determined by the teacher, each student works on an answer to the question, perhaps in writing, perhaps in jotted notes. (You could regard this as a built-in wait time.) At a signal, the teacher ends the think time and asks students to work now with another student to reformulate an answer to the question. The pairs can try out their original answers and deepen them by their collective thoughts. (The teacher might even ask these pairs to regroup with another pair in a foursome.) The final step invites the pairs to present their insights to the entire class, perhaps using a "go-around" or read-around with six or seven pairs reading their responses. The effectiveness of this model for thinking, talking, listening, cooperating, and demonstrating the variety of interpretations and answers depends to a great degree on the quality of the question.

Buzz. A buzz group is focused, student-managed, problem-centered, and time-limited. The name itself suggests the activity of working bees. That is the goal. Often, we name topics and let students quickly gather according to the topic of their choice and spend a designated amount of time sorting out their views before they report back to the whole class. The subjects for these quick discussions are typically immediate and topical. If computers are available with Internet access, so much the better. Teacher Benjamin Milner posts declarative position statements on different walls in his classroom and asks students to move to the statement with which they agree. Some call this "vote with your feet." When all students have chosen a place, the groups so formed (regardless of their size) work out fuller, more persuasive positions to present to the class.

Simulation (Role Playing). We will discuss the use of simulations more fully in later chapters on oral language and literature. Simulation invites students into an imaginative situation in which they construct and enact a role different from their own or solve an imaginary dilemma. Ideally, individuals and the group become immersed in the activity, adopt a personal perspective, and arrive at decisions seriously. Simulations provide powerful oral and dramatic opportunities for solving problems and for applying knowledge.

Literature Circles

One vital form of group work increasingly found in middle and high school English classrooms is reading or literature circles. Literature circles place students far from the teachers' direct instruction yet far from independent work as well. Reading or literature circles were originally designed to organize a whole class into small groups to discuss the same teacher-assigned text and/or to plan a project about it. The teacher assigned individual members to groups (often by reading level or ability), constructed discussion or activity prompts, and evaluated student performance. Often the groups, once constituted, did not change through the school year. Some still use the term generally to mean any small-group, collaborative discussion of literature as distinct from whole-class, teacher-led recitations and discussions. Literature circles are increasingly associated, however, with groups organized quite differently: The groups are often self-selected, and each group reads and discusses a different student-selected text rather than one teacher-selected text. Not only do students choose the book, often from a preselected menu of five or six choices, but they also determine their pace and pursue their own discussion questions. The requirements are simple and straightforward: Write a given number of open-ended individual responses per week (which often become the basis for discussion later) and actively participate in group discussion and work. Students have great autonomy and responsibility. The teacher's role shifts from that of a performer on center stage, where he or she presents, questions, assigns, and evaluates, to that of a facilitator in the wings, where he or she

- models reading as active meaning making
- answers organizational questions and secures access to books
- plans prereading, during-reading, and postreading activities as needed
- observes and validates individual progress
- observes individual and group problems and introduces alternative reading strategies
- interacts with the group (usually as codiscussant, rarely as expert resource)

- sets realistic individual and group goals
- monitors classroom norms of civility and productivity so that students can focus seriously and even passionately on the work before them
- constructs evaluation instruments that match literature circle practice
- evaluates students' developing skills
- evaluates current literature circles and makes decisions about how and what to teach next

Evaluation is multiple; it includes self-evaluation of group work and a teacher evaluation of a few individual responses, of group discussion contributions, and of a whole-group project.

Teachers Cindy Whetstone and Debra Warstler (1997) distribute literature circle guidelines to students as they initiate this activity (Figure 2–4). They sometimes include a list of novels from which their students choose, or they leave choices open. The actual work of the literature circle is suggested by Cindy Whetstone's handout (Figure 2–5). As you can see, much of the initiative for discussion is the personal journal. In fact, Warstler gives her students this hint: "It might be worth your while to take some time and reflect on the discussions in your journal following the times that your circle meets; return to your journal when it's time to write the paper."

FIGURE 2–4 Whetstone's literature circle guidelines

For the next several weeks we are going to be using a Literature Circle concept for the novels we have selected to read. I have designed groups consisting of 4–5 people who will be reading the same novel and sharing responses as they read. Each of you shares a responsibility in making this a rewarding activity. The following guidelines should help you get started:

Literature Circles are based on a "book club" philosophy. You have selected your own novel and are now responsible for deciding the reading/discussion schedule. Examine the calendar dates and divide the book into four sections. As a group, determine how far you will read for the first discussion day, the second, etc. Take into consideration the number of days in between each circle day so that you can all meet your deadlines. Agree that you will only discuss up to the page number you decide on; if you read ahead, be considerate of those who don't.

It is your responsibility to prepare for the discussions. Keep a journal as you read; this will give you something to draw on when you meet with the members of your group. Some suggestions for responses:

1. Short summaries to help you keep the plot line straight
2. Reactions to specific events, characters
3. Dialogue with the characters (talk to them)
4. Projections about future events
5. Connections to your own life—or the "real world"
6. Questions—these can stimulate discussion (What do you think about . . .)

At some point I will be collecting journal entries. This will tell me a great deal about your involvement in this activity.

Take advantage of class reading time. I value having a quiet time and place to be able to read; be sure that you are considerate of your classmates on these days.

My goal in this assignment is to give you an opportunity to read a piece of literature for enjoyment—but slow you down enough to allow for close reading. There's a difference in flying through a good book and truly becoming an involved reader. We're aiming for the latter.

At the end of this activity there will be an in-class writing and an extension project. It will be your choice whether you do a group project or work on an individual basis. Details for this will be given toward the end of our Literature Circle discussions.

Source: From "Literature Circles in One High School Classroom" by Cindy Whetstone, April 11, 1997, presentation at NCTE's spring conference, Charlotte, NC. Reprinted with permission.

FIGURE 2–5 Whetstone's literature circle requirements

LITERATURE CIRCLES:

Will decide how much to read for each discussion.
Fill out form and return to Mrs. Whetstone.
Record schedule in the front of your novel.
If you have not purchased book, have it for Tuesday's class.
Check class calendar for schedule.

RESPONSE:

Have your response journal with you every day that you are reading in class.
Stop and respond as you read, not when you have finished an entire section.
Date each entry and record the page number/chapter.
Concentrate on characters and plot.
Ask questions, make predictions, record quotations that affect you, consider the theme you are exploring, and/or relate happenings to your own experience.

EVALUATION:

You will be evaluated each time there is a literature circle discussion.
There will be a 25 point assessment for each of the 4 literature circles.
The evaluation will include your journal response and your discussion in the group.
It is your responsibility to come to the group prepared. Do not be absent on literature circle discussion days if at all possible.
You will be sitting in chairs for discussions. Bring your novel and your response journal with you.

GETTING STARTED:

Each person should share something from journal.
Include everyone in the group.
There should be no times when the conversation dies if everyone is participating.
A simple read around of journal responses is not a discussion.

Source: From "Literature Circles in One High School Classroom" by Cindy Whetstone, April 11, 1997, presentation at NCTE's spring conference, Charlotte, NC. Reprinted with permission.

Nancy Johnson (1997) suggests other activities that nurture and guide response in small or large groups and "encourage readers to respond other than 'academically.'" We mention three of her ideas.

Silent dialogue: Each student lists one question about the literary selection at the top of a sheet of notebook paper—a question he or she would like to pose during a discussion. While sitting in a circle, every student passes his or her question sheet to the reader on the right, who reads the question silently and then writes a response. After a few minutes, students again pass the question to the readers on their right. Encourage students to read the question and each of the responses prior to writing their response.

Sketch to stretch: After reading the literary selection, each student sketches what the selection means or what he or she made of the reading. Invite readers to experiment with interpretation through design, color, and shape rather than drawing an exact scene. In small groups, each reader shows his or her sketch and others speculate about what the artist is trying to say. After each hypothesized interpretation the artist gets the last word. If there's time, each group can create a group sketch to share with the whole class.

Quaker read: Readers first select a significant passage, line, or phrase from their reading. Then, seated in a circle, giving no explanation or rationale, one student reads his or her passage aloud. In no particular order, another reader adds his or her passage, and on and on. The key is to listen and consider how your passage connects to (or even contrasts with) the passage read. Remind students that lulls, pauses, and repeated passages are okay.

A Final Pitch for Group Work

Day Kennon (1992, personal communication) uses collaborative learning with young disadvantaged mothers so that they can pass a community-college entrance examination. In such a setting, she and three other colleagues might be expected to use a basic skills-and-drills approach; instead, however, they choose collaborative learning. Kennon describes the effect.

Students who feel they are within a community open to sharing ideas really do respond more openly and willingly.... The sharing with their classmates seems to involve and stimulate them to their highest potential for creative thinking.... Students with low self-esteem or those who do not feel their contribution to be important ... are motivated to interact only when they feel secure enough to share in the trial and error process of "talking an idea through." Speaking their thoughts about what they have heard—discussing and debating these with others—helps them consolidate what they learn.

Some of the students, though they may not realize it, become responsible for each other's learning. They spontaneously help each other understand mistakes or fallacies in their thinking. They become motivators to each other.

Clearly, effective group work does not happen accidentally or haphazardly; it develops from a teacher's organization, confidence, and patience and from students' practice. If group work, especially collaborative learning, succeeds, the rewards are significant. McClure (1990, p. 66) concludes that collaborative learning "is the most direct means of initiating [students] into participation in the active shaping of knowledge and meaning for themselves." We believe in this sort of learning—authentic, problem-solving, collaborative—as enumerated in the foundational work of John Dewey (1916). He believed that "A democracy is more than a form of government; it is primarily a mode of associated living, of conjoint communicated experience" (p. 87). As Michael Smith (2001, p. 278) reminds us, it is not enough for teachers to teach democratically in their courses. They must "enact democracy by creating a context where students work together on a common project in which differences are resources."

Invitation to Reflection 2-5

Through group work, other goals are also achieved that are good in themselves and instrumental to learning. Check those that strike you as persuasive reasons for this approach and add others.

1. enhances the motivation to learn
2. cultivates student curiosity and involvement
3. stimulates genuine peer interaction
4. instigates shared problem solving within the whole group
5. reduces the sense of alienation students feel in the chasm between their school life and their "real" life
6. invites students to move beyond their egocentrism and interact with others
7. develops students' confidence in themselves as learners
8. improves their attitude toward the subject at hand
9. gives opportunities for quiet and shy students to participate
10. allows for spontaneous exploratory talk, not rehearsed, self-conscious talk
11. develops a sense of audience and what is appropriate for different audiences
12. develops confidence in presenting to a larger group because of the opportunity to sort out ideas first with a smaller group

Free-write about reasons that group work is not as common in high school English classes as lecture or discussion is.

INDIVIDUAL WORK

An individual approach to learning might conjure images of silent monks at work in solitary cells. In fact, individual work in the high school classroom at its best more closely resembles a newsroom: A journalism class working to produce a biweekly student newspaper offers a recognizable school model for this mode of instruction. Students are working on different tasks as often as they are on the same assignment. Some may work in pairs (covering sports news) or large groups (analyzing an opinion poll), while others may work alone (writing feature articles). Central to this model is the release of students to choose and pursue their own projects and, in doing so, to grow self-reliant and self-confident as independent learners. The teacher sets up the circumstances but then steps off center stage to assume roles as material gatherer, coach, consultant, and rerouter. These roles are active, not passive, however. Individualizing instruction requires great energy and full attention from the teacher to organize and monitor projects or to be fully present for students as they work on short-term independent tasks. Even more than group instruction, individual instruction allows one-on-one moments between teacher and students and openings to focused, personal, authentic conversation. Individual learning opportunities can take many forms, but three are most common: independent study, workshop/conference, and individualized instruction.

Independent Study

Many call independent study the purest form of individualization. It frees students to work on a project that they select, monitor, and complete, all outside the classroom. The age, experience, and ability of students will determine their readiness for such independent work. McNees's (1977, p. 32) study of English independent-study programs identified four important structural elements:

Self-direction: Students are given much freedom in selecting and directing their own English study.

Interrelationship of fields: Students may relate English study to other disciplines.

Flexible scheduling: Students have schedules which allow them time outside the English classroom to conduct independent study.

Freedom of movement: Students are permitted to move from one area to another in the school (school library, English resource center, etc.) and outside of the school (community library, resource center, etc.) to work on particular study projects.

We add three additional elements that we consider to be essential:

Checklists of steps: Students have before them certain steps to be accomplished (detailed or general as the student requires).

Periodic conferences: Students meet at intervals with study groups and/or the teacher. The discussion that takes place during these conferences—a cycle of explanation, reaction, and response—is essential to students' developing ideas. Mentors who are experts in the field of study can also assist students, even arranging "internships" where students learn firsthand from their expertise.

Evaluation: Students report the results of independent study in a variety of ways determined by the nature of their inquiry and their cognitive styles.

Workshop/Conference

The workshop/conference classroom puts students on independent paths for extended periods of time, but the work is classroom-based and group-dependent. In writing workshops such as those proposed by Graves (1983a) and Atwell (1987, 1998), students work alone on their individual writing but collaboratively with peers and teachers on all stages of the composing process. (An initial motive of the writing workshop was to provide a responsive reader/audience for students through every phase of writing, a reader/audience that no one teacher could be for all students.) The size of each reading/responding peer group is small, usually from three to five. Its duration is varied—sometimes for the length of a single project, sometimes for an entire term. Although all of the students are working on personal projects, a basic working structure ties them together. Components of that structure include individual writing; peer group reading/responding; and teacher monitoring, conferencing, and presenting minilessons. Thus, some students may be working at word processors, others at tables in reading or editing groups, and others at desks in short conferences with the teacher. On entering the room, an observer might think that things are in disarray; the configuration and activity resemble those of an editorial room more than a classroom. Yet the structure of the work, the "discipline of the discipline," binds students to purposive and productive activity.

Individualized Instruction

Individualized instruction can take many forms, but essentially it invites students to work independently on a project whose timing, process, and even product they choose. This self-paced work may provide the basic structure of instruction for a class, or it may be supplemental and scheduled primarily for outside-of-class. In the 1970s, individualized instruction (sometimes called programmed instruction) grew in popularity in elementary and secondary schools and even in universities as teachers prepared handouts, publishers wrote and packaged modules, and computer programs took

students step by step through the mastery of a given subject. Students worked on small, sequential tasks; had immediate and corrective feedback (especially in the computer models); mastered a discrete segment of content; and demonstrated their new knowledge on measurable, objective scales. When students had achieved competence in a specific learning task, they moved to the next. Many educators dismiss this form of controlled content and mastery learning, but electronic programs have given it new legitimacy. The preponderance of high school English classes are now organized around whole-class activities, but individualized instruction still has a place in many English classrooms.

Appendix B contains an example of individualized instruction developed by Meiers (1990) for two and three weeks. This plan allows students to work alone on a large-scale but well-structured task. The activity starts with a newspaper article that especially interests students and builds on the interest created with many other genres: poems, cartoons, technical articles, letters, and pieces of personal writing. Meiers provides forms for daily checks of student progress and the criteria for evaluation.

If such individualized learning looks like a holiday for the teacher, it deceives. In fact, this kind of teacher-constructed instruction requires careful attention to individual needs, abilities, and interests; creative instructional activities; meticulous organization and structure; and attentive response to each student. Like independent study and workshops, individualized instruction relies on students' conversations with the teacher and with peers. Like them, too, it addresses individual differences in ability and interests and gives the teacher an opportunity to work closely with individual students. For ESL students especially, it diminishes the anxiety of exposing language deficiencies to their peers and allows teachers to address their language needs individually.

As heterogeneous mixed-track classrooms proliferate (they have been the staple in many poor and rural districts all along), individualized learning offers a strategy for dealing with the diversity and range among students in one class. Different texts can be chosen, and different projects can be undertaken whether students need enrichment or remediation. One of Applebee's findings that disappoints us is that students in nonacademic and mixed tracks are less likely to be asked challenging questions than their college-preparatory counterparts. Another Applebee discovery is that when students are grouped heterogeneously, teachers tend to make few adjustments to those changed circumstances. Individualized instruction provides an approach that lets you guide students toward a deepening understanding of literature and writing from whatever place they start.

All of these formats for individual work encourage student independence with a more self-chosen focus and pace. Some are explicitly structured and short-term; others are open and long-term. Each has potential power for organizing classrooms to meet the varying cognitive styles and abilities, multiple intelligences, and interests of its students and for equipping them to become independent, able, lifelong learners.

☞ LAYERING THE FOUR APPROACHES

These four approaches—lecture, whole-class discussion, group work, and individual work—comprise the usual organizational patterns within an English classroom. William James remarks in his *Principles of Psychology* that habits develop a dynamism of their own. Teachers often adopt approaches to instruction and styles of teaching early in their careers and elaborate on those through the lifetime of their teaching. We believe that the four approaches are most effective if no single one of them is the steady diet of a class. Many variables influence a teacher's choice of approach: student learning styles, class size and duration, class dynamics, subject matter, and teaching objectives. Lois Weiner (1997, p. 79) distilled what she had learned about planning during more than twenty years in high school English classrooms, insights that are crucial for prospective teachers to consider. One of two foundational schemas that she extols is Moffett's division of classroom activities into roughly the same organizational possibilities that we use: whole group, small group, pairs, and solo. Weiner articulates for her students the circumstances that favor the use of each:

> *Whole group:* The same information must be communicated to every member of the class—for example, "instructions for projects" or "discussions of classroom rules."
>
> *Small groups:* "[S]tudents need the maximum interaction they can get, to exchange ideas and clarify their thinking."
>
> *Pairs:* "[P]ractice and drill" profits from a partner; also useful when students share something that is "too personal" to communicate to more than one other person.
>
> *Solo:* Students are involved in tasks of assessment or individual writing or reading for which solitude is preferable. (Writing and reading could, of course, be done in one of the other three arrangements.)

In Weiner's recapitulation of the four basic modes of instruction, she also reminds her prospective teachers of the possibility of instructional variety and cautions them against relying too heavily on any one mode in their teaching.

Teachers need to open themselves to imagining a variety in their classrooms and to layering the four approaches within any one lesson. Our model is fluid and favors the teacher who swims between approaches. Teaching Activities 2–1 and 2–2 are examples of mixing several approaches. The "graphic literature" of *The Far Side* cartoons in Teaching Activity 2–2 offers an easily accessible tool for inquiry and generalization in a lesson that layers multiple instructional approaches. This activity comes just before a whole-class reading of George Orwell's *Animal Farm.* Possible follow-ups might involve learning centers or jigsaw groups that would explore common themes, author biographies, and other graphic and/or printed texts.

Learning Stations

One strategy that builds in multiple approaches falls between group work and individual work: learning stations. The idea of classroom learning centers arose from the world of primary education, where children were drawn to manipulatives because of their intrinsic interest and where educators were interested in the idea of students constructing their own learning, at their own pace, in their own style. This pedagogical structure was transformed into learning stations in middle and secondary classrooms as teachers there learned that the structure of stations makes learning more active and experiential, sometimes more social and collaborative, at other times more personal and reflective. Because secondary school environments are often highly structured, stations provide students with a chance to act with greater personal agency. Learning stations also economically manage scarce materials and equipment (for instance, tape recorders, CD players, computers, and books). Like group and individual work, learning stations promote independence by offering students their choice of subject, approach, and pace. They also allow teachers to have one-on-one time with students.

Physical Layout. Stations can be somewhat permanent classroom fixtures focused, for instance, on reading, writing, listening, talking, drama, art, and/or computers. In such stationary arrangements, a sign or banner typically hangs over the station to mark its boundaries and define its use. More typically, stations are temporary sections of the classroom marked out for work that is focused on a specific text or topic. Such a project might last from a few days to more than a week. All students work concurrently at multiple stations.

Practically, these stations must match the physical constraints of most classrooms. A permanent reading station, for instance, may simply be a revolving paperback rack in a corner. A permanent art station may be a grouping of pictures hung along or up an entire wall, or it could be a four-sided box mobile of pictures hung from the ceiling with a collection of art and graphics books on a desk

2-1 TEACHING ACTIVITY

Exploring Emily Dickinson

Individual Work

■ Read and reflect on four poems by Emily Dickinson.[2] Create three basic axioms about ideas important to and style characteristic of the poet.

1

"Hope" is the thing with feathers—
That perches in the soul—
And sings the tune without the words—
And never stops—at all—

And sweetest—in the Gale—is heard—
And sore must be the storm—
That could abash the little Bird
That kept so many warm—

I've heard it in the chillest land—
And on the strangest Sea—
Yet, never in Extremity,
It asked a crumb—of Me.

2

"Faith" is a fine invention
For Gentlemen who *see*—
But *Microscopes* are prudent
In an Emergency.

3

Immortal is an ample word
When what we need is by
But when it leaves us for a time
'Tis a necessity.

Of Heaven above the firmest proof
We fundamental know
Except for its marauding Hand
It had been Heaven below.

4

I never saw a Moor—
I never saw the Sea—
Yet know I how the Heather looks
And what a Billow be.

I never spoke with God
Nor visited in Heaven—
Yet certain am I of the spot
As if the Checks were given—

Small-Group Work

■ Compare each member's generalizations and decide on three axioms to present to the whole class.

---

underneath. With increased funding for educational technology, computers represent an increasingly predictable classroom station for writing and research. Permanent stations might also demarcate locales for writing (in which there are folders, portfolios, writing materials, dictionaries, thesauruses, grammar handbooks, and helpful Web addresses) and for reading (in which there are folders, books, dust jackets, bookmarks, author pictures, and author biographies). A temporary station for a week-long study of Hispanic American literature may be in boxes in the corner that are hastily resituated on desks between classes of freshmen and junior English. The reality, especially for young teachers, may be even more severe. If you do not have your own permanent classroom, centers may have to be flexible and mobile.

Organization. Organizing multiple stations is a challenge. Decisions regarding the learning activities at each station require a fine calibration that balances the needs

of the students and the subject. Those decisions will be influenced by other strategic variables.

Student choice: The teacher structures the array of stations; but inside that scheme, students elect the order of their work and the stations that interest them most. Typically, students select a designated number of stations and omit the ones that appeal to them least. (Certain key stations can be designated as necessary for everyone to experience.)

Station variety: The teacher, recognizing the diversity of student interest, style, and ability, constructs stations that provide a range of content and learning processes. These stations should be creative and unpredictable. A good benchmark for the development of stations is to have a mixture of the five language arts—speaking, listening, writing, reading, and viewing—and of the learning styles of multiple intelligences.

Whole-Class Work

- Have a "go-round" or read-around with each group contributing.

- Discuss the groups' different insights. Is there common agreement about the four poems' meaning and style?

- Examine a fifth Dickinson poem,

5

Apparently with no surprise
To any happy Flower
The Frost beheads it at its play—
In accidental power—
The blonde Assassin passes on—
The Sun proceeds unmoved
To measure off another Day
For an Approving God.

- Does this poem confirm or refute your generalizations?

Lecture

- Teacher offers a minilecture on Emily Dickinson's biography with emphasis on her religious sensibilities.

Individual Work

- As Emily Dickinson, write a letter to a friend who is experiencing religious doubts because of a recent natural calamity.

[2] Reprinted by permission of the publishers and the Trustees of Amherst College from *The Poems of Emily Dickinson,* Thomas H. Johnson, ed., Cambridge, MA: The Belknap Press of Harvard University Press, Copyright © 1951, 1955, 1979 by the President and fellows of Harvard College.

Interaction: The teacher must decide whether students can choose to work in pairs, in small groups, or individually. Variety can be incorporated with some stations that require partners and others that require individual work.

Once these basic decisions are made, the teacher has to write very clear directions that define the expectations of each station so that students can be self-sufficient and purposive. Whether these instructions are printed on posters or cards, programmed into a computer, or recorded on a video- or audiotape, they must set the students on a specific course of action and explain what students are expected to have accomplished by the end. The kind of evaluation for the stations also needs to be articulated clearly, whether it is self, peer, or teacher evaluation. The teacher must also determine how students will record their progress—through written records, check sheets, or maps—and whether these will be stored in

writing folders or turned in to the teacher. When all of these decisions are made, teachers must assemble the materials (books, magazines, newspapers, paper, pens, folders, technical equipment, and supplies) necessary to implement the stations. Front-end work is painstaking and replete with details and material gathering, but the rewards for students are great. With revision the stations can be basic resources in years to come.

Imagining the physical arrangement of a classroom into stations may be difficult for those who have never experienced them. Secondary classrooms are not commonly arranged with stations, so we have few models to help us envision this as a realistic organizational alternative. Also, stations require ambitious organization and a sturdy tolerance of confusion. In other words, attempts to use this approach to learning may meet with resistances. Therefore, working in conjunction with other teachers is especially helpful. In middle school, especially, and some high schools, stations can be integrated

2–2   TEACHING ACTIVITY

Exploring Graphic Literature

Individual

- Look at a student- or teacher-selected set of six Gary Larson cartoons.
- Jot down notes in answer to the following questions:
  - Does Larson amuse you?
  - Do you think he is making any comment about human beings through his cartoons of animals?
  - Is Larson's attitude toward human beings admiring or critical?
  - Is there any perspective that is repeated in more than one cartoon?
  - Name two human traits that he appears to satirize.

Pairs

- With a partner, examine each other's cartoons.
- Discuss your conclusions about Larson's views of human nature.
- Explore how your conclusions differ or agree.

Small Groups (pairs join another pair)

- Summarize your insights into Larson's cartoons.
- Discuss whether his use of animals is effective for his satiric purpose.
- Prepare to present two major conclusions about which you all agree to the whole class. State these in no more than two sentences.

---

with other subjects, especially social studies. We present concrete and elaborate examples of three sample stations in Appendix B: one textual and two topical.

Invitation to Reflection   2–6

In your second year of teaching, you observe that in your school teachers tend to be either tellers or askers, lecturers or questioners. In your first year you tried a different instructional approach, and you believe it failed. You had set up learning stations during American literature study on the American Dream that required group work. At first, many students, unaccustomed to group responsibility, either asked you for directions or talked discursively with their classmates. Most were willing enough, but unfocused. Your highly motivated students kept rolling their eyes and looking restless; your poorly motivated students seemed not only distracted, but frustrated. By the second day, teachers were beginning to notice a greater noise and movement level in your classroom. On the third day, you noticed that one of your least-motivated students had his head down on the desk, and one of your most conscientious students asked to be excused to see another teacher about a make-up test. On the fourth day, as several students moved aimlessly from station to station, you could not overcome your rising uncertainty and concluded that stations did not work in your classroom. What can you do to preserve your interest in stations (with the promise for collaborative learning and individual responsibility) and your hope for energized and purposeful work? How would you reform your plans?

∞ LEARNING WITH TECHNOLOGY

In his first column as editor of an *English Journal* feature devoted to "Learning with Technology," Trevor Owen (2000, p. 131) writes about integrating computers into his inner-city Toronto secondary school. In the mid-1980s, his interest in technology arose from a concern for his students' writing; however, that entry into the world of technology "would eventually lead me to reframe most of my thinking about learning and teaching." Many recognize that on a national, state, and local level, the integration of computer technology into classrooms during the past several decades has caused a significant educational shift.

Whole-Class Work

- The spokesperson from each group presents the group's conclusion.
- Through whole-class discussion, the class tries to distill all of the group ideas into two or three major conclusions.
- Listen to a reading of several short beast fables from Aesop, La Fontaine, or James Thurber.
- Discuss what the fables have in common with Larson's graphic work.
- If you find a "moral" in these fables and cartoons, would you prefer that the artists simply told you what they believed? Why or why not?

Individual

- Use three minutes to respond to one of four additional Larson cartoons presented on the overhead.
- Reread what you have written and bracket your favorite sentence.

Whole Class

- In a final read-around, read your favorite sentence when the teacher identifies you.

Lecture

- The teacher presents a definition of the concept of satire and/or fable and uses the students' insights as illustration. A few final cartoons (preferably ones that are more recent and timely) illustrate the nature of satire and/or fable and test the students' understanding of these concepts.

Although teachers have been using tools to aid their instruction since the time of the ancient pictographs, the development of electronic technology for educational applications has had relatively sudden and profound consequences. Barely fifteen years ago, in a history of the application of technology to schools since the 1920s, Cuban (1986) emphasized the influence of radio and television. In the decade after Cuban wrote, educators turned hopefully to other technological resources such as educational software for computer-assisted instruction (CAI) and then, around 1994, to the widespread use of the Internet. Remnick (1997, p. 214) has compared the Internet's emergence to "fire . . . more important than the invention of movable type." We cannot now foresee the next stage with certainty, but it is harder to foresee no change at all.

We have written these first two chapters almost as though the presence of technology has had no impact on middle and high school English teaching. In fact, we are convinced that, if carefully positioned and chosen, the ever-evolving hardware, software, and other computer-based systems provide teachers with tools that can significantly enrich their teaching and their students' learning. Consequently, we will scatter suggestions for specific technological resources (the tools) and projects for using

them (the process) in appropriate chapters to come. We present here general background information for technology as a resource for you as teacher and for your students as language and literature learners. Before we address these possibilities, however, please think for a moment about your own expectations for technology in your classroom.

 **Invitation to Reflection** **2-7**

1. Do you use electronic resources in your life as a student? Would you describe yourself as savvy about computers?

2. Do you anticipate using technology as an important tool for you as an English teacher?

3. What would you include as educational technology? Computer applications only? Hardware such as digital video discs (DVDs), digital cameras and camcorders, laserdiscs, handheld computers (personal digital assistants, or PDAs)?

4. Have you seen educational technology—computers, software, or hardware—used effectively in high school

or college English classes? What kinds of tools and processes were available?

5. Do you think of educational technology primarily as a vehicle to enhance your professional life of planning, developing materials, evaluating, and keeping records or as integral to student activity within your classrooms?

6. If the latter, how do you see technology being integrated into English study? (It is easy to see how it would enhance the study of social studies, science, or mathematics.) Does it have a natural place in the study of language or literature?

7. What are the challenges you might face if you want to bring technology into your language and literature classes?

Ten years ago Sheingold (1991, p. 23) identified the challenge you may be facing: "Teachers will have to con-front squarely the difficult problem of creating a school environment that is fundamentally different from the one they themselves experienced." As you will see, that environment has continued to change. We begin our brief overview with the actual presence of computers in United States schools today.

Technology in U.S. Schools

The U.S. Office of Technology Assessment reported a progression in the use of technology in teaching from 1982 to 1994 (as summarized in Table 2–3). More recently, the 2001 *Digest of Education Statistics* reports that in 1999 "the average public school contained 100 computers" and that 95 percent of schools had Internet access (up from 35 percent in 1994). Table 2–4 registers the increase of Internet access in public schools and instructional rooms from 1994 to 1999. Just in the short history of the textbook you now hold, the percentage of Internet ac-

TABLE 2–3 Change in instructional use of computers, 1982–1994

Year	Teachers Were Told To:	Rationale
1982	Teach students to program in BASIC.	It's the language that comes with your computer.
1984	Teach students to program in LOGO.	Teach students to think, not just program.
1986	Teach with integrated drill-and-practice systems.	Individualize instruction and increase test scores.
1988	Teach word processing.	Use computers as tools like adults do.
1990	Teach with curriculum-specific tools (e.g., history databases, science simulators, data probes).	Integrate the computers with the existing curriculum.
1992	Teach multimedia hypertext programming.	Change the curriculum—students learn best by creating products for an audience.
1994	Teach with Internet telecommunications.	Let students be part of the real world.

TABLE 2–4

Percent of all public schools and instructional rooms with Internet access, fall 1994 to fall 1999

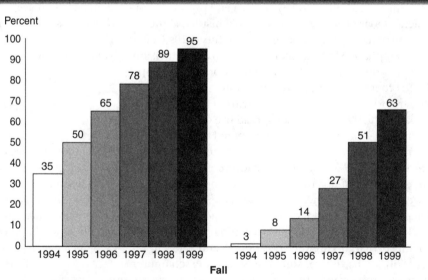

Schools with Internet access   Instructional rooms with Internet access

Source: U.S. Department of Education, National Center for Education Statistics. Fast Response Survey System. *Advanced Telecommunications in U.S Elementary and Secondary Public Schools:* Fall 1996, and *Internet Access in Public Schools and Classrooms: 1994–99.*

cess in classrooms rose from 3 percent (our first edition, 1993) to 63 percent (our second edition, 1999). The *Digest of Education Statistics* notes that "The total computer usage rate of students at school increased from 59 percent in 1993 to 69 percent in 1997." If the usage rate keeps pace with access, the use of computers rises steadily still.

Technology's Impact on Instruction.　Harrington-Lueker (1997, p. 4) has identified a natural progression that has evolved as English teachers grow more experienced with computers.

> *Entry stage:*　Teachers struggle to master the nuts and bolts of using computers.
> *Adoption stage:*　Teachers begin using computer-based activities daily but primarily for drill and practice.
> *Adaptation stage:*　Teachers typically use computers as a way to increase student productivity. For example, students can write better and faster using a word processor than they can by hand.
> *Appropriation stage:*　Teachers abandon their effort to simply computerize traditional practices.
> *Invention stage:*　Teachers begin experimenting with new instructional patterns, such as interdisciplinary and project-based instruction or team teaching.

In our present *invention stage,* new worlds of technology continue to unfold. Some of these offerings are merely bells and whistles—what Roblyer (1990) calls the "glitz factor"—that do not appreciably change or enhance student learning. Others provide something we can find nowhere else and many of these are congruent with constructivist, student-centered learning. Even before the presence of the Internet, Collins (1991, pp. 29–30) observed schools that had begun to use technology and found that computers had caused a significant restructuring of classrooms for teachers and students. This educator identified eight trends that differentiated these schools from traditional schools. Classrooms had shifted

- from whole-class to small-group instruction
- from lecture and recitation to coaching
- from working with better students to working with weaker ones
- toward more engaged students
- from assessment based on test performance to assessment based on products, progress, and effort
- from a competitive to a cooperative social structure
- from all students learning the same things to students learning different things
- from the primacy of verbal thinking to the integration of visual and verbal thinking.

More recently, Roblyer and Edwards (2000, p. 22) have identified two educational trends that are intertwined with trends in the use of technology. The first updates Collins's earlier conclusions.

1. Each of the opposed camps of direct versus constructivist instruction misses opportunities that technology provides to match specific tools and approaches to their educative purposes. The use of technology for "traditional, teacher-delivered" instruction (applications such as CAI) has a more established record because the completion of exercises and the taking of tests are easier to measure. However, technology can also be used for inquiry and speculation.
2. The debate over interdisciplinary versus single-subject instruction has been joined by technology. Although the debate has been waged quite apart from new electronic resources, these resources facilitate links among discrete traditional academic subjects such as English, history, government, and art.

Integrating Technology in the Language Arts Classroom.
With the bombardment of new technologies comes the temptation to start with them and accommodate your teaching goals to the tool rather than to select and integrate the tool into your teaching goals. Because at present so many educational reforms, expectations, and expenditures ride on computer technology, you will need to be deliberate and intentional in your planning in order to resist the belief that computers are an educational panacea. As our social studies education colleague, Raymond Jones, cautions (2002, personal communication), in all subject areas, teachers must carefully choose the tools best suited to their desired learning outcomes, whether technologically based or not. Wiske (1997) has similar advice: "Start Small. Keeping the focus on specific learning needs …is essential" (p. 3). Bjorklund (2000, p. 43) puts it simply: "The most important thing I have learned is that the computer can't drive the curriculum."

In imagining technology in your classroom, you should begin with your students' needs and your instructional objectives. Then you can ask, "Will the use of computer technology enhance what we are doing in the classroom?" As this textbook progresses, we will present our best thinking about language arts goals for students and instructional approaches for reaching them. Technology will be an instrument for achieving them, not a goal of its own. If our textbook has any suasion, you should begin to envision your teaching in terms of a broadening variety of general approaches and specific strategies and, at the same time, develop a sharper sense of what is appropriate to constructivist, student-centered, process beliefs about English education. Figure 2–6 contains a sequence of questions of the sort you would want to address as you plan for the unit or the next day's lesson, evolving only toward the end to the question: Which electronic tools are best suited for my classroom need? Read them now with the confidence that they will grow progressively clearer if read and pondered after each chapter of this book.

FIGURE 2–6 Teacher questions for lesson and unit planning

- What is required at this point in student learning: knowledge, comprehension, application, analysis, synthesis, or evaluation?
- Would my goals be better reached by the students working as a whole class, in small groups, or as individuals?
- Do I want to tap the students' imagination or their logic? Can I structure chances for using multiple intelligences?
- Should I organize instruction that requires students to work collaboratively or independently?
- Am I more concerned with the process of learning or the product?
- Do I want students to undertake a quick, spontaneous project or a more deliberate project that lasts over time?
- Do I want them to move outward to a wider context or focus more narrowly?
- Would a technology-based lesson engage students in a way that is not available with other means?
- Can technology be used to provide students with multiple representations of content?
- Would technology offer inquiry and critical reflection?
- Can I position technology as a forum for dialogue?
- Do I have time to extend the dialogue with students electronically before and/or after class time?
- Will it contribute to or detract from the conversation in the classroom?
- Can technology be used to provide multiple opportunities for students to express their knowledge?
- Can technology be an instrument for evaluation of student progress? Would it provide authentic assessment?
- Is this technology-based plan integral to reading, writing, talking, listening, and viewing; or is it a tack-on?

Three Types of Technology Tools

For the sake of clarity we identify three types of technology tools that offer rich possibilities for teaching and learning: hardware tools, software tools, and Web-based resources. We only hint at their promising classroom applications. We remind you, however, as our mentor on these matters, high school English teacher, now technology professor, Ann Cunningham (2002, personal communication) reminds teachers: Always keep your focus on the *application* of technological tools for educational purposes, not on the tools themselves.

Hardware Tools. We will discuss some of the possibilities of these hardware tools in our media chapter. We list them here to stake their claim on our attention:

- Laser discs (now evolving to DVDs)
- DVDs
- Digital cameras
- Digital camcorders
- PDAs (such as the well-known brand Palm Pilot)

Imagine the following activities made possible by these hardware tools:

- The teacher creates bar codes to select scenes from the DVD Academy Award–winning film *To Kill a Mockingbird* for discussions of character in Harper Lee's *To Kill a Mockingbird*. (As a bonus, this DVD production also includes a video to support the study of civil rights in the United States in addition to interviews with the producer, the director, and the citizens of Lee's hometown, Mon-

roeville, Alabama—the fictionalized Maycomb, Alabama, of the novel.)[3]
- A British production company, Ambrose, is putting all of the BBC productions of Shakespeare on DVD (www.ambrosevideo.com). Teachers and students of British literature can find, isolate, and easily retrieve scenes for the study of one Shakespearean play or several plays.
- Stuart Eagan (2002, personal communication) has acquired Palm Pilots for all of his students; and he communicates electronically during and after class in order to monitor their progress, prompt their discoveries, assign their homework, evaluate their work, nudge them to try again, and listen to their personal inquiries.

Software Tools. We will discuss the following software tools in later language and literature chapters. They open many creative possibilities—from teacher- and student-created PowerPoint and HyperStudio presentations; to the creation of concept maps and outlines with Inspiration; to the publishing of newsletters, class newspapers, or certificates with a desktop publishing program such as Microsoft Publisher. We mention the following general categories with some examples of their specific applications:

- presentation and multimedia authoring (PowerPoint)
- concept mapping/graphic organizers (Inspiration)

---

[3] Bar'N'Coder [Computer software]. (2000). Long Beach, CA: Pioneer New Media Technologies. *To Kill a Mockingbird,* collector's edition [DVD-video]. (1998). Universal City, CA: Universal Studios.

- desktop publishing (Microsoft Publisher)
- CD-ROM (compact disc–read only memory)
- Web editing software

In Appendix B, we include documents developed by Lisa Weaver (Braun, Feaster, Toth, & Weaver, 2001) for a unit on mythology. Employing Inspiration software, she used mapping at every step of her unit design, from the earliest planning phase to creating the semester exam for which a final concept map became the table of contents. With colleagues in her department, she further mapped her course with the courses of others.

In our earlier editions of *Bridging English,* we discussed the opportunities and pitfalls of computer-assisted instruction (CAI). Initially it held exciting promise for educators; but despite its valuable role, it has developed a mixed reputation. It has been used increasingly to bring low-performing students up to a standard. This remedial purpose often locked individual students into isolated, some say mechanized, skills-and-drills practice little different from former paper-and-pen worksheets. At present, integrated management systems (IMS) are replacing former CAI applications. Individual schools, school districts, or states can identify student needs, request software modules with the appropriate skills' instruction, put these on a school- or systemwide network, and with an integrated student management component, keep records of student progress and produce individual and group reports. The correlation between the instruction and standards has greatly increased the appeal of these systems. Similar service systems are becoming available via the Web.

If you have the resources, you will still need to determine for yourself whether the benefits warrant your use of specific software applications in your classroom. At the beginning of the educational technology boom, Dunfey (1989, p. 21) recommended criteria that English teachers should use to evaluate what software works best. The following questions remain pertinent:

- Is the program interesting to you?
- Does the thinking that the program requires seem worthwhile?
- Is the emphasis on thinking rather than on repetitive practice?
- Does the program involve two or more students at a time?
- Does the program introduce an activity or thought that is different from that provided by books or paper and pencil?
- Does the program allow the user to customize material?
- Can the program be used many times by a student and remain interesting and worthwhile?
- Does the program allow time for reflection?
- Does satisfaction in using the program come from the content itself?

Web-Based Resources. Roblyer and Edwards (2000, pp. 10–11) believe that, "As exciting and challenging as they were, the first 30 years of educational computing technology seem mundane compared to what occurred about five years before the new millennium. . . . Teachers joined the ranks of people in all areas of society in recognizing the power of the Internet: ready access to people and information, the ability to send and receive multimedia displays, and an increasingly realistic simulation of 'being there.' Educators who had never before been interested in technology began to envision the possibilities. The *Information Superhighway* became an expressway for education." We present classroom possibilities for using the Internet through teacher-created projects that we organize into small, medium, and large projects. Teachers can also use the Web for basic classroom organization; for instance, they could set up a Web platform on which they put a variety of materials such as a syllabus, assignments, links, and conversations.

Small Projects. The following might require a few minutes or a whole class period and involve individuals or groups:

- "As a lead-in to the *Canterbury Tales,* my seniors visit the Kingdomality site (http://www.kingdomality.com) and fill out a personality questionnaire that tells them what their job would be back in the Middle Ages" (Bjorklund, 2000, p. 45).
- British literature students research the United Kingdom on the Web and then, as Marr (2000, p. 123) suggests, use a desktop publishing program to "create a travel itinerary to the British Isles (or any setting in a novel)."
- Students "[c]ut and paste photos of characters from a *Lord of the Flies* on-line site to Microsoft Word or PowerPoint. [They] use it to supplement a lecture on characterization" (Marr, 2000, p. 123).

Medium Projects. These would take more class time and involve individuals and groups working on teacher set-up materials.

- Blasé (2000, p. 51) formed an academic e-mail link in order to expand the walls of her suburban, middle-class classroom and to help her students with the language of Zora Neale Hurston's *Their Eyes Were Watching God.* Through the Bread Loaf School of English and the National Endowment for the Humanities, Blasé's Cincinnati, Ohio, students began to communicate with a Bread Loaf rhetorician, Dr. Jacqueline Royster, and with classrooms in Vermont, Massachusetts, and Texas. The Cincinnati "hosts" initiated the e-conversations by sending greetings and constructing a Web site that created a cultural context for the 1930s and the novel and proceeded by studying and then responding to the messages of the students and the scholar. Blasé sums up the effects of this approach: "By examining both the literature and their own E-mail messages, students were able to profoundly feel the power of language. My students and I became collaborators, working together to establish the criteria by which they would be expected (and would expect themselves) to construct effective online response."

- Van Wyhe (2000, p. 62) and her students in Copper Center, Alaska, established a Pass the Poetry exchange with a Colorado teacher and students. Daily for ten minutes at the beginning of class, they read and reflect (both in writing and orally) on a poem. Students are responsible for "observing and recording what happens during our discussion time." Separated by 4,000 miles, each week the two classes read a common poem, and the week's researchers compile and post the "ethnographers' comments" on-line. This gives "all of us one more opportunity to compare opinions, interpretations, and ideas." They have even participated in on-line live "chats," with one student typing at the keyboard and the conversation being viewed on an overhead projector.

Large Projects. These can be assigned over a length of time and involve students working independently or in groups. These would have less teacher involvement and more student choice and decision making.

- In their study of the Harlem Renaissance, Claxton and Cooper (2000, p. 101) ask students to create a basic Web page to "look beyond the literature for contextual information (historical, social, cultural)." They read texts from the Harlem Renaissance as a whole class, divide into groups of four to choose a topic that interests them, and begin research in print sources and on selected Web sites (such as the Schomberg Center site entitled "Harlem 1900-1940" at http://www.si.umich.edu). This project provides students with both incentive and "a great venue for showcasing student learning."

These few examples suggest a range of possibilities for the wired English classroom, whether it has one computer or many or must travel to a school computer lab. We will include others in subsequent chapters.

Critical Internet Consumers. Your challenge in using the Internet for your teaching will be to sort out the good from the fair and the excellent from the merely good. James Greenlaw and Jazlin Ebenezer have written a useful guide to help English teachers negotiate the wealth of Web sites with basic information, suggested activities, and selected annotated sites: *English Language Arts and Reading on the Internet: A Resource for K-12 Teachers* (2001). These and other *English*

Journal recommendations targeted for language arts have cleared our students' paths through the World Wide Web.

Increasingly we read and hear stories of high school students who import erroneous fact and opinion into their class discussions and their writing from unsound Web sites. We also hear teacher concerns about student exposure to the commercial advertisements, hate speech, bigotry, and pornography from many search engines and Web sites. So your challenge is to help students separate the reliable from the unreliable, the educative from the distracting and harmful. Some English teachers have used the Internet thicket as a training ground to help students develop the critical skills to sort between acceptable and unacceptable sources. Students and teachers together establish criteria that students then apply as they make judgments of credibility. Kathy Schrock has collected excellent critical evaluation tools for the Web that you can find by going to http://www.discoveryschool.com and following the links to schrockguide.

Our Technology Recommendations. We have wavered between wanting to list technological resources that we and our students have found reliable and helpful and worrying that the information will lose currency and appropriateness. The technological world changes at such a rapid rate that we include specifics in this textbook as provisional, tentative suggestions or starting points from which you can work. We have checked each Web site, search engine, or software mentioned before press; yet we know some will be dated by the time you investigate them.

National Technology Standards for Teachers and Students

From the advent of computers, educators have been concerned that students learn *about* computers, not just *with* computers. Through the 1980s the skills for computer literacy were largely those of computer programming and word processing. In our state of North Carolina, some districts still require "technology literacy" skills, but elsewhere educators have moved away from an explicit set of skills as common to computer literacy.

National and international organizations have arisen as sources of information, discussion, and dissemination about instructional technology. The International Society for Technology in Education (ITSE) has developed technology standards for all K-12 students. The U. S. Department of Education understood that to prepare students to meet these standards they first had to prepare the teachers of these students. Under the Department of Education grant program, Preparing Tomorrow's Teachers to Use Technology (PT3), ITSE collaborated with the National Council for the Accreditation of Teacher Education (NCATE) to create educational technology standards for preservice programs. These two sets of standards articulate the performance indicators for students at specific grade levels, K–12, and the basic knowledge and skills requisite for teachers to use technology effectively in educational settings. If you are unfamiliar with the standards and would like more information, visit the ISTE Web site at www.iste.org. These standards explain what educators believe you and your students need to know about technology, but they also testify to the growing link between technological skills and the skills necessary to live and work in the twenty-first century.

SHAPING INSTRUCTION

Provoking, challenging, and engaging activities are what students remember about good teachers. What students may not know consciously, but do know intuitively, is that a master teacher welds these activities into a thoughtful sequence of instruction that gains power as multiple approaches work together.

We will discuss strategies for shaping these basic organizational patterns into effective learning in a later chapter. In our first two editions we located this present chapter toward the end of the book with the planning chapter. Again our decision of what to present first was difficult because the teaching act is richly complex and entry into the art is commensurately complex. What sequence is best? We decided to front-load these ideas because they provide some shape to your envisioning the students, classrooms, and learning to which we turn. From the beginning we want you to root your ideas about language and literature learning in the actualities of classroom organization. In this book's subsequent Teaching Activities, you will notice that we often structure our suggestions in terms of these four approaches. Just as potters must grow comfortable with the wheel and the clay before their pots can be thrown, so we introduce you to these basic components of instruction before, to borrow from C. Day Lewis, you begin to "fire the irresolute clay" (from "Walking Away").

Invitation to Reflection 2–8

Kagan's (1992) research into teacher cognition and teacher education suggested that the primary story with which teachers, associate and with which they plan their classrooms is their own personal story. Mindful of your unique history, reflect on the following questions.

1. Is it a good strategy to base your ideas of what makes language and literature meaningful to your students on what has made these meaningful to you? If not, how else are you to judge?
2. Sketch an original lesson plan in a thematic unit on "Matters of the Heart" or "No Ordinary Time" that would be effective with students who share the values and learning styles you had in high school. You can choose the grade, but the group is homogeneous.
3. When you are satisfied with your lesson, reframe your plans for students who are different from you.
4. Could the diversity of your students in terms of race, class, gender, ethnicity, language proficiency, track, and age affect what they value and how they learn?
5. Could you imagine using a mixture of these two plans for a class of diverse learners?
6. Can you imagine how their differences can become resources in your study, not impediments to it?

CONCLUSION

When students arrive in your class, they will enter the day's learning through lecture, discussion, group work, or individual work. Within those four approaches, you have many choices open to you. In his introduction to *Tom Jones*, Henry Fielding asks, "Where ... lies the difference between the food of the nobleman and the porter, if both are at dinner on the same ox or calf, but in the seasoning, the dressing, the garnishing, and the setting forth? The one provokes and incites the most languid appetite, and the other turns and palls that which is the sharpest and keenest." Fielding appears to believe that the subject is not as important as its presentation, which might be said for teaching as well. Our presentation makes much of the difference.

Centering on Language

The proper study of mankind is man, and there is nothing so basic to our humanity as our language.

James Sledd

Linguist S. I. Hayakawa has speculated that if fish were to examine their lives scientifically, the last subject they would study is water. He maintains that we have come just as belatedly to the study of language. Like water to the fish, language so surrounds and encompasses us that we hardly recognize it as a field for study. We fail to realize that our language habits are at the heart of how we experience our world. Language does more than reflect a world view for its user; it creates that view. It is the primary means by which we apprehend the world and the world apprehends us. Teachers and critics believe that our numbness to the importance of language is intensified by the constant bombardment of our "language-polluted and language-deadened environment" (Nelson, 1991, p. 17). In *House Made of Dawn,* N. Scott Momaday (1966) describes the destruction of the "magic of language" and its reduction to a "commodity." He believes that the dominant culture is "sated and insensitive" to language because "on every side ...there are words by the millions, an unending succession of pamphlets and papers, letters and books, bills and bulletins, commentaries and conversations."

Reflection on language is basic to our field of English. English educator George Henry (1986, p. 16) asked, "What is the nature of English education?" and answered that "the supreme art" of English instruction is "helping the self gain control of this peculiar medium called language."

The following questions will initiate our deliberations about language and language instruction:

1. Are you interested in language because of its ability to help you speak and write better or because you enjoy words, their sound and sense? Do you find more pleasure in written or spoken language?

2. How do you respond to variations from Standard English? Do you think of some forms of English as more socially prestigious than others? Do any forms stigmatize those who speak them?

3. Have you ever noticed and thought about a child's acquisition of language? Do you regard language as learned or inherited?

4. When you think of teaching language in an English class, do you think primarily of teaching English language users to improve their usage? Would you teach language differently if you had a number of non-native English speakers?

5. When you think of teaching language in an English class, do you think primarily of teaching grammar? Do you feel confident in your command of grammatical rules? Have you learned those rules indirectly through the experience of writing and speaking or directly through the learning and practice of those rules? Do they help you in your speaking and writing?

6. Is the study of language important to the study of literature? Is its primary importance to ensure that readers understand what a text literally says? Does it change or enrich that understanding?

7. Do you imagine teaching language not for practical applications but to awaken students to a delight in its structure and meaning?

Many middle and secondary English teachers confine the study of language to the study of rules of usage—remedial action against student errors of speech and writing. Many school critics pinpoint the failure of student performance on local and state writing tests to students' failure to understand grammar. The "back to the basics!" cry that arose in the 1970s, a time of societal shifts and skepticism about many public institutions, continues to be heard three decades later. English teachers are often reminded that student language needs to be standardized, homogenized, and corrected. Because the public so often assumes that the path to good writing and speaking is paved with rules of grammar, punctuation, and correct usage, the idea of language instruction is often synonymous with teaching grammar.

As an English teacher, you will be called upon to articulate your position on the teaching of grammar and to do so, you need a deepening understanding of the issues surrounding this instruction. Before we turn to those is-

sues, however, we invite you first to look at language from a more primary angle. Just as we must first *engage* students in their response to literature before we ask them to *analyze* it—to *care* about a poem, say, before they *study* its formal dimensions—so also with language study. We invite you to think about and play with the phenomenon of language before we ask you to consider the teaching of its structure. We recommend this sequence for engaging students in language learning as well. You will be building what Shirley Brice Heath (1987, p. 105) challenges language arts teachers to create: "a literate community learning together." "The search for understanding language is one in which teacher and students join as experts—all can use language, and yet all also join as novices in the exploration of ways to understand what it is" (p. 96). You will be entering Moffett's universe of discourse at its base.

AWAKENING AND BROADENING LANGUAGE CONSCIOUSNESS

Language consciousness raising is neither in the tradition of literary language study nor in the tradition of grammar, rhetoric, and composition. Not surprisingly, when students are taught language as literary analysis of others' linguistic virtuosity or as grammar drills, they often regard language study as a dull and passive chore. We would like to redirect their study and their perception of language. Our aim is not to make them linguists or literary stylists. British primary school education and children's book writer Neil Griffiths (2000) asks, "How does a child learn to read? Where does the journey begin?" He puzzles over two common answers: "with a stampede into phonics? with a scramble for grammar and punctuation?" He answers with a resounding "NO!" He invites the young into reading by setting up strategies so that the child has interest, motivation, a positive attitude, and a desire.

This section aims to interest and motivate you and, in turn, your students to view language study positively and to inquire about it further. To borrow from Robert MacNeil's (1989) account of his own childhood, we want to make you and students "wordstruck."

In his *36 Children,* Herbert Kohl (1967), a sixth-grade teacher in Harlem, presents a compelling testimonial to the potential of language consciousness. One day in the midst of Kohl's frustration at not getting through to his class, one student shouted to another, "What's the matter, psyches, going to pieces again?" (p. 23). While the class broke up, Kohl leapt on the word *psyches,* wrote the word on the board, and told them the story of Psyche and Cupid. Not satisfied with the story, they wanted to know what had happened to the history of the word. Not knowing the etymology and probably not willing to lose their interest, he asked them to think of all the English words that came from *Cupid* and *Psyche.*

> Leaping ahead, Alvin shouted, "You mean words change? People didn't always speak this way? Then how come the reader says there's a right way to talk and a wrong way?"
>
> "There's a right way now, and that only means that's how most people would like to talk now, and how people write now."
>
> Charles jumped out of his desk and spoke for the first time during the year.
>
> "You mean one day the way we talk—you know, with words like *cool* and *dig* and *sound*—may be all right?"
>
> "Uh huh. Language is alive, it's always changing, only sometimes it changes so slowly that we can't tell." . . .
>
> "Mr. Kohl, can't we study the language we're talking about instead of spelling and grammar? They won't be any good when language changes anyway." (p. 24)

Kohl reports that on that day he began what he called in his plan book "vocabulary" and "an enrichment activity" but what was actually "the study of language and myth, of the origins and histories of words, of their changing uses and functions in human life." His was not a continuous lesson but "a fixed point in each week's work," a point that sustained and deepened his students' original excitement as they became "word-hungry and concept-hungry" (p. 25).

Language Inquiry in the Classroom

We invite you into such fixed points of language inquiry through the concrete instructional ideas of two figures, selected Web resources, and, finally, four teaching activities. We hope that your imagining particular language lessons will demonstrate their "awakening potential" better than any telling could. These suggestions progress from general language queries (Figure 3–1), to a teacher's more articulated language lessons (Figure 3–2), and then to highly specific Teaching Activities (3–1, 3–2, 3–3, 3–4).

Figure 3–1 names language phenomena that might be developed to provide a quick class-ending bit of word play, a clincher for a class on editing, an examination of style in a novel or connotations in a poem, or an extended language lesson. You will need to supply the context and enlarge and sequence the activities for classroom use.

A teacher, R. Whitworth (1991), suggests a group of excellent classroom-tested language activities based on the text and spirit of S. I. Hayakawa's 1978 classic *Language in Thought and Action.* Figure 3–2 lists these activities, which he arranges in progressive steps for students, from those requiring "low language skills" to those requiring "complex language talents," and then divides them into the four traditional areas of general semantics (pp. 50–54). Although his suggestions are specific, Whitworth encourages teachers to allow students to "tinker with instructions" so that they can both envision more "fruitful ideas" and feel the pride and ownership in doing so.

Other promising sources of ideas that promote word play for K–12 students are two Web pages that contain links to other sites with ideas, activities, lexicons, even articles. Word Play (www.wolinskyweb.com) has more than 150 links.

FIGURE 3–1
Language phenomena

Frozen clusters	What governs the order of common clusters such as *pell-mell, ding-dong, helter-skelter,* and *willy-nilly?* Can you name other pairs?
Etymology	What are the word origins of common surnames, occupations, colors, animals, and natural phenomena? What are some common words that were originally proper nouns—for instance, *platonic, china,* and *quixotic?*
Idioms	Listen to the idioms of everyday life. List common expressions. Do they group themselves by region, age, socioeconomic status, or educational level?
Place names	Gather interesting place names in this country, and classify their origins. National history? Local history? Ancient history? Mythology? The Bible? Are any colorful and descriptive (Social Circle, Georgia)? A reflection of ideas (Providence, Rhode Island)?
Shortenings	Consider the origins of words that are shortened forms of longer words—for example, *ad, curio* (curiosity), *fan* (fanatic), *hood,* and *mike.* Consider why words are seldom lengthened.
Euphemisms	Recall euphemisms for human experiences, character types, occupations, and even profanity. List the words, for instance, that sportswriters use for *defeat.* Why do we use euphemisms? In what circumstances are they helpful? Harmful?
Language change	From 1914 to 1941, Monica Baldwin lived in a secluded convent. When she emerged, she found astonishing changes and had difficulty understanding much of the new vocabulary. She describes her experiences in *I Leap over the Wall* (London: Hamish Hamilton, 1949). Imagine that you, like Monica Baldwin or Rip Van Winkle, were absent or fell asleep for decades (in, say, 1960, 1970, or even 1980) and awoke today. What language changes might you find? What changes might you find if you awoke in 2050?

FIGURE 3–2

Whitworth's tested language activities

Source: From R. Whitworth (1991), A book for all occasions: Activities for teaching general semantics. *English Journal, 80* (2), 50–54. Reprinted with permission.

LANGUAGE AS A SYMBOLIC PROCESS

- Browse through Henry Dreyfuss's *Symbol Sourcebook: An Authoritative Guide to International Graphic Symbols* (1984). Discuss some of the unusual symbols such as hobo symbols, recreational signs, or semaphore signals. Or have students collect sporting symbols . . . and then have them create their own symbols for places and events around the school. (p. 51)
- Describe the body language of a person engaged in a telephone conversation that you cannot hear. Speculate on the gist of the content. What kinds of human behavior are displayed? Or tape a segment of a soap opera or sitcom. With the sound turned off, have students "read" the body language; then replay the tape with the sound on to verify student guesses. (p. 51)

MEANING OF WORDS IN CONTEXT

- Write a definition of *restaurant, theater,* or *cabin.* Compare the definitions to discover which attributes the group agrees upon and which are derived from personal experiences and biases. (p. 52)
- Research quotes from reviewers for inaccuracies and intentionally misleading statements in movie ads or on the flip side of paperbacks, especially those highly praised ones with suspicious omissions by use of ellipses. For example, one newspaper movie ad reviewer's quote—"Magnificent! . . . Made me cry!"—sounds like a winner, but the reviewer really wrote: "How can a director turn such a magnificent novel into such a stinker of a movie? What they've done to it almost made me cry!" Once students get the idea, have them find really rotten reviews and turn them into positive statements with the use of ellipses. (p. 52)
- Tape class discussions or alert students to note situations where the meaning of the words comes not through direct context but indirectly through "reading between the lines" of the context. Examples: "I know this sounds stupid, but . . ." or "This is just off the top of my head . . ." The intent of these disclaimers is often to soften criticism if it should occur. How many of the following nonquestion questions have occurred in your classrooms: "Are we doing anything in here today?" "Is this movie any good?" "Is there extra credit in this class?" "Isn't this grammar stuff stupid?" Why are such nonquestions raised in class? (p. 52)

REFERENTIAL (INFORMATIVE/FACTUAL) AND EMOTIVE LANGUAGE

- After a basketball game with a rival town's team, compare the local newspaper's write-up of the game with that of the newspaper from the rival town. What language variations are found in the two stories? (p. 53)
- Create a computer database of euphemisms and circumlocutions found in television commercials or political campaigns. Divide the entries into softeners, those which remove the harsh edge of reality, and impressers, fancy words for ordinary facts. Or use William Lutz's (1989) categories: euphemism, jargon, gobbledygook, and inflated language. (p. 53)
- Play the old Bertrand Russell game of Conjugating the Irregular Verb (e.g., "I am fastidious; you are fussy; he is an old fuddy-duddy" or the reverse: "He is broke; you are in debt; I am temporarily overextended") to show that although the basic meaning of the pivotal word remains the same, the value judgment changes. Bias often creeps into the language by our being very selective of words. The thesaurus often helps students to play the game effectively. (p. 53)

RELATIONSHIPS BETWEEN LANGUAGE AND THINKING (ANALYZING, SYNTHESIZING, INFERRING, AND EVALUATING)

- Collect contradictory folk proverbs (such as "Two heads are better than one" and "Too many cooks spoil the broth" or "He who hesitates is lost" and "Look before you leap"). Can the contradictions be reconciled? (p. 53)
- Using the tabloids, present a series of articles that seemingly prove a generalization (e.g., children of movie stars are wild; the rich and powerful are really miserable). Show how the generalization may be faulty. (p. 53)

Here are just two sample sites:

- AmeriSpeak is a repository of expressions used by our ancestors, catalogued by theme, such as "Advice & Life Lessons," "Character Traits," "Emotions," and "Statements & Exclamations."
- Malapropisms is a repository of malaprops beginning with those of the original, playwright Richard Sheridan's character Miss Malaprop—"She's as headstrong as an allegory on the banks of the Nile"—and ranging to more recent ones: "He's a legend in his own mind" and "We must try to emerge our viewpoints."

Wordly Wise Wordgames (www.hoadworks.com) also posts multiple links. Consider, for instance, a site we found there, William Safire's list of thirty "Never-Say-Neverisms" (www.mapping.com). Imagine a lesson on editing in which students work on the following advice from Safire, who has written numerous books and editorials on writing:

- Do not put statements in the negative form.
- Proofread carefully to see if you any words out.
- Avoid trendy locutions that sound flaky.

3-1 TEACHING ACTIVITY

Clichimiles

Individual

1. See how many of the similes you can complete using the common clichés of our culture. Ask five students and five nonstudents to complete these similes. (Try to question subjects of different ages.) Answer the questions that follow in light of your own and others' responses.

quick as a _____	crazy as a _____	dead as a _____
free as a _____	wild as a _____	late as a _____
sharp as a _____	fat as a _____	flat as a _____
happy as a _____	sly as a _____	slow as a _____

Small Group

1. Discuss:
   * What does the name for these bits of language—*clichimiles*—suggest about their character?
   * Why might these similes have frozen into clusters?
   * Does each of the ten phrases have a correct answer?
   * Which of the ten seems most solidified, or certain? Why?
   * Which is least solidified? Why?
   * What kind of society gave birth to these clusters?
   * In what sense have these clusters resisted change?
   * How have they been overcome by change?

2. Determine what central insight you gained from this exercise.

Whole Class

1. Chart the results of your individual and small-group data gathering on a computer or on paper.

2. Use the results to answer this question: What does our data tell us about language change and stability?

---

* A writer must not shift your point of view.
* Never use a long word when a diminutive one will do.

Teaching Activities 3-1, 3-2, 3-3, and 3-4 engage students in multiple dimensions of language, from etymology, dialect, idiom, and syntax to semantic context. The Internet site Word Play opens with an appropriate epigram from a surprising source, entertainer Eddie Cantor: "Words fascinate me. They always have. For me, browsing in a dictionary is like being turned loose in a bank." We hope lessons such as the following might bring language alive for students, acquaint them with its riches, and make them want to be turned loose in words.

Doublespeak

The concept of doublespeak possesses a natural interest for many students who have an instinct for political and social critique and delight in a vocabulary for articulating their insights. These ideas also provide an excellent example of the power of language in our lives. Kehl and Livingston (1999, p. 77) call doublespeak "an insidious practice whereby the powerful abuse language to deceive and manipulate for the purpose of controlling public behavior—the public as consumer, as voter, as student—by depriving us of our right to make informed choices." In 1949 George Orwell published the novel *1984,* in which he described "Newspeak," a manipulation of language that sanitized any thoughts that opposed the principles espoused by the government. Between 1972 and 1975, NCTE honored the ideas of Orwell with a series of initiatives that continue to alert us to the "pernicious social or political consequences" of our misuse of language:

1972: NCTE passed two resolutions decrying the misuse of language in public discourse and its effect on public policy.
1974: NCTE established the Committee on Public Doublespeak to enforce those resolutions actively.
1974: The committee began to publish a newsletter, now called the *Quarterly Review of Doublespeak,* which lists examples of doublespeak from government, business, medicine, and academia.

3–2 TEACHING ACTIVITY

Dialects on TV and in Film

Perera (1990) has reported that the surest way to gain a consciousness of a standard language is to inundate a classroom with examples of variants. It makes sense that one clarifies and more fully defines the other. When you hear TV Cajun chef Justin Wilson say that he likes the red wine because "it look more pretty" or explain "that is what I'm going to did," you are aware of a difference in the vocabulary, grammar, and pronunciation from Standard American English. The hearer might even recognize a Louisiana dialect used by French-speaking immigrants from Acadia (an early name for Nova Scotia). We recommend the following activity to raise the consciousness of variety in expression from one regional, national, ethnic, or social group to another and to diminish the stigma attached to any one variant (in this case, dialects) examined alone.

Individual

1. Select three characters from television or film whose speech is a clear departure from that of the mainstream characters who dominate sitcoms, soap operas, and drama.

2. Tape or transcribe examples of departure (at least one each).

Small Group

1. Read each other's samples aloud. Note any language samples that are similar or the same.

2. Discuss the group members' samples:
   - Are any expressions unfamiliar to you?
   - Which expressions have you heard in the everyday talk around you?
   - Do you regard any as archaic? Quaint? Stigmatizing? Stereotyping?
   - In your group's examples, what dialects are represented?

3. Choose your favorite examples to share with the whole class.

Whole Class

1. Have each group leader read his or her group's favorite examples.

2. Discuss the groups' samples as a whole set.
   - Does the language variant help to define and enliven the characters?
   - Does dialect make the character more or less appealing?
   - If you could substitute your speech for one of these dialects, which would you choose? Why?
   - Does the class as a whole favor one dialect over another? Why?

Individual

1. Free-write from the following prompt: "In examining different dialects, I have discovered . . ."

3–3 TEACHING ACTIVITY

New Words on the Street (or Slang)

The language of the adolescent experience provides a dynamic example of language change and rich possibilities for language investigation. Each generation coins words and idioms to secure its own separate identity and to differentiate itself from the adult world. Some have called adolescents the chief creators of slang in the culture. Semantic comparisons through time (with generations above or below them) or by community (with their own or other high schools or their own or other groups within their high school) can engage students in the shifting connotations of the vocabulary of their language. (Our own students learned, for example, that in one local high school "kicked to the curb" means to humiliate or put another person down; in another high school, ten miles away, the equivalent term is "wasted.")

3–3
continued

TEACHING ACTIVITY

Individual or Small Group

1. Identify words or expressions used by your peers that appear to be unique to a specific activity (used in your school, your grade level, your group of friends).
2. Ask others in locales or generations different from yours how they would refer to the same activity.
3. Compare the expressions of your own speech community with those of other communities or of years past.

Small Group

1. List all original expressions and variants that group members have collected.
2. As you consider your new expressions, do you find any that are especially appealing? Any that you would like to use? Why?

Whole Class

1. Share the group findings.
2. Create a lexicon of these expressions.
3. Submit them to your student newspaper for publication.
4. Create a survey form and collect and analyze a wider sample of verbal expressions.

3–4

TEACHING ACTIVITY

Semantics of Sex or Genderlects

Sociolinguists such as Deborah Tannen analyze everyday conversation and identify profoundly different ways in which men and women communicate. Tannen (1990) has written about one source of miscommunication between the sexes.

> If women speak and hear a language of connection and intimacy, while men speak and hear a language of status and independence, then communication between men and women can be like cross-cultural communication, prey to a clash of conversational styles. Instead of different dialects, it has been said they speak different genderlects. (p. 42)

Individual or Small Group

1. With their permission, tape conversations at lunch tables or at any other public place where people are talking freely. Record radio talk shows or television interviews. Fictional characters from print or film provide excellent subjects. For instance, a comparison might begin with a look at the sentences of John and Lorraine, who alternate as narrators in Zindel's *The Pigman,* or those of Harry and Sally in the film *When Harry Met Sally.*

2. Reflect:
   - Do you hear differences in the language of males and females?
   - Do these differences match your discoveries about the language around you? Note the most pronounced and the most congruent.
   - Are the differences in vocabulary? Subject matter? Volume? Tone?
   - Does one group seem to claim superior control over the conversation?
   - Do you hear different genderlects?

3. Discuss:[1]
   - Share Deborah Tannen's (1990) insights which follow.
   - Do these insights ring true? If so, find examples from your research or experience. If not, state your objections or your counterpositions to these generalizations.

   ° Women are believed to talk too much. Throughout history, women have been punished for talking too much or in the wrong way. Yet study after study finds that it is men who talk more—at meetings, in mixed group discussions, and in classrooms. (p. 75)

1974:   The committee began to award an annual Doublespeak Award for persons or groups who use public language that is "deceptive, evasive, euphemistic, confusing, or self-contradictory."

1975:   The committee established the Orwell Award for Distinguished Contribution to Honesty and Clarity in Public Language.

The committee undertakes other projects as well: a speakers' bureau; sponsorship of books in the field; and presentation of panel discussions, seminars, and workshops. Originally they also intended to initiate classroom instruction that would prepare students to confront and resist doublespeak in their lives. Kehl and Livingston, members of the NCTE Committee on Doublespeak, worry that the last goal remains unfulfilled. They recommend that teachers of English at every level should subscribe to "a linguistic equivalent of the Hippocratic Oath, an Orwellian Oath perhaps, whereby we commit to (1) use language clearly and responsibly ourselves; (2) combat doublespeak wherever we find it; and (3) seek effective pedagogical ways of making students sensitive to language and aware of linguistic vulnerability in all forms" (p. 77).

Before students can readily join in inquiry and data gathering, they must become sensitized to common forms of doublespeak. Figure 3–3 presents four of the most frequently read and heard forms. Examples of these and others, such as obfuscation and oversimplification, surround us—words, phrases, slogans, and sentences from advertising, the public media, and our private lives. The NCTE newsletter is a gold mine of detail. A few suggestions for class projects follow:

- Students in small or large groups compare samples they have gathered and analyze how they manipulate language to conceal or distort. Individuals examine which forms of doublespeak they most often encounter.

- Bonding through troubles is common among women . . . far less common between men. (p. 100)
- Women match troubles. Men mistake the ritual [feminine] lament [as] a request for advice. (p. 102)
- One situation that frustrates women is a conversation that has mysteriously turned into a lecture. (p. 125)
- Men, who do not typically encourage quieter members to speak up, assume that anyone who has something to say will volunteer it. (p. 145)
- The class clown, according to teachers, is nearly always a boy. (p. 91)
- Women's stories tend to be about community, while men's stories tend to be about contest. (p. 177)
- To most women, conflict is a threat to connection, [something] to be avoided at all costs. To many men, conflict is the necessary means by which status is negotiated, so it is . . . accepted . . . may even be sought, embraced, enjoyed. (p. 150)
- Nothing is more disappointing in a close relationship than being accused of bad intentions when you know your intentions are good. (p. 215)

Individual or Group

1. English is free of gender when compared with other languages such as French and Spanish that have masculine or feminine articles and endings assigned to words. Gather examples of gender indicators now in question, such as the suffixes -ess and -ette, and the gender-specific vocabularies they create (i.e., actor, actress, waiter, waitress, host, hostess).

2. Discuss:
   - Where are these distinctions changing? Where are they appropriate and necessary? Where are they offensive and pejorative?
   - What do you think should happen to gendered words in English? At some restaurants in big cities, waiters and waitresses are called "waitrons." Should all nouns and pronouns become neutral or common (neither masculine nor feminine)?
   - What do you think should happen to pronoun references in English, such as the use of *he* to refer to a generic person?
   - Some people have advocated for the use of *thou* instead of *he* to refer to a generic person. Do you agree? Why?

[1] Armstrong (1996, pp. 15–16) discusses how she used Tannen's insights to fathom her own miscommunication with a male student and then to lead a class discussion about different male/female styles of communication.

FIGURE 3–3
Doublespeak

Euphemisms	Words or phrases that soften unpleasant realities can be used to mislead or deceive, as when the phrase "unlawful or arbitrary deprivation of life" is substituted for "killing."
Jargon	The specialized language of members of a profession becomes doublespeak when used in addressing (and in fact, confusing) nonmembers. In its annual report to stockholders, an airline explained a $3 million loss due to a plane crash as "the involuntary conversion of a 727."
Bureaucratese	A sheer volume of words or complicated syntax can be used to overwhelm audiences. One bureaucrat, testifying before a Senate committee, stated, "It is a tricky problem to find the particular calibration in timing that would be appropriate to stem the acceleration in risk premiums created by falling incomes without prematurely absorbing the decline in the inflation-generated premiums."
Inflated language	This language makes the ordinary seem extraordinary, as when car mechanics are called "automotive internists" or electronics companies describe black-and-white television sets as units with "non-multicolor capability" (adapted from Dorney, 1988, p. 50).

- Students examine their own vulnerability or resilience to the effects of doublespeak. How do they react, for instance, to being told there was "a negative gain in measured academic achievement" in their school? Would their reactions be different if the announcement read, "There has been a drop in test scores"?
- Students examine their own writing for language that obscures; for abstract words when concrete words would clarify; and for euphemism, jargon, and inflated language.
- Students present their own Doublespeak Award to real or fictional persons. Remember Huck's struggle over Pap's explanation that he is "lifting" or "borrowing" watermelons, acts the Widow Douglas considers "but a soft name for stealing."

Humpty Dumpty rightly suggested the stakes in the use of language: power. In *Through the Looking Glass,* Lewis Carroll wrote:

"When I use a word," Humpty Dumpty said, in a rather scornful tone, "it means just what I choose it to mean—neither more nor less."

"The question is," said Alice, "whether you can make words mean so many different things."

"The question is," said Humpty Dumpty, "which is to be master—that's all."

Recognizing word manipulation will feel and be empowering to students. They may come to recognize the truth of C. J. Ducasse's observation "To speak of 'mere words' is much like speaking of 'mere dynamite.'"

In the hope that envisioning such classroom activities has stirred your curiosity and delight in words and the way in which they work, as well as your conviction in their power, we turn to two additional perspectives on language: (1) the story of the English language and (2) the study of language. We will remind you often in the course of this book that there is some knowledge you will need to possess but not necessarily to convey directly to your students. An understanding of the evolution of the English language might be such knowledge. It will resist an easy extrapolation to practice, but we believe it is integral to your consideration of that basic question facing our discipline: Why, how, and how much grammar should we teach? (We also, frankly, consider the subject of language to be fascinating in and of itself.) When you have finished this section, we hope that you and, in turn, your students might feel the affirmation and challenge in Ralph Waldo Emerson's words: "Language is a city, to the building of which every human being brought a stone."

THE STORY OF THE ENGLISH LANGUAGE

When we stop to consider the dawn of oral and then written language, our imaginations must stretch back toward those early human beings who used no speech; then toward those later people who developed utterance and painted signs to capture their history for their descendants; and then to those who made the early creative and cooperative attempts to develop vocabulary with which to name, syntax with which to communicate, and alphabets with which to write words. Our first hints of these efforts at language were found in caves that date from about 30,000 years ago; however, the story of the English language begins much later. Many date its beginnings only within the past 1,500 years and recognize it as a great amalgam of many languages mixed by successive waves of invasion and settlement of the British Isles. T. S. Eliot once remarked that English is the best language for a poet because it contains, for the poet's choice, the rhythms of many languages.

Although all languages stem from similar needs and purposes, they achieve their goals in a variety of ways. Apparently, no feature of grammar or syntax is necessary or universal. Some languages function satisfactorily with no fixed markers of syntax, while others operate within amazingly complex rules. Some languages manage without vocabulary that English speakers regard as indispensable. Bryson (1990, p. 35) notes, for instance, that "the Romans had no word for *gray*" and "Irish Gaelic possesses no equivalent of *yes* or *no.*" The number of languages in the world today is usually placed at about 2,700. New languages continue to be born, usually as combinations of two or more languages, as others dwindle and vanish. The last native speaker of Cornish, for instance, died two hundred years ago.

Even a brief history of the English language reflects rhythms of change and stability. The language originated in a historical migration, adapted continuously to other cultural upheavals, and consolidated only recently into its present shape. It began as a collection of Germanic dialects brought from the European continent to the British Isles by tribes who had no written language and consequently left no record. Scholars have painstakingly worked through linguistic comparisons to reconstruct its distinct origins and to verify that English, a relatively young language, is a member of a large Indo-European language family whose descendants once covered much of the globe. Its development was, of course, continuous; but linguists usually divide its history into three periods: Old English (A.D. 450–1066), Middle English (1066–1500), and Modern English (1500–present). Appendix C has a brief overview of those three periods. Here we describe a fourth historical category, American English (1620–present).

American English: 1620–Present

English became established as the dominant language in the United States only within the past three hundred years. The proclamations of the Continental Congress were printed in English, German, and French. Even when English had clearly gained preeminence in the United States, people as eminent as Thomas Jefferson, Noah Webster, and H. L. Mencken expected American English to evolve into a separate language from British English. Not until 1981, though, did a linguist and California senator, S. I. Hayakawa, make the first proposal for an amendment to the Constitution declaring English to be the official language. At about the same time (1983), a pressure group called U.S. English formed to lobby state by state for recognition of English as the sole official language of the United States. The English-only movement continues to keep the issue alive and to embody the belief expressed by Hayakawa (1987, p. 37) that "a very real move is afoot to split the U.S. into a bilingual and bicultural society." Not accidentally, perhaps, this merging of linguistic and political concerns originated in the 1980s, a decade when more immigrants came to the United States than in any

other time of its history, except for the peak immigration in the twentieth century's first decade.[2]

Our Mother Tongue

Despite these fears for our "mother tongue," English has grown to be not only our language, but also a global language. Bryson (1990) summarizes a few of the unique attributes that make the English language magnetic. It possesses:

- a staggeringly oversized vocabulary
- flexibility of word order
- simplicity of spelling and pronunciation
- a lack of complex inflection
- largely gender free nouns and modifiers
- a "tendency toward conciseness" (p. 19)
- nuanced complexity

Bryson calls the latter "the single most notable characteristic of English—for better *and* worse. . . . Nothing in English is ever quite what it seems. Take the simple word *what*. We use it every day—indeed, every few sentences. But imagine trying to explain to a foreigner what *what* means" (p. 19). About the "richness" of our vocabulary he notes: "*Webster's Third New International Dictionary* lists 450,000 words, and the revised *Oxford English Dictionary* has 615,000, but that is only part of the total. Technical and scientific terms would add millions more. Altogether, about 200,000 English words are in common use, more than in German (184,000) and far more than in French (100,000)" (p. 13).

∞THE STUDY OF LANGUAGE: LINGUISTICS

Scholars have long observed and speculated about the phenomenon of language. This study is called *linguistics*. We still like Postman and Weingartner's simple definition: "What is linguistics? It is conducting oneself in a particular manner—a scientific manner—when studying language" (1966, p. 16). This study can be divided into the different emphases and interests of linguists, but its earliest expression was in traditional scholarly grammar. The Greeks began to analyze the grammar of their language about 400 B.C., and Latin grammarians continued the method into the sixth century A.D.

---

[2] Bryson (1994, p. 364) answers these fears of the corrosive impact of foreign speakers with a 1985 Rand Corporation study which found that "95 percent of the children of Mexican immigrants in America spoke English, and that half of these spoke *only* English." He cites another survey in which "more than 90 percent of Hispanics, citizens and noncitizens alike, believe that residents of the United States should learn English." He concludes that history reassures us that "three things about America's immigrants are as certain today as they ever were: that they will learn English, that they will become Americans, and that the country will be stronger for it."

Medieval scholars carried on the tradition of studying classical Latin, as did Renaissance scholars. (Twentieth-century language scholars use this method to scrutinize the grammar of English to this day.) Appendix C describes four distinct areas of linguistic study that grew from these beginnings—historical, descriptive, psychological/sociological, structural linguistics—and then places these methods of linguistic analysis and description within a historic timeline.

In *Transformational Grammar and the Teacher of English,* Owen Thomas (1965, pp. 3–4) made a classic comparison of these four aspects of linguistics to the impulses that drive other academic fields of study:

> Some linguists, for example, are interested in cataloguing and describing various features of languages, just as some botanists prefer to catalogue and describe plants. Other linguists are interested in the history of various languages and language families, just as some anthropologists are primarily interested in tracing the history of various families of mankind. Still other linguists are concerned with the interrelationships between language and society, or language and learning, or language and intelligence, just as sociologists, educational theorists, and psychologists are interested in similar questions. And finally, some few linguists are interested in general theories of language, just as some physicists are interested in theories that explain the operations of the universe.

The differing perspectives of these linguists and grammarians suggest the richness of language study and the danger of dogmatic views of language. They open questions about the psychic and social effects of language; they prod us to consider how language is, to borrow a term from Postman (1995, p. 182), a "world-maker." They also influence decisions that English teachers must make about what we teach about language. Before we turn to different points of view in the debate about school language instruction, we must define two basic positions in this long-standing controversy: descriptive versus prescriptive grammar.

Descriptive versus Prescriptive Grammar

Linguists and grammarians distinguish themselves in their reaction to language change as either descriptive or prescriptive. Descriptive linguists look at the constant changes in the English language and the attrition of older forms as a natural characteristic of any live language. Latin is more regular and tidy than English is because no one speaks it in daily conversation. It remains "undefiled" by rock jargon or high-tech terminology. Descriptive linguists record the common tongue and watch dispassionately as many forces affect our language: status, access, new information, and cultural shifts. These linguists make some judgments about the efficacy and aesthetics of language, but largely they are permissive about what is brought into common discourse. They would agree with

H. L. Mencken that "stability in language is synonymous with rigor mortis."

Prescriptive grammarians, on the other hand, resist "the never-ending process of linguistic change" (Postal, 1968, p. 286). Their resistance is based on the assumption that we are headed for a "breakdown in communication" unless they oppose change. Their implicit belief about human language is that it is "a fragile cultural invention, only with difficulty maintained in good working order" (p. 286). They might quote from the preface to Samuel Johnson's *Dictionary:* "Tongues, like governments have a natural tendency to degeneration; we have long preserved our constitution. Let us make some struggles for our language." Consequently, prescriptive grammar tends to be interested in "correct English," to oppose "colloquial styles of speech in favor of more formal ones," and to accept "the curious assumption that it is necessary to teach 'grammar' in schools—that is, to the assumption that the child comes to school with no knowledge of grammar" (pp. 286–287).

Descriptivists usually define grammar as a physical phenomenon, a mechanism in the brain that forms and produces utterances, or, as Postal puts it, "an innate attribute of human nature" (p. 286). As Halpern (1997, p. 22) explains, "To call any recorded utterance ungrammatical, given this sense of the term, is to make a strange, almost meaningless statement: it is like criticizing the way the stomach produces digestive juices." Prescriptivists define grammar quite differently, as "the mechanism embodied in books and teachers that decided whether what you've said was correctly said." Given two such different viewpoints, it is no wonder that their debates are inconclusive and their "war," as Halpern calls it, is "a war that never ends."

Issues of Right and Wrong

The different views of descriptivists and prescriptivists are often perceived by the general public and teachers as issues of right and wrong language, of judgmental and nonjudgmental standards of correctness. *Learnt,* for example, is not commonly seen as an ancient form of English kept intact in isolated rural areas, but as bad language. Many English teachers bent on maintaining standards view *learnt* as poor grammar and censor it in their students' talking and writing. Many of these "language cops," as Robert MacNeil (1988) calls them, or "English Mafia," in Russell Baker's (1981) phrase, believe that a lack of mental capacity and a failure of will or discipline rather than geography, history, or economics are causes of this divergence from Standard English.

Such fears for the degeneration of the language and judgments of those who abuse it are so common that they seem natural to language itself. In fact, until the late Renaissance, a concern for correctness was quite rare; for a listener or reader to understand was enough. The notion that some usages and structures were more correct than others developed only gradually and culminated finally in the late seventeenth and early eighteenth centuries. In 1697 Daniel Defoe called for an academy to judge questions of right and wrong usage so that "it would be as criminal to coin words as money" (as quoted in McCrum, Cran, & MacNeil, 1986, p. 131). Jonathan Swift deplored the shortening of words, vogue words and phrases, and the chaos of English spelling. In 1712 he "proposed the only sure remedy against 'Manglings and Abbreviations' and against the innovations of 'illiterate Court Fops, half-witted Poets, and University Boys'—an English Academy" (as quoted in McCrum, Cran, & MacNeil, 1986, p. 132). Defoe and Swift had their counterparts in the United States, who, in the midst of the American Revolution, in 1780, called for an academy whose purpose, as John Adams wrote to the president of Congress, would be that of "refining, correcting, improving and ascertaining the English language" (as quoted in Bryson, 1990, p. 138). Much school time in the nineteenth and twentieth centuries was spent eradicating corruptions of language that prescriptive grammarians identified.

Correct English

The spirit of these concerns for correctness can be seen in a periodical published in the United States between 1899 and 1950 called *Correct English.* Gould (1987) explains that although the monthly publication resembled in some aspects *Reader's Digest, Saturday Review,* and *Writer's Digest,* its basic goal was to school its diverse readership "in the niceties of grammar, usage, diction, punctuation, and spelling....The fundamental aim of *Correct English* was to edify its readers—more specifically, to help them know how to conduct themselves in proper (i.e., elite) society" (p. 22). Its founder and editor, Josephine Turck Baker, not only was "unabashed about equating 'correct' English with social class and intelligence," but she also was dogmatic about the standard of correctness and implicitly equated correct usage with law and incorrect usage with crime:

> *Correct English* is now becoming the final arbiter of that which is correct....Under no circumstances does the editor express her private opinions, for when she indicates that which is correct her assertions are based, as in law, *upon the record....* As in law, so it is in language, there must be a final arbiter.... [Therefore,] when the editor makes a statement as to the correctness or incorrectness of certain forms, the reader is fully aware that the statement is authoritative, and that *Correct English* is the final Court of Appeal. (as quoted in Gould, p. 24)

Josephine Turck Baker has her more recent counterparts. Margaret Thatcher had a legendary assistant who would not read a memo if it had a split infinitive in it. More recently, George Will told the story of a grammarian whom he regarded as "one of civilization's friends." On his deathbed, the grammarian uttered these last words: "I am going to, or, I am about to, die. Either is correct."

Invitation to Reflection 3-2

1. Would descriptive or prescriptive best represent the linguistic philosophy of your former English teachers?
2. At this point in your career, where do you find yourself in this tug-of-war? What kind of linguistic position would you take into your classroom?
3. In what ways might you borrow from both positions in your teaching?
4. Consider the following statements. If they were used in speech or writing by your students, what would be your response?
   - I brung my textbook with me today, teacher.
   - I thought reading Rita Dove's poem was moving, and disturbing.
   - We owe a lot to Native Americans but I don't like to right about there stories because I get sad.
   - These crazy ideas comes to me all the time.
5. Does it make a difference if your student's error was written or spoken?

You may find yourself caught in the middle of this argument. You may be torn between thinking that you need to draw the line against the barbarians at the gate and that the dynamic energy and life in language must not be overly restricted by rules. You may see dangers at each extreme: relativism—the loss of standards—and dogmatism—the rigidity of standards.

THE INSTRUCTIONAL DEBATE

This contentious debate holds practical implications. As we turn now to consider language instruction, we will examine the arguments of four different perspectives in this debate: linguistic, political, psychological or biological, and practical. Each takes a different tack on the question "Should we teach English grammar to high school students?"[3]

We present these four perspectives in some detail because they raise complex issues of great practical importance for the choices you must make about language

---

[3] A more basic question might be, "*Which* grammar do we teach?" For years, traditional grammar as formulated by eighteenth-century grammarians was unquestioned. Increasingly, it came under criticism as being unscientific, inappropriately Latinate in its origins, and too prescriptive. The new structural, transformational, and case grammars, which emerged in the 1930s and 1940s and began to appear in textbooks in the 1960s and 1970s, were judged to be promising, but proved to be as unsuccessful as traditional grammar in making students language-proficient (Tabbert, 1984, p. 41).

instruction. Too many forces will push you toward teaching traditional grammar with traditional methods for you not to be fortified to meet them. We suggest only one teaching activity in this section because we present essentially a background briefing. We invite you to a number of Reflections, however, because we think it is essential that you take personal stock as you consider these matters.

The Linguistic Debate: Change versus Stability

If we believe that language is changing and that only dead languages behave grammatically, we might question the effects of teaching grammar. On the other hand, we may concede that language will continue to change and still argue that we have an obligation to introduce our students to the basic premises of a given language. Just because language is not absolutely frozen does not mean it is an unchecked flood.

You can actively enter these questions of language change and stability through your own inquiry. Teaching Activity 3-5 can provide a look (for you now, your students later) at what's happening at present to the past tense of five selected verbs. This simple survey can meet several instructional objectives, such as raising language consciousness, modeling language study, and introducing language issues. For our purposes just now, it imitates the linguist's data gathering and hypothesis making.

A linguist (or teacher and students) might reason as follows. These verbs were once strong, or irregular, verbs;

3-5 TEACHING ACTIVITY

Five Verbs

Individual

- Write down what you would use as the past tense of each of the following five verbs.

Present Tense	Past Tense
dive	_____
learn	_____
squeeze	_____
hang	_____
dream	_____

- Ask a group of ten friends and classmates to name the past tense they consider to be correct for each verb.

- Answer questions 1–6 below and then draw conclusions for a report that should answer question 7.

1. Can you immediately see a pattern to the responses?

2. Are both regular and irregular verb endings used?

3. Which are more prevalent?

4. How do you account for the concurrence of responses in some cases and the diversity of others?

5. If your respondents expressed ambiguity about *hang,* do you know on what basis they determined their final choice? On meaning? Sound? Experience?

6. Most people in England say *learnt* as the past tense of *learn.* How many of your respondents did so? How do we regard people in the United States who say *learnt?*

7. Does your sample register a trend toward regularity or irregularity?

Small Group

- Individuals present their data and hypotheses to the group.

- Compare the data and hypotheses of the entire group.

- Draw final conclusions based on your enlarged sample.

Whole Class

- Each group presents its conclusions to the whole class.

- The whole class tries to reach consensus on the strongest interpretation of the language phenomenon they have examined.

their past tenses were formed not by adding the regular -*ed* ending but by a change of spelling that often included a middle vowel shift (*hang* to *hung*, *squeeze* to *squose*, *dive* to *dove*) or an irregular ending (*learnt*, not *learned*; *dreamt*, not *dreamed*). These changes probably indicate a tendency toward regularizing such verbs. *Dived* is gaining strength every year, although the irregular form *dove* remains.[4] Mykia Taylor sums up the ambiguity of this phenomenon nicely.

> *Sneak—Sneaked, Webster*
>
> Into our language, a new work snuck
> When I wasn't looking.
> Into the dictionary I puck
> To see what was cooking.
>
> All through the s's I suck and suck
> But it wasn't there.
> Whoever the new word "snuck" has spuck
> Had better beware.
>
> When the purists' vengeance on you have wruck
> I'll give no defenses.
> My joints may have cruck, my voice have squck,
> But I've stuck to my tenses.
>
> *Mykia Taylor*

This dance of language—stability and change—produces many new words, pronunciations, and usages and, surprisingly, preserves others intact in isolated language communities throughout the English-speaking world.

Vocabulary. Wallace (2001, p. 43) reported that usage authorities once considered such presently acceptable words as *clever, fun, banter,* and *prestigious* to be "errors or egregious slang." In a cosmopolitan urban center, language is being created and modified every day by a rich blend of ethnic groups, a shifting set of social customs, and a variegated workplace. Special groups add vocabulary to the general fund at an accelerated rate. Physicists speak of "naked" and "clothed" singularity; rock groups move from "boss" to "bad" to "proper" in quick order. When the general culture catches up, the insiders shift to other terms that reinvigorate and reinforce their special worlds.

But in more isolated regions, the pace of change is less rapid. When an old-timer from the Appalachian Mountains

tells you he "holp" a stranger pull his car from a ditch, he's not mistaken or feebleminded. He is using the Old English form of the past participle of *help,* which still appears in the ancient carol "Holpen Are God's Folk So Dear." Peterson (1987) explains that the absence of the consonant sound /v/ in Old English might explain the use of *mighty* as an adverbial intensifier, as in "mighty good" rather than "very good." In Chaucer's Middle English, *right* was also used as an intensifier, as in "I awoke right early." Peterson describes the people of Appalachia as "a people whose linguistic heritage is rooted in orality and who have retained many of the older forms of usage" (p. 54). Similarly, the shrimper from the outer islands who still says "hit" for it is merely using a form of the pronoun that Shakespeare used in the beginning of the seventeenth century. It is perhaps mostly city dwellers who have reordered the King's English; those isolated speakers are maintaining forms that were standard and proper long ago. When their islands are bulldozed into beach condos and their mountains into ski slopes, the language of their children will change to fit the modern usage of the invading world. In the meantime, their failure to change or their extremely gradual change contributes to the diversity of the English language.

Peterson, speaking of Appalachian language, suggests the most important consequence of our understanding the sources of this diversity: "Learning about the changes that have occurred in the English Language, and learning at what stages in the evolution of language Appalachia has lingered and why, is certainly preferable to merely being left with the impression that the people use a corrupted or substandard English, with ignorance their only reason for doing so (p. 54)."

Pronunciation. Like vocabulary, pronunciation shifts must be measured like the movement of glaciers—over long periods of time. Two great vowel shifts are documented in the history of the English language: the first in Chaucer's day (1300–1450), the second in Shakespeare's (1550–1750). Linguists consider the first shift to be the more dramatic and often call it the "Great Vowel Shift." Vowels softened or shifted down so that endings that once rhymed no longer seem to do so. The final *e* at the end of words became silent. We experience this shift in hymns and poems written before that date. In fact, linguists think that this shift in pronunciation largely accounts for the inconsistency in the present English spellings of many words whose original spellings were fixed in the written language even as their pronunciations changed. Rhyming literature is the invaluable source of linguistic speculation about these oral shifts.

Other pronunciation differences originate in stress placement, not vowel sound, and distinguish, for example, the British gá-rage from the American ga-ráge, their con-tró-ver-sy from our cón-tro-ver-sy, and their la-bór-a-tor-y from our láb-o-ra-tor-y. In Old English, stress on the

---

[4] The clichimiles of Teaching Activity 3-1 provide another example. We reason that clichimiles have all frozen over time probably because they drew on common experiences for natural comparisons, were used repeatedly, and struck users and hearers as illuminating. As the homogeneous culture that produced them fades into a pluralistic society, they are heard and seen less. Consequently, they are strongest in older readers of books and weakest in younger watchers and listeners of TV and videos. That they once gained common currency testifies to language solidarity and to the slower pace of language change. Their gradual demise today is, paradoxically, a result both of the diversity in the American speech community and of the language uniformity that pervades our community through mass culture.

first syllable of two-syllable words was common and so can account for pronunciations such as gúi-tar and ré-ward in isolated areas of the United States.

Usage. Similarly, time has its way with usage, as we have demonstrated. Some teachers, on encountering an emerging form, think of the variant as wrong because they do not see that it is really part of a larger usage shift. The attempt to make our language inclusive of women necessarily situates us in awkward (and often reluctant) adjustments of language. But altering vocabulary—saying, for example, "police officers" rather than "policemen"—is easier than changing entrenched grammatical pronoun forms, particularly the singular he/his and she/hers. Thus, debate continues about the correctness of pronoun adjustments for gender inclusion. Does one say, for example, "Everyone ate dinner and returned to his room" or "Everyone ate dinner and returned to their rooms"?

MacNeil (1988, p. 18) celebrates the genius of English as "the tongue of the common person literate or not." He does not see English as "the special private property of the language police, of grammarians, or teachers, or even great writers." He agrees with Walt Whitman, who wrote that American English is not "an abstract construction of dictionary-makers, but is something arising out of the work, needs, ties, joys, affections, tastes of long generations of humanity and has its basis broad and low, close to the ground."

Perera (1990) questions how far variety in language can be extended before it becomes a new dialect or even another language. She praises the English language for providing the ever-more intermeshed world with an important common tongue. Our diversity becomes problematic only when it threatens the language community. Perera is saddened to think that we may meet the fate of the Portuguese and Brazilians, also separated by an ocean but no longer sharing a language. She wants to make room for both community and diversity.

Teachers of language are often torn between the desires to maintain the order and beauty of language and to celebrate the energy and vitality of its ever-new creations. Shakespeare alone coined more words than any writer before or since. Estimates are that he created 2,000 new words and countless phrases. How much poorer we would be without "one fell swoop," "to be in a pickle," "vanish into thin air," "go down the primrose path," "flesh and blood," and "foul play." Clearly, teachers must balance their caution with openness. Only a dead language lies perfectly still.

Invitation to Reflection 3-3

1. Would you describe yourself as tolerant or intolerant of language differences?

2. Did you arrive at college using the vocabulary, idioms, grammatical constructions, and pronunciation of a dialect different from the standard dialect of the academic community in which you operate?
3. Have you tried to hide that dialect?
4. Do you consistently speak Standard English?
5. Do you use slang? Vernacular expressions? If you do, do you regard these nonstandard usages as incorrect?
6. Does the larger culture project an image of "an ideal language, impossible to achieve, against which all usages are judged" (Wilson, 2001, p. 32)?
7. Do you operate with what Wilson calls the "linguistic insecurity that runs rampant in the general population"?

The Political Debate: Cultural Diversity

To answer the question of what we should teach about language, we must reach beyond linguistic considerations of language evolution. Language affects us in quite personal ways. It carries messages to our hearers or readers about who we are. Their reaction to our words can have a significant impact on our sense of self and on our social and economic achievements. Shuy (1982) argues that stigma or status can be conferred on speakers as they depart from the norms in three areas of speech: vocabulary, pronunciation, and usage, the same categories we used to illustrate language change and stability.

Vocabulary. When you hear a person say "griddle cakes" rather than "pancakes," you might perk up your ears but are more likely to regard the person as quaint rather than ignorant. George Bernard Shaw's most popular play, *Pygmalion,* has language at its heart. The linguist Henry Higgins sets out to demonstrate that language use can metamorphose a flower girl into a lady. In the *My Fair Lady* musical adaptation, at the Ascot races Eliza Doolittle urges her losing horse to "Move your bloody arse!" and thus exposes her aristocratic pretense. If, on the other hand, she had referred to the horse's derriere, no one would have thought that anything was amiss. The use of any of the common Anglo-Saxon four-letter words shocks members of polite society, whereas the use of their more cultured Latinate counterparts impresses them.

Pronunciation. When you hear a person say *aks* for *ask,* what do you assume about the speaker? On the other hand, when someone pronounces *about* so that it rhymes with *shoot* or *yard* with a long *a* and no *r* sound, what do you presume? In these cases, departures from standard pronunciation bring stigma to the first group and status to the second. The language of the second group is evaluated as socially prestigious and its members are thought to be Virginia tidewater aristocrats or New England intellectuals. In England, dialects stigmatize a speaker far more than in the United States. In fact, George Bernard Shaw observed

FIGURE 3-4

Walt Wolfram's usage levels

Source: Adapted from and printed by permission of W. Wolfram, "Standard English: Demythologizing an American Myth," lecture at Wake Forest University, Winston-Salem, NC (1983, April).

	WOLFRAM'S USAGE LEVELS		
	1	2	3
Substandard	It's mine, ain't it?	I thought they was stupid.	He does not supposed to do that.
Standard	It's mine, isn't it?	I thought they were stupid.	He is not supposed to do that.
Superstandard	It's mine, is it not?	I thought them stupid.	He is not to do that.

that "it is impossible for an Englishman to open his mouth without making some other Englishman despise him."

Usage. Pronunciation and vocabulary can earn stigma or status, but generally only to a moderate degree. The real social litmus test is found in usage. Usage more broadly influences the choices made in the use of language: words, expressions, and syntax.

Walt Wolfram (1983) has comprised a list of superstandard (status), substandard (stigma), and standard usage levels that make this point well. They are illustrated in Figure 3-4. The standard usage goes unnoticed, but people recognize the superstandard as the credential of high culture and view the substandard as unacceptable. Calvin Trillin once observed that we can't say *whom* "out loud without feeling just a little bit weird." Did you ever answer a fast-food server's question "Who gets the fries?" with "It is I."?

Language Diversity. The personal consequences of the failure to respect language diversity are movingly presented in Christensen's (1990, p. 36) personal account of a teacher's attempts to teach Standard English to all her students. She recounts her own struggle with social class bias in an English classroom:

> When I was in the ninth grade, Mrs. Delaney, my English teacher, wanted to demonstrate the correct and incorrect ways to pronounce the English language. She asked Helen Draper, whose father owned several clothing stores in town, to stand and say "lawyer." Then she asked me, whose father owned a bar, to stand and say "lawyer." Everyone burst into laughter at my pronunciation. What did Mrs. Delaney accomplish? Did she make me pronounce *lawyer* correctly? No. I say *attorney.* I never say *lawyer.* In fact, I've found substitutes for every word my tongue can't get around and for all the rules I can't remember.

Christensen explains other lessons she learned from Mrs. Delaney: "I learned early on that in our society language classifies me. Generosity, warmth, kindness, intelligence, good humor aren't enough—I need to speak correctly to make it. Mrs. Delaney taught me that the 'melting pot' was an illusion. The real version of the melting pot is that people of diverse backgrounds are mixed together, and when they come out, they're supposed to look like Vanna White and sound like Dan

Rather." It took Christensen years to shake off the sense that she was ignorant and recognize that "grammar was an indication of class and cultural background in the United States and that there is a bias against people who do not use language 'correctly.' Even the terminology 'standard' and 'nonstandard' reflects that one is less than the other."

The inward toll on speakers who learn to censor their own speech is significant. Christensen explains that, for her, the "problem is that every time I pause, I stop the momentum of my thinking. I'm no longer pursuing content, no longer engaged in trying to persuade or entertain or clarify. . . . These side trips cost a lot of velocity in my logic." She senses the same discomfort in her students who are self-conscious about their words: "When more attention is paid to the *way* something is written or said than to *what* is said, students' words and thoughts become devalued. Students learn to be silent, to give as few words as possible for teacher criticism" (p. 37).

In *The Color Purple* (1982), Alice Walker uses Celie as the spokesperson for those who struggle to learn the rules of Standard English. Celie reflects on Darlene's attempts to teach her how to talk:

> Every time I say something the way I say it, she correct me until I say it some other way. Pretty soon it feel like I can't think. My mind run up on a thought, git confuse, run back and sort of lay down. . . . Look like to me only a fool would want you to talk in a way that feel peculiar to your mind. (pp. 193-194)

In many communities, the recent arrival of great numbers of immigrants has created not just bilingual but multilingual classrooms in which students with widely different language proficiency and school experience must surely take mental and emotional "side trips" hour by hour, day by day.

Black English. Smitherman (1990) estimates that 80-90 percent of African Americans speak Black English. She believes that for too long teachers and textbooks considered speakers of Black English to have a language deficit. Labov (1973) presented landmark research that refuted this idea that nonstandard Black English is an inferior language system that must be corrected and eradicated by English teachers. He enumerated some of the basic, but erroneous, assumptions that people make about nonstandard variants of Black English and the people who use them:

Verbality: Black nonstandard speakers use inferior monosyllabic language that lacks subtlety and elaboration.

Verbosity: Black nonstandard speakers are nonverbal; they do not use rich language forms.

Grammaticality: Black nonstandard speakers have no complete mature grammar from which to generate language.

Logicality: Black nonstandard speakers use illogical constructions such as negative concord ("you ain't goin' to no heaven"), negative inversion ("don't nobody know"), and the invariant *be* ("when they be sayin") (pp. 21–22).

Linguistic environment: Black nonstandard speakers use a primitive, sloppy form of Standard English.

Clearly, these assumptions about speakers of Black English are broadened to label and stigmatize any nonstandard speaker or group of speakers. Aside from questions of racial, national, and ethnic prejudice, such assumptions are linguistically simplistic and naïve.

In 1974, NCTE's Conference on College Composition and Communication (CCCC) passed a strong resolution on African American language that addressed the diversity of American English and the need to respect and accept students' home language while they learn Standard English:

> We affirm the students' right to their own patterns and varieties of language—the dialects of their nurture or whatever dialects in which they find their own identity and style. Language scholars long ago denied that the myth of a standard American dialect has any validity. The claim that any one dialect is unacceptable amounts to an attempt of one social group to exert its dominance over another. Such a claim leads to false advice for speakers and writers, and immoral advice for humans. A nation proud of its diverse heritage and its cultural and racial variety will preserve its heritage of dialects. We affirm strongly that teachers must have the experiences and training that will enable them to respect diversity and uphold the right of students to their own language. (p. 1)

The resolution was affirmed almost three decades ago. Thus, you might expect consensus on questions of language diversity from teachers and scholars who are sensitive to nonstandard dialects. In fact, educators and laypersons continue to hold strong and differing opinions.

A young African American woman wrote a "My Turn" editorial to *Newsweek* two decades ago that captures the dilemma of African Americans who wish to remain true to their rich heritage and also thrive in a predominantly White culture. Jones (1982, p. 7) wrote:

> James Baldwin once defended black English by saying it had added "vitality to the language," and even went so far as to label it a language in its own right, saying, "Language [i.e., Black English] is a political instrument" and a "vivid and crucial key to identity." But did Malcolm X urge blacks to take power in this country "any way y'all can"? Did Martin Luther King, Jr. say to blacks, "I has been to the mountaintop, and I done seed the Promised Land"? Toni Morrison, Alice Walker and James Baldwin did not achieve their eloquence, grace and stature by using only black English in their writing. Andrew Young, Tom Bradley and Barbara Jordan did not acquire political power by saying, "Y'all crazy if you ain't gon vote for me." They all have full command of standard English, and I don't think that knowledge takes away from their blackness or commitment to black people....
>
> I know from experience that it's important for black people, stripped of culture and heritage, to have something they can point to and say, "This is ours, *we* can comprehend it, *we* alone can speak it with a soulful flourish." I'd be lying if I said that the rhythms of my people caught up in "some serious rap" don't sound natural and right to me sometimes. But how heartwarming is it for those same brothers when they hit the pavement searching for employment? Studies have proven that the use of ethnic dialects decreases power in the marketplace. "I be" is acceptable on the corner, but not with the boss.

Many African Americans have been the strongest advocates for a strict adherence to the standard language system in speaking and in writing. They say that we do not have Black language or dialect but good language or bad language and that middle-class teachers, White and Black, who do not carefully and rigorously correct the nonstandard language of their Black students are patronizing and ultimately damaging. They believe that children who do not speak correctly will have little opportunity to advance in society. They believe that standard language facility is closely associated with social acceptance and economic opportunity. Delpit (1988) and Reyes (1992) have criticized the writing process approach to writing (and grammar) because it does not give nonmainstream speakers enough explicit instruction in Standard English to give them access to higher education and to the workplace. Delpit writes:

> I suggest that students must be *taught* the codes needed to participate fully in the mainstream of American life, not by being forced to attend to hollow, inane, decontextualized subskills, but rather within the context of meaningful communication endeavors; that they must be allowed the resource of the teacher's expert knowledge, while being helped to acknowledge their own "expertness" as well, and that even while students are assisted in learning the culture of power, they must also be helped to learn about the arbitrariness of those codes and about the power relationships they represent. (p. 296)

♡ Invitation to Reflection   3-4

1. In what speech community were you raised?
2. Was it the dominant language of your classrooms in K–12 grades? In college?
3. Can you speak a second language?

4. If so, did you learn it at school? Do you remember the difficulty of learning it? If not, can you imagine the difficulty?

5. When you think of the students you will teach, do you expect them to be predominantly speakers of Standard English? (The U.S. Department of Education and the U.S. Department of Agriculture estimate that in 2000 38 percent of students enrolled in U.S. public schools were minorities. Does this change your expectations?)

6. Would you criticize Christensen's ninth-grade English teacher, Mrs. Delaney? How would you handle a student's choices of vocabulary, pronunciation, and usage if you know that they will clearly stigmatize the student?

The Psychological or Biological Debate: Language Acquisition

Understanding what linguists, psychologists, biologists, and educators know about language acquisition is central to our entering the debate over language instruction. When these researchers speak of language, they are not describing the etiquette of correct usage but "the system of rules governing the formation of words and the abstract relationships among words which generates the syntax of a language" (Sanborn, 1986, p. 74). In other words, Sanborn continues, grammar is "an abstract set of rules describing what we do with the elements of language to make *meaningful* utterances, not necessarily correct utterances."

Language Acquisition Research. Researchers have concluded that most students have acquired a natural, thorough, and unconscious understanding of English grammar by the age of five, when they normally enter school. They have achieved this competence not by learning the rules but primarily by listening and responding. Furthermore, they achieved it in a sequence timed to their developmental maturity. Dorothea McCarthy first conducted research in the 1930s on the speech of children between eighteen months and four years. She found, and subsequent researchers have validated, that the average vocabulary increased from ten to ninety-three words in those years. At eighteen months, half of these words were nouns; by four years, all parts of speech and most sentence forms found in adult speech were used (McCarthy, 1954).

Researchers speculate that language acquisition is an innate feature of the human species. Noam Chomsky (1968) believes that this specific linguistic ability causes infants to attend to speech sounds in the early weeks of life and to imitate those sounds and patterns throughout their infancy. Sanborn (1986, p. 74) compares our language-learning system to our digestive system: "we 'know' what to do with words just as we 'know' what to do with food.

Whether cognitive or visceral, the original response is innate."

Many believe that our inborn cognitive linguistic capacity is driven by a desire to communicate and by an environment rich in language. Behaviorist B. F. Skinner (1957) explains that children are conditioned to speech by their interaction with their primary caregivers. Competence in speech is determined by how often the infant hears speech and how well the child is reinforced for it. In fact, if the child is reinforced strongly for talking, verbal expression becomes reinforcing in itself.

Catherine Snow's work on mothers' speech places language acquisition in another social context. She suggests that language growth occurs as mother and child mutually seek a frequency on which they can communicate. Mothers adapt their own speech to the meanings of the child. Psychologists have catalogued and classified features of this baby talk or "motherese": a higher pitch than usual, fluctuations in intonation, simple and concrete vocabulary, and short sentences. Research in six languages found that these characteristics are true of the speech of almost all mothers (as well as fathers, other relatives, and strangers) in these speech communities (Ferguson, 1977). Snow and Ferguson conclude that adults skillfully adjust their speech to the child's level of comprehension and the child becomes more active in language acquisition as he or she attempts to make meaning of the world. Adults respond as though children are "viable communicators" (Kiel, 1998, p. 5). Stern (1977) calls the nonverbal behaviors that begin within the first three months of life and develop into language the "dance" that forms the basis for the child's interactive life. The dancers—adult and child—coordinate their linguistic dance because of a desire to communicate with each other.

The acquisition of language begins, then, in infancy and continues through a developmental sequence. But none of this learning is by direct language instruction or correction of errors. Some researchers, such as biologist Eric Lenneberg (1967), see talking as a biological development as dependent on physical maturation as walking is. More agree that language learning becomes rapid when a child reaches a stage of development in which he or she can see the connection between words and objects or actions. Carol Chomsky (1969) and other researchers found that, although children enter kindergarten with a basic grammar structure intact, they are constantly adding nuances of language to their repertoire. Milner and Elrod (1986) observed that some students did not acquire stress and other subtle communication features in their first six years of school.

Implications for Language Teaching. These observations about language acquisition suggest certain principles for the teaching of language. Rosen (1998) states a foundational principle: "*Learning to use the correct mechanical and grammatical forms of written language is a developmental process and as such is slow, unique to each child, and does not progress in an even uphill direction"* (p. 141, italics hers). We state four others:

- Teachers should encourage language experiences that enable students to produce language and to receive language that is accessible yet challenging.
- Teachers should teach language in the context of making meaningful sense of the student's world.
- Teachers should realize that students are still acquiring language through the school years, even though they have mastered basic grammar by age five.
- Teachers should not attempt to teach a consciousness of rules until the child has reached a level of abstraction that renders him or her capable of understanding them.

Sanborn (1986, p. 77) summarizes these observations:

Since students already know the grammar of their language unconsciously and since most of them cannot successfully take the steps of decentering and abstracting necessary to make the unconscious process conscious, I do not believe that we should attempt to teach grammar as early and as relentlessly as we do. It is valuable to understand the workings of one's own language but hardly necessary. Students who have not yet reached a level of formal operational thought or a level of ego development where they can step outside themselves should not be forced into grammar exercises that can have no meaning for them.

Sanborn does not dismiss the need for grammar instruction entirely. The biological model indicates "internal development may require an outside trigger." Students' readiness for that language trigger depends on their ability to think abstractly and to regard language as a means of social interaction. Although the timing of that readiness varies widely, Sanborn thinks most probably it does not arrive until the final two years of high school, when the exercise of language has been wide and constant.

It is important to understand that problems develop in language acquisition when stages are abbreviated and children are asked to operate at stages beyond their present stage. Further, difficulties arise when students are asked to grow conscious of what is for them an innate process. A story about W. C. Fields crystallizes the difficulty of making innate knowledge conscious: After reading an analysis of how he juggled, Fields could not juggle for six years.

The Practical Debate: Research and Experience in Grammar Instruction

Practical questions remain in the debate over secondary language instruction—namely, over the teaching of grammar. Much research has attempted to measure grammar's practical benefits. Is learning from direct grammar instruction transferred to actual oral and written use? These studies have been themselves the subjects of review and appraisal over many decades of the twentieth century.

The most noted critique, *Research in Written Composition,* by Braddock, Jones, and Schoen (1963, pp. 37–38), evaluated almost seventy years of research and reached a strong conclusion: "The teaching of formal grammar has a negligible or, because it displaces some instruction and practice in composition, even a harmful effect on improvement in writing." Within a decade of that critique, however, evidence suggested that this country's schoolteachers and students still devoted thousands of hours each year to grammar study. At that time, Wall (1971, pp. 1127–1128) asked why students "have to know their grammar" and found these answers:

1. To pass grammar tests
2. To "get into" college
3. To be able to write
4. To be successful
5. To have an educated person's understanding of how language operates

She refutes each of the first four answers as (1) "immoral," (2) a "lie," (3) a "cliché of our culture," and (4) "another lie, unless one includes grammar knowledge in his definition of success" (p. 1128). She translates the fifth as meaning "Learn grammar because it is there," and she finds this just a bit more justifiable. She says, "We learn about the pupil, cornea, and retina of the eye in a science class because it is knowledge educated people should at some time know, too. But we do not teach the technical aspects of the eye in every grade from fifth through twelfth; nor does one 'have to know' his eye in order to appreciate either the miracle of a cornea transplant or what he sees." Postman and Weingartner (1966) even earlier had listed and demolished other prominent claims on grammar's behalf. They use excerpts from the 1950 edition of the *Encyclopedia of Educational Research* to show that grammar does not (1) discipline the mind, (2) aid in the interpretation of literature, (3) improve writing and usage, (4) aid in the study of foreign languages, (5) improve reading, or (6) improve language behavior in general (pp. 63–74). These third and sixth claims remain the most persistent, disputed, and tested rationales for grammar instruction.

Two decades ago, Kolln's research (1981) concluded that Braddock's (1963) critique was severe in its claims of harm in grammar instruction. Many of the studies on which Braddock et al. based their conclusions did not meet research standards of the 1980s. Still, while not concluding that formal grammar instruction is as harmful as Braddock thought, Kolln's study and those of others are not optimistic (Sherwin, 1969; Elley, Barham, Lamb, & Wyllie, 1979). In the mid-1980s, Hillocks (1986, 1995) undertook a "meta-analysis," or "research synthesis," of five hundred previously conducted experimental studies of writing instruction. He selected sixty studies that he considered to be well designed and compared their results. He divided the writing instruction observed into four general methodological "modes of instruction" with six content "foci of instruction." Hillocks found the following six foci as "the dominant content of instruction" (1986, p. 219):

Grammar: Teachers teach traditional grammar concepts such as parts of speech and parts of sentences, not prescriptions for correct usage.

Models: Teachers present concrete models of finished writing for students to understand and emulate.

Sentence combining: Teachers ask students to put phrases, clauses, and sentences together in certain ways.

Scales: Teachers ask students to apply criteria to judge their writing and guide their revising.

Inquiry: Activities are designed to present sets of data and "to help students develop skills or strategies for dealing with the data in order to say or write something about it" (p. 211).

Free writing: Students write whatever they wish in journals as a means to discover their own ideas and voices.

We will discuss Hillocks's research further in our writing chapters, but we draw attention here to the first foci of instruction, grammar. In the 1980s his study found that it continued to occupy a prominent role in writing instruction, yet did not yield student gains in contrast to students whose teachers used the other five approaches (1995, pp. 219–223).

Often language arts teachers, confused by these inconclusive and even contradictory research claims, have gratefully ceased their attempts to teach grammar systematically or to fashion incidental lessons skillfully. Martinsen (2000, p. 123) calls the Braddock Report and the subsequent antigrammarian "war cry" a "virtual Woodstock in the English classroom: Abandon all the rules; free love and free grammar for all!" The rise of the process approach to writing instruction compounded the research implications and further depressed the concern with grammatical correctness. Writing instruction moved from a focus on correctness to composing, on product (the finished paper) to process (the sequence of acts undertaken to create the paper).

Recently, however, pressures have mounted on teachers to teach grammar—pressures from ideological shifts in linguistics and philosophy; from the standards movement; from local, state, and federal curriculum guidelines; and from end-of-course writing and grammar testing. Kolln (1996, pp. 29–30) believes "our profession has not been well served by the anti-grammar policies. . . . [Grammar] does have a place [and] . . . . the time has come to modify grammar in ways that clarify its place in our profession." After exhaustive research, Hairston (1981, p. 799) warned that teachers should not let students leave their classrooms with the mistaken notion that "surface features of discourse do not matter. They do."

Invitation to Reflection 3–5

- We ask you to participate in a research survey about why teachers teach grammar. Donovan (1990, pp. 62–63) surveyed all middle schools in three public school systems to determine language arts teachers' assumptions and practices about grammar instruction. Of those who responded to Donovan's study, 70 percent believed that mastering "grammatical terminology" was important for their students. She asked that they rank the following six reasons for teaching grammar. We ask that you too rank the following rationales.

____The more my students understand grammar, the better their writing will be.

____Students need to master English grammar as a preparation for studying a foreign language.

____The study of grammar will improve students' speech patterns.

____The study of grammar, like the study of mathematics, sharpens students' thinking skills.

____I want my students to do well on standardized tests.

____I personally find the study of language structures fascinating.[5]

- In the decade since Donovan's research, the public pressures to teach traditional grammar have intensified. Many school systems now publish curriculum guides that require teachers to teach particular grammatical constructions. (The directives often seem to carry the assumption that these will be taught in the "tried and true" methods of skills and drills.) Imagine yourself as a teacher who has just read these four perspectives on the instructional debate about grammar. What would you say to your colleagues in the English department meeting as they read the central office's directive and discuss how they should respond in their individual classrooms? Have you formed an answer to the question "Should I teach grammar?"

LANGUAGE INSTRUCTION

We have discussed competing sides of the debate over language instruction, but classroom teachers seldom have the luxury of debate for long. They must meet their students with practical plans for the day's learning. The simple conclusion we draw from these debates is that the laissez-faire approach to grammar of the 1970s and 1980s is as insufficient as the direct instructional approach it replaced. We position ourselves on this debate question—should I teach grammar?—with another balancing of tensions. We believe

---

[5] The teachers ranked their reasons for teaching grammar in the order in which they are presented here.

English teachers must teach their diverse students to use the language effectively but with approaches that fall between these extremes of direct versus contextual instruction. We turn now to examine those approaches. A look at the word *grammar* itself provides a good starting point.

Definitions of Grammar

The term *grammar* is highly loaded and means many different things to different people—linguists, teachers, students, parents, administrators, politicians. An important starting point for reducing this ambiguity and discussing what we should teach is to examine its multiple and diffuse meanings. Bill Gribbin (1996, p. 55) and others have divided grammar into three useful parts:

Grammar 1: Our unconscious knowledge of language that anyone using that language understands in order to communicate

Grammar 2: Our conscious knowledge of language that includes "concepts, terminology, and analytic techniques for talking about language"

Grammar 3: Our concern for proper usage or language etiquette

Too often in the debates about grammar instruction Grammar 1 is ignored and Grammars 2 and 3 are taken to be synonymous. When a student's unconscious knowledge of the language is unacknowledged, the teacher loses the opportunity to build language lessons on that scaffold. When Grammars 2 and 3 are intertwined, talking about language too often resembles rules of dos and don'ts. Using Grammar 2 to arrive at Grammar 3 ignores too much of what we know about language learning from research and experience. In an article entitled "Taking the G-r-r-r Out of Grammar," Stephen Tchudi and Lee Thomas (1996, p. 48) warn teachers to avoid these confusions of definition:

1. Don't say *grammar* when you mean *usage.*
2. Don't confuse "good English" (whatever that is) with "good," "proper," or even "correct" grammar.
3. Don't use the word "grammar" when you mean spelling or punctuation.
4. Don't equate knowledge of grammar with high morals or the Queen's English.
5. Realize that *everybody* already knows an enormous amount of grammar.

Grammar 1. Teaching Activity 3–6 will demonstrate to you, and later perhaps to your students, that Grammar 1 is present in their working language.

Most students, and even a majority of teachers, see sentence 1 as acceptable; however, *The Harbrace Handbook* tells students that a pronoun's antecedent should be a noun, not a possessive form of the noun. Nevertheless, most people accept the first sentence as grammatical and also at least the next two sentences. Some go all the way

to sentence 8 before drawing the line; but they won't accept *done* as a proper past tense of *did,* though it is widely used as such. For those who accept sentence 8, sentence 9 is insupportable because it does not complete a thought. Linguists, while admitting that many of these sentences are not acceptable to the general public, would say that only the last is clearly unacceptable and ungrammatical; this collection of words would not be spoken by anyone who grew up hearing the basic subject-verb-object grammar of English. This final "sentence" makes an important distinction. For a language to be understood as a single system, it must have a set grammar that all users, even those who use variants and dialectical differences, recognize in other speakers of the same language.

Most native English-speaking students will have the unconscious Grammar 1 knowledge just demonstrated. (Non-native speakers will, of course, have this knowledge in their first language.) John Skretta (1996, p. 66), a high school reading teacher whose students are classified as needing "skills remediation," wrote to protest what he regarded as a dehumanizing debate over grammar. He has a high regard for students' native language abilities: "Almost all of our students possess excellent grammatical strategies, despite our best efforts to make them conflicted, guilty, self-conscious, stuttering users of language." The recognition that students can communicate effectively in their native languages gives you, the teacher, a frame of reference on which to build language lessons without regard to conscious grammatical terminology. It also gives you confidence in your students as language users and then, if they are validated, confidence in themselves. However, will possession of Grammar 1 be sufficient for others? It probably will not. Grammar 3 will more likely be the concern of administrators and parents: How capable are your students in their written and oral use of English? If you are a teacher concerned about your students' abilities to communicate content that they value and wish to present to a variety of audiences, you will care about Grammar 3 also. Let's turn, then, to consider Grammar 3 before we try to answer the final question: How is correct usage taught? Can Grammar 2, the conscious knowledge of language, teach students to use that language correctly?

Grammar 3. Regardless of what specific decisions you make about effective methods, you will want to determine your students' actual usage. In a study by Hairston (1981, pp. 796–797), 101 professionals classified the grammatical or usage problems contained in 65 sentences from the most grievous, "status marking," to the most "minor or unimportant." Figure 3–5 lists the five categories and three examples of problems identified at each of those levels.

You may wish to simplify the number of categories; but whatever the number, you need a method to help you differentiate your students' level of usage. Ready-made diagnostic tools for language proficiency are available. Two

3-6   TEACHING ACTIVITY

Drawing the Line

Individual

- Read the following ten statements in order, and decide at what statement you would draw the line between its being an acceptable and unacceptable sentence. Circle the problem areas you perceive in each statement.

1. Jack's spontaneity often got in his way.
2. The drivers who failed to successfully complete the race were sent home.
3. Where is his car at?
4. Having leaped the chasm, a mere climb seemed easy.
5. Although we saw some bad spills, the race was different than the earlier ones.
6. He suggested that we might could meet on Wednesday.
7. None of the 163 students were finding their problems insoluble.
8. He never done any work in his life til now.
9. In spite of all that he did or failed to do.
10. Some the was home on and.

Pairs

- Compare where you drew the line.
- On which statement did you begin to question its acceptability as a sentence?
- Was there any statement that was clearly unacceptable? What made it wrong?
- Can you draw any conclusions about what is necessary in an English sentence?
- Share your conclusion with the whole class.

FIGURE 3–5

Hairston's levels of grammatical problems

Source: Adapted from Hairston, M. (1981). Not all errors are equal: Nonacademic readers in the professions respond to lapses in usage. *College English, 43*(8), 794–806.

STATUS MARKING
- Nonstandard verb forms in past or past participle: *brung* instead of *brought; had went* instead of *had gone.*
- Lack of subject-verb agreement: *We was* instead of *We were; Jones don't think it's acceptable* instead of *Jones doesn't think it's acceptable.*
- Objective pronoun as subject: *Him and Richard were the last ones hired.*

VERY SERIOUS
- Sentence fragment
- Nonparallelism
- Faulty adverb forms: *He treats his men bad.*

SERIOUS
- Dangling modifiers
- *I* as an objective pronoun.
- Tense switching

MODERATELY SERIOUS
- Lack of commas to set off an appositive.
- Failure to distinguish between *among* and *between.*
- Comma splices

MINOR OR UNIMPORTANT
- Use of a qualifier before *unique: That is the most unique city.*
- Writing *different than* instead of *different from.*
- Omission of the apostrophe in the contraction *it's.*

FIGURE 3–6
Levels of Usage

1. *Distract*
   - Nominative/objective selection: I/me; who/whom
   - Semantic content: good/well; may/can; to/too
   - Verbal misconstructions: dangling participles; split infinitives; prepositional closure
   - Usage variants: from/than; that/which
2. *Stigmatize*
   - Kernel rupture: he come; they helps
   - Semantic incongruity: she can't never; more better
   - Conjugational variant: he brung; she done; we knowed; they be
   - Reflexive excess: theyselves; John he did it
3. *Confound*
   - Lame particles: that he left home. John and Sue at their houses
   - Dual deep structure: The shooting of the natives was terrible. Ginny and Bob were wrapped in a bandage.
   - Open referent: John saw Paul and told Tom he could fly home with him.
   - Hyperextension: He went with John who could come but we never knew how his cousin was on the park bench.

common ones are (1) beginning-of-the-year tests of grammar rules and their applications and (2) students' past performance records as reported by former language arts teachers and/or end-of-course test results. We propose two teacher-made approaches that may come closer to the actualities of students' usage and engage them in the useful process of self-scrutiny.

Figure 3–6 is a scale we developed to help assess students' levels of usage. Do not be diverted by the idiosyncratic terms—one of us loves to categorize and entitle. We label our scale to suggest the effect of levels of usage on communication. Use the progression as a suggestion of a diagnostic movement from least to greatest hindrances to communication. Students can locate themselves on this scale through the sorts of ready-made tests and reports just mentioned, through self-report, through writing or speaking samples that the teacher assesses, or through a combination of these documents sorted out by teacher and student together.

Stella Beale (1997, personal communication) reports that she now asks her high school students to locate their usage difficulties on this schema. She found that their questions and her explanations helped them identify their common errors and understand why they made them. More important, the lesson defused their unease with grammatical correctness and eased grammatical tensions. Before she began to identify their language usage, their grammatical blunders felt to them like undifferentiated "sin." Afterwards, she and her students clarified the areas of real language need and directed their language study to the most serious departures from effective communication.

Middle school teacher Mitzie Renwick (1994) was so frustrated by the gap between grammar study and student usage that she took stock, rejected traditional grammar lessons, and significantly altered her classroom teaching strategies. Influenced by the work of Lindemann (1982), she became an astute observer and record keeper of her students' language use. She found the following to

be the top five areas of misuse in her South Carolina middle school classrooms:

1. irregular verb forms
2. *s, ed,* and *ing* endings
3. double negatives
4. pronoun usage
5. homophones[6]

Understanding her students' real usage allowed her to design language lessons—with no reference to grammar terminology or grammar rules—that could help them recognize their mistakes and select an alternative construction.

Erika Lindemann (1982, p. 116) believes that students do not need to understand grammatical principles (as English teachers do) in order to be effective writers and speakers. She does think, however, that English teachers can do much to create student awareness of their actual grammar usage and of the choices available between standard and nonstandard forms. The teacher's awareness of students' language deficiencies should form the basis on which to develop sound instructional plans. Students whose language is replete with departures from Standard English do not need intensive instruction on the dangers of split infinitives or preposition-ending sentences. To belabor these relative subtleties when other language deficiencies cripple communication would be like working on punt-return defenses with football players who know little about blocking and tackling. Instruction needs to be pitched where it is most needed. Nor do students whose usage is proper and effective except for one or two grammatical constructions (say, a common misuse of the personal pronoun following a preposition) need to conjugate irregular verbs or complete worksheets that distinguish between noun clauses and adverbial phrases.

---

[6] The most frequently misused verbs were *bring, ring, sing, think, drink, shrink, see, write, go, ride, do, run,* and *come.*

Invitation to Reflection　3-6

Imagine that you have identified the language usage level of each of your students. The question remains "How do I teach Grammar 3?" As you begin to imagine your specific approach to instruction, please consider the traditional strategies of language instruction below and answer the questions that follow.

These seven strategies move from the controlled and systematic to the natural and spontaneous, from the theoretical and abstract to the practical and concrete. They move, too, from work with writing to work with oral language. Finally, they move from distant to immediate connection to the everyday world. Some teachers would characterize them as moving from conservative to liberal.

Traditional Strategies of Language Instruction

____*Grammar rules:*
Make students aware of the basic rules of standard usage in our language system. Teach definitions of the parts of speech and more complex usage features such as gerunds and participles.

____*Conjugation of principal verb parts:*
Have students memorize the proper forms of verbs and the pronoun subjects that accompany them—for example, *I bring, I brought, I will have brought,* and so on.

____*Workbook/software drills:*
Let students practice and apply their knowledge of usage in fill-in-the-blank, multiple-choice, and other activities with electronic and paper texts.

____*Sentence diagramming:*
Write sentences as schematic diagrams to represent the relationship of their component parts to one another.

____*Writing response:*
Report problems in student writing by referring to grammatical rules or citing communication difficulties in commonsense language.

____*Oral transference:*
Use pattern drills and other means of code consciousness to encourage students to switch to standard usage, first in oral work and then in writing.

____*Modeling:*
Encourage standard usage through extensive reading of fiction and nonfiction and oral interaction with users of Standard English.

1. We are interested in the language instruction you received during your student years (K–12). Please check those strategies that you encountered.
2. Which of the seven was used most often in your high school experience?
3. Which most improved your actual usage?
4. Which strategy has dominated in the classrooms you have recently observed?
5. Have you observed other models in middle and high schools? Name them.
6. Which do you favor for your own teaching?
7. Which of the seven would seem least effective? Why?
8. Do you believe teaching grammar is a central or peripheral task for English teachers?

Grammar 2. Regardless of what method you use to teach Grammar 3, as a teacher you must have some grasp of Grammar 2 in order to present grammatical ideas efficiently, skillfully, and jargon-free. As repeated researchers and teachers have observed, articulating rules is confusing and ephemeral for most, even if students appear to want the knowledge. Patrick Hartwell (1985, p. 119) describes many of our technical explanations of error to students as COIK, "clear only if known." Yet we as English teachers need some conscious knowledge of the structure of language even if we avoid its technical terminology (and the trap of COIK) with our students. We must understand Grammar 2 thoroughly enough that we can convert it into practical application. We follow James Moffett's advice that English teachers should spend more time learning about language and less time having their students learn about language.

We recommend that you investigate the work of Rei Noguchi, who has provided a sort of middle ground between contextual grammar and traditional grammar that is comprehensive but easily accessible to students. In *Grammar and the Teaching of Writing* (1991, p. 21), he offers three reasons given for the "failure of formal grammar instruction to improve writing":

- Grammar is not adequately learned.
- Grammar is not transferred to writing situations.
- Grammar is not transferable to writing.

He considers that the first is merely the fault of the teacher, but professional training can help classroom teachers do better. The second is the fault of the student, but good teachers can help them do better. The third, however, is devastating because it accepts the idea that the learning *cannot* be transferred to writing: Good teachers, good students, good luck—nothing can help. Noguchi uses the majority of his text to fight that third battle by constructing a logical and relatively simple grammar.

Noguchi believes that "less is more" and is content to teach selected aspects of grammar, not the entire system of English. He believes that students have an "unconscious underlying knowledge" of language, Grammar 1, that cannot be articulated but can be brought to consciousness with good instruction (p. 45). He presents an initial lesson entitled "Underlying Knowledge of the Subject" in which students "locate the subject of a sentence easily" (p. 46). He asks them to turn basic statements into questions by adding tags: *Jim and Sal can ride our horses.* becomes *Jim and Sal can ride our horses, can't they?* Six-year-olds can make this transformation; and when they do, the teacher need only ask what *they* represents to enable them to find the subject. "Underlying

Knowledge of the Main Verb" uses the same substitution rule to locate the predicate. Building on the knowledge of the two earlier lessons, Noguchi moves on to "Underlying Knowledge of a Sentence" and then to more complicated constructions such as the "Presentence Modifier." He believes that this fundamental knowledge of such basic categories allows students to identify and correct many of their frequent stigmatizing errors.

Noguchi goes on to develop similar means for attacking run-on sentences and comma splices, using what he calls "five native speaker abilities":

1. The ability to distinguish a grammatical sentence from an ungrammatical one: e.g., *The cook put the soup on the stove.* versus *The cook put the soup* or *Cook the put soup the on stove the.*
2. The ability to produce and understand an infinite number of new sentences of potentially infinite length: e.g., *Jack went home, and he fixed himself a sandwich, and he cleaned his room, and he turned on his stereo, and …*
3. The ability to recognize ambiguous sentences: e.g., *My mother hates boring guests* (i.e., "My mother hates to bore guests" or "My mother hates guests who are boring").
4. The ability to recognize synonymous sentences: e.g., *Alice and Tom washed the car* versus *The car was washed by Alice and Tom.*
5. The ability to recognize the internal structure of sentences: e.g., *Julia is eager to help* versus *Julia is easy to help.* (In the first sentence, Julia does the helping; in the second sentence, someone helps Julia.) (pp. 65-66)

Noguchi systematizes this underlying grammatical knowledge to form a comprehensive framework; but he has done so not by the imposition of abstract rules but by active inquiry, discovery, and reflection.

There are other comprehensive approaches, of course. The essential principle is that language arts teachers should be familiar with the "concepts, terminology, and analytic techniques" of Grammar 2 without assuming they will pass that knowledge directly to students. We can avoid the COIK error by laying aside not Grammar 2 but grammatical terminology and by focusing on the students' attempts to communicate. Possessing such background knowledge without making it explicit and declarative requires constraint, patience, and good judgment. Other professionals exercise these virtues all the time; doctors act on a knowledge of the body, lawyers of the law, ministers of theology, politicians of government, and engineers of physics, without fully explaining the underpinnings that inform their actions to patients, clients, parishioners, citizens, or travelers.

Before we consider the indirect use of Grammar 2 in the classroom, we mention several print and electronic sources of grammar information for you and perhaps your students. Handbooks of grammar and usage can provide a valuable resource for your background knowledge, not a course of study for students. High school teacher Diana Purser (1996, p. 108) has developed an idiosyncratic and effective "visual-auditory-kinesthetic approach to tra-

ditional textbook grammar, usage, and mechanics concepts." She designed this graphic strategy to work "'twixt and in-between'" her writing instruction as a "systematic way to bring students' intrinsic background knowledge about grammar and usage to a conscious level." We include her two "visual graphic organizers"—"Grammar in a Nutshell"—and a brief description of how to use them in Appendix C. (Our students have found these helpful as a review for their classrooms and for their Praxis exams.) We also note two Internet grammar sites designed for grades 7-12 that may also be useful for you:

On-Line English Grammar (http://www.edufind. com/english/grammar/index.html): This site provides an alphabetical list of basic grammatical structures and links to other grammatical sites.

Guide to Grammar and Writing (http://webster. commnet.edu): This site provides a link to information about sentence, paragraph, and essay forms and other activities, including the ability to submit grammatical questions to Gramma(r) English in her rocking chair.

Contextualized Grammar

Many experienced teachers and researchers have a clear and urgent recommendation about a strategy of language instruction: Teach grammar in context. Lucy Calkins (1986, p. 204) reminds us that "English is a skill to be developed, not a content to be taught—and it is learned best through active and purposeful use." In *Teaching Grammar in Context*, Constance Weaver (1996a, p. 25) questioned formal prepackaged grammar instruction directed toward goals and objectives that did not take into account students' daily performance. Weaver believes teachers should experiment with other approaches to teaching grammar that do not require students to "analyze and label the parts of speech and various other grammatical constructions." Janet Emig (1980) has this in mind, we think, when she eschews the "magical thinking" surrounding grammar—that is, the assumption that students learn only *what* we teach and *because* we teach it. John Dixon (1967, p. 13) makes the same point in his classic observation that "language is learnt in operation, not by dummy runs." In Tabbert's (1984, p. 42) answer to the question "Why teach grammar?" he writes: "True literacy is more than the negative virtue of not making mistakes, and it cannot be attained primarily through analyzing sentences and memorizing rules."

Weaver (1996a, 1998) urges teachers to give up the role they have been too often trained for—to look for errors—and find new ways to help students with their language. She believes that students primarily need to learn certain grammatical concepts through using language in writing that they then revise and edit. To this end, she argues that we should teach only the relevant aspects of grammar, teach these within the context of writing, minimize terminology, target those aspects of grammar that are helpful in editing sentences for conventional mechanics, and emphasize those elements useful in helping students make sentences more effective. Weaver offers a useful list of specific alternatives to formal grammar that range from schoolwide changes to new ways of teaching language in the classroom:

- Restrict the teaching of grammar as a system to elective classes.
- Promote the acquisition and use of grammatical constructions through reading.
- Minimize the use of grammatical terminology and maximize the use of examples.
- Emphasize the production of effective sentences rather than their analysis.
- Teach not only "correct" punctuation but effective punctuation.
- Lead students in investigating questions of usage.

Weaver enumerates five key aspects of grammar to teach students that offer "a minimum of grammar for maximum benefits" (1998, p. 21). Each is relevant to writing, but they do not require a "conscious mastery of English as a complete grammatical system" (p. 21). She calls this "scope-not-sequence" because these concepts can be taught anytime between kindergarten and graduate school when students demonstrate their need and readiness. They do not require a mastery of the complete grammatical system of English. She estimates that teaching them will require no more than a dozen grammatical terms!

- Teaching concepts of subject, verb, sentence, clause, phrase, and related concepts for editing
- Teaching style through sentence combining and sentence generating
- Teaching sentence sense and style through the manipulation of syntactic elements
- Teaching the power of dialects and dialects of power
- Teaching punctuation and mechanics for convention, clarity, and style (pp. 21–23)

Weaver's key concepts are further articulated with specific instructional objectives that lead naturally to an extended set of classroom lessons that integrate grammar into writing instruction. She explains the nature of those lessons in her 1998 compilation of articles, *Lessons to Share:*

> The kinds of grammar lessons I suggest ... are *incidental* lessons, wherein (for example) grammatical terms are used casually, in the course of discussing literature and students' writing; *inductive* lessons, wherein students may be guided to notice grammatical patterns and derive generalizations themselves; teaching grammatical points in the process of *conferring* with students about their writings; *minilessons,* which present new and useful information (to a class, group, or individual) in a brief format . . . ; and *extended minilessons,* which typically involve students in trying out or applying the concept, brief and collaboratively, in order to promote greater understanding. (italics ours to emphasize the range of these lessons, p. 26)

You know the moment is ripe when, as Mina Shaughnessy (1977, p. 11) reminds us, students express a "healthy desire to control language." In Weaver's *Lessons to Share* (1998), Ellen Brinkley (p. 120) observes: "the grammar students learn 'for keeps' is grammar that is taught within conversations with student writers about crafting and editing their own work." Callies (1998, p. 110) suggests that the teacher should become an "interested reader, not a technical authority." Rosen (1998, p. 143) notes that, in contextual teaching, the role of teacher changes from "drill sergeant/error hunter to coach/helper." Newkirk (1990, p. 306) advises that grammar should be taught in "small doses." "If grammar is to be taught, it should be taught in mini-lessons of five to seven minutes at the beginning of some writing classes. The lesson should deal with an issue that relates to the writing that students are doing.... By relating grammar instruction to actual writing problems, the instruction has a better chance of sticking." In sum, Calkins (1986) cautions us to teach language as a skill, not a content.

The struggle for a middle ground by a middle-school teacher caught in the cross-claims of traditional skills-and-drills instruction and the permissive tolerance of writing workshops provides a concrete example of contextualized grammar in the classroom. She defined her student need: "to be able to write coherently, lucidly, and hopefully with some semblance of style and expression, observing the standard conventions as dictated by their purpose and audience" (van Zalingen, 1998, p. 13). She wrestled with her conflicts. "So when we insist on grammar exercises, determined to pound into young minds the difference between an adverbial clause and a noun clause, one has to ask whose interests are we really serving: our own comfort levels, or our students' future needs?" She established her ground for teaching effective usage. "By teaching usage, I mean teaching students to edit or proofread accurately because that is in fact how we ourselves catch our mistakes, and that is not a skill that one acquires by circling nouns and double-underlining predicates. A writing workshop setting affords the possibility of one-on-one instruction, catering to each student's specific needs and strengths. Students who write often necessarily have frequent opportunities to practice the skill of editing and proofreading, but there are also strategies that can be taught in mini-lessons to help students refine their editorial eye." Her essay is provocatively entitled "Sacred Cows Make the Best Hamburger!"

Critical Grammer

Christensen (1990, p. 38) provides another classroom test of a working relationship between Grammars 1, 2, and 3. Her approach reminds us of the daily need for affirmation of students' language, teaching some standard rules, and developing a critical consciousness about them. She affirms her "students' lives and language" as "unique and important" through the literature she selects, the history she teaches, and the use she makes of her students' own lives as "a content worthy of study." Yet she goes further to teach her students the rules of the dominant, standard language of our culture—what Jesse Jackson calls "cash language" (p. 37). She does not, however, teach grammar to one of her students, Fred, as she was taught, through humiliation and textbook drills. Rather, she reacts to the "text" of Fred's own writing. She also teaches him the politics of language: "I teach Fred that language, like tracking, functions as part of a gatekeeping system in our country. Who gets managerial jobs, who works at banks and who works at fast food restaurants, who gets into what college and who gets into college at all are decisions linked to ability to use Standard English" (p. 39).

Thus, Christensen teaches her students the rules of Standard English, but she goes beyond the rules to teach a critical consciousness about them. "Asking my students to memorize the rules without asking *who* makes the rules, *who* enforces the rules, *who* benefits from the rules, *who* loses from the rules, *who* uses the rules to keep some in and keep others out legitimates a social system that devalues my students' knowledge and language. Teaching the rules without reflection also underscores that it's okay for others—'authorities'—to dictate something as fundamental and as personal as the way they speak. Further, the study of Standard English without critique encourages students to believe that if they fail, it is because they are not smart enough or didn't work hard enough. They learn to blame themselves" (p. 40).

Glatthorn (1988, p. 49) advanced several practical reasons for teaching grammar. We want you to pay particular attention to his last. "Most teachers think it is important; most administrators and parents want it emphasized; a knowledge of some grammatical terms helps teachers and students talk about writing and literature." About this final point, he asks, "Why is it that science and math teachers never have to apologize for teaching the technical language of their disciplines?" John Wariner, a high school teacher whose *Handbook of English* has been a standard in the field since its first edition (1951), argues this same point: "the chief usefulness of grammar is that it provides a convenient and indeed . . . indispensable set of terms to use in talking about language" (as quoted in Tabbert, 1984, p. 40). One of the twelve NCTE/IRA (1996, p. 25) standards states the same rationale that "Students [should] apply knowledge of language structure, language conventions (e.g., spelling and punctuation), media techniques, figurative language, and genre to create, critique, and discuss print and nonprint texts." If we recognize that knowledge of language structure and conventions is a valuable tool, we can still choose how we teach it—the general approach, the timing, and the specific methods. This section has attempted to demonstrate that you can make Grammars 2 and 3 an integral part of your language and literature instruction—whether your approach is comprehensive, contextual, or a combination of the two—without abandoning your constructivist, student-centered approach to teaching.

Invitation to Reflection   3-7

Barton (1998) has written a critique of grammar teaching in our schools. He considers the students' lack of knowledge of what grammar is to be the scandal of late twentieth-century English teaching. Read his criticism and his suggestions and answer the questions below. He identifies the way grammar is commonly taught in English classrooms: (1) Grammar is taught as a detached series of exercises (which is akin to students' jumping through hoops); (2) grammar is taught in context (which can leave what is and isn't taught to chance—"a dangerously haphazard affair" [p. 111]) and, (3) grammar is not taught at all (always a temptation since most English teachers are literature folks at heart). He advocates connecting written, read, heard, and spoken language. He argues that it be regarded as the tool that gives you control in writing and the tool that connects aural rhythms of spoken language to conventions on the page. He would prefer that a teacher work on the sentence level so that students can internalize the rhythm of sentences, rather than concentrate on such abstract concepts as parts of speech. He sees this method as bridging the gap between skill and drill and contextual learning. He affirms its effect on his students: "[T]hey have gained greater confidence in their writing and a reassuring sense that writing skills can be learnt, rather than handed down at random by the gods" (p. 118).

1. Do his three points match your experience and observation?
2. Can you see how grammar instruction could be integrated with all the language arts?
3. Imagine that your students have demonstrated difficulty with grammatical usage of adverbs or appositives, say. Plan a lesson that integrates a particular grammatical concept over a week in which you are teaching literature that will culminate in writing.

Benchmarks for Evaluating Language Instruction

In later writing chapters, we will present other general approaches and specific activities for teaching grammar. Speaking and reading are the subjects of our next four chapters. Language instruction is fundamental to those enterprises as well, although grammar instruction will often arise indirectly as we attune students to the language craft of professional wordsmiths. Whatever your approach, we recommend five qualities of language instruction that are fundamental to the effectiveness of any approach. When you are buffeted by the suggestions available in grammar texts, workbooks, and the periodical literature and from experienced teachers, test your ideas against five qualities. Make certain your instructional plans are *concrete, inductive, personal, developmental,* and *contextual.*

Concrete. Concreteness is a basic tenet of Piagetian and Montessorian instruction for young children. It is equally important as a starting point with adolescents, most of whom are not fully formally operational in their thinking. Just as the abstractions of mathematics (even simple ones such as addition and division) are understood through the teacher's use of concrete manipulatives, grammar's abstract concepts (such as nouns and participles) are understood best when they can be expressed in concrete ways. For example, putting a band of British rock musicians under, over, in, around, by, beside, into, and beyond a red telephone booth is a concrete way to teach prepositions. Describing their preposterous stage presence would be a concrete way to understand adverbs.

Inductive. Donovan (1990) observes that the common approach of grammar texts is deduction: "definition of rule, example, practice." She contrasts that with the induction children use instinctively: "from the complex body of language which they hear, they construct their own set of rules" (p. 64). Thus, students explore how a sentence works to form meaning and discover in their deliberation that noun/subject and verb/predicate are the kernels of the English sentence. They examine pronouns, for example, and discern their role as substitutes or scrutinize conjunctions as links between features of a sentence. Such instruction starts with the concrete objects or examples and moves to theories, generalizations, or rules that cover all instances. When students create their own rules out of an accumulation of instances, chances are better that they will understand the rules and remember them.

Personal. S. I. Hayakawa, in the preface to *Language in Thought and Action* (1978, p. viii), states the case succinctly: "Often when students who are bored with studying grammar and diagramming sentences become interested in the content and purposes of communication, their hostility to linguistic instruction vanishes, and problems of grammatical and syntactical propriety are solved in passing." Caccia (1991, p. 55) notes his discovery as a teacher that "the only effective moment for introducing these distinctions comes in the midst of some breakdown that the students already care about."

Developmental. In the course of our own education, one of us was taught about run-on sentences at least seven times beginning in the fifth grade. He finally understood them not because constant repetition drilled the concept into his head but because he developed to a point at which he was able to understand what a sentence was and how a comma functioned. We should not expect grammar rules to make sense before a student has

developed the cognitive and linguistic maturity to understand the principles they exemplify.

Contextual. As early as 1898, Samuel Thurber, a teacher at the Girls' Latin School in Boston, wrote, "Language is acquired only by absorption from contact with an environment in which language is in perpetual use. Utterly futile is the attempt to give a child or youth language by making him learn something *about* language. No language is learned except as it performs the function of all speech—to convey thought—and this thought must be welcome, interesting and clear. There is no time in the high school course when language will be learned in any other way" (as quoted in Tchudi & Mitchell, 1989, p. 30, italics ours). A century later, Meyer, Youga, and Flint-Ferguson (1990, p. 66) echo Thurber's position. They conclude that the critical reason for the failure of traditional grammar instruction is that "it is given without any realistic *context.* . . . Language is often divorced from reading, literature, vocabulary, and spelling."

∽ CONCLUSION

This chapter's reasons for studying language range from the most expansive to the most particular, from the most idealistic to the most practical. We close our chapter with two broad rationales for the foundational importance of language instruction for the English teacher's "universe of discourse." While Owen Thomas's (1965) argument is particularly directed towards the usefulness of transformational grammar, we feel that it has broad applicability:

> English is no less a living subject matter than physics and chemistry. And teachers of English have a definite obligation to theorize about their subject matter. They have an obligation to develop the details of grammatical theories and to test them against the reality of experience and intuition. They have an obligation to keep their subject alive. And in fulfilling their obligations, they must make use of all the information that scholars provide about their subject. In short, they have an obligation to teach "living English." (p. 17)

Finally, Bradford Arthur makes an eloquent justification for the humanistic, not just the functional, value of language study in *Teaching English to Speakers of English* (1973):

> The study of language need not be justified by its effect on learning academic skills. If man needs or desires to understand himself and other human beings and if education helps satisfy this need, then the study of language does not have to be an aid to reading or writing, or to anything else. Our ability to think, act, feel, and interact as human beings is bound up with our ability to speak to and understand each other. In learning about language, a student is learning about himself; no further justification is necessary. (p. 150)

Developing an Oral Foundation

Talk underlies all subjects in school . . . For talk enters into the whole range of human interaction, and drama builds, from that interaction and talk, images of human existence.

John Dixon

We begin this chapter with a paradox. We believe that oral, not textual, language is the foundation of the language arts. Children talk before they write and listen before they read. Cultures likewise start with oral history centuries or millennia before alphabets and written messages appear. In some societies today, the fundamental communication tool is the spoken word. In many nineteenth-century English classrooms, oral addresses were prized above written compositions, as the organization of debating societies and the preeminence of valedictory speeches attest. The essay, which we value so highly today, was then regarded as a mere draft for the oral speech. Why, then, is oral language given so little instructional time or thoughtful attention in English classrooms? Why do many administrators value silent classrooms and suspect classrooms filled with talk? What place should talking and listening occupy in teaching English? Incidental only (from the teacher's giving public directions to the students' whispering private confidences)? Intentional? This chapter presents both an answer—English teachers should encourage active student talking and listening—and a conscious strategy—activities for introducing oral activities into the classroom. These activities, oral language exercises and creative drama, challenge passivity and stimulate movement, role playing, and performance.

Invitation to Reflection 4-1

1. In what context did most student talk occur in your own high school English classrooms: responses to teachers' questions; lesson-centered, whole-class or small-group discussions; or personal conversations?
2. What was the usual direction? Teacher to student? Student to teacher? Student to student?
3. What was the proportion of student talk to silence? Of student talk to teacher talk?
4. In 1965, Flanders (1965) found that almost 70 percent of talk in the average classroom is done by teachers (p. 1). Does that figure seem accurate for your high school years? Too high? Too low?
5. What have you observed in English classrooms today regarding student talk and teacher talk?
6. Why do you think oral language is seldom considered a serious part of the high school English curriculum?

CLASSROOM TALKING AND LISTENING

Consider the following common explanations given for the absence of instruction in oral language in secondary English classrooms.

- Talking and listening are natural acts that can be learned without adult help. Instructional time should be reserved for those skills and knowledge that must be taught, such as how to read and write.
- Talking and listening are too unwieldy to teach; we don't know how to help students learn much about this kind of language use. Teachers are challenged enough just preparing students to read and write without adding talking and listening.
- Talking and listening cannot be tested. We cannot afford to spend school time on skills and ideas that do not appear on school, state, or national tests.
- Talking and listening are taught in elective speech and/or communications class, not English.

These appear to be cogent explanations, but can our understanding of language and learning lead us to better conclusions? We believe so. Here are three counterpositions.

- Talking and listening in class develop the ability to clarify and understand the perceptions of others and of oneself. Talking and listening are essential to the individual's process of making meaning. Meaning is not simply received or discovered; it must be composed or produced.
- Talking and listening are the basic communication tools in most human lives. We are always negotiating the workplace, relating to friends and family, and expressing ourselves to others through talk.
- We must develop oral language skills because of their relationship to the highly tested skills of reading and writing. In their seminal discussion of the development of writing abilities, Britton, Burgess, Martin, McLeod, and Rosen (1975) argue that "of all the things teachers are now doing to make their pupils' approach to writing more stimulating, and the writing itself seem a more integral part of the manifold activities of the classroom, it is the encouragement of different kinds of talk which is the commonest and most productive factor." (p. 29)

These rationales alone (though we will uncover others) prompt us to suggest an expanded curriculum that deliberately includes talking and listening. Teachers, both veterans and new, might still protest: "Talk? Why, I can't keep my students quiet! All they do is talk! What do you mean by talk? I have a battle royale each day suppressing it. I have trouble getting my homework assignments *said,* much less *heard.*" In fact, teachers often arrive at a common solution to this dilemma of highly vocal students alienated by school and insistent on supplanting it with their own talk: silent work by individual students at solitary desks. One of our student teachers discovered with some dismay that, in her words, "The worksheet is the great student sedative." One of our most disheartening observations in the high schools we visit is the silence in many classrooms. Although these schools appear to be controlled and orderly to some, to us they appear to be impoverished. Inside the classrooms, what talk we do hear is often highly structured: Teachers give directions, students raise informational questions, and teachers answer. Often, even teacher-led discussions do not produce authentic animated talk. Too often the questions are serial: The teacher asks, a student answers, and the teacher evaluates the answer and, with the ball back in his or her court, directs a question to another student (the "Initiate, Respond, Evaluate" pattern mentioned in Chapter 2). The discussion resembles recitation, not conversation. This chapter suggests an alternative: lively, purposive talk and alert, perceptive listening. Perhaps we can show school administrators that oral language can be taught and even evaluated.

The common assumption is that classrooms, English classrooms particularly, center around language and therefore naturally involve all of the four traditional language arts—reading, writing, talking, and listening. Goodlad's (1984) in-depth observation of more than 1,000 American elementary and secondary school classrooms portrays a different reality. Table 4-1 is the "snapshot" that Goodlad and his researchers took inside the secondary classrooms that they visited. Although these observations are now almost twenty years old, they provide us with a frame of reference with which to consider

TABLE 4–1
Rank order of activities by probability of students' being observed participating

Senior High Activity	Percent Probability of Observation at Any Given Moment
Listening to Explanations/Lectures	25.3
Practice/Performance—Physical	17.5
Written Work	15.1
Preparation for Assignments	12.8
Student Non-task Behavior—No Assignment	6.9
Taking Tests	5.8
Discussion	5.1
Practice/Performance—Verbal	4.5
Use of AV Equipment	2.8
Reading	1.9
Watching Demonstrations	1.6
Simulation/Role Play	0.1
Being Disciplined	0.1

Source: From John I. Goodlad, *A Place Called School: Prospects for the Future,* New York: McGraw-Hill, 1984, p. 107. Reprinted by permission.

classroom talk and a picture that remains up-to-date in too many schools today.

In sum, Goodlad found that the typical high school classroom is organized around either a teacher before a whole class lecturing and explaining or students at their desks working on individual assignments: "Three categories of student activity marked by passivity—written work, listening, and preparing for assignments—dominate ... at all ... levels of schooling" (p. 105).

And how are these schools preparing their students for communicating in adult life? The National Communication Association (2001) commissioned a poll on how Americans communicate. The sample of adults over age eighteen were asked, "How well were you and most young people prepared in school to communicate effectively with others?" Their answers (Figure 4-1) demonstrate a greater optimism about the oral preparedness of themselves than "other young people."

In the United States, English teachers and educators are only beginning to formulate a rationale (why teach talking and listening), a subject (what kind of talking and listening to teach), and general instructional principles (how to teach them). By contrast, the British National Curriculum requires that all students be provided with a third of their language instruction in talking and listening activities. New Zealand elementary and secondary teachers have focused on oral language for some time and deliberately structure talking and listening into their curriculum. For instance, teachers have created oral genres that include poem reading, question posing, news telling, telephone conversations, introductions, object descriptions, team debates, giving instructions, prepared talks, and jokes and riddles. Listening activities also occur throughout the school year.

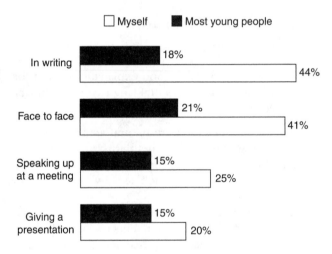

FIGURE 4–1 Poll on school effectiveness in teaching communications

Source: Copyright by the National Communication Association, 2001. Reproduced by permission of the publisher.

We know of no U.S. equivalent to New Zealand's or Great Britain's deliberate curricular approaches. Our high schools often offer courses in drama and speech; but these are typically removed from the regular English classroom, isolated as electives that concentrate on theater skills and showcase occasional student oral productions. Some state and local curricular guidelines or graduation standards are beginning to require demonstrated skill in speaking. On the national level, the fourth IRA/NCTE (1996) standard states that "Students adjust their use of spoken, written, and visual language ... to communicate effectively with a variety of audiences for a variety of purposes" (p. 25). Spoken language is first on this list of the language arts, and references to other oral language arts occur in nine of the twelve standards. The last one again begins with speaking: "Students use spoken, written, and visual language to accomplish their own purposes" (p. 25).

In response to these external criteria, secondary teachers are experimenting with specific instructional activities that promote oral language development in the general English curriculum. These activities, whether used for their oral language value alone or as integral to literature study, are part of a recognition of the essential importance of the spoken word.

The Relationship Of Talking, Thinking, Writing, and Learning

Beyond the current standards for oral skills stand years of research and theory about the essential connection between active language production and learning. According to Barnes (1992), teachers claim that children who have learned to value talk in their learning possess a greater understanding of the learning process and a greater repertoire of learning strategies. These students are aware of how language conveys knowledge, how they themselves acquire knowledge, and the purposes of acquiring specific knowledge. In addition, they explore beyond facts, seeking to identify causes, consequences, and multiple solutions; and they make connections among what they learn. Britton views talk as the sea upon which all other language activities ride. For instance, he argues that "the relationship of talk to writing is central to the writing process. It is no longer necessary to justify classroom talk as a means to anything else; it is properly valued in its own right, but this doesn't detract from our conviction that good talk helps to encourage good writing" (Britton, Burgess, Martin, McLeod, & Rosen, 1975, p. 29).

Vygotsky, the influential Russian psychologist, believed that thinking is essentially linguistic and social. He argued (1962, p. 126) that expressed speech begins in inarticulated, abbreviated inner speech. In order to say or write what we are thinking, we must elaborate upon that inner speech: "The structure of speech does not simply mirror the structure of thought; that is why words cannot be put on by thought like a ready-made garment. Thought undergoes many changes as it turns into speech. It does not merely find expression in speech; it finds its reality and form." Especially when a problem is at the boundary of our grasp, we are pushed to use our inner speech and to "talk our way through" difficulty.

Britton et al. (1975) articulate how talk more than any other variable operates to stimulate, integrate, and encourage other language competencies, as in the following case with writing.

Talk is more expressive—the speaker is not obliged to keep himself in the background as he may be in writing; talk relies on an immediate link with listeners, usually a group or a whole class; the rapid exchanges of conversation allow many things to go on at once—exploration, clarification, shared interpretation, insight into differences of opinion, illustration and anecdote, explanation by gesture, expression of doubt; and if something is not clear you can go on until it is. (p. 29)

Britton et al. contend that one of the great values of talk is that it "permits the expression of tentative conclusions and opinions" (p. 30). It allows thought to incubate and be tested.

Moffett and Wagner (1992, p. 75) describe the internal process of an individual's talk as it meets the talk of other speakers:

When talk teaches, the speakers are picking up ideas and developing them: substantiating, qualifying, and elaborating; building on, amending, and varying each other's sentences, statements, and images. All these are part of an external social process that each member of the group gradually internalizes as a personal thought process: he begins to think in the ways that the group talks. Not only does he take unto himself the vocabulary, usage, and syntax of others and synthesize new creations out of their various styles, points of view, and attitudes, he also structures his thinking into mental operations resembling those of the group interactions. Good discussions by groups build toward good thinking by individuals.

This intertwining of thought and language is essential to learning. Classrooms should be places in which thought can incubate through oral and written language before it takes flight.

Listening receives even less instructional attention than talking does. In too many classrooms, "listening" simply means to be quiet and pay attention to the teacher. These classrooms contain, as in the Simon and Garfunkel song "Sounds of Silence," "people hearing without listening." What we need to cultivate is active listening: attention, understanding, and response. Substantive talking is necessarily a reciprocal dance in which participants reflect back what is heard, challenge it or extend it, share observations and interpretations, and problem-solve and brainstorm. At such a point two or more minds are actively engaged. As Sheldon Kopp explains in *If You Meet the Buddha on the Road, Kill Him* (1973, p. 21), when we set out on our narrative journeys and begin to discover and tell our own stories, "there must be another there to listen."

A common concern about increasing classroom talk is that too often students are not focused and are not spending time on task but time on chat. Classrooms that value students' active oral participation are especially vulnerable to students' temptations for informal, discursive, small talk. When other classes are more structured, those conversations that are usually saved for the hallways between classes and the cafeteria at lunch seem irrepressible in a more open classroom.

In Chapter 2 we discussed specific strategies for creating a classroom environment that promotes meaningful talk and responsive listening. In 1985, NCTE's International

Assembly drafted a statement that encouraged teachers to enhance oral language use in their classrooms (Dillon & Hamilton, 1985):

- Be aware of the distinction between "learning through talk," and "learning to use talk," and provide opportunities to increase fluency in both areas.
- Consider students' own ways of talking—idiolects, dialects, and mother tongues—as linguistic resources that can enrich the language environment of the classroom.
- Involve students in a variety of class formats that encourage small-group discussions, dramatic improvisations, and conversations in order to discover the potential power of talk.
- Allow students to share their ideas with a variety of school audiences: different groupings of their peers, students of other ages, other adults in the school, visitors, parents, and others.
- Assist students in discovering what is valuable, powerful, and enjoyable in the way they use talk to explore ideas, to express and explain ideas, and to share a part of themselves.
- Ensure that students are provided with the opportunity to regard listening as an active component of conversations and discussions. Help them understand that participation does not mean holding the floor much of the time or ensuring that one's line of argument is carried along unmodified, any more than being a good listener means sitting quietly and passively out of the verbal arena.
- Encourage students to talk and to channel personal talk into more general concerns.

Common to these suggestions for creating talking-enriched classrooms is the teacher's focus on the student: The teacher takes seriously how students respond and work to construct personal meaning. Students are more inclined to risk talking where they feel valued. They are more likely to speak where they confront matters that engage their ready attention.

What of those increasing numbers of English-deficient or ESL students who may be reticent to speak in class? Fitzgerald (1995, p. 121) reported that in the last decade of the twentieth century, mainstreaming of non-native English speakers was the norm: "An estimated 85% of the ESL students in the United States' public schools do not participate in a program specifically designed for language minority learners." Kooy and Chiu (1998, p. 79) believe that "teachers tend to delay challenging ESL students with substantive language experiences until they are judged competent in basic English language skills." Sauvé (1996, p. 19) also believes that ESL teaching puts a "disproportionate emphasis on the structure of language": vocabulary exercises, grammar drills, reading comprehension skills. Kooy and Chiu regard language as "too complex" to "readily yield to 'how to' instructions or a linear process" (p. 79).

Young (1996, p. 20) suggests alternatives to direct instruction: ESL students "need multiple opportunities to practice" oral expression in their early experiences of language. This immersion in oral language can take many of the forms encouraged by NCTE's International Assembly. We will explore many promising oral activities in the course of this chapter, but we remind you here of the safe environment of small-group discussions and collaborative projects mentioned in Chapter 2. When talking occurs in small groups—especially those of mixed language proficiency that remain constant over time—ESL students not only have more chances to try out their emerging language, but they will do so under less pressure and with the help of their peers. As with proficient English speakers, the teacher's genuine, nonjudgmental interest in supporting their inquiry leaves students freer to try speech and surer of some degree of success. Tinajero (1994, p. 262) has these suggestions: Teachers should exercise "tact in error correction, provide liberal praise for L2 (second language) contributions, accept responses with grammatical deviations, and model appropriate syntax in a natural way."

In everyday classroom talk, teachers who trust in the importance of purposeful talk should engage in it vigorously. They should do so most obviously to lead whole-class and small-group discussion but also to greet students, negotiate class business, give directions, plan and execute projects, make decisions, brainstorm, introduce speakers, and part from students. It is here, in routine dealings with our students, that we may have our greatest impact on language. Upon reading one-page statements from former students and colleagues about his influence on them, Donald Murray, the legendary teacher and writer, wrote: "In reading the collection I am struck at how we teach most when we do not think we are teaching—in the corridor between classes, with the casual comment, the quick instinctive response, and by attitude more than subject matter" (Romano, 2000, p. 79).

Let us say a final word about creating an environment for talking and listening. One of the most defining characteristics of typical classrooms, which was conveyed to Goodlad (1984, p. 108) "loud and clear" by his data, was that "the emotional tone is neither harsh and punitive nor warm and joyful: it might be described most accurately as flat." Some days you *will* feel as flat as a cartoon coyote crushed by falling rocks (and the cause will seem to resemble just such a source). But your aim should be to create a more energized tone, one that expresses the enthusiasm of discovery and sharing, one that encourages talking and listening out of active interest and engagement.

ᐤ**ORAL LANGUAGE ACTIVITIES**

We integrate oral language throughout this book, but we focus here on possibilities for consciously and intention-

FIGURE 4–2
Oral language exercise schema

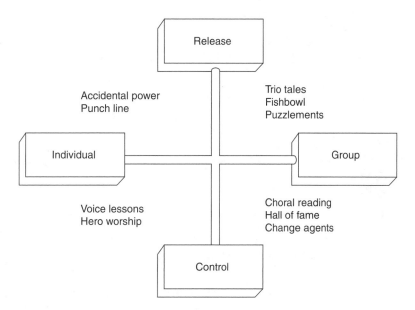

ally producing oral language (speaking) and for receiving it (listening). Figure 4–2 schematizes a range of activities that support, encourage, and extend important oral language experiences. When you are absorbed by the curricular demands of teaching textual interpretation, writing techniques, or even speaking skills, Figure 4–2 can be a quick reminder of effective oral approaches that promote language use for itself alone or in the service of other curricular requirements. It will help you seize opportunities to exercise oral skills.

The horizontal axis of the schema extends from individual to group expressions, the vertical from control to release.

Individual: Students are involved in solitary production (monologue or storytelling). In such singularity, personal creative talent, an authentic voice, and a singular syntax can emerge.

Group: Students work in collaboration that extends from pairs, to small groups, to large groups, to the whole class. Activities can be more elaborate, involving large casts and even simple costuming. Partners increase the need for talking and listening in preparation for the presentation.

Control: Students are speaking from a script or are improvising from highly structured or guided directions.

Release: Students are spontaneous. Their language is not guarded or guided by anything other than their own sense of appropriateness.

Activities: Individual to Group, Control to Release

We present activities in each of the four quadrants, moving from the most structured and controlled teaching sit-

uation (individual control) to the freest and most spontaneous (group release). Our movement through the four not only introduces you to many oral language possibilities but also invites you to imagine progressing incrementally from the predictable to the spontaneous, from stationary quiet to energetic movement, from behind the teacher's desk into every corner of the classroom. Many teachers find safe mooring in those desks or overhead projector stands. So do students. These initial activities will shove you and them beyond the shore to experience those multiple intelligences—spatial, bodily/kinesthetic, and musical—that Gardner believes are so often overlooked in English classrooms.

Voice Lessons (Individual, Control). In this activity, the teacher presents a collection of first-person poems and asks students to select one for oral interpretation. Figure 4–3 provides a list of first-person poems that we have used successfully with a range of students. We recommend that as you select your own texts, you look for ones that are short; have accessible diction; present concrete images, familiar situations, and rich voices; and appeal to the interests and abilities of the individuals in your class. The teacher's aim and the students' abilities determine whether students will read poems from a text, recite them from memory, or record them using sound and visual backgrounds. (Recording the production can make this task even more comfortable for students who are shy in front of a class.) The first-person point of view naturally places the students in the role of narrator so that they can more easily use their voices to bring their poems alive.

For many students, a prescribed and confined text makes public speech a bit easier. (We recommend this activity with literature other than poetry as well—short, vivid passages from short stories or novels. A colleague assigns tales from Chaucer's *Canterbury Tales* to each

FIGURE 4–3
First-person poems

William Blake (1757–1827)	"A Poison Tree"
Robert Browning (1812–1889)	"Meeting at Night"
Emily Dickinson (1830–1886)	"I'm Nobody"
W. S. Gilbert (1836–1911)	"The Modern Major-General"
Thomas Hardy (1840–1928)	"The Man He Killed"
A. E. Housman (1859–1936)	"The Carpenter's Son"
William Butler Yeats (1865–1935)	"He Wishes for the Cloths of Heaven"
Paul Laurence Dunbar (1872–1906)	"The Debt"
Robert Frost (1874–1963)	"Stopping by Woods on a Snowy Evening"
Carl Sandburg (1878–1967)	"Grass"
Elinor Wylie (1885–1928)	"Let No Charitable Hope"
	"Pretty Words"
Rupert Brooke (1887–1915)	"The Soldier"
e. e. cummings (1894–1963)	"Next to of course God America"
Langston Hughes (1902–1967)	"Dream Boogie"
	"The Negro Speaks of Rivers"
Theodore Roethke (1908–1963)	"My Papa's Waltz"
Olga Cabral (1909–1997)	"Life and Death Among the Xerox People"
Robert Hayden (1913–1980)	"Those Winter Sundays"
Karl Shapiro (1913–2000)	"Autowreck"
William Stafford (1914–1993)	"Traveling Through the Dark"
	"Judgments"
Paul Larkin (1922–1985)	"A Study of Reading Habits"
Donald W. Baker (1923–)	"Formal Application"
Maya Angelou (1928–)	"Life Doesn't Frighten Me"
Peter LaFarge (1931–1965)	"Vision of a Past Warrior"
Alden Nowlan (1933–1983)	"Aunt Jane"
Imanu Amari Baraka (1934–)	"Rhythm Blues"
Audre Lorde (1934–)	"Hanging Fire"
	"Coal"
Alice Walker (1944–)	"Women"
	"For My Sister Molly Who in the Fifties"
Susan Mitchell (1944–)	"From the Journals of the Frog Prince"
Katharyn Machan Aal (1952–)	"Hazel Tells LaVerne"

student to dramatize; another asks students to read and present favorite children's picture books; another suggests fairy tales.) We encourage you during your teacher preparation to begin a folder of first-person poems that appeal to a wide range of ages, abilities, and perspectives.

The flip side of talking—listening—is an important part of voice lessons. Student listeners as well as speakers should be sensitized to the ways in which volume, emphasis, tone, and other dimensions of the human voice can arouse interest, clarify ideas, and express emotion. Although another's text circumscribes this activity, it still provides considerable opportunity for creative individual presentation and engaged listening.

Hero Worship (Individual, Control). This activity invites students to read speeches and other documents that were originally written to be spoken and heard. From one or more selections, students extract short "sound bites" that capture the style and significance of the person who wrote them. When students find these passages, assemble them in chronological order, and arrange them by emotional color or by themes, they often develop a personal connection with the author. This identification can intensify the already heightened language. For instance, a dra-

matic sequence of Abraham Lincoln's words might be sequenced as excerpts from the following:

- the Lincoln-Douglas debates
- the First Inaugural Address
- public and private documents from his first term
- the Gettysburg Address
- the Emancipation Proclamation
- the Second Inaugural Address

Martin Luther King, Jr.'s life and influence might be rendered through excerpted passages from his speeches and writings:

- April 16, 1963, "Letter from Birmingham Jail"
- August 28, 1963, speech "I Have a Dream"
- 1964 Nobel Prize acceptance speech
- April 3, 1968, speech in a Memphis church the night before his death, "I've Been to the Mountaintop"

Maya Angelou's oral collage might begin with passages from *I Know Why the Caged Bird Sings,* move through poems such as "Life Doesn't Frighten Me," and conclude with lines from her 1992 presidential inaugural poem "On the Wings of the Morning." Though our examples are from actual lives, a hero worship activity could also include memorable passages from a novel or a play that capture the essence of a character and his or her development.

In activities in the top quadrant, individual release, students continue to speak as individuals but they improvise the words. Students can easily convert the hero worship activity to such a purpose by writing their own speeches as though they were real or imagined cultural heroes. Those speeches could be argumentative, as in a debate with a political opponent; persuasive, as in a rally speech by a social activist; conciliatory, as in an opening statement at a summit conference; or expressive, as in an acceptance speech at an awards ceremony. The student's task is to find interesting subjects and to create speeches that develop naturally, are authentic in character, and respond to the given situation.

Accidental Power (Individual, Release). This activity encourages improvisation within a structure as the teacher provides a context from which students can generate language. Dixon (1984) recommends a fail-safe context: a point of crisis so that speakers will have an almost inevitable linear direction, a narrative shape, and dramatic power that they would not otherwise possess. A simple classroom activity asks students to tell a story of an acute embarrassment, an accident, a personal or family crisis, or an experience with a natural disaster. The story can become more complicated and challenging when the speaker assumes a fictitious role. For instance, a student might imagine him- or herself as a president, a general, or a minister and hold a press conference in which student reporters fire questions as though a national disaster or an environmental emergency had just occurred. (The focus is on the interviewee, but the student interviewers also profit from this opportunity for active talking and, especially, listening.) The following roles have worked for our students:

- a survivor of an earthquake who is still lodged in a damaged building
- a mother whose three-year-old child is stuck in an abandoned well
- a Native American elder who must inform his community that the federal government has ordered the tribe onto a reservation
- Hansel or Gretel being questioned by their police rescuers at the home of the witch
- one of Cinderella's stepsisters interviewed on a talk show the day of Cinderella's wedding to the prince

When listeners are engaged with an account of an accident or a moment of serious crisis, they can become helpful respondents. After the oral exercise, they can critique the speaker's use of critical detail, elaboration, foreshadowing, suspense building, and other elements simply by explaining when they were most moved—anxious, frightened, troubled, or relieved—or most confused.

Such structured oral improvisation in response to a crisis can also enliven, personalize, and dramatize literary

study. Consider the impact of a spoken monologue by one of the five victims of the bridge collapse in Thornton Wilder's *The Bridge of San Luis Rey.* Such a dramatization often invites more entry into a character's personal world than a more traditional analytical discussion would, even if that analysis included a perceptive question such as "If this character had survived the fall, how might his or her life been changed?"

The concept from political theory of path dependency—the idea that even minor events can put you on a new path from which you cannot turn back—has proven useful for capturing such a moment. We ask students, particularly when studying longer works, to identify the juncture(s) that determined significant and irreversible new directions for one character. Then we ask them to assume the role of that character and talk to their biographer, their child, or a newspaper interviewer as they look back at their life just before its close and explain:

- What did that juncture mean to you?
- Describe the conflicts you were feeling.
- Tell us what you wrote in your diary on this day that changed everything.

Punch Line (Individual, Release). As its name indicates, this activity depends on humor. Because humor amuses us, it often seems simple; in reality, however, it requires tremendous verbal skill. Amusing stories, much like accident stories, depend on critical detail, elaboration, foreshadowing, timing, and other oral language skills to be effective. Ask students to recall an amusing incident or anecdote they have experienced, heard, or read. (Mark Twain provides some classic stories, Dave Barry excellent contemporary ones.) Then have them tell their stories to a partner or to two other students. The listeners critique the speaker based on their own genuine amusement. The pair or group can even rewrite or revise the humor, leave behind their intimate sanctuary, and try it on the entire class. The whole class provides an almost automatic evaluation with their response. Sometimes our students hold up scoring cards.

Although the activities thus far are individual projects, they require other people to serve as prompts (sometimes) and audience (always). The next activities are fashioned for groups, so the range of possibilities for verbal and nonverbal communication necessarily expands. A sense of classroom security and freedom is basic to the success of any activities involving performance, particularly spontaneous utterance. Trust between teacher and student and among students builds over time in a classroom, but these activities provide good starting points.

Choral Reading (Group, Control). Choral reading engages students in the presentation of a previously scripted text. One of the most effective readings we have observed both in terms of student learning and audience reaction was a reading of the Declaration of Independence by a group of twenty-five middle school students. The document itself, with its powerful and expressive arguments, was a charged vehicle for such a production; but the oral arrangements intensified its force. Students were assigned special lines and words so that their varied voices underscored the document's critical ideas and heightened language. Spatial arrangements of the presenters, language tempo, modulation, emphasis, and the number of single or choral voices all contributed to the impact. Teacher Lisa Fredenburgh used this approach to create a musical pastiche. She chose powerful words from our foundational political documents, which speakers would stand forward and read while a chorus hummed "America the Beautiful." When performed on special occasions before an audience, the effect and the learning involved are both intensified. Students sharpen their ability to project clearly and expressively to an audience. Effective sources can be found wherever strong and vivid language is present—in fiction, poetry, drama, and nonfiction.

Terry Ley (1995) presents clear suggestions for a group preparing a poem for choral reading:

1. Read through your poem once or twice. Then discuss it using these questions: What does the poem seem to be "about?" Does the organization of the poem help you to understand it better?
2. Divide your poem into several natural parts. (Stanza divisions may be helpful, but do not assume that they are the best divisions for an effective oral presentation of your poem.)
3. Make solo, duet, and trio assignments for the parts that you identify.
4. Decide how readers of each part should use volume, emphasis, speed, pause, and pitch to communicate meaning. Use symbols to mark copies of the poem so that they become scripts for performing the poem.
5. Rehearse performing your poem once or twice, revising the script to improve it.
6. Enjoy performing your poem for the class!

In addition to performing poetry for students, the group Poetry Alive publishes books that script poems for multiple voices and poses questions of interpretation and stage direction (Wolf, 1990). Chapter 6 presents an example of their work.

Hall of Fame (Group, Control). This activity relies more heavily on student initiative and converts the ideas of hero worship into a group project. Students select imposing or impressive statements made by a favorite president, public figure, or literary character to weave into a group collage of voices. A presidential collage might include Abraham Lincoln's "Four score and seven years ago our fathers brought forth upon this continent . . ." as well as Harry S. Truman's "The buck stops here" and "If you can't stand the heat, get out of the kitchen." A concluding collage of women's experiences in a unit on the War between the States or the horrors of war might include excerpts from the following:

> *Hospital Sketches,* by Louisa May Alcott, novel
> *A Diary from Dixie,* by Mary Chesnut, diary
> *A Journal of Hospital Life in the Confederate Army of Tennessee,* by Kate Cumming, journal
> "The Slave Mother," by Frances E. W. Harper, poem
> "The Loophole of Retreat" from *Incidents in the Life of a Slave-Girl,* by Harriet Jacobs, testimonial
> "Keeping the Thing Going While Things Are Stirring," by Sojourner Truth, speech

Group deliberation can determine the organizing principle among the quotes—chronology, theme, or personality, for instance. The possibilities are as varied as the political, national, ethnic, ideological, and vocational differences that distinguish humankind. Costumes, props, music, and art can be used to re-create and vivify the world of each speaker.

Change Agents (Group, Control). This activity creates a pastiche of voices of actual senior citizens and involves students in creating their own scripts through interviews. Each student interviews a person of seventy years or older about his or her life. The interviewer might ask what has changed most since the person's childhood years or what political event or personal crisis he or she remembers most vividly. Students listen carefully and record the essence of the interviewee's experience, noting memorable words or expressions. They return to their class or group and collaboratively decide how to arrange their acquired body of folk wisdom. We have sometimes structured the pastiche by asking each student to speak for his or her informant twice: first giving excerpted quotes and then the name, the date of birth, and sometimes the place of birth. We also have staged this activity: Students represent their interviewees by dress or prop; some are seated, while others kneel alone or in small clusters; some speak from their fixed positions, while others rise slowly to make their statements about change.

A former student reported a similar assignment for her university women's studies class. Her professor had her students talk with mothers, grandmothers, and great-grandmothers about their experiences as women—for instance, how many children they had, whether they worked, and what they expected of marriage. Students then made comparisons across the age groups. Your students might designate such specific groups and shape those interviews into an oral social history. In a thematic unit of nonfiction titled "Profiles in Courage," you could augment the subjects under study with the interviewed change agents.

Trio Tales (Group, Release). In trio tales, three students collaborate on telling a short tale. Although many students shrink from such creative oral assignments, trio tales provides a structure to aid them. They choose one element from each of three columns in a chart that provides the seed of a story idea that they then develop (Figure 4-4). The tone is left up to the tellers; some stories will be light and humorous, some ironic, and others tragic. (We sometimes intervene to influence tone by asking each group to flip a coin: heads, the tale is light; tails, it is serious.) Our instructional purpose determines whether we ask students to speak from a manuscript, notes, or memory and whether their telling will be live or recorded. Because it is usually more natural and effective for one person to spin a tale than three, the trio selects one member to tell the story. As that student tells the tale, the whole class listens, critiques, and suggests improvements.

One way to select the specific character, setting, and resolution on the chart is to use each trio member's birthday month. Each group member chooses one column and the item on the numbered line that matches the number of his or her birth month. For instance, in our sample chart, a June-May-October group would tell a tale about a spy who appears in the CNN newsroom and winds up with a promotion. Students can brainstorm the items in the lists, creating even greater student ownership and interest in the unusual combinations that result. We also use trio tales to conclude literature units by having students construct a chart with characters, settings, and resolutions from the texts they just read. Not only does this provide a good review, but it also secures students comfortably and playfully in their new learning.

Fishbowl (Group, Release). This activity requires yet more fluidity of talk and organization. It focuses not only on talk but also on listening. Four or five students take seats in the middle of the classroom to discuss and debate timely political or social or literary propositions. (The teacher can orchestrate a reliably animated discussion by mixing students who are impetuous and outspoken with those who are more deliberate and critical.) The other members of the class listen carefully and try to figure out where each of the discussants stands on the issue. When the teacher feels that the discussion has matured, become exhausted, or reached a predesignated time limit, the fishbowl discussion stops and a classroom discussion begins. The listeners recall or infer what each discussant said and describe the position of each. The discussants do the same. The class then can compare descriptions, those of listeners and speakers, to determine the level of clarity in listening and speaking. (Charts can be kept over the year in an oral language portfolio so students can mark their progress as listeners and as speakers.) If teachers anticipate topics and possible points of view, they can draw up position statements that focus and clarify this post-mortem.

The selection of issues for the fishbowl discussion is, of course, crucial. A fine line in good topic selection lies between those that are too close and personal and those that are too theoretical and distant. We work toward student-generated ideas about issues to which they have authentic, personal responses—for instance, "Is reality TV a fad, or is it here to stay?" or "Are adolescent females given more restrictive messages about ideal physical beauty than adolescent males are?" or "Does the school dress code violate students' freedom of expression?" We also prod students toward issues that they might not consider but should—for instance, "Are human beings fundamentally good or evil?" During the study of literature, issues raised within the selections themselves can be distilled as questions—for instance, in Paul Zindel's *The Pigman,* "Does Mr. Pignatti exploit John and Lorraine because of his own loneliness?" In S. E. Hinton's *That Was Then, This is Now,* "Should Bryon have turned Mark in?"

We also collect timely newspaper and magazine articles and editorials on topics such as capital punishment or the effects of media on the young, distribute these to

FIGURE 4-4
Trio tales

CHARACTER	SETTING	RESOLUTION
1. angel	school cafeteria	elopement
2. witch	riverbank	surgery
3. sailor	Iditarod	hysterical laughter
4. refugee	jail	firing
5. salesperson	CNN newsroom	explosion
6. spy	cemetery	starvation
7. hog	parade	inheritance
8. emperor	forest	surprise party
9. umpire	library	victory
10. time traveler	mall	promotion
11. spider	space station	remorse
12. dolphin	zoo	suspension

groups, ask groups to discuss their points of view, and select a spokesperson for the fishbowl. The discussants then enter the fishbowl with a more knowledgeable and nuanced position, and the listeners have a greater stake in the outcome. If clear sides are taken on an issue, teachers sometimes put all of those who are pro on the inside and those who are con on the outside. The pros and cons then exchange places to continue this "silent" debate. This activity demonstrates, without any teacher elaboration, how an interpretive community deepens individual perspectives.

Puzzlements (Group, Release). This exercise offers the ultimate in spontaneous group language exploration because the teacher poses puzzles for a group of students and then lets the students work them out alone. We have found puzzles to be almost universally self-motivating. The desire for cognitive closure makes most students want to find the solution. At the same time, the puzzles are difficult enough and sufficiently varied that most students will naturally seek the aid of others to arrive at an answer. Because we want their talk to acquire an authenticity and spontaneity often absent in class, we insist that the work be communal, not individual. Barnes, Britton, and Torbe (1990) note the consequences when students use language to discover, to collaborate, and to elaborate on learning. It becomes rich, real, and purposeful.

Students can chart or record their language in such groups and can listen afterwards to hear whether they are really collaborating and building on one another's ideas or merely trying to hold the floor and control the process, whether their problem-solving styles reflect gender differences, and whether they are using language as a way to discover meaning. If their group puzzle-solving discussions are recorded, students can listen to their own and other groups' tapes to make such observations and, later again, to see whether their talking matures over time. This activity can be used as a companion to examining dialogue in a text, especially a scene with conflict or a scene in which the characters are trying to solve a problem. Students can make comparisons between the characters' dialogue and their own.

Because English teachers appear to value games and puzzles, they provide good resources for material. The *English Journal* often poses verbal puzzles drawn from print and nonprint texts in a feature called "For Fun." NCTE published a book, *Inventing and Playing Games in the English Classroom: A Hand book for Teachers,* (Davis & Hollowell, 1977), concerned with designing and "running" games. Figure 4-5 is an example of prompts that require verbal, numerical, and spatial reasoning and that promote authentic, unself-conscious verbal collaboration.

Invitation to Reflection 4-2

On the basis of your reading about oral language exercises, respond to colleagues Pam Godfrey and Rick Roberts.

1. Fellow teacher Pam Godfrey has shared a number of her successes and difficulties with you since you both arrived at Kennedy High School. She is frustrated that her ninth-grade students cannot write simple narratives and admires your students' narratives hanging in the hallway. Pam asks, "How is it that your students write such great stories when you spend so much time in class on oral language activities?" How do you respond? What activities would you suggest to her?

2. Throughout the school year, you and Rick Roberts, another fellow teacher, have been discussing the difficulties his eleventh-grade students seem to have analyzing issues raised by the American literature they are reading. Rick recently attempted a discussion about contemporary American materialism in preparation for reading F. Scott Fitzgerald's *The Great Gatsby.* You find him at lunch despondent. He explains, "I was so surprised. This is a topic on which they are experts, yet they sat in silence. What can I do to get them talking?" What suggestions would you make?

CREATIVE DRAMA

Simply defined, creative drama asks students to put original words and actions together in a dramatic situation. Other comparable terms—*dramatic play, creative dramatics, improvisation, children's theatre,* and *role playing*—have shades of differences, but all describe essentially the same type of activity. A pioneer and early theorist in the field, Winifred Ward (1930, p. 3), in her struggle to have schools acknowledge the power of this new strategy, defined it in contrast to traditional drama study: "The term *creative dramatics* has grown up to distinguish this original dramatic work from the old formal study of ready-made plays." Since the 1930s, many have been drawn by the educative possibilities of creative dramatics and have elaborated on Ward's original work. In 1977, the Children's Theatre Association of America nicely defined the term as it had developed over almost fifty years:

> Creative drama is an improvisational, nonexhibitional, process-centered form of drama in which participants are guided by a leader to imagine, enact, and reflect upon human experiences. Although creative drama traditionally has been thought of in relation to children and young people, the process is appropriate to all ages. (as quoted in McCaslin, 1984, p. 9)

FIGURE 4–5
Puzzlement assignments

In small groups of four or five, solve the following problems in 20 minutes. You can move from one problem to another in any order you wish, but you must work as a group to solve the problems. You cannot assign individual tasks.

1. On a jetliner to Europe there are 9 boys, 5 American children, 9 men, 7 foreign boys, 14 Americans, 8 American males, and 5 foreign females. How many passengers are there on board? _____

2. Arrange the four pieces so as to fill in the block T below. Trace inside the T all sides of each of the four pieces so your answer can be checked.

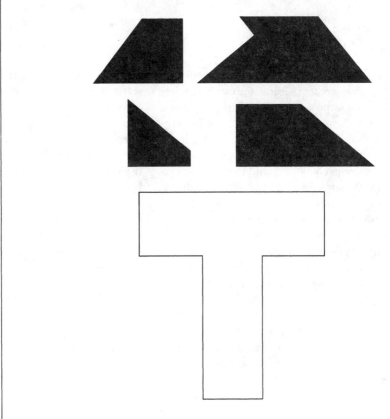

3. Find the next number in this series:
   7, 12, 27, 72, 207, _____

4. Change *bean* to *soup* by changing only one letter on each line in turn. Each line must be a word.

                    B E A N

                    — — — —

                    — — — —

                    — — — —

                    — — — —

                    S O U P

Creative drama occupies a place in the English classroom between oral language development and formal drama study and enjoys an established association with elementary language arts.

Many secondary English teachers are understandably reluctant to include it in their curriculum, however, because it departs not only from the "stand-up teaching" of the "talk and chalk" classroom but from text-based curricular requirements as well. It also challenges the teacher's traditional role as it frees students to imagine, think independently, develop their own ideas, and move closer to their emotions. Although teachers can assume varying roles—of coach offering suggestions from the sidelines, active participant in the drama, equal partner with the student dramatists—all of these involve some of the same risks as those students take. Creative drama loosens teachers' sense of predictable control. Gardner's (1983) theory of multiple intelligences may also explain teacher reluctance. He observes that linguistic and logical/mathematical intelligences dominate schoolwork; two of the other five, spatial and bodily/kinesthetic intelligences, dominate creative drama. While not deliberately suppressing these intelligences, teachers may not be comfortable with something relatively uncommon in English classrooms.

Content Goals

Two purposes seem uppermost in the plans of secondary teachers who advocate creative drama for content goals. First, it serves to teach important concepts in the curriculum. The American followers of British educator Dorothy Heathcote introduced creative drama as drama for learning. For instance, they have demonstrated how students might deeply and personally understand the religious life of the Incas or the principle of gravity by participating in their realistic portrayal. They use drama to impress important concepts into the memories of students, just as writing-to-learn proponents use writing. Under the spellbinding leadership of educator Betty Jane Wagner, we participated in a solemn dramatization of the Boston Tea Party. We took on the identities of citizens in the Boston community and, when we were confronted with matters of revolution, felt deeply conflicted. The personal learning was poignant and long-lasting. Heathcote exactly captured the differences between the knowledge that arises from creative drama and that which comes from the traditional transfer of a "body of knowledge." She characterizes drama as leading to the "lively interest of the 'stirred' individual who has become 'involved in knowing' rather than just knowing by memory alone" (in Johnson & O'Neill, 1985, p. 29). Drama is a means to an end beyond itself.

A second prominent purpose is to lead students into a deeper appreciation of formal drama written by playwrights for performance on the stage. While creative drama observes some of the conventions of formal drama, it leaves a great deal to the players' spontaneous creation. Formal drama is subject to diverse interpretations and performances; but the script has considerable authority over the actors, director, and audience. However, the two share common ground: They draw on the resources of language and action to put characters in motion before an audience. Playwrights and creative dramatists are bound by the same limitations and empowered by the same potentials. The word *playwright* comes from an Anglo-Saxon word meaning "a workman or craftsman," as in *shipwright, wheelwright,* and *cartwright.* It is related to a past-tense form of *work, wrought,* not to the verb *write.* Young creative dramatists learn experientially the work or craft of drama: the power of voice, movement, gesture, props, and scenery; their relation to the characters' roles; and their effect on others.

Personal Growth Goals

Dixon (1967) explains the potential of creative drama for personal growth: "To help pupils encounter life as it is, the complexity of relationships in a group and dynamic situation, there is nothing more direct and simple that we can offer them than drama" (p. 38). We will discuss five important aspects of creative drama's impact on personal growth: *language development, cooperative learning, risk taking, role playing,* and *creativity.*

Language Development. In creative drama students use language in simulated life situations and in concrete settings to interact with other characters. In authentic contexts, spontaneous speech replaces strangled, self-conscious classroom language. Furthermore, creative drama activities require collaboration in which students use language to plan, deliberate, negotiate, act, and assess their work. Dixon (1967) observes that "drama, like talk, is learning through interaction." In addition, the personal involvement of the teacher in the drama rearranges familiar classroom language roles, releasing new potential for language use by students and the teacher.

Creative drama activities, like those of oral language, have special benefits for the language development of ESL students. Gasparro and Falletta (1994, p. 1) observed the effects of dramatizing poetry on ESL students and found positive gains when they could "explore the linguistic and conceptual aspects of the written text without concentrating on the mechanics of language." They continue:

> Second language acquisition becomes internalized as a direct result of placing the learners in situations that seem real. The students use the target language for the specific purpose of communication. They experiment with non-verbal communicative aspects of language (body language, gestures, and facial expressions), as well as verbal aspects (intonation, rhythm, stress, slang, and idiomatic expressions), while interpreting the poems. The students begin to feel the language and gain the confidence to interact outside the classroom using the target language.

Cooperative Learning. Most of the creative drama activities that follow require cooperative work among actors, producers, stage managers, scriptwriters, and audiences. Group efforts behind the scenes make the performance possible. These cooperative acts produce immediate and intense interactions among students. As O'Neill and Lambert (1982, p. 13) observe, "Drama is essentially social and involves contact, communication and the negotiation of meaning." They explain some of the dimensions of this cooperation:

> Within the safe framework of the make-believe, individuals can see their ideas and suggestions accepted and used by the group. They can learn how to influence others; how to marshall effective arguments and present them appropriately; how to put themselves in other people's shoes. They can try out roles

and receive immediate feedback. The group can become a powerful source of creative ideas and effective criticism.

And we would add, the public nature of drama enhances students' motivation.

Risk Taking. Students who would be reluctant to enter into a full dramatic production of *Macbeth* can more easily participate in less-structured dramatic activity. Because their words and gestures are spontaneous and audience expectations are subordinated, students more comfortably take on roles that demand complex and emotionally compelling responses. Still, any performance before an audience daunts many students, even the dramatic extroverts. Creative drama challenges students to feel and express emotions that, particularly during adolescence, are volatile but tightly controlled. Growth in understanding often results from this challenge to customary perceptions and this projection into new ways of thinking and feeling.

Role Playing. Creative drama requires students to open themselves to other experiences, to imagine themselves in difficult situations, and so to enter others' personal perplexities. When students attempt to understand others— their histories, their characteristic behaviors, their motives, and their habits—they often receive sudden glimpses into other lives that challenge their existing assumptions and biases. In so doing, students can make significant advances toward genuine understanding of lives lived differently from their own. Young children play house to this effect. The role playing involved in creative drama can result in challenges to customary perceptions and imagining new ways of thinking and feeling.

Creativity. Within varying degrees of constraint, creative drama can free the imagination and encourage it to encompass new, open possibilities and transformations. Students are active, not passive. They become participants, not spectators, at an event that draws on their physical, mental, social, and even emotional capacities. Creativity and playfulness are the essence of this activity. We ask students to let go of the "brute facts" world momentarily, to suspend their self-conscious real selves, and to experience a moment of transforming play—moving "from surge to stage," as Eugene Ionesco says in the *The Bald Soprano*.

All of these effects of creative drama are captured in philosopher George Santayana's remark that play is the most serious thing we do. Yet the play of creative drama has some structure, and to enter it students must be willing to accept certain rules.

Rules of the Game

These rules of creative drama are not general and inflexible but specific and fluid, depending on the particular activity of the moment. O'Neill and Lambert (1982, pp. 1–12) establish a few basic ground rules. Students must be willing to

- make-believe with regard to objects
- make-believe with regard to actions and situations
- adopt a role
- maintain the make-believe verbally
- interact with the rest of the group

Even if students are willing, they may still be easily frustrated or remain shy and reluctant. Creative drama does not provide many hiding places for resistant students. It asks them to take risks and to act. Others can become giddy with unexpected freedom, unfamiliar assignments, and possible showmanship. Both the timid and the bold can defeat the enterprise. O'Neill and Lambert (p. 149) suggest building "certain safeguards into the work which can help to protect pupils against these risks":

- Establishing an atmosphere of trust and encouraging even the most limited contributions.
- Setting up work which has a clear focus and contains clearly defined tasks which are within the capacity of the class.
- Providing a model of appropriate behavior and commitment, most effectively perhaps by taking a role within the drama.
- "Distancing" material which may prove embarrassing to the pupils by setting it within an analogous situation.
- Offering constant reminders that the pupils are working in an art form which will legitimately permit them to explore thoughts and feelings through the safety of an adopted role.

Resources

Teachers must grow gradually in their confidence in such activities. The following resources can stimulate and supplement the teacher's imagination.

Books

Booth, D. (1994). *Story drama.* Markham, Ontario: Pembroke.

Duke, C. (1974). *Creative dramatics and English teaching.* Urbana, IL: National Council of Teachers of English.

Johnson, L., & O'Neill, C. (1985). *Dorothy Heathcote: Collected writings on education and drama.* London: Hutchinson.

King, N. (1993). *Storymaking and drama.* Portsmouth, NH: Heinemann.

McCaslin, N. (2000). *Creative drama in the classroom and beyond.* New York: Longman.

Morgan, N., & Saxton, J. (1987). *Teaching drama.* Cheltenham, UK: Stanley Thornes.

Norris, J., McCammon, L., & Miller, C. (2000). *Learning to teach drama.* Portsmouth, NH: Heinemann.

O'Neill, C., & Lambert, A. (1990). *Drama structures: A practical handbook for teachers.* Portsmouth, NH: Heinemann.

O'Neill, C., & Manley, A. (1998). *Dreamseekers: Creative approaches to the African American heritage.* Portsmouth, NH: Heinemann.

Spolin, V. (1967). *Improvisation for the theater.* Evanston, IL: Northwestern University Press.

Wright, S. (1991). *The arts in early childhood.* New York: Prentice Hall.

Web-Based Resources

- Drama Australia (www.ausdrama.gil.com)
- American Alliance for Theater and Education (www.aate.com)
- International Drama Education Association: (www.edyc.queensu.ca/~idea/)
- Arts-related resources and lesson plans (www.artsedge.kennedy-center.org)

Creative Drama Activities: Fixed to Free

In Figure 4–6 we present twelve specific activities that introduce creative drama into the English classroom. These activities range from having fixed structures to being almost wholly free.

Fixed: activities in which students are given a simple set of words or gestures to enact that do not require rehearsal, prior talent, or an immensely risky display of self

Free: activities based on improvisation from the teacher's prompts

The sequence—from games, simple dramatic activities, and short improvisations to extended improvisations—provides students with increasingly more challenging tasks. After this accumulated experience, they are ready to undertake complex improvisations of their own devising.

Freeze-Frames.   This activity requires active imagination but no action. Ask students to arrange themselves in the postures of sculptures, tableaux, monuments, still

photographs, waxworks, or statues to illustrate various human situations and emotions. These body sculptures can vivify the structure of literature, human experience, and even ideas under discussion. They can be instantaneous or preplanned. They require little space and demand little acting experience. Imagine what can be added to a class discussion when the following freeze-frames are enacted.

- During a thematic unit on families, a group creates a tableau representing the traditional rural family of 1810, while another group presents a tableau of the contemporary urban family of the twenty-first century. (According to the U.S. Bureau of the Census, 87 percent of the labor force was engaged in agriculture in 1810; by 1980, that figure had dropped to 3 percent.)
- While discussing Countee Cullen's poem "Incident," a group freezes in the posture of Baltimore citizens in the background and two children in the foreground just at the moment of insult and recognition.

Most students, if they work in groups, comfortably risk this bit of drama because no actions or words are required. However, they should be able to tell why they chose their particular poses and moments out of the range of possibilities inherent in the subject.

Chaos Drama.   In this activity, each member of the class draws a card that gives directions for a strange activity for that student alone to perform repeatedly. Following are a few representative performance cards that we have used:

- Walk to the nearest window or door and pretend frantically to try to open it. After a five-second attempt, cry out "Horrors! The air is streaming in on us!"
- Step up to a podium (or an imagined podium) and begin to recite the vowels with deep anger and great meaning in a loudspeaker voice.
- Skip slowly and gracefully about the room, stopping at any person who is not in motion around the room. Put both hands on this person's shoulders and say longingly, "It is so, so good to have you back home again."

FIGURE 4–6
Creative drama: Fixed to free activities

Freeze-frames:	stationary body poses
Chaos drama:	little snippets of a prescribed script
Faces, hands, and feet:	acting out words with a focus
Minidrama:	dramatic interpretation of a script
Personified poems:	acting out simple poems with gestures
Costume drama:	costumed groups produce a brief play
Bag act:	play devised out of the props placed in a bag
Nonstop triad:	two fast-talking antagonists and one arbitrator
When worlds collide:	elaboration of a fictive or historical event
Dramatic monologue:	students create a character through staged monologue
Four C's improvisation:	dramatic *c*onflict, *c*haracters, *c*ontext, *c*onclusion
Intervention drama:	strange characters in the midst of normalcy

When all students have been assigned a role to play, the entire class is told to act out the individual parts simultaneously until the teacher says, "Stop."

One point of the activity is to release individual dramatic energy that is acceptable, comfortable, and even liberating in a classroom in which every other individual is displaying equally bizarre behavior. The group effort minimizes the self-consciousness of the individual. Students have their words and their actions totally planned for them; they act in concert with everyone else. Yet despite the controlling script, there is room for improvisation and for idiosyncratic interpretation of whatever role is assigned. If the noise threshold of your classroom is an issue, all utterances can be whispered or merely mouthed.

Chaos drama is effective in textual study to invite students into the characters of a longer work and to set those multiple human beings in motion in ways a student might be too self-conscious to enact alone. We ask each student to choose a character and act as that character would at a particular point in a play or novel. Julie Peterson (2001, personal communication) adapted this activity after her students had read Gcina Mhlophe's short story "It's Quiet Now" about the riots in Soweto, South Africa. Students took on various roles—bus drivers, buses, passengers, children, the mayor and his family, police officers, sirens—to re-create the story's chaotic tone. (Students enacted rain by shaking newspapers.) With the anonymity of group performance, students can enter the imaginative world more fully and forthrightly. The synergy of many propels the one. (We must mention the following caveat: If you use this activity with an especially large, unruly, or excitable class, more than the drama may be chaotic. One option is to ask students to act out their roles in silence or in seated positions at their desks.)

Faces, Hands, and Feet. A further step toward an improvisational stage presence is concentration on a single element of the body's entire dramatic potential. A trio of students is asked to bare their toes and either recline with their feet exposed or sit at tables, head down, so that the feet can act in a normal foot posture. The three students are shown a card that contains a single word naming a human emotion or state of being—for instance, *anger, joy,* and *jealousy*—that they must portray using only their feet. The remaining students guess what the feet are suggesting. The acting job is, of course, a tough one; but the wordless, physical, and psychological distance of the actors reduces the risk. After the feet act out three or four words, the hands alone are placed above the tabletop and their owners receive a set of tougher words to act out, such as *anxiety, rage,* and *careful.* Because our hands are so fluent, they can usually convey words that the feet struggle to express. Consciousness of the role of actor gradually develops in these students, still with minimum risk involved. The final step passes the acting job to the face, our body's most expressive actor. The eyes, eyebrows, mouth, and all the other facial features act out difficult words, such as *savage, faithful,* and *bellicose.* Only the faces are allowed to appear, chins resting on a tabletop.

Although this activity can serve merely as an effective warm-up exercise, it builds an important sense of communicating ideas to an audience through nonverbal physical gestures on a stage. (A clip from a silent movie demonstrates the need for exaggerated gesture when words are not available.) During a unit on Greek drama, a colleague used this activity to help students understand the difficulties that Greek actors, who wore masks, faced in expressing emotion without the use of facial expression. Not only did her hands-feet drama increase her students' understanding of the body's dramatic potential, but it also served to build community in her classroom.

Minidrama. The missing ingredient in the creative drama activities discussed so far is language. Language controls our next activity, minidrama. As with a full-blown drama, a script provides students with a text to interpret through voice. Unlike most other dramatic texts, however, the script is so brief that students with poor memories or stage fright can comfortably take central roles. Pairs of students recite the lines as an exchange. Two possible scripts follow in their entirety in Figure 4-7.

The delight of the activity is that voice determines everything: situation, tone, mood, and outcome. In the first example, "So./So!" students can decide to let the words convey the sorrow of a final parting, the anger of a violent encounter, or the ennui of an uneventful conversation. In the second script, which begins "You're late," the scene could be played as if it involved two lovers, two spies, or a parent and child. Whatever the pairs choose,

---

SCRIPT 1
A. So.
B. So!
A. It's up to you.
B. Me?
A. Please.
B. Why?
A. It's inevitable.
B. That's what you think.
A. No, really.
B. I'll show you.

SCRIPT 2
A. You're late.
B. I know. Sorry.
A. I understand.
B. I knew you would.
A. I have something for you.
B. Really? What?
A. This!
B. Oh!

FIGURE 4–7 Two minidramas

each must consider and dramatize the lines so that an audience of peers can readily guess what's afoot. To do this, they must envision how they would feel in such a situation in real life and use volume, emphasis, inflection, speed, pauses, and pitch to convey their feelings. Gestures, movements, costumes, and props can be used to complicate and enhance the performance.

Teachers can create their own provocative minidramas. They can even use situations or lines from actual texts. The great payoff in this activity comes as different pairs present the same lines with striking variations. No explication is needed to teach the effects of dramatic choice. To explore technique, a simple question is usually sufficient: "How did the pair create its effect?"

Personified Poems. This activity, like minidrama, uses a script to which student actors add their dramatic gestures. (It is like the first oral exercise, voice lessons, but with gestures.) First-person poems, selected by the teacher or student, provide excellent texts (Figure 4–3). Those with pronounced rhyme and meter are easiest to commit to memory. The dialogue poems of Figure 4–8 invite the interaction of two or more students. Some of these require a third voice to read expository lines, almost like an ancient Greek chorus. Gasparro and Falletta (1994) have used the following poems successfully with beginner, low-intermediate, and high-intermediate ESL students:

"Love in Brooklyn," by John Wakeman
"Why Did the Children Put Beans in their Ears?," by Carl Sandburg

"Woodpecker in Disguise," by Grace Taber Hallock
"Read This with Gestures," by John Ciardi

Other poetic resources can be found in Chapter 6.

Costume Drama. This activity depends almost entirely on the effect that special garb has on the group's imagination. We use costume drama both as literature review and as dramatic experience at the end of a unit, a semester, or a school year. We ask every student to come dressed as a character or even a significant object from the literature the class has read together. We capitalize on the students' natural love of a mystery and a game by beginning this activity with a contest. Each student offers a line from the story or a clue of some sort to enable others to identify the character or object. After we guess the characters' identities (which makes an excellent review of the reading), we divide students into two groups and ask each to use the props and costuming they have assembled to create a short play with a title, a narrator (if desired), central and supporting characters, action, and a climax. The plays can be related to one of the familiar texts or entirely original.

Bag Act. This activity does not depend on prior reading but on a set of three or four bags full of hats, odd shirts, shawls, festive material, gaudy beads, ties, and assorted objects found in attics and yard sales. As before, students allow the props to ignite their creative powers. Teachers can, if they wish, guide the actors by offering a situation or conflict from which to work.

FIGURE 4–8
Dialogue poems

Anonymous	"Sir Patrick Spens"
	"Edward"
Thomas Nashe (1567–1601)	"A Litany in Time of Plague"
George Herbert (1593–1633)	"Love"
Anne Finch (1661–1720)	"Friendship between Ephelia and Ardelia"
William Blake (1757–1827)	"The Clod and the Pebble"
Percy Bysshe Shelley (1792–1822)	"Ozymandias"
John Keats (1795–1821)	"La Belle Dame Sans Merci"
Robert Browning (1812–1889)	"My Last Duchess"
	"Meeting at Night"
	"Parting at Morning"
Christina Rossetti (1830–1894)	"Up-Hill"
Lewis Carroll (1832–1898)	"Jabberwocky"
A. E. Housman (1859–1936)	"Terence, This Is Stupid Stuff"
	"Is My Team Ploughing?"
W. B. Yeats (1865–1939)	"For Anne Gregory"
Edwin Arlington Robinson (1869–1935)	"Mr. Flood's Party"
	"An Evangelist's Wife"
Paul Valéry (1871–1945)	"Asides (Chanson a part)"
Robert Frost (1874–1963)	"Out, Out—"
	"The Death of the Hired Man"
	"Telephone"
John Crowe Ransom (1888–1974)	"Piazza Piece"
Countee Cullen (1903–1946)	"Incident"
W. H. Auden (1907–1973)	"O Where Are You Going?"
Karl Shapiro (1913–2000)	"Doctor, Doctor, A Little of Your Love"
Henry Reed (1914–1986)	"Naming of Parts"

Mindi Fry (2001, personal communication) thought of the bag act for a group of ninth graders who needed a lift in their unit on *Romeo and Juliet* one Friday. She brought bags of miscellany to class, had students choose their own group, examine their props, decide on a scene to dramatize before the class, create their own skits, perform them, and peer-evaluate each other. Some groups retained Shakespeare's language; others converted the text into "ghetto slang." These contrasts initiated discussions about dramatic interpretation.

Nonstop Triad. A middle school teacher, Rick Carter (1991, personal communication) recommends this activity, which uses conflict with a twist to promote spontaneous drama. He assigns three students roles and a conflict situation. An authority figure has to try to arbitrate an intense conflict between two bitter adversaries: a policeman and two drivers in a major fender bender; or a principal and two students, one of whom has wronged the other; or from literature, a minister, Huck Finn, and the Widow Douglas just after Huck's flight for the island. The only stage direction the teacher gives is that the conflict is a bitter one—and this twist: The three participants should talk nonstop. Although they never cease talking, each is able to listen more than you might think. The triologue has produced for us amazingly authentic speech and inventive thinking. Improbable explanations and schemes arise frequently in these harried conversations. If the frenetic conversation is taped, groups can later transform it into a more traditional script as the core of a formal performance.

When Worlds Collide. This activity uses drama from the collision of two or three famous historic or fictional personages thrown together onstage without regard to normal historical constraints. Here we have character rather than conflict as the source of drama. Supply brief biographies or relevant Web sites. After students have become acquainted with these memorable persons, ask them to converse together in character. Imagine Moses, Sigmund Freud, and Helen Keller onstage responding to this simple prompt: "What do you think of women's contemporary roles?" Or consider the outcome of a conversation between literary characters: Holden Caulfield from *The Catcher in the Rye;* Cassie Logan from *Roll of Thunder, Hear My Cry;* and Huck Finn responding to the prompt "What's the hardest part of growing up?" or "Why do adults act the way they do?" We like to mix literary and historical figures. Imagine Abraham Lincoln and Okonkwo from *Things Fall Apart* discussing leadership or Rosa Parks, Cassie Logan from *Roll of Thunder, Hear my Cry* and Janie Crawford from *Their Eyes Were Watching God* talking about the difficulties of being southern African American women. Mere conversation gains dramatic scope and power. This transformation is heightened if the context also provides a particular, provocative

setting, such as an infantry trench, a television talk show, or a national political convention.

Dramatic Monologue. This activity provides an opportunity for the individual student to create and interpret a character first on paper and then through the telling of a story. Petrina McGowen (1997) explains the role of monologue in a traditional play: "To allow the audience some extra insight either into [character] or an [other] aspect of the play." McGowen sets tasks for her eighth-grade students that lead each to create a character (imagined, historic, or familiar) caught in the midst of a story. Each student must construct or select the following:

- a list of emotions (at least three)
- a list of physical attributes (at least three)
- a setting
- a conflict
- a secret (which they do not allude to; "it just helps deepen the structure" of the character)
- simple props (hats, ties, scarves, and so on) that help bring the character to life

After each student has visualized a character's attributes and imagined the character's story, the student tells the story to the class in the voice of the character. Students are not allowed to describe their characters' feelings or emotions but must bring these traits to life through the situation, mannerisms, props, voice, and setting.

Four C's Improvisation. In this activity, students use *character, conflict, context,* and *closure* to achieve full dramatic effect. To initiate the improvisation, the teacher gives brief descriptions of specific characters, their context, and the conflict they experience. With these three givens, students begin to construct a rising tension (complication), a moment of crisis and release (climax), and then the resolution (denouement). One of the most difficult things for students to achieve is satisfactorily clearing the stage, bringing the action to resolution and conclusion. They know that "and they lived happily ever after" does the job of closing fairy tales and "and they all died gruesomely hereafter" appears to close many horror stories. What is difficult is bringing dramatic action to a satisfying resolution of conflict. Student actors must do more than announce lamely to the audience, "That's all, folks!" They have to anticipate and plan their drama so that the audience knows when to clap or when to expect the curtain to fall. Students can give the audience signals that the play has ended by talking in slow or fast motion, freezing at the moment the last line is uttered, or turning slowly 180 degrees away from the audience; but the test is that the audience knows by word and by deed that there is nothing more that needs to be said, that the play is complete. When students have become adept at dramatic closes, they will know it because the audience's reactions will tell them so. Four C's improvisation provides the experience of planning, executing, and gauging one's success by the audience reaction. (Four C's provides a great prewriting activity for narrative writing as well.)

Intervention Drama. Our final creative drama activity satisfies all of the four C's but adds one new wrinkle. The teacher asks students to identify themselves as a group and then as individuals within the group and then to select a concrete context for interaction. They might choose, for example, to be an extended family at an out-of-doors reunion dinner. The teacher initiates a prompt for improvisation, one that incites, not resolves, a conflict. For instance, the crew of an Andromedean spaceship comes unexpectedly upon that family reunion. These intruders might be given distinguishing touches of costume or language so that the original players can identify them and know they are not from Savannah or Topeka. The conflict appears to be inevitable; but if it is not, the Andromedeans should be sure to create one. The challenge is for the student family to resolve the conflict and end the crisis—that is, to put the lessons on closure into spontaneous action. This activity can also be used as a prewriting prompt for students scripting scenes or plays themselves or as a pre-reading activity for an assigned text using actual characters, settings, and conflicts. (The author's decisions can then be measured against the students'.)

As we look back at these twelve creative drama activities, we see students enter the world of creative drama in the comfort of given directions. As they become more comfortable and confident in a dramatic role, students begin to experiment with what makes good drama. Students become aware of the body's potential for dramatic effects (and props and costuming, too). They can manipulate language for dramatic meaning. They sense the shaping force of character, conflict (issues and themes), and context (places and settings). In the final stage, improvisation taps students' personal imagination and intellect, develops stronger language arts skills, and prepares them for formal drama. Ideally, creative drama also provides delight.

McCaslin (1984, p. 22) provides a neat summary of the purposes and advantages of creative drama. She regards it "as a way of learning, a means of self-expression, a therapeutic technique, a social activity, or an art form. Children are helped to assume responsibility, accept group decisions, work together cooperatively, develop new interests, and—particularly in a classroom situation—seek new information. Drama is the most completely personal, as well as the most highly socialized, art form we have." Dixon (1967, pp. 42–43) summarizes the ways in which drama touches all four language arts for high school students:

- *improvising* talk appropriate to a vast range of situation and role;
- *listening and responding* in the fullest sense, while taking a role;

- *discussing* the approach to a theme, its possibilities, and finally the insights gained;
- *writing* scripts for one's own group;
- *reading,* learning and probing the meaning of a text—through private study, talk and enacting.

Dixon also recognizes the classroom context in which creative drama finds its greatest potential, not in a teacher's sustained and conscious development of actors and producers of school plays but in "an awareness among teachers of English of those moments in a lesson, or in a week's work, when what has been said or read moves naturally out to enactment with movement and gesture" (p. 42).

Invitation to Reflection 4-3

Swartz (1988) provides a frame of reference to use for planning additional possibilities for creative drama in the classroom (p. 10). Treat the schema (Figure 4–9) as a planning quartet tale, like the Trio tales discussed earlier. Select a variable from each column with which to shape a dramatic activity for the class—the sources, the components (or we might call them activities), the process to emphasize, and the group size.

STORY DRAMA

In describing these oral language and creative drama activities, we have included suggestions about their application to the study of texts. In the next four chapters, we suggest many other dramatic approaches to teaching fiction, poetry, and scripted drama. Before we leave this focus on oral language, however, we would like to elaborate on the great advantages of drama in the study of literature, particularly for low-achieving readers. Research studies such as those of Gambrell and Bales (1986) and Purcell-Gates (1991) suggest that lower-ability readers especially do not have strategies for imagining or visualizing fictive worlds. Dramatic activities can invite students to enter the story worlds of prose and poetry, an entry sometimes narrowed to the vanishing point by traditional classroom discussions. Less-proficient readers regard reading as a passive act of decoding words and receiving meanings, not as the active envisioning of characters alive in imaginary worlds and certainly not as the occasions for the constructing of meanings. They cannot arrive in what Bruner (1986) calls "the landscape of action," which the story triggers. Entering that landscape is a necessary prerequisite to reaching "the landscape of consciousness," where the reader begins to entertain and envision the characters and "what those involved in the action know, think or feel, or do not know, think or feel" (p. 14). Drama

FIGURE 4–9
Planning quartet tale

Source: Adapted from *Dramathemes* by Larry Swartz. Pembroke Publishers Limited, 528 Hood Road, Markham, Ontario L3R 3K9. Available in the U.S. from Heinemann Educational Books. Reprinted with permission.

Sources	Components	Process	Grouping
picture book	games	discussing	individual
novel	mime	planning	pairs
poem	tableau	improvising	small groups
script	movement	role playing	large group
short story	interviewing	problem solving	whole group
illustration	storytelling	decision making	audience
newspaper	choral speaking	questioning	
magazine	readers theater	reflecting	
properties	illustrating	persuading	
film	designing	summarizing	
song	writing	imagining	
our own stories	researching	describing	
	ritual/ceremony	challenging	
	performing	recalling	
	play making	instructing	
		reporting	
		informing	
		evaluating	

CLASSROOM POSSIBILITIES IN DRAMA

provides an equally effective ticket to facilitate ESL students' arrival in the story world.

In sorting out how to help his less-engaged and less-proficient readers, Jeff Wilhelm (1997) asked, "How might dramatic activity guide and support student efforts to fill textual gaps and to elaborate on and move around in textual worlds?" (p. 93). He turned to story drama activities in order "to evoke story worlds, to help them make inferences about characters and their situations, and thus find reading literature to be a rewarding experience" (p. 99). He drew on Heathcote's (1984, p. 44) idea that in drama you "put yourself into other people's shoes and by using personal experience to help you to understand their point of view you may discover more than you knew when you started." We summarize some of the activities that Wilhelm used to invite students to put on the shoes of story characters and to walk around in them. He calls the first, revolving role drama, the staple of the drama activity that he used daily.

Revolving role drama: Students are asked to assume the perspective of a character in the story, to "visualize the story world and enact movement and interaction within that world" (p. 100).
Dramatic play: Students are given a prompt or a situation (that may or may not come from the story) and are asked to assume the role of a story character and enact what would naturally follow from such a stimulus, remaining consistent with the psychology of the character.
To Tell the Truth Game: Students play the parts of characters, other students interrogate them about their lives, and the class judges who has "most convincingly 'become' that character" (p. 101).
Newscast: Students produce a videotaped news show that involves "interviewing characters, reporting on their activities, and editorializing on particular actions and decisions" (pp. 100–101).

Two-Sided Story: Students are asked "to act out a scene from their lives (real or projected) that in some way parallel[s] a scene from the book" (p. 108).

Wilhelm testifies to the impact of story drama on opening the world of literature for his low-achieving students. Story drama holds promise for ESL students as well. In a basic text on principles of second language acquisition, Krashen (1982) discusses an essential strategy for learning another language—"comprehensible input." The premise is that to learn language, the language must have meaning for the learner. Story drama can make literature more concrete, real, intelligible, and, in short, comprehensible. Story drama and many other creative drama activities employ nonverbal cues and verbal enactments to invite ESL students into the animated drama of characters and their stories. Seeing props, physical gestures, and even modest settings; hearing the give-and-take of interviews; becoming acclimated to a dramatic context; and watching scenes acted out pique interest, make words palpable, and clarify character, setting, and narrative.

In Chapter 2, we discussed the benefits of the smaller, more intimate environment of small-group work that provided more opportunities to talk and a safer context for testing language use. Oral language activities and creative drama activities appear to be more public and higher-risk settings in which the advantages of oral language development are compromised for ESL students and, in fact, for all but the most proficient language users. But the teacher can control the exposure of students to public embarrassment and can construct sheltered environments even when they are "on stage." We turn to a process of response to oral performance that provides both safety and critical response when oral language activities go public.

෨RESPONSE AND CRITIQUE

Many oral language exercises and creative drama activities require no formal feedback from the audience (teacher or classmates), but at times some form of response and even evaluation enrich and extend student learning. We enumerate an evaluative process that we have found pertinent to any form of creative expression and useful in whole or in part. A dancer and dance educator, Deirdre Smith, introduced us to a method of critical response that dancers Liz Lerman (1993) and Michelle Pearson (1997) developed as an alternative to the often-wounding critiques that dancers traditionally endure from their instructors and each other. We will discuss other evaluative methods in later chapters on writing and evaluation. We include this process here because we think evaluation is as integral to student learning of oral language as it is to their growth as readers and writers. Evaluation also serves to legitimate any subject of study. The process below serves the best of evaluative purposes in helping the learner understand audience reaction and reflect on that feedback. As you read, please consider the logic in the sequence of steps and the practical wisdom in individual parts of it.

Following any performance, a facilitator sits by the artist/performer to field questions from the audience in a sequence of steps.

Step 1: Affirmation

The facilitator solicits positive, affirmative responses from the audience with questions such as the following:

- What is working?
- What has meaning for you?
- What is unexpected?
- What was cool? What was invigorating?
- What was your favorite part?
- What should be definitely kept?
- What about this work "brought you something special"?

Step 2: Artist As Questioner

The performer next asks the audience more particular questions that critique the performance. The facilitator can step in to help the artist find the questions that are specific and essential. Usually, the facilitator steers away from general questions—"What do you think?"—and from general responses— "I thought it was interesting!" Specific questions yield more clarifying and productive insight: "Should the performers move to center stage at the conclusion?" or "Which prop or mannerism was most telling or expressive?"

Step 3: Responders As Questioners

Next, the facilitator asks the performer whether he or she is willing to answer the responders' questions and, if so, asks the responders to frame their opinions in questions that are neutral, that do not themselves make critical suggestions or statements. For example, rather than telling the performer, "The dramatic monologue didn't go anywhere," the responder might rephrase that into a genuine question: "What was the most essential character trait you were trying to communicate in your monologue?" and then "What details drove that trait home?" This rephrasing shifts the responder out of a superior position of authority and into a position as colleague and problem solver. In such a relationship, the artist is more likely to be open to what the other is saying than if she or he felt under attack.

Step 4: Opinion Time

At this point in the process, when some greater distance from the performance and greater ease with the audience have been established, the performer may be ready to hear direct opinions. Thus, during this fourth stage, the responders can actively state opinions or offer suggestions; but first they must ask the artist whether he or she is interested in hearing an opinion about the specific issue that concerns them. For instance, a responder might say, "I have an opinion about your timing. Do you want to hear it?" The artist can still control the situation by saying, "Yes," "No," or "Not at this time."

Steps 5 and 6: Subject Matter Discussion and Working on the Work

If the respondents and the artist are interested in continuing to talk, the discussion might broaden to the subject matter of the work. Often the content of this last discussion motivates and guides any rewriting or reworking of the original.

All of these steps could be used initially with activities involving large numbers of students, such as the costume drama or 4 C's improvisation. As trust builds and students grow familiar with the process, it can be used to reflect on the work of individual students. In addition to facilitating reflection and assessment, this process builds confidence by making the student artist the expert on his or her work; and it helps establish the tone of serious fun needed to make creative drama valuable as a learning experience in the classroom. Ideally, the steps of this process can become internalized for teacher, performers, and audience. It should become a perspective that provides specific, constructive response and nonthreatening critique, a habit that allows students to fruitfully examine their individual work and that of their classmates.

FIGURE 4–10
Interviewing matrix

Who \ How	Extensive	Intensive
Inside Out	Value Chat	Partner Probe
Outside In	Expert Query	Retrospective Talk

INTERVIEWING

Interviewing is another powerful way to make oral language come alive in your classroom. Interviews can be organized in a host of formats. We use a block matrix (Figure 4-10) to represent different possibilities. We borrow half of our matrix title from Kirby and Liner's *Inside Out* (1981). Students themselves are the interviewees for the "inside out" in the upper half of the matrix. Classmates interview them to learn what they know and feel and what they care to reveal. People who live beyond the classroom walls are interviewees for the "outside in" in the lower half. The matrix is also divided laterally. The left side calls for interviews that are extensive and informational, while the right side involves intensive, personal probes.

Value Chat

"Inside out" extensive interviews, like the value chat, invite students to take the catbird seat before the class and answer questions from classmates. Students use questions from an established list for the first six interview questions and then pose questions they have prepared for the remainder of the interview. We have used questions such as the following:

1. Does your family do anything together that is fun?
2. As you look at the world around you, what is something you sometimes wonder about?
3. Have you ever made a choice that surprised everyone?
4. Did you ever want to write a letter to the principal or a newspaper editor? What would the topic have been?
5. Of all the people you know who have helped you, name the one who has helped you the most? How did this individual go about it?
6. Where did you spend the best summer of your life?
7. Are there problems or injustices in your community you feel need attention?
8. Can you think of something that you would like to say to the whole student body that you think might be good for them to hear?

9. If you had an extra $5,000 given to you with no strings attached, what would you do with it?
10. What are three things at which you are good?

The student who is interviewed can ask for a pass on any question that is too tough or intrusive. When the interviewed student has had enough, he or she can merely say "Thank you very much," and the interview is ended.

Partner Probe

The intensive partner probe interview pushes deeper and is done in a less public fashion. Students interview each other in pairs to find out their deep thoughts and sensitive insights. You might compare the following ten questions to the value chat list. These questions grow more personal.

1. Do you look forward to coming to school each morning?
2. What is your favorite time of the school day?
3. During class, how often does your mind stray from the subject you are studying?
4. What are your favorite times at home?
5. What kind of people do you admire most?
6. Do you have any bold ambition or important long-term goals?
7. What makes life worthwhile for you?
8. Do you deal with success and failure pretty well?
9. What seems to be essential to a longtime friendship?
10. How important is work in your life?

Expert Query

The expert query of the "outside in" interviews involves asking interesting adults about career patterns, specialized skills, or political insights. Students can interview these outsiders, or they can ask them to attend class and let the whole class ask the questions. Preparing for these visitors with an intelligent sequence of questions develops students' sense of sequence and logic.

4–1 TEACHING ACTIVITY

Preparing for a Retrospective Talk

Interview someone whose life experiences are different from yours and who is old enough to cast a long backward glance at his or her life. Grandparents are excellent interviewees. Use these questions or variations of them.

1. Who are the best friends you ever had? Where are they now?

2. Do you celebrate your birthday? How? What other events do you celebrate?

3. Do you have any collections, favorite possessions, or hobbies? Describe one.

4. What people have taught you those things you regard as valuable lessons? Name one lesson you value highly.

5. Has there ever been a turning point in your life that made you a different person afterward? Describe it.

6. What was the greatest historic turning point for the nation or the world that you have experienced?

7. If you could choose another occupation for yourself different from your primary work, what would it be? Why?

8. Have you ever wanted to give advice to someone in a position of power and responsibility? What kind of advice? To whom?

9. What were the times in your life when you felt the greatest sense of accomplishment or joy and failure or hopelessness?

10. How would the people who know you best characterize you to a stranger?

Retrospective Talk

Students move outside the class again to interview grandparents or friendly elders with a set of questions that asks interviewees to reflect on what they have experienced and learned in the course of their lives. Teaching Activity 4–1 is a possible assignment sheet for such a retrospective.

Invitation to Reflection 4–4

In Invitation to Reflection 4–2, you helped two colleagues use oral language exercises to enhance students' writing and reading. We ask you now to address dynamics in your own classroom as you respond to the informal speaking problems you have noticed in some of your students. The problems of this small group were masked in class discussions and in oral language and creative dramatics activities because you have so many fluent talkers and eager performers. You have realized that about five of your tenth graders mumble, fidget, evade responses, use a lot of verbal stammering—"hmm, and uh, well, you know, uh"—and clearly are uncomfortable in any public role. Any direct attempts to draw them out only worsen their discomfort. You have a hunch these students are not poorly prepared or disinterested. You know you will have to define the problem more specifically before you can begin to address it through instruction.

- What questions would you ask yourself about how to help these few?
- What classroom observations would you make?
- Are there other resources you might seek to help identify the problem?

You consider three general strategies available to you: discussions (whole-class, small-group, pairs), oral language exercises, and creative drama activities.

- Do you turn to one or all three of these to help your students?
- Do you integrate your oral language instruction into study of the other language arts or isolate it in focused lessons?
- How do you manage the differences of oral language ability in your class?

After you have determined your approach and planned and implemented your lessons, you see progress. Quite outside your design, an opportunity arises for you to evaluate the students' progress in an authentic situation. Representatives of the State Department of Public Instruction are coming to observe how well English teachers are implementing the state language arts standards (based on the IRA/NCTE standards). The principal selects your tenth-grade class to demonstrate the steps the English department is taking to improve oral language.

- How will you plan a lesson for the visitation day that will involve all of your students, not just the achieving and proficient ones, in fluent talking and active listening?

☞ CONCLUSION

We have come quite a distance in this chapter, from taking our words seriously in ordinary classroom discourse to using a full range of oral expression to communicate effectively. Throughout, the focus of teaching has remained the same: the student as active word user. The many activities help students to find their own voices and to release their words and ideas, not to bury them. Britton (1970, p. 223) has fitting final words to remind us of the importance of bringing active talk into the classroom:

> Perhaps the most important general implication for teaching . . . is to note that anyone who succeeded in outlawing talk in the classroom would have outlawed life for the adolescent; the web of human relations must be spun in school as well as out.

5

Responding to Literature

At the center of the curriculum are not the works of literature . . . but rather the mind as it meets the book, the response.

Alan Purves and
Richard Beach

This chapter moves us from oral language to written text. In many English classrooms, after the roll is called, students settle into their desks and open their texts as predictably as some churchgoers settle into their pews and open their Bibles. *English* equals *literature*. Chapter 7 presents the historic reasons for literature's central position in the high school English classroom. For now, we address a more basic question: What can we learn from literature?

WHY READ LITERATURE?

We can begin to find an answer to this question in a common plea of children: "Tell me a story!" Young children, barely able themselves to form words into sentences, wait with eye-sparkling expectation to be told stories. The title of Robert Coles's book *The Call of Stories* (1989a) names this urgent allurement. People heard and responded to this call long before they had written language to record their tales. Why do very young children and humans throughout history call for a story? They do so to be entertained, to be instructed, to be enchanted, to be informed, to be thrilled, and to be comforted. Yet by the time we see children as adolescents, their zeal for stories has often diminished, sometimes to extinction. Literature holds no allure. Many approach classroom texts with leaden reluctance, as a burden to be borne until the bell rings. They do not read books outside of school. Their adult counterparts, too, more often turn to the television or the computer than to a book.

The Death of Literature

Alvin Kernan reports in *The Death of Literature* (1990) that his university students now assume that they are more likely to find something in the way of truth on their computer screens than on the printed page. Kernan believes that we are presently undergoing a number of cultural shifts that affect reading: (1) economic—in our marketplace economy, publishers no longer underwrite serious writers who don't sell; (2) social—we are an entertainment-driven society in which entertainment is pitched to a mass audience; and (3) technological—we are evolving from a print society to an electronic one. Writer Cynthia Ozick laments this "tyranny of accountants and computers" (Fraser, 1997). Independent booksellers are being replaced by large national chains whose displays feature best-selling money earners, not writers such as Ozick, and whose coffee shops are better staffed than their book aisles. Electronics challenge print partly because, as Sven Birkerts (1994, p. 188) explains, "The book dead-ends us in ourselves, whereas the screen is a sluice into the collective stratum, the place where all facts are known and all lore is encoded."

Some high school English departments have shifted their emphasis from printed literature to practical language arts skills (technical preparatory programs) in order to position their students to join this cultural stream. Yagelski (1994, p. 31) justifies this shift in our age of "inconceivable change." A focus on literature in high schools is "irrelevant to the challenges our students now face." He believes that we should remove literature from the center of our English curriculum and, if we must teach it, use it to "help students understand language and language use" (pp. 34-35). Yet because you have opened this book devoted to the teaching of English, we assume that you, too, must be drawn to books, the traditional subject of English study. If books are under threat at present, this challenge requires teachers of English to articulate just why we think reading literature is important. We need an answer for the question "What can literature teach us?"

The Life of Literature

Birkerts launches an eloquent answer to this question in his collection of essays *The Gutenberg Elegies* (1994). Birkerts calls us to recognize the loss we individually and collectively would suffer if the printed page inaugurated by Johann Gutenberg's movable-type printing press died. He asks, "Is literature offering us less?" and answers, "No." He continues, "Is it that what is offered is no longer

deemed as vital to our well-being?" and implies, "Perhaps" (p. 191). He reasons that the climate of late modernity may have rendered us less able to appreciate literature's relevance, but literature "remains the unexcelled means of interior exploration and connection-making. . . . So long as there is a natural inclination toward independent selfhood, so long will literature be able to prove the reports of its death exaggerated" (p. 197). Literature is "a way of talking about important and difficult aspects of our universal experience" (p. 191).

Elliot Eisner's book *The Enlightened Eye* (1990) elaborates what literature can teach by describing the interior acts it prompts. Eisner, who works at the intersection of art and education, explains that literature can help the reader do the following:

1. *Imagine new worlds:* envision new possibilities; create new visions
2. *Become seers:* look into what we have never seen; penetrate beyond what language tells; unveil the familiar, or, as Coleridge said, "call to our attention that which we have neglected"
3. *Stabilize the evanescent:* solidify the internal; grasp the fleeting; fasten the slippery thought
4. *Exchange our world with others:* glimpse another's world and acknowledge that reality; catch who we are and who we have been; enlarge our receptive sensibility
5. *Rely on judgment without established criteria or standards:* judge without received rules or predetermined interpretations
6. *See the universal in the particular:* see the significance in the slight; see metaphor's power
7. *Learn to play:* prompt the spirit of playfulness, nimbleness, and gamesmanship; refute Ciardi's observation "There is no poetry for the practical man."

In *The Developing Imagination* (1963, p. 58), Northrop Frye articulates the high stakes in the exercise of the imagination: "The ultimate purpose of teaching literature is not understanding, but the transferring of the imaginative habit of mind, the instinct to create a new form instead of idolizing an old one, from the laboratory of literature to the life of mankind, society depends heavily for its well-being on the handful of people who are imaginative in this sense."

Invitation to Reflection 5-1

1. Name one piece of literature, long or short, that touched you deeply.
2. Would you consider its effect on you to be worth inviting middle or high school students to experience? Would you recommend that particular book to a young adolescent?

3. Which of Birkerts' or Eisner's reasons for reading literature match yours? Check those that apply.

____to explore one's interior life

____to make connections

____to talk about significant aspects of our universal
experience

____to imagine new worlds

____to become seers

____to stabilize the evanescent

____to exchange our world with others

____to rely on judgment without established criteria or
standards

____to see the universal in the particular

____to learn to play

____your own reasons:

Goals and Methods for Teaching Literature

If you can find your mooring for teaching literature in
some of those reasons, you may be ready to consider goals
for instruction and methods for meeting them. Two
decades ago, Alan Purves (1981) surveyed thousands of
English teachers to answer this basic question: "What are
your goals for teaching literature?" His survey prompts
our entry into fundamental questions that the profession
still ponders. Table 5–1 lists his summation of the goals
for ninth- and twelfth-grade teachers (p. 29). The English
teachers surveyed appear essentially to agree on their
goals for teaching literature: Student self-understanding is
first; critical and analytical skills are second. Yet their answers to a question about how they plan to accomplish
those goals reveal significant differences. Teachers were
asked to rate each of seventeen questions that could be
asked about a literary text. Invitation to Reflection 5–2
poses Purves's questions for you.

Invitation to Reflection 5–2

Alan Purves (1981) poses seventeen questions that you
might ask students about a piece of literature. Rank the
importance of each for you on a four-point scale, from trivial (1) to very important (4).*

_____ 1. What literary devices did you notice in the work?

_____ 2. Is the work symbolic or allegorical? What is its
theme?

_____ 3. How would you describe the language of
the work?

_____ 4. What happened in the work? Who is narrating it?
What is the setting?

_____ 5. How is technique related to what the work says?

_____ 6. What is the structure of the work? How is it
organized?

_____ 7. Is the work well written? Does the form support
the content? Is it well constructed?

_____ 8. How would you interpret the character of this
person? What is the significance of the setting?

_____ 9. Did you find that any of these people are like
people you know? Did anything like this ever
happen to you?

_____10. Do any of the formal devices have any
significance? What symbols do you find in
the work?

_____11. What is the genre of the work? In what literary
tradition is it?

_____12. Does this work describe the world as it is? Do you
find the world like the way it is described in
this work?

_____13. What is the author teaching us? What is the work
criticizing?

_____14. What is the tone of the work?

_____15. What emotions or feelings does the work arouse
in you?

TABLE 5–1

English teachers' rank
order of goals of
instruction

Goal	9th Grade	12th Grade
To improve the literary tastes of students	5	6
To teach students the history of their literature	8	8
To acquaint students with their literary and cultural heritage	5	4
To help students understand themselves and the human condition	1	1
To develop students' ability to discuss the variety of literary forms that are around them	7	7
To develop the critical faculties and analytic skills of students	2	2
To develop students' ability to use their language	3	3
To show students the ways by which language affects their response to events	4	5

Source: From A. Purves, *Reading and Literature: American Achievement in International Perspective,* National Council of
Teachers of English, 1981. Reprinted with permission.

_____16. Is this work about serious things? Is it significant literature?

_____17. Does the work succeed in getting you involved in its situation? Is it successful in arousing your emotions?

*From A. Purves, *Reading and Literature: American Achievement in International Perspective.* Copyright 1981 by the National Council of Teachers of English. Reprinted with permission.

Purves found that teachers were more divided over the questions they would pose than the goals they had set. That division ran along a line that has been drawn and redrawn for decades between questions and classrooms that were text-centered and those that were reader-centered. English teachers have struggled between their sense of responsibility to the text and their responsibility to the students, their responsibility to matters of form and to matters of personal experience. That division is mirrored in a parallel line running between classrooms that are teacher-centered and those that are more student-centered. By joining our profession, you join these issues. In your classroom, will you focus on exploring the text in all of its historical, biographical, cultural, psychological, thematic, and formal richness or on exploring students' responses to the text in all of the historical, biographical, social, and cultural richness of those students? Will you assume the role of knowledgeable interpreter of the text's riches or as facilitator of student discovery?

This chapter, like others, attempts to bridge these lines and do justice to the claims of text and reader, teacher and student. We present our bridge as

- a three-phase cycle for teaching literature in the classroom—how we study texts
- a four-stage construct for reading literature that lies primarily inside the second phase of that cycle
- innumerable teaching activities pertinent to each of these four stages

Our teaching cycle and reading stages, like any construct that breaks something complex into segmented parts, will be misleading unless you understand, absorb, and then employ them as general models for your classroom planning. So we ask you to entertain the following discrete steps, knowing that to be an effective reader and teacher you must, in time, integrate them into an organic, seamless approach to reading and teaching literature.

∽THREE PHASES OF THE TEACHING CYCLE: ENTER, EXPLORE, EXTEND

Our three-phase teaching cycle provides a benchmark for the sequence of a class's approach to literature. It is not so much theoretical as practical. We use it to plan our in-

dividual literature lessons—how we get into and out of a text with our students. Its title alone suggests the direction, not unlike the way you would negotiate a creative project or an intellectual challenge or a visit to a foreign country or your national capital. Some colleagues refer to the same rhythm and movement with a title of prepositions: *into, through, beyond.* Borrowing from reading teachers, others call a similar teaching sequence *before, during, after.* Still others refer to the sequence as *prereading, reading, postreading.* Each of these names evokes an overarching strategy for opening texts with students. You might see it imagistically as a road map with which you can travel or a scaffold on which you can build your daily literature lessons or your thematic units. We will sketch each of the three steps with brief illustrations. The bulk of this chapter will be a more specific four-stage construct for reading literature, most of which nestles within the second phase of the cycle of classroom literature teaching. Both of our constructs describe something unique and important. Both should equip you to approach your classroom lesson planning with greater clarity and range so that when you walk in the room and find twenty-five students there, you will know what to do with them. The numerous teaching activities that illustrate our constructs are the bricks and mortar necessary to build that scaffolded structure. Figure 5–1 graphically represents the relationship of the two.

Enter

Whether our students are capable readers who arrive at a work with rich expectations or less proficient readers who can barely decode the words or picture a script in

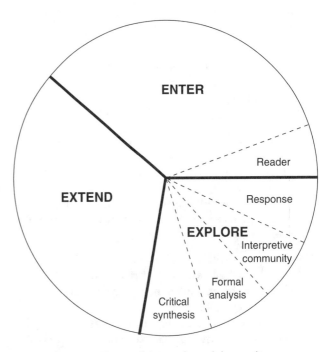

FIGURE 5–1 The teaching cycle and the reading stages

their heads, they are helped by activities that invite them to enter the ideas of the text. These invitations can take many forms; but all are designed to activate students' thoughts, experiences, and feelings about something essential in the text that follows or to build background knowledge necessary for reading it. (Such knowledge might include concepts of the genre that are new to these students or the text's context that is unknown.)

George Hillocks (1995) evokes a useful analogy when he calls prewriting strategies *gateway activities.* Similar activities in reading open a gate for students to make them ready and receptive for the text they are about to enter. So before reading excerpts from Homer's *Odyssey,* the teacher might consider activities such as the following:

Free Writing
- Free-write in response to a prompt:
  - List qualities you consider to be heroic.
  - Name one public person you would consider to be a hero and explain why.
  - Imagine you have just met your cultural hero. List five questions you would like to ask him or her.
  - Was your cultural hero female? Are the roles of female heroes different from the roles valued for males?
  - Write a letter to your cultural hero and ask him or her for advice about a problem you are facing.

Tree Diagram
- Think about someone you consider a cultural hero. Create a tree diagram in which you name the person (on the trunk) and name the qualities you admire (on the branches).

Think-Pair-Share
- With a partner, identify your hero and explain why you regard him or her as heroic.

Interview
- On the Internet, research the cultural hero identified above. Prepare yourself to assume the identity of your hero in an interview by your classmates.

Minilecture
- Briefly introduce students to Homer and his role as a *rhapsodist* (part oral historian, part entertainer). Discuss what was going on in Greece between 900 and 700 B.C. (when the *Odyssey* was composed) and the oral tradition surrounding the Trojan War. Ask students to research this author and period further via the Internet or encyclopedias.

Minilecture with Technology Follow-Up
- Introduce the names and a brief character sketch of several of the prominent heroes, gods, and goddesses students will meet in their reading. Ask students to research Greek mythology and legend on a Web site such as the following, select a favorite, and prepare a verbal sketch for the class's "Gallery of the Greeks":

The Encyclopedia Mythica (http://www.pantheon.org/mythica/): This site contains almost 5,000 articles, illustrations, maps, and genealogical tables of mythological characters from around the world.
The Book of Gods, Goddesses, Heroes, and Other Characters of Mythology http://www.cybercomm.net/~grandpa/gdsindex.html): This site has encyclopedic information about world mythological characters and lists of other mythology sites.

Wilhelm, Baker, and Dube (2001, p. 103) evoke another metaphorical connection when they refer to this phase of teaching as *frontloading.* They suggest a set of questions teachers might ask themselves as they consider and plan frontloading activities for a unit or a lesson. These questions include the following:

- How does your activity activate or build the students' prior knowledge or background information regarding your unit theme?
- How does the activity work to motivate students for reading and inquiry regarding the theme or driving question of your unit?
- How will the frontloading activity work to organize inquiry, set purposes, and consolidate learning about the theme throughout the unit? That is, how will it help students set purposes for their reading, focus their learning, clarify what they are coming to know, and help them monitor their learning progress?

Our first four strategies in the reader response stage of reading literature—*personal triggers, suppositional readers, conceptual readiness,* and *synergistic texts*—are especially designed as prereading activities, advance organizers, or anticipatory sets. Each invites students to anticipate the text, connect with it in advance, and prepare to integrate it with their previous experiences, both personal and cognitive. Unlike many advance organizers, however, they skirt the dangers of leading students toward a more knowledgeable teacher's foregone conclusion. Kelly (1992, p. 87) cautions that prereading activities, even the most carefully designed, can push a discussion in a prescribed direction and thus "inhibit divergent thinking." Our entering strategies focus the lesson on students and elicit their responses. By aiming at the personal, texts begin to resonate in students before they begin to make sense.

Explore

Once students are engaged, they are more confident, ready, and equipped to move through a work of literature. The bulk of this chapter presents different means for exploration through all stages of response, interpretation, formal analysis, and critical synthesis. In addition to the activities suggested here (thirty-two in all), throughout this textbook we present other strategies that advance exploration. Wilhelm (1997) enumerates ten dimensions of response to narrative literature that move through stages of reading similar to ours. The activities of exploring could be built on his scaffold. Wilhelm is concerned that after students enter the story world they then show interest in the story's action, relate to characters, see the story's world, elaborate on it, connect literature to life, consider significance, recognize literary conventions, recognize reading as a transaction, and evaluate the author and the self as reader. Appendix A of his "*You Gotta BE the Book*" provides a valuable outline of questions and activities for each of these dimensions (pp. 157–169).

One of the great challenges of teaching literature is to remain open to alternative approaches, to take the risks to try them, and to marshal the energy to critique them. The multiple demands on the teacher make the lure of the tried-and-true, teacher-directed, large-group discussions of literary interpretation or exercises of literary knowledge often irresistible. We were taught in such classrooms, quite different from those we choose for our students, so we must constantly align our planning with the principles of the teaching cycle and the reading stages that we will enumerate. Scholes (1985, pp. 24–25) explains how such principles alter the traditional role of teachers. The job of teachers is "not to produce 'readings' for our students but to give them the tools for producing their own. . . . Our job is *not* to intimidate students with our own superior textual production: it is to show them the codes on which all textual production depends, and to encourage their own textual practice."

McGonigal (1988) describes the unhealthy consequences of traditional teaching that relies on the vicarious literary analysis of others. The student "can understand literature in a third person impersonal sort of way, but dependence on a critic or on *Cliffs Notes* only strengthens a student's belief that literature belongs to others, that literature is somehow written in a foreign language comprehensible only to teachers and critics." On the other hand, when the reader's response becomes central, "wooden responses to literature give way to perceptions that literature, good literature, lives. But literature breathes and murmurs, cajoles and lambasts, laments and rejoices only when the reader makes it do so" (p. 66).

We find guidance once again from Louise Rosenblatt (1976), who provides a benchmark for our choosing just which strategies we will use in teaching literature. She cautions that we must

> be very careful to scrutinize all our procedures to be sure that we are not in actuality substituting other aims—things to do *about* literature—for the experience *of* literature. We can ask of every assignment or method or text, no matter what its short-term effectiveness: Does it get in the way of the live sense of literature? Does it make literature something to be regurgitated, analyzed, categorized, or is it a means toward making literature a more personally meaningful and self-disciplined activity? (p. 279)

Novelist Sue Ellen Bridgers (1997) goes to the heart of why literature is such fertile ground for exploration. She believes that "stories interpret the past and explain the present. They shape who we are and inform who we become. Of all the conscious acts we perform, the most important is claiming our own story. Stories matter more for the questions they raise than the answers they provide. Exploration and discovery lie at the heart of story."

Extend

If students have entered texts, explored them, and even, we hope, come to care about them, they are ready to extend them. Literature opens a way of seeing, of understanding more than our individual experiences might yield, of making sense of our world, of transforming the daily, and of discovering the significance there. Extending means taking the ideas, urges, and preachments of the text into our daily worlds. Yagelski (1994) envisions just such a classroom that takes literature study beyond traditional analysis and uses it to involve students in social, political, economic, and cultural questions. Thus, students might read Hemingway's *Fathers and Sons* to discover what his story reveals "about the complexities of parent-child relationships" before they go on to write narratives about their own relationships with parents and to explore related issues of "gangs, teen fashions, school reform, drugs, music" (p. 35). In one classroom, collaborative groups chose a project that involved both reading and writing. For instance, students concerned about their city's juvenile curfew ordinance read the ordinance, wrote letters, followed public debates, went to computers for information, polled local opinion, and finally wrote a report to the school board. Scholes (1985) explains that "the whole point of my argument" in *Textual Power* is that "we must open the way between the literary or verbal text and the social text in which we live." Rosenblatt (1969) sees the consequences of readers' personal involvement in the text in the trajectory of their entire lives: "Personal involvement in literature should reveal it as a life activity that has value in itself and that can offer [a reader] personal satisfaction, ethical and social insight. It can help him to develop a personal sense of values and to bring a human and humane perspective to bear on our mass civilization" (p. 1012). Moffett and Wagner's insight might be a useful mantra here: "Words on World."

Within these three phases of the teaching cycle, the explore stage will almost always be the longer and more elaborate. It will comprise the bulk of your teaching time. Yet the first and last stages are no less important for your students and make the vast middle matter to them. We have used the general models of classroom organization discussed in Chapter 2—lecture, whole-group discussion, small-group work, and individual work—to present most of our teaching activities. As your teaching plot thickens, you can see that in daily lesson planning these would need to be placed within the structure of *enter, explore,* and *extend*—our three-act classroom play. You might think of yourself as drafting a script for your classroom stage. You will want to organize each part of your lesson with a beginning, a middle, and an end in mind. As you become more experienced, your script may become less elaborate on paper, but you should not forget this general cycle of literature study.

We turn now to what has been the organizing design for the chapter in two previous editions. We have come to frame this within the three cycles just enumerated because we discovered the practical need to articulate our stages in terms of classroom realities. You may feel we are asking you to perform a dizzying bit of intellectual juggling to keep two constructs in mind at once. As we have said, the following four stages are primarily used at the exploration phase, but they have tremendous implications for entering and extending as well.

∞ FOUR STAGES OF READING LITERATURE

We base our four stages of reading literature on a conception of literature and on principles of personal and cogni-

tive development. This four-stage construct capitalizes on how people most naturally, effectively, and pleasurably read. Its general movement is from the concrete to the abstract, from the simple to the more complex, and from a precritical immersion in the text to a critical perspective on it. In this construct, consideration of a literary work begins in personal response and grows more studied and complex.

As we chart the four stages, each stage builds on the work of the preceding stage and prepares for the next. Students move from their personal responses as readers of texts to sharing and deepening those responses in the collective understanding of an interpretive community of other readers; to illuminating that understanding through formal analysis, and finally, for some, to synthesizing competing critical perspectives into their own interpretation. In actual practice, the movement is not rigidly sequential but recursive. The stages overlap. Different readers— some proficient, some less able, some eagerly engaged in literary experience, some hardly able to decipher the words on the page—move at different speeds. The individual reader moves back and forth between response and analysis. Some never arrive at critical matters. Figure 5–2 schematizes these four stages in terms of the reader's purpose, primary task, distance from the text, and types of questions about the text. The figure is not linear nor circular—very much like our classrooms.

FIGURE 5–2

Four stages of reading literature

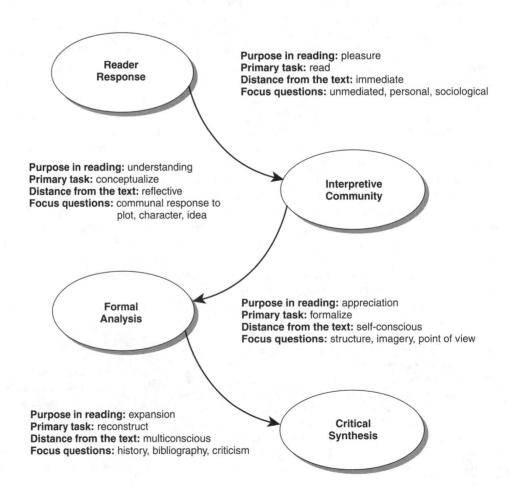

Reader Response

Purpose in reading: pleasure
Primary task: read
Distance from the text: immediate
Focus questions: unmediated, personal, sociological

Purpose in reading: understanding
Primary task: conceptualize
Distance from the text: reflective
Focus questions: communal response to plot, character, idea

Interpretive Community

Formal Analysis

Purpose in reading: appreciation
Primary task: formalize
Distance from the text: self-conscious
Focus questions: structure, imagery, point of view

Purpose in reading: expansion
Primary task: reconstruct
Distance from the text: multiconscious
Focus questions: history, bibliography, criticism

Critical Synthesis

Reader Response

All readers bring prior experience and knowledge of life and reading to any text. They are not blank tablets on which texts make unproblematic, predictable, definitive imprints. In the first stage, *reader response,* individual readers are face to face with the text. The center of our pedagogical concern is with the reader's unmediated, felt response to the text. The teacher's role at this level is to remove scholarly, historical, critical baggage and to free students for their personal, unencumbered encounters with the text. Reader response activities shift ownership for interpretation from teacher to student. They send the message immediately that studying literature is not a matter of a teacher's asking questions about a predetermined interpretation and the students' scurrying to find the correct answer. As Rosenblatt stresses, texts—the words on the page—differ from "aesthetic experience"—the reader's "living through" the text by entertaining it, imagining it, and entering its life.

Interpretive Community

When students have entered and responded to the world of the story or poem, they are ready to join a community of other readers. The *interpretive community* is reader response in chorus. We hope that the students' first impressions will generate enough momentum to carry these initial speculations and queries further. The notion of students' discussing ideas together and building on each others' ideas is not new, but the emphasis here remains on students' statements of their own responses and discovery of their own meanings. The chemistry for group work of such potential is delicate and builds over time or, with some students, not at all. But Langer (1995, p. 44) paints the compelling picture we envision. She is watching a group just beginning to gel:

> After getting to know one another better, the openness, willingness to assume others' perspectives, and willingness to disagree and confront one another increased greatly, but always with sensitivity and support. These are the types of discussions that students should learn to engage in, where they have room to explore topics that touch their lives, to use the text, related literature, and the author's life, as well as one another's and their own. What a preparation for life, if students can learn to interact in a community where their ideas can stimulate new awarenesses and possibilities, and where the reading of literature can assume a profound role in their human as well as cognitive development.

A community of readers—whether they be pairs, small groups, or whole classes—profit from these shared reactions. The individual perspective broadens, new insights are aired, multiple perspectives are entertained, tentative hypotheses are tried, the claims of the text are sharpened, and initial impressions gain a more considered shape. The ideal is that the classroom culture excludes no one, treats individual ideas generously, accepts dispute, balances impressions with reflection, and aims to arrive at meaning together.

Formal Analysis

In the third stage, *formal analysis,* students begin to explore the formal dimensions of the text more intentionally and to reflect on the author's craft more consciously. Questions of form should be reached only after the earlier stages of enjoyment, engagement, and conceptualization have commenced. For too long, literature study meant only an analysis of literary terminology and authorial craft. More recently, high school literature study has centered on a personal encounter with the whole text. We suggest you attempt both: personal response and, when students are engaged, careful formal analysis for some students. Some students may never move to this stage; their level of abstraction is insufficient, their engagement with the text too fragile, and their suspicion of literature as irrelevant too strong. With others, questions of literary knowledge such as conventions and literary terminology may arise naturally out of their push to understand texts more fully. If students care about what they are reading, they often realize on their own or with a little prodding that understanding the craft of the author deepens their understanding of the text. Students can appreciate literature in deeper, more nuanced, and more enduring ways. Their awareness of craft becomes part of their response to the next texts they read.

Critical Synthesis

In *critical sythesis* the reader takes a step further back from the text and regards it with a conscious, if rudimentary, knowledge of literary theory. Some of that theory arises from the natural generalizations that teachers and students develop from numerous particular observations. These might include what literary standards distinguish commercial from serious fiction or good from great poetry, why some texts are considered classics and others are not, and why English has a privileged position in many high schools as the one course required for all four years. Even a simple understanding of the approaches of various schools of literary criticism—historical, biographical, formalist, feminist, archetypal, or Freudian critical perspectives—can awaken students to the diverse ways in which a single text might be interpreted by a reader or literature generally might be understood by a culture. Although this stage may appear to be appropriate only for rare students, we have found it to be freeing and invigorating to students at all levels. Knowing a range of possible approaches to literature grants students a sense of ownership over their own interpretations. In time, such analysis deepens and complicates initial personal responses to texts.

Instructional Strategies/Teaching Activities

In this chapter we elaborate each stage of our construct with explanation and example.[1] We believe that instruction is most comprehensive and effective when it encompasses the first three stages for all students and all four stages for rare students and the teacher. But the movement through them is not linear or lockstep. The choice of stage and sequence will depend on the literature, the students, the day, and the moment in the term. In your classrooms, you may well use three or four strategies within one classroom period. Block schedules beg even more for such variety and diversity. We hope that the menu of the instructional strategies of the reader response and interpretive community stages (Table 5–2) will be one of the most used pages of this book when you become a teacher in search of a change in plans. A reader

of our second edition tells us that she has copied it and taped it in the front cover of her planning book as a quick reminder of possibility. Strategies for the formal analysis and critical synthesis are no less important than those of the first two stages, but they are harder to isolate and list on such a table. Although our examples in Chapter 5 are drawn mostly from fiction, our suggestions also apply to poems and plays.

☞READER RESPONSE

Our first stage invites students to the most personal engagement with literature—to an unmediated, felt response to the text. Often English students approach pieces of literature as dry, isolated academic events disconnected from real life. The strategies of reader response attempt to reconnect literature and life. They take what Rosenblatt (1978) considered the necessary first step of reading literature: paying close attention to what this particular group of words "stirs up within each reader" (p. 137). Although often the end-of-selection questions of literature textbooks influenced by reader response theory elicit general areas of association and emotions, the range of personal stirrings is far richer and more nuanced. Rosenblatt (1995, pp. 30–31) describes this interior experience:

> What, then, happens in the reading of a literary work? The reader, drawing on past linguistic and life experience, links

---

[1] Even if you do not consciously adopt this approach, you should find specific strategies and teaching activities to be useful. We illustrate our strategies with a handful of stories chosen because they are frequently read in high school English classes, include a range of different authorial voices, and are easily available to our readers. You can enter the exercises more productively if you have read the following: "Raymond's Run" (Toni Cade Bambara), "The Story of an Hour" (Kate Chopin), "A Rose for Emily" (William Faulkner), "The Sky Is Gray" (Ernest Gaines), "The Ones Who Walk Away from Omelas" (Ursula K. LeGuin), "I Stand Here Ironing" (Tillie Olsen), "Just Lather, That's All" (Hernando Tellez), and "Harrison Bergeron" (Kurt Vonnegut, Jr.). In Appendix D we list Websites that include author information, explorations, and other links of some of these writers. We also list two sites that offer full texts of many classic and contemporary short stories.

the signs on the page with certain words, certain concepts, certain sensuous experiences, certain images of things, people, actions, scenes. The special meanings and, more particularly, the submerged associations that these words and images have for the individual reader will largely determine what the work communicates to *him*. The reader brings to the work personality traits, memories of past events, present needs and preoccupations, a particular mood of the moment, and a particular physical condition. These and many other elements in a never-to-be-duplicated combination determine his interfusion with the peculiar contribution of the text. For the adolescent reader, the experience of the work is further specialized by the fact that he has probably not yet arrived at a consistent view of life or achieved a fully integrated personality.

Texts, for example, might arouse the responses and prompt the reactions shown in Table 5-3.

Although this first stage typically aims for students' independent reactions to a text, ones that are not controlled by teachers, we also know that some students need to be urged into response with approaches that are active without being controlling. We have culled our most effective reader response strategies from those of our second edition. We briefly describe the strategy and then delineate ten teaching activities so that you can more readily import them into your classrooms.

Personal Triggers

The basic intent of *personal triggers* is to connect students' personal experiences to the text. The basic strategy is to stir memory; to consider personal attitudes, beliefs, and values; and to revisit experiences or feelings that the text may echo. Many different activities—oral, written, individual, and group—might open these stirrings. We present four examples. The first two ask students to respond in their journals to carefully conceived prompts; the next polls student opinion via a questionnaire; the last records student memories.

Patricia Kelly and Robert Small (1993, personal communication) suggest the following prompt before ninth graders read "Raymond's Run" by Toni Cade Bambara:

You probably meet new people often in your life—new neighbors, new kids in school, new teachers. When you meet a new person, how do you decide whether you like that person? When do you decide? What makes the difference for you between liking and not liking someone? In your Reader Response Notebook write about meeting someone you quickly decided you liked a great deal. As you write, try to figure out how and why you decided you liked the person you chose to write about here.

Before Patricia Kelly (1992, p. 85) has tenth graders read "Words" by Sylvia Plath, she asks students to reflect in their journals about "a time when words hurt: When was it? What was the situation? Why do you remember it now? What did you learn?" Kelly's prompt can open sensitive subjects, so she protects students' confidentiality through their private journals. Before she reads the poem, she shares her own incident and invites their accounts as well, a constant point of reference in the subsequent discussion.

Mary Jo Schaars (1992, p. 147) will not let her eleventh-grade students "catch a glimpse" of Thoreau's *Walden* before she gives them a questionnaire that raises questions "about materialism, moral commitment, goals, lifestyle." The questionnaire elicits honest self-examination with questions such as the following:

- If you didn't have to worry about making a lot of money, what occupation would you choose? Why?
- When, during a routine day, do you find yourself happiest? Most bored?
- Do you believe you have too many, just enough, too few conveniences in your life? Explain, if necessary.

After students have examined their individual positions, the whole class discusses the issues raised before turning to discover how Thoreau might have answered similar questions.

Before reading Nikki Giovanni's poem "Nikki-Rosa," Carol Jago (2000, p. 144) asks her students "to describe what they envision when they say or hear that someone has had a 'hard childhood.'" She then suggests that the teacher "create a cluster on the board of all the features of this condition from your students' point of view." She continues the activity by asking students "to think about some of the things they experienced as children that might make someone feel sorry for them but that were actually pleasurable" (p. 145). The teacher makes a list of particular student responses on the board entitled "Childhood Remembrances" before initiating a discussion of Giovanni's apparently autobiographical evocation of childhood.

TABLE 5-3
Responses and reactions to literature

Responses	Reactions
A personal association	"This story reminds me of how Uncle Fred treats Aunt Clara."
An instinct about character	"I don't believe she would act that way."
The clarification of an idea	"Yes, that's exactly how one feels."
A reading memory	"This seems like a fairy tale plot."
An aesthetic judgment	"That passage says so beautifully what I have felt before."
Cognitive dissonance	"I do not agree with this character's point of view."
A strong emotion	"I get all tense inside when I see someone treated like that."

The danger of even the most carefully constructed personal trigger activity is that it leads students toward a preconceived and narrow reading of the text. Its virtue is that it engages students and offers them some personal stake in what follows. Its implicit message is that the teacher values readers and expects literature to connect with them and they with literature.

Suppositional Readers

Another effective entry into a text is to speculate about initial bits of available information or prior knowledge before reading begins. With a novel, the job is easy. You can ask students to examine the book's cover, its chapter headings, and its layout and to speculate about what these visuals lead them to expect in their reading. Frequently read classics possess a mystique and an oral tradition that you can tap by discussing questions such as "What have you heard about this book?" "Have you read anything else by this author?" "What do you remember about that book that you might look for here?" Teaching Activity 5-1 poses questions about a short story, which does not have as many visual or contextual clues as a novel. This activity might be done by the individual reader or by a group, by the teacher's oral directions or by a handout.

Such an activity can bring to consciousness what normally occurs on an unconscious level, in nonverbal flashes and feelings. It invites students to become active participants with the text, not passive receivers of it. Through speculation about the title and author and then in suppositions about the first sentence, paragraph, and page, students become creative partners in reading the full story.

Conceptual Readiness

This prereading exercise moves toward the story's conceptual center by examining its main idea in other nonliterary texts. Studies have shown that prior explo-

---

5-1 TEACHING ACTIVITY

Suppositional Prereading

Whole Class or Individual

- Consider the story "Harrison Bergeron" by Kurt Vonnegut, Jr.
- Does the title or author's name set up any expectations in your mind? What can you possibly predict from such a small bit of information?
- List your suppositions drawn simply from the title and the author's name.
- If you drew a blank and did not know what to suppose, consider these questions:
  - What assumptions do you make about a character named Harrison Bergeron?
  - What is the given name's relationship to the family name? Do they seem to go together?
  - Does his name seem stiff and formal or everyday? What do you make of that?
  - Do you recognize the author's name? Do you know of other fiction he has written? Can you describe a theme or style common to his other stories? Does your memory lead you to expectations for "Harrison Bergeron"?

(If these questions prompt an additional reaction to the title and author of the story, add to your original supposition list. Test this list against your reading of Vonnegut's tale. You have very little advance information here, but you may be amazed at what this meager amount will yield.)

- Now turn to the first sentence of "Harrison Bergeron" and consider where it might lead the whole text. If the title and author were hooks, the first line is bait: "The year was 2081, and everyone was finally equal."
- List what you suppose about the story from reading the first sentence.

(Once again, we have seemingly little to go on, but once again we may know more than we think. Your suppositions will likely be driven by information such as the date, the final word *equal,* the adverb *finally,* the use of the word *everybody,* and larger issues such as the tone set by the language. You might also speculate about where the story is set and how you are supposed to feel about the described state of affairs: everybodys being equal. Other features of the first sentence may cause you to speculate in other, more imaginative ways.)

ration of a concept that is important in a text enriches the reader's response to that text (Hayes & Tierney, 1982). These concepts might appear in a Miss Manners's column, an excerpted news or sports interview, lines of popular music, or a cartoon or painting. The idea is to draw out and articulate students' personal perceptions and, once they are primed, to connect them with what is relevant in the literary text. The best connections might not even be verbal but may appear as echoes or resonances of images and thoughts experienced before.

In teaching "Harrison Bergeron," we offer a short excerpt from John Stuart Mill's "On Liberty," an essay by conservative writer George F. Will (1978) selected from *The Pursuit of Happiness and Other Sobering Thoughts,* and John Lennon's song "Imagine" to help students focus on the central topic of Vonnegut's story: equality. We ask students to read and then compare these pieces; then we schematize the exercise on the sheet shown in Figure 5–3.

These comparisons can and should drive beyond an abstract discussion of ideas toward personal sharing and reflection on students' own experiences, values, and beliefs. When students have explored different views of the limits of freedom within democracy, they will be better prepared for "Harrison Bergeron." Our experience is that the discussions of ideas do not diminish the power of the fictive treatment but open and reveal it more fully. One potential danger is that you will lead students toward conclusions that you have reached and away from a free discovery of their own. Making sure that the surrounding works have different biases, however, helps to avoid this pitfall. Figure 5–4 presents a list of primary and prereading texts that we use to produce this enriching effect.

Synergistic Texts

Clearly, the breadth of students' experiences—literary and otherwise—has a great impact on how they read a literary text. The approach we call *synergistic texts* pair texts that challenge each other's basic premises. The teacher uses the natural appeal of contentious positions to engage students and draw out and provoke their opinions. When related or contending texts collide, the act of reading becomes more forceful and purposive.

Thus, we read "Harrison Bergeron" along with Ursula K. LeGuin's "The Ones Who Walk Away from Omelas." LeGuin's story looks not at the power of gifted individuals restrained so that the wretched can be equal (Vonnegut's concern) but at one individual made wretched so that all others can enjoy pleasure and prosperity. We pair these stories and ask students to keep a basic question in mind as they read them: How does LeGuin differ from Vonnegut on the question "How can a society promote the greatest happiness for the greatest number of its people?" or How would these texts respond to Abraham Lincoln's observation that "You cannot strengthen the weak by weakening the strong"? Such a matchup can be created with any pair of stories that focus upon a shared concern. The combined power of both texts can be far greater than the individual impact of one.

Matthews and Chandler (1998, p. 87) found that they needed prereading activities to prepare their eleventh-grade students for certain difficult stream-of-consciousness sections of Toni Morrison's *Beloved.* They showed excerpts of the film of Alex Haley's novel *Roots* to evoke the Middle Passage to which Morrison alludes and then asked students to simulate what they had seen. They asked volunteers to crowd under a row of desks and "imagine the smells and

FIGURE 5–3
Prereading "Harrison Bergeron"

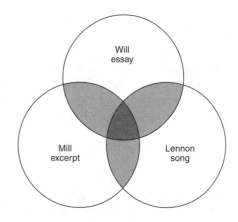

Full Agreement   Some Agreement   Difference

FIGURE 5–4
Primary and
prereading texts

PRIMARY TEXT	AUTHOR	PREREADING TEXT	CREATOR
Wuthering Heights (novel)	Emily Brontë	"Wuthering Heights" (song)	Kate Bush
"Where Are You Going, Where Have You Been?" (short story)	Joyce Carol Oates	"A Hard Rain's A-Gonna Fall" "It's All Over Now Baby Blue" (songs)	Bob Dylan
"Why I Live at the P.O." (short story)	Eudora Welty	Cartoons of sibling rivalry	Gary Larson
"The Circular Ruin" (short story)	Jorge Luis Borges	Drawing Hands Reptiles (etchings)	M. C. Escher
"Musée des Beaux Arts" (poem)	W. H. Auden	The Fall of Icarus (painting)	Pieter Brueghel
"A & P" (short story)	John Updike	"Heroic Fantasies, Nervous Doubts" (essay)	Phyllis Rose
"The Lamb" "The Tiger" (poems)	William Blake	"Both Sides Now" (song)	Joni Mitchell
		"Incident" (poem)	Countee Cullen
"A Rose for Emily" (short story)	William Faulkner	"The soul selects her own society" (poem)	Emily Dickinson

FIGURE 5–5
Synergistic texts

TEXT	AUTHOR	GENRE	CONNECTION
Their Eyes Were Watching God	Zora Neale Hurston	Novel	The growth of two heroines toward independence and self-assurance
The Color Purple	Alice Walker	Novel	
"Angel Levine"	Bernard Malamud	Short story	The responses of individuals to the appearances of an angel
"The Very Old Man with Enormous Wings"	Gabriel García Márquez	Short story	
"The Occurrence at Owl Creek Bridge"	Ambrose Bierce	Short story	How individuals face their execution
"The Secret Miracle"	Jorge Luis Borges	Short story	
"Everyday Use"	Alice Walker	Short story	Struggle in the relationship of men and women
"My Man Bovanne"	Toni Cade Bambara	Short story	

sounds of a slave ship" as excerpts from the novel *Roots* were read. To prepare students for the necessary close reading of Morrison's challenging text and for uncovering terrible events in that reading, they also read Shen Christenson's short story "Facts." Figure 5–5 shows other examples of texts that we have successfully brought together.

Associative Recollections

Bleich (1975, p. 48) believes that the reader's associations with the text are the "most complex but most useful form of expressing feelings about literature" because they reveal the pattern with which individual readers have organized "perception, affect, associations, [and] relationships" for themselves. *Associative recollections* prompt students to notice and harvest connections between their former experiences and texts. Teaching

Activity 5–2 is one possible exercise to prompt these associations.[2]

Appleman (1992, p. 96) introduces students to reader response theory in order to "bring to the reader's consciousness the values, assumptions, and beliefs brought to the text; it also helps to inform the teacher of the factors that affect these students' responses to the text." To begin her introduction, she asked eleventh- and twelfth-grade, college-bound students to read a group of poems and short stories selected for their interpretive ambiguity and openness. Students wrote and shared brief response papers and then discussed both the "general factors that can influence" a reader's response and the "specific factors

---

[2] Most public school districts rely on school-owned textbooks, and writing in them, even in pencil, is prohibited. An alternative is to have students write on separate sheets of paper or Post-it notes, noting their responses by page and line numbers. Both of these alternatives can be used in other teaching activities that suggest bookmarking.

5-2

TEACHING ACTIVITY

Associative Recollections

Individual Work

■ As you read, check moments in the story that feel familiar.

■ When you complete the story, return to your checkpoints and dwell for a moment on past associations evoked by your recent reading.

■ Record the associative recollections prompted by the two most powerful reference points in your journals or in free writing. Begin each recollection with a phrase, such as one of the following:
  - This character/event reminds me of . . .
  - The words here make me think of . . .
  - This part touches a general memory chord, which is . . .
  - This event awakens me to . . .

Small-Group Work

■ Present your perception of the story's two most powerful reference points to each other.

■ Discuss how these associations made their impact. Do the same incidents or characters touch others?

■ Do any think the impact is strong enough to make them remember this story (or character or incident) past this semester?

Individual Work

■ On the back of your cards record any final thoughts about your own or the group's recollections.

that were at play" in their own reactions to these texts. After she explained some of the basic tenets of Rosenblatt's transactional theory, she asked students to list the characteristics of both the text and themselves, characteristics that had influenced their responses to the texts read. After other prereading activities, including an anonymous survey to elicit their attitudes about suicide, they read Judith Guest's *Ordinary People* and completed a reader response diagram. This diagram records the personal characteristics they brought to the novel and also the textual characteristics the novel brought to them, an intersection that explains the transaction between the two. We adapt Appleman's diagram but use her examples in Table 5-4 (pp. 96-97). The reader's characteristics

and text's characteristics are independent of each other. They are joined here only to illustrate the rich transactional ground of the novel.

Comparing the emotional impact of a story on oneself with its impact on other readers can deepen a reader's individual response and remind the group of the critical impact of former experience on reading a text.

Co-Creative Authors

You can invite students to imaginatively confront texts through extending, elaborating, or revising the author's original work—that is, by assuming the role of author. Students can enlarge character, expand undeveloped

TABLE 5–4
Reader response diagram

Reader's Characteristics	Transaction (*Ordinary People*)	Text's Characteristics
Parents' divorce: "Suddenly the family was ripped apart. . . ." Relationship with parents: "don't get along with my mom." Thoughts of suicide: "The fact is I've thought about killing myself."		Realism: "People seemed like real life." Characteristics of protagonist: "Thoughts were some that I've thought." Setting: "You could relate it to our time."

situations, fill in gaps, and extend conclusions. Peter Adams (1987, p. 121), who coined the phrase "dependent authorship," believes that students "can discover and explore elements of their response to the work that they could not grasp or articulate in any other way." Teaching Activity 5–3 is an assignment sheet that prompts students to assume the role of authors and, in doing so, to become co-creators.

Anderson and Rubano (1991, p. 58) suggest several points to keep in mind while you lead this activity:

- The teacher's introduction to this exercise should stress that the writing must grow from the students' genuine curiosities about the text.
- Before students choose their writing project, they should list all the images they associate with the story. This will clarify the significance for students, which will "inevitably find its way into the writing."
- Students should list and share the "writing possibilities that lie within and around the text." Then they choose one of real interest to them.
- Their writing is "not treated as a piece of writing to be revised and polished."

We push students beyond the relative safety of writing to imagine and *perform* scenes between characters or debates within characters. While studying William Faulkner's first published short story, "A Rose for Emily," we ask students to present a minidrama in answer to a prompt such as the following:

- What was Emily's interior debate as she bought the rat poison?
- What did Emily and Homer say to one another on the fateful night as Emily made her final decision to poison Homer?

- What was the dialogue between them as she coaxed him to drink the poison?
- What were her thoughts the morning after this night as she lay in bed?

Students' minidramas often penetrate character and motive with far greater richness, depth, and empathy than their articulated responses to typical analytical questions such as the following, taken from an anthology of fiction:

- Who or what is the antagonist of the story? Why is it significant that Homer Barron is a construction foreman and a northerner?
- Explain how Emily's reasons for murdering Homer are related to her personal history and to the way she handled previous conflict.

Students in pairs, small groups, or whole classes can consider together whether their creative work as co-creators has given shape to aspects of the story that were implicit in it but not overtly stated by it. The following questions can promote such a discussion:

- Does the contemporary addition violate your sense of the characters and situations?
- Does it bring certain elements into clearer focus?
- Does it make you want to readdress certain other elements?
- Did you uncover richer insights that were not immediately apparent but that hover around the story's center, asking to be given form and substance?
- Does the original make it easier to write your additions?
- Does the original grant a richer significance to your work?
- If you departed from each other's sense of the text, where do the discrepancies lie?

5–3 TEACHING ACTIVITY

Co-Creative Authors Writing Prompts

■ Read the text and join the author's project by completing one of the following prompts:
- Write interior monologues in the persona of a chosen character at a particular point in a story.
- Write dialogues between two or more characters.
- Add asides or subliminal thoughts to existing dialogue.
- Write an epilogue to the text.
- Write a continuation of a scene or the whole text.
- Imaginatively reconstruct a gap in the text.
- Write a dream for one of the main characters.
- Add another episode.
- Rewrite the ending.

Imagine This

A first and almost instinctive response to reading a text is to reflect upon the actions, personalities, and motivations of its characters. We cannot believe that Iago can be so vicious with such flimsy cause; we are perplexed by Hamlet's failure to act on his own deep revulsion to the king. Readers have been puzzled for more than a century about Huck Finn's complicity with Tom Sawyer in harassing Jim at the Phelps's farm. Booth (1988a) believes that books draw us toward answering simple first questions: "What happened?" "Just who are these characters?" "Why do I like or detest them, trust or mistrust them?" and "Who are the good guys and bad guys?"

We can give students freer rein to entertain these characters through imaginative projection such as interior monologues, dreams, encounters, dialogues, and dual diary entries. The writing prompts of Teaching Activity 5–4 are invitations to students to respond imaginatively.

Polar Appraisals

This exercise sparks students' interest in characters by juxtaposing opposite characters and character traits and judging between them. It is especially helpful in the study of a long work because it requires a summing up of disparate parts. Both the notions of polarity and appraisal can invite oversimplification and judgment; but even if the activity begins in such gross appraisal, it can conclude in a deepening perception of complexity. Teaching Activity 5–5 presents an individual assignment after students have completed a novel.

Students may complicate this probe into character by comparing their lists of characters and qualities with those of other readers. If both students have selected the same pair, have them compare and discuss the chosen incidents and the qualities of character that they reveal.

Character Continuum

This exercise clarifies the relationships of characters, one to another, by locating them on different continua. The continua might be a movement from bold to cautious, from good to evil, from just to tyrannical, or any other extremes represented in the work under study. Ask students to place characters' names on a line that represents movement from one extreme to the other. Have students state a term or concept that guided their character placement.

5–4   TEACHING ACTIVITY

Imagine This Writing Prompts

- Write letters from one character to another in the same book or in different books.
- Keep journal or diary entries in the persona of a character.
- Make decorative suggestions for or bring in magazine pictures of how you imagine the houses and rooms of characters.
- Suggest a character's favorite songs or type of music. Play a selection.
- Write top-ten lists of characters' imagined attitudes, dislikes, and likes.
- Write yearbook entries for characters.
- Write a feature article for the local newspaper about a character.
- Write and deliver a speech in the persona of a character.
- Organize debates or panel discussions between characters on topics germane to the work or totally removed from it.
- Exchange gifts between characters in a text.
- Imagine a character from one book appearing at specific points in another book.
- Have a character visit a psychotherapist for a counseling session.
- Have characters go to family therapy together.
- Put characters on a talk show to discuss their struggles and dreams.
- Have a character apply for a job with a résumé, interview, and follow-up letters.
- Write epitaphs for characters.

5–5

TEACHING ACTIVITY

Polar Appraisals

- Choose two characters from the story or novel being studied. They should be rounded and illuminate one another when juxtaposed. One you should admire; the other should trouble you.

- Recall three incidents or situations that most clearly show why you chose each character.

- Name two qualities or characteristics reflected in each character's reactions to each of the three events.

- Review the list of six qualities or characteristics you have named for each character, and narrow those down to what you consider to be the most essential character traits.

- Consider these questions: "Do these qualities of my best character reflect my own ideals or values?" "Which ones do I identify with and which ones do I not?"

- Take the traits of the worst character and describe an opposite for each. Do these opposing values match your sense of yourself?

FIGURE 5–6

Character continuum on "The Sky Is Gray"

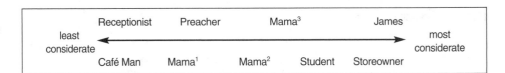

The character continuum in Figure 5-6 is based on Ernest Gaines's "The Sky Is Gray," a story with an assortment of strong characters: Mama, James, the Receptionist, the Storeowner, the Student, the Preacher, and the Café Man. This particular continuum is based on sensitivity; thus, James and the Receptionist are placed near the extremes. When a character stubbornly resists being placed in one spot, as Mama does on the sensitivity continuum, assign the character two or three places with notations of *1, 2,* and *3* to show the time order of their placement. Examine these ambiguous characters to see whether they actually change or whether we just gradually come to understand them better. Who were the two most difficult characters to place on the continuum? Why?

Teacher Shelley Hale uses individual character continua as a springboard to whole-class discussion. She asks one student to put a continuum on the board and explain his or her reasoning to the class. She then invites the whole class to respond: "Who agrees with this?" "Who disagrees?" "Did anyone put someone else first or last?" Hale reports that everyone becomes involved because everyone has just completed his or her own continuum. She also uses this activity as a marker of student reaction throughout a long text. Students chart several continua as they read. At the end of their reading, students have multiple continua with which they can trace their changing reactions to characters.

Teaching Activity 5-6 is another lesson for those who have just finished reading a novel.

Character Maps

An even more visually complex way for students to probe characters is to map them according to their relationships with each other. The aim is not to make comparisons so much as to uncover strong relationships between characters and understand how those are webbed together to create a whole story. The maps can be drawn with either a simple circle of characters or complex schematics. Patricia Kelly (1993) uses colored markers to color-code the "basic emotional relationships" in Ibsen's *A Doll House.* She asks students to choose the legend—for example, "green for jealousy, red for hatred, blue for love, yellow for distrust, or brown for dependency" (p. 132). Teaching Activity 5–7 can be used for an individual or small-group assignment and, in turn, for a whole-class discussion.

Maps can also clarify the reader's relationship to characters. Putting oneself at the center of a character map, a reader can draw lines to different characters and write his or her response to them at different vantage points in the reading of a text: Does the reader feel empathy for, distance from, or anger toward this character? For long works, the accumulation of graphs can prompt readers to reflect on their changed views of characters. Shelley Hale uses character maps to move a text even closer. After students identify relationship connections, she asks students to talk or write about a relationship in their own lives that is similar to a relationship in the text. This establishes the text's connection with students' lives and gives students an oppor-

5–6 TEACHING ACTIVITY

Character Continuum

Individuals

■ Place the key characters in the novel on a continuum of your choice.*

Pairs

■ Compare your choice of an organizing principle for your continuum and your placement of characters.

■ If your organizing concepts are the same, explore any specific differences in your responses to characters.

■ If your continua are different, examine differences and similarities. Do you ultimately share the same general concept of character, or do you have truly dissimilar views?

Whole Class

■ Discuss the impact these differences and similarities have on your basic understanding of the story.

* They may place the characters on the continuum without fully articulating what concept the two extremes represent. But having puzzled over which character belongs where, a concept that defines the continuum should begin to emerge. Good to bad, of course, can be such a starting point, but good or bad in what specific regard?

5–7 TEACHING ACTIVITY

Character Maps

■ List all the characters and place each name within a circle.

■ Connect the most obvious with lines between individual characters.

■ After a few such cliques are established, consider possible relationships between cliques so that all of the characters become visually connected in some fashion.

■ Select several major connections and label them to characterize the kind of relationships between characters and groups.

■ Share your mapped arrays with the class. How do the different maps agree or disagree in their portrayals of these relationships? Do the diverse ways in which the characters relate to one another shed light on the story?

tunity to be the experts (on their own relationships). She then asks students to trace the progress of these fellow characters through the story, consider whether they admire or dislike the relationship's development or outcome, and write about what they would do in their own relationships to emulate or avoid that outcome.

Focal Judgments

Focal judgments elicit readers' judgments of the text using commonplace language, rather than literary terms, and subjective response, rather than analytic critique. We ask readers to select the most important word, passage,

and aspect of the text. Bleich (1975) first introduced us to this strategy for transforming subjective reactions into what appear to be objective judgments without the paralyzing self-consciousness triggered by a request for literary, aesthetic discrimination. Such judgment is personal, which clearly implies that no single response is the "correct" answer.

Most Important Word. Selecting the crucial word for an entire work prompts students to think broadly about texts, especially short ones. The selection might be written or oral. In our classrooms, the question "What do you consider the most important word in this passage (or story or poem)?" is usually instantaneous in the midst of arriving at understanding.

Most Important Passage. The selection of a most important passage continues to elicit personal and diverse judgments of a text. Try an assignment such as the following:

- Read a story and note several short passages (of a sentence or two) that capture what you felt to be central to the text.
- Think through the story again and select the single most crucial passage.
- Reduce this passage to a three- or four-word phrase that captures the entire story.
- Compare your phrase with the work's title to see whether the two summon up the same meaning.

Most Important Aspect. The term *aspect* is left intentionally vague to allow more free play in the reader's mind and so evoke the most natural response. The very vagueness, uncomfortable for the teacher, often produces a great variety of responses. Have students select, distill, and justify their choices.

Shelley Hale sometimes uses a version of focal judgments on her literature examinations. She chooses significant passages and asks students to answer five questions about the text:

1. Who is speaking and to whom?
2. What is the context (when and where does it occur)?
3. Why is the passage important?
4. How does the passage relate to central ideas or themes in the work?
5. What does the passage remind you of in your own life experiences?

Opinion Survey

Opinion surveys are some of the most effective means we know of engaging students in a text. We merely ask students to respond to a set of strong, declarative statements related to the text. These statements can be drawn from general observation, the words of others, or an interpretation of the text. Straightforward statements appeal to students—they require only a simple, direct response. But although they invite quick, direct reaction, they can open rich possibilities for exploring the text, particularly when they raise points of uncertainty and expose honest differences of reader opinion. After students state their agreements and disagreements, we sometimes ask whether they think the author would agree with them. This shifts the argument beyond the class and invites students to project and to judge beyond their own points of view.

The following statements pose both textual and related issues. Concerning *Ordinary People* by Judith Guest, Deborah Appleman (1992) poses the following:

1. Most answers to problems lie within yourself.
2. Families that look perfect on the outside are not always perfect on the inside.

Of the short story "Where Are You Going, Where Have You Been?" by Joyce Carol Oates, teacher Ed McNeal poses the following:

1. People like Arnold Friend are prevalent in today's society.
2. Connie is wrong to let things get out of hand.
3. Most people, at first appearance, "judge a book by its cover."
4. Never trust strangers, even if they seem genuinely nice.
5. "Who isn't fascinated by evil?" (singer Marvin Gaye, 1985).
6. "Experience, which destroys innocence, also leads one back to it" (novelist James Baldwin, 1962).
7. "It [rock music] is *the* youth culture and there is now no other countervailing nourishment for the spirit" (critic Allan Bloom, 1987).

Of *The Chocolate War* by Robert Cormier, we pose the following:

1. You should always be an individual.
2. You should try to fit in after moving to a new place.
3. Small decisions can often greatly change your life.

After her students read *Romeo and Juliet,* Mindi Fry asks them to respond with yes or no to these general and specific statements:

1. I believe in love at first sight.
2. I believe that looks are a big part of liking someone at first.
3. I don't think it's right for parents to interfere in my relationships.
4. Family background will not matter to me when I fall in love.
5. Juliet was wrong to disobey her parents; family comes first.
6. Juliet's parents have her best interests in mind when they discuss her marriage to Paris.
7. It was wrong for Friar Laurence to become so involved in the romance.

Anna Milner asks students to answer true or false to the following opinion survey after they have read Machiavelli's *The Prince:*

1. I believe that a leader's moral character is as important as his political leadership.
2. A politician's job is to direct and represent public policies—his moral character and behavior are per-

5-8 · TEACHING ACTIVITY

Opinion Survey

Individual

- Complete the survey.
- Put an *X* in front of the two statements you found most difficult to answer and write a brief explanation of your ambivalence.
- Review the remaining statements and circle the two or three about which you feel certain.

Small Group

- Tally your members' three most certain statements.
- Explore areas of agreement and disagreement.
- Select the two statements that raised most ambivalence for members of your group and exchange ideas from your written explanations.

Whole Class

- Discuss each group's essential agreements and disagreements.

---

sonal matters irrelevant to the fulfillment of his duties.

3. In certain situations it is acceptable to bend rules, especially if it is for a good purpose.

4. All good rulers must, to some extent, be feared.

Teaching Activity 5–8 suggests how to incorporate individual opinion surveys into whole-class discussions.

Verbal Scales

A more nuanced kind of polar response asks students to rate the strength of their agreement or disagreement on a 5-4-3-2-1 (Likert-type) scale. Anderson and Rubano (1991) suggest using such a semantic differential or verbal scale throughout the reading of a text. For instance, they ask students to register their feelings after every stanza of Edwin Arlington Robinson's poem "Richard Cory" (pp. 31-32):

How do you feel toward Richard Cory?
    Like   1   2   3   4   5   Dislike

Anderson and Rubano observe that the scale not only elicits and clarifies an initial response but also makes the final stanza's "turn" more obvious for students. They use verbal scales for longer works as well—for instance, charting Hamlet's psychological state on a sane-insane scale or the symbolic geography of Huck's journey downriver on a civilized-uncivilized scale. A final example that they use for Zora Neale Hurston's *Their Eyes Were Watching God* shows two ways to ask questions to sharpen the reader's understanding of a central aspect of the story: Janie's "developing self-awareness and self-direction." An-

---

1

Who decides what Janie will do at this point in the story? (If it was completely the choice of the other person, circle 1; if it was completely Janie's choice, circle 7. Circling 4 means you think it was equally Janie's and the other person's choice.)

Other   1 2 3 4 5 6 7   Janie

2

At this point in the narrative, is Janie an active participant in the decision making, or a passive follower of the wishes of others?

Active   1 2 3 4 5 6 7   Passive

FIGURE 5–7   Example of verbal scale

Source: Anderson, P. M., & Rubano, G. (1991). *Enhancing aesthetic reading and response,* Urbana, IL: NCTE. Reprinted with permission.

derson and Rubano (p. 33) pose verbal scales repeatedly at particularly important points in the narrative, as Figure 5-7 illustrates.

Interrogative Reading

Since ancient times, philosophers have told us that education is not so much measured by the answers one receives as by the questions one raises. They encourage us to question the answers rather than merely answer the questions. Many teachers affirm the advantage of reading literature with pens or highlighters in hand, approaching the text interrogatively with questions to share later with students. Research findings have confirmed this wisdom for any reader: Students instructed to answer questions about texts were not nearly so conversant with the text

5–9   TEACHING ACTIVITY

Interrogative Reading

Individual

- Read a short story to get a total sense of it.

- Reread or review it, noting spots where you were uncertain or curious about plot, character, language, or meaning.

- Look over the work a third time, searching these checkpoints. Were your early questions resolved by the end? Do some puzzles still remain? Write phrases beside the checkpoints that you can later convert into full questions.

- Formulate five key questions from your initial curiosity, perplexity, or uncertainty or from later discoveries and associations—in other words, from points in the story where insights are emerging but doubts remain.

Pairs

- Take your five questions to a partner and compare your two lists. Can you answer any of each other's questions? Do so.

- Select which of your ten queries to pose to the whole class. These questions can guide you:
  - Which of your partner's questions converge with your questions?
  - Do your partner's questions lead you to any ideas that you had not considered?
  - Do they deepen your insight into the work?
  - Do your individual questions follow any particular pattern, such as clarifying details of setting, character, or situation? Puzzling over language? Interpreting meaning? Noticing formal patterns?

- Revise your own questions based on the discussion.

Whole Class

- Share your best questions with the whole class, both those that remain unanswered and any that lead you to new ideas.

- Consider the following: Were many questions the same? Has question asking revealed insights that were not present before? Have you generated still more uncertainties about the work, or has your sense of it settled?

---

as those who were asked to develop their own questions (Palinscar & Brown, 1984). The deep message of this strategy—using student-constructed questions for whole-class discussions and even tests and quizzes—is that students discover and develop confidence in their ability to take command of their own learning. Teaching Activity 5-9 is a lesson that engenders questions from students. With it, you and they can test the effectiveness of interrogative readings.

Jump Starts

Myers (1988) has devised twenty reader response questions that invite students to react personally to texts. She constantly revises the questions to sharpen her attempts to elicit the students' "perceptions, feelings, and associations"

(p. 65). These questions are based on the text, but they give students room to expand their ideas. They involve students with the text so that students cannot just angle to guess the teacher's opinion. These questions could be used as prompts for individual journal or free writing or as stimulants for whole-class or small-group discussions. They are good candidates for pasting in your literature textbook or on your lectern for your quick reference and adaptation.

Myers' Reader Response Questions

1. What character(s) was your favorite? Why?
2. What character(s) did you dislike? Why?
3. Does anyone in this work remind you of anyone you know? Explain.
4. Are you like any character in this work? Explain.
5. If you could be any character in this work, who would you be? Explain.

6. What quality(ies) of which character strikes you as a good characteristic to develop within yourself over the years? Why? How does the character demonstrate this quality?

7. Overall, what kind of a feeling did you have after reading a few paragraphs of this work? Midway? After finishing the work?

8. Do any incidents, ideas, or actions in this work remind you of your own life or something that happened to you? Explain.

9. Do you like this piece of work? Why or why not?

10. Are there any parts of this work that were confusing to you? Which parts? Why do you think you got confused?

11. Do you feel there is an opinion expressed by the author through this work? What is it? How do you know this? Do you agree? Why or why not?

12. Do you think the title of this work is appropriate? Is it significant? Explain. What do you think the title means?

13. Would you change the ending of this story in any way? Tell your ending. Why would you change it?

14. What kind of person do you feel the author is? What makes you feel this way?

15. How did this work make you feel? Explain.

16. Do you share any of the feelings of the characters in this work? Explain.

17. Sometimes works leave you with a feeling that there is more to tell. Did this work do this? What do you think might happen?

18. Would you like to read something else by this author? Why or why not?

19. What do you feel is the most important word, phrase, passage, or paragraph in this work? Explain why it is important.

20. If you were an English teacher, would you want to share this work with your students? Why or why not? (p. 65)

Title Testing

As we walk through art galleries, whether we are looking at the works of vaguely familiar old masters or unknown modernists, our irresistible impulse is to check a work's creator and title. The artist's name sometimes sets the particular work within a context of biography, history, or artistic style. But the title has far more impact. It can reform what we see; it directs our thinking and suggests a context that influences and even defines our sense of the work. With written texts, we are a little less aware of that telling effect because we always see the title before we read the whole text; and, for many of us, the words of the text are more leading than the line and color and composition of a painting. When we are baffled by a text or want a fuller understanding of it, the title is a natural place to focus our attention. We earlier discussed an exercise that asks students to speculate about the title *before* they read a text. Speculating about the title is an excellent strategy *after* reading as well. We often ask, "What light is thrown on this piece by its title?" "Does the ending of this story make you want to reconstrue the title?" Teaching Activity 5–10 is a more extended consideration of the

5–10 TEACHING ACTIVITY

Title Testing Whole-Class Discussion

■ After you have read Raymond Carver's "Neighbors," think about Carver's title with as much mental playfulness, creativity, and speculation as possible.

■ Write the word *neighbors* in the center of a circle and graph as many diverse connotations, suggestions, allusions, connections, and associations as you can. Figure 5–8 is an example of such a map.

■ Consider: Which word best matches your speculation about the story? Do others work to enrich your understanding of the story?

■ Invent story titles that you feel are better, more creative foci for the tale, such as "Invaders," "Love Thy Neighbor," or "Imagine."

■ Review the class suggestions and list several that seem to make good substitutes. Examine the power of the various titles to explain, compress, and focus the meaning of Carver's text. As a class, decide whether their effectiveness is greater or lesser than Carver's title.

Here is another option:

■ Create a short title of an editorial or philosophical essay that Carver might have written had he chosen nonfiction, rather than fiction, to capture his vision. Three suggestions might be "Modern Decadence," "Homeowner's Insurance," and "Good Fences Make Good Neighbors."

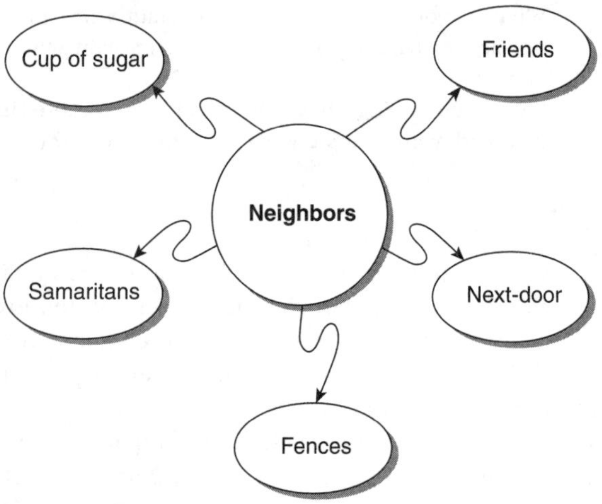

FIGURE 5–8   Title testing idea map

title of Raymond Carver's provocative short story about two young couples, "Neighbors."

Another provocative use of titles is to explain a title's history and to compare the effects of the final and earlier versions. For instance, Raymond Carver's working title for the brief short story "Popular Mechanics" was "Mine." Ibsen entitled his play *A Doll House*, but contemporary productions often call it *A Doll's House*. What is the difference between the two? What new light is shed by your comparison? Which do you prefer?[3]

Flynn (1986) describes three approaches to reading a text: dominant, submissive, and interactive. A *dominant* reading is detached and resists involvement; a *submissive* reading is involved and resists detachment; an *interactive* reading has the capacity to be both involved and detached, and it is a way to a meaningful interaction with the text. We have designed each reader response approach and teaching activity so that students might become interactive readers. We believe that the cumulative effect of literature on the reader is more powerful when students make connections between their experiences and the text. The more we can open them to seeing these links, letting literature live actively in their imaginations, the stronger they become both as readers and as people. The next step is to build on this individual involvement and response and enrich it by the shared work of a whole-class community. We invite students into a collaborative kind of learning.

---

[3] The importance of naming titles (and characters) can be illustrated by literary history. The working title of a first novel by an unknown Atlantan, a former magazine feature writer, was *Tomorrow Is Another Day*, and its heroine was named Pansy. The Macmillan editor who found Margaret Mitchell was not enamored of the title or the heroine, renamed both, and ordered a first printing of only 10,000 copies. By the end of its first year in print, 1936, *Gone with the Wind* had sold 1 million copies. Did the title and name make a difference?

Invitation to Reflection   5–3

Bleich (1975) raises some fascinating questions about the transition from private reading and personal response to public discussion and interpretation. He poses them as "lines of inquiry which might help a class to study some of the group functions of literary interpretation" (p. 104). We pose them to direct your thinking toward the act of group interpretation.

- If you read a story or a poem, and then tell no one about it, what effect does it have on you?
- What does the act of telling others do to your sense of the original experience? What kinds of things happen during a conversation that affect your sense of the reading experience?
- In real life, which people in your life would certainly hear from you about an interesting reading experience? Would you tell only people to whom you think the story is relevant?
- When you are in class, how much do you expect to learn from other students? Could you learn more from them or from the teacher? What effect might the opinions of unfamiliar peers (classmates) have on your own reading experiences?
- How many times have you read a book or seen a movie because others have and you want to be able to talk about it with them? . . . Of what benefit is it to a small group of people to read the same book and talk about it?
- When you are in a class discussion, do you feel you would somehow like to reach a conclusion that everyone should accept? If there is no exam on which you will have to write "answers," what kind of enlightenment could you expect from a class discussion of literature?
- To what extent do you use the occasion of literary discussion to find out what other readers are like as people? To what extent do you look forward to hearing someone's response just because you know he is an interesting person? Can a class be made to feel more like a group through a discussion of the same work of literature? . . . What would you say a classroom discussion about a story has in common with a . . . bull session? (pp. 104–105)

∞ INTERPRETIVE COMMUNITY

Students too often regard classroom discussions of literature as a way of bludgeoning texts into insensibility. For these students, it is murder to dissect. But there are alternative ways for students to talk collectively about literature. In this second stage of reading, we suggest activities that enable students to shape their personal responses into textual interpretation within an interpretative community.[4] A hidden agenda of the reader response stage was to prepare readers to take their personal responses confidently into a larger community, where they will be tested and sharpened. When students begin that communal sharing, the multiplicity of interpretations widens individual perspectives and unseats the idea that any one reading is the definitive reading. At this stage, students move to the company of others to explore their individual reactions, air their group differences, negotiate alternative perspectives, and enlarge their stakes in the text. Interpretive community clarifies their visions, strengthens their confidence in their personal ability to respond to literature, and kindles their respect for others to do likewise. Bleich believes that "each reader's responses . . . will take on full significance only when they are brought together and tested against one another in a communal setting."

At the Point of Utterance

Even before you invite student readers to bring their personal responses to the Interpretive Community for examination, a helpful way to encourage inexperienced readers is for you, as the most experienced reader, to respond to a work with which *you* are unfamiliar. Students can be asked to make the selection. We have found that something short enough for a quick in-class reading works best. You can read the story or poem slowly, offering at natural breaks in the text partial responses: questions, puzzlements, predictions, and hypotheses. At these points, you might invite students to add their responses—feelings as well as interpretations—in an attempt to fill gaps, refine small points, and even offer radically different readings. In other words, you invite them into your own interpretive exploration without the usual teacher's resources of textbook manuals, critical reviews, university course notes, and years of reflection. Such an experience allows less sophisticated readers to see that even a very experienced reader must struggle with a text to begin to forge an understanding that is coherent, comprehensive, and satisfying. Iser (1980, p. 62) delineates this internal process not as smooth and continuous but as one in which we readers "look forward, we look back, we decide, we

change our decisions, we form expectations, we are shocked by their nonfulfillment, we question, we muse, we accept, we reject." At the conclusion of the teacher's visible interpretive acts, you can include students in your active exploration. You may all agree that, although admirable, the reading was incomplete and the piece deserves further reflection.

This exercise has several effects. It demythologizes the notion that some people, namely teachers, have special interpretive gifts (almost genetic endowments) that most students can never match. It delivers a vital message to students to trust their intuitive responses. It may suggest, too, that the most satisfying and penetrating readings begin with individual subjective responses that are tempered by reflection and by the activity of the entire reading community. Jago (2001) calls this activity a "think aloud" and values it as a moment in which simple things can be sorted out and interpretation can emerge gradually without pressure. At the beginning of a text, it validates the idea that all readers are struggling readers. We believe that more than anything else, your students should get the message that the class cannot passively wait for the teacher to deliver the proper response to the text. Every member of the interpretive community—individuals, small groups, or the whole class—is vital to the work of interpreting texts.

Students can profit from being invited into the activity you have just modeled: saying their responses aloud as they read a text. Arnold (1987) suggests a variation, "subtexting," in which students in small groups or pairs read a few lines of a play, pause, assume the character whose lines they are reading, and articulate that character's thoughts and feelings about the situation at hand. However you invite students into these responsive acts, you prepare them for literary work as Walt Whitman and Umberto Eco understand it:

> The process of reading is not a half-sleep, but in the highest sense an exercise, a gymnastic struggle; that the reader is to do something for himself.
>
> *Walt Whitman*

> Every text, after all, is a lazy machine asking the reader to do some of its work.
>
> *Umberto Eco*

Proximate Reading

In this activity, short, student-selected excerpts of a text bring the subjective reading of individual students into the interpretive community. This exercise has some of the same effects as do abbreviated advertisements that appear on television as fragments of longer ones: The full ad enters your mind even though you only see a partial showing of it. Teaching Activity 5–11 instructs students about how to approach a communal reading of the text and then offers follow-up questions for you to pose

---

[4] Interpretive community is a concept used differently by a number of different people (Bleich, 1975; Fish, 1980; Scholes, 1985). Fish uses the term to mean a set of attitudes or conventions shared by a particular community that influences or dominates the interpretive acts of any of its members. Meaning is shaped or determined for individuals by those dominant beliefs and practices of the reading community to which they belong. We use the term in this book more broadly to mean a formal or informal gathering of students in which each student's personal responses are elaborated, informed, and enlarged by interaction with others.

5–11 TEACHING ACTIVITY

Proximate Reading

Student Instructions

■ Select two important short passages from the text: the one that you consider to be the most important passage and one that foreshadows it.

■ Write on a card the first one or two lines of each passage and the number of the page and line on which it begins and ends so that you can easily locate both.

■ Your teacher will collect all the cards, number them according to their proper order in the story, and redistribute them, two for each class member.

■ Read your two passages aloud sequentially so that all cards taken together will form an approximate reading of the whole text.

Follow-Up Questions

■ What was the cumulative effect of the proximate reading of the text?

■ What was the most important segment of the text for the community of readers?

■ Why did so many select it?

■ Were there any individual responses that diverged greatly from those of the majority of readers?

■ What were other students' reasons for selecting other passages?

■ Did other students choose the same or similar foreshadowing passages that you did?

■ Did your general understanding of the text improve with this exercise?

■ Did you find obvious differences in interpretation arising from the variety of the selected passages? If so, what were they?

---

in whole-class or small-group discussions or for journal reflections. In the selections students read, passages will likely be repeated and great gaps will appear, but those will both mark the power points in the text and offer another chance for the immediacy of the text to reach every reader.

Reconstructing the text and then reviewing it initiates talk about the text that opens it to the interpretive community and helps students open themselves to it as well. This activity can be especially useful with a long novel or drama or with a section of a long work.

Communal Judgments

In the focal judgments activity in the reader response stage, we suggested selection of the most important word, passage, and aspect to help individual readers focus and clarify their responses. Their choosing evolves naturally into communal discussions. Teaching Activity 5–12 suggests questions that bring individual judgments into a fuller group consideration. Its questions can be used with pairs or a small group. The activity could culminate in a

dramatic presentation to the whole class by clusters of pairs or small groups.

We have found the following criteria useful in sorting out and evaluating the strength of student selections:

• strength of rationale
• connection to important points of reference
• explanatory power
• comprehensiveness; breadth of understanding
• multiplicity of meaning
• appropriateness of tone

Defining Vignettes

Bleich (1975) and Holland (1975) believe that literature sets in motion differing interior responses in the reader and that we should capitalize on those idiosyncratic readings. Defining vignettes joins individual response to a group purpose. Students distill the essence of a longer text into a short, compact vignette. Teaching Activity 5–13 leads students from their individual readings of a work, to their imagining a crucial scene from it, to finally performing that short scene.

TEACHING ACTIVITY

Communal Judgments

After individual judgments of the most important word, passage, or aspect have been made, consider your choices using the following questions:

Most Important Word

- Do your individual choices bunch together? Or are they spaced throughout the text?

- Are they attached to certain characters?

- Are they associated with special events?

- Can lines be drawn to suggest connections between the three or four most often-selected words? What would these connections be?

- Are they connected with the title? Like the title, do the selected words shed new light on the whole piece?

- Do you differ in your interpretations of the text?

Most Important Passage

- What passages are selected repeatedly?

- What gives those passages their import, their significance?

- Do the different selections suggest diverse readings?

Most Important Aspect

- What term feels closest to your definition of *aspect?*

  theme_____   character _____
  setting _____   situation_____
  tone _____   plot_____
  structure_____   style _____

- Does the aspect comprise something central in the story?

- Do any of the aspects chosen suggest contradictory understandings of the story?*

* If the work is one that has already been filmed (Flannery O'Connor's "The Displaced Person," Ernest Gaines's "The Sky Is Gray," or James Joyce's "The Dead," for instance), showing excerpts from the professional version in class would allow students to compare their interpretation with another's.

TEACHING ACTIVITY

Defining Vignettes

Individual Work

- If you were filming this work, what four pictures or vignettes would you choose to capture the essential story?

Group Work

- As a group, study your individual selections and choose four vignettes to be the group's total sequence.

- In pairs, choose a vignette and develop a dramatic transformation of it, creating both dialogue and any narrated commentary.

- Reassemble as a group and appoint a script editor, a director, a prop manager, and a cast of characters in order to create a presentation of the total sequence.

Whole-Class Work

- Each group presents its vignettes for the entire class.

- React to the variety of vignettes and the interpretations each seems to represent.

Readers' Theater

This activity approaches a text through performance rather than discussion. Patricia Kelly (1992) makes a strong case for class dramatization of poems or prose and dramatic passages as "a way into meaning." Here is how she set up her lesson in a tenth-grade class whose students had enjoyed creative dramatics activities but were not experienced in readers' theater:

- Groups of students prepare to "perform" selected sentences in order to project specified moods and emotions (five minutes).
- As a whole class, the students guess the feeling being conveyed. (This exercise lets groups cohere, performers grow less self-conscious, and the class grow accustomed to conveying "with the voice an interpreted meaning to an audience.")
- In groups, the students prepare a performance of a poem (in Kelly's case, Sylvia Plath's "Words"), namely to "wrestle with the meaning of the poem and how [one] might present that meaning to an audience." (Each group reads the same poem.)
- As a whole class, the students enjoy the readers' theater performance of each group.
- As a whole class, they discuss the "readings" and consider this question: Why did you decide to present the poem as you did? (pp. 88–89)

Kelly describes the subtle, but crucial, benefits of the follow-up discussion:

These whole-class discussions following Readers' Theater presentations broaden students' understanding of the literary work because they hear the thinking that underlies different interpretations. The discussions are not a "reporting" of the group activity; neither are they like a class discussion of the poem. And therein lies their benefit. They are similar to an "expert" group approach because each group is an expert on its presentation, but the motivation is somewhat different. Each group wants the others, who have appreciated its rendering of the literary piece, to understand the uniqueness of its interpretation. Although they are teaching each other as "expert" groups do, students do not perceive the discussion in that way; they see it as an informal sharing. (pp. 89–90)

Several other advantages grow from this readers' theater: Less academic students can shine, both in their performances and in their "expert" perspectives on them; and students read the poem many times more than they would in traditional discussions as they try to understand its meaning, prepare their performances, perform, listen to other performances, and discuss. They may not address some difficult images or lines, but they seem to understand it "in a holistic way," a "sensing, emotional approach rather than an explicative one" (Kelly, 1992, p. 90).

Assaying Characters: Questions and Checklists

Perhaps our most compelling entry into literature is to treat it as lived life. Students assess, or assay, characters by regarding them like family members, next-door neighbors, classmates, or other people they know. Questions are essential for prompting students to uncover the human mysteries of motivation, personality, and interaction—in other words, to perceive characters as real people. The following questions have worked for us as discussion or writing prompts when posed to individual students or to the entire interpretive community.

Understanding the Central Person
1. What seems to drive this person to action?
2. What incidents tell us most about this person?
3. What acts affect your feelings about this person?
4. What are some basic character traits of this person?
5. What is the greatest strength/weakness of this person?
6. How does this person relate to other people?
7. What is special or important about this person's moral or religious life?
8. How does this person change or mature?
9. What personal insights enlighten this person?
10. What question would you like to pose to this character?
11. Would you be friends with this person?
12. Does he or she share any values with you?
13. Would you enjoy spending an evening together? Where would you go?

Exploring the World of Characters
1. What other characters draw your special attention?
2. What do they tell us about the central figure?
3. What special relationships are formed by these less central people?
4. What groups of people are associated in your mind?
5. Do some of these people or groups represent values or ideas beyond themselves?
6. Do any characters provoke your distaste or disdain? Which ones?
7. Which character is most mysterious and hardest to understand?
8. Which character could be most easily left out of this fictive world?
9. Do any of these other people seem to grow or change in the course of the story?
10. Does any character you don't know well play an important role?
11. Would you want to spend a Saturday or Sunday with any of them?

Imagining Characters in Our World
1. What serious matters could you talk about with this person?
2. What important values would you disagree about?

3. What would your parents think about this character?
4. What in our world would shock this character most?
5. What would make anyone know that this character doesn't fit in our world?
6. What social causes would this person support? To what charities would this person contribute?
7. What television program would be most appealing to this person?

Considering Any Discussion of Characters
1. Have we done justice to the complexity of this person in the text?
2. Has the text done justice to the world we know outside the text—that is, is the character believable?

Another strategy that invites students' personal connections presents checklists of character traits and the charge to connect the attributes with a character. The most successful checklists are constructed for the specific pieces of literature under study and articulate traits that students could not themselves express but trigger recognition. The possible points of connection between character and descriptor are numerous:

- distinguishing personality traits of the character
- crucial, tragic flaws
- contrasting traits between characters

- strengths or weaknesses of character
- needful traits that are absent
- intellectual, emotional, or behavioral habits when stressed or happy

Teaching Activity 5–14 was created by Patricia Kelly and Robert Small (1993, personal communication); it continues the class consideration of "Raymond's Run" begun as an individual personal triggers prereading activity. It provides a visual assay of character.

Psychological Profiles

One of the deepest appeals of fiction has always been, as Allen (1963, p. 12) stated four decades ago, the opportunity it offers of knowing characters "with a far greater intimacy than we can ever know actual human beings," many of them becoming "more 'real' to us, more comprehensible, than all but one or two of all the living people we know personally." There is a story about Charles Dickens's *The Old Curiosity Shop* that vividly illustrates the vital power of fictional characters. The novel was being printed in serial form in a London periodical; and when its final installment arrived on a ship in New York Harbor, thousands of people lined the wharves, crying out to anyone on board, "Did Little Nell die?"

5–14 | TEACHING ACTIVITY

Assaying Character

By the end of "Raymond's Run" you may have formed different impressions about Gretchen, Raymond, and Hazel from those you had at the beginning.

Small-Group Work

- Form groups of four people.

- Your group should make three character sheets by writing a character's name at the top of each of three separate sheets of paper. Then draw a vertical line down the center of each of the three pages. Label one side "First Impressions" and the other side "Last Impressions."

- With members of your group, list all the things you know or feel about each of the characters at the beginning of the story and then your views of them at the end. Consult the story for specifics.

Whole-Class Work

- For the whole-class sharing, have your group's "reporter" tell the other groups in turn an idea from your group's list of "First Impressions of Gretchen." If you hear good points offered by the other groups that are not on your group's list, add them. No information should be given twice.

- When all first impressions have been offered, begin telling ideas from your group's list of "Last Impressions of Gretchen" and add to your list in the same way. Follow the same procedure for the other two characters.

- Look at the class lists. Compare the first and last impressions of each character. Which character seemed to change most? Why do you think your perception changed?

When readers want to probe further into character, the study of human behavior becomes useful. We have found the work of developmental psychology especially helpful for deepening insights into literature. Theorists such as Erik Erikson, Lawrence Kohlberg, and Jane Loevinger chart the stages in a whole human life cycle along dimensions of personality, morality, and ego development. Their constructs possess significant explanatory power in themselves, but they also present abundant means by which to understand fictional characters—their natures and their actions. Appendix D outlines these three prominent constructs and ways to bring them into literary study: Erikson's stages of psychosocial development, Kohlberg's stages of moral development, and Loevinger's stages of ego development. Of course these brief explanations require your further study to integrate them into your literature classroom. We hint at the rewards of integrating ideas from another discipline with two teaching ideas.

Teaching Activity 5–15 solicits students' reactions to moral questions posed by Hernando Tellez's "Just Lather, That's All," the story of a revolutionary who tests the political position and will of a barber by extending his neck to the barber for a shave. Approaching the story in terms of Kohlberg's moral dimensions yields productive discussions of both the story and its ethical dimensions.

A young colleague adapted another construct, Kubler-Ross's grief cycle, for a final project with her eleventh-grade honors students who had just read Judith Guest's *Ordinary People*. Melissa McCabe asked students to write Dr. Berger's psychological reports of Conrad, Beth, and Calvin. The assignment was to describe the characters based on Dr. Berger's meetings with them, put forth a diagnosis, and make recommendations for final treatment. She encouraged students to use Kubler-Ross's stages of grief (that she had introduced earlier) and to adopt the unique dry-witted humor and voice of Dr. Berger.

Venn Diagramming

Ideas from neuropsychology are also instructive in literature study. Neuropsychologists have found that the asymmetrical brain functions in two basic ways. At times it moves in: It focuses carefully upon one instance or event. At other times it stands back: Its perceptual activity sprawls to include an entire field. In the study of literature, we might call the mind's work of focusing *analysis* and its more distant viewing *synthesis*. To use all of the reader's neurological potential in encountering texts, distant synthesis is needed as well as focused analysis.

Much of a student's study of literature focuses on one text at a time. That text may be placed in a historical context, set among pieces of the same genre, or even treated as part of a thematic unit; but typically one particular text

---

5–15   TEACHING ACTIVITY

Moral Choices

Read "Just Lather, That's All." Decide what action the barber should take. Then select the amount of importance the barber should attach to each of the questions that follow when he is deciding what to do.
_____ He should kill him. _____ I'm not sure. _____ He should not kill him.

Importance: Great Some Little No
_____ 1. Will I lose my effectiveness as a spy if I kill the lieutenant?
_____ 2. Can I get out of town before the murder is discovered?
_____ 3. Is it right to continue killing people to assert my political beliefs?
_____ 4. Is the lieutenant really planning to torture the newly captured prisoners?
_____ 5. Do I have any legal right to commit such a crime in the event of a U.N. settlement of the war?
_____ 6. Will the townspeople think me a coward if I fail to kill the lieutenant?
_____ 7. Are ideals ever worth killing for?
_____ 8. Should other, more well-trained guerrillas be asked to take on this difficult task?
_____ 9. Will my barber's shaving blade really kill the lieutenant?
_____10. Is the life of a grisly killer worth as much as that of any good man?
_____11. Whose army is most likely to be ultimately victorious?

From the list of considerations, select the four most important. Which stage of Kohlberg's moral development hierarchy does each represent?

will be analyzed before another is addressed. Venn diagramming, an approach from logic, uses the visual clarity of overlapping circles to compare and contrast texts, characters, events, or ideas within texts. Figure 5–3 is a model Venn diagram. When texts or elements within texts are charted in this visual way, their differences (white) and similarities (gray and black) become more apparent. Teaching Activity 5–16 presents instructions for a Venn diagramming activity.

A young teacher, Mindi Fry, used a mini-Venn in teaching *Romeo and Juliet*. She showed the same balcony scene from two film versions of the play. While students watched, she asked them to use a Venn diagram to compare the directors' interpretations and their own of each scene. This focused and active viewing left students with far richer impressions and insights for small-group and then whole-group discussions.

The ideas of the interpretive community promote reading literature collectively with angles of vision different from those of traditional analytical questioning. Crosman (1982, p. 214) describes what happens in the communal enterprise: "We go on learning, after we have read a text, by sharing our interpretation with others, and by letting their interpretations enrich our own." If we enter into dialogue with others after our personal encounter, the text becomes richer, deeper, and larger. The interpretive community thus becomes a resource not only of ideas but also of the processes by which ideas are formed and shaped.

5–16   TEACHING ACTIVITY

Venn Diagramming

Individual Work

■ Read three short stories (say, Ursula K. LeGuin's "The Ones Who Walk Away from Omelas," Hernando Tellez's "Just Lather, That's All," and Kurt Vonnegut, Jr.'s, "Harrison Bergeron").

■ List central concepts or impressions that each story raises for you (about ideas, characters, situation, or tone, for instance).

Small-Group Work

■ Compare your individual lists.

■ Select those concepts or impressions that your group agrees are most important to each story.

■ Draw three overlapping circles and assign a story to each circle. In the central portion where all circles intersect (*X*), list issues with which all three writers are concerned. Do the same for the issues common to pairs of stories, labeling these areas where two circles intersect *A, B, C*. Note any ideas that fall into the white portion as unique to one story only.

■ Discuss:
  • Do the authors have the same or different views about the issues they share?
  • Does one story develop a common idea more fully than another?
  • Do you find yourself agreeing with one author more than another?
  • Imagine the three authors sitting down to talk together. Write the questions they might pose to each other.
  • Which of the three would you most like to have lunch with?
  • List the one question you would ask that author.

Whole-Class Work

■ Discuss
  • Are the issues of the individual stories made stronger by considering them together?
  • Are issues of difference heightened?

Individual Work

■ Write a new conclusion to one story as your favored author might have written it, *or* write a letter the favored author might have written to another author or that author's character. (Make certain your writing expresses the perspective of both the author and the characters.)

FORMAL ANALYSIS

Students' journeys into literature could end at this point, midway through our four reading stages, and they would have touched the essential humanity of the fictive world. However, Rosenblatt (1968) reminds us that "the literary work is not primarily a document in the history of language or society. . . . As a work of art, it offers a special kind of experience" (p. 278). That experience is rich with personal meaning but with formal literary meaning as well. In this section we discuss ways in which to enlarge students' capacities to recognize, appreciate, and finally internalize dimensions of the special experience of reading literature. We suggest ways to sensitize them to the evolution of literary conventions, authors' creative variations on traditional techniques, their unique responses to textual and cultural challenges, and the literary effects of their completed works. We then hope to reconnect the students' first distinct responses in reading with their understanding of the literary context in which they occur. Our ultimate aim is that by enlarging their intellectual and emotional capacities to respond to literature, we also enlarge their capacities to notice and respond to their multilayered lives.

Our profession stands at an instructional crossroads between the forces of preceding decades: New Criticism, which is devoted to close formal scrutiny of texts and to discovering their meaning through formal analysis, and reader response, which is devoted to making textual meaning through associative and personal response. One considers knowledge of form to be essential, and the other struggles not to be drawn into formal matters. We believe a *technical reading* alone would omit the personal and communal steps that are essential for strong engagement with the text. A *personal reading* alone would omit much of the enrichment and delight of discovering how literature works and taking that knowledge to the next text and into many texts thereafter. We believe that English teachers need not choose one or the other but can address both the formal and the personal. Our four stages of reading validate and promote the revelations of both. As Elise Ann Earthman (1997, personal communication) says, we need ways to "move students from an initial free encounter with a poem toward the analysis that comes after the poem matters to them . . . to something deeper and more considered." Formal questions are part of that deepening: helping students to appreciate the craft of fiction, to understand how a work achieves its effects and thus often its meaning. Beginning teachers need to understand the "proper place" for formal analysis—"not as an end in itself but as a way of enriching and deepening one's growing interpretation" (Earthman, 1997).

English teacher, critic, novelist, and religious apologist C. S. Lewis (1961) was caught in a similar debate during the 1950s and 1960s. He writes of his own quandary: Should he read poetry only to experience its private effect, or should he read it to fathom the poet's intent? His answer identifies the interlocking power of both.

> The literary sometimes "use" poetry instead of "receiving" it. They differ from the unliterary because they know very well what they are doing. . . . "Why," they ask, "should I turn from a real and present experience—what the poem means to me, what happens to me when I read it—to inquiries about the poet's intention or reconstructions, always uncertain, of what it may have meant to his contemporaries?" There seem to be two answers. One is that the poem in my head which I make from my mistranslations of Chaucer or misunderstandings of Donne may possibly not be so good as the work Chaucer or Donne actually made. Secondly, why not have both? After enjoying what I made of it, why not go back to the text, this time looking up the hard words, puzzling out the allusions, and discovering that some metrical delights in my first experience were due to my fortunate mispronunciations, and see whether I can enjoy the poet's poem, not necessarily instead of, but in addition to, my own one? If I am a man of genius and uninhibited by false modesty I may still think my poem the better of the two. But I could not have discovered this without knowing both. Often, both are well worth retaining. . . . It is rather like revisiting a beautiful place we knew in childhood. We appraise the landscape with an adult eye; we also revive the pleasures—often very different—which it produced when we were small children. (pp. 100–101)

The debate over teaching literary form strongly resembles the debate over teaching grammar: The subject matter quickly becomes an end in itself in the English curriculum. At present, textbook makers, sensitive to calls for accountability from legislators and book selection committees, construct ever-more elaborate scope-and-sequence charts prescribing what and how the English teacher should present literary terms and concepts—their depth, their context, and their order. Their teacher editions, manuals, and glossaries make a skills-and-drills approach to literary vocabulary seem not only inviting but right. And testing literary terms is so easy: Matching, fill-in-the-blanks, and short answers are blessedly straightforward, easy to grade, and sometimes preconstructed! State-mandated, end-of-course tests of literary knowledge make teaching formal concepts and their chalk-and-talk presentation seem practical necessities. A basic principle, then, is to approach teaching formal matters carefully and intentionally.

Basic Principles of Formal Analysis in the Classroom

Organizing the classroom around students who are actively engaged in response and making meaning is as important to formal analysis as it is to the two preceding stages. Questions of form should arise after personal reflection on literary texts has already begun. We distill other important principles about how to lead students toward formal knowledge about literature.

- The scope of literary study should be based on what specific students can handle.
- Students must care about the text before they engage in formal study.
- Formal study should arise from texts being considered, not predetermined lists being presented.
- Literary terms should be regarded as language to help us understand and enrich our responses, not as terms used to catalog and pigeonhole.
- The author's creative acts should be regarded as active, live performances to be understood, not as demonstrations of static rules to be analyzed.
- Students can discover and construct, not simply receive, literary knowledge.
- As literary knowledge is gained and applied, it grows deeper, more sophisticated, and more integral to how students think and talk about literature. Learning becomes long-ranging and recursive.

The practical implication of approaching formal matters not as glossaries of terms to define but as structures of texts to understand is this: When you are actively engaged in a work of literature, seize the teachable moment. Teachable moments are usually construed to be those sudden points in a lesson when issues arise unexpectedly that can be immediately and effectively addressed. The term holds the sense of serendipity: seizing the unexpected, accidental moment and discovering something beneficial there. It also holds a more remote sense that a teacher is interrupted in a well-organized, prescribed lesson and departs from it for just a moment. We use the term to clarify the context in which formal literary knowledge is best acquired. If students have come to care about literature (reader response) and to communicate with each other about it (interpretive community), their deepening thoughts and their curiosity will ideally drive them to question form. You should be ready for that.

Langer (1995, p. 123) presents four particular situations that "provide environments for active thinking and learning" about formal elements. The four could be seen as levels of increasing readiness to explore the formal dimensions of literature:

- Students have neither the concepts nor the language to talk about them.
- Students have the concepts but not the language.
- Students have less complex understandings than their language implies.
- Students have the language and the concepts and are ready to think about them in more sophisticated ways.

In the midst of other instructional approaches, such as those suggested in the reader response and interpretive community sections of this chapter, when students are engaged in a thoughtful discussion of literature and their curiosity takes them beyond what they know, or when you sense that they have a tacit understanding but inadequate words for its expression, or when they are ready for a more sophisticated grasp, then seize the opportunity for exploring formal matters.

Beach and Marshall (1991, pp. 126–127) suggest that we gauge instruction in formal matters by noticing and reflecting upon, "unpacking," our own responses to a given text. If we realize that we need to know certain conventions in order to understand and interpret a piece, we should build a formal lesson around those conventions. If we encounter textual challenges in an assigned text, we must devise lessons that empower students to figure them out when they, too, are challenged. If, for instance, we realize that the author's or narrator's tone is crucial to understanding, we can sensitize students to tone by even brief oral demonstrations. Jago (2001) suggests that an easy way to teach tone is to read to students with a voice that carries the intonation, phrasing, and modulation that express the particular feeling or meaning of a writer/speaker. We have asked our students to utter to a partner or small group the simple query "Where are you going?" or "Where have you been?" or the direction "Come see for yourself" as though a parent or friend had uttered these with a range of emotions from anger to solicitousness to joy. (Even if students only speak these with a different emphasis on key words, multiple possible meanings become apparent.)

Our hope is that the concepts presented will become a part of the working vocabulary of subsequent discussions of literature and therefore become internalized, integral, and natural, not imposed, isolated, and artificial. The formal becomes embedded or integrated with the attempt to make sense of texts. Teaching Activity 5-17 is an individual or group assignment that uses the structure of Kurt Vonnegut's short story "Harrison Bergeron" to provide an entry into interpretation. It comes in the midst of a class's struggle to construct an interpretation of what the simple plot and strongly defined characters mean. Is the story more than a futuristic good guys/bad guys melodrama? Students sense the story is making a political point, but what?

If interest has been aroused, students will entertain this exercise with greater willingness; but more important, they will be more open to discovering that form can provide answers to genuine questions. In their next encounter with a text, they may be more likely to read with a consciousness that structure and meaning are interfused. In time, they might independently experience the pleasure of recognition that an author has created meaning through the interplay of character, plot, and structure.

5-17 TEACHING ACTIVITY

Structure as Meaning

- Place George, Hazel, Diana Moon Glampers, Harrison, and the beautiful ballerina on a continuum that moves from freedom to domination.

- List other polarities between freedom and domination in the story: images, settings, events, and political perspectives.

- Consider:
  - As you read this story, were you aware of polar opposites?
  - What are the two basic positions being contrasted?
  - How did you predict the conflict between freedom and equality would end?
  - Was Vonnegut subtle in this story?
  - What does he gain by these strong contrasts?
  - Does this structure help you make sense of the story?

Formal Discussion Questions

For several generations of college students, literature anthologies with teaching apparatus pitched their end-of-selection questions to form. A statement by the Committee on Response to Literature at the 1966 Dartmouth Conference (Squire, 1968) cautioned against the "dryness of schematic analysis of imagery, symbols, myth, structural relations, et al. [that] should be avoided passionately at school and often at college. *It is literature, not literary criticism,* which is the subject" (p. 26). These college texts that for generations defined what literature was all about are beginning to shift their focus a bit. Invitation to Reflection 5–4 asks you to respond to the questions asked in the three classic anthologies (listed in Table 5-5).

Invitation to Reflection 5–4

The questions in Table 5–5 are drawn from three highly respected college textbooks used in introductory literature courses. The questions reflect the typical organization of these anthologies around formal elements. We selected eight elements (and one general category) and ask that you read the questions within each element thoughtfully and check or highlight the questions that are most appealing to you as a reader. Then consider the following questions.

1. Which questions do you remember hearing from your own high school and college English teachers: the ones marked or not marked?

2. Can you identify what distinguishes the questions that appeal to you?

3. Do any prompt readers to reflect more deeply about craft by paying attention to their felt responses?

4. Do any appear to be knockout questions that might nail an interpretation or response to a text?

5. What is implied about the questioner?

6. Do these questions taken together imply that there is one best interpretation with which all enlightened readers will concur?

7. Can you imagine your posing these questions to your own students? If yes, which ones were your favorites?

We will return to these questions after you have read the next few paragraphs.

We will take the element of character in fiction as an example of the caution we must exercise in the way in which we approach formal matters in our literature instruction. John Dixon and Leslie Stratta (1989) criticize the questions we pose about fictive characters in class discussion, writing assignments, homework, examinations, and, we assume, in our literature textbooks. Questions such as "How would you describe the character of Stella in Sue Ellen Bridger's *Home Before Dark* or identify the changes in her as the novel progresses?" carry "tacit assumptions" or suggestions that "somehow or other, definitive answers are possible. It is not how you imagine a character that counts; instead it is your ability to describe something already existing and defined." These kinds of questions register in the student a belief that they are "a passive mechanism to which texts do things and that all readers by rights should think the same" (p. 26). The consequence of these sorts of standard questions is to "give

TABLE 5-5 Questions of form

	Literature: Structure, Sound, and Sense Lawrence Perrine	Bedford Introduction to Literature Michael Meyer	The Harper Anthology of Fiction Sylvan Barnet
Plot	Does the plot have unity? Are all the episodes relevant to the total meaning or effect of the story? Does each incident grow logically out of the preceding incident and lead naturally to the next? Is the ending happy, unhappy, or indeterminate? Is it fairly achieved?	What is the source and nature of the conflict for the protagonist? Was your major interest in the story based on what happens next or on some other concern? What does the title reveal now that you've finished the story?	Does the plot grow out of the characters or does it depend on chance or coincidence? Did something at first strike you as irrelevant that later you perceived as relevant? Do some parts continue to strike you as irrelevant? Does surprise play an important role or does foreshadowing?
Characters	What means does the author use to reveal character? Are the characters sufficiently dramatized? What use is made of character contrasts? Are the characters consistent in their actions? Adequately motivated? Plausible? Does the author successfully avoid stock characters?	Did your response to any characters change as you read? What do you think caused the change? Do any characters change and develop in the course of the story? How?	Which character chiefly engages your interest? Why? If a character changes, why and how does he or she change? Or did you change your attitude toward a character not because the character changes but because you came to know the character better? How has the author caused you to sympathize with certain characters, and how does your response contribute to your judgment of the conflict?
Setting	What contribution to the story is made by its setting? Is the setting essential, or could the story have happened anywhere?	Is the setting important in shaping your response? If it were changed, would your response to the story's action and meaning be significantly different?	Do you have a strong sense of the time and place? If so, how and at what points in the story has the author conveyed this sense? If you do not strongly feel the setting, do you think that the author should have made it more evident?
Point of View	What point of view does the story use? Is it consistent in its use of this point of view? If shifts are made, are they justified?	If it were told from a different point of view, how would your response to the story change? Would anything be lost?	Does the language help you to construct a picture of the narrator's attitude, strengths, and limitations? (Notice especially any figurative language and patterns of imagery.) How far can you trust the narrator? Why?
Tone		How does the author's use of language contribute to the tone of the story? Did it seem, for example, intense, relaxed, sentimental, nostalgic, humorous, angry, sad, or remote?	How would you characterize the author's tone? Whimsical? Bitter? Cold? Or what?
Style	What are the characteristics of the author's style? Are they appropriate to the nature of the story?	Do you think the style is consistent and appropriate throughout the story? Do all the characters use the same kind of language, or did you hear different voices?	How would you characterize the style? (You might begin by thinking about the vocabulary and the sentence structure. Are they fairly easy or rather difficult?) Is the style simple? Understated? Figurative? Or what, and why?
Theme	Does the theme reinforce or oppose popular notions of life? Does it furnish a new insight or refresh or deepen an old one?	Is the theme stated directly, or is it developed implicitly through the plot, characters, or some other element?	Suppose someone asked you to state the point—the theme—of the story. Could you? And if you could, would you say that the theme of a particular story reinforces values you hold, or does it to some degree challenge them? Or is the concept of a theme irrelevant to this story?
Symbol	Does the story make use of symbols? If so, do the symbols carry or merely reinforce the meaning of the story?	Did you notice any symbols in the story? Are they actions, characters, settings, objects, or words?	Do you feel that the writer wrote the story and then went back and stuck in the symbols? If you do have this feeling, which passages in the story seem stuck in?
General	Does the story offer chiefly escape or interpretation? How significant is the story's purpose? Does the story gain or lose on a second reading?	Do you think the story is worth reading more than once? Does the author's use of language bear close scrutiny so that you feel and experience more with each reading?	

Source: Excerpts from Lawrence Perrine, *Literature: Structure, Sound, and Sense,* 4th ed. (1983), pp. 338–340, Harcourt Brace & Company; M. Meyer, *Bedford Introduction to Literature,* 4th ed. (1996), pp. 259–261 (edited) New York: Bedford/St. Martin's © 1996 by Bedford/St. Martin's. Reprinted by permission. S. Barnet, *The Harper Anthology of Fiction,* Copyright ©1991 by HarperCollins Publishers Inc., Excerpt pp. 1250–1252. Reprinted by permission of Pearson Education, Inc.

students the messages that 'the character' is something that must be talked about in an impersonal way and in summary terms. Characters become bundles of traits, of 'points you make' in 'your answer' to a question" (p. 27). Dixon and Stratta (1986) indict how teachers and students discuss character in literature: It "blunts the edge of our perception of people. It treats the writing as a task, aimed at the production of a polished portrait, rather than an opportunity to search your own experience (or someone else's), reflect on it, and discover new meanings" (p. 57). These two educators have provided excellent guidelines that teachers might use to scrutinize their practice so that the study of literary characters and characterization does not elicit an arid discussion of technique but an imaginative engagement with the text.

1. Does the language of the assignment (or negotiated topic) indicate that the student is constructing a personal, imaginative experience, based on the printed text? Does it encourage students as they write to continue such imaginative work?
2. Does the topic or assignment allow the student to trace character(s) in action, to imagine people in relation to each other moment by moment? Is room left for narrative that comments and interprets from an imaginatively involved point of view?
3. Is there also an invitation to stand back and relate what happens in a specific scene (possibly chosen by students) to the way they now see the character in the action as a whole? Is there encouragement to keep any generalizations that emerge close to particularly telling moments in action?
4. Is there a further recognition that characters may be viewed as types (within a constructed social microcosm) as well as unique individuals? Is there room for an intelligent discussion of character as type? If so, are students aware enough of particulars to avoid overstereotyping and stock response?
5. Are there any opportunities for students who are at odds with the author and the way a character has been conceived? (Dixon & Stratta, 1989, p. 37)

We have seen that if we accept the reader response invitation to connect reader with the text, not any teaching strategy will do, not even one that appears to elicit vigorous reactions by students. Students readily adapt to the context that we as teachers set up. They become adept at operating within the ground rules we establish. Thus, if we pitch our discussion of form with questions such as "How does Jane Austen in *Pride and Prejudice* develop the character of Elizabeth Bennet in the context of the other females of her family?" or "How does Alan Paton in *Cry, the Beloved Country* transform the characters of Stephen Kumalo and James Jarvis?" students may be perfectly able to generate answers about the author's technique of characterization and even defend ideas with conviction and spirit. We expect more. Invitation to Reflection 5–5 invites you to fashion better questions.

Invitation to Reflection 5–5

Bearing in mind Dixon and Stratta's suggestions, read the following prompt constructed by one State Department of Public Instruction for the statewide tenth-grade writing test and then consider the questions below:

Literary characters often make major decisions that affect them and the people surrounding them. From the novels, short stories, full-length plays, and poems you have read, choose a work in which a character makes a major decision which has lasting results and affects him/her and the other characters. Using specific references from the work, explain what decision the character makes, how the decision affects the other characters, and the impact on the overall work. The work you choose must be from world literature other than British (England, Ireland, Scotland, and Wales) literature and American (United States) literature. Give the title and, if you remember, the author of the work.

1. Does this prompt approach literature as Dixon and Stratta suggest? Does it treat literary texts as the basis for constructing "personal, imaginative experience"?
2. Use their guidelines to critique the state's implicit assumptions about texts. Where do the test constructors succeed? Where do they fail?
3. Would you wish to alter the prompt to acknowledge that students can be more imaginatively involved in the text? In what way?
4. Imagine yourself a tenth-grade teacher who must prepare students for this end-of-term writing test. The stakes are high for you and the students. Their failure to do well will mean they fail your course and you receive censure and no raise. Choose a piece of literature you know well. Write questions that you might pose to a whole class or small groups to help them both respond to the text and prepare for the test. (All eight of the state's sample prompts revolve around literary terminology. Today you are focusing on character.) Sequence these questions to move students from reader response to formal considerations. Borrow from your work on Invitation to Reflection 5–4.
5. Expand your discussion of literary character by using one or two of the activities from either the reader response or the interpretive community sections of this chapter.

Literary Rules to Notice

As readers, we develop expectations for making sense of texts; and when repeated experience confirms our expectations, they solidify into rules. Thereafter, they structure the way we enter and respond to fiction. In *Before Reading: Narrative Conventions and the Politics of Interpretation*, Peter Rabinowitz (1987) has outlined characteristic strategies, or "rules," used by readers to read and interpret standard fiction: rules of notice, signification, configuration, and coherence. They have helped us to notice and clarify our interpretive strategies. As they inform our reading, they inform the kinds of questions and responses that we make to literature in class. These ideas do not need to be taught as terms to be learned but as concepts to be applied as we discuss our responses to fiction. In this indirect way, we help students grow more confident of their interpretive strategies. Mackey (1993) has helpfully summarized Rabinowitz's rules, and we include them as a reference in Appendix D.

In Chapter 2 we discussed Smagorinsky and Fly's (1994) suggestion that teachers model interpretive strategies so that students can internalize and apply them independently. Rabinowitz's rules are examples of such strategies. A better-known rule is the structure of a plot, often referred to as Freitag's triangle. We suspect this figure has gained such a common place in secondary English classrooms partly because of its simple, geometric precision. Yet it illustrates the danger as well as the potential of formal knowledge of literary schemata. Like literary form generally, it describes something valuable: the distillation of a repeated pattern in the narrative impulse. If used retrospectively and informally, it provides a useful vocabulary for articulating what students have experienced as fiction. If presented mechanically and used abstractly as a construct to be diagrammed or enumerated, it can become a paralyzing substitute for the involved, aroused emotions of literary experience. Anna Milner prepared Teaching Activity 5–18 for her tenth-grade

5–18 TEACHING ACTIVITY

Conventions of the Detective Novel in The Name of the Rose

Whole-Class Minilecture

■ Present the concept of a *convention:* a general agreement about basic principles or procedures; an established technique, practice, or device (as in literature or theater).

■ List examples of detective or mystery novels and short stories students have read or films they have seen.

■ Were there any typical patterns they could discern in the whodunits they have read or seen? Discuss some of those patterns.

Whole-Class Project

■ Create a detective novel (in general outline) on the board. Consider each of the following questions and list the answers.
  • Who are the primary characters?
  • What will the setting be?
  • What is the incipient/inciting action?
  • What is the process of detection?
  • Is a detective brought in?
  • Who is the villain?
  • What clues are left behind for the detective to use in unraveling the crime?
  • How will the villain be discovered?
  • What are the understood/unstated rules of the "detective world"?

Whole-Class Discussion

■ If we know what will happen, why are these narratives so compelling?

■ Do you like to have the crime explained?

■ Did the investigation of the crime interest you as much or more than the details of the crime itself?

■ The years between World War I and World War II have been called the golden age of the detective story. Why might the genre have been popular at that time?

■ Does Eco play by the rules in *The Name of the Rose?* How so? How not?

■ In a classic convention, called a "red herring," the author introduces some clues that mislead the reader and conceal other more significant clues or patterns. Did Eco use this convention?

■ What commentary is he making about detective novels? About us as readers?

■ Some believe the appeal of this genre lies at the end of the story, when the narrator or the author makes the seemingly inexplicable appear clear and the mysterious appear natural. Does Eco achieve that effect for you?

students after their summer reading of Umberto Eco's *The Name of the Rose*. By considering a familiar literary genre—detective or mystery novels or whodunits—her lesson provided points of entry into and departure from this complex novel.

We turn now to four approaches that bring consciousness of form into the middle school and high school class. All three operate within Purves, Rogers, and Soter's (1990, p. 84) caution: "Literary terms can be used to scaffold and bolster responses, but not to build them."

Intertextuality

Literary scholars emphasize that no writer writes without a consciousness of preceding texts. Rabinowitz's rules of interpretation arise from the general expectations we carry from one text to the next. More specifically, one text may contain a mention of another, for instance, or a quotation from or citation of an earlier text. It may be a translation of another, an imitation, an adaptation, a satire, or a parody. Less obviously, texts often build on character or situations in earlier pieces. The ideas of intertextuality are important to scholars as they trace original sources and subsequent borrowings.

Henry Louis Gates, Jr., (2002a, pp. 104–108) has written a *New Yorker* article about an unpublished, handwritten, 1850s manuscript entitled "The Bondwoman's Narrative by Hannah Crafts, a Fugitive Slave, recently Escaped from North Carolina." He enlisted the advice of an "investigator and historical-document examiner" to establish its authenticity. Their close examination of the manuscript's "fragile, yellowing," 301 pages (the investigator with "visual, chemical, and microscopic criteria" and Gates with textual, historical, and literary criteria) made them believe that it was a fictionalized account of the life of an actual fugitive slave in the 1850s. Gates has traced the author's roots back to a North Carolina legislator and slave owner, John Hill Wheeler. Gates and other scholars heard echoes in Crafts's prose of Harriet Beecher Stowe, Frederick Douglass, and "the conventions of nineteenth-century sentimental and gothic fiction" (2002b, p. 5). The recent discovery of a catalog of Wheeler's library offers the possibility of more precisely tracing the literary influences on the author. Meanwhile, readers of the article wrote to document other passages borrowed from Charles Dickens's *Bleak House*. Gates (2000b, p. 5) responded to the readers without defensiveness, explaining why intertextuality should be acknowledged as a phenomenon of power and importance:

> No doubt, further study will uncover other instances of influence and borrowing. But the image of a fugitive slave turning to the greatest English novelist of her day—a novelist known for his vivid descriptions of poverty and powerlessness—to help fashion her story carries with it at least

one lesson: that the republic of letters has always transcended the bounds of identity.

Intertextuality is important for teachers for reasons beyond the enrichment of reading. The web of connections among texts can ensnare curiosity, enlarge interpretation, and release playfulness. In addition, as students read material that has been creatively reworked, questions naturally arise about why an author makes certain decisions to change the material. Juxtaposing two texts nudges the curiosity naturally. The more texts that students read, the more questions of form will bubble up and the more their knowledge of form will be activated and reinforced.

The term *intertextuality* refers not only to one author's references to another but to the reader's use of other specific texts and the literary conventions of all texts to relate to the present text. Reading many texts becomes important to enlarge students' frames of reference. We often ask students to reflect back on how a character or a situation, say, is like something they have experienced before. Reading is also a part of their history. So we might ask, for instance, "Does this character remind you of a character you have encountered before?" As we build experiences of literature into their lives, they have more history to tap and more understanding to bring.

Contemporary texts are especially useful in clarifying intertextuality and many other literary conventions. Many modern and postmodern writers, particularly experimentalists and satirists, overturn our common expectations of literature to achieve their effects. In this jolt to the reader, our implicit expectations are exposed. For example, after we read fables by Aesop (620–560 B.C.) and La Fontaine (1621–1695) with students, we read some of the *Fables for Our Times* by James Thurber (1894–1961). The fable, one of the oldest written forms, achieves its effect by surprising the reader with its resolution, or moral. Thurber adapts this fabulist tradition to comment on the midtwentieth century by surprising the surprise ending. The incongruity of the old form put to a sophisticated new purpose disarms our expectations and thereby throws fabulist conventions into clearer outline.

Teaching Activity 5-19 is a lesson that requires students to use the conventions of one of the oldest literary genres, the fairy tale, in their reading of three poems. (The activity can also be used to teach literary elements such as point of view and authorial tone.)

Students Write

When students write fiction or drama or poetry, they face the same choices authors face. Rosenblatt (1995, p. 48) acknowledges that "One of the best ways of helping students gain this appreciation of literary form and

5-19

TEACHING ACTIVITY

Intertextuality

Whole-Class Work

- Recall the story of the frog prince.

- Discuss these questions: What has always been your reaction to this story? Have you experienced another "and they lived happily ever after" kind of moment? Did you think of the frog as having been rescued from a cruel fate? Was it a triumphant story of goodness rewarded (the princess's) and evil overturned (the witch's)?

Small-Group Work

- Read each of the following poems:
  - Kathryn Machan Aal, "Hazel Tells LaVerne"
  - Susan Mitchell, "From the Journals of the Frog Prince"
  - Stevie Smith, "The Frog Prince"

- After all three have been discussed individually to clear up confusions and approach meaning-making, consider these broad questions:
  - Does the (modern) poem change your point of view?
  - Does it enlarge your sensibilities?
  - Does it make you want to reevaluate the original?
  - Does it spoil the enchantment? How does it leave you feeling?
  - Which version attracts you most?
  - Which kind of world would you rather inhabit: a world in which magic is present, good and evil are clearly defined and rewarded, and people live happily ever after; or a world that uncovers romantic sensibilities, is securely grounded in reality, and recognizes that happiness is tenuous?
  - Why do these or other collections, such as the popular series *Politically Correct Stories,* appeal to readers today?
  - Psychologists and social critics have discussed the reasons that the traditional fairy tales are both appealing and instructive for young readers. Have we lost anything of cultural and personal value when these tales are presented to the young with a modern irony?

Individual Work

- Write a continuation of this sentence in your journal:

  I liked the traditional/modern version of the frog prince story because. . .

---

artistry is to encourage them to engage in such imaginative writing." They wrestle with questions of form as practical matters, not as theoretical ones. After students have written their own stories, they are positioned to consider what they did and, in turn, to more consciously understand the choices authors make as well. Teaching Activity 5-20 presents a writing assignment for a Halloween unit on suspense that begins with several Edgar Allan Poe short stories and concludes with students' own tales of suspense. The formal aim of the activity is to make students aware of point of view. This may appear a sophisticated or esoteric concern,

but it is central to making students aware of the "author" behind the many texts (print and nonprint) of their lives.

Authors Speak

Writers *of* literature are also inveterate writers *about* literature. We often use authors' words to make students conscious of craft. The words are often memorable; they have credibility because they come from practicing writers; they often carry the punch of heightened language;

5–20 TEACHING ACTIVITY

Students Write

Individual Work

■ Write a suspense story to be read to the class on Halloween. Create a new tale or adapt one of Poe's stories by changing the point of view of the narrator.

Paired Work

■ Read your stories to each other.

■ The author should ask the following questions of their partners:
  • Who is telling the story?
  • What is unique about the voice of the narrator?
  • Does the voice sound trustworthy and reliable?
  • What made you believe it? Name those telling moments in the story that establish the narrator's reliability or authority?
  • How does the narrator's voice compare to the voices of the characters presented in the story?
  • What is the relationship of the narrator to the tale and its characters?
  • Does the narrator's voice ever reach barriers or limits to the telling?
  • Would you have responded differently if the story were told by someone else? Would anything have been lost?

Whole-Class Work

After your paired discussions, answer these questions together:

■ Can you give any examples of how point of view provides clues to Edgar Allan Poe's or your classmate's story?

■ Does the point of view conceal or reveal the author's purpose?

■ What is the relationship of the teller to the listener?

■ What is the relationship of the teller to the tale and its characters?

■ Has your sense of the importance of point of view changed at all through this lesson?

Individual

■ Rewrite your story using a different point of view.

---

they arise naturally at teachable moments. Figure 5-9 contains some of our favorites.

We clearly do not regard formal analysis as contrary to the aim of personal response if it is addressed to students who can handle it and is integrated into literature study. If the study of literary concepts and terminology is the first or most privileged or the only approach to literature in the classroom, it dampens or swamps the personal. Yet it need not do so. Astronomers do not lose their sense of wonder at the cosmos because they understand the process by which galaxies are formed. Biologists do not grow dulled to the remarkable complexity and order of the human body because they have completed the genome project. Like painting, which has line, texture, and color, and physics, which has space, time, and mass, literature has its own basic elements. Understanding how the fundamental elements of literature work together can be as enriching to a reader as knowing proportion is to a painter and statics is to an engineer. If they were left with such formal emphases only, painters would never paint, engineers would never construct bridges, and readers would never respond. Combined with the personal, a formal approach can deepen our responses and our meaning-making. But it has a supportive, not the starring, role in this drama. Consider the knowledge of literary concepts and vocabulary as part of what allows us to clarify, deepen, and enlarge our initial responses to literature. Form can increase our thoughtfulness, understanding, and self-reliance as readers.

FIGURE 5–9
Authors speak about craft

Character	"It is . . . one of the most startling and effective devices in fiction to take characters out of one setting and put them in another, where different facets of their personality come to the fore." *Orson Scott Card*
	"Habits not only make the character more realistic, but also open up story possibilities—a change in pattern might show an important change in the character's life; other characters might take advantage of her habits; curiosity about or annoyance at a habit might lead to an interesting relationship between characters." *Orson Scott Card*
	"Remembering that of all these different ways of getting to know people—and therefore getting to know characters—the most powerful of them, the ones that make the strongest impression, are the first three: what the character does in the story, what his motives are, and what he has done in the past." *Orson Scott Card*
Dialogue	"Speech is what the characters do to each other. . . . Each piece of dialogue *must* be something happening." *Elizabeth Bowen*
	"Writers should use dialogue with restraint, because dialogue forces the reader to hear, to see, to supply the right tone and to fill in the background from what the characters say without any help from the author . . . [Dialogue requires] the reader to do rather more than his share of the work of creation." *Virginia Woolf*
Idea	"Art itself may be defined as the single-minded attempt to render the highest kind of justice to the visible universe by bringing to light the truth, manifold and one, underlying its every aspect." *Joseph Conrad*
	"The obligation of the artist is not to solve the problem but to state the problem correctly." *Anton Chekhov*
	"There is no story written that has any value at all, however straightforward it looks and free from doubleness, double entendre, and duplicity and double play, that you'd value at all if it didn't have intimation of something more than itself." *Robert Frost*
Setting	"If your feet aren't in the mud of a place, you'd better watch where your mouth is." *Grace Paley*
	"If a gun is hanging over the mantel in the opening scene, it had better go off by the last." *Anton Chekhov*
Symbol	"In good fiction, certain of the details will tend to accumulate meaning from the action of the story itself, and when that happens, they become symbolic in the way they work." *Flannery O'Connor*
	"You can't give a great symbol a 'meaning,' any more than you can give a cat a 'meaning.' Symbols are organic units of consciousness with a life of their own, and you can never explain them away, because their value is dynamic, emotional, belonging to the sense-consciousness of the body and soul, and not simply mental." *D. H. Lawrence*
Comedy	"The true test of comedy is that it shall awaken thoughtful laughter." *George Meredith*

Purves, Rogers, and Soter (1990) explain both the origin and dangers of formal language:

> The critical language that developed came from people's need to classify and categorize their experiences. It came from the same impetus that has led to the elaborate classifications of plant and animal life. In one sense, education is the learning of these classificatory schemes, but too often the learning of the names of plants has replaced looking at them, smelling them, enjoying them. The same thing happened to the teaching of literature. (p. 57)

Formal analysis must be done within the clear context of readers responding and communities reflecting on texts. Remy de Gourmont's observation captures the academic attraction to formal labels and categories and reminds us of the need to resist it: "We live less and less and learn more and more. I have seen a man laughed at for examining a dead leaf attentively and with pleasure. No one would have laughed to hear a string of botanical terms muttered over it."

A final principle for the effective teaching of literary knowledge is that the teacher should be alive to literature. This third step, formal analysis, should originate in your own considered pleasure and understanding of the way in which literature works. In *How Does a Poem Mean?* poet and critic John Ciardi (1959) tells a story of W. H. Auden that reiterates our hope for your literary knowledge and understanding:

> W. H. Auden was once asked what advice he would give a young man who wished to become a poet. Auden replied that he would ask the young man why he wanted to write poetry. If the answer was "because I have something important to say," Auden would conclude that there was no hope for that young man as a poet. If on the other hand the answer was something like "because I like to hang around words and overhear them talking to one another," then that young man was at least interested in a fundamental part of the poetic process and there was hope for him. (p. 667)

Auden's advice to the prospective poet is the same as our advice to prospective teachers. Years of our reading and teaching have steadily increased our own pleasure in literature—its delights and riches. As Birkerts (1994) reminds us, "reading changes across the trajectory of the reader's career" (p. 87). Yours will too, we hope. Your teaching will profit from that increase as you grow more confident about how language and literature work. We encourage you to grow familiar with formal elements, play with them, and use them to deepen your own discoveries about literature. Do not make them rigid definitions on their way to a final exam. Do not leave them as formal abstractions but as formal endowments that will intensify student insight and enjoyment of literature and the life it celebrates.

⌘ CRITICAL SYNTHESIS

With a secure grounding in reading that has become personally owned, communally interpreted, and formally considered, why now step into literary criticism? We, too, have asked this question. We observe that periodicals published for secondary English teachers often offer different critical theories implicitly in their many pedagogical ideas and activities; but these theories usually remain tacit and applied, not defined and articulated as theory. Textbooks also offer much prereading space to historical and biographical perspectives and postreading apparatus to formalist and, increasingly, reader response questions. Applebee's (1993) national survey of literature instruction found that the critical approaches that were cited by teachers "as influencing their teaching of a representative class were New Criticism (50 percent of the teachers in the random sample of public schools) and reader-response (67 percent). . . . Teachers reported that recent alternative approaches, including feminist criticism, had had little influence on their instruction." In fact, Applebee found that 72 percent of the teachers he surveyed in the schools with reputations for excellence "reported little or no familiarity with contemporary literary theory" (p. 122).

Different critical perspectives produce very different approaches to texts and generate very different questions about them. When critical theory remains relatively unexplained, students have difficulty developing a coherent framework for comprehending the field of literary study and individual pieces within it. One day they are asked, "What did the author intend?" The next day they are asked, "What does the literary history reveal?" The next question is "What is the plot structure, and how does it contribute to unity?" Then they are queried, "How do you feel about this book?" No sooner is one critical perspective implied as central than another possibility is introduced that challenges it. The consequence deepens the common student error of attempting to arrive at an authoritative, usually reductive, interpretation of a text. Students do not develop the useful tools that are available for approaching any text. They are left to wonder on what criteria literature is to be understood and judged and conclude that only the wise, learned, or especially gifted can know.

We proceed to introduce critical theory cautiously, however. Until students are comfortably and personally engaged and are confident of their own immediate and considered responses, they should not be asked to make their considerations more studied. If formal analysis is a stretch for students, critical synthesis will be a longer one. Yet psychologists tell us that one of the characteristics of the young adolescent's intellect is metacognition, the ability to think about one's thinking. Many adolescents have moved beyond concrete stages of intellectual development and are capable of abstract reasoning. Piaget did not believe that cognitive development could progress without this ability to reflect abstractly. Critical synthesis invites students to that level of abstraction. Formal analysis began such a standing outside and observing how the textual elements functioned as parts of a whole. Critical synthesis takes a further step back from the text to look at the whole field of literary study. If students are curious, if they pose critical questions about the ground rules for a good interpretation, and if they are moving to metacognitive perspectives, then perhaps the time is ripe.

Those who can take this step discover a whole new way of seeing. Appleman (2000) articulates some of the benefits of understanding alternative critical perspectives: "They bring into relief things we fail to notice. Literary theories recontextualize the familiar and comfortable, making us reappraise it. They make the strange seem oddly familiar. As we view the dynamic world around us, literary theories can become critical lenses to guide, inform, and instruct us" (p. 2). These "critical lenses" alert us to different perspectives and give us the ability to recognize complexity, not only in literary texts, but also in the world. Desai (1996) observes that "literary theory reminds us that we do not live in isolation nor do we read and interpret in isolation. We understand what we read through some combination of our selves as readers and the text with which we interact, but this is never free of the multiple contexts that frame us" (p. 169). Bonnycastle (1996) believes theory can be a guard against single-minded authority: Studying theory "means no authority can impose a truth on you in a dogmatic way—and if some authority does try, you can challenge that truth in a powerful way, by asking what ideology it is based on" (p. 34). Critical theory, then, can have a clarifying and a deepening impact on our ability to read literature and ourselves. At its best, theoretical knowledge will become intertwined with and enrich personal response.

Early Critics and Eleven Critical Approaches to Literature

Since the time of the early Greeks, literature has been attended by a parallel body of critical thought. In *The Mir-*

ror and the Lamp, M. H. Abrams (1953) distinguishes three possible foci for the critic: art, the artist, or the audience. In contemplating those three, critics have articulated elaborate theories about how literature works, how authors write, and how audiences or readers respond. Opinion differs about what portion of this is important for high school students to know. (Thirty years ago, Purves [1971, p. 751] named the handful of those theories that college-bound high school students might be expected to know: "Aristotle's definition of tragedy, something of the system of genres, something of the new critical method.") When students have demonstrated interest and readiness, we introduce this parallel field simply and concretely (and wait hopefully to see if they ask for more.) We present eleven of the most prominent critical approaches, which share common assumptions about texts and readers and about methods with which to read texts. These approaches originate in the earliest thinking about literature in the western world, and they animate current academic debates. We name these general approaches *schools of literary criticism* and schematize our summary of them in Table 5-6.

We begin with a description of two of the earliest critics of literature, Plato and Aristotle, and then describe a few basic theoretical principles and characteristic techniques of each of these eleven schools. Each has many and varied practitioners. For a fuller explanation of these schools specifically and literary theory and criticism generally we recommend several print guides and Web sites:

Books

Abrams, M. (1993). *A glossary of literary terms* (6th ed.). New York: Harcourt Brace.

Carey, G., & Snodgrass, M. E. (1999). *A multicultural dictionary of literary terms.* Jefferson, NC: McFarland.

Childers, J., & Henzi, G. (1995). *The Columbia dictionary of modern literary and cultural criticism.* New York: Columbia University Press.

Gates, H. L., Jr. (1988). *The signifying monkey: A theory of African-American literary criticism.* New York: Oxford University Press.

Groden, M., & Kreiswirth, M. (Eds.) (1994). *The Johns Hopkins guide to literary theory and criticism.* Baltimore: Johns Hopkins University Press.

Macey, D. (2000). *The Penguin dictionary of critical theory.* New York: Penguin.

Magell, F. N. (Ed.) (1987). *Critical survey of literary theory.* Pasadena, CA: Salem.

Makaryk, I. R. (Ed.) (1993). *Encyclopedia of contemporary literary theory: Approaches, scholars, terms.* Toronto: University of Toronto Press.

Peck, J., & Coyle, M. (Eds.) (1993). *Literary terms and criticism.* London: Macmillan.

Web Resources

IPL Online Literary Criticism Collection (http://www.ipl.org/ref/litcrit/)

Literary Criticism of the Web (http://www.geocities.com/Athens/Crete/9078/)

The Johns Hopkins Guide to Literary Theory and Criticism (http://www.press.jhu.edu/books/Hopkins_guide_to_literary_theory/)

Literature and Literary Criticism (http://www.stcc.cc.tx.us/main/litsearch.html)

Much of what follows may remain background knowledge for you and enter your classroom only indirectly and wordlessly. A clear understanding of the field will ground you more confidently in it and will protect you from being prey to literary assumptions and judgments that you cannot locate or name. If students encounter literary theory directly, they should be invited into the "manifold possibilities" (McGuire, 1973, p. 3) that it opens, not into one or another dogmatic position. Figure 5-10 poses characteristic questions that each school of thought might ask of Tillie Olsen's short story "I Stand Here Ironing." We encourage you to consider these questions as you read the description of each school and observe whether your response and insight changes and deepens with each.

Early Critics: Plato and Aristotle. We introduce our survey with the story of these two seminal thinkers for three reasons:

1. Western literary criticism begins with them. They establish comprehensive and profound views of art.
2. Many contemporary positions are based on their thoughts or certain vestiges of them.
3. The argument between these two thinkers suggests that such reasoning about literature was taken seriously by eminent minds and that their conflict was understandable and inevitable. What we believe about literature is greatly influenced by

TABLE 5–6

Prominent schools of literary criticism

Early Critics	Traditional	Textual	Psychological/ Sociological	Postmodern
Plato	Historical/biographical	Formalist	Freudian	Deconstructivist
Aristotle	Moral/philosophical	Rhetorical	Archetypal	Reader response
			Feminist	New Historical
			Marxist	

SCHOOL OF LITERARY CRITICISM	QUESTIONS
Moral/Philosophical	• Whom should we judge most critically for Emily's plight: the social institutions during the American Depression, Emily's mother for her decisions, or Emily's father for his desertion?
Historical/Biographical	• What social and economic forces at work in the 1930s Depression could explain what caused Emily's father to leave and her mother to struggle? • Tillie Olsen was born in 1913 and lived through the poverty of working class families in the mining towns and farms of the West. Because she was raising four children, working, and struggling to make ends meet, she could not concentrate on writing until she was forty. Could these experiences have influenced this prize-winning story?
Formalist	• Who is the narrator? Do you consider the narrator reliable or unreliable? Does this point of view give the story unity? • Is this story anything more than a sociological or psychological case study or a list of personal difficulties? It violates many principles of short story writing as it summarizes nineteen years of a person's life. What makes this story "literature"? (Pay special attention to its narration, its language, its structure, and its imagery.)
Rhetorical	• With which characters are you in greatest sympathy? • How did the author manipulate your feelings? • Did she "load the deck" for some and against others?
Freudian	• What particular events in Emily's life do you consider most influential in the development of her personality? • Could this story be a psychological case study? Does the pain and guilt of the mother influence the way she sees the world of her child? What is the effect of reading this story of self-blame and self-justification on you?
Archetypal	• This story has become a classic of the modern American short story. Do you find any mythical patterns here that would explain its lasting appeal? Could you identify the mother with one of the archetypal characters such as the good mother or bad mother, or the heroine struggling on her personal journey through motherhood? • Would you have preferred that this story have more of a fairy tale ending, like *Cinderella*, in which Emily suddenly tries on the glass slipper, transcends her difficult childhood, and dances happily and wholly with the prince?
Marxist	• The mother clearly feels powerless to control her life and that of her daughter. Where do you lay blame for this, on the individual or the society of which she is a part? • What are the economic and social structures that create Emily's mother's terrible struggle? Does class have any bearing on her life?
Feminist	• What conclusions can we draw from the fact that the mother is never named? She seems to feel as though she had little control over her own or Emily's life. Why might that be so? • What role do the two fathers play in Emily's life? How do they fulfill the expected parenting roles for males at the time of the story? Which of the three adults, the fathers and the mother, would you judge most harshly as a parent?
Deconstructionist	• Do different members of the class have different interpretations of the narrator? Does her narrative contain contradictions that might lead to divergent interpretations? • Can you reconcile the narrator's exclamation—"She is so lovely. Why did you want me to come in at all? Why were you concerned? She will find her way."—with the last two paragraphs?
Reader Response	• Imagine an incident of behavior that might have caused the guidance counselor to call Emily's mother. Imagine Emily's reaction when she learned that the counselor had called home. Imagine how your mother would react to such a call. • Is there any incident or situation in your early life that you consider crucial in forming who you are? Have your parents ever spoken with regret about that time? • Did you feel more sympathy for Emily or her mother? What would be your advice to each?
New Historical	• Find images from newspapers, magazines, or films from the era of the Great Depression and World War II. Can you find any clues in them of the social pressures that surrounded Emily's family and shaped their actions? • There is more than one historic context for "I Stand Here Ironing." The history on which we focus is influenced by our present histories. The story was published in 1961. Do we read it differently from the way that readers of that cultural moment would?

FIGURE 5–10 The Critics and Tillie Olsen's "I Stand Here Ironing"

what we believe about reality. In other words, Plato's and Aristotle's disagreement prepares students to appreciate a critical pluralism in which two minds equally intent on truth arrive at two different conclusions.

Plato faced a dilemma. He himself was a poet, but he had a critical view of poetry (or art). He believed that not only is art far removed from the truth, but it also appeals to an inferior part of the human faculties, namely the passionate and fitful temper, not calm and wise reason. Thus, as a practical moralist, Plato concluded that poets must be banned from the ideal society—the proper environment for nurturing the good citizen—the republic, because poets undermine the discipline that all citizens need to bring to their lives.

Aristotle answered Plato's objections. Aristotle believed that the best literature is that which best imitates the universal laws. Because of its universality, poetry is, in fact, superior to history. Furthermore, the artist, rather than being dominated by passion, is admirably in touch with the universals. Poetry, rather than harming its audience by inflaming the passions, gives benign and even therapeutic purgation to the passions.

The first two schools of literary criticism in our survey, moral/philosophical and historical/biographical, can be seen as outgrowths of this classical argument between Plato and Aristotle about the purpose, function, and disposition of literature. Traditional early approaches to the teaching of literature centered on literature as the vehicle for arriving at another, more serious, intellectual or moral field. It was not explored as a subject in itself but for what it illustrated of history (the author's, the work's), of biography (the author's, the character's), or of moral virtues (implicit and explicit in the work itself). The function of literary study was to inform or to instruct.

Moral/Philosophical.

Standard American texts from well before the twentieth century—*The New England Primer* (c. 1686-1690), Webster's *Blue-Backed Speller* (1783), and McGuffey's *Readers* (c. 1836)—identify schooling with moral and religious instruction. In *Tradition and Reform in the Teaching of English: A History,* Arthur N. Applebee (1974, p. 5) states that these "early educational giants . . . provided a common background of culture and allusion, a common heritage for a nation too young to have any other." Although their explicit text was reading, their implicit text was personal and civic virtue. From grade schools to colleges, literature study served skills acquisition but also moral instruction in what was good and virtuous. A nineteenth-century educator, William Riley Parker, observed that the typical professor of English at midcentury "was a doctor of divinity who spoke and wrote the mother tongue grammatically, had a general 'society knowledge' of the literature, and had not specialized in this or any other academic subject" (as quoted by Graff, 1987, p. 24). For instance, as Graff notes, "of the twelve professors of English appointed by the University of North Carolina between 1819 and 1885, nine were ministers."

The implicit assumption, then, of these scholars and critics is that literature is a secular scripture that needs to be explicated to the general public. Literature as an aesthetic or personal experience with claims to be taken seriously for its own intrinsic or its personally deepening sake would arouse in such teachers the same consternation that imaginative poetry awakened in Plato. For moral and philosophical critics, literature is the vehicle for arriving at more serious intellectual and moral matters. Texts are chosen to serve the ennobling agenda of the culture. Works that describe a more pedestrian, even debased, view of human affairs are not selected. Today's debate over cultural literacy has its roots in an old and admirable tradition. These critics ask, "What picture of human experience does this text depict? What does it teach us about how to live our lives?" Teachers in this tradition ask students to search the text for its "moral," usually articulated as a "theme,"—one central, authoritative meaning.

Historical/Biographical.

Historical/biographical critics and teachers regard a literary work chiefly, if not exclusively, as a reflection of its author's life and times or the life and times of the characters in the work. Literary texts provide a different window into the past than any other sources do, and history can also provide clear windows into literature. In fact, often history—of the author or of the times—shapes the work. For historicists, an enriched reading of a work depends on knowledge of what is happening in the world at the time the work was written: the intellectual currents, the artistic trends, the economic situation, the politics, and the writer's private life.

The history of our profession partly explains the tenacious hold of this point of view. English was attempting to establish itself as an independent academic department in colleges and universities in the second half of the nineteenth century. Graff (1987, p. 74) reports that, particularly in the new American research universities, departmental status was purchased at the high price of making literature susceptible to "scientific observation and formulation." This resulted in historical literary scholarship, a search for sources and parallel references as an equivalent to the hard research being done in other departments. These early English departments tried to train readers just as others trained biologists.

We do not minimize the richness of such knowledge. With young students of literature, regardless of their age, the historical and biographical surroundings can envelop a text in greater meaning and the reader in greater confidence and certainty. The problem with this contextual approach is twofold. First, it may overlook the work of art itself. Literary study becomes history, a record of the past, rather than something "lived through" (Rosenblatt's term) in the present. Second and more significantly, such an approach, particularly in an academic setting with students who are initiates, can make responding to literature a privileged occupation, divorced from contact with the work itself. It reduces literature's potential for making meaningful sense in the life of the common reader.

Still, the vestiges of this approach are evident in most basic literature textbook series, particularly those with a national/cultural organization. These books are often presented chronologically with introductions to units and selections replete with surveys of history and biographies of authors.

Formalist. In England and the United States in the 1920s and 1930s, the group of scholars, critics, and writers who made the first and most powerful challenge to the established moral/philosophical and historical/biographical traditions were called variously agrarians, fugitives, formalists, and New Critics. These New Critics felt that any work of great art is an organic whole, united by its form, complete within itself, and written for itself alone. This organic form—that is, the necessary interrelationships of the parts of a literary work—animates and organizes it from within. So organized, a literary text becomes an autonomous or independent verbal artifact and can be scrutinized without regard for the traditional concerns of its historical, biographical, or cultural context. All essential information is contained within the work itself. Criticism is primarily concerned with unity—the kind of whole that the literary work forms or fails to form and the relation of the various parts to each other. The analysis of an individual text is complete only when everything in the work has been accounted for in terms of its overall form: How do the internal operations of the text—its language, images, tone, and so on—create intelligible structure and meaning? Are any of the elements in tension with each other? How are these resolved to produce a final unity? Cleanth Brooks (1947/1968) summarizes: "There is surely a sense in which anyone must agree that a poem has a life of its own, and a sense in which it provides in itself the only criterion by which what it says can be judged."

Thus, the hallmark of a formalist or New Critical approach is intensive, close reading of the text itself. The first question to be asked of literature is not *what* does the work mean but *how* does it mean. Nothing external to the text is necessary to answer this. Archibald MacLeish's poem "Ars Poetica" begins "A poem must not mean/But be . . ." The formalists' motto for poetry is "Trust the poem, not the poet." One of their principal proponents, Cleanth Brooks, made a famous declaration: "I have tried to read the poem, the *Horatian Ode,* not Andrew Marvell's mind." In an influential essay, "Technique as Discovery," Mark Schorer (1948) explained the new focus of the formalist critic:

> Modern criticism has shown us that to speak of content as such is not to speak of art at all, but of experience; and that it is only when we speak of the *achieved* content, the form, the work of art as a work of art, that we speak as critics. The difference between content, or experience, and achieved content, or art, is technique. (p. 67)

Different formalist critics give different emphases to what is the central principle in all texts: tension, paradox, irony, or ambiguity. But all share a belief that close scrutiny of technique leads the reader to the discovery of the text's definitive "statement" or its "insight into essential truth" (Brooks, 1947). New Critics trust that their criticism can lead them to "grasp the subject most thoroughly and deeply." Such insights are far more than opinions about literary taste or paraphrased statements of moral judgment.[5]

Rhetorical. Just as Plato's problems with imaginative literature invited Aristotle's response, so the formalist position prompted a group of critics to differ. R. S. Crane and others at the University of Chicago were troubled by the formalists' rejection of historical/biographical analysis, their assertion of subjective judgments as though they were objective, and their focus on poetry to the exclusion of prose and drama. Wayne Booth (1961), in *The Rhetoric of Fiction,* theorized that even if art is an autonomous, organic whole, as the New Critics believed, it is still not the world of experience. It is a conscious creation of an artist whom we must not forget or fail to notice. Despite the attempts at objectivity in art, authors can never excise themselves from their fiction. They can take on different disguises, but they are always there, attempting to persuade us. (*Rhetor,* the root of *rhetoric,* comes from Greek and Latin sources meaning "orator.") Just as we listen to orators with critical consciousness, we need also to scrutinize the implicit world view or value system being expressed by an author through his or her work. Booth's intent was to examine "the art of communicating with readers—the rhetorical resources available to the writer of epic, novel or short story as he tries, consciously or unconsciously, to impose his fictional world upon the reader." Thus, the question is not "What is the organic unity of this piece?" but "What is the connection between the author and the creation?"

Paradoxically, Booth suggested that our critical consciousness would lead us to trust an artist more if we trusted ourselves as readers as well. But we need to equip ourselves for our task. For a rhetorical critic, the formalists' tools of close reading provide the basic method. Booth developed several additional tools as well:

- the notion of an authorial "voice" or an "implied author" whose attitudes and perspectives the reader deduces from numerous elements of the text
- the separation of "reliable" and "unreliable" narrators in which the first is closest to the values of the "implied author" and the latter often deviates from it

Reading and interpretation need always to be conducted with a consciousness of a creator at work. Is the

---

[5] The formalist influence began to be disseminated beyond the concerns of academics and scholars, first to college students and then into the high schools, largely due to the impact of such respected college texts as Cleanth Brooks's and Robert Penn Warren's *Understanding Poetry* (1938) and *Understanding Fiction* (1943), John Ciardi's *How Does a Poem Mean?* (1959), and Laurence Perrine's *Sound and Sense* (1956) and *Story and Structure* (1959). These books and their subsequent revised editions were texts for generations of college students who began to teach and influence secondary English students in the 1950s. Their techniques of close reading remain pervasive.

authorial voice reliable or unreliable? To what is it persuading us?

The first four schools of thought assume that literary texts possess an objective reality that readers, for all their different perspectives and biases, interrogate and appreciate. Twentieth-century critics of these schools appear to be the inheritors of nineteenth-century poet and cultural critic Matthew Arnold's "profound, almost reverential regard for literary works themselves" (Selden & Widdowson, 1993, p. 10). Arnold even proposed that religion and philosophy would be "replaced by poetry" in modern society. He was joined in this century by poet, dramatist, and critic T. S. Eliot and Cambridge academic and critic F. R. Leavis, who believed that great works of literature (called the "tradition") were the repositories or "vessels" in which humane and civilized values survive. They are our "weapons" in the battle of culture against barbarism. Yvor Winters viewed poetry as "moral statement"; Kenneth Burke regarded literature as "equipment for living." Yet even as these critics prized texts and disputed with each other as to the best approach to a text's vital life, ideas from the fields of linguistics, philosophy, psychology, sociology, anthropology, and even physics and economics reached the field of literature and yielded perspectives that opened entirely new ways of viewing it. We turn now to four of these perspectives drawn from the social sciences of psychology, sociology, and economics.

Freudian. Critics who respect the theories of Sigmund Freud (1856-1939) have found in literature a perfect source for exploring the inaccessible world of the unconscious—that of writer, of character, and of reader. Freud believed that a literary work was to its author as dreams are to a dreamer: a rich source of insight into the psychology of the individual, a rich manifestation of unconscious desires, fears, and fantasies. In turn, characters themselves, in the hands of sensitive writers, give expression to the personality dynamics to which we are all heir. Finally, readers' responses to literature reveal perspectives on their subjective experience.

High school students from vastly different backgrounds are usually prepared to name and appreciate basic Freudian insights because they have absorbed them unconsciously through our culture. An outline of some primary concepts awakens in students a latent understanding, even though the concepts have not been explicitly taught before. That outline generally includes the following:

- the levels of consciousness: conscious, preconscious, unconscious
- the theoretical structure of the psyche: the id, the ego, and the superego
- the influence of defense mechanisms on personality, especially those of repression, reaction formation, projection, rationalization, displacement, and regression
- the presence of certain key personality syndromes such as the Oedipus and Electra complexes
- the nature and interpretation of dreams

Our reading of literature has benefited from this animating sense of its latent and ambiguous meanings, as if it were no less alive and contradictory than the artist who created it and the characters who populate it. Freud believed that art revealed more than science about the human heart or, as Shakespeare called it, "the mystery of things." Freud himself used literature to show the applicability of his theory. (In a questionnaire on reading, he ranked the poems and plays of the following as the "most magnificent works" and the ones that provided his "best illustrations" of psychoanalytic theory: Homer, Sophocles, Goethe, and Shakespeare.) The analysis of the latent psychological content of language, characters, images, metaphors, and plots influenced readers through the work of early Freudian critics Ernest Jones (1879-1958), Otto Rank (1884-1939), and Ella Freeman Sharpe (1875-1947). Yet some psychoanalytical criticism reduces literature to a clinical case study of author, character, or readers. Ruthven (1979) sees the consequences of simplistic applications of Freudian theory: "any work of literature inspired by unconscious projections is likely to record little more than the spontaneous overflow of powerful neuroses" (p. 65). Such simplification greatly compromises literature's complexity and power. Psychological interpretation can easily become a superficial parlor game and Freudian literary criticism a silly search for sexual symbols. It deserves to be recognized, instead, for the provocative and rich insights it can yield.

Archetypal. Archetypal criticism is based on insights dating back at least to Plato. For centuries, philosophers and theologians observed that identical characters, images, situations, and ideas occurred in the literature (particularly myths, religion, art, and folklore) of cultures widely separated by time and space. No explanations of cultural transmission or basic human nature could account for the repeated occurrence of these universal human experiences. In the twentieth century, psychologist Carl Jung (1875-1961) hypothesized about these universals, and his theories have been enormously influential in the way in which we understand human history and read literature. He called these images, motifs, or patterns *archetypes of the collective unconscious.* Repeated experiences of our species shaped these archetypes and myths, religion, dreams, fantasies, art, and literature expressed them. They reflect the deepest experiences and meanings of the human race. The archetypal critic examines literature in terms of these archetypes, reasoning that to recognize them puts us in touch with the deepest meaning of the text. The power of certain texts resides just here, in the presence of archetypes that resonate deeply within the reader.

One of the fascinating pieces of twentieth-century cultural history is the falling out between Freud and his disciple Jung on a transatlantic trip to the United States in 1909. Students enjoy hearing the story and recognizing, as with Plato and Aristotle, the clash of powerful personalities and positions. Their original disagreement was due both to differences in theory and to Jung's dislike of Freud's reaction to disagreement. Their theoretical differences included the nature of the unconscious, the nature of the artist, and the responses of the reader to literature.

Freud believed that the unconscious is a blank tablet at birth on which imprints are made from one's earliest experiences. It becomes the repository of repressions and memories that cannot be recalled but that influence personality and behavior. Particularly for individuals who have had trouble in their psychosexual development, the unconscious can be troubling and destructive. Jung, on the other hand, believed that beyond our own personal conscious and unconscious is a more universal unconscious, the same for all members of the species. We inherit this collective memory of our past by being born human beings. The content of this collective unconscious consists essentially of archetypes or patterns formed by the repeated experiences of human beings during their entire history. Figure 5-11 is a schema of common archetypes. (The term has been traced to Plato; *arche* means "original" and *typos* means "form.") Jung adds to Freud's system of the psyche what he calls "a second psychic system of a collective, universal, and impersonal nature which is identical in all individuals. This collective unconscious does not develop individually but is inherited." Jung believed that being connected with these universal archetypes is health-producing, while being unaware of them is destructive. He wrote, "It is only possible to live the fullest life when we are in harmony with these symbols (the archetypes of the collective unconscious); wisdom is a return to them."

Freud believed that art is produced out of neurosis that arises as an artist's conscious and unconscious struggle for expression. Jung held that art is created by an artist who possesses a special sensitivity to archetypal patterns and a gift for speaking in primordial images. He explains that "the work of the poet comes to meet the spiritual need of the society in which he lives." Although Freud, like Plato, was sensitive to literature and acknowledged that it can have a therapeutic effect on the audience by releasing mental tension, he also called art a "substitute gratification," "an illusion in contrast to reality," and "a narcotic" with which to escape reality or protect against unpleasant reality. Jung, on the other hand, thought of literature as enriching. In fact, he has helped explain the powerful impact that it can produce in the reader as its archetypes strike deep, primordial chords.

The danger in an archetypal approach to literature is the same as that of the Freudian interpretation: When knowledge exterior to literature (even though it is intuited first and articulated later) becomes central to its interpretation, ordinary or inexperienced readers feel excluded and distrustful of their own responses. The critical apparatus can overcome a personal reading. Yet the approach has been productive for high school students because the idea of archetypes is stirring and the archetypes themselves are easy to understand from one's own experience. At its best, an archetypal perspective can deepen and complicate students' responses to texts.

Other perspectives from the field of psychology do not comprise schools of literary criticism that have systematic theories about art, the artist, and the audience; but many have provided rich practical insights into particular works of literature, their creators, and their readers. For instance, developmental theory such as that worked out by Erikson, Kohlberg, and Loevinger has been used to understand character definition, motivation, and growth. These constructs enrich the reader's understanding and appreciation of individual works. Furthermore, the writer's underlying assumptions or personal biases can be helpfully situated in the cycle of personality, moral, or ego development. While archetypal criticism flowered in the 1960s and 1970s, by the 1980s its influence was felt most in a new direction: feminist criticism.

FIGURE 5–11
Archetypes

IMAGES	CHARACTERS	MOTIFS/PATTERNS	LITERARY GENRE
Water: sea, rivers	The earth-mother	Creation	Spring: comedy
Sun: rising sun, setting sun	The good mother	Initiation	Summer: romance
Colors: red, green, blue, black, white	The terrible mother	The hero's journey	Fall: tragedy
Numbers: 3, 4, 7	The soul mate	The quest/journey/search	Winter: irony
Garden	The fatal woman	Transformation: physical, spiritual, social	
Tree	The old man	Prophecy and fulfillment	
Desert	The scapegoat	Immortality	
Circle: manila, egg, yin yang	The alter ego		
	The serpent		

Feminist. Feminist criticism originated in the 1960s from the sociopolitical movement that arose to name and combat the gender divisions that affect the legal, economic, and social lives of women. These early modern feminist critics drew on the liberatory energy and know-how of the social movements of that decade and on the insights of women who have spoken over the centuries about the subjugation of women. Simone de Beauvoir (1949) wrote that woman "is defined and differentiated with reference to man and not he with reference to her. . . . He is the Subject, he is the Absolute—she is the Other" (p. xvi). She continues: "The categories in which men think of the world are established *from their point of view, as absolute. . . .* A mystery for man, woman is considered to be mysterious in essence" (p. 257). Yet as Jane Austen's heroine Anne Elliot says in *Persuasion* (1818/1966, p. 202), "Men have had every advantage of us in telling their story. Education has been theirs in so much higher a degree; the pen has been in their hands."

Feminist critics concur. They are especially sensitive to the image of women characters in texts written predominantly by men, the place of women writers in the canon, the differing responses of women and men to literature, and the differing ways that men and women use language. What constrictive roles did many of the conventions of fiction assign women, for instance, in the fairy tale, the gothic tale, the romance? Did women characters ever have a leading role? Did any destiny present itself for female heroines other than securing a husband? Was the woman's existence always anchored in another person? Did she ever find an identity for herself not defined by attachment to a man? Did any women characters possess independent, active, original, expressive souls? Heilbrun (1979, p. 175) says outright of American literature: "American male novelists have always been notoriously uninterested in female destiny."

They also raise questions about the different treatment of male and female writers. One example will suffice. Showalter (1971, p. 341) describes the tumult over the author's identity when *Jane Eyre* was published. "Many critics bluntly admitted that they thought the book was a masterpiece if written by a man, shocking or disgusting if written by a woman." Ellmann (1968, p. 29) summarizes: "Books by women are treated as though they themselves were women, and criticism embarks, at its happiest, upon an intellectual measuring of busts and hips."

Feminist critics regard most schools of literary criticism as expressing a predominantly male perspective. They are attempting to correct these imbalances and present a more balanced view. The practical exercise of their criticism employs tools from many disciplines: history, psychology, linguistics, anthropology, and sociology. Lynn (1990, p. 268) reports that his university students take to feminist criticism enthusiastically, perhaps, he reasons, because of its "simplicity"—they "need only read as a woman." However, that perspective requires "the reader

to dismantle or discard years of learned behavior," and the result is striking. The feminist perspective "quickly turns out to have a profound effect on the reader and the text—an effect that hardly can avoid being political."

Marxist. Marxist critics apply Marxist theory to literature, just as Freudian critics apply psychoanalytic theory. They, like the psychology-based critics, are critical of the New Critics for being too narrowly focused on literature as art rather than as a reflection of its social, cultural, and political milieu. They see art as a projection of social history. George Watson (1986, p. 203) describes Marxist criticism as "inevitably historicist, and in a special sense, since it judges all contemporary literature in relation to its political effect, and all past literature in relation to its social setting." Thus, although Marxist critics overlap with historical critics, the Marxist's emphasis is on the social forces that shape people and culture.

Marxist critics differ from historical or biographical critics in the use of literature as well. Their interpretation attempts to expose the explicit and implicit assumptions of the writer and the times. They are especially concerned with issues of social and economic justice: Does the writer demonstrate a sensitivity toward the exploitation of the poor? Does the text support prevailing power relationships or challenge them? Meyer (1996) explains that Marxist critics "argue that criticism, like literature, is essentially political because it either challenges or supports economic oppression. Even if criticism attempts to ignore class conflicts, it is politicized, according to Marxists, because it supports the status quo" (p. 2013). They are scornful of New Critics, who make literature a precious and elitist aesthetic form; and of historians, who treat art as important to the transmission of the general culture; and of psychological critics, with their emphasis on the individual rather than on the social context that defines the individual. They fear literature's role as an opiate, lulling readers away from their natural grievances and social judgments. Selden and Widdowson (1993, pp. 93–94) explain:

> The critic must dismantle received notions of 'literature' and reveal their ideological role in shaping the subjectivity of readers. As a socialist the critic must 'expose the rhetorical structures by which non-socialist works produce politically undesirable effects' and also 'interpret such works where possible 'against the grain,' so that they work for socialism.

Literature possesses this potential for promoting a critical consciousness of culture, a first step toward liberating the reader.

Many high school juniors and seniors have absorbed the same sort of working knowledge of Marx that they have of Freud, and they like to interpret "against the grain" with his ideas. The challenge is to deepen their understanding of social theory, to call them to more than a parody of Marxist principles, and to push them toward the questions that matter to a Marxist critic: What does literature say about our culture—the writer's time, the book's time? What can literature be and do in our society?

Despite their differences, the first eight schools of literary criticism share a concern for mastering the text and opening its secrets. Three prominent critical schools that developed toward the end of the twentieth century believe that these critical projects were based on a fundamental error. These later critics do not accept the idea that texts have definitive meanings. Their theories and practices reflect another twentieth-century phenomenon: the relentless assault on objective certainty in every area of human life and learning.

Deconstructionist. Deconstruction is not generated by extraliterary theories of psychology, politics, or sociology but by those of philosophy and linguistics. Deconstructionists, strongly influenced by French linguistic theory, believe in a social construction of reality. They believe that language is not a precise instrument. It can never express exactly what we intend it to mean. It has no absolute connection with anything outside itself. All language is metaphoric. The world provides us with a series of signs to be read that have nothing to do with truth or what is real. Language should be properly understood as an elaborate word game. Because language and communication are indeterminate, we must relinquish the notion that we can arrive at a right or correct reading of any literary work. Texts have no fixed boundaries, no simple, solitary meanings.

Although the schools of deconstruction and formalism have widely different purposes, they share the same method of textual analysis: close reading. Whereas New Critics examine a text to arrive at a final, fixed reading of the work, deconstructionists examine a text to expose it as indeterminate. While New Critics try through close reading to stabilize the meaning of a text, deconstructionists aim through close reading to destabilize it. While New Critics try to account for all of the gaps and paradoxes in a text, deconstructionists exploit those paradoxes to undermine our assumptions of a solitary interpretation. Deconstructionist scrutiny aims for the logical or rhetorical inconsistencies between the explicit and implicit meanings of words, images, characters, plot, and theme. Deconstructionists will also demonstrate how these confusions are disguised by the text. Jonathan Culler (1982, p. 86) explains that "to deconstruct a discourse is to show how it undermines the philosophy it asserts, or the hierarchical oppositions on which it relies." Barbara Johnson (1980, p. 5) describes the method as "the careful teasing out of warring forces of signification within the text itself."

Steven Lynn (1990, p. 263) enumerates a three-step process of deconstructive criticism:

1. a deconstructive reading must note which member of an opposition in a text appears to be privileged or dominant . . .

2. the reading shows how this hierarchy can be reversed with the text, how the apparent hierarchy is arbitrary or illusory . . .

3. a deconstructive reading places both structures in question, making the text ultimately ambiguous.

Hillis Miller divides readings of texts not into right or wrong, but into weak or strong. "Strong interpretations" are those that display creativity, cleverness, and ingenuity. No one interpretation is privileged above others. (Deconstructionists explain that the close reading of the New Critics just wasn't close enough. Others call deconstructionists' techniques, close reading with a vengeance.) Lynn (1990, p. 263) locates the value of deconstructionist readings for his university students just here: "It encourages creativity" and, as a bonus, careful "scrutiny" of the text. We will elaborate further on the effects of deconstruction on teaching in Chapter 7.

Reader Response. We used the term *reader response* to define the first stage of our four-stage approach to reading literature. The term is used more broadly to define a body of critical theory that centers on the major concern of that first stage: what readers experience as they read a text. (Other terms are also used: reader theory, audience theory, and reception theory.) Bleich (1975, p. 4) begins with this assumption: "The role of personality in response is the most fundamental fact of criticism." Reader response critics all agree with several principles:

- The text has no literal meaning outside the reader's acting upon it. It is not ever a finished product with a fixed, "correct" meaning. Its meaning depends on the reader's activity.
- The reader actively constructs the meaning of a text, not simply discovers it there.
- The interest of a critic is on *how* the reader creates meaning and *what* influences that reading. As Meyer (1996, p. 2017) explains, "we get a reading of the reader."
- The contexts that influence readings are personal and social and include the reader's past and present history, psychology, past experiences of literature, and knowledge of literary convention.

If the reader's response is central, it follows that these critics are not just interested in printed texts but in texts from a variety of media—all stimuli for response. They have thus broken down the boundaries that separate literary study from other disciplines. Television soap operas and historical documents are legitimate texts for critical study. They have further challenged the evaluative standards with which readers and critics judge literary quality. Texts do not have unvarying literary status. The distinctions between escape and serious, popular and literary texts no longer apply. Radway (1984), for instance, criticizes traditional academic judgments of romance novels (just as others reassess westerns, spy novels, and mysteries). She explains that the cultural importance of those romances depends on the meaning ascribed to them by their readers, who approach texts with very different strategies of interpretation.

One technique of reader response that illustrates its major principles is to imagine how someone with an entirely different perspective would regard a text. Consider, for instance, how "Harrison Bergeron" would have been differently received had it been published in *The Village Voice* or *Pravda*. Meyer (1996, p. 2019) imagines "The Story of an Hour" read by readers of *Ms.* or *Good Housekeeping*. He asks, "What assumptions and beliefs would each magazine's readership be likely to bring to the story? How do you think the respective experiences and values of each magazine's readers would influence their readings?" Appendix F provides a list of books about reader response as a critical approach and a pedagogical strategy.

New Historical.   New Historicism is a style of literary analysis that arose in the 1980s to challenge "the dominance of Deconstruction and the legacy of New Criticism" (Macey, 2000, p. 270). New Historicists have used the notion of an indeterminate text to reintroduce a historical dimension to literary study, what Selden and Widdowson (1993, p. 162) call "the interconnections between the literature and the general culture." But they are not simply using literature to illustrate the events of the past or those events to illuminate literature—the old historical/biographical approach. They view history as "narrated" stories about past events but never as a stable and definitive body of facts that we can observe and ascertain with detached objectivity. Nor is history a neutral backdrop for the literary text. We construct a view of history from previously written texts; but our vision is always partial, determined by the particular historical context of those authors and ourselves, the readers. The New Historicists explode the notion of texts as reflecting a unified and coherent world view of their epoch. They offer new perspectives on traditional readings of the past. Louise Montrose (1989, p. 3) describes the concern of New Historicist critics as "the historicity of texts and the textuality of history."

Part of their technique is to enlarge the different kinds of texts that previous literary historians left to others. They refuse to consign literature to a precious aesthetic realm removed from other forms of cultural expression. Stephen Greenblatt (1990, p. 14) explains their "intensified willingness to read all of the textual traces of the past with the attention traditionally conferred only on literary texts." For instance, they have opened what once was considered "popular" literature to serious scrutiny. They attempt to know the culture of a period in multiple dimensions: social, economic, political, and aesthetic. Jane Tompkins (1985) suggests, for example, that the nineteenth-century sentimental novel critiques American society with far more devastating insight than those written by the better-known literary giants such as Hawthorne and Melville.

The New Historicists present an array of procedures for reading texts. They begin with a rejection of the previous assumptions that literature is an autonomous entity and that the society mirrored by that literature is stable and coherent. Then they revisit literature and reinterpret the culture reflected there and how literature influences readers to yield to this culture. They have been ingenious in tracing what appear to be trivial anecdotes and passages to reveal the organizing beliefs and codes of whole societies. They are especially interested in exposing dominant ideologies and resistances to them. That delineation of power and of resistance to it, a kind of cultural dialectic, is a hallmark of New Historical criticism.

A critical approach that overlaps with New Historicism arose in the 1990s, when critics raised questions about feminist theory partly because of deconstruction's belief that binary oppositions such as male/female and hetero/homosexuality are unstable. Macey (2000, p. 321) explains, for instance, that "masculinity can be demonstrated to be an unstable cluster of fears about effeminancy and repressed homosexual or homosocial desires, rather than the 'simple' opposite of femininity." This approach to texts is sometimes called queer theory or gender theory and is regarded as a "general defense of minority cultures" (p. 321).

∞ CLASSROOM STRATEGIES

Many students enjoy entering into discrete, self-contained systems. They readily understand the organizing principle of different schools of thought because they experience just such organization of politics by political parties and religion by denominations and sects. They enjoy standing outside the field and uncovering principles that have been implicit but unstated in classroom discussions. Furthermore, they like to see how different schools grow from and relate to each other. The points of difference animate them. The students who profit from this introduction seem to feel both relief and release. They discover a way to recognize, tolerate, and respect differences of literary interpretation. They can sample from this array to define their own unique approaches to literature.

For those students who seem ready, we introduce the individual theories, gradually working from definition in brief minilectures to application of that perspective in textual interpretation. We continue to move back and forth between brief explanation and extended illustration and application. For instance, after we have discussed feminist criticism, we might ask of *The Adventures of Huckleberry Finn,* "How is Twain characterizing all of these nineteenth-century women? What would a feminist critic like to say to him? To us, his readers?" As students ask questions or probe more deeply, we return to central ideas of each school of thought or to additional levels of complexity.

Here are four group activities that have helped our students to solidify and exercise their understanding after they have encountered at least four or five of the different critical schools. They represent major teaching activities, three set in class and one set outside of class. We hope they will answer Eagleton's (1983) critique of those "who complain that literary theory is impossibly esoteric—who suspect it as an arcane elitist enclave somewhat akin to nuclear physics" (p. vii).

Small-Group Questions. We assign students to small groups and ask the groups to generate questions that a critic of each school studied might pose about a particular text. These group questions are then answered by the small group and later posed to the whole class. Beyond interpretation, the questions can promote an awareness of the usefulness of multiple critical points of view. Possible discussion prompts include the following:

- Which questions took you closest to an encounter with the text? Were they the ones you characteristically ask?
- Which yielded your deepest discovery about this literature? The author's position? The story's craft? The story's connection to you?
- Were all of the questions text-centered? Did any stir your thinking beyond the text?

The questions of Figure 5–10 on Tillie Olsen's story "I Stand Here Ironing" were culled from small-group work of our high school students.

Jigsaw Groups. Again, the class is divided into small groups, each representing a different school of criticism. Each group discusses the work being studied from its particular critical perspective. At a signal, the groups reconstitute themselves, each new group comprised of representatives from a different original group. In this new group, each individual discusses the work as a critic from the particular school of criticism that he or she represents.

Role Playing. Students are each asked to represent a critic from a particular school of criticism with consistency, depth, and enthusiasm during a whole-class or small-group discussion. Sometimes we ask students to play their roles incognito. (The mysteries created are engaging.) Oddly, while critical analysis would seem to distance readers from the text, readers actually seem sometimes to grow closer because they have a conscious means for moving into it and a cover for moving around in it. We have found that discussions of literature fired by strong competing viewpoints do not grow more cerebral. Often interpretation becomes more clearly defined, and nuances that are easily submerged surface. Alternative or oppositional views take readers deeper into a text than an easy consensus could. (What would an archetypal critic say about the Mississippi River in *The Adventures of Huckleberry Finn?* How would you respond to that position?) Texts can be transformed from something inert into something vital enough for people to discuss them seriously and passionately.

Battle of the Book Critics. This ambitious project culminates the smaller attempts at absorption and application. We divide students into eleven schools of literary criticism and ask them to approach a text as a critic of that school would. Then we invite other classes to come in for a discussion of a selected piece of literature. Ranged in front of the visitors, our students sit under banners that declare their perspectives. A teacher/convener begins a discussion of a short text with the uninitiated students. The student-critics gradually start to make interpretive comments based on their particular points of view. The presence of an audience energizes them and encourages their more defined and contentious articulation of their perspective. The animated and competing viewpoints startle the audience into a lively examination of the text. This presentation never fails to generate strong responses in both performers and audience and a quickened awareness of the enlivening richness of literature. We often follow these group assignments with individual work—for instance, writing an editorial, a letter to the author, an essay about a text from the point of view of one critic, or a rebuttal of another critic.

A Plea for Pluralism

Academics debate whether to ask students to commit themselves totally to a single, consistent critical position or to employ and mix the methods and insights of different schools of thought. We favor the latter, pluralistic approach for high school students, their teachers, and ourselves—with one caveat. Critic and teacher Wayne Booth (1979, p. 21) makes an important distinction in *Critical Understanding* between eclecticism and pluralism. He explains that eclectics "deliberately hack other critics' works into fragments, salvaging whatever proves useful" for their purposes. He finds, though, that such ransacking does not do justice to the original positions and is often used in the service of an entrenched position. It appears to conform to the "dictionary sense" of "rejecting a single, unitary and exclusive interpretation, doctrine or method" (p. 346). But what appears to be open and inclusive might often just mask a rigid and monistic perspective. "In practice the attitude quickly resolves into a raiding of ruined edifices in search of bricks and straw useful in a preconceived building program" (p. 24). Such raiding or even borrowing keeps the reader unfocused, confused, and inconsistent and undermines the reading done and the conclusions drawn. Pluralists, on the other hand, "claim to embrace at least two enterprises in their full integrity, without reducing the two to one" (p. 21):

> Ideally, the pluralist will examine the question each critic has chosen to ask, the critical language he employs, and his characteristic way of seeking evidence and reasoning with it. He will have been forced into pluralism by his discovery that when he has taken at least two critics' reasoning with as much seriousness as they did themselves, more than one mode emerges intact, irrefutable, viable, and not reducible or totally translatable into some other, superior mode.
>
> In practice, he will expect that some controversies will lead to a both/and resolution rather than an either/or. Having learned in at least one case that, when conflicting conclusions were related back to their intellectual sources, sharply contrasting modes proved both sound and in no final sense contradictory, he suspects, and indeed works for, further experiences of the same harmonious kind. (pp. 27–28)

We saw just such a difference of basic assumptions and therefore critical conclusions with Plato and Aristotle and with Freud and Jung. We hope that you have been emboldened, not baffled, by the discovery. As John Stuart Mill (1859/1989) observed in *On Liberty* in the nineteenth century, "in an imperfect state of the human mind, the interests of truth require a diversity of opinions" (p. 51). Mill gives a further explanation of the advantages of pluralism: "the conflicting doctrines, instead of being one true and the other false, share the truth between them" (p. 45). Booth's (1979) way of approaching literature embodies our hope in presenting this multiplicity of perspectives: "It is more a way of living with variety than of subduing it. It thus begins in what might better be called an attitude than a critical position: methodological pluralism" (p. 3).

Exposure to schools of literary criticism need not make students narrow dogmatists with a single-minded approach to literature. If students move into one camp or another, it is only temporarily. The direction of their exposure to the eleven schools of criticism should ultimately drive them toward a personal synthesis. In the final sentence of *Critical Assumptions*, Ruthven (1979) says, "the supreme critical act is not evaluation but recognition" (p. 202). We agree absolutely.

Invitation to Reflection 5–6

1. Did you have any explicit introduction to literary criticism in your high school or college English classes (other than a course in literary criticism)?
2. Has literary criticism in any way deepened or enlarged your understanding of and response to literature?
3. Do you think that literary criticism has a place in high school English classes? If you believe it has a place, is it appropriate for all students or only those who are in the upper grades or in AP or college-bound classes?
4. Are some schools of criticism more appropriate to study with adolescents than others? Which? Are some schools easier to teach and apply than others? Which?
5. Do you believe that understanding the multiple perspectives of literary critics provides a resource that would enlarge students' understanding of themselves and others?

CONCLUSION

A crucial first step toward your becoming an effective teacher of literature is that you, the teacher, read gladly and openly and that you find delight, enrichment, and illumination in your reading. That is your best hope for introducing others to literature's possibilities. Only when you have found works that take "the top of your head off" will you be able to help others envision and know a similar experience. Then you and your students can begin to share those texts together, to work out interpretations through attention to the new collective understandings, to form, and to other critical insights. At the end of this process of responding to literature, perhaps you and they can arrive at some appreciative sense of the work and say with Rainer Maria Rilke (1954, p.29) that "Works of art are of infinite loveliness and with nothing so little to be reached as with criticism. Only love can grasp and hold and be just toward them."

Celebrating Poetry

A poem refreshes a world.

Wallace
Stevens

Poetry is like nothing else we teach. In describing what a poem should do for its readers or hearers, T. S. Eliot used the verb *interrupt*. Ntozake Shange (1978) points to the same effect:

> quite simply a poem should fill you up with
>   something
> cd make you swoon, stop in yr tracks, change yr
>   mind,
> or make it up, a poem shd happen to you like cold
>   water or a kiss. (p. 57)

But many high school students barely notice poetry; occasionally they will consent to a handshake with it but rarely to a kiss. In fact, our students often bring strong biases to poems, and those biases are often more negative than positive. So we begin most classroom poetry encounters with many student resistances.

Yet nursery rhymes are the delight of childhood reading. The child is rare who does not respond to the rhythm and rhyme of this poetry with pleasure and even enchantment. How can we explain this dramatic decline? After all, music is at the heart of adolescence. What converts rhyme-loving youngsters and rhythm-loving youths into poetry-resisting students? To begin to answer this question, think for a moment about the place poetry has occupied in your own life and learning.

Invitation to Reflection   6-1

1. Which descriptor best characterizes your personal response to poetry?
   - devotion
   - keen interest
   - mild interest
   - uneasiness
   - dislike
2. What were the major influences in your feeling about poetry?
3. Which emphasis best describes how you were taught poetry in your high school English classes?
   - oral reading
   - historical context
   - authorial biography
   - analysis of form
   - discussion of ideas
   - connections with personal experience
   - performance
4. Was it taught differently in your college or university courses? In what way?
5. Did your high school English teachers or those you've observed more recently
   - seem to prize and relish poetry?
   - celebrate the pleasure of sound and rhythm by reading poetry aloud?
   - select and teach poetry beyond what was contained in English textbooks?
   - emphasize the formal aspects of poetry over personal response to it?
   - favor their own analytical, even private, interpretations over students' reactions?
6. What has been the best experience of poetry, in or out of the classroom, that you have ever had?
7. Do you have a poet to whom you often turn?
8. Do you ever select a poem to read for pleasure before a novel, short story, or drama?

Chapter 5 articulated four stages of reading literature that are as applicable to poetry as to prose. But poetry has unique properties that make a separate chapter both desirable and necessary. Before we discuss how poems work for meaning making, we need to consider how poems engage us for pleasure. Our initial teaching strategies address the diverse reading/writing development of students and the playful pleasures and possible meanings of poems. The suggestions of our first three sections bridge the personal world of the student with the possibilities that lie within the poem. The order of our sections does not necessarily represent the order in which you should approach poetry with your students. Writing (what we call *forging*) poems might well be the final response to encounters with poems. What they all seek to do is avoid a trap described by Natalie Goldberg (1986) in *Writing Down the Bones:* "Poems are taught as though the poet has put a secret key in his words and it is the reader's job to find it." She suggests an alternative approach: "Instead we should go closer and closer to the work. Learn to recall images and lines precisely as the writer said them. Don't step away from their warmth and fire to talk 'about' them. Stay close to them" (p. 31).

Some students will never cross even the thresholds of poems, some will timidly move into the vestibule, and some will find themselves exploring the whole poetic house and, if not wanting to reside there, at least hoping to visit often. But we like at least to welcome all of our students to its door. Table 6–1 lists our welcoming moves described in this chapter.

FINDING POETRY

Our discussion starts at a place that we have found to be an excellent beginning: letting students *find* poetry in the world around them. Poetry can be found in innumerable places if one knows how to look. Found poems begin as unintentional utterances discovered in

TABLE 6–1   Celebrating poetry

Finding Poetry	Forging Poetry	Reading Poetry	Talking Poetry
Nonliterary Prose	Templates	Definition	Adolescent readers
Music	Fixed forms	Choice	Selecting poems
Advertising	Limericks	Personal response	Listening to poems
Radiant images	Sonnets	Enactment	Discussing poems
Figurative language	Haiku	Visualization	Poets talk
Compressed language	Cinquains and diamantes	Synthesis	
Bumper stickers	Folk ballads		
Unexpected places	Other verse formulas		
	Open forms		
	Found poems		
	Concrete poetry		
	Wild cards		
	Poetry trap		
	Dictionary magic		
	Magnetic poetry		

nonpoetic contexts such as newspapers, advertisements, conversations, and product instructions. Found poetry has enjoyed a recent vogue, beginning with the publication of two anthologies, *Pioneers of Modern Poetry* (Peters, 1967) and *Losers Weepers: An Anthology of Found Poems* (Hitchcock, 1969). But earlier practitioners such as William Carlos Williams have experimented with its power. His long poem *Paterson* quotes statistics and historical documents. In a letter, Williams says that prose can be a "laboratory" for poetry: "It throws up jewels which may be cleaned and grouped."

Finding poetry promises the delight experienced with most found treasures. And the poetic search and discovery involve all the language skills: listening, talking, reading, and writing. Our specific intentions in introducing students to found poetry are

- to awaken students to the everyday
- to expose in it unexpected realities and significances
- to discover how poetry uses words and images to startle us into an uncovering and recognition of meaning
- to move to more traditional forms of poetry with a new degree of attachment and understanding.

We discuss here poetry found in locations common to our everyday lives: nonliterary prose, music, advertising, bumper stickers, and even less expected places.

Nonliterary Prose

Devotees of found poetry make claims for it that take us to the heart of the questions "What is poetry?" "What distinguishes it from prose?" "How are the poet's perceptions and craft unique?" In the preface to *Search for the New Land: History of Subjective Experience,* Lester (1969, n.p.) explains: "We are so accustomed to reading horror in each day's newspapers, the news columns bordered by ads, that we have become insensitive to that horror. By taking news articles and arranging them as poems, what was mere news in one context becomes the human experience it really is."

Gorrell (1989) enumerates a three-part lesson that begins with a found poem, "Parents," by Julius Lester and grows to an exploration of the nature and effects of poetry. That lesson will be explanation enough for our belief in the power of found poetry. Read, as Gorrell's students do, the following poem.

Parents

Linda failed to return home from a dance Friday
   night.
On Saturday
she admitted she had spent the night
with an Air Force Lieutenant.
The Aults decided on a punishment

that would "wake Linda up."
They ordered her
to shoot the dog
she had owned about two years.
On Sunday,
the Aults and
Linda
took the dog into the desert
near their home.
They
had the girl
dig a shallow grave.
Then
Mrs. Ault
grasped the dog between her hands and
Mr. Ault
gave
his daughter
a .22 caliber pistol
and told her
to shoot the dog.
Instead,
the girl
put the pistol
to her right temple
and shot herself.
The police said
there were no charges
that could be filed
against the parents
except possibly
cruelty
to
animals.

Julius Lester[1]

Students' shock and horror immediately provoke a discussion of the narrated events. And the class quickly arrives at an urgent question: "Did this really happen?" At this point Gorrell distributes the following article from the *New York Times* (1976, Feb. 7, p. 29):

Coed Kills Herself to Spare Pet Dog Doomed By Father

PHOENIX, Ariz., Feb. 6 (AP)—Linda Marie Ault killed herself, policemen said today, rather than make her dog Beauty pay for her night with a married man.

"I killed her. I killed her. It's just like I killed her myself," a detective quoted her grief-stricken father as saying.

"I handed her the gun. I didn't think she would do anything like that."

The 21-year-old Arizona State University coed died in a hospital yesterday of a gunshot wound in the head. The po-

---

[1]From SEARCH FOR A NEW LAND by Julius Lester, copyright © 1969 by Julius Lester. Used by permission of Doubleday, a division of Random House, Inc.

lice quoted her parents, Mr. and Mrs. Joseph Ault, as giving this account:

Linda failed to return home from a dance in Tempe Friday night. On Saturday she admitted she had spent the night with an Air Force Lieutenant.

The Aults decided on a punishment that would "wake Linda up." They ordered her to shoot the dog she had owned about two years.

On Saturday, the Aults and Linda took the dog into the desert near their home. They had the girl dig a shallow grave. Then Mrs. Ault grasped the dog between her hands, and Mr. Ault gave his daughter a .22-caliber pistol and told her to shoot the dog.

Instead, the girl put the pistol to her right temple and shot herself.

The police said there were no charges that could be filed against the parents except possibly cruelty to animals.

New York Times

As students sort out the differences in the two accounts, they naturally begin to consider why Lester left out certain details and then to speculate about the difference in news reporting and poetry writing. In a gradual, broadening progression, students work toward important definitions of the nature of poetry. Gorrell nudges them with her own perceptions. She writes: "I point out how the poem enabled us to 'be in Linda's shoes'—to experience the moment with all its choices and inexplicable emotional textures. I suggest that the poem, unlike the news article, enabled us to participate in the event. Lester skillfully leads us to place anger and blame. I stress that poetry should be evocative, empathetic, and experiential" (p. 32). She moves then to discuss how poetic language works to this end, not by the presence or absence of "meter, rhyme, stanzaic form, sound devices, and figurative language" but by its intensity, precision, and concision (p. 33).

Gorrell says that she concludes her first poetry class with "the most appropriate response to poetry—writing our own." She capitalizes on students' enthusiasm for the poem "Parents" with an assignment that allows them to be "enthusiastic seekers having acquired a new sensibility—to feel and think poetically." Teaching Activity 6-1 presents two individual found poetry assignments: Gorrell's verbatim, with numbers added (p. 33), and an alternative version.

6-1 TEACHING ACTIVITY

Found Poetry Writing

I

1. Search newspaper and magazine articles, editorials, textbooks, instruction manuals, catalogues, labels, personal and want ads, "notes left on paper bags"—any nonliterary source—for hidden poetic potential.

2. Lift and isolate at least three consecutive lines from the text and arrange to expose new meanings.

3. Keep the words in the same order. Do not add words to change the original material.

4. You may add a title and space and break lines and words any way you wish to create new meanings or sound effects. Search for hidden ironies, puns, and incongruities. The result may be serious, shocking, ironic, sarcastic, clever, or humorous.

5. After you have written your poem, write it on an overhead or a ditto master so that it may be duplicated for the class. Include a copy of the original source, including a complete citation. Have fun finding poetry in all the "wrong" places!

II

1. Find any prose sentence or passage (in a newspaper, magazine, catalogue, textbook, or advertising copy) that has poetic potential.

2. Copy it into lines of poetry, placing what you consider the most interesting words at the ends of lines to give them greatest emphasis.

3. Strip out unnecessary, prosaic words.

4. Rearrange syntax, compress phrases, and repeat key words—anything but add words, the one rule in found poetry.

5. Repeat key words. Gather words to create a refrain.

Gorrell summarizes the effects of finding poetry in nonliterary expository prose, articulating the power that we, too, think it possesses for students:

> In sum, found poetry is an ideal tool or starting point for teaching poetic response. It lets students connect to what excites, outrages, inspires, and provokes them in the real world. It starts where they are, and lets them respond with passion. It provides a vehicle for attitudinal change—poetry is everywhere to be discovered. It makes students active observers and seekers developing their own poetic sensibilities. And last, it inspires students to write their own poems—the final and perhaps most important way of responding. (p. 34)

Jeff Morgan asked his high school sophomores to write poems based upon "a recent, actual event in the news." He collected these poems into a book, *Reality into Art: Selected Current Event Poetry by Watauga High School Sophomores: 1996,* and published it on the W. H. S. Web page. In Norway, Borge Ousland later spotted one of its poems, "The Trek," as he searched his name on the Web. Ousland responded via e-mail to the poet—a great novelty in that time and place.

The Trek
Borge Ousland did what no one else had done
He skied to the North Pole by Himself
And
He skied to the South Pole by himself without any
Assistance
Then he tried to go across The White Wilderness the
same way
But, alas, he failed.
"No
Matter"
Says he.
He says,
"Skiing alone for so long gives you a different
Perspective
on
Life, you
Really understand what a small piece you are in
Nature's Greatness,"
His son painted his skis various colors so Ousland had
Something
To Concentrate on
While crossing a
White
Wilderness.

Andrew Tillman

More recently, Jeff Morgan used found poetry to absorb the catastrophic news of the September 11, 2001, terrorist bombings. When he learned of the attacks during his morning planning period, he downloaded graphic Internet news stories and immediately photocopied several accounts. After he discussed the breaking news with his students, he asked them to use the reporters' vivid words to write a found poem, a small but powerful stay against despair.

Music

Music provides another entry into poetic understanding and pleasure and helps us become aware that poetry is "not a thing far removed from the ordinary sphere of human experience, but a thing at the center of our lives" (Pichaske, 1972, p. xxvi). We have mentioned that the sounds and rhythms of spoken language awaken children's earliest delight in poetry. Adolescents are rapt with the rhythms and rhymes of popular music. Allan Bloom (1987) believes that music "is *the* youth culture and there is now no other countervailing nourishment for the spirit." Kennedy (1976) observes that "most poems are more memorable than most ordinary speech, and when music is combined with poetry the result is more memorable still" (p. 556). Songwriters, like poets, choose "words for sound as well as meaning" and use "the sound as a means of reinforcing meaning" (Perrine, 1983, p. 666). The goal of Teaching Activity 6–2 is to help students begin to make these connections between music and poetry.

Some students will need the teacher's prodding or direction to see the relation between music and poetry. But this teaching activity usually prompts students to realize that they have rediscovered some of poetry's essential elements:

- *Rhyme:* Two or more words that sound the same are repeated.
- *Meter:* The words and music create a kind of beat or pulse, a rhythm.
- *Images:* Vivid and concrete objects and experiences are presented by an appeal to the senses.
- *Figures:* Unexpected comparisons are used.
- *Symbols:* Some words feel special; they seem to represent something beyond themselves.
- *Refrain:* Some phrases or whole sections that look alike are repeated.

You may wish to invite students to present additional songs whose sound and sense strike them as poetry. Many will need help in developing criteria for selecting lyrics that reflect depth of observation or insight and attention to the language that expresses it.

Nowhere is the relationship between traditional elements of poetry and music more apparent than in rap, with its heavy reliance on cadence, rhythm, rhyme, and compression. The appeal of this music for the young affirms our sense of poetry's original pleasures. We have found students of all abilities absorbed by rap and deeply interested in playing it in class. One poem that neatly bridges the space between the poetry of class discussions and the rap of solitary headsets is Maya Angelou's "Harlem Hopscotch." Imagine as you read the poem a classroom presentation in which two students read the

6–2   TEACHING ACTIVITY

Lyric Elements

Whole Class

Play a song that has printed lyrics available, selected by you, a student, or a group. Classic rock songs that have been instructionally effective for us include the Beatles' "Eleanor Rigby," Simon and Garfunkel's "Sounds of Silence," Don McLean's "American Pie," Leonard Cohen's "Suzanne," Crosby, Stills, and Nash's "Southern Cross," Sting's "Fields of Gold" and "Fortress Around Your Heart," Natalie Merchant's "Carnival," and the Dave Matthews Band's "Satellite." These songs have lyrics that are rich, textured, nuanced, and challenging yet not overly elusive and rhythms, meter, sounds, repetitions, and even rhyme that are akin to what is central to poetry.

Individuals

Ask students to look at and listen carefully to the lyrics two or three times. Ask them to momentarily ignore the music's content (story or idea) as they enumerate the lyrics' formal features and elements. Student lists will likely include items such as the following:

1. Two or more words repeat the same sound.
2. The words and music create a kind of beat or pulse that repeats with variations.
3. A few vivid, concrete objects or experiences are presented.
4. Unexpected comparisons are made.
5. Some words feel special; they seem to mean a lot.
6. Some phrases or lines are repeated at intervals.

Small Group

Have students listen to several student-selected songs and then examine sets of lyrics and determine whether those same elements are repeated in the additional songs.

Whole Class

Each group reports its conclusions. Ask students whether any of the musical elements that they have found resemble the terms they remember from earlier discussions of poetry.

---

poem aloud as one or two pantomime the action of this familiar game and one or two others mime the clapped rhythm of hopscotch bystanders.

Harlem Hopscotch
One foot down, then hop! It's hot.
Good things for the ones that's got.
Another jump, now to the left.
Everybody for hisself.
In the air, now both feet down.
Since you black, don't stick around.
Food is gone, the rent is due,
Curse and cry and then jump two.
All the people out of work,
Hold for three, then twist and jerk.
Cross the line, they count you out.
That's what hopping's all about.
Both feet flat, the game is done.
They think I lost. I think I won.

Maya Angelou

Dawn Potter, poet, musician, and music teacher, finds rap "hugely successful with [her] music students—getting them to *absorb* rhythm as a physical element" (2002, personal communication).

Music can also be introduced as an accompaniment to poetry. Hutchinson and Suhor (1996) encourage students to make connections between words and music that animate each other. Their practical guidelines for a performance of the two together suggest alternative sequences of poetry and music:

- Music begins, then poetry enters;
- Poetry first, music entering at appropriate point;
- Alternation of short poems and short musical vignettes;
- Short sections within a longer poem . . . with interspersed musical vignettes or phrases;
- Musical backdrop of one or more tunes for a string of short poems on a common theme. (pp. 80–81)

Sato (1995) uses this fifth sequence as she accompanies individual poems with music selections such as "Nocturnal

Sounds" by Kattie M. Cumbo, "Latest Latin Dance Craze" by Victor Hernandez Cruz, and "Piano Man" by Joyce Carol Thomas.

Music and poetry profit from being heard and read together. Many older English ballads began their lives as songs. Shakespeare scattered songs throughout his plays. Many of his contemporaries wrote original poems to fit existing tunes. Few of the melodies survive, but these survivors have power: Ben Jonson's "To Celia" ("Drink to me only with thine eyes") and the anonymous Scottish ballad "Bonny Barbara Allan." In the United States, practically every schoolchild knows the Kentucky mountain song "On Top of Old Smoky" and the ballad "Frankie and Johnny." Modern composers have written powerful choral music based on poetry and poetic prose as well, following the example of Beethoven's choral finale to the ninth symphony based on Schiller's "Ode to Joy." The following are samples:

Benjamin Britten	*Hymn to St. Cecilia*	W. H. Auden
Frederic Rzewski	*De Profundis*	Oscar Wilde
Ralph Vaughan Williams	*Jerusalem*	William Blake

Whishaw (1994) used the linguistic variety in her classrooms to teach the music of language and poetry (and the rewards of collaboration with someone from another language family). During a poetry-writing unit, she had her students write poems in their first language and then pair with a speaker of a different first language to translate the poem. Poet and translator read the original poem and its translation before the entire class. Whishaw asked students to listen for the music of the translation regardless of the words' meaning. Collom and Noethe (1994) suggest asking students who are acquainted with second languages to write poems that mix languages in the same poem in order to pick up the "sonorities" of language even when meaning is only barely grasped (pp. 158–159). (Modern poets Ezra Pound, T. S. Eliot, and Robert Lowell shuttled among languages, even ancient ones.)

Advertising

We may not choose to attend to advertising as we do music, but we cannot escape it. Because it is so pervasive and perceived as so ordinary, we do not recognize it as a craft in its own right. Yet some of our most inventive minds work in this field. Their challenge is akin to the poet's. Advertising agencies, constricted by space (print media) or time (broadcast media), must make words and images count to achieve their effects. If poets, as Emily Dickinson says, "tell all the truth but tell it slant," advertisers sell their truth but sell it "slant." If alerted, students are natural critics of these slick sells, as we will discuss in our media chapter. Studying the carefully crafted language of advertising can serve poetic purposes as well because advertisers use, among other techniques, three elements that

are basic to poetry: *radiant images, figurative language,* and *compressed language.*

Radiant Images. A close scrutiny of advertising can heighten students' consciousness of the power of visual and verbal imagery to evoke a place, a person, a situation, or an idea. If students perceive the graphic connections professional advertisers craft between objects and ideas, they may see and appreciate these same skillful choices made by poets. Students may also, by inference, understand the importance of using sharp, vivid images for the success of the poetic as well as the commercial enterprise. One classic Coca-Cola TV ad features a group of attractive, culturally diverse young people who are standing on an idyllic hillside, smiling, lifting their Cokes, and singing together for the camera. The radiant connection between Coca-Cola and brotherhood is clinched by their song, "We'd like to teach the world to sing, in perfect harmony." Perrine (1983) could have been describing the skill of the advertiser when he describes the skill of the poet who must seek "concrete or image-bearing words in preference to abstract or non-image-bearing words" (p. 563). Holman (1980) elaborates on the power of such images in literature: "The *image* is one of the distinctive elements of the 'language of art,' the means by which experience in its richness and emotional complexity is communicated. . . . The *image* is, therefore, a portion of the essence of the meaning of the literary work, not ever properly a mere decoration" (p. 223). Ezra Pound (1954) wrote that "it is better to present one image in a lifetime than to produce voluminous works" (p. 4). Advertising careers are made by creating just such singular imagery.

Figurative Language. Observing advertising also can be instructive for introducing and playing with figurative language—specifically *metonymy,* the figure of speech in which a significant aspect or part of one thing is used to suggest its whole or something associated with it. Metonymy functions in poetry to make the abstract concrete. Similarly, metonymy is at work in most advertising as advertisers contrive ways for consumers to associate a product with a desirable outcome. Thus, if we wear a certain brand of basketball shoes, we can play like, or be, a superstar. A standard Christmas beer commercial assures viewers an experience of holiday cheer—even the old-fashioned, mythical cheer of horse-drawn, bell-jingling sleighs gliding over the snow—if they drink a certain brew. As Scholes, Comley, and Ulmer (1988) suggest, these commercials aim to establish a "metonymic connection" between good times and a particular product, "hoping the viewer will accept a further metaphoric connection and finally a cause-and-effect connection: the beer *is* good and a *cause* of good times" (p. 122). The verbal imagery of poetry and the visual imagery of advertising transform abstractions into concrete sensuous or sensible objects.

Teaching Activity 6–3 invites students to explore these corrections.

Compressed Language. Concision is important in both advertising and poetry. The images and language must be concise and concentrated in both so that readers, hearers, and viewers have their attention arrested and quickly satisfied. Korg (1966) explains that "in poetry, as in every art, the limitations of the medium provide the artist with his most exciting opportunities. Just as a sculptor may shape hard stone into the soft-looking curves of a body or a painter may produce the effect of depth on a flat canvas, so a poet works with language to overcome its natural deficiencies. He does this not by using a special vocabulary of unusually high-powered words, but by using more or less ordinary words in special ways" (p. 22). The creators of billboards, magazine ads, and radio and TV spots are confined by space, time, and audience attention and therefore must carefully select their visual and verbal imagery. As Emerson said, "Poetry teaches the enormous force of a few words." Teachers can illustrate that same lesson through the contemporary medium of advertising, which in 1999 poured $215,229,000,000 into a few words (*Statistical Abstract of the United States,* 2000, p. 579). (For updated data, go to http://www.census.gov/statab/www.)

Bumper Stickers

Even more than poetry and advertisements, bumper stickers rely almost exclusively on compressed words to make their mark. And like poetry, bumper stickers often attempt to sell an idea rather than a tangible product. Gunslingers, choice protectors, and lovers of states and all sorts of creatures use a small space to deliver a strong message. Many bumper stickers reflect neither insight nor cleverness, but students can scavenge for original ones and examine the way in which the words work— rich connotations, sharp images, imaginative juxtapositions, and ironies—to arrest our split-second vision.

6–3   TEACHING ACTIVITY

Advertising

Individuals

- Bring print advertisements to class from any source (newspapers, magazines, broadsides, or fliers) or audio/video advertising (selected clips recorded from radio or TV).

Small Groups

- Examine these ads. Select the ones that you consider to be the most effective in their use of vivid imagery and compressed and figurative language.
- Can you see why the ad creators made the choices they did?
- Do they use radiant images? Figurative or compressed language?
- Discuss what made the ad successful for you.

Whole Class

- Present these selected ads to the whole class and explain why they are effective. Choose several class favorites.

Small Groups

- Reconvene and read one or two short poems (student- or teacher-selected). Scrutinize words or images for their effectiveness, just as you did with advertisements.
- State what image or language you like in each poem.
- Choose the poem you find most striking in its imagery and language.
- Post the selected poem on the classroom walls or bulletin boards.

Individuals

- Look at and read the posted poems as you would a billboard. Write about the one that first grabbed your attention and explain why.

"America—Love It or Leave It" may not represent your idea of tolerance, patriotism, or respect for the individual; but this sticker was once so commonplace that we suspect its appeal is more than political. The language itself is appealing: its compression, alliteration, word and sound repetition, and approximate rhyme of *love* and *leave*. *America*, followed by the two visions balanced one against the other, is bold.

"Give Peace a Chance" is a powerful slogan of just four words that originates at the other end of the political spectrum. Its power comes from its direct appeal, its compression, and the strong, concrete verb and nouns: *give, peace,* and *chance*. "Save the Baby Humans" is stark and direct also, but it draws its force from an ironic juxtaposition; it is a play on the original slogan "Save the Baby Seals." Anti-abortion advocates want a reader to be shocked into remembering the original version and realizing that the life of a baby human should be even more precious than a baby seal's. The bumper sticker would not be as effective without the allusion. One of our favorite bumper sticker parodies derives its punch from the original slogan "Preserve Your Right to Bear Arms." The parody has all of the poetic elements we've mentioned: concrete image, figurative (nonliteral) language, and compressed language: "Preserve Your Right to Arm Bears." In addition, this bumper sticker possesses one of poetry's most winsome qualities: playfulness.

Whatever the message may be, bumper stickers provide a useful introduction to the compressed and vivid language of poetry. Scrutiny of bumper stickers that fail can be equally instructive in uncovering how words work. Students enjoy collecting and sharing the bumper stickers they see ("poetry in motion"). They also enjoy making their own, a much less daunting task than writing a poem. Like ads, bumper stickers help students express the human predilection to play with language ("visualize whorled peas").

Unexpected Places

We also suggest finding poetry in less expected poetic corners: children's books, student literary magazines, and other noncanonical sources. Easily accessible poems written for younger readers recall high school students to the world of poetry. High school teachers and librarians have long appreciated the appeal of Shel Silverstein's books *Where the Sidewalk Ends* and *The Light in the Attic* to attract and delight students. Table 6–2 lists twenty titles of accessible and appealing poems found in children's literature anthologies. They merely serve as exemplars of the resources available. They have reminded some of our most reluctant poetry readers of their childhood pleasure in verse. When these students enjoy and affirm these poems, they become more receptive to, comfortable with, and understanding of the poetry in their secondary and college texts. Teacher Julia Neenan asked her tenth graders to bring children's poetry to class to illustrate formal poetic elements. Their sharing brought them back to the origins of their experience of literature,

TABLE 6–2
Poetry from children's anthologies

Author	Poem
Anonymous	"Poor Brother"
Richard Armour	"Money"
Hilaire Belloc	"Henry King"
Richard L. Callienne	"I Meant to Do My Work Today"
Lewis Carroll	"The Crocodile"
Arthur Hugh Clough	"'There is no God' The Wicked Saith"
Ebenezer Elliot	"On Communists"
Bret Harte	"At a Reading"
Ralph Hodgson	"The Bells of Heaven"
Maxine W. Kumin	"Sounds of Weeds"
Vachel Lindsay	"The Moon's the North Wind's Cooky"
John Masefield	"Sea Fever"
E. L. Mayo	"The Mole"
David McCord	"Books Fall Open"
David McCord	"Cocoon"
Theodore Roethke	"Praise to The End!"
Dr. Seuss	"Too Many Daves"
Shel Silverstein	"The Loser"
Shel Silverstein	"Skinny"
Karl Shapiro	"Manhole Covers"
R. L. Stevenson	"The Land of Counterpane"

and they discovered that they knew and felt more than they thought they did.

One high school librarian points out that it is a discouraging but clear indication that students like a book when it is "ripped off" repeatedly. She cannot keep Mel Glenn's books on the shelves. He is a high school teacher who writes biographical poems and even attaches pictures of students. We include his titles in Table 6-3 with other anthologies that teachers and librarians have found that pitch even reluctant readers headlong into poetry.

French author and artist Jean Cocteau (1969) describes the nature of poetry's impact on the reader and thereby explains our hope for the impact of found poetry on the student:

> Suddenly [in poetry], as if in a flash, we *see* the dog, the coach, and the house for the first time. Shortly afterwards habit erases again this potent image. We pet the dog, we call the coach, we live in a house; we do not see them anymore. . . . Such is the role of poetry. It takes off the veil, in the full sense of the word. It reveals . . . the amazing things which surround us and which our senses usually register mechanically. (pp. 179-180)

Poet Marianne Moore calls this moment at which the mind apprehends "the lion's leap." We believe that we often underestimate poetry's appeal to young adults. Perhaps that is true because many have not received such cordial invitations to it. The Found Poem of Teaching Activity 6-4 is such an invitation.

∽ FORGING POETRY

Inviting students to create poetry is another essential step toward student engagement with and response to poetry. The word *poet* derives from the Greek *poietes,* which means "one who makes." (William Carlos Williams referred not to *writing* a poem but to *making* a poem.) Georgia Heard (1989) and Jack Collom and Sheryl Noethe (1994), poets and teachers themselves, suggest many sound and creative ideas about setting a stage and inspiring students to write poetry, whether in elementary, middle, or high school. The physical arrangements of a room—its organization and furnishings—influence what goes on there, whether it be poetry writing, reading, listening, or discussing. Heard says she sometimes thinks that "the information about how to write a poem is less important than the atmosphere of the room. There are places that give me an excited urge to write, places that feel rich and warm, where time slows down and whatever I want to do is possible"

TABLE 6–3 Noncanonical poetry anthologies

Arnold Adoff	I Am the Darker Brother	1968
	All the Colors of the Race	1982
Steve Dunning, Edward Lueders, and Hugh Smith	Reflections on a Gift of Watermelon Pickle	1967, 1995*
Paul Fleischman	Joyful Noise: Poems for Two Voices	1988
Betsy Franco, editor	You Hear Me? Poems and Writing by Teenage Boys	2000
Mel Glenn	Class Dismissed! High School Poems	1982
	Class Dismissed II: More High School Poems	1986
	Back to Class	1988
	My Friend's Got This Problem, Mr. Chandler: High School Poems	1991
Ruth Gordon	Under All Silences: The Many Shades of Love	1987
Paul Janeczko	Postcard Poems: A Collection of Poems for Sharing	1979
	Don't Forget to Fly	1981
	Poetspeak: In Their Work About Their Work	1983
	Pocket Poems	1985
	Preposterous: Poems of Youth	1991
Paul Janeczko, editor	A Poke in the I	2000+
Kenneth Koch	Rose, Where Did You Get That Red?: Teaching Great Poetry to Children	1973, 1990**
Kenneth Koch and Kate Farrell	Sleeping on the Wing: An Anthology of Modern Poetry with Essays on Reading and Writing	1981**
	Talking to the Sun: An Illustrated Anthology of Poetry for Young People	1985**
Myra Cohn Livingston	A Circle of Seasons	1982
	There Was a Place and Other Poems	1988
Frances McCullough	Love Is Like the Lion's Tooth	1984
Lillian Morrison, editor	More Spice than Sugar, Poems about Feisty Females	2000+
Naomi Shihab Nye	Words Under the Words	1995
Jon Stallworthy	A Book of Love Poetry	1974

*About one-fourth of the material in the first edition has been cut and replaced with new poems.

**These valuable texts contain poems and suggestions for how to teach children, or, we would add, anyone, to read and write them.

+These anthologies are illustrated and may be found in libraries or bookstores shelved with children's literature.

6–4

TEACHING ACTIVITY

Teaching Found Poetry

Whole Class

Have you ever read a newspaper account that caught your fancy and made you want to share it? Here's what Ursula K. LeGuin read in the Associated Press and what she did with it. She included the AP report in her poem, entitled "Found Poem." Read it first silently, then aloud.

Found Poem

However, Bruce Baird, Laguna Beach's chief lifeguard, doubts that sea lions could ever replace, or even really aid, his staff. "If you were someone from Ohio, and you were in the water having trouble and a sea lion approached you, well, it would require a whole lot more public education," he told the Orange County Register.

Paul Simon, for AP, December 17, 1984

If I am ever someone from Ohio
in the water having trouble
off a continent's west edge
and am translated to my element
by a sudden warm great animal
with sea-dark fur sleek shining
and the eyes of Shiva,
I hope to sink my troubles like a stone
and all uneducated ride
her inshore shouting with the foam
praises of the freedom to be saved.

Ursula K. LeGuin*

Small Group or Whole Class

- If you were drowning in the ocean, would the approach of a sea lion worsen your situation? Would it confound you?

- Did the AP account strike you as containing provocative material?

- Which would you prefer reading, the news report or the poem?

- What one line of the poem is most indebted to the news account? Which strays the furthest from it?

- What is the effect of altering the news story?

- What is the effect of arranging the newspaper account in lines? Is the meaning or language enhanced by this change?

- Does the arrangement of individual lines point out any particular image or meaning?

- Do any details take on additional depth?

- If you had written this poem, would you have published the source of the poem alongside the poem itself? What is the impact of reading the prose and poetry together?

- Do you consider the poet less creative because she found the poem outside of herself?

Individual

- See Teaching Activity 6–1.

*From "Found Poem," copyright © 1986 Ursula K. LeGuin; first appeared in Buffalo Gals and Other Animal Presences; reprinted by permission of the author and the author's agent, Virginia Kidd.

(pp. 21–22).[2] For a classroom to possess this necessary richness, it must have "books standing on the table, poems on large paper displayed all over, quotes by poets on the walls, kids writing everywhere, intently" (pp. 22–23).

With such a stage set, Heard then turns to effective stage directions for poetry-writing projects, whether they are spontaneous or calculated, brief interludes or class-long. Her list of things for teachers to remember as they begin to teach poetry writing includes

- *Prepare the soil.…*
- *Let students decide what they want to write about.…*
- *Create an open, trusting environment.* When students are willing to write about what's really on their minds, their poetry is extraordinary. As a teacher I'm aware that every time I choose to listen instead of control, every time I encourage, and every honest self-revelation I'm brave enough to make bring the classroom closer to being the kind of environment where good poetry can flourish.
- *Spend enough time.…*
- *You don't have to be the expert.* (pp. 34–35)

No matter how she begins, Heard "keeps in mind these lessons my own writing has taught me":

- *Poems start with a feeling, and an image is one powerful way to convey feeling.…*
- *Poets write about what they can't help writing about.…*
- *It's crucial not to censor, especially at the beginning.* (pp. 32–34)

Collom and Noethe (1994) are poets experienced in organizing poetry-writing sessions around a classroom hour. Their book is filled with effective poetry-writing activities for that hour as well as general advice about leading these sessions. For instance, they suggest an organization of time that is divided equally between an introduction to the session, poetry writing, and oral reading of the new poems. They advise encouraging students to be playful with language, to experiment, to be concrete, and to allow significance to emerge naturally, not by reaching for the "big idea." They believe that teachers should "speak of the mechanics of poetry as naturally as you'd speak of fixing a broken shoelace." They think that teachers should insist that student writers reread their poems and revise them instantly while they are "still in the flow and feeling of the poem." They recommend that teachers not criticize student poetry when it is first read but give praise that is genuine and concrete (pp. 1–9).

Appendix E contains other books that we have found useful for teaching poetry. We discuss here four strategies for encouraging poetry writing that move from the most scripted to the most free: *templates, fixed forms, open forms,* and *wild cards.*

Templates

A *template* is a mold or pattern from which a new object or idea is formed. Poetic templates provide a form into which students pour their own words. They are effective with young writers because they provide a structure that does not require what traditionally would be considered poetic utterance. Students can be engaged in careful word choice without the consciousness or intimidation of usual poetic elements such as meter and rhyme. And the template can begin with simple, structured patterns and later move to more complex, freer ones. The templates that follow are comfortable starters for students because they invite them to work from familiar material: themselves.

The first templates result in a brief biography, called a *bio-poem,* and have been circulated for so many years that no one knows their precise origin. They have been effective for us with students of all abilities. Some students have already encountered them in junior high; but because they are undergoing such accelerated changes, they write fresh, new poems even though the templates remain constant. The two templates shown in Figure 6-1 consist of partially completed lines that students finish.[3]

Sears (1987) offers yet another pattern, which we adapt here, set up as an exercise that invites reflection and expression about oneself. Students pick one of the moods listed in Figure 6-2. They brainstorm ways that the mood does not feel, then ways that the mood does feel. They cull from their lists to write a poem, using the following pattern:

1. required line (select your own mood)
2. an example of how your mood *does not* feel
3. another example of how your mood *does not* feel
4. another example of how your mood *does not* feel
5. required line (another way of describing the mood)
6. an example of how your mood *does* feel
7. another example of how your mood *does* feel
8. another example of how your mood *does* feel

The following student poem demonstrates the effect of Sears's template in guiding young writers to choose concrete images to convey specific feelings—important learnings at the heart of poetry.

---

[2] All excerpts adapted by permission from: *For the Good of the Earth and Sun: Teaching Poetry* by Georgia Heard. Copyright © 1989 by Georgia Heard. Published by Heinemann, A division of Reed Elsevier Inc. Portsmouth, NH.

---

[3] We ask anyone who knows the identity of the teachers who originated these two templates to write us care of the publisher. We will be happy to give full credit in subsequent editions of this book.

FIGURE 6–1

Bio-poems

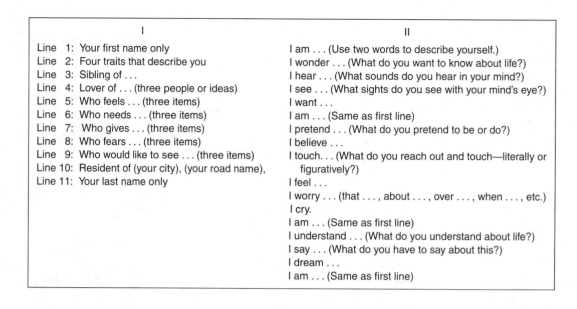

	I		II
	Line 1: Your first name only		I am . . . (Use two words to describe yourself.)
	Line 2: Four traits that describe you		I wonder . . . (What do you want to know about life?)
	Line 3: Sibling of . . .		I hear . . . (What sounds do you hear in your mind?)
	Line 4: Lover of . . . (three people or ideas)		I see . . . (What sights do you see with your mind's eye?)
	Line 5: Who feels . . . (three items)		I want . . .
	Line 6: Who needs . . . (three items)		I am . . . (Same as first line)
	Line 7: Who gives . . . (three items)		I pretend . . . (What do you pretend to be or do?)
	Line 8: Who fears . . . (three items)		I believe . . .
	Line 9: Who would like to see . . . (three items)		I touch. . . (What do you reach out and touch—literally or
	Line 10: Resident of (your city), (your road name),		figuratively?)
	Line 11: Your last name only		I feel . . .
			I worry . . . (that . . . , about . . . , over . . . , when . . . , etc.)
			I cry.
			I am . . . (Same as first line)
			I understand . . . (What do you understand about life?)
			I say . . . (What do you have to say about this?)
			I dream . . .
			I am . . . (Same as first line)

FIGURE 6–2

Feelings that people have, but fail to identify

Abandoned	Crushed	Frightened	Kind	Piteous	Stingy
Adamant	Culpable	Frustrated		Pitying	Strange
Adequate		Full	Laconic	Pleasing	Stuffed
Affectionate	Deceitful	Furious	Lazy	Pleased	Stunned
Agitated	Defeated		Lawful	Precarious	Stupefied
Agonized	Delighted	Glad	Left out	Pressured	Stupid
Almighty	Desirous	Good	Lifeless	Pretty	Suffering
Ambivalent	Despairing	Gratified	Lonely	Prim	Sure
Angry	Destructive	Greedy	Longing	Prissy	Sympathetic
Annoyed	Determined	Grieved	Loving	Proud	
Anxious	Different	Groovy	Low		Talkative
Apathetic	Diffident	Guilty	Lucid	Quarrelsome	Tempted
Astounded	Diminished	Gullible			Tenacious
	Discontented		Mad	Raging	Tense
Bad	Distracted	Happy	Maudlin	Rapt	Tentative
Beautiful	Distraught	Hateful	Mean	Refreshed	Tenuous
Betrayed	Disturbed	Heavenly	Melancholy	Rejected	Terrible
Bitter	Divided	Helpful	Mellow	Relaxed	Terrified
Blissful	Dominated	Helpless	Miffed	Relieved	Threatened
Bold	Dubious	High	Miserable	Remorseful	Thwarted
Bored		Homesick	Mystical	Restless	Tired
Brave	Eager	Honored		Reverent	Trapped
Burdened	Ecstatic	Horrible	Naughty	Rewarded	Troubled
	Electrified	Hurt	Nervous	Righteous	Turbulent
Calm	Empty	Hysterical	Nice		
Capable	Enchanted		Niggardly	Sad	Ugly
Captivated	Energetic	Ignored	Nutty	Sated	Uneasy
Challenged	Enervated	Immortal		Satisfied	Unsoiled
Charmed	Envious	Imposed on	Obnoxious	Scared	
Cheated	Evil	Impressed	Obsessed	Screwed up	Vehement
Cheerful	Exasperated	Infatuated	Odd	Servile	Violent
Childish	Excited	Infuriated	Opposed	Settled	Vital
Clever	Exhausted	Inspired	Outraged	Severe	Vivacious
Combative		Intimidated	Overwhelmed	Shocked	Vulnerable
Competitive	Fascinated	Isolated		Silly	
Condemned	Fawning		Pained	Skeptical	Weepy
Confused	Fearful	Jealous	Panicked	Sneaky	Wicked
Conspicuous	Flustered	Joyous	Parsimonious	Solemn	Wonderful
Contented	Foolish	Jumpy	Peaceful	Sorrowful	Worried
Contrite	Frantic		Persecuted	Spiteful	
Cruel	Free	Keen	Petrified	Startled	Zany

I'm mellow
   Not a go lay in a sunny field
      smoking a cigarette mellow
   Not mellow enough to give a bum
      all my money
   Not mellow enough to sit on an
      ocean yacht and drink lemonade
But just a sit in the air-conditioned
   living room watching reruns mellow
   Mellow like a nothing to do Saturday
      morning
   Mellow like watching your cork from
      the banks of a cool country pond
   A do what I want mellow that takes
      no effort or planning.

Jimmy O'Daniel

Templates can be more open, based on less restrictive patterns. We have found other poems to be effective templates. Each of the following has a distinctive structure or idea that invites adaptation:

Richard Armour	"Money"
Elizabeth Barrett Browning	"How Do I Love Thee?"
Adelaide Crapsey	"Triad"
Rudyard Kipling	"If"
George Ella Lyon	"Where I'm From"
Marcia Lee Masters	"April"
Harold Monro	"Overheard on a Salt Marsh"
Karl Shapiro	"Manhole Covers"
Stephen Spender	"What I Expected"
William Stafford	"Fifteen"**
Wallace Stevens	"Thirteen Ways of Looking at a Blackbird"
William Carlos Williams	"This Is Just to Say"
William Carlos Williams	"So Much Depends"

Linda Christensen (2000), a teacher deeply committed to grounding English study in the actual lives of students and teaching them to pose essential and critical questions about their society, uses George Ella Lyon's "Where I'm From" to position students to know and affirm themselves. Lyon's free-verse stanzas begin with "I am from" or "I'm from" and then name images of things around the house, things in the yard or neighborhood, the names of relatives or those we consider family and the images or habits associated with them, and family sayings. Christensen believes that classrooms should be "laboratories for a more just society" and that her heterogeneous, multicultural students must first affirm themselves as unique individuals before they can begin to reflect on the world around them. Lyon's template initiates that self-reflection.

The following is English teacher Lezlie Laws Couch's (1987) poetic confession. She mimics Williams's "This Is Just to Say" to reflect on why she changed her teaching method from a formalist to a response-based approach to poetry:

This Is Just to Say[4]
I'm sorry to have
guided you poorly

To have burdened you
with schemes and
trophes

And meter and form
Long before you
were ready

Forgive me
I didn't know
how to begin . . .

Lezlie Laws Couch

Rock music provides many templates that are provocative and have the additional appeals of being musical, rhythmical, and connected with the familiar and desirable in the worlds of our students. Lyrics that have worked well for us with students include Paul Simon's "These are the days of miracles and wonders . . .," Billy Bragg's "I don't want to change the world, I'm not looking for New England, I'm just looking . . .," and ". . . said the firefly to the hurricane, said the falling rain to the open plain." Students can add new verses or create new refrains using similar patterns.

Grossman (1991) presents broad but personal templates to her students with titles such as "When I Grow Up," "The Rooms We Live In/The Rooms We Leave Behind," and "I Am Not Who You Think I Am." Collom and Noethe (1994) enumerate many poetry-writing exercises based on loose templates. The exercise titles alone suggest a creative range of possibilities for patterned poems:

- acrostics
- acrostics from phrases
- chant poems
- declarations
- definition poems
- geometry poems
- "going inside" poems
- "last words" poems
- list poems
- "my soul is . . ." poems
- recipe poems
- spelling list poems
- "things to do" poems
- used to/but now poems

Harmston (1988) suggests a relatively open template and a method for encouraging spontaneous, not mechanical, response. Figure 6–3 presents Harmston's lesson verbatim. Mary Beth Braker says that this page of *Bridging*

---

[4] From Lezlie Laws Couch, "So Much Depends . . . On How You Begin: A Poetry Lesson," *English Journal*, November, 1987.

FIGURE 6–3

Harmston's lesson on impromptu poetry

Source: From "Impromptu Poetry" by D. Harmston, 1988. In F. A. Kaufman (Ed.), *Ideas Plus: A Collection of Practical Teaching Ideas. Book Six.*

Sometimes an apparent constraint can serve to free the imagination. In this activity, students stretch their creativity and their understanding of metaphor as they write to beat the clock. With adaptation, this approach could be used at all grade levels.

I designate each row of students as a separate team and give each team a metaphor from the list below.

Sleep is a stone	Dreams are hollow logs
Belief is a doorway	Anger is a palace
Fear is cold water	People are windows
Evening is a crooked highway	Loneliness is an empty streambed
Parents are blankets	Love is a fountain
Friendship is a seesaw	Morning is a bridge
Summer is a sleepy turtle	Anger is a rope
Amazement is a mirror	Fear is a hummingbird
Jealousy is a razor	War is an old car

Working individually, students are to build and extend the metaphor by adding four additional lines. The result will be a five-line poem from each student.

In round one, students each have three minutes to complete a five-line poem. The students who finish their poems in the allotted time are asked to read them aloud. I comment briefly on interesting images and effective use of language in students' poems.

If students need help starting their poems, I suggest that they begin the second line with "that" or "when"; they can then develop answers to how, where, and why in the remaining lines. If some students are still having trouble developing poems quickly, they might simply describe the concrete object mentioned in the first line. The metaphorical connection established in the first line will be carried through the brief image students compose.

In round two, each row receives a new metaphor. This time, students have two minutes to complete a five-line poem. Again the students who complete poems read them aloud.

The third and final round proceeds in the same way, except that students have only one minute to complete their five-line poems.

As the time for writing is reduced, students have less time to plan what to write; with one minute of writing time, students end up jotting down whatever images or phrases spontaneously pop into mind. This may not create great poetry, but it does have a freeing effect, and the results sometimes contain fresh and original images.

Here is an example of a poem written for this activity.

> Belief is a doorway
> Opening, Closing
> Always thinking
> You have the truth
> But not really knowing

Teams with the most completed poems for each round may be recognized at the end of the activity. One appropriate way of rewarding students might be to let the winning team choose several poems by their favorite authors for the class to read and discuss.

English is particularly tattered because she uses Harmston's exercise with every level of students—general, college preparatory, and honors—several times a year (1997, personal communication). She reports that she and her students are always amazed at the intimate, concise poetry this exercise sparks.

Fixed Forms

Some students like to play with traditional fixed forms, patterns that strictly govern a whole poem. Adrienne Rich explains that writing within predetermined form was part of her early writing discipline: "like asbestos gloves, it allowed me to handle materials I couldn't pick up bare-handed." The limerick and sonnet are the most common fixed forms in English poetry. The haiku from Japan, the more obscure five-line cinquain and seven-line diamante from France, the folk ballad, and the ode are progressively freer fixed forms. Some of our students feel uncomfortably constrained by such arbitrary prescriptions and write grudging and mechanical verse. But others enjoy the constraints of composing within an established tradition. They even sometimes discover why these poetic conventions survived centuries; that is, they come to appreciate the relation between the structure and the thoughts or feelings. Perrine's (1983) explanation of the challenge of form for the serious poet is pertinent to students as well, even those who are reluctant writers and readers of poetry:

> The inferior poet, of course, is often defeated by that challenge: he will use unnecessary words to fill out his meter or inappropriate words for the sake of his rime. The good poet is inspired by the challenge: it will call forth ideas and images that might not otherwise have come. He will subdue his

form rather than be subdued by it; he will make it do his will. There is no doubt that the presence of a net makes good tennis players more precise in their shots than they otherwise would be. And finally, there is in all form the pleasure of form itself. (p. 723)

Ronald Gross (1967) produces found poetry from the prose of newspapers and traffic signs, yet his discovery of poetry in prose underscores Perrine's point: "As I worked with labels, tax forms, commercials, contracts, pin-up captions, obituaries, and the like, I soon found myself rediscovering all the traditional verse forms in found materials: ode, sonnet, epigram, haiku, free verse. Such finds made me realize that these forms are not mere artifices, but shapes that language naturally takes when carrying powerful thoughts and feelings" (p. 2).

Limericks. The limerick is probably the most popular fixed form because of its association with playfulness and bawdiness. (Although the limerick's formal pattern is five anapestic lines—three syllables, two unaccented, one accented—that usually rhyme *aabba*, it can be grasped almost instantaneously simply upon hearing it.) Its form demands only two end rhymes, and it has a catchy metric pattern that almost every secondary student knows; furthermore, its tone and content are almost exclusively irreverent and humorous, which students relish. Most limericks are anonymous, having passed into the oral tradition so readily that their authors went unnoticed. The name of a friend or one's school or town provides a good beginning for limericks. Teacher Becky Brown enjoys asking her seniors to write limericks after they read *Oedipus Rex.* Her students wrote the following two examples:

> There once was a king that was wise,
> who conquered a sphinx of great size.
> He went on a date,
> And met the wrong mate,
> And ended up losing his eyes.

> *Sally Wilson*

> There once was a king called Rex
> Upon whom the gods laid a Hex.
> He did a bad thing
> With mom had a fling
> And developed an awful complex.

> *Jonathan Milner*

Sonnets. In English poetry, the sonnet has almost no rivals in popularity and durability. The English imported the form from Italy in the middle of the sixteenth century and almost immediately gave it their own rhyme scheme. Kennedy (1966) notes that "so great was the vogue for sonnets in England at the end of the sixteenth century that a gentleman courtier might have been thought a boor if he proved unable to write a decent sonnet when

a lady demanded one" (p. 183). More recently, Robert Bly observes that "the sonnet is where old professors go to die." Sonnets are quite complex; but that very challenge may be what draws some students, just as it has many courtiers, poets, and professors. Wordsworth captures that interest in the final lines of his sonnet "Nuns Fret Not at Their Convents' Narrow Room":

> In sundry moods, 'twas pastime to be bound
> Within the sonnet's scanty plot of ground;
> Pleased if some souls (for such there needs must be)
> Who have felt the weight of too much liberty,
> Should find brief solace there, as I have found.

> *William Wordsworth*

The two forms of the sonnet provide students with some alternatives: the abrupt surprise of the English, or Shakespearean, form (with its three quatrains and concluding couplet) and the clear smoothness of the Italian, or Petrarchan, form (with its eight- and six-line division). In both forms, the divisions of the lines often correspond with divisions of thought. Many modern poets have revitalized the sonnet by writing variations of it. Maya Angelou's "Harlem Hopscotch," presented earlier in this chapter, is one surprising variation. Part of the challenge for the modern poet, we might imagine, is the same for our students: putting an old form to immediate and everyday use. The following sonnet was written by high school senior Julie Dunlop and published in *Heritage* (Spring, 1991, p. 58), the James Madison High School (Vienna, Virginia) student literary magazine.

> *Resonance: An English Sonnet*
> A brightly colored patchwork offers me
> warm refuge from the chill of mountain air—
> I lie in Mother's childhood room and see
> out-dated photos—Mom with long, curled hair!
> The pale blue ceiling tempts me, and I think
> of wriggling through its cracks to find a bit
> of airborne thought and dreams to build a link,
> for that is how tomorrow's hopes are lit.
> Cold rain is spiking hard against the tin
> roof. I am reminded that we all
> are a part of life's sweet melodies (and din)—
> whose notes our sleepy, silent minds recall.
> The past is churning in a hoary brew
> just like a river when the rains are through.

> *Julie Dunlop*

Haiku. The haiku is an attractive form for young writers. Its structure is straightforward and manageable; and the content calls for simple, stark, sensory images. In its Japanese origins, it consisted of three lines of five, seven, and five sounds (like English syllables); American practice has taken some liberties with these. The first line sets up a concrete image, usually from nature, and the subsequent lines juxtapose another image (or "vortex," as Ezra Pound called it) on top of the original. The classic haiku moves from the concrete detail of a specific moment in the first line to that image's universal and spiritual implications in the last. Haiku depends on careful, precise observation and a sense of the meaning unleashed by the observed object. It possesses one of the virtues of poetry generally: An image can convey—in a flash—meaning beyond itself. An abstraction is understood through the senses. In effective haiku, the reader arrives at that suggested meaning with surprise and recognition. As with the limerick, a good introduction to writing haiku is reading haiku. Two good reference books are Cor Van Den Heuvel's (2000) *The Haiku Anthology* and William J. Higginson's (1989) *The Haiku Handbook: How to Write, Share, and Teach Haiku.*

Cinquains and Diamantes. Heard (1989) calls the haiku and the cinquain "the hamburger and hot dog of American poetry classrooms" (p. 96). The cinquain and a similar form, the diamante, are far more obscure than limericks, sonnets, and haiku; but they provide an accessible, somewhat flexible form for the student writer. Surprisingly perhaps, personal topics can be shaped with these forms. The familiar and personal material reduces the intimidation of the structure; the structure shapes the stuff of memory and reflection. Figure 6-4 outlines the two.

Folk Ballads. The folk ballad is an inviting form because it is a simple narrative not limited by either length or rhyme scheme. (Common four-line rhyme schemes are *abba, abab,* or *abcb* in which only two lines rhyme.) Ciardi (1959) explains the nature of this oral, often musical, folk tradition and enumerates its appeal to our students as readers and writers as well:

> It is easier to remember the high spots of an action than to remember all the connecting detail: so the folk ballad leaps from peak to peak of the story's action, skipping the incidentals. It is easier to remember an action than it is to keep straight the moral comment upon it: so the folk ballad tends to consist of action for its own sake, and to avoid moralization. It is easier obviously, to remember an effective image, phrase or detail than it is to remember an ordinary or ineffective one: so the folk ballad, its weak points weeded out, has become a treasury of a sort of poetry that English-speaking people have found unforgettable. Finally, the folk-mind is most likely to be attracted to larger rather than smaller kinds of action: so the folk ballad is full of tales of life and death— of tragic loves, of bloody betrayals, of heroic deeds; and so the action tends to be direct and uncomplicated by subtleties and minor motives. (p. 685)

FIGURE 6–4   Cinquain and diamante

CINQUAIN

title
describe   title
action   action   action
feeling   about   the   title
title

Line 1: A word for the title (two syllables)
Line 2: Two words to describe the title (four syllables)
Line 3: Three words to express action (six syllables)
Line 4: Four words to express feeling (eight syllables)
Line 5: The title again, or a word like it (two syllables)

DIAMANTE

noun
describing   describing
action   action   action
transition   nouns   or   phrase
action   action   action
describing   describing
noun

Line 1: noun
Line 2: two adjectives
Line 3: three participles
Line 4: four nouns or phrase
Line 5: three participles indicating change
Line 6: two adjectives
Line 7: contrasting noun

You can invite students to write ballads from personal experience, from news stories, or from their own imaginations. The familiar form, the strong story line, the simple language, the repetition—all make this form accessible for the student writer. Although folk ballads are usually anonymous, Pete Seeger, Johnny Cash, Bob Dylan, Kenny Rogers, Joan Baez, Bruce Springsteen, and many other modern songwriters compose and sing their own narrative versions of the traditional forms. The melody and rhythm of existing ballads may supply a musical template for students' compositions. (Many famous ballads are simply new lyrics composed to the tune of an old familiar melody.) Or students can compose music for the ballads they write. As Hall (1987) predicts, "When a harrowing story is told in rhymed and delicate verses, the tension between form and content, story and music makes a dreadful energy" (p. 518). Here are some questions to be asked of ballads—anonymous, poet-made, or student-made:

- What has happened here? Can you see why these events attract a balladeer?
- What are the feelings that rise from this action for the characters? For you, the reader?
- Could any of the stanzas be omitted? Do they build to a climax?
- Are important things implied, not stated? What is gained by what is *not* told?
- If there is repetition, what is its effect on you? Does it add to suspense or emotional intensity?
- How does music reinforce the tone?

Other Verse Formulas. Many other established poetic designs provide patterns. Pantoums, rondels, sestinas, troilets, and villanelles are based on more complex patterns of rhyme, meter, and repetition. You might present one of these traditional patterns and examples to illustrate it or ask students to read an example and sum up the rules that govern it. After discovering the poetic rules, a good next question is "What does the poet gain by casting ideas and feelings in this fixed form?" (One of the most familiar is Dylan Thomas's poem to his aging father, "Do Not Go Gentle into That Good Night," in the fixed form of the courtly French villanelle. A number of poems are entitled by their form: Jean Passerat's "Villanelle," Elizabeth Bishop's "Sestina," and Ezra Pound's "Sestina.")

Heard (1989) has distilled suggestions that give students a clear entry into the particulars of a given form. Her suggestions for a villanelle serve as models for effective teaching tips:

- Begin with a subject that's important, something crucial; then write the two rhyming lines that will repeat throughout the poem.

- It's easier if the two rhyming lines are big and open; if they're concrete, with specific images, it will be harder to keep hearing them again and again.
- After the two repeating lines are written, play around with the others; it's like working a puzzle. Patience and persistence pay off. (p. 95)

If stricter constraints frustrate students, they might respond to more open forms, those defined by intent and mood, such as the ode, lyric poem, and elegy. We have found the following references to be useful for other fixed forms:

Paul Fussell, *Poetic Meter and Poetic Form*, 1979
Preminger, Warnke, & Hardison (Eds.), *Princeton Encyclopedia of Poetry and Poetics*, 1965
Ron Padgett (Ed.), *The Teachers and Writers Handbook of Poetic Forms* (2nd ed.), 2000
Lewis Turco, *The Book of Forms: A Handbook of Poetics*, 1968

Poetic Forms, hosted by Ron Padgett, consists of ten thirty-minute audiocassette discussions of ten basic poetic forms: free verse, haiku, ode, ballad, acrostic, list poem, sonnet, prose poem, villanelle, and blues poem. Each tape gives an informal definition and illustration of the particular form and lively advice about reading and writing poems in that genre.[5]

Hullet (1991) borrowed an idea from Grossman (1982) about a way to prompt her students to write an ode. Although it is not as circumscribed by meter and rhyme as other forms are, an ode is constrained by some conventions of manner and form. Teaching Activity 6–5 adapts Hullet's lesson, which is based on Pablo Neruda's "Ode to My Socks."

Open Forms

Like templates or fixed forms, open forms invite students to play within constraints. Robert Frost defined freedom as "moving easy in harness." We have always thought that this perfectly defined poetry as well. Open forms provide a fairly easy harness, but they are not without restraints. They do not necessarily use traditional meter, rhyme, and stanzas; but they still rely on a heightened use of language—word choice, repetition, and rhythm—and line arrangement to achieve poetic effects. Frost distrusted open forms; he said, "writing free verse is like playing tennis with the net down." But

---

[5] The tapes can be ordered through Teachers and Writers Collaborative, 5 Union Square West, New York, NY 10003-3306, 1-888-BOOKS-TW, phone, 1-212-675-0171, fax, and www.twc.org.

6–5

TEACHING ACTIVITY

Forging an Ode

Whole-Class Minilecture

Explain that the topic of an ode is often serious and its tone formal. Odes tend to be more public than private. They often include lofty sentiments, spoken with dignity. They are longer than most lyric poems are. Common topics elevated enough for an ode are initiation, beauty, truth, freedom, love, the meaning of life, and death. One of the best-known odes in English literature is Wordsworth's "Ode: Intimations of Immortality." Read a few of its familiar lines. Have students jot down topics that they consider to be of high seriousness that might be fit for an ode.

Whole-Class Reading and Discussion

- What topics did you write down?

- Do they conform to the usual seriousness of odes?

- Listen now to Pablo Neruda's "Ode to My Socks," (Figure 6-5). (If a student reads, that student needs to be alerted in advance in order to provide an effective reading with the proper seriousness.)

- Did Neruda's poem fit your expectation of lofty sentiment and high poetic purpose?

- Does the language fit the way you talk about the socks you wear?

FIGURE 6–5
"Ode to My Socks"

Ode to My Socks

Maru Mori brought me
a pair
of socks
which she knitted
herself
with her sheepherder's
hands,
two socks as soft
as rabbits.
I slipped my feet
into them
as though into
two
cases
knitted
with threads of
twilight
and goatskin.
Violent socks,
my feet were
two fish made
of wool,
two long sharks
sea-blue, shot
through
by one golden thread
two immense
blackbirds,
two cannons:
my feet
were honored
in this way
by
these
heavenly socks.
They were
so handsome
for the first time
my feet seemed to me
unacceptable
like two decrepit
firemen, firemen
unworthy
of that woven
fire,
of those glowing
socks.
Nevertheless
I resisted
the sharp temptation
to save them
somewhere
as schoolboys
keep fireflies
as learned men
collect
sacred texts.
I resisted
the mad impulse
to put them
into a golden
cage
and each day give
them
birdseed
and pieces of pink
melon.
Like explorers
in the jungle who hand
over the very rare
green deer
to the spit
and eat it
with remorse,
I stretched out
my feet
and pulled on
the magnificent
socks
and then my shoes.
The moral
of my ode is this:
beauty is twice
beauty
and what is good is
doubly
good
when it is a matter of
two socks
made of wool
in winter.

Pablo Neruda
(*Translation by*
Robert Bly)

- What lines let you know the value of the socks to him?

- Does it seem a waste of good images and metaphors to go on so about socks?

- If you were Maru Mori, would you be pleased?

- Now that you know what an ode is, do you think that Neruda's title adds anything to his poem?

- Here is a letter that Neruda might have written to the knitter Maru Mori (Hall, 1987, p. 463). Which would you have preferred receiving: the poem or the letter?

  Dear Maru Mori,
  Thank you ever so much for your kind gift of a pair of socks. They are very pretty. They are warm. They fit me perfectly. I will wear them all the time. Mrs. Neruda likes them too. Thank you again. Yours truly, Pablo Neruda

Individual

Choose your favorite article of clothing to write a poem about. Make a list or a cluster of the characteristics of this piece of clothing. (Show students the cluster of characteristics illustrated in Figure 6–6.) Include all of the information in the sample cluster and anything else you feel is important about it. Then select details that are especially striking. Use Neruda's poem as your model to write your own ode.

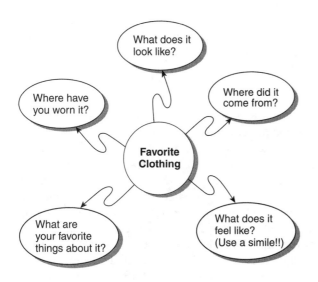

FIGURE 6–5   Cluster of characteristics

many modern poets and earlier poets such as Walt Whitman played poetry quite effectively without the traditional nets.

Found Poems.   The found poems discussed earlier are most often open poems. They rely on white space, line breaks, indentations, and repetitions as well as selected (intensified) words for their effect. An exercise that reveals the poet's purpose is to take any open poem and rewrite it into lines (even paragraphs) of running prose. Read it aloud, letting punctuation dictate pauses and stops. Then consider: What did the poet gain by arranging these words as poetry?

Concrete Poetry.   Concrete poetry is arranged so that its words show visually what they render verbally. They are shape poems. They make designs out of the arrangements of letters and words. Elementary children delight in "picture poems," but serious poets such as George Herbert in the seventeenth century and e. e. cummings and John Hollander in the twentieth also have played with this form. On the next page is a modern poem for the eye, "Kitty and Bug." As you read it, consider whether it is anything more than an ingenious exercise. Does the visual trimming of lines point out meaning? Does it mean less than meets the eye? Does it entertain eye and ear?

Kitty and Bug

```
        I              a
      cat      who
      coated   in   a
      dense shadow
      which I cast
      along myself
        absorb the
          light you
        gaze at me
       with can yet
      look at a king
      and not be seen
      to be seeing any
      more than himself
      a motionless seer
      sovereign   of   gray
      mirrored    invisibly
      in  the  seeing  glass
      of air Whatever I am
      seeing is part of me
      As you see me now my
      vision  is  wrapped  in
      two  green  hypotheses
      darkness    blossoming
      in  two  unseen  eyes
      which pretend to be
        intent on a spot of                    bug
          upon
            the
          rug
      Who
      can
          see
            how
              eye
                can
      know
```

*John Hollander**

As you can see, what concrete poets try to achieve is an "eye pun." Poetry collections of concretists such as John Hollander, Richard Kostelantz, and Mary Ellen Solt give a range of examples that provide a good starting point for students. Students should begin their own attempts at a concrete poem with a particular or tangible concrete image. This is an instance in which freedom of paper, time, and imagination is essential.

Wild Cards

These strategies are freer and may attract students who are uncomfortable or annoyed by templates, fixed forms, and even open forms. They draw attention to poetry's playfulness and delight in words. The exercises discussed here are *poetry trap, dictionary magic,* and *magnetic poetry.*

Poetry Trap. This activity provides more structure than that imposed by the other templates or fixed forms. *Poetry trap,* adapted from a method used by a Vassar College teacher, supplies students with a list of words and four fairly common poetic forms:

1. *Blank verse:* unrhymed iambic pentameter—the best-known, repeated one-line pattern in English verse, which Shakespeare used for most portions of his plays
2. *Enjambment:* a run-on line in which the sense of the line carries into the next line
3. *Internal rhyme:* rhyme in which final-consonant sounds are the same but vowel sounds differ, as in *rover* and *lover*
4. *Slant rhyme:* an imperfect or near rhyme.

If the terms are unfamiliar, we define and illustrate them so that students can recognize and use them, not simply label them. Teaching Activity 6–6 demonstrates how a poetry trap works to move students from words to meaning rather than the usual sequence, from meaning to words. The trap of the title comes to suggest engagement in the playfulness of poetry making, not imprisonment. The structure can be altered to meet your own goals and to interest your students. You could, for instance, require other poetic forms and select words studied in literary selections or vocabulary study.

Magnetic Poetry. Poet-musician Dave Kapell devised a method to help him through writer's block: He cut words from magazines and arranged them to form lyrics. Because he has allergies and his sneezing badly dislocated his songs, a roommate gave him magnets with which to secure his words. So successful was the project that Kapell developed and began marketing magnetic poetry kits (Heller, 1996, p. 125). Each kit contains more than four hundred magnetized words and word fragments. Although they are most commonly seen on refrigerator doors, they can also work on classroom surfaces: stationary file cabinets, portable cookie sheets—any steel surface. Something in the play of words against surfaces, of preselected words immediately before you, of the words themselves, encourages poetic play by individuals, pairs, or groups. The popularity of magnetic poetry has led the 1990s president of the Academy of American Poets, Jonathan Galassi, to speculate that "America's youth is bored with the way technology tends to suppress the imagination" (p. 125). Former U.S. poet laureate Robert

---

[6] From *Harp Lake,* copyright © 1988 by John Hollander; first appeared in *The New Yorker;* reprinted by permission of Alfred A. Knopf, Inc.

6-6 TEACHING ACTIVITY

Poetry Trap

Individual Assignment

Write a poem in blank verse using at least thirteen of the following words. You must use at least three verbs, four nouns, and two adverbs. The blank verse should include one instance of enjambment, three internal rhymes, and two or more slant rhymes.

rent	whimper	apt
becalm	shunt	somber
tinge	spent	woefully
rancor	cudgel	throe
nor	already	shun
fleece	mince	trip
awful	meagerly	haze
spot	bubbly	vixen
balk	hoax	shore
gloat	nave	eagerly

Hass calls magnetic poetry "one-man scrabble and the prize is insight" (p. 125).

Dictionary Magic. The most adventurous of these divergent forms is dictionary magic. This exercise asks students to fill a form—a template, fixed form, or wild card—with words drawn randomly from the dictionary or preselected word banks. It is like formal verse without attention to the usual concern for meaning. Individual students or a group can assemble a verse in this way. It may appear to take poetic play headlong toward verbal chaos, but with some students it frees delight. The arbitrary construction is energizing, and the final production often invites a sense of wonder at its novel and surprising juxtapositions.

Whether you are asking students to find or forge poetry, the goal is the same: From poetry play comes poetry ease, enjoyment, and understanding. Poet and teacher Donald Hall (1992) in an essay about Dylan Thomas writes, "All poets start from love of words and wordplay. Then they learn to love poetry as well" (p. 69). Another poet and teacher, Dawn Potter (2002, personal communication), believes that strategies for inviting students to play with poetry are "analogous to the way in which we learn to speak and read prose: from word, to phrase, to complex phrase, to sentence, to paragraph. . . . and the line moves endlessly outward. It's hard to understand why so many teachers want to start with the huge—that is, formal close reading—

when their students have not even begun to master the language of the small." Some students will continue to feel poetry's essential difference from their everyday prose and their everyday lives, but some may come to identify with Holden Caulfield's younger brother Allie in J. D. Salinger's *Catcher in the Rye.* Before he becomes ill with leukemia, eleven-year-old Allie writes poems in his baseball mitt so he will have something to read while he waits in the outfield for fly balls.

⌘ READING POETRY

We believe in giving students the poetic license to find and create poetry but also the poetic liberty to look at poetry in ways that are not strictly analytical. In *How Does a Poem Mean?* John Ciardi (1959) distinguishes different approaches to the study of poetry. One is represented by Charles Dickens's character, teacher Thomas Gradgrind, in his School of Hard Facts. After a student, "girl number twenty," gives a deeply felt definition of a horse based on her own experience of the living animal, Gradgrind turns to a boy for a proper definition.

"Bitzer," said Thomas Gradgrind, "your definition of a horse."

"Quadruped. Gramnivorous. Forty teeth, namely twenty-four grinders, four eye-teeth, and twelve incisive. Sheds coat in the spring; in marshy countries sheds hoofs too. Hoofs hard, but requiring to be shod with iron. Age known by marks in mouth." Thus (and much more) Bitzer.

"Now girl number twenty," said Mr. Gradgrind, "you know what a horse is."

from Hard Times, *by Charles Dickens*

Ciardi describes a similar attempt at classification of literature by a "recent anthologist who wrote that the inspection of a poem should be as certain as a chemical analysis" (p. 665). Ciardi senses danger when "the language of classification" is used to define something that should be approached by "the language of experience." He wants to see the reader of poetry become "alive to it by natural process," as Dickens's girl was to the horse (p. 666).

We present here six classroom strategies that engage students personally and experientially. We have drawn on the insights of reader response educators in naming this section "Reading Poetry." These educators define reading as more than deciphering, recognizing, and understanding words on a page. Reading is the dynamic discovery of connections that lie between three points: the text, the context of the text, and the context of the reader. We welcome students into the dynamics of reading a poem with our six nonanalytical strategies: *definition, choice, personal response, enactment, visualization,* and *synthesis.* In the cycle of classroom literature study, these activities could fall anywhere in the progression of *enter, explore,* or *extend.* What they have in common is response without "close reading"—that is, without analysis line by line.

Definition

The first strategy camouflages as traditional analysis, but it is not. We start with a poem that does not have the look of serious poetry. A concrete poem, such as e. e. cummings's "1(a" is perfect:

l

1(a

le

af

fa

ll

s)

one

l

iness

e. e. cummings[7]

[7] "1(a". Copyright © 1958, 1986, 1991 by the Trustees for the E. E. Cummings Trust, from COMPLETE POEMS, 1904-1962, by E. E. Cummings, edited by George J. Firmage. Used by permission of Liveright Publishing Corporation.

The appearance alone of "1(a" prompts students to ask elemental questions:

- What is this? Is it a poem?
- What does it mean?
- Why does cummings arrange this on the page as he does?
- Has there been some terrible typo?
- Why doesn't he just write "a leaf falls"?
- Why not write the letters "loneliness" together?
- Is "1(a" more or less of a poem than Wordsworth's "Lines Composed a Few Miles above Tintern Abbey?"

Natural curiosity drives these questions and arises out of the shock of the unexpected. Students try to align the words before them with what they have come to expect from poetry. These are the sorts of questions that engage students in the very act of defining the art form. By thinking at this level, some open themselves to a broader and more confident sense of what poetry can be and do. When students consider how an individual poem does or does not conform to their expectations of what a poem is, they may shake free from notions of poetry as remote and formal. They may begin to discover for themselves the special game poetry plays with language and experience—so different from our everyday use. They may discern that the stuff outside the parenthesis—"loneliness"—and that inside—"a leaf falls"—form the two basic components of a poem: the universal and the concrete. They may understand Edwin Arlington Robinson's observation: "Poetry has two outstanding characteristics. One is that it is undefinable. The other is that it is eventually unmistakable."

Choice

We have found that asking students to make a choice about a preferred poem or poet or interpretation, without analysis, creates an opening for response to poetry. Also, adolescents love to vote on things. Several settings for choice are possible both during a particular lesson and during an extended unit of study.

Selecting Among Poems. We present a set of short poems (six to eight) by an individual poet and ask students to volunteer to read each poem aloud. After all have been heard and before discussion begins, we ask students to state their individual preferences and their reasons for their choices. Of course, the objective of the activity is not a poll but involving students in hearing a variety of poems and talking about their preferences. Those who would be reluctant to analyze a poem can be caught off guard as they articulate their choices.

A less ambitious variation is to read two poems and ask students to state a preference. For instance, after reading Emily Dickinson's different views in "I Never Saw a Moor" and "Faith Is a Fine Invention," some side with her adamant faith, while others are drawn to her skepticism. In either case, the exploration of differences invites students to entertain questions of idea and form indirectly and to act on these impressions by taking tentative positions.

Choosing Between Poets. We ask students to choose between a few representative poems from two poets. For example, a perfect partner for Langston Hughes's "Hold Fast to Dreams" is Gwendolyn Brooks's "Kitchenette Building." We ask, "With which voice do you identify or agree?" Then we might press further: "Why?" For instance, do Hughes and Brooks differ on the hard facts of life or on the need for dreams? With a claim thus staked, students enter these poetry worlds unaware.

Debating over Ideas. A final choice can be set up between differing interpretations of one poem. Does one interpretation make more sense than another? For instance, does Frost's "Mending Wall" suggest that those who continually try to maintain walls between people are foolish? Or consider Montgomery's (1962) interpretation: Walls are essential for maintaining a communal civility. Which is more satisfying?

Poetry Anthologies. Scimone (1999) used choice in an extended poetry project to energize his passive tenth-grade students. He explains that nothing that he teaches requires the restraint that teaching poetry does. He believes that his "students' general lack of familiarity with poetry formed a vacuum that I was sorely tempted to fill. And yet, if I believed that literary discovery rather than literary information was at the center of imaginative learning, I would have to allow even unsophisticated readers to make some of their own choices" (p. 78). As a consequence, he asked students to construct poetry anthologies, "books" that would be "published" and public. The contents were (1) a preface stating the book's theme and, more important, the student's reasons for the choices made; (2) poems, between five and ten (the "core of the book"); and (3) some discussion of at least three of the poems. These discussions were to be simple and to contain an interpretation, examples of "figurative language, tone, and diction that the students thought were especially effective," and a personal response to the poem. These discussions could appear together after the poem or in any order the student judged to be most effective. Scimone also hoped that the students would enhance their books with visual appeal (pp. 78–79).

During the three to four weeks that students were researching, drafting, revising, and publishing, he was able to "present my own favorite poems and 'model' what I wanted them to do" (p. 79). In addition to the surprising poetic content and commentary of the student-created books, "what distinguished these 'books' from the flat, pro forma poetry papers I had assigned in previous years was a student voice that was richer, more genuine, and more engaging" (p. 80). In the all-important synthesizing preface, "many students ar-

rived at an apprehension of poetry as the best way to express certain kinds of human experience" (pp. 79–80).

Presenting students with choice promotes unexpected understanding of and excitement about poetry. Because talk, action, and reflection are necessary for personally owned choice, students are primed to regard poetry as living, not petrified. The only position that is unacceptable in this choosing is an uninvolved one.

Personal Response

When we ask advanced-placement English students in our local school system (Winston-Salem/Forsyth County, North Carolina) what they cherish most in their English language and literature classes, they almost invariably answer "the poetry responses." Each fall, teacher Becky Brown makes a long-term poetry assignment, often to disgruntled and disbelieving students.[8] By the spring this weekly writing task has become a chosen pleasure. The continual introduction of new poems, the absence of grading, the encouragement of personal response, the unusual use of the journal, and the teacher's accepting and encouraging return responses combine to open students to a personal discovery of the rewards of poetry. Brown teaches able, highly motivated students; but the exercise may be adapted for a range of classes. Her assignment, which she struggles each year to "get right," may enrich students at all skill levels. Appendix E contains two versions of her assignment as well as a list of poems that Brown has selected and that students have found inviting. She chooses poems that are pertinent to her classes, to the time of year, and to other literature being studied. Each year Brown also distributes sample poems and student responses as models for her current students. Figure 6–7 shows an example of one such model.

Andrasick (1990) suggests a strategy that has elements of Brown's poetry response applied to a whole-class reading of the same poem. She asks each student to keep a process log, which records the student's response, engagement, and interpretation of a poem in preparation for a whole-class discussion. Specific steps of her strategy include the following:

- reading the poem carefully for a general "understanding of the subject of the poem and the author's attitude"
- writing a brief (one- or two-sentence) statement about what the student thinks the subject is
- a second, more deliberate, reading with a reconsidered sense of the poem's core
- a rereading of step 2 and then rewriting or approving the first impression
- free-writing about the process of reading the poem

---

[8]Brown has adapted this project from an original idea by professor and poet Lawrence Raab of Williams College.

FIGURE 6–7

Student poetry response

Source: From *Poems 1960–1967* by Denise Levertov. Copyright © 1964 by Denise Levertov Goodman. Reprinted by permission of New Directions Publishing Corporation.

The Secret

Two girls discover
the secret of life
in a sudden line of
poetry.

I who don't know the
secret wrote
the line. They
told me

(through a third person)
they had found it
but not what it was,
not even

what line it was. No doubt
by now, more than a week
later, they have forgotten
the secret,

the line, the name of
the poem. I love them
for finding what
I can't find,

and for loving me
for the line I wrote
and for forgetting it
so that

a thousand times, till death
finds them, they may
discover it again, in other
lines,

in other
happenings. And for
wanting to know it,
for

assuming there is
such a secret, yes,
for that
most of all.

Denise Levertov

STUDENT RESPONSE

I like the poem, "The Secret," because it deals with the so-called secret of life. I believe in this great secret, and I believe that poetry, even one line, can make you realize the secret, if only for a brief moment. Sometimes I'll hear or read a poem that makes me realize something that I'd never thought about before, or that shines light on my thoughts about life and how it should be lived. If it is a poem I read in class, I'll think about the idea then, but later in the day or week it becomes lost. It is easy to forget the things you learn. Realizing a secret of life can be like a New Year's resolution, you swear that you will remember the secret and live by the secret, and I believe that some, but not many, can find it. I think I know the secret a lot of times, but other times I lose it. I would like to have the secret with me always, although it is fun to keep rediscovering it in new and exciting ways.

Marla Vaughan

This final step is crucial to the student's becoming aware of the process of reading—initial feelings, questions, confusions, and meanings. Her instructions for the process log are "Do not be concerned if you have questions and uncertainties; simply try to identify them as specifically as you can. You are trying to describe HOW you read and understood as well as WHAT you read and understood" (pp. 59-60). Andrasick poses questions to guide student reflection:

- What questions did you have [after your first reading]?
- What words/phrases were confusing?
- What words/phrases helped your understanding?
- What words/phrases seemed to have particular importance? Can you tell why?
- As you read the poem a second time, marking it, what insights did you have? (pp. 59-60)

Nelms (1988) recounts an incidental lesson that encourages just this personal response to poetry. She seized the moment of her students' early springtime restlessness and their pleas to have class out-of-doors. She had them go outside without talking or throwing Frisbees, read the poetry designated, and "take time to reflect in their quiet places, and then write in their journals for ten minutes before returning to class at the end of the hour" (p. 23). Then, in perfect synchronization with her lesson and her students' feelings, she saw them off by reading Wordsworth's "The Tables Turned." We include the whole text here because Wordsworth's short poem contains our same warning about shutting the doors of perception.

The Tables Turned

Up! up! my Friend, quit your books;
Or surely you'll grow double:
Up! up! my Friend, and clear your looks;
Why all this toil and trouble?

The sun, above the mountain's head,
A freshening lustre mellow
Through all the long green fields has spread,
His first sweet evening yellow.

Books! 'tis a dull and endless strife:
Come, hear the woodland linnet,
How sweet his music! on my life,
There's more of wisdom in it.

And hark! how blithe the throstle sings!
He, too, is no mean preacher:
Come forth into the light of things,
Let nature be Your Teacher.

She has a world of ready wealth,
Our minds and hearts to bless—
Spontaneous wisdom breathed by health,
Truth breathed by cheerfulness.

One impulse from a vernal wood
May teach you more of man,
Of moral evil and of good,
Than all the sages can.

Sweet is the lore which Nature brings;
Our meddling intellect
Mis-shapes the beauteous forms of things:—
We murder to dissect.

Enough of Science and of Art;
Close up those barren leaves;
Come forth, and bring with you a heart
That watches and receives.

William Wordsworth

Enactment

Chapter 4 presented many activities that use poems as the vehicle for dramatic action in the classroom. Drama can also "carry" poems. Narrative poems and ballads are clearly effective as drama, but practically all poems have a dramatic tension that students can enact. When a male and a female read Yeats's "For Anne Gregory" aloud or

John Wakeman's "Love in Brooklyn," the dramatic tension is palpable. The serious disagreement between Booker T. Washington and W. E. B. Du Bois in Dudley Randall's "Booker T. and W. E. B." comes vitally alive when spoken. In William Blake's "The Clod and the Pebble" and Ralph Waldo Emerson's "The Mountain and the Squirrel," two opposing points of view are represented by inanimate objects. As you read the following, imagine staging it.

The Clod and the Pebble
"Love seeketh not Itself to please,
　Nor for itself hath any care,
　But for another gives its ease,
And builds a heaven in Hell's despair."

So sang a little Clod of Clay,
　Trodden with the cattle's feet;
　But a Pebble of the brook
Warbled out these metres meet:

"Love seeketh only Self to please,
　To bind another to its delight,
　Joys in another's loss of ease,
And builds a Hell in Heaven's despite."

William Blake

The group Poetry Alive! performs poetry in schools and encourages teachers to organize poetry performance in their classrooms. Their teacher's edition of *Something Is Going to Happen: Poetry Performance for the Classroom* (Wolf, 1990) gives basic tips for poetry performance, fifteen scripted poems, director's notes, and additional learning activities. Figure 6-8 is their scripting of Leigh Hunt's poem "The Glove and the Lions" and their questions to

FIGURE 6-8
Script and sample questions for "The Glove and the Lions"

Source: From *Something is Going to Happen: Poetry Alive!* by Allan Wolfe, 1970, 48, 49 & 50. Asheville, NC: IAMBIC Publications. Reprinted with permission.

**THE GLOVE AND THE LIONS
BY LEIGH HUNT**

Suggested cast:
voice 1: the lady
voice 2: the knight
voices 3, 4, & 6: the court
voice 5: the King

voice 1	The Glove and the Lions
voice 2	by Leigh Hunt
voice 3	King Francis was a hearty king,
voice 4	and loved a royal sport,
voice 3	And one day as his lions fought, sat looking at his court;
voice 5	The nobles filled the benches,
voice 6	with the ladies by their side,
voice 3	And 'mongst them sat the Count de Lorge, with one for whom he sighed:
voice 1	And truly 'twas a gallant thing to see that crowning show,
voice 2	Valor and love,
voice 1	and a king above,
voice 2	and the royal beasts below.
voice 5	Ramped and roared the lions,
voice 6	with horrid laughing jaws;

FIGURE 6–8
continued

voice 1	They bit,
voice 2	they glared,
voice 3	gave blows like bears,
voice 4	a wind went with their paws;
voice 6	With wallowing might
voice 5	and stifled roar
voice 1	they rolled on one another,
voice 3	Till all the pit
voice 2	with sand and mane
voice 6	was in a thunderous smother;
voice 5	The bloody foam above the bars came whisking through the air;
voice 6	Said Francis then,
voice 5	"Faith, gentlemen, we're better here than there."
voice 6	De Lorge's love o'er heard the King,
voice 2	a beauteous lively dame,
voice 1	With smiling lips
voice 4	and sharp bright eyes,
voice 3	which always seemed the same;
voice 6	She thought,
voice 1	the Count my lover is brave as brave can be;
	He surely would do wondrous things to show his love of me;
	King, ladies, lovers, all look on; the occasion is divine;
	I'll drop my glove to prove his love; great glory will be mine.
voice 3	She dropped her glove,
voice 6	to prove his love,
voice 4	then looked at him and smiled;
voice 3	He bowed,
voice 6	and in a moment leaped among the lions wild;
voice 2	The leap was quick, return was quick,
voices 4–6	he has regained his place,
voice 4	Then threw the glove,
voice 2	but not with love,
voice 1	right in the lady's face.
voice 5	"By heaven,"
voice 3	said Francis,
voice 5	"rightly done!"
voice 4	and he rose from where he sat;
voice 5	"no love,"
voice 3	quoth he,
voice 5	"but vanity, sets love a task like that."

QUESTIONS TO CONSIDER

Character

1) The characters in this poem are members of the King's court. How would they act? What mannerisms can you adopt to let your audience know that you are a member of royalty?

Setting

2) What is the setting of this poem? How could you arrange your stage area and use available props to communicate this setting to your audience?

Action

3) This is your chance to really ham it up. The action of this poem should be purposefully overdone. How could you portray the count's jump into the lion's pit?

4) Consider, at the appropriate moments, changing roles from court attendants to blood-thirsty lions. You don't necessarily have to get down on hands and knees to do this. What are some alternative ways of portraying a group of ferocious lions?

Meaning

5) While this poem is a lot of fun, it also offers us a lesson. What is this lesson? Can you think of any moments in your own life when you "set a task" like the woman in the poem? Has someone ever asked *you* to do something undesirable just to test your loyalty?

consider for staging it. Their Web site contains other materials designed to help students become poetry performers: http//www.poetryalive.com/products.html.

A less ambitious activity teams a narrator/reader with mimes. In presenting Frost's "Home Burial," for instance, as one student reads the poem, two miming students, as the wife and husband, change places on stairs as the poem reveals their opposite but equal reactions to the death of their son. A more direct enactment stages the poem as a play with the words spoken in dialogue between two or three players.

Whether the enactment remains bound by or freed from the text, the spatial and kinesthetic properties of drama enliven the poems; the concrete gestures lend vitality to the read word. If drama is not possible, ask students to read the poems aloud with feeling, gesture, and emphasis. The ear and eye together can find delights of sound and sense that one alone would miss. If you have fluent speakers of other languages, urge them to read non-English-language poems *not* in translation. Table 6-4 contains poems that have been vitalized by dramatization.

TABLE 6–4
Poems for enactment

Author	Poem
Jonathan Swift (1667–1745)	"A Description of the Morning"
Percy Bysshe Shelley (1792–1822)	"Ozymandias"
John Greenleaf Whittier(1807–1892)	"The Farewell: Of a Virginia Slave Mother to Her Daughters, Sold into Southern Bondage"
Walt Whitman (1819–1892)	"A Noiseless Patient Spider"
Matthew Arnold (1822–1888)	"The Last Word"
Emily Dickinson (1830–1886)	"I'm Nobody! Who Are You?"
Lewis Carroll (1832–1898)	"Jabberwocky"
A. E. Housman (1859–1936)	"When I Was One-and-Twenty"
James Weldon Johnson (1871–1938)	"Since You Went Away"
Paul Laurence Dunbar (1872–1906)	"When Malindy Sings"
	"We Wear the Mask"
Walter de la Mare (1873–1956)	"The Listeners"
Robert Frost (1874–1963)	"Out, Out"
Carl Sandburg (1878–1965)	"Chicago"
D. H. Lawrence (1885–1930)	"Piano"
Ezra Pound (1885–1972)	"The River-Merchant's Wife: A Letter"
William Rose Benet (1886–1950)	"Stage Directions"
Archibald MacLeish (1892–1948)	"The End of the World"
Edna St. Vincent Millay (1892–1950)	"Oh, Oh, You Will Be Sorry for That Word"
Robert Graves (1895–1985)	"Traveller's Curse After Misdirection"
Arna Bontemps (1902–1973)	"A Black Man Talks of Reaping"
Langston Hughes (1902–1967)	"Ballad of the Landlord"
	"Harlem (A Dream Deferred)"
	"Minstrel Man"
Countee Cullen (1903–1946)	"From the Dark Tower"
	"For a Lady I Know"
C. Day Lewis (1904–1972)	"Walking Away"
Phyllis McGinley (1905–1978)	"Portrait of Girl with Comic Book"
W. H. Auden (1907–1973)	"O What Is That Sound"
Karl Shapiro (1913–2000)	"Autowreck"
Mari Evans (1923–)	"And the Hotel Room Held Only Him"
Maya Angelou (1928–)	"Africa"
	"Prescience"
Marge Piercy (1936–)	"A Work of Artifice"
Pat Mora (1942–)	"1910"
William Hathaway (1944–)	"Oh, Oh"
Alice Walker (1944–)	"Women"

Visualization

Teachers who have appealed to the eye's intelligence in their classes say that the study of poetry profits from it. A simple guided exercise, Teaching Activity 6–7, can connect students with imagery by asking them to imagine through their senses and then capture those impressions through their writing.

We can use art to prompt such visual imagining. We like to ask students to write poems inspired by photographs or paintings. Hollman (1989) explains the effects of taking her students to the library, giving them time to "re-experience the art books," and then quietly saying, "Find something in one of these that you're willing to spend some time with. I'm hoping a poem will come out of your time" (p. 24). The poems that emerged were remarkable: "These poems bristle with particulars, surprise the reader, focus on the moment rather than unarticulated longings or greeting card platitudes" (p. 27). Her account of the success of the assignment and the poems it produced is a strong rationale for linking the visual and the poetic:

> The art itself accounts for a lot. First, the writers' choices are generally powerful "stuff," and *they* choose it, to the extent it is reproduced in the library's collections. In these paintings, sculptures, or photographs, they encounter a piece of the world already shaped. Order has been imposed, details chosen; the undifferentiated landscapes of the world in which we see and feel have been particularized, composed, if you will. This frees the writer to confront the feeling, to enter the landscape, to concentrate on language to respond to or describe that world. The art, and perhaps the questions and talk which preceded the writing, seem to model a way of seeing, or organizing, experience so it can break out again in the poems. (p. 27)

Portraits, subject pieces, landscapes, and photographs provide excellent beginning points for many of our students: basic elements around which narrative, descriptive, or lyric poems can be imagined. (We have never encouraged epics!) If students are dubious, remind them that Stephen Crane based *The Red Badge of Courage* on Matthew Brady's pictures of the American Civil War. Hemingway borrowed ideas from Cézanne's landscapes to create passages in his fiction. Ray Bradbury credited his ability to write screenplays to his love of comic book illustrations as a child (Weaver, 1998, p. 155). Pop art and abstract art also stretch the imagination and invite students to see the world with fresh vision.

To open her unit on literature of peace, prejudice, and the Holocaust, Gorrell (2000) uses the photograph of a little Polish boy with arms upraised before Nazi machine guns and the poem written by a Holocaust survivor, Peter L. Fischl, in response to it. After her students imagine the reaction of a survivor to this picture, she tells them the real story of the photograph's and the poet's history. Without comment, she asks them to write "their own poems to the little Polish boy or anyone in the photograph. Keeping the instructions open and simple, I pose the following questions:"

- If you could speak to the little Polish boy, what would you say?
- If you could speak to anyone in the photograph, what would you say?
- If you could imagine any of the subjects speaking, what do you think they would say?
- On a new page in your journals, write any poem reflecting on your viewing of this photograph. You may reread your wonder questions and reflections to help you get started. (p. 35)

6–7 TEACHING ACTIVITY

Guided Imagery

Whole Class

1. Imagine that you have lost your eyesight (or any of the senses).

2. Close your eyes and try to bring into your mind's vision some of the sights (sounds, smells, tastes, or touches) that you believe you will most miss.

3. Can you remember past experiences in which your vision (hearing, touch, etc.) was heightened? At such times, did you seem to sense everything more clearly and vividly?

4. Choose one sight (sound, etc.) that you would greatly miss.

5. Jot down ways you would describe it to others.

Individual

Gather your impressions into a poem. Focus on the sensory image that you selected in step 4. Use your impressions (step 3) and descriptions (step 5) to render this particular sense.

After ten minutes, she has them read their poems in progress and, without any discussion, reflect in their journals what they "hear" in each poem, what each reveals about "the nature of violence, genocide, or human behavior." They can also write "wonder questions"—"What are you wondering at this moment?" (p. 35). Her final long-range assignment asks students to search for a "photograph, piece of art, monument, or sculpture that profoundly affects or inspires you" and then write a poetic response to this piece that includes

- describing what you see in detail
- addressing a subject in the piece
- assuming the "identity/persona of a subject in the work" and trying to imagine what that subject is saying, or thinking, or contemplating doing.
- reflecting upon the visual piece and your feelings when you first saw it.

Finally, students display their art pieces and present their poems to the class (p. 38).

Our students have also been delighted by those rare paintings that were the sources of poems. Poetry written in response to or as an interpretation of visual art, such as Fischl's "Little Polish Boy," is called *ekphrastic* (sometimes spelled *ecphrastic*) poetry. The most striking examples we know are six poems based on Pieter Brueghel's *The Fall of Icarus:*

Dannie Abse, "Brueghel in Naples"
W. H. Auden, "Musée des Beaux Arts"
Edward Field, "Icarus"
Michael Hamburger, "Lines on Brueghel's Icarus"
Joseph Langland, "Fall of Icarus: Brueghel"
William Carlos Williams, "Landscape with the Fall of Icarus"

Three other fairly accessible examples are X. J. Kennedy's "Nude Descending a Staircase," based on Marcel Duchamp's modern painting, *Nude Descending A Staircase, No. 2;* William Carlos Williams's "The Great Figure," based on his friend Charles Demuth's painting, *I Saw the Figure Five in Gold;* and Williams's "The Dance," based on Pieter Brueghel's *The Kermiss* (also called *Peasants Dancing*). (Williams has an entire volume inspired by Brueghel.) Inspiration can also flow from poetry to painting. Artist Larry Johnson has collaborated with poet Nikki Giovanni to illustrate her 1968 poem, "Knoxville, Tennessee," which Scholastic has published as a children's picture book. Brown (1992) corroborates the findings of Cage and Rosenfield (1989), who analyzed students' classroom reactions to ekphrastic poetry: "When the relationships between the poems and paintings are acknowledged, students' emotional and intellectual engagement with the texts is extended to new dimensions; the poem encompasses more and there is more to respond to simply because another art form is integrated into the literary text" (p. 44).

The following are useful books that link paintings and poems:

Abse, D., & Abse, J. (Eds.). (1986). *Voices in the gallery.* London: Tate Gallery.
Adams, P. (Ed.). (1986). *With a poet's eye.* London: Tate Gallery.
Benton, M., & Benton, P. (1990). *Double vision: Reading paintings...reading poems.* London: Hodder & Stoughton.
Hollander, J. (1995). *The gazer's spirit: Poems speaking to silent works of art.* Chicago: University of Chicago Press.

As Abse and Abse explain in their introduction, "The poet, through a personal vision and expression, brings to the subject a wider, sometimes entirely unexpected dimension, which in turn evokes new visual images" (pp. 11–12).

We can also connect specific works of art with particular poems. We can ask students to select and present art to match the poems they are reading. We can display paintings that are contemporary to a text to illustrate the wider historical and cultural context in which the writer was working. Questions of form and structure arise naturally and become more comprehensible when those techniques are demonstrated in another media. ESL teachers report that ESL students especially like using art as a prompt for writing or responding to literature. The visual allows a moment's pause from the verbal and supplies a common focus.

Synthesis

Our final approach begins in a reading of several poems that converge in structure or idea. We ask students to listen to the individual poems and then listen for echoes among the poems. Our directions for reading the following three poems are these words: "Enter the worlds of four insects, a mole, and a caterpillar and the three poets who observe them. Can you find any similarities in these accounts? Do the lives of these creatures converge in any way?"

An August Midnight

I

A shaded lamp and a waving blind,
And the beat of a clock from a distant floor:
On this scene enter—winged, horned, and spined—
A longlegs, a moth, and a dumbledore;
While 'mid my page there idly stands
A sleepy fly, that rubs its hands. . . .

II

Thus meet we five, in this still place,
At this point of time, at this point in space.
—My guests besmear my new-penned line,

Or bang at the lamp and fall supine.
'God's humblest, they!' I muse. Yet why?
They know Earth-secrets that know not I.

Thomas Hardy

The Mole

When the mole goes digging
He never meets a soul;
The stars are inattentive
To the motions of the mole.

He digs his frantic tunnel
Through chalk and clay and slime
His never-ending tunnel
A mouthful at a time.

Alone: no planet bothers
To tell him where to dig:
For moles are very little
And worlds are very big.

And when his tunnel ceases
The little mole lies stark,
And at his back is dimness
And at his head, the dark.

So to the mole all honor
And the labors of the mole,
With doubtfulness for tunnel
And ignorance for goal.

E. L. Mayo[9]

Cocoon

The little caterpillar creeps
Awhile before in silk it sleeps.
It sleeps awhile before it flies.
And flies awhile before it dies.
And that's the end of three good tries.

David McCord[10]

Students could, of course, analyze the structure and idea of each of these three poems individually and arrive at insights. A traditional classroom hour might center on just such careful, close scrutiny of single poems and not seem complete until all the details of that poem are accounted for. Our approach arrives at insight more broadly by asking students to suspend close reading and open themselves to the general impression that several poems make. A synthesizing approach requires no special knowledge or experience of poetry, just an open mind. Like analysis, it, too, uncovers meaning but without intimidating the reader, particularly the poetically timid or resisting reader. One poem sounds a theme, subsequent

poems repeat that theme or variations of it, and the cumulative effect is greater than one poem alone might achieve. The ideas take hold. After this approach is established, we ask the students to find poems that converge. To these three, for example, have come the mouse under Robert Burns's plow in "The Mouse," the worms under the battlefield in Thomas Hardy's "The Dynasts," and the beetle in John Hall Wheelock's "The Beetle in the Country Bathtub." Table 6–5 lists other groupings that we have used successfully.

☜ TALKING POETRY

These ideas for finding, forging, and reading poetry can stir students into caring about and responding to poetry in ways that the more traditional close reading of individual poems does not. After these initial encounters with poems, when poems matter to students and when they have a heightened sense of the way poems work, they can move toward considering and deepening their responses. As our discussions in Chapter 5 suggested, New Criticism (Formalism) is no longer the predominant critical approach to literature; yet it still has a mighty hold on the actual practice of high school and college classrooms. Whenever poetry is the class subject, poems are in danger of becoming individual specimens to be analyzed and the analysis is not complete until the poem's meaning has been explicated and its inner workings explained. All of that meticulous accounting for meaning and meter can enrich our reading if we have grown to care about the poem. But we cannot assume that high school students do. We must consider the question "What is the best way to talk about poetry together?"

Adolescent Readers

Let's visit those text-bound and teacher-centered classrooms. Here is a common scenario:

- The poem is read, aloud or silently, one or perhaps several times.
- The teacher guides students through a series of questions about the poem, soliciting their reactions and interpretations.
- The students' challenge is not to make sense of the poem for themselves but to figure out the definitive answer that the teacher or any literary scholar generally expects.
- Finding students' initial, often fumbling, answers inadequate, the teacher supplies the right answer (based often on years of reflection and research).
- The teacher moves to the next question or to a neat summing up of the final interpretation.
- The teacher's inward suspicion is confirmed: These are immature or disinterested readers who don't

---

[9] From Collected Poems, "The Mole," by E. L. Mayo, 1981. Reprinted with the permission of The Ohio University Press/Swallow Press, Athens.

[10] From *One at a Time*, by David McCord. Copyright © 1949 by David McCord; first appeared in *The New Yorker.* By permission of Little Brown & Co.

TABLE 6–5
Poetry groups: Duos, trios, quartets

African American experience
  Imamu Amiri Baraka   "Rhythm Blues"
  Countee Cullen   "Yet Do I Marvel"
  Langston Hughes   "The Negro Speaks of Rivers"
  Audre Lorde   "Coal"
Dreams
  Gwendolyn Brooks   "Kitchenette Building"
  Nikki Giovanni   "Revolutionary Dreams"
  Langston Hughes   "A Dream Deferred"
  William Butler Yeats   "He Wishes for the Cloths of Heaven"
Children and fathers
  Raymond Carver   "Photograph of My Father in His Twenty-Second Year"
  Robert Hayden   "Those Winter Sundays"
  James Reiss   "¿Habla Usted Español?"
  Theodore Roethke   "My Papa's Waltz"
The deaths of insects
  Karl Shapiro   "Interlude"
  John Updike   "Mosquito"
  John Hall Wheelock   "The Beetle in the Country Bathtub"
The deaths of mammals
  Maxine Kumin   "Woodchucks"
  William Stafford   "Traveling Through the Dark"
  Richard Eberhart   "The Groundhog"
The deaths of other living things
  Richmond Lattimore   "The Crabs"
  W. D. Snodgrass   "Lobsters in the Window"
  Miller Williams   "The Caterpillar"
Neighbors
  Robert Frost   "Mending Wall"
  A. R. Ammons   "Winter Saint"
The sinking of the Titanic
  Thomas Hardy   "The Convergence of the Twain"
  David R. Slavitt   "Titanic"
Springtime
  A. R. Ammons   "Eyesight"
  e. e. cummings   "spring is like a perhaps hand"
  William Wordsworth   "I Wandered Lonely as a Cloud"

like poetry and don't have a clue about how to unlock its riches.

• The students' inward self-doubt is confirmed: Poetry is too remote or arcane for me ever to figure out. Only English teachers can make sense of it. Well, let them!

Dias (1996) thinks an important first step to reforming such a classroom is to understand this central question: "What happens in the transaction between adolescent readers and poems?" He believes not all students respond to poetry in the same way. Dias sensitively describes the four patterns of response that are common in the high school classrooms he studied (Figure 6-9). These are not static, inviolable patterns; they are changing and dynamic ones. As readers try to make sense of poetry, they develop working strategies based on what they can comfortably do and what they infer their teachers expect. Dias enumerates these strategic patterns, not as narrow categories with which to label and judge students but as sympathetic attempts to understand what happens within adolescent readers when they encounter a poem

(pp. 49-72). His description provides insight and holds implications for our approach to poetry in high school English classes.

Readers of any age might find themselves identified with one group more than another. An awareness of these types of readers is an important beginning step toward helping students to become more responsive, independent, committed readers. Imagine the difficulties of a problem-solving reader who is confronted by fellow readers who are paraphrasers, thematizers, and allegorizers ready to dismiss many details of the text and to settle as quickly as possible on a solitary meaning, finish the reading, and move on. (Imagine that the thematizer were the teacher!)

Leggo (1991) worries "that students frequently reflect their teachers' reading orientations. In other words, students learn to read poetry from experiencing the way teachers read poetry, and teachers are often paraphrasers, thematizers, and allegorizers intent on revealing the meaning . . . and closing down the transaction with the text" (p. 58). Billy Collins's poem "Introduction to Poetry" vividly captures the difficulties of introducing poetry to

	READER'S EXPECTATIONS	READING APPROACH	READER'S CLOSURE
Paraphrasers	To restate the text in one's own words discloses meaning (usually one of several stock themes)	To work out meaning from the sentence or word level often directed by an impression based on the initial reading	To close soon after a first or second retelling even if gaps appear; sometimes to add a moral or lesson
Thematizers	To find the simple theme—a statement or generalization about life—which underlies the poem	To use any means available—a series of different probes—to arrive at a meaningful statement of theme	To set the poem aside as soon as a satisfactory theme is discovered or to abandon the search if no coherent account emerges
Allegorizers	To uncover the poem's extended statement about life—to work out the "equivalence between the poem and the real world"	To work from an initial feeling or intuition about the poem and align its details to that generalization	To rest when a complete sense of the poem has developed even if there are gaps or flaws in this interpretation
Problem Solvers	To explore several possibilities of meaning and connections to one's own experience	To approach a poem as a complex artifact and so to try a variety of strategies to test tentative hypotheses	To delay closure until difficult aspects of the poem can be accommodated; to realize that a poem continues to unfold its meaning

FIGURE 6–9   Dias's four kinds of adolescent poetry readers

students when what they want to do with a poem is "tie" it "to a chair with rope/and torture a confession out of it" (p. 16). Rather than trying to reconstruct all students as problem solvers, Dias suggests various strategies so that students can develop confidence in their own individual resources as poetry readers and entertain alternative ways to read. Central to his reforms is the provision that teachers help students grow as independent readers.

The first three sections of this chapter aimed at setting students loose to find poetry, to write it, and to approach it without the teacher's analytic mediation. That focus on students' response permeates the fourth section as well: talking about poetry. As poet Octavio Paz (1956) reminds us, "Now, the poem is just this: a possibility, something that is only animated by the contact with a reader or a listener. There is one note common to all poems, without which there would be no poetry: participation. Each time the reader truly relives the poem, he reaches a state that we can call poetic. The experience can take this form or that, but it is always a going beyond oneself, a breaking of the temporal walls, to be another" (p. 14).

Selecting Poems

Selection of the poems for class is crucial. We have reiterated throughout this chapter that we often begin with short, contemporary poems. These have several advantages:

- The vocabulary and allusions are usually within the grasp of students, so the teacher does not have to become the more knowing expert and explainer.
- The poem's context is more likely known or accessible to students.
- The brevity reduces poetry anxiety and focuses attention on a manageable number of lines.

- Much contemporary poetry uses language, subjects, and tone that are familiar to students and so breaks down stereotypes of poems as formal and elevated.
- Dias (1996) suggests that "students will come to realize that their own experiences are relevant to uncovering the experiences presented in the poem" (p. 85).

Heard (1989) explains another criterion for choosing: "I don't just pick poems that I think my students will like; I choose poems that I like, that I can share. If I read kids poems that don't interest me, it shows in my voice; I've had to take the time to search for words that satisfy us both" (p. 5). We add another criterion: Choose poems that are still fresh and intriguing for you as the teacher. Goldberg (1986) tells the story of hearing Galway Kinnell read his just published *Book of Nightmares,* a reading in which he "sang those poems." Six years later, she heard him read the same poems again, and this time the "air was no longer electric." As a poet herself, she recognized that for Kinnell "there was nothing dangerous for him in them anymore" and that for any poet, and we would say any teacher of poems, "it is very painful to become frozen with your poems, to gain too much recognition for a certain set of poems" (p. 33). A final criterion is to select from a variety of poets who in their difference will touch diverse kinds of experience and craft.

After choosing, prepare students to read a poem more than once. As Meyer (1996) reminds us, "like a piece of music, a poem becomes more pleasurable with each encounter" (p. 607).

Listening to Poems

We have discussed poetry's appeal to the eye and to the ear. The sounds of words—vowels, consonants, rhyme, alliteration, meter, and rhythm—create pleasure, produce effects, and contribute to meaning. Silent or prior reading may be necessary for longer poems. But if poems are shorter, reading aloud is important. In addition to the pleasure that the sounds bring, listening to poems can also uncover sense. Often, passages that have resisted understanding suddenly fall into place.

Lucy Calkins (1986) writes of prose: "It is listening that creates a magnetic force between writer and listener. The force of listening will draw words out; writers will find themselves saying things they didn't know they knew." Listening is equally, perhaps more, important to poetry. Heard (1989) quotes Stanley Kunitz: "Above all, poetry is intended for the ear. It must be felt to be understood, and before it can be felt, it must be heard. Poets listen for their poems, and we, as readers, must listen in turn. If we listen hard enough, who knows—we too may break into dance, perhaps for grief, perhaps for joy" (p. 8).

The brown bat in Randall Jarrell's *The Bat Poet* (1965, p. 15) says to himself, "The trouble isn't making poems, the trouble's finding somebody that will listen to them." Often an anxiety about time, an impatience to move to the next text, and an uncertainty about students' genuine interest become the great enemies of oral reading and even silent rereading in the classroom. We counsel ourselves and others with this reminder: If you have done the work to create an environment in which students are enthusiastic about poems, trust what the sound will yield and trust the students to be willing to be still and listen.

Audio resources can provide a new voice, and often a professional one, to animate poetry study. Textbook publishers frequently include in their teacher resources audiotapes of skillful readers, even the poets themselves, reading poems. If you do not have your own resources, scour textbook rooms and ask other teachers about them. We have found the following sources helpful:

Bill Moyers: The Power of the Word [11]
PBS Video
1320 Braddock Place
Alexandria, VA 22314

The Academy of American Poets
588 Broadway
Suite 1203
New York, NY 10012
212-274-0343
http://www.poets.org/

Bill Moyers: The Language of Life: A Festival of Poets
PBS Video [12]
1320 Braddock Place
Alexandria, VA 22314
800-424-7963

The Atlantic Monthly Group [13]
77 North Washington Street
Boston, MA 02114
617-854-7700

The Writer's Center
4508 Walsh Street
Bethesda, MD 20815-6006
301-654-8664
http://www.writer.org/gallery/gallery.htm

Modern Poetry Association
60 W. Walton Street
Chicago, IL 60610
312-255-3703
http://www.poetrymagazine.org/toc_mpa.html

Discussing Poems: Setting, Approaches, Questions, Sequences

If our aim is to encourage autonomous readers, small-group discussions hold clear advantages. They remove the teacher from the position of expert and transfer the responsibility for response and interpretation to the students. They also allow students to sort out their reactions without the fear of failure that whole-class, teacher-led discussions often invite. In this process, students are more likely to discover positions that differ from those they thought were self-evidently correct and to reconsider their original views. They also might be more likely to talk about the personal experiences that the poem evokes. In the freer pull and haul of a small group, students gain confidence in their responses.

Whether you organize small-group or whole-class discussions, you will profit from the advice of other poets and teachers. We turn now to five of them. National and regional poets at New Jersey's East Brunswick High School Poetry Celebration (Lockward, 1994) gave sound suggestions to teachers:

Poets' Advice on What Not to Do with Poetry

- Do not explain the poem to students.
- Do not give tests on poetry.
- Do not be overly concerned with techniques.
- Do not approach a poem with historical matters.
- Do not impose the critics on students.

Poets' Advice on How to Teach Poetry

- Expose students to beautiful, powerful language.
- Allow time for multiple oral readings of a poem.
- Lead discussions that encourage a personal relationship with a poem.
- Teach contemporary poetry first and then go backwards in time.
- Teach poems you don't fully understand.
- Teach poems that are accessible to students.

---

[11] Bill Moyers's six-part videotape series. Tapes and teaching kits are also available.

[12] This video series is available for purchase through http://ww.amazon.com or at 800-257-5126. A companion book has been written for this program that contains brief introductions, pictures, interview segments, and from three to sixteen poems of thirty-four contemporary poets.

---

[13] In addition to comments, reviews, features, and appreciations, *The Atlantic Monthly's* online Poetry Pages also list audio soundings.

- Allow students to sometimes choose their own poems.
- Provide opportunities for students to write poetry. (pp. 65-70)

We like an analogy that Meyer (1996) uses to introduce readers to poetry:

> Come to it, initially at least, the way you might listen to a song on the radio. You probably listen to a song several times before you hear it all, before you have a sense of how it works, where it's going, and how it gets there. You don't worry about analyzing a song when you listen to it, even though after repeated experiences with it you know and anticipate a favorite part and know, on some level, why it works for you. Give yourself a chance to respond to poetry. The hardest work has already been done by the poet, so all you need to do at the start is listen for the pleasure produced by the poet's arrangement of words. (p. 589)

First comments or questions can set the tone and direction of the class. At the poetry celebration Lockward (1994) describes, poet Craig Czury suggested a number of questions that he would like readers and listeners to ask of his own poems:

- What does the poem remind you of?
- What did you think about while listening to it?
- Where did your mind go?
- Has anything been said in the poem to remind you of something in your life?
- What pictures did this poem give you? And what feelings do you get from those pictures?
- Does the poet bring up ideas you'd like to ask him or her about? Ideas you've often thought about yourself?
- How does the poem make you feel? And what has ever happened in your life that has left you with a similar feeling? (p. 67)

Golub (1994) suggests an effective sequence for discussing poetry that allows students to be "responsible for their own meanings" rather than passive discoverers of "a predetermined meaning imposed on the poem by the teacher" (p. 102). He suggests that a poem be introduced in this manner:

1. Read the poem aloud.
2. Ask students to "write down three questions they have about the poem."
3. Divide the class into small groups and instruct each group to answer the questions raised.
4. For the whole class, a recorder from each group summarizes the group's questions and conclusions.
5. The entire class adds its responses and interpretations. (p. 103)

Leggo (1991) asks students to respond to poetry by writing questions about individual poems. Then he and they decide whether or not to try to answer them. As he explains, "too many students grow up with the mistaken notion that all questions have answers. . . . The advantages of doing nothing with the questions are multiple: the poem remains open, the questions hint at tantalizing ideas and experiences and people and places to pursue, and the questioner remains open" (p. 60).

Poets Talk

One of the pleasures of exploring poems and the poets who write them is reading these poets' prose reflections on their art. The concision and playfulness, observation and insight that they bring to poetry makes for memorable prose as well. We have found a number of quotations useful at serendipitous moments in our teaching. Many of these are scattered through this chapter. Some of our favorites are gathered in Figure 6-10.

FIGURE 6–10
Poets on poetry

W. H. Auden	"Of the many definitions of poetry, the simplest is still the best: memorable speech."
Gwendolyn Brooks	"Poetry is life distilled."
Samuel Taylor Coleridge	Poetic faith is that "willing suspension of disbelief for the moment."
Ralph Waldo Emerson	"Poetry must be as new as foam, and as old as rock."
Robert Frost	"Poetry is that by which we live forever and ever unjaded. Poetry is that by which the world is never old."
Christopher Fry	"Poetry has the virtue of being able to say twice as much as prose in half the time, and the drawback, if you do not . . . give it your full attention, of seeming to say half as much in twice the time."
A. E. Housman	"Experience has taught me, when I am shaving of a morning, to keep watch over my thoughts, because, if a line of poetry strays into my memory, my skin bristles so that the razor ceases to act."
Josephine Miles	"I like the idea of speech—not images, not ideas, not music, but people talking—as the material from which poetry is made."
Percy Bysshe Shelley	Poetry is the "record of our own best and happiest moments." "Poets are the unacknowledged legislators of the world."
Wallace Stevens	"Poetry is a search for the inexplicable." The poet is "the priest of the invisible."
Wei T'ai	"Poetry presents the thing in order to convey the feeling. It should be precise about the thing and reticent about the feeling."

We conclude this section on reading poetry with Robert Frost's moving analogy between a poem and love. In the preface to his 1939 *Collected Poems,* Frost draws a parallel between the shape of love and "the figure a poem makes": "It begins in delight, it inclines to the impulse, it assumes direction with the first line laid down, it runs a course of lucky events, and ends in a clarification of life—not necessarily a great clarification, such as sects and cults are founded on, but a momentary stay against confusion." Frost (1973) wrote to Edwin Arlington Robinson about an ambition not unlike ours that runs through all of these suggestions and activities: "The utmost of ambition is to lodge a few poems where they will be hard to get rid of" (p. 126).

✑ PLACING POETRY

We turn finally to consider an essential question: Where does poetry fit in the curriculum? The approaches and activities of this chapter have focused so intently upon poetry that you may have begun to envision teaching poetry as a separate unit all its own. Particularly when the course of study is organized around genres, the temptation to teach poetry only as an isolated subject is great and sometimes necessary. When students are more comfortable with prose, it is tempting to plan a quick poetry unit around a holiday or during the dog days after exams. A separate unit may seem necessary when state end-of-course tests emphasize the vocabulary of poetic craft and when national writing exams favor the use of longer prose works. But just as language, writing, or, we will argue later, nonfiction profit from being taught in conjunction with other subjects, tasks, or genres, so does poetry.

We have found the integrated study of poetry and prose to be synergistic. Those unique poetic qualities—radiant images, figurative and compressed language—make it a highly transportable and effective ally for delivering that knockout punch to a period, whether as an entry, an exploration, or an extension of other literature and language. Especially if a long work is under study—a novel, novelette, or drama—poetry can highlight, enrich, and enlarge a fictive element or idea whose shape can become diffuse during the sprawl of extended reading assignments. Logistically, poems can richly fill a period while students are spending their homework or even some in-class time reading the longer work.

Some of these classroom links between poetry and prose are essentially stylistic. F. Scott Fitzgerald's editor, Maxwell Perkins, in commenting on *The Great Gatsby,* said: "The manuscript is full of phrases which make a scene blaze with life." A scholar observed that Fitzgerald "merges the craft of the novelist with the craft of the imagist poet." Fitzgerald is not alone among novelists, which

may explain why novels are excellent resources for the imagery of found poems. Mitchell (1995) has students reread parts of a novel with attention to those places that evoke vivid pictures in their minds. They then arrange them "poetically" on a page. She reports that students who might resist a discussion of the novelist's use of language willingly share their poems and respond to their classmates'. One example of a poem created from Stephen Crane's *The Red Badge of Courage* demonstrates the power of the lesson:

> The blue smoke-swallowed line
> curled and writhed
> like a snake stepped upon
> It swung its ends to and fro
> in an agony of fear and rage. (p. 67)

Such a discussion of language use might prove the truth of Mark Twain's classic comment on the power of the chosen word: "The difference between the right word and the almost right word is like the difference between the lightning and the lightning bug."

In Teaching Activity 6–8, we adapt the lesson of a teacher who asked students to find the poetry in a prose passage from John Steinbeck's story "Flight." The virtues of any passage of well-written prose can be isolated and illuminated by this activity. It is essentially what William Butler Yeats did when he edited the *Oxford Book of Poetry* in the early twentieth century. He chose to begin the book by breaking a passage from Walter Pater's "The Renaissance" into poetic lines.

Jeff Morgan directs his students from poetry to prose in order to sharpen their understanding of basic characteristics of each—poetic narrative and newspaper exposition. His sophomores read "Parents" by Julius Lester and "Out, Out" by Robert Frost and then convert the poems into newspaper articles. Morgan believes that operating between the two genres reveals more about the uniqueness of each than considering one alone could possibly show.

Teachers also link specific prose texts and particular poems because of the interplay of "a sense or idea." Mitchell (1994) uses Mel Glenn's (1982) *Class Dismissed!* to introduce Paul Zindel's *The Pigman.* She reads aloud the poems "Dora Antonopolis," "Rickie Miller," "Benjamin Heywood," "Jason Talmadge," and "Faith Plotkin" and then discusses their common expression of alienation. Next, small groups list ways in which adolescents feel alienated at home or in school and sometimes create "a story, script, or poem that in some way illustrates alienation" (p. 79). When the class turns to John and Lorraine, they empathize more readily with the characters' distance from their families. (Teachers also find Mel Glenn's volumes to be excellent leads into the study of Edgar Lee Masters's *Spoon River Anthology.*)

Zitlow (1995) reports on the poetry connections made by teachers and students to three young adult novels: Bette

6–8

TEACHING ACTIVITY

Tone Poems from Prose: John Steinbeck's "Flight"

Individual

- Select a page of prose.

- Choose ten nouns, ten verbs, ten adjectives, and (if you wish) five adverbs. List these words in four columns. Look for unusual or powerful words or just words that particularly strike your fancy. (*Teacher:* on the board, make four columns, one for each of these parts of speech.)

- Select one or two of the most striking words from your list for the columns on the board.

Whole Class

- Each class member may write one of his or her "best" words in the appropriate column. (The number allowed will vary according to the class size.)

Individual

- Attempt your own tone poems. You are free to use any of the board words along with your own list. You may also compare notes with a neighbor, borrowing any words that seem attractive.

- (*Teacher:* Hand out models of poems composed by other classes if they are available or ones you created using this model. *Tip:* It works best if you choose a model from a different source. Otherwise, the models can be limiting.) Keeping the models in mind, combine the words on your lists in any fashion you choose. Look for unusual combinations and striking images.

Greene's *Summer of My German Soldier* (ranging from Emily Dickinson's "I'm Nobody" to Myra Cohn Livingston's "The Secret"); Bruce Brooks's *The Moves Make the Man* (Arnold Adoff's "We Are Talking About" and "Trilingual," John Updike's "Ex-Basketball Player," and Mel Glenn's "Neil Winningham"); and Gary Paulsen's *Hatchet* (Jean Toomer's "Banking Coal" and Felice Holman's "Loneliness"). These connections were not simply to a central idea but to the novels' settings, moods, situations, and characters. The students mirror "what proficient readers and writers do: make comparisons to prior reading, read a variety of literature and consider different points of view, make and defend interpretations and judgments, listen to the ideas of other readers" (p. 110). Some links are even more direct. Golub (1994) connects Ray Bradbury's short story "There Will Come Soft Rains" and Sara Teasdale's poem "There Will Come Soft Rains." We link Maya Angelou's *I Know Why the Caged Bird Sings* with Paul Laurence Dunbar's "Sympathy" ("I know what the caged bird feels, alas!").

As you know from your study of literature, many writers wrote extraordinary prose *and* poetry. Even when they are remarkable in both genres, mixing an author's genres delights students and illuminates and enriches both texts. Some of our favorite authors of prose, poetry,

and drama include William Shakespeare, Herman Melville, Stephen Crane, Thomas Hardy, T. S. Eliot, Jorge Luis Borges, Carlos Fuentes, Maya Angelou, Raymond Carver, John Updike, and Alice Walker.

You may also have students use poetry templates to describe fictional characters. Such imaginative play often uncovers deeper insights than students realize they possess. Robert Hamm's two students wrote this bio-poem about Dr. Heidegger of Nathaniel Hawthorne's "Dr. Heidegger's Experiment."

Doctor
Eccentric, curious, singular, old
Friend of Medbourne, Killigrew, Wycherly,
   Gascoigne,
Lover of Sylvia, magic, a rose,
Who feels isolated, alone, old,
Who needs friendship, experimentation, love,
Who gives medicine, free champagne, second
   chances,
Who fears his own youth,
   Who would like to see results, happiness,
      common sense,
   Resident of Massachusetts,
   Heidegger.

And of course, poetry templates can provide a scaffold for students' capturing *their* response to a text.

Resources. The following Internet sites are teacher-recommended for the poems, activities, and poetry resources they present and for the numerous creative links they include.

Playing Around with Poetry (http://www.english. unitecnology.ac.nz/resources/units/poetry/home. html): a list of helpful poetry Web sites (appropriate for elementary as well as secondary)

Poet's Corner (http://www.galegroup.com/free_ resources/poets.htm): authoritative biographies of more than twenty poets, activities, a timeline, and other poetry resources

Poetry Pals Resources, Activities & Lessons for Teachers (http://www.geocities.com/EnchantedForest/ 5165/pages/lessonplans.html): lesson plans, activities, and assessment ideas for K–12, including a rubric that can serve as a model for your own assessment plans

The Atlantic Online Poetry Pages (http://www.the atlantic.com/unbound/poetry/poetpage.htm): a multimedia feature devoted to poets and poetry, both classic and contemporary

American Verse Project (http://www.hti.umich.edu/ a/amverse): a searchable electronic archive of American poetry prior to 1920

Poetry for Everyone (http://dent.edmonds.wednet. edu/imd/poetry.html): a compiled list of useful poetry links for K–12

Poetry Index of Canonical Verse (http://eserver.org/ poetry): poetry links from the Carnegie-Mellon English server; also essays, humor, and other links

Creating Drama with Poetry: Teaching English As a Second Language Through Dramatization and Improvisation (http://www.cal.org/ericcll/digest/ Gaspar01.htm): two teachers, Marie Gasparro and Bernadette Falletta, with excellent ideas for helping ESL students "explore the linguistic and conceptual aspects of the written text"

Of course, you can use a search engine to search by specific categories. There are a growing number of home pages of specific poets—from the established, such as Emily Dickinson, to the little known. The Modern Poetry Association (MPA), a nonprofit organization, publishes *Poetry* magazine. Its Web page explains that it "also sponsors educational programs, readings, and other events to promote understanding and appreciation of the art of poetry" (http://www.poetrymagazine.org/toc_mpa.html). Appendix E lists books on poetry and teaching poetry that we have found helpful. Appendix E also lists poets who have held the position designated "Consultant in Poetry to the Library of Congress" from 1937–1986 and as "Poet Laureate Consultant in Poetry" since 1986. These poets present excellent starting points for you and your students as explorers of new verse.

Two weeks after the September 11, 2001, catastrophe, *USA Today* tapped the five most recent poet laureates for a poet's response because the editors felt "war and poetry have come together since Homer sang of the Trojan War in the *Iliad*" (Donahue & McKelvey, 2001). Poet Adam Zagajewski explains that people turn to poetry in hard times because, "for a while, they don't seek entertainment but a different solace: poetry; even the most 'modern' poetry, doesn't shun the tragic vision—and there's sometimes a moment when people's needs and poetry's vocation do overlap" (as quoted in Donahue & McKelvey, 2001, p. 1D). Billy Collins, the 2001–2003 poet laureate, also explains in this issue how poetry "has always accommodated loss and keening": "It's not that poets should feel a responsibility to write about this calamity. All poetry stands in opposition to it. Pick a poem, any poem, from an anthology and you will see that it is speaking for life and therefore against the taking of it. A poem about mushrooms or about a walk with the dog is a more eloquent response to Sept. 11 than a poem that announces that wholesale murder is a bad thing" (p. 13A).

Invitation to Reflection 6–2

1. Wormser and Cappella (2000) report that "at the beginning of the twentieth century, poetry comprised a full 50% of the reading material in standard school texts; today it is less than 3%" (p. 341). Speculate on why the amount of poetry has plummeted. In your ideal textbook, would you devote more than 3 percent to poetry? Why?

2. Return to your answers to Invitation to Reflection 6–1 that began this chapter. As you have begun to imagine your own classroom, has your answer to question 1 shifted or intensified?

3. Look at your characterization of your former teachers in questions 3, 4, and 5. As you read this chapter, did you find some alternatives to the strategies they used to teach poetry? If your teachers had used these, would it have made a difference in your experience of poetry in school?

4. Name any teaching ideas from Chapter 6 or from your observations of middle and high school teachers that are new to you and seem promising for students.

5. Think of yourself as a first-year teacher whose eleventh-grade students have typically been taught by teachers who are paraphrasers, thematizers, and allegorizers (Dias, 1996). They are used to moving quickly through several poems in a class period after they have answered the essential question for each one: What does this poem mean? Design a lesson that nudges your students toward developing confidence in themselves

as poetry readers and delight in poems as rich sources for their reading. Include some of the teaching ideas you named in question 4.

6. Design a lesson that brings poems into your study of a particular thematic unit or prose text. Reconstruct at least three activities suggested in this chapter for your purposes.

∞ CONCLUSION

We present these strategies to help our students enter and explore poetry and to extend it into their lives. As Meyer (1996) explains, "we read poems for emotional and intellectual discovery—to feel and experience something about the world and ourselves. The ideas in poetry— what can be paraphrased in prose—are important, but the real value of a poem consists in the words that work their magic by allowing us to feel, see, and be more than we were before" (p. 595). We hope that some of these activities can cause students to fall into Robert Frost's poetry trap. He says, "My poems are all set to trip the reader head foremost into the boundless."

In many *English Journal* articles, teachers attest to their own faltering approaches to poetry that began in traditional formal analysis and moved, in despair, to experiments with experiencing poetry. One such teacher, Lott (1989), explains that she resorted to traditional approaches out of her own private delight in poetry and her unwillingness to risk the students' rejection of it. When she tried alternative strategies of "not teaching" poetry, she remembered "why I had wanted to be a teacher in the first place: to share what I love with those who are growing" (p. 68). She then draws an analogy that we like: She compares introducing her students to poetry with introducing her mother to her husband-to-be. "I didn't say to her, 'Look at the symmetry of his legs,' or 'Do you hear that special note in his voice?' Instead, I muttered, 'Mom, I want you to meet Gary,' and sat there petrified while she looked at him through her eyes and asked him her questions" (p. 68). And, she concludes, "analysis comes after recognition, and it rarely precedes love, maybe because we all have our own set of questions that we formulate only after something matters to us" (p. 68).

We hope that our approaches to poetry—finding, forging, reading, talking, and placing—provide you with ideas for just such an introduction for your students. Perhaps someday one of them may even bring to poetry feelings similar to those of Emily Dickinson:

If . . . it makes my whole body so cold
no fire can warm me, I know that is poetry.[14]

---

[14] Reprinted by permission of the publishers and the Trustees of Amherst College from THE POEMS OF EMILY DICKINSON, Thomas H. Johnson, ed., Cambridge, Mass.: The Belknap Press of Harvard University Press, Copyright © 1951, 1955, 1979, 1983 by the President and Fellows of Harvard College.

7

Opening
Texts

⟳ *The debate over the literary
canon has taken on great
importance because it
embodies most of the key
educational issues of our time:
the knowledge that is most
worth teaching, the teacher's
role in fostering independent
thinking, the extent to which
schools will reproduce the
social order or create a new,
equitable order.*

Anne Ruggles Gere,
Colleen Fairbanks, Alan
Howes, Laura Roop, and
David Schaafsma ⟳⟳

The last two chapters considered the process of teaching
texts. This chapter focuses on the selection of those
texts. As recently as thirty years ago, such a chapter
might have concerned itself with an introduction to the
great western tradition of classic novels, short stories,
plays, and poetry. In fact, as a young teacher, one of us
lived constantly with a haunting sense that she had not
read the classics and, more worrisomely, could not exactly identify them. No sooner would she read one "masterpiece" and become a bit more secure in the field than
two more books would appear with claims of equal urgency to be read. Today, with an expanding canon, the
young teacher has an even more daunting task. The battleground of text selection is one of the most contested
in English education. We want to prepare you for the fray.
We turn first to identify the classics and then to defenders and challengers of this established canon.

⟳ THE CLASSICS

The term *classic* was originally used to designate the literature, art, and culture of ancient Greece and Rome, revered
for centuries by western scholars and educated people. It
was then extended to include any piece of literature that
by common consent was considered superior—that is,

189

which achieved the high quality of Greek and Roman masterpieces. The term itself, according to Funk (1978), has a "slight touch of snobbery about it, for the roots of *classic* are in the Latin word *classicus,* which meant 'of the first rank' and was applied to the upper and better classes of Rome" (p. 309). Thus, before *classic* became used for everything from late-model cars to mass-produced hamburgers, it meant "to be in the first rank of literature."

And what standards distinguish the first rank? In *The Western Canon: The Books and School of the Ages,* Harold Bloom (1994) has his own "ancient test for the canonical [that] remains fiercely valid: unless it demands rereading, the work does not qualify" (p. 30). T. S. Eliot believed a classic was "a work of art that does not yield up its secrets easily." Samuel Johnson gave the common answer: A masterpiece is a work that has stood the test of time. An aggregate of masterpieces has come to be assumed as the heritage of any educated person, a literary tradition to be passed from one generation to the next. That body of individual masterpieces is called the *canon.*

Historical Roots of the High School Canon

In his history of the teaching of English, Applebee (1974) examines an important question for the secondary English teacher: How did the high school literary canon evolve? He delineates the role of college entrance requirements in determining both that canon and, more importantly, English as a field of study in its own right. In fact, he sees these entrance requirements as the "moving force" of the rapid evolution from no formal instruction in literature in 1800, to its introduction into schools as a "handmaiden of other studies" by 1865, to its almost universal presence as an important study of its own by 1900 (p. 30).

In the late nineteenth century, college applicants were not assessed on the basis of SAT scores or common applications but on entrance examinations constructed by each college. Colleges announced topics in advance and thus dictated the preparatory school's curriculum for the year. Literature first became established in the college entrance requirements as a vehicle for demonstrating competence in nonliterary fields such as philology, rhetoric, and grammar. Applebee places a "real milestone" at Harvard's 1873–1874 requirements, in which literature was to be studied for the purpose of writing a short composition on a subject to be taken from "one of the following works: Shakespeare's *Tempest, Julius Caesar,* and *Merchant of Venice;* Goldsmith's *Vicar of Wakefield;* Scott's *Ivanhoe,* and *Lay of the Last Minstrel.* This requirement institutionalized the study of standard authors and set in motion a process which eventually forced English to consolidate its position within the schools" (p. 30).

As other colleges and universities set their own examinations and as these changed from year to year, preparatory schools were severely taxed. By the early 1890s, their call for uniform requirements produced regional and then national conferences and commissions whose work resulted in the clarification, unification, and validation of various aspects of English instruction within American schools and colleges. The most influential of these bodies, the conference commissioned by the nationally appointed Committee of Ten, issued their statement of the purpose of English studies in 1892:

> The main objects of the teaching of English in schools seem to be two: (1) to enable the pupil to understand the expressed thoughts of others and to give expression to thoughts of his own; and (2) to cultivate a taste for reading, to give the pupil some acquaintance with good literature, and to furnish him with the means of extending that acquaintance. (quoted in Applebee, 1974, p. 33)

Contained within this statement are central issues that remain sources of definition and debate more than one hundred years later: the processes of English study as understanding, expression, and appreciation and the subject of English study as good literature.

Texts in the High School Canon

In 1892, as now, works considered to be "good literature" were passed from one generation to the next, often by unspoken consensus. Over time, some works dropped from reading lists and classrooms as others were added. To orient you to what contemporary high school English teachers and educators consider to be good literature, we mention several lists of the most frequently selected long works by anthologizers, teachers, and Advanced Placement (AP) test constructors. They will demonstrate the evolution from Harvard's 1873–1874 list.

Arthur N. Applebee's 1988–1989 Study. In the late 1980s, Arthur N. Applebee (1993), director of the federally sponsored National Research Center on Literature Teaching and Learning, undertook four separate but interrelated studies designed to produce a comprehensive picture of the content and approaches to the teaching of literature in U.S. high schools.[1] The sample for the survey of required book-length works was large and diverse: public ($n = 322$), Catholic ($n = 80$), and independent ($n = 86$) schools with classes that were noncollege preparatory, college preparatory, and mixed-track in grades 7–12 in urban, suburban, small-town, rural, and mixed communities. In Tables 7–1 and 7–2, we list his findings of the most frequently required books (grades 7–12) and authors (grades 9–12). In public school grades 9–12, 64.7 percent of these long works were novels, 25.5 percent were plays, 7 percent were nonfiction, and the remainder were collections of poems and short stories.

---

[1]Several other comprehensive studies of the teaching of English have been conducted since the early 1960s: Lynch and Evans (1963), Anderson (1964), Squire and Applebee (1968), and Applebee (1978, 1981, 1984).

In Table 7-1, note that in these top twenty-seven only two authors are women and none are minorities; four works are by Shakespeare, three are by Steinbeck, and two are by Dickens. Table 7-1 also compares 1988 titles with a 1963 study conducted by Anderson (1964). Only *Silas Marner* disappeared from the list (from being third on the list, taught in 76 percent of schools, to being taught only in 15 percent). Table 7-2 shows the data compiled by author. Because the ranks were based on the number of times a work by an author was taught, the figures reveal the magnitude of emphasis on the most popular authors. The majority of required texts were from the twentieth century (61 percent in public schools, for instance). Twelve percent of those texts were published since 1960. The results were almost identical for public, Catholic, and independent schools.

Applebee also examined the seven most commonly used literature anthologies (as cited by schools in his national survey). The forty-two volumes with 1989 copyrights came from the following publishers: Harcourt Brace Jovanovich; Scott, Foresman; Holt, Rinehart, and Winston; McDougal, Littell; McGraw-Hill School Division; Prentice Hall; and Scribner Laidlaw (pp. 228–229). Table 7-3 lists the most frequently anthologized long fiction, excerpts from long fiction, and plays.

Advanced Placement Lists, 1981–2001. A list of titles that have been used on AP literature exams between 1981 and 2001 appears in Appendix F. This list might be regarded as unrepresentative, produced by college and secondary teachers sensitive only to college-bound high school students far removed from the majority of secondary English classrooms. Still, while targeted for one segment of students, its influence reaches other segments as AP courses proliferate and their courses of study affect book selection in nonacademic classes

TABLE 7-1

Titles of book-length works required in 30% or more of the public schools, grades 7–12

Title	Author	Percent of Schools 1988 (n=322)	1963 (n=222)
Romeo and Juliet	Shakespeare	90	14*
Macbeth	Shakespeare	81	90*
Huckleberry Finn	Twain	78	27*
To Kill a Mockingbird	Lee	74	8*
Julius Ceasar	Shakespeare	71	77
Pearl	Steinbeck	64	15*
Scarlet Letter	Hawthorne	62	32*
Of Mice and Men	Steinbeck	60	<5*
Lord of the Flies	Golding	56	<5*
Diary of a Young Girl	Frank	56	6*
Hamlet	Shakespeare	56	33*
Great Gatsby	Fitzgerald	54	<5*
Call of the Wild	London	51	8*
Animal Farm	Orwell	51	5*
Separate Peace	Knowles	48	<5*
Crucible	Miller	47	<5*
Red Badge of Courage	Crane	47	33*
Old Man and the Sea	Hemingway	46	12*
Our Town	Wilder	44	46
Great Expectations	Dickens	44	39
Tale of Two Cities	Dickens	41	33
Outsiders	Hinton	39	0*
Pigman	Zindel	38	0*
Death of a Salesman	Miller	36	5*
Tom Sawyer	Twain	32	10*
Miracle Worker	Gibson	32	<5*
Red Pony	Steinbeck	31	5*

Source: From Applebee, A. N. *Literature in the Secondary School: Studies of Curriculum and Instruction in the United States.* NCTE, p. 71. Copyright © 1993 by the National Council of Teachers of English. Reprinted with permission.

*Percentage significantly different from 1988 sample, *p.* < .05.

TABLE 7–2
Ten most frequently required authors of book-length works, grades 9–12

Author and Cumulative Percent of Titles Required					
Public Schools (*n* = 322)		**Catholic Schools** (*n* = 80)		**Independent Schools** (*n* = 86)	
Shakespeare	364	Shakespeare	358	Shakespeare	334
Steinbeck	150	Steinbeck	140	Steinbeck	101
Dickens	91	Dickens	108	Twain	76
Twain	90	Twain	96	Dickens	69
Miller	85	Miller	83	Miller	61
Orwell	70	Hemingway	76	Hawthorne	56
Lee	69	Sophocles	75	Fitzgerald	53
Hawthorne	67	Hawthorne	73	Sophocles	51
Hemingway	60	Lee	67	Homer	47
Fitzgerald	54	Orwell	66	Lee	47
Golding	54				

Source: From Applebee, A. N. *Literature in the Secondary School: Studies of Curriculum and Instruction in the United States.* NCTE, p. 72. Copyright © 1993 by the National Council of Teachers of English. Reprinted with permission.

TABLE 7–3
Most frequently anthologized long fiction, excerpts from long fiction, and plays

Most Frequently Anthologized Long Fiction

Title	Author	Appearances						
		Total*	7	8	9	10	US	UK
The Pearl	Steinbeck	7	0	1	0	6	0	0
Great Expectations	Dickens	5	0	0	5	0	0	0
The Call of the Wild	London	5	1	3	1	0	0	0
A Christmas Carol	Dickens	4	3	1	0	0	0	0

Most Frequently Anthologized Excerpts from Long Fiction

Title	Author	Appearances						
		Total*	7	8	9	10	US	UK
Le Morte d'Arthur	Malory	7	0	0	0	4	0	7
Frankenstein	Shelley	6	0	0	0	0	0	6
Gulliver's Travels	Swift	6	0	0	0	0	0	6
A Journal of the Plague Year	Defoe	5	0	0	0	0	0	5
Moby Dick	Melville	4	0	0	0	0	4	0
The Adventures of Huckleberry Finn	Twain	4	0	0	0	0	4	0
The Adventures of Tom Sawyer	Twain	4	4	0	0	0	0	0

Most Frequently Anthologized Plays

Title	Author	Appearances						
		Total*	7	8	9	10	US	UK
Julius Ceasar	Shakespeare	7	0	0	0	7	0	0
Macbeth	Shakespeare	7	0	0	0	0	0	7
Romeo and Juliet	Shakespeare	7	0	0	7	0	0	0
Our Town	Wilder	7	0	0	0	2	5	0
The Miracle Worker	Gibson	6	0	2	4	0	0	0
Pygmalion	Shaw	6	0	0	0	0	0	6
The Diary of Anne Frank	Goodrich and Hackett	6	0	5	0	1	0	0
Antigone	Sophocles	4	0	1	1	2	0	1

Source: From Applebee, A. N. *Literature in the Secondary School: Studies of Curriculum and Instruction in the United States.* NCTE, p. 233. Copyright © 1993 by the National Council of Teachers of English. Reprinted with permission.
*Total means number of series out of seven. This may be less than the sum of the individual grade levels.

through teachers' talks with each other, their familiarity with selections, and the availability of texts. At the least, these titles represent the works that AP examiners consider what American colleges expect of the educated student.

☞ THE CANON WARS

When you begin to consider whether particular works exist that should be read by all high school students, you are on the boundary of an academic battleground in the canon war. Implicit in such a question is the notion that there is a body of writing that all literate or educated people should have read.

∞ Invitation to Reflection 7-1

1. Have you ever wondered why teachers seem to choose to teach certain literary texts over and over again?
2. Can you explain how a book becomes assigned to the following hierarchy of literary value?
   - literary masterpiece
   - minor classic
   - popular classic
   - ethnic literature
   - women's literature
   - regional literature
   - escapist fiction
   - trash
3. Think of the most recent novel you have read, classic or contemporary. Under which category would it fall? How would you explain your categorization?
4. Why are bestsellers so often excluded from classrooms as not fit to be read?
5. Do you assume that this hierarchy (its definition and selection) has been formed by natural, objective evolution (survival of the fittest) or by biases (historical and cultural)?
6. Do you think that there is general consensus among the most literate readers about what makes a literary work great?
7. Do you assume that those in academic literary circles generally agree on the criteria of greatness?

Cultural Literacy

In the last decades of the nineteenth century, Matthew Arnold, a school inspector, critic, and poet, was the most influential spokesperson for the "tradition," the "best that is known and thought in the world," a shared bulwark against forces threatening civilization. The American who perhaps most embodied and articulated Arnold's views of cultural education was Horace Scudder, a member of the Cambridge, Massachusetts, school committee; chief editor at Houghton Mifflin; and later editor of the *Atlantic Monthly*. His argument for acceptance of English

study in American schools was that literature (namely the classics) had the effect of "spiritualizing life, letting light into the mind, inspiring and feeding the higher forces of human nature" (as quoted in Applebee, 1974, p. 24). Another pioneer in English education, Fred Newton Scott, the first president of the National Council of Teachers of English (NCTE) and the only president to serve two terms, made similar claims. He, in fact, identified the debate over a common core of literature as one of the two crucial problems facing English teachers in NCTE's first year. In his 1912 NCTE presidential address, Scott (1913) responded to a suggestion for making literature study more vital and interesting by substituting current magazine essays and stories for the "obsolete," "outworn" classics:

> What will the readers of the current magazines remember a few years hence? Still more important, what that is worthwhile will they remember in common? One of the best things that can be said about the old classical education is that it created a community of interest in something great, noble and finely wrought. I believe that we must continue to teach in the school and the university what cannot be learned by ordinary students under ordinary conditions in the street and the shop, namely, the ideal values of men and things in society. For this purpose a certain detachment from the commonplace will always be necessary, and this is supplied by the fittest survivals of man's past expressions and communications. To make modern ears sensitive to the music of bygone ages will never cease to be one of the noblest of the teacher's functions. When we abandon that hard task for the easy appeal to current superficial interests, we rob the student of the best gift which it is ours to bestow. (pp. 8-9)

Mortimer Adler, Robert Maynard Hutchins (both at the University of Chicago), and Mark Van Doren in the 1930s and 1940s echoed this same sentiment in their quarrel with progressive education. Adler saw reading as "a means toward living a decent human life." He introduced his list of the "Great Books," a collection of the seminal works of the western tradition, as the only reading worth doing. Hutchins called the tradition that passed knowledge from one thinker to another the "Great Conversation." Van Doren critiqued progressive education's neglect of this tradition of "the deep resemblances between human beings, calling for a fixed program of learning which no child may evade, and the importance of the past" (as quoted in Applebee, 1974, p. 186).

Two influential books in the 1980s, Alan Bloom's *The Closing of the American Mind* (1987) and E. D. Hirsch, Jr.'s, *Cultural Literacy* (1987), intensified this debate. Bloom critiques university faculties that lack purpose and students who lack understanding of themselves and knowledge of literature and philosophy. He explains the consequence: Our culture is failing to learn from the tradition of the great thinkers of the past who projected a prescription for the present and a vision of the future.

Hirsch believes that this shared background, this "network of information that all competent readers possess" (p. 2), is necessary to create a common culture. In order to communicate and to engage in literate discourse, citizens must share a core of common knowledge. In an appendix to *Cultural Literacy*, Hirsch, Kett, and Trefil actually offer a preliminary and provisional list of 5,000 names, places, dates, terms, quotes, and concepts that they believe all literate Americans should know. Scholes (1998) calls these the "infamous list of cultural nuggets" (p. 80). Other books and reports that appeared in the 1980s captured American uneasiness with the education of the young. Bennett (1984), Ravitch and Finn (1987), and Cheney (1987) all point to the failure of education to halt and reverse what they see as the intellectual and cultural impoverishment of students. Their solution for the nation's teachers, and high school English teachers specifically, is to become more rigorous in teaching the classics of our culture—its language and its literature.

◯◯ Invitation to Reflection 7–2

1. What explicit and implicit notions of the literary classics were present in your high school and college English classes? Which of the following seems to have been the characteristic assumption of your teachers?
   - Literary classics are texts to be covered and lists of authors, works, literary conventions, and timelines are to be mastered for admittance to colleges and universities.
   - Literary classics connect you to what is noblest and most enduring in human history.
   - Literary classics are a means to a deepening understanding of yourself and your world.
2. Teachers often use the following rationales to explain their choice of texts. Check any that you were told in school. Star the most persuasive rationales for your choice of teaching texts.
   - These books are classics, masterpieces, or exemplary examples of literary greatness.
   - Everyone studies them.
   - They are something everyone should know.
   - They are centered around timeless or universal truths.
   - You'll need to know them in college.
   - They will probably be on your AP, SAT, or ACT exam.

Teaching the Tradition

The rationale for teaching the classics often carries with it an implicit pedagogical approach. The "best that has been thought" has the authority of decades, even centuries, and therefore can be transmitted only by the authorities who have come to possess and understand this knowledge. Because these works have such a revered place in our culture, some teachers assume that their interest will be immediate and their meaning self-evident. In fact, because most were written in times and with language different from our own, and many are long and challenging to read, students feel especially unqualified and uninspired to read them. Indeed, parallel teaching materials, *Cliffs Notes*, and school traditions so surround the most commonly read masterpieces that they often become mystified for teacher and student alike and thus removed from the easy reach of novices.

Brazilian educator Paolo Freire (1970) sees a dangerous analogy between education and banking in which education is "an act of depositing," the students are "the depositories," and the teacher is "the depositor." "Instead of communicating, the teacher issues communiqués and makes deposits which the students patiently receive, memorize, and repeat" (p. 58). Even though the students have become mere receivers, filers, and storers, teachers continue to "fill" students with "contents which are detached from reality, disconnected from the totality that engendered them and could give them significance" (p. 57). Ironically, "the more meekly the receptacles permit themselves to be filled, the better students they are" (p. 58). Teachers are vulnerable to this banking system. Because they themselves have been chastened and inspired by the weight of decades of critical analysis and interpretation of the classics, they believe that their deposits of knowledge in the empty accounts of their students' minds are necessary and significant: This *is* education. And the most efficient banking method often appears to be the lecture.

Renewing the Canon

Canon defenders such as Bloom, Hirsch, and Bennett use it as a kind of secular scripture, a frame of reference that dogmatically affirms or denies certain expressions. Wielding the canon, they appear to wall off literature and culture into a protected preserve approached only by a narrow path, which they have marked. Poet, artist, scholar, and teacher Jack McMichael Martin (1991) explains the tradition in another way—as an inheritance handed down from one generation to another that has within it seeds of a message to those who follow. The seeds are fertile and have great power for growth, but they are only a beginning. These classic seeds are unfinished and wait for our use to flower. They are forerunners only and tell us not to take their words as absolute but to use them "to release the word not yet realized." They have the "fecund power" of the past responding to the present and preparing for the future. Hutchins's metaphor of the Great Conversation captures the same dynamic. Knowledge, when passed to another, does not remain immutable but is modified, altered, and refined.

Martin (1992, personal conversation) explains something about how the conversation goes. He sees the author as sender and students as receivers. The young are apprentice readers, and their apprenticeship is active and toilsome. Martin sees reading as an attempt to "gain what the work has that is beyond oneself. This is the most active reading of all because it involves an imaginative leap beyond one's self-shackling urgencies and drives. Teachers must teach the young the virtue of contemplation, a listening for echoes and resonances within the integrity of the text. The strength of their reading is in the strength of their response to that which they are not and which surpasses them."

Postman (1995) adds a final frank and practical point about the dynamic of the canon:

> As to the legitimacy of canons, the word simply refers to agreed-upon examples of excellence in various genres of creativity. Any canon can be added to, modified, or even discarded if it no longer serves, in part or whole, as a model of excellence. This means that any canon is a living, dynamic instrument, and it is certainly not limited to those artists who are dead, and long dead. The long dead dominate for the obvious reason that their works have given pleasure and instruction to diverse people over long periods of time. They have earned, so to speak, their place. To the extent that teachers believe in the importance of conveying a sense of continuity in artistic creation, they must give respectful attention to the long dead. But, of course, teachers must not be reluctant to include models of excellence produced by living artists. (pp. 168–169)

❧ FIVE CHALLENGES TO THE CANON

Challenges to a canonical approach to literature—its content and its method—appear from several different directions. We turn first to three challengers from the fields of educational reform and literary criticism. The first, critical pedagogy, grows in part from a historical/sociological critique of culture and education. You will recognize the second and third, deconstruction and reader response, from Chapter 5.

Critical Literacy Challenge[2]

In *Textual Power,* Robert Scholes (1985) reasons that students must learn to make personal meaning out of texts because they must come some day to make personal meaning out of the world. "If wisdom, or some less

grandiose notion such as heightened awareness, is to be the end of our endeavors, we shall have to see it not as something transmitted from the text to the student, but as something developed in the student by questioning the text" (p. 14). Richard Shaull makes just that distinction between using texts to integrate students into "the logic of the present system" or to liberate them through "the practice of freedom" (Freire, 1970).

Greene (1978) grounds the practice of freedom in the everyday challenge to shake fully awake and to "transcend passivity." For teacher and student alike, the pursuit of freedom depends on the individual's changing awareness and consciousness. Schools should be places where teacher and learner practice what it means to be authentically human: not a static state but a dynamic one; not a fixed state but a process of continual becoming; not something ready-made or preexistent but something created and re-created. Our realities are not fixed and predetermined but are perpetually emerging and becoming more varied "as more perspectives are taken, more texts are opened, more friendships are made" (Greene, 1988, p. 23). Greene reminds us that we create ourselves by reaching beyond what exists at present to bring something new into being. Education aids that project when it becomes "a process of futuring, of releasing persons to become different, of provoking persons to repair lacks and to take action to create themselves" (p. 22).

Critical pedagogy does not leave the individual to practice freedom in reflective isolation outside of a social context. Self-understanding is grounded in a social understanding of the self in the world. Critical reflection becomes possible if we consider the world, not as an inevitable and unchangeable given but as something upon which we can act. We are not passive pawns in the grips of predetermined, unfolding destinies. We are creatures of will, intentionality, and responsibility. If we animate students' sense of agency, we necessarily invite them to care about and respond to the world around them. Critical pedagogists would say that their daily round of existence is the proper text for school.

These theorists quarrel with the canon because it distances students from their authentic experience and is usually taught by the banking method that Freire describes. In an English classroom, "lifeless and petrified" texts do not inform students about their own experience in memorable ways or empower them to act on that experience. Instead, these texts alienate them from their own abilities to choose as self-regulating human beings. Giroux and Simon (1988) see the conservative model of education as legitimating "forms of pedagogy that deny the voices, experiences, and histories through which students give meaning to the world and in doing so often reduce learning to the dynamics of transmission and imposition" (p. 10). Critical theorists contend that schooling has refused to admit the most important components of students' real lives and has included only a narrow definition of what is appropriate

---

[2] We use the terms *critical pedagogy* and *critical theory* to refer to the perspective of a group of scholars from several fields (sociology, history, and education) who pose a serious critique of the fundamental structure of human society. They feel that the schools reflect the culture, especially its preoccupation with "hierarchy, conformity, success, materialism, control" (Purpel, 1989, p. 20). Critical theorists include, among many others, Michael Apple, Henry Giroux, Maxine Greene, David E. Purpel, Kathleen Weiler, and, most notably, Paolo Freire.

for education. Freire (1970) believes that, apart from inquiry, human beings "cannot be truly human. Knowledge emerges only through invention and reinvention, through the restless, impatient, continuing, hopeful inquiry men pursue in the world, with the world, and with each other" (p. 58). If the works of the canon are central to the English classroom, the danger is that the gulf widens between class life and the real life lived outside of class. Critical theorists, like deconstruction and reader response theorists, would broaden the criteria for selection of texts for study and toughen the questions raised in that study.

Invitation to Reflection 7-3

Linda Christensen (2000), a teacher you met back in Chapter 3 reflecting on her struggle over the pronunciation of "lawyer" in Mrs. Delaney's ninth grade, believes in critical literacy as moving "beyond a description of society and into an interrogation of it. . . . Critical literacy questions the basic assumptions of our society" (p. 56). She uses a basic format to organize her units of study. Read her four basic steps and then plan a lesson or unit of study using this paradigm.

1. a question that provokes the examination of historical, literary, and social "texts";
2. the study and involvement of students' lives;
3. the reading of a variety of texts, ranging from novels to historical documents, to first-person narratives, to movies, speakers, role-plays, and field trips; and
4. a final project that opens the possibility for students to act on their knowledge. (p. 56)

As a model, here is a brief sketch of Christensen's unit for a course called "Contemporary Literature and Society" (pp. 53–67):

1. *The question:* Is language political?
2. *Students' lives at the center:* Student experience is central to every aspect of study, but one early activity involves their writing a poem using the template discussed in Chapter 6 based on George Ella Lyon's poem "Where I'm From."
3. *Samples of the assignments for reading the word and the world:*
   - *Wild Meat and Bully Burgers,* by Lois Ann Yamanaka (1966)
   - *Pygmalion,* by George Bernard Shaw (1914/1951)
   - "How to Tame a Wild Tongue," by Gloria Anzaldúa (1987)
   - "Achievement of Desire," by Richard Rodriquez (1982)
   - *Brothers and Sisters* (segments), by Bebe Moore Campbell (1994)
   - *Talkin' and Testifyin',* by Geneva Smitherman (1997)
   - *Rethinking Schools* (ebonics issue), by T. Perry and L. Delpit, editors (1997)

4. *Writing the world and moving beyond classroom walls:* After the readings and viewings, discussions and debates, students write essays—not essays "that demonstrate a close reading of a novel" or an "evaluation of the text" but that "tackle larger social issues that have urgent meaning in their lives" and that use their words to "affect other people" (pp. 62–63).

After you complete your unit, consider Christensen's final appeal for critical literacy in school. Do you agree or disagree?

Language arts teachers need to explore more than the best practices, the newest techniques in our profession; we need to explore and question the content as well. Too often, the work of critical literacy is seen as necessary in inner-city schools or in schools where students of color represent the majority of the student body, but it is deemed unnecessary in schools where the majority of students are of European descent. I would argue that critical literacy is an emergency in these schools as well. How else are students who have only been exposed to the status quo going to recognize and resist injustice? Students must learn to identify not only how their own lives are affected by our society, but also how other people's lives are distorted or maligned by the media and by historical, literary, and linguistic inaccuracy. (pp. 64–65)

Deconstructionist Challenge

We discussed deconstruction in Chapter 5 as an influential critical perspective at the end of the twentieth century. Its preeminence in academic circles has been challenged by other approaches—"the next wave"—but deconstruction continues to influence attitudes toward the canon. Deconstructionists quarrel with basic assumptions about definitions of greatness. We summarize their position briefly with an often-told baseball anecdote:

A seasoned umpire was behind home plate and a young hitter was at bat. The tension was high for the young player. He was sweating with every pitch. After a fast ball whizzed over the plate, the umpire paused in his calling of balls and strikes. The hitter, puzzled, turned and said, "Well, what was it? A ball or a strike?" The umpire gazed directly at him and slowly said, "Sonny, it ain't nothin' till I call it."

The player assumes that balls and strikes are brute facts that enjoy an independent existence in the world. The umpire refuses to acquiesce to this common assumption of a world of preexisting facts that he must recognize and name. He understands that balls and strikes are not independent of his verbal actions. What we take to be real and indisputably there is the product of our way of thinking. Deconstructionists point out that the umpire is operating as they are: with a social construction of reality.

The traditional view was that nature exists outside of us and waits to be interrogated and described by our activity. The deconstructionist view is that we are continually making and remaking our world. Those things that present themselves as inevitable and natural are, in fact, constructed. Nature and—even more pertinent to us—literature are products of human activity. Thus, to the question of whether, for example, Pat Conroy's *The Prince of Tides* is a masterpiece, popular fiction, or trash, deconstructionists answer: "Sonny, it ain't nothin' till I call it."

Whereas before 1965, credentialed experts answered such questions definitively and, purportedly, with an unbiased appeal to objective criteria of greatness, today deconstructionists contest the authority of anyone's making such literary value judgments. They assume that the text is re-created by every reader and are suspicious of anyone's making an authoritative claim of "classic." They have scrutinized and challenged the established masterpieces in traditional university curricula. They have shaken literary assumptions about greatness and have empowered readers to make their own interpretations. The following are two effects on the selection and teaching of texts:

- Deconstructionists look for the historical or political motives of canonization. For instance, they note that Shakespeare's place in the canon evades scrutiny because he has become a well-merchandised commodity and the profit motive sustains mistakes. They point out that Hawthorne was included in the canon because he had influential connections—he roomed with a future U.S. president at Bowdoin College—and had children devoted to preserving his memory who persuaded the *Harvard Classics* editors to include his work in the first edition of the series, where he has been canonized ever since. Some call deconstruction a "technique of trouble" as adherents undermine our certainty in the primacy of certain literary texts. It opens the curriculum to a variety of print and nonprint texts, including westerns, romance novels, and soap operas.
- Deconstructionists unsettle our confidence in the inherent and transcendent meaning of certain texts. They demonstrate, as Eagleton (1983) observes of Paul de Man, "that literary language constantly undermines its own meaning" (p. 145). We sometimes suspect that their inclusive selections are appealing because they are easy targets for the deconstructionists' "ironic, uneasy business, an unsettling venture into the inner void of the text which lays bare the illusoriness of meaning, the impossibility of truth and the deceitful guiles of all discourse" (p. 146).

Reader Response Challenge

Reader response is both a critical and a pedagogical approach to literature that emphasizes experience *through* literature rather than experience *of* or *with* literature. Like deconstruction, such an approach defines how any reader reads an individual text but also how any teacher selects texts to be read. The classics present particular difficulties for teaching and selection. They have become so deified and mystified by the public, teachers, and even students that their reputations can interfere with the central focus—not the work itself but the intimate personal response of the reader, what Rosenblatt (1978) calls "the web of feelings, sensations, images, ideas that he weaves between himself and the text" (p. 137). An established text can sink the reader beneath the weight of its title alone. It can too easily become an inert set of meanings waiting to be deciphered. Reader response critics believe that literature lives and is re-created by the reader's action upon it. Meaning is born in the transaction between the reader's active mind and the words of the text. Rosenblatt (1968) writes that "all the student's knowledge about literary history, about authors and periods and literary types, will be so much useless baggage if he has not been led primarily to seek in literature a vital personal experience" (p. 59).

Rosenblatt understood that her emphasis on the response in the reader would meet with much resistance and would require new teaching approaches to be realized. In her view, the primary role of teachers of literature "is to foster fruitful interactions—or, more precisely, transactions—between individual readers and individual literary works" (pp. 26-27). She believed that "sound literary insight and esthetic judgment will never be taught by imposing from above notions of what works should ideally mean" (pp. 33-34). Instead, she suggested some principles for the sort of instruction that would arouse, challenge, refine, and enlarge the reader's response to literature:

- First, is the necessity not to impose a set of preconceived notions about the proper way to react to any work.
- Scrutinize all practices to make sure that they provide the opportunity for an initial crystallization of a personal sense of the work.
- [M]aintain the conviction that it is important to place the discussion of the text in the matrix of personal response. . . . [K]eep the discussion moving along consistent lines by eliciting the points of contact between different students. (pp. 66-71)

Basic to this approach is "to reject the routine treatment of literature as a body of knowledge and to conceive of it rather as a series of possible experiences" (p. 74). We must remove literature from a privileged shelf that only teachers and academics can reach and that students must passively gaze at.

If classics are selected, they should be read with the reader in mind, not the tradition. When the criteria for selection shifts to the reader, then other texts become more desirable. Classics are not privileged choices for teachers. Clearly, some texts are not suitable for students at particular stages of their development, even if they are in the canon. If the canon has no work that is age and stage appropriate, the teacher should feel free to look at a wider range of genres. Science fiction might engage some; young adult novels might engage others. With the emphasis on the student's response, the range of choices becomes broad.

Invitation to Reflection 7-4

1. Imagine that you are teaching average high school juniors in a large urban high school. Convinced by the arguments of reader response advocates, you decide to build a modern American poetry unit around the "poetry" of rap music. A parent calls to complain that this is her child's only chance to read the giants of modern American poetry. She wants to know why you are not teaching Robert Frost, e. e. cummings, and Langston Hughes. You try to explain your reasons and use as a final clincher that, in the fall of 1997, the University of California at Berkeley taught a course entitled "The Poetry and History of Tupac Shakur." She is not appeased. Her child can hear rap on the street. You need a stronger rationale. How would you respond?

2. Imagine that you have been chastened and have decided to plan a more conventional unit with two poems as centerpieces of your discussions: a Robert Frost poem, "The Road Not Taken," and a Langston Hughes poem, "Mother to Son." You resolve to remain true to a reader response approach in your teaching of these poems in class. Consider these questions:
   • Does a reader response approach imply that you should turn students loose to make any interpretation they want of a text?
   • Are there an infinite number of possible interpretations roughly equivalent to the number of readers?
   • Do readers have interpretive autonomy free of any textual constraints?
   • Are the author and the reader equally creative?

3. The irate mother calls back: "If you encourage young readers to make any interpretation of the text they want, you are allowing students to miss the message of the most powerful visionaries of the culture." How do you answer?

4. Imagine now that you want to organize this poetry unit with your primary emphasis on the ideas of critical pedagogy. How would you structure your classes to do the following?
   • place students at the center of study
   • invite critical reflection about the world
   • use texts to discuss the students' experience and the world's condition
   • use texts to question the status quo
   • enlarge students' thinking about their own life hopes
   • challenge the tradition of a literary canon

5. Finally, imagine planning the unit with the ideas of deconstruction paramount in your mind. The following are questions that deconstructionists might ask themselves as they approach texts. Read them and decide whether they represent ideas with which you are comfortable.
   • How can I encourage students to question the established structure and language of these poems?
   • How can I help students to expose the biases and assumptions of the poet?
   • How can I help students to expose the hidden and silenced ideas here?
   • How can I help them to uncover the contradictions in the text and to dismantle its pretense to a solitary and fixed meaning?

(We confess to a worry about deconstructivist practices in high school and think to ourselves: Aren't many secondary students unconscious deconstructionists anyway, who regard literary texts as unsubstantial fictions, easy marks on the page, sitting ducks open for anyone's playful instincts rather than serious subjects for inquiry? Do we not undermine our basic attempt to engage students through literature by raising deconstructive questions?)

We turn now to two final challenges. These two embody the practical consequences on text selection of many of the philosophical and political ideas of the first three. In the last quarter of the twentieth century, nothing had more impact on the texts taught in middle school and high school English classrooms than an appeal for young adult fiction and multicultural literature. These two challenges to classic texts are a part of the same call we hear in the first three—an appeal for greater openness to texts and responsiveness to students.

Genre Challenge: Young Adult Fiction

One response to the call has been to open classrooms and criticism to a greater variety of literary genres. Before we consider the resources of young adult fiction—the genre that has had the most revolutionizing effect on English classrooms—we reflect on the distinction often made between "high" and "popular" culture. This culture difference burst into public notice in October, 2001, when

Jonathan Franzen, author of *The Corrections,* a novel that had glowing reviews, a nomination for a National Book Award (which it later won), and a place on *The New York Times* best-seller list, was chosen for Oprah's Book Club. So great is the effect of Winfrey's seal of selection that his publisher immediately increased the initial 90,000-copy print run to 500,000. But Franzen, naïve and inexperienced with the press he has claimed, demurred. He said that he was afraid being chosen would make him "misunderstood": "I feel like I'm solidly in the high-art literary tradition. . . . She's picked some good books, but she's picked enough schmaltzy, one-dimensional ones that *I* cringe, myself, even though I think she's really smart and she's really fighting the good fight" (as quoted in Giles, 2001, p. 68). Winfrey rescinded her invitation that he participate in her televised book club discussion and implied that her viewers might as well stop reading the book. Editorialists and commentators led a chorus criticizing Franzen's literary snobbism. Jacquelyn Mitchard, whose novel *The Deep End of the Ocean* was Winfrey's first book club selection, said, "It confirms everything that people already believe about serious writers, which is that they're pinch-nosed and ivory-towered. And that's terrible for writing and terrible for quote-unquote serious books. If you have disdain for *any* reader, then to heck with ya" (pp. 68–69).

High Culture/Popular Culture. One powerful assumption of traditional school selection of texts rests on just this contrast between high and low or popular culture. Chambers (1985) defines *high culture* as "cultivated tastes and formally imparted knowledge," which call for "particular moments of concentration, separated out from the run of daily life" (p. 5). Popular culture, on the other hand, "mobilizes the tactile, the incidental, the transitory, the visceral" and is not grasped by contemplation but by informal "distracted reception" (p. 5). Jameson (1983) sees the breakdown of the division between high and low culture as distressing to academics who have "traditionally had a vested interest in preserving a realm of high or elite culture against the surrounding environment of philistinism, of schlock and kitsch, of TV series and *Reader's Digest* culture, and in transmitting difficult and complex skills of reading, listening and seeing to its initiates" (p. 112). Kellner (1988) acknowledges the "unique pleasures and enticements" provided by traditional high culture but believes that its enshrinement and canonization serve to exclude and marginalize "precisely those phenomena which most immediately engage most individuals in our society" (pp. 32–33).

For these critics, the canon is a device of exclusion—exclusion of students from their own experienced lives and exclusion of popular culture from serious scrutiny and discussion. Culture, they say, can also be defined as how people live, interact, and change. Rouse (1989) describes students in the classroom studying Shakespeare who feel perhaps "a sense of pious satisfaction for having done their duty before returning with a sigh of relief to their usual entertainments. Outwardly conforming, they inwardly resist the imposition of our cultural authority and the implied denigration of their own taste" (p. 87). Rouse believes that if we are to engage students in reading literature, we may have to relinquish our "promotion of 'art.'" He argues that we can do this "in good conscience" because the separation of high and popular culture is not necessarily "built into the nature of things." Shakespeare, after all, was the most popular dramatist of his own time and in the nineteenth-century United States. And, Rouse concludes, any work that will "engage the feelings and thoughts of young people, and help us shape the interior world by which they interpret their experience, is artful enough for our purpose, whether admired by the cognoscenti or not. The great themes are not found only in the great books" (pp. 87–88).

This redefinition of culture expands the English curriculum to genres that would have formerly been laughed out of school: detective stories, mysteries, romances, westerns, science fiction, fantasy, and even comics. (Interestingly, the university curriculum seems to have been most open to this diversity of forms.) In addition to these once-excluded fictional genres, English study has also opened to include many genres of nonfiction, not as ancillary texts in the study of literature or writing but as valuable in themselves. We will devote all of Chapter 9 to the richness of nonfiction.

We turn now to literature that many would put at the opposite extreme from the classics: young adult fiction. The designation itself is of recent origin. It was once used to refer to slight, formulaic stories about adolescents turned out by sentimental hacks. Today it designates a body of work that not only centers on adolescent protagonists and is marketed for young audiences but also possesses literary distinction. Until the publication of Louisa May Alcott's *Little Women* (1868), very little was written for American adolescents. The young, when they graduated from school texts, read adult literature—classics and popular fiction. Indeed, until the late nineteenth century, the age divisions in the human life cycle were simple and straightforward: children and adults. Formerly, when children reached the ages of fourteen or fifteen and could begin to work and contribute to their families, they began to be considered adults. *Adolescence,* as a term used to describe an age of unique stages of cognitive, psychological, sexual, social, and even moral development set apart from both childhood and adult life, is a relatively recent designation.

The Expansion of Young Adult Fiction. Literature featuring adolescents as protagonists grew in popularity at the end of the nineteenth and the beginning of the twentieth century. This literature was read by adults and the young alike, and it became noted primarily for its serialization and its sentimentality. As its writers moved toward greater realism at the mid-twentieth century and its publishers moved toward more specialized publishing and marketing efforts (spurred especially by the rise of paperbacks), it attracted an increasing number of talented authors and a corresponding number of interested young readers. Many of its writers did not consciously begin to write for the young. Donelson and Nilsen (1980) tell of Robert Cormier's initial reaction to becoming a young adult author: "shock followed by a month-long writer's block" (p. 6).

Some of these writers remain ambivalent about being pigeonholed by publishers, booksellers, and librarians in this category. Others find that their adolescent characters can become involved with many of the same dilemmas as those faced by protagonists of classic literature, and they engage in other age-specific issues that are equally as life challenging. The adolescent reading audience is also distinguished by its hospitality to new ideas and to divergent styles. It is generous in its expectations of fiction. Many adolescents, of course, expect and demand certain predictable character types, plots, and ideas. (Books about Nancy Drew and the Hardy Boys remain in print.) But many others have a tolerance and playfulness about literature and the time to read it. According to writer S. E. Hinton, the adolescent reading audience is open to "all kinds of writing."

Robert Small (1992) enumerates characteristics unique to young adult novels that clearly explain their appeal:

- The main character is a teenager.
- Events and problems in the plot are related to teenagers.
- The main character is the center of the plot.
- Dialogue reflects teenage speech, including slang.
- The point of view presents an adolescent's interpretation of events and people.
- The teenage main character is usually perceptive, sensitive, intelligent, mature, and independent.
- The novel is short, rarely more than two hundred pages.
- The actions and decisions of the main characters are major factors in the outcome of the conflict. (pp. 282–283)

Gallo (1989) listed the results of a poll of past and present officers of NCTE's Assembly on Literature for Adolescents (ALAN). Figure 7–1 lists the eighteen young adult authors that they named as most important. Ted Hipple (2000) surveyed members of ALAN about the best young adult novels of the 1990s. A decade earlier, he had informally polled English teachers, English educators, and present and past officers of ALAN to "identify the ten adolescent novels they wanted all English teachers to know about" (1989, p. 79). Figure 7–2 includes both lists.

FIGURE 7–1

Important authors of young adult literature

S. E. Hinton	Judy Blume	Norma Klein
Paul Zindel	Sue Ellen Bridgers	Scott O'Dell
Richard Peck	Virginia Hamilton	Paula Danziger
Robert Cormier	Madeleine L'Engle	Norma Fox Mazer
M. E. Kerr	Robert Newton Peck	Paula Fox
Katherine Paterson	Robert Lipsyte	Zibby Oneal

FIGURE 7–2

Hipple surveys of top adolescent novels

2000 Survey	
1. *The Giver*	Lois Lowry
2. *Out of the Dust*	Karen Hesse
3. *Holes*	Louis Sachar
4. *Make Lemonade*	Virginia Euwer Wolff
5. *Ironman*	Chris Crutcher
6. *The Watsons Go to Birmingham*	Christopher Paul Curtis
7. *Harry Potter and the Sorcerer's Stone*	J. K. Rowling
8. *Walk Two Moons*	Sharon Creech
9. *Staying Fat for Sarah Byrnes*	Chris Crutcher
10. *Freak the Mighty*	W. R. Philbrick
11. *When She Was Good*	Norma Fox Mazer
12. *Deliver Us from Evie*	M. E. Kerr
1989 Survey	
1. *The Chocolate War*	Robert Cormier
2. *The Outsiders*	S. E. Hinton
3. *The Pigman*	Paul Zindel
4. *Home Before Dark*	Sue Ellen Bridgers
5. *A Day No Pigs Would Die*	Robert Newton Peck
6. *All Together Now*	Sue Ellen Bridgers
7. *The Moves Make the Man*	Bruce Brooks
8. *Jacob Have I Loved*	Katherine Paterson
9. *Words by Heart*	Ouida Sebestyen
10. *Dicey's Song*	Cynthia Voight
11. *Summer of My German Soldier*	Bette Greene

Many teachers welcome these well-crafted books. They say that these texts "make readers" of their students. They appeal to a wide gamut of reading interests. They reflect all of the genres of adult fiction: realism, romance, adventure, suspense, science fiction, fantasy, westerns, mysteries, historical fiction, utopias, and even horror. Students are clearly drawn toward the range of texts, from the mythological quests of fantasy to the excitement and thrill of suspense. Many of these genres attract a cult of devoted readers who haunt bookstores and libraries for new titles. Most important, as Rosenblatt (1983) understood, "Like the beginning reader, the adolescent needs to encounter literature for which he possesses the intellectual, emotional, and experiential equipment" (p. 26). "Books must be provided that hold out some link with the young reader's past and present occupations, anxieties, ambitions" (p. 72).

Content. Since 1972, the staff of the University of Iowa's Books for Young Adults Program has annually polled tenth- through twelfth-graders about their reading choices, based on initial appeal and subsequent enjoyment. Consistently, the most popular books are those in the category of contemporary realism. The choices of these young readers, then, suggest an interest in their fictional counterparts involved in all of the perplexities and excitements of growing up. Young adult fiction encompasses the experiences and feelings peculiar to the age of its adolescent protagonists: overriding issues such as personal identity, separation from family, identifications with groups, cliques, age mates of both sexes, and developing moral clarity and commitment. Formerly, boys' identity issues were tied to occupational choices and girls' to marriage choices. Those gender-specific benchmarks are no longer as predictable. Both sexes are engaged in what Freud believed is the crucial resolution for mental health: one's ability to love and to work. And all of these issues are negotiated in the turbulent context of a fluid and changeable identity that engenders an overwhelming self-consciousness. For instance, the fifteen-year-old protagonist of Colin Neenan's sensitive and witty first novel, *In Your Dreams* (1995), is convinced he is hideously ugly and impossibly in love with his older brother's girlfriend. The words on a *Peanuts* poster that we saw on the wall of an English classroom exactly capture the feelings of this character and of so many high school students: "As soon as I get up in the morning, I feel like I'm in over my head."

Books that reflect these experiences can reassure adolescents that they are not alone in being "over their heads" and that their clamor for emotional, intellectual, behavioral, and moral balance is normal. Many young adult novels deal with current, topical issues: child abuse; substance abuse; the turmoil of parental tensions, separation, and divorce; estrangement from families, friends, and community; confusions of sexual identity; running away; and date rape. These novels have a strong appeal for adolescents who are personally or vicariously caught up in similar traumas and tensions. Furthermore, the egocentrism so characteristic of adolescents can be nudged to include others. They can acknowledge and empathize with stories other than their own personal narratives of anxious hope and imagined glory. Adolescents often create imaginary audiences who watch and judge their appearance, behavior, and career; through reading young adult novels, they become the audience for others. There is reassurance and affirmation in such a role and a widening sense of possibility in the world.

Because students do personally engage with the fiction, they seem eager to share their responses to it, just as they commonly share their reactions to movies, sports events, and rock concerts. Small (1972) points to the power relationships common to secondary classrooms: The teacher is perceived as authority and students as less knowing. He notes that teaching young adult literature changes that knowledge balance. Students become the more knowing in responding to the lives and situations of the adolescent protagonists. "Students can justifiably be said to speak from a greater authority than their teacher" (p. 226). Because this literature touches their authentic experiences, it engages students more actively and encourages the sharing of responses, feelings, ideas, and reactions—in short, the work of the interpretive community.

Form. If teachers like the appeal and impact of this type of reading on their high school students, they also value its style. Teachers welcome the expanded possibilities for the young to read writing that rises above the mediocrity of earlier juvenile literature and in fact often challenges the honesty and craft of adult fiction. Adolescent literature is usually easily accessible to students in its straightforward narrative, its recognizable characters, its uncomplicated syntax, and its approachable vocabulary. It is free of the obscurity and incomprehensibility of many texts. Often those texts, so highly valued by critics and academics, appeal to a highly literate elite and in so doing exclude the uninitiated reader. Young adult writers, perhaps more conscious of their audiences, exercise care in making their fiction readable. Where they experiment, they do not exclude the reader from the possibility of comprehension. Thus, the young reader becomes more readily involved in imagining fictive worlds. Students reading this fiction are likely to embark on Rosenblatt's (1978) transaction with the text: "The reader envisions the characters, participates in their uttered thoughts and emotions, and weaves the sequence of events into a plot" (p. 68). Students do so because these characters are struggling in the context of dilemmas they, too, are experiencing *and* because the prose invites the reader to comprehend it.

These works also allow teachers to teach form effectively—often better than with traditional classics. Students have a firmer grasp of the works and therefore more control over the material and more confidence in discerning the craft with which it is written. Small (1977) comments on this potential for formal analysis by analogy. He notes that we would not try to teach novices about the steam or internal combustion engine by taking them to visit a large-scale generating plant or to inspect a highly sophisticated car. Instead, a good teacher would start with a "simple steam engine, a one-cylinder engine, a working model, where each part was one of its kind and its functions clear. The junior novel is, for all purposes, that simple but working model of the adult or classic novel." For instance, students quickly understand difficult concepts such as irony when reading *The Chocolate War* (Robert Cormier, 1974); multiple perspectives in *A Hero Ain't Nothin' but a Sandwich* (Alice Childress, 1973) or *The Lord of the Rings* trilogy (J. R. R. Tolkein, 1967); narrative voice in *The Pigman* (Paul Zindel, 1968); psychological complexity in *Home Before Dark* (Sue Ellen Bridgers, 1976); poetic prose in *Out of the Dust* (Karen Hesse, 1997); and the influence of culture on individual identity in *Homeless Bird* (Gloria Whalen, 2000).

Appeal.   Young adult fiction is appropriate for students at all reading levels. Grimes (1991) tries to find the special books that will lead reluctant readers of low or high ability to the "big breakthrough" to reading enjoyment. She describes this search for the "all-important breakthrough book" as "one of the reading teacher's most important contributions" (p. 45). And she finds these books in young adult fiction. She describes introducing some of her "toughest nonreaders" to a love of reading through Arthur Roth's "adventure-packed survival stories" *Trapped* (1983) and *Avalanche* (1989). She discusses the novels that led a snarling, problem-beset student to discover that other people have problems that she could compare to her own: Deborah Hautzig's *Second Star to the Right* (1982), Frank Deford's *Alex: The Life of a Child* (1983), Lois Lowry's *Find a Stranger, Say Goodbye* (1978), and Robyn Miller's *Robyn's Book* (1986). This same student explained that at first she had entered class hating to read; in fact, her deepest wish was "to pick up a book and throw it!" (p. 45).

Rakow (1991) is equally devoted to sharing young adult fiction with an entirely different student population: gifted students. She explains that teachers and parents often unwittingly deny these students valuable experiences and insights by insisting that they read the classics. She observes that teachers "frequently offer honors students fewer opportunities than their nongifted peers to explore through reading, writing, and discussion how modern literature addresses questions of growing up. Conditioned to seeking answers to questions and solutions to problems through books, these youngsters are

cut off from a significant source of insight and support when they are discouraged (even forbidden?) from reading YA literature" (pp. 48–49). Rakow believes that "certain life experiences and developmental needs are shared by all students, and giftedness is not an inoculation against the pain and confusion of adolescence. Gifted teenagers . . . need young-adult books to help illuminate and validate their own experiences. They need books that can help them explore how others feel and function in the day-to-day teenage world in which they so often feel alien" (p. 48).

Young Adult Fiction and the Classics.   Other teachers use adolescent fiction as a bridge to adult fiction or the classics. Spencer (1989) brings young adult novels into her AP classroom. Before teaching Jean Paul Sartre's *No Exit* and existentialist philosophy, she asks that her students read Chris Crutcher's *Running Loose* (1983) or his *The Crazy Horse Electric Game* (1987) or Norma Howe's *God, the Universe and Hot Fudge Sundaes* (1984). She regards these three novels as excellent catalysts for discussions of the various aspects of existentialism that concern Sartre: alienation, chaos, personal choice, and commitment. She reports her reasoning: "An advanced-placement student devours an adolescent novel in a single evening; change of pace, ease, and interest level provide new accessibility to the difficult, cold philosophy of existentialism" (p. 46).

> Adolescent literature in an advance-placement classroom connects classics to the present. Even those students who read Nietzsche on their own find relevance and pleasure in sharing the lives of fellow teenagers Louie, Willie, or Alfie. If the purpose of a unit on philosophy in literature is to ask students to think more deeply about life, death, and their place in the universe, then this succeeds: perfunctory discussions dissipate. Personal, passionate, probing exchanges vitalize literary discourse. (p. 46)

Others have found connections between young adult fiction and the classics to be powerful. An *English Journal Booksearch* (March, 1989) asked, "What adolescent novel do you use to introduce students to a literary classic?" The responding teachers indicated that they used young adult fiction both before the classic, to "help readers make that leap of understanding," and after, to "clarify for young readers the meaning of more difficult selections" (p. 82). Figure 7–3 records these connections as well as those from other sources.

We have found two resources to be especially helpful in connecting young adult literature and the classics. These volumes are filled with ideas for thematic connections and detailed lesson plans for units of study:

Herz, S. K., with Gallo, D. R. (1996). *From Hinton to Hamlet: Building bridges between young adult literature and the classics.* Westport, CT: Greenwood.

ADOLESCENT NOVEL	AUTHOR	PAIRED CLASSIC	AUTHOR
The Island	Gary Paulsen	*Walden* *Civil Disobedience*	Henry David Thoreau
Z for Zachariah	Robert O'Brien	*Hiroshima*	John Hersey
Dove	Derek L. T. Gill	*The Odyssey*	Homer
The Wild Children	Felice Holman	*Animal Farm*	George Orwell
Bless the Beasts and Children	Glendon Swartour	*Lord of the Flies*	William Golding
Summer of My German Soldier	Bette Greene	*Anne Frank: The Diary of a Young Girl*	Anne Frank
The Chocolate War	Robert Cormier	*The Oxbow Incident*	Walter Van Tillburg Clark
The Witch of Blackbird Pond	Elizabeth George Speare	*The Scarlet Letter*	Nathaniel Hawthorne
The Homecoming[1]	Cynthia Voight	*The Odyssey*	Homer
		The Adventures of Huckleberry Finn	Mark Twain
A Hero Ain't Nothin' but a Sandwich[2]	Alice Childress	*As I Lay Dying*	William Faulkner
The Island of the Blue Dolphins[3]	Scott O'Dell	"Ninth Sketch" in *The Encantadas*	Herman Melville
Soldier's Heart	Gary Paulsen	*The Red Badge of Courage*	Stephen Crane

[1]This idea is from teacher and writer Julia Neenan and librarian and writer Colin Neenan.
[2]We have had able students who were fascinated by *As I Lay Dying;* however, we regard it as too difficult for most high school students.
[3]Sandy Benedict recommends the benefits of reading and comparing these two accounts of the same historical incident from two perspectives.

FIGURE 7–3   Adolescent novels as complements to the classics

Kaywell, J. F. (Ed.). (1993). *Adolescent literature as a complement to the classics.* Norwood, MA: Christopher-Gordon.

A list of recommended young adult works prepared by high school librarian Sandy Benedict in 1992 appears in Appendix F. She compiled this list of novels to strike a balance between literary merit and compelling subject matter. She included some genres, such as science fiction, that have great appeal to high school readers, especially males. Other resources for selection include annual awards and book lists chosen by school librarians, professors, and professional reviewers and published by the *School Library Journal* (a December award), *Booklist* (a January award), and the *American Library Association* (a spring award).

The ISLMC's Children's and Young Adults' Authors and Illustrators: This site provides biographical, bibliographical, and instructional resources for an extensive list of children's and young adult books.

Random House's Alphabetical Title Index of Young Adult Literature Guides (http://www.random-house.com/teachers/index.html): This site provides a list of instructional resources for about one hundred young adult novels.

Young Adult Literature Library (http://www.uiowa.edu): This site has summaries and reviews of more than thirty young adult novels.

The Assembly for Literature for Adolescents (http://www.alan-ya.org/): This is the home page of ALAN, with information about *The ALAN Review* and its articles about young adult literature.

 **Invitation to Reflection   7–5**

James Marshall (1999) has reported provacatively on U. S. reading habits. Read and reflect on some of the details he and others have amassed. Carl Kaestle (1991), in *Literacy in the United States,* found that 20–25 percent of the population reporting say they read books regularly (p. 185). (These books range from literature, of whatever kind, to *any* trade book.) James Twitchell (1992), in *Carnival Culture: The Trashing of Taste in America,* found that in the 1980s three authors were responsible for 50 percent of the fiction sold in the United States: Tom Clancy, Stephen King, and Danielle Steele (pp. 72–73). Marshall (1999) notes that the publishers of Silhouette and Harlequin Romances proudly report that their books account for 20 percent of all book-length fiction sold in the United States. Michael Smith (1995), in a study titled "Adult Book-Club Discussions: Toward an Understanding of the Culture of Practice," found that "participants were far more likely than students in classrooms to relate personal experiences, talk about important ethical issues, and share their emotional experience of reading. Participants felt free to offer tentative ideas and to disagree with one another, though in interviews they reported that they rarely did either of these things when they were students" (quoted in Marshall, 1999, p. 186). Janice Radway (1987), in *A Feeling for Books: The Book-of-the-Month Club, Literary Taste, and Middle Class Desire,* attributes the popularity of the Book-of-the-Month-Club to its editors' conscious selections of books "with a particular form of experience, a reading experience that was, above everything else, characterized by the pleasure it gave. The particular experience referred to again and again in reader's reports . . . was always bound to a certain extent with a feeling of immersion, a sense of boundaries dissolved" (p. 114).

1. Most of these habits would discourage classicists. How would genre challengers regard these details? How do you regard them?
2. Is there any lesson for the English teacher in the success of the book club editor's selections and in the members' experiences of book discussions?
3. What genres would you consider appropriate for middle school and secondary students?

science fiction	fantasy	detective stories
romance	horror	spy stories
mysteries	westerns	comics

4. Have you been convinced that young adult fiction could find a place in your classroom? If yes, what was the most persuasive argument for you? If not, explain why.
5. Where do you draw the line at what is not acceptable for study?

⌒ MULTICULTURAL CHALLENGE

Many women, people of color, and non-Europeans argue that the canonical texts have largely been written by white European males and thereby reflect a predominantly Eurocentric masculine consciousness. They note that the editors, the critics, and the academics who select and evaluate these texts have, until very recently, reflected the same cultural experience; yet their ultimate praise for works that they designate as classics is the accolade *universal.* Multicultural challengers remind us that these classics often do not, in fact, reflect universal experiences. They overlook the significant intellectual, artistic, and social perspectives and contributions made by many diverse groups. These challengers sometimes remind us of Huck Finn's remark (regarding Moses) that he "didn't take no stock in dead people."

Applebee's (1993) research on the characteristics of anthologized authors validates those claims. Historically, the high school canon reflected "a mainstream Anglo-Saxon tradition," but in the past few decades anthologizers and teachers have tried to provide more balanced selections. In grades 7–10 especially, 26–30 percent of the pieces contained in 1989 textbooks were written by women and 18–22 percent were written by minority, nonwhite authors. The selections for the anthologies of national literature usually taught in grades 11 and 12, namely American and British literature, were less diverse. In the British literature texts, only 8 percent of the selections were written by women and 1 percent by minorities, even when these texts included Com-

monwealth writers. The American texts were somewhat more diverse: 24 percent of the pieces were written by women and 16 percent by nonwhite minorities. When all of the selections of these texts were summed by national literary traditions, North American and United Kingdom writers accounted for 93 percent of the selections, European writers for 4 percent, and writers from other areas of the world just a smattering (pp. 93–96). The canon clearly needs to include texts by and about women, African Americans, Native Americans, Hispanic Americans, Asian Americans, Europeans, and non-Europeans. Their experiences should not be excluded. Most multicultural challengers do not propose to trash the classics but to open readers to a broader view, to a variety of perspectives. After all, as Table 7–4 and Figure 7–4 show, the United States and its schools mirror just such variety.

Women. In *A Room of One's Own,* Virginia Woolf (1929) retold the dilemma of women imaginatively. Finding so few remnants of women's lives in recorded history, she created several biographies herself. One of these imagined women is William Shakespeare's "wonderfully gifted sister," Judith. In relation to William, Judith "was as adventurous, as imaginative, as agog to see the world as he was. But she was not sent to school. She had no chance of learning grammar and logic, let alone of reading Horace and Virgil. She picked up a book now and then, one of her brother's perhaps, and read a few pages. But then her parents came in and told her to mend the stockings or mind the stew and not moon about with books and papers" (p. 49). Eventually Judith escaped to London, found no place for herself in the theater, was pitied by an actor-manager, became pregnant with his child, and, in "the heat and violence of the poet's heart when caught and tangled in a woman's body," killed herself (p. 50). The social role and political power of the ordinary Elizabethan woman were severely restricted; for an imaginative rebel such as Judith, they destroyed talent and vision.

Women throughout history have left their written traces in the letters and journals of their assigned domestic sphere, but in the past these were often discarded as ephemeral. In *Silences,* Tillie Olsen (1978) offers a moving explanation and convincing evidence of the constricting impact of women's traditional roles on their creative possibilities. She explains the literary achievement of a nineteenth-century writer, Rebecca Hardin Davis, who, after her excellent *Life in the Iron Mills* (1863), married and never thereafter wrote as well again; that decline "was the price for children, home, love" (p. 107). According to Maxine Greene (1988), "it was, most often, the infinity of small tasks, the time-consuming obligations of housework and child care that narrowed the spaces in which [women] could choose" (p. 60). Few could choose an education (women's education being

TABLE 7–4   2000 census data on U.S. population, in millions

Population by Race and Hispanic/Latino Status	Census 1990 Number	Census 1990 Percent of total population	Census 2000 Race alone[1]	Census 2000 Race alone or in combination[2]
Total population[3]	**248.7**	**100.0**	**281.4**	**281.4**
White	199.7	80.3	211.5	216.9
Black or African American	30.0	12.1	34.7	36.4
American Indian and Alaska Native	2.0	0.8	2.5	4.1
Asian	6.9	2.8	10.2	11.9
Native Hawaiian and Other Pacific Islander	0.4	0.1	0.4	0.9
Some other race	9.8	3.9	15.4	18.5
Hispanic or Latino (of any race)[3]	22.4	9.0	35.3	35.3
Not Hispanic or Latino[3]	226.4	91.0	246.1	246.1
White	188.1	75.6	194.6	198.2
Black or African American	29.2	11.7	33.9	35.4
American Indian and Alaska Native	1.8	0.7	2.1	3.4
Asian	6.6	2.7	10.1	11.6
Native Hawaiian and Other Pacific Islander	0.3	0.1	0.4	0.7
Some other race	0.2	0.1	0.5	1.8

Source: U.S. Census Bureau, Administrative and Customer Services Division, Statistical Compendia Branch, http://www.census.gov/statab/www/part1a.html.

Note: Because individuals could report only one race in 1990 and could report more than one race in 2000, and because of other changes in the census questionnaire, the race data for 1990 and 2000 are not directly comparable. Thus the difference in population by race between 1990 and 2000 is due both to these changes in the census questionnaire and to real change in the population.

[1]One of the following six races: (1) White, (2) Black or African American, (3) American Indian and Alaska Native, (4) Asian, (5) Native Hawaiian and Other Pacific Islander, (6) Some other race.

[2]Alone or in combination with one or more of the other five races listed. Numbers for the six race groups may add to more than the total population and the six percentages may add to more than 100 percent because individuals may indicate more than one race.

[3]Hispanic or Latino population may be of any race.

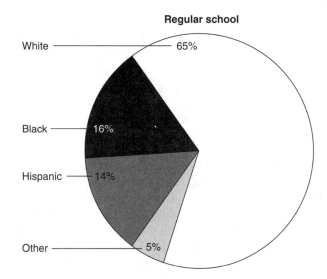

Regular school

White — 65%
Black — 16%
Hispanic — 14%
Other — 5%

FIGURE 7–4   2000 census data on U.S. school population

more concerned with general learning and specific domestic arts) or a profession. And if they wrote, despite these odds, few could find a publisher or a public willing to take them seriously.

When women began to compose in the established genres—poems (Anne Bradstreet and Phillis Wheatley), essays (Mary Wollstonecraft), and novels (Jane Austen)—they met with suspicion and rejection from critics, academics, and the public. Many became publishable only by assuming male pseudonyms. Woolf (1929) reflects on the bias against women's voices and women's concerns:

> It is obvious that the values of women differ very often from the values which have been made by the other sex; naturally, this is so. Yet it is the masculine values that prevail. Speaking crudely, football and sport are "important," the worship of fashion, the buying of clothes "trivial." And these values are inevitably transferred from life to fiction. This is an important book, the critic assumes, because it deals with war. This is an insignificant book because it deals with the feelings of women in a drawing room. (pp. 76–77)

If women's roles were constricted and their powers to choose and to act were limited, their power to understand themselves and to be understood were also compromised. Only at the end of the twentieth century did theorists begin to study and enunciate critical differences in the way in which women understand and respond to the world, differences that for centuries have simply been considered as being oddly female. These theorists have explored a distinct emotional, cognitive, linguistic, and moral development that grows from the particular historical, social, biological, and psychological experience of women. Donovan (1985) sees women's consciousness as being shaped by their roles in the domestic sphere and their biological and psychological experiences, particularly of giving birth and nurturing children. These experiences distinguish how women *know*—a knowing that is personal, private, intuitive, and subjective rather than more public, rational, and objective.

Carol Gilligan's (1981) *In a Different Voice* raises a serious challenge to the male emphasis on autonomy and principled decision making as the highest stages of moral development (Kohlberg) and as superior to the female value on the bonds of human connection. Gilligan differentiates between women's choices within the context of "mutuality and concern, of ongoing dialogue and conversation, of cooperation" and male choices within the framework of "competition" and gamesmanship (Greene, 1988, p. 84). Rather than focusing on their individual rights in human encounters, Gilligan believes that women are more prone to think in terms of responsibility to others. Many others point out that, until recently, the range of a woman's sphere was severely limited to falling in love, getting married, and having children.

In this difference in experience lies the great motive for an expanding canon that embraces women. If we want our classrooms to be places in which students actively explore their own lives, the fictive lives they encounter need to reflect the full range of human experience, not just half of it. Particularly in adolescence, when the young are actively seeking to arrive at self-definition, they need to be presented with accounts of the nature of their unique experiences and possible hopes. Barker (1989) recognizes that literature classes commonly approach that need in their young male students: "High school classics such as Miller's *Death of a Salesman,* Hemingway's Nick Adams stories, and Faulkner's "Bear" provide all sorts of opportunities for boys to make connections with their own lives—football, fishing and hunting, fathers and sons, and the like." Young women need the same provisions: "We always want our students to relate to what they're reading and bring their own experiences into discussions and essays; making sure that all students—girls included—are involved equally is not hard, but it requires conscious effort on the part of the teacher" (p. 42). Howe (1982) addresses the same issue: "Women must have a place in the curriculum that will allow them images of achievement and inspiration comparable to those the curriculum has generally afforded at least to white middle-class males" (p. 12).

Guilford (1985) reminds us of how literature might start to correct that constricting consciousness. She writes that in selecting literature for her classes around the "lives and problems of women," she wanted "stories to illustrate that women, like men, are sometimes major characters in the situations and problems of daily life. I also wanted stories that would identify some of the unique qualities that women represent" (p. 24). These expanded views serve our male as well as our female students. Segel (1986) concludes that literature is useful in a gender-divided society to reduce the alienation between men and women. She wonders whether men might become more understanding and easy with women "if they had imaginatively shared female experience through books, beginning in childhood. At the least, we must de-plore the fact that many boys are missing out on one of fiction's greatest gifts, the chance to experience life from a perspective other than the one we were born to—in this case, from the female vantage point" (p. 183).

Appendix F presents a list of novels and collections of short stories written by women and other excluded authors. We have limited what could be a very long list by including only books that we or colleagues have taught to high school students and that do not appear prominently on other lists in this text. One of the vexing contradictions that we experienced as beginning teachers was not wanting to assign or suggest books that we had not read yet not wanting our students to be confined by the limits of our own reading. (Those anxieties assert themselves here again as we compile these lists for you.) The problem eases in the course of a teaching career as the teacher has time to read more widely, profit from the suggestions of colleagues (in school or in professional resources), and gain confidence in introducing students to unknown texts. Teachers also learn pedagogical perspectives and organizational strategies for teaching longer works that do not require a teacher to be an authority on every work read or at the center of every discussion.

African Americans. African Americans also chafe under a canon that excludes their writers and ignores their unique cultural experience. Baker (1980) has observed that the men and women viewing the New World for the first time from the decks of the *Mayflower* saw a very different world from those seeing this same continent for the first time from the holds of a slave ship (p. 156). On their arduous and deadly passage into slavery and onto American soil, African men and women brought an oral tradition that spoke and sang of personal experience, religion, history, geography, and a long cultural heritage. The newly arrived African slaves were severed from ties to their former homelands—people, language, customs, and rituals—and faced a desperate struggle to survive. The slaveholding culture acted systematically to eradicate indigenous African values and practices, especially in the agricultural deep south, where education was prohibited, families divided, and individuals cruelly exploited. Even when slavery was abolished, African Americans continued for another century in narrowly defined, constricted, and stifling roles, living largely in the depressed and poverty-stricken south. Discrimination against ex-slaves and their progeny was sanctioned by "separate but equal" laws and often enforced by violence. African Americans then began another defining exodus in search of unskilled and semiskilled employment in northeastern and midwestern urban industrial centers.

A written literature began even during the days when slaves were officially forbidden to read and write. The literature that followed gave voice to a unique and defining experience, and it sprang from unique sources: an oral tradition, slave narratives, blues and spiritual music, jazz, signifying, and African and African American history.[3] The black writer also wrote from a perspective of marginality—of the outsider looking in with a different perception of reality, unique historical and psychological experiences, and distinctive sociopolitical aims. James Baldwin sums up the content of those texts: "For a tradition expresses, after all, nothing more than the long and painful experience of a people; it comes out of the battle waged to maintain their integrity or, to put it more simply, out of their struggle to survive."

Theologian and philosopher Cornel West (1982) suggests two different perceptions of African American history: African Americans as "passive objects" of a history of continual political, economic, and cultural degradation and of "ceaseless attempts to undermine Afro-American self-esteem" and African Americans as "active subjects" of a history of gallant persistence and struggle against "white paternalism," segregated capitalist opportunities, and "pervasive denigration" (pp. 69–70). Literature reflects both perspectives. West describes four traditions of thought and action that arose in response to that experience:

- One tradition claims a unique and exclusive African American culture and personality that is exceptional because of its history and culture.
- A self-effacing tradition depends on assimilation with a white culture to break its cycle of political oppression and social and psychological pathology.
- A marginal tradition emphasizes the confinement and restriction of the African American and therefore the need for individual rebellion and revolt.
- A humanist tradition projects an image of African Americans between these extremes.

We believe that West's humanist tradition provides a promising context for the study of African-American literature in our classrooms.

> The humanist self-image of Afro-Americans is one neither of heroic superhumans untouched by the experience of oppression nor of pathetic subhumans devoid of a supportive culture. Rather, Afro-Americans are viewed as both meek and belligerent, kind and cruel, creative and dull—in short, as human beings. This tradition does not romanticize or reject Afro-American culture; instead, it accepts this culture for what it is, the expression of an oppressed human community imposing its distinctive form of order on an existential chaos, explaining its political predicament, preserving its self-respect, and projecting its own special hopes for the future (West, 1982, p. 85).

Both African-American students and their non–African-American counterparts need to be opened to what Cobb (1985) describes as "the communal wisdom of a culture, the survival strategies, hero-images, women-images, social

---

[3]*Signifying* is an indirect use of language not necessarily to exchange information or explanation but simply to maintain connection with another in a hostile environment.

ordering, and authority symbols that ultimately determine values" (p. 256). Thirty years ago Turner and Stanford (1971) offered an appeal for this inclusion that remains relevant. They believed that for African American students the need is especially urgent:

> Growing up in a racist society which systematically conditions him to think negatively of his own racial group, the Black child develops a negative self-image. At school this negative self-image is further developed when he attends a class that is supposedly about general literature or American Literature and finds that the moral and social values, heroes, world view, and literary heritage of his own community are excluded. (p. 6)

D. Johnson (1990) observes:

> African-American youth live in a society and in a world in which the "happy ending" does not constitute a realistic model. Their realities must be represented, explored, and interpreted in the literature that they read. "Realistic" does not of necessity mean "bleak." It means only that the literature must be inclusive of a multitude of experiences. Fortunately, these include experiences of dreaming and imaging other realities, other worlds, and possibilities. (p. 2)

Our concern about the inclusion of African American literature in the English class arises from our concern that students of all races be given the personal freedom of imagining different possibilities for themselves, an imagining that is at the heart of reading and writing literature.

Appendix F contains a list of works that provide such an introduction. We include them as a testament to the remarkable literary achievements of African Americans and as starting points for those of you who are unfamiliar with this literature. We are indebted to many teachers for their suggestions of works that appeal to and are suitable for high school students, but especially to Mary Helen Washington (1991) and Angelene Reid (personal communication, 1992 and 1997).

Native Americans. Historians estimate that when the Pilgrims landed at Plymouth Rock in 1620, 4 to 8 million people, with five hundred distinct native cultures, each speaking its own language, were living in what is now the continental United States (Lincoln, 1983, p. 15). By the mid-twentieth century, that number was estimated to be eight or nine primary cultural groups.

> About seven hundred thousand native Americans survive as full-bloods or "bloods," to use the reservation idiom, mixed-bloods whose parents derive from different tribes, and half-bloods or "breeds" with one non-Indian parent. Another half million or more blooded Indian people live as whites. Over half of the Indian population now lives off the fifty-three million acres of federal reservation lands. (p. 15)

No voices in our culture have been more severely silenced or deserve more to be heard than those of Native Americans. The history and culture of these first known Americans have been repressed and nearly destroyed by centuries of the dominant culture's blind misunderstanding, deliberate cruelty, and misguided attempts to "civilize" or assimilate Native Americans. When Native Americans have entered the dominant literature, they have been either romanticized or villainized. Bruchac (1987) writes, "From before Fenimore Cooper, the major presence of the American Indian in the writings of non-Indians has been as one of two opposed, yet complementary, incarnations: the murdering red skin and the noble savage" (p. x). Even those "objective" eighteenth- and nineteenth-century recorders of Native American narratives often distorted the accounts and made subjective moral observations about their subjects. White writers who were raised or worked among Native Americans and wrote of their experiences often judged these cultures naïvely and unsympathetically.

European newcomers usually classified Native Americans as primitive. Velie (1979) explains that when "whites first came in contact with many tribes, the Indians had a Stone Age technology. . . . The whites equated civilization with level of technology, and therefore judged them as backward" (p. 4). In fact, their culture was rich and varied. Lincoln (1983) sees that variety reflected in the geographic origins of the different tribes: "forest, prairie, river, valley, seacoast, mountain, tundra, desert, and cliff-dwelling peoples. They have lived as farmers, food gatherers, fishermen, and hunters inseparable from the land" (p. 16). In this diversity, however, common traditions remain. "Native American peoples acknowledge specific and common inheritance of the land. They celebrate ancestral ties. They share goods and responsibilities, observe natural balances in the world, and idealize a biological and spiritual principle of reciprocation. Personal concerns lead into communal matters" (p. 16).

Velie (1979) describes their literature as "an organic part of everyday life, not a thing apart to be enjoyed by a highly specialized class":

> In former days, all members of an Indian tribe listened to tales, and in many tribes virtually everyone composed and sang songs. . . . [L]iterature was . . . functional. Myths and tales were educational tools that taught the younger generation the beliefs and history of the tribe. Many songs were good medicine; others were morale builders sung before battle. Songs were sung to increase the fertility of the fields, to assure a successful hunt, to gain power over a recalcitrant lover. Oratory played an important role in political decisions. . . . Ritual was a form of sacred drama filled with poetry, song, and dance; it acted out on earth events taking place in a more important realm. (p. 7)

As with most oral traditions, retelling over centuries honed those words, narratives, and perceptions to their essence. Until they came into contact with white settlers, Native Americans needed no written language. Their spoken voices embodied and transmitted the culture.

In the late nineteenth century, the U.S. government adopted policies toward Native Americans that had almost as devastating an effect on the culture as the periodic massacres had. In order to assimilate and "civilize" Native Americans, they systematically removed the young from their tribes, thereby separating them from the center of their material and spiritual existence, and sent them to boarding schools, first in the east, and then in states all over the union. Supporters of these schools argued that the children's native identities had to be suppressed and replaced with White values of hard work, ambition, and individualism. Most of the children returned to the reservation, or "back to the blanket" as it was called, but they returned feeling alienated from both worlds, victims of Whites' misguided, if well-meant, intentions. Larson (1978) describes this period (between 1880 and 1920) as "one of humiliation and defeat, above all one of hopelessness. The lessons of the recent past had taught them that the Native American was a dying breed—that survival (if one could call it that) could only be achieved by accepting the values of the white man's world" (p. 10). When the government reversed its policies in the 1930s, closed the schools, and urged Native Americans to reclaim their languages, the damage to Indian culture seemed irreversible.

In recent decades, however, attempts have been made to affirm Native American history and culture, not as anachronistic oddities but as remarkable testaments of endurance and wisdom. Young writers who at one time may have had difficulty finding voices, publishers, or readers have been the beneficiaries of a changing history. Many Native Americans left the reservations during World War II and began to establish their separate identities; therefore, they were primed to respond to the political activism of the civil rights movement and the anti-Vietnam War protests of the 1960s and 1970s with their own counterparts. The National Youth Council (1960) and the American Indian Movement (1969) challenged the assumption that the Native Americans' demise was inevitable. Bruchac (1987) quotes the reaction of Louis Oliver, a Creek poet: "We were always taught in the schools that the Indian was doomed to be absorbed into the American melting pot and that all of our old ways were only memories. Before I met some younger American Indian writers, I was just like that old ground hog. I had crawled in my hole and just accepted that I was forgotten" (p. xi). Larson (1978) senses among the younger writers "the desire to articulate a new national awareness" (p. 12). A young Native American poet, Wendy Rose, explains that she was not raised to speak her native language, live on her lands, or know her native literary tradition; so she is now engaged in discovering it. With a similar affirmation, a whole new generation of poets and writers have emerged to claim their identities and give written and visual expression to their experiences. Their flourishing has been called a renaissance. Others explain that, in fact, the "oral tradition has been central to every form of expression, and as Simon Ortiz argues, 'in that sense the literature has always been there; it just hasn't been written, with its more contemporary qualities and motives' " (Coltelli, 1990, p. 6).

As a simple matter of justice, we should make a place for Native American oral and written literature in English classrooms. We should acquaint our students with this deep and vital tradition that predated the one that European settlers brought and adapted. "When the Pilgrims arrived in the New World, the Indians already had an oral tradition of storytelling and ceremony which integrated all of life" (Stensland, 1979, p. 3). Furthermore, English teachers need to directly dispel the negative stereotypes that are products of both print and nonprint literature: the images of the noble red man, the warring savage, the drunkards and idlers, the murderous thieves, the reservation derelicts, the taciturn women, the passive victims, and the rootless drifters. Such stereotypes are tenacious, but one means of dispelling them is to read and discuss more accurate portrayals of three-dimensional individuals.

There are even deeper arguments for the inclusion of Native American literature. Stensland (1979) explains that "American Indians—with their spiritual oneness, their concept of the sacred hoop—have much to teach modern youth, many of whom find their own world dreary and materialistic. The Indian's problem of trying to live in two worlds also strikes a responsive chord in teenagers who are in search of self-realization" (p. 3). Teacher Cary Clifford sees Native American literature as possessed of the "magic quality" of a story told late at night around a campfire. Because it is not limited to the written word and is "lived literature" consisting of song and dance and oratory, it has the quality of individual action and communal participation, which draws students to it. She feels that for most secondary students, "leaving the classroom and coming into the natural world is an act of joy" and that they find a "natural bond with these people who told their stories under the stars and sang their prayers in the open dawn (1992, personal communication)." Although some were hunters and others farmers, some wanderers and others cliff dwellers, they seem to share a spiritual sense of the oneness or roundness of life; a strong loyalty to the tribe (and most often to the family); a valuing of honesty, endurance, acuteness, and bravery; a sense of the earth and nature as ever-present and sacred.

Appendix F includes a list of literature written by Native Americans and by Whites who seem to have done justice to the culture they sought to describe. The usual genre categories are restrictive for Native American literature, made up, as it is, of myth, legend, oratory, biography, autobiography, and history. Here are two Web sites with resources about Canadian and American "First Nations" authors:

Native American Authors (http://www.ipl.org/ref/native/): The site has biographies and detailed book catalogues of four hundred authors.

The Index of Native American Electronic Text Resources (http://www.hanksville.org/NAresources/): The site includes essays, poems, and short stories by Canadian and American writers.

Hispanic Americans. Hispanic Americans are the fastest-growing minority in the country. Some census estimates predict that, within the first decades of the twenty-first century, one-fifth of our population will be Spanish-speaking. An increasing number of immigrants and native Spanish speakers are entering our schools. These Hispanic Americans experience the difficulties of all latecomers in their struggle for economic security and cultural stability. One of the predicaments for a minority culture, especially one that is largely immigrant, is whether to reject its cultural history and personal memories in order to be assimilated into the dominant culture or to hold on to that heritage and risk standing on the outer boundaries of its new society.

Reading factual or fictional accounts of individuals bound by similar language, experience, and history is liberating for the young who are caught in such cultural perplexities. Richard Rodriguez's (1981) autobiography, *Hunger of Memory: The Education of Richard Rodriguez: An Autobiography,* is a testament to just that dilemma. His early promise was identified by teachers who conscientiously opened him to an awareness of intellectual and cultural possibilities but, in so doing, alienated him from his family and the culture that bore and sustained him; his parents were even discouraged from speaking their native language to him at home when he was a boy. Most of today's schools seem more sensitive about dividing students from their sources of identity and nurture. Nevertheless, mainstream images are presented so continuously as the norm that minorities need to have their alternative perspectives affirmed. In Applebee's (1993, p. 94) study of 1989 textbook anthologies for grades 7–12, only 2 percent of selections were by Hispanic writers.

Hispanic students are enriched in their understanding and deepened in their sense of themselves by reading Sandra Cisneros's (1989) novel *The House on Mango Street,* a coming-of-age tale about a young Hispanic girl growing up in Chicago, or Nicholasa Mohr's novel *Nilda* (1973), the story of Nilda Ramirez, who lives in El Barrio of New York City and experiences the tensions of being urban, poor, and Spanish-speaking. This kind of literature, reflecting honestly, perceptively, and unapologetically on their shared experiences, allows minorities and immigrants to envision life within a dominant culture without forsaking the customs and traditions of their origins.

Members of the dominant culture as well as other minority cultures also gain from learning about the experiences of Hispanic Americans. It frees all from the restrictions of ethnocentric perspectives, exercises empathy, defeats stereotypes, and enlarges literature's boundaries. Oliver and Bane (1971) have said that the young "need the opportunity to project themselves in rich hypothetical worlds created by their own imagination or those of dramatic artists. More important, they need the opportunity to test out new forms of social order" (p. 270). Hispanic social orders are rendered in literature from three sources:

1. Hispanic writers born here but torn between two cultures
2. writers native to Mexico and countries of the Caribbean, Central America, and South America, who have immigrated to the United States and whose works are translated for English readers
3. non-Hispanic writers who write with an understanding and appreciation of Hispanic culture

Reading the works of these three groups has what Maxine Greene (1988, p. 131) calls "emancipatory potential" for Hispanic and non-Hispanic students alike.

Appendix F includes fiction written by authors who are Hispanic American (born or having immigrated to the United States) and Latin American (born in, living in, and writing about Mexico or countries in Central America and South America). Worthy of mention are two U.S. authors who are sympathetic to Spanish culture and highly teachable to high school students. Barbara Kingsolver, in her novels *The Bean Trees* (1988), *Animal Dreams* (1990), and *Pigs in Heaven* (1993), includes and affirms Hispanic characters and their dilemmas, not as isolated cultural oddities but as integral to the variety and complexity of American life. When she was more than seventy years old, Harriet Doerr wrote two novels about Americans living in small Mexican villages, *Stones for Ibarra* (1984) and *Consider This, Senora* (1994), that capture the sudden discoveries and insights that arrive when we leave the familiar expectations of home and open ourselves to the wisdom of a different culture.

Asian Americans. Japanese American David Mura (1988) explains the gulf he sometimes feels between himself and white friends: "I point out to them that the images I grew up with in the media were all white, that the books I read in school—from Dick and Jane onwards—were about whites and later, about European civilization. I point out to them the way beauty is defined in our culture and how, under such definitions, slanted eyes, flat noses, and round faces just don't make it" (p. 137). Chinese American Amy Ling, born in Beijing, brought to the United States when she was six years old, and educated in American schools from first grade through a Ph.D. in comparative literature, describes the same experience: She never in her schooling encountered any Chinese American authors or characters except in a humiliating poem, Bret Harte's "Heathen Chinee." When she first read

Maxine Hong Kingston's autobiography, *A Woman Warrior,* and Nellie Wong's book of poems, *Dreams from Harrison Railroad Park,* she was "thunderstruck": "Here were people like me creating moving and artistic literature from our shared Chinese American experience. They expressed the struggle for personal balance that is the experience of every American of dual racial and cultural heritage, but, specifically, they wrote with pride and affirmation out of our common Chinese American background" (Ling, 1990, p. xi). Mura's experience leads him to conclude that "multiculturalism, for a member of a racial minority, is not simply tolerance, but an essential key to survival" (1988, p. 141).

Amy Tan's novel *The Joy Luck Club* (1989), the intermeshed first-person stories of four Chinese immigrant mothers and their American-born daughters, struck an imaginative nerve in the general American reading public. The story introduced the traditions and heritage of an Asian culture and the difficulties of assimilation for its first-generation children alongside the recurrent dilemmas experienced by all human beings. If Asian Americans benefit from validating and enriching their experiences through works by and about other Asians, so mainstream readers also profit from a deepening understanding of another culture and, by contrast, of their own. Applebee (1993) estimates that about 1.1 percent of the 1989 anthologies' selections are by Asian writers.

Other books, written in English by ethnic Asians and Eurasians and published in the United States for a general readership, have had appreciative audiences and have been recommended to us for high school students. They include *Farewell to Manzana,* Jeanne Wakatsuki Houston and James D. Houston's (1973) autobiographical novel of Jeanne Wakatsuki's experience in a Japanese American internment camp during World War II; Yasunari Kawabata's *Snow Country* (1981, 1996) or *Thousand Cranes* (1981, 1996) (he was the first Japanese writer to win the Nobel Prize in Literature); Maxine Hong Kingston's second book, *China Men* (winner of the 1981 Obie Award for Best New Play) and her *M. Butterfly* (1988 Tony Award winner for Best New Dramatic Play); Carolyn Lau's poetry collection, *Wode Shuofa* (1989 winner of an American Book Award from the Before Columbus Foundation); Frank Chin's short story collection *The Chinaman Pacific and Frisco Railroad Co.* (another 1989 American Book Award winner); Cynthia Kadohata's *The Floating World* (1989); Karen Tei Yamashita's *Through the Arc of the Rain Forest* (1990); John Okada's *No-No Boy* (1957, 1990); Lydia Minatoya's *Talking to High Monks in the Snow* (1991 winner of the PEN/Jarard Fund Award); Amy Tan's second novel, *The Kitchen God's Wife* (1991); Gish Jen's *Typical American* (1991); Chang-Rae Lee's first novel (which many regard as the Asian immigrant's version of Ralph Ellison's *Invisible Man*) *Native Speaker* (1995). Monica Sone's *Nisei Daughter* (1979) and Yoshiko Uchida's *Journey to Topaz*

(1971) are based on the authors' experiences in the Japanese American internment camps in California during World War II. Although this list includes mainly works by Chinese and Japanese Americans, whose immigrant history in the United States is longest and most complex, immigrant groups from Korea and Southeast Asia can be expected to swell this number. A law teacher, Lan Cao, has published a fine first novel, *Monkey Bridge* (1997), the autobiographical account of the difficulties of Vietnamese immigrants in the United States. Several anthologies, while old, provide good starting points for a search of Asian American works: Kai-yu Hsu's (1972) *Asian American Authors;* Frank Chin, Jeffrey Paul Chan, Lawson Fusao Inada, and Shawn Hus Wong's (1975) *Aiiieeeee!: An Anthology of Asian-American Writers;* and David Wand's (1974) *Asian American Heritage.* For critical studies, see Elaine Kim's (1982) *Asian American Literature,* Amy Ling's (1990) *Between Worlds: Women Writers of Chinese Ancestry,* and Cynthia Wong's (1993) *Reading Asian American Literature.*

Canadians. Canadian literature reflects a unique cultural history and experience that U.S. students and teachers profit from knowing. Gregory (1998) observes that "any reader interested in exploring world literature, learning more about other peoples and America's influence would be remiss not to read Canadian Lit." Canada is, after all, "America's largest trading partner, closest and friendliest neighbor" (p. 8). Its literature reflects the full scope of human experience set within a specific geography and history of frontier and settlement; rural and urban life; and Native American, English, and French languages and customs. We are most familiar with contemporary English-speaking Canadian writers and mention a few whose short stories, novels, and poems are rich resources in our classrooms. Several stories by Margaret Atwood, Mavis Gallant, and Alice Munro are staples; they never fail to engage students with their frank realism and astute insight. Munro's stories of adolescent life, such as "An Ounce of Cure" and "How I Met My Husband," are centerpieces of units that we teach on friendship and love—issues of critical concern to high school students. We have recommended to avid and curious readers Robertson Davies's portrayal of Canadian life in the novels of *The Deptford Trilogy* and *The Cornish Trilogy.* Canadian and U.S. teachers have extolled the success of teaching Margaret Lawrence's (1966) *A Jest of God,* W. O. Mitchell's (1947) *Who Has Seen the Wind,* and Mordecai Richler's (1959) *The Apprenticeship of Duddy Kravitz,* Carol Shields's (1994) novel *The Stone Diaries* (winner of the 1995 Pulitzer Prize, the National Book Critics Circle Award, and the Governor General's Award of Canada), which portrays a completed life cycle that spans residence in Canada and the United States, and Margaret Atwood's (1996) *Alias Grace* based on a true nineteenth century murder mystery. The poems of Michael Ondaatje (bet-

ter known as the author of the Booker Prize–winning novel *The English Patient*), Leonard Cohen, and Alden Nowlan are arresting. Canadian teachers have explained why Canadian literature is so rich in poems: More poetry than fiction is published in Canada. In all of the genres, Canadian writers have produced abundant literature that portrays all of the positive and problematic aspects of human life. This literature has a combination of the familiar and the foreign that intrigues and enriches those of us in the United States. Here are two Web sites that open the rich resources of Canadian literature:

Northwest Passages: Canadian Literature On-Line (http://www.nwpassages.com/): This encyclopedic site has connections to more than two hundred Canadian authors' pages and links to other Web sites on Canadian literature.

The Canadian Literature Archive (http://www.umanitoba.ca/canlit/): This site has biographies of Canadian writers and reviews of their books.

South and Central Americans. The South American writers that we teach—the prose of Isabel Allende (Chile), Jorge Luis Borges (Argentina), Gabriel García Márquez (Colombia), and Julio Cortazar (Argentina) and the poetry of Pablo Neruda (Chile) and Carlos Fuentes (Mexico)—reflect some of the same divisions of cultural identity that are so prevalent in Hispanic North Americans. Their lives and literature express a dual character based on the history of an indigenous population invaded and conquered by Europeans. Over centuries of cultural collisions and intermarriage, questions arise for many: Who am I? What is my proper role? Fuentes (1992) speaks of that catastrophic encounter of two cultures—when the Europeans came to Mexico and conquered and almost vanquished an Indian civilization with its own moral and imaginative universe. Although he acknowledges that the conquest was catastrophic, he does not regard it as sterile. From the merger of the European, the Indian, and the African came an Afro-Indo-Iberian new world that we can celebrate in the midst of economic disasters and cultural discontinuities. The European conquest interrupted the destiny of the indigenous civilization, but there is creative life in the tension between competing values and alternative possibilities.

Many South and Central American writers give expression to this tension. Borges, one of the first Spanish American writers to achieve an international reputation, was preoccupied throughout his prose and poetry with just this constant striving for elusive, unknowable truth that is inevitably frustrated. He and his fellow countryman Cortazar often resort to games, riddles, and puzzles as a kind of reenactment of their personal and cultural labyrinths. Both men, Cortazar in *End of the Game and Other Stories* (1963) and Borges in *Labyrinths* (1962,

English translation), wrote many short pieces that students relish for their cleverness and insight. Nobel Prize winner García Márquez puzzles over the same important questions of meaning but in an entirely different way. His longer novels, such as *One Hundred Years of Solitude* (1970, English translation), the novella *Chronicle of a Death Foretold* (1981), and his collections of short fiction such as *Leaf Storm* (1972) and *No One Writes to the Colonel* (1961), present life in a small coastal town, Macondo, and draw our students almost unfailingly into them because of their realism and magic. Finally, Isabel Allende, in "Two Words," a story our students invariably choose in their top-ten lists of short fiction we read together, imaginatively projects the power of language to answer the power of guns. She reminds us of the truth of Fuentes's affirmation of the imagination: We can only discover what we have first imagined.

Non-Europeans. The political and social challenges to the canon extend beyond those American populations with interest in their gender, tribal, national, or ethnic heritages. The world's diverse peoples have left oral and written traditions that, from ancient times, have been rich with the variety of human experience. American students benefit from access to these divergent traditions. But world literature selections and courses, while becoming more common in high schools, still tend to center on the experiences of ancient Greece, Rome, and Israel and Western and Eastern Europe. Applebee's (1993) estimates of the major anthologies, grades 7–12, show representation of authors from the following national traditions (p. 94):

North America, 59.2 percent
United Kingdom, 33.7 percent
Western Europe, 3.6 percent
Russia and Eastern Europe, 0.8 percent
Africa, 0.8 percent
Central and South America, 0.5 percent
Asia, 0.6 percent
Other, 0.7 percent

There is a need for greater inclusion of, say, 1968 Japanese Nobel prize laureate Yasunari Kawabata's *Thousand Cranes* (1947, 1965) and *Snow Country* (1937, 1960); Chinese Lu Hsum's (1972/1990) *The True Story of Ah Q*; New Zealander (Maori) Keri Hulme's *The Bone People* (1984, the 1985 Booker Prize recipient); Nigerian Chinua Achebe's *Things Fall Apart* (1967); Botswanan Bessie Head's *Maru* (1972, 1988); Egyptian Nobel prize laureate Naguib Mahfouz's *Midaq Alley* (1981); and South African 1991 Nobel prize laureate Nadine Gordimer's *July's People* (1981). (Additional suggestions are included in Appendix F.) The following Web site opens the literature of many countries, among them South Asia, Australia, New Zealand, India, Japan, and Turkey:

Literature Resources—Other National Literatures (http://andromeda.Rutgers.edu/): This site provides links to the literature of many countries.

In "Saving the Life That Is Your Own," from *In Search of Our Mothers' Gardens,* Alice Walker (1983) talks about the impact of reading diverse literature on the artist and, we would add, on all of us: "The absence of models, in literature as in life . . . is an occupational hazard for the artist, simply because models in art, in behavior, in growth of spirit and intellect—even if rejected—enrich and enlarge one's view of existence" (p. 4). Students profit from knowing a great range of peoples. They move further toward a recognition that ours is not the only or even the best arrangement of institutions, ideas, and values. They are in a position to grow and be challenged from a variety of perspectives, to open their cultural habits to scrutiny and their cultural understanding to a sense of wider possibility. Such study has the potential to develop our tolerance, enlarge our sensibilities, and deepen our appreciation of others and ourselves. It tests the idea that to go deeply into the particular opens up the universal. Poet and essayist Kathleen Norris (1996) calls maturity "the slow process of the heart's awakening" (p. 80).

೨ CLASSROOM CHALLENGES IN TEACHING NONCANONICAL AND CANONICAL TEXTS

This chapter has focused primarily on expanding literacy through expanding the choices of texts that are taught. This section presents instructional strategies that expand the allowable ways we teach our chosen texts. We add these organizational choices and teaching activities to those presented in Chapters 5 (fiction) and 6 (poetry). Although we don't place them within our teaching cycle or reading cycle, they express again our interest in student-centered, interactive classrooms.

Multicultural Literature in the Classroom

The multicultural challenge for the high school English teacher is significant and the resistances to it are many. Many English teachers have themselves been schooled in the Western European classics. These are the texts that they know and love as friends. Many enter the field with the impulse to share what has meant so much to them, what they love. The following are some of the difficulties that English teachers face in trying to expand the canon:

- Selecting appropriate new texts requires teacher reading time. Many English teachers struggle constantly against the longing to read more and the guilt of not having time to do so. Opening the canon broadens the arena for teacher guilt.
- Dilg (1995) names a more subtle hesitancy that arises from the awkwardness and tension of speak-

ing of cultural differences in multicultural classrooms. She quotes the author of *Black and White Styles in Conflict,* Thomas Kochman, who has noted that "as a culture we lack 'the public etiquette to talk about difference'" (p. 21). As a consequence, we avoid such uncomfortable conversations. The language alone with which we designate different groups is problematic, partly because it is constantly changing. If we speak of groups different from our own, we are never sure what language is most acceptable to their members. Dilg uses as examples the uncertainty of the preference for "Chicanos" or "Mexican Americans" and the evolution of preference for "Negroes," "Blacks," "Afro-Americans," and "African-Americans" (p. 21). We don't have language or models for talking honestly in dialogue with others about differences of history, perspective, life experiences, expectations, and language.

- Dilg (1995) also points out that "multicultural classes embody the unresolved tensions of the larger culture" (p. 22). These emerge not only in students but also in the teacher. Teachers who talk about groups different from their own run the risk of not understanding those groups or, in assuming to do so, appearing to "speak from a position of hypocritical loftiness" (p. 23). To reach a balance is difficult.
- Even if teachers meet these personal obstacles to an expanding canon, practical school-based obstacles remain. Students acculturated to predominantly White, western literature struggle to understand the assumptions, contexts, language use, and inferences of multicultural texts. Multicultural students in American schools challenged by western literature have an even harder task as they encounter yet another cultural expression.
- Course syllabi, curriculum guides, critical resources, reading lists, textbooks, and school bookrooms and libraries all stock the classics. The availability of noncanonical texts, especially in poor districts and those not served by community or neighboring college and university libraries, may be limited.
- Instructional time presents another problem. To introduce a new selection into your study is necessarily to omit another. Limited class time necessitates limited selection.
- Other teachers, administrators, and parents equate English with established literary traditions.

Each of these obstacles can be hurdled; but each requires patient, hopeful effort. You must have the conviction that you need to add a variety of voices to those of the classics. We turn now to strategies intended to introduce literature into your classroom that will promote resistance to cultural stereotyping, sensitivity toward cultural difference, empathy for individual experiences, sympathy for common ground, and awareness of the struggles and achievements of all humankind. They may encourage what Postman (1995) considers the purpose of public education: "to help the young transcend individual identity by finding inspiration in the story of humanity."

Classroom Environment. On the simplest visual level, the classroom creates the stage for an openness to many cultures. If you display author pictures and biographies on bulletin boards and wall displays, the authors should be drawn from a variety of races, genders, and cultures. If you have writers' quotes or images of cultural heroes, they, too, should reflect diversity. Newspaper clips, maps of the world, or maps and cultural artifacts of specific foreign countries can open students to imagine other people, other places. Athanases, Christiano, and Lay (1995) affirm the value of the visual to "communicate to students that members of all groups are welcome, supported, and encouraged here" (p. 27).

Of course, creating a receptive classroom environment is far more complicated than hanging wall decorations. The arrangements of desks; the position of the teacher in the room; the openness of the students to respond to texts and work through them together; and group tolerance, empathy, and curiosity all contribute to an environment that welcomes differences.

Literature Selections. We need to select literature that sensitizes students to cultural differences, promotes empathy for others, and opens points of connection. Because introducing new works into an already tight curriculum is difficult, the temptation is to remain with the tried-and-true anthologies or school bookroom lists. Barker (1989) explains the struggle: "The only problem is that if you start to get really serious about balancing your curriculum, it means dropping a man for every woman you add. For me, that meant putting *Huckleberry Finn* aside to make room for stories by Sarah Orne Jewett, Charlotte Perkins Gilman, and Kate Chopin. These are tough decisions, and you have to be creative" (p. 39).

Selecting a high quality of literature from the array of multicultural possibilities multiplies the difficulty: Teachers don't have the usual sanctioned texts. The American Library Association (Hayden, 1992) recommends five broad guidelines for selecting multicultural literature:

1. Look for a quality of reality that gives the reader a chance to experience something.
2. Try to determine the author's commitment to portray cultural groups accurately.
3. Avoid materials that sensationalize, enumerate unusual customs, or practice reversed stereotyping.
4. Be sensitive to emphasis on cultural differences at the expense of similarities.
5. Whenever possible, use the same critical criteria appropriate for all types of literature—distinctive language and appropriate dialogue, style, relevance and potential interest, clear-cut plots, and believable characterizations. (p. vi)

Four multicultural anthologies that provide a range of shorter works appeared in the 1990s:

Applebee, A., & Langer, J. A. (Senior Consultants). (1993). *Responding to literature: Multicultural perspectives.* Evanston, IL: McDougal, Littell.

Appleman, D., Reed, M., & the Minnesota Council of Teachers of English. (Eds.). (1991). *An anthology of multicultural American writing.* St. Paul: Minnesota Humanities Commission.

King, L. (Ed.). (1994). *Hear my voice: A multicultural anthology of literature from the United States.* New York: Addison-Wesley.

Purves, A. C. (Ed.). (1993). *Tapestry: A multicultural anthology.* Paramus, NJ: Globe.

We also have found *The Graywolf Annual Five: Multicultural Literacy* (Simonson & Walker, 1988) to be a useful resource. It contains essays that articulate what *truly* literate persons need to know. It also provides an alternative to Hirsch, Kett, and Trefil's famous multicultural reference list, with its male and European bias (in Hirsch, 1987).

Alternative Organization.

Jay (1991) offers an alternative to the traditional thematic or chronological divisions of American and English literature. He observes that "themes, like periods, derive from and are determined by a previously canonized set of texts and authors. The classic themes of American literature—the Virgin Land, the Frontier West, the Individual's conflict with society, the City versus the Country, Innocence versus Experience, Europe versus America, Dream versus Reality, and so on, simply make no sense when applied to marginalized texts and traditions" (p. 276). Jay suggests that we alter the usual division of seventeenth- through early nineteenth-century American literature into colonization, building a nation, and New England renaissance. We should not organize instruction around historical moments or even the conscious themes of a privileged, literate few but around what he calls "problematics." These problematics represent the intersection of cultural events and modes of coping with them. Jay describes them as indicating "how and where the struggle for meaning *takes place.*" He suggests raising the problematics and discussing texts that deal with them from different cultural perspectives. His own examples of problematics include "(1) origins, (2) power, (3) civilization, (4) tradition, (5) assimilation, (6) translation, (7) bodies, (8) literacy, and (9) borders" (p. 277).

Some high schools have cracked the canon by creating electives on minority writers. These have the advantage of focus and of not having to bump established classics as new works are added. Nevertheless, although we acknowledge the difficulties of adding to an already overtaxed curriculum, we strongly prefer integrating the study of diverse literature into the mainstream English course. Our preference originates in practical concerns (that is where most students are taught English), political

belief (the experience of other genders and cultures is not something novel or exotic to be segregated from the culture's dominant experience), and personal conviction (such classroom integration exactly matches the necessary cultural struggle of our nation and world today). Writing by women, people of color, and people of different national traditions need not be regarded as incidental, isolated, and peculiar to one group. Instead, it should be treated as positive and integral to the experience of our diverse national and world culture—not as an anomaly but as a rich, vital, and beautiful tradition.

Pairing.

We pair works by writers with diverse cultural perspectives. The pairings are especially effective when other elements remain constant, as with a similar genre or theme. Consider, for instance, comparing novels of initiation: Ralph Ellison's *Invisible Man*, Mark Twain's *The Adventures of Huckleberry Finn*, or F. Scott Fitzgerald's *The Great Gatsby*; or of autobiography: Benjamin Franklin's *Autobiography*, Frederick Douglass's *Narrative of the Life of Frederick Douglass*, or Harriet Jacobs's *Incidents in the Life of a Slave Girl.* When examined together, the differences between the two writers' experiences and sensibilities become apparent and almost teach themselves. Many students also find that they have more impressions to discuss when they compare and contrast two works rather than talk about one alone. Figure 7–5 presents pairings of male and female authors that we and other teachers have used (Barker, 1989; Carlson, 1989; Hale, personal communication, 1997; Lake, 1988; Moore, 1989; Reid, personal communication, 1992).

Resistant Reading.

Resistant reading is a reading strategy that approaches texts with a heightened critical consciousness. We ask students to observe and uncover stereotypes of gender, race, ethnicity, and nationality in the texts they read. In *Playing in the Dark: Whiteness and the Literary Imagination*, Toni Morrison (1992) lists several rhetorical strategies used by writers to manipulate perceptions of African Americans. Goebel (1995) translated Morrison's ideas from an African American context to a Native American one. He summarizes her strategies as follows:

1. *economy of stereotype*—physical and cultural descriptions of individuals and groups that are so brief as to render them caricatures with no unique distinctions between them;
2. *metonymic displacement*—where a single image, action, or object is used to represent an entire group of people—such as large lips or slanted eyelids to represent African Americans or Asian Americans;
3. *metaphysical condensation*—reducing a people's language, religious beliefs, and values to simplistic description—for example a multilingual Lakota Indian's speech might be reduced to "Ugh!" and "How";
4. *fetishization*—focusing attention on images or acts that evoke erotic desires or fears, such as miscegenation or cannibalism;

MALE AUTHOR	TITLE	FEMALE AUTHOR	TITLE
Martin Luther King, Jr.	*Letter from Birmingham Jail/I Have a Dream*	Harper Lee	*To Kill A Mockingbird*
Henry D. Thoreau	*Walden*	Annie Dillard	*Pilgrim at Tinker Creek*
Richard Wright	*Black Boy*	Maya Angelou	*I Know Why the Caged Bird Sings*
James Baldwin	*Go Tell It on the Mountain*		
Walt Whitman	*"Song of Myself"*	Emily Dickinson	*"I'm Nobody!"*
	To a Locomotive in Winter		*"I Like to See It Lap the Miles"*
Mark Twain	*The Adventures of Huckleberry Finn*	Willa Cather	*My Antonia*
		Cynthia Voigt	*Homecoming*
Uri Orlev	*Island on Bird Street*	Anne Frank	*Anne Frank: The Diary of a Young Girl*
Scott O'Dell	*The Island of the Blue Dolphins*	Jean C. George	*Julie of the Wolves*
Edgar Allan Poe	*The Black Cat*	Charlotte Perkins Gilman	*"The Yellow Wallpaper"*
Thomas More	*Utopia*	Charlotte Perkins Gilman	*Herland*
Eli Wiesel	*Night*	Etty Hillesum	*An Interrupted Life*
James Baldwin	*If Beale Street Could Talk*	Ann Petry	*The Street*
Gordon Parks	*The Learning Tree*	Mildred Taylor	*Roll of Thunder, Hear My Cry*
Alex Haley	*Roots*	Margaret Walker	*Jubilee*
August Wilson	*Fences*	Lorraine Hansberry	*A Raisin in the Sun*
Stephen Crane	*The Red Badge of Courage*	Grace King	*Bayou L'Ombre*
T. S. Eliot	*The Wasteland*	H. D. (Hilda Doolittle)	*"Trilogy (The Walls Do Not Fall)"*
John Steinbeck	*The Grapes of Wrath*	Willa Cather	*O Pioneers!*
		Harriette Arnow	*The Dollmaker*
Henry James	*Daisy Miller*	Edith Wharton	*The Age of Innocence*
Frederick Douglass	*The Narrative Life of Frederick Douglass*	Buchi Emecheta	*The Slave Girl*

FIGURE 7–5 Pairings of literature by men and women

5. *dehistoricizing allegory*—describing groups as though they were somehow removed from a specific social, political, and historical moment. (p. 44)

Goebel demonstrates that these devices are effective in stereotyping any discrete groups and the individuals within them. Students can be primed to look for these strategies in the texts they read. Direct questions can also help uncover these stereotypes. For instance, if you read texts not written by African Americans, pose questions such as the following:

- How are African Americans portrayed?
- Does the author use stereotypes: lazy field hands, Black Mammy, Aunt Jemima, Uncle Tom, contemporary absent fathers, and menacing drug-addicted ghetto youths?
- Are there explicit or implicit expressions of racial prejudice?
- Are the portraits two-dimensional?
- Are the African Americans marginal to the main action?
- Could African American characters be substituted for the main characters?
- As Wallace (1988) might ask, "Has Tonto walked away from the Lone Ranger yet? Has Rochester handed Benny his notice?" (p. 164).

Students also can look for counterexamples of stereotyping that demonstrate understanding and application of cultural pluralism.

For texts in which women are nonexistent, Barker (1989) has his students raise issues of gender. "What are the implications of Billy Budd's being described in feminine terms? . . . Could *A Separate Peace* have been written about a girls' school? Is the reason that girls give up swinging on "Birches" the same as it is for boys?" (p. 41).

Davis (1989) uses another type of resistance to intensify her students' insights into gender issues. She teaches American classics such as F. Scott Fitzgerald's *The Great Gatsby* and Arthur Miller's *Death of a Salesman* but uses "feminist scholars" in her interpretation rather than the "traditional explications" of male critics (p. 45). Barker (1989), in a "covert" attempt to create a "learning situation more responsive to the needs and interests of *all* students," focuses "discussion and writing topics on areas in which female students are authorities" (p. 39).

Student Assays. Like the polar responses discussed in Chapter 5, student assays can engage students before they read and discuss texts and can prime them to pay attention to stereotyping. Barker (1989) queries students by a variety of means to make them aware of their assumptions about gender. He takes quick votes. Could the situation in Charlotte Perkins Gilman's "The Yellow Wallpaper" happen today? He asks students to list the "qualities they perceive women and men expect from relationships" (p. 41). Lawrence (1995) prepares students for stories or novels that may have atypical gender roles by asking students to designate which gender is associated with particular activities, such as "washing clothes, doing dishes, vacuuming, mowing a lawn, cleaning out flower beds, fixing a bicycle, cleaning toilets, playing baseball, playing football, a career in ballet, a career in nursing, a career in engineering, etc." Then she asks them to respond to this writing prompt: "Which of the above categories do you believe women should not be involved in? Why? Which of the above categories do you believe men should not be involved in? Why? Do you believe it is harder to be a male or female in our society today? Explain" (p. 82). Activities that ask students to state their assumptions and then to examine them can do much to uncover their bias about the "other."

Perspective Taking. To uncover bias is an important step; to enlarge empathy for individuals and groups different from themselves is a crucial one. We present a number of different strategies that teachers have used to help students creatively project into the experiences and perspectives of another. Within another's world view, they can first discover differences and then perhaps, similarities.

For a unit on Robert Cormier's *The Chocolate War* and William Golding's *Lord of the Flies,* Samuels (1993) suggests a prereading activity to tie the novels to the students' own experiences, a plan that helps students project into the world of the other in any context. Samuels's suggestion goes like this:

> Have small groups role play a situation in which most of the students are part of the "in group" (they wear buttons that say "cool" or wear special hats) and one or two students are part of the "out-group." As we well know, middle and high school students are often organized in cliques or groups. The role play should involve some aspect of school life today. For example, the "in group" tries to convince the others to do something that is not acceptable according to the standard rules (i.e., cheating, wearing particular clothes, shunning a particular student, drinking alcohol, smoking, etc.). Discussion should follow with questions like the following:
>
> • What makes a group "in"? What makes a group "out"? How does the "in-group" in a school identify itself? Who identifies the "out-group"?
> • How does the "in-group" keep their power? What tools do they use to convince others to follow them?
> • Are "in-groups" good or bad for a school?

> • What are the "in-groups" at your school? What are the "out-groups" at your school? How can they each be identified? (p. 200)

Higgins and Fowinkle (1993) suggest a dramatic activity that forces students into the perspectives of others and thus to "greater insight into a person's psyche" (p. 47). When all students have read the same novel and are working in groups, they assign a group role play in which students assume "another's position and psychological perspective" (p. 47). They ask each person in a designated group to "choose a character in a novel and play out a scene (or several scenes). Each person should try to assume the character's position and perspective as much as possible" (p. 47).

Lawrence (1995) offers a number of ideas to help students understand gender issues from the opposite perspective (p. 82). We list a few:

Collages. She asks students to make a collage "of magazine pictures that shows how their gender is being encouraged to look and dress." She then asks them to write about "what the pictures tell females/males they should look like."

Adopting the opposite gender's point of view. "Have students try writing a story from the point of view of the opposite gender about a very gendered issue such as being rejected in a dating relationship or asking someone out or getting ready for a big dance. Then ask them to write a reflective paper on which parts of the story were hard or easy to write and what they think they learned or realized about the opposite sex."

Collecting compliments. "For a period of two weeks, ask students to collect compliments they hear or overhear from teachers, parents, peers. Categorize comments by gender and then look at what each gender is complimented on or appreciated for."

Athanases does a similar thing when he asks students "to write narratives and poems from the points of view of people involved in current crises in the news and to role play characters from literary works involved in imaginary scenes. In these ways students voice and embody others' experiences" (Athanases et al., 1995, p. 32).

Kelly (1993) suggests using passages from a text to prompt students to consider specific issues of gender or ethnicity. With Sue Ellen Bridger's novel *Permanent Connections,* she distributes the quotations in Figure 7–6 and asks students to write about each of them; select one to explore more deeply before class discussion; and, in a small group, discuss ideas and feelings stirred by the chosen quotations. Kelly explains that the small group creates a safe environment in which to encounter new, sometimes sensitive issues and to "formulate ideas and attitudes" (p. 136).

FIGURE 7–6
Statements from Sue
Ellen Bridger's *Perma-
nent Connections* asso-
ciated with feminist
issues

How might each of the following statements be associated with feminist issues? Write briefly on each one, but choose one to explore your thinking in some depth.

1. [Ginny says]" . . . lately I have been trying to take care of myself. That's what women are most afraid of, you know. Being selfish. It's the ultimate sin." (p. 91)
2. "I am afraid, too," [Ginny] whispered in the darkness. "Hear me, Coralee Dickson, while you are curled like an animal in a hole away from sky and wind and sun. The demons that devour women are all the same." (p. 92)
3. "I just thought I'd reach the time when I didn't have to take care of nothing but me," Coralee said. "I want to have that feeling one day before I die." (p. 117)
4. "I thought that, too," Ginny said. "I married because of it. I did everything I was told because of it. But in the long run being safe meant being in prison. It took a long time, but I came out of it. I guess I thought for years somebody had to open the door for me. I was waiting for that. But the truth is, the door was locked from the inside. Nobody could open it but me." (p. 134)
5. [Leanna says] ". . . Travis wants us to get married. He says it will make college easier . . . He's got in his head how we'll have this cute little apartment instead of living in the dorm . . . but I don't know. I was sort of looking forward to being with girls, talking and all like we're doing. . . . I have to do things on my own sometimes." (p. 151)

Enactment. We have suggested performance through role play and visualization. We focus here on dramatically entering an oral tradition out of which the original texts were created. Native American literature lends itself to active reading or performance because so much of it was originally oral and ritualistic. If students have selected works appropriate to the communal circle, they should read them encircled by their fellow students, preferably out of doors, but at least on the floor of a classroom illumined perhaps by natural, not artificial, light. Percussion instruments and flutes can add authenticity to the reading. Or students may enact an event. For example, imagine what students might do with "The Deathsong of White Antelope." White Antelope of the Cheyenne tribe died at the 1864 Sand Creek Massacre "with the dignity expected of and befitting a war captain of some fifty years. With folded arms, he stood singing his death song as he was killed" (Sanders & Peek, 1973, p. 285):

> *The Deathsong of White Antelope*
> Nothing lives long
> except the earth
> and the mountains.

Students may choose to enact what Lincoln (1983, p. 47) calls the "Navajo Night Chant":

> *Navajo Night Chant*
> May it be beautiful before me.
> May it be beautiful behind me.
> May it be beautiful below me.
> May it be beautiful above me.
> May it be beautiful all around me.
> In beauty it is finished.

The art and film of the places and peoples of any of these cultural groups extend students' imaginative entry into other worlds. For instance, there are numerous books on aspects of Native American art—paintings, architecture, pottery, weaving, silver, crafts—as well as collections of photographs spanning Native American history from the nineteenth century to the present.

Tackling Stereotypes. Multicultural literature is built on cultural differences and thus is often politically and culturally charged. Such issues prompt envisioning and then understanding and often produce strong feelings. Dilg (1995) observes that fictional works by writers of color are "more complicated to address than are works with greater psychological or historical distance" (p. 24). Ideally, when political or cultural content enters your classroom, you will have built an ease and empathy within students and the language for talking honestly about these issues.

Athanases et al. (1995) face stereotyping head on in both our culture and their students. They introduce texts (print and nonprint) that present stereotyping in overt and subtle ways, and they structure class activities that open these questions to student reflection and discussion. Christiano asks students in a unit of his U.S. literature/history class to examine their "impressions of racial and ethnic groups." A portion of this unit is described in Figure 7–7. He reports that this deeper understanding of the larger social and political picture helped students begin to see the value of moving beyond divisiveness to unity among people of color and others interested in combating racism" (p. 30).

We confront serious questions about the dominant culture's treatment of Native Americans via the oratory

In studying Latino culture and experiences, students read an excerpt from Piri Thomas's *Down These Mean Streets* (1967), poetry by Pat Mora (1985), historical texts, essays by Carlos Fuentes; and view a slide presentation of California Chicano murals and films such as *Nuestro Pueblo* (a 1991 documentary about Chicanos in Northern California) and the Hollywood feature film *Zoot Suit* (1991). In groups, students explore cultural assimilation and the phenomenon of feeling lost between two worlds.

To culminate this unit, students who identify themselves as Latinos answer questions that tap personal responses:

- How do your views of your ethnic identity differ from what you see as the general, popular impressions?
- What do you consider to be the most prevalent stereotypes about Latinos and to what extent do they accurately reflect the prevailing attitudes, behavior, and values of your culture?

Non-Latino students respond personally to questions such as these:

- When you hear the terms "Mexican," "Chicano," "Latino," or "Hispanic," what kind of image comes to mind?
- What is the source of this image (how did it form in your mind)?

While the first question asked of non-Latino students invites them to reveal whatever cultural notions they hold, however stereotypical, about Latinos, the second pushes them to examine how such notions developed. Students also answer questions such as these:

- What are some stereotypes you've come across having to do with Latinos?
- To what extent do you believe that these stereotypes have any truth to them?

FIGURE 7–7 Christiano's unit on tackling stereotypes

Source: From Athanases, S. Z., Christiano, D., and Lay, E. "Fostering Empathy and Finding Common Ground in Multiethnic Classes." *English Journal, 84* (3), 26–34. Copyright © 1995 by the National Council of Teachers of English.

and written correspondence between Native Americans and those who were negotiating their removal or demise. For example, Chief Joseph of the Nez Percé, in "An Indian's Views of Indian Affairs," written for the *North American Review* (April 1879), eloquently explained his arduous and honorable attempt to save his tribe from encroachment, coercion, and destruction. These documents can be found in anthologies and then orated and debated. When students assume the roles of Native Americans and whites, drama and intensity build.

Goebel (1995) has his students examine excerpts from the journals of Christopher Columbus with attention to the literary devices used to register his regard for the Native Americans whom he met on his arrival. Goebel's class uses Toni Morrison's list of rhetorical strategies as their guides. They also explore the accounts of these events in current junior high and high school textbooks for racial and cultural bias and stereotyping. Finally, they return to fictional and poetical accounts of the same event to see whether these accounts give them greater access to the people who received Columbus. Michael Davis's (1992) young adult novel *Morning Girl* tells the story of one such family, both their daily lives before the Europeans arrived and their impressions of their arrival. Goebel reports the impact of reading this novel after reading the nonfiction accounts: "the reader can no longer take [Columbus's] words as objective truth, but rather as one perspective in a complex web of human interaction" (p. 48).

Athanases et al. (1995) say that two questions underlie their multiethnic classes. Their carefully designed teaching allows students to openly grapple with these tough issues.

- How can we understand or come to terms with differences within and between various groups such as those defined by race, culture, gender, or sexual orientation?
- How can these differences in identity expand rather than restrict the potential for human life and democratic possibilities? (p. 31)

Perrin (1999) wanted to address gender issues in his classroom but could never find the proper entrée until he discovered Marge Piercy's poem "Barbie Doll." This text provided the opportunity for students to discover multifaceted meanings—not meaning—for themselves. Through vivid images and rich language, this twenty-five-line poem builds on the stereotypes that confine young girls and women. After the class explores these issues, Perrin raises powerful gender distinctions in a series of remarkable questions that imagine the same stereotypes applied to males:

- What toys are foisted upon boys during early childhood, with what sorts of social, personal, and psychological implication?
- What kind of comment from a classmate can undermine a boy's self-concept?
- What adolescent qualities that seem positive in a neutral context are the bane of a young boy's existence?
- What would he feel obliged to apologize for or dismiss?
- What implicit advice does "everyone" give young men?
- What behaviors are they encouraged to engage in?
- What would make a boy's good nature wear out, and what contrasting image would replace the fan belt?
- What ceremonial image of a young man would the undertaker create? (p. 84)

Perrin appeals to teachers to search for selections and devise activities that enable students "to extend, elaborate, and create meanings for themselves. For we cannot, it seems to me, *teach* gender awareness. We can, however, help students *learn* about the power that gender has in our lives" (p. 85).

Invitation to Reflection 7–6

Creating a culturally responsive classroom that identifies, embraces, and celebrates differences clearly involves more than the selection of multicultural texts for study. Consider the following questions based on your experience as a high school learner or on your more recent observations of middle or high school classrooms. We ask you to enter this classroom as an observer.

1. Do the walls have visuals that represent diverse cultures?
2. Is the natural, self-selected grouping of students prone to divisions by race, gender, cultural tradition, or ability?
3. Does the organization of the class engage all students? Are any students habitually excluded by the characteristic structure of the lessons? What patterns seem to work to include all students?
4. Does the talk of the classroom invite all in the class to speak and respond?
5. Are alternative voices allowed and validated? Do you hear oppositional positions encouraged and taken?
6. What features of the class successfully build a diverse learning community? What features are problematic?
7. Do the literary texts selected for study reflect diverse authorship and experience?
8. Does your own reading reflect diversity? Do you believe your experience of language and literature prejudices your choices for your future students? What steps have you taken to broaden your own reading of multicultural literature and your understanding of diverse cultures?
9. Do your observations suggest ways in which you might build your own culturally responsive classroom?

Expanding the Teaching of Literature

We turn now to questions of classroom strategy for teaching long works. (The majority of these strategies and activities are effective with shorter texts as well.) Most of the works considered classic are lengthy, which creates special challenges such as the following:

- A novel represents a large reading commitment. In diverse classes, how can one novel appeal to the authentic interests and the reading abilities of many different students?

- If one novel is chosen and all students read in advance of classroom talk, the work can lose its compelling vitality by the time it is finally addressed. Your talk of it often ends up *summarizing* rather than *experiencing* the novel. It has lost its fresh, living reality.
- If you talk about novels before they are finished, readers are at different points in their reading; therefore, discussions are problematic. Fast readers can't use insight gained by completion; slower readers don't want the story spoiled by knowing its development prematurely.
- If the class is engaged in reading many different novels, coming together as a whole class dictates only the most general discussion and reduces the benefits (necessities for most of us) of working in an interpretive community.

In Chapter 2 we discussed an approach to these challenges that has revolutionized many high school English classes—literature circles. The suggestions that follow can work with literature circles or with single texts read by an entire class. We organize our suggestions here around five of Gardner's (1983) multiple intelligences, those most often overlooked in our verbal and logical/mathematical schooling: spatial, musical, bodily/kinesthetic, interpersonal, and intrapersonal (Table 7–5). Many of these ideas originate in the suggestions of classroom teachers presented at the annual NCTE convention's Concurrent Sessions and Idea Exchanges and in the *Ideas Plus* series, which compiles the best of those ideas. We will take most of our extended examples from those works that we designate as classics, but these activities represent good teaching practices for any literature. Many of the strategies were developed by classroom teachers. We include them as models even when they use texts that a decade ago were common school fixtures and today are problematic in our multicultural classrooms. They represent good (and generalizable) practice.

Response Chart. Chapter 5 discussed the use of verbal scales to chart student reaction to literature. Kelly (1993) devised an assignment that elicits students' initial reactions to characters in a novel and then provides a continuing benchmark for their evolving impressions. Figure 7–8, her response chart, is based on Sue Ellen Bridger's (1987) *Permanent Connections*. Kelly distributes a list of characters to whom the students respond in their reader's logs.

Character Circle. Another visual presentation of characters that is especially helpful in long works in which characters and subplots multiply is a simple character circle. One of our student teachers named this a character bull's eye because it focuses students' attention on important

TABLE 7–5 Expanding literacy through multiple intelligences

Multiple Intelligences	Teaching Activities	Thinking Process*	Instructional Strategies*	Teaching Activities* (examples)
Spatial	Response chart Character circle Story quilt Mobile Guided imagery	In images and pictures	See it, draw it, visualize it, color it, mind-map it	Visual presentations, art activities, imagination games, mind mapping, metaphor, visualization, etc.
Musical	Song search	Via rhythms and melodies	Sing it, rap it, listen to it	Superlearning, rapping, songs that teach
Bodily/kinesthetic (drama)	Impromptu drama Reading between the lines Classroom drama	Through somatic sensations	Build it, act it out, touch it, get a gut feeling about it, dance it	Hands-on learning, drama, dance, sports that teach, tactile activities, relaxation exercises, etc.
Interpersonal	Imitations of life	By bouncing ideas off other people	Teach it, collaborate on it, interact with respect to it	Cooperative learning, peer tutoring, community involvement, social gatherings, simulations, etc.
Intrapersonal	Response journal	Deeply inside themselves	Connect it to your personal life, make choices with regard to it	Individualized instruction, independent study, options in course of study, self-esteem building, etc.

*Definitions of the Thinking Process, Instructional Strategies, and Teaching Activities from Thomas Armstrong (1994). *Multiple Intelligences in the Classroom*. Alexandria Association for Supervision and Curriculum Development. (pp. 27, 52).

characters and graphically indicates their distance from center. Students are given the following directions:

- Draw a circle in the center of a sheet of paper and write the name of the central character in that circle.
- Draw concentric circles around the center circle, one for each character connected to the central character. Write the name of the secondary character closest to the protagonist in the next-to-center circle. If two characters are equally close, put their names in the same circle.
- Add character names, moving to those with increasingly distant relationships as you move from center.

Story Quilt. Warstler (1997) and Whetstone (1997) introduced us to this visual and tactile activity to culminate the reading of a text.

For the discussion of *My Name Is Asher Lev* we will be building a story quilt. Using the paper I provide, make a quilt square to represent the chapter assigned to you. Identify one quotation that seems to sum up the focus of the chapter and allow that to inspire the creation of your square. Each square must reveal artistically the idea you wish to convey. Think carefully which artistic medium will be most effective. In addition to the quotation (which must appear on the quilt), design a border that is appropriate for the novel. It may reflect the individual chapter you are using or the novel as a whole.

The selection of the quotation (similar to the activity in focal judgments) and the presentation through art are instructional enough; but the work in assembling it, the discussion while students work, and the display and scrutiny of the completed quilt carry perhaps the final educative payoff. Displaying the quilt can continue to

FIGURE 7–8

Kelly's response chart

Source: From Kelly, P. P. (1993). *Reading from a female perspective: Pairing A Doll House with Permanent Connections.* In J. F. Kaywell (Ed.), *Adolescent literature as a complement to the classics* (pp. 127–142). Norwood, MA: Christopher-Gordon.

As you are reading this novel, you will naturally have reactions toward characters, much as you do in real life when you meet new people. As you interact with new acquaintances on a regular basis, however, your views of them often change. At the points indicated in the novel, stop your reading and make decisions about how you feel about the characters. Give at least one reason why you have made your choice.

| Chapters 1–15 Why? | like | 1 | 2 | 3 | 4 | dislike | no reaction |
| Chapters 16–30 Why? | like | 1 | 2 | 3 | 4 | dislike | no reaction |

evoke the work long after class discussions of it have ceased—a pleasing after-image.

Mobile.   Another visual project that can both sum up a book and leave it hanging is a mobile of significant quotations from a text. Students individually or in groups select quotations, attach them to heavy paper, then to strings, then to wire (a coat hanger will do), and suspend them. Students write a brief explanation of their choices—why they are important to them, why they are important to the entire text—and then distribute or post these for others to read, in the manner of gallery fliers in an art museum. Images can be used along with quotations—either students' own visuals or clipped magazine art. Mobiles make an arresting public display of students' personal responses and of the book's heightened moments.

Guided Imagery.   Through deliberate oral suggestions, students can be led to imagine places, characters, or situations. In our impromptu and planned exercises of this sort, we usually ask students to close their eyes or we dim the classroom lights to focus the mind's eye on the images we suggest. Shuman and Wolfe (1990) use guided imagery to lead students through a hot summer's walk down a city street and then down a dusty country road in preparation for reading R. Baird Shuman's poem "Citykid." Students enter the poem with heightened openness and energy, having just visualized its setting and character imaginatively. Group work follows in which students create a visual design that illustrates the central dilemma for the boy in the poem.

Figure 7–9 is a more elaborate guided imagery assignment, without the eyes closed, created by Mary Abbott (1990). She carefully leads students into the spatial arrangements of a text. For students who think in images and pictures and who love to draw, design, or even doodle, guided imagery is a boon.

Song Search.   We ask students to listen to music that reiterates the ideas or characters of a work of literature. For instance, teaching Edwin Arlington Robinson's "Mr. Flood's Party" or Seamus Heaney's "Mr. Bleaney" with the Beatles' "Eleanor Rigby" deepens the understanding of the loneliness of all three characters. We also employ music that captures tone, mood, or situation to set the stage for discussion, oral reading, or improvisation. (We don't always pause to listen but have the music playing as students arrive and settle in their places.)

FIGURE 7–9

Abbott's guided imagery assignment

Source: Abbot, M. (1990). Idea exchange: *To Kill a Mockingbird. North Carolina English Teacher, 47*(2), 16–17.

To Kill a Mockingbird is on our high school's core list and one of my favorite novels to teach. Last year, however, for the second year in a row, I was having trouble getting my general (below average) level 10th grade students "into the novel." The first chapter is especially difficult. Scout, the narrator, starts out discussing her family's history which seems long and detailed to low attention span students. She then goes into even further detail in describing her neighborhood as she remembered it as a child. These details are essential to the novel's setting and take on more importance as the story progresses. It finally occurred to me that my students just weren't imagining the "old neighborhood" described by Scout well enough.

Believing I had identified the problem, I thought perhaps I could create some sort of visual to help my students. So I re-read chapter one and started trying to map out Scout's neighborhood from what Harper Lee had written. Suddenly I noticed gaps in the description. That got me thinking, "how well could I remember my own childhood neighborhood?" Not too well, but certain things stood out just like they did to Scout, particularly those "crazy" people who became neighborhood legends and were the subject of many childhood rumors.

The next day, I passed out pieces of blank white paper to my students. I asked them to draw a map of the neighborhood they lived in when they were about six years old. I started out by drawing a portion of my old neighborhood on the board and describing some of the local characters. Some students said that they couldn't remember back that far and chose to draw their maps from the perspective of nine or ten years old, instead. The point was that the kids began to look back and think what their lives were like at another age and how they viewed it at that time.

After about 15 minutes of drawing, I asked students to hold up their maps and tell us about them. This turned out to be exceptionally fun! Many of the students in the class had known at least one other student as a small child, and the stories about the "old neighborhood" began to come out. Students who rarely spoke to each other suddenly were sharing experiences and remembering their past connections. Described were many boundaries—houses beyond which the children were not allowed to wander—just like with Jem and Scout. There were also the "scary" houses and the unusual "Boo Radley" type characters. In this discussion there was a lot of laughter as the students recalled their childhood fears and perspectives.

We finished up the hour by re-reading aloud the sections from chapter one in which Scout describes her childhood neighborhood and boundaries. We mapped out as much of her street as possible on the board and conducted many other activities to relate the novel to students' own lives, but I believe it was this particular activity that got our experiencing of this novel off to a good start.

NOTE: There were, of course, many differences between Scout's era and neighborhood life that children today experience (apartment complexes, etc.). Those comparisons added to the discussion and, for them, helped students understand the narrator's perspective.

After the American Civil War, a committee was formed to find a song that could become the country's unifying national anthem. The observation of one committee member is pertinent to the introduction of music into English classrooms: "Music is the universal language of emotion. Men will sing what they will be shamefaced to say." We angle to move in the course of a term from our selecting the music to the students' initiating and bringing their own suggestions. Blanscet (1988) suggests an assignment that leads students to make connections between music and literature (Figure 7-10).

Impromptu Drama. We ask students to role-play characteristics of specific characters or the relationships between different characters, using their bodies in mime or nonverbal drama. We also ask them to use body sculptures to demonstrate personal traits of specific characters or critical relationships between characters at certain moments in the work. We often interrupt the flow of discussion and have students move into such postures according to their interpretation, as the whole class directs them, or as the author's words, read aloud, dictate. Because no words are spoken, this exercise is especially kind to less verbal students.

Reading Between the Lines. We have adapted an idea from Jeff Wilhelm (1998) for helping reluctant readers create the visual scripts that engaged and proficient readers habitually produce when they read. Wilhelm observed in many of his less-able readers what reading specialists have described: that these readers do not understand that the words in printed texts represent people, places, and things in action in the everyday world. They cannot visualize settings, imagine scenes, or empathize with characters. This contributes to and confounds their sense that school is dumb and reading even dumber. Wilhelm asks students to dramatize scenes that do not exist in the written text in order to breathe life into characters and the difficulties they face. The teacher or an expressive reader reads the text to the class and stops at pivotal points to let students act out invented scenes. Each student is assigned to be a member of an *A* or *B* group, which are given temporary group roles throughout the exercise. Within the two groups, each student has a number. The pairs created from both groups (*A2* and *B2*, for instance) dramatize the assigned vignette simultaneously with the other pairs. The students are active in imagining and speaking within character. Everyone has a part. No one faces the discomfort of a solo performance before the rest of the class. We have adapted Wilhelm's ideas for "readings" for a short story, "The Fan Club," written by fifteen-year-old Rona Maynard, which originally appeared in the magazine *Read*. In the story Laura struggles to fit into a new group of students, to overcome her embarrassment in algebra class, and to remain true to her childhood friend Rachel.

Teaching Activity 7-1 presents the directions that a teacher would give to the two groups of students. The numbers in the activity correspond with stops in the story. Although these dramatizations were developed for less-proficient readers, we have used them with students in a range of grades and reading levels, and their responses have been universally engaged, energetic, and insightful.

Classroom Drama. Dixon (1967) believes that drama provides a means of "doing, acting things out rather than working on them in abstract and in private" (p. 43). We do not here suggest drama as theater, the staged production of professionally written plays. Instead, Figures 7-11, 7-12, and 7-13 present dramatic lessons that require forethought and preparation but not scripts with predetermined dialogue or stage directions. All three were constructed by teachers for the study of three American classics. As you read them ask yourself, "Will these dramatic approaches to classic texts enhance or change student response? Do they forge new ways of understanding established literature? Could I adapt them for other texts?" Coffin (1988) proposes a debate on some of Benjamin Franklin's aphorisms (Figure 7-11), Ditzian (1990)

FIGURE 7–10

Blanscet's song search

Source: Blanscet, K. (1988). Themes in stories and songs. In F. A. Kaufmann (Ed.), *Ideas plus: A collection of practical teaching ideas, book 6* (pp. 31–33). Urbana, IL: NCTE.

*Blanscet lists these especially effective student connections: the idea of premeditated murder in the Police's "Murder by Numbers" and Edgar Allan Poe's "The Cask of Amontillado" and the use of vignettes in Gordon Lightfoot's "The Wreck of the Edmond Fitzgerald" and Twain's *The Adventures of Huckleberry Finn*.

I begin by asking students if they can think of any songs whose words originated in literature.* Typically cited are Iron Maiden's version of "The Rime of the Ancient Mariner" and the Alan Parsons Project's album entitled "Tales of Mystery and Imagination—Edgar Allan Poe," the latter of which sets several of Poe's well-known stories to music. I then challenge each student to find a song that he or she likes and that has the same theme or idea as one of the literary works we have studied. (It's best to use this strategy during the latter part of the school year to ensure that students have a bank of literary works from which to draw.) To complete the assignment, I ask each student to prepare and turn in the following items:

1. a recording of the song on a cassette tape
2. the words of the song written out in stanza form (often found on the jacket sleeves of albums)
3. preliminary and final drafts of a short paper discussing (a) the main theme or idea in the song and the theme of the literary selection and how they relate; (b) the effect of the style of music on the theme; and (c) the reasons why the student chose the song and the literary selection
4. answers to these questions: May I share your paper and/or idea with other classes? Would you rather I did or did not use your name?

7–1

TEACHING ACTIVITY

Reading Between the Lines

1. Laura seeks support

    A. *Laura:* Tell how you felt about the algebra class, Mr. Knowles, and your "friends" after class on Friday.

    B. *Neutral friend:* Listen to Laura and encourage her. But be sure to protect Diana and Terri and the back-row crowd a bit, too.

2. Shopping center encounter

    A. *Laura's mother:* Ask about how Laura is doing at school, what's going wrong, why friends aren't stopping by the house lately.

    B. *Terri:* Try to let Laura's mother know that the algebra teacher was a creep for humiliating Laura.

3. Granny's bedroom

    A. *Rachel:* Because you sense you are losing your friendship with Laura, you let your guard down with your grandmother, who seems to understand you better than your parents do.

    B. *Grandmother:* You listen to Rachel and try to make her understand that being young is always very tough.

4. Ripping Knowles

    A. *Laura's mother:* You go to school to let Mr. Knowles know just how you feel about his humiliation of Laura.

    B. *Mr. Knowles:* You listen to Laura's mother without empathy and only reiterate that Laura is almost flunking algebra.

5. Guardian angels

    A. *Laura:* You feel pretty unsure about your report and what Patti, Diana, and Steve are planning.

    B. *Guardian angel (circle the room):* You each stop at Laura and encourage her with a brief positive phrase. You circle once more and offer another word of support.

6. Radio talk show
    Interview Laura's English class on the question "What do you think of Laura's main point—that we are all prejudiced in quiet ways?"

7. Vote with your feet
    Move to the side of the room to show your opinion:

    Laura is right ◄———► Laura is wrong

8. Laura's alter ego: Mixed emotions

    A. *Laura #1:* What was your honest feeling when you saw the yellow index cards?

    B. *Laura #2:* What do you think you should feel when you see the cards?

9. Deep letters

    A. *Rachel:* Write a letter to Laura telling her how you are feeling about her now.

    B. *Laura:* Write a letter to Rachel trying to explain yourself.

10. Best-phrases poem
    Underline your favorite phrases in your letter and read them antiphonally as a Laura-Rachel strophe/ antistrophe or line up the phrases to make a poem.

FIGURE 7–11

Coffin's microdebates of Benjamin Franklin's *Moral Perfection*

Source: Coffin, E. (1988). Idea exchange: Microdebates of Benjamin Franklin's moral perfection. *North Carolina English Teacher, 45*(2), 7–8.

Pro—Prepare a short speech (only 1½ minutes) developing one, possibly two, strong pro or affirmative arguments for Franklin's advice.
Con—Brainstorm and try to find telling arguments against Franklin's advice. Play devil's advocate! Have fun! You'll have to respond to what the affirmative speaker argues so anticipate what a pro speaker might say.

1. SILENCE
   Speak not but what may benefit others or yourself; avoid trifling conversation.
2. ORDER
   Let all your things have their places; let each part of your business have its time.
3. RESOLUTION
   Resolve to perform what you ought; perform without fail what you resolve.
4. INDUSTRY
   Lose no time; be always employed in something useful; cut off unnecessary actions.
5. SINCERITY
   Use no hurtful deceit; think innocently and justly, and, when you speak, speak accordingly.
6. MODERATION
   Avoid extremes; forbear resenting injuries so much as you think they deserve.

FIGURE 7–12

Ditzian's child custody hearing: *Black Boy*

Source: Ditzian, M. (1990). Idea exchange: A child custody hearing: *Black Boy. North Carolina English Teacher, 47*(2), 14–15.

When I taught *Black Boy* by Richard Wright to sophomores in my American literature class at Marshall High School, I was amazed at the energy and sense of purpose with which my students threw themselves into reading a fairly long novel. At that time I was still operating on the model: read a piece of literature—write an analytical essay. My main thrust in writing instruction for these students was to get them to use evidence to support a thesis. My students had been responding so personally to this book, though, that I felt it would be inappropriate for them to remove themselves and dissect the work.

Rather than assigning a straight character analysis, I brought up the topic of parenthood in class. I asked my students what makes a good parent? What must a parent provide for a child? What makes a bad parent? We spent a whole period discussing these questions in depth. Everyone had plenty to say on the subject. The next day, I asked my students to form groups of four and gave each group the following memo, assigning each group a different character from the novel.

December 5, 1989
To: Investigative team
Re: Child custody hearing

The Department of Children and Family Services requests your expert investigation immediately. It has been brought to our attention that there is some question regarding the fitness of _____ (fill in character name) as guardian of the child of Richard Wright.

Your team has been given one week before the hearing into this matter to make regular visits to _____'s home and/or work place, and to assess his/her behavior in general and particularly as it relates to the child.

Be prepared to state your findings at a hearing Tuesday, December 13. At that time the court will also receive a written version of your assessment. It is of the utmost importance that your findings be based solidly on the evidence you gather. Judge _____, who will hear this case, will award custody of the aforementioned child based on the findings of your team.

Sincerely yours,
Maxine Assignment
D.C.F.S. Director

Groups were told earlier that they would share the work and the grade. When the court date arrived (actually, it took three days because we allowed courtroom observers to question the investigative teams after they had made their statement), we audiotaped the proceedings. All of a sudden my sophomores were using evidence to support an argument and doing it well. Aside from meeting my educational objective, this assignment allowed students the opportunity to respond personally to a novel.

convenes a child custody hearing (Figure 7–12); and Bickford (1991) calls a town meeting (Figure 7–13).

Imitations of Life. Here are several projects that prompt students to enter texts imaginatively and to work cooperatively in pairs or small groups:

- Interview book characters or authors.
- Write letters to characters responding to their dilemmas, advising them, or criticizing their actions.

Figure 7–14 is a note-writing exercise developed by Rogers (1990, pp. 12–13).

- Place characters in a high school annual and imagine their high school histories. Find an appropriate picture and caption it with lists of activities, awards, favorite quotations or subjects, characteristic expressions, plans for the future, superlatives, and teacher and classmate testimonials.
- Imagine how characters would respond to altered events in the text or to new phenomena that you

FIGURE 7–13

Bickford's town meeting

Source: Bickford, S. (1991). Idea exchange: Huckleberry Finn town meeting. *North Carolina English Teacher, 48*(2), 27–28.

Huckleberry Finn is a good novel to assign for summer reading for students entering 9th-grade honors English. To encourage students to complete summer reading, I usually try to devise alternative methods of testing to determine that all students have read the novel assigned. Following is the evaluation method that I have found to be most successful with *Huckleberry Finn*.

I introduce the unit by telling the class about town meetings and their importance in the nineteenth century. Then I tell them that they will participate in a town meeting which might have taken place in St. Petersburg, Missouri, when Huck and Jim return after their "adventure." The town meeting is held to determine what should be done with Huck. Huck wants to be left to his own devices because he believes he has proved himself capable of surviving on his own. Aunt Sally wants to take him into her home to "civilize" him. Some other members of the town believe he should be sent to a school for wayward boys.

After this brief introduction, everyone in the class assumes a role of one of the characters from the novel who could be present at the meeting. We add characters so that everyone can participate. Of course, there must be a mayor, a sheriff, some constables, schoolteachers, store owners and clerks—even Pap might show up. (We do not really have proof that he is dead, and after all, this is a "fictional" assignment.)

Preparation for the town meeting involves having each student (1) develop a character sketch of his character and (2) write a letter to a friend explaining his or her opinion of what should be done with Huck. The character sketch must include physical and personality characteristics and must be written down in two well-developed paragraphs. Students who wish may draw their version of their particular character. The letters must be written in correct personal letter form. These two preparatory assignments give me an opportunity early in the year to assess students' writing abilities.

While the students are writing their character sketches and letters, we devote one day in class to studying the basics of parliamentary procedure. One of the constables "volunteers" to be the parliamentarian for the meeting.

On the day of the first town meeting (of course, this meeting cannot be completed in one session) students dress "in character." If possible we try to hold the meeting in the auditorium to get out of the classroom setting. The entire meeting is videotaped and made available for student purchase.

FIGURE 7–14

Rogers's Half a Note

Source: Rogers, M. L. (1990). Idea exchange: Writing half a note. *North Carolina English Teacher, 48*(1), 12–14.

This is a completion exercise which requires students to make inferences and then develop an idea based on those inferences. In addition it gives students the opportunity to show their understanding of particular characters within a novel.

Write half of a note on the board or on an overhead projector.* Give students time to complete the note and to share their writing with the class.

```
To the most
Thanks so much for your
last week. It made me realize
without you. Life would be
I beg you to please
to upset you.
to the time when we'll
the problems we've had

    All my
```

The first example is based on *The Crucible*, the second on *The Scarlet Letter*.

To the most outstanding witch-hunter around—Rev. Hale,
Thanks so much for your help getting the trials started last week. It made me realize how hard it would have been without you. Life would be still teeming with sin in Salem. I beg you to please help us condemn the rest of the witches, and we'll lock them up so they won't be around to upset you. I look forward to the time when we'll round up all the hateful witches and watch them die. It will solve the problems we've had in Salem.
   All my heartfelt thanks,
   Danforth

To the most beautiful and kindest woman I know—Hester,
Thanks so much for your words that were spoken to me last week. It made me realize how strong you are and how I would have faltered without you. Life would be nonexistent without you to hold me up secretly and quietly. I beg you to please forgive me, because I have so much guilt that I couldn't stand to upset you. I shall pray and wait until Judgment Day, to the time when we'll stand together as a family and take our punishment together. After that glorious day of freedom, the problems we've had will vanish and no more will we be judged.
   All my prayers and sorrow are for you,
   Arthur Dimmesdale

*This idea was developed with a colleague; the half-note itself is original.

imagine. The excerpts in Figure 7–15 are from an activity Belgard (1987) uses to provide a framework for such imagining.

- Write and illustrate a children's book that connects with the core text. Read it to a partner or a small group with the animation you might bring to a listening child.
- Arrange a television talk show that substitutes writers or literary characters for the usual personalities. An amusing model for the satiric effects of such a juxtaposition is Woody Allen's (1991) piece "If the Impressionists Had Been Dentists," which records imaginary letters from Vincent van Gogh that speak of molars, Novocain, and other dental matters.
- Stage a sort of Academy or Emmy Awards for Literature. Categories might include the following:

most long-winded author	most romantic heroine
most decisive protagonist	most readable novel
most chauvinistic character	most astute writer
most imaginative author	most opaque text
most personally compelling character	most likely to succeed

Simply imagining the categories for the rewards stirs divergent thinking and a proper playfulness with texts.

Response Journals.   In preceding chapters, we have alluded to the benefits of response journals in studying literature and we will return to their advantages in the writing chapters. We want here to consider their use in reading longer works. Response journals can provide opportunities to free-write about literature *before* any group discussion has occurred and opportunities for reflective writing *after* students' initial reactions have met and been informed by other students' responses. These free writes should be private, protected pages that a student shares only voluntarily. They can provide memorable stops and points of reference in the course of reading a long work.

Many teachers assign double-entry journals. Students draw a line down a page and on the left side record passages (page numbers and whole lines or key words or phrases) that especially struck them (puzzled, disturbed, moved, or delighted them). On the right, students write down how the passage affected them. Some teachers call this process *note taking/note making*. Students can even make subsequent notes as their views change and as hypotheses are proven or negated. They can share entries with the interpretive community and use them to track their gathering understanding. (These entries also can serve as a source book for story quilts, mobiles, and formal writing.)

Ericson (1993) recommends literature logs, in which students respond daily to any topic or question about the book provided by the teacher. Following are some of Ericson's prompts:

1. Describe one character's problem or a choice to be made. What advice do you have for the character?
2. Explain why you think a character is acting as he or she is.
3. Copy a provocative/interesting/important/enjoyable passage and comment on it.
4. From what you have read so far, make predictions about what could happen next, explaining the reasons for your predictions.
5. Explain why you would or would not like to have a particular character as a friend.
6. Explain why you would or would not like to have lived in the time and place of this novel.
7. Write questions about a part you had difficulty understanding. Choose one question and explore possible answers.
8. Examine the values of a character you like/dislike.

FIGURE 7–15

Belgard's contemporary Huck Finn

Read each of the following statements and circle the letter that best completes the statement in terms of what you think would fit the character of Huck Finn. Be prepared to defend your answer with reasoning based on evidence from the book.

1. If someone approached Huck Finn with drugs, his reaction would be:
   A. he'd take them
   B. he'd refuse but not tell anyone
   C. he'd refuse and report the dealer
   D. he'd try to convince the dealer to give it up
2. If Huck got a traffic ticket, he'd probably:
   A. rip it up
   B. go to court and argue with the judge
   C. pay the fine
   D. leave town
3. On a typical date Huck would probably go:
   A. on a picnic
   B. to a rock concert
   C. to the movies
   D. to a museum

9. What real-life persons or events are you reminded of by characters or events in the story?
10. Reread your entries to date and discuss what your main reactions to this book seem to be so far. (pp. 5–6)

Ericson asks students to select entries to share in group discussions in order to hear the reaction of others. Once or twice a week, she skims the entries and writes *her* response to theirs in order "to encourage thoughtful reading and responding" (p. 6).

Roseboro (1994) gives the following specific prompts for texts by writers from cultural/ethnic minorities to enlarge students' sense of difference and similarity. She asks students to write about a half page after each reading.

- It surprised me that . . .
- Before I thought . . . ; now, I know . . .
- When I read . . . , I began to understand . . .
- This author writes (comment on style, subject matter, structure) . . .
- What new information did you learn about the specific cultural/ethnic group?
- Were any stereotypes demystified for you?
- How similar/different to yours are the emotions expressed in this reading?
- In what way is this story alike/different from those you usually read? (p. 15)

Finally, Schneider (1994) speaks of journaling as the most "significant change in her teaching" in the past decade. She has created "a special kind of journal that keeps kids close to the readings, involves all students in thinking, and promotes frequent writing." She describes how she organizes her journals and how they affect her students' reading of novels.

The journals are just cheap notebooks with about thirty sheets of paper. Students create a cover page, an ongoing table of contents, and a title page for each new section of the journal (when we start a new novel). Students' writing is of several kinds. "Thought pattern" questions, as Mina Shaughnessy called them, ask students to describe, explain, define, summarize, illustrate with examples, and compare and contrast. Open-ended questions ask students what they found most interesting or important in the reading. And creative-writing projects use something in the reading to fire students' imaginations. We may read aloud a dialogue which presents a conflict, and then students try their hands at showing conflict through dialogue. After reading Rosemary Sutcliff's *Dragonslayer,* students rewrite a scene from the monster's point of view. Often, at the end of the novel, I have students choose a character and have that character tell about a moment or event in the story. From these monologues, excellent poems can develop.

Typically, students write at the beginning of class, and their responses are a fine way to initiate discussion. Some of the writings are taken through drafts, but many are one-shot responses. All drafts are kept in the journal, so the journal becomes a growing body of work, something students have to show for their work. (p. 88)

A Reader's Bill of Rights. French author Daniel Pennac has written a best-selling book, *Better Than Life* (1994), that addresses a paradox we, too, have pondered in this text: How do children who find magic and pleasure in books read to them before they start school, become indifferent and reluctant readers after they enter it? In a succession of short chapters, Pennac evokes the problem and, quite surprisingly, offers remedies for home and school, parents and teachers. The force of his critique of schools is directed at practices that focus too much on comprehension and too little on pleasure and response. He quotes Flannery O'Conner: "If teachers are in the habit of approaching a story as if it were a research problem for which any answer is believable so long as it is not obvious, then I think students will never learn to enjoy fiction" (p. 46). He invites us to issue young readers invitations to read, grant them certain rights as readers, and then step back and mimic his own models, those "few adults who gave me the gift of reading"—that is, who "let their books speak and never once asked if I had *understood.*" He calls these rights and privileges a "Reader's Bill of Rights." Although we might not have drawn our bill of rights quite as Pennac does, his views seem fitting for a chapter concerned with fresh challenges to a tradition that, unexamined, might grow inert but, when examined and expanded, startles us with its new life.

1. the right not to read
2. the right to skip pages
3. the right to not finish
4. the right to reread
5. the right to read anything
6. the right to escapism
7. the right to read anywhere
8. the right to browse
9. the right to read out loud
10. the right to not defend our tastes

Chris Crowe (1999), in an open letter to English teachers, asks that they "work consciously" to help his own children "become readers, not just readers of school assignments, but independent readers, the kind who will continue reading on their own after they've finished school" (p. 139). He knows that teachers' suggestions of good books alone will not help them; teachers' actions are required. Among his recommendations to teachers, he includes Pennac's list, even though he knows that his oldest child, a high school senior who "despises" reading, would gladly claim the first right for any assigned school text. Crowe suggests the following for the teachers of his three children: "Maybe you can simply use Pennac's Bill of Rights as a spring board for a discussion about reading, how it works, and why it's important. I'm convinced that whatever you do to help my children understand and exercise these rights will contribute to their becoming life-long readers" (p. 140).

∽CENSORSHIP

The IRA/NCTE document that articulates the first national language arts standard, "Students read a wide range of print and nonprint texts," goes on to ask, "What criteria should be used to select particular works for classroom study?" When those works fall within system-selected textbooks, the question is answered with reference to student ability, interest, and maturity and to curriculum sequence. When the work is supplemental to a basic text and teacher-influenced or -chosen, the questions raised are often shadowed by concerns about censorship.

Pressures mount on English teachers to select texts and instructional programs that are acceptable to all of a school's constituents. The media frequently report incidents of censorship and court cases that result from them. New and veteran teachers describe both external and internal attempts to censor what they teach: the superintendent's, the principal's, the department chair's, or their own self-censoring. Individual parents and collective pressure groups assume adversarial positions. Suhor (1997) explains the actions of a typical protester:

- Objects to particular passages or pages, oblivious to context or the overall theme of the work
- Circulates photocopies of the offensive snippets or reads them aloud at public meetings
- Has been given the opportunity to have his/her child read a substitute work, but insists on a total banning of the book
- Assumes that the author, the teacher, and the school are endorsing the profanity, sexual activity, ethnic slurs, violence, or other offensive depictions in the work (p. 26)

Suhor names "the usual suspects" in censorship cases: "violence, profanity, sexual content, and supernatural themes" (p. 26).

Two examples will suffice to demonstrate the predicament for English teachers. Teacher Marion McAdoo Goldwasser (1997) was disciplined for choosing Clyde Edgerton's (1988) *The Floatplane Notebooks* for her two "unenthusiastic 'general' (low-level) eleventh grade" classes. Attacked by a radio evangelist for her choice, she was summoned before administrators, who withdrew the book and promised the vocal complainants that it would not be taught again. The district expected Goldwasser to accept these compromises quietly, but she chose to fight, asking, "Should professional opinion and judgment be cast aside whenever any individual voiced complaints? And if so, where would the complaints stop?" (p. 35). She insisted that the complainants argue the merits of her choice through the procedures established. She came to regard herself and the novel's opponents as representing two opposing educational philosophies: "They believed school should teach facts, traditional conservative values, neat handwriting, and respect for teachers, who should fill students with the same knowledge the opponents themselves had received. I believed that students needed to be exposed to many and varied ideas, learn to analyze, synthesize and formulate their own opinions. Students needed facts to solve problems not as ends in themselves. Teachers helped students adapt to a changing world and gave them the tools to be effective thinkers and learners" (p. 41).

Cissy Lacks (1997) was disciplined because she had asked her eleventh-grade language arts students to write a dramatic script in which they remembered the playwright August Wilson's advice "to write about things important to them and to write from authentic voices they heard in their lives" (p. 31). Not surprisingly, the scripts that they performed and taped to analyze dialogue contained profanity. The issue of censorship became clouded by other, clearer issues that administrators raised as less problematic grounds for their disciplinary action. Administrators shifted from concern over particular book selections and focused instead on Lacks's failing to follow district procedures. She was fired finally because she "supposedly disobeyed an appendix to a student discipline code, a Type II Behavior which includes a list of minor misbehaviors by a student to disrupt a class or show disrespect to a place" (p. 31).

The experiences of Goldwasser and Lacks read like cautionary tales. You might be ready to resolve to follow the old rule: When in doubt, leave it out. We present their stories to acknowledge the difficulty, not to paralyze you. Young teachers especially can become so terrified of offending someone that they choose only texts sanctioned by the tradition, the anthologizers, and years of safe teaching. Our culture does appear to be divided and acrimonious, and thus the teacher of the young is vulnerable to attack. We think you need to be aware that problems may arise but equally that you have strategies to prevent censorship issues from occurring and methods to handle complaints if they do. Researchers Brown and Stephens (1996) report that the best defense against censorship is to develop proactive strategies and multifaceted support systems.

Community Standards and School Policies

Most schools have experienced teachers and administrators who can orient you to the students and parents that your school serves. Even anecdotal accounts from wise practitioners can forewarn you of potential areas of sensitivity. Of course, even the safest materials and methods may trouble and offend someone, but you will at least know the cultural context in which you are working.

Many schools have stated policies governing the selection of texts and even procedures to follow if one is challenged. Teacher Kenneth L. Zeeman (1997) and the entire English department of which he was chair were engaged in a fight over John Gardner's (1971) *Grendel* for twelfth-grade students. He observes that the literature on censorship indicates "that censors most often win when there are no procedures for selection of materials and for curriculum design, or for reviewing the same when someone challenges them" (p. 48). He enumerates two of his English department's guards against censorship battles: "In addition to educational justification for the literature we taught, we had specific procedures for adopting new texts:

1. The teacher who introduced *Grendel* presented and defended it to her peers. During that defense she cited sound educational objectives supported by the book.
2. Her peers read the book and engaged in further discussion with her.
3. The department voted on the adoption.
4. The purchase request was reviewed by the district language arts supervisor and approved.
5. An alternate book was offered to students who, in consultation with parents and the teacher, found the book objectionable for justifiable reason. (p. 48)

These procedures didn't prevent the parental objections to *Grendel,* but they allowed Zeeman to demonstrate the good faith and considered judgment with which he and his teachers were operating.

Many teachers construct their own procedures. A common practice is to prepare a clear rationale for the texts you want to teach, give students choices of long works, send an annotated list of choices home to parents, and provide a phone number so parents can call and discuss choices with the teacher. Yet even careful plans cannot always protect you. Before studying Robert Cormier's *The Chocolate War,* a North Carolina teacher sent a parental permission sheet home that itself initiated a censorship struggle. Ted Hipple (2001) surveyed *English Journal* readers about such a permission request. Hipple thought that "such action may awaken potentially censorious parents (somnolent bulls) who, without such notification, might be content that their children were reading something, indeed anything" (p. 17). Survey respondents were evenly divided about the permission request, but one teacher suggested another strategy: Send parents "a September syllabus listing all the major literary works to be covered during the year, inviting them to read these books and contact the teacher for an alternative assignment if the parents were concerned" (p. 17). Center on English Learning and Achievement researcher Agee (1999) notes that a veteran teacher at the opening of school sends parents a list of films that might be shown in her course, which is titled "Film as Text." If parents and students are uncomfortable with the list, the student can drop the course. This openness and willingness to communicate about students' learning can't prevent all fights, but it makes them less likely and equips you better to face them if they come.

Allies

Zeeman (1997) praises his department's defense against the censors, but he acknowledges that the resolution to the crisis was reached largely because of the support of his community. He and his teachers had long demonstrated their sensitivity and integrity in teaching the community's young. They were themselves moral people. Parents came forward in good faith to defend the teachers. He regards "parental and community involvement [as] the key to insuring that censors do not win" (p. 49).

Zeeman also was helped in his battle by turning to others for information, advice, and aid: NCTE, the Utah affiliate of NCTE, and People for the American Way. Teachers who find themselves under attack are not without support. People for the American Way (1995) observes that "when teachers or administrators are left to battle censorship groups on their own, the chances for the worst outcome increase dramatically. But when a community comes together and forms alliances that include parents, business leaders, clergy and educators, the censors are hard-pressed to prevail" (p. 11). People for the American Way maintains a toll-free censorship hotline and "offers a variety of technical and legal assistance" (p. 48). The National Coalition against Censorship (http://www.ncac.org) monitors censorship issues and publishes a newsletter. Their 2000 greeting cards featured *New Yorker* cartoonist Roz Chast's "Read-AT-YOUR-OWN-RISK Bookstore" with a front door warning "Caution: Words Ahead." Placards in the window caution further: "WARNING: Reading has been known to cause thinking in humans"; "Management Not Responsible for Post-Book feelings"; "Contents have not been PASTEURIZED, HOMOGENIZED, or STERILIZED."

NCTE provides help through SLATE (its intellectual freedom group) and the NCTE Committee on Censorship. Suhor (1997), an NCTE officer, explains that "in many cases . . . we can and do actively support teachers on matters like the literary quality, teachability, and general suitability of the challenged work, and also support their thoughtful use of controversial teaching methods, from journals to guided imagery, that are grounded in theory and research" (p. 28). NCTE also publishes a number of free or inexpensive pamphlets and statements to aid teachers: *The Students' Right to Read; Guidelines for Dealing with Censorship of Nonprint Materials; Guidelines for Selection of Materials in English Language Arts Programs, Selection and Retention of Instructional Materials—What the Courts Have Said; Statement on Censorship and Professional Guidelines;* and *Common Ground.* Another resource is the American Library

Association's *Newsletter on Intellectual Freedom.* Appendix F provides a list of other full-length treatments of censorship, especially those cases involving schools.

Censorship issues involve English teachers in more than political battles with parents and pressure groups (from the political right *and* left, according to the People for the American Way). Ken Donelson (1997) hints at the deeper range when he points out the powerful connection between literature study as meaning making and censorship issues (pp. l6–20). We would do well to consider deeper questions raised by censorship, such as those posed by Noll (1994):

- What are our individual and collective responsibilities in advocating our students' intellectual freedom?
- In what ways do we support and silence our colleagues' freedom of expression?
- What are our beliefs about the roles and responsibilities of schools as institutions of a democratic society? (p. 64)

We leave this subject with the wise admonition of Charles Suhor (1997). We think he would caution us to choose our censorship battles wisely, but he would also charge us to "work with equal zest on the messy stuff, trudging inventively through the grounds that surprise and resist us" (p. 28).

Invitation to Reflection 7–7

In a speech given to a university English department that was experiencing conflict just short of open warfare, Wayne Booth (1988b) cast some of his remarks as a mimicked debate between the Ancients and the Mods (Moderns). Read the arguments he makes for both sides, and then choose which position more nearly represents your present perspective on your purpose in reading and studying texts.

Booth's Ancients
English appears to be the chief heir and last hope of a once-glorious liberal arts tradition. . . . We do not justify our requirements by saying to Secretary of Education Bennett, "We're filling in those cultural gaps that you seem to care more about than whether students can function in the world." We justify them by doing something *for* students that ought to be done. In short, we hope to educate readers who will write back or speak back profitably to demanding texts, people who can engage in a kind of discourse that is by no means shared by all cultures or by all within our culture, a precious exchange of ideas that, just because it is not by any means essential to bare survival, is always in danger of being lost. The hard fact is that most American students, graduate and undergraduate, will receive little or no liberal education, little or no liberation from the provincial dogmas of our increasingly crass culture, unless they get it from us. (pp. 78–79)

Booth's Mods
What we call "English" should be considered the most important subject in the curriculum because . . . English classes are the only place where students can be freed from their natural tendency to slavish dependence on whatever texts fall into

their hands, or ears. In teaching them how to read productively, creatively, rather than in mere passive reception, in teaching them how *not* to accept texts as givens and classical hierarchies as fixed, in teaching them to recognize just how subtly and oppressively standard readings and reading lists can impose norms of behavior and thought that are entrapments of the spirit, we can hope. . . (p. 79)

Here Booth drops off to summarize the hopes of a multitude of critical positions for freeing students from impositions of gender, class, racial, or ethnic bias and, philosophically, from "all solidities, all notions of presence, all binary oppositions of sex, class, quality, or genre" (p. 79).

- If you talked over Booth's ideas with your own high school English department or with high school English teachers you have recently observed, which side would they support?
- With whom would members of your college or university English department side?
- Which position do you favor?
- What would E. D. Hirsh say about your position? If he disapproves, what could you say to him in response? Do you think he would be convinced by your arguments?
- Try your arguments with Paolo Freire. What would he say?
- What position would a deconstructionist take?
- Would Louise Rosenblatt agree with you? Virginia Woolf? How could you answer these thoughtful persons?

CONCLUSION

Our introduction to the traditional classics and their modern challengers involves you in an important debate going on in our field and our classrooms. All professions have their politically sensitive issues. "Back to the Basics" and "Expand the Canon" are two rallying cries often heard in ours. The first assumes weaknesses in American students and the educational solutions for remedying them. It calls for invigorating doses of classics teaching in literature study. The second sees weakness in our traditional English subject matter and methodology and calls for an expansion of both. Our hope for you is this: that understanding the history, assumptions, and values of competing claims for the English classroom will enable you to select literary texts and teaching strategies while standing confidently on some ground between traditionalists and challengers.

We clearly hope you will turn to texts that sound a variety of authorial voices, critical issues, and unexpected genres. But we also hope that when you approach canonical texts, you do so with a broadened consciousness. Applebee (1974) suggests such an approach:

> Any definition of a literary heritage in terms of specific books or authors distorts the cultural significance of a literary tradition by failing to recognize that what the Great Books offer is a continuing dialogue on the moral and philosophical questions central to the culture itself. The usefulness of the heritage lies in the confrontation with these issues which it provides; any acquaintanceship which avoids the confrontation is both trivial and irrelevant. (p. 248)

Martin (personal conversation, 1991) also offers a vision that embraces tradition and challenge. He finds something indispensable in the continuum of reflected experience passed from one generation to another. He envisions this heritage as a baton passed from one runner to the next, necessary for both runners, happily offered, and eagerly grasped in order to run the race. In his analogy, we not only receive a cultural inheritance but also act upon it through our own exertions. And the runner not only carries on the baton but carries it further and with energies that those who transmitted it could not have supplied.

So it is not Shakespeare who is universal but what he reveals when we ask the right questions. The wrong question is "What value does *Hamlet* have?" *Hamlet* becomes valuable when we as teachers and students relate personally to it. The charge is not to enshrine the classics, nor to trash them, but to remain open to new and different perspectives and to relate personally to those we read. This shared past can awaken us to present realities and future possibilities.

Jack McMichael Martin, a sculptor, artist, poet, and friend, has joined our attempts to articulate the ideas in this chapter over the past decade and, as is his nature, wrote a poem for this book. We close our chapter with it.

The Voices of These Masters

The voices of these masters
enjoin us to go farther

that is, to surpass them
and ourselves

we, who've taken their voices
into our own

as we must do,
we, their apprentices

to have done with them
and to go on.

That's their admonition
borne down the generations

on the wind that scatters them
and carries them to us.

Jack McMichael Martin

8

Understanding
Drama

There are two reasons why people become actors: one is to hide themselves, the other is to reveal themselves

Sir Ralph Richardson

Whuen students have experienced the full continuum of creative drama, they have accomplished much in terms of speaking and moving publicly, collaborating in groups, taking risks, and exercising empathy and creativity. What they begin to understand about formal drama is also of great importance. By the time they perform a 4 *C*'s improvisation, they have seen essential elements of drama firsthand. They begin to appreciate the expressive force of facial expression, gesture, and speech. They appreciate the power of objectifying human dilemmas in the spoken interaction of characters. With this felt or experienced conception of drama, they are better prepared to meet and greet formal drama.

Our focus shifts now toward the oral language of theater. The learning goals of classroom talking, oral exercises, and creative drama are put into play as they give life to the powerful scripts that are housed in texts but are meant to be acted out to the witness of a live audience. Chapters 5 and 6 suggest approaches to teaching any literary text and present numerous specific classroom activities for exploring them. We discuss here classroom strategies that are especially apt for drama and that are active (not as dependent on teacher talk or whole-class discussion) and social (involving pairs and groups of students). These strategies have a common aim: to lift drama texts from page to stage and to shift students from passive spectators to active creators and performers. At first, we set students in motion simply by reading scripts that professional writers have transformed from well-known fiction. Then students begin creating their own scripts from short stories and poems. With those moorings in place, we approach the plays of esteemed writers by absorbing entire dramatic productions and then participating in reflective activities that deepen students' appreciation of plot, character, theme, and form. Finally, we consider how any dramatist's text can be more deeply understood when students actually perform significant parts of it.

∞ TRANSFORMING TEXTS

Ready-Made Plays

Creative drama prepares students to translate simple stories into dialogue and narrative descriptions into sets, props, and stage directions. A fine way to start their dramatic writing and performing is with material that has already been translated from story to dramatic form. Scholastic's *Literary Cavalcade* publishes easily accessible examples. This publication has transformed the works of young adult novelists such as Paul Zindel, Bette Greene, and S. E. Hinton as well as those of classic short story writers such as Edgar Allen Poe and Arthur Conan Doyle into short, engaging, easily readable drama for classroom use. *Literary Cavalcade* also publishes timely international dramas and screenplays, such as *A World Apart* by South African playwright Shawn Slovo. Because this drama is concrete, immediate, and dynamic, it appeals to a wide range of students. Students who have not been energized by anything else in the traditional English classroom often respond to even uninspired dramatizations of these novels and short stories. Productions do not have to be elaborate. You can merely assign parts and ask students to read their roles from their desks. We have witnessed moving readers' theater performances on spare classroom stages as well as costumed performances on classroom-adapted sets, with lines well rehearsed and even memorized. Both types of staged performances elicit students' lively interest. The simplicity and authenticity of characters speaking for themselves as they move and act on the stage draw these students nearer to fictive art than any silently read texts do. The brevity and simple language capture even unenthusiastic readers.

Student-Created Drama

As both audience and participants in these transformed dramas, students may come to understand how plays work and how they are transformed from fiction. That understanding will help them in the next step: initiating the transformation from text to theater themselves. We suggest that you begin slowly with brief scenes between pairs; progress to longer scenes with several players and perhaps a subplot; and culminate with two scenes that manage to move characters on and off stage, to link incidents, and to elaborate on the plot. Practice is required for this progress.

More ambitious dramatic transformations are outside the scope of this text. O'Neill and Lambert (1982, p. 25), however, suggest specific strategies that teachers might use to establish a dramatic context and so give students a "stronger sense of purpose and motivation":

Provide a starting point for inquiry: Groups prepare a short scene encapsulating their particular viewpoint on a chosen theme or topic—for example, emigrants, young offenders, or a woman's place (p. 25).

Provide evidence and information: Various aspects of a theme, life-style, or problem can be illustrated in a number of different scenes in order to build up a fuller picture of a particular way of life—for example, the differences between rich and poor in Victorian times (p. 25).

Present an alternative reconstruction of events: Each group shows a different version of the circumstances leading up to a situation in which events are open to interpretation—for example, what exactly happened when the child's bedroom was wrecked? (p. 26).

Provide alternative courses of action: Groups illustrate a suitable solution to a problem with which they are concerned—for example, different versions of how the runaways can be reconciled with their parents (p. 26).

Provide a means of reflection: Each group prepares a short scene or series of scenes summing up the most significant areas of their work on a particular theme—for example, the struggle of women for the vote (p. 26).

Once students negotiate these small steps, they are better prepared to construct a larger production. The resources for concrete and manageable ideas are the same as for oral interpretation and creative drama: poems, visual art, MTV videos, and television commercials. Our students have also elaborated and staged narrative ballads and poems such as Robert Browning's "My Last Duchess" or Robert Frost's "Out, Out." A more ambitious project is to transform short stories or novels into performances. We have found that stories with strong but concentrated action, dramatic tension, and clearly developed characters are especially accessible to production—for example, Hernando Tellez's "Just Lather, That's All," Leo Tolstoy's "God Knows the Truth but Waits," Gabriel García Márquez's "The Very Old Man with Enormous Wings," or Zora Neale Hurston's "Snake" and "The Gilded Six Bits." A half step toward such full transformation of a short story is to read a piece of very short fiction such as Stuart Dybck's "Sunday at the Zoo" (in Shepard & Thomas, 1986) and then have pairs write dialogue between the drinking couple before or after their visit to the zoo. Moving on, a whole class might undertake a longer work, such as vignettes from Sandra Cisneros's *The House on Mango Street*. One modest kind of staging is for a student to read selected passages that others enact in tableau or pantomime.

We have seen dramatization used successfully with ESL students. Teachers ask small groups to select a favorite scene from a longer work, convert it to oral language, learn parts, and enact and videotape it. The whole class then assembles the scenes in chronological order and presents the tape to themselves and other classes. The performance gives motive to their work, yet the camera also places a distance between them and their audience. Converting scenes to written and then spoken speech in this way can bring the formal words to life.

The work of transformation can awaken students to a clearer sense of the dramatic. Just as performing musicians become more acute and sympathetic listeners to music, so even amateur dramatists become more alert and responsive theatergoers. They can sense when characters are not well defined, when they are too predictable. They feel the presence of dramatic tension or the lack of it. They see how the context works to define conflict and whether a satisfactory resolution is achieved at the play's conclusion. (The four *C*'s—character, conflict, context, closure—can be used as checklists to guide or critique the basic components of good drama.) Thus, students learn through dramatizing much as writing-to-learn students expose what they know and don't know about science as they explain a chrysalis. Although it is impossible to guarantee that drama will have depth and integrity, acts that produce those results are most likely to occur when the class and the teacher are working together spontaneously (O'Neill & Lambert, 1987). Then students begin "to question, accept challenges, make decisions, realize implications, go beyond stereotypes and alter their perspectives. If the class is working with belief, commitment and integrity the pupils may even achieve the kind of change in understanding which is at the heart of educational drama" (pp. 27–28).

⬧ENGAGING DRAMA

By transforming texts, many students move toward a sensitive awareness and deeper understanding of drama. You may still want to secure your students' grasp through traditional classroom strategies. An alternative approach asks students to explore drama through active engagement rather than passive reading and discussion of scripts. We argue for this approach not because we devalue the vital language and story of dramatic texts but because we

value the story in action. Playwrights intend their plays to be understood in terms of their live performance. We should exploit this unique characteristic and ask students to be not only readers but also spectators and actors.

⬧Invitation to Reflection 8-1

1. What particular plays do you remember studying in high school or college? Were they all written by professional playwrights?
2. How were these plays taught?
3. Did your teachers approach them in ways different from their approach to other nondramatic literature?
4. Have you ever written a play? If so, was it performed before an audience?
5. What is your favorite experience as a spectator of drama on stage? Why was that moment memorable? Can you imagine re-creating a vestige of such a moment in a middle or high school classroom?
6. Have you ever acted in a play? If so, how was performing the play different from reading it as you would a narrative poem, short story, or novel?
7. Chapter 4 introduced approaches to drama through oral language exercises and creative dramatics. This chapter imagines students as playwrights, spectators, and actors. Do you find yourself comfortable with moving words (and students) from the page to the stage?

We believe that analysis can and should be brought to bear on the powerful dramatic works of professional playwrights; but we know that the stage, not the page, is where drama belongs. So we argue that your students can analyze drama's quality and appreciate its artistry better if they encounter it as live drama first. To this end, we suggest a host of reflective exercises that focus on four dimensions of any drama:

Plot: what
Character: who
Theme: why
Form: how

These four are intricately meshed in drama, but separating them helps many students understand plays more readily and explore drama more deeply. We enumerate exercises that will help students understand drama apart from strict classroom analysis of it. Figure 8–1 makes these suggestions more visible. Once students have entered the what, who, and why of drama, they might then be ready for our final consideration of form—the how of drama.

Plot

The first question asked of any story is "What happened?" Before readers or viewers can appreciate character or

FIGURE 8–1

Active exercises for drama appreciation

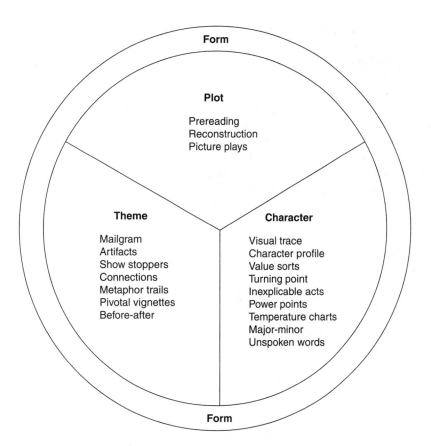

theme, they must first comprehend the sequence of incidents and the causal connections between them.

Prereading. One approach to plot centers on the play's first scene. We suggest that before students read or see an entire play, they see this scene, act it out themselves, or hear it read by a group of strong readers. Then we ask students to speculate on the possible middle and end that issue from this beginning. Not only are potential confusions cleared up at the outset, but curiosity is piqued and a sense of some dramatic conventions and continuities is sharpened.

Reconstruction. One of the best means of understanding the play's action is to have pairs of students recount major events of the play to each other. The sequence might be as follows:

- In pairs, students construct a simple narrative by jotting down key words that capture the action, characters, and/or setting of major incidents.
- A pair of students shares with the whole class its list of the first five incidents at the play's beginning.

With most classes, the invitation will evoke a hail of changes and rearrangements. This activity does not simply recount facts but sorts out understanding, interpretation, and even criticism. After settling the beginning, a second pair can be asked to recount the middle and a third the end. Everything, including the point at which they stop, gives clues to their sense of plot and even the play's structure.

We have also used two-page summaries to stimulate students' thinking about the plot. The class is divided into groups (one for each act) and asked to underline the event in their act's summary that seems most significant to understanding the play. When the small group reaches consensus, it informs the entire class. Then the whole class considers the one event whose omission would change the meaning of the play. Plot in this fashion comes to be more than a string of incidents. It is marked by relationships. The same groups can explore those relationships, and each group can link its scene to the act before and after it. By linking the adjacent acts, the groups with the first and last acts connect both ends of the play as well. When these underlined events are linked to the surrounding events, a clearer sense of the entire play's interrelated structure emerges. This is a simple beginning that lets the entire class start on a sure footing. We move from comprehending events to perceiving significance in the events and finally to understanding the relationships among them.

Picture Plays. In addition to these two verbal methods of comprehending plot, we can capitalize on the playwright's use of the visual and concrete image to depict character and conflict. The clues for what these props, scenery, gestures, stage movements, and stage positions mean are in the dialogue. Exploring students' physical presentation reveals how they have picked up those clues. Students are asked to visualize the play and capture crucial moments in drawings, schematics, or props. Some depict groups of characters in sociograms; others have brought in props such as a dagger for *Macbeth* and a unicorn for *The Glass Menagerie*. A more ambitious task is for individuals, pairs, or small groups to create a schematic of the events of the main plot or the defining incidents for the main character. Arriving at the play's plot through concrete objects or drawings often anchors and secures students' understanding. Interestingly, when students see other students' pictures and hear their explanations, they tend to reflect upon, and usually sharpen, their own sense of what happened. Here, too, we teachers gain a much surer understanding of what students have comprehended in the play.

Understanding plot, the most elementary dimension of the play, is essential to developing a deep understanding of the more complex notions about character, theme, and form that follow. The first step should be sure, but it must also be enlivening. It must build interest in the human, personal events at the heart of the dramatic story. It nudges students toward creating a vivid and precise performance in their minds' eyes.

Character

Character is what draws us to a play. We see an individual who "struts and frets his hour upon the stage"; he is concrete, alive, among us—almost. The curtain between life and art is thin. Characters are like us. They are people, living out a crisis through action and spoken dialogue with each other. Even if the crisis or plot seems contrived and unconvincing, we can be diverted by the human beings involved in it. We are witnesses. In class discussion, we can focus our questions and our uncertainties on character, and generally students will respond. But we also can focus, sharpen, and enlarge our responses to character through nonanalytical experiences. We recommend nine exercises that depart from the traditional formal analysis of character.

Visual Trace. Visual trace is a means of using videotape to trace the growth stages of a character.

Major Character. In Chapter 10 we enumerate an exercise involving the central character in the 1979 film *Norma Rae*. We excerpt a series of brief segments from the film and ask students to respond to each segment by noting the qualities of the central character as she changes in the course of the series. We also ask students to mark the most blatant change and the one that captures the most subtle shifts. These response sheets become the concrete prompts to small-group and then whole-class discussion.

Character study based on familiar film media always intrigues our students. We propose the same kind of analysis for staged drama. Select a play that is available on DVD. Ask students who have read or seen the play to choose and then analyze a set of six to eight bar-coded DVD excerpts that trace the movement of a character such as Antigone or Hamlet. Small student groups select their set of steps in a character's development and submit their sequence to the entire class; the awareness that comes from watching and noting is also developed by the act of selecting. Both reception and production work are valuable.

Character Pairs. The analysis of a single character's development can be broadened to the scrutiny of two major characters. We ask students to isolate and watch the crucial interactions of pairs of characters as they relate to one another through the course of the play. Each scene in which they talk together can be taped and a growth chart used to examine the changes that transpire. For instance, we may sense shifts in the relationship between Tom and Amanda in *The Glass Menagerie;* but when we study their exchanges more intently, free of other characters and other plots, we can understand what has come of it, the subtle ways in which it changes. Through this piecing together, we drive more deeply toward understanding them as both individuals and family members.

Minor Character. The kind of growth that is evident in a central figure is rarer in minor characters and is often perceptible in only small gradations of change. The distinction is useful here between characters who are *static,* or unchanged by the action in the play, and those who are *dynamic,* or developing as a result of the action. To help students gain a clearer sense of the play's lesser characters, we ask individuals or small groups to select a minor character, chart his or her growth, and then present that character in a parade for the whole class. Students organize the parade in progression from the most one-dimensional and unchanging to the most intricate and dynamic.

Observer or Narrator. The playwright's spokesperson is not always present or evident, but we ask students to search for the character who seems to present a consistent and collected perception of the unfolding events or to act as an outside observer of the play's action. The Stage Manager clearly serves this purpose in Thorton Wilder's *Our Town,* but characters such as York in Shakespeare's *Richard II* also present themselves, through their words and placement in the drama, as the voice of the playwright. York, for instance, is always present at moments of crisis to comment almost omnisciently. Students can look for such authorial voices in other plays and videotape or record their key statements to look at how certain characters illuminate the meaning or theme of the play. Playing these recordings for the class provides a dramatic culmination.

Character Profile. Writing character profiles is a simple way to involve students with the major players of a drama. Give each student two concrete measures of response to a character: (1) a list of five statements about a single character to be acknowledged as true or false—for example, "Amanda is more realistic than Tom" and "Hamlet does not love Ophelia"; and (2) an adjective checklist to be checked for descriptive terms that capture the character. Making your own specific checklist is best; a general list of feelings appears in Chapter 6 (Figure 6–2). An alternative is to ask students simply to list characterizing adjectives. These can be explored in small groups or with the whole class. When students stake claims and clarify reactions through these simple responses, they are more likely to be engaged by discussion of the differing readings or viewings. A key to developing good exploratory conversations is to offer statements that address the ambiguities and uncertainties in the plays.

Characters can also be understood by exploring serious conflicts between them. Jill Snyder (2001, personal communication) created a lesson that highlights Macbeth and Lady Macbeth. She asks students to take the roles of the famous husband and wife and speak separately to their marriage counselor about the difficulties they are facing in their marriage. Similar roles can be taken by Hamlet and Ophelia, Julius Caesar and Calpurnia, Othello and Desdemona, and many other pairs. Teaching Activity 8–1 is the assignment that Snyder gave to her students.

Value Sorts. Value sorts encourage students to consider the value systems of characters in the play and to compare them with their own. In this activity, which moves from individual to partnered to small-group work, students are asked to do the following:

- Select the characters that you consider to be the play's most admirable and least admirable.
- State three virtues and three vices of this polar pair, or select them from a list we provide.
- Discuss those values with a partner.
- Circle three of your worst character's values and invert each to see how closely those inverted values may lie to your own.

Where these conversations expose differences of literary and personal opinion, they gain energy and authenticity. This exploration of character can be connected more strongly to the text by asking students to cite specific lines, actions, or scenes to support their ideas. When students must hunt for evidence for their opinions, they give the text a deeper reading and acquire a more thoughtful interpretation of the play.

An alternative to the best-worst comparison is to ask students to rank a list of four or five characters drawn from several plays from most to least admired. When the stock of shared plays is limited, well-known film characters can work amid the play casts. Qualities are again enumerated for the most and least admired, and these rankings are discussed in small groups. We also find benefits in reporting these conclusions to other classes. Students enjoy hearing how other classes voted in these

8-1 TEACHING ACTIVITY

Marriage Counseling for the Macbeths

You (Macbeths and Lady Macbeths) are attending your usual marriage counseling session. Every Thursday you and your spouse meet at Dr. Sylvia Smoothover's office for an hour-long joint session. But once a month you come in separately for individual sessions to talk with the good doctor about the ups and downs of married life with your partner. There have been many significant events that have happened in your household recently, and you are eager to discuss them with the psychologist. Your spouse's actions since the end of war with the Norwegians have been interesting, to say the least.

You enter the office, sit down, and the doctor greets you. Your spouse has just finished his or her session in the office. Now the doctor looks at you, sees that you have a lot on your mind, and tells you to let it all out.

Explain your view of your spouse and his or her actions to the counselor in a written page. Support your views with at least three examples from the text. (Choose one example each from Acts I, II, and III.) First, choose significant examples of your spouse's behaviors, actions, or words and then formulate your story for the psychologist. Describe the examples to the doctor as you are sharing your side of the story, but make sure you also cite the examples by referring to scene and line numbers in parentheses as you write. Remember, the marriage counselor is a psychologist and is very interested in how your partner's actions make you *feel*.

informal polls, and we like expanding their sense that literature is a subject of lively inquiry and speculation.

Turning Point. Another way to measure growth and understand character is through the simple device of a time line that marks major events and crucial turning points. The teacher alone or, better, the class together draws up a plot time line, perhaps on long rolls of paper. Each student then marks the point on the time line at which the major character or characters makes a crucial choice or engages in defining action. Next, students explain why these decisions or actions are formative. A nice benchmark is the freedom that existed before that point and the dwindling options available after it.

Inexplicable Acts. Postman and Weingartner (1969) state that the only questions that should be asked are those authentic ones for which the teacher has no ready answer. In this exercise, those are the *only* questions asked. First, ask students to keep a running list of actions and scenes that can't be satisfactorily explained, that leave them confused, or that might easily perplex others. Here are some examples:

Why doesn't Hamlet kill Claudius?
Is there method or madness in Hamlet's actions?
Does Polonius deserve Hamlet's scorn?
Is Polonius merely a meddlesome moralizer?

Then poll students for their list of inexplicable acts and write them on the board, a transparency, or a sheet of paper. The class rates the list to find their top five most inexplicable scenes. Small groups or the entire class then attempt to find at least two plausible interpretations. A jigsaw discussion would be excellent here: Give a question to each group to discuss; then, when time is called, each student goes to a new group composed of one member from each of the original groups, and students discuss the answers to each of the questions. Students need to know that understanding character is never a settled business: Their questions have puzzled audiences and critics for centuries, much as the persons in our lived lives perplex us. They need to see that careful reflection can unravel some characters but that others seem to become more perplexing. They need to see that thoughtful questions don't always have ready answers.

Power Points. The powerful soliloquies of Hamlet and Macbeth and other gripping utterances of Shakespeare's characters can be brought together in one precious heap so that students can move to a heightened awareness of the craft and power of Hamlet's tedious internal arguments or Henry V's stirring battle speech. Small groups in your class are given responsibility for carefully examining one of Hamlet's soliloquies, selecting a most important line, and choosing one of the group to deliver it to the

class. When the lines are delivered to students who have seen them in the total context of the professional production, they can gain a clearer sense of Hamlet's move to resolution and action.

Temperature Charts. A helpful way to see characters is in their relationship with one another. This is especially true when they are "mighty opposites"—a protagonist (the chief character or contender) and an antagonist (a rival or opponent of the protagonist). Ask students to select two closely related characters and locate a number of contact points throughout the play when the two express their feelings for one another or respond to one another's actions or words. Their feelings for each other are likely to be synonymous, but occasionally they differ. With contact points established, we ask individual students or groups to label each point according to the strength of feelings between the two. Students can create their own terms to characterize the attitudes or use a ready-made list such as the following scale of rising (negative) temperatures. For each of the agreed-upon contact points, the groups must come up with a temperature or term to define the positive or negative heat of the relationship. Differences are as instructive as agreements; students begin to analyze characters more intently and see their relationships more clearly.

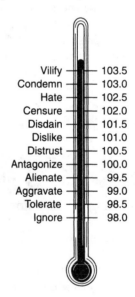

Vilify	103.5
Condemn	103.0
Hate	102.5
Censure	102.0
Disdain	101.5
Dislike	101.0
Distrust	100.5
Antagonize	100.0
Alienate	99.5
Aggravate	99.0
Tolerate	98.5
Ignore	98.0

Major-Minor. This exercise lets students explore the parallels of two characters of unequal importance to the play. Here the major character's main actions throughout the play are listed on a time line; on a parallel line below it are those of a minor character. The study of the actions and feelings of minor characters at important times of the play, as they compare to and refer to those of the major figures, is enlightening. This is particularly true of Shakespeare. We can see the craft of the playwright at work with an unexpected clarity: Minor characters create foils, character definition, tone, foreshadowing, and recurrent motifs.

Unspoken Words. Our final entry into character asks students to use their imaginations to write soliloquies, asides, or dialogues that characters might have spoken. Imagining and then performing the inner thoughts of, for example, Laura Wingfield, Willie Loman, or Juliet open students to insights into those characters that reveal and expand their depth of understanding.

Theme

Perceiving the play as action and character are the first steps to understanding dramatic art. But we must also invite students to see deeper significances, or we short-change them as students of both life and literature. We have to remember that abstract, formal-operational thinking is not the natural province of most secondary students, who are largely caught in concrete, literalistic thinking. Thus, we need to nudge our students, use what Piaget called disequilibrium, to raise their thinking to the level of theme.

When we ask students to tell us what a play is about, the common response is to recite a list of significant incidents of plot. Few will understand these actions as embodying ideas. We need to work hard to help students see the abstractions that action encapsulates.

Mailgram. One strategy for helping students develop their sense of the central thrust of a play is to compress the play's action into the sixty words of a mailgram. When they compact a play such as *Our Town* into these few words, the next step—deciding what those actions really mean—is a little easier to achieve. Groups can work to strip away excess until the major sixty words are found. The next step is finding one word—an abstraction such as *community, realization, fate,* or *transformation*— to stand for all of those actions. Once the groups have settled on a single abstraction, they can post their one word and debate with the other groups the capacity of their choices to sum up the whole play. Those same groups, having explained their single word, are more able to look from that general abstraction to a single short sentence that further explains their words. These sentences can then be expanded to identify the center of meaning in the play. The conceptual movement is like an equation:

> concrete actions = single abstraction = abstract statement

The transformation is less difficult when the steps are made more explicit. Those who deal best with concrete palpable events and things are more likely to make the shift to a general statement by using specific steps to get there. It is the shift from the concrete summary to the single abstract word that makes the entire process work. This activity can be easily varied. For example, during the study of Shakespeare's *The Tempest,* teacher Julia Neenan (1992, personal communication) asked small groups of students to sum up the political platform for each of the play's contenders for leadership or power. The student groups distilled aphoristic phrases from those platforms to put on posters plugging their candidate.

Artifacts. Another starting point is to use highly charged props or scenery to begin to articulate theme. We ask students to list three objects from the play that stand out as special and loaded with meaning beyond themselves. For *The Glass Menagerie,* a student might list *coffin, glass unicorn,* and *blue roses.* After these objects are selected, the three are translated into a word that captures the meaning behind each:

Object	Idea
coffin	death
glass unicorn	uniqueness
blue roses	unreality/imagination

The student then takes the transformed objects and tries to connect them in a sentence that captures the essence of the play. As with the mailgram activity, when an earlier distillation has occurred, the transformation takes place in the single word.

Show Stoppers. Another approach that translates actions and objects to theme centers on those lines we immediately know are significant when we hear or read them—those lines that catch us and perhaps urge us to write them down. A student's selection of a line suggests it has power for him or her as a reader. Students select four they like best and then translate these power statements into encapsulations of the play's central ideas. Beck (1988) makes a game of students' awareness of Shakespeare's greatest lines by using both the cooperative learning of teams and the fun of competition between them. He suggests that you select quotations that connect the crucial points in the play and represent the most prominent themes. So while his students are enjoying themselves, they are coming to understand the basic meaning of Shakespeare's works.

Connections. Herz's (1996) *From Hinton to Hamlet* offers an effective way to clarify and further define themes shared by Shakespeare's plays and today's adolescent fiction. She lists some of the major themes in *Julius Caesar* and *Romeo and Juliet* that are illuminated by books such as Greene's *Summer of My German Soldier,* Zindel's *The Pigman,* Peck's *Remembering the Good Times,* and Avi's *The Confessions of Charlotte Doyle.* Such connections can clarify ideas and bring the familiarity of everyday life into relationship with the more difficult idiom of Elizabethan times.

Metaphor Trails. Shakespeare and other fine dramatists deepen the thematic thrust of their play by using particularly poignant metaphors and repeating similar images. You can point out the clothing images of *Macbeth* or the dark-light images of *Romeo and Juliet* or let students gather them. Metaphors such as "sleep that knits up the ravell'd sleave of care" can be located, replayed on DVD or tape, and examined carefully for cumulative effect. Robano and Anderson (1993) offer a thoughtful approach to Shakespeare's metaphors and other figures of speech in their idea for character journals, where they ask students to keep careful watch over the metaphors from Act I to Act V as these figures of speech subtly define theme in plays such as *Macbeth*. They believe this awareness moves students from efferent to aesthetic readers.

Pivotal Vignettes. Focusing on significant, well-defined moments in the play can also help students make the leap to understanding theme. When these moments occur, we usually sense them; they possess a heightened intensity. If students can respond to and identify such moments, they are on their way to knowing what the play is about. The characters seem to be set up on stage as in a frieze, and students are asked to mimic these captured moments. Other students can walk around and reflect on this pivotal scene as they would an actual frieze. Rare teaching moments can occur as teachers help students puzzle over the meaning, much as good docents do with visitors to art galleries.

Before-After. This exercise works not with one pivotal scene but by comparing an early with a late scene in which a character is noticeably altered. Almost any character will work: Shakespeare's Macbeth, Richard II, or Lear; Ibsen's Torvald, Nora, or Hedda; Williams's Amanda or Blanche. Students can focus on these stark contrasts and then complete the following:

_____ moves from _____ in
  (character)   (early quality)

_____ to _____ in about
  (act and scene)   (final quality)

_____ .
  (act and scene)

Students will find different words for the character transformation, but that change process will probably lie near the center of those ideas the playwright wishes to embody.

Form

Form is even more distant and abstract than theme is, but for some it is the key to appreciating drama and the goal toward which preceding discussions of plot, character, and theme have aimed. The active considerations of plays should have opened students to a sense of the play as a structure with formal, defining conventions. Other exercises can help students learn to recognize form, which may not have been apparent to them as less sophisticated readers, audiences, or actors. The play's form is its art or its *howness:* what the playwright has done to shape the meaning of the story. Because considerations of form in the high school classroom always verge on the analytical and distanced, it must be taught very carefully. Chapter 5 discusses the common pitfalls of formal discussions and suggests positive ways to avoid them.

⌒ TEACHING SHAKESPEARE

When you hear that Shakespeare or other powerful dramatists are being taught in an English class, you usually expect to find students conscientiously reading the texts of those plays. This approach seems particularly proper to most of us, who have studied the great plays as read literature. English essayist and critic Charles Lamb, who had a clear understanding of literature and a particular love for Shakespeare, is said to have held the deep personal belief that his plays should always be read rather than seen on stage. He approached them almost as poetry, which profits from careful scrutiny of its compressed sound and sense on the page. Some would say that a play that is read is almost a different genre from a play that is watched. Many teachers agree, arguing that the plays are too rich and complex to hurry over. The language and the deeper meaning of the play, they fear, will be lost on uninitiated or untrained student audiences. They believe that rather than killing drama, careful reading vitalizes it; savoring a play over time yields deeper appreciation.

Performing Shakespeare

In the past fifteen to twenty years we have seen this belief challenged. A strong contingent of English teachers urges us to turn to the stage, not the page, to introduce students to Shakespeare. They contend that his plays, and those of other dramatists, were made for audiences to watch and hear in their full three-dimensional power; plays are aural and visual events, not private textual ones. These drama advocates might characterize the difference as analogous to studying a series of football plays in a coach's playbook rather than watching the athletes perform on the field. Styan (1965, 1980) and others observe that when students see a whole play enacted by a company of flesh-and-blood characters, it becomes tangible and meaningful rather than abstract and impenetrable. Styan (1993) further argues that analysis is not lost in performance; the reverse is true. "Nothing comes between the play and the students" (p. 62). When Kent and Gloucester are joking about Edmund's linage in *King Lear,* students watching the play have to come to terms with Edmund's reaction to this crude treatment of his bastardry. We know from Piaget and other psychologists that knowledge of wholeness helps us recognize parts better and that the sensory world is understood long before the symbolic word. MacKail (1970) agrees, saying that Shakespeare and almost all drama is meant for the stage, not the study: it is stuff for actors; it is whole, not fragmented; it is sensory-rich, not abstract.

When students read a play over time, especially when that time extends over three or four weeks, they lose the power of the whole play, dramatic and unbroken. When we merely read it, we substitute verbal and symbolic code cracking for primary contact with the characters in action onstage. Encountering Shakespeare through performance rather than print is analogous to using manipulatives to help students understand math concepts rather than just teaching the abstractions of mathematics. We argue, perhaps hyperbolically, that if you tried to create a scheme for destroying these great plays, it might well involve a too familiar classroom scenario— reading them slowly over a few weeks' time, analyzing them piece by piece, and focusing on the form and context rather than the meaning and content.

We need to capitalize on those qualities that set plays apart as dramatic performance in front of an audience. We must approximate this performance condition in any way possible: to let students see it live if possible, in its entirety if possible, as unbroken and enveloping if possible. DVD, videotape and film are the more common nonprint alternatives for introducing students to plays. Two Internet sites offer excellent resources for teaching Shakespeare as well as multiple links to other sites.

> *The Shakespeare Resource Center* (http://www.bardweb. net/) This site has links from all over the world wide web to enhance Shakespeare instruction: his life, his works, his time, his critics, and much more.
>
> *The Folger Library* (http://www.folger.edu/education/ teaching.htm) Besides resources about Shakespeare, his life, his works, his time, this site provides monthly updated lesson plans, a lesson plan archive, festivals and workshops, links, and even shopping for Shakespeare items.

This struggle between stage and page may be taken one step further to suggest that students not merely become the play's audience but its actors as well. The move is from seeing to being the play. Frey (1993) argues that even teachers who plan to teach literary analysis should give a hefty amount of class time to letting students see the impact of intonation, gestures, and blocking as they perform a small part of the script. He believes that the stage versus page conflict comes from vastly different concepts of learning and assessment. Muir (1984) has said that "to act any part is to understand." When we move to this performance extreme, we are using John Dewey's axiom that we learn what we do. Performance becomes interpretation, a visible "reading" of the play.

The student who seriously acts and becomes Polonius onstage knows Polonius because he has entered his consciousness.

Seven Shakespearean Activities

We briefly explore here seven simple ways you might help your students enact Shakespeare's plays, from ad-libbed vignettes to well-polished dramatizations of crucial scenes.

Beyond Memory. Brown (1981) suggests a simple approach that encourages students to understand Shakespeare's or a more contemporary playwright's works by standing inside the world of drama. He urges teachers to enlarge the assignment of memorized speeches from *Julius Caesar, Macbeth,* and *Hamlet.* He asks that we push students past memorizing the famous lines to performing the lines in dramatic fashion. Beyond mere memory, students work on the gestures, the posture, and the movement of their character's bodies. When they reach deeply into their chosen lines, they will begin to see "the clues to performance that lie within the text" (p. 97). This deeper understanding pushes students to experiment with gestures and facial expressions as they master the text. A performance based on understanding can communicate a deep knowledge of the lines to the entire class. Brown lets his classes gain a sense of the dramatic by having the class read a biblical text and then watch the same passage enacted as a part of a miracle play. He argues that students come to a realization about drama that can be communicated in no other way.

Interestingly, this and other performance approaches mediate the controversy between stage and page. To work well on the stage, the text has to be given even greater attention than it normally receives in the traditional pedagogy of the classroom. The movement from reading to seeing to doing brings the process full circle.

Absorption Exchange. Hawkins (1984) and Halio (1977) take this performance approach a step further. Hawkins urges fellow teachers to have students rehearse speeches and even scenes in plays so that they will develop a deeper sense of the dramatist's intentions and will communicate that to classmates through both performance and reflection. Halio refines the process. He suggests that teachers ask groups of five to seven students to select a fifteen- to twenty-minute scene from any play to perform for the class. The troupes are given sufficient time to develop a serious, well-wrought performance. They can choose to add simple scenery and costumes, but they are required to memorize their parts and must present their scene to a live audience. Here again, we get the double value of live performance absorbed by audience and absorbed also, in the deepest sense of the word, by those who have performed. This depth of understanding can be explored and communicated when performing students talk about the textual discoveries each has made.

Language Shifts.

O'Brian (1984) has developed a performance method that helps students attend to the language in Shakespeare's plays, especially the shifts from prose to poetry. She suggests that pairs of students work on a scene in which a shift occurs and discuss how to affect the shift and where the problems arise in this change. Students who perform these shift scenes become very much aware of what is going on metrically and so become more attuned to the structure as well as the meaning of the play.

Diverse Productions.

Newlin (1984) recommends the combined use of the Royal Shakespeare Company's nine videotapes and live student performance. Actor Ben Kingsley talks in one of the excellent teaching tapes about a specific scene and then offers three distinct versions of the scene as his company performs it. The relationship between performance and interpretation comes clear for students who are faced with diverse renditions of the same scene. Similarly, student groups can perform the same monologues or dialogues but with very different interpretations. In both instances, penetration of the text is more likely in the dramatic version than in a simple reading or even viewing of the play.

Intense Scrutiny.

Swander (1984) suggests another approach to performance in which two students are given ten class days or more to develop a two-person scene of twenty-five to fifty lines. Before they produce it on stage, they give the other students in the class a copy of the text to study briefly. The students perform the scene and answer questions from their student audience. Students further internalize the drama by writing a short paper on their performance and the experience related to it. Not acting but thinking about the play is central to this entire process. Understanding develops because the creators care, other students challenge, and they all reflect on the experience.

Concrete Details.

A dramatic routine suggested by Fuller (1989) is similar. His idea is simple: more rehearsal of fewer lines rather than quicker reading of more lines. He urges teachers to choose a scene and make it become important to students. He believes that a diverse group of students will respond to this approach better than to lectures on Elizabethan times or discussions of imagery. He knows that the humanity of the live production is compelling to all students and thinks they will come alive when they contend about concrete questions of dramatizing: where characters stand, who they look at, how they gesture, what tone of voice they use. He allots less time than some of the other advocates of the perform-

ance approach, but he urges the teacher to coach students by stressing the following:

- observing closely
- analyzing action and effect
- asking strategic questions of actors
- listening carefully to their answers
- trying different ways to perform a scene
- reinforcing performances or challenging them

Students work in small groups to produce these scenes and then interact with their classmates to explore them more deeply.

Mannikin Motion.

Brown (1981) suggests a final performance approach that combines reader's theater and puppet drama. The students are not given time to memorize lines but practice reading for meaning and understanding. They use mannikins with character labels or crudely defined dolls and move them about on the stage. The complication comes in asking another set of students to position the mannikin characters according to their understanding of the lines being read for that character. The mannikin movers are then challenged by students in the audience about why their character looks in a particular direction, moves toward a certain character, withdraws, or moves in any specific way. Actions must be defended and explained.

These exercises build involvement, expand insight, and deepen understanding of Shakespeare. They do not ask that you become a drama teacher to use them; but they do require more risks than do the traditional lecture, scene-by-scene reading, or discussion of plays. Mallick's (1984) book is repeatedly cited as the text that offers teachers the most insightful ways of enriching student performance. He focuses on students' deep understanding of brief vignettes before their performance and then on students' intense work on selected scenes rather than helter-skelter performances or long ineffectual readings.

Ꮼ CONCLUSION

Whether your students are transforming text into scripts, witnessing plays come alive on stage, or performing dramatic scenes, they will be ushered into a deeper care and clearer understanding of the power and craft of dramatists. You must merely be willing to rely on your imagination, your empathy, and your invention. You must move from behind a desk or lectern. In other words, you must rely on the same arts a dramatist uses. With practice, you will be ready to "take this show on the road" or at least confidently into class!

Assaying
Nonfiction

But fiction represents only a part of our literary legacy. . . . Nonfiction—with its stirring language, its compelling subject, and its impressive abilities to provoke thought and challenge beliefs—has shaped philosophies, societies, and individuals.

Richard Abrahamson and
Betty Carter

*L*ike young adult fiction, nonfiction has had to struggle to find a place in secondary English classrooms. Aidan Chamber, an English critic, defines traditional literature as the "holy three": fiction, poetry, and drama. Abrahamson and Carter (1991) document the rule of this triumvirate. They report that the most popular high school literature textbooks devote, on the average, 88 percent of their total content to fiction and that most "awards and prizes for both children's and young-adult literature" go to fiction (p. 52). Yet Ellis (1987) estimated that nonfiction accounts for at least 50 percent of the total reading done by high school students. Carter (1987) found that 49 percent of books checked out of the junior high libraries that were studied were nonfiction. Caswell, Villaume, Johnson, Butler, and Barnett (2001) have estimated that 90 percent of a student's reading after high school will be informational reading. On annual lists of titles recommended for young adult readers, such as those published by *School Library Journal* and the *English Journal,* 25–50 percent are nonfiction.

Despite what Purves and Monson (1972, p. 169) call "a general tendency away from fiction to nonfiction" in the secondary school years, English faculty members, textbook publishers, and workshop organizers continue to operate as though fiction were the overwhelming choice of high school readers. High school literature and writing textbooks are apt indicators. In the genre and thematic anthologies of the first high school years, nonfiction occupies a decidedly narrow spot compared to fiction. Texts organized by geographic identity (American, British, and world literature) scatter a few nonfiction entries among the predominant fiction and poetry selections. Teachers, particularly those in schools with compressed block schedules and/or end-of-term standardized exams, report to us that covering literature is difficult enough and that nonfiction textbook selections are the ones they usually omit.

Nonfiction has traditionally been chosen for a more functional purpose in writing textbooks: to display a variety of rhetorical models for students to emulate. As student writing has grown more personal, expressive, and informal, however, even the formal nonfiction models have become less pertinent. The very idea of a model is less valued as students try to find their own unique voices. In sum, nonfiction has an established, if modest, place in the English curriculum: a quiet accompaniment to fiction, poetry, and student compositions. But often in the accelerating pace of a school year, the position of nonfiction in English classrooms fades out of sight.

Invitation to Reflection 9–1

1. Do you remember reading nonfiction in secondary English classes? If so, list any names of nonfiction authors or pieces that you recall.

2. Do you tend to make a distinction in the books that you read between "literature" and "nonliterature"? If so, how do you make the distinction?

3. When you select reading material out of choice, not assignment, what percentage is fiction? Nonfiction?

4. Where do you most frequently encounter nonfiction?
   newspapers periodicals letters Internet
   books anthologies speeches other

5. When you write for school or out-of-school purposes, what genre do you most frequently use—fiction or nonfiction?

6. Which genre, fiction or nonfiction, best serves the following purposes in your reading?
   enjoyment insight
   information inspiration

7. Have you been in high school or university classes that assume that fiction deserves a more serious reading than nonfiction does?

8. Have you read nonfiction whose language or style struck you as powerful—that is, whose subject was measurably enhanced by the power of its presentation? If so, can you name a few titles or authors?

WHY TEACH NONFICTION?

The strongest reason for teaching nonfiction is pragmatic and has already been introduced: It forms a significant portion of what students actually read. We should capitalize on the reading that naturally interests students; to ignore these texts is to miss an opportunity. Omitting nonfiction from our classroom notice and discussion denigrates their chosen texts. The student may wonder, "Is my reading not worth a teacher's notice? If it does not deserve teacher scrutiny, does it deserve my critical attention? Should I keep my reading a private, guilty pleasure, removed from public attention?" We need to openly acknowledge, address, and validate students' reading choices. We need to encourage students to approach nonfiction with the same comprehending, responsive, and critical minds that they bring to fiction. We need to ask ourselves if the reason for our neglect is connected with our lack of knowledge about it and/or how we might teach it.

Another justification for teaching nonfiction is simply that the boundaries between it and fiction are indistinct. As early as 1722, Daniel Defoe (c. 1659–1731) published *A Journal of the Plague Year* as though it were an eyewitness account of the Great Plague of 1664–1665 when in fact he was only five years old when the epidemic occurred. In the twentieth century, journalistic fiction has done much to dim those lines. Novels such as Truman Capote's *In Cold Blood* (1965) and Norman Mailer's *Armies of the Night* (1968) and *The Executioner's Song* (1979) are based on real people and events and are written with the novelist's attention to voice, character, narrative, and conflict. Tom Wicker, a political editorialist, wrote a fine novel about the Civil War, *Unto This Hour* (1984); and Tom Wolfe, a social critic of wit and insight, wrote the highly acclaimed comedic novel *The Bonfire of the Vanities* (1987). Novelist and essayist Kathryn Harrison published *The Kiss* (1997), a story of incest between a daughter and father, as fiction. A year later, she reissued it with the subtitle *The Kiss: A Memoir* (1998) and called it nonfiction, a claim her father denies. Maimon, Nodine, and O'Connor (1989) believe that "we live in an age of 'blurred genres'" (p. xx). In fact, many of the techniques that students use to analyze and interpret literature apply to nonfiction as well and can be used with nonfiction as readily as fiction. Welcoming nonfiction into the English classroom enlarges our definition of reading to encompass the act itself, not just particular acts of "high literature."

Invitation to Reflection 9-2

Two decades ago, Donelson and Nilsen (1980, p. 342) asked English teachers to recommend ten adolescent and ten adult novels as "worthy of young adult reading." The following nonfiction titles appeared on the fiction survey answered by three hundred teachers.

- Read the titles that follow. Would you make the same "mistakes"?

  Piers Paul Read, *Alive,* 1974
  James Herriot, *All Creatures Great and Small,* 1972
  Robin Graham, *Dove,* 1972
  Peter Maas, *Serpico,* 1973
  Doris Lund, *Eric,* 1974
  Alvin Toffler, *Future Shock,* 1970
  Maya Angelou, *I Know Why the Caged Bird Sings,* 1969
  Dee Brown, *Bury My Heart at Wounded Knee,* 1970
  Claude Brown, *Manchild in the Promised Land,* 1965
  Eldridge Cleaver, *Soul on Ice,* 1968
  John H. Griffin, *Black Like Me,* 1961
  Carlos Castaneda, *Journey to Ixtlan,* 1972
  Vincent Bugliosi and Curt Gentry, *Helter Skelter,* 1974
  Studs Terkel, *Working,* 1974
  Pat Conroy, *The Water Is Wide,* 1972
  Henry David Thoreau, *Walden,* 1854
  Eliot Wigginton, *Foxfire* (the series), 1972
  N. Scott Momaday, *The Way to Rainy Mountain,* 1962
  Lorraine Hansberry, *A Raisin in the Sun,* 1959
  Annie Dillard, *Pilgrim at Tinker Creek,* 1974

- Name other books published in the past twenty years that have blurred the lines between fiction and nonfiction.

A third reason for teaching nonfiction flows from those challenges to the canon—deconstructionist; reader response; and political, social, and aesthetic critiques of the tradition—discussed in Chapter 7. These postmodernist critics contend that any sharp distinction between "good texts" (which tend to be fiction) and "bad texts" is an arbitrary distinction—a human construct based more on cultural/historical/political norms than on objective standards of excellence. In *Textual Power,* Scholes (1985) explains that university English departments have divided the field into two categories: "literature and non-literature" and "mark those texts labeled literature as good or important and dismiss those non-literary texts as beneath our notice. . . . The proper consumption of literature we call 'interpretation,' and the teaching of this skill, like the displaying of it in academic papers, articles, and books, is our greatest glory" (p. 5).

By contrast, the consumption of nonliterature is called reading and is left to elementary and secondary English teachers. Scholes believes that the bias against the serious study of nonliterature is based on the perception that it is "grounded in the realities of existence, where it is produced in response to personal or socio-economic imperatives and therefore justifies itself functionally. By its very usefulness, its non-literariness, it eludes our grasp. It can be read but not interpreted, because it supposedly lacks those secret-hidden-deeper meanings so dear to our pedagogic hearts" (p. 6). Scholes asserts that "all texts have secret-hidden-deeper meanings, and none more so than the supposedly obvious and straightforward productions of journalists, historians, and philosophers. . . . And who is to say that Locke or Gibbon is less valuable than Dryden or Gray?" (p. 8).

Annie Dillard (1988) makes the case that, in earlier centuries, fiction writers struggled to have their work regarded as nonfiction in order to maintain respectability:

> In the eighteenth and nineteenth centuries, some literary folk considered fiction *ipso facto* trash. Serious writers tried to weasel out of that genre. Fielding originally titled *Tom Jones* "The History of a Foundling," to lend it the artistic dignity that nonfiction alone was then thought to possess. Melville's *Typee,* a work of pretty outrageous fiction, masqueraded as fact in its day; so did *Omoo.* Poe published *The Narrative of A. Gordon Pym* as nonfiction. Twain's first title for his novel was "Huck Finn's Autobiography"—to distinguish it from a mere romance, and thereby to plead for serious reading. (p. xiii)

In the twentieth century, the reverse became increasingly true. Writers often consider fiction the more "intellectually respectable" and fudge on the genre "as if fiction were not descriptive but honorific, as if fiction didn't mean fabrication but artfulness" (p. xiv). Thus, writers today call their "closely autobiographical narratives fiction": Henry Roth's *Call It Sleep* (1934), James Agee's *A Death in the Family* (1957), Norman MacLean's *A River Runs Through It* (1976), Stratis Haviaras's *When the Tree Sings* (1979), J. G. Ballard's *Empire of the Sun* (1984), and Harriet Doerr's *Stones for Ibarra* (1984) (p. xiv). Dillard's point is obvious enough: If the standard of good literature is as plastic as to have almost completely reversed itself in the past centuries, why discredit nonfiction today?

Abrahamson and Carter (1991) suggest a final rationale for nonfiction in the classroom. They argue that nonfiction has the potential to provide some young readers with a vital personal encounter with a text that is unavailable to them in fiction:

> While a general love of literature may be shared by many individuals, the realization of that passion is always intensely personal. It begins when readers encounter an author whose theme, or subject, or language speaks directly to them, when they experience a moment of self-realization, or discover a piece of themselves in a particular work, or see ideas and actions they hope to emulate. For many teenagers, fiction introduces these incipient responses.

But for just as many, nonfiction triggers the same reactions. (pp. 53-54)

Abrahamson and Carter reason that we cannot "afford to prescribe their responses by deciding for them" that fiction leads to an enlarged aesthetic response and nonfiction to a narrowed efferent one. We must present students with a wide and free choice of texts so that they, sampling among them, can decide for themselves. We should not be dogmatic about the relative importance of one type of text as opposed to another. No one can be sure for someone else—especially those as young and varied as today's high school students—just where the most telling and eloquent voices may be heard.

Teaching Activity 9–1 surveys student experience and opinion as a prelude to a nonfiction unit or selection.

∽NONFICTION GENRES IN THE CLASSROOM

Nonfiction print genres have burgeoned to include essays, diaries, journals, reviews, memoirs, letters, autobiographies, biographies, aphorisms, lists, interviews, epigrams, dictionaries, proverbs, testimonials, and speeches. If we add nonprint genres, the list grows longer. Each of these has a singular power of purpose, subject, and language. Examination of a few will illustrate how their study can enliven and enrich the English classroom.

Essays

We turn first to the essay, the most frequently anthologized nonfiction genre for high school readers. The genre

---

9–1   TEACHING ACTIVITY

The Place of Nonfiction

Individual

■ On a piece of paper, respond to the following statements by writing a number 1 (wholeheartedly agree) through 10 (strongly disagree).
1. The term *literature* designates nonfiction as well as fiction.
2. In my literature classes, we read more fiction than nonfiction.
3. I have read fiction pieces that have made a strong impact on me.
4. I have read nonfiction pieces that have made a strong impact on me.
5. Fiction deserves a more careful reading than nonfiction does.
6. The language of fiction is more impressive than that of nonfiction.
7. The books that I like to reread tend to be fiction.
8. The books that I like to reread tend to be nonfiction.
9. If I could choose, in English class I would prefer to read nonfiction over fiction.
10. If I were stranded on the proverbial desert island with one book, I would like it to be fiction.

■ Look at Donelson and Nilsen's (1980) survey of teacher mistakes in categorizing novels. (Teachers can use this survey in Invitation to Reflection 9–2 and/or add new titles of their own.) Do you know these titles? Are you confused about any of them?

Small Group

■ Look together at your individual responses to each of the ten items. Are there any strong agreements among you? Any strong disagreements?

■ Sum up your responses to each item. Under numbered columns on the board, list the magnitude of your group's response.

Whole-Class Discussion

■ On the basis of the survey, what is the class's preference for reading?

■ Do English classes typically satisfy that preference in the texts that they study?

■ If few nonfiction texts are studied, how can you explain that absence? Why would English classes have a prejudice toward fiction?

■ Does the survey suggest any change that needs to be made in the selection of class texts?

is far more flexible and expansive than its formal name connotes. Kathleen Norris (2001, p. xv) calls the essay "a welcome open space in the crowded, busy landscape of American life. A place to relax and take a breather." When French philosopher Michel de Montaigne (1533-1592) retired from active life, he devoted himself to reflection and began to collect and publish both the aphorisms popular in his day and an explanation of his reasoning about them. He is considered the first modern essayist, and he established characteristics that still distinguish the essay today: personal, informal, and intimate. He followed his own advice: "We must remove the mask." In fact, the root word of *essay* means "to attempt," and essays are just that—attempts merely to address issues, not attempts fully to cover a subject or instruct readers as treatises do. And as Edward Hoagland (1999, p. 17) reminds us, Montaigne wrote his *Essais* a quarter-century before Cervantes's *Don Quixote,* which many regard as the first novel.

Since the time of Montaigne, essays have become such a popular means of expressing an opinion that anyone interested in looking for good essays finds an appetizing variety. In the eighteenth century, essays became extremely popular in England and one can easily find a wealth of terse and pithy pieces about the day, ranging in authorship from Joseph Addison (1672-1719) to Sir Richard Steele (1672-1729). In the nineteenth century, essayists such as Charles Lamb (1775-1834), William Hazlitt (1778-1830), Thomas De Quincey (1785-1859), Thomas Carlyle (1795-1881), Thomas Macaulay (1800-1859), John Ruskin (1819-1900), and Robert Louis Stevenson (1850-1894) ruminated on their personal experiences rather than on public life (as their predecessors had done) in a form that was as relaxed as it was lengthy. In the United States, two of our earliest literary forbearers, Emerson and Thoreau, were essentially essayists. Even Washington Irving, Edgar Allan Poe, and Mark Twain contributed significantly to the genre. Distinguished and popular essayists from the early part of the twentieth century included English wits such as G. K. Chesterton (1874-1936) and Hilaire Belloc (1870-1953) and U.S. writers such as William Dean Howells (1837-1920) and H. L. Mencken (1880-1956).

Dillard (1988) explains that the "essayist does what we do with our lives; the essayist thinks about actual things" (xvii). Yet today, some consider the essay a bit stilted and old-fashioned. They prefer the article—a piece that is usually informative, timely, and impersonal and more concerned with covering the subject than with style. The essay, by contrast, possesses a more consciously literary style and offers a more personal distillation of and reflection on the subject at hand. Atwan (1988) suggests a reason for this bias against the essay: Despite the radical changes in other forms of twentieth-century literature, essayists "broke no new ground; . . . resisted no rules; . . . violated no conventions" (p. i).

Yet the essay's status is changing. Its place is more assured in literary quarterlies and general magazines. Serious writers are exploring its imaginative and narrative possibilities—pushing its border with fiction and poetry. Writers of proven fictive and poetic ability turn more and more to writing essays, including Louise Erdrich, William Gass, Elizabeth Hardwick, Jamaica Kincaid, James A. McPherson, Joyce Carol Oates, Cynthia Ozick, Robert Stone, and John Updike. Collections of individual writers occasionally appear—for instance, Sven Birkerts's (1994) *The Gutenberg Elegies* and Barbara Kingsolver's (1995) *High Tide in Tucson: Essays from Now or Never.* Publishing houses such as Oxford University Press and W. W. Norton publish essay anthologies. The collection *The Best American Essays* was first published annually in 1986 and has a guest writer-editor each year whose introductions provide a running commentary on the state of the literary essay. In 2000, Houghton Mifflin published a hundred-year retrospective, *The Best American Essays of the Century.* In it the guest editor, Joyce Carol Oates (2000), stakes a claim for the unique power of the essay:

> Here is a history of America told in many voices. It's an elliptical tale, or a compendium of tales, of the American twentieth century by way of individual essays that, fitting together into a kind of mobile mosaic, suggest where we've come from, and who we are, and where we are going. . . . The essay, in its directness and intimacy, in its first-person authority, is the ideal literary form to convey such a vision. (p. xvii)

Figure 9-1 lists a few of the periodicals in which essays of substance and style often appear. In addition to these literary magazines, English teachers have long used magazines written specifically for students, such as *Scholastic Magazines' Voice, Sprint, Action, Scope,* and *Literary Cavalcade; U.S. Express,* written for ESL students in grades 6-10; and *Writing!, Merlyn's Pen, Challenge,* and *International Readers' Newsletter.*

FIGURE 9-1
Periodicals that publish literary essays

The American Scholar	Encounter	Northwest Review
The American West	Esquire	The Paris Review
Antioch Review	The Georgia Review	The Partisan Review
Antaeus	Harper's Magazine	The Sewanee Review
The Atlantic	Hudson Review	Shenandoah
Audubon	Kenyon Review	Spectator Magazine
Civilization	Natural History	Village Voice
Community Review	The New Yorker	The Virginia Quarterly Review
DoubleTake	North American Review	Witness

Essays can provide opportunities for teaching both reading *and* writing. They can be used as companions for literature study, as sources of rich ideas, as tools for teaching reading skills, and as models for writing. We will consider here what they can contribute to the study of literature and then suggest how they can enhance reading and thinking. In the following Chapters 11 and 12, we discuss the different characteristics of specific essay genres (for instance, the critical literary essay; the personal, reflective essay; the autobiographical essay; the persuasive essay; and the research essay) and explore ways in which these genres serve as tools for writing instruction.

Essays to Enhance Literature Study. Essayists often address ideas directly without weaving them indirectly through narrative and character. Although essays can enhance the study of literature at any point in the teaching cycle, we use them most often at the entering phase. We choose essays to sound ideas and associations before students encounter them in other literary texts. (Correspondences can also be drawn in style, narrative technique, character development, and tone.) Chapter 5 has already shown their usefulness in the reader response stage. For example, in Figure 5–4, Phyllis Rose's (1984) delightful essay "Heroic Fantasies, Nervous Doubts" is listed as a prereading text for the primary text, John Updike's short story "A & P." Rose's short essay strikes a deep chord in students. The title alone indicates the connection with human experience and fiction—our uncertainties about ourselves in the midst of our stubborn hopes—ideas that resonate in "A & P." We have even found essays such as Russell Baker's (1980) "Schlemiel" that imaginatively respond to literature, in this case to Woody Allen's (1977) short story "The Kugelmass Episode." As Dillard (1988) reasons, "in some ways the essay can deal in both events and ideas better than the short story can, because the essayist—unlike the poet—may introduce the plain, unadorned thought without the contrived entrances of long-winded characters who mouth discourses" (p. xvi). Hoagland (1999) explains, "Essayists, in dealing with the present tense, are stuck with the nuts and bolts of what's going on" (p. 20). This makes them invaluable for priming ideas and associations and prompting predictions, questions, and brainstorming before we begin to read other literature.

At the explore and extend stages, multiple texts and approaches enable students to move around in fictive worlds in order to experience and understand those worlds and themselves. Hoagland reminds us that the essayist is "not a puppet master or ventriloquist" (p. 17). Essays do not require us to do the interpretive work required by fiction and poetry.

When the *English Journal* asked teachers, "What works of nonfiction do you recommend for the English Classroom?" (Teacher to Teacher, July, 2000), Mary Buckelew (2000) answered with the names of four essayists:

Gloria Anzaldua, Paul Auster, Susan Bordo, and Alice Walker. She has found that their work "inspires great discussion and writing in the high school classroom" (p. 36). She reports that Anzaldua's "Entering into the Serpent" and "How to Tame a Wild Tongue" from *Borderlands/La Frontera* (1999) introduce concepts of "borders, traditions, religion, language and race"; Auster's "The Invisible Man" from *The Invention of Solitude* (1988) prompts thoughtful self-reflection; Bordo's "Hunger as Ideology" from *Unbearable Weight: Feminism, Western Culture, and the Body* (1993) provokes discussions about "self-image, gender relations, popular culture, and music"; Walker's "Beauty: When the other Dancer is the Self" also inspires discussions on "self-image" (p. 36). Think of works of literature that these ideas might illuminate and enrich.

The essay also aids in exploration and extension through its use of many tools essential for the craft of writing. One feature that is especially distinctive in the essay is authorial voice. Hoagland (1999, p. 17) defines essays by voice: "Essays are how we speak to one another in print—caroming thoughts not merely in order to convey a certain packet of information but with a special edge or bounce of personal character in a kind of public letter" (p. 17). Oates (2000) makes a similar emphasis:

> Of course there are crucial distinctions between the art of the essay and the art of prose fiction, yet to the reader the immediate experience in reading is an engagement with that mysterious presence we call *voice*. Reading, we "hear" another's speech replicated in our heads as if by magic. Where in life we sometimes (allegedly infrequently) fall in love at first sight, in reading we may fall in love with the special, singular qualities of another's voice. (p. xix)

The voice of the essay is usually that of the author without the fictive mediation of a narrator or characters. Oates calls this its "directness and intimacy, . . . its first-person authority" (p. xvii). Our students often quickly become attuned to the essayist's voice. If they can hear the voice behind the public text and even discover a voice they love, they will be well on their way to understanding a crucial element of all speech and writing. We realized with delight that the voice we love in Kathleen Norris's writing was echoed in all of the essays she selected as guest editor for *Best American Essays, 2001,* each a small gem.

Essays to Enhance Reading and Thinking. We present three teacher-tested tools used originally with essays (but applicable to other prose) to sharpen reading comprehension and thinking skills. The first is an approach that draws on the Quaker reading discussed in Chapters 4 and 7. Teacher Katie Moulder (personal communication, 1998) adds questions and discussion to the Quaker reading. She has students read a passage aloud with the understanding that if anyone in the class has any question about the words or ideas, that person will interrupt and pose his or her question. Students often have to practice interrupting and publicly acknowledging confusion. In time, though, readers approach seriously and deliberately this chance for shared working through a passage. They often discover that they are voicing the queries of others. Moulder reports that progress can be slow but also active and engaging. Students arrive at the conclusion with a deeper understanding. Norris (2001) writes:

> An essay that is doing its job feels right. And resonance is the key. To be resonant, the dictionary informs us, is to be "strong and deep in tone, resounding." And to resound means to be filled to the depth with a sound that is sent back to its source. An essay that works is similar; it gives back to the reader a thought, a memory, an emotion made richer by the experience of another. Such an essay may confirm the reader's sense of things, or it may contradict it. But always, and in glorious, mysterious ways that the author cannot control, it begins to belong to the reader. (p. xvi)

Middle school teachers have introduced us to other tools for improving reading skills and comprehension of the essay (or any prose). Debra Butler (Caswell et al., 2001) has developed a "note-taking system" that "gives the reader a way to construct and extend the meaning of text." She bases her system on bookmarks. When she assigns nonfiction reading for her eighth-grade language arts students, she also passes to each a half sheet of copy paper (colored paper, if possible, to "add to the novelty"). We adapt her instructions to students as follows:

- Write responses on the bookmark, including the pertinent page number of the text.
- Responses can include, but are not limited to, the following:
  ○ points of importance/interest/confusion
  ○ favorite parts
  ○ connections to personal experiences
  ○ predictions

Butler often removes the texts so that students rely on their bookmarks for their discussion. Not only does this system aid their reading comprehension and their discussion skills, but it sharpens their note-taking abilities.

Another eighth-grade teacher, David Barnett (Caswell et al., 2001), has developed a similar approach to help his students comprehend essays. He uses a number of prereading activities that anticipate the text; activate prior knowledge; and transfer to readers a sense of purpose, confidence, and ownership. He asks students as they read to take marginal notes or (because the books must be reused by others) to write on Post-it notes and leave them in the margins. (He keeps a huge stockpile of Post-it notes as an essential part of his classroom supplies.) He asks students to include the following in their marginalia:

- questions
- comments
- paraphrases of important ideas
- questions about the need, validity, or purpose of the information
- personal connections
- text connections

Clearly, the essay provides a vital resource for literary study and for improving reading skills. (We will say more about the essay in our writing chapters.) There are many excellent contemporary essays with familiar dialect and subject matter that you can use to catch your students' attention and interest. But "the ideal essay, in any case, is as timeless as any work of art, transcending the circumstances of its inception. It moves, as Robert Frost says of the ideal poem, from delight to wisdom, and 'rides on its own melting,' like ice on a hot stove" (Oates, 2000, p. xxviii).

Biographies

Our earliest independent reading was of little orange-backed biographies written for children. We never got over our delight. Biographies serve the same goal we expect of imaginative literature—that we stretch ourselves, travel from our narrow personal perspectives, and enter the lives of others with empathy and broadened sympathy. A well-written biography possesses the same virtue as well-crafted fiction: It renders a person who is recognizable but distinct and individual. For young students just starting out on their own life careers, biographies can provide useful views into different lives and offer compelling alternative visions. Biographies can trace the formative people, events, and places in a subject's life. They can track significant changes, recurring patterns, or repeated themes over time. They can illuminate the private experience of public acts. They can shed retrospective light on crucial moments in a life and uncover the wholeness of a completed life history. Biographies offer the comforting solidity of that completed cycle. Encountering the lives of others illuminates not only those lives but also our own.

Standard biographies present figures significant for their contributions to literary and civic life. The celebrity biographies of sports heroes and entertainment stars take a substantial portion of the biography shelves in bookstores. Those lives can grab the attention of our students and even lead to their exploration of the lives of weightier subjects. We also find excellent biographies in shorter form. Lytton Strachey's (1918) *Eminent Victorians* is an early twentieth-century example that still reads easily, although students might not recognize his iconoclastic treatment of the Victorian heroes and heroines of his day. Phyllis Rose's (1983) *Parallel Lives: Five Victorian Marriages* and Howard Gardner's (1985) *Leading Minds: Anatomy of Leadership* are examples of collections of shorter biographies that are accessible to high school students. Shorter profiles also appear in book reviews of full-length biographies and in periodicals such as the *New Yorker.* The Internet is another resource for biographical information, which students can themselves use to piece together a portrait.

As you read the teaching activities that follow, notice the variety of creative ways in which these teachers approach biographies—some as a subgenre worth studying for itself alone, some as a biographical enrichment to literary study, some as an approach to particular stories or to the general elements of fiction, and some as a way to learn skills.

Keating (1996) was frustrated with the limitations of her seventh-grade students in identifying qualities that they admired. The list focused on "NBA stardom or a Grammy Award. . . They had limited exposure to other creative, dedicated, talented, original, or brave people outside of the realms of music and sports." She decided to introduce students to the genre of biography in order "to fill this void." The unit began with brainstorming on "the definition of admirable qualities." Those qualities were posted in the room, "to be added to as students read biographies and discovered other qualities they admired" (p. 66). Following this discussion, students were required to complete the following tasks:

- Read a self-selected biography.
- Complete a biography report form.[1]
- Create a biography project.
- Make a presentation to the class in the character of the subject of their chosen biography.

Suggested biography projects included the following:

- Create a timeline of the subject's life. Include significant events in the subject's life, as well as notes on world events and the lives of those connected to your subject.
- If your subject is deceased, write at least a one page obituary including the following: important events in the subject's life, accomplishments, survivors at the time of death, a charity the subject might want people to contribute to as a memorial.
- Write at least ten journal entries your subject may have written. They can all be related to one time period in your subject's life, or they may skip around and address different events.
- Create drawings, newspaper clippings, mementos, recipes, etc. that your subject might have included in a scrapbook.
- If your subject was a creator, try to imitate his/her creation. For example, try to produce an art piece similar to your subject's, write a short story if your subject was an

author, compose a song if your subject was a composer, or design an invention if your subject was an inventor (p. 69).

The unit ended "by referring back to our original list of admirable traits and adding characteristics of which students were now aware after reading biographies" (p. 69).

Johnson (1986) introduces his biography unit by having students read short biographies. He then asks them to write or speak about their subjects in response to his informal, spontaneous questions: Would the subject "make a good friend"? Were there times when the subject was "not courageous"? He says that these prompts "lead the students into thinking of these biographical figures as real people—people they might know, like, or sometimes dislike." He then asks students to write short stories in which they meet their subjects and answer the following questions: "How do your lives interact? Are you close friends? Rivals?" (p. 27). Johnson concludes by having each class member write a three- to five-page biography of a classmate, whom he assigns and whom they must interview. The value chat interviews in Chapter 4 could provide the structure for such interviewing.

Bowen (1991) encourages her students to try a variety of forms for expressing their insight into their subjects: "dialogues, poems, and newspaper articles. Obituaries, songs, and letters also work" (p. 53). For instance, one of her students, interested in Eric Clapton, took on his persona and wrote a letter to Clapton's friend and fellow musician Muddy Waters. Bowen asks her students to keep what Romano (1987) calls "research journals" (which note "details as well as impressions") and to write in them a "dozen questions they would ask their subjects if they were to meet them" (as quoted in Bowen, 1991, p. 54). She checks their journals often and adds her own questions. As they write their larger biographies, she also uses small in-class assignments to encourage their creative thinking about biography's multiple possibilities (Figure 9–2).

Wahlenmayer (1991) also found in students' genuine questions an alternative to the deadly biography reports that used to haunt her classroom. She lists on the board questions that they would like to ask their chosen subjects, combines them, deletes duplicates and highly specific ones, and uses the remaining questions as the core of a ten-question oral interview. The students' assignment is to select a subject and become so familiar with that person that they can talk of his or her life "comfortably and in some detail" (p. 56). An interviewer (the teacher or one of the students) randomly picks ten of the questions in Figure 9–3, plus an additional two submitted by students, and asks them to the student/subject. Students not only more authentically enter their subjects' lives, but the listening students do so as well.

Hogarty (1991) conceived of an audacious activity that set students up as IRS auditors. He gathered as

---

[1]This form has space for the usual information—title, author, publisher, page numbers—but also poses seven questions, such as "What problems did the subject overcome?" (p. 68).

FIGURE 9–2

Bowen's in-class biographical writing prompts

Source: Bowen, B. (1991). A multi-genre approach to the art of the biographer. *English Journal, 80*(4), 54.

- Free write for ten minutes as though you were the subject.
- Make a list of twenty-five important things in the subject's life (titles, objects, people, etc.).
- Choose a date in the subject's life and write a diary entry.
- Write a dialogue between the subject and someone else.
- Answer these "quiz" questions—What is the subject's favorite leisure activity, favorite place, most regretted incident, best assets (personality and physical), and the like?
- Write a letter from a friend of the subject or from yourself.
- Write a descriptive paragraph about the subject.
- Using the strongest words and images from one of the previous assignments, develop poetic phrases and write a couple of lines of verse.

FIGURE 9–3

Wahlenmayer's biography questions

Source: Wahlenmayer, C. W. (1991). Ray Charles has been in my classroom. *English Journal, 80*(4), 55.

1. Why would someone want to write a book about you?
2. What was the place where you grew up like?
3. How much of your life is covered by this book?
4. Tell me something important about your parents.
5. How did you prepare for what you became famous for?
6. What was the happiest period in your life?
7. What is the most difficult situation you ever faced?
8. Describe yourself emotionally.
9. Tell me about a turning point in your life.
10. Tell me about your family since you've been an adult.
11. Do you have any idiosyncrasies or trademarks?
12. What was the source of your motivation to accomplish what you did?
13. Tell me something about yourself that's not commonly known.
14. What part has romance played in your life?
15. How do you like to spend your free time?
16. Who was a very influential person in your life?
17. Explain whether your fame has brought you happiness or unhappiness.
18. How do you feel you were portrayed in this book?
19. What is something you'd like to be remembered for?
20. Was the time you lived in important to what you did?
21. Describe your death.
22. Tell me more about that.

many different IRS forms as he could find and asked his students to fill out forms for imaginary persons who might exist. Other students audited them and wrote the biographies and autobiographies of these characters. In his more direct approach to biography, Hogarty does not try to distinguish fiction from nonfiction. He uses excerpts from Gore Vidal's (1988) historical fiction *Burr,* for instance, to "provide a marvelous counterpoint to the typical history text treatment of that figure" (p. 58). Further, he uses William Carlos Williams's (1956) essay about Aaron Burr, "The Virtue of History," because "it is definitely nonfiction and obviously literature" (p. 58). He also links Vidal's historical fiction and Carl Sandburg's biography to textbook accounts of Abraham Lincoln. His students appear to be able to operate comfortably between what purports to be fiction and nonfiction. They see, for example, what historical fiction can do to compensate for the "squeezing out of the man" that occurs in many history textbooks. They ponder the discovery that "Wolfe's astronauts in *The Right Stuff*

(1979) lived different lives from those portrayed in many newspapers and magazines of their time. Why? What gives?" (p. 58).

Mitchell (1996) uses biographies as she would literature. While at one time she approached the genre unenthusiastically, with a focus on the "facts of a person's life," she now organizes her biography lessons around the traditional "elements of literature":

Setting: Students "create a visual representation of the places the character lived or visited and . . . indicate . . . the importance of each place" (p. 75).

Plot: Students create a "time line illustrating what they perceive to be the most important actions and events in the character's life and represent them with words or pictures" (p. 75).

Characterization: Students discuss "which characters came to life for them, which . . . they would like to meet, and which actions of characters seemed hardest to understand." She elicits the same responses to biographical characters as she does for fictional ones. Students "write letters to them, find poems the character would like, and create conversations with them" (p. 75).

Theme: Students discuss the recurring issues of their subjects' lives, the common problems they confronted, what they learned from their struggles. The class sometimes creates a word collage from individual students' suggestions of what the most persistent issues or themes were.

Point of view: Students consider how the perspective on the subject would have changed "had the book been written by the subject's parents or friends or even an enemy" (p. 75). Students test that hypothesis by writing brief character sketches of themselves, one written by someone unsympathetic and another by someone sympathetic toward them.

Teaching Activity 9-2 suggests questions that you might pose to students to make connections between biography, history, and/or fiction of the kind that Hogarty (1991) made. Although the activity emphasizes analytical questions, it could culminate in the freer expressions of art, music, drama, or creative writing. The questions can be used for whole texts or selected excerpts; for oral or written work; and with individuals, small groups, or the whole class.

Autobiographies and Memoirs

Autobiographies, like biographies, take us into the lives of others but at closer, more intimate range. We are eyewitnesses to actual events; we are introduced to real people. Often in the course of our reading, we develop a partnership with the narrator-subject as we receive the self-disclosure and willing confidences that are so hard-won in our everyday friendships. Like knowing a mystery's successful conclusion before we begin reading, we read with the trust that struggles have been overcome and order has been achieved. Autobiography, then, often snags the adolescent's natural curiosity about the lives of others and offers the reassurance that childhood and youth, particularly, can be negotiated and life commenced successfully.

Autobiography has other attractions. It provides models for high school students involved in their own personal writing. We design much of what we do in the English class to encourage students to explore and compose their own lives. In his introduction to his novel, *Dandelion Wine,* Ray Bradbury (1983) discusses a secret that allows his ideas to flow, a secret that is also the source of both autobiography and of students' personal writing.

> I was gathering images all of my life, storing them away, and forgetting them. Somehow I had to send myself back, with words as catalysts, to open the memories out and see what they had to offer.

9-2 TEACHING ACTIVITY

Biographical Comparisons

Compare a historical account, a biographical account, and/or a fictional account of the same person and then answer the following questions:

- Which left you with a sharper, more well rounded sense of the individual?

- Did the authors' methods of characterization differ?

- Did they favor authorial summary or enactment in scene and dialogue?

- Was dialogue used in each? How did it differ?

- Which had the kind of interesting and defining detail that gives a character a lively uniqueness?

- Which created the richest sense of setting? Was it a backdrop to the events or instrumental to them?

- Did one account give you a sense that it was more accurate or authoritative?

- Did the authors seem biased about the subject? Positively? Negatively?

- Oscar Wilde observed that every great man has his disciples and it is usually Judas who writes the biography. Is that true of any of your accounts?

- Which text best helped you answer the question "Would I like to spend an evening talking to this character?"

- Which text did you enjoy the most?

- From which did you learn the most?

So from the age of twenty-four to thirty-six hardly a day passed when I didn't stroll myself across a recollection of my grandparents' northern Illinois grass hoping to come across some old half-burnt firecracker, a rusted toy, or a fragment of a letter written to myself in some young year hoping to contact the older person I became to remind him of his past, his life, his people, his joys, and his drenching sorrows. (p. viii)

Another compelling form of autobiography is memoir. Memoirs do not attempt to comprehend a whole life but reflect on and render only a portion of it. "Unlike autobiography, which moves in a dutiful line from birth to fame, omitting nothing significant, memoir assumes the life and ignores most of it. The writer of a memoir takes us back to a corner of his or her life that was unusually vivid or intense—childhood, for instance—or that was framed by unique events. By narrowing the lens, the writer achieves a focus that isn't possible in autobiography; memoir is a window into a life" (Zinsser, 1987, p. 21). Alice Walker's (1988) four-page "Am I Blue?" from *Living by the Word: Selected Writings, 1973–1987* is a wrenching memoir evoked by her empathy for the feelings of a stallion that is separated from his mare, feelings similar to the narrator's life in the south. Dillard (1995, p. ix) calls the memoir "a powerfully fixed point of view." In a useful collection, *Modern American Memoirs,* editors Dillard and Conley (1995) excerpt passages from thirty-one classic modern American autobiographies to capture the memoirist's fixed viewpoint. Dillard explains that these writers celebrate, as Charles Wright does in one of his poems, "all the various things that lock our wrists to the past." The following titles are just a sampling of the rich autobiographies and memoirs available.

A Sample of Autobiographies.

Classic examples of moving autobiography, the gradual unfolding of a life in all of its remembered particulars, include Helen Keller's (1902) account, written when she was twenty-two, of her struggle to overcome blindness and deafness: *The Story of My Life;* Zora Neale Hurston's (1942) *Dust Tracks on a Road: An Autobiography;* Thomas Merton's (1948) *The Seven Storey Mountain;* Mary McCarthy's (1957) *Memories of a Catholic Girlhood;* Margaret Mead's (1972) *Blackberry Winter;* Harry Crews's (1978) *Childhood, The Biography of a Place;* and Russell Baker's (1983) *Growing Up.*

Autobiography also offers deeply personal and moving global perspectives. In *Facing Mount Kenya,* Jomo Kenyatta (1962) begins the account of his remarkable life with his ancestors, the Gikuyu, telling how they became oppressed and how he, their son, became the first president of an independent Kenya. In *From Emperor to Citizen,* the last emperor of China, Aisin-Gioro P'U Yi (1960), detailed his life from becoming emperor at age three under a regent, to his isolated life in the walled Forbidden City, to his years as a citizen deposed by the Chinese Nationalists, to an observer of Communist rule under Mao Zedong. Mark Mathabane (1986) wrote *Kaffir Boy,* whose subtitle tells it all: *The True Story of a Black Youth's Coming of Age in Apartheid South Africa.* In *When Heaven and Earth Changed Places: A Vietnamese Woman's Journey from War to Peace,* Le Ly Hayslip (1990) writes movingly of her traditional Buddhist childhood in a Vietnamese farming family; the nightmare of war, which began when she was twelve; her decision to fight as a Viet Cong; her struggle to survive in Saigon; her marriage to an American; and her return to Vietnam as a Vietnamese American. *Angela's Ashes* is Frank McCourt's (1996) remarkable account of growing up Irish, Catholic, and poor in Limerick, Ireland. Jill Ker Conway's two books, *The Road from Coorain* (1989) and *True North* (1994), present lucid but lyrical accounts of her life as she moved from the Australian outback on a sheep station, to provincial post–World War II Sydney, to graduate school at Harvard University, to an academic appointment at the University of Toronto, and then to the position of first female president of Smith College. Conway has also edited two anthologies of autobiographical writing by other women: *Written by Herself: Autobiographies of American Women* (1992) and the second volume, *Women's Memoirs from Britain, Africa, Asia, and the United States* (1996). These shorter fragments of lives have the appeal of brevity for student readers.

A Sample of Memoirs.

One classic memoir is *Black Elk Speaks,* in which John Neihardt (1932, 1988) records (with some changes, we now realize) Black Elk's vital account of the Lakota tribe's customs and world views both before and after the tribe was forced onto reservations. More recently, a former U.S. president, Jimmy Carter (2000), has written a moving memoir, *An Hour Before Daylight.* Hellman (2000) reports that her seventh graders were absorbed by Melba Patillo Beals's (1995) *Warriors Don't Cry,* "the powerful, compelling story of the Little Rock Nine and their fight to integrate Arkansas' Central High School in 1957" (p. 33). *Black Ice* by Lorene Cary (1991) appeared on Nilsen and Donelson's annual adolescent honor lists. In it Cary describes her experience as a student from West Philadelphia sent on a scholarship to a prestigious prep school in New Hampshire. *Making Waves: An Anthology of Writings by and about Asian American Women* (1989) contains memoirs (as well as poems, fiction, and essays) organized around themes such as immigration, war, work, and generations.

Author's Stories.

Not surprisingly, many writers have written autobiographies of their lives (sometimes veiling these as fiction) and memoirs of brief segments of their lives. We especially like James Thurber's (1933) *My Life and Hard Times,* Eudora Welty's (1984) *One Writer's Beginnings,* and Reynolds Price's (1988) *Clear Pictures: First Loves, First Guides.* In *Self-Consciousness: Memoirs,* John Updike (1989) candidly and sensitively takes us inside the boy and youth, troubled by psoriasis, stuttering, dentists, and Vietnam, who became one of our finest novelists. Following his near-fatal accident, Stephen King (2000) wrote a lucid account of writing, an essential part of his recovery: *On Writing: A Memoir of the Craft.* Interviews of authors often appear in educational magazines: *Language Arts, Instructor, Learning,* and *Creative Classroom.* Barbara Kiefer (1991) has compiled some of these in *Getting to Know You—Profiles of Children's Authors Featured in Language Arts.* Eve Shelnutt has edited the writing memoirs of living male and female writers: *The Confidence Woman: 26 Women Writers at Work* (1991) and *My Poor Elephant: 27 Male Writers at Work* (1992). Linda Gray Sexton (1994) has written about life with her mother, poet Anne Sexton, in *Searching for Mercy Street: My Journey Back to My Mother, Anne Sexton.* These volumes shed an autobiographical light on active authors that will humanize their works for students and personalize the career of writing. Kai Erikson (1989) edited *Encounters,* a brief series of eighteen portraits, each of an encounter with a literary figure written by another literary figure. For instance, John Hersey worked as Sinclair Lewis's secretary, describing him as someone who "could no more stop telling stories than he could stop his hair growing."

Figure 9-4 lists other teacher-recommended autobiographical pieces that deal with issues vital to today's students.

Holocaust Literature. Some of the most compelling memoirs of our time are those of Holocaust survivors. One survivor, Elie Wiesel, eloquently explains the need to give witness to these catastrophic events. In our teaching of this tragic moment in history, we rely primarily on letters, diaries, and memoirs, although we supplement with historical accounts and with fiction, drama, and poetry. *Anne Frank: Diary of a Young Girl* (1952) is well known by many students coming into high school. Anne's adult counterpart, twenty-seven-year-old Etty Hillesum, also kept a diary during these years. That diary, *An Interrupted Life: The Diaries of Etty Hillesum, 1941–1943* (1983), and Hillesum's subsequent letters from the last deportation center before Auschwitz, *Letters from Westerbork* (1986), are absorbing. So, too, are Primo Levi's accounts of his ten months in Auschwitz, *Survival in Auschwitz* (1959) and *The Drowned and the Saved* (1986), and Elie Wiesel's (1960) memoir *Night.* A more

recent memoir by Robert O. Fisch (1994), a Minnesota pediatrician and visual artist, *Light from the Yellow Star: A Lesson of Love from the Holocaust,* combines his art (on the cover and each page of text), quotations from the gravestones of the memorial concentration camp cemetery in Budapest where his father is buried, and his personal narrative. Fisch opens his memoir with words that capture both our motive and our challenge in teaching this literature. "I have been thinking for quite a long time whether any medium is appropriate to describe the scope of the tragedy of the Holocaust. How can sorrow, suffering, and atrocities of this magnitude be expressed?" Gorrell (1997) describes in detail how she and her high school juniors read and learned from Fisch's memoir.

In addition to the gripping first-person accounts of nonfiction are autobiographical poems, art, stories, and novels. Excellent bibliographies are available on Holocaust nonfiction and fiction for adolescent readers. The Internet has multiple sites with annotated references. We have found *A Teacher's Guide to the Holocaust* from the University of South Florida especially helpful. Kaywell (1993) has an excellent annotated list of general reference sources and specific books for young adults (pp. 13–35). The U.S. Holocaust Memorial Museum publishes a teaching resource with instructional guidelines and a detailed bibliography called *Teaching about the Holocaust: A Resource Book for Educators.*

Memoirs in One English Classroom. Gillespie (1991) uses memoirs to prompt her seventh-grade students to write their own memoirs, allowing each to become "the editor of his own life" (Zinsser, 1987, p. 24). Gillespie introduces memoirs with a brief overview and reads aloud the first few paragraphs of selected memoirs. The oral reading prepares students to write their own memoirs and, at the same time, to select someone else's memoir to read. Figure 9-5 includes twelve memoirs (Gillespie, 1991, p. 50). She reminds students of Calkins's observation that "what appears to be an ordinary event can be meaningful" (pp. 48–49). She uses Romano's ideas of "percolating" as students select a viable personal topic by saving ideas from their own lives, events that, upon reflection, might reveal something important.

Not only do autobiographies and memoirs introduce the lives of others and help us to compose our own, they raise speculative questions about how we write about

FIGURE 9–4
Autobiographies

I Dream a World (1989)	Brian Lanker
Bloods: An Oral History of the Vietnam War by Black Veterans (1984)	Wallace Terry
Voices from the Future: Our Children Tell us About Violence in America (1993)	Susan Goodwillie, Ed.
Freedom's Children: Young Civil Rights Activists Tell Their Own Stories (1993)	Ellen Levine
Warriors Don't Cry (1994)	Melba Pattillo Beals
Lives on the Boundary: The Struggles and Achievements of America's Underprepared (1989)	Mike Rose
The Hunger of Memory: The Education of Richard Rodriguez (1981)	Richard Rodriguez
Personal History (1998)	Katherine Graham

FIGURE 9–5
Gillespie's memoirs for students

I Know Why the Caged Bird Sings (1970)	Maya Angelou
A Girl from Yamhill: A Memoir (1988)	Beverly Cleary
An American Childhood (1987)	Annie Dillard
Homesick: My Own Story (1982)	Jean Fritz
China Homecoming (1985)	Jean Fritz
The Endless Steppe (1968)	Esther Hautzig
ME ME ME ME ME: NOT A Novel (1983)	M. E. Kerr
The Woman Warrior: Memoirs of a Girlhood Among Ghosts (1976)	Maxine Hong Kingston
Little by Little (1987)	Jean Little
West with the Night (1983)	Beryl Markham
Blue Remembered Hills (1983)	Rosemary Sutcliff
One Writer's Beginnings (1984)	Eudora Welty

ourselves. Here are some questions that might follow student writing:

- Was I comfortable writing a complete account of my entire life or highlighting crucial events of my life?
- How accurate and complete a picture is my autobiography/memoir?
- Can I now remember other ordinary events that in retrospect appear meaningful?
- What conclusion might readers draw about me from reading what I write?
- How much do I want my reader to know?
- What writing techniques do I use or not use to expose or conceal myself in my writing?

Testimonials

Carey-Webb (1991) defines testimonials as "edited oral narratives collected from people who by their circumstances cannot write about their own experiences firsthand" (p. 44). Many of the narratives of African American slaves; Native Americans; Holocaust victims; and survivors of natural catastrophes, airplane crashes, shipwrecks, and dam collapses come to us through testimonials. The breadth and variety of their human experiences and the immediacy of their presentations make compelling reading. Librarians report that one of the most popular nonfiction books for high school students (on *The New York Times* best-seller list for seven months) remains Piers Paul Read's (1974) account of the Uruguayan airplane crash in which only sixteen of forty-six passengers (most of whom were members of a rugby team) survived. That book, *Alive: The Story of the Andes Survivors,* is based on Read's interviews with survivors, their families and friends, and rescuers. Carey-Webb describes *I Rigoberta Menchu* (1984), the story of a courageous Guatemalan Indian woman told to a French anthropologist, as one of the "most moving books I have ever read." He sees such testimonials as a "sort of Third World 'autobiography' that brings to the center the experience of the unlettered, marginalized, and oppressed. They are ideal texts in which students and teachers alike attempt to hear the voice of the voiceless, investigate cultural and social differences, and raise questions about

what it means to be 'culturally literate' " (p. 44). Carey-Webb's annotated list of these compelling nonfiction testimonials includes the following (adapted from pp. 45–46): *Life Among the Piutes: Their Wrongs and Claims* by Sarah Winnemucca Hopkins (1969), an account of the nineteenth-century encounter between the Piutes and white settlers in Nevada, Oregon, and Washington; *Let Me Speak! Testimony of Domitila, A Woman of the Bolivian Mines* by Domitila Barrios de Chungara and Moema Viezzer (1978), the memoir of the wife of a Bolivian miner who witnessed the upheaval created by labor organization among some of Bolivia's poorest citizens; *Rachel and Her Children* by Jonathan Kozol (1988), the story of homeless families in New York City; and *Fire from the Mountain* by Omar Cabezas (1985), a Sandinista guerilla's story of revolution and struggle.

Whole- or small-class discussions can focus on the subject of the testimonial with the same kinds of questions that we ask of fiction.

Character: Did you like the subject? Could you identify with the subject? Did you know enough to understand and predict how he or she met difficulty? Would you like to have known more? What details helped you empathize most? Find sentences that you think are especially important in revealing the central character. Did you know enough about other minor characters? Were they well-enough developed to become individuals? Did your regard for any of the characters change as you read?

Setting: Was the setting important to the action? What details helped create the sense of place for you? Did you have enough details? Can you imagine this story happening in another time or place?

Plot: Did the narrative hold your attention? How did the writer create interest and suspense for you? Did you find the events predictable? Where were you surprised? Did you want to know more about what happened? Did the testimonials reach a satisfactory conclusion?

Point of view: Would you have reacted differently to the story had it been told by an objective observer? Would you have liked it better had someone shaped the events and characters of the testimonial into fiction? Did the teller have a voice you like? Did it ring true?

Significance: Did the story seem worth telling? Does it add to your understanding of human experience? What ideas came to you as you read it? When you had concluded it? Would you recommend it to others?

Testimony by its nature raises excellent speculative questions for personal writing or discussion:

- What would you consider to be the most difficult crisis the subject describes?
- What do you think you would have done in such a situation? Would you have acted differently?
- What is the greatest fear you have ever known or the gravest crisis you have ever faced?
- Is it easy for you to accept help from others? Would you accept help in a crisis?
- With whom would you like to face a crisis in your own life?
- Would you rather face a sudden, severe crisis or multiple smaller difficulties that linger over time?
- Do you admire or censure how the subject acted in his or her crisis?
- What is your worst nightmare?

Students can use testimonials as spurs to record oral histories of those around them who have endured traumatic events. Veterans, survivors, and ordinary people who experience car accidents, urban unrest, rural disasters, tornadoes, and floods live in most communities and are often willing interviewees. (Almost everyone is willing to tell a story in response to the question "What was the most challenging personal catastrophe you ever experienced?") The individual testimonies can be transcribed and written as character sketches, dialogues, or short biographies. A collage of testimonials with photographs or music can become a project for the whole class. Reading the testimonials of others also can provide scripts for readers' theater (Chapter 5) or situations for an accidental power exercise (Chapter 4).

Diaries and Journals

Diaries and journals are two other nonfiction sources infrequently studied in English classrooms, but they are well worth exploring. They can provide glimpses into lived lives that novels only aspire to. More than autobiographies, which are written at some reflective distance, and testimonials, which usually are spoken accounts to others, diaries and journals take us to immediate experience. They also are a particularly important resource for access to the experiences of people who have lived in the domestic rather than the public sphere, such as most women. Whether kept during a lifetime or through a significant segment of personal or world history, diaries guard their writers against the loss of perishable events,

impressions, and reflections. *Diary* (from the Latin *diarium,* meaning "daily allowance") connotes a greater privacy, while *journal* (from the Latin *diurnalem* and the Old French *journal,* both meaning "daily") suggests a greater public importance; both, however, seek to preserve the rapid passage of experience before it sinks into oblivion. Anne Morrow Lindbergh (1971) provides another motive: "My diaries were written primarily, I think, not to preserve the experience but to savor it, to make it even more real, more visible and palpable, than in actual life. For in our family an experience was not finished, not truly experienced, unless written down or shared with another" (p. xvi).

Students are surprised by the variety and sheer number of published and manuscript diaries kept over the centuries and are more surprised still to discover their gripping interest. They often will have encountered the two best-known English diarists: Samuel Pepys (1633–1703), known for his accounts of major seventeenth-century events, and James Boswell (1740–1795), remembered for his picture of eighteenth-century man of letters Samuel Johnson. They bear immeasurably valuable witness to public and private history. But other diarists, such as Reverend John Wesley, Dorothy Wordsworth, Elizabeth Barrett Browning, Charles Darwin, Queen Victoria, and Virginia Woolf, kept daily records of their lives that offer candid glimpses of exterior and interior events. John Quincy Adams kept a diary for about sixty-eight years, which historian David McCullough calls one of the treasures of American literature and history.

We mentioned as memoirs what were originally journals written by Anne Frank and Etty Hillesum. A remarkable diary was kept in Brazil by Carolina Maria de Jesus (1913–1977). She lived a life of wrenching poverty, had only two years of formal education, wrote on notebooks she found in the garbage, and struggled to support herself and her three children by selling scrap paper and metal that she collected. A reporter discovered her diaries by chance and had them published serially in the newspaper and then later as a book entitled *Child of the Dark* (1962), which became the best-selling book in Brazilian history. Anne Morrow Lindbergh's diaries and letters—*Bring Me a Unicorn* (1971) and *Hour of Gold, Hour of Lead* (1973)—chronicle her childhood, her youth, her meeting and courtship with Charles Lindbergh, her participation in aviation history, and the tragic loss of her first child. She explains that she was encouraged to write an autobiography of her life and times but instead went to her diaries. Her adolescent diaries cause her particular embarrassment because they are often "self-conscious and self-centered, immature and sentimental." But "if one eliminates adolescence from life and records, how much is suppressed: youth, hope, dreams, impractical ideals, falling in love with countless 'not impossible He's,' gaiety that spurts up for no reason, despair that is gone the next morning, and a foretaste of the inevitable tragedies of life along with one's early confused attempts to understand or meet them" (1971, p. xxv). Lindbergh's justification for using her diaries to tell her story is ample testimony to the power of such personal writing.

Diaries and journals are valuable to the English classroom as records of actual events played out in history and literature and as personal testaments to the whole range of human experience. Their immediacy and rare self-disclosure can bedazzle our critical faculties and leave us simply to savor the individual before us and share favorite passages. Like biographies, autobiographies, and testimonials, however, they can be approached with the same questions we raise about literature, especially those surrounding character. Prompts for discussion or writing might include the following:

- This entry exactly described something that I have experienced myself: . . .
- I felt most pain at this entry, because . . .
- I was most uncomfortable at this point because . . .
- If I could enter this life as the subject, I would want to experience this day . . .
- If I could travel with the subject to one time and place, it would be . . .
- If I could ask the subject one question, it would be . . .
- If I could give the subject one bit of advice, it would be . . .
- I envy the subject this one thing: . . .
- I would like to change this one episode or event: . . .

Diaries and journals can also validate, encourage, and model the journal-keeping instincts and possibilities that we value for our students.

Letters

Although they are written to an audience, the language of letters is "perhaps the closest to natural speech and represents that casual spontaneity we associate with conversation, which makes letters a good form of writing to use with reluctant writers and beginning writers" (Dittmer, 1991, p. 24). Even though we delight in writing and receiving letters and treasure the published letters of others, we taught literature for twenty-five years before we talked formally about letter writing. Mail is so common in our lives, letters so rare. The two get confused. Letters are often treated as impersonal mass-produced announcements or as personal ephemera. We want students to pay attention to the possibilities in letter writing. We assume that most of our students are or will be writers and receivers of letters. We ask them to attend to the unexpected richness of language put to everyday use. We want them to discover what American writer Thomas Bailey Aldrich felt: "There's a singular and perpetual charm in a letter."

Teaching Activity 9–3 illustrates our linking of this private writing to the experiences of students. We have used this activity successfully with high school students of all ages and abilities. You will observe that it teaches more than insight into letters by linking letter writing to the private writing of students as well as to the literary letters of others.

Many teachers find letters engaging as focuses of study in themselves and as supplements to other units of study. Dittmer (1991) suggests a letter writing assignment that he says has produced some of the best writing he has received from students. He asks them "to write a letter in which they confirm or reestablish a relationship. They can write to someone real or imaginary, living or dead, animal or human, and if appropriate, they should consider sending it to the party to whom it is written" (pp. 21–22). Becky Brown (personal communication, 2001), after the tragic events of September 11, 2001, asked her students to write a letter to their grandchildren to explain the events and emotions of that fateful day. Teachers report the popularity of a collection of letters from American soldiers, *Dear America: Letters Home from Vietnam* (1985). The letters range from the tragic to the humorous, from the bitter to the patriotic. Shaw (1991, p. 25) testifies that these letters give students "a perspective not available in traditional history textbooks." Shaw intensifies the class reading with an HBO film by the same title, which provides a visual backdrop against which many actors read hundreds of letters. Perrin (1991, pp. 30–32) used his junk mail to teach lessons about analyzing audience, searching for "poetic" language, identifying persuasion, analyzing meaning through close reading, developing vocabulary, and writing synopses. We have used letters both to clinch discussions and to provide a more public audience for writing. At the end of an integrated unit on war poetry and persuasive writing, during which students research and position themselves on a current topic, we ask them to present their strongest ideas in letters to the local newspaper editor. We know teachers who use letters for another motive: informing and communicating with parents. They ask students to write periodic letters home about what they are experiencing in English.

Miscellaneous Nonfiction Books

Many full-length nonfiction books fall within the categories of biographies, autobiographies, memoirs, testimonials, and published diaries; but the array of other categories extends from Bruce Catton's histories of the American Civil War to David Macaulay's illustrated books, such as *Cathedral* (1973), *Motel of the Mysteries* (1979), and *The Way Things Work* (1988). Abrahamson and Carter (1987) describe attending a convention where adolescent nonfiction reading interests were being discussed and observing that the librarians/media

9–3

TEACHING ACTIVITY

Letter Writing

We begin our lesson with caution. We are aware of the danger of drawing attention to something that is very personal and, we hope, spontaneous. We don't want to spoil the natural and introduce self-consciousness and contrivance. But we try to demonstrate that the promise outweighs the danger. After this disclaimer, we ask students to complete the following survey. While we ask them to commit their responses to paper, we assure them that we will use those responses for discussion only with their permission. We begin with the individual letter writing survey in Figure 9–6. We then discuss the written answers to these personal questions with the whole group. With the class sensitized and conscious of letter writing, we move to the students' own writing. Here is the sequence of our in-class assignments and our instructions. They move back and forth between work that is individual, paired, and whole class.

Note to a Classmate

1. Begin by writing a note to a partner, a note about anything that's on your mind at this moment, the kind of note you might write in any given school day. Be candid. A public reading of your note will be undertaken only with your approval.

2. Now send your note, read your correspondent's note, and respond on the back. Return the note to its origin.

3. Talk as a class about what just happened. If I were to spy on your note writing and say, "All right, Leah, is that something you'd like to share with the class?" would you be embarrassed? Is your communication that confidential? What delights you in writing the note? In receiving it? What kind of message does it contain? What was the best note you ever remember receiving in a class? If you are not a note passer, have you ever envied those who are?

Postcard to Your Family

1. Shift your location from the classroom to home. Imagine that your family is away for two weeks and you find a postcard from them in the mailbox. Here is what it says:
   Everything is going well. The food is great. The company is enjoyable. I wish you were here. I want to hear from you. Please write.

2. Write a postcard responding to this request.

3. Exchange cards with another student and talk together about what you've each written to your family.

4. How do these cards differ from notes written to a classmate? Which interested you more? In which was the writer the most spontaneous? Which had the greater specificity? Substance? Imagination?

5. Would any of you read your postcards to the class? If you were the family member reading this account, would you have additional questions that you'd like to ask of the writer?

6. Cartoonist Gary Larson has a number of cartoons featuring letters. (We distribute several *Far Side* cartoons involving letter writing between animal families and friends.) Do you notice anything in these cartoons that reminds you of your experiences with letters?

Letters to a Friend

1. Imagine now that a friend, rather than your family, is away. Write a letter or postcard back to that friend.

2. Don't share this correspondence. Is there any difference between it and what you wrote to your family? If so, what?

3. Consider this observation of German philosopher Arthur Schopenhauer: "If you want to discover your true opinion of anybody, observe the impression made on you by the first sight of a letter from him."

Published Letters

1. Read the excerpt from a seventeenth-century letter written by Madame de Sevigne (1626–1696) (Figure 9–7). She was writing to her daughter about a royal house party during which a disconsolate cook took surprising action. (Many other letters, of course, would serve for this activity.)

2. Does Madame de Sevigne describe the scene sufficiently for you to imagine it? Can you imagine a cook or a restaurant owner in our day becoming equally as distraught as Vatel over the food and the service? How were Vatel's circumstances different from ours today? Have you ever been so publicly embarrassed or privately guilt-stricken for letting someone down that you despaired? Are you surprised by the reaction of the court to his death?

3. Imagine that you are a friend of Vatel and that you observe his misery on this night and want to write something that will comfort and calm him. Write that note.

4. A contemporary of Madame de Sevigne once said, "When you have read one of Madame de Sevigne's letters you feel a slight pang, because you have one less to read." Can you see in this excerpt why she was valued by her contemporaries?

5. Does this letter interest you now, more than three centuries after it was written? Does it provide any insight of value to you? What impresses you about it?

6. Model Madame de Sevigne by describing an event or situation in your recent life. Can you imagine what someone in three hundred years might make of what you are describing?

We go on to read and discuss a variety of published letters. They include a range of writers—Lord Chesterfield, John and Abigail Adams, Abraham Lincoln, Emily Dickinson, George Eliot, Rainer Maria Rilke, Anne Morrow Lindbergh, H. L. Mencken, Etty Hillesum, Flannery O'Connor, and Leslie Marmon Silko—and of letter types—anecdotal, reflective, satiric, humorous, and literary. Our approach to these letters varies. Often we give groups a number of letters and ask them to select those that they want to share with the whole class.* Discussion easily follows the groups' oral reading. Questions that readily open discussion include the following: Had you received this letter, how would you have responded? Have you ever gotten such a letter? Does it make you want to write back?

Letters to the Teacher

The unit concludes with student letters to the teacher in which they explore their reaction to the unit. (If the easy spontaneity of the other activities is threatened by this final letter, we would advise against this assignment.)

---

*The published exchange of letters between correspondents adds the dimension of a dialogue. Reading the give-and-take between two minds resembles eavesdropping (which may account for the power of these collections). For instance, some of our students have been entranced by a slim volume of letters between the poets Leslie Marmon Silko and James Wright (1986), *The Strength and Delicacy of Lace.* Our students have also been intrigued with fictional letters. C. S. Lewis (1959) wrote a robust batch, *The Screwtape Letters,* between an older devil, Screwtape, and his apprentice nephew, a fledgling devil, Wormwood, to present a theological argument about the nature of the human struggle between good and evil.

FIGURE 9–6

Letter-writing survey

1. Do you ever write notes in class to other classmates?
2. If so, why? If you will see the person later, why take the risk? What drives you to write notes?
3. Do you receive electronic mail? How often? Is personal e-mail more like a note or a letter for you?
4. How many letters have you received in the last month? From whom have you heard?
5. How many letters have you written in the last month? Are you writing to anyone out of town, or do you write letters to those you could just as easily call?
6. What prompts you to write letters? Is the motive like your motive for writing notes? Do you see them as anything more than an occasion to pass along information?
7. What other kind of writing do you do that is not assigned by a teacher?
8. Which is more important to you, a letter written to you from someone you know and value or a well-written story by an accomplished writer?
9. What do you think is the most common form of writing for the average adult?
10. Think for a moment about any of your adult friends or family. What occasions prompt them to put a pen or pencil to paper?
11. Have you ever seen sections of your English textbooks devoted to the writing of letters?
12. Do teachers ever discuss letters as an important form of writing? If so, do they emphasize business letters or personal letters?
13. What does your work in class lead you to conclude is the premier genre of writing? Novels? Short stories? Poems? Personal memoirs? Diaries? Journals? Letters?

Paris, Sunday, April 26, 1671

This is Sunday, April 26th, and this letter will not go out till Wednesday; but it is not so much a letter as a narrative that I have just learned from Moreuil, of what passed at Chantilly with regard to poor Vatel. I wrote to you last Friday that he had stabbed himself—these are the particulars of the affair: The king arrived there on Thursday night; the walk, and the collation, which was served in a place set apart for the purpose, and strewed with jonquils, were just as they should be. Supper was served, but there was no roast meat at one or two of the tables, on account of Vatel's having been obliged to provide several dinners more than were expected. This affected his spirits, and he was heard to say, several times: "I have lost my honor! I can not bear this disgrace!" "My head is quite bewildered," said he to Gourville. "I have not had a wink of sleep these twelve nights; I wish you would assist me in giving orders." Gourville did all he could to comfort and assist him; but the failure of the roast meat (which, however, did not happen at the king's table, but at some of the other twenty-five), was always uppermost with him. Gourville mentioned it to the prince, who went directly to Vatel's apartment, and said to him: "Every thing is extremely well conducted, Vatel; nothing could be more admirable than his majesty's supper." "Your highness's goodness," replied he, "overwhelms me; I am sensible that there was a deficiency of roast meat at two tables." "Not at all," said the prince; "do not perplex yourself, and all will go well." Midnight came: the fireworks did not succeed, they were covered with a thick cloud; they cost sixteen thousand francs. At four o'clock in the morning Vatel went round and found every body asleep; he met one of the under-purveyors, who was just come in with only two loads of fish. "What!" said he, "is this all?" "Yes, sir," said the man, not knowing that Vatel had dispatched other people to all the sea-ports around. Vatel waited for some time; the other purveyors did not arrive; his head grew distracted; he thought there was no more fish to be had. He flew to Gourville: "Sir," said he, "I can not outlive this disgrace." Gourville laughed at him. Vatel, however, went to his apartment, and setting the hilt of his sword against the door, after two ineffectual attempts, succeeded in the third in forcing his sword through his heart. At that instant the carriers arrived with the fish; Vatel was inquired after to distribute it. They ran to his apartment, knocked at the door, but received no answer, upon which they broke it open, and found him weltering in his blood. A messenger was immediately dispatched to acquaint the prince with what had happened, who was like a man in despair. The duke wept, for his Burgundy journey depended upon Vatel. The prince related the whole affair to his majesty with an expression of great concern; it was considered as the consequence of too nice a sense of honor; some blamed, others praised him for his courage. The king said he had put off this excursion for more than five years, because he was aware that it would be attended with infinite trouble, and told the prince that he ought to have had but two tables, and not have been at the expense of so many, and declared he would never suffer him to do so again; but all this was too late for poor Vatel. However, Gourville attempted to supply the loss of Vatel, which he did in great measure. The dinner was elegant, the collation was the same. They supped, they walked, they hunted; all was perfumed with jonquils, all was enchantment. Yesterday, which was Saturday, the same entertainments were renewed, and in the evening the king set out for Liancourt, where he had ordered a *medianoche;* he is to stay there three days. This is what Moreuil has told me, hoping I should acquaint you with it. I wash my hands of the rest, for I know nothing about it. M. D'Hacqueville, who was present at the scene, will, no doubt, give you a faithful account of all that passed; but, because his hand-writing is not quite so legible as mine, I write too; if I am circumstantial, it is because, on such an occasion, I should like circumstantiality myself.

FIGURE 9–7   Madame de Sevigne's letter

coordinators in the audience were nodding knowingly, while the English teachers looked bewildered (p. 104). Librarians, who respond to student queries and check out their book selections, often know more about the reading habits of students than those of us in English classrooms surrounded by novels, poems, and plays. From librarians/media coordinators we have heard the strongest appeals to address the students' desire to know how to survive in this world and their eagerness to read those books that give them clues. They point to the popularity of informational books on topics of importance to them, such as the relationships between men and women, families, music, sports, work, college admissions, suicide, and drugs. Popular titles themselves reflect those interests: Richard Moll's (1985) *The Public Ivys,* Clifford J. Caine's (1985) *How to Get into College,* and Torey Hayden's (1980) *One Child.*

English Journal "Booksearch" features in 1984 and 1990 and a Teacher to Teacher feature in 2000 asked its readers: What books of nonfiction have you found useful in the classroom? As shown in Figure 9–8, teachers suggested books that take the reader through centuries, from the second and third crusades; to the American Civil War; to the twentieth-century Russian Revolution, the sinking of the *Titanic,* the Holocaust, and Hiroshima; and on a post-Vietnam walking tour of the United States. The editors of the *English Journal* (Booksearch, 1990b) wrote that in "nonfiction we see how events shape people's lives, and we learn about our own" through "narratives of lives and events as intriguing as any work of fiction" (p. 91).

Figure 9–8 merely suggests the range of titles and subjects available; but they are enough, we hope, to validate reading that you, too, may have enjoyed and to encourage you to consider it for your classrooms. Of course, no externally provided list of texts will be as good as the ones that individual teachers make through wide reading and sensitive awareness of the students before them. We en-

courage you to start immediately to collect nonfiction pieces of any length that attract you because of their interest as stories, their grace of expression, or their keenness of insight. The following are writers that we have found especially compelling. We suggest them merely to celebrate the craft of these nonfiction writers and to encourage you to begin your own list.

Sven Birkerts (culture critic and essayist)
Freeman Dyson (physicist)
Roger Ebert (movie reviewer)
Loren Eiseley (scientist)
Adam Gopnik (essayist)
Meg Greenfield (editorialist)
Stephen Hawking (astronomer)
Carolyn G. Heilbrun (literature critic)
Etty Hillesum (diarist)
Gerald Johnson (journalist)
Primo Levi (chemist)
C. S. Lewis (medieval scholar)
Margaret Mead (anthropologist)
H. L. Mencken (social critic and writer)
V. S. Naipaul (writer)
Lewis Thomas (medical doctor)
Barbara Tuchman (historian)
E. B. White (journalist and author)

If reading full-length works is not feasible, we encourage you to use excerpts from longer books. Some feel that such borrowing violates the original source. Certainly an argument can be made that the intention and force of the original is compromised. But our concern for what the text provokes for the student overrides these reservations. Indeed, high school students often can enter the writer's world more easily with a short piece than with one that stretches the limits of their reading time. We cull and save newspaper articles and editorials, books of aphorisms, lines of biographies, paragraphs of history, phrases from published letters, captions of cartoons, and single words

Hiroshima (1946)	John Hersey
A Night to Remember (1955)	Walter Lord
The Dog Who Wouldn't Be (1957)	Farley Mowat
Night (1960)	Elie Wiesel
Travels with Charley (1962)	John Steinbeck
Ishi: Last of His Tribe (1964)	Theodora Kroeber
Growing Up Female in America: Ten Lives (1971)	Eve Merriam, Ed.
The Hiding Place (1971)	Corrie ten Boom
Gone for a Soldier: The Civil War Memoirs of Alfred Bellard (1975)	David Herbert Donald, Ed.
Dove (1978)	Robin Lee Graham
First Person Rural (1978)	Noel Perrin
A Walk Across America (1979)	Peter Jenkins
Queen Eleanor: Independent Spirit of the Medieval World (1983)	Polly Schoyer Brooks
From Russia to USSR: A Narrative and Documentary History (1985)	Janet G. Vaillant and John Richards II
One Writer's Beginnings (1985)	Eudora Welty
Under the Eye of the Clock (1987)	Christopher Nolan

FIGURE 9–8   Teachers' choices: Books of nonfiction

that strike us as *right* anywhere we find them. We encourage our students to be their own savorers as well.

Newspapers

In an editorial in our local *Winston-Salem Journal* (May 6, 2001), George Will identified the difference between journalism and literature: Journalism is "the opposite of literature, which is writing that deserves to be read twice." Nelms (1990) explains that "magazine and newspaper columnists can help wake up our students; columns bring them into the world of current events and issues, and challenge them to observe and reflect on the world around them." Students experience the pleasure of thinking, "so someone else has felt that." These columns create the effect of having "us look at life and at ourselves as we live it" (p. 79). Mitchell (1996) observes that newspapers naturally appeal to students and are filled with a variety of types of writing. She asks students to examine newspapers in order to review and connect ideas in the literature the class has been discussing. Before she arrives with the papers, she lists with students what they have read, viewed, discussed, and written in the two preceding weeks. She brings enough copies of her daily newspaper so that each student can look for articles about "any issues or ideas we have touched on in the last two weeks" (p. 78).

We like to bring editorials from the morning paper to class because their recognizable and compelling subjects engage students. The editorialists' observations often pull students toward insights that they would not entertain on their own and toward the power of language to express those insights. The *English Journal's* "Booksearch" feature (1990a, pp. 79–82) asked readers to name syndicated newspaper columnists that had been effective in their classrooms. The columnists included Erma Bombeck, D. L. Stewart, Dave Barry, Mike Royko, Bill Stokes, Anna Quindlen, William Safire, and Bob Greene. We add to that list some of our favorites, influenced, of course, by the choices of our local paper's editors: Thomas Freidman, Ellen Goodman, Molly Ivins, and George Will. Several editorials on a single issue that present divergent positions can enlarge and deepen perspectives. Because differences of opinion attract student enjoyment of a good fight, these editorials are natural prompts for engaged thinking. They also can model a rarity in our civic life: honest disagreement about an issue that doesn't resort to the personal. One assignment that grows from these comparisons asks students in pairs to construct a pro and con editorial page on a selected issue.

∽ NONFICTION IN THE FICTION CLASSROOM

We have described links that we make between fiction and nonfiction, links of subject matter and style. We also use nonfiction models to create fictional responses to literature. Of course, the nonfiction texts discussed in this chapter arise in a historical context, not an imaginative one. We don't wish to blur genre boundaries and confuse students. But nonfiction genres can promote creative writing that enlivens any literature under study. The activities suggested below do not require students to write nonfiction but to use what they know about nonfiction to write fiction.

1. *letters* of advice, counsel, condolence, and outrage to characters, to authors, and between characters and authors
2. *interviews* of characters or authors by students or other characters and authors
3. *dialogues* between characters from different books
4. *epitaphs* of characters
5. *journal or diary entries* of characters
6. selecting what might be the favorite *proverbs* or *maxims* of characters
7. selecting *aphorisms* that could be drawn from having read a piece of literature
8. using Ambrose Bierce's *The Devil's Dictionary* as an example from which to write *definitions* of qualities as the book's author or characters might write them
9. imaginative *speeches*
   - Mae Tuck of *Tuck Everlasting* being the keynote speaker at the national convention of the American Association of Retired Persons (AARP)
   - Huck Finn, testifying before a congressional committee on runaways
   - Stella Willis of *Home Before Dark* explaining to her guidance counselors why she chooses to live alone, apart from her family
   - Ishi from *Ishi: Last of His Tribe* talking to a group of anthropologists
10. lists of characters or authors studied in categories of the class's own making.
    - superlatives (best athlete, most likely to succeed, and so on)
    - top-ten lists (most like to spend a vacation with, most one-dimensional, most like me) or top-ten selections of literature studied
11. newspaper articles about an event in a work, a feature story about a character, an editorial about an idea, and an obituary of a character

∽ CONCLUSION

In sum, nonfiction can be a valuable resource in any lesson at any time. Like devotees of the "holy three," many of our high school students (often those most partial to English) at first devalue nonfiction as a poor relative of fiction and consider our use of it to be "a holding pattern" until we land again with serious literature. Simply on the level of language, however, it provides invaluable lessons. Language is set apart from imaginative story and character, and thus it can sometimes be scrutinized more directly and its power perceived more keenly than in literary analysis. Considering style apart from literary genre springs students free from literary categories and biases. It provides a more generic demonstration of how the skillful presentation of any subject can dramatically increase its power. Enthusiasm about individual words, the way in which phrases are put together, how sentences work, how an argument moves, how an image crystallizes, how a caption functions—all enthusiasms over nonfiction—can teach a great deal about the pure play and potential of language.

Then students do not so easily mistake carefully crafted language as isolated only in a pristine enclave called "literature," written by rare geniuses and accessible primarily to "elected" scholars and critics. Rather, the skillful use of language surrounds us and can surprise those with the confidence and openness to recognize it, even in our morning newspaper and magazine cartoons. Exploring the vital world of nonfiction can be accomplished with many of the tools we use for the exploration of fiction or even poetry and drama. Some of these approaches are noted in this chapter. But the overriding pedagogy is captured by Moffett's axiom: the best way to comprehend is to compose. Let students read great letters and then try their hand at writing one. The same can be said for essays or autobiographies or even journals. Invert the process and see your students' interest rise and their understanding deepen.

Students often ask English teachers for recommendations of good books. We believe that teachers need to base their answers not on a sorting operation of their personal library shelves but on taking stock of the individuals before them. As we have mentioned during our early years of teaching, one of us was often made miserable by the very question she should have welcomed because she was never sure that the stock of novels that she had read would appeal just to this or that student. Only when she began to trust her pleasures in nonfiction (and the necessity to recommend books she had not actually read) did she have a wide-enough inventory from which to pull promising titles.

We believe that high school English teachers should take nonfiction into their teaching. The divisions between literature and nonliterature are imposed on students by texts and teachers, and they harm both those who love literature and those who feel it to be alien. Embracing both without disparaging one and extolling another frees students to appreciate what the printed word brings to their lives wherever they find it. Nonfiction may even bring some to a discovery that eluded them in the more traditional genres of fiction, poetry, and drama.

Making Media Matter

A major new medium changes the structure of discourse; it does so by encouraging certain uses of the intellect, by favoring certain definitions of intelligence and wisdom, and by demanding a certain kind of content—in a phrase, by creating new forms of truth-telling.

Neil Postman

Sven Birkerts (1994) speculates that the book world may be in its death throes: The fast-paced world of media will bury books as we know them. Does he have cause for concern? Oscar Wilde offered his view of the new media of his day: "There is much to be said in favor of modern journalism. By giving us the opinions of the uneducated, it keeps us in touch with the ignorance of the community." Should English teachers share Wilde's disregard for the media and the general public or embrace media as offering something essential and enlivening.

The word *media* is so common in contemporary life that we use it without precisely understanding its meaning. To arrive at a working definition of the term, we must start by thinking of as many media forms as possible. When we enumerate the different media—CD player, VCR, DVD, telephone, slide projector, television, bumper sticker, radio, overhead projector, e-mail, newspaper, CD-ROM, and billboard—a definition begins to emerge. Can you see a central purpose in these disparate forms?

Invitation to Reflection 10–1

Before reading this chapter, answer these questions about media in the classroom and in your own life. Some may be questions to pose to your own students.

1. Have media other than books ever been a part of the English instruction you have known as a student?
2. If so, how were they used:
   - to enrich the study of written texts?
   - to vivify a lesson?
   - to examine each medium as a separate form of popular art?
   - to explore the impact of media on our culture?
   - to prompt writing?
3. Which of these media do you find most inviting and promising for classroom study?

television	film	magazines
newspapers	radio	comics

   art (painting, prints, photographs, sculpture)
4. Do you make a distinction in this list between forms of media for mass consumption and those with a rarer, more artful purpose? Which on the list do you consider high culture and which popular culture?
5. Do your own personal interests and style suggest media approaches that ought or ought not to be undertaken?
6. Do you think that the study of media itself is
   - relevant to English classrooms?
   - important in understanding our culture?
   - important in understanding ourselves?
   - a capitulation to mass culture?
7. Do you consider the media in your life to be a source of entertainment? Education? Liberation?
8. Which of the following technical means of access to media do you frequently rely on in your daily life?

television	VCR	tape recorder
radio	CD player	movie theater
computer	DVD player	

9. What media form do you turn to for leisure? Do you seek that resource before talking with a friend, writing in a journal, or reading a book?
10. When you are alone, how often do you fill the silence with music or TV: 25, 50, 75, or 100 percent of the time?
11. Does television or film influence your assumptions and aspirations about your life?
12. Do you think that you are influenced in your desires by advertising?
13. Through what source do you get your information about the news of the world?
14. Do you consider some media less biased, more straightforward, and more objective than others?
15. When you go on a trip, do you feel frustrated if you do not have a camera with you to record your experience?
16. If you have ever been at a stadium or a coliseum with a wide screen, have you ever found yourself watching the screen as well as the event before you?
17. Do you know anyone (perhaps even yourself) who finds some media form more real than lived life?

Figure 10–1 is a graphic representation of media's classroom possibilities. The lower level of the matrix contains concrete products of media: student-created productions (*enact*) and professional creations (*entertain*). At the upper level, process, students consider the craft of various media (*examine*) and encounter serious critiques of the media (*expose*).

When the matrix is sliced vertically, *produce* is on the left side and *receive* on the right. The lower left side of the matrix invites students to create productions based on the media models that flow through their daily lives. The upper left side asks students to make their own analysis of how media work. Students might look at the audience of the various ads on television to determine how special groups are being targeted, or they might consider the difference between the top-ten pop hits of 1980 and 2000. The lower right side, *entertain,* employs the powerful appeal of media's carefully constructed language, sound, and images in the classroom. Multiple versions of the opening scenes of *Macbeth* on CD-ROM, Beatles's music that nicely parallels Edwin Arlington Robinson's poetry, and videotapes of the ten best American commercials all invite students to react to the artful craft of verbal, visual, and auditory images. On the upper right side, *expose,* students become aware of the impact of various media.

Each of the four quadrants can stake a strong claim for use in the English classroom. Your choices will be based on a number of variables: you, your students, your

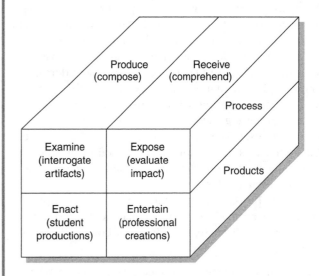

FIGURE 10–1 Media literacy

resources, and your environment. As you consider the teaching possibilities in these four approaches to media, consider Susan Sontag's (1967) warning in *Against Interpretation:*

> Ours is a culture based on excess, on overproduction; the result is a steady loss of sharpness in our sensory experience. All the conditions of modern life—its material plenitude, its sheer crowdedness—conjoin to dull our sensory faculties. What is important now is to recover our senses. We must learn to see more, to hear more, to feel more. (pp. 13-14)

We believe that all four approaches need to be a part of an English teacher's repertoire to help us awaken our students. But we want to begin with those that lie at the lower level because they are the most useful in developing our students' language.

⟡ ENACT: STUDENTS AS PRODUCERS

The initial approach to media offers students a chance to create and produce TV programs, newspapers, magazines, cartoons, comics, drawings, and photographs. We are not suggesting that English teachers mimic highly technical and ambitious media productions in their regular English classrooms. What we suggest more modestly involves students in media production in the service of language enrichment. Our objective is to harness the power that the visual and the auditory dimensions of media bring to the spoken and written word.

This kind of media production has a natural appeal: It brings a cultural phenomenon to the classroom that is familiar, persuasive, and powerful in the lives of most students. They know this world intimately and can quickly understand and manipulate media for a variety of purposes. Beyond its natural appeal, though, asking students to be producers invites them to be active language users. Thompson (1988) summarizes the power of this expressive use: "Perhaps the best way to be an active learner and to exercise all mental abilities is through *expression*—actually producing videos rather than watching television, for instance. The formulation of an expression demands very complex mental activity, in which all the impressions that have been gathered . . . are utilized" (p. 49). Students are putting "words on world," as Moffett and Wagner counsel. They are acting, not passively receiving. Using media as a structure for production of student work gives a natural push toward students' lively interaction with their worlds.

Teacher Teresa Regina (1988) provides an example of the kind of learning by experience that media production opens up. She discusses the effects of composing a TV sports report on her students:

> It gave the opportunity to introduce style and format of presentation. Indeed, a review of the football season, which had not been very eventful, would have been boring if recounted

game by game. However, as students became more familiar and comfortable with editing, they saw that segments could be selected from the season and placed to music. Those who spent much time on the project found sequences with similar actions or camera positions and enhanced the sound tracks by inserting interviews or players' comments. (p. 50)

She continues:

> As words and sentences are placed in an order and in a particular form to reveal style and tone, so sound and visual images must be ordered. The process of selection, of deciding what is to be included or excluded, continues throughout the production process. If composing involves talking, reading, writing, thinking, and communicating, then video production is composing in a most exciting and creative way (p. 52).

Students who engage in those acts of composition deepen their awareness of language as well as the artistry of professionals who work in these media.

Figure 10-2 presents thirteen activities that ask students to produce media events. We intend these activities primarily to prompt your creative ideas, to provide examples of varied possibilities for production, and to illustrate the range of language experiences that are possible through production projects. We think that they may carry our message better than an extended explanation of the potential of media to stimulate language play and production in the classroom. Each prompts students to borrow from a format that is well known to them to produce a facsimile in the classroom. We will enumerate each activity in broad outline and suggest uses to which it may be put. Figure 10-2 presents in its left column language arts skills that many of the activities promote. We have not checked which skills might be learned in each activity nor articulated how the activity builds the skills. We invite you to consider those connections and to note others. Several of these thirteen have entered our text earlier and appear again because we believe they warrant emphasis.

Juxtaworlds

Students are asked to juxtapose the words and images of poetry with the images of advertising and thereby create an original piece. Students may work in groups or as individuals to connect single lines, a group of lines, or an entire short poem with advertising images. Their original pieces can be presented to the class as either the visual ads of television with poetry voiced-over the original script or the print ads of magazines or newspapers with the oral accompaniment of poetry.

The commercial images of advertising reflect the sophisticated work of professional advertising people and photographers. They are usually targeted toward a specific audience with the single-minded aim of persuading that audience to buy a product. Consequently, most ads are short, vivid, carefully focused, richly connotative, original, and memorable. The quality of these commercial

FIGURE 10–2
Media activities

Language Arts Skills	13 Classroom Activities												
	Juxtaworlds	Madison Avenue	Rock review	Piggyback Pop	Jacketeering	Rock market	Anchor people	Radio head	Crisis interview	Pilot making	Class magazine	Classy comics	Bumper stickers
Playing with words													
Discerning an audience													
Recognizing a dramatic context													
Developing a character													
Compressing language													
Selecting richly connotative words and images													
Combining the unexpected													
Selecting and organizing material													
Sequencing ideas													
Shaping an argument													
Summarizing													
Creating and producing a piece													
Manipulating methods of persuasion													
Comprehending a position													
Choosing appropriate language for a context													
Exercising the imagination													
Posing questions													

images can be profitably discussed during this project. Their success can be measured with some of the same standards with which the images and impact of poetry are assessed.

An interesting side effect of this exercise is that the words of the poetry and the power and vitality of its imagery can be reinforced every time its newly juxtaposed commercial ad appears on the screen or in print. For example, Walt Whitman's "Song of Myself" can be set to the Coke ad "I'd Like to Teach." The melody and images of the song may come to evoke Whitman's words as well as cans of Coke. Or in a more somber example, the ironic juxtaposition of Wilfred Owen's antiwar poetry with the Army's "Be All That You Can Be" might make it difficult to hear that advertisement uncritically.

This exercise can enrich, enliven, and clinch the study of a single poet or poem, a number of poets or poems in a unit, or selected poets or poems from a whole term.

Madison Avenue

In this activity, students are challenged to use their imaginations and their skill with words and actions to create a new product and develop a thirty-second commercial for television. The imagination demanded to create a new product is paralleled by that needed to develop the advertisement that will market it. Students complete this activity best in stages. A successful approach that we have used follows.

1. Teams of seven or eight students are given a plastic soft-drink bottle, a plain paper box, or a cylinder packet and asked to come up with a new product.
2. After each of the teams has come up with its product, students use crayons and paper to create a label for the container.

3. The group then develops the action and script for a thirty-second commercial with actors, product, jingle, and announcer.
4. The groups take turns videotaping their creations.
5. The teams' ads are presented to a panel of advertising professionals for review and comment or to another class that ranks the ads using a set of criteria developed by the original class.

Rock Review

Rock music is one of the most powerful media for adolescents, and its capacity to promote language can be demonstrated by a number of projects. One approach is to let trios assume studio production responsibility for a local rock station; they must create a script for a two-hour broadcast. (Students more devoted to country, classical, or classic rock music could organize competing programming.) A series of fifteen to twenty recordings with thirty seconds or less of commentary for each is the goal for the eight or so groups in the class. The productions are judged on the basis of their selections, the sequence they form, and the language that is used to promote them. All members of the audience (teacher and students) critique them. (Each group is allowed to play only one song during its "broadcast.") If the class is energized by the project, students might collapse the best scripts and present them to a local station.

Piggyback Pop

Another approach to the domain of rock music is to add lyrics to existing songs. A song such as John Lennon's "Imagine" promotes imaginings of additional lines or verses. In Lennon's song, the first verse deals with religion, the second with politics, the third with economics, and the last is a coda, or conclusion. A new fourth stanza could be added to extend Lennon's basic philosophy by imagining that which is not, but ought to be, in the world we know: education, friendship, or peace. (To provide interest and clearer thinking, dissenting students could write a satirical set of stanzas that stand Lennon's ideas on their head.)

Jacketeering

Another approach to music is to ask students to draw up a list of forty or fifty titles of what they consider to be the best music being played today. Small groups of students are then given the list and asked to categorize the music by its thematic center. Some songs defy categorization, of course, and can be discarded or assigned to a miscellaneous category. The groups are then responsible for selecting two or more of the categories they developed to create a thematic album of fifteen to twenty songs. The students create a title for the album and a jacket cover that explains the special collection and comments on each of the songs in it.

Rock Market

Just as a pilot TV show tries to anticipate trends and project a marketable theme for a soap opera or sitcom, this project asks students to locate an audience, develop a core idea or thrust for a song, and create lyrics that make sense for that context. The selection of an audience should be somewhat specific at first—for example, pop, rock, blues, country, progressive, rap, or heavy metal. That selection will rule out certain themes and encourage others. Can you imagine, for instance, the Beatles singing a Willie Nelson ballad? Once a few general themes are considered (students working alone or in large groups can do this), a set of lyrics needs to be written. To help ideas flow, the class could be asked to list eight to ten words that would likely be associated with each of the musical categories. Each group then tries to use two or three of these as key words in its lyrics. Putting words together with feeling and sense is the goal.

Anchor People

Another direction to take with television is spawned by the slightly more serious world of news broadcasting. Consider a current story of national or international urgency. If a class is large, two stories might be used, with half the students being given the first and the other half the second. Each of these groups is in turn divided into as many groups of four as possible. Each of the quartets takes its story and, in pairs, fashions a strong liberal or vigorous conservative bias into a forty-second news story. Each pair writes its script and creates stick-figure visuals that punctuate the script. Then the two pairs actually produce a videotape of that forty-second slot for an evening news program. The other students critique the news spots after they have viewed them. They might even continue in a television idiom by expressing their reactions in a point-counterpoint or news talk-show format.

Radio Head

Talk shows dominate the AM radio dial. You can put this argumentative forum in motion in your classroom by selecting three or four polemical statements that can be used by students who take roles as initial callers or guests on the show. The host should respond boldly to the first callers and then invite class members to call in their opinions. The callers post names and hometowns they assume on placards on their backs. They sit in class with their eyes closed facing away from the host and contribute to what can become a rich conversation.

Crisis Interview

This is one of the most reliably successful pieces of media mimicry. The interview should be recorded on audiotape or even videotape if students dress for it and create a proper backdrop and props. The focus should be on language, however, not on the physical objects. A designated reporter interviews onlookers at the scene of a catastrophe or an unusual event. The questions and responses of all participants are spontaneous. Here are scenarios that have worked for us:

- tourists at the scene of a hot-air balloon crash at the rim of the Grand Canyon
- Chicago firefighters at the site of a conflagration caused, it seems, by a gas explosion at a restaurant
- a trio of pedestrians at the foot of Radio City Music Hall, where an unidentified woman threatens suicide on a ledge sixteen floors up
- a group of rodeo clowns who have just discovered that an unidentified novice has entered the bull-riding contest on a dare
- the community and family of the boy killed in Robert Frost's "Out, Out" or of Richard Cory in Edwin Arlington Robinson's "Richard Cory" or of Emily Grierson in William Faulkner's "A Rose for Emily"

The special nature of each place and crisis makes it easy for the reporter to ask strong questions. Because these are well-defined crises, the respondents find it very easy to build spontaneously a shared story; and the language that flows from the vignette is almost always authentic and bold. Students do not plan it; it just moves. Because students are projecting into a critical life event, the language matures to meet the expectations of that particular situation. The episode is recorded on tape and thus can be easily transcribed into a dramatic scene with directions and rewritten as a radio play. After reshaping it, another group can rehearse and finally perform it. Students can then compare the original and the revised versions to decide which is most powerful, most true.

Pilot Making

Students know a great deal more about soap operas and sitcoms than about Chaucer and Dickens. Their literacy in the media world can help them create a pilot for a new dramatic series that might introduce them to elements essential to the study of a story—elements, say, of character, dramatic conflict, and plot. The students' task is not actually to make the pilot but to create the general format for the entire project.

- We ask students working in pairs or as larger teams to come up with a set of two or three characters who are delineated in such a way that conflict naturally occurs between and among them.

- A context for their relationship must be established as well: the kitchen of an exclusive restaurant, the office of an elementary school, or a life-guard station at the beach. A novel situation is preferable.
- Students are asked to imagine the nature of possible conflicts that would arise from *these* characters in *this* setting.
- When character, context, and conflict are formulated, all the ingredients to generate drama are available; what we don't know is the conclusion. The shape of the conflict between the characters will shift for each episode and will demand episodic conclusions or resolutions. Each team is responsible for summarizing a set of four episodes that spell out specific conflicts and resolutions as well as for creating a final climactic conclusion.

If you have used the combined power of cooperation (the groups at work learning together) and competition (each group's sense that others are equally engaged in this work), you may wish to select the most promising by popular response, just as networks do. When a pilot is selected from those presented, the class might set out to develop the dialogue for a few of the shows and even move toward production with props and costumes. This final development of the dialogue can offer the crucial test of its effectiveness. Whether or not you take the pilot into production, students learn a great deal about turning daily language into dramatic dialogue. More important, perhaps, their sense of how character, conflict, and context work together will be a step toward better understanding fiction as well as drama.

Class Magazine

Ask students to create their own class magazine, a one-time commemorative issue designed to express something fundamental about the class's experience, spirit, or nature. Working in small groups, have students brainstorm about the nature of the magazine. What would be most expressive of the class: a news magazine, a literary magazine, a tabloid, a human interest magazine, or a wildlife publication? The range is wide. Each group selects the most promising idea and writes up an outline of its format. The whole class hears each group's suggestion and votes on the class choice. Serious production roles, assignments, schedules, and necessary materials are decided with a student chair and the groups collaborating together. The production activities are done by individuals, small groups, and the whole class. When the magazine is "published," each student is asked to select two nonclass members, perhaps parents, to read and respond to it. That public response can be combined with the students' assessment for evaluation.

Classy Comics

Ask students to render any narrative literature as frames of a comic strip with dialogue bubbled in. No painterly skill is needed; stick figures will do. The simplifying of plot, character, and language is the essence of the exercise. The visual delight for the class is the secondary side effect. Another way to use graphics with literature or language is to juxtapose professionally drawn comics or cartoons with students' words or captions. When the additions are relevant to class studies, the benefits of the exercise are greater. Our chunky *Far Side* calendar pads, along with *New Yorker* and newspaper cartoons, have been rifled like this for years.

Bumper Stickers

The bumper sticker, like the billboard, provides a quick message. The drivers who see the message usually glimpse it for a limited time. The medium thus dictates certain characteristics such as brevity, cleverness, and a logocentric style. Show students facsimiles of some classic stickers and discuss what makes these examples effective. Then challenge students to produce equally good ones that address current issues. Ask students to come up with a political issue such as antismoking legislation and to work in small groups to create bumper stickers that support or attack the issue. The wordplay and compression central to success in this medium make it an excellent connector to poetry. This activity also can be used as the beginning point or as a clincher in exploring topics that will be used for extended debate and discussion and in expository and persuasive essays.

Invitation to Reflection 10-2

1. Have you ever been involved in these kinds of projects in English classes?
2. Which of the thirteen was most immediately appealing to you?
3. Which was least appealing?
4. Can you imagine actually initiating such an activity with a class?
5. Do you believe that having students produce media would teach them anything about media that a discussion would not?
6. Because some of these projects are uncommon in traditional classes, to achieve them demands energy, vision, and toughness. If you think their production is promising, what obstacles to trying them can you imagine?
7. How can you overcome these obstacles?

⏁ ENTERTAIN: STUDENTS AS LISTENERS AND VIEWERS

Invitation to Reflection 10-3

1. Do you associate visual images and musical sounds with the study of literature or language?
2. What classroom media experiences have touched your work as a reader or writer?
3. Are those experiences especially vivid?
4. Did you ever experience dramatic enactments of the plays being studied in your English classes? Did you ever view film adaptations of novels or short stories?
5. If so, did you respond differently to seeing or hearing them than to reading them?
6. Have you ever used still pictures to augment your texts?
7. Do you ever find correspondences between music you hear and literature you read?
8. Would you be more likely to introduce a literary character or theme by discussion or by a picture?
9. Would you more likely prompt writing by verbal explanation, pictures, or music?

When we focus our attention on the bottom right quadrant of Figure 10-1, students turn from composing to comprehending CDs, videos, film, and other media that bring vivid sounds and sights to the classroom. Before we discuss using professional media productions in the classroom, we want to establish some general guidelines for the best use of two of the most prominent forms, music and film. We believe that the use of both is enhanced by careful selection and incorporation of excerpts—seldom whole pieces—of film (or videotape) or long pieces of music. Fehlman (1987, p. 84) calls excerpting brief passages of film "quoting films." He is convinced that films provide rich texts that prompt lively interpretation because these texts and their language are familiar to students. But film is traditionally brought into the English classroom so that students may view entire adaptations of the classics, usually after reading the originals. "Often the film is shown without explanation (a mere 'treat,' to see an audio visual representation of what was written). The follow-up to viewing consists of criticizing the film for not being faithful to the original" (p. 86). Fehlman believes that a more productive exercise is to select particular film segments that augment specific points of classroom discussion.

Nathanson (1992, pp. 88–89) elaborates the productive classroom use of film in a list of twenty guidelines for viewing videotapes (see Figure 10-3). Kearns

FIGURE 10–3
Nathanson's guidelines for using videotape

1. The videotape segment, after motivating discussion and direct teaching, is from ten to twenty minutes in length, not a full-period component.
2. The videotape segment is used to develop appreciation by providing rapid plot exposition when covering a difficult or complex work such as a Shakespearean play.
3. Students have already read or previewed the material which is covered by the videotape segment.
4. A directed reading/writing question precedes the viewing of a particular video segment; discussion of that question follows viewing.
5. The aim of the lesson is not "to watch a videotape."
6. All students have a clear instructional purpose in watching the video segment, not passive viewing or time-killing. The objective in viewing is product or task oriented.
7. Active viewing is checked by the teacher via a writing assignment, worksheet, small-group activity, or other evaluative means.
8. As a meaningful homework assignment, students are urged to compare, contrast, evaluate, or perform some critical thinking or writing task related to the videotape lesson.
9. Careful summary notes are provided by the teacher so that absentees can still grasp the essence of the videotape lesson, or obtain a sense of continuity.
10. New and unfamiliar material is not introduced by the videotape; introductory, technical, or background material related to the unit of study may be provided via videotape.
11. The teacher reduces the light in the room for greater visibility; however, a dark room is not necessary; lit rooms may actually be preferred for outlining or other note-taking activities done while the video segment is on.
12. Videotape, as opposed to audiotape, versions are used because seeing and hearing are more appropriate to the lesson than simple audiotape.
13. Consecutive class periods are not devoted to the showing of a videotape; serialized viewing is not teaching.
14. Videotape is not a daily lesson component nor a one-time special event. It is effective if used frequently, used to present material which is to be tested later, and elevated to an importance equal to that of print material.
15. Video segments have been carefully previewed and screened for potentially offensive or controversial material, technically poor copies, and other problems.
16. Video segments have been carefully cued to minimize loss of instructional time from fast-forwarding or rewinding.
17. Sufficient time has been built into the lesson for student questions and comments following the viewing experience. Viewing does not end at the bell, the lesson does.
18. Teachers make clear their expectations concerning student viewing behavior; respect, politeness, and courtesy are stressed before, during, and after the viewing experience.
19. During the viewing the teacher circulates and actively supervises the class, answers individual students' questions, and insures task-orientation.
20. The teacher avoids sending unintentional—but destructive—double messages through performing clerical tasks during the viewing session.

Source: From Steven Nathanson, "Guidelines for Using Videotape: A Checklist for Educators," *English Journal,* March 1992. Reprinted by permission.

(1997) recommends several texts for analyzing and teaching film:

Boggs, J. M. (1985). *The art of watching films.* Palo Alto, CA: Mayfield.

Bone, J., & Johnson, R. (1991). *Understanding the film: An introduction to film appreciation.* Lincolnwood, IL: National Textbook Company.

Perkins, V. F. (1993). *Film as film: Understanding and judging movies.* New York: Da Capo.

Resch, K. E., & Schicker, V. D. (1992). *Using film in the high school curriculum—A practical guide for teachers and librarians.* Jefferson, NC: McFarland.

Watson, R. (1990). *Film and television in education: An aesthetic approach to the moving image.* Bristol, PA: Farmer.

Using Film

The study of electronic texts opens the study of literature in several directions. As Fehlman notes, the most tradi-tional use of media for literary study is in the comparative analysis of classics and their film adaptations. Many plays, novels, and short stories have been dramatized in excellent productions. The shared experience of watching these in class can greatly intensify students' experience of reading them. The emotional charge of having been engaged by the drama heightens viewer/listener response. Films of plays, using the original medium of the *spoken* word, restore power that is lost in reading. Furthermore, older plays, notably Shakespeare's, can be made more comprehensible when speech is clarified with gestures, props, and setting. Veidemanis (1988) explains that the best purpose of such comparisons "is not to elevate one medium over another or even to win consensus. Rather, the goal is for students to come away more secure in articulating their own judgments and responses and fortified to continue the imaginative performance of classic literature on their own" (p. 57).

Films promote an imaginative involvement with literature with many of the same strategies found in a reader response approach. Films promote students' visual participation and emotional involvement in the text, their ability to fill gaps in the text, and their appreciation of multiple interpretations. Griffin (1989) explains that he uses video to teach Shakespeare because he finds that "unless our students visualize a play as they read, the words can seem disembodied and devoid of meaning" (p. 43). He describes the ways in which videos complement the literary text:

- Videotapes can help students perceive the atmosphere of a play.
- Videotapes can help students understand the subtext of a scene . . . those ideas and feelings not stated directly in the dialogue but implied by the way characters look, move, and talk to each other.
- Videotapes can help students see that the same scene can be validly interpreted in different ways. At the very heart of the reader-response approach to literary works is the premise that they can be interpreted by various readers, actors, and directors in different ways. One way to encourage students to experiment with different interpretative possibilities for the same text is to show them how it has been interpreted in different productions. (p. 42)

Fowler and Pesante (1989) demonstrate the power of multiple interpretations of texts by having their students view the same scene performed by different actors. For instance, the same scene from at least five productions of *Hamlet* and *Jane Eyre* (see appendix G) can be shown and students asked to respond to the different versions: How do they differ? Does the difference alter your interpretations of character or idea? Do you have a preference? Does that preference correspond with any bias you bring to the works? Fowler and Pesante then ask their students to read specific scenes in class and draw on their own interpretations for their reading. They even talk through the interpretive possibilities: "For example, would you really play Polonius as a fool as he makes one of the most memorable speeches, his advice to Laertes?" (p. 28).

Fehlman (1987) suggests another use of segments from adapted films: to view "additions to or alterations of the original" and to reflect on what is gained and what is lost. Changes are necessarily made as print is converted to film, but some of these, "rather than undercutting the original, expand ideas inherent in it" (p. 86). Fowler and Pesante (1989) believe that such imaginative projections allow students "to interact in more provocative ways not only with contemporary texts (including television programs, commercials, comic books, music, movies) but also with classics and myths" (p. 28). They have their students read Tom Stoppard's contemporary play, *Rosencrantz and Guildenstern Are Dead*, after *Hamlet*, not as an example of existential or absurdist theater but to enlarge *Hamlet* and invite students to play with the original text. They report that what "initially engages students is how Stoppard creates an entirely new work, using two characters who, in the students' earlier reading of *Hamlet*, were seen simply as Hamlet's friends" (p. 29). Student speculation on that reversal of perspectives, as Rosencrantz and Guildenstern move to the foreground and Hamlet shifts to the background, brings them to question the gaps in any author's text and the important and imaginative role of the reader in filling them. These teachers capitalize on students' reflections by asking them to do for *Hamlet* what Stoppard did—that is, to fill gaps in *Hamlet* creatively. They give as examples of students' writing a short piece of dialogue between Gertrude and Claudius in their bedroom, a dialogue between Hamlet and Ophelia before the death of the king, a description of the gravedigger and his wife at home, and an essay on Hamlet and the jester when Hamlet was young (pp. 29–30).

Fehlman (1987) uses film quotes in yet another way: "to contemporize literary classics by demonstrating similarities in themes, especially those expressed in parallel scenes from book to film" (p. 85). There are several provocative illustrations of his strategy: "after my class reads Conrad's "The Secret Sharer," I have used a scene from Hitchcock's *Strangers on a Train*, in which Bruno first announces to Guy that they share the guilt of Miriam's death. Both narratives deal with shared identities: thus, they can be discussed together, one helping to clarify or verify the message in the other" (p. 85). Other connections he makes are in the keeping of dead bodies in Faulkner's "A Rose for Emily" and Hitchcock's *Psycho;* the singular pursuit of a compelling and alien phenomenon in *Alien, Jaws,* and *Moby Dick;* and the gathering of travelers in the opening scene of John Ford's *Stagecoach* and Chaucer's *Canterbury Tales* (pp. 85–86).

Similarly, we have used clips from the 1974 film *Monty Python and the Holy Grail* to teach aspects of the medieval concept of chivalry. Basic assumptions about royalty can be hilariously grasped in a sequence in which King Arthur talks with members of an anachronistic medieval communist collective. The exploration of the causes of chivalry's decline, for instance, can be capped by a viewing of the entrenchment of the two knights who duel until one has lost both arms and legs yet is still challenging the other.

Film can vivify many literary units as extensions or recapitulations of setting, character, plot, tone, and idea. We ended a unit on diaries, memoirs, short stories, and poems of the Holocaust with a 1988 French film, *Au Revoir les Enfants,* based on writer-director Louis Malle's childhood memories. Set in 1944 in a Catholic boarding school in Nazi-occupied France, the film centers on the friendship between two bright adolescents, one a Jewish student. Our students' understanding of the subtleties of the film was much deepened by their prior reading. The dimensions of the Holocaust's horrific tragedy were personalized in the character of the Jewish schoolboy and his classmates and thus left an imprint that summed and held all the suffering we had met.

Excerpted clips abound for a unit on satire—for instance, scenes from Woody Allen's 1973 *Sleeper* (filled with satirical scenes of 1970s American life) and Robert Townsend's 1987 *Hollywood Shuffle* (a personal protest against black movie stereotypes). Students readily understand satire's critical laughter in *Sleeper* when the Allen character is asked to identify 1970s relics such as Howard Cosell: "When people committed great crimes, they were forced to watch that." In *Hollywood Shuffle*, a black actor's school trains African American aspirants with impeccable British accents to speak like field slaves and muggers.

Finally, film contributes to the study of literature as what Fehlman (1987) calls a "textbook" for teaching literary technique and craft. Students, drawn to the compelling and immediate visual and auditory drama of this "film text," transfer an understanding of the technique of the director to an appreciation of the craft of the author of a "printed text." Directors achieve with picture and sound what authors must achieve solely with words. When students begin to think analytically about technique, they must consider the tools of the craft in order to articulate their insights. "[M]ost all literary terminology is applicable to film, so narrative terms like 'setting' and 'conflict,' along with more poetic terms like 'imagery' and 'figures of speech,' can be identified, defined within a film segment, either directly or as an offshoot of the discussion of the film as text itself" (p. 84). Nathanson (1992) reminds us that music videos are also helpful in analyzing poetic imagery. He asks students to match the visual images with "the lyrical and musical text of a rock video!" (p. 89).

In one successful classroom exercise, we use clips from the films *Norma Rae* and *Dead Man Walking* to ex-

plore how authors or directors lead us to their perspective through carefully selected detail (visual imagery, evocative music, and spoken dialogue). We use the list and the sequence shown in Figure 10–4 with *Norma Rae*. The ideal setup is to use selected scenes from *Norma Rae* so that you do not have to hold students through the awkward fast-forwarding process. We have used this exercise with individual students, small groups, and the whole class. On one side of a sheet of paper we list the nine sequences from *Norma Rae* with blank lines following each. The directions, shown in Figure 10–4, are on the reverse side.

Using Music

Music as well as film enriches literary study. We have linked music and literature already in this text. We make that connection here again with a story we teach. Joyce Carol Oates's chilling "Where Are You Going, Where Have You Been?" has the influence of mass culture on adolescents at its heart. Connie, its fifteen-year-old protagonist, is deeply absorbed in the lyrics of the popular songs of her culture; they form the basis of her best and deepest hopes, but they badly deceive her. The fulfillment of the idol promised in her songs turns out to be a threatening sham, probably a rapist, perhaps a killer.[1] Centrally important in suffusing the story with additional meaning and import is noting the story's dedication ("For Bob Dylan"); tracking the title back to its musical source,

---

[1]A made-for-TV movie, *Smooth Talk*, is based on this story and appears to have captured its characters, plot, and cumulative tension. Thus, it vivifies the story except for several telling details. A discussion of the differences between the story and the movie intensifies appreciation of both.

FIGURE 10–4

Viewing *Norma Rae*

CLIPS		
Sequence	*VCR setting*	*Duration (seconds)*
1. Theme song	013–094	150
2. Setting	095–115	60
3. Noise, Mamma	116–173	138
4. Organizer	174–219	120
5. Bulletin board	220–265	120
6. Norma Rae joins union	265–284	50
7. Letter and fight	284–330	120
8. Letter and the law	330–396	190
9. Fired	396–472	240

FOCUS

Record (using numbers to guide you) your sense of each scene by writing about
1. dominant images, sounds, and feelings of the scene
2. what Norma Rae is feeling and thinking about her world
3. what the director wants us to think and feel about the world of a textile worker

SPRAWL

1. Write a short response to the entire film clip. Pay particular attention to the important shifts in Norma Rae's development as a worker and as a person.
2. Write a brief comparison of the consciousness the artist-director is hoping to develop in his audience. Pay particular attention to the ways in which he elicits the audience's sympathies.

"It's All Over Now, Baby Blue," or to another Dylan song, "A Hard Rain's A Gonna Fall"; listening to the songs; and tracing their imagery to Oates's story. Possible questions to be raised include the following:

- How is Oates's story an answer to the question posed in its title? What happens to Connie?
- Which is more horrific, the story's or the song's vision?
- If you had written a story in response to Dylan's vision, what kind of plot and characters would you have imagined?
- Although Oates clearly worked imaginatively on her material, she said in an interview that the "story came to me more or less in a piece" after reading a story about a killer in a southwestern state and thinking about old legends and songs about "death and the maiden." Write your own newspaper account of the events in Oates's story.

One of our students, Susan Quinn, was so interested in the interactive effects of music and literature that she began to collect correspondences between them. We list several of those connections, as well as those of other students who followed her, as examples that you might introduce into the classroom and of connective work that your students might undertake (Figure 10-5).

Using Paintings, Prints, and Photographs

In our chapters on teaching literature, we discussed the enhancing possibilities in the still visual imagery of paintings, prints, and photographs. We have found visual print media to be instructionally powerful as enrichment, clarifier, clincher, and extender of literature.

We discussed how the study of W. H. Auden's "Musée des Beaux Arts" is greatly intensified by showing the painting that inspired it, Pieter Brueghel the Elder's sixteenth-century work *The Fall of Icarus*. Writer Jorge Luis Borges acknowledges a particular indebtedness to art: "To a painting by Watts, done in 1896, I owe 'The House of Asterion' and the character of its sad protagonist." That painting, *The Minotaur*, in the Tate Gallery in London, invites viewers, as Borges does readers, to redirect their sympathies toward the lonely, isolated creature so commonly reviled in myth, story, and picture. (Many other sculptures and paintings, such as Maggi Hambling's 1986-1987 *Minotaur Surprised While Eating*, present the conventional view of the minotaur as rapacious monster and thereby provide a perfect contrast to Watts's and Borges's imaginative reversal.) After the riddle of the story is solved, our students move with sympathy into the minotaur's perceptions and unconscious suffering. Examining the painting reinforces that surprising view as well as the imagination of both artists to conceive it.

Many M. C. Escher prints are perfect visual foils for Borges's verbal games, riddles, and puzzles. Both the Dutch artist and the Argentinean writer concern themselves with the creative and enigmatic interplay between the logic of everyday realities and the vision of infinite possibilities. The fiction of Raymond Carver and the paintings of Edward Hopper present stark, hauntingly similar perspectives on human experience. The motives and art of each of these four creative artists become far more accessible when they are examined together.

We also teach short stories with cartoons. In Eudora Welty's 1941 short story "Why I Live at the P.O.," for instance, the jealousy and resentment of the narrator, Sister, towards her younger sister, Stella-Rondo, is basic to the story's plot, characters, and idea. Four Gary Larson cartoons of insect and fish siblings locked in jealous and acrimonious domestic combat invite students to both laugh at and take seriously this common and corrosive experience. The visual art used to teach literature, however, need not be titled, professional images found in museums or books. We have used students' own searches and selections of faces in periodicals as springboards for discussions of characters in literature.

Wendy Ewald, a MacArthur Award winner, has developed a program called *Literacy Through Photography* (Stainburn, 2001). Her program prompts students to gain a new measure of self-understanding through a combination of photographs and writing about matters that are close to home: self-portrait, family, community, and dreams. Ewald's work in two domains illuminates students' initial ideas and evokes vital writing and deft photography.

FIGURE 10–5
Connections between literature and music

Beneath the Wheel, Herman Hesse	"The Wall," Pink Floyd
The Stranger, Albert Camus	"Killing an Arab," The Cure
Their Eyes Were Watching God, Zora Neal Hurston	"Crossroads," Tracy Chapman
"Richard Cory," Edwin Arlington Robinson	"Richard Cory," Simon and Garfunkel
Romeo and Juliet, William Shakespeare	"Romeo and Juliet," The Indigo Girls
To the Lighthouse, Virginia Woolf	"Virginia Woolf," The Indigo Girls
"What Are Years?," Marianne Moore	"The Sound of Silence," Simon and Garfunkel
The Glass Menagerie, Tennessee Williams	"Father and Son," Cat Stevens
Wuthering Heights, Thomas Hardy	"Wuthering Heights," Kate Bush
A Raisin in the Sun, Lorraine Hansberry	"For Emily, Wherever I May Find Her," Simon and Garfunkel

Jane Marshall (1991) believes that the visual world can open students to literature because the visual world dominates their lives. She discusses Jules Prown's (1982) three-step methodology for analyzing the visual dimensions of artifacts: description, deduction, and speculation. Beginning with close observation of art and artifacts anchors her students' responses; moving to inferences about a particular piece extends those responses; ending with creative reflection about it drives viewers toward new insight. Prown categorizes visual objects from the portentous (museum masterpieces) to the pedestrian (Brillo boxes) and urges that the process be applied across his continuum.

Portentous ◄——————————————► **Pedestrian**

Art	Diversions (books, performances)	Adornments	Modifications	Applied Arts	Devices (vehicles, machines)

By using Prown's analytical steps, Marshall moves her students from exploring paintings, to films, to photographs, and to television (from the arty to the everyday). Students claim jokingly that she has ruined their enjoyment of films: "I can't go to the theater and just let it happen. I notice everything." She knowingly concurs; that was her hope.

Using Comics

Few forms of writing are taken less seriously than comic books. However, comic books have grown up; and many have turned from the simple superhero-versus-supervillain scenario to more complex plots, characters, dialogue, and ideas. Many are even regarded as literature. Some comic books, published as graphic novels, involve a complex sense of philosophy, history, and current events as well as possible futures.

Teachers have long appreciated the seductive appeal of comic books, with their vivid pictures, limited verbal descriptions, sparse dialogue, strong plots, and predictable, almost formulaic ideas. In fact, in our high school generation, classic comics were as much an anathema to English teachers as *Cliffs Notes* often are today. But even traditional comics have been allies of teachers concerned with engaging reluctant, limited, or ESL readers with printed texts. This new generation of comic books has drawn more English teachers to it because the pictorial appeal remains but with far richer narrative, character, and theme. Students become engrossed in the graphic story and emerge with characters well worth pondering and ideas well worth discussion. Admittedly, many teachers see these pictorial stories as points of entry on the way to mature nonpictorial literature, the kind of progress expected as children move from simple, illustrated nursery rhymes toward robustly pictureless college poetry anthologies. Comic book pundits would like

to see even that snobbery erased and the pictures in comic books viewed as exciting enhancements to good literature, not coverups for poor writing. One such devotee, our former student Matt Wood, directed our attention to several. In the following paragraphs, he and we describe them as an introduction to this genre.

Among the earliest of the serious graphic novels is *The Watchman* by Alan Moore. It is a book about a world that is changed by the existence of superheroes, most of whom are merely men in masks. Some are noble of heart, strong of arm, and empty of thought; but others are characters who can be taken seriously. In addition to superheroes, Moore explores the minds of a diverse range of ordinary people: frightened little men and grandiose dreamers. He enters the mind of a frustrated New York City detective as well as a lonely newspaperman and an exasperated psychologist. It is a book that looks at a world on the edge of the end and the ways in which people cope with the fact that they may soon die.

Alan Moore has also written a ten-part miniseries, *V for Vendetta,* set in a totalitarian society that springs up in England after World War III. The hero, a man called V, decides that England would be better off with no government. He proceeds to dismantle the existing government and attempts to usher in an age of voluntary, rather than imposed, order. Whether he succeeds or not is not revealed to the reader, nor is it important. Moore's depiction of a complacent society, a government's power, and an individual's responsibility go to the heart of the important political issues of our time. V is a philosophical man; but his most important belief is that the time for education, the time for knowledge, and the time for freedom is now and forever. Dangerous as they are, they must never be repressed. The author appears to share those beliefs and to write his books for an audience that might be persuaded otherwise.

Several comic books have historical resonances. One is Art Spiegelman's graphic novel *Maus: A Survivor's Tale.* This book does to the Nazi Holocaust what Orwell's *Animal Farm* did to the Russian Revolution. It is the personal account of a survivor of the Holocaust, and the reader reexperiences the horrors of Nazi Germany, but not through human characters: All the characters are animals. Neil Gaiman's *The Sandman* is an ongoing series of comic books that touch upon history through the main character Morphers, the Lord of Dreams, who has existed for as long as dreams have and will not disappear until they do. Often the book touches upon history that he has altered. One of the story lines, entitled "Distant Mirrors," deals entirely with the effect that he has had on the shaping of the world. For instance, Morphers appears in a conversation with Augustus Caesar that determines the fate of Rome and in action that contributes to Robespierre's fall in the French Revolution.

Other comic books worthy of mention include Steve Gerber's *Foolkiller,* which takes a difficult look at our society and its problems; *Classics Illustrated,* which makes graphic, faithful versions of many classic stories; Guy Davis's *Baker Street,* which details the adventures of Sharon Ford, a modern-day detective modeled after Sherlock Holmes; and Scott Beadestadt's *Trollords,* a book with silly characters and serious themes.

Comic strips, too, are extremely popular with adolescents and deal with the basic issues of our time. Comics such as *Dilbert* and *Bloom County* offer relevant social commentary. They appeal to adolescents because of their cynical look at the established order. Black's (1997) study of comics found that students responded to them more positively than to short stories and were able to deal with them in a more sophisticated fashion in their writing.

Our discussion of the challenge to the canon in Chapter 7 presented some of the arguments for a breakdown of the divisions between high and low culture. Never has that breakdown been more apparent than in the open admission of comic books into the English classroom. We suggest that you take a look at them before you close your door to their benefits.

Developing Film Literacy

A number of teachers apply film to the teaching of literature; a smaller number believe that film should be taught for itself alone. Even if film were an inferior art form composed only for commercial entertainment, some teachers would feel that it still warranted attention because of its importance to youth. Gallagher (1988) observes that it "is not entirely coincidental that videocassettes resemble, in shape and heft, books, nor that, despite their sometimes sleazy and usually tacky atmosphere, videotape rental outlets function very much like the commercial lending libraries of old. The fact is that film and literature, particularly in terms of narrativity, share a great deal. Clearly, today's students are 'reading' films at the rate English teachers have always wished they would read books" (p. 59). This magnetic attraction for students gives us strong reason to include film in the English curriculum. The same claims for making students critical readers, alert and awake to the printed text, apply to this filmed text in which they are absorbed. Instructional attempts should be to enhance students' viewing and to make it more selective, not, as sometimes happens, to spoil their viewing through tedious analysis and to make it overly self-conscious.

Teaching film per se has claims for study that rest with the medium itself. An expanding canon validates such study; the creative collaborative work from directors and screenwriters to actors and actresses provides rich material and justifies close critical attention. William Arrowsmith (1985), a renowned classicist, believes that if Sophocles were alive today, he would be making films. The technology of DVDs, with their digital precision and their ability to move quickly and precisely to preset scenes in the text, facilitates this study. Teachers can make easily programmed sequences of character development, imagery, and structure. Gallagher (1988) predicts that the "new technology, because it permits and so encourages a concentration on the 'micro-skills' of visual analysis, will bring the study of film and of literature closer together. Film segments can now be analyzed in all their detail and not just for the overall impression they create" (p. 58). He goes on to suggest that "we need to give students the names, and so the ability to speak critically, of those devices whose basic use they already comprehend but about whose structure and formal operations they remain ignorant" (p. 59).

Griffin (1989, pp. 40–41) enumerates some of the vocabulary of film, the range of "theatrical, cinematic, and film signs" that a study of videos introduces to students (see Figure 10–6). Gallagher (1988) mentions another motive for the learning of film vocabulary (roughly parallel to learning the vocabulary of fictional elements):

> We might also note that there is a growing reciprocity between film and modern literature, not only in that about half of American films are derived from some literary source or other, or even that some modern authors (like Norman Mailer) are involved in filmmaking, but also in that a number of authors—Joan Didion is a particularly striking example—have been strongly influenced on a *structural level* by the motion picture. Film devices like jump cuts, lap dissolves, fades, and track-ins are part of contemporary "signifying practices" and are regularly approximated in much contemporary literature, particularly fiction. (p. 59)

Teasley and Wilder (1997) have developed some extremely useful and insightful ideas for using film in English classes. For example, they focus students' initial perceptions as they watch the first ten minutes of the film *Pathfinder* with questions that link what they have seen and heard to a deepening understanding of how setting, character, and theme merge. Then they show five clips of poignant moments in the film and ask another set of questions about the meaning of what students have watched. This punctuation of watching with questions keeps their interpretive minds awake as they soak up the vital sounds and sense before them. The process is intended to lead students toward habits of active viewing of the films that are so important in their lives. Teasley and Wilder suggest a list of six questions that can be used with any film:

1. What changes did you notice in the film as you watched? What changes did you notice in your feelings or opinions as you watched?
2. Go back over your viewing guides looking at your "visual images" and "sounds" notations. Do you notice any patterns emerging? (For example, do you see the same images again and again? Do you hear musical phrases or lines of dialogue repeated?) What do you think the director was trying to communicate by using these patterns?

FIGURE 10–6
Griffin's vocabulary of film

THEATRICAL AND CINEMATIC SIGNS

Body: the actor's voice, facial expression, physical gestures, bodily posture, physical movement, size and shape, make-up, hairstyle

Costume: its color, texture, weight, cut

Space: its size and shape and its relationship to the auditorium

Set: whether realistic or symbolic; how related to movements of the actors; the colors, shapes, textures, and weights of all its stage properties

Lighting: whether obtrusive or supportive only, warm or cold, sharp or gentle, bland or emotional

FILM SIGNS

Shot types: whether long, medium, close-up, or deep focus

Camera angles: whether bird's eye, high, eye-level, low or oblique

Lighting: whether high key, high contrast, or low key

Color: whether cool or warm, advancing or retreating

Frame areas: whether pictorial elements are located at the center, top, bottom, or on the edge of the frame

Composition: how pictorial elements such as contrast, weight, line, planes, and proxemic patterns are used

Camera movement: whether pan or tilt shots, dolly or tracking shots, use of zoom lens

Editing: how shots are used to establish a scene, how they are joined into sequences through cuts, dissolves, and wipes

Sound: how the sound track, including music, is used to underscore, parallel, or counterpoint an image or scene

---

3. Make a list of all the things that this film is about.
4. Make a list of all the conflicts you have seen in this film.
5. What characters, incidents, or objects in this film remind you of other stories you have read or movies you have seen?
6. In your opinion, is this film neutral, or does it clearly take a position on a particular issue? (p. 65)

Like the questions in their viewing guide, Teasley and Wilder's six questions prompt students to view with depth of thought as well as feeling. To these methodological suggestions they have compiled a list of one hundred films (see Appendix G) that are extremely effective with adolescents (Teasley & Wilder, 1996).

Burmester (1983) summarizes the history of film instruction in American classrooms after its initial awakening, when McLuhan gave "respectability" to mass-media study: "There was a brief 'golden era' in the late 1960s and early 1970s when it appeared that film and television courses might find a permanent niche in the schools, but 'back to basics' and budget problems put an end to such optimism" (pp. 95–96). At present, most film study occupies a tight place in an already overtaxed study of the printed word. But some curricula have electives. Franza (1984) describes one he offered called "The Art of Film." His course goals articulate a thoughtful and balanced regard for an art form often overwhelmed by glamour and hype; his aim is

1. taking no movie for granted,
2. being aware of the collaborative effort in filmmaking,
3. focusing attention on directors rather than on actors and actresses,
4. knowing a bit about the history of movies,
5. realizing that other people make movies besides Americans,
6. knowing some of the technical aspects of moviemaking, and
7. being aware that movies are conscious, carefully planned, creative and expensive undertakings. (p. 40)

Whether we integrate the study of film into the regular English literature and language course or teach it as an elective, Franza (1984) reminds us of our basic motive. He quotes what Joseph Conrad said of his purpose in his novels: "My task, above all, is to make you *see*" (p. 40). That should be our purpose also in the study of film.

Locating Materials

We have found nothing so helpful in locating media materials as experience coupled with awareness. As we grow more familiar with what we teach, we search more efficiently and freely for relevant collateral material. We ransack libraries, art museums, periodicals, television listings, and advertisements for media that connect, enrich, and extend language and literature. Students themselves, when alerted, can enter the search via the Internet. The next immediate source of materials after your own experience is your school, municipal, or nearest accessible college or university library. Departments of media are becoming common in all types of libraries.

In Appendix G, we suggest some general resources for you as a beginning teacher left to your own solitary search. These resources can provide access to film, TV programming, radio drama, and books on tape. Ongoing rapid developments in the electronic world make a list of specific sources quickly dated; this list, however, of names and addresses of periodicals can acquaint you with upcoming live events and the range of nonprint productions, from verbatim reading and acting of novels and plays to interviews, analyses, and documentaries. The list also includes the names of distributors of film, videotapes, and recorded books as well as several video series that we have used in whole or part with great success.

⌒EXAMINE: STUDENTS AS ANTHROPOLOGISTS AND LITERARY CRITICS

To examine media is to look at them in terms of how they work and how each is shaped differently. In this quadrant, we ask students to behave as archeologists or anthropologists digging carefully through these cultural phenomena in order to understand more specifically how they touch us. Then we suggest ways in which skills of literary analysis are also useful tools for examining media—not as artifact but as art.

⌒Invitation to Reflection 10-4

1. What is your hunch about people who watch more than four hours of TV a day? Are they males or females? Young, middle-aged, or old? College educated or not? Low-, medium-, or high-income level? Urban or nonurban?
2. Do you receive news any differently from TV, newspapers, or periodicals? Which is more likely to satisfy the need for logical, sequential analysis?
3. Do you assume that national news coverage on TV is unbiased? Liberal? Conservative?
4. Do you think of TV news more as information or entertainment?
5. Does advertising more often inform you or persuade you?
6. Do you often encounter print or nonprint advertising with no pictures, just words?
7. Do soap operas present a picture of American culture with which you are familiar in your own life?
8. Do you ever interrogate the lyrics of popular music?
9. Can you imagine using your critical tools of literary analysis on mass-media forms such as TV or film?

Interested students might enrich their understanding of how TV works and how it affects the viewer or listener by reading the results of demographic studies. At the University of Pennsylvania's Annenberg School of Communications, Gerbner, Gross, Morgan, and Signorielli (1982) have conducted meticulous research on prime-time TV viewers each year since 1967. Table 10–1 provides a demographic picture of TV viewing in the United States using data for 1977, 1978, and 1980.

If you were using this professionally polled data with students, you might ask them to notice especially where the greatest discrepancies lie—for instance, in the educational level of medium and heavy viewers: Does this lead you to wonder what attracts this disproportionate number of women, non–college-educated, and lower-income viewers? And what picture of life do they see?

These researchers' delineation of prime time's skewed picture of American social life is instructive also. Even though their research was conducted two decades ago, we excerpt parts of it to reveal how professional media

TABLE 10–1
Relationship between amount of television viewing and demographic variables (%)

		Television Viewing*		
		Light	**Medium**	**Heavy**
Sex				
	Male	50	46	37
	Female	50	54	63
Age				
	18–29	24	24	31
	30–54	51	46	34
	55+	25	30	36
Education				
	No college	54	67	82
	Some college	46	33	18
Income				
	Low	31	33	49
	Medium	35	37	33
	High	35	30	18
Region				
	Urban	45	43	43
	Nonurban	55	57	57

Source: Adapted from G. Gerbner, L. Gross, M. Morgan, and N. Signorielli (1982), Charting the mainstream: Television's contributions to political orientations. From *Journal of Communication, 32*(2), 100–127. Copyright © 1982, *Journal of Communication*, Oxford University Press, Inc. Used with permission.

*TV viewing: light = 0–1 hours per day; medium = 2–3 hours per day; heavy = more than 4 hours per day.

watchers draw conclusions. We might use such an analysis after asking students for their interpretation of data.

> The world of prime time as seen by the average viewer is animated by vivid and intimate portrayals of over three hundred major characters a week, mostly stock dramatic types, and their weekly rounds of dramatic activities.

> Conventional and "normal" though that world may appear, it is in fact far from the reality of anything but consumer values and social power. The curve of consumer spending, unlike that of income, bulges with middle-class status as well as middle age. Despite the fact that nearly half of the national income goes to the top fifth of the real population, the myth of middle class as the all-American norm dominates the world of television. Nearly seven out of every ten television characters appear in the "middle-middle" of a five-way classification system. Most of them are professionals and managers. Blue-collar and service work occupies sixty-seven percent of all Americans but only ten percent of television characters. These features of the world of prime-time television should cultivate a middle-class or "average" income self-designation among viewers.

> Men outnumber women at least three to one. Most women attend to men or home (and appliances) and are younger (but age faster) than the men they meet. Underrepresentation in the world of television suggests the cultivation of viewers' acceptance of more limited life chances for women, a more limited range of activities, and more rigidly stereotyped images than for men.

> Young people (under eighteen) comprise one-third and older people (over sixty-five) one-fifth of their true proportion in the population. Blacks on television represent three-fourths and Hispanics one-third of their share of the U.S. population, and a disproportionate number are minor rather than major characters. . . . Weigel, Loomis, and Soja (1980) show that although blacks appear in many programs and commercials, they seldom appear with whites, and actually interact with whites in only about two percent of total human appearance time. The prominent and stable overrepresentation of well-to-do white males in the prime of life dominates prime time. Television's general demography bears greater resemblance to the facts of consumer spending than to the U.S. Census. . . .

> But threats abound. Crime in prime time is at least ten times as rampant as in the real world. An average of five to six acts of overt physical violence per hour involves over half of all major characters. Yet pain, suffering, and medical help rarely follow this mayhem. (pp. 443–445)

These researchers do not suggest causal relationships between prime-time content and viewer attitudes, but they do find correlations. For instance, among TV viewers versus their non–TV-watching counterparts, the study found the following:

- "stronger prejudices about women and old people"
- heightened "perceptions of danger and risk"
- "an exaggerated sense of mistrust, vulnerability, and insecurity" (p. 445)
- susceptibility to "simplistic appeals to law and order" (p. 412)

Such an analysis of this commonplace phenomenon holds natural interest for most students and serves as a model of critical scrutiny. It can also be a precursor to their own data gathering and interpretation.

Morris (1989) explains her design for moving her students from being "couch potatoes" to "informed critics." She asks them to "practice three kinds of analysis in [her] classes: (1) individual detailed logs of text, (2) group dialogue about TV programming, and (3) researched essays documenting and interpreting details of television programs." Her first step is "to ask students to keep their own individual written logs of program content. I describe these viewing/writing homework assignments as being similar to anthropologists' field notes" (p. 35). She moves toward speculation only after these concrete details are gathered and recorded. She says that students learn that "intellectually sound and worthwhile criticism depends upon the employment of accurate language and documentation" (p. 36). Their discussion is based on reading aloud from their logs.

Morris cites studies that "indicate that alarmingly high numbers of regular television watchers believe TV content is primarily transmission of unmediated and direct imagery, when, in reality, television production results from selection, arrangement, and emphasis of countless textual elements by authors for specific purposes and from their own viewpoints" (p. 39). Because television content is so familiar to students, Morris feels that she must help them "acquire sufficient distance" to form discriminating responses to different kinds of programming; to the producers', directors', and actor's choices; and to the cinematic influences on viewer reactions. She believes that asking students to exercise their critical abilities through television analysis helps them develop "analytical methods that further their thoughtful interpretations" (p. 40). She also poses provocative questions to her students to help "break their habits of casual acceptance of texts and, instead, think anew about meanings of television's messages: How [are] society and people's roles in it being portrayed? What values, attitudes, and conceptions of pleasure does this program promote? What responses might this program elicit from viewers who are watching from differing situations and circumstances than your own?" (p. 41).

Another teacher, Lorraine Lewis (1984), involved students in "visual research and observation." Her assignment was less structured than Morris's. She did not tell students what to look for; rather, they were "to observe the topic area and draw conclusions about the nature of the media" (p. 52). Here is a list of her topics:

- advertising and audience appeal in specialized magazines
- objectivity and news magazines
- broadcasting time in relation to commercials and content

- lyrics as social statements
- ways to interest teens in news shows
- how children, teens, women, minorities, the elderly, and social classes are portrayed in news broadcasting and programming
- point of view in news writing
- liberal versus conservative media recognition
- rescheduling weekly TV programming to increase ratings
- emotion and advertising as shown in the slogans for brand-name products
- the future of cable (p. 52)

Her classes did discuss the implications of their observations, but they also demonstrated their eye-opening insights by becoming "media manipulation experts" themselves. They wrote biased news stories, stereotypical macho or sultry or all-American commercials, and satirical cartoons; and for their final evaluation, they divided into three groups and produced "a television show that would elicit specific emotions. They also had to include two commercials appropriate to their target audience, radio 'spots' announcing the show's premiere, and ads prepared for newspapers and magazines urging readers to watch" (p. 53).

Teacher Margo Sorenson (1989) describes several journal-writing prompts that set up her classroom activities for using television to develop critical viewing and writing. The first is a prewriting assignment to introduce the unit.

- How does TV influence your life?
- Write about your favorite and least favorite commercials, listing your reasons for your opinion. Remember to consider viewpoint and tone in your reasons.
- Watch two TV programs. List the main characters, their major actions during the show, and what other types of people are shown on the program. List what you like about the show.
- Does TV control people, or do people control TV? (pp. 42–45)

Thoman (1998) offers a guided tour through resources for teaching media literacy. We name just a few major references:

Considine, D. (1994). *Visual messages: Integrating imagery into instruction.* Libraries Unlimited.
Davies, J. (1997). *Educating students in a media-saturated culture.* Technomic.
Masterman, L. (1989). *Teaching the media.* Routledge.
Worsnop, C. (1994). *Screening images: Ideas for media education.* Wright Communication.

Examining the News

We suggest six ways to involve students in examining the news.

1. Replicate the kind of study done by a New York group, Fairness and Accuracy in Reporting (FAIR), and log several weeks' worth of guest lists on a variety of Sunday news interview shows, such as CBS's *Face the Nation,* NBC's *Meet the Press,* ABC's *This Week,* and CNN's *Late Edition.* What kind of racial, sexual, and political representation is present?
2. Log in the pictures of world leaders and politicians that appear over a designated span (at least six months) on the covers of news magazines such as *Newsweek* and *Time.* Chart the racial, sexual, and political point of view that each represents.
3. List *all* pictures of individuals on these magazines' covers. What are the proportions of famous to ordinary persons; of individuals from entertainment, business, politics, art, academia, and religion; and of world and United States citizens?
4. Explore this question: Is the mass media an adequate source of public information? You and your students might answer this question with the following instructional sequence.

   Small-group assignment: In a thirty-minute segment of a national news program, monitor the minutes and seconds given over to
   - reporting of national events
   - reporting of international events
   - reporting of legislative deliberations
   - investigative reporting
   - in-depth news analysis, commentary, and discussion
   - interviews
   - unrestricted questioning of public officials
   - debates
   - human interest stories

   After you have gathered your data, consider their implications. Do the national networks provide us with the kind of news coverage that gives us accurate, unbiased information with which to know our world and live responsibly in it? Where does news reporting verge on entertainment? Can you discern strategies the program uses to attract viewers? How much of its thirty minutes are used for news and how much for advertising?

   Whole-class activity: Small groups report and discuss their findings and their conclusions. This information might be discussed generally or used as background for classroom debates or panel discussions that revolve around these questions: Do our mass media provide us with an adequate source of information? Do our national media bias our perceptions of the world around us?

   Individual writing projects: This data gathering, speculation, and discussion leads, we hope, to individual students' arriving at personal judgments. Ask students, as a clincher for this work (and possibly the evaluation of it), to articulate their judgments in forms of their own choosing: letters to the editor, editorials, satires, or parodies of the network news shows.

5. Have students use the form shown in Figure 10–7 to scrutinize the lead news story carried by each of the major networks on the same evening's news. Small groups could be assigned to watch one of the presentations of the major story and to enumerate very specific features and details that will allow them to make cross-network comparisons.

6. Help students see how news is packaged to win audience share. PBS analysis of the major network coverage of the horrific September 11, 2001, terrorists attacks on Washington, D.C., and New York City suggests that the logos established by each network were attempts to package their coverage in such a way as to enlarge market share. ABC's *Challenge to America* was cautious in its analysis and response, while CNN was more aggressive in its logo, *America's New War,* and its coverage. Students could review footage from coverage of September 11 or look for the labels and accompanying coverage in future national or international catastrophes.

Examining Advertising

Here are five ways to take a critical look at advertisements.

1. Have students bring in print or video ads that show our culture in positive ways and, conversely, ads that are embarrassing. After students have presented their selections, list on the board those qualities they are proud of and those they are critical of. Do they disagree? (We have asked students to arrange these visual images and words into bulletin board collages or box collages, which we suspend as mobiles from the ceiling.)

2. Have students log the ads for a whole segment of programming. We asked students to record each of the ads during a Superbowl game and then to arrange them by type. They reported that the project became more exciting than the football game. They formed a new awareness of the extent of advertising time (in comparison to game time), of the values and predispositions of those whom advertis-

ers targeted, and of the values that the advertisers wished to impose on them. Questions related to such a list include the following:

- How are these advertisers appealing to the viewer: through rational analysis, emotional persuasion, or subliminal suggestion?
- Of what social class, race, or sex are most of the subjects of the advertisements?
- What image of American culture is presented?
- Do any ads represent products or services that fill genuine human needs or only manufactured needs?
- Do they employ the idiom of our culture in their pitch?
- Are there any hidden messages about American life in our advertising? What are they?

Another strategy that explores the propaganda techniques of advertising is to find ads of the same product marketed to different audiences.

3. Political advertisements pose other important issues. Have students view political ads and answer these questions: What is the visual image behind the words that the candidate is selling to the public? Are these characteristics and the words uttered related to the office being sought? Do they appeal to reason? Emotion? Logic? Fears?

4. Sorenson (1989) describes a unit on advertising that examines how advertisers analyze their audiences and persuade them through emotional appeals and statistical manipulations. As a culminating event, she asks students to write and perform an advertisement and the class audience to analyze its methods of persuasion. The following is her checklist of emotional appeals:

patriotism
affections (love, hate, friendship)
security
personal honor
family life
better life for the future
fair play
power

FIGURE 10–7
Comparison of network evening news

Observations	Networks			
	ABC	CBS	NBC	CNN
Total length of time				
Anchor frame time				
Correspondent time				
Visual variety				
Coloring language				
Inflectional bias				
Balance of opinion				
Depth of background information				
Other				
Shift time				

motherhood
fear
self-preservation
preservation of society
ego (social prestige, recognition)
better life for your children
progress

5. Postman (1985) observes that commercial messages "defuse the import of the news, in fact render it largely banal. . . . We have become so accustomed to its discontinuities that we are no longer struck dumb, as any sane person would be, by a newscaster who having just reported that a nuclear war is inevitable goes on to say that he will be right back after this word from Burger King. . . . One can hardly overestimate the damage that such juxtapositions do to our sense of the world as a serious place" (pp. 104–105). He especially worries about the impact on youthful viewers who look to TV for clues about "how to respond to the world" (p. 105). Ask students to watch TV news and record the juxtapositions of emotional tone and content of news and commercials. After the whole class compares notes and their own emotional reactions, discuss Postman's proposition: Do these juxtapositions teach the young that the difficulties of our world are "not to be taken seriously or responded to sanely" (p. 105)?

Scrubbing the Soaps

Burmester (1983) uses a feature on soap operas from a PBS series, *Media Probes,* to prompt students to examine the daily and prime-time soap operas. His students "contrast the life shown on the soaps with their own lives" and with the communal life of this country. They speak of soap operas as mirrors, "perhaps distorted, funhouse mirrors, but mirrors nonetheless," of "our hidden selves" (p. 96). We suggest that students work again from their own gathering of data. Use the follow-up discussion and writing questions listed here, or develop your own.

- Did these characters and their stories seem believable?
- If they distorted life as you observe and experience it, describe the distortion.
- Does the life on these soaps seem more vivid or heightened than your own?
- Is there a range of characters that reflect different social classes and ethnic, racial, and age groups?
- Was there anyone your age? Could you identify with that person's life situation?
- Could you affirm the implicit values and overt behavior of these characters?
- Have you ever known a "soapaholic"?
- Burmester says that "the media are makers of myths and molders of opinion" (p. 96). Do the soap operas bear out his observation?

A final examination of media might use the tools of literary analysis for media analysis. Each media form has its own elements, conventions, and standards. Literary analysis sensitizes students to the author's intent and technique. This same sort of critical consciousness can be applied to the creators of media and their persuasive strategies, which Vance Packard (1957) called the "hidden persuaders" that are practiced on us, the viewers and listeners. Some of the analytic tools that can transfer comfortably from printed text to media text include point of view, setting, characters, style, plot, and tone. These can all be used to penetrate TV drama. Consider, for instance, a show's plot: Is it formulaic or imaginative, focused on strong physical action or more psychological? Are the characters stereotyped or original? Flat or round? Dynamic or static? Does the point of view (the camera's eye) focus on one character with frequent close-ups, or is its angle of vision usually long shots of many characters? Is the tone of the show upbeat? Melodramatic? Somber? Does the whole show break with tradition in this genre, or is it conventional? Genre distinctions such as the following can also provide useful frames of reference for analysis: drama, realism, tragedy, comedy, melodrama, serials, westerns, detective stories, musicals, fantasy, action, documentaries, and romance. Evaluative questions about the quality of a show mirror those critical questions that we asked of literature in Chapter 5.

Analyzing Magazines

A teacher (whose name did not survive this handout's long use) set up guidelines for magazine analysis that combine several of these anthropological and literary approaches to media. The directions can guide the work of individuals or small groups of students and require three to five successive issues of a magazine.

Part 1: Design. Analyze the design of the magazine, section by section, and include cover specification, color usage, column design (it may differ from section to section), type styles, headline styles, graphics, photography, and special effects. Be sure to look for anything that unifies the magazine as a whole, such as logos or catch phrases. Also be sure to look for things that unify the individual sections.

Part 2: Content. Analyze the content of the magazine. Include feature and/or news coverage as well as any regular features, such as editorials, letters, and reviews. Based on the content you find, decide on the magazine's intended audience. What is the magazine's purpose?

Part 3: Business. Who is the publisher of this magazine? What other major publications does this publisher produce? Who is the editor of this publication? Find out who advertises in the magazine regularly and what the advertising rates are. (Include classified advertising rates, if applicable.) What are subscription rates, and what is this magazine's circulation? (Often, there is an 800 number listed in the masthead. If not, locate the publisher and dial the 800 information number to see if there is a number for this publication. If not, you will have to drop a postcard or letter in the mail or find an e-mail address.)

Part 4: Politics/Philosophy.   What is the ethical stance, political perspective, and world view expressed in this magazine? Who would be its presidential choice; what is its view on controversial issues; and how does it picture women, men, and family?

Final questions might include "Would you subscribe to this magazine? Would you recommend it to someone else? Who?"

Examining Public Service Announcements

This activity bridges the examination of media as artifact and art and the exploitation of media in student productions. Have students take a cause such as drunk-driving legislation and devise a public service announcement that will be broadcast in each of five different media: television, billboards, radio, magazines, and bumper stickers. Students should shape their announcements to the requirements of the form. After students present their announcements, the whole class might clarify the basic characteristics of each of the five media and the technique required for communicating effectively in each.

Analyzing Viewing Styles

Our emphasis in exploring the medium of television may have seemed negatively biased. Formerly a high school English teacher and now a television researcher, Patricia Gillard (1994) reminds us of a very different story. In her research on television with children and adolescents, she says that she "tapped a reservoir of energy and enjoyment and a desire to share their TV experience. Perhaps they are surprised that an adult is interested. They 'love' TV. They know it well and celebrate it in the playground, but keep it to themselves around disapproving adults" (p. 82). Gillard believes that TV viewing is not the same for all adolescents and that teachers need to appreciate those differences before they disparage the viewing habits of their students. She summarizes some of the differences that were re-

vealed in her own research. (She uses the term *children* to designate an age group spanning from elementary through high school years.)

- The more TV is on, the more likely children are to engage in other activities as they view. This suggests that children adapt to their TV environment. How they view may be the most important aspect of TV viewing, because it differentiates between children in the ways that they "see" and therefore, presumably, what they learn from what they see.
- A definition of TV viewing as watching particular *programs,* rather than a continuing activity taking place with other events, assumes a particular style of viewing which is typical of families who structure their time and generally have more leisure options.
- This pattern is probably typical of many teachers as well. The view that TV is an inferior use of leisure time and that other media such as books are superior, is associated with this particular program-related definition of television.
- Families where TV is a major source of leisure and where it is switched on for much of the time are less likely to perceive the need for "control." On the other hand, viewing is more likely to be a shared activity and a part of being "at home."
- Where TV is a major source of leisure there is likely to be less difference between what adults and children view.
- In families where women work away from the household, alternative ways of dealing with TV will usually be adopted, such as discussion with children of program content, and deliberate co-viewing with children. (p. 79)

Teachers need to be sensitive to the family context in which students watch TV before criticizing it. Gillard reiterates our sense of the importance of locating students' experience and of building our instruction from that. She reminds us, too, of the probable error in assuming that their experience is like ours. Thus, she gives four cautionary "don'ts" to teachers before they begin to discuss television media:

- Don't measure the time spent viewing TV with the purpose of encouraging students to reduce it.
- Don't list programs viewed by students and exhort students to watch better programs.
- Don't set television viewing in opposition to other preferred uses of leisure time, such as reading.
- Don't prohibit students from doing homework in front of the TV.

She does not ask that we be noncritical of television, just that we don't impose our biases and thus silence and shame students about their own and their family's daily habits. The chances of students' thinking critically are much greater if they are not defending themselves. Then both teacher and student might be open to explore and discover in television what is creative and vital and what is stultifying and false.

☞ EXPOSE: STUDENTS AS SOCIAL CRITICS

In this quadrant, we are exposing media's impact on the culture. As we begin to look at the possibilities in our classrooms, we want to understand and articulate the power of media in our lives. Aronowitz (1977) maintains that "in the last half of the twentieth century, the degree to which mass audience culture has colonized the social space available to the ordinary person for reading, discussion, and critical thought must be counted as the major event of social history in our time" (p. 468). Can you imagine a day in your life without those media that we have come to regard as necessities? Media have so pervaded our lives that we are barely conscious of their impact. Raymond Williams (1980) observes that viewers have grown so accustomed to receiving one-way "talking-head" content from television speakers who cannot be interrogated and images that cannot be slowed down that they do not even ask questions about it. Salomon and Leigh (1984) observe that past experience and TV's unchallenging programming lead viewers to expect to exercise little mental effort in processing television content and so to put little into it.

Postman (1979a) argues that we must actively resist turning our youth over to the "entertainment media: television, film, records, radio," and that we must actively resist them in the classroom. He enumerates four media "biases which are in special need of opposition by the schools" because they disregard or undermine essential skills, values, and behaviors that schools should promote in the young: The media are (1) "attention-centered," with their main goals being to capture and hold their audience's attention; (2) entertaining and so must not be too "demanding or disturbing" or they will lose their audience; (3) image-centered and so work against sustained thought or language development; and (4) narrative, rather than expository, and so make "the systematic presentation and development of ideas" alien to students. Postman suggests counterbalancing strategies with which these seductions might be resisted: "This would imply that the schools stress, for example, subjects that require students to understand and express themselves in words; that require them to pay attention even when they are not being entertained; that require them to evaluate and criticize ideas; that demand concentration and a confrontation with complexity."

Postman's emphasis here is on reinforcing teachers' confidence in a curriculum that is "sharply differentiated from other cultural institutions such as movie theaters, rock concert sites or playgrounds." Other educators join his struggle and suggest the focused study of media as another strategy. Aronowitz (1977) believes that media study is necessary but difficult; it asks students to run in the face of accepted realities:

> The teacher must persuade students of the significance of the study before the study will be meaningful to them. The objects of mass-cultural perception, particularly rock music and televi-

sion, are so close that achieving critical distance from them requires even more intellectual and emotional effort than literature or math, which are sufficiently distanced by their historical character and academic legitimacy to make them easier to study. Mass-cultural forms have colonized the leisure time activities of youth so completely that giving up, through analysis, the pleasure one gets from them may be painful. . . . Having successfully demystified media content and seen how certain forms such as popular music provide only spurious satisfaction, students are still left to face daily life. (p. 470)

Despite these resistances, Aronowitz suggests that an examination of media be undertaken to free and exercise critical thinking. He believes that teachers must first be willing to examine media as a legitimate subject "in order to criticize and transcend it—or to discover whether genuine expressive forms are repressed within it" (p. 469). We have, in this chapter, presented concrete exercises that do that.

We conclude with five common concerns about the impact of the media. We propose them as questions that you might ask students to examine. An assignment might include the following:

- Choose one of the five concerns about media or propose a concern of your own.
- Gather evidence from specific media (for instance, designated shows on TV, popular songs, or advertisements in specific magazines or on the Web).
- Reflect on the data through free writing, discussion with others, writing again, testing your hypothesis with further data collection, and reading the opinion of experts on media.
- Develop a position you can support in answer to your question. Write a position statement in which you present your answer and support it with analysis and detail.
- Prepare to answer the questions raised by classmates about your position in a class debate or a fishbowl or a jigsaw discussion.
- As a culminating task, choose a model from some form of media and use it to make your position public.

Our explication of each of these five questions draws on the insights of media critics. We present strong positions for your reading because these critiques are well developed and run counter to cultural norms. We do not intend to persuade students to our position but to persuade you of the importance of raising critical questions about this crucial subject. As you read these critiques, however, imagine how you can use them to help students develop their own critical skills.

Do the Media Corrupt Cultural Morality or Mirror It?

One of the most common complaints in the popular press is that the media have corrupted our morality with their graphic portrayals of violence and sex. Social and behavioral scientists in laboratory and real-life studies have discredited some of the most inflammatory charges and the anecdotal evidence of copycat crimes and seriously harmful antisocial acts. But some researchers (such as Milgram & Shotland, 1973) have convincingly demonstrated a correlation between the viewing of violent programming and aggressive behavior. Further, social critics identify the source of corruption not only as absorbing content but as also deadening sensitivity to real-life suffering and violence. Because violent programming dulls the reaction to the experience of the media itself, media must escalate violence to assure the same degree of viewer interest and excitement.

Do the Media Falsify Expectations of Life or Create a Sense of Possibility?

Many social critics identify media's impact as even more subtle and pervasive. In *Teaching as a Conserving Activity,* Postman (1979b) claims that the media now serve as "a surrogate for reality." He gives the amusing example of a popular hospital-set TV drama of the 1960s, *Marcus Welby, M.D.* Not only did Robert Young, the actor who played Marcus Welby, receive more than 5,000 letters a week seeking his medical advice, but the American Medical Association actually invited him to one of its annual conventions as the keynote speaker. Postman acknowledges that long before the electronic revolution, reading played a significant role in encouraging a fantasy life and that many nineteenth-century novel readers probably found more pleasure among fictional characters and places than with the people and situations of their actual lives. But today the power and frequency of experiencing life removed from actuality, life filtered through a technological screen, is tenfold.

We read with our students the poem "Reel One" by Adrien Stoutenburg, which speaks of the same sort of impact in film. After a young couple watch an action-packed, Technicolor movie "like life, but better" in which "the screen shook with fire," they walk home through falling snow, which, disappointingly, isn't "blue in the drifts" and is so silent that the "sound track" seems dead. The young people are startled when life turns out so differently from the controlled and heightened projection on the screen. Can you see the handicapping of the young's ability to face their real lives: You expect, don't you, that "reel two," the flesh-and-blood experience of the two moviegoers, will seem diminished? They have no soundtrack; no screenwriter providing dialogue; no camera selecting the important scenes; and no ability to see, interpret, and validate their own lives for themselves.

Do the Media Reinforce Passivity or Promote Action?

Many other social critics join Postman in his alarm at the media's encouragement of passivity and the attendant retreat of reason. Aronowitz (1977) characterizes the impact of media on students: "Most students go through their classes as if in a dream. They are bemused by daily interaction as if it were the unreality. Many of them live for the spectacle of the blockbuster film, the rock concert, and other mass-cultural activities. The spectacle appears as the real world in which they wake up and participate in the process of living; their nonmedia life is the fiction" (p. 469).

Bloom (1987), although he is quite different from Aronowitz in his general critique of the culture, observes a similar phenomenon in the effects of rock music on the young.

> It is *the* youth culture and . . . there is now no other countervailing nourishment for the spirit. . . . It makes conversation impossible, so that much of friendship must be without the shared speech that Aristotle asserts is the essence of friendship and the only true common ground. With rock, illusions of shared feelings, bodily contact and grunted formulas, which are supposed to contain so much meaning beyond speech, are the basis of association. None of this contradicts going about the business of life, attending classes and doing the assignments for them. But the meaningful inner life is with the music. (p. 75)

Do the Media Undermine Critical Reasoning Capacity or Promote Thoughtful Reflection?

For Aronowitz (1977), this absorption in media assaults "the capacity to engage in critical thought as a meaningful form of social discourse" (p. 463). He believes that TV, film, and photography have restricted "the capacity of persons to make inferences, to offer arguments, to develop explanations of social events that may counter those that are considered authoritative" (p. 468). He locates the educational crisis today not in the decline of the skills that the back to the basics movement addresses but in this loss of critical thinking. This numbing of reasoning is exacerbated by the one-way communication of the media. Individuals are the passive recipients of messages to which they have no power to respond. Sorenson (1989, p. 42) sees English teachers as embattled with a piece of "talking furniture—the television set." Postman (1985) cites the effects of our movement from a print-based to a television-based culture: "We are getting sillier by the minute" (p. 24).

Postman believes that schools are the last bastion of processing the world through letters and numbers; that is, we are a part of the Gutenberg galaxy now being threatened by a technological galaxy. When we read a book's print, he argues, we are forced to distance ourselves from the reality it represents; we must transform letters to words and words to mental pictures. We are three steps from reality (see figure on this page).

(word)	(idea)	(thing itself)

tree   *tall, leafy oak tree*

With some distance on reality, Postman argues, we are more analytical about it. We cannot be so easily manipulated when we are three steps removed. Graphic processing is not the same; it is immediate and stirs us in a way that Postman says is akin to magic or religious rites. We are not allowed any distance from the reality it presents. We are moved to action or internal response with very little or no reflection. In a sense, the analysis, objectivity, and progress (or decline) that print brought us in the sixteenth century are now being foreclosed by the lack of mentality ushered in by the visual media.

Do the Media Promote Consumerism or a Consumer Protection Mindset?

Beyond stunting the mind and dulling the imagination, critics point to another impact of the media on our lives: It manufactures false needs that obscure authentic ones. The vast media system we live under manipulates our needs and persuades us to become uncritical buyers of an endless supply of commodities. Citizens step onto a treadmill of consumption, are never quite satisfied with the life promised by purchase, and so purchase more in an endless cycle of phony promises and disappointed hopes. Kellner (1988) observes that "[a]ds work in part by generating dissatisfaction and by offering images of transformation, of a 'new you' " (p. 43). Kellner traces the geometric expansion of advertising expenditures from 1950 (about $6.5 billion a year), to 1970 ($40 billion a year), to 1980 ($56 billion), to 1988 ($102 billion). In Chapter 6, we reported that in 1999 advertisers spent over $215 billion. "When one considers that an equal amount of money is spent on design, packaging, marketing, and product display, one grasps that a prodigious amount of money is expended on advertising and marketing. For instance, only eight cents of the cosmetics sales dollar goes to pay for ingredients; the rest goes to packaging, promotion, and marketing" (p. 48). Individuals are being bombarded by sponsors intent on enticing them to buy. It is no wonder that they cannot distinguish between needs and wants, between the genuine and the spurious, and between the important and the trivial.

Invitation to Reflection 10–5 invites you to evaluate your own understanding of these five critiques of media. It can serve as a model for a student survey at the end of your critical media study.

Invitation to Reflection 10–5

One way to explore media is with an interest in exposing their power over the culture. We enumerate five consequences of that power. Rate the strength of your concern for each from 5 (most concerned) to 1 (not concerned). Then check which of these critiques you would consider bringing into your classroom.

_____ Mass media corrupt the morality of the culture with tolerance for violence, sexism, and stereotyping of minorities.

_____ Mass media falsify life and set up unrealistic expectations for it.

_____ Mass media reinforce a passive reception of life rather than active engagement in it.

_____ Mass media undermine the capacity for critical thought as well as analytic and synthetic reasoning.

_____ Mass media promote consumerism, not self-reflection and self-discovery.

We have summarized the critical perspectives on media in order for you to grasp the position of many social critics. If you choose to teach this material to your students, you will be attempting to shake students awake to a part of their culture that is so intertwined in their lives that they are hardly conscious of its impact. We do not recommend, however, that you teach by polemic but by student inquiry into their own experience of media. Their "text" surrounds them. McLuhan (1964) spoke prophetically of the importance of such exploration for the purpose of exposing media: "Just as we now try to control atom-bomb fallout, so we will one day try to control media fallout. Education will become recognized as civil defense against media fallout" (p. 305).

∽CONCLUSION

We have suggested four ways in which the secondary teacher might use media in the classroom. We think that all students need to confront these powerful phenomena as more than means of entertainment and information. Students need to understand media more critically, to appreciate them with greater subtlety, to be warned of dangers, and to be encouraged in the enjoyment of potential delights. Whether your perception of the classroom study and use of media is positive, negative, or neutral, you must make decisions about how to employ them in your classroom. We believe that we can appropriate media's power to deepen our students' experiences, to enliven their study, and to energize their language production. The possible roles are challenging but well within our students' range: producers, consumers, anthropologists, and social critics.

11

Inspiring Writing

CO *While speech is the medium of home and neighborhood interaction, writing is largely or completely the medium of the school, and the child whose school writing is stultified has little else to draw on. . . . A sense of the social system of writing has so inhibited and overawed many teachers that they have never given a pupil the feeling that what he writes is his own.*

John Dixon

*I*n no area of English teaching is there more theorizing, experimenting, and researching than in writing pedagogy. And in no area are English teachers more vulnerable to the public's recent outcry about the failure of schools to teach elementary skills and their need to return to the basics. Shuman (1985) explains that "because one's use of language, whether spoken or written, is much more public usually than one's use of a subject like mathematics, the secondary school English curriculum has been criticized more than most for not teaching students basic skills" (p. 324). Laypersons who consider English classrooms deficient often point to the failure of students to learn the structure of the language (grammar), the mechanics of expression (spelling and punctuation), and appropriate usage (conventions of correctness). Those within the profession criticize writing instruction for stymying the expressive and communicative needs to write and for inculcating, instead, the dull and lifeless language of many school classrooms. LaBrant (1934) recognized more than half a century ago "a large gap between natural expression and the stilted performance which passes as school composition" (p. 62). Macrorie (1970) named this "phony, pretentious" language "Engfish." Mayher (1990) characterized typical writing instruction "as a kind of civil defense preparedness drill that most of us had in school: something we might have to use in some future emergency, but of no real consequence to our current lives" (p. 227).

Elbow (1973) believes that "the ability to write is unusually mysterious to most people" (p. 12). He observes that our lives are full of mastering difficult tasks, but "few of them seem so acutely unrelated to effort or talent" (p. 12). Various explanations are given for this inscrutable mystery: Writing is a special faculty or a force of inspiration or a capacity for "having something to say." Elbow captures our basic misconception about the process of writing in a parable:

> Once there was a land where people felt helpless about trying to touch the floor without bending their knees. Most of them couldn't do it because the accepted doctrine about touching the floor was that you did it by stretching upwards as high as you could. They were confused about the relationship between up and down. The more they tried to touch the floor, reaching up, the more they couldn't do it. But a few people learned accidentally to touch the floor: if they didn't think too much about it they could do it whenever they wanted. But they couldn't explain it to other people because whatever they said didn't make sense. The reaching-up idea of how to touch the floor was so ingrained that even they thought they were reaching up, but in some special way. Also there were a few teachers who got good results: not by telling people how to do it, since that always made things worse, but by getting people to do certain exercises such as tying your shoes without sitting down and shaking your hands around at the same time. (pp. 13–14)

Teachers, both experienced and new, feel that teaching writing is as mysterious as writing itself and far too complicated to be unguided. This chapter introduces several foundational theories of writing instruction and the teaching activities that follow from them, activities that are more than exercises in which students take out paper and shake their hands around. We are building on the work of others. What little direct writing instruction we experienced was traditional, teacher-directed, product-centered, and grammar-based. We became teachers of high school classrooms at a time when these traditional writing approaches were being challenged. During the past thirty years a process approach to writing articulated by advocates such as Donald Murray (1968/1985), Donald Graves (1983a), Lucy Calkins (1986/1994), and Nancie Atwell (1987/1998) promised a miraculous transformation of tradition. But in the 1990s, after years of classroom experience and teacher reflection, some of the basic assumptions of process writing and writing workshops have themselves been questioned. A new postprocess approach was signaled by Atwell's (1998) second edition of her 1987 *In the Middle*. Before you enter these discussions about teaching of writing, however, we would like you to look inward for a moment to consider the assumptions about writing instruction that you bring to this chapter.

Invitation to Reflection 11–1

WRITING ASSUMPTIONS AND PROCEDURES SURVEY

Write *D* (disagree) or *A* (agree) before each statement in the survey.

_____ 1. In teaching writing, correctness and organization should be emphasized more than clarity and substance of thought.

_____ 2. Grammatical conventions (including punctuation and spelling) should be emphasized only in the final edited version of a piece of writing.

_____ 3. Usage problems such as noun-verb agreement should be corrected through workbook exercises to instill the rules of grammar.

_____ 4. Students should be asked to write about their own experience and to develop their own ideas about what they wish to write about.

_____ 5. Writing is best generated by assigning topics on which students can write well.

_____ 6. Most of a student's writing time should be spent in the initial writing and proofreading of a paper.

_____ 7. Students are of little help in responding to other students' work.

_____ 8. Teachers should grade everything that students write.

_____ 9. Students should spend as much time in creative, expressive writing as in analytical, expository writing.

_____10. Grammar instruction is essential to the writing progress of secondary students.

FIVE INTERLOCKING WRITING CONSTRUCTS

This chapter presents a circular pattern of five interlocking writing constructs, shown in Figure 11–1, that encompass a total approach to writing in the English classroom. Each of the five constructs provides answers to basic questions about the teaching of writing and appropriate classroom practices and writing activities.

Developmental tasks are the cognitive tools required to accomplish successively more difficult composing tasks. "*When* do students have the cognitive capacity to write in different discourse modes?"

Process model is the process used to write. "*What* are the necessary steps in the writing process?"

Writing workshop is the context in which students write. "*Where* are different writing tasks undertaken and completed?"

Portfolio work influences the roles of the teacher and students. "*Who* is responsible for writing in the classroom?"

FIGURE 11–1 Five writing constructs

Authentic assessment is the evaluation of writing. "*How* do teachers assign and evaluate writing to meet the communication needs of the everyday world?"

We turn first to some foundational assumptions about language that underlie all five constructs. One of the best known and most influential challenges to the primacy of classical writing instruction has come from James Britton and his research team from the British Schools Council Project. Britton, Burgess, Martin, McLeod, and Rosen (1975) acknowledge their indebtedness to Piaget and Vygotsky, who regard words as a means of expressing thoughts that are prior to language. (We discussed the relationship between words and thought in Chapter 4.) These rhetoricians do not assume that words will always be used to achieve a single purpose. Traditional writing instruction has too often regarded teaching writing as helping students write out their thoughts with clarity, coherence, correct usage, and forceful style. Britton et al. describe not one, but three categories of how language functions:

Transactional: language used to "get things done: to inform, to advise or persuade or instruct people"
Expressive: language used to think "aloud on paper," to "record and explore the writer's feelings, mood, opinions, preoccupations of the moment"
Poetic: language used to create "phonetic, syntactic, lexical and semantic" patterns depending on the requirements of the writing (pp. 88–90)

The user, audience, and purpose are interrelated differently in each of these categories. Language users can assume the role of participants (transactional language) or of spectators (poetic language). Participants are trying to get things accomplished; spectators are rendering "real

or imagined" experience "without seeking outcomes in the actual world" (pp. 79–80). The spectator role is more detached from immediate experience. The user might be either participant or spectator when language is used for an expressive function. In written discourse, writers are situated differently depending on their function and their relation to the subject.

Britton et al. explain that writing also differs according to its audience; they maintain "that one important dimension of development in writing ability is the growth of a sense of audience, the growth of the ability to make adjustments and choices in writing which take account of the audience for whom the writing is intended. This accommodation may be coarse or fine, highly calculated or totally intuitive, diffused through the text or explicit at particular points in it" (p. 58). Teachers have traditionally initiated the writing task and nominated themselves as the audience. The role of one-person audience is not neutral either; the teacher becomes "the sole arbiter, appraiser, grader and judge of the performance" (p. 64). Thus, school writing has required students to make elaborate judgments about how to satisfy the teacher's demands as audience rather than about how to explore and express their ideas. Applebee's (1981) observations, interviews, and surveys of American secondary school writing also found that the most common one-person audience for student writers was the teacher as examiner (pp. 46–58).

The implications of Britton et al.'s observations for writing instruction are clear. If language use originates in an expressive impulse for forming meaning, and if the making of meaning remains central to English classrooms, opportunities for expressive writing should be frequent. Yet Britton et al. found in their examination of British high school seniors that 84 percent of the writing was transactional, less than 7 percent was poetic, and less than 4 percent was expressive (p. 165). (Five percent was distributed among additional and miscellaneous categories.) Britton et al. propose that we alter this emphasis: In the early stages of writing, children write a form of "written-down expressive speech. . . . As their writing and reading progress side by side, they will move from this starting point to . . . broadly differentiated kinds of writing" (p. 10).

Moffett (1968), in *Teaching the Universe of Discourse*, explains a progression that moves from conceptualization to oral language to text language and observes a similar movement from egocentric communication to public discourse. He believes that our instruction should progress through a sequence of writing tasks from the familiar and personal to the more distant and impersonal, the *I-you-it* we have mentioned before. Moffett's (1992) *Active Voice* invites students to write at different levels of discourse, to move from the personal writing of inner speech to monologues, dialogues, and narrative before reaching the formal essay. When we couple all these developmental ideas about language with Piaget's concept of intellectual development from infancy to adolescence, a new model of writing instruction emerges.

∞ DEVELOPMENTAL TASKS

Piaget's observations and speculations provide a fruitful way for understanding how a developing mind structures knowledge in the period from infancy to late adolescence. Piaget described four stages of cognitive development through which he believed all people move in the same progression (Figure 11–2). Each stage is distinguished from the next by certain operations that the individual masters—new ways of seeing the world and thinking about what happens in it. We build from one stage to the next as capacities consolidated in one stage give way to and are synthesized into the maturing of the next stage. These four stages have been questioned and studied since Piaget first conceptualized them. Research has confirmed the stages as being sequential (higher stages always emerging out of lower ones), invariant (people do not regress or progress in nonsequential ways), and universal (valid in all cultures).

When linked to writing, Piaget's cognitive development theory forms three postulates that serve as the foundation for a developmental writing construct:

1. Writing is built on talking and listening, both of which grow from thinking.
2. If thinking is the basis of talking and writing, it follows that writing has developmental stages built on or parallel to those of cognitive development.
3. Writing tasks or stages that require more complex, abstract procedures follow those that are more concrete.

But as LaBrant (1957) reminded us long ago, "Knowing *about* writing and its parts does not bring it about, just as owning a blueprint does not give you a house" (p. 256). We turn now to the tools for constructing a productive, vital writing program. Of course, few high school English teachers will have the luxury of a stand-alone course in

writing. For now, however, we isolate writing instruction for clarity even though in practice it will be integrated with the other communicative arts.

Developmental Sequence

The instructional conclusion from this theory is developmental. Teachers should try to understand a student's stage or level of writing comfort and ability and challenge him or her to move to higher stages, whether this movement occurs within a class, over a year, or through the entire K–12 curriculum.

We begin our discussion by describing a six-stage developmental writing sequence, which is illustrated in Figure 11–3. We find these six stages to be useful as a scaffold or organizing principle for instruction and long-range planning. They are most beneficial as a general sequencing device, not as an invariant order. Writing at each of the six stages requires progressively greater cognitive complexity and competence. Students need control of the cognitive skills required at one stage to write at the next higher one. Preceding stages will be revisited as new ones are entered. Growth within each of the last five stages will be ongoing.[1]

Two complementary Piagetian concepts are important to helping your students move through these stages: *decalage,* the complete mastery of a new cognitive capacity, and *disequilibrium,* the lack of balance resulting from being poised between two cognitive capacities. Piaget observed that children move into the concrete operational stage and master its tasks one at a time until all are under control. Similarly, students must undertake each writing stage so that they feel certainty and comfort in that stage before rushing on to the next. Students who are beginning to understand a higher stage of thought become less satisfied with working only at the former stage. They are off

---

[1] James Moffett, James Britton, and other English educators have suggested their own useful progressions. We have discussed Moffett's I-You-It sequence and Britton's taxonomy of transactional, expressive, and poetic language use. Ours is another developmental option; but even if you do not use our exact sequence, the suggested teaching activities (11-1 through 11-4) have proven themselves useful in other contexts.

FIGURE 11–2

Piaget's cognitive stages

age thirteen	*Formal operations:* Ideas, categories, and logic flourish without need of concrete objects as ability to deal with abstraction grows.
age six	*Concrete logical operations:* Rules, categories, sequences, and the ordering processes develop in company with concrete experience as capacity for symbolic representation of concrete experience develops.
age 2	*Preoperational:* Language begins to represent things, so the child can learn more quickly and efficiently. Word and thought unite.
birth	*Sensorimotor:* Instinctual reflex activities interacting with the world teach us rudimentary cause and effect. Human learning is not dependent on language yet.

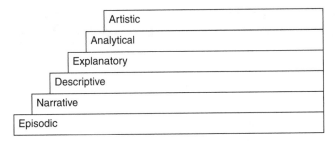

FIGURE 11–3 Developmental stages of writing

balance, caught between two worlds, which may be the signal that they are ready to move to another stage. Teachers must walk a fine line with their students. They need to allow students to work at each stage until they are very comfortable with it, but they also must nudge students into disequilibrium so they can move to the next higher stage. The six-stage developmental sequence corresponds conceptually to Piaget's stairsteps of cognitive development.

Episodic (Nonsequential). Episodic writing is usually the first produced by children and probably is seldom encountered in secondary schools. An amazing percentage of children entering school believe that they can write, even though their essentially episodic writing may not be easily understood by others. Giacobbe (1982) and others merely give children writing materials and tell them that they are expected to write in their books.

Narrative (Temporal Events). A philosophical comic once said that "time is Mother Nature's way of not letting everything happen at once." Stories use time to do that. Narration is the simplest form of writing, and children who first shape their words tell stories. Most of them use the structure of their daily lives. Giacobbe (1982) calls these "bed-to-bed stories": "I woke up this morning, put on my jeans, and ate some runny eggs for breakfast. Then I went with Uncle Fonzo to the farmers' market where we saw some gooses and. . . . My stomach was hurting so much from Uncle Fonzo's yellow candy chickens that I could hardly get to sleep at night." The child merely has to recall the correct order of events to tell a story. When adult friends gather or families reunite, stories are often the discourse that connects them. They do not generally turn to analysis, which is a more complex cognitive process and brings more distance to the language at hand.

Narration is a simple and natural form; and teachers can evoke it, enliven it, and empower it. Chapter 4 provided prompts for oral stories, including the accidental power, trio tales, four Cs improvisation, and intervention drama exercises. Look at the elliptical bed-to-bed story and consider how a teacher can help students shape a more interesting story. What would be the effect if a teacher circled the crisis event—the stomach ache from Uncle Fonzo's yellow chickens—and asked students to look for any earlier event

that should be emphasized so that the reader could recognize the cause of the stomach ache? Sophisticated narratives that involve dialogue, varied and complicated characters, and a rich and ingenious plot with narrative suspense can be developed by young students.

Descriptive (Spatial Sweep). Description leaves sequential, chronological order behind. Students must impose their own order on the world around them. The palpable external world keeps the descriptive task in the concrete operational range. The difficulty for writers is choosing and following an ordering device for their description. This task touches on abstraction itself: going from near to far, significant to trivial, or large to small. Teaching Activity 11–1 presents two writing activities that together can help students develop the perception, precision, and perspective needed for excellent description.

Explanatory (Temporal-Spatial). When students move into the explanatory mode of discourse, they are still dealing with physical objects and sequences but are working with the two at once. Narration and description deal only with one; two makes the task tougher. In addition, the sequence is not remembered from past experience, as in temporal narration, but must be established by the composer to produce an intelligible system. Studies have shown that explanation is a difficult task for elementary children because they can't see a whole system made up of disparate parts (Milner & Elrod, 1986). Asking students to write explanations will help develop this systematic thinking. We have found that the best assignments avoid subjects that are familiar to the reader. It is better to ask students to develop explanations that can be tested by the performance of an uninformed apprentice. The articulation of an unfamiliar process requires clarity and precision, hallmarks of good explanatory discourse, or the apprentice will fail. Teaching Activity 11–2 is an example of such an assignment.

Analytical (Categorical-Logical). This mode of discourse parallels the formal operational ability to depart altogether from the concrete world of space and time, the everyday familiarity of persons, places, and things. In analysis, students explore topics categorically and build arguments logically. Abstractions provide the structure at this level of discourse. The difficulty is that teachers often ask students to approach a complex analytical problem when students have not arrived at a cognitive stage at which they can do so with ease. Few average ninth graders are ready to analyze Shakespeare's use of irony in *Romeo and Juliet*. If we expect them to have success at such a task, we must teach the kind of thinking that lies at the foundation of analysis from the very earliest years in school. Wiltshire's primary teachers prepare six-year-old students by asking them to place baskets or buttons in separate piles and then label each pile. Concrete objects are thus turned into abstract concepts. Teaching

11-1 TEACHING ACTIVITY

Descriptive Exercises

The Small Shell Game

Find eight to ten small conch shells that closely resemble each other and discreetly number each shell on its inner fold. Divide the class into teams of two or three students (one team per shell). Ask each team to write a precise description of its particular shell and give it an exotic place name as a title for its description (the Auckland Shell, for example). Record the name and number on a master list and distribute each of the descriptions to a new team. Display the conch shells and have each team study all of the shells using the description in hand. Each team then must decide which of the numbered shells is being described. Consult the master list to see which team descriptions are apt enough to enable readers to identify their shells. The descriptions are thus given reality testing; precision and perception pay off.

Cultural Artifacts

Ask students to look at the sheet of penny heads shown in Figure 11–4 and select the one that most closely resembles the actual coin. Having warmed up with the commonplace penny, ask students to extract a single square cheese cracker from a pack of snack crackers, examine it more closely than they have examined pennies all their lives, and write a one-page detailed description of this ordinary artifact. This exercise involves solitary exploration in which an individual's careful attention to detail will lead to exacting writing.

FIGURE 11–4
Pennywise

Activity 11-3 encourages analytical thinking using the concrete objects that are part of a shipwreck (Kahn, 1984). Taba's (2001) thinking skills model is used in writing to move students from brainstorming information, to categorizing items, to identifying categories, to developing generalizations. The model promotes the kind of thinking that is the foundation of analytical discourse.

Artistic (Concrete Universal). Most of us do not expect to nurture professional artists in our classrooms, but we can help free students to give expression to their own creative impulses. Our suggestions about "right writing" in Chapter 12 will elaborate this encouragement of the artistic. For now, one of the most obvious ways to shape student ideas and experiences is to center on the metaphorical or analogical. Teaching Activity 11-4

11-2
TEACHING ACTIVITY

Explanatory Exercise

Game Plan

Ask groups of four students to create a new board game based on characters and events from a book that they have read. The game should have a board with pieces, moves, tokens, complications, obstacles, and ways to win. Bring the games and directions to class and let groups try to play them. The games need to be creative and fun, but the explanation must be quite precise and complete to allow the game to be played. After the games have been played, the creators should rewrite their explanations to ensure that any new players will play the game correctly. A simpler task requires a group of students to explain in writing how to play the card game Hearts. A group of students who do not know the rules begins to play the game while another group whose members know the game serve as monitors to see how well the rules are understood.

11-3
TEACHING ACTIVITY

Analytical Exercise

Survival Dilemma

Your ship is sinking, but you have managed to board a lifeboat with twelve other people. Most of the people were not able to reach the cabins to get warm clothing, so they are in street clothes. One woman is in a bathing suit. The ship is in the North Atlantic, and the temperature is near freezing, with strong winds and high waves. The lifeboat is an open wooden craft with no motor, so it must be rowed. You may have to spend several days at sea, depending on when the boat is spotted. The ocean is very foggy with low, heavy clouds. Because the boat is dangerously overloaded, and you *must* remove sixty pounds of weight in order to keep safely afloat. Decide which items you will remove. For safety reasons, you cannot suspend any items from the lifeboat. You cannot remove any of the people. You must choose from among these items:

- three wet suits, each five lbs.
- a two-gallon container full of water, fifteen lbs.
- four wool blankets, each two lbs.
- a large S.O.S. flag, three lbs.
- thirty cans of tuna (flip tops), each one lb.
- eight oars, each five lbs.
- first-aid kit, ten lbs.
- five slicker raincoats with hoods, each two lbs.
- battery-operated signal light, eight lbs.
- two buckets for bailing, each three lbs.

We ask students to make thoughtful individual decisions about which sixty pounds are to be tossed overboard before we ask groups of five to agree on the best solution to the problem. Each student writes a paragraph listing and justifying his or her choices; each group selects the best and combines them into a single document. When all groups have had enough time to collaborate, we call on one group to list the items selected to be jettisoned and their reasons for tossing them. We then invite other groups to challenge this group's selections and offer better lists. These exchanges usually lead us to question what these expendable items represent beyond themselves. Categories of items begin to emerge: oars and flag used like a sail represent movement or mobility; tuna and water represent sustenance; signal light and flag represent communication; and oars, wet suits, and blankets represent protection.

This classification facilitates discussion. And as the categories are refined and ordered, material and motive for writing develop. Hillocks (1986) found that these kinds of activities developed prewriting skills, which are the building blocks for good analytical writing. Exercises such as these, which pique analytical reasoning and give it a concrete and engaging context, energize thinking and therefore writing.

11-4

TEACHING ACTIVITY

Artistic Exercise

Parables

Explain to students that a parable, or fable, is a story that relates a series of concrete events to suggest an abstract moral lesson that means more than the mere description of those events. Ask students in groups of four or five to recall the details of the African fable "The Tortoise and the Hare" and the biblical parable of the talents (provide texts if needed). Have students individually write on note cards what each story means and as a group compare interpretations. Then discuss the similarities in how the two work as stories and how they are different from ordinary narratives. Finally, ask students to read "The Parable of the Lord's House" and write down what the story means.

The Parable of the Lord's House

A young boy passed through his years of tender ease in a household of safekeeping where all about him seemed good and sure. Many was the time he was told of a fine lord's house to which he must make a journey. Its riches and splendor were often made known to him. So it seemed quite well to him that he should journey to that house some day.

And indeed one day he set forth on his journey and the road was long but the path was soft; and the ease of rest and the bounty of his sustenance made the journey seem no longer than the twinkling of an eye. And when he came upon the house of the lord, his eyes were pleased, for it appeared as his father had said—its riches and splendor seemed more than could be told.

He dwelt there in that house which his father had spoken of so often, and it seemed as if he were almost dwelling there as his father and not as he himself. And while he was dwelling in that house he was coming of age. And his feet began to wander on paths that led away from the lord's fine house. And on some days he would journey forth and sojourn for a night or more before returning to the lord's house. And on those days away from the house, he began to rest his eyes on many a strange sight and his ears heard many a troubling tale. And at times he would forget that he had traveled forth from the lord's house and would stay many a night away before awaking to the vision of the lord's house of which his father had spoken. And he would rise and journey to that house again. But the way was never easy as it had once been in his youth.

Then on one of his sojourns away from the lord's house, he came upon a wise man who knew the paths upon which he had wandered and who knew the lands which lay beyond those paths. And this wise man explained many new things to the youth which made his head spin with zeal. He told him that the lord's house from which he had wandered was not a house at all but only a facade which fooled his senses. Such counsel was so strong that the youth continued to dwell in the land of the wise man for many a day and explore its many paths and tangled ways.

After dwelling in that land for so long a time the aging youth felt a strong power begin to grow in his heart which made him want to return to the lord's house. So he set forth on a curious, labored journey which brought him to that house. And when he gazed upon it his heart felt full. It seemed good and just as he remembered it from his father's words. But as he drew closer upon that house the loathsome thought came to him that what he saw was merely what his father had taught him to see. And though he felt good he did not feel at peace. For his mind troubled him all the more.

Discuss various readings of this parable and then consider whether it works as the previous ones do. Once students have examined the three parables in their groups and have determined some of their basic features, have each group try to create a parable—one that uses characters (people or animals), events, and objects to represent truths or ideals that lie beyond these ordinary matters. Use the following questions to see how well students have developed their parables.

1. Does the story make sense as a simple story?

2. Does the story have a simple meaning that most readers could recognize?

3. Do characters, objects, and events clearly represent something beyond themselves?

4. Do the characters have characteristics that reinforce the idea of the story?

5. Do all of the events fit together to work toward a unified meaning of the story?

When you have checked out the workings of each group's parable, have the students read it to other groups. Let them first judge it by these same standards and then write down its simple message.

introduces a natural way to enter into this world by asking students to write parables. Parables and fables are often thought to be more simple and moralistic than artistic. Their very directness, however, can encourage young writers to a simple shaping of their own deeply held convictions.

In addition to parables and fables, students can attempt other, more elusive kinds of stories. Some of the suggestions in the "apprentice writing" section of Chapter 12 are helpful in creating this sixth step of developmental writing in which the events of a story represent (symbolize) more than themselves.

The National Assessment of Educational Programs' (NAEP) *Writing Framework and Specifications* (1998) embodies the concept of writing stages built on cognitive tasks. It designates three major genres of writing (narrative, informative, and persuasive) and briefly explains the increasing "cognitive complexity" of the sequences: "Each writing assignment may also be categorized according to the major form of reasoning required." This national initiative confirms our view that the cognitive tasks underlying writing vary greatly and that a teacher's awareness of their range and relationship to different genres of writing provide crucial knowledge for understanding students and their writing progress.

Invitation to Reflection 11–2

1. Is your writing largely transactional, expressive, or poetic?
2. Who is its audience?
3. Do developmental constructs correspond with your sense of how human beings mature?
4. At what stage was most of your writing in grades K–6?
5. Did the focus change in middle school? in high school?
6. Which stage seemed most left out of your writing experience?
7. How would you use stages in a high school writing program?

PROCESS MODEL

Process means "becoming," not "being." In writing pedagogy, it acknowledges the protracted work involved in any authentic and thoughtful writing, whether that of thirteen-year-old students or mature writers. Even professional writers require an extended period of time for prewriting, writing, and rewriting. Some extremely able writers are able to complete this extended process entirely within their heads. Mozart, for example, is said to have composed music by just writing it down perfectly

the first time, "as if," according to Leonard Bernstein, "it were phoned in from God." Most of us, however, struggle to frame our thoughts and capture and express them in words. For most young writers, it helps to separate discrete parts of the writing process, although they are by nature recursive. We will enumerate these steps in the process, but first we present some basic assumptions that are the foundation for these steps.

Basic Assumptions

The original process approach to writing as articulated by Atwell, Calkins, Graves, Murray, and others rests on foundational assumptions that include these eight:

1. *The writer is an autonomous self-starter who has a need to explore meaning and to communicate.* The writing process approach reflects a deep-seated belief in the nature of humans as communicators and writing as a basic means of satisfying this need. Whether the need is to make and express a story, self-discovery, or play, assigning topics only perverts the direction of that natural motion. Writing process phrases such as "everybody has a story to tell" and "no more writers' welfare" affirm that all students have something to say and that teacher-suggested topics lead to dependence and misdirection. Graves (1983b) argues that students have become dependent on teachers' topics because they believe that they have nothing to say. He has found that teachers who make the least assignments receive the most writing. Writing serves multiple purposes and these purposes direct how the writing works.

2. *Writing is an extended process that includes prewriting, writing, and rewriting (revising and editing).* The idea that such a thing as the writing process can be reduced to a neat formula, be laminated, placed on a classroom wall, and carefully imitated is antithetical to the complexity and mystery of good writing. Many good lists have emerged, but none is definitive. Some simplify writing to the three foundational stages of prewriting, writing, and revising. Figure 11–5 elaborates more of the steps taken even as we acknowledge Anderson's (2001) warning that a codified set of steps can obscure rather than clarify, turning what should be a natural process into an unnatural act.

3. *All modes of written discourse are equally respected.* The idea that school writing takes only one shape (analytical, expository writing) is too narrow a view of writing. Graves (1983b) honors narrative in talking about "stories to tell," and Murray (1977) makes a convincing case for student narratives' exhibiting all of the composing skills developed by any other mode of discourse. Teachers need to challenge students to move through all

FIGURE 11–5

Extended writing process

Inventing	brainstorming, listing, webbing, and nonstop writing to discover ideas for writing
Arranging	looping together the best ideas into patterns and structures that make sense
Drafting	writing at top speed so that composing tries to keep pace with thinking
Uniting	rereading a draft all at once to see how it can be made to move forward in a purposeful way
Proofreading	reading a paper slowly after some time has elapsed since drafting to find the mistakes
Peer reviewing	partnering to get an outsider's view of the writing
Revising	reviewing the writing to see if it does what it was intended to do and reshaping it to do just that
Editing	reading of the writing by a more mature writer so that important help can be offered
Refinishing	using the help of an editor to revise and proof so that the writing best meets the writer's hopes
Evaluating	assessing the worth and status of the writing by the writer and/or teacher
Publishing	putting the writing forward in the world so that it can reach its fullest audience

modes of discourse and to provide enabling structures that support them to do so.

4. *Students are expected to write and are given responsibility for shaping their own writing.* Primary teachers give first-grade students writing books and ask them to write in them. Writing process teachers empower older students to take into account advice about their writing from many sources through a series of drafts. Portfolios contain tangible evidence of the stages of the writing process in one place—the writer's efforts along with the responses of many readers. Writing grows out of students' insights and the reactions of other readers and matures when they take full responsibility for its final shape.

5. *Conferencing with student writers is a basic feature of instruction.* The teacher who teaches best reads students' writing with great attention and shows deep respect for the writer. Conferencing means listening carefully to a student's intention in the writing, reading the draft itself, questioning the student about the next step, and offering suggestions. It means finding out what students are discovering they want to say and helping them reflect on effective ways of saying it. Conferences are often brief and suggestive rather than lengthy and directive.

6. *Student writers need many readers to respond to their work.* If teachers are the only people who read their students' writing, students feel that their words are not touching the real world. They learn to write to the teacher's tastes and beliefs. They need more responses to their work than any one person can offer. They need to see that a story judged as confusing by a teacher may be judged as both confusing and uninteresting, or as coherent and engaging, by another reader. Furthermore, if students are active writers, teachers cannot read everything they write.

Multiple readers aid the composing process and allow teachers to give careful attention to the best work, writing that students "own" because they have labored over it.

7. *Ownership of writing begins with selecting a topic and extends to giving writing a public platform.* When students write out of their own choices, ownership is under way from the start. It then must be maintained by the way in which writing is handled. Students should stay in charge of their pieces even when they submit them to other readers for help. Readers honor students' work by how they question it, recommend alternatives, suggest other readers, and reveal honest quandaries about the piece. This encouragement should continue until the work is published in some form. This public platform compels more risk and investment in the early and middle stages of the process and now rewards and completes that effort.

8. *Writing is a whole process whose parts are not easily divisible but are recursive one with another.* Whether a teacher recognizes three or eleven steps in the writing process, those steps are not discretely set apart but are naturally recursive. A rocking back and moving forward are always at work. Writers plan as they revise and revise while they write. While a word is checked for its spelling, an unintended strong right turn in the thrust of the piece may present itself. Writing proceeds, but new plans race ahead and some of those are revised in turn. At the same time that we recognize the power of this recursive process, we sometimes intentionally blunt it to cause students to focus on writing at full speed (waiting to check on the spelling of a difficult word) or concentrate on arranging a large clump of ideas (waiting to reconsider an embedded idea.)

The comparison of the process approach to writing to the more traditional product approach can throw both into sharper focus. In Figure 11–6 we add a post-process approach that reflects how the basic process approach has revised, a revision we discuss in the following pages.

The Teacher's Role

We consider here a fundamental difference between the product and the process models: the teacher's role. Murray (1968, 1980, 1982, 1985) sees teaching writing as a matter of responding to student writing. Teachers not only set up the conditions for writing but respond through mini-lessons, conferences, and whole-class meetings. The emotional tone of all of these encounters is encouraging, facilitating, and guiding. In responsive teaching, the student acts and the teacher reacts. The range of reaction is extensive and diverse because an individual teacher is responding to an individual student and the student in turn is passing through an ever-changing process of discovery through writing. Here is a closer look at the steps of response that Murray encourages:

The student writes. Do not respond until there is at least a primitive text—lists, notes, drafts, attempts at writing. Instruction given before writing may limit or interfere with the student's writing.

The student responds to the text or to the experience of producing it. The student must learn to evaluate a draft to produce a more effective draft. The teacher must know what the writer thinks of the draft to know how to read it because the teacher's job is to help the writer make increasingly effective evaluations of the evolving draft.

The teacher listens to the student's response to the text and watches how it is presented. The student teaches the teacher the subject matter of the text and the process by which the text was produced. In teaching the teacher, the students teach themselves.

The teacher reads or listens to the text from the student's perspective. What the student thinks of the text is the starting point for learning and teaching. The teacher will understand where the student is in the writing process if the teacher frequently experiences the process of writing.

The teacher responds to the student's response. The teacher attempts to give the minimal response that will help the writer produce increasingly effective drafts. The teaching is most successful when the teacher helps the student realize what the student has just learned: first the learning and then the teaching.

When Atwell (1987, p. 11) began to incorporate process ideas into her writing instruction, she had to learn new structures for sharing responsibility with her students. As Figure 11–6 demonstrates, Atwell (1998)

Product Approach	Process Approach	Post-Process Approach
1. Topics are assigned.	1. Writing is self-initiated: everybody has a story to tell.	1. Writing is sometimes self-initiated and sometimes teacher-assigned.
2. Expository essays are the staple of school writing.	2. All modes of writing are respected equally.	2. All modes of writing are respected equally, but teachers will intervene to make certain many genres are undertaken.
3. Grammar study, handbook rules, and exercises lead to good writing. Mini-lessons and student-teacher conferences are the primary means of direct instruction.	3. Prewriting, writing, and rewriting produce good writing.	3. Prewriting, writing, and rewriting produce good writing. Mini-lessons and conferences are still primary, but mini-lessons may be longer and more sequenced.
4. Good writing is based on models and formal guidelines.	4. Meaning precedes and determines questions of form.	4. Teachers may intervene more directly than in a process model to tell writers what works and does not work.
5. Teachers are the single audience for student writing.	5. Writing should be read like literature by a diverse audience.	5. Writing should be read like literature by a diverse audience.
6. Teacher-corrected papers are central to the teaching effort.	6. Conferencing with students and organizing other readers is central to the teaching effort.	6. Conferencing with students and organizing other readers is central to the teaching effort.

FIGURE 11–6 Three approaches to writing instruction

has continued to revise *In the Middle* and reposition the teacher to a more central role. She puts a new emphasis on the teacher as a knowing expert who takes a more active part in establishing direction for writing assignments and in intervening to tell writers what does and doesn't work. From the first, high school teachers have adapted Atwell's middle school model to their older student population with more particular teacher expectations for writing with different genres, audiences, and necessary writing conventions. The idea of a student apprenticeship with a more expert teacher is a model both middle and high school teachers can share. As Atwell (1996) explains:

> Instead of removing myself from the equation—functioning as a facilitator of the process who coordinates the workshop—I have come on like gangbusters in terms of teaching and expecting a lot in writing and reading workshop. And instead of diminishing or silencing their voices, I think that raising my voice, in the company of students in the workshop, has had the effect of strengthening theirs. (p. 48)

Giacobbe (1982) builds on the work of her writing teacher, Donald Murray, to list variables central to the teacher's new role in a process writing approach. They catch the spirit of these classrooms. As you read, consider how a post-process approach might revise them.

Motivation: I assume everyone wants to understand his or her own life, to make meaning out of experience, to share this meaning.

Assumptions: All of my students have the potential to write something worth writing. They come to me with experience, language, and the human need to use language to order, evaluate, and communicate experience.

Method: I teach a process of using language to discover meaning in experience. My students do not necessarily learn any specific form or how to respond to any specific writing task. They learn a discipline of thinking in writing, which they can apply whenever they need it.

Discipline: Writing is one of the most exciting things I do, yet I avoid it unless forced by external or internal deadlines to write. I do not think this should be so, but it is; and I assume my students are like me.

Ethos: Writing is a craft before it is an art. All writing is experimental; therefore, the writing course must be failure-centered or at least failure-accepting, for trial and error is the process of discovery through which subject, form, and language are found.

Content: I have no content to teach in the writing course, nothing to say before writing. I am a coach who attempts to help each student develop his or her own subject and own voice.

Energy: My students' papers provide the energy upon which the course runs. They motivate the students to write and me to teach.

Relationship: My students teach me how to teach writing. In the conference I listen to what they say about their own writing and help them hear what they are saying.

Attitude: I am a mirror in which the student will see his or her own potential, but the mirror image I project must be honest. I cannot reflect a potential in which I do not believe.

Goal: I am a success when I am unnecessary. My goal is to underteach. I try not to teach my students what they already know or what they do not need to know at this particular moment. It is my responsibility to create a climate in which my students can teach themselves.

One anecdote impresses us with the power of Murray's embodiment of these ideas. In *The Art of Teaching Writing*, Lucy Calkins (1994) describes the importance of her conferences with the Pulitzer Prize–winning Murray for her growth as a writer. For her fifteen-minute conference with Murray, she would drive two and a half hours each way (p. 15)!

Invitation to Reflection 11–3

Giacobbe (1982) has distilled Murray's view of seven basic steps in the writing process. Read through the steps below. Check those you have experienced as a student of writing instruction. Did you omit any? Do you believe you skipped something essential? Would you omit any as you anticipate establishing your own writing instruction? Would a writing process approach be feasible in your high school literature classes?

Prewriting

1. *Collect.*   Writers know effective writing requires an abundant inventory of specific, accurate information. The information is collected through reading, interviewing, observing, remembering.

2. *Connect.*   Meaning begins to be discovered as pieces of information connect and evolve into patterns of potential meaning. The writer plays with the relationships between pieces of information to discover as many patterns of meaning as possible.

3. *Rehearse.*   In the mind and on paper, the writer follows language toward meaning. The writer will rehearse titles, leads, partial drafts, and sections of a potential piece of writing to discover the voice and the form that lead to meaning and communicate that meaning.

Writing

4. *Draft.*   The writer completes a discovery draft, usually written as fast as possible, often without notes, to find

out what he or she knows and does not know, what works and does not work. The writer is particularly interested in what works since most effective writing is built from extending and reinforcing the positive elements in a piece of writing.

Rewriting

5. *Develop.* The writer explores the subject by developing each point through definition, description, and especially documentation, which shows as well as tells the writer, and then the reader, what the piece of writing means. The writer usually has to add information to understand the potential meaning of the drafts and often has to restructure them.

6. *Clarify.* The writer anticipates and answers all the reader's questions. At this stage the writer cuts everything unnecessary and often adds those spontaneous touches we call style. They produce the illusion of easy writing, which means easy reading.

7. *Edit.* The writer goes over the piece line by line, often reading aloud, to make sure that each word, each mark of punctuation, each space between words contributes to the effectiveness of the piece of writing. The writer uses the most simple words appropriate to the meaning; writes primarily with verbs and nouns; respects the subject-verb-object sentence; builds paragraphs that carry a full load of meaning to the reader; and continues to use specific, accurate information as the raw materials of vigorous, effective writing. The writer avoids any break with the customs of spelling and language that do not clarify meaning.

∽ WRITING WORKSHOPS

When an idea such as writing workshops enters the world of English education with such force, we want to know where it came from and why it is so appealing. Workshops grew in the nurturing soil of middle-grade classrooms that were being redefined as less cozy than elementary classrooms but less driven by subject matter than high school classrooms. Thus, with less ground to cover, writing and other subjects had time to move at a slower pace. Because process writing does not lend itself to students' sitting in neat rows, writing workshop teachers such as Nancie Atwell restructure their classrooms so that they look like an artist's studio or a newspaper office where everyone is working alone or in teams on different projects. Bromley (1998) reasons that the writing process does not lend itself to whole-class, teacher-led arrangements because the steps in the writing process are elongated and individual. The places where students might be at any one time both mentally and physically are numerous and unpredictable. When topics are assigned and students write individually without much time to plan before they write or revise after they write, there is little need for anything other than a traditional arrangement of desks.

Writing Workshop Principles

A set of principles undergirds the workshop approach that starts process ideas in practical motion.

1. Writers need regular chunks of time.
2. Writers need their own topics.
3. Writers need response.
4. Writers learn mechanics in context.
5. Young writers need to know adults who write.
6. Writers need to read.
7. Writing teachers need to take responsibility for their knowledge and teaching.

You can see from these principles that the class is decentered in more than its physical arrangement. The work and the responsibility for writing shifts from the teacher to the students. In the middle schools especially, writing time is given primacy and is scheduled generously so that deliberate, intentional writing can be undertaken. Atwell (1987) reports that her students' newly found devotion to writing comes not only from the freedom to choose but from "the time to exercise that freedom" (p. 21). About the crucial second principle, choice, Atwell says, "all the strong feelings and raging enthusiasms of adolescents get directed toward ends that are meaningful because students choose them" (p. 43). Although she has become more directive about her assignments, Atwell still values choice. She now links choice with teacher knowledge and insight into broader rhetorical requirements. We will become more specific about teacher response later in this chapter.

These seven principles require a variety of specific teaching acts: helping writers discover topics; talking to students about writing in effective ways; showing them how to confer with one another productively; teaching them how to control mechanics and conventions; and offering ways to make their work reach beyond the classroom walls. Because this kind of teaching represents a significant departure from what many of us have experienced as students, the entire procedure needs to be clearly explained. We will describe it as it is used in upper elementary classes and middle schools. Its incorporation into the high school curriculum requires adaptations that we discuss in closing.

Writing Workshop Proper

The writing workshop proper (that is, the specific class time spent on intense individual writing) is a place for students to work full-tilt on their own writing with increasingly greater independence. It provides teachers a chance to step back and watch students at work and then move in closer for one-on-one conferences. Teachers usually allocate a large part of class time for serious writing, at least thirty minutes or more, during which students can become seriously engaged in their writing and the teacher can have time to confer briefly with most of them. Some teachers fear this apparently loose structure, but Atwell (1987) responds, "it is a tight ship . . . but a different kind of ship" (p. 56). Brock and Mirtz (1994) believe that three axioms provide the structure for that ship: Keep it real, provide time, and provide reflection. Giacobbe (1983) lists similar and crucial ingredients for successful workshops: *time, ownership,* and *response.* Each of these three must be given serious attention.

Time.   Time is needed to consider and reconsider what students have written. When teachers use most of a day's or a period's time for writing, students see that it is valued. The time also must be used to confer with students and to keep track of where students are in their latest projects. Time is necessary for students to get serious writing under way. The more time students are given to write and the more often they are given an extended period of time in which to write, the more they will have something to write about. Regular and frequent writing time helps writers grow. There is no instant writing—not even in our quick-fix culture.

Ownership.   Ownership is vital for adolescents who are caught between childish dependence and mature autonomy. They need to claim things as their own partly because they choose them. Atwell (1987) says that she made a huge change when she carted "her stuff" home and allowed students to make the class their room. She told them, "This is your room. That's your bulletin board. Feel free to fill it up" (p. 63). Many materials for writing must be present to make writing work; but when all of this material is explained and located and students have free access to it, those, too, become theirs. When students are involved in decision making, experimentation, and independence in their writing, a sense of ownership rides in on that tide. Because students in this workshop environment do not wait for teachers to prompt them at every step in their writing, they are more likely to develop a deep feeling that the work is truly their own.

Response.   Response is another vital ingredient. Fernan (1993) believes that the focus on reflection through feedback is what truly distinguishes writing workshops. Teachers, peers, and adults provide this for students; but the coaching, conferring, and consulting affirmed by Moffett and Wagner are very different from the pushing, prompting, and prodding that students experience in more traditional classrooms. Teachers are not useless because they

are not the apparent driving force. The conferences provide an opportunity for what Murray describes as a time for students to teach the teacher about their writing and for teachers to help them "discover the meaning they don't yet know" (p. 68). When students are set in motion and writing is going well, teachers use workshop time for one-on-one conferences that are unavailable otherwise.

Work of the Writing Workshop

We turn now to four components of the writing workshop proper that promote the growth of individual writers and the class writing culture: *teacher/student conferences, mini-lessons, group share,* and *status of the class conference.* The act of writing occupies the central workshop position, but these four provide a structure for the learning that is taking place.

Teacher/Student Conferences.   Brinkley (1998) has a comprehensive list of the various purposes of teacher/student writing conferences (Figure 11–7). The conferences can be short or long, simple or complex, planned or spontaneous, depending on student need or the teacher's purpose.

Atwell (1987) suggests some simple but effective guidelines:

- Keep conferences short.
- See as many writers as possible.
- Go to the students so you can control conference length.
- Make eye contact with the writers.
- Don't tell writers what should be in their writing.
- Build on what writers know and have done.
- Resist making judgments about the writing.
- When questioning students, ask about something you're curious about.

Questions play an important role in conference success. Atwell names her favorite open-ended questions: "What are you up to here?" and "How's it coming? Any problems?" Most experienced teachers have developed favorite responses, whether they are questions, problem-related statements, or prompts:

- Tell me more about that.
- I don't understand that.
- Read it to me again.
- What's the most important thing you're trying to say?
- What's your favorite part? How can you build on it?
- How could you find out more about your topic?
- Is all this information important? What parts don't you need?
- Why is this significant to you?
- Does this lead bring your reader right into the piece?
- What do you want your reader to know or feel at the end of your piece?

FIGURE 11–7

Brinkley's varied reasons for teacher/student conferences

Source: From E. Brinkley (1998), Learning to use grammar with precision through editing conferences. In C. Weaver (Ed.), *Lessons to share on teaching grammar in context* (pp. 120–136). Portsmouth, NH: Boynton/Cook Publishers, Heinemann. Reprinted by permission.

- Conferences allow students to test their writing on a real audience and to discover new ideas as they think aloud about their writing.
- Conferences provide individualized instruction that can be tailored to an individual writer's learning style and that is always based on the writer's own needs and interests.
- Conferences help writers generate ideas, discover a direction, keep going mid-draft, rethink and revise, and edit an almost publishable piece.
- Conferences provide intervention for all students, especially for those who need it and for those who seek it.
- Conferences allow teachers and students to know each other in a personal way often not possible in whole-class activities.
- Conferences build confidence in insecure writers.
- Conferences help student writers become more articulate in describing themselves as writers and their own writing processes.
- Conferences help teachers understand the logic of students' thinking about their writing.
- Conferences help teachers recognize what student writers know already and what they still need to learn.
- Conferences help students understand the source of their difficulties with writing and recognize what they still need to learn.
- Conferences nudge students to become confident, independent writers.

Moffett and Wagner (1992) offer prompts for students in small workshop groups as they help their peers rethink and revise writing (pp. 204-205):

- What would be a better title for the piece?
- What seems to be the main point of the writing?
- What uncertainties do you have about the piece?
- What would happen if key words or main ideas were changed?

Giacobbe (1982) has an effective list of questions that help students look at their writing in such a way that they can bring a fresh mind to its revision.

- Do I have accurate information?
- Do I have enough information to satisfy the reader?
- Do I have so much information I will confuse the reader?
- Is there a pattern of meaning in the information?
- Does each piece of information lead toward that meaning?
- Is the meaning worth communicating?
- Are the reader's questions answered when they will be asked?
- Is the most important information emphasized?
- Would the information be better presented in a different genre?
- Is each part of the piece of writing developed effectively?
- Do the parts of the piece of writing add up to a pleasing and effective whole?
- Does each paragraph carry a digestible amount of information to the reader?
- Does each sentence carry information or its meaning to the reader?
- Does each phrase and each word, especially verbs and nouns, clarify information or its meaning for the reader?

- Does the entire piece of writing have a consistent and appropriate voice?
- Have I been honest?

With questions like these, students are urged to extend the process and deepen the content of their writing.

Brinkley (1998) frequently uses a handout (Figure 11–8) titled "Editing = Polishing Writing" as a "reference and reminder" for students and teachers about the necessary focus in the final editing phase of the writing process. Although high school students often address grammar and surface features throughout the writing process, these issues receive greatest attention at the end, when writers prepare their compositions to be published.

Mini-Lessons. Mini-lessons offer both direct instruction on procedures in the workshop and techniques on writing itself. The procedural guides to the workshop can range from models for how to confer to where various writing materials can be found. Atwell's list of writing techniques includes ways to develop leads, strategies for revision, methods for editing, and various crafts that shape writing. Tompkins (1990) offers her own list of ideas that should be considered as topics for mini-lessons (pp. 562-564):

- Teach the stages of the writing process.
- Teach writing workshop procedure.
- Identify new topics.
- Explain a writing workshop schedule.
- Explain and model conferences.
- Demonstrate group share process.

Mini-lessons should not be developed without regard to the classroom context; they should be the result of particular needs and gaps detected in the students' writing during the writing workshop. Even those short sessions

FIGURE 11–8

Brinkley's "Editing = Polishing Writing"

Source: From E. Brinkley (1998), Learning to use grammar with precision through editing conferences. In C. Weaver (Ed.), *Lessons to share on teaching grammar in context* (pp. 120–136). Portsmouth, NH: Boynton/Cook Publishers, Heinemann. Reprinted by permission.

Editing is

- Rereading and anticipating a reader's response
- Listening for precision of language
- Tightening and linking
- Clarifying and sharpening
- Smoothing out and reordering
- Listening for pace and rhythm
- Creating or refining a title
- Finding ways to engage and support a reader
- Anticipating a critic's attention to detail
- Noticing and correcting

Editing means making changes, when needed, to

- *Words:* seeking words with the precision that will express exactly the meaning the writer intends
- *Length:* paring away redundant words and phrases or adding telling details that extend and enrich meaning
- *Pacing:* creating short, quickly read sentences that add emphasis or drama; adding transitions that show relationships between ideas; slowing the pace so that the reader can make connections; or untangling long convoluted sentences
- *Emphasis:* underlining, italicizing, boldfacing, capitalizing, or bulleting
- *Spelling:* using computer spell-checks and dictionaries for every word the writer isn't sure about
- *Punctuation:* selecting punctuation options to clarify and to convey the desired level of formality
- *Capitalization:* consulting a handbook to check conventional usage
- *Paragraphing:* indicating logical sequences and relationships between ideas
- *Verb tense:* creating consistency for the reader's sake
- *Person:* considering who potential readers are in order to decide how best to address them by using first, second, or third person
- *Grammatical constructions:* noticing and correcting lack of agreement between subjects and verbs, or between pronouns and antecedents; lack of parallel phrasing; lack of complete sentences (some computer grammar checkers will help highlight these problems)
- *Visual presentation:* deciding on font and point size, margins, graphics, spacing, and arrangement

---

should not be filled with teacher talk; they are most effective when techniques and strategies are demonstrated. Calkins (1994) talks about the effect of these whole-class sessions as they "add information to the class pot" (p. 200).

Group Share. The central idea of group share is that everyone stops work and gathers at the center of the classroom, where two or three students read their writing and receive responses from the other student writers. Atwell (1987) believes that two things are always accomplished by these plenary sessions: They "bring closure to the workshop" and "allow you and other students to find out what writers in the workshops are up to" (p. 85). This forum (along with the status of the class conference) brings accountability and purposefulness to the entire enterprise. The simple rules are that everyone but the reader puts down his or her paper, listens carefully, watches the face of the reader, and comments after the reader finishes if comments are sought. One effective strategy pairs two pieces that have some relationship to each other—for example, how the writers used leads or how they generated body and texture for their topics. Sometimes every writer may be asked to read a lead or a

close so that a general sense of what might work best in those techniques can emerge. Megyeri (1996) believes that group share is extremely important, so she offers a set of useful rules (pp. 73-76):

- The speaker should not begin reading until the listeners are ready.
- The speaker should wait for the audience to react before moving on.
- The speaker needs to make eye contact often with the audience.
- The reading rate must be slower than in conversation.
- The presenter needs to speak in a loud, clear voice.
- The speaker should use facial expressions: smile, frown, gasp.
- The reader must bring enthusiasm and energy to the performance.

This segment of the writing workshop is extremely important to the success of the entire process because such rules breed courtesy and respect for writing.

Status of the Class Conference. The other task for teachers as they move about the room observing or conferring is to fill out the day's status of the class chart. It is the key to the organization and ongoing progress of students' writing. A simple model such as the one shown in Figure 11-9 helps solve organizational problems and is easy to fill out during the workshop. Whatever its shape, the chart is the essential means for keeping teacher and students aware of progress, purposiveness, and difficulty.

Physical Arrangements and Workshop Rules

The physical arrangement and materials of a workshop have a great impact on the workshop's ongoing effectiveness. A variety of floor plans are possible, but most proponents agree that things flow smoothly when the workshop provides the following:

- Counter space for materials
- Stack trays for writing ready to be edited and writing to be photocopied
- File cabinet (one drawer per class) for portfolios
- Quiet-zone corner table: no talking, students' backs to the class
- Center desks: to write and confer
- Conference corner: away from quiet zone
- Group sharing area: carpeted or comfortable sitting area

The working rules of the workshop space should be posted. Simple rules that allow students to produce their best work as developing writers might include the following:

- Don't erase; strike through.
- Use one side of the paper only.
- Save everything.
- Date and label everything.
- Speak quietly.
- Work really hard.

Block (1997) believes that the rules that guide students during a writing workshop need to be focused on developing student independence. She finds four rules indispensable in creating this attitude (p. 42):

- No one interrupts individual conferences.
- Leaders resolve team needs and record them for next workshop.
- Students assess their own work at the close of the workshop each day.
- Students work in groups or alone while the teacher is conferencing.

These guidelines not only control the noise level and promote on-task behavior, but they also contribute to students' reflecting on their writing.

Advocates and practitioners of the writing workshop approach have made modifications to its structure over the years, as evidenced in Atwell's (1998) second edition of *In the Middle,* 70 percent of which is new. However, her revisions leave the essential principles of process writing and writing workshops intact. The track record of writing workshops includes high test scores, students who become devoted and skilled writers, and students who read and write for pleasure in ways they never did previously. Moffett and Wagner (1992) sum up the natural power of the writing workshop: "When a workshop works well, everyone's personal performance improves, and individuals learn from it how to function well independently" (p. 202).

Research on Writing

As director of the federally sponsored National Research Center on Literature Teaching and Learning, Arthur Applebee has provided reliable and nuanced pictures of writing and literature instruction in U.S. secondary schools during the last decades of the twentieth century. Applebee (1981) and his research team visited some three hundred classrooms to observe what was taking place in writing instruction. Although the researchers'

FIGURE 11–9

Status of the class chart

| Names | Dates | | | | | | | | |
	4-1	4-2	4-3	4-4	4-7	4-8	4-9	4-10	4-11
Adam	5,6	7	7	8	8	8	8	8,9	9
Brittany	1	2	3	3,4	3,4	4	4,5	6	6,7
Emily	8,9	9	1	2	2,3	4	4,5	6,7	7,8
Joshua	9	6	8	8	8	9,1	1	2,3	3
Phillip	8,9	9	9	9	9	1	1	1,2	3,4
Sara	1,2	2	2,4	5,6	8	9,1	1,2	2,3	3,4,5
Troy	4	4	4,5	5,6	6,7	7,8	8	9,1	1,2,3

Code:
1 = Invent   *4 = Proof*   *7 = Edit*
2 = Draft   *5 = Peer*   *8 = Print*
3 = Confer   *6 = Revise*   *9 = Publish*

purpose was descriptive, they were experienced teachers and consequently began to form impressions of those classes that worked especially well. They were not interested in the lessons that failed but in "the differences between lessons that gave the impression of a pleasant and effective teaching situation, and those in which that pleasant atmosphere of competence was transformed into something more exciting" (p. 104). Invitation to Reflection 11-4 presents these researchers' model of good, better, and best writing programs.

Invitation to Reflection 11-4

Reflect on Applebee's (1981) evaluation of good, better, and best programs (pp. 104–105).

Good Lesson

- There is an ordered variety of tasks for students to perform.
- Assignments are clear and their purpose evident.
- Students perform teacher-designated tasks.
- Grades are used as the primary motivation.
- When assigned, writing is used as a measure of student knowledge or performance.
- The predominant teaching technique is teacher-led class discussion.

Better Lesson

- Students are actively involved in teacher-designed tasks.
- The teacher maintains a high level of student interest.
- The teacher encourages a free flow of give-and-take.
- The teacher incorporates student experiences into the lesson.
- The predominant teaching technique is teacher-led class discussion—but student-led discussions are encouraged.
- Students are prepared for writing assignments with prewriting activities such as audiovisual presentations or modeling.
- There is a climate of trust between teacher and students.

Best Lesson

- Students assume an active role in their own learning.
- The teacher encourages students to explore and discover but seldom dominates the class.
- Students' own experiences are freely incorporated into class discussions.
- Students are enthusiastic about their work.
- Writing is viewed as a means of learning and emerges naturally out of other activities.

1. Which of Applebee's three classroom models most resembles the writing instruction you received in high school English classes?

2. As you read the descriptions of each, which class most attracts you as a student? As a teacher?
3. Are you surprised at the researchers' evaluation of the three?
4. Can you see a connection between their best lesson and the principles of our first three writing constructs? How would our three constructs contribute to creating the best lesson?
5. Make a quick list of actions you could take to create such a "best" classroom.

The final principle of the workshop approach challenges teachers to seek the same credibility and autonomy in their professional growth that Atwell prizes for her students in the writing workshop. Teachers cannot know what to do with their classes unless they keep up with best practice and current research. But even more important, teachers cannot know writing unless they write; and they cannot know teaching unless they find ways to observe their students and examine what works and what does not. Interestingly, the writing process has always emphasized teachers themselves writing and through that discipline, teachers have become more conscious of the need for changing and adapting the original model.

PORTFOLIO WORK

Our first three writing constructs emerged one after another because each naturally requires the next to fulfill its possibilities. When teachers begin to elongate the actual process of students' writing, loosen the lockstep linear schedule of writing, and then rearrange the room, the necessity for portfolios becomes apparent. Ironically, because portfolios can be so readily simplified and adapted to more traditional forms of writing instruction, their use has become widespread and more popular than the pedagogies that spawned them. We speak of them here as an integral part of the writing process; we return to them in Chapter 13 as an alternative tool of writing assessment.

Portfolios make explicit what the process approach and writing workshops only imply: Students, not teachers, are now in charge of writing. Elbow (1991) defines portfolios in terms of student capabilities. He believes that the portfolio is an invitation: "Can you show us your best work so we can see what you know and what you can do—not just what you do not know and cannot do?" (p. 16). Kneeshaw (1992) regards portfolios as vehicles for measuring the "cumulative success of individuals over time." Their use carries a conception of writing as "living pieces": working drafts, holding drafts, and final drafts. Sorting out their own writing gives students the responsibility of differentiating between those pieces that need a great deal more effort, those that seem hopeless, and those that seem well composed.

Sunstein (2000) says that portfolios cause her students to *collect* (gather samples of their literacies), *select* (decide what will best represent them), *reflect* (write and talk about their decisions), and *project* (set goals and work to meet them). They cause her students to treat writing as works in progress and thus to enlarge their sense of themselves as writers. When these pieces are assembled and are kept over time, they "offer teachers a focused observation tool" that allows teachers, students, and parents to monitor writing progress and accomplishments. Applebee's (1984) research found that portfolios allow students to represent a broader spectrum of performance than can ever be sampled in an examination situation (p. 44). Schools are realizing more than ever that the student-parent portfolio conference during open-house nights is one of the best drawing cards for parents. Some schools that were once lucky to attract sixty parents to a PTA meeting now regularly draw three hundred or more because of these conferences. Some of this success is due to the developmental nature of this approach to students' academic achievement. It is more concerned with what steps (for example, spelling growth, use of proper punctuation in dialogue, control of voice, and use of tone) students have taken from month to month or semester to semester than with students' individual scores on achievement tests.

Portfolios have another benefit. Their transfer of responsibility allows writing teachers to lay aside their overbearing burden of responding to every piece of student writing and students to take some measure of responsibility for the quality and appraisal of their work. A legitimate part of the popularity of this approach may be this relief from the paper load it provides.

Variety of Contents

Bromley (1998) believes in portfolios that require students to choose what writing they will include. She also argues for a variety of portfolio content: skills' checklists, learning logs, self-assessment pieces, creative writing, letters, poetry, reports, and a number of other kinds of writing. Other teachers promote a variety of discourse modes that include narrative descriptive writing and analytical pieces. Some portfolio advocates urge students over the course of a year or over a span of two or three years to use each of the traditional modes of discourse, from narrative to exposition to poetry. When students attempt and save a range of writing, their strengths and weaknesses in each can be tracked. Porter and Cleland (1995) enumerate that kind of inclusive list: journal entries, bookmarks, written conversations, multiclass book responses, "sketch to stretch" visual entries, reflections on discussions, and photographs of students at work writing.

Morrow (1997) also places in portfolios a multidimensional range of writing added to other kinds of evidence of ongoing performance in class: observation checklists, daily performance samples, anecdotal notes, audiotapes, teacher-made tests, and standardized tests. Her concept of the portfolio brings personal artifacts and external evidence together for student, parent, and teacher to gain a full-bodied sense of performance. Purves, Quattrini, and Sullivan (1995) argue that two portfolios are needed: One they call a working portfolio, which houses evidence of the work in progress with the final draft; the other they call a presentation portfolio of final, finished pieces. This compromise allows the process to be kept alive and manageable instead of falling into a product-presentation trap. Porter and Cleland (1995) found after a time that they had been too directive and controlling about the kinds of items that needed to be included in portfolios and the kinds of questions they appended to it. Experience taught them that students needed greater flexibility and freedom. Luce-Kapler (1996) reached a similar conclusion: "They wanted the opportunity to explore their fictional worlds without being given a road map. Some students didn't want any guidance for the writing process while others appreciated suggestions in the way an adventuresome traveler would welcome an occasional road sign" (p. 47).

Raines (1996) builds the same argument using the metaphor of a house becoming a home. In an ethnographic study she found that transformation occurs when writers develop comfort about their portfolios and a sense of ownership about what belongs there.

Works in Progress

Writing portfolios embody the idea that a piece of writing is a work in progress and that the process extends beyond assigning, writing, and correcting. Mondock (1997) suggests a three-step procedure that ensures that writing is ongoing, is archived, and moves forward toward completion. The three steps are part of what Mondock calls the "story behind" the writing. Each step is composed of questions that call for a return to the work as writing in progress. The first set comes after the first draft of a piece of writing and focuses on the prewriting process.

Step 1 questions. Students answer the three questions on an index card and then use the comments to revise the work in progress.

- What is your focus/purpose of writing?
- Are you satisfied with your topic and ideas so far?
- Is there anything that you need to change to make your topic/focus/purpose clearer or more interesting for the reader?

Step 2 questions. The next set of questions asks students to review and revise their work once again.

- What significant changes are you going to make or have you made in your piece to improve the focus?
- Could anything still be improved through revisions?
- Are you satisfied with your piece to date?

Step 3 questions. When the writing is complete, a third set of questions is used to reconsider the writing, even though it is a finished piece.

- Are you satisfied with your final piece?
- What did you like about your piece that you think will appeal to your reader?
- How could you improve your piece if you write about this topic again?
- How did the class respond to your writing and publishing? (pp. 61–62)

Mondock poses such questions to push students to think further about the writing at hand, but it is students' attitudes toward returning to the writing that makes it an ongoing process. In time, those questions and thoughts about additional work on the writing should be internalized for students; they will no longer need to be prompted by teachers. There is a zone of proximal development at work here in which the added support of the teacher's enabling structure prompts students to do more than they might have done without the thoughtful intervention.

Student Responsibility

The portfolio clearly nudges writers (and teachers) into accepting a wide range of writing and to understanding writing as an ongoing process. Portfolios promote those two characteristics beyond what might occur if only the process approach and writing workshops existed. But the third characteristic of portfolios adds a dimension to writing that is truly unique and would not exist without them. They carry students far beyond what could be expected in their writing without that final concept. As Graves and Sunstein (1992) argue, "If we want to help them become independent learners, then we *must* nurture self-evaluation of writing" (p. 60). Portfolios offer a panoramic view of the writing process rather than a snapshot of the final product; they offer an entire time line rather than a mere time capsule.

A student who is troubled with vocabulary choices early in the year may use his or her portfolio to understand how that problem is being solved or remedies that may need to be taken. A student who almost always writes narratives can use the portfolio to gain awareness of the repetition and narrowness of his or her writing. Similarly, students who are making progress in handling troublesome connections or in developing a unique voice can be given that same kind of awareness by thoughtful use of portfolios. Mondock (1997) believes that portfolios that contain the total record "accumulate more evidence of student growth than may be possible from the final product" (p. 63). A small aid to students' thoughtful and accurate scan of their own work is a simple date stamp that Raines (1995) requires all of her students to use on every piece of writing in their portfolios. Porter and Cleland (1995) put it succinctly: "reflection made possible by portfolios allows learners to see changes and development over time" (p. 48). Mondock (1997) affirms the reflection process of portfolios and what comes of it:

> By reflecting regularly on their portfolios, students soon realize that they have not simply collected evidence from the process but that this evidence is first-hand feedback for their self-directed improvement in future efforts. In this way, the students put their collections to work to serve as a guide or goal for improvement of the process, and ultimately for the final product. Thus, a higher-quality process leads to a higher-quality product. (p. 59)

Raines (1995) supports this line of reasoning and draws from it three important qualities that a portfolio contributes to students' writing growth and learning:

- Portfolios help to extend the amount of time that students spend in practicing authentic writing.
- Portfolios provide important evidence of students' evolving learning experiences and useful information about the unique literacy development of each student in our classes.
- Portfolios encourage and nurture collegial relationships between students and teachers.

Robbins, Brandt, Goering, Nassif, and Wascha (1994) prompt this reflection through a required essay in which students respond to seven issues that call on them to carefully think through their writing and the procedures that prompted it:

- What you selected and why.
- What you learned about writing these pieces and how.
- Improvement, strengths and weaknesses in your writing.
- Piece of writing that best represents your work and why.
- Aspects of the class or particular assignments that were most helpful in your writing.
- Types of assignments that you would like to do more of.
- Assignments that you particularly disliked and why. (p. 74)

A similar list is used at the end of the year by students to write about their writing:

- What does your portfolio say about you as an individual with hopes, dreams, beliefs, and values?
- What have you learned about your ability to read and write this year?
- What was your best piece this year? Why was it your best?
- What steps did you use to develop it?
- How does your best piece compare to your other writing?
- What causes you to do your best writing?
- When your writing has not been your best, why was that?
- How does your writing at the end of the year compare with the beginning?
- How does your portfolio help you understand your strengths and weaknesses? (p. 76)

Raines (1996) attempts to provoke this same kind of global reflection with a list of simple questions:

- What are your writing goals?
- In what ways have you achieved those goals?

- What still needs to be done?
- What is your best work?
- Why do you believe that is your best work?
- Why did you include a specific piece in your portfolio?
- What changes do you see in your work over time?

Krest (1990) believes that students need to differentiate low-order and high-order concerns so they will not be overwhelmed by the unfocused charge to revise. All of these prompts to reflection and revision combine to suggest a powerful spur to students' growth as independent, self-critical writers.

Accomplishments

There are numerous reports of portfolio successes, including the following:

- They encourage students to identify specific elements of good writing.
- They help students set specific writing goals based on those elements.
- They provide them with specific models for achieving those goals.
- They cause students to assess their success in them.

Burch (1999) found many advantages in using portfolios, but the two most impressive were students' more positive attitude toward writing and their intensified sense of the need for revision. Tierney and Clark (1998) offer eleven strong positive findings from their research on portfolios. The most impressive focused on the changed role of the teacher and the fuller images of student performance. Purves et al. (1995) offer a stunning list of some of the specific contributions of portfolios:

- Portfolios are particularly appropriate vehicles for metacognitive awareness. Both students and teachers can see a term's work and can hardly resist reflecting on what has happened over a period of weeks. Such metacognitive awareness is basic to further learning.
- Portfolios are used for remarkably similar reasons, even though the portfolios and the systems in which they are embedded may differ greatly.
- The standards for portfolio evaluation grow out of teachers' own interactive experiences with one another and with their students; standards are not imposed from the outside.
- The specifics of individual portfolio systems are important to their authors; one assumes that this is because these specifics encode intentions, goals, and ideas unique to individual schools.
- And, finally, portfolio assessment inevitably involves its users in larger issues of teaching, learning, institutional goals, and student individuality. Portfolios enable assessment, but they also reach out beyond assessment and engender changes that could not have been foreseen. (p. 23)

It may be helpful to balance our vision of the portfolio by looking at a few of Bromley's (1998) qualms and then her celebration of portfolios. On the liability side of the ledger, she points to the sense that feeling is given more attention than thinking is; that writing becomes more individualistic than social; writing feels too loosely structured for some students and many teachers. Her list of assets clearly overwhelms those qualms:

It is student-centered. This approach validates student experiences and ways of knowing.

It celebrates individuality. It focuses on the student rather than the teacher or the text.

It promotes independence. Since each individual is given the freedom to make independent choices in this approach, decision-making capacities are strengthened.

It promotes creativity. This approach emphasizes each student's creative potential and encourages students to discover themselves and to invent their own worlds.

It values feeling. Often neglected in other approaches, students' and teachers' emotional responses to literature and life are the starting point of this approach.

The pluses are the stuff of real teaching success and justify thoughtful and inventive ways of defusing the negatives.

∽ AUTHENTIC ASSESSMENT

Just as each of our first four constructs arises from the preceding one, so authentic assessment arises naturally when portfolios are used to promote independence and self-assessment in writing. The authenticity of both process and product leads logically to a need for the authentication of the next step: assessment. We deal here with constructing clear connections between what is being taught and what is being assessed and with constructing and applying clear rubrics with which to judge the outcomes. Chapter 12 will present many practical suggestions for authenticity of writing assignments.

Writing Tasks Assessed, Writing Tasks Taught

Authentic assessment assures students and parents that the writing tasks required of students for assessment are those that are being taught in the classroom. It is performance-based. Lauren Resnick (1987) has championed this new kind of learning assessment for many years. Her expertise in the field of cognitive science, her leadership of the New Standards Project, and her specific contribution to the advancement of performance-based learning (the driving force in the New Standards Project) make her endorsement compelling. Her central thrust has been the promotion of a kind of learning that is measured by real-world performance of students. In that framework, teaching and learning are inextricably linked to the manner in which students' performance is assessed. Applebee (1994) defines this new approach as direct assessment and argues that NAEP has "played a major role in legitimizing direct writing assessment" (p. 41). Ability or knowledge is assessed by performance, much as a musician is assessed by a highly skilled judge who is screened off from the performer. Assessment is more direct and thus more authentic and valuable. Resnick (1987) believes that we need to move to this totally new way of assessing students' work. Whereas certain disciplines' standards might appear to be a bit vague or fuzzy (Milner, 1997), the process that Resnick offers for assessing performance has a hard edge. In the assessment she envisions, real-world tasks are assigned and then assessed by clearly delineated criteria that are defined by a six-level rubric. When this kind of assessment is in place, the testing tail will truly wag the instructional dog; and for once that will be proper because the tests will be a measure of real writing ability.

State-Initiated, Performance-Based Assessment

Virginia was one of the first states to develop a rubric for writing assessment, although it did not link class practice to the process. The Virginia Literacy Testing Committee established five domains for assessment that are weighted in favor of composing features rather than conventions:

Composing: building a message for the reader
Style: shaping the message to engage or affect the reader
Sentence formation: how the sentences are made
Usage: how the paper sounds
Mechanics: how the paper looks

The five domains are not as well defined as best practice would require, but the state's definitions attempt to offer specificity within each domain (see Figure 11-10). Along with the indicators in the five domains, there is a lengthy clarification of the five domains for teachers. The three-paragraph statement says, for example, that style is the second-most important domain and includes "appropriate vocabulary selection, sentence variety, voice and tone." The domains are each "evaluated holistically" according to the "extent to which the features appear to be under the control of the writer." The rubric for control (Figure 11-11) has four levels. These do not offer definitions of what control entails, but we must remember that Popham (1997) has warned us that highly complex rubrics can become so mentally taxing that teachers will not use them in their classrooms (p. 23).

Some proponents of authentic assessment believe that there are problems in multidomain rubrics. Thus, they have developed a simpler assessment rubric that ranges from a high of 9 to a low of 1. The top papers (8-9) are well defined (Figure 11-12), while the low papers (2) are described by negative comments (Figure 11-13).

Duke and Sanchez (1994), working in Pennsylvania, were aware of the insufficiency of these two options and helped develop the Pennsylvania State Assessment System, a six-point rubric that has five domains, or traits, with a "range of quality within each trait" (p. 50). While their rubric (Figure 11-14) solves some serious problems, two still exist. There are only three distinct scores for each domain, and the rubric is not specific to the mode of discourse assessed.

FIGURE 11–10
State of Virginia's domains and definitions

COMPOSING: (C) WEIGHTED ×3
- Central idea
- Elaboration
- Unity
- Organization

STYLE: (S) WEIGHTED ×2
- Vivid vocabulary
- Selected information
- Sentence variety
- Tone
- Voice

SENTENCE FORMATION: (F) WEIGHTED ×1
- Completeness
- Non-enjambment
- Expansion through standard coordination and modifiers
- Embedding through standard subordination and modifier
- Standard word order

USAGE: (U) WEIGHTED ×1
- Standard inflections
- Agreement
- Word meaning
- Conventions

MECHANICS: (M) WEIGHTED ×1
- Capitalization
- Punctuation
- Formatting
- Spelling

FIGURE 11–11
Rubric for control

<table>
<tr><td colspan="2" align="center">*Consistent Control*</td></tr>
<tr><td>4 =</td><td>The writer demonstrates consistent, though not necessarily perfect, control of almost all the domain's features.</td></tr>
<tr><td colspan="2" align="center">*Reasonable Control*</td></tr>
<tr><td>3 =</td><td>The writer demonstrates reasonable, but not consistent, control of most of the domain's features, indicating some weakness in the domain.</td></tr>
<tr><td colspan="2" align="center">*Inconsistent Control*</td></tr>
<tr><td>2 =</td><td>The writer demonstrates enough inconsistent control of several features to indicate significant weakness in the domain.</td></tr>
<tr><td colspan="2" align="center">*Little or No Control*</td></tr>
<tr><td>1 =</td><td>The writer demonstrates little or no control on most of the domain's features.</td></tr>
</table>

FIGURE 11–12
Rubric for top papers (8–9)

- Developed a good introduction.
- Maintained an appropriate point of view throughout the paper.
- Employed precise, apt, or evocative descriptive vocabulary.
- Did not shift in tense or person.
- Organized ideas effectively and provided an introduction, some closure, and an orderly progression from one idea to another.
- Varied sentence structure and length.
- Used effectively the conventions of written English—spelling, usage, sentence structure, capitalization, punctuation.
- Used at least three examples with specific supporting details.
- Used at least three of five senses.
- Wrote legibly.

FIGURE 11–13
Rubric for low papers (2)

- Has no sense of organization.
- Shifts constantly in tense and person.
- Shows little or no development of ideas; lacks any focus on specific and related details.
- Distorts, misreads, or ignores the topic.
- Contains disjointed sentences, lacks sense of sentence progression and variety, and contains many sentence errors.
- Shows serious faults in handling the conventions of written English to the extent of impeding a reader's understanding.
- Has no discussion of the five senses.
- Handwriting cannot be read easily.

California has also sought to construct an authentic assessment model. Dudley (1997) reports that as early as 1987, English teachers in her state began to develop the California Learning Assessment System (CLAS). The teachers, by dint of their own efforts, selected the types of writing, the prompts, and the assessment criteria that would help teachers throughout the state participate in authentic assessment of writing. They later added reading to CLAS; but the politics of division entered the fray in 1994, when the governor ended the project with a veto of funding.

Because education reform networks are so intimately related (McCollum-Clark, 1995), it is no coincidence that performance-based learning promoted by the New Standards Project has become a priority initiative for states that have strong connections with the education reform movement and that they would adopt strong, cutting-edge assessment measures. North Carolina's work on au-

thentic assessment has been led by its Education Standards and was driven by then Governor Hunt's connection with the National Board for Professional Teaching Standards. The state sponsored assessment workshops in large population centers across the state, where teachers worked with national consultants to develop precise rubrics that would prod writing instruction in this new direction.

Two salient features of North Carolina's approach to instruction and assessment set it apart: It creates tasks for students to perform that are quite similar to tasks in the workplace and the real world, and the levels of performance are defined by performance rubrics that are clear and well understood by students. One of North Carolina's performance-based writing standards is a real-world task that might be undertaken by a president, a prophet, or any thoughtful person: the memoir. The task places students inside the real-world context

Focus

6/5 • establishes and keeps a clear purpose
   • maintains a clear purpose most of the time
   • shows clarity and originality of ideas
4/3 • maintains a clear purpose most of the time
   • varies occasionally in keeping a single point of view
   • ideas are generally clear but not especially original
2/1 • shows uncertainty about task and audience
   • has no clear sense of purpose
   • has difficulty in holding a single point of view or role
   • lacks clarity or originality of ideas

Content

6/5 • shows sophisticated thinking and ideas
   • provides well developed examples and explanations related to topic and purpose
   • selects information appropriate for audience and situation
4/3 • presents ideas somewhat lacking in sophistication
   • provides examples and details related to the topic but they may be uneven in development
   • selects information appropriate for audience and situation
2/1 • presents under-developed and unsophisticated ideas
   • provides examples and details as listings without development and not always relevant to topic and purpose
   • shows little awareness of the audience's needs

Organization

6/5 • maintains a logical order/sequence
   • focuses on one subject in each paragraph
   • provides logical transitions within sentences and between paragraphs
   • offers a clear introduction and conclusion that frame the topic under discussion
4/3 • maintains a reasonable order/sequence
   • focuses most of the time on one subject per paragraph
   • provides logical transitions within sentences and paragraphs but is not always consistent in their use
   • offers an adequate introduction and conclusion but without much clarity or originality
2/1 • displays inconsistent order/sequence
   • exhibits difficulty in maintaining focus on one idea in a paragraph

   • shows inconsistency in use of transitions within sentences and paragraphs
   • offers little in the way of a controlled introduction and conclusion

Style

6/5 • shows precise language use
   • exhibits effective word choice that suggests originality and a sophisticated vocabulary
   • offers a consistent voice and tone appropriate for the topic, purpose, and audience
   • demonstrates control over variety of sentence structure, types, and length
4/3 • shows fairly precise language use
   • exhibits appropriate word choice
   • offers somewhat inconsistent tone and voice or selects voice and tone inappropriate for audience and purpose
   • demonstrates control over basic sentence structure but appears uncertain about variety, types, and length
2/1 • shows little precision in language use
   • exhibits little originality in word choice and some choices may be inappropriate
   • offers an inconsistent voice and/or inappropriate voice/tone
   • shows little control over sentence structure, variety, types, and length

Conventions

6/5 • exhibits few if any errors in spelling, punctuation and capitalization
   • demonstrates control of appropriate forms of usage—pronoun reference, subject/verb agreement, etc.
   • displays a control of sentence completeness (absence of run-ons and unnecessary fragments)
4/3 • exhibits a number of repetitive errors in spelling, punctuation, and capitalization but not severe enough to interfere significantly with reader's understanding
   • shows inconsistency in appropriate choice of usage
   • displays inconsistency in control of sentence completeness
2/1 • exhibits repetitive and frequent errors in spelling, punctuation, and capitalization that interfere with the reader's understanding
   • shows inconsistency in choice of appropriate usage
   • displays lack of understanding of sentence completeness

FIGURE 11–14 Pennsylvania State Assessment System rubric

of a memoir submitted to a magazine that will be judged by its editor on the basis of three criteria: It must be engaging, clear, and insightful. The content standard of the task is spelled out in a succinct paragraph for teachers:

> Content Standard: writes for extended periods of time; writes imaginative and personal narratives that have a coherent, logical, and organized structure; writes imaginative narratives with sufficient, related detail that revolve around an event and have a resolution; expresses main idea and supporting detail in descriptive writing; edits written work for errors in sentence formation, usage, mechanics, and spelling. (p. 41)

The interest in control of conventions such as spelling, punctuation, and usage is present; but other, more complex dimensions of writing are highlighted. The assignment itself is directed to the student and spells out much more than a simple topic:

> *Cricket* magazine is collecting memoirs of students to include in a special spring edition of the magazine. It will focus on memorable moments in their lives. They have sent out a call for submissions. You decide to submit. The editor of *Cricket* has indicated that the submissions must relate to one memory, and will be judged on how *engaging, clear,* and *insightful* they are. In judging how clear the memoir is, the editor will be looking at *main idea, supporting details, organization,* and *coherence.* (p. 41)

The assignment also promotes a real-world demand for revision because it includes a note to the writer warning that the editor will return the submission with editorial marks that need attention: "After you make your submission, the editor writes back expressing enthusiasm for your work but suggesting revisions. With the confidence of a 'soon-to-be-published' author you complete the rework and submit it again" (p. 41). Wyngaard and Gehrke (1996) report that among other things the use of rubrics in memoir writing produced stronger awareness of audience in student writers.

Tied to Daily Instruction

The instructions for the teachers reinforce the authentic nature of the task because they are based on writing instruction that takes place in the classroom daily. Teachers are reminded, "you must remember that during the completion of this task, you are an assessor, not an instructor/ coach. What you are interested in is finding out what the students can do independently." Smede (1993) believes that the opportunity to practice the tasks in class and the specificity of the tasks promote both fairness and student participation: "Part of assessing student work fairly according to the beliefs of performance gurus is to let them know exactly what you expect before they begin. In essence, this is just a part of good teaching" (p. 21).

For instance, as Smede suggests; during instructional time, teachers might help students understand "what a memoir is," which is, in this case, defined "as a piece of writing that is personal, has action, contains a 'lesson' learned (or insight made) in the situation remembered, and is written in the first person." Along with this definition, the student writers are given a number of memoirs to read so they can learn by example as well. Teachers then show their students how the rubrics for being engaging, clear, and insightful will be used to assess their writing and encourage them to look for and discuss these qualities in the exemplary memoirs. As a final instructional task, teachers ask students to write about a shared class memory that individual students later turn into their own memoirs. These are collected in a book and sent home so that parents become a real audience for their children's writing. The cycle of definition, production, publication, and reflection is imprinted on these students so that the final assessment of their ability to write a memoir will be a fair test of a real-world skill that is used to perform an authentic task.

Constructing Rubrics

Dudley (1997) speaks about what such rubrics mean for instruction: "We were seeing the scoring guide not only as an assessment tool but as a set of coherently and precisely articulated expectations that were grounded in classroom reality and that would help us to be better teachers when we returned to our classrooms on Monday morning. So as a scoring guide developed, there was a constant revision process, until we felt it reflected not only what many students had achieved, but what more, with good instruction, could be expected to be achieved" (p. 17). Burch (1997) adds to this an unintended positive consequence for students when they develop rubrics: "Working together to construct the rubric helps students accommodate their strengths as learners and creates a more democratic classroom by engaging them in the process for assessing their work" (p. 56). For each of the criteria that students use as standards for evaluation, there is a set of performance rubrics that includes six well-specified definitions of criteria accomplishment. For the first criterion, the CLAS (1996) rubric for clear writing, shown in Figure 11–15, lists six levels of performance. The levels are neatly delineated so that each represents ever greater performance of the criterion as the rubric level ascends from 1 to 6. The shift from "no evidence . . . of an intended message or meaning" (level 1) to "The work is insufficient to communicate the message or meaning" (level 3) to "The work reveals a well-thought-through message or meaning"

FIGURE 11–15
Rubric for clear writing

6. The communication is usually clear. Language is sophisticated and precise, the work is thoroughly and logically developed, and the message or meaning is unambiguous. The work reveals an unusual control over form and content in the service of intention.
5. The communication is clear. Language is apt and precise, the work reveals a well-thought-through message or meaning, and good control over how to convey it best.
4. The communication is mostly clear. Language is apt but not always sufficiently precise. There are some instances of ambiguity, vagueness, or otherwise hard-to-discern meanings (especially concerning the more subtle or complex ideas). The work suggests, however, a thought-through message or meaning.
3. The communication is somewhat clear. Language may be inadequate, not always apt or up to the demands of the task. There are major instances of ambiguity, vagueness, or otherwise hard-to-discern meanings throughout. Key ideas are insufficiently developed or explained. The work is insufficient to communicate the message or meaning effectively AND/OR the work suggests an insufficiently worked-through intended message or meaning.
2. The communication is unclear. There are many places where intended messages or meanings cannot be discerned. Language may be too imprecise, inappropriate, or immature to convey the intended message AND/OR the work suggests an insufficiently thought-through message or meaning.
1. The communication is difficult if not impossible to decipher. OR there is no evidence in the work of an intended or deliberate message or meaning.

(level 5) offers assessors a refined way to classify the performance of the memoir writer. The level attained not only allows teachers to come up with a qualitative score but also tells the student writer just where the problem or proficiency lies in his or her piece. Language use, likewise, which helps define clarity, shifts from "imprecise" (level 2) to some instances of "ambiguity, vagueness" (level 4) to "sophisticated and precise" (level 6).

The rubric for insight, which is an even tougher criterion to calibrate in a six-level rubric, is shown in Figure 11–16. The features that define the six levels of the rubric are perception, lessons learned, impact, and originality. Each

of these features is more evident in the writing as the rubric rises from "blah" to "wow!" Because the writing tasks are like those of daily life and are assessed using clear-cut criteria, students begin to view writing less as a mystery and more as a job that they can perform. This does not mean that writing becomes mechanical and arid but that it advances to new levels of excellence.

Burch (1997) reports on how an individual class developed a very useful two-tiered portfolio that awarded 60 percent credit for the quantity of its contents and 40 percent credit for its quality as determined by a rubric that the students and teacher established. The two-tiered portfolio is presented in Figure 11–17.

FIGURE 11–16
Rubric for insight

6. The memoir is unusually perceptive. The writing contains keen insights of discovery or self-discovery beyond the particulars of the episode(s) but thoughtfully and ably derived from them. The writing has great impact: significant lessons have been learned and shared through reflection and writing, insights that speak to readers, not just the writer.

5. The memoir is perceptive. The writing contains insights beyond the particulars of the episode(s), but thoughtfully and ably derived from them. The writing has impact: lessons have been learned and shared through reflection and writing.

4. The memoir contains thoughtful reflections beyond what is recalled and described, but the message is somewhat obvious or restricted. The writing has somewhat limited impact. Lessons have been learned and/or offered, though they may speak more to the writer than the readers (due to weaknesses in drawing insights from the memories or limits in the richness of what has been recalled).

3. The memoir contains reflections beyond what is recalled and described, but the message is somewhat obvious, restricted, ambiguous, or unwarranted. The message amounts to little more than a restatement of the facts OR involves leaps to conclusions somewhat unwarranted by the facts presented. Lessons may well have been learned and/or shared, but the exact nature or importance of the lessons remains somewhat unclear.

2. The memoir does not go much beyond recall OR the writer jumps to a simplistic conclusion that may or may not be warranted by the facts presented. The lack of warranted insight may be due to EITHER a lack of rich detail in the memoir AND/OR an inability to draw thoughtful conclusions from experience.

1. The writing does not amount to a memoir, containing merely facts and descriptions without any apparent meaning or value to the writer (as revealed by the absence of deliberate reflection or meaning-making).

FIGURE 11–17
Two-tiered portfolio

A. Contents of Portfolio
(60% of portfolio grade)
Writing (40) Points

_____ 1. _____ [Name of piece]
_____ 2. _____ [Name of piece]
_____ 3. _____ [Name of piece]
_____ 4. _____ [Name of piece]

Metawriting/Reflection (15 points)

_____ 1. _____ [Name of piece]
_____ 2. _____ [Name of piece]
_____ 3. _____ [Name of piece]

Peer Writing (5 points)

_____ 1. _____ [Name of piece]
_____ 2. _____ [Name of piece]

Writer's Choice
(up to 5 extra points: not required)

_____ 1. _____ [Name of piece]
_____ 2. _____ [Name of piece]

B. Quality of Portfolio
(40% of portfolio grade)
You must allot 3–12 points to each criterion, for a total of 40 points. Write your allotments in the bracketed spaces.

_____ 1. Voice—distinctness of style, creative   [ ]
expression and arrangement, personality

_____ 2. Organization—logical, orderly arrangement,   [ ]
ease of movement within portfolio

_____ 3. Reflection—thoughtfulness, awareness of self   [ ]
and teacher in metawriting

_____ 4. Development—fullness of contents, full   [ ]
explanations, adequate detail

_____ 5. Mechanical and Usage—spelling, punctuation,   [ ]
_____ word choice, usage

Contents points ( ) + Qualities points ( ) = Total score ( )
Comments about the portfolio

NAEP Framework

NAEP's (1998) work on rubrics has a far broader influence and its work is more enduring than that done in the states. Its belief in the power of rubrics is manifest in the process of rubric construction suggested in its *Writing Framework and Specifications* and presented in Figure 11-18. In addition, the publication offers a set of useful guides for developing rubrics to promote better writing through authentic assessment (Figure 11-19). Both NAEP contributions make it more likely that such

new means of assessment will be adopted by states, districts, and individual teachers. North Carolina has just turned to an informational essay for its state writing assessment, and its construction is deeply embedded in the rubrics developed by NAEP.

Rubrics and the Paper Load

Using rubrics for assessment is not a necessary component of process writing, writing workshops, and portfolios, but

FIGURE 11–18
Suggested process for rubric construction

- Convene a group of writing experts and classroom teachers to discuss the nature of the assessment (e.g., number and nature of tasks, time allowed).
- Read a wide sampling of field test papers, looking for special characteristics of the *students* contained in the sample as these characteristics will influence the level of complexity in the information specified by the rubric. Also, look through the student responses to get an idea of the *diversity of responses and levels of achievement* to identify the characteristics and content that should be included in the rubric.
- Consider the level of discriminations necessary for the purpose of the test. Consider the length of time the student has had available to respond to the task.
- Read all the papers and divide them into piles that demonstrate the characteristics of writing that are described in the rubric for each score point.
- Write descriptors for each pile of papers. Consider what characteristics distinguish the top papers from the lowest levels. Then, assess what categories these characteristics fall into. In assessing writing, for example, the categories of most rubrics fall into purpose, audience, idea development/ support, organization/structure, sentence structure, and word choice, voice, and mechanics.
- Write rough drafts of descriptors for each score point.
- Consider the rubric to be a "draft in process" until after the field test results have been evaluated.

FIGURE 11–19
General characteristics of writing by mode

NARRATIVE
Understands the narrative purpose.
Develops character.
Maintains focus.
Has satisfying resolution.
Has appropriate ordering of events.
Gives attention to audience when appropriate to the prompt.
Uses elaboration and details.
Handles direct and indirect discourse.
Demonstrates control of mechanics.

INFORMATIVE
Understands the informative purpose.
Has clear and complete information.
Conveys messages, instructions, and/or ideas.
Uses sufficient detail.
Uses coherent and logical organization.
Shows efficient relationships between and among ideas.
Gives attention to audience.
Fulfills the demands of the task.
Uses language level appropriate to the topic and voice desired by the writing.
Demonstrates control of mechanics.

PERSUASIVE
Understands the persuasive purpose.
Takes and retains a position.
Supports and develops a position through examples, details, statistics, and supporting evidence.
Has coherent and logical organization.
Gives attention to audience.
Uses language level appropriate to the topic and voice desired by the writing.
Demonstrates control of mechanics.

they are closely associated because process teachers by necessity have appropriately transferred much of the assessment and revision responsibility to students. Even more important, because proponents of process writing argue that students should spend more time working seriously on a few good pieces rather than churning out multiple mediocre pieces, the approach is associated with the movement to reduce teachers' paper loads. LaFontana (1996) commented on her experience: "As I pondered these questions, I had to admit that the martyr approach just wasn't working. I was spending an inordinate amount of time with only a slim hope of effecting any improvement in student writing" (p. 71). Assessment with rubrics is swift because teachers do not have to offer justifying comments, and it is more objective because judgment is tied to standards. Wiggins (1997) has added another important reason for using rubrics and authentic assessment; he believes task specific standards are the only available means of incorporating broad national standards into the realities of the classroom.

Whether they are the collective effort of an association of English teachers, the initiative of a state governor, the suggestion of a respected national testing body, or the good work and will of a single teacher, rubrics for assessment can be created that are similar to everyday writing tasks used in class; are cooperatively established; and provide fair, well-defined measures of incremental success. This is a difficult, time-consuming, and sometimes politically dangerous next step to take; but it seems to link the circle inexorably. It is a compelling approach to writing. Most states, of course, will not encourage teacher-developed assessment systems such as the one California teachers created, nor will they fund training for assessment as North Carolina did for a time. Most of the strength of this new movement will have to emerge from the bottom up.

Invitation to Reflection 11–5

Our basic assumptions about writing are presented in the following list. Check those that you claim as being important to you, altering and expanding them to match your own vision. Add two or more additional assumptions of your own.

_____*Holistic, not partial.*   All writing should be communication in the real world. Workbook dummy runs don't make sense to students. Contrived assignments don't ring true.

_____*Organic, not formulaic.*   All writing takes some form, but form should follow meaning. Communication should lead; rules and methods should follow.

_____*Inclusive, not exclusive.*   Writing should move across many modes of discourse and touch many dimensions of life. Analysis of literature is important, but it is only a small segment of the whole writing continuum.

_____*Developmental, not static.*   Writers grow as they develop through many stages. Teachers need to be aware of those developmental paths and praise their students for the growth they see.

_____*Foundational, not isolationist.*   Writing is built on the foundation of thinking. It should be integrated into a full language curriculum in which students move from thinking to speaking to writing and in which reading is seen as reciprocal to writing.

⌘ CONCLUSION

The five constructs of teaching writing are linked in such a way that they continuously reform the circle; each one naturally leads to the next. They are affirmed by best practice and current research but have varying degrees of acceptability and status in today's secondary schools. The process approach is almost old hat, while portfolios are becoming highly acclaimed in reform-centered schools. Writing workshops are much rarer but still are attractive curriculum models for teachers who like challenges. Atwell's (1998) new edition of *In the Middle* has taken some moderating stands on ownership and other critical positions that will make her approach easier to adopt in high schools. Authentic assessment still has tremendous support from important reform sources; but its complexity is inherently problematic, so the vote is not yet in on that promising approach. The developmental model is traditional in the modes of discourse it includes, while it is somewhat progressive in relating those modes to the thinking process. The five constructs work together as a dynamic cumulative model for writing instruction. By the close of this century's first decade, we might well see these constructs as fixtures rather than cutting-edge pedagogy. They may, in fact, become so commonplace that innovative teachers will begin to develop new constructs in the ever-evolving attempt to teach writing.

12 ∽

Enabling
Writing

∽ *It's the head-to-page trip that is so frightening and difficult for writers. Acting as coaches of writing, teachers can assist students by helping them understand the strategies they are using and suggesting others they might use, by raising questions and more questions as the text emerges, and by encouraging and supporting student decision-making throughout the growth of the piece.*

Dan Kirby, Tom Liner, and
Ruth Vinz ∽

*Y*ou may wonder why we need another chapter on writing when we have presented basic writing approaches in Chapter 11, ideas about teaching grammar in context in Chapter 3, and writing assignments scattered throughout the book. As with our multiple chapters on teaching literature, numerous approaches, genres, and activities are available to put your philosophy of writing instruction into everyday operation. To do justice to this complex and challenging task, we continue to discuss enabling structures that we have found helpful, that are not in common use in many middle and high schools, and that would have swelled other chapters past comfort. The recommended writing texts in Appendix H contain the structures of others.

We introduce you here to further theories about teaching writing (collaborative writing, right writing, writing to learn, elemental variation, and apprentice writing), to genres of writing (environmental journalism, journal writing, research writing, writing about literature, dependent authoring), and finally to tools that enable students to undertake any writing assignment (code switching, sentence combining, vocabulary growth, and style developing). These fourteen chapter sections may appear as randomly organized as groceries thrown into a shopping cart—good and needful items but assembled in no apparent order. Teaching writing coheres for us around the first principles discussed in Chapter 11; but there are other approaches, genres, and tools with which to build effective writing instruction. We hope these ideas will become part of your planning repertoire and be ready for particular moments, particular students, and particular needs. They all conspire toward what Britton et al. (1975) reminds us is our purpose in preparing students to write: "work in school ought to equip a writer to choose his own target audience and, eventually, to be able, when the occasion arises, to write as someone with something to say to the world in general" (p. 192).

We present these fourteen sections as a means of fulfilling four critical needs in student writing that will shape any writing program you may construct: *substance, skills, structure,* and *style.*

∞ FOUR BASIC NEEDS

Substance

Substance, or content, is the fundamental need. To get writing started, we must help students find the subject of their thoughts and bring that thinking to consciousness on paper. Fluency is what is wanted. We hope to find ways to let students express themselves. We need to know how to offer an invitation to writing that is provocative and genuine. Further, we need to construct enabling structures that nudge students beyond their starting points. We need to call on students to express themselves and then to explore their experiences and ideas through writing. Substance is richest and flows most easily when students write about what they know best and when it follows thinking and talking.

Skills

Skills are naturally acquired through repeated practice, but they are also consciously mastered. They come about because students are absorbing them all along *and* because teachers are helping students gain consciousness of them. Vocabulary, spelling, and punctuation are some of the basic skills that students must master to write well; and students value these skills most when they care about what they are writing. These skills become more complex as writing itself becomes more complicated. Usage, which most people call grammar, describes how words relate to one another. Its basic components are the relationships between major features such as the subject and predicate of a sentence: *she runs; they run.* Similar but less crucial relationships are those between pronouns and their referents: *He is the man whom you seek; Mary said that it was her book.*

Relationships in form are least noticeable: splitting infinitives and using prepositions at ends of sentences are only mildly unacceptable for some. Style can sometimes override relationship, and social concern can outweigh form as with the questions of gendered pronouns we discussed in Chapter 3.

Structure

Structure is the architecture of composing. It is the macro form rather than the microlevel of design and relationship. We know that form and organization should arise from the content at hand, but we also try to provide some organizing structures to help students mold and shape their content. We fail them when we insist on only one way to organize writing: Metaphors and graphic patterns can inform organization as well as a five-paragraph or comparison-contrast structure can. Coherence has to do with making the sentences and paragraphs fit together. Connectors and other function words (*and, but, therefore*) provide complex ways to direct, redirect, and calibrate the directions of a writer's thinking.

Style

Style is the most subtle element. It is founded on all of the other four elements, but it goes far beyond them. It can be created by the vocabulary of the writer; through the variety and aptness of its use; by the inventive use of images and actions that represent something beyond themselves; and by metaphors, symbols, and extended figures of speech. Style's most sophisticated language dimensions are related to syntax: the arrangement of words. The maturity of syntax and the ability to juxtapose stark simple utterances and lengthy complex ones are central here. Voice is even more difficult to cultivate and nourish. Murray (1985) explains its crucial importance in writing: "Voice allows the reader to hear an individual human being speak from the page. . . . Voice is the quality, more than any other, that allows us to recognize exceptional potential in a beginning writer; voice is the quality, more than any other, that allows us to recognize excellent writing. . . . Voice gives the text individuality, energy, concern" (p. 21).

Each of the writing strategies we recommend has the power to meet some or all of these four critical needs. Figure 12–1 indicates the fourteen strategies that we suggest and a measure of their effectiveness in meeting each of the four critical needs. Before we turn to these fourteen sections, we present examples of the kind of middle ground we attempt to traverse through all of these approaches, genres, and tools.

FIGURE 12–1
Basic needs matrix

● Profound Effect   ◯ Moderate Effect   ○ Slight Effect

	Substance	Skills	Structure	Style
Collaborative writing	●	◯	◯	◯
Environmental journalism	●	◯	◯	○
Right writing	●	○	○	●
Journal writing	●	○	○	●
Write to learn	●	◯	◯	○
Code switching	○	●	◯	○
Sentence combining	◯	○	◯	●
Vocabulary growth	○	●	○	●
New research	●	◯	●	○
Elemental variation	◯	○	●	◯
Lit. write	●	◯	○	●
Dependent authors	●	○	◯	●
Apprentice writing	●	◯	◯	●
Practical stylist	◯	◯	○	●

✑ MEDIATED INSTRUCTION

Fearn and Farnan's (1990) *Writing Effectively* addresses the fundamentals of writing. They acknowledge that a balanced writing program is composed of multiple dimensions, but they limit their attention to the basic conventions of writing. They place all instruction inside the context of whole pieces of writing; but for them, "the unit is always a sentence" (p. 6). This simple context gives them great control of what they want students to master. They believe that for teachers to be effective they must develop a systematic approach to the host of major writing problems suffered by a majority of students; they fear that incidental or spontaneous teaching directed to the problems that happen to appear in students' writing will not solve the problem. They opt for a kind of direct instruction that they believe will achieve maximum effectiveness in minimal time.

In the same fashion Kystron (2001) has developed an electronic handbook that covers parts of speech, sentence structure, Standard English grammar, and much more. Because it grows out of his writing project experiences, it has a constructivist orientation. One of its unusual features is that users are taught language conventions in a fairly ordinary fashion, but they are then asked to teach the ideas and skills they have acquired to an imaginary student. It is this teaching that places the approach on a middle ground between direct and process-based instruction and so qualifies it as mediated instruction.

Middle Ground

Hillocks's (1986) *Research on Written Composition* has been a landmark in the field, but he has recently updated his research, broadened his pedagogy, and raised further questions about process writing. He seems to have positioned his work (as we do) between two extremes: the traditional presentational teacher who explains everything in a lecture or relies on workbook drills and the strict constructivists who rely on the hope that students will discover everything for themselves. He believes that traditionalists will fail because "the abstract rules and formulas of such teaching exclude the self" (p. 23), yet he is not willing to abandon some form of direct instruction. He uses a simple rite-of-passage incident as an analogy to the failures of these extremes and his own success:

> Consider learning how to use the clutch on a standard transmission. My dad's explanation, by itself, would have done little good. His explanation, combined with my trying (and stalling the car fairly frequently) and his coaching, finally did the trick by the end of our second session. On the other hand, had he chosen simply to demonstrate, I would have been in trouble. It would have taken a long time to perceive exactly what the relationships of the pedals had to be. (p. 122)

Explanation and demonstration are insufficient; only learning by doing together with careful coaching will get the job done. Hillocks says that his scrupulous planning and exacting arrangements for student interaction brings about the desired results, moving students through Vygotsky's zone of proximal development. He calls his pedagogy "environmental instruction" because its successes are due to the structures he crafts. He believes that his theory for teaching composition will "draw upon knowledge from a variety of sources" (p. 41) and thus overcome the paradigm split between the positivists and the constructivists.

Hillocks's Lesson

Hillocks offers a sample lesson that illustrates the complex interactions between teacher and students in writing instruction. Hillocks and his graduate students meticulously planned how groups would be composed and the directions for their activity. He lists four important principles of sequencing in his plan that are essential for an activity to work effectively (pp. 180–82):

Fun: Begin with enjoyable work at the early stages as a way to establish interest.

Building: Use earlier simple knowledge to create more complex understanding later.

Integration: Pull together standard activities to engage and complete gateway activities.

Independence: Learn to use appropriate and fruitful strategies at the students' discretion.

Hillocks and his team used the following sequence of activities, which embody his four principles, to help their students develop a personal narrative:

1. *Initial writing sample.*   Students write about an experience important to them.
2. *Examples of personal narrative.*   Students talk about similar works by professionals and other students.
3. *Idea sheets.*   Students write a few sentences about their own experiences.
4. *Introduction to using specific detail.*   Students describe shells in teacher-led session.
5. *Details about people and places.*   Teacher-led talk about an interesting drawing or photograph of a person in action or in a mood.
6. *Describing sounds.*   Teacher-led talk about recording of various sounds.
7. *Writing about bodily sensations.*   Students write briefly about what they feel.
8. *Writing about the "dumpster scenario."*   Students write what they see, hear, and feel as an ominous man approaches.
9. *Pantomime of characters in emotional states.*   Students write details for an audience who did not see the person.
10. *Invention of dialogue.*   Students talk about two or three examples of dialogue from professional and student pieces.
11. *Individual work on dialogue from idea sheet scenario.*   Students read aloud to groups for feedback and revision.
12. *Punctuation of dialogue.*   Teacher demonstrates simplest dialogue form on overhead.
13. *Workshop.*   Students select an incident to develop from their idea sheets, to work on drafting, and to revise.
14. *Class publication.*   Students choose which pieces to include.
15. *Final writing sample.*   Students compare first and final writing. (pp. 178–179)

Much more can be learned from Hillocks's complex and provocative strategy. It breaks new ground and avoids the difficulty of insufficient options from those on either side of his centrist position.

Another Middle Way

Collins and Collins (1996) take the same centrist position, describing their approach as "strategic instruction for struggling writers." They offer four clear steps for such writers that help them gain strength and independence:

- identifying a strategy
- introducing and modeling it
- helping students use it
- repeating practice to achieve independence

Collins and Collins explain their position clearly: "The strategic writing approach asks teachers to add instruction in procedural knowledge to their work with writers, especially procedural knowledge in the form of self-regulatory strategies, ways of thinking about writing which help students control the writing process by setting goals and monitoring progress toward achieving them" (p. 55). They use goal setting, double-entry note taking, read-think-summarize-interpret revising strategies, and heavy-line marking of students' writing for analysis (p. 56). They help students understand the sense of sentences by carefully looking at ways of connecting referents and strengthening coherence. Other educators are turning to this kind of intensive work with students in order to develop a rigor and power in their writing that is sometimes missed in other approaches.

We turn first to an approach to writing instruction that is basic to the theories of Chapter 11.

☙ COLLABORATIVE WRITING

When students aren't able to start writing, one of the most successful ways to bypass that block is to turn to collaboration. Very little research has been done on writer's block, but Rose (1984) finds that the best explanation is a psychological resistance to putting anything on the table that might be embarrassing. Rose cites Minninger, Goodman, and others as researchers who believe that the child in the writer has a block because of a fear of meeting disapproval (pp. 13–15). When students work together, their talk can be used to produce a confidence and a fluency in their writing that they do not possess when working alone. In the early grades, three students taking turns at a computer keyboard can turn halting utterances into extended narratives. Uncertain individual thoughts gather assurance as they are aired and refined in a small group of peers. When a trio of secondary students compose a bizarre story using a list of items from three columns labeled *character, conflict,* and *conclusion,* the same collaborative power is unleashed. The social fun derived from such interaction makes the language flow. Dale's (1994) research shows that collaborative writing groups become better than other student groups at taking conversational turns because they learn together, are better focused on the task at hand, and are better able to handle productive disagreement. Senge's (2000) compelling work on the fifth discipline shows that students in school as well as adults in the business world can learn to work in groups in this same productive fashion. He describes the process of dialogue and discussion and explains how these skills can be learned in ways that maximize productive group effect.

What Vygotsky tells us about the social construction of language helps us see how language is unlocked in a social situation. We have also observed that the most repeated research finding about effective writing strategies is that talk promotes writing best. Dale (1997) thinks of the collaborative process as co-authoring and lists a set of activities that work well when students write in groups (Figure 12–2). Each of these ideas calls on group members to think for themselves, talk about their differences of opinion, analyze the problem or phenomenon together, and compose a forceful position statement that has a real and well-defined audience. Dale says that the advantage of the topics and procedures is their strong appeal to students. They deal with contemporary issues that fully engage adolescents' political and social interests.

Because most secondary students are moving toward formal operational thinking, they are intellectually and psychologically ready to measure the realities of the world around them against the ideals that they are formulating in their minds. The world of *ought* rather than *is* is the ground they occupy. That is why parents and adults who are seemingly inured to the unsettling facts of daily life are often alien to them. Adolescent literature works so well with them in part because it focuses on the tension between being a dependent child and an independent adult.

FIGURE 12–2
Co-authoring activities

- Write a letter to a school official which defines a problem that you think exists in this school.
  - Propose a solution.
  - Detail the feasibility of that solution.
  - Ask members of another group to edit the draft.
- Write a questionnaire and survey classmates about an issue that you know your classmates are talking about.
  - Conduct short interviews.
  - Characterize the views at your school.
- Name your generation.
  - Support your stance.
  - Draw from the experiences of all members of the group.
  - Protest the labeling of your generation as Generation X.
- Think of a trend in society.
  - Combine your experiences.
  - Explore the underlying causes.
  - Explain why this trend exists.
- Satirize a phenomenon in society.
  - Choose a specific subject.
  - Show what is mildly to very irritating.
- Analyze a particular advertisement.
  - Describe the ad's script and visual message.
  - Investigate the product or the target audience for the ad.
  - Analyze the ad for its underlying social message.
- As a group, analyze a movie you view together.
  - See a recently released film.
  - Discuss the movie.
  - Compose a movie review.
- Use a political cartoon as a visual prompt.
  - Bring to class political cartoons.
  - Objectively describe the cartoon in one or more paragraphs.
  - Write a description of the cartoon using slanted language.
  - Present these short papers orally to the class.

Source: Adapted from H. Dale (1997) *Co-authoring in the classroom* (pp. 63–65). Urbana, IL: NCTE.

Adolescence is a self-searching and self-defining time that makes students ripe for teaching, especially the kind of teaching that provides them with the opportunity for intellectual dissent.

Cognitive Conflict

Dale's (1997) report on the research on cognitive conflict is compelling (pp. 8–9):

1. "Cognitive conflict occurs with the recognition that one's ideas are different from another person's or are incompatible with new information" (Daiute & Dalton, 1988).

2. "Students in groups restructure their thoughts by comparing new information with information previously acquired and modify or replace existing concepts or attitudes if that seems necessary" (Webb, 1982).

3. "Some cognitive conflict is an inevitable part of the process of collaborative writing because students must negotiate differences of opinion in order to arrive at consensus" (Dale, 1994).

4. "A number of studies find that cognitive conflict is a vital component of successful collaborative writing" (Burnett, 1994; Daiute & Dalton, 1988; Dale, 1994).

5. A strong correlation occurs "between the quality of written work and the amount of substantive engagement in the collaborative writing group" (Burnett 1994).

6. Cognitive conflict is "one of the most important factors in separating a model group of writers from a typical or problem group" (Dale, 1994).

Verbalization

All of the research that Dale (1997) cites about verbalizing in groups and writing together also speaks clearly about its effectiveness. Four findings about verbalization are especially provocative and appropriate to the kind of writing we suggest here (pp. 6–7):

1. Verbalizing is "the biggest factor behind the success of collaborative learning in all its forms" (Brown & Palincsar, 1989; Gagne & Smith, 1962; Johnson & Johnson, 1985).

2. Verbalizing about what they're learning helps students comprehend fully; and "the more explaining a student does, the more benefits that student receives" (Cohen, 1994).

3. "Requiring verbalization forces students to think of reasons for the choices they make as they think through a problem or issue" (Gagne & Smith, 1962).

4. "The social context allows students to think out loud, which, in turn, provides an opportunity to think not only about the ideas involved, but also about writing itself" (Daiute & Dalton, 1993; Dale, 1994).

Benefits of Collaboration

Dale (1997) concludes that the general benefits of collaborating are very powerful (pp. 55–56):

- It socializes the writing process.
- It shifts the responsibility for good writing to students.
- It helps students see each other as resources, not competitors.
- It removes the loneliness of writing.
- It encourages cognitive growth.
- It helps students plan more.

All of the benefits that Dale lists are significant, but one that has additional punch is that working in teams is so commonplace in the work world that students need solid preparation for working together rather than alone. Goodman (1980) introduced collaborative writing to teachers in ten city school systems from California to Mississippi at the Excellence in Teaching English Institute. He arranged the outstanding teachers into teams that responded to a request for proposal for a biplane by completing an extended written proposal. His exercise demanded the same kind of group discussion and decision making of teachers before writing their proposals that Dale calls for in her text. The completed team proposals were full of strong writing because of the rigorous discussion that led to the writing. They were matched against a real-world activity almost one hundred years old, the Wright Brothers' submission to the patent office as they worked on the dunes at Kitty Hawk to manufacture a vehicle that would provide sustained flight.

Gillis (1994) developed a collaborative writing plan that emerged as "young writers [were] paired with writers in the community outside the school." They wrote at first about life at their school but began "to experiment with a range of writing" (p. 64). The group discussion and decision making that take place before writing in Dale's project is absent here. But the knowledge that a real partner who shares your interests is reading what you write and is thinking over your ideas creates some of the same reflection and cognitive dissonance that is generated by group writing. We have entered into a similar project with our students and those at Peking University, and Dilworth and Wilde (1979) and Pope (1998) also have created partnered writing experiences of this same sort. Each project has proven such collaboration to be an effective way to initiate writing and to provide forward steps in skills, structure, and even style because students are learning so much from each other.

Computers and distance learning have been credited with helping promote collaborative writing. Stock (1980) found that when students did not discuss or produce poetry face to face but electronically, they became more involved in the conversation, were more comfortable and skilled in their responses, and were less inhibited socially. Neff (1998) found that composing electronically at a distance had a profound impact on students in that the teacher's role changed abruptly. The classroom became decentered; student groups were given a little more space in which to rely on each other and themselves. Changing the context of writing had a powerful effect on the students' attitudes and their ownership of the work. Langer (1997) used collaborative peer groups in working with her New York students from the Dominican Republic. They had limited English proficiency; but by working in revising and composing groups, they gained a confidence that increased their proficiency remarkably as they progressed through the school year.

Graves (1996) reminds us of the power of collaborative writing but cautions us that able lifetime writers all share a common need—the desire for solitude, a place to write alone. We need to help students with fluency at times by using collaborative writing but must remember the place of individual invention and solitary revision in the writing process.

✎ ENVIRONMENTAL JOURNALISM

This approach to writing has deep roots in the life of the community that surrounds the English classroom. Mining the local environment for lively information is an approach conceived and given notoriety by Eliot Wigginton (1985) through his *Foxfire* books. In the midst of his attempts to solve common classroom problems, he hit on the idea of setting his students loose to explore their native ground, the North Georgia community of Rabun Gap. What Wigginton found was that he had shifted the responsibility for writing from the teacher to the students and so had changed his classroom from a place where he presided to one where all worked together as in a workshop. English teachers from urban centers to small coastal towns, from elementary schools to colleges, from classrooms of gifted students to those of slow learners have tried his strategy and found similar success. Three features of the *Foxfire* writing model are constant: student control and responsibility for the project, student interaction with the community, and student publication of their journalistic research. The community provides both resources and reasons for writing. Outstanding examples of environmental journalism have been created even in settings that seemed to possess minimal allure and support. Brunwin (1985), for example, brought his own brand of this approach from England to a sixth-grade class, which collectively wrote a historical novel about nineteenth-century gold mining in their small town of Concord, North Carolina.

Foxfire's Lessons

Students learn at least five important lessons from this writing model. They represent sequential stages of dis-

covery for those engaged in such projects, a chain reaction that drives the process toward strong writing:

- awareness of writing's public nature
- understanding of requisite detail
- sense of community
- investment of self in writing
- desire to develop a rich, well-finished product

Public Nature. The public nature of environmental, or cultural, journalism awakens students to the realization that writing can be located in a concrete world of real people and consequential events. Students base their writing on material from their known worlds and return that writing to the world by publishing it for the public. That public audience may be the class, the school, the school administration, or the community at large. Students begin to feel that the written word is more than an insular academic exercise, read and evaluated by one reader only. Writing concerns itself with a concrete reality in the world beyond the classroom and elicits the attention of the same people who read the local paper or a national magazine.

Requisite Detail. Writing based on oral histories drives the writer toward specific and detailed content. The available material is as rich as the students' genuine interest and curiosity. With sensitive and probing questions, anecdotes of community history and folklore open onto a more personal and nuanced history. Student journalists may even begin to realize others' intrinsic interest in the material and their responsibility to the person interviewed. The challenge then becomes to distill the personal account into a cogent and effective form.

Sense of Community. Because of their natural ties with their subjects in the community, students often feel more invested in their own communal history. As they publish their findings to that community, a cycle develops. Students discover an interest in people and events that they once did not know or notice, and they find a way to express that interest. The broader community, through the interviews and their publication, intensifies its interest in the work of the school. This interest prompts students to take themselves and their work more seriously.

Self-Investment. When students know their past, care about the people who are the repositories of that past, and tender it in the present, they write with a greater certainty of purpose. As they engage in the actualities of real lives and invest themselves in the project, writers develop a personal stake. The product of environmental journalism grows from individual and collective sources, but it has a good chance of being personally *owned* by each contributor to it.

Finished Product. When the first four steps are thoroughly undertaken, the final step naturally follows. If the writer's investment has become deep and personal, then review, revision, and proofreading are self-motivated. When writers know that their representation of a part of the community will return to the full community, they want to get it right. As for students in a play or concert, rehearsal goes on outside class time. Environmental journalism provides a rare opportunity for English students to perform. Their performance is important and provides strong motive for doing it well.

Interviewing

Interviews are at the heart of environmental journalism. What might students seek in such interviews? One common answer is a record of the crafts and tools of the past. A list of other topics that explore a community's rich lore include the following:

- lost customs
- famous visitors/infamous local citizens
- mysterious occurrences
- ornery folk/wily characters
- games/entertainment
- old wives' tales/magical cures
- religious observances
- transportation
- famous romances/infamous feuds
- clever tricks/practical jokes
- local idioms
- natural disasters

Most students know little or nothing about these topics, and the community at large knows very little more. Students' families and older acquaintances can be rich sources of other topics. Many communities have a briefer or less picturesque history. Cussler (1987) had her sophomores do an oral history of the Vietnam War, an event of which they had "no memory and little knowledge" (p. 66). We know teachers who have used the school culture as the historical source, interviewing administrators, cooks, custodians, secretaries, teaching assistants, and teachers.

Examples and guidelines for interviewing can be found in Wigginton's (1985) book about his *Foxfire* experience, *Sometimes a Shining Moment; Sea Chest,* an award-winning publication from the Cape Hatteras School (Buxton, North Carolina) about life on North Carolina's outer banks; Earl Seidman's (1991) *Interviewing;* and sources from the field of radio and television journalism. Useful beginning interviewing points for students include the following:

1. *Preview.* Learn as much as you can about the topic and the respondents before the interview.
2. *Plan.* Develop a loose strategy for the sequence of small topics you will cover with your respondent.
3. *Engage.* Demonstrate your personal interest in the respondent and the material explored in the interview process.
4. *Narrow.* Move from the beginning point that is personal and general to an examination of particular detail.
5. *Record.* Remember details and special phrases and use tape recorders when they do not interfere with the relationship.
6. *Transcribe.* Turn the recording or the remembered details into an accurate, progressive, and readable narrative or a smooth question-and-answer column.
7. *Transform.* Change the narrative or question-and-answer format to an essay that uses essential details to create an exposition of the topic.

In one example of environmental journalism, teachers Louella Caison and Phyllis Younts at Farmer School, in Randolph County, North Carolina, and their classes came up with the idea of creating a calendar featuring twelve senior citizens of the month, with brief biographies based on student interviews. They expected the calendar to sell because of its self-evident usefulness and, more important, because of its community interest. Other writing uses could also be made of such material. Students could be asked to read over the entire group of twelve biographies and write an essay on cultural change, language, or the collision of past and present. In this manner, the discrete portraits could be transformed into an expository essay rich in texture and detail.

Wigginton's temporary experiment to engage and energize his rural students turned into a learning strategy applicable to any population. Krueger (1988) attributes its wide-ranging success to its adaptability to different geographical locations, the flexibility of its products (from single experiments to ongoing publications), its transferability to diverse age groups and ability levels, and its crossdisciplinary appeal. Invitation to Reflection 12–1 offers you the opportunity to imagine your own class in environmental journalism.

Invitation to Reflection 12–1

You wish to use environmental journalism in a two-semester class of tenth-grade average English students. You plan to publish a journal of community pieces. How do you imagine designing this course? Make your choices by answering the following questions (modified from Krueger [1988]).

1. Will you, the editors, or the entire class make publication decisions?
2. How will production decisions be made in the publication of your journal?

3. Will you, students, or the community come up with ideas for articles?

4. What are the most likely sources for the articles in your journal?

5. Will interviews, libraries, or community research be the source of information?

6. How will the students gather information for their articles?

7. What techniques will your students use before they begin to write an article?

8. How much of any given article will be written in your classroom under your supervision?

9. Will you use peer editors before writing begins, during writing, during revision, or only for final publishing?

Contemporary Excavations

Stock's (1995) *dialogic curriculum* changes the students' investigations from looking into the past to questioning the present. Nelms (2000) reports that students interrogate their own community and then "tell their own stories" by "identifying issues, conducting investigations, reporting results, and publishing their products" (p. 54). As a result, alienation and cynicism are transformed into genuine concern. Nelms has such respect for this new approach to writing that he lists Stock's idea as one of the five richest contributions to the field of English education in the last decade.

Recently Chiseri-Strater and Sunstein (1997) and others have added an anthropological dimension to the environmental approach to writing. Their student ethnographers invade a town, truck stop, or shopping mall to take the measure of that particular culture and report it in a compelling narrative. Zollo (1997), for example, has a piece entitled "Friday Night at Iowa 80" that explores the "texts" of a lively truck stop that has become a culture center for interstate truckers. "Strike a Pose" (Downing, 1997) offers readers a close look into the world of "Photo Phantasies" that includes a collection of twelve artifacts (including a map of the store, a promotional flyer, a poem posted on the proprietor's wall, and transcripts of a conversation with a customer) that collectively spell out the nature of the culture. *Field Working* (Chiseri-Strater & Sunstein, 1997) presents a detailed description of this new step in the environmental approach to writing; Moffett would call it "words on world." The world as it is becoming is the focus of writing—not just the world as it was. The responses of the anthropologist to our shimmering world carry us beyond the means of the archeologist in exploring the wonders of our past. Some teachers believe that such a broad definition of text takes us just a bit further down the slippery slope that negates serious texts altogether and leaves us doing the work of social studies teachers. Others see this development as the perfect way to enliven a classroom.

◌ RIGHT WRITING

When Piaget looked at the mind, he saw it through the eyes of his zoological training; he saw it as a growing organism. Neuropsychologists such as Ornstein (1972) have looked at its structure and its ways of processing information to come up with another understanding of the mind. Rico (1983) wants teachers to employ the "talent of the two hemispheres in their proper sequence and in their proper interplay" (p. 10). She calls the left (analytical) hemisphere the *sign mind* and the right (artistic) hemisphere the *design mind*.

Left Hemisphere	Right Hemisphere
Parts (Sign)	*Connectedness (Design)*
explanation	images, rhythm
clarity	recurring pattern
sequence	metaphor

Rico identifies the artistic design mind as the "stepchild" of schools. She believes that through simple processes, she can bring most students in her classrooms into contact with the right hemispheric wholeness found in the writing of children and poets. Her major working tool comes from an associational linking of ideas and images in a roadmap-like design she calls *clustering*. She claims that clustering can help students write with greater ease and authenticity because it works toward wholeness. The fragmented use of grammar, the frustration of mechanics, and the isolation of most vocabulary study are all products of left hemisphere–dominated approaches. She believes that both hemispheres must work in harmony but that the right hemisphere's search for connections and patterns must be allowed to work freely and first. Without both minds at work, writing will fail; but writers must turn off the nagging sign mind at some point in the process, or it will wholly quell the design mind.

Rico Clusters

Rico's (1983) book of exercises propels students toward whole-mind writing. Two exercises—clustering words alone and clustering with art—suggest her approach. In the first, she sets the design mind free by asking students to focus on a kernel word, such as *popcorn* or *revenge* (it can be concrete or abstract), and then begin to allow associations to rise out of the focal point. Figure 12–3 records the associations that arose when one of us played with *popcorn*. The design mind has run free here. (It's run amok, you might say, but that would be your sign mind talking.) Rapid responses are important. Rico promises that the process "unfolds from a center like ripples." She considers it most important that the process begin with a word at the center of a blank page. She recommends doodling or darkening lines if the free association process slows down. The artistic play relaxes you and lets you exhaust the mind's store momentarily. When the

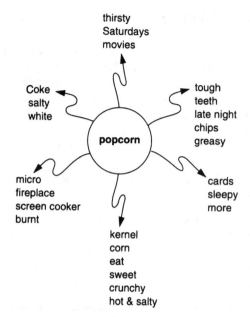

thirsty
Saturdays
movies

Coke
salty
white

tough
teeth
late night
chips
greasy

popcorn

micro
fireplace
screen cooker
burnt

cards
sleepy
more

kernel
corn
eat
sweet
crunchy
hot & salty

FIGURE 12–3 Focal point associations

process is completed, Rico says you'll sense what the mind maps tell you to write. Glance at the cluster a few seconds and then write away. No stopping. The mental footwork has charted a course that you cannot know but that will lead to something.

An even more productive technique of clustering juxtaposes the process with evocative art such as that of Cezanne, Giacometti, Klee, van Gogh, Turner, Rembrandt, or Whistler. New works exhibited in a local art gallery can have the same power. In this exercise, Rico tells students to let the design mind pore over the work of art until a dominant impression is formed. With a painting such as Goya's *The Third of May, 1808,* that impression might be fear, death, tyranny, or even darkness. Her instructions are to relax and let the eyes play over the painting. After scanning it, students take the feeling or dominant impression and use it as the nucleus from which they generate a cluster of images. She tells them to look at the central word and return with it to scan the picture. Then, after a short period, a sense of what to write about will emerge. At this point, she has students write nonstop for eight to ten minutes. Rico reports that some of the very best results she has had were from a class of tough, nonverbal ninth graders. The right writing approach makes the unthinkable happen.

Other Paths

The world of graphic organizers and concept maps makes use of the power of the right brain to help students understand and then express themselves. Character relationships, arrangement of arguments, and structural elements of novels can be made vivid by use of such graphic organizers. Senge (2000) creates a whole host of graphic organizers that help people present ideas in writing and even prompt clarification of complex constructs. Behavior over time graphs, causal file diagrams, and other nonlinguistic representations provide real insights for students confronting complex relationships, as he demonstrates by charting the young boys' progressively brutal behavior in *Lord of the Flies.*

Dellinger (1982) offers another extremely effective way to reach the design mind through the use of photographs of striking people. In the prospector and the child activity, each student is given a photo of an old prospector or a sad child (or any other dissimilar and provocative pair). Working with a partner, each student writes a monologue as if he or she were the child or the prospector. Students paired as prospector and child read their monologues to each other. They talk about how they see the characters in the monologues. Then, as a team, they write a dialogue in which they find a common ground and speak to each other. After they read the dialogue, they plan a story line for a vignette in which the two talk in the context of the events of a story. Finally, the students read the story and discuss their sense of what it is about. They explore ideas, the characters, and the tone. Then each student writes an essay that locates something universal or public in the relationship of the pair: loneliness, differing views of time between the very old and the very young, or healing grief. Thus, students move from monologue to dialogue to story to essay. Student-selected photographs of interesting characters provide a similar structure for writing alone and then in tandem.

Wood (1985), a knowledgeable but healthily skeptical neuropsychologist, believes that much of what has been drawn from the hard research in his field has been overextended by the popularizers and practitioners. He argues that our basic tendencies toward either flight or fight are the only ones we can count on as the consequence of bilateral asymmetry. Wood characterizes those whose cognitive style is to sprawl as "cowboys"; those who focus and pinpoint are caricatured as "librarians." Those who sprawl see the big picture. Those who focus move in close to the reality at hand, dwelling on detail. Wood pictures the coordination of these brains as the left hand (right-hemisphere cowboy) holding the nail and the right hand (left-hemisphere librarian) placing a well-aimed blow to its head.

We can find a pedagogical analogy here and apply it to interpretation and writing about literature. We will use as our example Shakespeare's Sonnet 116 (page 11 in Chapter 1). You may have looked at this poem through the lens of imagery, structure, persona, metrics, or other analytical frames. You may be unaware of these tools and still have made use of them. When you examined the poem, you may have noted the metaphors of time and space that compare love to exploration and hazard; you may have been struck by the prohibitionary *not* and *never;* you may have been conscious of the writer-lover who understates in each venue. The nature of the examination appears to be to look at the particular, the discrete. Focus upon detail often seems the essential task when we analyze literature for a writing assignment.

Henry (1974) presents an alternative in his brief but explosive book *Teaching Reading As Concept Development.* His idea is to look big instead of small in reading literature. Rather than exploring only Shakespeare's sonnet, he uses it and two other poems that circle roughly the same topic: love. He selects also W. B. Yeats's "For Anne Gregory" and Anne Sexton's "The Farmer's Wife." Teaching Activity 12–1 demonstrates his method of exploration with a whole class, small groups, or individuals. We suggested other groups of two, three, and four poems in Chapter 6. We believe that this shift to the right side of the mind provokes rich and plentiful insights. Seeing three visions at once can clarify all three. Shelly Hale (1997, personal communication) was taken with this idea in her student teaching and developed other trios. She suggests the following grouping around marriage.

Adrienne Rich, "Aunt Jennifer's Tigers"
Ezra Pound, "The River-Merchant's Wife: A Letter"
e. e. cummings, "if there are any heavens my mother
   will (all by herself) have"

How many times can you recall discussing literature using such a synthetic method?

Right-Left Continuum

A last writing strategy centered on neuropsychological insights moves students from writing about concrete objects to writing about texts (Milner, 1976). It, like Hillocks's (1995) *Teaching Writing As Reflective Practice,* looks at the power of sequence and progression in writing. In hemispheric terms, this strategy invites students to begin with concrete materials (those that appeal to the global imagination and intuition) and conclude with written texts (those materials that are processed linearly, analytically, and logically). See the box below.

Cultural Artifacts. Writing in this sequence begins at the far right with seeing. Just as the artist is said to paint with the eye, not the hand, the new writer can be urged to look more closely, to write with the eye. Prime cultural artifacts (such as cheese crackers) can be set before the student to respond to with visual acuity and then verbal

Far Left	Near Left	Center Left	Center Right	Near Right	Far Right
short fiction	dramatic verse	dramatic performance	film, TV	visual arts	everyday objects, artifacts

12–1   TEACHING ACTIVITY

Exploring Common Ground

Consider Henry's three suggested poems as a unit: Shakespeare's Sonnet 116, Yeats's "For Anne Gregory," and Sexton's "The Farmer's Wife." A Venn diagram may be helpful as you explore what is common to two (*A, B,* or *C*) and what is central to all (*X*).

Common ground among the poems might emerge through questions such as the following:

■ Do you find any aspect of love upon which all *three* poets agree (*X*)?

■ Do any *two* poets perceive common qualities in the love relationships between men and women (*A, B,* or *C*)?

■ Which poets appear to have more realistic views of love? Which have more idealized views?

■ Are any cynical?

■ Which view of love appeals most to you? Why?

■ Do you sense a dialogue in any of these poems? Whom is the narrator addressing?

■ Imagine all of the narrators gathered together. What would you say to them together and as individuals?

■ Which of the other two narrators might Sexton choose for her husband?

■ Which poem would you send to someone you loved? Why do you make that choice?

precision. When such a limited visual space is established, response is intensified. Such graphic concentration builds a reportorial confidence that infuses the student's writing. Most students know that their eyes are as sharp as anyone else's and that they do not have to make any ingenious interpretation beyond their range of vision.

Visual Arts. Visual arts lie at the near-right position, so the global process is still primary. Ideas and generalizations take a back seat to sensorial experience. The object is processed immediately; the mind goes from line, shape, and color directly to meaning. Students who have not studied or even seen the memorable still lifes of American painter William Harnett's work (1848–1892) can catalog many of the tricks the artist has massed to convey the sense of reality in his canvas.

Film and Television. Film and television are dominated by visual immediacy, but they also have a left-brained verbal element. Not surprisingly, these are the media that are compelling to most adolescents. Students easily respond to the visual intensity; yet because of the verbal intrusion, these media function as a halfway house in the move from right (visual) to left (verbal).

Dramatic Performance. The kinship between dramatic performance and film (or television) is obvious. It is close kin to textual literature because it is read as well as seen, but it is distinct from literature because there is no author who mediates the reality or compounds the complexity. This right-brained quality makes us use it before other textual forms in this composition continuum.

Dramatic Verse. At near left, perhaps surprisingly, comes what we call dramatic verse. This readable poetry, which adds voices and action located in particular time and space, comes before fiction because it is more immediate and intense. Students can respond to a reasonable and provocative poem almost as they might to a work of visual art; it stands before them all at once. In all poetry, the spatial quality is more significant than it is in fiction. But because most poetry is highly condensed, intense, and intellectual, it requires left-brain processing and thus resides near the extreme edge of the continuum.

Short Fiction. Fiction, on the far left, requires full left-hemisphere attention; but it can be used to promote writing that ignores formal matters at first—writing that attends primarily to emotional response and meaning. The Aristotelian premise of beginning with one's emotive response to the work does much to keep that focus. Centering on what Fowler (1981) refers to as "faith issues" (essential questions related to one's world view) or using developmental constructs such as those of

Kohlberg or Erikson prompts the writer to respond initially in terms of character and theme rather than more formally. When writers do write about formal concerns, students should be urged to consider them in relation to personal response and meaning. It is then that they occupy the whole of the continuum.

With this hemispheric strategy, we need neither eschew literature nor wholly adore it. Both the visual and the literal can be used at the appropriate juncture. We need merely to locate our students' places on the continuum and then offer the appropriate materials from which their writing may most freely and powerfully flow.

JOURNAL WRITING

Fader and McNeil (1968), in *Hooked on Books: Program and Proof,* describe how daily journals were used at the Maxey Training School in Michigan and resulted in students' becoming freer about expressing themselves, discovering that they had much to say, and developing confidence in their ability to do so. What was novel in the 1960s has become a growing educational phenomenon: journal writing. Other terms are used almost synonymously: *diaries, commonplace books, writing notebooks, daybooks,* and *thinkbooks.* Journals have become almost as popular in biology and math classrooms as they have in English classrooms. The downside of this popularity is that a common student complaint has become "I have to keep a journal in four of my five classes!" Why have journals become so popular with teachers? They may appear to be faddish, but their use is based on sound pedagogical principles.

Invitation to Reflection 12-2

1. What additional types of journals have you heard of being used or can you imagine using?
2. Which of these journal types do you think would best serve students' *personal* uses? Which would best serve *pedagogical* aims?
3. Consider the following list of possible purposes to be served by journal writing. Which seem important and useful? Why?
   - to make connections between personal experience and the class material at hand
   - to recapitulate the course material through identifying what has been learned, what is confusing, and what needs further study
   - to assess learning
   - to collect observations, responses, and data
   - to practice writing
   - to experiment with voice
   - to examine the self

- to clarify values
- to have an ungraded forum for writing
- to provide information about a student's feelings and understanding
- to be a repository for writing ideas and materials
- to have a chronological record of student thought and opinion during a term
- to have prompts for classroom discussion

The research of Britton et al. (1975), described in *The Development of Writing Ability, 11–18,* analyzed writing in all subject areas in British secondary schools where extended writing occurred. Two writing dimensions that Britton and his colleagues describe in detail have import for journal writing: the relation of the writer to the audience and the purpose of writing (discussed in Chapter 11).

NCTE has formulated guidelines for journal writing in most school settings that provide concrete, practical suggestions for their positive and efficient use. It suggests that students write in loose-leaf notebooks so that they can submit only the pertinent pages and keep more personal entries private. It also recommends that every time students write in class, teachers "do something active and deliberate with what they have written. For example, have volunteers read whole entries aloud, have everyone read one sentence to the whole class, have partners share one passage with each other, etc. (In each case, students who don't like what they have written should have the right to pass.) Sharing the writing in this manner gives credibility to a non-graded assignment." NCTE guidelines also suggest that in lieu of qualitative grading, teachers should quantitatively count student journals in some way, perhaps "a certain number of points, a plus added to a grade, or an in-class resource for taking tests." The guidelines advise teachers not to write a response to each entry but to skim and respond to selected entries. NCTE's final proposal is that at the end of a term, teachers "ask students to put in (a) page numbers, (b) a title for each entry, (c) a table of contents, and (d) an evaluative conclusion. This synthesizing activity requires journal writers to treat their documents seriously and to review what they have written over a whole term of study" (quoted in Newkirk, 1990, p. 276).

The promises of freedom, confidentiality, and respect all enhance the possibility of students' moving toward deeply probing journals. These three conditions deserve brief explanation.

Freedom is what drives students toward depth because when they trust that constraints and possible disapproval are removed, they may write about what truly matters. What matters is what creates good writing. They write for the purpose of expression, not transaction.

Confidentiality guarantees students' right to privacy. With this guarantee they will more likely risk writ-

ing about private thoughts and feelings. Students are often caught in the paradox of wanting total privacy with their thoughts and perceptions but, at the same time, wanting a trusted, sensitive other who knows these inner thoughts. Some teachers resolve the paradox by allowing secret journals or "flopped" journals, in which students review their writing and select pieces that they especially want a trusted teacher to read.

Respect means prizing the student with no thought of evaluating or selecting only those features that appear to be good and dismissing those that seem bad. The teacher's response can approach in the classroom what Rogers (1957) believes to be the necessary conditions for therapeutic change in the counseling encounter: genuineness, empathy, and a high level of positive regard. Journal writing removes many of the barriers between students and teachers—namely, barriers of teacher-dominated assignments and grading.

Journal writing can be particularly effective with ESL students who are hesitant to speak in class. Kooy and Chiu (1998) help ESL students overcome their language difficulties in literature study by having them first write out their thoughts about a text in reading logs. "As students read or listen to texts, they regularly stop to 'pause and think' by sketching, diagramming, listing (un)familiar words, asking questions, or stating a fact about a character or event." The reading logs "provide opportunities for bringing students' thoughts, predictions, guesses, or questions forward" (p. 83). Kooy and Wells (1996) discuss two advantages of reading logs for ESL students: (1) they allow an active, private use of language with which to consider the world of the texts; and (2) they acknowledge and validate the students' abilities to interpret and understand texts (p. 115). Kooy and Chiu (1998) believe that "[r]ecording their thinking also gives ESL students 'rehearsal' time before any discussions take place as well as a literary vocabulary that admits them to literary discussions and communities—incredibly important to newcomers to English" (p. 83).

We conclude this section with specific suggestions for journal assignments that suggest the diversity and complexity of this approach. They address two dilemmas in journal writing: how to encourage greater depth of reflection, and how to encourage experimentation and risk taking without compromising spontaneity.

Intense structures such as that developed by Progoff (1975) have been designed to promote a deep level of self-understanding. Nelson (1991) asks students to write their thoughts in two major territories: the subconscious world of dreams and fantasies (kept in a pink notebook) and the conscious world of observation and insight (kept in a yellow notebook). The two worlds are separate, but they can be fused by reading the pink and then the yellow. From the juxtaposition, students create a new journal (a blue one) and a new reality.

The choices presented in Teaching Activity 12-2 shake students from journal writing that has become too pat and invariant. For instance, a student who is always aloof and distant might be drawn toward more personal writing when dreams, aphorisms, encomiums, myths, and introspections are ordered up by fate or by date. For the sentimental writer, polemics, sarcasms, critiques, and sophistries may turn the tide. The swift rotation from mode to mode and form to form is enlivening and, once sustained for a time, can lead to exploration and discovery for a young writer.

Specific prompts for journal writing arise out of many different purposes. Probst's reader response questions posed in Chapter 2 could be used as points for reflection about specific texts, for instance. The following general writing topics are selected from those that Neenan (1989) found to be provocative with her students.

- Describe a time when you felt afraid. How did you deal with that fear? What was the outcome?
- Write a letter to God.
- Cite an instance when you have been disappointed about something. Why were you disappointed? How did you show your disappointment? Was there anything you could have done to change the situation? Explain. Who or what disappoints you the most? Why? How?
- You awaken one morning and find you have turned into an animal. You have the same mind but a different body. What animal are you? Describe your day.
- What cruelty have you seen or experienced? How did you feel about it? Are children more cruel than adults?
- What are five ways you personally exercise control or power over people or situations? Describe how you feel when this happens. Evaluate your method of control and tell whether it is negative or positive. How? Consider how you feel when others exercise control over you; also consider how you feel when you are in control of yourself. What feels best? Why?
- Write a letter to yourself today as though you were eighty. (pp. 7-12)

For some students, school writing has been so tedious and arid that reaching into the personal dimensions of emotion and imagination is the only way to remove the block to writing. Somewhere in these journaling suggestions lies a new pathway for writing for those students. They might find themselves like Frank McCourt, author of *Angela's Ashes,* who wrote: "I learned to recognize the significance in my insignificant life."

12-2　TEACHING ACTIVITY

Experimental Writing Logs

Have students make log entries three times a week during time assigned in class or as homework. Suggest a specific question or ask students to free-write. As a departure from explanatory prose forms, suggest that students experiment with one of the following forms. Collect the logs periodically every four or five weeks. Respond to, but do not grade, the work.

1. dreams	16. fantasies
2. satires	17. sarcasms
3. aphorisms	18. axioms
4. reviews	19. critiques
5. conceits	20. analogies
6. essays	21. editorials
7. polemics	22. diatribes
8. encomiums	23. panegyrics
9. fables	24. parables
10. allegories	25. myths
11. lyrics	26. verbosities
12. analyses	27. epiphanies
13. meditations	28. introspections
14. narrations	29. yarns
15. commercials	30. sophistries

∞ WRITE TO LEARN

When a history or biology teacher becomes interested in writing across the curriculum, that zeal has probably been spurred by a desire to have all students write better: fewer errors, better organization, greater clarity. At a time when teachers see all too many errors and all too few writing virtues, such enthusiasm is understandable. What they champion is learning to write, but what is even more important in schools is writing to learn. If you turn the concept around and think of writing as a tool for stronger and clearer thinking (Langer & Applebee, 1987), you can see that it is a powerful instrument for instruction in all subject areas. And because it is an instrument that will improve achievement in all subjects, it is easier to sell to all of your colleagues in history and biology.

Figure 12-4 summarizes assumptions about the connections between language and thought that have clear applications here. These assumptions suggest why writing is as relevant to a science class as it is to an English class. If math teachers can be shown how to make use of writing to help their students solidify and expand their grasp of basic or sophisticated math concepts, they will listen to your ideas and employ writing in their classes. But if you ask them to take on the job of making students write better, all but a few will politely disengage from the conversation. They may ask what you've done lately for numeracy if you ask them to help with literacy. Tierney (1990), Griffiths (1991), Fulwiler and Young (1982), and others have demonstrated countless ways to make learning deep and long-lasting through the use of writing across the curriculum. We offer two ways to use writing as a tool for learning: one from basic math and one from AP biology.

Math and Science

U.K. headmaster Neil Griffiths uses tiles to help students understand mathematical patterns and sequences. He asks students how many square tiles will be needed to surround a central tile and then how many tiles would be needed if another tile is added to the center. After each query, he directs the students to think about the problem and write down their answers. Some are confused; some challenge him about what he means by *surround* (he encourages that kind of care with words); others quickly figure the answer to be two. He then asks them how many tiles would be needed to surround the central tiles if a third tile were added. At this point he asks them to explain their answers. Some give simple answers; some see it visually; some few see it as a mathematical pattern and explain it in those terms. He uses their writing to provide a picture of their thinking so that he can identify problems and students can profit from a comparison of their thinking with their peers'.

In his AP biology class, Bob Tierney uses writing in a different way but to the same purpose: to increase understanding. He says that he never lectures longer than eight minutes because more would be lost on his students. Instead, he uses writing. During a lecture, he asks each student to take notes on the lefthand page of a spiral-bound notebook. After Tierney has completed his brief explanation and the students' pages are filled, he asks each student to divide the righthand page into a top and bottom half. On the top half he asks students to put into their own words what they have just learned. Then he asks them to divide the lower half into two equal right and left sides. The left side is to be used to answer the question "So what?" and the right side is to be used to sketch out a diagram or graphic representation of the concept just encountered. Figure 12-5 shows what the whole spread looks like in a physics lesson on volume and mass. Using all four steps to capture concepts takes longer than the traditional lecture and note-taking method does. Less ground can be covered. But Tierney's (1990) research and that of others shows that although the traditional method of lecture and note taking develops performance equal to that developed by Tierney's methods at end-of-course testing, the results two and three years later are significantly greater for those who use Tierney's methods of writing to learn.

Writing to predict what will happen in experiments, writing to capture very accurate observations, writing to define abstractions such as angles, writing to connect course concepts with personal experience, writing to express tentative understanding of a poem, writing to capture the conversation of a small group exploring why

---

FIGURE 12-4

Assumptions about language and thought

1. When people *articulate connections* between new information and what they already know, they learn and understand that new information better (Bruner, 1966).
2. When people *think and figure things out,* they do so in symbol systems commonly called languages, which are most often verbal but may also be mathematical, musical, visual, and so on (Vygotsky, 1962).
3. When people *learn,* they use all of the language modes—reading, writing, speaking, and listening; each mode helps people learn in a unique way (Emig, 1977).
4. When people *write* about new information and ideas—in addition to reading, talking, and listening—they learn and understand them better (Britton et al., 1975).
5. When people *care* about what they write and see connections to their own lives, they both learn and write better (Moffett, 1968).

FIGURE 12–5
Tierney notebook

Lecture Notes	Student Notes	
	So What	Graphic
	M	Boat in a lock
	↓	
	V	
	Volumn over Territory	

port cities are laid out differently from river cities, and writing to explain what the saying "a rolling stone gathers no moss" means and what the language intends—all of these uses of writing enhance learning and solidify concepts for your students. Mitchell (1996) offers a list of interesting writing tasks that support learning across the curriculum. We report a few of her best suggestions, which you can use to build a larger repertoire of your own.

- What would your life be like if calcium were absent from all foods?
- Which planet, aside from Earth, seems to you to be superior?
- What if your heart had only three chambers instead of four?
- In math, students could give awards to the most important formula.
- What three words best describe the Bill of Rights?

Difficult Problems

The fact that we sometimes talk our way through difficult problems illustrates the power of writing to learn. The basic idea in all of the problems posed in Figure 12–6 is to use writing to deepen the way in which students conceptualize what they are learning. Each of the tasks assigned is difficult and encourages talking and writing to solve the problem. In writing to learn, you may find your-

self working with colleagues in other disciplines; and this will have the unexpected benefit of helping you integrate the power of the full curriculum into your teaching of English. You also will find that, although you are selling writing across the curriculum as a way to help students learn, they also will learn to write because they are writing about things that they come to understand deeply. Foster (1992) calls taking writing seriously in other disciplines "the first step in the student writer's discovery that writing is purposeful human activity, not just academic labor. Personal writing subjected to serious inquiry and feedback will take on value for writers themselves, as a reflection of its value for others" (p. 174.)

CODE SWITCHING

The field of sociolinguistics provides an approach to writing instruction that addresses the issue that concerns many English teachers and an ever-larger segment of our population: that of determining "good" and "bad" grammar. Many teachers, and the public at large, want young people to speak and write inside the bounds of standard usage. They see current usage as a corruption of the norms of educated language; the teacher's charge is to teach students Standard English. As we discussed in Chapter 3, among many educators, linguists, and public figures, there is a counterargument. This group reasons

FIGURE 12–6
Write to solve

1. The captain of a Dutch cargo vessel was concerned that the water level in the canal lock was too low for his heavily loaded vessel. He was not sure what to do when the lock commandant, who spoke a language he did not understand, tried to offer a solution. A young deckhand finally came up to suggest a solution: Toss the two extremely heavy but worthless lead cylinders overboard. Should the captain follow the suggestion? If he does, will the water in the lock rise, remain the same, or fall? Explain your answer in a clear written statement.
   Use two baking tins, two batteries, water, and a pencil to test your previous thoughtful response. Be sure that the larger tin is almost 3/4 full when you start your experiment. Write your new explanation of what will happen if your experiment proved something different from what you wrote previously.
2. A camper has 3 fish to cook on her campfire and must cook each of them for 2 minutes on each side. Because she has a small grill, she can only cook 2 fish at a time. Explain in writing the most efficient sequence for cooking the 3 fish.
3. Find the next number in this series: 7, 12, 27, 72, 207, ____.
   Explain in writing how anyone can find that answer.
4. Three baskets sit on a high ledge with signs over them that correctly mark their contents: Apples, Pears, Mixed. A clever child mixes up the signs so that none of the signs correctly indicates what is actually in the basket below. The orchard owner decides to make a game of it by allowing you to reach into one of the baskets above you and, without being able to see what is in the basket, pick out one piece of fruit. The reward is that if you then can put all the signs over the correct baskets, you can have all three baskets without charge. Explain in writing how you might beat the orchard owner at this game.

---

that students have a right to their own language and the dignity that accrues to that language. Their underlying assumption is that language has no fixed and permanent rules because it is constantly changing. The criterion for judging usage is not "Is it correct?" but "Does it work in the context in which it is used?"

Program Requirements

Smitherman (1989) enumerates three standards that all strong and pluralistic language programs should embody:

- All teachers should know enough about linguistics to understand that all languages are equally effective in communicating ideas.
- All students should have their own variants from the standard affirmed while they are given an opportunity to learn the standard or mainstream language.
- All students should be required to learn a second language (for example, Spanish, Chinese, or German) from their first years in school through graduation.

Smitherman believes that second-language learning is extremely important to the cognitive development of all students; those who are Standard English users will better understand the complexity of language and the variety of languages. Furthermore, she argues, they will struggle with the same challenge posed for non–Standard English users who are asked to acquire a second language. Both groups will share the common ground of an acquired language. Her program affirms non–Standard English usage on practical and psychological grounds while acknowledging the need for using Standard English in a culture in which it is the dominant language.

Smitherman's standards offer a theoretical context for a four-step plan developed by Elifson (1977) for the Atlanta Public Schools and the employees of Coca-Cola.

Like Smitherman, Elifson's first step requires that teachers who adopt this program be well informed about the nature of the English language, its variability, and its changes over time. They must then make students understand that all language systems work equally well, although somewhat differently. They must affirm the language of all students and encourage or permit them to use that language with confidence and energy. This step must be treated seriously and handled deliberately. Varied methods should be used—for instance, a study of concrete examples of variability (sampling, polling, and interpreting the results). It is important, too, to discuss freely the value of pluralism and of a standard language system. The rewards and losses for those who do and do not have the ability to use Standard English should be explored. Elifson sees three important realities that must be affirmed in such a program:

- All language users switch dialects to fit the setting in which the language is being used.
- All languages are equally effective in transmitting ideas.
- Standard language helps to open the paths of opportunity for all students; inability to switch to the standard code in certain settings penalizes students.

With this framework of attitudes in place, students can elect to move toward possession of a second language system or dialect. They can embrace rewards of this language learning without having to disown their first language.

Switching Principles

Elifson sets up four principles to guide the process of code switching. Each is important and integral to the next:

- Select target areas in which to work.
- Make the transition to Standard English in oral, not written, language first.

- Move from wholly controlled language drills to ones that allow spontaneity of language.
- Develop the ability to switch codes by creating exercises in which students can develop consciousness of their language.

Unless attention is given to a few points at which the differences between the nonstandard and standard are most notable, students will be frustrated by the size and difficulty of the task. (In setting up a program of this type at a local high school, we used student papers as our source for sentences that departed from Standard English.) Because oral language is our most fundamental language, basic code switches can be made most readily and most lastingly if they are begun at the oral level. If students begin to talk in the standard code, their writing will likely follow suit. The reverse is not true.

Program Outline

The program begins with rather strict controls on the oral productions of students. Students hear a sentence read that was written with nonstandard usage—for example, *Rony ate a whole nother dinner.* Students then repeat the sentence by "correcting" it to standard usage using guidelines provided by the teacher. Gradually, the language under scrutiny moves from short memorized parts in plays, to planned and recorded speeches, and finally to almost wholly spontaneous talk. Control for the analysis, critique, and change also moves from teacher to student. The progression of Elifson's activities is as follows:

- pattern drills
- short, memorized dramas
- planned speeches
- unmemorized, planned skits
- planned oral speeches
- controlled discussion
- role playing
- impromptu speeches

For the program to work, consciousness must develop. If language change and variability are explored with openness and without judgment, language has a chance to become interesting to students. If, however, it is treated in an entirely prescriptive way, as rules to be mastered, a healthy consciousness of language may well be stymied and experimentation stifled. Students are left with no interest, desire, or method for exploring their own language. Rather, they become self-conscious and silenced in the presence of those they consider to be grammarians.

Four principles undergird the work of the class: target areas are well selected, transitions are oral, control is released, and consciousness of language is developed. In our teaching we have adapted Elifson's progression. We laid the groundwork in discussions of language change and variability, discussed honestly the power of all languages to communicate, explored the value of code switching, and then began a regimen of five-minute pattern drills. Each day began with a short drill based on eight sentences in the target area, such as the following:

1. Braden come home last night.
2. Willy run fast.
3. Mozelle done eat.
4. Jack and Fred they can't stay tonight.
5. Sally bes mad at me.
6. Wanda ain't going with us.
7. Felisha ain't got none.
8. We might could find some.

A sample week of lessons is presented in Figure 12–7. Through this series of five days, each student works in the target area; moves from oral to written language; works with controlled and then somewhat more spontaneous language; and develops self-consciousness by the repetition, the emphasis, and the markings. The short version of this program used in our schools proved to be remarkably effective in a period of weeks. It resulted not only in control of standard features but also in greater confidence in writing. While the success of such programs has been remarkable, the need to approach them with deliberate organization and care is imperative.

FIGURE 12–7
Pattern drill

Monday. The teacher gives each student a list of ten Standard English sentences with the target area underlined. The teacher has the same sentences, but the target areas are nonstandard expressions. The teacher says the same faulty sentence, and students respond by saying the sentence emphasizing the underlined standard form.

Tuesday. The teacher reads the same faulty sentence, and the students respond using a new sheet with the ten Standard English sentences but without the targeted area marked. Again they respond by emphasizing the area of correction.

Wednesday. The students have no sheet but respond to the faulty sentence emphasizing the correct usage as they have on the first two days.

Thursday. The students have a sheet with the nonstandard feature underlined and are asked to write the sentence correctly above the faulty one.

Friday. On the final day, the students have the same sheet but with unmarked nonstandard sentences. They write standard versions above the nonstandard sentences.

SENTENCE COMBINING

In the middle of the twentieth century, at about the time that structural grammar was moving into classroom textbooks, another system for understanding the English language was developing. This system, known as *generative* (or *transformational*) *grammar*, moved from describing syntactic structures to understanding the deeper structure that produced them. By delineating the mental processes underlying the transformation, which could produce an infinite and varied number of sentences from a few basic structures, grammarians sought to explain the intricacies of language.

Noam Chomsky's (1957) *Syntactic Structures* gave the most prominent description of the formal structures of the English language as something we acquire or absorb without training: All sentences originate as simple declarations or "kernels," which comprise the deep structure of those sentences. The basic kernel is S-V-O: Rain (*subject*) pelts (*verb*) sidewalks (*object*). Various transformations of these kernels, through negatives, appositives, and possessives, for instance, produce more complex surface structures. The basic task for generative or transformational grammar was to articulate the rules by which the basic kernel sentences could be transformed into all the possible sentences of English. Roberts (1956), for example, in *Patterns of English,* distilled from the English language a set of twenty basic sentences.

English teachers were faced with an uncomfortable question: Which grammar should we teach, traditional or generative? Many teachers and educators, reluctant to be drawn into a grammarians' war, found much traditional grammar clear and useful yet discerned possibilities for writing instruction in generative grammar. Linguistic research (Chomsky, 1968) suggested that students at a certain stage of maturity (about fifth grade) have acquired a template for comprehending complex sentences by merely having heard them repeatedly. They understand syntactic complexity *before* they use it.

Sentence combining was the classroom application of these new grammatical insights. Some teachers believed that students might be taught to use a wider repertoire of sentence structures imprinted on them to improve the syntactic maturity of their writing. Although its original popularity has declined, it remains an effective teaching strategy for encouraging syntactic growth. It invites students to *build* rather than *repair* sentences.

Christensen (1967) experimented with having students generate strong sentences from basic sentence structures. Mellon (1969) suggested rules for transforming two or three simple sentences and then combining them into one sentence. Strong (1973) and O'Hare (1975) simplified the process by dropping the rules and merely asking students to combine sets of kernels to form new complex sentences.

Strong Kernels

"Motorcycle Pack," shown here, is a typical set of Strong's (1973) kernels. Individuals or groups can combine the short sentences within each cluster by adding coordinating and subordinating structures or by embedding modifiers.

Strong's Kernels: Motorcycle Pack*

1. We could hear them coming.
2. They were way off in the distance.
3. They were winding down the road.
4. The road was through the mountains.
5. The road was east of town.

6. The sound made us think of power saws.
7. But the sound was more sustained.
8. The sound was deeper.
9. The sound got louder.

10. The first one broke into view.
11. He was at the edge of town.
12. The edge is where the brush is thick.
13. The brush was full of shadows.

14. The others swarmed behind him.
15. The others rapped their pipes.
16. The others brought the noise.
17. The noise was like a wave.

18. The leader geared down.
19. The gearing down was at the grocery store.
20. The leader set the pace.
21. The pace was swaggering.
22. The pace was through the middle of town.
23. The leader did not glance to the side.
24. The leader did not acknowledge the people.
25. The people watched from the sidewalk.

26. The leader personified seriousness.
27. The leader personified bravado.
28. The seriousness was leather.
29. The bravado was chrome.

30. The others stared at his back.
31. The others tried to imitate him.
32. The others tried their best.

33. He lifted his right hand.
34. The lifting was at the highway.
35. The highway belonged to the state.
36. The highway intersected Main Street.

37. The pack leaned to the right.
38. The pack followed him.
39. The pack accelerated toward the road.
40. The road was open.

---

*From W. Strong, 1973, *Sentence combining: A composing book.* New York: Random House. Reprinted with permission.

41. Exhaust ripped the air.
42. The exhaust was from motorcycles.
43. The exhaust was like an insult.

44. The air healed.
45. The healing took all day.

Teaching Activity 12–3 is an example of how sentence combining might be organized as a class activity using Strong's "Motorcycle Pack."

Other Sources

The manuals of Strong and others are obvious sources for interesting kernel sentences that engage students. In *English: Writing and Skills,* Winterowd and Murray (1985) used sentence combining in a general language arts text. They combined aspects of traditional, structural, and generative grammar that they considered to be most helpful in enabling students to understand how the English language functions. They also included exercises that encourage sentence variety and fluency by the joining of sentences. Like the best of generative grammar, Winterowd and Murray's strategy leads students to ex-

plore the deep structure of the language, the mental processes at work in their organization of thoughts into language, and ways to connect their thoughts more clearly and fluently.

Teachers and students themselves can provide sentence kernels that appeal to the special interests of the students who use them. For instance, a teacher might present a work of art, such as van Gogh's *Self-Portrait,* and ask students to note its details:

- The man's eyes are glazed.
- His ear is bandaged.
- His chin is covered with a light beard.
- His hair is very wavy.
- The coat buttons are bright red.

Once their observations are noted, they are asked to combine their list into one sentence. Or more personally still, a teacher might ask students simply to describe what they observe in the classroom or during an athletic contest or pep rally. (This exercise also encourages close observation of detail and the use of clear, precise language and requires a more active engagement in the kind of thinking so important to writing.) After students have

---

12–3   TEACHING ACTIVITY

Sentence Combining

Small Group

- Divide students into trios.

- Each individual in a trio takes the simple, choppy, unmodified sentences of each cluster in "Motorcycle Pack" and combines them into one complex sentence.

- The trio selects the most appealing sentence of each cluster. (In one trio, for example, the first student might arrange the first cluster like this: *We could hear them coming from far off in the distance winding down the mountain road east of town.* The second student might come up with another sentence: *From a distance we could hear them winding down the road through the mountain east of town.* And the third might write yet another: *We could hear them coming way off in the distance as they were east of town winding down the mountain road.*)

- The trio reads the three sentences and decides which it likes best.

- They then combine the ten extended sentences to create a compressed and rich narrative about the motorcycle pack.

Whole Class

- Each group reads its narrative to the whole class.

- The class compares the stories for their fluency and complexity.

Individual

- Individuals write several sentences that use their own content but imitate the structure of their favorite combined sentences.

recorded their observations, they can take the simple sentence constructions and turn them into mature complex sentences.

Teachers have another source of kernel sentences in students' own writing. If students overuse simple constructions, a string of their own sentences (or just two) can help them realize the power of the approach for improving their fluency, clarity, and style. Hillocks's (1995) meta-analysis of sixty-five studies of writing instruction cites sentence combining as more effective than any other strategy except inquiry. (The use of rubrics was the only other instructional method that was its equal.) Other quantitative research, such as that of Combs (1977) and Daiker, Kerek, and Morenberg (1986), indicates that sentence combining produces improvement in sentence complexity across all ages measured. It provides a strategy that many students need and a concrete skill that all students can learn and confidently apply. Sentence combining also demystifies questions of rhetorical style and allows inexperienced writers a point of entry into talking about it.

Teachers can also use the technique to sensitize students to the constructions of professional writers. We have seen teachers decombine interesting or important sentences from the text under study and then have students recombine and compare theirs with the original. Another technique asks students to choose several memorable sentences written by the professional and to imitate the structure of those sentences with content of their own. Another strategy is to abridge the sentence of such a writer, mark the deleted phrases, and ask students to expand the sentence at those marks. We know a teacher who even has her students recombine Hemingway's sentences!

⌾ VOCABULARY GROWTH

Writing skills that promote organization, development, and coherence are essential to the deep structure of a piece of writing. Other features seem far less essential and are sometimes left out of the equation of good writing. (These are sometimes called surface features and receive surface attention.) We know, however, from the Hairston (1981) study of usage that a preponderance of professionals who read the sentences in her survey were troubled by problems of usage, punctuation, and vocabulary. Vocabulary can significantly enhance or diminish writing, and it can be improved by good teaching.

A student's vocabulary growth can be seen as a natural process that continues as he or she moves through all of the school years. We know, however, that vocabulary growth depends on the student's environment: It can flourish or wither. The six-year-old brings as many as 6,000 words to school that are clearly not the result of direct parental instruction (de Villeas & de Villeas, 1978); rather, they are gleaned from the word world that surrounds the child. We know that voracious readers gather the strongest vocabularies. Students who live in talk-rich environments in which new words are used repeatedly in lively and enticing discourse will also grow robust vocabularies. The consciousness awakened by seeing words in print may give some edge to the early readers; however, seeing words in print enables any secondary student to respond more to informed vocabulary instruction. Adolescent learners are developing a new consciousness of themselves and of language that was not a part of their elementary years.

Our basic question is, then, "How shall we best contribute to this natural process during the secondary school years?" We know that our contribution to the process will not be large as a percentage of total vocabulary, but it can be important. Although the public's ire about low standardized test scores has prompted serious work in this area of the secondary English curriculum, that attention has often resulted in a one-dimensional approach to teaching vocabulary. Educators are developing better ways to improve the vocabulary of adolescents.

Moffett's and Wagner's ideas about reception and production of language (discussed throughout this text) are seminal here. Students have a reception or decoding vocabulary that differs from their production or encoding vocabulary: One they understand only partially; the other they feel free to use. What they risk in one situation, they won't risk in another. Our job, as with sentence combining, is to help them move the larger *reception* vocabulary over to *production* so that they will risk using newly incorporated words to empower their utterances, private and public, oral and written. The following four strategies for vocabulary development grow out of this belief.

Acquisition

The span from acquisition to semantics moves from unconscious collection to playfulness with language. Acquisition is influenced by three important conduits for new language: texts, talk, and television. While written words are the only way to acquire spelling power, the two other modes can be engaged to propel vocabulary growth. And because we believe that meaning precedes form, we also believe that when students find new words they want to use, they more readily incorporate them into their working vocabulary. All three domains should be enlisted to help students find words that attract them. It is important to think in the broadest terms in considering texts. Books ranging from William Steig's and E. B. White's rich children's literature to Stephen Jay Gould's nonfiction to E. Annie Proulx's contemporary novel *The Shipping News* are loaded depositories. Because poetry is semantically rich, new words are plentiful there, as they are in any compressed language. You can urge your students to read insurance policies, bonds, users' manuals, and guarantees to see if this mundane world of print does not also yield unexpected word dividends.

Text print is important, for it may imprint vocabulary more deeply than the other two modes; but the other two conduits are livelier sources for most students, so attachment is strong when they, too, are used. To make acquisition most available for your students, oral interaction is essential. This can include the fascinating world of television talk shows, where guests, hosts, and callers provide a potpourri of language; but it is probably best that your students glean vocabulary from talk with each other and with people outside the classroom. The process of acquiring new vocabulary is natural, but you can promote the natural process by the opportunities you give students to confront new and engaging language. The list of people who can provide that enrichment is endless, but four likely ones are elders, specialists, creators, and outsiders. The best class formats are probably similar to those presented in Chapter 4 and others that make sense to you and engage your students with these people and their language. Elders have a rare language by dint of time spent with it and a different set of experiences and circumstances. Even their special vocalization makes their language memorable. Specialists obviously must speak with some general, popular language terms; but their specialties as doctors, pilots, or electronic engineers make new language inevitable. Creators, with their inventive styles, will likely use creative language; and outsiders such as libertarians, the Amish, sports heroes, and other fascinating people who don't conform make fine language bearers.

Television, film, and other modes in which words and pictures are combined offer your students many occasions to encounter new language. This is especially true when the material is less narrative and more analytical. *Nova, 60 Minutes, Larry King Live,* and many other shows offer goldmines of new words. But film adaptations of books also work well, as do the animated zany Dr. Seuss stories, especially when they are faithful to the author's language.

Morphology

This is a more abstract process; but you can move your students to a consciousness of some of the core features of the language around them, and they will then be more sensitive to it, understand it, and adopt it. It is true that many students do not do as well with parts as with wholes; but if this approach were productive with no more than 25 percent of your students, it would still be worthwhile. The idea is to work with two primary techniques and two basic elements to expand students' vocabulary: roots and stems. If you give your students a

sense of words' antecedents in classical language, they are given a key that unlocks many verbal treasure chests. For instance, the root words *pose, geo, scribe,* and *bio* are basic language features that refer to the hard reality of the nouns and verbs *lead, earth, write,* and *life.* If your students can transpose what they can guess into clear and useful knowledge, they take command of a sizable list of words. It won't be sheer memory work. With this logical root knowledge, as well as knowledge of stems, they can begin a growing list of words. The stems are not central, as are the roots, but they are the inflections or redirections of words, which, along with roots, create the semantic load of the word at hand. Prefixes and suffixes, the two stem types, are almost never interchangeable. Understanding the word *interchangeable* itself is a perfect example of morphological knowledge, with its double stem on either side of the root *change.*

Two primary techniques that are useful parts of this analytical process are analogies and context clues. Students unconsciously use these two techniques from birth to soak up language; but they can be made explicit, like the use of morphology, to further activate this process. Students can be taught to use analogies and parallels to guess what words mean. These can cut across cultures or can reside in the same language. By the same token, students can look at the context to predict what a word may mean. Such prediction works increasingly well when students see the same words in different contexts because the contexts let them rule out some guesses and bolster others. These techniques and their features of analysis are bits of prior knowledge that your students possess and that you can bring to consciousness to help them develop their vocabularies more effectively.

Immersion

This is the simple technique of being dunked into a new culture so that language is acquired and mastered as a means of survival, of getting through the day. It is like the acquisition strategy but with an added dose of consciousness and even mastery to ensure that students come into contact with words.

Word Dots. This may be an approach that some of your students have already developed on their own, but most students need to be prompted. You merely ask your students to keep a pocket dictionary with them at all times so that they can place a dot in front of every new word that they hear or see, whether it is on TV or in a book. You can ask small groups to take a few minutes each week to compare notes from their dictionaries or ask the whole class for spectacular words that they've dotted during the past seven days. You can ask them to make a bimonthly checkup whereby they make a count of dots over a specified ten dictionary pages to see which student or group has the most collected.

Class Webster. This is a delegated approach to word collection in which you appoint or students elect a word hawk from the class who keeps a list of all of the new words that pop up in class or out of it. This is a communal approach in that it is a collective list, one that all students contribute to and is the same for all students. The advantage is that all or parts of the list can be used by students as they write group stories or imaginary letters to the editor, or make some other interesting use of the word collection. The disadvantage is that it is not a list made by individual students. A compromise that works is to let groups of five or six appoint their own word hawk to collect a slightly different set of words.

Semantics

The semantic strategy is a potpourri of ideas tied together by the basic notion that words represent meaning beyond themselves and that meaning is, after all, what is most attractive about words. With this in mind, we present in Figure 12–8 a sample of semantic descriptors that generate and create consciousness about words. (See Chapter 3 for more discussion of this idea.)

We believe that students who become engaged in looking at language in these challenging and interesting ways will, with your help, noticeably increase their vocabulary and, more important, their interest in gleaning and using new language in their everyday discourse. We believe that each of the four strategies makes sense, but what makes the most sense is the managed use of the entire set of strategies. Eclecticism is not a fault when the strategies are not mutually exclusive or contradictory but reinforcing.

⏤STUDENT RESEARCH PAPERS

Our profession has long debated the proper role of the research paper in the English classroom, but you may pause to ask the prior question: Should it have any place at all? It requires careful research, in fact, to locate articles in the *English Journal* advocating traditional research papers. Many secondary English programs have either dropped the requirement or turned all but the mechanics over to other subject areas. For decades even its marginal place in the English curriculum has been questioned by those who argue that secondary "students are not equipped to carry on meaningful literary research" and that "reasonably correct and creative writing—the goal of instruction in composition—cannot be developed by teaching students to regurgitate the thoughts of others" (Taylor, 1965, p. 126). Even more critically, Stevenson (1972) sees these long papers as "a rite of passage" that is in fact "an exercise in deception" because of the woeful lack of emphasis on primary materials (p. 1030). We add to this older critique the fear that made-to-order research papers only line the pockets of e-business hucksters.

In spite of these ample hesitations, the research paper's credentials as an instrument of instruction are defensible if its essential shape rather than its superficial form is kept in view. Its role in encouraging critical thinking and the close examination of fact is compatible with the instructional design of any English classroom. Schroeder (1966) offers a slightly different approach, arguing that the two defining components of the research paper are "library research techniques and intellectual investigation of a subject" (p. 898). He goes on to break down the development of the necessary skills into a

FIGURE 12–8
Semantic awareness

1. *Etymology:* finding the origins of words and phrases (*dope, stole my thunder, kitty-corner,* and *becoming*)
2. *Hobble de Hoy:* creating multiple fanciful or realistic definitions of words that have dropped out of the language since the 1933 edition of the OED (*yamph, gumple-foisted, tic-polonga*)
3. *Doublespeak:* listing examples of euphemistic pleasantries and obfuscating bureaucratic language and discussing their intent as insidious or salutary (*passed on, sorties, misspoke*)
4. *Jargon:* exploring the language of special groups and its necessity or pretension (*throughout, spin doctor, burnout*)
5. *Limpids:* investigating bland basal verbs and their loss of power, and offering helpful replacements (*do, have, eat, run*)
6. *Place names:* explaining the unusual names of towns, rivers, and other geographic entities (*Paris, Texas; Buffalo, New York; Mt. Rushmore*)
7. *Superchargers:* examining hyperbolic journalistic language to replace it with neutral and opposing language (*rabble, crowd, throng*)
8. *Synontinuums:* creating lists of almost-equivalent words that students put on their own continuums (*happy-glad-joyous-ecstatic-peaceful-content*)
9. *Faces-hands-feet:* acting out words with one of these three parts of the body for classmates to guess (*bellicose, anxiety, jealous*)
10. *Slanguage:* noting language that has passed from unacceptable slang to public parlance (*bounds, snooze, narc*)
11. *Amphibonyms:* locating words that are spelled the same but that shift from verbs to nouns when the stress moves forward or the vowel lengthens (*record, permit, bow, lives*)
12. *Technese:* noticing language that has invaded our daily lives by way of the high-tech world (*interface, leverage, fax, deplane*)

four-year continuum: ninth-grade library skills, tenth-grade paraphrasing and documentation, eleventh-grade controlled research, and twelfth-grade topic restriction and free research. Others have suggested an intensive six-week period of instruction on the conventional research paper to address matters such as limiting the topic, taking an argumentative stance, and learning the art of documentation. Some have suggested more unconventional research strategies such as audiocassettes and mixed-media presentations as possible alternatives to the traditional format. But are these manipulations of the surface rather than suggestions for research papers that differ at a more essential level? We suggest the following six models for the research paper that we believe differ in kind and might be appropriate for secondary English students.

Controlled Sources Research

This approach has been one of the most popular in English classrooms, for it allows the teacher to thoroughly survey the source material and ensures that all students come into contact with a wide range of usable materials. The approach makes use of texts such as the Norton Critical Edition of *Moby-Dick,* which contains raw historical material (letters, analogues, sources, reviews, and criticism), and more narrow casebooks such as the Merrill text of "A Rose for Emily" and Macmillan's *Huck Finn and His Critics,* which contain critical essays without the other historical paraphernalia. Because these texts can be expensive, many teachers have turned to teacher-made casebooks as an alternative. No matter which of these you employ, your students will encounter the disadvantage of failing to get involved in original research. On the other hand, they will learn how to extract, evaluate, and synthesize materials, which may be more essential research components for secondary students to engage in initially.

Textual Analysis

This approach offers students the opportunity to locate and carefully examine a definable body of writing so as to discern differentiations, comparisons, or progressions within that corpus of material. Such examinations can be performed on both literary material (for instance, a short story collection such as Malamud's *The Magic Barrel,* selected poetry of the Harlem Renaissance, or the fiction of *Redbook* magazine) and nonliterary material (for instance, Franklin Roosevelt's inaugural addresses, four standard American dictionaries, George Will's editorials, or Elton John's lyrics). The emphasis is on primary materials and students' ability to assess them. This analytical approach allows students' interests to be expressed in the research they select yet makes it possible for students in all but the most isolated

locales to engage in the *search* part of research. The Internet can diminish even that isolation.

Historical Synthesis

This approach demands an even more complete range of source materials, but it allows students to uncover both primary and secondary sources as a means of arriving at an informed answer to a given question. Students might, for example, be asked to investigate the details (who, when, where, how, and why) of an isolatable event in history, such as the death of Hitler. They might be asked as well to make use of varying kinds of sources and to become involved in evaluating the reliability of those sources. Even when they work with a limited supply of sources, students have the chance to be confronted by the researcher's most essential tasks: locating, evaluating, and synthesizing material.

Contemporary Issues Research

This kind of research offers students even more topical subject matter to investigate, but it also broadens the scope of the research, thus decreasing teacher awareness of the material under consideration and placing greater demands on students in locating source material. Students involved in research of this kind might be found probing local problems such as zoning, child abuse, or allocation of funds by the school board. They use interviews, public records, questionnaires, Internet sites, and other research tools to gather their data. Torsberg (2000), Sharka (2000), and others report amazing success stories when their students use the Internet to research problems such as no-fault insurance, gun laws, or gender discrimination in the workplace. Students are involved in consulting governmental reports, current periodicals, countless public documents, as well as other primary source materials. Another important part of this process is students' growing capacity to evaluate the various sites' data. When assessment is rigorous, both the final product and the analytical process are greatly improved. Both conventional and electronic research consume much time and energy, but the payoff in enthusiasm and understanding of the research process is sizable.

Scholarly Research

This approach offers an alternative for more advanced students. It is the most traditional and earns the most prestige in some settings because it seems to be the purest, most original kind of quest. In imitation of scholarly research, it asks students to search for relationships, connections, analogues, and influences in both nonliterary and literary topics. Because this kind of research activity demands a more comprehensive library and a greater measure of sophistication than can be generally expected, some teachers save students' time and energy by offering them lists of possible productive investigations. This short-circuits some of the originality but also greatly reduces anxiety and frustration. A topic such as the influence of Eugene Zamaitin's *We* on George Orwell's *1984* offers solid potential and at the same time much room for student initiative.

Fabulous Analysis

Romano's (1995) *Writing with Passion: Life Stories, Multiple Genres* created this category if it did not already exist. His much-acclaimed multigenre research paper is a kind of search-and-analysis process that ignites secondary students when no other work in this area will: "Its amalgam of poetry, prose, drama and nonfiction capitalizes on the cognitive benefits of each genre, and, most importantly, recognizes that there are many ways to see the world" (Bencich, 1996, p. 92). Romano says that his method is ever-changing—evolving through constant negotiation with his students: "The multi-genre research paper was born out of my own literacy pursuits, the dynamic connection between my students' needs and development and my own wonder and delight with literature and writing" (p. 128). His method is described painstakingly in *Writing with Passion,* but it is basically a class production in which a fictive character's artifacts from a wide range of genres (thus the name) are brought together to flesh out the details of that life. A favorite gift from a dying grandfather, a program from a rock concert, notes from a biology class with telling romantic doodles, a fragment from a speech of a radical politician, a letter from an angry brother, three well-worn children's books, and divorce papers from a first marriage are assembled, annotated, and analyzed by individuals or small groups to bring together a kind of analytical biography. The energy generated from both imaginative and analytical thinking and writing makes this a powerful winner.

As a student teacher, Karen Haymes (1988, personal communication) developed an extended writing-and-research project for five small groups of six or seven students. Each group developed the life story of a fictive character who grew up in their city years earlier. The biographical research included materials from five major periods of the character's life: childhood innocence, adolescent struggles, early adult adjustments, midlife achievements, and aging reflection. Like Romano's students, Haymes's were asked to build the story around artifacts from their character's life. The finalé was not so much a paper, although there was one, but a kind of dramatic production that centered on a table that featured all of the critical artifacts with carefully composed legends that explained each artifact and its place in the character's life.

Brunwin's (1985) work with class-developed historical research is similar to Romano's process, but it uses real historical events and artifacts to produce a historical novel. His students follow the trail of an incident that occurred nearly one hundred years ago. He shows his students how to seek details from their city's or region's past, attack in small groups the stubborn historical record, and as an entire class develop not a research paper but a historical novel. Lively and credible stories of goldmining, extortion, and illegal ventures by offshore island pirates have resulted from such class projects and the research and analysis that the project demands are every bit as solid as those provided by less exciting tasks.

Cameron (1994) suggests a number of effective ways to use superheroes from television and the comics to promote writing. One that could be adapted for imaginative but careful research involves concepts about the hero drawn from Joseph Campbell's (1988) *The Power of Myth.* Students begin by listing favorite superheroes and reviewing powerful attributes of mythic heroes:

1. Gives his or her life to something bigger than oneself, to some higher end.
2. Performs a courageous act either physical or spiritual.
3. Feels there's something lacking or something has been taken away.
4. Embarks on a series of adventures to recover what is lost or to discover some life-giving information.
5. Moves from conventional safety to undertake the journey.
6. Undergoes trials and tests of courage, knowledge, and the capacity to survive.
7. Achieves satisfaction.
8. Journeys from a departure, to fulfillment, and return. (Adapted from Cameron, 1994, p. 92)

Using this authoritative list of heroic qualities, students select a set of six superheroes and analyze them. After researching each superhero's words, thoughts, deeds, and the wonders attributed to him or her, students can develop a careful analysis using all of the rigorous paraphernalia of a bona fide research paper.

All of these approaches to the research paper may be both suitable and effective preparation for your students, but none alleviates the dreaded burden of writing the paper itself. As you consider this reality, you may decide to use an alternative. Ask your students to create a chart that will be used to develop a class discussion that will enact the basic research ingredients of locating data and synthesizing it to develop a thesis. The basic categories of information (who, when, where, how, and why) may be used as column headings; list below these the source materials that provide information in each category. The discussion can start with students' presenting their findings to small groups and creating a synthesis. The findings of each group can be compared, with the teacher urging students to look carefully at each source and scrutinize the inferences developed by each of the groups. With a few hours' work out of class and an intensive hour's work together, a group of students may discover more about the nature of research than many others do in days of writing and hours of teacher time evaluating long papers. This is an alternative worth considering.

☞ELEMENTAL VARIATION

Winterowd (1981) argues, and research supports him, that we can help students expand their consciousness of what he calls the full rhetorical context. A distillation of the six elements that he identifies (pp. 66–69) as being fundamental to rhetoric is presented in the box below.

Each of the elements is important to writing, and their complex union brings the writer to new levels of writing maturity. We use a game, rhetorical topology (Figure 12-9), so that students can experience the effect of Winterowd's powerful scheme without having to remember the intricacies of his textbook definitions. Notice also that the medium, or form, of the composition departs from the usual rhetorical forms of school writing.

Topology Procedures

Students in a typical classroom are divided into groups of six. Each member of the group is assigned an element and rolls a die to select one of the six choices within each element. For instance, if the first student (WHO) rolls a four, the persona is an inventor; if the second (WHAT) rolls a five, the topic is popcorn. This continues until all group members have explicit rhetorical definitions. Individual group members write using the fated full rhetorical context of their group within a set amount of time, read their papers to other members of the small group, respond, and even select one or two to read to the whole class.

If the writing assignment seems too difficult with all six elements, begin with three or four of them. The items in the matrix can easily be tailored to the ability level of the students you teach. Both abstract and concrete items can be used as they are here, or a different matrix also can be composed by students. A matrix of literary characters, settings, titles, authors, and periods generates interest, imagination, and energy. The topology encourages the free and expansive play of the mind with the literature. For instance, personas for a writing assignment after a unit study of modern American drama might include Amanda Wingfield, Laura Wingfield, Willy Loman, Stanley Kowalski, Emily Gibbs, and the Stage Manager. The possibilities for audience after a unit on Greek and Roman myths and legends might be Zeus, Aphrodite, Hercules, Theseus, the Medusa, and Atalanta. Students become collaborators in the creative enterprise of literature as they extend these characters imaginatively. Tchudi, Estrem, and Hanlon (1997) used the idea of rotating facets of writing to help students gain consciousness of them. Changing an essay to a letter, totally reshaping an introduction, switching points of view, and shifting dialogue were all used to give students better control of these significant dimensions of a piece of writing. A film instructor at North Carolina's Governor's School (Larsen, 2001) used a similar topology composed of themes, genres, styles, characters, and techniques to prompt students to engage the full power of these features in producing films. The parallel is exact, and the results were especially mature.

Becky Brown (1999, personal communication) used rhetorical topology but substituted fixed, though provocative, writing configurations. One of her best evoked the response shown in Figure 12-10. Common to these suggestions is our sense that the rhetorical topology reinforces the complexity of writing and inspires both creative expansion of texts and creative iteration of other concepts under study.

Element	Interrogative	Definition
Persona	Who?	The voice the reader hears from the page.
Topic	What?	The subject of the piece.
Medium	Where?	The form through which the writing is achieved.
Purpose	Why?	The author's intention in writing.
Tone	How?	The flavor of the piece.
Audience	Whom?	Those who will read or listen to the piece.

WHO *Persona*	WHAT *Topic*	WHERE *Medium*	WHY *Purpose*	HOW *Tone*	WHOM *Audience*
Congressman	Frogs	Bumper sticker	Election	Sarcasm	Senior citizens
Accident victim	Nepotism	Radio spot	Conversion	Precision	Ministerial association
Murderer's mother	Global warming	Public letter	Excuse	Pity	Little League managers
Inventor	Elevators	Editorial	Congratulations	Elation	Veterans
No. 1 draftee	Popcorn	Poem	Praise	Pride	Chamber of commerce
Retiring miner	Ambition	Mediation	Compromise	Chastisement	Beloved uncle

FIGURE 12-9 Milners' rhetorical topology

FIGURE 12–10
Brown's literary topology

Topic	Persona	Audience	Tone	Purpose	Medium
"Royal Rumble"	Beowulf, Arthur, and others	National TV viewers	Intimidating	To entertain	Pro wrestling match

Announcer: In this corner, the legendary Celtic hero and world champion King Arthur. And in this corner, the challenging hero from the wild wastes of Scandinavia, Beowulf! Gentlemen, the fight is without armor and to the death or at least severe bodily mutilation! Begin!

Arthur: You're nothin! man! The Intercontinental Belt is mine, man; I've got all the Knights of the Round Table on my side, and all you've got is that little punk, Wiglaf.

Beowulf: Yeah, just send in your knights to fight for you the way you always do. You never even got off your butt to find the Holy Grail; you just sent your knights out to do it! It didn't matter when I was king, man! I still went out to fight.

Arthur: Yeah, well if you're such a big hero, how come you never had a woman?

Beowulf: What?! All you even had was Gwynevere, who was sleepin' around anyway! You're dead!

Wiglaf: Come on you punk Catholic king. You ain't nothin' man! I'm right witcha, Beowulf.

Arthur: That's it, man! Lancelot, Palomides, Tristram, get in there and show him what the Round Table boyz can do.

(Beowulf trashes all three of the knights, and he tosses them out of the ring.)

Beowulf: (pointing) All right, man, I want YOU!

Arthur: (He runs in and puts Beowulf in the Cranium Crunch.) Right makes might, you punk Scandinavian!

Wiglaf: I'm right by ya, Beowulf! (Wiglaf takes Arthur down in a figure-four leg lock and breaks Arthur's legs.)

Beowulf: This right makes might, dude! (Beowulf delivers a right cross that crunches Arthur's mandible.)

Announcer: It's over, baby! Arthur has tried to let his knights do the work as usual. But Beowulf comes out on top because whereas Arthur leads by claim to kingship, Beowulf leads by example. Beowulf is the stronger warrior and leader of men! That's it, folks, I'm outta here.

Evaluation

Mastery of the topology can be evaluated fairly straightforwardly. Portfolios of writing activities over a quarter or a semester should be kept to measure growth in consciousness of the five elements other than topic. Students can look at their own work or that of other students and measure the effectiveness of a piece of writing by seeing how faithfully each of the six elements is handled in the piece. A person from an outside group (or the teacher) can look at the paper and try to locate which of the choices under each element was selected by the roll of the die. At a more advanced level, the reader could try to name the six pieces of the configuration. If all are located, able writing has begun. In a known configuration, each of the elements might be rated on a four-point scale (excellent, good, fair, weak) so that scores can range from sixteen to four. Invitation to Reflection 12–3 gives you an opportunity to evaluate the idea of rhetorical topology and to construct your own.

Invitation to Reflection 12–3

1. What has been the typical emphasis in English writing assignments that you had in high school and college? (Circle all that apply.)
   a. topic   c. persona   e. tone
   b. purpose   d. medium   f. audience
2. After reading Winterowd's theory and our application, which of the six elements in the full rhetorical context seem to you important enough to include in making writing assignments?
3. Which one(s) seem not important enough to articulate and assign to your students?
4. Now fill in the following matrix as a final writing project in a comparative study of two literary works or two literary periods. State your general subject and fill in the thirty-six blanks in the box below.

		Rhetorical Topology			
WHO	WHAT	WHERE	WHY	HOW	WHOM
Persona	Topic	Medium	Purpose	Tone	Audience
1. _____	_____	_____	_____	_____	_____
2. _____	_____	_____	_____	_____	_____
3. _____	_____	_____	_____	_____	_____
4. _____	_____	_____	_____	_____	_____
5. _____	_____	_____	_____	_____	_____
6. _____	_____	_____	_____	_____	_____

ᴥ LIT. WRITE

Writing about literature is the most venerable yet possibly the most contemporary writing strategy in the field. It was the staple of secondary English classrooms until the early 1970s. Literature was what students wrote about then. Applebee (1993) notes that "Historically the relationship between writing instruction and literature has always been a close one" (p. 155). His research shows that a decade ago 73.8 percent of writing in public schools was about literature (p. 161) and that 75.2 percent of English teachers reported that writing about literature was their primary approach to composition (p. 167). More recently, states such as California have returned to literature as the focal point of an integrated curriculum in which all of the modes of discourse are unified. States such as North Carolina have followed.

Applebee (1993) praises Kathleen Andrasick for showing us how to use process writing to teach literature (p. 1). Newkirk calls her book *Opening Texts* (1990) "a conservative book" yet an "innovative book" (p. xii) because it retains the rigor of the "critical tradition" and the personal response of the journaling approach. Andrasick shows us how to urge students to turn their initial exploratory responses into elaborated pieces of analysis that have none of the formulaic emptiness of five-paragraph themes. Andrasick explains ways to help students "change and/or enlarge the angle of vision" to become "critical reader[s]" who are "able to distance self from text" without killing the initial personal contact with it (p. 5). She shows us how to help students "recognize and *value* their personal connections and initial readings" through students' writing and talking (p. 6). After this initial contact and exploration, she nudges students toward imitating, transforming, and acquiring texts so that they become adept at the following tasks:

- enjoying literature on levels beyond simple comprehension of narrative line
- exploring literature for questions and insights interesting to them
- composing meanings from texts
- knowing how they understand literature
- expanding the ways in which they compose meanings from texts
- making connections between and among texts
- learning to trust their responses and critical assessments

Andrasick regards the different ways in which students read and annotate texts as a prelude to true collaboration, where the crucial mental event is "abandonment of a position we hold" (p. 22).

Her procedure for teaching an understanding of imagery in *The Red Badge of Courage* demonstrates her method (p. 24):

Objective: Students learn to question a repeated image for patterns and emerging meanings.
Procedure: Students trace a particular image through a novel. They work in groups to validate and extend their findings. They analyze and report to the class the significance of patterns. They repeat the process independently using a new image.
Evaluate: Students discuss an image not covered by class work in a final essay.

Andrasick also shows us how she prompts students to plunge deeply into a discussion of the main character's expectations. She begins with a quote from critic R. W. Stallman (1976): "Everything goes awry; nothing turns out as Henry had expected" (p. 201). She asks her students to "identify and define Henry's expectations about war, himself and his behavior and briefly detail how they go awry" (Andrasick, 1990, p. 26). She lets them think, search, and write for twenty minutes. She then asks them to read their lists, which she uses to forge a discussion. In that exchange, she participates only by asking for clarification and prompting students to make connections; at the same time, she creates a graphic representation of their points to use later.

Andrasick uses two process writing strategies to deepen insights for writing about literature: dialogue journals, and process logs. The dialogue journal is a double-entry journal in which students first enter jottings, excerpts, and brief summaries of the text on the left page of their journals and on the opposite page respond with their interpretation and feelings about them. The second step is rereading their entries and writing on another page as many questions as they can generate about their responses. They use the other side of the second page to group questions, answer them, and locate areas of central importance for general inquiry. Students use the questions in a general class discussion and then elaborate a central question for their personal investigation and use all of their journal entries to compose their responses.

Andrasick uses process logs to help students "identify the analytical strategies they use with particular texts" (p. 59). The process log helps students explore a poem by asking them to respond to questions such as the following:

- What did you understand, feel, think after your first reading?
- What questions did you have?
- What words/phrases were confusing?
- What words/phrases seemed to have particular importance?
- As you read the poem a second time, marking it, what insights did you have?
- What areas are still confusing to you?
- What meanings do you feel the poem is expressing? (p. 60)

She emphasizes that she is asking her students to describe *how* they read and understand as well as *what* they read and understand. She ends the section on process logs by reminding us that "we are not teaching skills but awareness of the thinking process." She believes that these two formats "show us how we can teach students to use language to distance themselves from their perceptions, feeling and thoughts about a text" and thus produce fresh insights and strong writing (p. 67).

Even though some teachers, school districts, and states are returning to literature as a focal point of an integrated curriculum, literature will not likely occupy the dominant place in writing it once held. Teachers and students now have many other genres to explore. But literature's usefulness as a vehicle for writing and writing's usefulness as a vehicle for response to literature should not be ignored.

∞ DEPENDENT AUTHORS

Writing about literature has been an important part of the English curriculum for a long, long time. Writing about good writing makes sense because students are provided with richly fabricated events to interpret and analyze. But writing that imaginatively extends a text also works extremely well as a way to energize student writing. The concept of dependent authors, in which teachers ask students to add vignettes to a novel, short story, play, or even poem, coupled with Murray's belief that narratives require all the composing skills displayed in exposition, have convinced us that inviting students to be co-creators with professional writers produces effective growth.

Roles Around

We begin this writing activity by looking into a narrative form used by Faulkner, Childress, and other twentieth-century writers: the multiple first-person monologue. The teacher starts with a quick drawing activity that demonstrates the concept of relativity, the scientific foundation of these works of fiction. A student assumes an unusual posture in the center of the room while the other students encircle the model and use broad-stroke crayon markings on newsprint paper to capture their perspectives of the figure before them. After a quick rendering of their varied perspectives, students move to the left one space and view the figure's representation there, then they continue moving left to each of the positions until they return to their starting position. Then the teacher or a student reads a sentence from Faulkner's *As I Lay Dying,* which describes Addie's coffin as a "cu-

bistic bug." A cubist picture visually captures what the verbal describes. A brief discussion follows around the question "How do multiperspective drawings, the passage, and the painting connect?" Once such speculations are entertained, students read aloud the first paragraph of one of the interior monologues of the eleven characters in Childress's *A Hero Ain't Nothin' but a Sandwich.* When all eleven of these voices have been heard, the students are told the following true story about a tragic school incident:

> Ronnie Morse has had a tough time in school. His dad works on two-week-out-of-town shifts, so he lives alone with his mother, Ann. Last week he had a run-in with his science teacher about dangerous behavior in the lab. That turned into a pretty nasty encounter, and he was eventually suspended from school by Dave Gratton, the assistant principal. Three days later he came to school at the end of the day and walked up to Gratton, who was standing at a bus door, and shot him. Gratton reached for the gun so was hit only in the right shoulder, but he fell to the ground looking pretty dead. Ronnie took about three steps back from the bus, pointed the gun at his head, and pulled the trigger. When nothing happened, the students who had gathered nearby laughed. When Ronnie heard that, he took another two steps toward them, put the gun to his head again, fired, and fell to the ground dead.

After students have absorbed this sad story, they are asked to look over the following list of names of people who knew Ronnie Morse and write a monologue from the perspective of the person checked on their list.

Ronnie's World

Mr. Teeder (principal)	Piggie Morrison (best friend)
Ann Morse (mother)	Reverend Bly (Morses' minister)
Blake Morse (father)	
Jill Nicholls (girlfriend)	Jelk Jimson (cousin)
Dave Gratton (assist. principal)	Tom Wise (superintendent)
Richard Greene (bus driver)	Melinda Jumps (cheerleader)
Artis Gilson (science teacher)	Ray Toms (Ronnie's boss)
	Norma Nelson (school nurse)
Jim Nicholls (Jill's father)	Ron Phife (sheriff's deputy)

Because students become fully aware of the uniqueness of a special perspective and are touched by the poignancy of the suicide, they write remarkable monologues. Figure 12-11 presents two such monologues that we've collected. We clipped this story from our local paper and elaborated upon it. Any striking story from your local paper holds the potential for equally fine writing.

FIGURE 12–11
Two perspectives

DAVE GRATTON (ASSISTANT PRINCIPAL)

Ronnie Morse is nothing but trouble. I feel sorry for him. He has gotten in with the wrong crowd. He is abusive to the teachers here at our school; he comes to class high, and just last Friday he openly threatened me. He said he'd kill me. I was a bit worried but not too much. I get threatened a lot. You see, the principal and I decided the only disciplinary action left was to expel Ronnie. We have tried many different punishments such as in-school and out-of-school suspension, reports, etc. Nothing works. As the assistant principal, it is my duty to administer these various punishments. A great job, huh? I know the kid doesn't like me, but hey, he ain't exactly my favorite person either. So we kicked him out and good riddance. He was a bad apple. Today is Monday, and the day has been fairly calm, I am on bus duty and am getting on to some boys who are horse playing. It is then that I feel a terrible pain shoot through my shoulder and hear a shot simultaneously. I've been shot. I hear laughter, sick laughter, and I know it's Ronnie Morse who has shot me. He made good his threat. I don't move for fear he'll shoot again and then another shot and then I lose consciousness.

MR. TEEDER (PRINCIPAL)

If all days were like yesterday, I would have to retire from principalship. A terrible tragedy occurred that could have easily been prevented by communication and self-control. I have tried my best to be a good principal—to be objective, fair, but follow through with my decisions. My assistant principal was shot today. Yes, shot! The young man who fired the gun then turned it on himself, the gun failed to fire at first, and despite the pleading of his friends, he tried again . . . and this time succeeded in taking his own life.

His mother was in my office, discussing his suspension with me at the time of his death. He was suspended from English for insubordination and then cursing at the teacher and other students in the classroom. We had come to a decision pertaining to the work he would miss. I think he could have graduated on time if he had stuck it out. Why? Why? How could he take his life? He was not a totally bad kid. He had friends and family who loved him, even if they weren't always present in his life. I'm concerned about how this will affect the student body. Some professional counselors will be on campus tomorrow.

Other Dependencies

Cameron (1994) prompts his students to allow superheroes to enter a work of fiction in the same way the fairy godmother enters the life of Cinderella. (His examples are taken from the fictive world of Jay Gatsby and the real world of Malcolm X.) Walker (1997) borrows from authentic assessment's basic axiom that school writing must look like writing in the real world to connect with the ideas in Thoreau's "Civil Disobedience" and those of other essayists. As town planners or members of citizens' groups, students carefully construct a plan or proposal that puts Thoreau's and Emerson's ideas into play. Walker's five requirements, presented in Figure 12–12, are exact and demanding; yet they allow students to extend the authors' ideas into a real-world context.

Dixon (1984) used two samples of student writing in response to the powerful antiwar poem "Dulce et Decorum Est" by Wilfred Owen to demonstrate the effectiveness of dependent authorship. An earnest and sensitive student produced only a faltering essay about the terror of the gas attack for the individual soldier or the univer-sal sickness of war, while a similar student wrote a poignant and deeply sensitive narrative that captured both. When he presented the two writing pieces to a group of Michigan teachers, the narrative was so much more compelling that some concluded that they would try dependent authors a good part of the time; others said that they would sometimes allow students a choice of the two forms; and still others said that they would consider using dependent authors as a step toward better expository writing.

∞ APPRENTICE WRITING

Many professional writers attribute their writing abilities to cutting their composing teeth on the works of the masters; as aspiring writers, they painstakingly copied the masters' work until something of their genius seeped through. Formerly, classic models were basic to instruction in rhetoric. Although textbooks often continue this approach through collecting model essays, the method has lost credibility in today's classrooms. For some teach-

FIGURE 12–12
Walker's planners

1. Describe the problem in at least fifty words, including why they feel it is significant.
2. Propose a specific solution to the problem in one to three sentences.
3. List three print and/or human resources that would give useful information for designing and implementing the plan, explaining why each would be helpful.
4. List in complete statements at least five specific steps they would take to implement the plan in the order the tasks should be accomplished.
5. Write an explanation of at least one hundred words to tell how Emerson and/or Thoreau would view their proposed plan, basing their explanation on what they know about transcendentalism from the readings and citing at least two supporting quotes.

ers, however, the rationale remains: Writers learn their craft by striving to meet standards set by reading good models. In *The Anxiety of Influence,* Bloom (1973) argues that unconscious apprenticeships are always served in the lives of great writers. Annie Dillard agrees: "the writer studies literature. . . . he is careful of what he reads for that is what he will write." Some of that same process can be useful for all writers, not just those who want to make writing their craft. In the realms of style and content, models can give uncertain students training wheels that keep their forward motion from faltering. More important, modeling can help students evolve their own original voices. We present four steps that can be taken in this apprenticeship. Each step is more difficult and takes more effort and independence than the preceding one. The individual imagination must be kept alive at each stage or the process will sink into tedious, stupefying, and even harmful work.

Copying (Duplicating Exact Texts)

When children hear parents read a bedtime story over and over, they seem almost able to read it themselves. They have so absorbed the tale that its rhythms and sounds become embedded in their memories. Researchers tell us that children learn much about reading from this repetition. Secondary students might learn much about writing with just such attention to and reproduction of the words of others. (You will find as you teach the same works over time that certain lines, phrases, and words insinuate themselves into your thoughts and speech. Harold Bloom, in a television interview, spoke of his poetry seminars that centered on students' fond recitation of parts or all of the poems they studied.) The following exercises call for a close attention to key words, phrases, and sentences and a heightened repetition of them. The purpose is to acquaint students with the power of another's writing and to encourage their identification and ownership of that language. They first reproduce the original and then impose their own interpretation, verbal or visual, on it.

Little Snippets. Each student selects prized phrases from a favorite writer, copies those snippets onto posterboard, and surrounds the words with related visual images. These collages can be presented to the class visually as students recite the snippets from memory or from carefully rehearsed reading. The emphasis here is on the words. The visual imagery and spoken words together deepen a student's proprietary identification with the author's consciousness and expressiveness.

Write Out and Draw In. Students combine art with writing in this exercise. They each choose and transcribe a personally meaningful poem or prose extract. We find

that short passages work best. Students then paint, draw, or paste together a picture or collage that rises from their reading of literature. We are asking students to connect to the words of the artist. Not all students feel artistically capable; but as long as care is given to both the transmission of the poet's words to paper and the creation or selection of the accompanying artwork, the power of the process is secure. Figure 12–13 is an example of one such personal connection between the imaginations of two former students, Cary Clifford and Benjamin Milner, and lines from Wallace Stevens.

Paraphrasing (Translating Passages)

Paraphrasing moves in a new direction. We are trying to help students believe in themselves as writers, as people with something to say to others. We know that we all have something to say; Graves (1983b) convinces us that everybody has a story to tell. Unfortunately, not all of our students believe this. Many of them have little faith in themselves as communicators. Two exercises follow that invite original writing by providing a preformed structure. The teacher furnishes the form to free students to find their own meaning. Our examples are taken from poetry, but other forms can work as well: aphorisms, famous passages from speeches, and even bumper stickers or advertising slogans.

Translation. Translation prompts students to rewrite poetry in their own words. The process may seem reductive, but students who have little self-confidence often create written prose statements that are penetrating and satisfying to themselves. After each student develops a working paraphrase of a poem, groups of three students read their translations to one another, comparing their prose with the poem's original meaning and with its greater economy of words.

Official Plagiarism. Such paraphrasing can take place after students have developed a feel for the use of another writer's words. They can select a poem already studied in class and restate or reorder it in their own words. Students give their poems titles and display them under their own names, with the original poet's name and the poem's real title on the back. (To add interest and reward for the paraphrasing authors, class members might read the poems closely and identify the sources of the new titles.) This appropriation leads students to trust themselves a bit more. They can trust the original author's structure and thereby gain trust in their own words.

In these two instances of paraphrasing, writing masters have become what John-Steiner (1987, p. 37) calls "distant teachers." Paraphrase is not done in the old, reductive attempt to pinion literature into a simple declarative statement. Rather, it is used to help students see how the stylist carefully shapes meaning with special

FIGURE 12–13
Copying (duplicating exact texts)

Source: Poem from COLLECTED POEMS by Wallace Stevens. Copyright 1923 and renewed 1951 by Wallace Stevens. Reprinted by permission of Alfred A. Knopf, Inc.

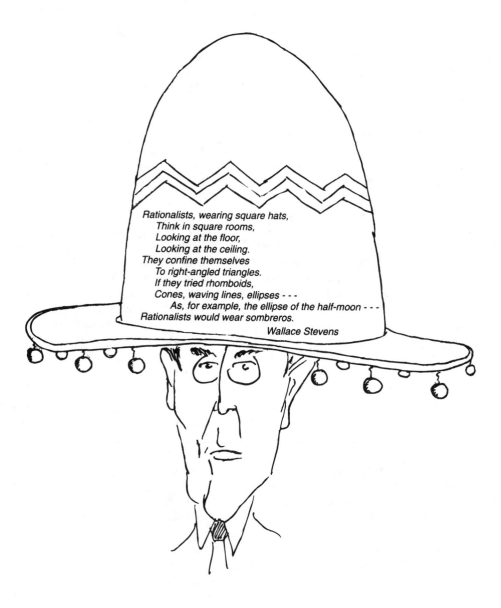

Rationalists, wearing square hats,
Think in square rooms,
Looking at the floor,
Looking at the ceiling.
They confine themselves
To right-angled triangles.
If they tried rhomboids,
Cones, waving lines, ellipses - - -
As, for example, the ellipse of the half-moon - - -
Rationalists would wear sombreros.
Wallace Stevens

arrangements of words and to release students to trust their own voices to carry their own insights.

Modeling (Employing a Template)

Modeling evokes student writing while allowing students to borrow form and pattern from master word crafters. All elementary teachers make use of this in some fashion, but the process can be equally successful for secondary students. Brooks (1973), in her essay "Mimesis: Grammar and the Echoing Voice," proposes carefully composed exercises that encourage her students to find their own unique styles and to learn specific grammatical points by using what she calls "persona paraphrase." She asks students to give conscious attention to the professional writer's medium and to use that writer's words to discover their own voice and style. She uses established writers to free young writers to the possibilities of writing for their own purposes. In a similar effort, in Chapter 6 we dis-

cussed using single poems or fixed poetic forms as templates from which students can develop their own poems.

Building Conceits. This model develops a piece of writing around one powerful comparison, as the poet Karl Shapiro does in "Manhole Covers." Lines such as "Mayan calendar stones" and "like medals struck by a great Kahn" make us transform the everyday object into a larger-than-life artifact from an exotic world. Students can use this model to build poems of their own from a conceit. Rather than just telling them to come up with a comparison, you can give them a method for coining such metaphoric constructions. We ask students to think of a mundane object such as a hammer or a slide and then list attributes such as shape, size, use, color, and material; from that list, they try to shape an extended conceit.

The Creature. This template encourages students to use their eyes to write well. The enabling structure that releases this poetic writing is a nature study. Students visit a zoo or an aquarium or merely set out to watch a creature in nature closely: a dimpled spider, a buzzing fly, a beetle trapped in a bathtub, a harmless snake in the grass, or a twitching wren. Students watch this creature carefully and record as would a naturalist its attributes, actions, colors, habits, and dwelling. Then they use the template (Figure 12–14) to slot in the features they like best and add the personal or metaphorical connections made possible by their choices for the poem. Although the template is fairly tight and may seem to constrain the autonomy and creativity of writers, most students experience a good feeling when their animal springs to life and takes on a significance that did not previously seem inherent in the creature.

Imitating (Mimicking the Masters)

This final stage of stylizing cuts the student free from copying, paraphrasing, and using models. They remain on a leash of sorts, but a long one. We ask them to make their own decisions in mimicking a master. They need both a sensitive consciousness of another's style and the ability to play with an imitation. The following three exercises demonstrate this method.

Public Parody. In this initial activity, students write and tape-record the verbal style of a well-known public figure. These recordings are played; and students are asked to note their impressions of the voice and syntax, the vocabulary and the rhythm. Students then determine which aspect is nearer the defining center of that person's public utterances.

Literary Caricatures. From this pure parody, students may move to caricaturing literary figures whom they have studied and whose styles are distinctive, such as Edgar Allan Poe, Emily Dickinson, Ernest Hemingway, Langston Hughes, or William Faulkner. These written pieces might be exaggerated so as to emphasize characteristic styles. They are half-fun and half-serious. Other students can try

to guess each caricature. From the exaggeration of these extreme characterizations, students can turn to more serious imitations of childhood favorites such as William Steig, Dr. Seuss, and Maurice Sendak. These writers are supposedly simpler and, more important, are removed from students' present reading menu. To capture Sendak in an unpublished chapter of *Where the Wild Things Are* takes great effort but teaches much about the writer's craft.

Emulate Masters. Ask students to read, reread, and listen on tape to writers such as C. S. Lewis, John Updike, Alice Walker, Eudora Welty, and E. B. White to soak up their styles. Choosing from a diverse stylistic range will provide appeal to a wide array of students. Those who can absorb this work deeply can begin to note authors' tricks and slowly appropriate them in their own writing.

We must never forget that we are trying to invite students into genuine literary activity—writing comfortably and frequently for their own purposes and reading confidently and frequently from the vast array of written texts. Modeling masters was once the primary means of teaching rhetoric. We have come to understand the importance of many other modes, but we can still profit from acquainting our students with the successful craft of others and with validating an apprenticeship to them. The success of any apprenticeship is in its releasing the learner from imitation to independent craft.

Invitation to Reflection 12–4

Have you ever yourself experienced writing instruction by copying, paraphrasing, modeling, or imitating? These four instructional modes are arranged on a continuum from most model-dependent to least model-dependent. Write under each category titles, authors, or passages that you believe have distinctive styles worthy of imitation.

Copying → Paraphrasing → Modeling → Imitating

FIGURE 12–14
The creature

The _____ _____ and _____ .
          creature   action   action

Its _____ _____ _____ .
     color   attribute   action

Never does the _____ disappoint* us!
               creature

Its _____ , its _____ , its _____ astonish* us.
   attribute   attribute   attribute

We behold it and the _____ _____ our imaginations.
                   connections

Aye, it is the _____ of our collective souls.
        connections

TEMPLATE PROTOCOLS
1. Enter your creature, its actions, attributes, associations, and color in the spaces indicated.
2. Each of the words marked with an asterisk may be replaced by a better one of your choice.

⌒ PRACTICAL STYLIST

Style is elusive and, as we pointed out earlier, very difficult to teach. We believe books on style do exist that are worth looking at; their good ideas can help your students work at this goal. Copying texts is how many of the finest writers began. Some writers, such as Abraham Lincoln, who were limited to the few books they could find, may have developed into master stylists because they repeatedly read exceptionally crafted texts such as the Bible. We believe, however, that exposure to a number of fine writers and excellent texts that explain the secrets of the craft of writing is the best way to help writers develop mature and idiosyncratic styles.

Three Style Books

Williams's (1990) *Style: Toward Clarity and Grace* is the complex work of a thoughtful linguist. His thinking is as comprehensive as any in this limited but important field. He says that he wants to go beyond the mere "high-mindedness" about style that is typical of standard works; he argues that his book "explains how to achieve those ends" (p. ix). Williams deals carefully with seven central features of style: clarity, cohesion, emphasis, concision, length, elegance, and usage. He offers some examples of bad writing (too many prepositions; complex, unfamiliar concepts at the beginning of sentences; and confusing use of negative verbs), explains their negative impact, and shows how to correct them. He speaks insightfully about metaphors. He shows how they can add elegance and power to writing but how, if ineptly posed, they can confuse a reader and undermine the writer's intent. In his usage chapter, he sanctions the split infinitive and clarifies the use of *shall* and *will,* showing how turning to *will,* though it may be unconventional, adds the force of intent to writing. His book is full of instruction for more clarity and grace in everyday writing.

Romano's (1995) *Writing with Passion* is famous for its chapter "The Multi-Genre Research Paper," but we are also fond of his chapter "Breaking the Rules with Style." In that chapter he (like Williams) teaches writers to intentionally break the conventions of writing as a way to establish a style and a voice that are both noticeable and attractive. He honors unmentionables such as fragments and extended, involuted sentences. The brash brevity of the fragments and the droll, desultory nature of the extended sentences break the rules of length at either extreme. Robust and witty writers like Mark Twain and H. L. Mencken use unsanctioned brevity to great effect. Other stylists use repeated phrases or even seemingly redundant passages to capture their readers. Romano tells us, too, how to build a recognizable voice with labyrinthine catalogs, spelling aberrations, double discordant voices, and verbal collages. He uses the glories and peculiarities of literature to demonstrate the way in which stylists violate the norm in beautiful and clever ways to entrap the reader. In *Writing with Passion,* learning new ways to encourage bolder style in student writing becomes a treat.

Collette and Johnson's (1993) *Common Ground* is not as familiar as are the other two. It is not the work of a linguist or an English educator; however, it is rich with detail and stout with insight. It is replete with thorough explanations and apt demonstrations. The opening chapter appropriately is titled "Reaching the Reader." Details, analogies, and anecdotes are some of the authors' hooks. In discussing anecdotes, they show the need for a balance of uniqueness and typicality; bright ideas such as these are commonsensical yet fresh. Collette and Johnson discuss Howard Nemerov's essay "On Metaphor," which offers the jewel "if you want to see the invisible world, look at the visible one" (p. 18). They show us how to exercise our metaphoric powers by making a passage "metaphorically richer by working on the verbs" (p. 22). They show writers how to search for metaphors to explain, not express, a feeling or emotion to someone else. Their other chapters pore over such specific matters as finding a common ground via humor, setting, and special perspectives. It becomes clear that comic wordsmiths such as Woody Allen, Stephen Wright, and Dave Barry must have learned such lessons somewhere to achieve their delightful way of getting us to move into their worlds. The authors further show writers, in the chapter titled "Movement," how to achieve focus or energy, how to make "paths," and how to "move through the whole." In a highly stylistic chapter titled "Discourse," they, like Romano, show us how to go about "changing the rules" (p. 140) and then move on to finely articulated chapters titled "Roles and Relations" and "Voice, World and Authority." In the latter, they show how cadence in prose can be recognized and then developed (pp. 224–234) and how to mix and shift voices (pp. 241–248). All of this is done with economy, straight talk, and verve. It is not a methods book, but it is full of methodology. It is worth any teacher's time. One thing more: Although it may be seen as a creative writing primer, the lessons on style are not confined by genre or discourse mode but are transferred across all.

Others

Phillips (1997) adds a nice touch about style—more specifically, voice. She discovered through her ethnographic study of a young African American female that poetry allows her to find a voice because it provides the comfort of a natural rhythm that gives her the confidence that allows her to write about her life. Stetson (1996) believes that assigned topics, prescribed structures, and formulated steps in writing snuff out the student voice and replace it with a cool, unembodied institutional voice. Style is, as we said, difficult to teach; but we can at least know what we ought not do so that it can mature without being squashed.

We have listed other recommended writing textbooks in Appendix H. In the course of our careers, we have treasured writing books for a time and kept them on privileged places on our desks before we found another and drew from it. For some years, we opened Donald Hall's (1973) primer for students *Writing Well* for quick nourishment; later we turned to Murray's (1985) *A Writer Teaches Writing, Second Edition.* Intermittently through all these years one of us kept the thin third edition of Strunk and White's (1979) *The Elements of Style* by the bed for reading pleasure. E. B. White revised his old Cornell professor's privately printed volume on style because when he reexamined it forty years after he graduated and had become a fine professional stylist himself, he found it contained "rich deposits of gold" (p. xi). Strunk and White have fallen out of favor with some English educators, partly because of the virtues White found: "Professor Strunk was a positive man. His book contains rules of grammar phrased as direct orders. . . . [T]hese rules and principles are in the form of sharp commands, Sergeant Strunk snapping orders to his platoon. . . . 'Use the active voice.' (Rule 14) 'Omit needless words.' (Rule 17) . . . Each rule or principle is followed by a short hortatory essay, . . . followed by . . . examples" (pp. xii–xiii). We treasure *The Elements of Style* for similar reasons, "its sharp advice, . . . the audacity and self-confidence of its author" (p. xiv). Even instructional books on writing can possess style and a voice. We hope you will find your own valued writing books. A wealth of material is available for building writing; and when young writers start to care about style, you know they are moving in free flight.

Summary of Research About Writing

In Chapter 11 we looked at five major approaches to writing and suggested a structure for bringing these approaches together. In this chapter, we offered a broad array of instructional strategies that fulfill critical needs in writing. These are not wedded to a single ideology but are affirmed in current research and best practice. It may be that the best assessment of writing comes from a close look at the environment in which it is taught. Consider classrooms you have seen and the one you hope to construct and rate each item in Invitation to Reflection 12-5.

Invitation to Reflection 12-5

Consider classrooms you have seen and the ones you hope to create for effective writing instruction. An ethnographer attempting to record the dynamics of such a class might use the chart (Figure 12–15) as a checklist of its artifacts, arrangements, and behaviors. For your real and/or imagined classroom, rate what you consider to be the importance of each item for effective learning.

We close this chapter with five summary reports that give us a general sense of what is presently considered best practice in writing. The research of Hillocks and his associates (1986) looked at six important writing strategies as we described in Chapter 3. They found that grammar instruction had little or no positive effect on writing and that free writing was only slightly more effective as an instructional strategy. The use of models was more effective but was not as powerful when used exclusively. Sentence combining was very effective, twice as useful as the free-writing approach. Generally, Hillocks found that carefully planned and systematic writing strategies were most effective. Attitude and good feeling were necessary, but they were not sufficient.

Zemelman, Daniels, and Hyde's (1993) *Best Practice: New Standards for Teaching and Learning in American Schools* presents eight essential practices in writing:

- Teachers must help students find real purposes to write.
- Students need to take ownership and responsibility.
- Effective writing programs involve the complete writing process.
- Teachers can help students draft and revise.
- Grammar and mechanics are best learned in the context of actual writing.
- Students need real audiences and a classroom context of shared learning.
- Writing should extend throughout the curriculum.
- Effective teachers use evaluation constructively and efficiently.

We believe that the general approaches we presented in Chapter 11 and in this chapter embody these standards and the specific strategies will help you meet or exceed them in your writing instruction.

Two summary documents—William Bennett's Department of Education's (1986) *What works* and the National Commission on Teaching and America's Future's (1996) *What Matters Most*—both report that the writing process is the essential ingredient for effective writing. Success comes when teachers develop a sequence that includes prewriting, writing, and revising. The reports also note that when writing programs extend across the curriculum, student's performance improves.

The National Assessment of Educational Progress (NAEP) publishes highly respected and influential research findings.[1] The goals and achievement levels for

---

[1]When the National Assessment of Educational Progress received federal funding, it moved its operation from Boulder, Colorado to Washington, DC and was renamed the National Assessment Governing Board.

FIGURE 12–15
Writing ethnography

Artifacts, Arrangements, Behaviors

	Abundant (4)	Strong (3)	Present (2)	Absent (1)
Students talking about writing successes with classmates				
Students writing to accomplish tasks outside school				
Students writing collaboratively				
Teachers reading their writing to students				
Teachers writing alongside student writers				
Students working on various stages of writing				
Teachers conferencing with students about writing				
Students reading their writing to small groups				
Teachers moving about all areas of the classroom				
Adult writers visiting class				
Students using various writing instruments				
Walls displaying student work				
High-quality texts posted around room				
Challenging vocabulary displayed around room				
Word walls displaying essential words				
Environment integrating all areas of the curriculum				
Models featuring emphasized writing skills				
Movable chairs and tables				
Interactive seating arrangements				
Variety of media accessible to students				
Open book shelves, magazine racks				
Accessible computers				
Up-to-date, student-friendly software				

writing published in the NAEP's *Writing Framework and Specialization: 1998* are worth comparing with what we have outlined in these two chapters on writing to see whether we are speaking to those national standards. The NAEP's five goals are terribly broad:

- Students should write for a variety of purposes: narrative, informative, and persuasive.
- Students should write on a variety of topics and for many different audiences.
- Students should write from a variety of stimulus materials and within various time constraints.
- Students should generate, draft, revise, and edit ideas and forms expressed in their writing.
- Students should display effective choices in the organization of their writing. They should include detail to illus-

trate and elaborate their ideas, and use appropriate conventions of written English. (p. 27)

The NAEP's writing achievements (basic, proficient, advanced) for grades eight and twelve are more precise and thus give us a good sense of the mark that our students must achieve. These are presented in Figure 12-16.

∾ CONCLUSION

Teaching writing is one of the English teacher's essential charges. Nowhere does the dual sense of teaching as art and craft seem more pertinent. In the course of these two chapters, we trust that you have found some theories and

PRELIMINARY ACHIEVEMENT LEVEL DESCRIPTIONS FOR GRADE 8 WRITING

These achievement levels are proposed for first drafts, not final or polished student writing, that are generated within limited time constraints in a large-scale assessment environment.

BASIC

Students performing at the basic level should be able to:
- Demonstrate appropriate response to the task in form, content, and language.
- Maintain a consistent focus.
- Respond appropriately to the task.
- Use supporting detail.
- Demonstrate sufficient command of spelling, grammar, punctuation, and capitalization to communicate to the reader.

PROFICIENT

Students performing at the proficient level should be able to:
- Create an effective response to the task in form, content, and language.
- Express analytical, critical, and/or creative thinking.
- Demonstrate an awareness of the purpose and intended audience.
- Have logical and observable organization appropriate to the task.
- Show effective use of transitional elements.
- Use sufficient elaboration to clarify and enhance the central idea.
- Use language (e.g., variety of word choice and sentence structure) appropriate to the task.
- Have few errors in spelling, grammar, punctuation, and capitalization that interfere with communication.

ADVANCED

Students performing at the advanced level should be able to:
- Create an effective and elaborated response to the task in form, content, and language.
- Express analytical, critical, and/or creative thinking.
- Have well-crafted, cohesive organization appropriate to the task.
- Show sophisticated use of transitional elements.
- Use varied and elaborated supporting details in appropriate, extended response.
- Begin to develop a personal style or voice.
- Demonstrate precise and varied use of language.
- Use a variety of strategies such as analogies, illustrations, examples, anecdotes, and figurative language.
- Enhance meaning through control of spelling, grammar, punctuation, and capitalization.

PRELIMINARY ACHIEVEMENT LEVEL DESCRIPTIONS FOR GRADE 12 WRITING

These achievement levels are proposed for first drafts, not final or polished student writing, that are generated within limited time constraints in a large-scale assessment environment.

BASIC

Students performing at the basic level should be able to:
- Demonstrate appropriate response to the task in form, content, and language.
- Demonstrate reflection and insight and evidence of analytical, critical, or evaluative thinking.
- Show evidence of conscious organization.
- Use supporting details.
- Reveal developing personal style or voice.
- Demonstrate sufficient command of spelling, grammar, punctuation, and capitalization to communicate to the reader.

PROFICIENT

Students performing at the proficient level should be able to:
- Create an effective response to the task in form, content, and language.
- Demonstrate reflection and insight and evidence of analytical, critical, or evaluative thinking.
- Use convincing elaboration and development to clarify and enhance the central idea.
- Have logical and observable organization appropriate to the task.
- Show effective use of transitional elements.
- Reveal personal style or voice.
- Use language appropriate to the task and intended audience.
- Have few errors in spelling, grammar, punctuation, and capitalization that interfere with communication.

ADVANCED

Students performing at the advanced level should be able to:
- Create an effective and elaborated response to the task in form, content, and language.
- Show maturity and sophistication in analytical, critical, creative thinking.
- Have well-crafted, cohesive organization appropriate to the task.
- Show sophisticated use of transitional elements.
- Use illustrative and varied supportive details.
- Use rich, compelling language.
- Show evidence of a personal style or voice.
- Display a variety of strategies such as anecdotes, repetition and literary devices to support and develop ideas.
- Enhance meaning through control of spelling, grammar, punctuation, and capitalization.

FIGURE 12–16   NAEP's writing achievements

strategies around which you can begin to practice the craft. We hope, too, that you have felt some connection with the art that is also necessary for teaching writing.

Dawn Potter (2002, personal communication), our copyeditor and a very fine writer and teacher herself, reminds us of a fundamental aspect of writing and, we suggest, of teaching writing: "the willingness to let the observation—the lived life—leave its mark. We cannot write unless we are first open to experience." Poet and memoirist Kathleen Norris (1996) embodies this willingness as she struggled to write a personal narrative "that seemed too personal, too painful to ever see the light of day. Sitting with my notes around me, gazing at a blank computer screen, I tried to forget that a deadline loomed, and I was still spending hours just sitting and brooding, letting the thing work itself out inside me" (p. 351). Just as your students may be stuck before their writing project, you may find yourself also paralyzed before the year's curriculum design or your next day's lesson plans. I think Potter's and Norris's advice to you would be to remain with the struggle, keenly open to your experience and your students', acutely aware of the wealth of advice available about teaching writing— perhaps even writing in your journal about your quandary or listing wise suggestions or possible lessons—but also confident that plans are forming within you out of this active openness and tension. Potter sent us the words of novelist Graham Greene (1951/1999), who captures this moment for the writer and, we believe, for the writing teacher:

> So much in writing depends on the superficiality of one's days. One may be preoccupied with shopping and income tax returns and chance conversations, but the stream of the unconscious continues to flow undisturbed, solving problems, planning ahead: one sits down sterile and dispirited at the desk, and suddenly the words come as though from the air: the situations that seemed blocked in a hopeless impasse move forward: the work has been done while one slept or shopped or talked with friends." (pp. 19–20)

Teacher Bill Stifler provides a fitting close for the chapter as he muses on the art and craft of teaching writing.

On Writing

I've tried to think what I could tell you,
about the way words feel, the sound
they make when they touch, the way
words fight you, fall flat, clattering
like pans to a kitchen floor or the slap
of a tire limping, only you know all
this, and I wonder if there's anything
I could tell you, or tell myself,
because words make their own way,
play by their own rules, and all we do,
if we're lucky, is find them.

Bill Stifler

13

Evaluating Learning

Evaluation should not dictate, distort, or displace what it measures.

James Moffett and
Betty Jane Wagner

More than a decade ago, Purves, Rogers, and Soter (1990) reported that the "United States has been called test mad" (p. 161). Tchudi and Mitchell (1989) observed that "grades have so permeated the school system that everyone has become addicted to their use" (p. 384). During the last decade of the twentieth century and into the first of the twenty-first century, external pressures on schools and teachers to test students have intensified further. Persistent calls come from the general public and their policymakers, first to establish educational standards that students must meet and then to assess the students', teachers', and schools' abilities to learn, teach, and meet those standards. Proponents of standards and testing claim there is an educational emergency in the country. For them, tests are the best means to maintain standards, motivate teachers and students, and achieve educational excellence. Many other educators believe the overemphasis on testing is not a solution to these difficulties; it has become the emergency itself.

No methods text would be complete without inviting you to consider the connection between what we teach and how we evaluate—that is, to think about evaluation very carefully. In the first and second editions of this textbook, our evaluation chapter concentrated on teacher-designed and -administered assessments of students. At present, our national conversation about evaluation is driven by external concerns. Consequently, we ask you first to consider those tests developed, normed, administered, and scored by agencies outside of individual schools and used by outsiders to judge students, teachers, and schools. Then we will move to the more immediate context of assessment in particular English classrooms.

STANDARDIZED TESTS

We begin this chapter with standardized tests because teachers operate within a cultural context overwrought with testing. Laypersons and legislators point to lower test scores as proof of the decline of American education, of our losing ground in a competition with other countries or with our own former educational achievement. Perhaps this sentiment explains the popularity of two 1980s films, *Stand and Deliver* (1988) and *Lean on Me* (1989), inspirational stories of academic betterment that reflect the hegemony of tests in our culture. Both are accounts of real teachers and principals struggling with troubled, mostly minority high schools. The success of these schools and the students and teachers within them is measured by student achievement on statewide proficiency and college placement exams. The viewer, exhilarated by the novel stratagems of Hispanic teacher Jaime Escalante and the authoritarian tactics of African American principal Joe Clark, may applaud the dramatic turnarounds of both schools without questioning the final measure of the achievement: test scores. These films attest to the cultural confidence placed in scores on one or another standardized assessment instrument.

District- and State-Mandated Tests

Since the 1970s and 1980s, concerns about the nation's schools have mounted. The approach to school reform taken by many local, state, and national education entities has been to establish minimum standards that all students must meet in order to complete grades or school. On the heels of these standards have come initiatives to administer standardized tests to determine if the standards themselves have been successfully met. By the end of the century, forty-nine states and many urban districts had established standards for their students. According to Wolk (1998), a third of these required students to take tests and achieve a designated score for a passing grade. Systems were answering the charge to get tough and be accountable.

These mandated tests have produced mixed results. There are school critics who believe the accountability initiatives have brought welcome school reform—a standardization of curriculum and higher test scores. We turn to the testimonies of English teachers from urban and suburban high schools in New Jersey and Massachusetts who report other effects.

Impact on Teachers and Students. Students in two Camden, New Jersey high schools are now required to pass state proficiency exams (in reading, math, and writing skills) to graduate from high school. In *Savage Inequalities,* Jonathan Kozol (1991) describes the impact on students and teachers. Students are given preliminary tests in eighth grade. According to one English teacher, 80 percent fail; and these failing students enter ninth grade, where the entire year becomes test preparation to be ready for the state exams in April. The teacher continues, "Then, if we are lucky, we have two months left in May and June to teach some subject matter. Eight months for tests. Two months, maybe, to enjoy some poetry or fiction" (p. 144). If students fail the test, they retake it in tenth grade and, if they fail again, in eleventh grade. Camden High School principal Ruthie Green-Brown explains the results: "We are preparing a generation of robots. Kids are learning exclusively through rote. We have children who are given no conceptual framework. They do not learn to think, because their teachers are straitjacketed by tests that measure only isolated skills" (p. 143). Six hundred students enter ninth grade at Camden High School. The number drops to three hundred by eleventh grade (p. 146). In Camden's other high school, Woodrow Wilson, the dropout rate is 58 percent (p. 149). Although Kozol (p. 137) describes Camden as the fourth-poorest city of more than 50,000 people in the United States and with the highest rate of child poverty, many observers see a connection between these tests and the classrooms that prepare for them and the number of students leaving school.

Luna and Turner (2001) interviewed Massachusetts teachers from urban and suburban high schools, and they report similar consequences from the Massachusetts Comprehensive Assessment System. The test's "immediate effects" were to undermine the confidence and self-esteem of students and teachers and to threaten "the solidarity of the school community" (p. 84). The teachers' experiences bear out research.[1] They are " 'teaching to the test,' not only through specific test preparation activities and changes in the content of their curricula, but, more diffusely through pervasive changes in their pedagogy. . . . Overall, they seem to reflect a shift away from 'thinking' and 'exploration' toward 'drilling' and 'naming' " (p. 83). As one urban teacher "lamented": "It's stifling creativity, it's stifling depth, it's stifling thinking" (p. 83). Other losses include "time spent on teaching and learning, in-depth exploration of literature, curiosity, creativity, inventiveness among students, projects, coverage of supplementary information, and field trips" (p. 86). A teacher explains more specifically the impact on teaching writing: "we're not really teaching them how to write. We're teaching them to follow a format. . . . It's like, you

---

[1] Luna and Turner's (2001) citations include Cooper and Davies (1993) and Wideen, O'Shea, and Pye (1997).

know, they're doing paint-by-numbers. . . . We're putting the numbers down and they're filling in the colors. There's no creativity involved at all" (p. 83).

The stakes are high indeed. The Massachusetts teachers regard high-stakes testing "as a wrecking ball, poised to demolish their school and destroy their students' life chances" (p. 81). Kozol (2002) calls testing the "sword that hangs forever above the teachers' heads." Adkison and Tchudi (2001, p. 43) report "a steady encroachment on classroom autonomy by the forces of external assessment." In a lecture entitled "Raising the Scores, Ruining the Schools," Alfie Kohn (2002), one of the country's most outspoken critics of testing, says that accountability has come to mean control of classrooms by those who are not in classrooms. Like a stone thrown in a lake, the consequences ripple out to curriculum and pedagogy, to teaching and learning. Furthermore, students can lose promotion to the next grade; teachers can lose salaries or jobs; schools can lose credibility and funding.

Lessons Applied. Many believe that it is not the tests that distort our best educative purposes but our responses to the tests. The reactions of school districts, schools, departments, and individual teachers to the challenges of standardized testing vary. In the two schools in Luna and Turner's research, the administrative response was strikingly different. One group "panicked" and tightened the controls on its teachers. For instance, the principal initiated "department-wide final exams modeled" on the state exam. All students in a grade level had to pass this same exam (p. 81). The principal also promised students that if they achieved a proficient score on the state exam, they would be exempt from their teacher's exam in that subject. But the other high school's administrators reacted more collaboratively, asking teachers to analyze the state exam and to figure out how the school should respond. Some of the teacher initiatives added clarity to their curriculum and test-taking proficiency to their students without altering or disrupting the essential work of their classrooms.

Fischetti (2001) speaks directly to English teachers' tensions between meeting the demands of high-stakes testing and engaging students with best-practice teaching. He reports on a Kentucky classroom where skill-and-drill routines dominated English classes throughout the year in the name of high test scores. When the tests were over in April and spring vacation ended, most classrooms became saturated with feature films and other fillers to occupy students until the end of the school year. Fischetti praises a team of teachers who took a different tack. In these few months, they used an integrated approach in their classroom, not test-driven instruction. The results were irrefutable. Attendance, which typically goes down at that time of year, went up; tardiness went down. Students' attitudes were turned around and grade-point averages were markedly improved.

Many committed, energized, and creative teachers counsel others to teach as effectively as they know how throughout the year without regard to end-of-year tests. "Students taught and assessed via a theory-based, multiple-measures pedagogy will, in the end do as well if not better on standardized tests than those whose curriculum has been limited to the implied lowest common denominators of blanket standards and impersonalized tests" (Adkison & Tchudi, 2001, pp. 43–44). Able teachers have found that if they teach (and evaluate) their students effectively, the students will perform well without direct coaching. One such teacher, Janet McClaskey (2001), has tried various approaches to standardized tests in various schools—to ignore, embed, or embrace them—but she has always consistently taught with commitment and verve.

> The threat of standardized tests becoming the culture of our schools—the method by which we evaluate intelligence, success, and self-worth—is an issue of personal teaching philosophy not of legislation. I simply don't believe that a paper test, taken with pencils and Scantron forms, can measure any of those qualities, and I refuse to allow my students to buy into that scheme, either. I know, and they know that their sum total is much more than a score on a standardized test, no matter how much significance society places on the number. (p. 95)

Standardized Achievement Tests

A more familiar type of standardized testing has been a part of U.S. schooling for decades. Publishers or private agencies, such as the Educational Testing Service (ETS) or the Advanced Placement (AP) Program, have carefully constructed, administered, scored, normed, and interpreted standardized achievement test results for generations of students applying to colleges, universities, and other special programs. These tests are not commonly used for school purposes; however, they, too, affect schooling indirectly and, on rare occasions, directly.

Jones (2001, pp. 51–52) reports that two-thirds of U.S. high schools offer at least one AP course. In 2000, more than 300,000 students paid to take one of the two AP English exams. From the outset of these exams in 1956, the English exam has been "among the most popular" with students. The English exams are composed of multiple-choice questions (given in one hour for "45 percent of the test's value") and three essay questions (given in two hours for "55 percent of the test's value"). Jones believes these tests drive the curriculum of AP and other comparable courses with a multiple-choice format that is far removed from "complex ideas in speech and writing" (p. 53). Furthermore, the exam questions—multiple choice and essay—are inappropriately rooted in "a New Critical approach to literature and a 'product' (as opposed to 'process') approach to composition" (pp. 53–54). He quotes White (1995, p. 37): "Every assessment defines its subject and establishes values."

Like critics of state-mandated tests, Moffett and Wagner (1976, p. 433) warn that standardized testing "overfocuses on a few, easily testable skills and ignores what is hardest to teach and ultimately most important." But the testing behemoths disarm criticism. They give the appearance of scientific accuracy and empirical proof. Scores are precise and appear to be infallible. The testing industry is so large, its products so sophisticated, its administration so rigorous, and the interpretation of results so commonplace that the individual teacher finds critique difficult to wage convincingly. Even when test items do not match what is actually taught in school, when the norming groups do not match the students being tested, and when norms are interpreted as standards for all students, teachers have a hard time being heard. Moffett and Wagner (1976, p. 416) suggest a cardinal principle for keeping language arts evaluation sane: "Each party should do his own evaluation." We suggest that you clarify your own possible use of standardized tests and if they are used at all, it is simply for diagnosis of students.

Invitation to Reflection 13–1

1. Do you remember being tested by standardized achievement tests or state- or district-mandated tests during your schooling? Were you tested never, once, often, or many times?
   elementary school
   middle or junior high school
   secondary school
   college or university
2. Did you assume that the purpose of such testing was to measure learning for you, the student?
   your family?
   your teachers?
   your school administrators?
   your school system?
   state educational agencies?
   state or national legislatures?
   college admissions officers?
3. Which of the following describes your feelings about taking standardized tests?
   disliked
   preferred classroom tests
   neutral
   liked the testing environment
   enjoyed the challenge
4. Can you tell a personal story about your experience with standardized testing?

The best critiques of high-stakes testing raise fundamental questions about what learning and schools are all about. Prospective teachers must enter this debate. If you do not question the present system and establish a bal-

ance and direction with which to navigate it, you, too, might be swept into the testing flood. A special issue of *English Journal* (September, 2001) devoted to testing seems aptly named "Assessing Ourselves to Death."

We turn our attention now to the teacher as evaluator in his or her own classroom.

GRADING AND EVALUATION

Many terms are used almost synonymously in talking about evaluation: *measurement, assessment, appraisal, grading,* and *testing.* Although some prospective teachers will have taken courses on evaluation and be familiar with its concepts, we will begin our focus on classroom evaluation by defining these general terms. Our purpose is to inform those who are less familiar with this material and to establish and clarify our usage for those who are more familiar with it. The most important distinction is between evaluation and grading. Figure 13-1 demonstrates our sense of that crucial difference of purpose.

The distinction between grading and evaluation is fundamental. Grading is more closely aligned with what Chapter 1 described as a traditional approach to teaching in which teachers transmit knowledge to students who receive and absorb it. Testing measures the level of that absorption. Evaluation represents a pedagogy in which the teacher helps students construct knowledge by reorienting, reframing, and rethinking their present knowledge. Evaluation measures that unfolding process of construction.

Grading looks at specific work at a discrete moment in order to assign a mark to it. Evaluating, with a more student-centered developmental perspective, considers the relationship of students' performance to their earlier efforts and future possibilities. Grading tends to compartmentalize, label, rate, and rank students, while evaluation tends to engage students in a continuing process of self-assessment and growth. Grading often serves adults in their needs to assign students to groups, classes, grade levels, or colleges or to inform parents, administrators, or school systems. Evaluation primarily serves students because it focuses on the students' growth and learning.

Grading is so endemic to our culture that we can hardly conceive that it has not always been a part of education. In the United States, grading was introduced at Yale University in the 1760s and spread slowly. A hundred-point scale began in the 1830s and letter grades in the 1880s. The growth of universities and their desire to admit qualified applicants occurred simultaneously with the expansion of public school education. As grades became instrumental to higher education, they began to influence all schooling, finally becoming inseparable from the learning enterprise. Although elementary schools have occasionally resisted, for the most part our institutional arrangements have supported and legitimated

FIGURE 13–1
Evaluation versus grading

EVALUATION	GRADING
Happens anytime self- or group reflection about learning occurs.	Happens at discrete moments usually of oral or written production.
Measures a developmental process.	Measures a concrete product.
Is integral to instruction.	Occurs after instruction.
Offers a qualitative explanation of value judgments.	Offers a quantitative enumeration of value of individual performance.
Is experienced as a supportive learning activity.	Is often experienced as a judgmental activity.
Attempts to engage students' process of self-assessment.	Informs students about the teacher's perception of progress.
Reinforces students as active agents in this process.	Reinforces students as passive receivers of the teacher's marks.
Can involve teacher and student collaboration.	Is essentially teacher-directed.

grading; and it now seems inextricable from those arrangements. But grading was attacked by reformers of the 1960s such as John Holt (1967, 1969): It removed all intrinsic value from the process of learning, it absorbed too much instructional time and energy, it was biased against minorities, and it dictated too many educational decisions. "At best, testing does more harm than good; at worst, it hinders, distorts, and corrupts the learning process" (Holt, 1969, p. 53). Kirschenbaum, Napier, and Simon's (1971) *Wad-Ja-Get? The Grading Game in American Education* satirized the grading process as equivalent to a government inspector's role in the beef industry. They considered such labels alien to the education process, undermining the self-esteem of students for the sake of a consumer mindset.

Yet thirty years ago and increasingly today, grading has its defenders. The idea that grades are extrinsic to the learning process does not necessarily mean that they are toxic to it. Measuring one student's performance against others with concrete and unequivocal marks can present a realistic gauge of how well the student is doing and what kind of life work he or she might aspire to. Grading provides reality testing for students who must enter a competitive culture. It also can motivate students to a higher level of achievement.[2] Grades inform other interested parties (colleges or employers, for instance) about how the student has performed in school and might perform hereafter. Adkison and Tchudi (2001) pose "The Case for Evaluation as Pedagogy," in which they argue that assessment "need not be a killer of innovation if it is consistently linked to teaching; that is, assessing student work is a neutral and important part of teaching and makes good classroom sense when devoted to information-gathering rather than simply to proving to outsiders that we are competent" (p. 43). Invitation to Reflection 13–2 invites you into this debate.

---

[2] As we have said, politicians today see tests as the means to motivate teachers and schools as well. In an increasing number of states, student scores now influence teacher salaries. Even legislators who might not regard testing as a panacea for school reform vote to mandate and fund it in order also to fund programs that can influence student learning.

Invitation to Reflection 13–2

1. Following are the charges hurled between camps. Read and reflect on each.
   - Evaluators indulge themselves and students; graders enjoy cracking the whip.
   - Evaluators waffle on the hard decisions about student performance; graders make students toe a rigid line.
   - Evaluators are too student-centered; graders are too teacher-centered.
   - Evaluators are preoccupied with students' constructed knowledge; graders are preoccupied with teachers' transmitted knowledge.
   - Evaluators are naïve idealists; graders are brutal realists.
2. Do you recognize these criticisms?
3. Have you heard them before?
4. Can you see difficulties in both positions? Can you see justifiable ideas in either?
5. With which do you most identify?

Grading advocates often resort to a final argument: Grading is so interwoven with schooling that a wholesale abandonment of the process is impossible. The debate often breaks down at this point. Yet some compromise is necessary for the classroom teacher who might be drawn toward an evaluation model but must work in the context of school systems that require grading. We have found that grading is the common expectation of parents, students, administrators, and politicians when they speak of evaluation. Grading seems not only a routine part of instruction but also a necessary part. Consequently, if you do not sharpen your own perspective, you will be drawn into the prevailing testing culture of your school. Nothing you decide about your teaching will have more immediate impact on your daily action in class and your interaction with your students than how you evaluate. We want you to formulate your own position along the continuum from evaluation to grading. We encourage you at the outset to remember other principles of teaching that you have begun to construct and to try to envision evaluation that is consistent with those deepest aims. We believe some form of evaluation is central to our concern with the aims of English instruction. But you must work out the alignment between your curriculum and your assessment. This chapter should help you decide how.

Definition of Terms

Figure 13–2 schematizes the relationship between evaluation and grading and other terms commonly used in psychometric parlance. As you can see, measurements can be used for evaluation or for grading. Measurement instruments include far more than the traditional tests or exams. Self-evaluation instruments, portfolios, contracts, and observations are all used to measure student progress and performance. Appraisal is used at times to mean either evaluation or measurement. It carries connotations of the value or worth of its subject, the sort of estimation a jeweler makes about the quality of a gem.

Purposes of Evaluation

Measurement or assessment instruments are constructed to serve many different purposes. The first four that follow are most prominent in English classrooms. The last describes the purpose of many national standardized tests.

Descriptive: to describe the present status of students on any chosen variable. Example: A beginning-of-the-year worksheet to show how accurately students use semicolons or a survey of their understanding of formal elements in literary texts.

Diagnostic: to determine the strengths or weaknesses of a student in a specific area in order to make instructional decisions for the student. Example: A beginning-of-the-year test on knowledge of five formal elements of fiction (setting, plot, characters, point of view, and tone).

Formative: to monitor student progress in small increments during a term. Example: Periodic checks in the writing process during the early stages of prewriting, writing the first draft, and rewriting.

Summative: to measure mastery of a body of knowledge at the end of a unit or grading period. Example: A comprehensive test on all key texts and concepts in a six-week unit on "Coming of Age in America."

Predictive: to predict the future performance of students and their likelihood of success. Example: The Scholastic Aptitude Test (SAT) and the American College Test (ACT) as indicators of college/university performance.[3]

Invitation to Reflection 13–3

1. List at least three adjectives that capture your attitude toward the process of evaluation.
2. How do you distinguish between grading and evaluation?
3. Recall one positive and one negative experience that formed your attitudes about grading and evaluation.

---

[3] These standardized tests are often taken to be absolute measures of ability, but a more modest interpretation is more accurate: They predict only. The use of such predictive tests for descriptive, formative, or summative purposes threatens the integrity of these tests and, more important, the students who take them.

FIGURE 13–2

Relationships among common terms used in evaluation

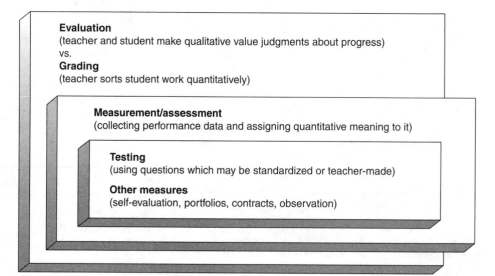

Evaluation
(teacher and student make qualitative value judgments about progress)
vs.
Grading
(teacher sorts student work quantitatively)

Measurement/assessment
(collecting performance data and assigning quantitative meaning to it)

Testing
(using questions which may be standardized or teacher-made)

Other measures
(self-evaluation, portfolios, contracts, observation)

4. How is evaluation in English different from that process in other subjects?
5. Consider the five basic evaluative purposes below to the kinds of classroom assessment that you have experienced:
   a. descriptive
   b. diagnostic
   c. formative
   d. summative
   e. predictive
6. Which of the five purposes motivated most of the assessments you remember in your College English classes?
7. Have you ever been in a class in which only summative evaluation was used? Did you feel that provided a fair reflection of your work? Did it help you discover something about yourself as a learner?
8. Have you ever had your SAT or ACT scores used as final statements of your ability and worth rather than as indicators of possible college performance?
9. Have you ever considered the evaluations of your school career as assessment *for* learning rather than assessment *of* learning?

Learning Possibilities to Be Measured

Recognizing one's principal purpose in evaluation is essential. An awareness of the range of learning variables is also important to sound evaluation. We have touched on all four of the following variables elsewhere in this text. We here summarize them and explore their relevance to the way in which we evaluate.

Bloom's Taxonomy. A group of university examiners (Bloom, Englehart, Furst, Hill, & Krathwohl, 1956) at-tempted to systematize the possible educational objectives for student behavior. Although they divided objectives into three domains—cognitive, affective (attitudes, interests, and values), and psychomotor—the cognitive objectives have received the most attention. Figure 13–3 lists the six major categories in Bloom's cognitive domain. Notice that they are arranged in a hierarchy of behavior (or objectives) from simple to complex. As with other stage theories, work at Bloom's higher levels of understanding depends on completing preceding stages. Thus, without knowledge of the short stories of Edgar Allan Poe, no analysis of his Gothic technique can occur, nor a comparison of his fiction to contemporary horror movies, nor judgments of the value of the macabre as a form of entertainment or enrichment.

A general consciousness of these different levels of cognition can be useful as a gauge to evaluation strategies. In evaluation, for instance, if you are interested in determining whether your students have read an assigned chapter in Amy Tan's *The Joy Luck Club,* you might administer a short-answer quiz. If, on the other hand, your class discussions of the novel have built from comprehension toward a final consideration of the difficulties in the relationships between immigrant parents and their first-generation American children, you would not evaluate learning by a true/false exam. You want what you measure to be consistent with what you have valued in your lessons. Your awareness of the variety of cognitive levels should guide your choices about appropriate evaluation. Table 13–1 schematizes those different levels in possible evaluative questions of Shakespeare's *Romeo and Juliet.*

Gardner's Intelligences. Gardner (1983) examined evidence from a large and diverse group of resources and

FIGURE 13–3
Bloom's taxonomy of cognitive educational objectives

1. *Knowledge:* the ability to recognize or recall previously learned information and processes. Knowledge is usually defined more broadly; here it merely involves remembering information.
2. *Comprehension:* the ability to understand what is being communicated, but at a basic level. The student knows the meaning of information or ideas, but may not necessarily be able to relate it or apply it to other material or see its implications.
3. *Application:* the ability to use learned knowledge in particular and concrete situations. The student can apply rules, principles, and concepts in new and appropriate contexts.
4. *Analysis:* the ability to break down information into its component parts.
5. *Synthesis:* the ability to put together elements or parts so as to form a whole. The student arranges and combines pieces to form a pattern or structure that was not clearly evident before.
6. *Evaluation:* the ability to judge the value of materials, methods, or ideas for a given purpose. This represents the highest level of intellectual functioning and is difficult for even the brightest students.

TABLE 13–1

Evaluation of reading literature based on Bloom's cognitive objectives: Shakespeare's *Romeo and Juliet*

Level of Objective	Teacher Questions	Typical Questioning Verbs Used
Knowledge	Name the two feuding families.	*Define, draw, repeat, record, recall, recite, recognize, identify, write,* * *describe, label, list, name*
Comprehension	Describe the consequences of their hatred on the relationship of Romeo and Juliet.	*Classify, compare, contrast, describe, discuss, interpret, translate,* * *explain, give examples, summarize*
Application	How is the predicament of Romeo and Juliet similar to other thwarted romances you know of personally or in other literature?	*Apply, calculate, complete, demonstrate, illustrate, practice, solve, use,* * *predict, show*
Analysis	Human experience: Why do we feel Romeo's and Juliet's deaths more keenly than Mercutio's and Tybalt's? Literary: Why does Shakespeare open the play with Romeo's infatuation with Rosaline? How does Shakespeare use other characters to underscore the tension surrounding Romeo and Juliet?	*Analyze, classify, discuss, divide, explain, infer, inspect, separate, sort,* * *diagram, outline*
Synthesis	What is the effect on the audience of all of these contending characters and events? How do they affect our sense of the tragedy? If you could view either *Romeo and Juliet* or *West Side Story,* which would you prefer? Why?	*Arrange, combine, construct, create, design, develop, generalize, organize, plan, predict, prepare,* * *categorize, compile, rearrange, revise*
Evaluation	Are Romeo and Juliet equally mature in their love for each other? If not, how do they differ? Does Shakespeare's dramatic reflection on human experience have value for our lives almost 400 years later?	*Appraise, assess, critique, estimate, evaluate, grade, judge, rank, rate, recommend, test, value,* * *justify, interpret*

*Guerin and Maier (1983, pp. 63–64) listed these verbs by cognitive levels in a table on which ours is loosely based.

isolated seven ways in which human intelligence is expressed. (In the late 1990s he began to articulate additional intelligences—namely, intelligences attuned to the natural and the spiritual worlds.) Just as a range of instructional strategies enable students to exercise those diverse intelligences, so alternative means of evaluation allow students to reflect that diversity. Traditional testing favors linguistic and logical/mathematical intelligences; alternative models can measure and validate other intelligences. For students whose best abilities are linguistic and logical/mathematical, alternatives provide new possibilities for self-discovery and self-expression. And when evaluation strategies encourage collaboration, students can benefit from the differing intelligences of others.

We borrow from Peter Smagorinsky's (1991, p. 2) helpful distillation of Gardner's ideas to define his first seven intelligences.

Linguistic: a sensitivity to the sounds, rhythms, and meanings of words, and to the different functions of language

Logical/mathematical: a sensitivity to and ability to discern logical or numerical patterns, with the ability to follow or generate long chains of reasoning

Musical: the ability to produce and appreciate rhythm, pitch, and timbre or an ability to appreciate the structure and forms of musical expression

Spatial: the ability to perceive the world in visual-spatial terms and to re-create things after seeing them

Bodily/kinesthetic: the skillful use of the body to solve problems and of the hands to fashion a product

Interpersonal: the ability to discern and respond appropriately to the moods, temperaments, motivations, and desires of other people

Intrapersonal: the ability to achieve self-knowledge demonstrated in its highest form by the great ascetics, such as the Buddha, but also achieved by highly reflective individuals who have achieved great personal insight

Table 13-2 enumerates evaluative strategies that capitalize on, exercise, and validate Gardner's five less ac-

TABLE 13–2
Evaluation and testing via Gardner's multiple intelligences

Intelligence	Strategy
Linguistic Logical/mathematical	Later chapter sections, "Evaluating Knowledge and Response to Literature" and "Evaluating Writing" discuss evaluation approaches for these first two intelligences.
Musical	Select music or write lyrics for a song that expresses the mood or situation of a piece of literature (poetry, fiction, or drama), or that elaborates a theme. Neenan (personal communication, 1992) has students compile a series of pop songs to reflect stages of a character's growth. Assemble or compose soundtracks for a found or student-scripted play.
Spatial	Diagram settings or map character relationships. Present photographs or pictures that suggest characters. Create sets, props, and staging for poems, dramatic monologues, and plays. Create a Web page to advertise a novel with appropriate art for characters, setting, and events.
Bodily/kinesthetic	Perform dance or mime that expresses ideas or feelings from literature studied. Arrange tableaus or body sculptures that capture the essence of a literary piece or a central episode, situation, or theme. Act out the gestures of a character as another student reads a dramatic passage from a poem or play.
Interpersonal	Collaborate on projects anywhere from productions to artistic displays that distill the most important insights from a single or a group of literary pieces. Conduct interviews with persons whose experiences touch the subject at hand and write these up as dialogues, character sketches, dramatic monologues, or productions. Work with another individual or small group to complete projects or write essays and tests jointly.
Intrapersonal	Through journals, free writes, or discussions reflect personally on literature and connect it to personal experience. Take these inward acts seriously.

knowledged intelligences. These suggestions serve the purpose of descriptive, diagnostic, formative, or summative evaluation; they can be used as primary evaluative procedures, as adjuncts, or as alternative choices. They are posed as directions to students who are engaged in reading and responding to literature.

Gardner's theories have another important implication for evaluation. Because students' aptitudes and strengths vary widely, individuals can bring different gifts to a group evaluative project. Traditional one-size-fits-all strategies prejudice one form of intelligence over others. Group evaluation activities allow each student to make a valued contribution to creating a product or to solving a problem.

Hemisphericity.   Chapter 12 presented Rico's (1983) chart of the differing talents of the brain's two hemispheres. The following example is another version drawn from Moffett and Wagner (1976), who credit Ornstein (1972).

Left Hemisphere	Right Hemisphere
intellectual	intuitive
analytic	synthetic
linear	holistic
verbal	nonverbal
sequential	simultaneous
temporal	spatial
digital	analogical
explicit	implicit
literal	metaphorical

Sensitivity to the features of both hemispheres is important to your instruction and evaluation. Students should be evaluated in work that honors more than simply left-brained, school-honored work. For instance, students can reflect on poetry with art that they create or with art masterpieces that they select. They can match a literary period with its music. They can discuss a novel by imagining themselves to be a character in it and composing letters, diary entries, lists of gifts for other characters, New Year's resolutions, and a scrapbook. If learners are asked to transfer impulses from one hemisphere of the brain to the other, they are in touch with a far greater range of responding capacities than is traditional. The dominant side within school and our culture is the left side. Postman (1979b) believes that schools should serve as a kind of corrective to the one-sidedness of everyday life. But whenever there are cuts in school budgets, you can usually expect music, art, and drama teachers to receive the first pink slips. The challenge to the teacher is to keep the right half of our students' brains awake in both teaching and assessment.

Dynamic and Contextual Views of the Mind.   For some time, cognitive scientists and learning theorists have explored other models of thinking and learning to determine the "kinds of basic processes that underlie intelligent performance" (Resnick, 1976, p. 4). They reject traditional views that focus on the mind as a passive storage container; a solitary machine working independently; or a composite of smaller parts, each doing an isolated task. (They also reject the corollary, of course, that knowledge exists as a separate entity and learning occurs when this knowledge is transferred to and acquired by the learner.) From the first chapter, we have contrasted the more traditional conception of learning with a more constructivist one based on a dynamic view of the cognitive conditions for learning. Without presenting any one cognitive system as the final revelation, we borrow from a number to indicate the lively scope of alternative views of the mind.

Resnick and Glaser (1976) define intelligence as "the ability to acquire new abilities under less than optimal environmental conditions, conditions where the appropriate solution routines are not directly prompted or specifically taught" (p. 228). They envision a more complicated model of the mind's weaving back and forth in a dialectic between basic skills and higher-order thinking. They are concerned about transitions in cognitive competence" and particularly in the "acquisition of new competence" without the influence of direct instruction (p. 6).

Ebel (1982) sees the interdependence of knowledge, thought, and performance and the insufficiency of one without the other. We must acquire knowledge in order to have something to think about; but without thinking, such knowledge remains inert and useless. "Acquiring knowledge and learning how to think thus would seem to be identical goals. . . . A mind stuffed with memorized facts possesses very little useful knowledge" (p. 269). Ebel believes that performance provides opportunities to convert this knowledge into action. Myers (1991) also conceives of thinking as embedded within situations and subjects. He sees school-acquired knowledge as so decontextualized that we do not expect it to help us make sense of the world. Vygotsky (1978) believes persons do not learn in isolation but help each other to make meaning. Learning occurs as a dynamic dialectic in which the expert (a more knowledgeable other) guides the learner (or novice) to insight, to problem solving, and finally to initiatives that demonstrate learning.

These dynamic and contextual conceptions of the mind contain implications for evaluation as well as instruction. They recommend evaluation that requires *using* knowledge rather than *having* knowledge. Evaluation methods should include opportunities for applying knowledge in a new context or in new ways. Furthermore, evaluation should assess students working in groups, not in isolation, and the process of their work, not the final product. In other words, evaluation should mirror instruction. Often teachers teach from constructivist assumptions but test from traditional ones. Teachers who value dynamic and contextual views of learning and who attempt to develop genuine understanding in their students should use a variety of assessment instruments or schemes, not simply traditional paper-and-pencil texts. They should also use evaluation to support, not simply to measure new learning. If learning is dynamic, feedback is a powerful tool to clarify how the student has success-

fully met learning expectations or how the student can improve his or her achievement.

We turn next to consider alternative evaluation methods that recognize these diverse perspectives on learning. They provide concrete ways to align your curriculum with your assessment. Although these methods are associated with constructivist learning, they can also be used to measure the outcomes of traditional direct instruction. As you read each, imagine how it can be used for "evaluation as pedagogy" (to borrow a phrase from Adkison and Tchudi).

☞ ALTERNATIVE METHODS OF EVALUATION

Later in this chapter we discuss traditional evaluation with some specificity. We assume that you are experienced with its general outline. Traditional assessment approaches are largely teacher-controlled. Just as teachers determine the curriculum and present it, they test students' mastery of it. Students have little or no choice. Standards are set and met; homework assignments, class reports, writing assignments, quizzes, and tests determine whether or not the student has mastered the essential curriculum. Individual exceptions and departures have little place in this heavily prescribed system.

The four alternative strategies that follow—*self-evaluation, portfolios, contracts,* and *observation*—can serve the purposes of evaluation or grading. They do encompass, however, patterns of evaluation that respect and encourage the individuality and autonomy of the student, the professional skill of the teacher, and the unique nature of English study.

Self-Evaluation

Because we are concerned about the development of students as reflective, self-aware individuals, we believe in teaching and modeling self-evaluation strategies. Students need opportunities to assess their work habits, learning strategies, progress, and achievements. Because schooling has traditionally located evaluation outside of the student—in the teacher, the parent, the school, and the school district—students have learned to depend on others for identification of their weaknesses or confirmation of their achievements. We need to relocate some of that responsibility. Furthermore, we know that students who are prompted to gain a metacognitive awareness of their own thinking learn to think more deeply and creatively.

Whether as a primary evaluation strategy or as an adjunct to the primary teacher-based evaluation, the benefits of student self-evaluation include the following:

- It more solidly anchors evaluation within the individual as opposed to making it a series of impersonal verdicts handed down by outsiders.

- Educational goals and individual progress become clearer to the student and are more personally owned.
- Processes of learning become more important than the products.
- Students "gain an authority in the classroom otherwise reserved for the teacher" (Schwartz, 1991, p. 72). Their self-esteem rises simply through their empowerment.
- Students can sometimes identify areas of strength or weakness that the teacher might not observe.
- The importance of grades can be mediated by shifting focus to the student's self-perceived progress.

Teachers who shift to even modest forms of self-evaluation encounter challenges from prevailing student and parent expectations, but they affirm the benefits of their efforts. An experienced teacher, Schwartz (1991), describes moving to a new school and trying to change traditional practices in a classroom in which the teacher typically controlled grading and evaluation with teacher-made reading quizzes, cumulative tests, and assigned writing topics. In incremental steps he began to ask students to assess their own learning. His midyear exam reflected that refocusing. He posed the question "In what central area of your writing have you made most substantial progress?" (p. 69). He asked that they write a two-part essay, the first a "summary of central strengths and weaknesses" and the second "an in-depth analysis of one central area of their writing" (p. 69). His summation of the rewards of the project included a more subtle consequence of it: "By having to synthesize patterns in their work over time . . . they are gaining additional practice in how to read literature. . . . Most important, by identifying strengths and weaknesses, and by taking control over their own processes, students are becoming more independent learners, always the most important goal of my classes" (p. 72).

An *English Journal* "Roundtable" feature (November, 1989) queried middle and high school teachers about successful initiatives to involve students in the evaluation of their own work. Figure 13–4 contains four teacher ideas. We describe in greater depth four other promising forms of self-evaluation: *self-assessment inventories, learning logs, student-maintained records,* and *teacher-parent-student conferences.*

Self-Assessment Inventories. Inventories of student attitudes, prior reading, preferences, reading and writing habits, and interests can be administered at any time in a term

- to sensitize yourself to your students
- to aid instructional planning
- to promote student self-analysis
- to gather baseline data with which to assess the gains of study
- to measure progress or the attainment of established goals

Figure 13–5 is a self-assessment inventory that we administered during a six-week literature course for eighth and ninth graders. We had just completed a three-week study on the topic "The Wisdom of Fables" that concluded with selections from James Thurber's *Fables for Our Times.* Because much student and teacher effort had been spent in adjusting to new classroom expectations and arrangements, we felt that such a self-evaluation would reinforce and clarify our expectations and would prompt student reflection on theirs. Because students were primed for end-of-unit tests and were accustomed to taking them seriously, we assumed that they would apply themselves to what *looked like a test.* It had exactly

FIGURE 13–4
Teacher initiatives to promote student self-evaluation

TECHNIQUE	DESCRIPTION
Student-generated rubrics	Students working in small groups with anonymous sample drafts establish five standards by which a paper is to be graded and the weight of each of them. The whole class agrees on the criteria and they guide the revision and evaluation process of compositions, posters, speeches. (Kathleen T. Choi)
Weekly peer evaluation	Each Friday the class circles the desks to read a journal assignment made on Monday. After each reader, every person comments on the writing, at first via sentence opening teacher prompts, but progressively from suggestions the listeners initiate. Readers make notes and submit a revision for teacher evaluation. (Phyllis Parypinski)
Tell me a story	With each finished piece of writing, students turn in a "process log," which tells the story of their composition. "Because process logs emphasize the most important reader—the writer—they can produce richly revealing biographies of the writing process". (Susan Kimball and Susan Grotewold)
Learning from the process	Disappointed with an essay exam, the teacher discussed the problem with students, set up grading criteria, assigned points, and weighted possible responses. Students got their tests, evaluated them and defended points they think they deserved. In class, two students read and evaluated each test. The three scores were averaged. (Marilyn Cole Wenzel)

FIGURE 13–5
"The Wisdom of Fables": Self-evaluation

Please evaluate your work this week during the study of fables. Circle the number that best describes your work.					
5—Strongly agree 4—Agree 3—Neither agree nor disagree 2—Disagree 1—Strongly disagree					

POSITIVE BEHAVIORS

	5	4	3	2	1
I listened actively to the class discussions.	5	4	3	2	1
I was prompt in focusing on the work at the beginning of class.	5	4	3	2	1
I completed homework assignments.	5	4	3	2	1
I tried to enter into the class conversations about fables by either offering my interpretations or listening to others.	5	4	3	2	1
When my mind wandered, I tried to bring it back to the literature.	5	4	3	2	1
I was open to new ways of approaching this literature.	5	4	3	2	1
I participated in the oral reading.	5	4	3	2	1
I did not distract others from learning.	5	4	3	2	1
I did not introduce unrelated topics.	5	4	3	2	1
I did not use class time for private chats with friends.	5	4	3	2	1
I contributed constructively to small-group work.	5	4	3	2	1
If my family had been silent witnesses to this week's English classes, they would probably have been quite proud of my work.	5	4	3	2	1

Total self-evaluation score _____

Extra points (one each for your serious response to the following questions) _____
What are the two most important learnings for you in this week's study?
If you were the teacher, what fable(s) would you omit from study? Why?
If this unit on "The Wisdom of Fables" had been eliminated, what would be lost?
Describe one thing you did well in English class this week.

Total points _____

the effect that we had hoped: Students, in the heightened moment of self-scrutiny, paused to take stock of themselves, to ask penetrating questions of our intentions, and then to settle more solidly into our new routines and purposes.

We also use inventories on the first day of new courses to survey student reading and writing preferences or experiences from which we construct a tentative course agenda. Our classroom inventories usually have the side effect of alerting students to our interest in their personal experiences. This seems to promote individual reflection, excitement about the subject, and group sharing.

Learning Logs. Learning logs differ from journals by focusing on students' reflections on their own learning. Entry topics can be student- or teacher-generated. We list here specific sample prompts that focus on different aspects of learning.

Learning Styles
- Do you prefer to study alone or with a group?
- What do you do first when you are assigned out-of-class reading?

- What kinds of questions do you most enjoy considering in class discussions?
- When you do not understand something in class, what do you do?
- If you think the teacher is incorrect, what do you do?

Strengths or Weaknesses
- Describe one thing you do well (need to improve) in this class.
- If you could strengthen one thing about your work in English, what would it be?
- Tell a story about something you have done in class this year of which you are proud (or embarrassed).

End of Unit
- What are the two most important things that you learned in this unit?
- What topics, if any, would you wish to pursue?
- What did you find confusing?
- What skills or concepts do you wish to improve?
- If you were the teacher, what would you omit in the unit? Add?

Purpose
- If this unit were eliminated next year, what would be lost?

A Finished Piece of One's Own Writing[4]
- How did your idea for this piece originate?
- Why did you choose this form?
- What new techniques did you try?
- What problems cropped up and how did you solve them?
- Which lines or sections do you consider the best? Which still don't satisfy you?
- What surprises came during your writing?
- How does this work compare to previous writing you've done?
- What did you learn in the process?

Student-Maintained Records. Students can be encouraged to do their own record keeping. The purposes of such recordkeeping are multiple: to gather in a central place (student folders, for instance) a summary look at goals and performance; to encourage students to take responsibility for their own work; to provide an opportunity for them to revisit that work as they log it in; to prompt students to reflect on their past learning, their progress, and their next plans; and to free the teacher from this time-consuming task. The simplest log is merely a list of all the novels (or plays, stories, or poems) read during a term; stages or end products of writing and oral productions may be documented as well. When they are available, computers can make record keeping more efficient for students and response simpler for teachers. Teachers can even make electronic comments. The particular purposes to which you and your students put such records will determine their exact shape. This process holds greatest potential when learning goals are clearly articulated and progress in achieving them is conscientiously recorded.

Teacher-Parent-Student Conferences. We tend to envision the parent-teacher conference as a meeting of adults to resolve a student's classroom problems, often with "last resort" connotations. But if we refashion this image as a productive collaboration of all parties—parent, teacher, and student—we might disengage the punitive implications of these conferences and find something more potent. Try to imagine the conference as a natural extension of a student's self-evaluation in which his or her input is sought and valued. The experience becomes a joint discussion about an individual's learning—strengths and weaknesses—rather than what may seem to the student to be a conspiracy of fault-finding adults. When multiple measures enlarge the teacher's awareness of a student's learning, he or she can present far richer, more nuanced data to students and parents than a simple comparison of scores on tests can. Anthony, Johnson, Mickelson, and Preece (1991, pp. 161–174), remind us that, with careful

planning, students can be asked to share the responsibility for describing and interpreting for parents their classroom performance. All three parties can then discuss the setting of new goals and tasks. (Chapter 15 discusses other strategies for engaging parents in the work of the classroom.)

Portfolios

Our second alternative strategy, portfolios, have been common in fields other than English education for centuries. Whether they are documents carried by ministers of state, financial papers of investors, or paintings of artists, portfolios represent a comprehensive collection of somebody's hard work. The educational portfolio is no different: It is a gathering of student work in an ongoing, dynamic process. Portfolio assessment has been common in English schools for some time but has come only recently to the United States. Teachers here have embraced it because portfolios promise to match new instructional perspectives: to do greater justice to the student as a growing learner and to the teacher as collaborator, not examiner; and to align student work with real-world writing and authentic situations students will face when they leave school classrooms.

As we discussed in Chapter 11, although their contents and purposes differ from classroom to classroom and from district to district, educational portfolios are the natural consequence of a student-centered process approach to learning that focuses on the development of individual students, not on the end results of that learning. If portfolios can be instruments of instruction, they can be tools of assessment as well. If the emphasis in writing instruction, for example, is on how students compose, traditional assessments based on finished compositions are inadequate. If, in literature instruction, the concern is with developing breadth of reading or depth of response and reflection, multiple-choice exams or even traditional essay questions limit students' demonstration of learning. If the teacher values a personally engaged collaborative relationship with students, not a distant, judging one, then portfolios are a resource. For the sensitive teacher, these situations beg for an opportunity to sift through a portfolio and witness the evolution of a student's grapplings.

Writing Portfolios. Some teachers include all of a student's writing in the writing portfolio. Other teachers prefer to keep the bulk of student writing in writing folders and use portfolios for selected pieces. Common selection criteria include

- a specified number of pieces (usually three or four) representing the student's best writing
- one best piece of writing with all of the stages of composition represented: drafting, review, revision, editing, final piece

---

[4] This final list on writing is adapted from Kimball and Grotewold (1989, p. 76).

- best pieces chosen to represent different writing modes: exposition, persuasion, narration, description, argumentation, expression
- a number of best pieces chosen from the term and one in-class composition written without feedback or revision
- a number of best pieces chosen by the student and one selected by the teacher
- pieces that demonstrate the student's "best work as well as any experiments . . . attempted in order to extend and diversify . . . [the] portfolio" (Graves, 1991, p. 168)

In addition to this collection of student writing, other contents might include the following:

- a table of contents
- a statement of the writer's personal goals and/or the class goals for the period covered by the portfolio
- an introduction to the portfolio to provide a context for the reader
- a letter to a reader
- a cover sheet for every piece that reflects on the writing process and acknowledges any help received
- a writing checklist devised by the teacher or, better, by the teacher and student in concert
- writing learning logs or writing process checklists
- a rationale for selection of a best piece or all of the pieces chosen

Herter (1991, p. 90) regards portfolios as the most powerful form of writing assessment because they can "involve students in assessing the development of their writing skills by inviting self-reflection and encouraging students to assume control over their writing." She argues for this approach as the most thorough way to promote students' knowledge about their own writing. She sees portfolios as the recorded history of the semester's learning.

Reading Portfolios. Graves (1991), in describing the literate classroom for younger students, suggests that reading portfolios

> require a broader interpretation than writing portfolios. The objectives for reading portfolios are similar, to show both range and depth. But in the reading portfolio, the child will include favorite books, authors, and characters. It should also contain evidence that the child is experimenting with various kinds of reading. . . . The key element in the reading portfolio is the opportunity it affords the child to demonstrate good thinking about books, especially books that have had a significant impact in the child's life. (p. 170)

Secondary reading portfolios might include the following:

- an introduction to the contents of the portfolio with a statement about what the student has learned as reflected in the portfolio pieces

- lists of novels, stories, drama, and poems read; favorite characters, authors, settings, fictive events, and ideas
- lists of nonfiction or nonprint texts
- written compositions about literature
- journal entries, quick-writes, or other brief personal reflections on reading literature
- annotated lists of collateral reading about literature
- clippings of book reviews or biographies of favorite authors
- glossaries of vocabulary learned from reading or terms learned and demonstrated in reading
- evidence of intertextual correspondences
- descriptions of epiphanies while reading

Duration. Time lengths for reading or writing portfolios vary from a unit, to a term, to a year, to a school career depending on the purposes of the portfolios and the nature of the students. Older, more mature students seem more able than younger ones to profit from work collected over extended periods.

Evaluation Strategies. If portfolios are used for assessment across grade levels, the process and product remain unfinished. One of the most promising features of portfolios is their sense of a dynamic ongoing cycle. In many schools, teams of teachers grade portfolios. Elbow and Belanoff (1986) report that "the only way to bring a bit of trustworthiness to grading is to get teachers negotiating together in a community to make some collaborative judgments. That the portfolio promotes collaboration and works against isolation may be, in the end, its main advantage" (p. 338).

Krest (1990, p. 31) uses portfolios not only to promote writing production and progress but also to encourage risk-taking explorations on papers that will not be graded traditionally. She assigns two grades on her portfolios:

1. a "portfolio grade," which reflects the amount of revision, risk taking, and changing they do on *all* papers
2. a "paper grade," which reflects the outcome of *one* final product.

Her rubric for evaluating student papers is as follows (p. 31):

High-order concerns: focus, development, organization, and voice
Middle-order concerns: style, sentence structure, and sentence variety
Low-order concerns: spelling, punctuation, and usage

A great advantage of Krest's strategy is that the teacher can adapt the system to the personal needs of students and to the broader aims of an individual classroom. The teacher weighs the portfolio grade and final paper grades differently, depending on the circumstance. Krest enumerates four consequences of adopting portfolios in her writing workshop classes. Three involve questions of evaluation.

- I lightened my paper load.
- I began spending most of each semester coaching rather than grading students.
- I began looking forward to grading students' papers (at least I became excited about how an idea or revision turned out).
- Most important, I watched as previously unmotivated writers became motivated to work for a grade they desired and at the same time to improve their writing. (p. 29)

Assessment Tips. Here are a few final suggestions to aid portfolio assessment:

- Determine intervals for collection, selection, and submission and then announce them clearly.
- Vary the suggested contents of the portfolio to reflect your instructional aims.
- Keep the entire portfolio in the classroom (except for removal of single pieces).
- Date everything that goes into the portfolio.
- Give all responsibility for keeping track of the portfolio to the students.

Portfolio assessment has its defenders and detractors. Dudley (2001) affirms portfolios as a "valuable classroom practice" but rejects them as tools of assessment. Another teacher, Kent (1997) has written a book, *Room 109: The Promise of a Portfolio Classroom*, about the revitalization of his classroom as he reoriented his teaching toward student-centered practice and portfolio evaluation strategies.

Other teachers make other claims for the consequences of portfolio assessment. They:

- encourage students to become conscious, reflective, independent, and responsible learners
- promote students as self-evaluators
- document growth over time and sequence that growth
- provide a collection of writing of which students are proud
- make students "more aware of their experiments and their specialties" (Graves, 1991, p. 169)

This focus on the developing student, whether reader or writer, places portfolio assessment outside of the norm-referenced tradition of sorting and distributing individuals along a normal distribution curve. Elbow and Belanoff (1986, p. 337) observe that "the portfolio process . . . assumes that the ideal end product is a population of students who have all finally passed because they have all been given enough time and help to do what we ask of them" (p. 337). It also promises to diminish the separation between learning and evaluation.

Contracts

Contract assessment, our third alternative strategy, invites students to establish an independent course of study in collaboration with the teacher and to determine their grades by choosing the amount and quality of their work. As with legal agreements between people or parties, educational contracts involve negotiation and agreement. Although the teacher maintains important control in initiating the contract and establishing its terms, individual students gain choice and responsibility for their work.

Most contracts begin with a teacher presenting work options for the entire class. For both specific and broader contract choices, the criteria by which each item will be judged should be clearly enumerated. Ideally, the teacher confers with each student individually about how to structure his or her learning and to assess outcomes. The teacher helps each student set realistic goals (while pushing those goals beyond the most obvious boundaries) and then collaborates with the student during the process to unravel snarls, suggest additional resources, and encourage follow-through. When the teacher has supported and facilitated all stages of the contract, grading should be straightforward and without surprises. Some teachers believe that contracts should offer students an opportunity to revise and resubmit work that fails the requirements of the contract.

Contract work can be time-intensive for the creative and attentive teacher; thus, we recommend scheduling it strategically. Often, contracts make ideal vehicles for culminating a unit of work, such as the contract in Figure 13-6 that concludes a unit on short fiction. We have used contracts with the study of other genres, literary themes, literary periods, and even literary conventions (such as satire and metaphor). Some have been open; others present a range of possible options. They allow students to pursue personal interests and to express their discoveries in idiosyncratic ways. They make use of knowledge gained with the whole class and then extend and personalize that knowledge. The amount of work to be done is the most natural place for grade demarcations—"You must do this for a *C,* more for a *B,* and even more for an *A*"—but the teacher must relentlessly advocate for the good quality of that work regardless of the quantity.

Contract assessment attempts to engage students in evaluation decisions and to make grades secondary to the work achieved. Like portfolio assessment, they make students' intentions, plans, progress, and achievements more visible. But contracts can sometimes drive students to gun for grades alone: they can become preoccupied with productivity, not learning. The role of the teacher is crucial in keeping the focus on the progress of students' work. Simply asking questions of process and content rather than number of contract items achieved can redirect students to their own learning.

Observation

Like the first three alternative assessment strategies, observation can serve many purposes: description, placement,

FIGURE 13–6
Short-fiction
contract

I _____ contract to complete the following assignments by
    (student's name)

_____ .
        (date)

                                        _____
                                              (Author)

I will:

1. Read _____ short stories by my author.
2. Read _____ pages of biographical material about my author.
3. Read _____ essays about my author's fiction.
4. Record in my journal my thoughts and feelings as I
    a. read the stories.
    b. read the author's biography.
    c. read the literary criticism.
5. Submit a bibliography of my reading.
6. Find another person who has read works by my author, conduct an interview about his or her responses to those readings, and write a report of that meeting.
7. Research and list available public resources (school and public libraries, bookstores) for my author's stories.

I will choose any _____ of the following, but one must be a written account for the teacher and my reading group and another an oral or visual presentation for the whole class:

1. Compare narrators, techniques, or ideas in my author's stories in a three-page response paper.
2. Write an imitation or a parody of my author's style.
3. Compare or contrast my author with another author whose works we read in class.
4. Find nonfictional material (editorials, news or human interest stories, cartoons, music, comic strips, TV programs, movies) that remind me of my author's stories (character, theme, setting, tone) and present those correspondences imaginatively.
5. Dress as my author or a character and deliver a 4-minute monologue about other characters and arrange music to accompany it.
6. Create a visual impression (collage, illustration, Web site) that would entice my classmates to read my author's works.

For the satisfactory completion of the above work I will be awarded a grade of _____

_____   _____
Student's name   Date

_____   _____
Teacher's name   Date

instruction, evaluation, and reporting. It is an integral part of teaching. The interest in human experience that draws many to the study and teaching of English may explain why English teachers are often excellent intuitive observers. If you focus your attention, perhaps even systematizing your observations, you can develop a useful tool to augment other evaluation strategies. (Seldom in the typically large, diverse English class can observation be the sole strategy.) When observations are systematic and documented, they possess great explanatory power. We discuss here a few common means of observation that are useful in English classrooms.

Anecdotal Records.   These consist of records of unanticipated student behavior or events. Our colleague Becky Brown prepares a separate notebook page for each of her students at the beginning of the school year. Each day after school, she records memorable anecdotes of individual students. She uses these primarily to prepare her letters of recommendation for students, but we suggest that you use the technique also to clarify and solidify your

impressions of a student and to illustrate your sense of the student during conferences.

Participation Charts.   Participation charts list behaviors in a group context. These can be elaborate—"What kinds of questions are raised by students? What are characteristic responses to discussion?"—or simply counts of how often a student speaks. Because of the teacher's time constraints, they will often be done intuitively. We have tallied participation most often to answer questions about students who are quiet and seldom speak. These silent students are easy to lose in a classroom of their more vocal peers. Sometimes we can sense cliques building or antagonisms growing; participation charts help clarify our intuitions and guide our strategy for negotiating them.

Checklists.   Checklists record the presence or absence of individual behaviors or attitudes. These can be made by you, an outside observer, or by students. Checklists can be lists of expected behaviors or of actual behaviors. Figure 13-7 is a list of questions that Probst (1988b,

FIGURE 13–7
Questions about
student progress

1. Does the student seem willing to express responses to a work, or is she cautious and constrained?
2. Does the student ever change her mind, or is she intransigent?
3. Does the student participate in discussions, listening to others, considering ideas offered, and presenting her own thoughts?
4. Does the student distinguish between the thoughts and feelings she brings to a literary work and those that can be reasonably attributed to the text?
5. Is the student able to distinguish between fact, inference, and opinion in the reading of a literary work?
6. Is the student able to relate the literary work to other human experience, especially her own—that is, can she generalize and abstract?
7. Does the student accept the responsibility for making meaning out of the literature and the discussions? Or does she depend on others to tell her what works mean?
8. Does the student perceive differences and similarities in the visions offered by different literary works, or is she unaware of the subtleties?

To record our observations of students more easily, we might recast our list of questions as dichotomous pairs. The first question, for example, might simply be:
open .... closed

Others might be:

speaks willingly... speaks reluctantly
enjoys the reading .... dislikes the reading
relates work to self... remains distant
listens to others .... refuses to hear other ideas
rational .... emotional

Locating students on each continuum may give the teacher useful information about their habits and inclinations.

Source: From Robert Probst, (1988). *Response and analysis: Teaching literature in junior and senior high school.* (p. 228). Portsmouth, NH: Boynton/Cook.

p. 228) suggests as a way of monitoring students' learning styles, classroom habits, and actual progress.

Rating Scales. When checklists record frequency or quality, they become more quantitative and might be called rating scales. These scales can count the errors made in writing or the number of pages completed in reading. They are useful when a straightforward tally clarifies performance.

Chronologs. A chronolog is a detailed report of a student that records all that the observer sees and hears during a specified learning event. Teachers attempt chronologs only infrequently, but sometimes they need comprehensive data from which to draw conclusions. When we have had serious difficulties with students, having a colleague come and quietly keep a chronolog has helped us form keener impressions and take more positive remedial steps than would have been possible without this objective record.

Whether you rely on informal observation or try to incorporate formal observation into your evaluative plan, these principles can help guide you. Observation

- should not intrude or disrupt instruction
- should "take place in authentic situations—those that are part of normal instruction" (Anthony et al., 1991, p. 30)
- should be directed toward answering questions about individual students or whole-class learning
- becomes more productive when those questions are specific and the observations are single-minded

- should reflect a range of processes and a variety of products
- can involve collaboration with students, parents, and colleagues
- may be more important to understanding some students and classes than others

Purves et al. (1990) discuss an evaluation-of-literature strategy based on observation. Their concern is not to evaluate students' memory of previous "passive" learning but the "processes of thinking, feeling, responding, and imagining they can bring to bear on a new experience" (p. 174). They suggest that the teacher halve the class; present the groups with a new literary selection; ask them to discuss it; and record their discussion through notes, an audiotape, or a videotape. Following the discussion, the teacher and/or the observing students assess the "performance and process" orally or in a written "marking," even playing the tape back. Here are their specific suggestions: "As you listen to the class or the recording, make notes about where you think the students might have checked something, where you think a student did a particularly good job picking up on somebody else's ideas, where you can suggest another example, and so forth" (p. 174).

Rudd (1990) provides a detailed account of her list-keeping strategies as an English teacher. She uses multiple copies of her classroom roster to catalogue things such as a student's implementation of writing skills (use of sensory details or vivid verbs, for example), employment of new vocabulary, misspelled words, and variety of sentence structure. She finds that it is often "desirable for students to be involved finding the samples themselves" but suggests that the teacher limit the number of characteristics to be observed, perhaps even to one.

∽Invitation to Reflection 13-4

1. Have you experienced any of the four alternative evaluation strategies in your career as student? If so, which?
   self-evaluation
   portfolios
   contracts
   observation
2. In comparison with other forms of evaluation, what was the proportion of time given to these alternatives?
3. What was the impact of alternatives on you? Did you like them? How? Prefer them? Why?
4. Did they allow other dimensions of your abilities to be expressed?
5. Do any of these seem more aligned with your developing ideas about teaching than traditional approaches are? How are they more consistent with constructivist, process-oriented assumptions about learning and instruction than paper-and-pencil measures are?
6. Can you find in these an approach that uses assessment *for* learning, not just *of* learning? Do any help students to take the next steps in their learning?

We have begun with these alternative evaluation models because they are less common and we want to draw your attention to them. We consider now the more traditional means of assessing student mastery of the four traditional language arts: reading, writing, speaking, and listening. Each presents its own assessment requirements and challenges. We pose the challenges, and then common solutions.

∽EVALUATING KNOWLEDGE AND RESPONSE TO LITERATURE

Many critics deplore the reductive nature of reading and writing tests that tend to concentrate on questions that are testable: questions of content, questions of passive (or remembered) knowledge, and questions with simple answers. They believe that tests of literary knowledge should be tied to our deepest perceptions about student reading and learning. They worry that the more measurable the content, the more trivial our teaching. Teaching purposes should determine our testing rather than our testing determining our teaching purposes. Purves et al. (1990, pp. 165–166) locate the dilemma of testing students' knowledge and response to literature in the dis-

tinction that Rosenblatt (1968/1978) makes between reading undertaken to experience a text personally, sensually, and viscerally (aesthetic) and reading undertaken to gain information or instruction (efferent).[5] "The current reading tests only measure efferent reading and by implication signal to students that it is the only kind of reading that is to be valued." Mayher (1990, p. 256) believes that testing the complex process of reading for meaning is flawed because "if we want to know how well someone has read something, what we are concerned with is how well they understood it. This doesn't depend on how they have decoded it, which can be assessed by a right answer format" (p. 256).

Psychiatrist, writer, and literary and social critic Robert Coles (1989a) tells a story that captures the dilemma well. He described his childhood questions about his parents' habit of reading literature aloud to each other. His father politely tried to explain to him that "novels contain 'reservoirs of wisdom' out of which he and our mother were drinking. . . . 'Your mother and I feel rescued by these books. We read them gratefully' " (p. xii). Indeed, his mother had a particular passion for the Russian writers Chekhov, Dostoevsky, and Tolstoy, reading and rereading their works throughout her life. She therefore was excited that her son was studying Russian novels in his undergraduate days at Harvard and asked eagerly about his first exam. He explained that his reading had been tested by fifty multiple-choice questions. She was dismayed and exclaimed, "Tolstoy would be horrified" (p. xv). Coles (1989b) says that she also suggested, "Robert, Robert, pray for your teacher."

Applebee (1993) gives us a more textured picture of how English teachers are assessing high school students' learning in literature study (pp. 131–137). He asked teachers to rate how frequently they used particular assessment techniques with specified classes. Table 13-3 indicates that quizzes, unit tests, and essays (interpretive and response-based) dominated teachers' formal evaluation of progress in literature (p. 135). Assessment, however, differs among the three tracks (nonacademic, mixed, and college prep). The largest differences occurred in essay writing of all sorts, with nonacademic students being assessed by essays far less often than their college-prep counterparts were. These nonacademic students were more likely to be assessed via quizzes and worksheets. Teachers used group or individual projects in mixed classes more than in any other (perhaps in accommodation to individual differences within the classes). You will notice that, overall, teachers rated "participation in discussion" as the most frequent measure of progress.

Earlier we addressed evaluation alternatives that could replace the old standbys of literature evaluation: the test

---

[5] Britton (1970) uses the terms *poetic* and *transactional* to make the same distinction. Bruner (1986) speaks of "a good story and a well-formed argument" (p. 11).

TABLE 13–3
Means of assessing student performance in literature in a representative class, by track

	Non-academic (n = 27)	Mixed (n = 106)	College Prep (n = 231)	Chi-Square (df = 2)
Essays focusing on				
Literary analysis	33.3	58.9	82.7	42.29***
Student responses or interpretations	59.3	75.9	86.6	14.99***
Major themes or comparisons among texts	34.6	55.6	78.8	33.70***
Activity-based assessments				
Participation in discussion	81.5	77.6	84.1	2.09
Brief written exercises	77.8	72.9	72.2	0.38
Group or individual projects	40.7	75.9	65.5	12.49**
Journal responses	48.1	43.5	34.6	3.64
Role playing or dramatization	29.6	31.8	31.5	0.05
Tests				
Quizzes	81.5	86.0	73.5	6.83*
Unit tests	66.7	70.8	77.9	3.07
Study guides or worksheets	59.3	57.4	42.9	7.63*
Commercially available standardized tests	11.1	23.4	16.2	3.45
Department or district exams	18.5	12.1	12.3	0.88

Source: From *Literature in the Secondary School: Studies of Curriculum and Instruction in the United States* by A. N. Applebee. Copyright © 1993 by the National Council of Teachers of English. Reprinted with permission.

[a] Ratings of 4 or 5 on a scale from 1 (not at all) to 5 (regularly).
* $p<.05$
** $p<.01$
*** $p<.001$

or writing assignment taken simultaneously by all the students of a class. Although many would urge you to use these traditional strategies seldom or never, we know you will at times find them appropriate or required. Thus, we conduct a brief tour of the traditional evaluation strategies to encourage your selection and construction of the best possible test for your purposes.

Think of the testing possibilities as ranging between the two major types—commonly called objective and subjective (essay)—with a variety of formats for each along the way. Many psychometricians question whether any item is objective (Wiersma & Jurs, 1990, p. 41). A teacher's selection of what to test, how to phrase items, and how much time to allow introduces subjectivity regardless of the appearance of unbiased precision in the standard scoring key. Thus, psychometricians have replaced the designations *objective* or *subjective* with *se-lected-response* (a student choosing from two or more options presented by the teacher) and *constructed-response* (test takers write their own responses). Figure 13–8 presents that assessment continuum. Within constructed-response, we distinguish between questions that are limited (more open than selected-response and less free than constructed-response) and open-ended. We also include the traditional terms associated with testing: *objective* and *subjective.*

Selected-Response (Objective)

Four common types of selected-response questions are *true/false, matching, multiple choice,* and *analogy.* They appeal to teachers because they can

- be administered quickly and efficiently
- be scored quickly and reliably

FIGURE 13–8
Types of test items

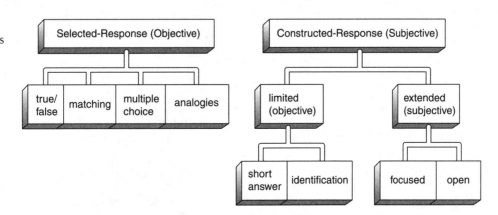

- cover an extensive body of content because they can be quickly answered by the student and scored by the teacher
- check reading or concept comprehension and leave class time for writing or discussion of larger issues
- prepare students for taking other selected-response standardized tests (especially multiple choice)

Their disadvantages are that they

- are often constructed to test the most limited mental process—recall of facts
- cause evaluation to rest on a single measure
- include only the most trivial content of learning
- (if timed) test speed, not thoughtfulness

We suggest guidelines for the construction of such questions so that teachers can enjoy the advantages and avoid the disadvantages of selected-response questions. With time and care, test items can be written that avoid trivia and invite application, analysis, and synthesis as well as basic recall and comprehension. If these are combined with multiple and varied measures, you also diminish the harm of a single measure that gives speed an advantage.

True/False. Of the four selected-response question types, these items, which simply ask students to identify a declarative statement as true or false, seem to be the most resistant to testing anything but simple memory. They also are often ambiguous and as confounding to the reflective student as to the unprepared one. Because the student has a 50 percent chance of being correct, they also can encourage unthoughtful guessing. These questions can work in literature study as gauges of a student's reading or comprehension of the simplest and most direct statements of plot, character, or setting; however, testing interpretive matters with true/false items can discourage the kinds of reflective acts and personal empowerment that our book encourages. Cautionary guidelines include the following:

- Make statements unambiguously true or false.
- Do not lift such statements directly from expository texts (students will infer the importance of memorization).
- Do not write trick statements.
- Avoid the trivial.
- Write statements that require higher cognitive processes than recall (for instance, comparison or synthesis).

Matching. Matching formats commonly present two columns and ask students to find the best associative relationships between them. Teachers like this format for several reasons: It requires students to discover relationships or definitions; the teacher does not have to write plausible distractors; its compression of content allows

students to take it quickly and cover a large amount of content. Cautionary guidelines include the following:

- Make matching items neither tricky nor simplistic.
- Write both columns with clear and parallel structure.
- Avoid lists with longer than ten entries, or students waste time trying to sort out responses.

Some teachers include more options than can be matched to the list of stems to eliminate the confounding problem of one bad answer creating other answers that also must be incorrect.

Multiple Choice. Multiple-choice questions usually consist of an introductory question, or stem, and four or five statements, one of which best completes that stem. Well-written possible answers, called *distractors,* can engage students in a process of making finer distinctions than can true/false or matching questions. Furthermore, if you analyze the distractors that are most seductive to students—that is, those that many mistakenly choose—you have useful diagnostic information about students' confusions. Cautionary guidelines include the following:

- Write questions that invite application, comparison, analysis, and synthesis.
- Make the distractors parallel in structure and length.
- Write plausible distractors.
- Construct stems and distractors that are simple and compact.
- Avoid distractors that are so close to the correct answer that to choose between them is to split hairs.

Review the following multiple-choice questions to see whether you note the difference we are trying to establish between recall and recognition of significant facts and retrieval of trivia.

When Huck visits the Phelps farm, he
    a. dresses like a girl
    b. helps Tom escape
    c. pretends to be Tom
    d. turns Jim over to Mr. Phelps

At the Grangerford's funeral, the undertaker returned from the basement
    a. with the money in his hands
    b. saying a rat was there
    c. to have a snort of whiskey
    d. after the service was over

In the first question, the distractors contain seeds of other important actions of the story (Huck pretending to be a girl, believing he should turn Jim in as a runaway slave, being overwhelmed once again by Tom's romantic folderol in helping Jim "escape"). The correct answer is a small yet significant detail: Huck takes on Tom's name and his foolish characteristics during this episode. It is a detail that you hope any insightful reader would attend to. The second question probably separates a very good memory from a less facile one but tells you little else about reading and interpretive skills. You can assume that most of the details an author selects are well considered and are thus of some significance, but some are clearly more important than others; they are the ones we need to select. These more significant details are ones that students can infer if they know the work rather than merely draw out of their memory bank.

A difficult form of multiple-choice question, which presents students with the challenge of making finer discriminations, is one that allows for more than one answer to be correct:

> Huck's love of mystery and disguise is suggested by which of the following?
> 1. He dresses as a girl.
> 2. He pretends to be a sheriff's deputy.
> 3. He dresses Jim as an Indian.
> 4. He pretends to be Tom Sawyer.
>
> The correct response to the preceding question is
> a. all of the above
> b. 1, 2, and 3
> c. 1, 2 and 4
> d. 1, 3, and 4
> e. 4 only

Analogies.   Analogies are another way of asking students to think in terms of relationships of characters, events, places, and objects. Simple analogies can set up three parts of a paradigm and ask students to complete the relationships by selecting one answer from a group of four. Because this format is uncommon and difficult, we recommend that you give students an example and an explanation of why the correct answer is best among the four. A variant of this format centers on relationships, but it asks students to look over a list of paired relationships and select the one that is unlike all the others. An example of this format, Figure 13–9, is taken from a test on ten adolescent novels: *Home Before Dark; The Princess Bride; Tuck Everlasting; Ordinary*

People; The Summer of My German Soldier; The Contender; That Was Then, This Is Now; A Hero Ain't Nothin' but a Sandwich; The Chocolate War; and *House of Stairs.*

Constructed-Response (Subjective)

By constructed response, we mean those questions that require students to construct their responses rather than select them. We wish to distinguish a range of constructed test questions—from those in which test takers have limited options to those in which test takers can generate and expand their answers.

Limited.   Limited-option questions (short answer and identification or association) have some of the virtues of both selected-response and constructed-response questions.

- easy to score
- quick to take
- not as difficult to construct as good multiple-choice and matching questions
- do not reward random guessing
- require a limited expansion of answers
- often test a higher level of cognition than selected-response questions do

Short Answer.   Short-answer questions are in a middle land between clear-cut objective items and subjective essay responses. They are objective enough to call for fairly definite answers yet open enough to challenge more than recall or recognition. Cautionary guidelines include the following:

- Avoid ambiguity.
- Favor a question format rather than a fill-in-the blank or supply-the-missing-words format. Questions usually provide a clearer idea about what is being asked.
- Write questions that have only one unique, correct response but that test more than recall.

FIGURE 13–9
Analogies test on ten adolescent novels

I. CHARACTER AND THEME
Which relationship or action is unlike that of any other in the group (circle the letter)?

1. a. Ann and Stella
   b. Count Rugen and Westley
   c. Berger and Conrad
   d. Mr. Tuck and Winnie
   e. Ruth and Patty
2. a. Inigo and six-fingered sword
   b. Patty and family ring
   c. Winnie and vial of water
   d. Alfred and alarm wire
   e. Bryon and Charlie's car
3. a. Bryon and Mark's pills
   b. Yellow Suit Man and Music Box
   c. FBI and initialed shirt
   d. Stella and shotgun house
4. a. Butler's wait at detox Center
   b. Stella's move to Maggie's house
   c. Jerry's advice to Goober
   d. Peter's refusal to dance
   e. Calvin's backyard embrace

Lifting sentences directly from the text encourages reading for trivial test items. To guard against this, we sometimes ask students to summarize two or three examples of a designated principle or fact. For example, you might ask students to name three examples of false identification in *The Adventures of Huckleberry Finn* or three important references to children in *Macbeth*. This requires a good, working grasp of central issues in the works.

Identification. Identification or association questions, while requiring constructed responses, actually rely strongly on memory because students must supply the missing identity. The stem or descriptor is present, but no identity list is offered. For instance, in assessing students' reading of a play or piece of fiction, a quote is given and students are asked to identify the speaker or even the place, time, and addressee. The answer is indisputable, like those in the four selected-response formats; but the task of answering is more difficult for students, who must recall rather than merely select, and a bit more taxing for teachers, who must grade without simple grading keys.

English teachers commonly use identification of quotes or passages, especially longer excerpts, to check students' knowledge of the work; to query students about the elements of fiction, poetry, or drama; or to test broad interpretation. These passages or excerpts should be representative of or important to the work or the literary element under study; otherwise, students are frustrated and learn to treat testing as a capricious game. One variation on the use of quotes is to ask students to state the central idea or theme among two or three passages. Another is to present in random order a set of five passages that show the linear development of a character such as Cassie Logan or Macbeth and ask students to place them in a chronological sequence of development. This order of development might also be used for progression of theme in a longer literary piece. A variant on this strategy lists a set of four or five passages, one of which does not carry forward the theme found in the other passages, and asks students to circle the passage that is not congruent with the others and then name the theme embodied in the other four. Cautionary guidelines include the following:

- Make certain that identifications are of significant material.
- Write clear instructions about how students are to respond to what is being identified.
- Be certain of your testing purpose. If it is to distinguish those who have read a work, for instance, obscure passages are not necessary.

Invitation to Reflection 13–5 offers you a short-answer test on literary terms to take and evaluate.

Invitation to Reflection 13–5

Following is a list of definitions of literary terms. Write the term defined in the space provided.

_____ 1. the context in time and place in which the action of a story occurs

_____ 2. the central idea or unifying generalization implied or stated by a literary work

_____ 3. the angle of vision from which a story is told; "the physical vantage point" occupied by the narrator in a story and the device by which the writer establishes the "authority" for the fiction.

_____ 4. a character whose distinguishing moral qualities and personal traits are complex and many-sided

_____ 5. a character whose distinguishing moral qualities and personal traits are one-dimensional

_____ 6. a character whose essential nature does not change in the course of the story

_____ 7. a character whose experiences cause a change in attitude and behavior so that he or she emerges a different person at the conclusion of the work

_____ 8. the attitudes toward the subject of the story and toward the audience implied in a literary work

_____ 9. a method of writing that describes the procession of a character's uninterrupted, varied, and disjointed flow of mental and emotional impressions

_____ 10. a situation or a use of language that implies some discrepancy or incongruity

Evaluate the test design.

1. Did taking this test require you to reflect on literary conventions? Did it require anything more than simple recall? What?
2. Which of the brain's two hemispheres did it favor?
3. Can you imagine a classroom context in which it might be useful?
4. Did it violate any of the cautions given previously for limited-response tests?
5. Is it parallel in structure?
6. Is it stated clearly?
7. Design a test of literary terms that applies knowledge to a related task.
8. Which of Bloom's cognitive objectives did your test evoke?
   knowledge
   comprehension
   application
   analysis
   synthesis
   evaluation
9. Which of Gardner's intelligences and which of the brain's hemispheres did your test require?

Extended. Extended evaluation designs assign projects or pose questions that invite a wider latitude of response.

We will begin with questions and then move to more open evaluation alternatives. Extended questions range from the focused to the open. They can be single questions or a group of questions from which students choose a selected number. They can be assigned ahead or presented in the moment of testing. They can be answered with or without notes and within or outside of a designated hour. They can be undertaken by a single student or groups of students. Our pedagogical bias favors open choices. But some situations (for instance, a curriculum that intends to prepare students for standardized test taking or needs to certify that all students have covered the same material) and some students (those especially who need teacher encouragement or have difficult out-of-school environments for writing) may dictate traditional, in-school testing with students working individually at their desks.

Regardless of the setup for posing extended questions, they offer the advantages of

- measuring a range of cognitive processes from recall to evaluation
- inviting students' use of multiple intelligences
- encouraging freer self-expression of attitudes and values
- presenting the possibilities of problem solving or applying knowledge to new situations
- allowing the possibility of group work
- mirroring the kind of organization and expression more typical of adult life

Focused. The most common college and university testing format is the focused essay question. (It is also common in academic secondary classes.) Students structure their own answers to teacher-made questions, but they usually set forth a central idea and develop it with some detail and at some length. Traditionally, such questions elicit an expository, argumentative, or persuasive essay. Many teachers are presently moving to questions that encourage a greater rhetorical range that encompasses description, narration, and expression.

The focused essay question, for instance, might ask students to respond to a broad idea: ambition and fate (*Macbeth* and *Othello*), the harsh side of nature (Emily Dickinson), the harsh side of society (Gwendolyn Brooks), or the rootlessness of migrant workers' children (Bridger's *Home Before Dark*). The question requires knowledge and comprehension of particulars but at the same time provides freedom of response that allows individual and creative thinking. Dixon (1984) poses questions that are somewhat similar but offer more freedom of response. A few of his examples follow:

- In Chapter 19 of *Great Expectations:* What do these farewells tell us about the boy Pip at this stage of the novel? Bearing in mind how he develops later, how do you feel about Pip at this point?

- In act 3, scene 2, of *Macbeth:* In what ways do you find Macbeth and Lady Macbeth behaving characteristically, and what do you find unexpected in their behavior, attitudes, and language? (You will need to think back to their earlier scenes together.)
- In Chapter 34 of *Jane Eyre:* What does this scene between St. John Rivers and Jane add to your understanding of him and what he thinks is important in life?

These questions each focus on a specific incident in the work, but they open up the work and students' responses by asking students to explore the entire work imaginatively in terms of the change undergone by a character.

Further departures still are questions that are based on the text but move away from it. L. H. Willey (1991, personal communication) has eighth-grade students read *The Diary of Anne Frank* as part of a unit on courage. She then poses a series of textual questions that require students to know the text but then to move imaginatively, speculatively, and personally beyond it:

- Explain why this work is appropriate for this unit.
- Compare and contrast the courage displayed by Anne with the courage displayed by a character in one of the readings (a, b, c).
- Everyone who resided in the Secret Annex died except Otto Frank. Considering the sacrifices, the lack of privacy, the deprivation, and other restrictions, was it worth it to go into hiding for that extra twenty-five months of life?
- Thoroughly describe Anne and Peter's relationship. Then answer this question: If they had survived to live again on the outside, what would have happened to their relationship?

Two primary disadvantages of focused questions concern us. These questions often come in the form of essay assignments, which rely on writing skills that may be tangential to the original evaluative intent. Spelling, vocabulary, grammar, and penmanship may become too instrumental in essay writing. If writing as a process has been critical to a classroom organization, in-class essay examinations may be confounding because they are timed and thus do not allow for prewriting, rewriting, and editing. Slow writers especially are handicapped in such testing.

A strategy that aids weaker writers with their organization and expression is to pose questions with a built-in structure for the response. Such a question may be quite focused:

Describe one incident in which Huck grows close to Jim and learns from him and then another in which he is more distant and ruptures their relationship. Give your interpretation of why he acts so differently in the two incidents and explain how this relates to the central intent of the novel.

Some teachers might even place a *1* after the phrase "learns from him," a *2* after the phrase "ruptures their relationship," a *3* after the phrase "the two incidents," and a *4* after the phrase "intent of the novel." The four phrases would create a content outline that would be difficult for many students to construct without such guidance. This format gives students guidelines for their responses, prods them to think about things in terms of relationships, and enables teachers to make better judgments about the quality of their understanding. Some latitude for the student response is provided but this kind of enabling structure promotes student independence. The answers build on each other so that thought, too, builds to higher levels. The structure also makes it easy for teachers to allot points for nuances of response so the cumulative total test score shows more recognition of the students' understanding of the text. Finally, such a structured question makes key choices for students so they don't have to stew over them.

Scoring is the second disadvantage of focused questions in terms of both teacher time and scorer reliability. (We discuss English teachers' paper load and six scoring alternatives in the next section of this chapter.) Purves (1971) presents excellent guidelines for the constructor of essay questions:

> The general rule for the writer of the essay question is . . . to do what he advises his students to do: narrow the topic. He will point his students in the direction he wants them to go, in terms that they can comprehend; he is not putting them in the desert without a compass. It may be that a teacher will want to give an assignment or a test that forces the student to do his own narrowing, particularly as a first assignment to see what sort of focus a class might have, or as an invitation to the class to consider the part of the course that they found most fruitful or relevant. These types of assignments, however, differ from the general purposes of summative evaluation, which will be best served by specific questions. (p. 728)

We add these cautionary guidelines:

• Construct questions that are not too broad, nor too specific, nor too cumbersome.

• Write questions that lead students toward high-level cognitive processes or invite them to use multiple intelligences. Use words such as *compare, contrast, analyze,* and *imagine.*

• Connect the question to the outcome you wish to measure.

• Imagine diverse and creative possibilities for writing.

• Consider asking questions in a way that structures the answer and makes it manageable.

• Calibrate the time that students will require to answer the question and use only those questions that can be comfortably answered in the allotted time.

• Frame broad, contextual questions to ask "the student to apply the works to the context, rather than the context to the work" (Purves, 1971, p. 728).

Teacher Becky Brown field-tests her essay questions. She constructs her essay topics and then answers them as though she is one of her students. Only then, she says, can she appreciate the hidden difficulties and pitfalls in her questions.

Open. The open test does not present a set of focused prompts for student response, nor is there an expected answer. It provides students with more freedom of response than even the most open essay does. Its aim is a creative, idiosyncratic synthesis of the material in question; its method is to create a loose structure in which students operate. For instance, students who have studied Native American writers might be given a culminating "test" in which you tell them to imagine a book about Native American writers and have them include the following:

1. title
2. cover design (rough sketch)
3. preface (2-3 pages)
4. table of contents (5-15 chapter titles)
5. chapter introductions (2 chapters, ½-1 page each)
6. illustrations: photographs, drawings, paintings (with captions)
7. notes for the treatment of three pieces
8. book conclusion about the importance of its contents

Working from step 1 to step 8 allows students to develop their final generalizations from all of the specifics that they have amassed. You may wish to reverse the order, moving from 8 to 1. This option asks students to focus on the importance of their material first. The particulars (1-7) are then selected with a clearer, more coherent sense of purpose and direction. Each of the parts of this "test" is working at a progressively more detailed level. Each depends on the other. Students are given choices within a large structure, but they must have a sense of the whole to develop the parts they select. Creating a book design could easily be converted to creating a Web site on Native American writers with equivalent requirements, one of which would be proposed links to other sites.

Schaars (1992, p. 153) suggests an essay question that culminates the study of Thoreau. She credits the idea to Tom Romano (1987, pp. 156-157):

> Through the miracle of 1980s technology, young Henry David Thoreau (same character, personality and principles) has been transported to the present. He is seventeen years old and living in Central Wisconsin. In an essay *describe six things he possesses* that reflect his personality, character, and concerns. Explain what each possession reveals about him.

In two recent award winning children's picture books, *Henry Hikes to Fitchburg* (2000) and *Henry Builds a Cabin* (2002), D. B. Johnson adapts Henry David Thoreau's writings to tell an engaging story in vivid pictures and spare words. After a unit on "American Crosscurrents" or "The Concord Sages" students might be presented with these books and asked to explain how closely they come to capturing the spirit of Thoreau or to create their own picture book based on other passages but designed to communicate the spirit of *Walden* to children.

A 1987 *English Journal* "Our Readers Write" feature asked readers "What's a new and interesting way to test students?" Figure 13–10 contains five suggestions that impressed us with their imaginative openness.

Like the test proposals of Figure 13–10, the test design of Figure 13–11 expands evaluation in two essential ways: (1) work is done by groups of students and (2) the work exercises the full range of intelligences. This open assessment was written and reviewed by NCTE members involved in examining alternative approaches to assessment under the auspices of the New Standards Project of the Learning Research and Development Center (University of Pittsburgh) and the National Center on Education and the Economy (University of Rochester). *The Council Chronicle* (November, 1991, p. 1) published it.

We close this discussion of open assessment with the ideas of Horn (1988), who taught the *Iliad* in a unit on heroes to a reluctant group of students; some were "learning disabled, some [were] foreign students struggling to learn English, some [were] slow learners, some [were] discouraged learners, underachievers, or on the five-year plan" (p. 25). Her imaginative instruction culminated in three evaluative projects.

- She asked students to "cartoon a story strip of *Days of Our Greeks.* Results were graded on completeness of plot, its being turned in on time, and effort."
- She assigned them to "write on one of six essay options ranging from 'Discuss one of the heroes studied in this unit' to 'Write a letter to a personal hero' and 'Imagine that you are a hero in the future. What did you do and why?' "
- And, our personal favorite: Horn wrote the *English Journal* article and then "gave it to small groups . . . to edit and revise. The article was not only a review of the unit but a lesson in editing and a statement to students about their value in the learning situation" (p. 26).

FIGURE 13–10
Teachers' testing suggestions

> *Sociograms.* Have students think about the relationships among characters in a novel or play and draw sociograms (tables of interpersonal relationships) describing and schematizing those characters. These work especially well in literary pieces with small casts. (Joanne K. A. Peters)
>
> *Decision making.* Use the dilemmas of literary works to provide a context in which to reflect on characters outside that work. For instance, in James Hilton's *Lost Horizon,* the characters at the end must decide whether to return to their former civilization or remain in Shangri-La. Have students write about how another character such as Wang Lung from Pearl Buck's *The Good Earth* would react to that situation. (Carl Carlsen)
>
> *Talk shows.* Ask students to assume "the hosting duties of their own talk show" and write the "transcript" of a given number of interviews of characters encountered in the course "including a person inside a poem or a poet." The results have been imaginative within a "familiar and comfortable" context. "In almost all transcripts, the dialogue discussed major themes embodied by the characters, and in many cases, the hosts were challenging, asking their character/guests probing questions exploring both sides of a motivation or decision. And, because they were transcribing speech, students used speech patterns and vocabulary appropriate to a chosen character/guest." (Carl Carlsen)
>
> *Newspapers.* Ask students to write news stories about events in a book. The assignment can be directed to a certain audience—general, sensational, liberal, or conservative—or, we would add, to a specific type of column (for example, editorial page, feature article, obituary, or advice column). (Sharon Snyder)
>
> *Children's books.* Have students write "an original story or even a children's story or nursery rhyme as a naturalist like Dreiser or Crane (using any literary philosophy under study) might have, or as told by someone like Holden Caulfield in *The Catcher in the Rye* or McMurphy in *One Flew over the Cuckoo's Nest.*" (Sharon Snyder)

FIGURE 13–11
Open assessment instrument

> Imagine that four of the characters from the literature you have read this year have gathered in one place. Work in groups of four. Each group will do the following:
>
> - Choose the four characters and the setting.
> - Develop an interesting script that reflects the personality of the characters. The script will deviate from the plots of the works where the characters originally appeared.
> - Prepare to perform this script in front of your classmates.
> - Consider casting, staging, scenery, costuming, and props.
> - Perform your scene for your classmates.
> - Evaluate the scenes of other classmates.
> - Write a reflective essay about your experiences in this project.

Invitation to Reflection 13–6

1. How much of your high school teacher-made evaluation of your knowledge of literature was devoted to the following?

   Selected-response (objective tasks)
   - true/false
   - matching
   - multiple choice
   - analogies

   Constructed-response (limited tasks)
   - short answer
   - identification or association

   Constructed-response (extended tasks)
   - focused (essay questions)
   - open (holistic possibilities)

2. Would your answers differ for your college/university English classes?

3. Does any one of these strategies predominate in your memories of high school?

4. Which has been the type of evaluation you have preferred for yourself?

5. Have you had any teachers who have mixed these strategies?

6. Have any of Bloom's cognitive processes or Gardner's multiple intelligences predominated in your experiences of testing? If so, which?

7. If you plan to use any of these traditional means of assessment, would you use them differently from how your teachers used them?

8. Return to your test design in Invitation to Reflection 13–5. Push that design further from traditional testing than you did earlier. (Select another testing subject if you wish.)

EVALUATING WRITING

Like literature, writing needs to be carefully evaluated to assure that we do not undermine the deepest aims of our teaching. Assigning grades itself is dangerous. Mayher (1990) rightly sees the negative consequences when the writer's goal becomes getting the best grade: "[It] takes the responsibility for choosing how to most effectively compose a piece away from the writer and cedes it to the teacher/grader. Experimentation is therefore restricted, and everyone sticks as carefully as possible to those pre-structured genres of antiwriting which have proved themselves the safest paths to good grades" (p. 239). The way in which those grades are assigned complicates these dangers.

The most common classroom practice in evaluating secondary students' writing is for the teacher to read student papers, mark errors, comment on strengths and weaknesses, and assign a letter grade. Several problems arise from this tradition, beyond the harried and oppressed teacher: Teachers' comments often address only an end product, not the process that preceded it; focus on the narrow, easily graded issues of mechanics (spelling, grammar, and penmanship) rather than on student meaning; justify the grade rather than respond to the writing; and hinder students' ability to assess their own writing. But what alternatives do we have? Chapters 11 and 12 addressed some of them—namely, authentic assessment and writing portfolios. We now turn to others.

Outside the Classroom

Alternatives have been tried outside the classroom whereby schools, districts, states, and the nation make major educational decisions on the basis of writing evaluation. Early attempts to assess writing on a large scale were based on multiple-choice grammar tests. Reforms of that process have been attempted. Two prominent attempts were in the writing portion of the National Assessment of Educational Progress (NAEP) and in the College Entrance Examination Board's Achievement Test in English Composition. In addition to multiple-choice questions, AP English Literature and Composition and English Language and Composition exams use essays to evaluate the writing skills and literary insights of college-bound students. All three—NAEP, SAT, and AP—ask students to write for a short time on an assigned topic in a formal testing situation. Graders assemble, determine criteria for grading, test their scoring consistency, and read and score papers holistically. State and school districts have followed these models in developing their own assessment instruments for the purposes of making student placement decisions, determining student competency, and evaluating programs and schools. (Myers [1980] wrote a concise guide for constructing such a test—selecting topics, writing directions, scoring, and reporting.)

Although these evaluation methods are clearly superior to earlier multiple-choice tests, they still run counter to a student-centered process approach to writing. The genre (essay) is preset, topics are assigned, and the elaborate writing process is constricted; only the final product is evaluated. Dyson and Freedman (1990) observe that "writing for a test has little function for the student writers other than for them to be evaluated" (p. 8).

Inside the Classroom

Although these national writing tests may well influence your work in the classroom, our major concern is with what you do with your own students. You will remember that in Chapter 11, we expressed our biases for a writing program that is holistic, organic, inclusive, developmental, and foundational—best embodied in a writing process approach. One of the cornerstones for such an approach is the use of student portfolios. We think that the most promising present writing evaluation alternatives rest with portfolio assessment. But having suggested that process for assembling pieces of writing for purposes of evaluation, we still must address how selected pieces might be assessed.

We discuss here six evaluation strategies available to you, some probably familiar from your classroom experiences and others less visible in your experiences with state and national exams. We do not present them as contestants for your final winning choice but as viable alternatives given the needs of your students and the aims of your instruction.

- crucial-errors scoring
- rubric scoring
- holistic scoring
- student, peer, and teacher collaboration
- personal-response appraisal
- cumulative-process tallying

These six are not always mutually exclusive. Features of each can be merged, or different strategies can be chosen at different times to meet your instructional (and assessment) aims. As you consider each, evaluate it in terms of your purpose, your style, and your total approach to writing. Then turn your attention to the instructional potential of feedback and the challenge of paperload in writing assessment.

Crucial-Errors Scoring.

In many English classes, writing instruction has been a three-step sequence: classwork on grammar, student writing on assigned topics, and teacher grading of completed papers. The old three-step method often centered on surface features as the tool of evaluation: two misspellings, three comma flaws, and a single subject-verb agreement problem could mean a failing grade. Crucial-errors graders often determine the failing point by a certain number of errors (usually grammatical or mechanical). Sometimes these teachers enumerate targeted features of composition, each of which has an established weight for grading purposes. Summing and weighing the parts determine the final grade. Kirby, Liner, and Vinz (1988) acknowledge the advantages of this technique in focusing graders as well as writers: "Such guides, when carefully shared and explained to students, can demystify the final grade and highlight strengths and weaknesses in their writings. The guides also ensure that certain surface features in the piece (handwriting, spelling, pronunciation) do not influence the rating of the piece out of proportion to their importance to the piece's effectiveness" (p. 224).

North Carolina's NCTE affiliate journal, *North Carolina English Teacher,* used the rather general set of idea-centered criteria shown in Figure 13–12 by which a panel of referees assessed the value of a manuscript submitted for publication. Interestingly, the referees had an amazing concurrence on their ratings of individual manuscripts. Appendix I contains an analytic scale carefully developed by Diederich and his colleagues for the Educational Testing Service's SAT essay exam. We do not recommend it as your sole writing assessment method, but it is an effective model to be used occasionally.

Some teachers keep individual convention logs (Figure 13–13) which let students see and chart their most frequent and flagrant errors. With these logs students can recognize their habitual errors without becoming so cautious about grammar and usage that they stop paying attention to content. They can be kept at the front of a

FIGURE 13–12
Criteria for manuscript evaluation

| NCET | REFEREE: _____ |
| ESSAY NO. _____ | TITLE: _____ |

_____ A. PERTINENCE:	On-Target		Loosely Connected		Largely Tangential		Left Field	
	8	7	6	5	4	3	2	1
_____ B. SUBSTANCE:	Very Informative		Interesting		Somewhat Clichéd		Bland	
	8	7	6	5	4	3	2	1
_____ C. FORM:	Very Talented		Quite Competent		Somewhat Flawed		Inept	
	8	7	6	5	4	3	2	1

_____ TOTAL EVALUATION POINTS

REJECT   REVISE   PRINT   (Circle One)

REJECTION COMMENTS: _____
_____
_____

REVISION COMMENTS: _____
_____
_____
_____

DATE RECEIVED: _____   DATE MAILED: _____

FIGURE 13–13
Convention log

Convention	Paper # Title and Date	1	2	3	4	5	6
Problem areas							
Comma flaws							
Misused semicolons							
Sentence fragments							
Run-on sentences							
Omitted apostrophes							
Lost antecedents							
Dangling modifiers							
Nonparallel construction							
Quotation mark flaw							
Subject-verb agreement							
Other							

portfolio, placed on file in the classroom, or kept in students' notebooks. Other teachers keep error-count charts for a set of student papers to track central writing issues that need to be addressed with the whole class.

The adoption of other approaches to writing has brought with it new means of assessment. The surface of any piece of writing is important to communication; but in the process approach to writing, it represents only the final step in editing and revising, not the central concern. Crucial-errors scoring focuses on problems not specific to the writing assignment at hand. Critics of this means of assessment fear its paralyzing consequences. Diederich (1974) judges its negative effects by his remedial college students' fear and dislike of writing. He explains their self-disparagement: "All their teachers looked for were mistakes, and there are so many kinds of mistakes in writing that their students despair of ever learning to avoid them" (p. 21). Graves (1986) believes that such avoidance of errors undermines risk taking and is the cause of bad, not good, writing: "The biggest misconception is that children learn to write by not making mistakes. . . . Putting words on paper involves enormous risk-taking. If the words appear to be a crude form of English, parents and teachers may be tempted to overcorrect. But writing is

thinking you have things to say, and having an audience to say them to. Grammar and spelling are not as important as content."

Beyond its crippling effects on the composing process, crucial-errors scoring reduces response to a totaling of countable errors, hardly a nuanced reflection of the paper's merit.

Invitation to Reflection 13–7

Diederich (1974) tells the following story:

Professor Edward Gordon of Yale tells about an examination he once conducted for the College Board. He explained and illustrated the scale of five points that was to be used and had the readers practice using it by grading copies of a set of sample papers.

When the actual grading began, he noticed that one military-looking gentleman—an instructor from West Point—was obviously not using the scale. His grades were all two-digit numbers: 53, 71, 83, and so on.

"How do you get these numbers?" asked Dr. Gordon.

"Well, Dr. Gordon," replied the military gentleman, "I'm too old a dog to learn new tricks like that new-fangled scale you wanted us to use. So I went back to my usual way of grading papers, knowing that you're smart enough to translate my grades into any scale you please. I just count the number of mistakes and subtract that number from 100 percent."

"But what do you call a mistake?" asked Dr. Gordon.

The man's astonishment was obvious. "Why surely, Dr. Gordon, you know what a *mistake* is!" (p. 29)

What mistake do you see being made here?

Rubric Scoring. Teachers who are not primarily interested in the general writing mechanics of crucial-errors scoring but are still concerned that student writing meet established criteria for a given assignment have turned to rubric or primary-trait scoring. This analytical approach identifies the presence or absence of traits required by a particular writing assignment and often joins a concern for writing conventions with an expectation of significant content. The two—the surface and deep structure—can be represented by a set of traits that scorers rate as present or absent.

Table 13-4 is a writing assessment instrument developed by a state educational agency in which traits are articulated for each of several domains. Surprisingly, when the matrix was used by forty North Carolina Writing Project teachers to evaluate a large set of papers, the intergrader reliability for the rhetorical elements was stronger

TABLE 13-4 Writing assessment matrix *(continues on following page)*

	Rhetorical Elements			
Assessment	**Quality of Ideas**	**Expression of Ideas**	**Organization of Ideas**	**Maturity of Syntax**
Unacceptable	Operates on a literal level in which the thinking is clichéd and simplistic; the ideas lack soundness or insight; the thought is stale and exhibits no originality; the ideas are not developed in any detail, little or no elaboration of concepts is present.	Cannot communicate ideas; the logic of phrasing is inconsistent and the idea communicated unclear; often awkward or flat word choice; a personality and voice are never established.	Neither states nor implies a point; little or no movement or focus is found in the writing; no structuring features are present; no segmental markers are evident.	Uses only simple sentence structure; has no variety in the sentence patterns.
Weak	Occasionally rises above literal level of clichéd and simplistic thought; the ideas are sound at points and exhibit some insight; the thought is occasionally fresh and original; the ideas are not developed in any detail, little or no elaboration of concepts is present.	Occasionally conveys ideas to audiences other than the self; the logic of the phrasing is often questionable and the idea communicated is somewhat uncertain; word choice is rarely rich or enlivening; a mild sense of personality or voice is evident.	Makes the main idea discernible but it is wholly unstructured; some sense of movement or focus is found in the writing; few or no structuring features are present; no segmental markers are evident.	Typically uses simple sentence structure although there is some use of complex sentence structure with embedded phrases and clauses; has some variety in the sentence patterns.
Satisfactory	Generally rises above the literal level to communicate important ideas; much of the thinking is sound and insightful; the ideas are developed in some detail, some elaboration of concepts is present.	Communicates to audiences other than the self, but not always in a stylistic and sophisticated manner; the logic of the phrasing is most often sound and the idea communicated is generally understood; word choice is at times rich and enlivening; a sense of personality or voice is fairly consistent.	Develops the main idea in an incomplete or loosely structured fashion; a general sense of movement or focus is found in the writing; some structuring elements are present; a few segmental markers are evident.	Often uses complex sentence structures; frequently uses a variety of sentence patterns.
Excellent	Consistently is able to communicate fresh and important ideas in depth; the ideas are sound and insightful; the thought is generally fresh and original; the ideas are developed in great detail, elaboration of concepts is rich.	Consistently is clear and elaborate in communicating ideas in a style acceptable to a literate audience; the logic of the phrasing is rigorous and the idea is communicated clearly; word choice is consistently rich and enlivening; a sense of voice and personality is strongly established throughout the writing.	Fully develops and structures the main idea implicitly or explicitly; a strong sense of movement or focus is found in the writing; structuring elements unify the entire piece of writing; segmental markers are effectively used throughout the writing.	Uses a variety of sentence patterns and sentence structures.

TABLE 13-4 (continued)

	Conventional Features 1		
Assessment	Capitalization	Spelling	Punctuation
Unacceptable	Fails to apply basic rules of capitalization such as first words in sentences, personal names and the pronoun "I."	Frequently misspells simple common words.	Fails to use end punctuation correctly.
Weak	Applies basic rules of capitalization correctly; often fails to apply other rules of capitalization.	Spells common words correctly; frequently misspells more difficult ones.	Uses end punctuation correctly; rarely uses internal punctuation correctly.
Satisfactory	Correctly applies basic capitalization rules; usually applies other rules correctly.	Rarely misspells even difficult words.	Always uses end punctuation correctly; generally uses internal punctuation correctly.
Excellent	All rules of capitalization are applied correctly.	Spells all words correctly.	Uses all forms of punctuation correctly.

	Conventional Features 2	
Assessment	Usage	Vocabulary
Unacceptable	Constantly makes basic usage errors such as lack of subject-verb agreement, use of double negatives and use of improper verb forms.	Constant misuse of basic words.
Weak	Controls basic usage with frequent problems in less important usage areas such as pronoun antecedents and misplaced modifiers.	Control of basic words; Frequent misuse of more sophisticated language.
Satisfactory	Makes occasional errors in less important usage areas.	Control of basic words and more sophisticated language; occasional misuse of the latter.
Excellent	Has full control of all conventional usage.	Full control of basic words and more sophisticated language.

than those on the conventional features; capitalization, spelling, punctuation, usage, and vocabulary. Such a rubric can help students better define and focus on the many elements that must be mastered to produce fine writing.

Holistic Scoring. For many teachers, looking at the writing style and mechanics *and* at the conceptual content of a piece is a schizophrenic process. Some teachers compromise by assigning one grade for content and one for form, thus recognizing the importance of both. But in recent years (perhaps encouraged or validated by the College Board's scoring of writing samples on its tests), teachers have been attracted to the idea of seeing writing as a whole, not as the sum of its faltering or successful parts; reading it for a single impression, not for itemized stylistic errors or conceptual blunders; and assigning a total response to it rather than trying to enumerate the components that give it strength or weakness. Myers (1980, p. 2) concurs: "Even though one can list all of the characters of a good piece of writing (clarity, coherence, complete sentences, smooth transitions, good spelling and punctuation), the best way to identify a good piece of writing is to ask people to select typical samples which they rate highly." He feels that "the whole of a piece of writing is greater than the sum of its parts" (p. 1).

The procedure for holistic scoring can involve the individual teacher or teams of readers. Neenan (1992, personal communication) explains that she draws twenty papers randomly from her pile, reads them quickly, constructs her scale based on her impressions of those sample papers, and then begins to read and evaluate deliberately. If two or more teachers work together, usually before grading, these readers establish both criteria (which describe the writing features paramount to a particular writing project) and sample anchor papers (which demonstrate what is considered to be high, middle, and low quality). The AP program of the College Board has been conscientious in developing grading standards and rigorous in assuring that the AP readers understand and use them carefully. In fact, three to seven hours of the five-to six-day exam-reading period are devoted to the readers' review of the standards and to their practice of consistent application of them. As Jensen (1987) reports, the scales themselves are carefully developed to "avoid the problem, on the one hand, of too few points, allowing only coarse distinctions, and, on the other hand, of too many points, requiring overly refined, often meaningless discriminations. Because the standards and their accompanying scales are tailored to the individual questions, they allow each answer to be appropriately ranked" (p. 3).

Kirby et al. (1988, p. 221) point out that holistic scoring has the advantage of being accomplished "more quickly, more consistently, and more pointedly." It provides significant help with English teachers' paper load as teachers read more rapidly without stopping to mark errors, make suggestions, and explain their responses. Many teachers also report that papers seem fresh to them without the burden of their own extensive note writing. Reader consistency grows from the establishment of effective writing criteria and model anchor papers.

Diederich (1974), who has been deeply involved in implementing this strategy, describes what happens to teachers who have used holistic scoring for two years:

> After two years (at most), they move easily and naturally into the use of standard scores as a quicker and easier way to indicate their judgment of the general merit of a paper. We call this "ratings on general impression," but it is no longer a blur: it is a quick summing up of characteristics that determine whether a paper is high, medium, or low in general merit. The teachers also have a common vocabulary for discussing the merits and defects of papers on which their grades disagree. (p. 55)

⟨⟨ Invitation to Reflection 13–8

Diederich tells another story:

> John Stalnaker, long president of the Merit Scholarship Foundation, recalls this incident from his early days as Examiner in English at the University of Chicago. In one of his experiments he had a few hundred papers to grade. He called in four of his most experienced readers and told them, "I want you to grade these papers but not on your regular scale of A to F. I know that you all have different ideas about what those letters mean. Just sort these papers into five piles in order of merit. Then mark the highest pile 4, the next pile 3, and so on down to 0."
>
> They agreed to do so, but about a week later they came to his office and said, "We're sorry, John, but we could not do what you wanted. It turned out that there weren't any "4" papers. But we did the best we could. We sorted them into five piles, but we had to mark them 3, 2, 1, 0, 00." (p. 49)

Into which pile should these readers' logic be put?

Student, Peer, and Teacher Collaboration.
Crucial-errors, rubric, and holistic scoring can be done by a classroom teacher acting alone, by groups of teachers, by teachers and students, or by teacher and writer. The most common experience of students is of evaluation done by the single classroom teacher. The AP model is of groups of teachers reading, collaborating, and scoring. Teachers have experimented with involving students—the writers' peers or the writers themselves—in writing evalua-

tion. Experience has demonstrated that students can be effective readers if they have been involved in establishing effective writing criteria, have been trained carefully, and have gained some experience. Kirby et al. (1988, p. 222) "learned the hard way that evaluation by peers must be thoroughly structured and patiently implemented," but they also learned the advantages of engaging peers in evaluation when such steps are taken:

- Students come to recognize that "the grade represents a reader's estimate of the worth of the piece. A grade is simply a calibrated personal response."
- They become sensitized "to problems in their own papers" and thereby become their own teachers.
- They "use peer papers as creative sources for borrowing ideas, rhetorical and syntactic strategies, and even vocabulary" (p. 230).

Many strategies for collaboration are possible. Writing process ideas of individual and group conferencing, peer collaboration and review, and small-group and whole-class workshops are easily adapted for this purpose. We especially like collaborative strategies that involve readers and writers sitting down together to read and discuss the effectiveness of a piece. Beaven (1977, p. 137) believes that a climate of acceptance and trust is essential to the developing writer and discusses kinds of responses that teachers have refined to create that environment.

- A teacher may ask for more information.
- A teacher may mirror, reflect, or rephrase the student's ideas, perceptions, or feelings.
- A teacher may share with the student times when he or she felt, thought, or behaved in a similar fashion. (p. 139)

Beaven quotes Cazden's (1972) research, which found that "adults who respond to the content and ideas of the child and carry on a 'conversation,' regardless of the child's grammar or syntax, are reinforcing positive language development, the motivation to talk, the desire to have 'something to say,' and the ability to experiment with language, stretching it to accommodate an expressive need" (Beaven, 1977, p. 137).

Our experience in teaching composition is that the most teachable writing moments occur in our discussions with individual students as we struggle together over a composition. Evaluation can be incorporated into such immediate and personal moments if it is done with care. Kirby et al. (1988) agree. They "believe that the only consistently helpful and effective evaluation of student writing comes as the two of you sit down with the piece of writing, focusing directly on what's on the page. Extraordinarily successful teachers of writing have one thing in common: they spend very little time in isolation, reading and marking papers, and a great deal of time responding and discussing student writings with the writers themselves" (p. 235).

Personal-Response Appraisal. Teachers who believe that writing conventions are less important than self-expression have tried to diminish the threat of correction. A focus on form and correctness paralyzes the personal. They use free writing, personal journals, creative writing, and field reporting to provide opportunities for personal response. They ask students to focus on what they know, what they are discovering, and what matters to them, not on conventions of composition. In a developmental sense, they are starting at home, beginning with Moffett's *I* rather than *it* or even *you.* They are freed from the common caution in school writing to efface themselves; adopt an impartial, objective voice; and remove the *I.* With this approach the *I* returns, and the world at hand—the daily concerns of students—appears at school.

To switch to this approach is not easy for students and teachers accustomed to a traditional style, and one of the impediments to change is the problem of assessment. Bleich (1975) defines the dilemma of subjective-response approaches to literary study:

> Since we are not dealing with questions of objective truth or falsity, but rather with questions of emotional and social viability, the authority of the teacher is experiential, not evaluative. One cannot set up a standard of response for the class to meet which will not, in application, result in the judgment of the student's character. A student will have real grounds to think he is a "C" person if his emotional responses receive that letter grade. (pp. 105–106)

Clear-cut objective criteria about writing conventions afford teachers an authority that assessing students' subjective responses does not. Teachers who invite self-expression sometimes designate criteria for assessment such as originality, interest, and clarity and claim that these are not a big departure from real-world judgments about writing. Bleich (1975) discusses the "viable compromise" he worked out "between the evaluative methods demanded by the response process and the need for a letter grade created by competitive admissions policies." Without denying the difficulty and subjectivity of his method, he explains two grading principles that he has worked out for his own classroom: "(1) the amount of work produced by the student, and (2) the seriousness of purpose in the production of that work" (p. 107).

Self-evaluation of writing is a common goal of a personal-response approach. Self-evaluation is consistent with taking one's own thoughts and feelings seriously. It internalizes evaluation and helps students accept responsibility for their own writing. Two practical advantages are that it can be initiated at any time during the stages of writing or the course of a term, and it does not consume large amounts of class time. Following are Beaven's (1977) questions, which form the basis of her self-evaluation procedures. She believes that students grow weary of the same questions; therefore, teachers need to vary them "from week to week, adding questions related to the current work of the class" (p. 143).

1. How much time did you spend on this paper?
2. (After the first evaluation) What did you try to improve, or experiment with, on this paper? How successful were you? If you have questions about what you were trying to do, what are they?
3. What are the strengths of your paper? Place a squiggly line beside those passages you feel are very good.
4. What are the weaknesses, if any, of your paper? Place an X beside passages you would like your teacher to correct or revise. Place an X over any punctuation, spelling, usage, etc., where you need help or clarification.
5. What one thing will you do to improve your next piece of writing? Or what kind of experimentation in writing would you like to try? If you would like some information related to what you want to do, write down your questions.
6. (Optional) What grade would you give yourself on this composition? Justify it. (p. 143)

Cumulative-Process Tallying. A cumulative process of grading can resemble a performance system in which students get a grade simply by completing an assignment. No evaluative judgments are made about a work's quality, good or bad. Teachers still read and respond to writing, but no error counts are made or holistic scores given. The responsibility for the grade rests solely with the student's willingness to do the assigned work.

The cumulative approach can fit nicely with a process approach to writing. Rather than evaluating the final written product, teachers assign credit to each of the steps (whatever the number) in the writing process. Students are awarded points for their prewriting, drafting, peer editing, and revising. The evaluation of many of these parts of the total process may be straightforward: Points are automatically awarded for completing a particular part. Or a balance can be struck between points awarded for productivity and those awarded for quality of performance. Newkirk (1990) has suggested an evaluation strategy that assigns grades while maintaining a workshop approach to writing. He believes that only the students' selections of their best writing should be evaluated for a grade—a "real incentive for revising." He then suggests a combined quantitative and qualitative evaluation:

> At the end of a marking period a student might be evaluated as follows. All students who complete a satisfactory volume of writing—those who worked regularly and met deadlines—should get a base grade, perhaps a C. This base grade can go up if the student has made major improvement on a skill identified at the beginning of the marking term or if the quality of the selected pieces of writing is superior.
>
> This system rewards productivity; a student who writes several thousand words in a marking term does not, in my opinion, deserve a D, even if there are substantial difficulties in that writing. The system also rewards quality; excellent writing gets an excellent grade. The system penalizes sloth—and that's the way it should be. (pp. 156–157)

Invitation to Reflection 13-9

crucial-errors summing
rubric scoring
holistic scoring

peer and teacher collaboration
personal-response appraisal
cumulative-process tallying

1. In your schooling, which of these evaluative strategies have you experienced?
2. Which predominated?
3. Which kind of writing evaluation did you most enjoy receiving?

4. Do you remember any of these strategies that you experienced negatively?
5. Recall a personal story about writing evaluation that had a happy ending. Recall one with a sad ending.
6. Which of these strategies can you envision using most often in your own high school classroom? Next most often?
7. Figure 13–14 contains the written, in-class responses of three ninth-grade students to the prompt "Write about the effect of watching television on young children." Consider how you might evaluate these three using the

FIGURE 13–14
Student writing samples: The effect of watching television on young children
(continues on pp. 386–387)

Watching television is somewhat harmful to young children. The shows on television set examples for the children to follow. Some shows have too much violence in them which may affect young children and lead them to violence in later years. Violence on television may also scare a young child and lead him to be afraid that others may hurt him as the people on television have been hurt. Another thing that is exposed too much on television is sex. When a child sees sexual activities on the television he may think nothing is wrong with it because he does not see all there is to it. He may try it out with someone of the opposite sex a few years later and will think nothing of it. Televised sex may not be the main cause of teenage pregnancies, but it may be a benefitting factor. Some controls should be set on the intensity of violence and sex shown on television so that it will not harm the young children of our nation.

FIGURE 13–14
(continued)

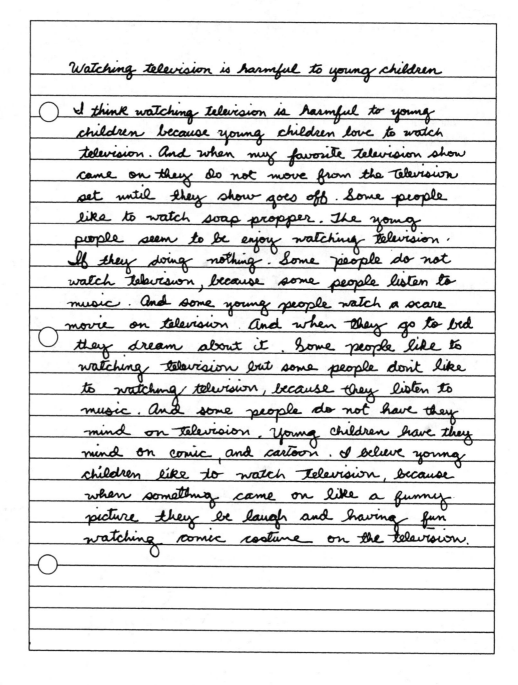

Watching television is harmful to young children

I think watching television is harmful to young children because young children love to watch television. And when my favorite television show came on they do not move from the television set until they show goes off. Some people like to watch soap propper. The young people seem to be enjoy watching television. If they doing nothing. Some people do not watch television, because some people listen to music. And some young people watch a scare movie on television. And when they go to bed they dream about it. Some people like to watching television but some people don't like to watching television, because they listen to music. And some people do not have they mind on television. Young children have they mind on comic, and cartoon. I believe young children like to watch television, because when something came on like a funny picture they be laugh and having fun watching comic costume on the television.

strategy that you most prefer and the strategy that you least prefer. Do you arrive at different conclusions about the students' work?

8. Figure 13–15 is a character sketch written out of class by a college-bound senior. Evaluate it with the strategy used by your twelfth-grade English teacher. Then consider whether you have discovered any better alternatives to that method.

These six alternatives, or variations of them, offer compromises that allow you to remain true to your best aims in teaching students to write and to your need to supply a grade to school administrators. Cutting across all

six alternatives is an issue that Lorrie Shepard (2002) has brought clearly into focus for us: the issue of feedback.

Feedback. Quite apart from the assigning of a grade, feedback is essential to promoting students' learning. Shepard believes in building new knowledge on old knowledge, exercising student understanding in new contexts, and telling students how they are doing so they can take the next step in learning. The key role of the scaffolder of learning is to summarize progress made and point out behaviors that lead to success. She cites numerous studies that demonstrate the benefits of feedback for positive learning gains. For instance, students grew dramatically when feedback focused on specific errors and

FIGURE 13–14
(continued)

Watching television could not be harmful to young children. With proper supervision the television can be used as a learning tool as well as an entertainment center. By watching such shows as Sesame Street, Captain Kangaroo, and Mister Rodgers, children can learn important facts about the world around them. While watching cartoons and adventure shows gives them strong imagination will to do things and sometimes an idol to look up to and learn about.

articulated how to improve inadequate or poor learning strategies. In other words, feedback was effective when it made a distinction between performance and an ideal. Researchers in the United Kingdom found other feedback variables to be compelling to the teachers who tried them:

- making sure students knew what the learning task was and what they were to learn from it
- sharing the criteria for success (i.e., rubrics)
- focusing on how each student had improved and how far each was from reaching his or her target
- leaving tangential things until later
- paying attention to what marking strategies engaged students and improved their learning and what strategies did not

Shepard believes that effective feedback is tied to the teacher's clear answers to the following questions:

- What do I want my students to learn?
- What learning do I want to assess?
- How do the assessment tasks relate to what we have been studying?
- Are these tasks an effective way to measure the students' gains?
- Will feedback on this assessment permit my students to learn further?

(After the assessment, teachers should ask other questions of the assessment event itself and prepare to change their approaches based on their self-scrutiny.) Shepard

FIGURE 13–15
Student writing sample:
Character sketch

SIDNEY CARTON

Of all the many characters in Dicken's novel, <u>A Tale of Two Cities</u>, there can be none who so drastically changes as Sydney Carton. Nor can there be one as influential to the story. Finally, there cannot be one who is such a sorry example of a human being, then becomes as loving a hero as ever there was. Carton too is so controversial in that he is once so down and out and then so caring. So with all this change and contrariety, did Dickens create a realistic character in Sydney Carton? The answer is yes, for all this change occurs for love, a power man cannot, and never can, overcome. Love for Lucie is so strong, that he later trades his life for that of his rival to Lucie.

Carton's change is obvious and sudden, but nevertheless realistic. At first Carton is the epitome of a bad person. He is a sharp-tongued French assistant lawyer and alcoholic who defends the most wretched and lowly prisoners imaginable. However, Carton turns out to be the model hero whose immortal last words are some of the most memorable in literature.

"It is a far, far better thing that I do, than I have ever done;
It is a far, far better rest that I go to, than I have ever known."

He proclaims this as he is about to die in place of his friend and rival, Charles Darnay, who was imprisoned and sentenced to death. But through this switch, it is Carton (who looks very much like Darnay) who will die. Through these last words he shows his willingness, and even gladness, to die in place of a friend.

Thus, Dickens has masterfully created a change in which an "unlikely alcoholic" gradually, and believably, progresses into a dazzling hero. He is a hero who twice risked his freedom and his life to allow a friend to live and thus a love to continue. The sacrifice is made more poignant by its involving saving a man to love the woman whom Carton himself loves.

This character and his change are fundamentally important to the story in that they allow the main character to live and to continue his relationship with his mistress. In my eyes, there can be no greater hero than Carton. Carton has given up his two most valued things, his love for Lucie and his life, all to allow his friend to live and love Carton's favorite thing in the world, Lucie.

believes that feedback will not only improve the way we measure students but will help shape students' attitudes toward assessment. Students will no longer regard evaluation as a means to measure and grade and "catch them out" but as an integral part of learning that will help them grow.

Paperload. We close this discussion with a note about the consequences of writing evaluation on the English teacher—one of those everyday issues that is sometimes overlooked but that may be of paramount importance to you in your teaching career. One of the fundamental diffi-

culties for English teachers from middle school to high school is the paper load. When English teachers face 120 or more students each day, they can easily find themselves buried under five class sets of papers each week. Even at ten minutes per paper, reading them requires 1,200 minutes, or twenty hours, every week. It is no wonder that many school reforms start with reducing the English teachers' work loads—fewer classes, fewer students per class. Such a reduction is so expensive that the reform is seldom seriously considered, but less costly remedies must be found.

Approaches to writing that involve the writing process and writing portfolios can have a significant (and more realistic) impact on the challenge of an English teacher's paper load. A writing workshop structure means that more class time is dedicated to writing. The teacher is free during some class time to work with students in conference to address surface and deep-structure writing snarls. Each student will spend more hours on and make more of an investment in a single paper and thus produce fewer but higher-quality papers during a term. When other students have read and responded in the revision stages of the process, they give the writer a much wider audience than the teacher can alone. These additional readers are not solely judges but can help the writer tune ideas, voice, and mechanics. Teachers become resources, not evaluators. Furthermore, writers are challenged to become their own best assessors. Thus, the teacher will respond to fewer papers of higher quality, whereas in the past, teachers provided the only feedback to students and marked many mediocre papers.

In the portfolio approach, all of the students' work has response and revision brought to it; but only a few selected pieces serve as the means of final evaluation. With both strategies, parents, students, and teachers can readily see the progress through the term; but much less out-of-class time is spent grading papers. They also avoid what Kirby et al. (1988) call perhaps the "most seriously damaging habit we get into as 'theme graders' . . . mindlessness. The sheer volume of papers and their frequent drabness have a kind of hypnotic effect that can rob the evaluator not only of objectivity but sensitive and insightful reading. If student papers are important enough to be graded, they deserve the best reading we can possibly give them" (p. 219). What is most important is that students know both how writing will be evaluated and that different means of assessment will be brought to all parts of the writing process.

⌗ EVALUATING ORACY

Evaluation of the most fundamental dimensions of language—speaking and listening is even less discussed and researched than is evaluation of knowledge of literature and performance in writing. As we discussed in Chapter 4, U.S. teachers have been hesitant to teach talking and listening. Student talk is natural, a given of life outside of school and in classrooms. It is often considered an interruption or intrusion, not part of the learning itself. Furthermore, classrooms neglect talking and listening because they are not easy to evaluate and almost no tests exist to do so. As sports announcer Skip Carey might say, the situation is a "vicious circus."

Traditional oral productions—book reports, brief speeches, debates, oral interpretations, and poetry recitations—have long been used in class to help students learn to "speak on their feet" and have been traditionally evaluated with the kinds of holistic or analytic instruments used for writing products. Seldom, however, has process been assessed. A federally funded project from the National Basic Skills Improvement Program to our local Winston-Salem/Forsyth County schools expanded those traditional genres of speaking and listening. A committee of teachers enumerated oral communication skills necessary not simply for occasional speeches but for everyday life. The project resulted in a book of researched, conceptualized, and tested lessons and activities to help students improve their speaking and listening skills (Barlow & Stankwytch, 1982). Appendix I includes five of their evaluation instruments: an oral communications activities log to keep track of an individual student's oral activity; two inventories that sample student self-assessment of oral language use; an evaluation form for discussion (used by teachers, peers, and students); a rating scale for the group discussion form; and a teacher evaluation form for a talking activity that is rarely addressed in classrooms but is common in life—announcements.

Instruction in and evaluation of a wider variety of speech acts have had only incidental support in most English classrooms. Particularly overlooked is the active, exploratory talk that does not report on learning but does produce it. When classrooms are teacher-centered and students speak only to clarify the teacher's ideas or to answer the teacher's questions, such exploratory talking seldom occurs. But in classrooms where students are central, talk that grows from questioning, probing, defending one's own position, and narrating experiences becomes essential to the learning of content or language systems and processes. Evaluating such talk is as difficult as separating the filaments from a spider's web to grade the quality of its weaving.

After examining the best theories, research, and practice in the area of oral language development and its evaluation, Harrison (1991) created a set of seven general criteria useful in curricular activities and assessment of oracy (Figure 13–16). These seven features go far beyond what most schools articulate and foster. But further work still needs to focus on the components of each of the genres to create an appropriate nomenclature comparable to that used in writing. Of course, much of writing's terminology is well suited for oral production, although many holistic thinkers would rue the day that we dissect speaking. They fear that we would disable students' talking, as we may have their reading and writing, by the close analysis of component parts. The fishbowl conversation of Chapters 2 and 4 provides a model of how talking (formal and informal) is best evaluated: holistically, contextually, nonthreateningly, recursively, as a process (not one product), by listeners (students and teacher), and by the talker.

FIGURE 13-16

Harrison's seven criteria
of oracy

Source: Adapted from L. R. Harrison
(1991). *Speaking and listening are
much used but little taught:
Incorporating oral language into the
high school English curriculum.*
Unpublished Master's Thesis. Wake
Forest University, Winston-Salem, NC.
Used by permission.

Articulateness. Does the student express him or herself with clarity and fluidity? Does he or she speak coherently? Does the speaking or talk make sense?

Effectiveness. Does the speaker achieve his or her purpose? Does the speaker do what he or she sets out to do? For example, if the student is delivering a persuasive speech, is it persuasive? Or if the student is telling a story, is the telling believable or credible?

Register. Is the talk appropriate for the particular audience? Does the language used fit the context and the purpose? How well does the student adjust language and delivery to suit the purpose and context? Is the student able to use the very best and exact word where necessary?

Delivery. How well does the student make use of voice, pitch, tone, volume, eye contact, and body language? Is the voice range too high or too low? Does it reach the listeners? Does the speaker's stance help or hinder his or her communication?

Collaboration. How well does the speaker relate to others? Is the speaker able to involve and interest the audience? How well does the student function with others in the group (applicable to group activity)? How well does the speaker listen to them, and how sensitive is he or she to their responses?

Diction. Does the student use correct speech? Is the diction acceptable? Do the diction or the pronunciations irritate the listener or detract from the effectiveness of the talk?

Fluency. Does the student overuse stabilizers *(er, mm, you know, sort of, ah, um)?* Does the student speak at a suitable speed, allowing pauses where necessary? Is the student able to elaborate adequately? Is the amount of talk suitable (especially applicable to dialogues and class discussions)?

∞ALTERNATIVE GRADING CHOICES

Few schools in the United States have abolished grades entirely. Thus, whether teachers use traditional or alternative evaluation strategies, they still wind up having to assign one letter or number to represent student learning. Table 13-5 enumerates the traditional range of grades. To shake the anxiety-producing and stigmatizing effects of numerical grades or their equivalent letters, some schools have shifted to the alternative systems shown in Figure 13-17. Nevertheless, whatever our attempts to downplay or negotiate around grading's negative consequences, grades seem to remain hierarchical and summative. Inertia erodes our best attempts at change. Some systems simplify to pass/fail, but even these are often corrupted into high and low passes. Two of the advantages of such systems—that students are more relaxed about their work and are freed to take greater personal risks with it—are lost as the hierarchical ladder forms itself again. (Credit/no credit systems can avoid these pitfalls and remove the stigma of failure, but in traditional schools they still require the judgment of an authority who is not the student.)

The following ten polarities contain other choices that teachers can make about how they grade (Figure 13-18). For clarity, we draw the contrasts sharper than they appear in school life. One of Downie's (1967) basic principles about the contentious nature of testing is pertinent: "In a democracy every form of appraisal will have critics, which is a spur to change and improvement" (p. 9). After we describe our ten polarities, we invite you to place yourself at some spot along a continuum between the two extremes. Such a placement between competing claims may spur you to understand and improve both.

TABLE 13-5   Traditional grading schema

Numerical Range			Letter Grade
95–100	93–100	90–100	A
88–94	85–92	80–89	B
81–87	77–84	70–79	C
75–80	69–76	60–69	D
0–74	0–68	0–59	F

FIGURE 13-17

Alternative grading systems

A	Excellent	Excellent	G (good)	H (high pass)	✓+
B	Good	Shows improvement	S (satisfactory)	P (pass)	✓
C	Fair	Needs improvement	U (unsatisfactory)	L (low pass)	✓–
D	Poor	No improvement			
F	Fail	Failing	F (fail)	F (fail)	F (fail)

Quantitative	Qualitative
Aware	Blind
Absolute	Relative
Objective	Subjective
Incidental	Cumulative
Holistic	Partial
Independent	Individual
Bound	Open
Formative	Summative
Cooperative	Competitive

FIGURE 13–18 Ten poles of grading

Quantitative-Qualitative

One of the most troubling questions about grading for beginning teachers is "How much should I take the personal lives of my students into consideration in my evaluation?" The quantitative teacher looks at performance objectively, sums scores on graded events, and assigns her students grades. Although the quantitative teacher's strict time lines and unyielding standards may send a harsh message to students, they encourage independence and responsibility. Students are asked to manage their own affairs.

The qualitative teacher accepts knowledge about the private lives of students as pertinent to evaluation. Such personal knowledge can be instrumental in encouraging the developing student. Response to the individual student is paramount to the efficient functioning of the whole class. However, just as too little sympathetic awareness of individual students is problematic, so, too, is over-involvement with students. For teachers negotiating five classes of 115 students, being as open to the nuances of individual lives as they might want to be is complicated if not exhausting. Furthermore, students who are shy, self-sufficient, or distrustful of school authorities can be given less consideration than they deserve. No teacher can be all knowing, and students are not equally self-disclosing.

Aware-Blind

This dichotomy also relates to the matter of judging student responses. In addition, it returns us to the question of teacher omniscience. You can read students' responses knowing who wrote them or offer students a measure of anonymity. If you prefer the latter, you can let students make codes that only they can identify using birth dates and middle initials or social security numbers. Students often feel a greater sense of fairness in grading when their work is judged anonymously. Even if you intend to have an objective approach to scoring, biases may creep in. With blind grading, no prior assumptions or grade stereotypes can be carried from one testing event to the next.

Absolute-Relative

The dilemma of absolute and relative standards arises when you consider whether grades are established strictly by meeting set criteria (identifying nine of ten quotes from *Macbeth* earns a student an *A*) or whether the grade assigned depends on the performance of the entire group. If seven correct identifications are the best performance in the class, that student earns an *A*, not a *C* as he or she might in an absolute grading system. Seeing the individual's performance with respect to a group's performance (grading on the curve) can be rather sophisticated (as detailed in statistics and tests and measurements courses) or appear to be somewhat quixotic and cavalier (as determined by the charity of the grader). These polar positions are usually referred to as criterion-referenced versus norm-referenced interpretations of performance.

Objective-Subjective

Many students regard grading as the basic way to label a teacher as either an objective or a subjective grader. Students themselves enjoy the comfort of counting on the straightforward, unbiased, public verifiability of the objective test, especially when essay questions are poorly conceived and articulated. In addition, the objectivity brings with it a consoling certainty about what is the right and wrong response. But this exactitude is problematic in English, where certainty in all dimensions of language is evasive and where teachers ask students to operate at the most challenging boundaries of their abilities.

Most teachers and students operate with a more fluid, less exact approach to language and literature; but they realize that open-ended evaluative strategies are difficult. The constructed-response questions of essay tests or long-answer exams are dreaded by students because they are so broad and the teacher's grading of them can be idiosyncratic. Beyond the issue of teacher reliability across many papers is the question of what teachers define as the skill or knowledge that they are evaluating. In having students write about literature, for instance, teachers often are not themselves sure whether they are interested in the writing skills of literary analysis or in the analytical or imaginative skills of literary interpretation. Essay items by definition involve language and writing skills; thus, they handicap the less-able writer, vocabulary user, and speller and those whose handwriting is poor.

A further dimension of this split is the type of marks that the two poles tend to generate. Most objective grading has the appearance of exactitude and can be quantitatively established: 33 out of 40 correct true/false responses yields an 82.5 percentage. At the other extreme, a very strong essay on nature in Native American chants, an acceptable comparison between Buck's *The Good Earth* and Bertolucci's *The Last Emperor,* and a rather weak examination of Lady Macbeth's metaphors can all come to a *C+* in a qualitative system in which grader reliability is hard to achieve.

Incidental-Cumulative

Most beginning teachers think of the grading process as assigning grades to each of the tests, papers, or other assignments completed in a term. The grading events typically stand alone, and their total at the end of a grading period (with various weights assigned to quizzes, tests, class contribution, and long or short projects) forms the final grade. Beginning teachers often adopt this incidental approach because it is the grading system that they have experienced. When little or no system exists, averaging isolated grades is the system that prevails. It is further reinforced by the traditional, seemingly commonsensical assigning of an absolute grade to each student product.

The cumulative, or incremental, approach puts all of the grades into a system so that each event is assigned a clear value in a total evaluation process. It requires that all assignments be given some weight and that the sum of those weights equal the grand total, usually 100 or 1,000. It is a planned economy, though, not a free market. Because the cumulative approach requires planning for the entire term or the year, those who are teaching a course for the first time and have little time to plan or those who make their plans as they move through the year find it more difficult to use. It is also an alien concept for those whose experiences as students are the basis for their approach to evaluation. But it is an approach that you might find useful as you gain greater confidence and mastery of your classroom. There is a final reckoning, at which point the person with, say, 93.4 points receives an *A* while another with 87.3 gets only a *B*. Moreover, the weights for each of the assessed components and a knowledge of what part of the total is needed for an *A, B, C, D,* or *F* must be clearly spelled out at the beginning. Such careful system building has some disadvantages, but certain advantages argue for its use:

- It avoids the student ego struggles with teachers over whether a paper or test is an *A* or a *B*. The use of numerical weights undercuts that contest.
- It opens the grading process so that mysteries and quixotic obstructions are generally eliminated or at least diminished.
- It gives students the sense that even small daily contributions add up to a grand total controlled by their own choices rather than by fate.
- It generally encourages the creation of multiple, small, manageable grading events rather than a few overwhelming blockbusters.

The third advantage is especially useful in awarding grades for increments of the extended writing process: Every step that students take is rewarded by a small number of points.

Holistic-Partial

This dichotomy relates more narrowly to how the teacher reads or grades a test. For essay tests particularly, the teacher can read each individual student's complete test or read all student responses to the same question and then repeat the process through each successive question. Typically, teachers appear to grade each student's entire test, one after the other. A grade is assigned based on the summing of points for each answer or on the teacher's more general impression of quality.

A partial approach has benefits worth considering as an alternative. When you read an entire class response to a single question, you have the advantage of greater clarity about how a student responds to the question because of your focus upon that question and answer. Almost like an assembly-line worker, you economize and clarify the operation by repetition of it. You also do not as easily carry your judgment of the student from one question to the next because of the time interval between questions. (We also reshuffle the pile after each question.) Every response of every student to every question is dealt with in a fresh way.

Independent-Individual

Independent work places students on different learning tracks of their own making, while individual instruction (programmed instruction) puts all students on the same learning track but with different timetables. With individualized learning, because performance is fixed and only time is variable, evaluation of students occurs at different times but not necessarily in different forms. Programmed instruction features sameness and objectivity; like the hamburgers at McDonald's and your bed at Holiday Inn, there are no surprises. All student work moves toward a common objective standard, although at differing paces. Assessment of the mastery of these objectives simply requires the teacher to choose from the array of traditional and nontraditional measures.

Independence opens students to choice and invites them to take off in directions of their own choosing. Consequently, an assessment of mastery of content is difficult, and even an assessment of common skills or methodologies (for instance, using the semicolon, varying point of view in a narrative, or identifying rhyme schemes in poetry) is hard. The joy and independence of learning, a general consciousness of language or literature, and the successful completion of chosen tasks might become the most salient features to be evaluated. The idiosyncratic evolutions of free-style student learning will challenge the teacher during assessment, but its possibilities for discovery and growth may make the challenge worth accepting.

Bound-Open

Embedded in the question of independent versus individual assessment is the question of time. Most of our classrooms are bounded by strict time limitations in their curricula, instruction, and assessment. An open approach might begin with the freedom of time allowed by programmed instruction, but it should run deeper. Bloom's (1968) mastery learning asks teachers to allow students the time they need to do their work well rather than hustling them onward whether or not they have fully understood their lessons. Such hurry breeds in students and teachers alike a lack of concern for the idea at hand, whether it is constructing simple sentences or contrasting narrative styles in *The Pigman.* Those who are uncertain about the former in the fourth grade will be totally defeated by the latter in the tenth grade.

But an open approach can suggest something more than allowing students to complete a computer-assisted instruction program at their own rate. An open classroom allows the time that most of England's elementary schools give children to complete serious, high-quality, unhurried work. English grading relies on a portfolio type of assessment, which does not report 87s or even *A*s, but contains detailed notes about, for example, the way a student handles narration as opposed to analysis in written composition. In U.S. schools, an open approach could mean more time to do things well and less pressure on tests to spill everything out in one burst. If most testing must be conventionally built on speed, perhaps a part of our grading could be as time-free as possible. Take-home exams or tests that generally take half a period, with the remainder to be used by quick students for silent reading or writing would be useful to both the speedy and the methodical. The extended writing process, of course, signals the switch from fifty-minute writing assignments to those that require parts of many days with much time for reflection. A totally open approach to instruction and assessment is hardly conceivable; everything we undertake has finite time limits placed upon it, and the most intractable of time constraints—the school year—limits any assignment's ultimate due date.

Formative-Summative

These terms refer to both the timing and the purpose of testing or evaluation. In timing, formative testing or evaluation is done over time, usually in small increments such as weekly quizzes. Summative testing is done, as the term implies, at the conclusion of instruction; it gives a more summary picture of performance, as with final examinations. In purpose, formative testing monitors student progress and often tests modest instructional objectives. It is used frequently to diagnose individual problems with learning. It is also valuable for questioning students' attitudes toward their work and their engagement in it. If

teachers discover negative drifts during the year, they can act to correct them. Sampling student response at the end of a term or year does not yield profitable, course-altering information for that group. Summative testing more often provides information about whether the student has achieved a desired final outcome of instruction. Formative testing has a narrow focus; summative has a wider vision.

Some teachers use formative testing predominantly and even sum such testing for final grading. Others rely more on large, end-of-unit examinations in which students rise or fall on their performance on one day. We employ both for different purposes and in acknowledgment of different student styles. We use formative evaluation to keep track of basic skills or knowledge and to reward those students who try hard and perform best on small, discrete tasks such as quizzes of reading. (We find that it works as both a motivating force—to keep students honest—and as a reward.) We deploy summative examinations to allow students to work at Bloom's higher levels of analysis, synthesis, and evaluation. We are deeply interested in students' work in progress, but we also want students to have the opportunity of making broad kinds of judgments about a larger body of material.

Cooperative-Competitive

Some teachers work constantly to undermine the competition that seems so basic to our culture, while others assume that competition is both natural and useful and therefore exploit it. Nowhere do students learn competition more readily than in school testing. They quickly see in the elementary and middle grades (before athletics intercedes to introduce physical prowess into the equation) that the rewards schools provide—"grades, honors, recognitions, affection"—are conditioned on individual achievement (Purpel, 1989, p. 35). As testing is established in individual classrooms, schools, systems, states, and our nation, students are often pitted against each other. We erect ladders that move up from failure to success and then arrange students along them. We assume that students arrive at their rungs by their own choices, by the quality of their performance. We fail to acknowledge our own determining part as test constructors of those ladders. We overlook the individual differences of the students whom we expect to climb them. Sadly, we also fail to notice the negative consequences on those who can never progress past the bottom rungs.

But whether we accept competition and hierarchy as inevitable or learned, we can still decide whether to encourage or discourage them. Ways to discourage competition among students and encourage a sense of community purpose in learning range from the construction of group tests to the abandonment of testing altogether. In the former, pairs of students, small groups, and whole classes can be given problems to be solved together. The same mark is given to all members of the group, or individuals can be given their own baseline score with bonus points for the class's or their group's attainment of a specified goal. At the latter end might be a move to portfolio evaluation. But even if the most traditional instruments are used in common ways, teachers can influence a class sense of individual competition versus communal purpose by their professed attitude toward grading. When teachers use grades to punish, cajole, and praise or to single out high achievers and shame low achievers, students become alienated from each other and protective of their own performance. When grading events are treated more casually—high achievers are not publicly extolled, low achievers are not scolded—the corrosive effects of individual competition can be mitigated. Lower achievers also can be praised for specific strengths and successes and the unique contributions that they make to a class. If you provide structured opportunities for expressing multiple intelligences, everyone achieves at some time.

These dichotomies represent a range of choices that individual teachers can make in developing whole systems, designing questions and assignments, or marking them. The choices rest within prior decisions about curricula and instructional approaches. We encourage you to make your evaluation consistent with your instruction. We would not expect, for instance, that an exploratory lesson on *The Scarlet Letter* (which asks students in groups to speculate on the moral values of Hester, Dimmesdale, and Chillingworth) be tested by matching or multiple-choice questions. We further encourage your fitting the evaluation strategy to the students before you. As you establish your classroom, you may wish to review this list of polarities and decide which of them will be important to consider seriously. You will want to experiment with some and try different points along these continua to see how you and your students respond. We feel that such wrestling with alternatives is critical to the effectiveness of your teaching and your students' learning. As Downie (1967) reminds us, such struggle spurs us to imagine better possibilities.

Invitation to Reflection 13–10

1. Review the ten poles of grading and decide where you stand on each of them (Figure 13–18).
2. Would your former high school and college English teachers fall at places different from you on the continuum?
3. Do you find any evaluation possibilities in these ten that are new to you? If so, which?
4. Do you feel strongly about any evaluation stances? Do you hope to incorporate any of them into your own classroom? Which? Why?
5. One of psychologist William James's Harvard students was the writer Gertrude Stein. Barzun (1983) tells the

story of Stein's having gone to too many operas and "finding herself mentally vacant in front of the final in James's course. . . . She addressed James on the blue book, saying she did not feel like writing philosophy that day. As she remembered it after thirty years, the next day, she had from James a postal card: 'I understand perfectly how you feel. I often feel like that myself.' He passed her then, but his sense of justice to others exacted an 'exit' examination [from the university later]" (p. 278). How do you evaluate James as an evaluator?

All of the contending means of assessment will likely continue to stir questions as you become an experienced teacher. We hope you will keep these alternatives in mind as you observe experienced teachers and note where they fall along these continua.

CRITIQUE OF TRADITIONAL GRADING

We want to become more specific about our critique of traditional grading. We have struggled to be fairminded in articulating traditional approaches and hopeful in suggesting creative alternatives to them. We discuss here a few final cautions about the dangers of grading in general and the pitfalls for the English teacher in particular.

Pedagogical Dangers

Too often, traditional grading compromises the deeper aims of English education. It focuses on the product of learning, not the process; on the adult's need, not the child's; and on teacher control, not student empowerment. It makes little accommodation for the developmental experience of the individual student. It imposes an adult's authority on the personal authority of the child and thereby takes initiative and responsibility from students. Too often, assessment becomes an external rather than an internal event, discouraging self-reliance. Some critics even see grading as subverting the basic aim of schooling. Purpel (1989) writes that grading "is also antiintellectual in its irrational and arbitrary character, and it is a serious barrier to the true educational process of inquiry, sharing, and dialogue" (p. 120).

Psychometric Dangers

Testing often invites learning on the most basic level. Moffett and Wagner's (1976, p. 416) second cardinal principle opened this chapter: "Evaluation should not dictate, distort, or displace what it measures." Often, teachers "teach to the test," and the adage is proven again: "Those who control the tests control the curriculum." Consequently, if a low order of mental activity is being tested, that activity comes to dominate the class. If assessment of reading comprehension extends only to literal recall of plot and character, for instance, students will study that and teachers will teach it. The scope of what is possible in a classroom is restricted and trivialized.

Furthermore, if grading is narrowly conceived, it comes to determine what students will take seriously. If, for instance, a teacher extols the value of class participation yet grades only written quizzes and exams, students quickly devalue their classroom discourse. Even students motivated by a serious interest in the subject matter become calculating and strategic in their study, particularly if they are pushed in other courses.

Finally, the construction of "objective" measures that are fair and valid and "subjective" measures that are reliable and efficiently scored can be done but only with care, some knowledge, and much time. Few English teachers have that training or time.

Personal Dangers

On a personal level, grading is problematic because it is most often based on comparative criteria, which leave some students feeling worthless and without dignity. Even those who often score well come to depend on external measures to motivate their action and to validate their worth. Students who consistently fail struggle with self-esteem. They learn to depend on the teacher's evaluation of them rather than on their own evaluation. Because schools are the dominant field of activity through the formative years of students' lives (usually ages five through eighteen), the consequences can be life altering.

Another personal effect of grading students is that they are diverted from intrinsic or personal learning and spend their energies on grades. Purpel (1989) enumerates the consequences: "students come to worry more about grades than meaning; and both teachers and students respond to these problems by developing techniques (e.g., multiple choice tests, cramming, memorizing) which are at best distracting, and at worst counterproductive to serious learning. The concern for grading produces anxiety, cheating, grade grubbing, and unhealthy competition" (p. 8).

Cultural Dangers

Purpel (1989) sees technical discussions of testing as distractions from the crucial cultural and moral discussions:

> To value grading is to value competition and to accept a society of inequality and a psychology that posits external behavior rather than internal experience as more important.

> Grading is primarily a technique for promoting particular social, moral, and political goals, and it is those goals which should be debated rather than the technical and misleading questions about the value of essay vs. objective testing or whether to use grade point averages or standardized tests as the basis for college admission. (p. 9)

Our culture tends to structure its thinking around hierarchies, ladders, and pyramids. Greene (1985) observes that teachers "have a habitual tendency to see students in terms of superior and inferior, high up—and lower down—on a scale." She wonders if even Piagetian thought has given legitimacy to hierarchy: "It is simply assumed that development occurs sequentially, that analytic capacities are 'higher' than holistic ones, that the abstract is more worthy than the concrete" (p. 144). Such a ranking makes us tolerate the inevitability of failure in some and success in others. Teachers need to question this basic assumption in our culture.

Moral Dangers

Dangers multiply when standardized tests are introduced to judge and rank students, teachers, and schools. All three are at risk and may suffer damaging consequences. Schools and districts have wide variance in per-pupil expenditure, socioeconomic levels of children, conditions of schools, and experience of teachers. Nevertheless, all students take the same test. Kozol (2002) has heard the justification for these tests: We live in a world that will test us in a thousand ways, and we must prepare our students to face those tests. But he answers that *tests without equity* are bludgeons with which to hit children and humiliate their teachers. In *Savage Inequalities,* Kozol (1991) quotes Ruthie Green-Brown, the principal of Camden High School, on the consequences of testing in poor school districts:

> The state requires test results. It "mandates" higher scores. But it provides us no resources in the areas that count to make this possible. . . . If they first had given Head Start to our children *and* pre-kindergarten, *and* materials *and* classes of 15 or 18 children in the elementary grades, *and* computers *and* attractive buildings *and* enough books and supplies *and* teacher salaries sufficient to compete with the suburban schools, and then come in a few years later with their tests and test-demands, it might have been fair play. Instead, they leave us as we are, separate and unequal, underfunded, with large classes, and with virtually no Head Start, and they think that they can test our children into a mechanical proficiency. (p. 143)

We encourage you to be wary if high-stakes testing encroaches on your choices of curriculum or pedagogy, if it intrudes on your autonomy as a teacher, and if it prejudices the education of diverse students. Of these three, the moral danger lies most threateningly in the last.

Invitation to Reflection 13-11

Imagine that you are a first-year teacher in a consolidated rural county high school, the youngest and most inexperienced member of an established faculty. You decide to take some new curricular and evaluative ideas into your eleventh-grade English classes; namely, you want to set up a process-centered curriculum and an assessment program based primarily on portfolio grading and self-evaluation. Because your students are amazed and then energized by this departure from tradition, a majority of them put considerable time and energy into their work and achieve *A* grades. After the first quarter's grades are reported, the guidance counselor notes the "disproportionate" number of *A*s, hears from parents of highly competitive students in other classes who wonder about the devaluation of their children's grades, and talks with the principal. The principal also has heard from disgruntled older teachers whose students are either jealous of their peers' good fortune or incredulous that other students are earning *A*s so easily. The principal values your new instructional approaches but calls you in to talk about your grading. How will you answer the concerns of parents, teachers, and students?

Unique Difficulties for English Teachers

Beyond these difficulties in evaluation and grading, English teachers have unique, specific burdens. Our field itself—the receptive and creative study of oral and written language—is resistant to narrow measurement. When we define our educative purpose as opening students to the responses and possibilities that are uniquely their own, we falter at the use of grading to measure that personal openness. We find it hard to reduce a novel to a multiple-choice exam. Not only is the richness of any novel worth teaching reduced, but so is the richness and ambiguity of personal response and interpretation. It is harder still to reduce the individual response to any criteria- or norm-referenced standard of excellent, good, fair, or unacceptable. The dilemma reminds us of the American composer Charles Ives's reaction to an award for his composing: He said that giving a prize to a composer is like offering a prize to the curate who loves God the most.

Dixon and Stratta (1989) have observed the reductive consequences of the kinds of questions that we pose about literature in classroom discussions, in out-of-class assignments, and on examinations. They find that these questions betray "false assumptions about the act of reading, the kind of knowledge to be derived from literature, and the kinds of writing that help to articulate it" (p. 30). They explain: "To be specific, these exercises assume that you do not create a character in your imagination as you read; that you do not feel sympathy or antipathy to those

personae on the screen, that you never test their reality against life as you know it, that you can't read the play as a metaphor for parts of your own life, and that you won't challenge the author's conception of people and society" (p. 26). Because what we aim to teach in the English classroom is complex, measuring it is a risky business.

CONCLUSION

We must engage in evaluation with resistance to those evaluative acts and attitudes that stymie or harm the individual's making of meaning and with openness to alternative means for expressing understanding. We need also to be clear about the uses of evaluation. Moffett and Wagner (1976) articulate five functions served by language arts evaluation that address each of the constituents of schools. Evaluation should indicate

- to the individual student how effectively he is communicating,
- to the parent how much the student is learning in school,
- to the teacher the needs of the student, for diagnosing and advising,
- to the administrator how good a job the teacher is doing, and
- to all parties how effectively the curriculum and materials reach their goals. (p. 415)

We take each of these seriously and, as we have discussed, feel that different forms of evaluation must address each need. Parents are perhaps the most overlooked of these five. Greene (1985) vividly identifies the range of parents whose particular mindsets come to bear on schools:

There are middle class parents worried about SATs, insisting on high achievement, whatever the cost. There are poor parents frightened by persisting illiteracy, people who want an exclusive emphasis on the three Rs for the sake of job training and survival in the mainstream. There are academic parents who purport to know more about education than do the teachers; there are zealots who want human relations "experiences" and non-cognitive play; there are fundamentalist parents afraid of certain novels, or of evolutionary theory, or of sex education. It becomes increasingly clear that students, parents, teachers, and the general public have different and competing ideas about how schools should be judged. Their assumptions differ; their values differ with regard to what good schools ought to be. (p. 153)

Greene does not try to provide simple answers to this dilemma. Struggle is inevitable if we attend to those complexities. But we should be anchored in our attention to the student. In the life of the classroom, evaluation is, quite simply, interpretation of the student by the teacher. That interpretation needs to be generous. In fact, we have observed that often the best teachers are those who were not the best students. Their youthful difficulties appear to sensitize them to the feelings of discouragement, anxiety, and shame experienced by their students.

Psychologists G. B. Berenson and Robert Carkhuff (1967) reason that all human encounters work for good or ill. No encounter is neutral. Nowhere is this more true in teaching than in evaluation and grading. To render judgment of process or products too often fore-closes on the student's dynamic life processes. We need to recognize the personal and idiosyncratic nature of reading, writing, and speaking and to provide evaluation strategies that give them expression. We should work towards Greene's (1985, p. 154) hope that "evaluation may some day serve the cause of growth and constant learning."

$\mathscr{14}$

Planning the Lesson

One of the commonplaces of any profession is the need to exercise judgment in the presence of the unexpected and the uncertain. Experience occurs when design and chance collide. This happens every time a lesson plan encounters a child. We wouldn't need professionals otherwise; they are professionals who reason and intuit, decide and discern.

Lee Schulman

Most of our readers are in the unusual position of having to put the suggestions of a textbook into immediate practice. *Bridging English* is both an academic text and a practical guidebook. Thus far we have presented many theories, general approaches, specific methods, and texts (print and nonprint) that critically influence what goes on in English classrooms. But a gap falls between discussing why, how, and what to teach and actually teaching students. We want to fill that gap by articulating the intermediate steps that we and others take to transform theories about English teaching into practice. Beginning teachers need to be able to conceptualize their purposes in teaching but also to implement those purposes in classroom lessons that are energetic and confident. We want young teachers to talk as teachers and act as teachers. At some time in their schooling careers, most prospective teachers have been good students and willingly followed at least a few teachers whom they admired. You are about to become a classroom leader for others.

Provoking, challenging, and engaging activities are what students remember about good teachers. What students may not know consciously, but do know intuitively, is that a master teacher welds these activities into a thoughtful sequence of instruction, one that makes the interesting pieces all the more powerful as they work together. Research has shown that teachers who develop long-range plans are those whom students see as most able (Zimpher, 1988). Teachers are regularly engaged in four basic types of planning: yearly, unit, weekly, and daily. (Occasionally, they also are asked to deliberate over school- or systemwide curriculum planning, but this is rare for young teachers.) Each type of planning is important for effective instruction; and each needs to be worked out within the context of your own abilities, your students' needs, and your sense of how learning best occurs. Owen (1991) likens teaching to composing and sees planning as "similar to pre-writing, the stage of the writing process which precedes the first draft" (p. 57). She sees the planning process as "a rehearsal in which the teacher prepares for teaching," as Murray (1980) says, "in the mind and on the page" (p. 62).

We turn first to four common models that can be used for planning any unit of instruction—lessons, units, or the course-long curriculum—which are based on *creative process, conversations, objectives,* and *content.* After we consider lesson planning, we then highlight issues that teachers should address as they plan the unit. (These, too, can be generalized to the lesson.) We then explore planning for the week and the entire year's curriculum. (We discuss weekly planning briefly because weeks do provide predictable, if less significant, learning benchmarks.) Next we look at classroom variables that should influence any instructional planning, particularly those constant structures and concerns that af-

fect the everyday classroom stage on which those plans will be enacted. Figure 14-1 illustrates the four models and some of the prominent variables that will affect your planning.[1]

LESSON PLANNING

Our former student, now a teacher, Stella Beale (1997, personal communication), describes her anxieties as a student teacher and in so doing explains the need to consider practical suggestions for planning, the need that prompted us to write this chapter of *Bridging English:*

> I was about three weeks into my student teaching. It was 2:00 in the morning, and the hard knot of anxiety which had been centered in the pit of my stomach rose to my throat. Choking back tears, I cried out to no one in particular: "I don't have anything to do tomorrow!" Hastily, I threw something together—some wisp of a plan, and stumbled to the bedroom.
>
> Several weeks later, at a dinner organized by my methods teacher, I somewhat hesitantly asked a first-year teacher and former graduate of the master's program at Wake Forest, "How do you plan?"
>
> I'd been teaching for over a month and I still didn't feel confident about my ability to plan effective lessons. I was just beginning a unit centered around *Grimms' Fairy Tales,* but I could no more tell you what would happen tomorrow in the classroom than I could predict the weather. It wasn't that I didn't have any ideas. In fact, quite the opposite was true. I had thousands of ideas, and no effective method for translating these ideas into 50-minute lessons. My wise friend didn't chastise or scorn me; instead she offered me a simple solution.
>
> "Go home," she said, "and write down all of your ideas. Don't monitor your writing, just get it all down on paper. When you've finished, take one of those ideas and, on a separate sheet of paper, write as much as you possibly can about that particular concept. Do the same for all of your ideas. Each sheet of paper represents one lesson."
>
> Her idea was simple but effective. And, as time passed, I combined her technique with other hints and strategies. I realize today that there are many effective ways to plan and that there is no need to adopt one indiscriminately. I have stopped looking for a recipe or formula for planning; I have not, however, stopped searching out the experience of other, more experienced teachers; I have not stopped asking: "How do *you* plan?"

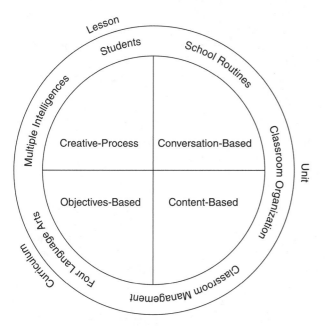

FIGURE 14-1 Planning models and variables

[1]As we have discussed, *viewing* has recently been added to the traditional four language arts. In this chapter we refer to four models because those are the strands in most common use, but we remind you of the power of *viewing* as well.

Invitation to Reflection 14-1

1. Have you been responsible for planning lessons or programs in your school life?

2. Have you ever known the kind of blind panic that Stella Beale describes?

3. What strategies have you developed to resolve that panic and approach planning productively?

4. As you observe experienced teachers, do they appear to plan using curriculum guides, their former lesson plans, the ideas of others, electronic sources, or sudden inspiration?

5. When and where do they appear to plan? At school? At home? During planning periods? The night before? On the drive to school?

6. What seems of paramount importance in their planning? Individual students or classes? Content that must be covered? Curriculum concerns from outside their own classrooms? The expediency of their personal circumstances?

7. Do they write out their plans in detail, in a jotted outline, in planning books, in notes in the text, or not at all?

Hawkey (1995) observes that "teachers must integrate public and personal knowledge in the complex task of learning to teach" (p. 176). To learn any complex and difficult human activity, we must draw heavily on the experience of those who know it better. Lesson plans occupy a central place in the daily lives of teachers, from the experienced to the novice. They are especially important for new teachers so that they can enter classrooms with ease and launch lessons energetically and confidently. In considering how to plan a lesson, we turn first to recent planning schemata. The first systematizes the suggestion made to Stella Beale—a creative process-based model. Then we consider a model clarified by Arthur Applebee's research that was new as we wrote our second edition and that has gained experience since—a conversation-based model for planning. We conclude this section with two other models, the first—an objectives-based model that teachers, educational psychologists, and teacher educators have advocated—and the final, a model that is the oldest and most common, the one found in innumerable English classrooms—a content-based model. Please note that these models can be used for lesson or unit planning.

Creative-Process Model

One of the reasons for the inadequacy of most planning schemata is that their simplicity does not match the more complicated reality of the process itself. The common six-step lesson plan described later implies that we arrive at lessons through an objective progression, an entirely logical chain of events. Cognitive taxonomies make teaching appear to be almost scientific in the classification and application of objectives and skills. Lois Weiner (1997) cautions that "most formulas for solving teacher problems reduce the challenging, creative decision-making of lesson planning to a banal, anti-intellectual endeavor. Just as importantly, the formulas frequently don't accomplish their ostensible purpose because classrooms and teaching are too unpredictable for one-size-fits-all solutions" (p. 78). Not only will each of your classes be different (whether or not they share course name and number) but a single class's dynamics might shift from day to day. Cain's (1989) proposal of a creative planning model comes nearer to the complex dance of many variables that planning appears to be for Weiner and for us. We liken Cain's creative-process model to the writing process, with its preplanning, planning, and postplanning, and the teacher-planner to a creative designer, not an industrial engineer.

Cain (1989), in her work with preservice teachers, found the "rational means-end" planning model developed on the behavioral goals-and-objectives rationale to be inadequate. It produced in her students "unit plans characteristic of the old-world instructional routine . . . giving the reading assignments for homework, discussing the questions at the end of the text, taking the quiz" (p. 5). She wondered, "Why not construct a planning model that would help preservice teachers think creatively about their 'worldmaking,' about their educational designs? Why not help them see more clearly that they are creating an educational environment, a new classroom culture, instead of just objectives that need to be met and tested?" (p. 6). She examined research on planning and creativity and writing-to-learn theory for ideas for a creative planning model, which she then articulated and tested. Her design imagines teachers to be like architects, sculptors, and other creative people who must consider many design variables when thinking about their projects. These variables remain active points of consideration for the teacher through three planning stages: *preplanning, planning,* and *postplanning.* Cain's planning model (Figure 14–2) includes the three planning stages, design variables that are active in each, and design evaluation questions.

Preplanning. Writing process theory suggests that writers do not begin with their thesis statements first because that diminishes their thinking. Similarly, teachers do not begin with a statement of measurable behavioral objectives as they compose a lesson/unit plan. Otherwise, they limit their thinking.

Planning. In traditional expository writing, when the thesis statement is established, the writer's task is simply to elaborate and neatly conclude that thesis. In planning

FIGURE 14–2

Cain's process-based model

Source: From Beatrice N. Cain, "With Worldmaking, Planning Models Matter," *English Education,* February 1989. Reprinted by permission of National Council of Teachers of English.

PREPLANNING	**PLANNING**	**POSTPLANNING**
Brainstorming	Organizing	Experimenting and testing by teaching
Researching	Sequencing	Evaluating
Collecting	Visualizing	Reorganizing
Generating	Integrating	Internalizing
Collaborating	Designing	Storing away
		Creating sound methods

DESIGN VARIABLES

1. Physical characteristics of classrooms and ideas for their use.
2. Other available school space and ideas for its use.
3. Number of students.
4. Number of periods.
5. Pupil characteristics.
6. Philosophy of education.
7. Theories of learning.
8. Learning activities.
9. Curriculum and resource materials.
10. School objectives and/or standards of learning.
11. Current social events that may impact on classroom content or activities.
12. Evaluation procedures.
13. Classroom management strategies (example: quick way to break students into small groups).
14. Executive management strategies (example: way to collect information about authors).
15. Personal teaching refinements (example: want to use more metaphors to illustrate ideas).
16. Professional goals (example: want to publish article on experimental method).
17. Goals for making instructional environment beneficial and stimulating for students.

EVALUATION OF EDUCATION DESIGN

Does form follow function?

Is the total educational design beneficial and stimulating for students? (p. 8)

---

by objectives, a similar pattern often occurs: The objectives are established, the enabling activities are planned, and the lesson or unit is summed up. No recursive reworking is necessary. The whole paper or lesson is neatly concluded. Cain follows no such straightforward blueprint but considers the mental activities necessary for envisioning one's unit of instruction.

Postplanning. Cain's model, like the writing process, keeps the teacher reexamining and refining the unit of study. In her own research, the young teacher using the creative planning model kept a journal of her thoughts, and they reflect a consciousness of what the students needed and how she was meeting their needs. "The creative planner created a learning community that eventually became what she hoped it would be: a place where teacher and students could learn and grow together." Her concerns always seemed to be related to the question "Is the plan well suited for my group of students?" whereas the rational means-end planner's concerns were with whether "the objectives she established for the unit would be met by the students" (Cain, 1989, p. 23).

Creative-Process Model in Operation. How would Cain's model operate in the daily planning of teachers? In her model, the final written lesson plans would be only the tip of the planning iceberg. They follow much internal work that can occur at any place, at any time. Preplanning teaching ideas and rehearsals can be recorded in notes jotted in a lesson plan book, questions noted in the margins of textbooks or the borders of handouts, detailed outlines, or revisions of previous lessons on computer disks. These ideas originate in an active mental process that can be outlined as follows:

1. *Generate* as many ideas as you can for a lesson. The active "doing" verbals of Cain's preplanning suggest generative sources. Conversations with other teachers are one valuable source. Concept maps are another. The story is told of English essayist Walter Pater's composing trick of placing a small pink paper at the center of his desk with a core idea, then writing related ideas or activities on blue paper and arranging them around the pink. This chapter began with Stella Beale's description of a similar technique. She compares this generation of ideas to a hawk circling, appraising what lies below it before it descends to strike.

2. We necessarily *cull* some of the ideas, save others for a better time, and *center* on the most promising.

3. When we have arrived at central ideas, we may then need to *expand* them or combine them with previous ideas. Again, look at Cain's verbals in the planning stage (Figure 14–2).

4. Finally, we begin to *arrange* them into a framework or sequence for a lesson.

Teaching Activity 14–1 simulates how you must apply your theoretical knowledge to practical decisions. You

14-1 TEACHING ACTIVITY

Contemplating a Bathtub-Bound Beetle

We present a poem by John Hall Wheelock and scattered ideas about how to teach this poem. We ask you to apply a creative planning process to the suggestions made as you prepare to teach a class of diverse ninth graders. After you cull unpromising ideas, expand what is left with ideas of your own and arrange them in a sequence for a lesson.

The Beetle in the Country Bathtub*

After one more grandiloquent effort he slips back—
Slumping? Oh no, he may be down but he's never out
(Probably wishes he were); now, pondering a fresh attack,
He wheels his slender, simonized bulk about,

Fumbles at the slippery surface until he has come to grips,
Mounts, very slowly, with ever-increasing hope, and then
Mounts, more slowly, with ever-increasing hope—and slips
All the way down to the bottom of the tub again;

Lies there, motionless, pretty discouraged perhaps? not he—
It's dogged as does it, keep your chin up, don't take
No for an answer, etc.—he plots a new strategy,
The oblique approach. This too turns out to be a mistake.

The enamelled surface of his predicament
Resembles those pockets in time and space that hold
Sick minds in torture, his struggle is a long argument
With a fact that refuses to be persuaded or cajoled.

Midnight finds him still confident. I slink to bed,
Worn out with watching. The suave heavens turn
Blandly upon their axis, overhead
The constellations glitter their polite unconcern.

Toward morning, hounded by anxiety, slumberless,
I post to the scene. Where is he? the enamelled slopes below,
Vacant—the uplands, vacant—a bathtub full of emptiness,
The insoluble problem is solved! But how? Something no
    one of us, perhaps will ever know.

Unless he went down the drain?
                                    John Hall Wheelock

---

are at the point that critical theorists call *praxis*—not the test but that place where ideas and action must necessarily intersect.

Conversation-Based Model

Research undertaken and conclusions drawn by Applebee (1996, 1997) have ramifications for planning. Applebee (1997) and his team of researchers collected case studies of elementary, junior high, and high school teachers designated as "expert" in order to investigate teachers' decisions about "what to teach and when." They examined the tacit assumptions that influenced teachers' decisions, the classroom results of those decisions, and the curriculum that evolved from them. They were especially interested in "the kinds of choices that led to teachers and students experiencing a sense of coherence and continuity in the curriculum" (p. 26). The results of the

Potential Teaching Ideas

_____ 1. Examine the symbols in the poem.

_____ 2. Bring a live beetle to class and watch it try to escape from a ceramic bowl.

_____ 3. A student reads the poem aloud to the class while two other students mimic the actions of beetle and narrator.

_____ 4. A student conducts an interview with the beetle as he struggles to ascend (accidental power activity of Chapter 4).

_____ 5. Students write poems that use other animals to comment on human existence. (Some illustrate them with a drawing or clipped magazine pictures.)

_____ 6. Identify the meter, rhyme scheme, and imagery of the poem. Discuss how they contribute to the effectiveness of the poem.

_____ 7. Ask students to read the poem and two others: Thomas Gray's "Ode: On the Death of a Favorite Cat Drowned in a Tub of Goldfishes" and Robert Frost's "Departmental." Compare the lessons learned from the animal kingdom in these three poems.

_____ 8. Ask students to write a letter from the cartoon cat Garfield, the president of the United States, or a leading sports figure that states his or her opinion of the poem.

_____ 9. Ask students to pretend to be the narrator of the poem, who is telling his best friend what he felt about the beetle.

_____10. Discuss how the person watching the beetle is like God watching humankind in its struggle.

_____11. Journal prompt: Have you ever experienced a predicament from which you could not remove yourself? Describe what you felt in that difficult situation.

_____12. Journal prompt: If you had been the narrator of this poem, what would you have done?

_____13. Journal prompt: Have you ever observed an animal and drawn comparisons between animal life and human life? Describe the connection(s) you made.

_____14. Discuss the impact of the final line on the meaning of the poem.

_____15. Imagine, script, and perform a dialogue between the struggling beetle and the watching narrator.

_____16. Fishbowl prompt: Two students debate the actions of the narrator. One could be the beetle and one the narrator. (The listening students vote for the one who makes the most persuasive argument for or against his actions.)

_____17. Write a letter from the beetle (now escaped and literate) to the narrator.

_____18. Debate the question "Would this be a good poem to read at an exterminator's convention?"

_____19. Debate the question "Would a religious person be offended by this poem?"

_____20. Debate the question "Do you believe a man or a woman is the narrator of this poem? Why?"

_____21. Add your own ideas.

*Reprinted with the permission of Scribner, a Division of Simon & Schuster, Inc., from BY DAYLIGHT AND IN DREAM: NEW AND COLLECTED POEMS, 1904–1970 by John Hall Wheelock. Copyright © 1970 by John Hall Wheelock.

study caused Applebee to propose a rethinking of the language arts curriculum in terms not of content or objectives but of students engaged in sustained and interrelated conversation.[2]

The teachers under study clearly worked to reconcile two different frames of reference: constructivist, integrative, reader-centered with traditional text-centered. These teachers engaged students in exploring the different voices of others in print and nonprint texts in order to enter conversations with and about them. The conversations were crucial. As the researchers observed classrooms across grade levels, they distilled a view of the most effective curricula—"that is, of those that were most successful in providing a sense of continuity and coherence, maintaining student interest and engagement, and

---

[2]The idea has echoes of Jay's (1991) proposal for organizing instruction around a "problematic," discussed in Chapter 7.

helping students enter into culturally significant domains of conversation" (p. 29). For instance, many English teachers organize their planning around genres. Applebee (2000) observes: "But conversations about genre—where they come from, how they differ, why they matter—are quite rare. Instead, most classrooms revert to teaching individual works in isolation from one another" (p. 1). While framing the planning in terms of genre might work as an organizing device for the teacher, "it fails to support stimulating conversation" (p. 1).

A Conversation-Based Classroom.

At this point, you might think that you hear a strange ringing in your ears, as though E. D. Hirsch is peacefully planning a curriculum with Louise Rosenblatt. Their different perspectives represent the conflict that we see Applebee (1997) bridging, a bridgehead he has gained because he has observed classroom teachers struggling with and reconciling these very issues. He uses one teacher, Tony Harrison, as an example. Harrison inherited an established tenth-grade American literature survey course that had evolved into five units, each anchored by a novel:

The Scarlet Letter (Puritan literature)
Billy Budd (transcendentalism)
The Red Badge of Courage (the Civil War)
The Adventures of Huckleberry Finn (realism, we imagine, but later eliminated because of controversy)
The Great Gatsby (modern literature)

Although the English department's concern about multiculturalism had caused revisions—*I Know Why the Caged Bird Sings* had replaced *Billy Budd*, Twain had been dropped, and a Native American literature unit now introduced the course—Harrison inherited this still-traditional shape and approached it with the skills of textual analysis refined by the New Critics.

As Harrison adjusted to additional selections, he found that he had less and less time for discussion; so he reorganized the course around a focus: the clash of cultures. Applebee explains that "initially this was simply a new template within which he continued to emphasize textual analysis, but gradually the template began to influence the questions that he and the students asked, and Harrison began to think of the course as an exploration of the question, 'Who chooses the canon?' " (p. 28). These changes caused a fundamental shift in the way in which Harrison thought of the curriculum. He now saw it not as helping students "solve the puzzle of the text" (with himself as the final verifier of the "appropriate solutions") but as "helping students participate in a set of living conversations" (p. 28). Texts became appropriate or interesting, not in and of themselves, but because of the questions they engendered and the kinds of discussions they generated. Harrison broadened his instructional approach from a primary reliance on whole-class discussion to leading "the class toward a shared set of understandings" that would eventually create "room to explore multiple interpretations and diverse points of view" (pp. 28–29).[3]

Implementing the Conversation-Based Model.

Applebee's conversation-based model defines a central and coherent domain for all language arts. It helps us unite issues of curriculum (content) and instruction (process). Applebee recognizes that his model is a shift from established traditions, and he offers suggestions about how to make it work in English classrooms. He presents (1997) four touchstones, or principles, for planning an effective curriculum:

Quality It must be built around episodes of high quality.
Quantity It requires an appropriate breadth of materials to sustain it.
Relatedness It must have interrelated parts.
Manner It must gear instruction to helping students enter into the curricular conversation. (pp. 29–30)

He also suggests several concrete steps to take in initiating such a change within the profession at large:

- to develop examples of domains for conversation that will be appropriate at different grade levels, domains whose topics and experiences will be sufficiently compelling to engage students in extended curricular conversations . . .
- to develop a rich repertoire of appropriate topics that teachers and departments can adapt to fit their local circumstances . . .
- to demonstrate its effects on students' learning . . .
- [to] learn from the disappointments that also always occur amidst the complexities of schools and classrooms. (pp. 30–31)

In sum, Applebee's conversation-based model presents a focus for planning that carries out many of the teaching approaches we believe in and that we have explored in this text. As Applebee (2000) explains, "the most effective learning contexts engage students by encouraging them to participate in the debates and activities that give any field its interest. In such contexts, students are asked to *engage* in rather than *learn about* issues that matter" (p. 1). The practical planning questions you would raise with this model include: "Are [my] materials and activities structured to foster interesting conversations about issues that matter? Will the students participate in conversations rather than being told about conversations other people have already had? Will students learn from their engagement in these conversations?" (p. 8).

---

[3]Applebee's (1996, 1997, 2000) model reconciles the opposed positions of traditionalists (Hirsch, Bloom, and Bennett) and reformers (Freire, Giroux, and Levine) by recognizing the tradition as "knowledge-in-action." As we learn to participate in these traditions, to draw from them "alternative and complementary ways of knowing and doing," we gain the knowledge and confidence to "reject or to change them" (1997, p. 26).

Objectives-Based Model

Many educators identify the central mission of schools with mastery learning and the central means of attaining that learning with the implementation of goals and objectives. Goals (the general aims or purposes of the curriculum) are generally stated in terms of broad concepts, such as *understand* and *appreciate,* and objectives (the desired changes of students' thoughts, actions, or feelings as a result of a particular lesson) are stated in terms of measurable outcomes of instruction, such as *enumerate* or *recognize.* The work of Madeline Hunter (1976) has had a great impact on the development of a model for mastery learning. She describes her model (1989) as a "teacher decision-making model" that employs "research-based, cause-effect relationships between teaching and learning . . . to escalate all students' achievement" (p. 16). The decisions center around what the teacher's goals are for instruction, what knowledge or skills students need to learn to achieve these goals, and how the teacher can facilitate that achievement. She outlines three planning questions that a skilled teacher must address.

1. What will these students be able to do as a result of their time today, or at the end of several days (not daze) in this class?
2. What information or skills will students need to achieve that goal?
3. How will the teacher artistically use research and intuition to make students' satisfactory achievement more probable? (p. 16)

She recommends that teachers answer these questions by "task analysis," which "enables the teacher to identify knowledge, skills, and processes that can accelerate or, if not present, inhibit learning" (p. 16). You will understand why many call an objectives-based model a "rational approach" to curriculum planning.

We borrow here from a well-respected general methods text by Grambs and Carr (1991) to enumerate the six component parts of planning by objectives that must be addressed in this model:

1. Scope—how much content is to be covered? (And consequently, how much time is required?)
2. Sequence—in what order are the elements of the content to be studied?
3. Objectives—what learnings are to be achieved?
4. Learning activities—in what day-to-day experiences will students engage that will allow them to achieve the objectives?
5. Materials—what things will teachers and students need to examine and use to complete the learning activities?
6. Evaluation— (a) how successfully did the teacher perform? and (b) how successfully did the students perform? (pp. 138–139)

The Six-Step Lesson Plan. After parts 1 and 2 have been determined, Hunter's model arranges a lesson structure (parts 3, 4, and 5) that is widely called a six-step lesson plan. Such a step-by-step process appeals to a sense of deliberate organization and good order. The six-step lesson plan not only sets this agenda but also prompts the teacher to assemble all of the necessary components for the plan: objectives, subject matter, instructional activities, materials, evaluation instruments, time estimates, and assignment schedules. Other miscellaneous materials for noninstructional classroom business can be easily inserted, such as library notices, special announcements, or papers for return. Our colleague, Leah McCoy, has distilled the six steps of this model (Figure 14–3).

Proponents of education by objectives list these advantages in its favor:

- It establishes a sense of control and order.
- It originates in the observations of specialists and experts who generated hypotheses about education and tested them.
- It is based on learning theory, educational psychology, and research about best practice.

FIGURE 14–3
The six-step lesson plan

1. *Objective(s)*—The objective of a lesson is a statement informing the student what he or she will be able to do by the end of the instruction.
2. *Focus/review*—The anticipatory set consists of those activities that prepare the student for learning by
   - focusing the student's attention
   - providing very brief practice on previously achieved and related learning
   - developing a readiness for the instruction that will follow.
3. *Teacher input*—This involves the dissemination of new information and activities necessary to achieve the stated objective. It may include modeling or demonstrating the acceptable finished product or process and checking for understanding (often by oral questioning) as the lesson progresses.
4. *Guided practice*—The instructor closely monitors and directs the student as he or she practices the task for the first time.
5. *Independent practice*—The student continues to practice the task without the instructor's monitoring and guidance.
6. *Closure*—The lesson concludes with reviewing and reinforcing the major points and helping students organize their knowledge.

- It has overtones of both a scientific and an engineering model.
- It provides a model, for the inexperienced teacher especially, that is systematic and inclusive. It presents an image of education under control, guided by authorities who know what is best for students.
- It corrects for a teacher's random choices in planning and aimless drift in teaching.
- It is more and more widely used by school systems to govern teachers' instruction and evaluate teachers' effectiveness.

In sum, observation has defined and research has demonstrated the correct approach to educating the young, and skillful technicians have constructed efficient plans and devices for achieving it. Education by objectives even has within its system a way of testing the hypotheses because it lays heavy stress on measurable behaviors that can be readily evaluated. Many educators consider Hunter's behavioral-objectives approach to lesson planning to be the quintessential model. More than three decades ago, Kliebard (1970) observed that using behavioral objectives for instruction has almost attained the status of "revealed doctrine" (p. 256).

Despite these claims, critics consider this approach seriously flawed for the following reasons:

- It overlooks the individual learner whom it purports to teach.
- It does not allow for variation among individuals.
- It separates persons from their behavior.
- It ignores the cultural context of learners in its attention to the intellectual context.
- It fails to attend to the whole person.
- It caps the possibilities of learning as though there were clearly definable limits.
- It reduces the possibilities of serendipitous discovery within the classroom.
- It overlooks learning outcomes that cannot be stated in easily measurable terms.
- It is based on a scientific model, not an artistic one.

Among its harshest critics are more experienced teachers. They believe that it confines their knowledge of students and the field and limits their creative designs for class time. When it is used as a rigid model from which teachers cannot deviate, it discourages and punishes teacher creativity and spontaneity, the very hallmarks of teaching that we celebrate. Milner's (1991) research revealed the consequences of its three-year use in the classrooms of one school system: a 50 percent decline in suppositional questions asked by teachers in each year of the study. Particularly in the field of English, which values the subjective and personally felt response, many teachers believe that the model doesn't fit their subject. The objectives that many teachers most value—

appreciation, valuing, discovering, and understanding—are suspect. The whole realm of subjective response to literature resists the narrowing statement of objectives with verbs describing observable actions or products that can be measured: *identify, list, compute, locate, explain,* and *analyze.* Some of those intellectual acts should be part of an English class but not the bulk of the work done there. An objectives-based model reduces what English teachers attempt to teach and restricts their styles of doing so.

Hunter (1989), whose work is closely identified with this narrow rigidity, is clearly answering those critics when she writes her own rebuttal in an article for the *English Journal:* "There is no one best way to learn; it varies with content, situation, and learner" (p. 16). She explains: "teaching is surely an art, but it is based on science, as are all arts. Using that science separates the competent from the incompetent teacher. Translating the science into artistic performance identifies the virtuoso" (p. 17).

Bloom's Taxonomy.   There are other planning schemata that follow an articulated, though more flexible, design. These models revolve around classification schemes that establish teachers' expectations for student learning and their choices of activities and texts for meeting their expectations. In Chapter 13 we discussed the most influential of these schemata—Benjamin Bloom's (1956) taxonomy of educational objectives for the cognitive domain (Figure 13–3). Bloom's taxonomy is a frequent accompaniment to a goals-and-objectives approach to teaching. He offers a guide to a sequential progression of learning from the most basic cognitive level—knowing—to the most challenging—evaluating. With his taxonomy as a planning guide, teachers can identify the cognitive level that they want for their students' work and select appropriate texts and activities that invite that level. His taxonomy is frequently cited as the ultimate heuristic that enables teachers to determine whether they have included a reasonable range of cognitive processes in their plans. The taxonomic divisions provide teachers with a clear question: "Have I included opportunities for a student to progress through all the six levels of the hierarchy: to know, to comprehend, to apply, to analyze, to synthesize, and to evaluate?" If the answer is no, teachers can adjust their plans to ensure that a range of skills and abilities are developed. Bloom's devotees believe that his taxonomy is especially important as a reminder to include higher-order cognition in lessons that can too easily focus on the more basic levels of knowledge and comprehension. It assures that no crucial level will be inadvertently omitted.

Many English educators consider Bloom's taxonomy as inappropriate for the English classroom as Hunter's six-step lesson plan is. The natural progression from one level to another does not match the realities of classroom life. The cognitive levels are mixed as students in a discussion of a short story, say, move back and forth between questions of plot (knowledge) and connections with another story (synthesizing); among interpretation of character (comprehension), a comparison of that character with another fictional character or with an actual friend (synthesis), and a return to plot for clarification. Such an interweaving of levels in a discussion would be defeated by an imposed set of questions moving from low to high. An authentic conversation does not move in such order, and to impose it compromises the conversation's authenticity. These divisions in the teacher's train of thought can divert the spontaneous questions (teacher's and students') that should ideally arise from an animated discussion. A high consciousness of Bloom's taxonomy also can directly or subtly undermine the teacher's attempts to encourage greater student autonomy. It sets up the notion, despite its denial, that some questions are of a higher order and some questions are inferior and that the teacher holds the key to identifying each. Also, despite disclaimers, Bloom's hierarchy can rigidify the work of the class and reduce the flexibility to pursue unforeseen directions suggested by student interest or contributions.

The objectives-based model has as many detractors as defenders; but we present it because, at this date in American education, we think you need to be familiar with it. It may be an ally at first, particularly if it is not applied too rigidly. It will give you a frame of reference for broad planning—What will be the overall outcome of the lessons?—for intermediate planning—What do these students need to learn to achieve them?—and for specific planning—What activities will facilitate students' learning of this knowledge and these skills? It is straightforward and orderly in the midst of the many initial ambiguities and uncertainties of student teaching. Just as a driver's manual provides direction for the beginning driver and a dictionary and grammar handbook are necessary for the learner of a foreign language, so does a six-step lesson plan offer guidance to the beginning teacher. It codifies some classroom strategies that experienced teachers do instinctively. We know teachers who simplify it into a formula: *presentation, practice, production.* It gives the hope that even something as complex as teaching can be mastered and its uncertainties subdued if we approach it as a logical chain of cause and effect.

We present this model, finally, because administrators often use it as their rubric for teacher evaluation. Even the current sample *English Language, Literature, and Composition: Pedagogy* section of the Praxis exam has identifying "an instructional objective" as the first item on each of the six levels of the scoring guide. From the highest (6) to the lowest (1), the scoring rubric also includes whether the examinees wrote a full, thoughtful, and clear explanation of how classroom activities related to the objective.

Content-Based Model

Goodlad (1984) found that in American high schools English and language arts "formed the backbone of the curriculum" and "occupied more . . . teachers at the secondary level (combining both junior and senior high schools) than any other subject" (pp. 204–205). More specifically, "in English, there was still a substantial emphasis on the basics of grammar and composition—punctuation, capitalization, sentence structure, paragraph organization, word analysis, parts of speech. . . . The most commonly offered courses in English at the high school level were those combining mechanics with some literature, courses only in literature, and courses in grammar and composition—in that order. These formed the core of the required English in our high schools. Beyond this core were electives in journalism, speech, and creative writing" (p. 205). Applebee's (1993) study broke down the time allocation to different components of representative public school English classes: literature, 48.3 percent; writing, 26.8 percent; language, 15.4 percent; speech, 6.9 percent; and other, 3.2 percent (p. 35). Because of the interrelated activities in speech, writing, language, and literature, another survey question yielded a higher estimate of literature-related class work—78.3 percent. Commonly, teachers anchor their lesson or unit planning by content and most often that content is literature.

Literature. Whether you will be working with a curriculum in which literature predominates or is integrated with language instruction, literature study often revolves around divisions set by textbooks. Consequently, a look at the literature programs of six major textbooks can ground planning in actual practice. Applebee's (1993) survey found that the most typical course of study is organized around genres in grades 7–10, American literature in grade 11, and British literature in grade 12. World literature is increasingly being offered at either grade 10 or 12. Particularly in poor districts and schools, these textbooks include all the literature that will be taught. Whatever the organizing principle of these books— *genre, theme,* or *chronology* of national literatures— each has advantages and disadvantages.

Genre. Genre study splits the year into units of poetry, drama, fiction (short stories and novels), and occasionally nonfiction, usually biography or essays. Often, within these general categories, stories are arranged by elements of fiction or poetry, such as plot, character, point of view, imagery, or figures of speech. Many states have begun standardized tests of just this literary terminology and so have given a rationale for a genre approach. This organizational arrangement directs attention to form and the more aesthetic dimensions of literature, which is often poor timing in the developmental progress of students. The arrangement by elements also further distances literature as whole works and carries the false implication that particular works have one element primarily or only and that by knowing the element we have read the work. Moffet has a kinder word for this organization. He advises us that if we must teach something in an anthology, we should teach genre. It is the freest of teacher dogma and prejudice. The lesson can't suddenly jump into history or become a thematic ax to grind.

Theme. Thematic organization of the curriculum has had periods of both acceptance and disrepute. Major texts for a time were providing alternative tables of contents so that teachers who wanted to approach the text thematically could have a ready-made guide. Thematic study gains favor with those who want to relate literature to the lives of their students, explore compelling ideas, instill the best ideas in a culture, or use literature as cautionary tales. Thematic study was a stronger phenomenon in the 1960s and 1970s than it was in the 1980s and 1990s. (Perhaps the back-to-basics movement discouraged it.) Fewer textbooks are arranged by thematic content these days. But some signs of regeneration of interest in theme or topic are appearing in the trend toward integration or whole language in the elementary grades. Teachers in American elementary schools who work by topics or themes (an established tradition in British and New Zealand schools) are increasingly enthusiastic, and their students' performance on tests has been as strong or stronger than that of students in traditionally taught classes. One explanation for this achievement may lie in research-based reports that the power of graphic, connective memory (triggered by topic or thematic organization) is far greater than rote memory (O'Keefe & Nadel, 1990).

Chronology. Anthologies used in eleventh and twelfth grades typically focus on national literature, and the units are set up chronologically by periods. These texts generally include a three- or four-page introduction of the literary and cultural history of each period of literary history. The various sections of the chapter present authors of the period, who are usually introduced with some biographical material, a part of which often ties a figure to the intellectual, cultural, or political history of the period. These anthologies (and often parallel reading in novels) determine the sequence and scope of study. The danger of the chronological approach is that the exactitude of dates, titles, and other historical generalizations can become a terrific temptation for teachers and students alike. The course easily begins to emphasize knowledge of the national literature and history. This approach can so concentrate on the literary history that a study of Shakespeare's England, Dickinson's Amherst, or Hughes's Harlem can take the place of a full encounter with the texts.

In the 1960s, Lynch and Evans (1963), two literary scholars, called for teachers to abandon the chronological approach. Applebee (1997) explains that the American literature course entered U.S. high schools after World War I in reaction to the national fervor of the era and the growth of the field of American studies in universities.

As it became institutionalized, it became a "chronological survey of works by major Americans (*not* of major works by Americans, thus adding many relatively minor works to the syllabus)" (p. 27). As the course evolved, it lost the power of patriotism with its legends of national destiny, its "myths of the frontier and the American Spirit," and turned instead toward "the internal character of works" (p. 27). Applebee sums up the results of this "disarray": American Literature courses "spend too much time on works that students don't like and lack a real tradition of conversation into which students can enter" (p. 27).

On the other hand, apologists explain that the chronological approach helps students see connections among texts, authors, and culture. Students can participate in what T. S. Eliot calls *the tradition.* They can make connections themselves between, say, the romances of Nathaniel Hawthorne and Flannery O'Connor rather than have them explained by the teacher. Intertextuality can be a serendipitous affair and create a sense of literature unfolding.

Grammar and Composition. The third most common classroom structure that Goodlad (1984) found in secondary school English classes is organized around units of grammar and composition. Chapters 11 and 12 presented multiple strategies for teaching writing, and many of these strategies could form effective individual units. But there are assumptions about organizing writing instruction that are more basic than questions of strategy. Traditional classrooms presented writing and grammar instruction as they did literature—as a body of knowledge (grammar or rhetorical rules) to be comprehended and mastered. A process/workshop approach is organized out of quite different assumptions and in a far different structure. One of the central structural differences is that whole groups, small collaborative groups, partners, and individual students working at solitary tasks are on center stage, not the teacher.

∽Invitation to Reflection 14–2

1. How were your four years of high school English organized in terms of content?
   grade 9 _____ 1. literature and grammar/composition
   grade 10 _____ 2. literature
   grade 11 _____ 3. grammar/composition
   grade 12 _____ 4. integrated
2. Was your language study essentially grammar, composition, or both?
3. How was literature study organized?
   grade 9 _____ 1. genre
   grade 10 _____ 2. theme
   grade 11 _____ 3. chronology
   grade 12 _____ 4. other
4. Which organizational plan did you find most beneficial?

Creative Planning with the Text. Our text is dedicated to the proposition that what teachers do in classrooms should center on their perceptions of the students before them. Thus, any curriculum begins with an estimate of the students. Characteristically, texts, especially textbooks, provide an organizing structure. Often, schools or school systems have written curriculum guides or tacit curriculum expectations, which accompany textbooks to shape what individual teachers do in the classrooms. But extending instruction beyond what is found in even the most creative texts and most solid teacher handbooks promises richer experiences than simply using the texts alone. We suggest two ways in which you might impose your order (and ardor) on traditional texts. We then summarize other suggestions that are scattered throughout this book.

Turned Tables. Turned tables is a simple way to re-create the text by revising its table of contents or altering its sequence. If the text is arranged chronologically, the simplest revision is to move through it in reverse order. (In Chapter 6, we discussed how starting with a contemporary idiom and era that students know experientially can engage them initially in a more confident approach to poetry.) Chronologically organized texts can be rearranged by genres. Sonnets, for instance, can be extracted from the Renaissance, the Romantic period, and the twentieth century and studied together. Thematic topics can be regrouped historically in units on a history of ideas. A look at the yearning for individual freedom or liberties can be traced chronologically in the American experience through the works of Thomas Jefferson, Sojourner Truth, Kate Chopin, W. E. B. Dubois, Langston Hughes, and the adolescents before you. Your best rearrangements and additions will be based on your perceptions of students' needs and styles and even on your collaboration with them on how they would like to structure the course. In such classes, the text will be uncovered, not merely covered.

Immediate Texts. Immediate texts are those that you can print on the board, project on an overhead projector, or hand out on a sheet of paper to evoke an immediate response. "1(a" by e. e. cummings is just such a poem: It is brief, arresting, and engaging. The short-short story has almost the same effect. It is so brief that it can be read in a few minutes and responded to immediately. One anthologist calls it "sudden fiction," and it does have the effect of startling with its condensed brevity. Beyond their specific virtues, immediate texts gain emotional power from being shared by students in one sitting. Our aim in searching for short, compressed pieces is to engage students and enlarge an idea under discussion (for instance, a philosophical or social question; a matter of form; or a characteristic of an author, period, or literary convention). Often our aim is to enrich, but it should also be to enliven.

Table 14-1 lists other ways in which teachers can enliven district- or state-mandated content while being responsive to the individual learners before them. We gather them from throughout the text.

✎ UNIT PLANNING

Clark and Yinger (1979) report that many teachers identify their most important planning as unit planning.

TABLE 14–1
Extending learning beyond the text

Strategy	Description	Chapter Location
Transformed texts	Take a simple poem or short story and put it into a new dramatic form	4—Oral 6—Poetry
Literary surprises	Read children's literature as oral reading or as accessible works for analysis of theme and form	6—Poetry
Home stories	Invite parents to class to read and explore their favorite writing, poem, story, letter, or editorial, or ask students to read their parents' selections	15—Professional
Feature film	Watch full-length or selected segments of films (adaptations of classic literary works or original films)	4—Oral 10—Media
Literary listening	Listen to recordings of short stories, poems, or selected parts of novels read by the authors or actors	5—Fiction 10—Media
Art watch	Use art or graphics as a prompt for writing; explore its connections to literary texts, authors, and periods	5—Fiction 6—Poetry
Musical methods	Find and listen to music as an extension of ideas, a prompt for writing, an illustration of literary periods, an illumination of literary works, or a connection with students' experiences	5—Fiction 6—Poetry 10—Media
Thinking heads	Periodically work on creative problem solving to isolate and focus upon the process of students' thinking	4—Oral

Teachers commonly define a unit as a series of lessons or experiences related to one central topic. Its length varies, but units are seldom less than two weeks long or more than nine. High school English classes are usually organized around units of literature or language. Some school systems, schools, and teachers even divide the year neatly so that one semester is devoted to literature and the other to language. Very often, writing instruction and literary study are integrated. Literature serves as a prompt for writing; writing serves to teach and evaluate literature.

Focused or Integrated Units

Both literary study and writing instruction lend themselves to one of two kinds of organization: integrated, in which the two mesh and reinforce each other; or focused, in which literature is central for a period and then writing instruction assumes prominence. We have seen and experienced difficulties in the focused approach. Of course, when teaching is text-centered, teachers do have the advantage of moving crisply from one text to another. Units are clearly distinguished from each other. As one subject area is mastered—say, the theme "Human Hopes and Dreams"—the class moves to the next, "Composing the Paragraph." The organization is simplified, and students are focused. Tests and evaluation are concentrated, and the measures of achievement are precise and straightforward. The problem we see in such focus is that each unit suffers from not being approached by the full power of all four language arts.

This book has offered specific strategies and general approaches to teaching English that move back and forth among the four traditional language arts: reading, writing, talking, and listening. Gere, Fairbanks, Howes, Roop, and Schaafsma (1992) have described four integrative approaches to teaching language arts based on four quite different assumptions about language (Appendix J). Integration, being key to our instructional strategies, is basic to our organizational strategies as well. We have continually suggested the advantage of a variety and diversity of strategies and approaches, and the integrated approach provides just that. We have repeatedly proposed that instruction address the multiple intelligences and learning styles of students, and an integrated approach has a chance of meeting those student differences. We also have placed the student at the center of our planning—not the text, the curriculum guideline, or even the teacher. The integrated approach offers more possibilities to focus on students and to plan the curriculum around them. Even if book and material shortages circumscribe planning and dictate a focus on literature or language in turn, teachers can integrate instruction in each day's learning.

Many prospective teachers feel more comfortable with planning an individual lesson than with shaping lessons into whole units. Research shows that what separates able teachers from excellent teachers is the latter's ability to develop long-range plans. Teachers who design their work for a semester or a year usually build with unit plans. Lessons do not stand alone. They work in consort with other lessons on a shared topic.

As we have just discussed, traditionally the organizing principle for upper-level high school English classes has been literature by genre or chronology. (Some English teachers become history teachers in practice because they fall into the habit of teaching lists of works and dates, focusing on literary periods and emphasizing the context of literature rather than the literature itself. Genre study likewise can end up as a study of the formal elements of literature at the expense of responding to the ideas and feelings found in texts.) Elementary and middle school teachers have long recognized the power of another planning principle; they organize their units of study around a theme. Many high school teachers are turning to themes because they draw students into more engaged and authentic participation in study. A growing number of teachers and some school districts are turning to thematic units because they also encourage an integrated curriculum. We suggest a few guidelines to help you produce strong and effective thematic units.

Topic Selection and Quality Control

Topic selection controls all that you plan, just as a thesis sentence controls a well-composed essay. A strong unifying idea is essential. We favor topics that raise broad questions, that matter to your particular students, and that are versatile and open a rich store of literature and language arts on which to draw. Once a topic is selected, it will serve as a lens by which to focus and control all of the activities selected for the unit. Selecting those activities is a second important dimension of planning. To make sure that instruction is excellent, we suggest four standards that should govern topic selection and activities development.

Significance and Pertinence. The first and most important standard is selecting a topic that has both pertinence and significance. We distinguish pertinence from relevance. *Relevance* generally means that adolescents are naturally attracted to the idea. *Pertinence* means that the topic is connected to the students' interests, although that connection may not be immediately obvious. *Significance* tugs us in the other direction; it requires that a topic be not only personally attractive but also in some sense important. This is a tough standard, but it will help you avoid the opposing pitfalls of banal fluff and academic disconnection.

Diversity. The second standard, diversity, reminds the planner to shape the activities selected so that multiple intelligences and multiple learning styles are engaged. In addition, the four language modes—talking, listening, writing, and reading—should all be used. It also naturally asks us to develop a wide range of materials that draw upon the riches of different cultures and social perspectives.

∞ Invitation to Reflection 14–3

Cooke (1989) has suggested a thematic unit for high school seniors that moves students from the known to the barely grasped with a rich variety of texts. Figure 14–4 contains his unit "The Stranger." In addition to Cooke's texts, we suggest the following texts: the short film *Neighbors*, Spike Lee's film *Do the Right Thing*, Frost's poem "Mending Wall," Hinton's novel *The Outsiders,* and Seidman's *Lifeline* interview. List other texts on this theme that would meet standards of significance, pertinence, and diversity on the theme of "The Stranger". If you wish, select another theme and list texts for diverse students.

Balance and Challenge.

The third standard, balance and challenge, depends on the teacher's view of learning. When teachers work to establish a balanced and accepting approach to the topic, students feel free to explore. Challenge is essential as a way of inviting students to examine their assumptions and open their minds to new possibilities. But teachers must walk a narrow line between questioning student assumptions and implying teacher opinion. Teachers who take strong positions, particularly about current issues, can silence students and leave them in entrenched positions. Teachers are then not teaching but preaching. Author bell hooks (1998), who does not shy away from tough issues, says that teaching must involve a "radical openness" that balances, for example, a classic novel with a work by Toni Morrison. We are all biased and can never achieve a fully neutral classroom, but we need to consider how openly we approach each topic that we encounter.

Patricia Grace's story "Butterflies" illustrates this point briefly and beautifully. In it a young farm girl in New Zealand is sent off to school by her adoring grandparents, who stay home to tend their fields of cabbages. When she leaves for school, her grandfather reminds her to "Listen to your teacher, do what she say." When the young girl returns home that afternoon, her grandfather asks her about her day. She softly replies that she wrote a story in her book and sadly reports that when her teacher saw that she had written "I killed all of the butterflies," the teacher told her, "Butterflies are beautiful creatures. . . .

The butterflies visit all the pretty flowers. . . . You don't kill butterflies." Her grandfather listens to her report and after a pause says, "Because you see . . . your teacher buys her cabbages at the supermarket, and that's why." The teacher has a narrow view of life that sees butterflies only as beautiful creatures. She cannot imagine that any of her students might see them as life-threatening pests. Similarly, we teachers cannot be aware of all of our misconceptions or narrow ways of understanding, but we can try hard to make room for all reasonable and civil perspectives in our classrooms.

Depth and Discovery.

The fourth standard, depth and discovery, makes sure that a unit increases depth and a sense of discovery. Students need to move from a naïve, unexamined, and simplistic sense of a topic to one that grows more complicated and multilayered. It must start with their own personal experiences and ideas but should move them far beyond those by consistently challenging them to rethink old assumptions and explore new possibilities.

Steps of Unit Development

A third dimension of unit building involves the process of generating the basic ideas and activities that will, when finally assembled, create a sound unit that will engage students and help them to grow. The three steps in this process are similar to writing a paper: one starts with a barrage of ideas that loosely gather around a central proposition and ends up with a well-organized and tightly sequenced set of activities that constitute two to three weeks of instruction. It also resembles the creative-process design that we recommended for daily lesson planning.

Brainstorm.

The first step is to brainstorm as many ideas as you can come up with in a brief period of time. Scribble these hastily on a piece of paper or on the board if a number of teachers are working together. Self-adhesive notes are helpful in group planning because they allow everyone to work individually but to post their ideas for group use. Group and self-criticism are important; but if they come too early, they can stymie the production of strong ideas. Piggybacking on your initial wild ideas or those of

FIGURE 14–4
Unit for upper-level high school students

Billy Joel	"The Stranger"	popular song
Robert Heinlein	*Stranger in a Strange Land*	science fiction
Albert Camus	*The Stranger*	existentialist novel
Joseph Conrad	"Amy Foster" or *Lord Jim*	modern fiction
New Testament	Parable of the Good Samaritan	parable
Old Testament	Psalm 146	psalm poetry
Mary Shelley	*Frankenstein*	quasi-science fiction

Selection(s) from the work of anthropologist Mary Douglas or historian of religion Mircea Eliade others is what is important here, not subjecting them to premature scrutiny.

Cull and Expand.

The second step is two directional. Good ideas need to be expanded; unproductive ones must be culled. In this step, you might circle all of the activities that seem truly promising and consider ways in which they can be expanded. Elaboration and intricacy of structure almost always enrich learning. Rearranging our mindsets helps us open up so many new ideas that it needs to be mentioned as an isolated move in this second step. Here we think of ways to explore a unit topic, such as happiness, by opening up the concept in three specific ways.

The first of these is to consider synonymous concepts that broaden and deepen the original topic. For instance, happiness might be reframed as joy, peace, contentment, or bliss. Working with contentment rather than happiness may automatically deepen the exploration. Second, an inversion of the concept may widen and deepen students' understanding of the general concept of happiness. Dickinson's "Success is counted sweetest by those who ne'er succeed" is a poignant reminder of how the inversion of the concept can make a unit's activities stronger and more challenging. A third way to deepen the topic is to make sure that the egocentric circle is broken so as to take in ever-wider perspectives. Looking at the views of people well beyond the age of students, asking the opinions of citizens of different socioeconomic status, and considering the role of other ethnic groups can also add greater depth and challenge to the unit.

Arrange.

Once the many different kinds of activities have been developed, the third step in planning involves arranging them so that those that are most obvious and natural are used first and those that are culminating and call for reflection occur at the end of the unit. In the middle, you will need strong activities that look toward the deeper ones at the end and create a smooth and solid transition from the beginning steps.

Using this sequence, our education students developed the unit on happiness in Teaching Activity 14–2, pp. 413–414. It is skeletal and unpolished, but it has some excellent ideas. Invitation to Reflection 14–4 invites you to amend or extend these ideas with your knowledge and then shape them into a unit using a single model or a combination of the four planning models discussed earlier.

Invitation to Reflection 14–4

1. Read the following first sketch of a short ten-day unit on happiness. (In practice, each day's lesson would be more fully designed and articulated based on the students' daily and cumulative responses to the unit.)

2. Using the *creative-process* planning model, brainstorm about these ideas. Delete unpromising suggestions. Add others. Alter some. Sequence your lessons into a unit of instruction.

3. Now reorient your plans using a *conversation-based* planning model. Name some of the central topics around which you might organize conversations that would engage students and turn something that seems simple into something they might discover to be complicated after all. Can you identify topics that would allow you to uncover less obvious angles on and implications about happiness?

4. Try framing the unit with an *objectives-based* planning model. Think of yourself as teaching ninth-grade students with diverse abilities and backgrounds. They have just entered high school, and the happiness unit begins their study of English literature and language. What might be some of your learning goals for them?

5. Which of these models leads you to the most satisfying planning? Which helped you plan the most engaging unit?

6. This proposal does not have an evaluation component. How would you evaluate student work on your unit? Would your evaluation plan differ according to your planning model?

Appendix J contains ideas about teaching Shakespeare— a subject that practically every English teacher will one day teach. We invite you to read these teacher-generated ideas and shape them into a coherent unit, just as you have done for the thematic unit on happiness.

Planning as a Recursive Process

We want to suggest other means of grounding your planning in student interests and abilities. As Cain's (1989, p. 5) research demonstrates, if we are concerned about "designing new versions of classroom life" and with the individual's making meaningful sense of our classes, we get a head start if we plan with them in mind: their styles, their interests, and our perception of their academic and social needs. We can even engage them directly in the process, surveying their ideas, responding to their suggestions, and conferring with them about the next step. Taking students into active, rather than indirect, decision making is most effective when the students are older and have confidence in the group process. Above all, we can pay attention and listen to students.

Furthermore, we can plan for students by leaving the unit fluid, with enough flexibility to accommodate the unexpected. Cox (1991) explains how that flexibility works on a daily, quarterly, and yearly basis: "I cannot plan my daily lessons too far in advance. My quarterly and yearly plans give me general ideas for weeks; I set aside tentative dates for projects and assignments, but in doing so, I always make myself aware of the need for fluidity, informing my students from the beginning of the quarter that those dates may change" (p. 35). This flexible openness, while rewarding, has its price. Coon (1991) summarizes the dilemma exactly:

> I struggle constantly to strike a balance between planning carefully structured assignments and allowing room for my students—and me—to follow a promising idea wherever it leads us. Both sides of this balance contain pitfalls. With too rigid a structure, I find that students only go through the motions, giving superficial responses and not involving themselves in their work. With too much latitude, some will respond with excellent work while others wander off course in directions that aren't as productive as I would like. (p. 28)

Owen (1991) reports on a ninth-grade teacher for whom "teaching is like writing, a constant pull between freedom and structure" (p. 57). Despite the struggles of this tension, keeping the focus on students makes the tension necessary and worthwhile.

Your deliberate and intentional planning, no matter how carefully weighed and implemented, can still produce a unit that has flaws. Your planning and execution of a unit should always allow for evaluation of that unit. If you are observant and critical, you will discover ways to restructure your lessons as you go along. But at its conclusion, you can reflect with the greater insight that a completed event discloses. Again, the analogy

14–2   TEACHING ACTIVITY

A Unit on Happiness

Day 1: Introduction

1. *General expectations.*   Brainstorm with students about what they think happiness is (using connective words, word etymologies, and so on).

2. *Introduce the topic.*   Explain what the focus of the unit is; give some specific details and pique their interest.

3. *American dream.*   What does society say happiness is? Break up into small groups. How does Hollywood paint happiness? Name one television show or one movie as an example of your view. What words from our brainstorming exercise does Hollywood's picture include? What is the American dream? Is it equally accessible to everyone? What groups have had trouble obtaining it? Why?

4. *Journal assignment.*   What does happiness mean to you?

5. *Long-term assignment.*   Interview someone who is fifty years old or older and have the person describe the experience that gave him or her the most happiness. The assignment is due on the ninth day of the unit.

Day 2: Paintings
Look at reproductions of the paintings *Ecstasy* by Maxfield Parrish, *The Kiss* by Gustav Klimt, *Water Lilies* by Monet, and assorted paintings by Matisse. Draw or color a representation of where you find happiness or describe the happiness in one of the paintings.

Day 3: Media

1. Watch a comedy routine by a comic such as Robin Williams or Steven Wright.

2. Break into small groups. Write a short stand-up routine about happiness or how comedy affects parts of life. Volunteers perform stand-up routines.

3. Watch a clip from a television show such as *Good Times.* Discuss the show's implied view of happiness. For instance, in the case of *Good Times,* consider the irony in the title of the show. Does an accumulation of wealth make one happy? Can happiness occur without reference to wealth?

4. Watch the final wedding scene and a bantering scene between Beatrice and Benedict from *Much Ado About Nothing.* Discuss what seems to be Shakespeare's idea of happiness throughout the play.

Day 4: Blues Music

1. Have blues music playing as students enter the classroom. Write down three feelings evoked by the blues. Hand out lyrics to two songs. Play the songs, read the lyrics, and discuss them.

2. *Assignment.*   Bring in written lyrics and a cassette or CD of a love song for the next day.

Day 5: Song Lyrics

Look at the written lyrics of several of the students' love songs. Discuss the relationship between the song lyricist and a poet. How does the lyricist use rhythm, words, and sounds (like a poet) to convey a message? Why does music evoke such strong feelings and memories?

Day 6: Poetry

1. Compare and contrast Wordsworth's "Surprised by Joy" and Keats's "Ode to Melancholy." Are both happiness and melancholy worthy of being poeticized? How is sadness a part of happiness and vice versa?

2. Read "We Wear the Mask" by Paul Laurence Dunbar. What emotions do we try to hide in order to put up a facade to the outside world? How and why do we hide these emotions?

3. Draw a mask expressing an emotion you would like to show to the outside world. On the back of this mask write the emotion you are attempting to hide and why and under what conditions you would hide this emotion.

Day 7: Stories

1. Read a children's book—such as one of Maira Kalman's "Max the Dread Dog" stories—aloud to the class. In this example, talk about dreams and how dreams relate to happiness. Was Max's happiness fixed to his dream? Were the Stravinskys happy? How about Max's best friend?

2. Talk about how children's stories and fairy tales often seem to end with "And they lived happily ever after." Is that realistic? Why or why not? Are the endings of most stories happy?

3. Read Aesop's fable about the man, his son, and the donkey. Discuss how we go out of our way to make other people happy. How do we sometimes forsake our own happiness to ensure others' happiness?

4. Read aloud Chaucer's "Wife of Bath's Tale" from *The Canterbury Tales*. What would make the Wife of Bath happy? Would finding the perfect mate make her happy? What characteristics would the perfect mate for you have? If you found this person, would he or she make you happy? Can you be happy without this person?

5. Talk about how sometimes the thing we think would make us the happiest is unattainable. Write in your journal about what would make you happiest. Would you still strive for it if others said it was unattainable?

Day 8: Festivals and Holidays

1. Decorate the room in the style of holidays and festivals from different cultures (Easter, Christmas, Hanukkah, Kwanzaa, and so on).

2. Read Rosetti's "The Birthday." Examine Marc Chagall's painting *The Birthday* (1915). Discuss, in pairs, students' most memorable birthday (good or bad). Ask for volunteers to discuss their birthday memories.

3. Look at clips of a production of *A Midsummer Night's Dream* and May Day celebrations. Discuss holidays that allow for activities and behaviors not ordinarily allowed.

Day 9: Interviews

1. Conduct interviews in pairs or small groups about a happy occasion. Write a snippet (1–3 sentences) expressing the interviewee's feelings and perceptions during this happy event.

2. Perform this snippet in character. The teacher is the audience. This dramatic presentation may even be videotaped and viewed later by students to critique their performances.

3. *Reminder.*   Complete journal entries and interviews.

Day 10: Conclusion

1. Reread your journal entry on happiness from the first day of the unit. Write a response to that entry about how your perception of happiness has changed. What part of this happiness unit altered your perceptions about happiness the most? What was the most meaningful activity?

2. Devise a list of fifty things that make you happy.

between planning and writing can be helpful. Cox (1991) finds that if

> teaching resembles writing [then] planning is the prewriting stage where attention must be given to the connections among the teacher/writer, students/audience, and the needs and goals of the two. It is also recursive, involving revision not only after an initial delivery of a lesson but also during the act of teaching itself. In fact, planning for the present always requires looking back to the previous year and being ready to adjust ideas to past experience (p. 33).

We suggest that you begin with fresh plans for any new group of students in order to be true to their unique abilities and interests. But you can profit from your past units if you use them retrospectively as field tests.

WEEKLY PLANNING

Weekly planning is not as strategic to your instructional decisions as unit and lesson plans are, but it is not without its importance. In fact, although a week is an arbitrary though clearly marked block of instructional time, in many schools administrators require teachers to submit weekly lesson plans each Friday afternoon. Students often mark their school time by weeks. In many schools, specific days of the week are designated for different subject tests (for instance, all math tests are on Tuesday, science on Wednesday, and English on Thursday). Assemblies, pep rallies, and altered class schedules are often predictably scheduled by days of the week. Many teach-

ers anticipate student affect and behavior around weekly rhythms, beginning with dazed Mondays and ending with distracted Fridays. Thus, calibrating your instruction around a weekly calendar has some merit.

You may choose to use a weekly calendar to chart the nature and variety of your instruction. Figure 14-5 displays graphically the kind of blueprint that can help ensure variety in your classroom. Plan and monitor each day's lesson by checking which of the four language arts or Gardner's multiple intelligences will be engaged by your work. Other variables can be substituted or added, such as the four teaching approaches introduced in Chapter 2.

CURRICULUM PLANNING

Many teachers are called upon to help formulate broad curriculum goals and objectives for their schools, districts, or even states. Although these advisory and collaborative assignments seldom go to new teachers, they, too, are affected by this planning. They absorb the implicit assumptions of curriculum planners and teach within the structure set by their decisions. And they may one day be asked to think about the broader context in which they teach. For that reason, we mention a few issues to alert the novice teacher.

As a beginning teacher, you will be amazed by and preoccupied with learning about the protocols of your school—attendance forms, hall passes, and copying schedules—but you will soon adjust to the daily routines

Days of the Week	Four Language Arts				Gardner's Multiple Intelligences					
	Reading	Writing	Listening	Talking	Logical/Mathematical	Musical	Spatial	Kinesthetic	Interpersonal	Intrapersonal
Monday										
Tuesday										
Wednesday										
Thursday										
Friday										

NOTE: Talking is both a language art and part of Gardner's schema (linguistic) and is thus placed under both headings.

FIGURE 14–5 Weekly planning guide

of school. You will probably simultaneously crave specific ideas and suggestions to keep your head above water in your classroom. The shock of the sudden immersion in daily, weekly, unit, and yearly planning will claim your attention and energies. When some of the urgency of the newness begins to settle, you will be ready to look around and take stock. You can become more aware of the contexts in which you teach, both the explicit expectations of the educational establishment and what has been called the hidden curriculum: beliefs, mores, norms, and values that, although not articulated directly, communicate themselves to students through both course content and the social arrangements of school and classroom. Then you can begin to observe the wider context of the student and community culture. Curriculum planning becomes unrealistic if it is not anchored in such a framework; it seems random if it is not seen in a context.

As you become aware of your individual classroom as part of a wider educational and cultural world, you want to remain open to thinking creatively about your classroom possibilities. Curriculum planning is more than a problem-solving process. It calls for a critical reexamination or reevaluation of what you consider to be worth teaching. Doing it with others is creative. If teachers share their individual hopes, aims, and struggles rather than compare pros and cons of educational objectives and grind out solutions, the result is likely to be wiser, richer with diverse meanings, and more commensurate with the complexity of human lives. What is required, then, is openness, imagination, inquiry, intellectual rigor, aesthetic sensitivity, and creative free thinking. The paradigm that often exists for curriculum planning is mechanistic and controlling—What are our objectives? How will we implement them? How will we measure their achievement?—and rooted in a cluster of assumptions that are hard to understand and recognize. Purpel (1989) encourages us to "squeeze as much humanity and sanity as can be found in existing arrangements" and then to think creatively of alternatives (p. 140).

∞ VARIABLES IN ANY PLANNING

You are at the point that critical theorists call *praxis*, where ideas and action must necessarily intersect. We would like to review some of the variables that we think you would do well to consider as you enter that intersection. We begin with what we consider to be the most important variable in your planning, without which other variables become mechanical tools rather than inspiriting ideas; that is, we turn first to students.

Students

Haberman (1995), in his book on teachers of the urban poor, identifies the crucial characteristic of star teachers

as their strong personal relationships with students. When we asked Becky Brown, a teacher whom we greatly admire, what would be her advice to young teachers about planning, she said without hesitation, "Listen carefully to students. Pay attention." She says that she really learned to teach during her most difficult teaching assignment—an eight-year tenure at our city's toughest high school—because there she had to begin listening to the students. No amount of energetic teaching of texts or skills that she had successfully taught before worked with these disaffected students. Only by being in touch with their lives, concerns, pursuits, and abilities could she construct lessons that would matter to them.

If we intend to factor students into our planning, we need more than profiles of adolescent characteristics or lists of personality syndromes or learning disabilities. We must talk to the adolescents before us openly and continually; we must read and respond to what they write. Becky Brown tells a story of trying to find some hook that would cause disinterested seniors to take writing seriously as something that mattered in their lives. She asked them to bring in any ideas about writing projects that would demonstrate their writing skills. One student brought her his only writing of the term—a perfectly written business letter to a mail order catalog to order a fake I.D.

Individualization, Interaction, and Integration

Lois Weiner (1997), in distilling what she learned about planning in more than twenty years in high school English classrooms, names two formulas for developing effective lesson plans. Both originate in the work of two experienced and creative educators, James Moffett and Betty Jane Wagner (1992), and are basic to what we do in English classrooms. In the first chapter we discussed Moffett and Wagner's three *I*'s: individualization, interaction, and integration. These educators believe that all three must be present in order for students to "master the full power and range of language." Although the three *I*s no longer represent completely novel ideas, Weiner believes that the formula helps prospective teachers recall that "*all* are essential" (p. 78).

Individualization calls for students to construct their own individual meaning from the activities in which we engage them. This *I* reminds us to plan lessons that "deepen the individual's desire and ability to communicate" (p. 79). Remembering the *I* of interaction "reminds us to consciously apply our understanding of students so that instruction exploits the desire to communicate, rather than attempting to suppress it." She notes what anyone who has stood for an instant before an adolescent audience knows feelingly—that "students usually have a great deal to say to one another, but frequently the conversation doesn't focus on the teacher's instructional goals." Integration requires planning lessons that tap "the entire range of skills and forms in communicating and receiving messages" (p. 78). For integration to occur, any lesson must meet these two requirements:

1. At some point students should be listening, speaking, reading, and writing.
2. The product or process should involve authentic communication that taps life outside the classroom. (p. 78)

Weiner's student teachers critique their lesson plans for the presence of these three *I*s and, with this formula, can spot and correct problems. For instance, one student, frustrated with the response to her carefully designed poetry unit, applied the formula and realized that all three *I*'s were absent. "That night she generated an entirely different approach: students would bring in poems of their choosing and read them to the class. On copies of the poems, students marked literary terms they had studied with color-coding schemes. The poems were then put on the bulletin board for classmates to read and inspect for accuracy of coding" (p. 79).

Four Modes of Classroom Organization

In his *Interaction* series (1973, now out of print), Moffett divided activities into roughly the same organizational possibilities that we do in Chapter 2: whole group, small group, pairs, and solo. Weiner (1997) articulates for her students the circumstances that favor the use of each (p. 79):

Whole group: when the same information must be communicated to every member of the class—for example, "instructions for projects" or "discussions of classroom rules"

Small groups: "when students need the maximum interaction they can get, to exchange ideas and clarify their thinking"

Pairs: when "practice and drill" profits from a partner and when students share something that is "too personal" to communicate to more than one other person

Solo: when students are involved in tasks of assessment or individual writing or reading for which solitude is preferable (writing and reading could, of course, be done in one of the other three arrangements)

Weiner's recapitulation of the four basic modes of instruction also reminds her prospective teachers of the possibility of instructional variety and cautions them against relying too heavily on one mode in their teaching.

Sequence, Variety, and Flexibility

You should gauge your sequencing of activities by your students' interests, abilities, and learning styles. Some stu-dents thrive on varied activities and pace within a class period; others are jangled by such animation. When students are willing, resist the predictable patterns. Most students profit by the surprise and energy created by variety. We estimate and note the probable duration of each activity in a given lesson. That timing provides a realistic gauge and a temporal structure, but we remain open to the serendipitous possibilities that may arise. We try to tailor our plans to the particular students in a particular class and to the given class size and allow that class of students to determine our progress. When planning time is limited and three classes are studying the same subject, we are drawn to the economy of sharing one preparation among them. But we try to resist squeezing all students into the same mold. We want *what* we bring to class to match *who* we find there. We don't want to force the closure of a lesson for one group because another worked at a different rate. Because all of these differences confound and complicate planning, we note what each class has accomplished while the memory is fresh. Given the urgencies of your time constraints, however, when preparation time is terribly squeezed and keeping classes together becomes necessary, we believe that it is better to omit activities to synchronize classes than to herd students mechanically through lessons.

During her first year of teaching, Stella Beale addressed this need for flexibility (personal communication, 1997): "I frequently have to remind myself not to be so rigid. Once I have a plan in mind and on paper, I often find myself unable to relinquish control in the classroom. I find myself unwilling to risk going in a new direction. Plans should not be written in stone. Planning is important, but once inside the classroom, the students, not the plans should be central. I struggle to allow myself to follow the students' lead, to perceive and seize the teachable moments, to referee instead of control discussion, and to let discussions have their own evolution."

John Dixon (1967) believes that a unitary rather than a fragmented approach to English "permits the flow from a prepared activity to one relatively unforeseen" (p. 33). He does not reject careful preplanning but cautions against the kind of abstract planning of curriculum guides and textbooks that organize class activities around different foci—moving, for instance, from a lesson about talk to another about drama to others about writing, each completed in turn. Dixon envisions a variety of activities in English classrooms unified by a focus on some "theme or aspect of human experience" around which all work centers (p. 33). Other learning, while important, is secondary to "effecting insight into experience" (p. 33). His example of planning with this focus in mind illustrates how issues of sequence, variety, and flexibility intersect.

A teacher who is planning flexibly needs to consider beforehand *many* possible avenues that his pupils may discover in the course of a lesson, so that whichever catches their enthusiasm he is aware of its possibilities. The more active the part pupils are given, the more difficult to predict all that they will find and uncover: thus the need for a flexible teaching strategy rather than rigid lesson plans, and for teachers confidently able to move with a class for instance from reading *My Childhood* to discussing old people they know or to acting encounters of youth and age. (p. 33)

A Common Danger

Britzman (1991), in a book about learning to teach called *Practice Makes Practice,* discusses a common fear of new teachers: that they do not know enough about literature, methodology, and theory. He believes that this fear arises from a cultural myth about the teacher as expert and from a conception of the knowledge taught as "a set of discrete and isolated units to be acquired" (p. 228). A planning error of young teachers grows from this very fear. In preparing to teach literature, they rely too much on their research into the literary interpretation of the texts. They expect to teach in the same way many of their college professors taught them: through whole-class lecture or discussion that formally analyzes literature. They have not experienced a reader-response approach to literature themselves, so they rely on finding the "correct" interpretation from the critical books and articles of academics and scholars. Finally, they assume that everything they studied in their preparation needs to be somehow passed on to their students.

Every chapter of this text has prepared you to resist this error. You can also avoid some of these difficulties if you concentrate on the question that Cain (1989) discusses: How can I create a learning community in which my students and I learn together? Or you can remember Applebee's model: Which texts are most likely to stimulate a real conversation with students about issues that matter? Then turn to frame the kinds of questions you would genuinely like to explore with your students.

Writing Out the Lesson

When you have solidified your ideas for the daily lesson plan, we suggest that you write down your outline for the day. Such an outline is far more than numbers of textbook pages or titles of selections to be covered. It is detailed with classroom organization and the actual questions that you will use in whole-class or small-group discussions—at least the initial question, what Kozol (2002) calls the "combustible question" which will start a chain reaction, or Christenbury and Kelly's (1983) dense question—or the precise tasks that you will ask small groups to complete. You do not have to worry about form or neatness. What you are preparing is a personal script for the day. You will depart from it, of course. Teaching is improvisational. But you will depart more confidently if you have a framework from which to work.

One of our repeated surprises is the impact of written instructions that we distribute to students for any task that requires independent or small-group work, particularly work that is nuanced or multilayered. With rare exceptions, our students like to hold directions or assignments in their hands, to mull over them, to question them, and to write on them. A printed assignment seems to possess an imprimatur that dignifies the task and intensifies students' work in tackling it. We are not recommending that all assignments be distributed in writing. We use paper sparingly and strategically, recycle always, and cut assignment sheets into halves or fourths to preserve paper. Many schools do not have funding for such handouts. But when they do and when we judge the moment to be opportune, we carefully prepare sheets in the confidence that they will appreciably increase the effectiveness of the assignment and student work. (Overhead projectors and black boards are good backups if paper is unavailable.)

We suggest that you put your lesson plans on paper that can be filed in a binder or placed in folders, perhaps by units. Add any pertinent handouts, texts, or evaluation instruments. We advise also that you evaluate the lesson and that you write on the lesson plan directly to make it immediately revisable for future use.

Planning with Discipline and Inspiration

After more than three decades of teaching, we still cannot sleep without a written plan for the morning's classes. We do not find teaching a profession that we can wing. It requires the same sort of deliberate planning for public performance that might characterize a lawyer's brief before a judge, a senator's questions at a hearing, or a minister's sermon to a congregation. We agree with Leila Christenbury (1994) that "part of your job as a professional is to come to class prepared; relying on inspiration is a sloppy way to run your teaching life" (p. 42).

Still, we are also open to inspiration. Usually, our best lesson plans do not arise as the logical conclusion of a deliberate thought process but from reflection about a student, a text, or an idea that has struck home in a class. Sometimes a flash of insight arrives unexpectedly to throw a new light on what we had planned, to clarify a strategy, or to remind us of a related text; suddenly, in the morning shower or on the drive to school, we see the lesson more richly or clearly. Without the careful groundwork of lessons planned, though, that inspiration cannot find sure footing and can scatter our plans and our lessons beyond rescue. Inspiration resembles the desperate more than the divine. Thus, our advice to our students is to pay attention to inspiration but don't fail to plan.

∽ CONSTANT CLASSROOM STRUCTURES AND CONCERNS

In addition to your planning lessons with these critical variables in mind, you will be considering other influential structures and concerns. We mention a few that you may have studied in general methods courses but that are crucial and deserve reiteration.

Routines and Emergencies

Daily planning must accommodate and fit within an established context that partly reflects your idiosyncratic habits, partly your school's, and partly your students'. Teachers rely on these established routines for instruction and management. The word *routine* has negative connotations, but actual routines can free our minds to think about other things. They also make the classroom predictable for students. If the roll must be completed and absentees' notes must be checked always at the beginning of class, the wise teacher schedules the first five minutes of each day for free writing. If assignments always appear in the same corner of the board, students get used to checking there.

You can establish predictable resources for yourself as well. As we have mentioned previously, we have discovered that some of our students photocopy and laminate pages from this text and tape them to their podiums, grade books, or textbooks so that they always have ideas or questions available to draw on. We also suggest that you have a repertoire of alternative routines or procedures to consult. Many teachers keep games, short projects, discussion topics, and writing prompts in their files to pull out when they discover that their planning has left them with a space of time or when they suddenly lose their voices or the sixth period overwhelms their spirits. Chaotic days will occur when half of a class is on a field trip or thirty minutes are taken up by a fire drill or only half of the classes meet because of an early-dismissal schedule. We have found the following books' suggestions for self-contained and impromptu plans to be helpful.

Brandvik, M. L. (1990). *Writing process activities kit: 75 ready-to-use lessons and worksheets for grades 7–12.* Upper Saddle River, NJ: Prentice-Hall.

Brandvik, M. L. (1994). *English teacher's survival guide: Ready-to-use techniques and materials for grades 7–12.* West Nyack, NY: Center for Applied Research in Education.

Powell, D. (1981). *What can I write about? 7000 topics for high school students.* Urbana, IL: NCTE.

Motivation

Too often, education relies on motivation that is extrinsic to study: rewards, emphasis on the pragmatic value of learning tasks, and competition. When lessons are calculated to address the range of students before you and when variety and dynamic movement are present, then the motivation becomes intrinsic: It originates from within the learning environment. Teachers who establish a classroom of energized, engaged students are sometimes suspected of not being serious about their teaching. We find that those classes are usually taught by the teachers with the highest expectations for themselves and their students. They are realistic, but they challenge students to reach just beyond their given grasp. Students have greater confidence in what they are learning because they feel tangible growth. When teachers identify themselves as partners in learning, students have role models for learning. Such a classroom of learners provides greater opportunity for genuine communication and conversation that engages students. Enthusiasm and energy attract students and secure their commitment. A sense of humor also spices any environment. We have found that wit often graces those who love language and literature, as both arise from a need to lighten the human spirit. Thus, if you are responsive to wit, you will find it in your subject matter.

Finally, we return to Goodlad (1984) for a necessary quality within the classroom if students are going to find a motive there for their allegiance and hard work. We have mentioned that he and his associates found in the classrooms that they visited an "emotional tone . . . neither harsh and punitive nor warm and joyful; it might be described most accurately as flat" (p. 108). He describes such classrooms as having a "constrained and constraining environment" (p. 109). That flatness needs to be contoured by a positive and encouraging spirit. That spirit will usually originate with the teacher. Then if structures encourage it and students respond to it, this spirit can spread.

Classroom Management

Amid all of their uncertainties, our prospective teachers worry most about control of the classroom. Experienced teachers offer much sympathetic advice: "Make a clear list of classroom rules. Post it. Enforce it." "Don't let them ever see you addled." "Rule with an iron fist." "If you give an inch, they'll take a mile." "Don't even smile until Thanksgiving." Many colleges and universities, anticipating the challenges of high school classrooms, make courses in classroom management imperative for education students. We believe that you should enter a classroom with a plan for meeting its many challenges to purposeful order and meaningful activity, but we do not have space to address the issues with any depth in this text. In lieu of an exploration of alternatives, we mention a viewpoint that dissents from the advice to be hardnosed first and foremost, a viewpoint that our students have found compelling and that falls within our bias toward active, student-centered learning.

Martin Haberman (1995) has worked tirelessly in urban schools populated by "children and youth consumed by the tension that comes (and never fully abates) from having unmet basic human needs for physical safety, adequate nutrition, decent health care, freedom from pain, and the nurturance of secure adults who provide care and love" (p. 2). He has observed teachers in those schools and noted especially those whom he calls "star teachers"—those who function confidently, productively, and positively with students. He explains that these teachers place little emphasis on discipline. They spend most of their time trying to understand the difficulties of their urban students and to find ways to connect with their students' daily lives. Haberman calls into question the habits of traditional teachers: lectures, worksheets, unrevised lesson plans, an emphasis on running a tight ship, and a readiness to quell unruly behavior. Star teachers "expect problems as part of their normal workload." They never make the assumption that if only this student or that were removed, the classroom could function as they want it to. They don't see discipline as "a set of procedures that must be put in place before learning can occur, and believe that few of their problems with discipline emanate from the way they teach" (p. 3). Their normal teaching involves them in a great deal of personal interaction with students that revolves around learning tasks, and these natural relationships allow these teachers to "anticipate, prevent, or ward off many emergencies." Their strong personal connections don't form around serious problems; they don't wait for trouble to arise. When it does occur, star teachers "assume problems are the reason for needing skilled practitioners" (p. 2).

Donald Graves's (1986) practice is in agreement with Haberman's. Graves believes that the ties to our students' lives are the essential hope for effective teaching. More specifically, he shows how teachers should consciously work to know their students, find out what their interests are, and relate to them in some significant way outside of class. Rob Slater, an experienced teacher, asks our student teachers to spend their first three days at school, not watching him teach but interviewing each of his students. This takes time, but it pays rich dividends when our prospective teachers stand before classes of these students and begin to teach. Engagement with students takes careful planning as well as time and energy, but these educators mark it as the essential job of teachers and the first step in managing a classroom. All other steps follow.

Assignments

Nowhere is your attention to the individual students you teach more essential than in the area of homework assignments. Some students operate within such tight economies of time and such constrained economies of home that most homework assignments are burdensome or impossible. Other students eagerly seek to read more and to work harder. Their evaluation of a course may in fact be based on how hard it makes them work. Still, a vast middle ground of students are so distracted by the attractions of our culture or so seduced by their particular adolescent subculture that they do not wish to be bothered by out-of-class assignments. Experienced teachers in your school should know the general group of students that you teach and can help you decide what you can fairly expect from their work outside of class.

Advantages. Clearly, the work of the English class is enhanced when students read and write before coming to class. The enhancement is more than simply not having to devote class time to individual work and thus being able to read, write, or collaborate more. Out-of-class work provides private, relatively chosen moments when students can respond and create alone. Such work has the power to develop those independent, committed habits of reading and writing at which we aim. The private moment sometimes yields a kind of autonomous, personal response that collective work cannot.

Advance Organizers. One important spur to homework or any long-term project is an advance organizer. Advance organizers anticipate the new material or ideas that the student will encounter and prepare the student for that newness. They put the anticipated work in a frame of reference or a context. Mayer's (1979) study demonstrated that "when learners have clearly established goals and when they can organize information around key concepts, they retain more of what they learn" (p. 168). Advance organizers also arouse curiosity and pique interest in the work to come. They are particularly effective when they tie the assignment to personal experience or to prior reading—for example, a personal question that will be central to the text; a group reading of the first paragraphs of a story followed by the question "What do you think will happen next?"; or a photograph or picture that touches on the character, setting, or situation to come followed by the question "What comes into your mind when you see these images?"

Teacher Response to Homework. Two uses to which homework should never be put are punishment and busywork. Whatever your motive in making an assignment, if the work is worth student effort, it deserves the teacher's or the class's attention. You have many ways to respond to student work, but you should respond in some way. We tell our students, "Use up everything: Nothing goes unheard or unread."

Block Scheduling

For classes of any length, a variety of activities within a period keeps you and your students alert and energized. That variety is an absolute necessity with the ninety-minute classes of block scheduling. Proponents of block scheduling like the concentration that a few subjects offer students rather than the scattered focus over five or six subjects. They also applaud the opportunity to extend lessons over a long span of concentrated time so that students can immerse themselves in a subject deeply rather than lose impetus and time with numerous stop-and-start classes. Block scheduling has created a challenge to teacher planning, however. Some teachers have been slow to adjust and merely extend their customary fifty-minute classes to sixty or sixty-five minutes and leave the remainder of the time for working on homework assignments. Many other teachers have felt a compression of total course time and have responded with panic about coverage of material. They believe that they must teach with great efficiency in this abbreviated time and thus make lessons less student-centered and more text- and teacher-driven. Much that is gradual, gracious, and spontaneous falls before the need for speed and efficiency.

We recognize in these new circumstances a need for careful planning more than controlled planning. We present many ideas for one or more lessons on satire in Figure 14.6. Use these ideas to practice planning for a ninety-minute lesson.

Invitation to Reflection 14–5

Plan a ninety-minute lesson for eleventh-graders on satire. Use some of the ideas about teaching satire in Figure 14–6 and create some of your own. Because of the length of the period, using varied instructional approaches and activities

will be important. We suggest that you place an estimated time beside each activity. As you work or when you have finished, evaluate your plans according to Moffett and Wagner's three *I*s and Moffett's four modes of classroom organization. Consider Dixon's (1967) perspective. Can you construct this lesson so that the notion of satire becomes secondary to a primary focus on insight into human experience? What question could you raise to start the sort of conversation Applebee (1997) encourages?

Paper Load

Debating each night whether to evaluate and respond to papers or plan for the next day's lesson is rugged, dispiriting work. It is often tempting to let the planning go as you grade paper after paper, hoping to get to the bottom of the stack and satisfy students who are clamoring for your return of their essays or tests. They assume, as you might come to, that the plans will take care of themselves. Resist that assumption. When faced with the choice, we recommend that you plan the next day's lesson. The burden of evaluation can grow heavy and sink you in anxious gloom, but a worse gloom descends when you and your students are dissatisfied with your lesson. (Alternatives to teacher-graded papers are discussed in other parts of this book.)

FIGURE 14–6
Ideas for a lesson on satire

Individual	writing	Write definitions of satire.
Small group	talking	Read individual definitions and revise the ideas into one best definition.
Whole class	talking	Discuss the groups' definitions and write a class definition on the board.
Individual	thinking	Examine four teacher-selected cartoons to determine which of the four is satiric.
Individual	reading	Bring in examples of satiric cartoons or editorials from magazines and newspapers.
Pairs	talking	Select your favorite satires from those brought and present to the class.
Whole class	talking	Discuss reactions to pieces and determine whether or not this piece is satiric. (Your students will probably discover that satire has no one solitary identification. Opinions differ.)
Whole class	listening	To identify satiric tone, listen to three examples of satire: brief excerpts from Ambrose Bierce (*The Devil's Dictionary*), H. L. Mencken, and Woody Allen.
Whole class	viewing	Watch film excerpts from Monty Python's *In Search of the Holy Grail*
	talking	What is being satirized? What makes us laugh?
Individual	writing	Respond to this prompt: What is this excerpt satirizing? *Tip:* Use concrete details from the film to explain and elaborate your ideas.
Pairs	writing	Write a satiric letter to the editor of your school or community paper criticizing something about the school.
Individual	writing	Complete this prompt: "I do/do not enjoy satire because . . ."

Advice from Experienced Teachers

One of the difficulties of planning as a new teacher is knowing where to turn for advice about a complex activity such as teaching. Many friends and family members will willingly share their impressions and opinions of you and your students, but you may wonder how you can approach experienced teachers who understand your situation better. In his first year of teaching, our son Benjamin, a physics and math teacher, commuted with three others—an English teacher, a physical education teacher, and a counselor—on a forty-five-minute drive to a remote high school in tidewater Virginia. He was first shocked, then shaken, then devastated by the school culture and his inability to influence his students to want to learn or even to attend. On certain days, quite apart from his difficulty in making simple instructions heard, he could not even be heard when he asked students to quiet down. He regarded the problems first as his weakness and then as his failure. As disheartening as his daily classroom struggles was the nonsupport of the faculty members to whom he turned for help. When he began to articulate his perplexities and misery and ask for advice from the colleagues in his carpool, he often heard, "Well, he doesn't act that way in my class," or "No, I've never had any problems like that." His gloom deepened as his resources for help narrowed.

Often, approaching experienced teachers for advice is difficult: They are busy, competent professionals; they have developed effective techniques of classroom management; they have gained reputations that students anticipate and respect; and they have increasingly taught highly motivated and older students and have forgotten the quandaries of the beginning teacher. Their competence alone can intimidate the novice, who is pained by his or her sense of insufficiency. Turning to professional literature can be just as disheartening. Journal articles, for instance, are usually written by those who have succeeded with some technique or strategy. If these articles admit to frustration and failure, they are failures overcome. Understandably, stories of triumph are the norm. Jason Farr (1997) sought consolation in the narratives of teachers in the professional literature and met the same sort of success stories that were at odds with what he was experiencing. He confesses that they "seemed utterly out of my reach. I was dealing with students for whom realistic expectations might involve merely coming to class most of the time" (p. 107). Ben Nelms (1992), a past editor of the *English Journal,* reflected on the predominance of such idealism in the journal and acknowledged that "such stories do not always convey the uncertainty, the ambivalence, the apprehension, the misgivings that are a normal, even necessary, part of every teacher's life" (p. 43).

We agree with Farr (1997) that what is needed is "a balanced picture of our profession: quite high-minded goals, perhaps, but tempered by realistic expectations" (p. 108).

He concurs with Robert Inchausti (1993) that the stories of teachers are crucial to the professional development of beginning teachers. Yet as Inchausti says, "Most teachers, I found, seldom admit to the psychological horrors in their classrooms or to misgivings about their teaching skills to anyone but a few trusted souls" (p. 26). For this reason, Farr values Mike Rose's (1989) *Lives on the Boundary: A Moving Account of the Struggles and Achievements of America's Educationally Underprepared.* Rose and Inchausti acknowledge that a balance is needed—not of arriving at "some bland middle ground, but of affirming extremes of success and failure that teaching truly presents" (p. 108). All teachers—experienced and new—must work toward this honesty. If you have no one at present who can help you, you do have a resource in your own reflections, which we now address.

Learning from Mistakes

Janet Allen (1995) believes that the real success stories often come after struggle and even failure. "We never really learn anything without experiencing unsettled thoughts. If that is true, I no longer have to wonder why this year of almost constant disequilibrium was the most significant learning experience in my life" (p. 154). New teachers will, of course, make mistakes. No one should expect to master a profession of such complexity quickly. Student teaching and the first several years of teaching that follow are a period of apprenticeship and formation. Our colleague Bob Evans's most frequent admonition to his prospective science teachers is this: "It will take two to three years for you to become the teacher you envision for yourself. You are starting on a long road, and you should be patient with yourself as you move down it. You are not going to become the excellent teacher you want to be quickly."

Evans assists his students in meeting their difficulties directly and honestly. He asks them to enumerate daily the good things they did in any period of the day. He insists that they also restrict the time they worry about the things that did not go well. He helps them train themselves to separate the good times from the bad. He advises students to worry only during a defined time. (He recommends that they let their worries surface as they exercise so that they can burn off their negative emotions. When they finish exercising, they are to quit worrying.) Then they can address the question "What can I do tomorrow to be better?"

Student judgments of the teacher also must be resisted. Students often assume that good teachers are born with special endowments and sort teachers accordingly. They can be especially tough on new teachers. You might begin to accept their valuation. Resist it. It won't do you or them justice. Hawley (1979) exactly captures the difficulties of teachers' daily public performances:

Human beings generally dread the prospect of speaking authoritatively before a group. The dread is greatest when the group being addressed is not particularly receptive or welcoming, when they do not anticipate being pleased. Teachers play to tougher houses than actors do. They also play to them in more intimate settings, and the scheduled run is generally long regardless of the reviews. An actor, often with reason, may blame a flat performance on his material. Teachers are less able to do this; it is rarely Euclid's or Melville's fault that a class has fallen flat. Teachers move among their audiences, address them, converse with them. Any inattention, boredom, hostility is clearly visible before them. Because there are normally no co-stars or supporting players, the experience of teaching imperfectly is essentially a private matter. And again, because failure is by nature humiliating, we tend to keep it to ourselves. (p. 597)

We still have teaching experiences that leave us with a terrible sense of desolation and insecurity. All our confidence in ourselves as teachers capable of teaching these students totters. At those times, we regard teaching as the best school for humility that we know of. But even these blunders or failures can be used for profit if we work on understanding what they teach us about ourselves. In time their impact is blunted. Sometimes we can and do function as teachers with wonderfully little to go on, without all that we at first believed indispensable, in the knowledge that this is a profession dedicated to change and growth in ourselves as well as our students.

∞ CONCLUSION

Planning daily lessons and extended units is both hard and joyous work. If teachers remain alert and attentive to their students and to developments in the field, planning will remain active and challenging. Like so much of teaching, though, as you become more experienced, its challenges appear less formidable. At present, you will often be pulled in many competing directions. You will negotiate between two poles: between a keen awareness of the personal needs of your students and the demands of textbooks, curriculum guides, English departments, and other teachers; between a desire for a classroom environment that grants students space in which to think independently and respond authentically and one that possesses an order in which a whole class can work productively and creatively; between the establishment of your own authority and your belief in students' autonomy; between finding energy and time to plan lessons and finding the time to treat yourself kindly; between the calls of expediency and creativity, of safety and risk. These pulls are still active in our teaching careers. Sometimes, although we want a definitive solution—that is, we want to pitch ourselves in one direction or another—we take solace in Virginia Woolf's words in *To the Lighthouse:* "The great revelation had never come. The great revelation perhaps never did come. Instead there were little daily miracles, illuminations, matches struck unexpectedly in the dark."

15

Becoming a Complete Teacher

In every lucky life there is one teacher who places a finger upon our soul.

William Gibson

e have arrived at the final chapter, and we know that you are anxious to put your ideas to work in the classroom. Calkins (1983) quotes Erikson as saying, "We are the teaching species." She goes on to say that "human beings need to teach, not only for the sake of those who need to be taught but for the fulfillment of our identities, and because facts are kept alive by being told, truths by being professed" (p. v). We hope this book has helped you arrive at greater certainty about those facts and truths, where to find them, and how to profess them. But before you launch into the world of real students and actual classrooms, we want you to stop to consider three important concerns that are part of the context of teaching. All three appear to lie outside the immediate realm of instruction, but each is intimately related to your growth as an English teacher. The first concerns defining yourself in a setting of teachers and schools, the second building relationships with your students through your connection with their parents and the community, and the third developing as a member of your profession.

DEFINING YOURSELF AS A TEACHER

In almost every aspect of your professional life, you will need to work between competing claims that will not allow for easy answers or quick solutions. Like Robert Frost, whose poems acknowledge the rightness of both introspection in snowy fields and movement toward town duties, the virtue of walls and the value of openness, we have to live in the tension between contending possibilities. You will certainly face some difficult alternatives; we hope you will embrace or resolve them rather than polarize them as either good or evil.

As a beginning teacher, you may have doubts about your role as an authority with your students and your place as an equal with colleagues, administrators, and your students' parents. That lack of ease will dissipate as you gain experience and confidence. Confusion and uncertainty often arise from the tension between finding your comfortable teaching style and experimenting with alternatives. You have much to do in discovering what pedagogy—traditional or new—works best for you and your students. Classroom research can help you see which new directions make sense and what established approaches warrant continued use. But your zest for particular content (the magical realism of Spanish American writers, for example) and modes of discourse (whole-class discussion, perhaps) is also important to recognize and enlarge. In planning, you will need to keep alive this same healthy tension between understanding your course's place in the state, system, and school curricula and establishing learning sequences that depart from those norms. The authorized texts and the adopted curricula may sometimes seem to represent tame conformity, but they also are reservoirs of tested content and practice that may merit a place in the classroom. At the same time, departures that recognize the needs of the particular students you teach and that promote genuine involvement make sense as their complement.

You must find middle ground between working for curricular change and avoiding fads. For example, questions raised about the canon will have a serious impact on new texts and on the decisions of curriculum committees. Reconsidering what literature we will teach must be undertaken with a consciousness of the integrity and worth of much of the established tradition and the rich and urgent new literature that also deserves to be read. Likewise, computers can be powerful vehicles that enlarge your students' reach or expensive classroom tools that function as electronic worksheets. DVDs of Shakespearean plays can enliven study of that master or deaden it if they are poorly used. As a new teacher, you are called upon to evaluate these new ideas. Rather than seeing internal dialogues between strong pedagogical voices as aberrant, we see them as signs of an alert and critical consciousness at work. Too much self-doubt can, of course, be paralyzing; but too little questioning also can be deadening. You are doing nothing less than composing yourself as a teacher. As Bateson (1990) says of life, "Each of us has worked by improvisation, discovering the shape of our creation along the way, rather than pursuing a vision already defined" (p. 1). You have been brought to teaching by some vision of your own, but all you know for certain about the terms of that actual teaching is that they will be challenging. We acknowledge the legitimate and neces-

sary struggles that are part of the profession when you are aware of your surroundings and awake to yourself.

One teacher's fantasy of teaching may remind you of the possibilities of a classroom awakening as well as of the inevitable challenges and frustrations in achieving it. Even if you don't aspire to a class that is taking notes and parsing parts of speech, you will recognize this teacher's tenacious dreams. We suggest that you read Edwin Romond's "Dream Teaching" now and later, after you have entered your own classroom and met your own Ernies and Cindys, as a reminder of the shared struggles and hopes of our profession.

Dream Teaching[1]

I am first in line for coffee
and the copier is not broken yet.
This is how dreams begin in teaching high school.

First period the boy who usually carves skulls
into his desk raises his hand instead
to ask about *Macbeth* and, for the first time,
I see his eyes are blue as melting ice.
Then those girls in the back
stop passing notes and start taking them
and I want to marvel at tiny miracles
but still another hand goes up
and Butch the drag racer says he's found the
    meaning
in that Act III soliloquy. Then more hands join the
    air
that is now rich with wondering and they moan
at the bell that ends our class and I ask myself,
"How could I have thought of calling in sick
    today?"

I open my eyes for the next class and no one's late,
not even Ernie who owns his own time zone
and they've all done their homework
that they wave in the air
because everyone wants to go to the board
to underline nouns and each time I turn around
they're looking at me as if I know something they
    want
and steady as sunrise, they're doing it all right.

At lunch the serpentine food lady discovers smiling
and sneaks me an extra meatball. In the teachers
    room
we eat like family and for twenty-two minutes
not one of us bitches about anything.

Then the afternoon continues the happiness of
    hands
wiggling with answers and I feel such a spark
when spike-haired Cindy in the satanic tee shirt
picks the right pronoun and glows like a saint.
And me, I'm up and down the room now,
    cheering,
cajoling, heating them up like a revival crowd.

---

[1]Reprinted with permission from *English Journal*, 80(4), 96.

I'm living only in exclamatory sentences. They
    want it all
and I'm thinking, "What drug are we on here?"
Just as Crusher Granorski screams, "Predicate
    nominatives
are awesome!" the principal walks in
with my check and I almost say, "That's okay,
you can keep it." When the bell sounds
they stand, raise lighted matches
and chant, "Adverbs! Adverbs!"
I drive home petting my plan book.

At night I check the weather without wishing for a
    blizzard
then sleep in the sweet maze of dreams
where I see every student from years of school days:
boys and girls, sons and daughters who're almost
    mine,
thousands of them stretching like dominoes into
    the night
and I call the roll and they sing, "We're all here,
    Mr. Romond!"
When I pick up my chalk they open their books,
look up, and with eager eyes, ask me to teach them.

Edwin Romond

Invitation to Reflection 15–1

1. Return to the first Invitation to Reflection 1–1. Have any impressions of your own schooling altered or deepened in the course of reading this book?

2. Reread and rethink your answer to the last question in Invitation to Reflection 1–1. Has your sense of the profession of teaching English changed since you first answered that question? Have you changed your sense of why you want to become an English teacher?

3. As you anticipate teaching, where do you feel yourself to be within the tensions we just mentioned?

Defined, confident, established, traditional
Self: _____
Teaching style: _____
Teaching content: _____
Planning: _____
or

Fluid, open, experimental, unknown
Self: _____
Teaching style: _____
Teaching content: _____
Planning: _____

4. Does our acknowledgment of our sense of necessary struggle unnerve you or relieve you?

∞ DEFINING YOURSELF IN A PROFESSIONAL CONTEXT

Any self-definition has to begin with a close look at the way we teach and the core beliefs that are foundational to that teaching. Beyond that personal examination lie broader questions of how we see ourselves as part of a profession and how the world sees us as teachers. Nothing says more about that broader self-definition than the issues and concerns of our profession. Many serious issues are out there, but five will serve as examples of the national and local political context in which teachers work: *community support, discipline, class size, funding,* and *high-stakes testing.*

Teachers today feel community support eroding; disengagement from the schools seems pervasive. The school-neighborhood connection has nearly been severed, PTAs have withered, and the number of taxpayers with children in schools has been cut in half since the 1960s. *The Metropolitan Life Survey* (Axelrod, 2000) reports that almost half (45 percent) of secondary school parents feel left out of things at school.

Discipline is a major problem for teachers that is directly tied to the school-community disconnect and societal upheaval. *The Metropolitan Life Survey* (2000) reports that school safety is ranked as the second most important issue in schools. Glazer (1997) credits the terrific turnaround in the crime rate in Boston and New York City to the application of George Kelling's "broken windows" theory: The crime rate drops when small-time offenders receive swift and certain judgment (p. 29). Former mayor Rudolph Guiliani's use of this theory in restoring order in New York City by arresting turnstile jumpers might well be applied in the schools. However, neither Glasser (1990) nor Haberman (1995) believes that swift punishment for small misdemeanors is the answer. They believe that connecting with students is the solution to unacceptable behavior in class and at school. Something of both responses is clearly needed.

Reducing class size is central to many school reform plans; but dropping the average class size by even two students would cost millions at the state level. The solution may reside in the nationwide allocation of school personnel reported by the U.S. Department of Education (Figure 15–1). In nations with less heterogeneous populations, teachers comprise almost 75 percent of their total school staff. If the percentage of teachers in U.S. schools could be raised substantially above the current 52 percent level, the teacher-student ratio could be improved without huge additional funding.

The lack of funding might appear to be closely related to teacher attrition, but the NCES (1998) found that teacher satisfaction showed a "weak relationship with salary and benefits." Issues related to autonomy, time to reflect, and respect for the profession seem to be more crucial. Legislative intrusions and poor school leadership

FIGURE 15–1

National allocation of school personnel

Source: U.S. Department of Education, National Center for Education Statistics, Common Core of Data, *State Nonfiscal Survey.*

Note: Details may not add to the total due to rounding

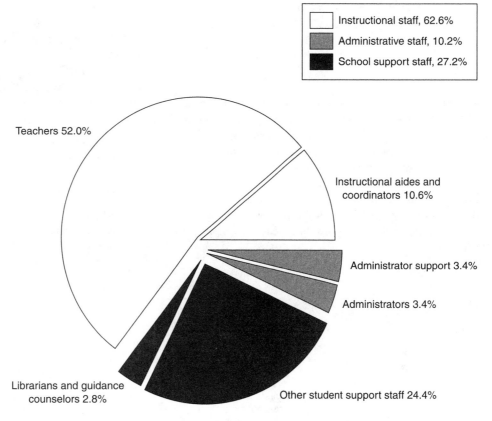

Instructional staff, 62.6%
Administrative staff, 10.2%
School support staff, 27.2%

Teachers 52.0%

Instructional aides and coordinators 10.6%

Administrator support 3.4%

Administrators 3.4%

Librarians and guidance counselors 2.8%

Other student support staff 24.4%

have had a large negative impact on these important factors. A more positive public regard for schools and an enlightened kind of leadership are key to improving the factors that make teaching a joy rather than a burden. With a greater demand for new teachers and more emphasis on school-based decision making, teacher autonomy has a real chance to flourish. NCES (1998) reports that "the teachers with greater autonomy show higher levels of satisfaction than teachers who feel they have less autonomy" (p. 1).

High-stakes testing is named last but probably is most timely as we discussed in chapter 13. Olson (2001) and many others complain that tests were intended to be part of the standards system, but they now dominate: Teachers absolutely teach to the test. A host of voices challenges our testing preoccupation, saying that weighing the pig every day does not make it grow heavier. Grasmick (2001) goes further to argue that high academic expectations and harsh consequences for those who fail to meet the standards require adequate interventions and serious funding to make the performance possible. Marlowe and Page (1998) make the final point that the battered teacher syndrome won't work. They show that teachers who have standards and testing imposed upon them will subvert the process—that only surface changes will result.

School Critics

For many years now, an outspoken group of critics has unrelentingly attacked the public schools by claiming that students' academic performance is lackluster and that discipline is a joke. A vociferous detractor in North Carolina recently claimed that the high schools award diplomas for eighth-grade work that is equivalent to that done in Third World countries. He added that we should once again let adults rather than students run the schools. George Will, who is usually careful with his words, has said that this is the first American generation whose schools are not as good as those that their parents attended. William Bennett, Chester Finn, and Diane Ravich have spent a good part of the past two decades thrashing the public schools. In the past several years, Berliner and Biddle (1995), Bracey (2002), and others have returned fire, saying that the myth of failing schools has been manufactured as part of an effort to privatize K–12 education. Popular films have not been part of any orchestrated effort; but they have, according to Burbach and Figgins (1993), presented negative images of "incompetence and buffoonery" (*Ferris Bueller's Day Off* and *The Breakfast Club*) and positive but romantic images of the "youthful idealist" and "tough love teacher" (*Dead Poets Society* and *Stand and Deliver*). Some educators believe that negativism and ambivalence are a result of stiff resistance to a paradigm shift from the traditional to a contemporary approach to pedagogy, which Doyle and Pimentel (1993) propose (Figure 15–2).

Defining Yourself for Schools

As you consider this paradigm, you will naturally reflect on where you stand, where the high school you attended stood, and where your future employers might be positioned on this pedagogical split. An immediate test of your stance will come when you interview for a position as an English teacher. You can get a sense of your employers' perspective when you think about the top-ten dilemma questions and the top-ten topics during interviews (as surveyed and reported by Head, 1990, pp. 2–3). See Table 15–1.

The positions of the ten interview topics and dilemma questions change from year to year. Most are generally used to let prospective teachers define themselves for the interviewers.

This extended look at self-definition includes a recent study that focused on teachers, not structures. Ward (1997) reported that the top teachers at thirty excellent schools shared four basic characteristics:

- high teaching expectations
- respect for students and their cultures
- teaching driven by research and theory
- classroom experimentation and action research

The first two characteristics speak of these teachers' care for others; the latter two indicate that they are reflective about their practice and their role as teachers.

FIGURE 15–2
What's in and what's out?

OUT	IN
inputs	outputs
innate ability	effort
rote learning	mastery
autocratic	autonomous
seat time	accomplishment
student as learner	student as worker
teacher as lecturer	teacher as manager of instruction
longevity	competence
administrator as master	administrator as servant
centralized bureaucracy	decentralized management
technology: bells and whistles	technology: productivity enhancer
school board: micromanagement	school trustees: stewardship
time: periods, semesters, years	time: flexible
schools: teacher proof	schools: teacher friendly
diploma = seat time/age	diploma = mastery/accomplishment
superintendent = dictator	student = choreographer
taxpayer	shareholder
standardization	standards
true-and-false tests	authentic assessment
blue collar	professionals
uniform salary schedule	pay for scarcity; pay for performance
education: school's business	education: everyone's business
school = building	school = learning

TABLE 15–1

Top-Ten Tough or Dilemma Questions	National Top-Ten Interview Topics
What is your philosophy of education?	classroom management
How do you handle discipline in your classroom?	student teaching
What are your strengths?	personal strengths
What are your weaknesses?	personal weaknesses
Describe in detail a lesson you taught.	hypothetical situations
How would you develop . . . skills in your students?	teaching style
How would you set up a program in . . .?	future plans
What if . . .?	employment history
Tell me about yourself.	motivational theories
Why should I hire you?	health history

✆ BUILDING PUBLIC TRUST

As a new teacher, you cannot help thinking about the day-to-day urgencies of teaching: "What will I do Monday?" Developing home-school connections is not likely to be an immediate concern. But those connections provide an essential support on which your classroom teaching will flourish. Conservative and liberal educators alike agree on one thing about education: Classrooms that work best have strong bonds with the homes of the students they serve. These bonds are all the more important at a time when homes are fragile and schools are drawing more and more criticism. When more than one-fourth of our children come from one-parent families, when the population of students that the school serves is racially underrepresented by the teachers who help them learn, when an ever-slimmer portion of the taxpaying population has children in public schools, when the parents of some students are little more than children themselves, then the odds against strong parental support for teachers' work are very high. At this time, then, the need to build relationships with students' families is especially important.

We suggest three fair and effective ways to build a relationship with parents: *include* them, *inform* them, and *involve* them in all that you do. These three *I*s are basic and can be accomplished with little expenditure of effort yet exceptional profits to you and to your students.

Include

Many parents have had negative experiences themselves with schools and feel antagonistic to or alienated from them. With a new approach, they can become allies instead of aliens. Neil Griffiths, former headmaster at Westlea School in Wiltshire, England, began working with his parents more than a year before their children entered his school. He invited them to come to school for a meeting and let them know that he would visit them in their homes if they did not attend. You cannot go that far perhaps, but you can let parents know what you expect of their sons and daughters and what you plan to accomplish during the school year. This is a beginning point: an oral or written word of welcome, an invitation to become partners, and an agenda for the term. Too much talk with too little action will not impress any parent, but words that lead to action can invite parents to reappraise their relationship to school. If they see useful skills, important knowledge, and personal growth as the end result of your class, the possibilities for a good home-school relationship increase. If, in the attempt to include them, you offer your agenda but also invite parents to express their hopes and fears, the effect of reaching out may rise sharply. If you are able to gather parents together, they can meet you and come to see you as a person. Many teachers are using e-mail to build a relationship with parents and to keep them informed about their children's progress. Not only are the chances greater that they will encourage their children's efforts in English, but if you must meet them to discuss an academic problem, they will know you. Without that initial contact, parents can easily become defensive or hostile. In addition to this preliminary letter, meeting, or conference, we recommend that you establish other times when parents can come by to review their children's work or actually visit class for a period. PTA meetings and scheduled open houses are also times when strong connections can be forged.

Inform

Periodic teacher-student-parent conferences (often held at the end of grading periods) can be very effective means of describing and displaying student work (portfolios, writing folders, homework, and tests) and explaining the curricular agenda for the coming term, especially when you are able to ground talk of the student's progress in concrete particulars. Parents want to see the kind of substantial work that shows the true progress of their children.

Perhaps an even more useful tool for cohesion is student performance. Student-conceived, written, and produced presentations can draw on all of the language arts skills. Professionally scripted drama, which can remain inert if it stays in the pages of a textbook, can come alive in student productions. Literature is enlivened for students as classrooms are enlivened for their parents. These productions provide evidence of both student involvement and their recently acquired knowledge.

A less public way to inform parents is to use Tierney's (1990) concept of a class assignment monitor. A log of all out-of-class assignments can be kept by a no-nonsense student whose job includes providing a record for absent and returning students of exactly what they missed during that time. When parents look at the log, they can see just how much is going on in class and how much congruence exists between a son's or daughter's assessment of the workload and the record of the actual work.

In addition to telling families about plans for the school year, some teachers send home periodic lists of supplemental readings. If you also ask parents to offer comments and suggestions, you will be both informing them and mitigating the threat of their censoring responses later. This approach becomes even more effective when you include a brief statement about your rationale for choosing the literature and your willingness to discuss any of the texts on the list. Other kinds of lists presented at meetings or in conferences also inform parents of your goals and expectations for your students: lists of skills to be learned, topics to be covered, major due dates to be anticipated. Because the goals, pedagogy, strategies, and content of English education change over time, parents need to become more comfortable with the basic philosophy of your program. When they see little of the activity that was central to their school experience, knowing what is transpiring will assure them that an important kind of learning is taking place. When both your rationale and activities are simply and clearly communicated to parents, they can become allies with you and their children.

Involve

The lines between each of these three components of strong parent-school connections are not always sharply delineated. Including and informing parents ideally will involve them in the life of the classroom. With some, that involvement might lead to active partnership with the teacher. You will come to imagine ways to initiate and solidify that activity. One of the simplest and least threatening for parents is the role of guest or interviewee. Most adults who are willing to come to class to talk about their lives—vocations, avocations, continued learning, parenting, and life stories—will be able guests to interview. Those with unusual vocations might talk about them or serve as panel members about life work. Parents are more likely to participate if they know that others are involved. (Industry, medical institutions, and public service agencies have become more willing to support this kind of partnership with schools.) Another role for a few is actually to teach or talk about fiction, nonfiction, or poetry that they particularly like. Others are willing to volunteer as relief teachers for your occasional times away from the classroom. In each of these approaches, you are supported, the parent is involved, and students are enriched.

An approach that requires less parental time yet still allows parental expression about the work of your class is to survey their opinions. They might be asked about their language use (idioms, colloquial expressions, sayings), reading habits, television viewing or music preferences, and favorite books. Surveys are especially effective when the results of all parental responses are handled anonymously and reported enthusiastically. Tact and common sense are crucial here to protect against awkward self-disclosure. But if you use care, incorporating surveys into the work of the class to enlarge literature is engaging for all: to provide writing ideas, to prompt discussion, or to provide stories for dramatic activities such as choral reading or change agents (Chapter 4).

Another way to involve parents is to use their talents and experience to help as editors of their children's writing. Not all parents are able to write, and some who can don't think of themselves as able writers; but all can help—even by listening and making oral suggestions. Because they attend to content better than to form, parents may be valuable deep-structure revisers. An even larger extension of this approach is used as papers progress through many drafts; such response is freed of the relia-

bility and consistency problems of grading. The parent becomes another active reader. Some schools even pay these paraprofessionals a small stipend.

On another level, parents can be asked to support your goal that students read and write outside school and beyond the compulsion of assigned texts and topics. You can ask parents to give you ten minutes of two nights each week to provide a period of uninterrupted, silent, sustained home reading or writing. Research increasingly demonstrates the value of this practice (Gardiner, 2001). They might find it a pleasure and a bond, not a tax on their patience and time. For families in which parents are struggling with basic literacy skills themselves, you can try to locate or even develop a tutoring program.

James Comer at Yale and David Perkins at Harvard agree that smart schools are, above all, ones that reach out to parents and make the school seem to be an extension of the family. Epstein (1997), at the Center on School, Family, and Community Partnership at Johns Hopkins, has identified six important reciprocal types of cooperation between school and home:

1. Parenting: Families must provide for the health and safety of children, and maintain a home environment that encourages learning and good behavior in school.
2. Communicating: Schools must reach out to families with information about school programs and student progress.
3. Volunteering: Schools should create flexible schedules, so more parents can participate, and work to use the talents and interests of parents.
4. Learning at Home: With the guidance and support of teachers, family members can supervise and assist their children at home.
5. Decision-making: Schools can give all parents meaningful roles in the school decision-making process.
6. Collaboration with the Community: Schools can help families gain access to support services offered by other agencies. (p. 4)

The National PTA (1989) has been more directive in its recommendations to teachers and schools. It provides a list of ten things that parents wish teachers would do:

- build students' self-esteem by using praise generously and avoiding ridicule and negative public criticism
- get to know each child's needs, interests, and special talents as well as the way each child learns best
- communicate often and openly with parents, contacting them immediately when academic or behavioral problems occur, and be open and not defensive when discussing these problems
- assign homework that helps children learn and advise parents how they can assist their children with this learning
- set high academic standards, expecting all students to learn and helping them to do so
- care about children since children learn best when taught by warm, friendly, caring, and enthusiastic teachers
- treat all children fairly

- enforce a positive discipline code based on clear and fair rules that are established at the beginning of each school year; reinforce positive behavior rather than punish negative behavior
- vary teaching methods and make learning fun
- encourage parent participation by reaching out to involve parents in their children's education, showing them how they can help their children at home and remembering that parents want to work with teachers to help their children do their best

All of this adds up to what the U.S. Department of Education calls rebuilding social capital. The responsibility stretches from a welcome at the front door of the school to your thoughtful reflection on students' progress as you listen with parents or guardians as students using their open portfolios and explain the headway they have made in their writing over the course of the year.

The list of ideas for including, informing, and involving parents is as long as your imagination and must be tied to your understanding of your particular circumstances. Exactly what you do is not as important as communicating to parents that you care about their children and that you are reaching out to them to promote purposive and successful learning.

Invitation to Reflection 15–2

1. How important do you consider the connection between teachers and parents to the learning of the classroom: *Very important? Somewhat important? Important? Unimportant?*
   to the teacher
   to the student
   to the parent
2. Which of the strategies for building public trust appeals to you most?
   For including and informing:
   teacher-student-parent conferences
   student performance
   logs of assignments
   lists of Supplemental Readings
   For involving:
   guests or interviewees
   surveys
   editors
   home reading
3. Do you remember your parent or parents coming to your middle or high school? If so, what were the occasions?
4. Were they included or involved in the life of your classes?
5. Would it have made a difference if they had or had not been?

∽PROMOTING PROFESSIONAL GROWTH

Thinking about your long-term professional growth may seem quite distant and therefore unimportant to you at this time; but along with seeing your place in the community of English teachers and making connections with parents, it is an essential indicator of excellence in teaching. You may have heard the old distinction between the teacher who has twenty years of experience and the teacher who has had one year of teaching experience twenty times. We want you to grow with your years in this profession. We believe a profession is defined as a community of practitioners that possesses a complex body of knowledge and skill that rests on theory and research and is constantly tested and refined by experience. Professionals, then, not only understand the universal or the general but also learn from the particular and the situated. By this definition, your growth in teaching becomes proof of your being a professional. We explore seven steps that will promote your growth as an English teacher and as a person who seeks self-knowledge and acts on professional commitments: *goal setting, self-evaluation, peer review, external assessment, action research, guild building,* and *association membership.*

Goal Setting

The first of these steps may be prompted by departmental or schoolwide initiatives, but more likely you will provide your own prompt for setting goals for yourself as a professional. These can clarify and name specific and/or general areas to explore and accomplish. They can govern curricular directions that you take and instructional choices that you make. They can serve as an index of new measures adopted and areas accomplished toward professional growth. The goals you set may be as personal as working toward a close relationship with a small number of students or as public as increasing the number of attendance days for at-risk students. Some goals may be pedagogical (trying to add two new approaches to literature instruction) or content-centered (reading four new texts by non–European authors.) The goals may have to do with professional efficiency (reading all short papers within three days of their completion) or personal efficacy (leaving every Saturday completely open for a non-school–related activity). Such goal setting can enable you to focus your energies, to experiment with new possibilities, and thus to grow professionally. The goals should be few, important, and attainable. You should review them periodically and check the results at the end of every year. If you can convince your colleagues in the English department to set goals for the entire group, that will reinforce your own and lend cohesiveness to the work of the department.

Self-Evaluation

Student evaluation provides an important measure of the success of these goals. If you are alert and open, you can sense much about your teaching through informal observation and self–reflection. But to assure comprehensive and objective assessment, you should let students speak through an evaluation instrument that you devise or select from available ready-made forms. Developing or selecting a form that measures what you think is important about teaching is critical. If you believe that student participation and construction of knowledge are essential, then you need to develop an evaluation form that can measure these accomplishments. Learning about students' perceptions of your teaching through description is useful too. Asking what they regard as the percentage of class time involved in collaborative writing, say, or asking them to rank order the time allotted for talking and listening, reading, writing, and viewing can enrich your understanding of students' experiences in your classroom. We recommend that your format also provide some space for short responses, open or guided, such as three adjectives that best describe the course, two problems with the course, or two topics that should be omitted. Invitation to Reflection 15–3 prompts you to consider this type of evaluation by examining a form used to evaluate both an entire course and its teacher.

Invitation to Reflection 15-3

Review the following end–of–course evaluation form and explain its strengths and weaknesses.

Course: _____

Teacher: _____

Circle your response to the statements below and offer comments where helpful.

Excellent   Good   Average   Below Average   Poor

1. Preparation and organization of the subject matter
   10 9 8 7 6 5 4 3 2 1
   Comment: _____
2. Intelligence and insight brought to subject matter
   10 9 8 7 6 5 4 3 2 1
   Comment: _____
3. Scholarship and knowledge of the field of inquiry
   10 9 8 7 6 5 4 3 2 1
   Comment: _____
4. Enthusiasm for and communication of subject matter
   10 9 8 7 6 5 4 3 2 1
   Comment: _____
5. Ability to stimulate thought and provoke inquiry
   10 9 8 7 6 5 4 3 2 1
   Comment: _____
6. Sensitivity to and concern for student response
   10 9 8 7 6 5 4 3 2 1
   Comment: _____

7. Openness to and reception of divergent points of view
   10 9 8 7 6 5 4 3 2 1
   Comment: _____
8. Accuracy and fairness of evaluation of students
   10 9 8 7 6 5 4 3 2 1
   Comment: _____
9. Availability for academic help and personal counsel
   10 9 8 7 6 5 4 3 2 1
   Comment: _____
10. Adequate class time spent to cover course material
    10 9 8 7 6 5 4 3 2 1
    Comment: _____
11. General evaluation of total effectiveness as a teacher
    10 9 8 7 6 5 4 3 2 1
    Comment: _____
12. General comments about strengths and weaknesses:
    _____
    _____
    _____

Two important parts of this process are the students' security and your receptivity. We think that students' comments are most honest when they are assured full anonymity and when they are assured that grades will be recorded before the evaluations are read. With students thus protected, you will need to protect yourself from disappointment at student evaluations while opening yourself to listen to their responses, no matter how harsh. One way to elicit thoughtful reflection is to let students know that you will take their perceptions seriously and that you have adapted your teaching to improve it based on the suggestions of former students. Ideally, your year's or semester's work with your classes will establish a partnership of learning for which a final evaluation is a natural and promising conclusion, not an occasion for vendettas and airing gripes. If such a partnership has not been created, treating the event seriously may help. You will, of course, need to make your own judgments about students' responses. Some things that they may want are not what is best for the class as you envision it. Some of their remarks may be personal and excessive. They may arise from anger or disappointment or arise from profound admiration, but they need to be taken seriously. One of our university colleagues assures his own receptivity to student evaluations by waiting for a year, just before planning for the evaluated course, to read evaluations.

Peer Review

Many schools have established mentor teachers to serve as guides for first-year teachers. If you do not find a mechanism in place for help from an able teacher, we strongly recommend that, even in the crowded schedule you will face as a first-year teacher, you try to find an experienced teacher on whom to rely. In actuality, the hard part is not finding time but establishing trust. We suggest a concrete plan for such a process, an ideal to which you will undoubtedly make personal accommodation.

- Find a partner, someone you like and feel you can learn from.
- Work out a schedule in which you will use part of your planning period once a week to visit the partner's classroom.
- Reciprocally, the partner comes to one of your classes once a week and in brief after-school meetings gives you impressions of the things you were doing very well. Keep the focus on strengths and capabilities at first before moving to more problematic observations and questions about the class session. These questions need not imply negative judgments but your departures from what was expected or what the partner might have done. The result is greater reflection on diverse ways to accomplish the same learning.
- After four of those sessions, include explanations about things that the partner might have done differently or accomplished in a different order. This leads to fuller exploration of pedagogy and a more honest sense of differences.
- In the next four sessions, add the exploration of content and method that might have been used but were not. Here, a broader repertoire of method and content is injected, pushing you toward deeper and broader questions of teaching.
- Finally, discuss problems and difficulties in the lesson openly.

The peer review sequence, then, involves a slow progress through these stages:

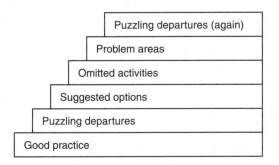

| Puzzling departures (again) |
| Problem areas |
| Omitted activities |
| Suggested options |
| Puzzling departures |
| Good practice |

This pace, a slow movement toward a thorough critique, is necessary or even the sturdiest and most self-confident new teacher will become defensive. The option of taking each of these steps in writing first, before they are taken orally, may help to ease the pain of growth. But when all the steps are taken with a colleague you trust and admire, the time spent will be repaid many times over in terms of what you learn about your teaching. You may not now believe that you can afford that ex-

penditure, but we believe you will not consider using that weekly thirty minutes any other way after completing ten sessions.

External Assessment

These personal assessments of your teaching progress will be extremely beneficial to your growth and long-term success as a teacher, but there are other ways in which you will be evaluated by outsiders that will also have an impact on your career. In the past, external assessments were infrequent and marginal features of the teaching profession; but in these times of public demand for school accountability, you must be prepared for encountering many kinds of assessment.

Teaching Portfolios. Teachers in many states are now facing school and individual evaluations based on student-gain scores on standard achievement tests. This is part of the shift from considering input to considering output (noted in the Doyle-Pimentel paradigm shift), but many school leaders complain that the measures of achievement are not authentic and that many confounding and contaminating variables are ignored. An assessment model that responds to those inequities is the *teaching portfolio,* which provides a thoughtful means for evaluating ourselves and at the same time presents a solid vehicle for external evaluations. Wolf (1996) explains the process and its merits for teachers at any level. He describes five steps that lend credibility and usefulness to the portfolio.

- Explain your educational philosophy and key principles that underlie your practice.
- Choose specific features of your instructional program to document. Collect a wide range of artifacts, and date and annotate them.
- Collaborate with a mentor and other colleagues to discuss your teaching and your portfolio.
- Assemble your portfolio in a form that others can readily examine.
- Assess the portfolio. Assessment can range from an informal self-assessment to formal scoring. (p. 36).

Wolf also provides a list of contents that lend credibility to a teaching portfolio.

- Background Information
  Résumé
  Background information on teacher and teaching context
  Educational philosophy and teaching goals
- Teaching Artifacts and Reflections
- Documentation of an extended teaching activity
  Overview of unit goals and instructional plan
  List of resources used in unit
  Two consecutive lesson plans
  Videotape of teaching
  Student work samples
  Evaluation of student work

Reflection commentary by the teacher
Additional units/lessons/student work as appropriate
* Professional Information
List of professional activities
Letters of recommendation
Formal evaluations (p. 35)

These are a part of standard practice in many schools today and are the basis for the certification process of the National Board for Professional Teaching Standards. Both of our institutions' teacher education programs require that each graduate prepare an electronic portfolio that includes running commentary on i-Movie clips of instruction, classroom artifacts, and a stated philosophy of education that parallels the structure and requirements of the National Board examination. We believe that this way of demonstrating performance provides a solid account of what a teacher intends to happen in his or her classroom and what does in fact happen. This descriptive account can be used by schools and boards to evaluate, by prospective employers to hire, and by teachers to scrutinize and enlarge their teaching.

General-Knowledge Tests. Some of the major forms of evaluation that are becoming more widespread include both once-in-a-career tests and those that are administered annually. The teacher achievement tests developed in several states are typically taken by a teacher only once. They are not based on performance or knowledge about classroom pedagogy but focus on content knowledge. They set minimal passing scores that teachers have to achieve no matter how long or how successfully they have taught. Some focus on a teacher's specialty area, but most are tests of general knowledge. These tests seemed to be prompted by public perceptions that teachers are not well educated. Some critics blame this perceived insufficiency on undergraduate education—an overload of professional coursework or poor general education—and others blame the shift in the population of students who are entering teaching. Whatever the reason, the tests have been used, and some very effective teachers have suffered.

Classroom Performance. A second wave of teacher evaluation has centered on teaching performance rather than teacher knowledge. It pleases those who feel that the knowledge tests are superficial and reductive, but its simplistic format has created a new set of adversaries. Its critics range from classroom teachers to think-tank theorists who assail its failure to account for the skillful blend of content and pedagogy that effective teachers are able to create. And while some teacher groups have called for a moratorium on such evaluation instruments for all but novice teachers, other educators defend them as primitive but necessary first steps. Some have said that these performance-based instruments need to be balanced with another measure based on a very different

sense of how knowledge is best discovered and integrated (Milner, 1991). The first three items are drawn from an objectives–based evaluation:

* The teacher asks questions and assigns tasks that students handle with a high rate of success.
* The teacher begins the lesson with a review of previous material.
* The teacher summarizes the main point(s) of the lesson at the end of the lesson.

A second three are taken from an evaluation based on very different teaching values.

* The teacher uses words of supposition such as *perhaps, maybe, then again, one wonders, inexplicably, might,* and *possibly* in his or her discourse.
* The teacher actively encourages students to question propositions and theses developed by the teacher and by other students.
* The teacher makes it clear that knowledge is uncertain, that "facts" can change.

Madeline Hunter speaks for the first; Jerome Bruner is a proponent of the second.

Specialty Performance. The National Teacher's Exam had for many years been the major paper-and-pencil test for prospective teachers—the gatekeeper for entrance into the classroom for many states. It was akin to the teacher achievement test mentioned earlier, but it also tested pedagogical knowledge. As the Educational Testing Service sensed the evolution in evaluation, it began to develop a new test, Praxis, which is more performance-centered but provides the content sophistication lacking in the state-developed teacher performance tests. It is discipline-specific and makes use of technology to offer a more authentic assessment of teaching. To date, the results have been mixed. Most methods teachers support the pedagogy central to the test, but the norming procedures in certain states have caused real difficulties.

Student Achievement. A recent revolution in evaluation has been toward student performance as the final test of teaching effectiveness. Such a measure doesn't look at philosophy, pedagogy, or even content knowledge; it doesn't care about teaching style or the student-teacher relationship. It evaluates teachers straightforwardly on how well their students perform. If your students perform well then you are considered successful. Some states allow the teachers at a particular school to designate a quantifiable dimension of student performance to be evaluated (attendance, for example); and if progress is discernible (the average daily attendance rises), rewards are forthcoming. These evaluations appear at first to have a clear, objective quality, but on second glance their defects become more apparent: They often fail to take into account contextual factors, which may radically skew comparisons; and they rely primarily on easily measurable variables. They may not reflect gain scores, for instance, in schools with high-risk students. They may also compromise long-term goals for teaching, such as student attitudes toward the subject at hand. Instead, instruction hammers away at the test but excludes almost everything else. This approach could eventually turn teachers into assembly-line workers and students into their widgets.

Board Certification.   The most promising form of evaluation may be the voluntary kind promoted by the National Board for Professional Teaching Standards (1994). Its model is the National Board examinations in medicine, which certifies physicians as specialists in medical fields such as neurology, pediatrics, and pathology. The National Board for teaching invites experienced teachers to be examined to qualify for board certification in specialty areas such as middle school language arts (the first area developed). The exam includes various components, such as portfolio review, classroom simulation, and a look at content.

Teachers standing for examination have to demonstrate a high level of knowledge, skills, dispositions, and commitments reflected in the five core propositions of the National Board.

- ***Teachers are committed to students and their learning.*** Board-certified teachers are dedicated to making knowledge accessible to all students, act on the belief that all students can learn, treat students equitably, adjust their practice as appropriate, and understand how students develop and learn.
- ***Teachers know the subjects they teach and how to teach those subjects to students.***   Board-certified teachers have a rich understanding of the subject(s) they teach and appreciate how knowledge in their subject is created, organized, linked to other disciplines, and applied to real-world settings.
- ***Teachers are responsible for managing and monitoring student learning.***   Board-certified teachers create, enrich, maintain, and alter instructional settings to capture and sustain the interest of their students and to make the most effective use of time, command a range of generic instructional techniques, know how to engage groups of students to ensure a disciplined learning environment, and understand how to motivate students to learn and how to maintain their interest even in the face of temporary failure.
- ***Teachers think systematically about their practice and learn from experience.***   Board-certified teachers are models of educated persons, exemplifying the virtues they seek to inspire in students—curiosity, tolerance, honesty, fairness, respect for diversity, an appreciation of cultural differences, and the capacities that are prerequisites for intellectual growth.
- ***Teachers are members of learning communities.*** Board-certified teachers contribute to the effectiveness of the school by working collaboratively with other professionals on instructional policy, curriculum development, and staff development and find ways to work collaboratively and creatively with parents. (pp. 6–8)

Some states and a few schools are supporting accomplished teachers who want to earn this national certification. The hope of the enterprise is to bring the art and science of teaching together for a rigorous look at best practice.

These three—Praxis as a gatekeeper to beginning practice, the induction period as a passageway for licensure, and the National Board for field certification—form a natural set of steps to full professional standing. If these steps remain meaningful and distinguish those who are truly master teachers in their fields, the profession will be enriched, those who are outstanding will be recognized and rewarded, and excellent teachers will become the mentors of our profession.

Invitation to Reflection 15–4

1. Rank your reactions to each of these evaluative strategies from positive (10) to negative (1) or by order.
   - teaching portfolios
   - general-knowledge tests
   - classroom performance
   - specialty performance
   - student achievement
   - board certification
2. How do these forms of assessment make you feel about being an English teacher?
3. Which ones seem most promising?
4. Which seem reductive of teaching?
5. Which seem to acknowledge the complexity of teaching?
6. Which are consistent with your sense of the profession?

Action Research

The act of classroom research is perhaps the most productive and least used tool of self-evaluation. It is the tool of growth for excellent teachers. When you teach awareness of language and self-consciousness about the human condition, it is not surprising that you bring similar antennae to your own teaching life.

That consciousness can help you grow in teaching through informal posing of questions about what is going on in your classroom. You may sense, for example, that your students are responding more intensely in their writing when they select their own topics. Because that intensity is important, you may want to make two explorations. You could start with alternating self-selected and assigned topics for a term. Or you might even alternate with two classes so that one is working in complete freedom one week while the other is given a topic; the next week reverse the procedure.

You may want to use a more ethnographic approach in looking closely at a particular group of students assigned to a long-term project. For instance, does the subject selection or voice differ significantly in the journal writing of males and females? In-depth interviews of the kind Seidman (1991) describes can also be used in searching to discover what makes learning most effective in your classroom.

You can develop even more formal designs for your classroom, such as the ones a student teacher created when she examined the effectiveness of film and text versions of the same story. She let her students engage the story in its two forms during a regular class period. One class read it; one class saw it. She used adjective checklists and a variety of content questions to establish the students' emotional engagement and comprehension of the two versions of the story. Her study was a formal, empirical study; but it did not really violate her teaching style, and it allowed her to gain an insight into a question that had real meaning for her and the teaching community as a whole. The study was particularly meaningful to her and her mentor teacher because he had strong reservations about using film in the English classroom.

Action research is a challenge that more and more young teachers are accepting. Graduates of our teacher education program become involved in ethnographic research on key features of the teaching act. These prospective teachers focus on a particular dimension of teaching, such as "Student Response to Global and Focal Questions" (Ochs, 2001), "The Effect of Teacher Proximity and Touch on Student Achievement" (Morris, 2001), "Teacher Response to 'Wrong Answers'" (Orser, 2001), "Teacher Strategies to Promote Gender Minority Responses" (Cole, 2001) and "Using Literary Criticism to Prompt Student Response" (Vonnegut, 2001). All of these studies bring greater consciousness to teaching and increase our students' sense of themselves as reflective professionals.

Guild Building

We suggest this simple but beneficial act for beginning teachers: Join local groups of English teachers who gather to share experiences central to their discipline and the art of teaching it. Members of such collegial associations often work cooperatively on common concerns and become instrumental in influencing administrative decisions about the curriculum. If such a group does not exist in your area, you should consider founding one. If logistical matters such as dues and organization are kept to a minimum, if meetings are regular and focused, and if learning from one another is paramount, the group will flourish. All professionals increasingly realize that continuing education is the cornerstone of their success.

Pathologists who do not read and take part in seminars are soon outdated. In the medical profession, the decline of competence is quickly observed by colleagues and even clients; but in our field, where the stakes are not as overtly crucial, English teachers are just as surely approaching professional rigor mortis if they do not create guilds or networks to nourish themselves.

Robert Putnam's (1999) *Bowling Alone* affirms the importance of social capital. Putnam (2000) believes that our social networks reinvigorate us and make us more productive. An ethic of reciprocity develops that is an asset to the individual and the community. (He says that going to meetings actually lowers our stress level—a finding some teachers might dispute—and joining a group increases our longevity substantially.) Bowling was once the biggest participant sport in the United States, but league bowling has plummeted. U.S. bowlers now bowl alone. (Putnam reports that the number of Americans living alone increased by 50 percent between 1977 and 1999.) Teachers do not have to work alone; they can build sustaining and productive guilds.

Association Membership

Whereas local guilds are best when their organizational structure is minimal, the complexities of organization are essential and even helpful for national and international professional associations. NCTE and most state affiliates are huge organizations that have the same function as the local guilds, but they address a broader range of issues and support a broader spectrum of English teachers who cannot meet on a regular basis. The executive committees, which deal with the structure and substance of the associations, the committees that focus on crucial and timely issues such as censorship, and the editorial boards that publish the journals and texts that articulate professional issues for those who are rarely able to attend annual meetings are all essential components for perpetuating the life of the organization and the profession it serves. These associations nurture individual teachers and provide possibilities for service and leadership that allow English teachers to clarify, express, and practice what they believe.

We strongly urge you to take advantage of the tremendous range of resources offered by NCTE, its state affiliates, and the National Writing Project. Specific professional organizations and their publications address particular interests such as media, reading, and drama. There are many resources available to augment, enliven, and deepen your ideas about teaching. One pleasant discovery for the young teacher is the body of instructional materials surrounding literary works (particularly certain commonly taught classics) that is shared by teachers informally and through the professional literature and meetings. Appendix K lists the associative and periodic resources that we have found to be most valuable.

⌒ PROFESSIONAL LEADERSHIP

A culmination of all of these ways to grow professionally is the act of leadership that begins in the classroom and can extend to the whole profession. Leadership means internal locus of control and personal autonomy. It means teachers moving away from the qualities yield to directives and control of others to Glasser's (1990) leadership qualities (survival, love, power, fun, and freedom) that promote student autonomy and well-being while increasing achievement (p. 43).

Wolfe and Antinarella (1997), in *Deciding to Lead*, describe fifteen ways in which English teachers can take the lead in worthwhile reform.

- Don't coerce.
- When asked, help.
- Relate to colleagues as you relate to students.
- Suggest agenda items for faculty gatherings.
- Resist reform strategies you don't believe in.
- Conduct classroom-based research and share it.
- Join a National Writing Project site.
- Don't say "no" to leadership opportunities.
- Promote cross-visitations in teachers' classrooms.
- Get to know influential people who can help.
- Communicate regularly with parents.
- Promote/organize teacher-led seminars.
- Invite nonteaching staff to participate in classrooms.
- Build a reputation as the best listener in your school.
- Work visibly. (pp. 112–116)

Each suggestion is insightful and specific enough to make our call to lead more tangible. Wolfe and Antinarella chart a leadership growth path in the careers of all teachers. Only the very best achieve the final stage.

Emulation/Control   In the first stage, the teacher is highly self-conscious, survival-oriented, and sensitive to his or her every word and action and to students' reactions. The teacher does little in the way of profound self-reflection.

Experimentation/Discovery   In the second stage, the teacher initiates conversations with colleagues about professional subjects, reads some professional literature, attends a few professional conferences, and analyzes classroom dynamics.

Facilitation/Resource   This stage tends to be philosophy and theory driven, with the teacher as facilitator and resource person, an active learner.

Research/Innovation   In the final leadership stage, the teacher knows how to lead, attract, and win over students to a view of school as a welcoming place, always thinks several shots ahead, is able to stand apart from himself or herself and watch with a critical eye what goes on in the classroom, and is an active researcher. (pp. 96–99)

All of this lies far ahead of you; but as you try on some of the leadership roles in the coming years, you will begin to feel yourself move up the developmental path that Wolfe and Antinarella outline for us.

All of these means of personal growth will not be at your disposal immediately. You will leap into some because you need them and wait on others because you may feel overwhelmed by the day-to-day pressures of teaching. But the old axiom "an ounce of prevention is worth a pound of cure" is repeated and remembered because it is true. The ounces you give to these elements of professional growth will certainly relieve you from pounds of professional difficulties and the tendency toward burnout. Where there is conscious and supported growth, burnout is less likely.

⌒ CONCLUSION

There are many senses in which this book has worked at *Bridging English*. It has attempted to serve as bridge between competing voices within the English profession—those of teachers, researchers, scholars, theoreticians, scientists, humanists, pragmatists, and idealists. We have tried to be fair to the legitimate claims of many. We have also attempted to span those distances between you as you are now, you as a student in the past, and you as a teacher in the future. William James (1907) has clarified our sense of how any individual obtains new learning and changes old opinions into new. His description of the process is that the individual "tries to change first this opinion, and then that until at last some new idea comes up which he can graft upon the ancient stock with a minimum disturbance of the latter, and some idea that mediates between the stock and the new experience and runs them into one another." He calls this new truth or idea a "go-between" or a "smoother-over of transitions," which marries old opinions to new facts "so as ever to show a minimum of jolt, a maximum of continuity" (p. 396). As this new truth enters into a person's working knowledge, it, too, becomes the "old ideas" ready to be challenged and changed in turn. Thus, we must always be ready for some new arrangement of our beliefs—and nowhere more than in teaching.

If *Bridging English* has had the role of helping you to new understandings with a "minimum of jolt," it will have been the bridge we hoped. Despite these many pages of ideas and activities, we believe that you will compose yourself as a teacher as you compose yourself as a person. Bateson's (1990) sense of life as an "improvisatory art" is apt here. We know that after we explain language development, say, or learning theory, reader response criticism, canon challenges, writing process, and portfolio evaluation—all important in themselves—we will only have begun to initiate your entry into teaching. It is in the actual work of the classroom, where you struggle to teach and to learn, that you will become a teacher. To borrow from Henry James's sense of art, we might say that in that classroom you will engage in the teaching art: "a braving of difficulties." Glatthorn (1975) reminded us more than a quarter century ago that good English teaching does not necessarily involve "a teacher-proof curriculum, an open classroom, or a learning package," but occurs in the act of "an authentic individual who is able to stay real in a very artificial world." Glatthorn says of English teachers with their students: "We teach in our own way, speak with our true voice, search for a deeper self. . . . In our own becoming we touch them and help them come alive again" (p. 39).

Appendix A

POSSIBLE LITERATURE LESSONS ON SHAKESPEARE'S SONNET 116

Whole-Class Lecture, Discussion, and Viewing

The teacher presents the concept of the chivalric ideal of courtly love and its embodiment in Elizabethan sonnets. The concepts are enumerated and illustrated with visual images (from paintings) and with narratives from history and literature. The final example is Shakespeare's Sonnet 116. The teacher asks a student to read it aloud. The teacher, through focused questions, guides students to identify elements of courtly love in the sonnet. Finally, the teacher shows two excerpts from the Ang Lee movie *Sense and Sensibility* (1995), in which Sonnet 116 figures prominently: the first occurs at the initial meeting of the two young lovers; the second occurs as the young woman laments her lost love.

Whole-Class Mini-Lecture and Discussion

Following the teacher's brief lecture on different sonnet types and poetic conventions, students are asked the following questions:

1. What kind of sonnet is this: Italian (Petrarchan) or English?
2. Does the meaning of the poem break into the standard three quatrains of the English sonnet? How does this form help clarify the poem's meaning? What is the effect of the final couplet on the ideas presented in the three quatrains? Does it provide a fitting conclusion?
3. Consider Shakespeare's use of metaphor. Name and locate the metaphors active in this poem. What single word unifies the two controlling metaphors of the poem?
4. Two important figures of speech are *metonymy* (in which one thing stands for another associated with it) and *synecdoche* (in which a part stands for a whole). Which figure does Shakespeare use when he refers to "rosy lips and cheeks"? To "bending sickle's compass"?

Small-Group and Individual Work: Comparison with Contemporary Works

The teacher assigns the following tasks to small groups after the whole class has read Shakespeare's Sonnet 116.

1. Read two other poems about love: Li Po's "Written in Behalf of my Wife" and John Frederick Nims's "Love Poem." Do these poems' ideas match or differ from Shakespeare's views about love? How is their tone similar or different? Do they reflect historical or cultural or gender differences among the Chinese (701-762), the English (1564-1616), and the American (1914-) poets? (Remember Li Po writes in behalf of his wife.)
2. Of the three poets, whose attitudes toward love and marriage appeal to you most? If Li Po, Shakespeare, and Nims joined your group, with which of the three would you like to discuss any problems you have experienced with friendship and love?
3. Listen to the old folk ballad "Frankie and Johnny." How is the song's view of love and relationships different from or the same as those of the three poets? Does the song jangle your sense of love?
4. Listen to John Lennon and Paul McCartney's "Eleanor Rigby." Why is Eleanor Rigby first pictured as picking up the rice thrown at someone else's wedding? Why is this image used in a song about human loneliness?
5. With which of the three subjects of song—Frankie, Johnny, and Eleanor—do you feel most compassion? Do the culture's images of love play a role in their lives?
6. Individually, free-write for five minutes from this prompt: "This discussion made me wonder about. . ."

Independent Group Project

Choose one of the following assignments:

1. Your task is to find personal connections between Shakespeare's sonnet and the world you know. Connect the poem to your own life, to happenings in school or in the community, or to love stories you have seen or heard from others. The connection may be an illustration of or a rebuttal to Shakespeare's view of love. Present the connections you think are most powerful to the rest of the class.
2. Your task is to develop a list of questions about Shakespeare's sonnet that you might want to discuss with the rest of the class. Don't worry too much about details. Try to help your classmates talk about the big ideas about love presented in the poem. Usually, the best discussions arise from your genuine reactions—thoughts and feelings—as you read. Connecting those to a story or a song you have seen, heard, or experienced or quandaries about love you have known might also prompt an animated discussion.
3. Your task is to present the poem dramatically to the class. The purpose is to convey with your voices and staging an interpreted meaning to the audience. You can organize a choral reading or a mimed reading. You can use music, visual art, clips from movies or TV, and/or other connected poems in your production. Make certain each member of the group has a part in the presentation.

Appendix B

MEIERS' INDEPENDENT PROJECT FOR ENGLISH: COLLECTING AND WRITING A PERSONAL ANTHOLOGY

1. Find a newspaper report about a subject that especially interests you. Here are some suggestions:

transportation	sports
the future	conservation
work	animals
war	people
new technology	robots
medical developments	computers

2. Keep a note of the date and name of the newspaper in which you found the article.

3. Discuss the article you have chosen with me, and then use it as the first piece in a personal anthology about the subject you have chosen.

4. The collection *must* include the following:
   - a title page
   - An introduction that explains your interest in this subject
   - a table of contents listing, in order, every piece of your collection and the name of the writer of each piece
   - a conclusion (see item 12)
   - twenty different pieces, made up of five short pieces of your own writing, and at least one of each of these kinds of writing:

poems	technical articles
short stories	factual information from
newspaper reports	various sources
cartoons	magazine articles
writing by other	letters
students	extracts from novels

   - The five pieces of your own writing should include different kinds of writing, too.

5. No photocopied material is to be included. Newspaper articles and cartoons must be cuttings taken directly from the newspaper (note the date and source). All other writing must be copied neatly in your own handwriting or on a word processor.

6. Marks will be given for presentation—cover, title page, headings, general neatness, illustrations, use of special features such as graphics and calligraphy, etc.

7. You can use looseleaf sheets bound into a special file, a special scrapbook, or a folder with plastic inserts.

8. In assessing your work, special attention will be paid to the accuracy of spelling, punctuation, setting out of dialogue, sentences, and paragraphs.

9. All class time until (due date) will be spent on this project, and you will also need to work at home. Some classes will be booked in the resource center (RC).

10. The newspapers in the RC are available as a source of materials. Check with the librarians about those that can be cut up.

11. Report regularly to me on the progress of your anthology, and ask for help whenever you need to. Make sure you check the first draft of your own writing with me.

12. When you have finished making your collection, write a short conclusion expanding what you learned while working on this project.

TEN TEXTUAL LEARNING STATIONS: MARK TWAIN'S *THE ADVENTURES OF HUCKLEBERRY FINN*

Each of these stations offers a different approach to the novel's life and ideas. Most will take a student or a group more than a period to complete. Each student will be required to complete six of the ten, and none can omit the first station. (More than any other, it brings the whole novel together for students.) We'll outline the activity of each station for considering Twain's *The Adventures of Huckleberry Finn*.[1]

1. River Chart

Your first station, river chart, is the only one that all of you will encounter in your two-week journey into Huck Finn's world.

1. Create a map of Huck's journey from the Widow Douglas's house in Missouri to the Phelps's farm in Arkansas.

2. For every recognizable spot on that river map, draw out a quote from Huck that explains how he feels about one person he encounters there. For instance, you might choose this quote concerning the Widow Douglas.

   That is the way it is with some people. They get down on a thing when they don't know a thing about it. Here she was bothering about Moses, which was no kin to her, an no use to anybody.

3. Tag the quote with your sense of what it says about Huck and his growth as he moves down the river.

4. After other maps are completed, compare your quotes to see how different readers trace the development of the main character, where he is at his best, and where he fails his own sense of himself. (Students who are taught Jane Loevinger's stages of ego development might use these concepts to mark Huck's developmental growth.)

2. What If . . . Huck Finn?

In Chapter 7 we presented a sample portion of an exercise that imaginatively placed Huck in the present. If you used that activity here, you might ask students to work alone and imagine Huck in the contemporary world. Here is another imagina-

---

[1] Parents and school districts have objected to the language and characterizations of Twain's novel since 1957 when the NAACP charged that it contained "racial slurs" and "belittling racial designations." We use it as illustration because it has a place in U.S. classrooms if its context is carefully established and because it is a novel with which most of our readers are familiar.

tive activity, which leaves Huck in his own nineteenth century and asks a group of students to speculate on his journey.

1. With a small group, brainstorm several pivotal moments in Huck's journey.
2. Discuss these questions about each pivotal moment: What if Huck had decided differently or the event did not take place or was replaced with another event? How might the story have ended?
3. As a group, rewrite Twain's novel by altering a decision or event and telling how the journey would have ended. For example, what if Huck had not gotten the raft back in Chapter 15? What would have happened to Jim?

Because this activity is intended as an explanation of the journey motif, your group's story should indicate how "your" journey influenced the development of Huck's character. Is the Huck at the end of your story the same person as the person Huck is at the end of Twain's story? If not, how is he different and why?

Remember that this story is a group effort and everyone must contribute. Have at least three people serve as secretary during the writing process.

3. Jim's Diary

1. Work alone with a tape recorder to try to capture what Jim might have been thinking and feeling as he moves along the river with Huck.
2. Focus on six specific incidents or locales.
3. Gather your thoughts and make a diarylike recording of your feelings about Huck, river society, and the day at hand.

These personal oral utterances should try to capture Jim's "voice," not in its oral dialect as much as in his own unique view of the world. (Remember that, tragically, teaching slaves to read and write was a crime in most states of the Confederacy.)

4. River Talk–Shore Speak

At this station you will have a chance to look at two kinds of language in Twain's dialect-rich book: river talk and shore speak. River talk is the language Huck uses when he is most touched by nature. We see it early in the text—not when he's on the river but when he is alone in his room at the Widow Douglas's and says,

> I set down in a chair by the window and tried to think of something cheerful, but it warn't no use. I felt so lonesome I most wished I was dead. The stars were chinning, and the leaves rustled in the woods ever so mournful, and I heard an owl, away off who-whooing about somebody that was dead, and a whippoorwill and a dog crying about somebody that was going to die; and the wind was trying to whisper something to me.

But it comes more often and more deeply when he's on the river alone or with Jim. In contrast, his language is less natural when he's on shore:

> Buck said she could rattle off poetry like nothing. She didn't even have to stop to think. He said she would slap down a line, and if she couldn't find anything to rhyme

with it she would just scratch it out and slap down another one, and go ahead.

This language misleads the credulous Huck. The shore folk often incriminate themselves with their own words.

1. Select four pairs of utterance from significant points along the journey downstream representing these two different forms of language.
2. Put them on a chart.

Twain's Words

River Talk	Shore Speak
1.	
2.	
3.	
4.	

3. Next, on this same chart, try to decide the difference between the two language styles.

Description of Language Difference

River Talk	Shore Speak
1.	
2.	
3.	
4.	

4. Assume the language style of these characters and complete the chart by writing your reaction to the opposite character's language.

Your Imaginative Response

River Talk About Shore Dwellers	Shore Speak About Huck
1.	
2.	
3.	
4.	

5. Now focus on Huck's famous dialect. Research by Shelley Fishkin (1993) suggests that Twain modelled Huck's voice on a ten-year-old black servant he called Jimmy. Twain himself said that the models for Huck were a poor white boy from Hannibal, Missouri, named Tom Blankenship and his brother Bence. The debate raises the possibilities of another language exercise.

Your final task is to look at Huck's language very carefully and determine whether it is closer to that of Jim or that of Tom or any of the other white boys in the novel. Look at the vocabulary, syntax, rhythm, and idiom to see how Huck's voice is similar to and different from the novel's white and black characters. State your conclusion in a paragraph. Support it with specific examples.

5. Women's Portraits

1. Select the novel's most interesting female.
2. Project her and Huck or another character into a new scene in the novel.
3. Dramatize this scene in your mind. Study the woman carefully to imagine how she would react in a new situation. Reread the section of the novel where you will insert your vignette.

4. Share your ideas with another student. Discuss with your partner which of your ideas would work best.
5. Develop a written script together, revise it, rehearse it, and enact it in costume for the whole class.
6. After your enactment be prepared to discuss the following questions: Which delighted you? Deepened your sense of the novel? Enlarged your sense of the female character? Would your class's collaborative sense of women have been comfortable to Twain, or does it reflect a twenty-first-century consciousness?

(You can see that this extension of women's portraits requires a much longer expenditure of time. More important to its success is a teacher's energy and enthusiasm. Its payoff is equal to its risk, though: to invite students to become creative collaborators with Twain.)

6. Scams

1. List as many scams—tricks, disguises, costumes, playacting—as you can remember in the novel.
2. Compare your list with at least three other classmates'.
3. Review the lists by yourself or with others and come up with two positive and two negative meanings that these acts of foul play and ingenuity may have for Twain's reader.

7. Aristocracy-Democracy

This station requires a tape recorder and a recorded dramatic reading of speech.

The Boggs-Sherburn incident is a landmark in Twain's novel. Their clash serves as the focal point for this station.

1. Listen to the spoken tape of Sherburn's speech to the crowd (Chapter 22).
2. Enumerate strategies of rhetoric that Sherburn employs. Name the persuasive technique and illustrate it from the speech.
3. Discuss the effect of his rhetoric on his audience.
4. List scenes in the novel that present the conflict between the natural, unspoiled American person and the restrained, socialized, and tradition-bound citizen.
5. Conclude this station by reflecting on this dilemma, which runs deeply through the entire text. To which of these two groups are you more drawn? Which group can you more easily imagine as being your friends?
6. To which group does Twain seem most sympathetic?

8. Mark Twain's Humor

This station requires two videotape clips, described below. This activity explores aspects of Mark Twain's humor. As you participate in this activity, you need to keep in mind these two definitions.

Burlesque—a ridiculous or devisive exaggeration of content or form

Parody—an imitation of a work of art for comic or critical purposes

1. Play the clip from *L.A. Story.* Then play the clip from *Hamlet.* If you wish, you can play the clip from *L.A. Story* again.
2. Decide whether the scene from *L.A. Story* is a burlesque or a parody. Write out your answer and explain your reasoning.
3. Now compare the Duke's version of Hamlet's soliloquy with the original text. Underline or note words and phrases that are in both speeches. Allow about three minutes for this activity and then play the next clip, which dramatizes this soliloquy.
4. Discuss these questions with others:
   • Is the Duke's version a burlesque or a parody? Why?
   • What do the words *bodkin* and *fardel* mean? Does the Duke preserve the meaning of the speech?
   • What is Huck's reaction to the Duke's rendition? Is this reaction typical of Huck? What is the significance of Huck's response?

9. Authentic Slave Narratives

1. Read excerpts from two authentic slave narratives: Frederick Douglass's (1845) autobiography, *Narrative of the Life of Frederick Douglass* and Harriet Jacobs's (1861) *Incidents in the Life of a Slave Girl.*
2. Reflect on the following questions: What were the ways Douglass and Jacobs resisted slavery? Do you think Jim's accommodation to slavery—"wearing the mask"—is wrong-headed and demeaning? Can you understand the differences in these three, all of whom lived in mid-nineteenth century America?
3. Imagine a conversation between Douglass, Jacobs, and Jim. They have just heard the song—"Nobody Knows the Trouble I've Seen." Write down what they might have said to each other as the song concludes.

10. Religious Professions

This final station uses Twain's "The War Prayer" as a guide to his regard for his character's religious beliefs.

1. Read Twain's short piece.
2. Pick out three characters in the novel who *appear* to be religious but may be less than devout.
3. Write down what those characters have said and, beside their words, the secret prayer they may in fact be uttering.

All private prayers might be collected, read orally by students, and developed into a pastiche of impious petitions.

FOUR TOPICAL LEARNING STATIONS: UTOPIA

The topical learning station may seem to be the stuff of humanities electives or social studies classes: investigations of myths and rituals, utopias, or ambition and identity. In fact, these topics on ideas which draw students into acts of reading, writing, talking and listening, and material (print and nonprint literature) are central to the goals of any expansive English curriculum.

We take the topic of utopias as an example of how stations might be developed to meet the goals of English teachers and the needs of their students. Each of four stations engages students in considering the ideal state: personally, socially, politically, and philosophically. Four teams of four to six students explore each. After completing them, each group is responsible for constructing a new utopia station. Each group must then complete two from this set of new stations. They move in graduated steps from the personal and immediate (their school) to the more distant (their culture and politics) to the universal (all life in all cultures). We leave that progression for students to discover for themselves after the total investigation of utopias is completed.

1. Draw a School

Draw the floor plan for the secondary school of tomorrow within the approximate limits of a school of today. Label the use of its different spaces. Try to imagine not just new architectural possibilities, but new ways of organizing the way we learn in school.

2. Brave New World

Divide into two groups with one or two observers. Choose one of the following two debate topics. Each group should make as strong an argument as possible using a rough debating format: two five-minute statements (pros, cons) followed by two-minute rebuttals (cons, pros).

1. Parents must pass courses in child development before they become licensed so as not to inundate society with children who are unprepared to become productive members of society.
2. Children should be inoculated with mood-stabilizing drugs to eliminate manic and depressive swings (both the source of psychic distress and, studies show, creativity).

3. USA II

1. Each of you works alone to list five possible major changes that might be made in our government or political system (for example, six-year presidential terms).
2. Pass your lists around your group so that each list is read by all members.
3. On each list you receive, check those suggestions that are the same as yours. Put a *1* by the suggestion you consider most important.
4. As a whole group, discuss the one or two proposals you would like to present to the whole class. Enumerate good reasons for the proposed changes. Brainstorm all the possible repercussions or results brought on by such a change. What does your chosen reform contribute to a more ideal country?

4. Imagine

Listen to John Lennon's song "Imagine" and discuss the ideal world that he envisions. Does his view of possessions, religion, or government make sense to you? If it does, add a verse about a new topic that is compatible with his ideas. If you don't like his ideas, write verses to a song that satirizes his personal utopia.

DAVIS'S LEARNING CENTERS: FAMILY[2]

I once created learning centers for high schoolers that allowed students to think about and create responses to vari-

---

[2]Teacher Meg Davis sent us a description of an example of learning centers that she had created and shared with another teacher through NCTE's Listserve. The teacher had asked for ideas about a culminating activity for a unit on family.

ous meanings, shapes and forms of family. I wonder if a similar culminating activity would be helpful for your students.

The setup included a constellation of four centers through which students moved and worked. The centers included a station in which students wrote a "recipe" for a family. I placed sample recipes and dictionaries and other word sources there. Each student created a sort of poem that combined his/her notion of family ingredients. The variety of these poems testified to and celebrated (and sometimes lamented because everyone's notion of family isn't positive) the myriad of ways we and literature conceptualized family.

Another center required students to listen to taped music that suggests various aspects of family. Carole King's or James Taylor's "You've Got a Friend," Rockapella and the Persuasions' "My Home," and Tracy Chapman's "Behind the Wall" were a few of the pieces to which students listened. After listening, students listed the various images of family in each of the songs.

Still another center invited students to make a human knot and to "untie" it by cooperating, listening, and acting to untangle it. A description of this activity is in the *New Games* book that came out in the 1980s. After participating in this exercise, students discussed the qualities required to make the untangling process work—qualities that are vital for the survival of a healthy interactive group (i.e., family).

At the fourth center, I spread a huge canvas (bulletin board paper) on the floor. Around the sheet, I placed many paints, colored pencils, construction paper, etc. for students to use as they created a class collage with their images and/or words of family.

We used this activity to introduce the unit on family. The experiences provided us with a wide range of ways to conceptualize family, so they served as reference points as we discussed various texts about family. This kind of activity could serve as an anticipatory introduction to a unit on family or it could be a summing up for students.

MAPPING YOUR WAY TO UNDERSTANDING: MYTHOLOGY

Teachers Elizabeth Braun, Sharon Feaster, Melissa Toth, and Lisa Weaver (2001) have demonstrated the power of concept mapping for curriculum design and development: planning and implementing an interdisciplinary course, mentoring between experienced and novice teachers, providing an alternative assessment for an inquiry-based project, and integrating technology into the curriculum. We present Weaver's creative ideas about using concept mapping for a unit on "Mythology" (Ten Steps to Mythology Mapping). Using Inspiration software (*www.inspiration.com/book/cm.html*), she and her students created the final concept map for their study (Weaver's Course Overview Map). Weaver's second of her ten steps uses an assessment of knowledge strategy she describes as K-W-L. She (2002, personal communication) describes the strategy as follows:

K What do students *know?*
W What do students *want* to know?
L (At the conclusion of the study) What have students *learned?*

She even sometimes uses large butcher paper to hang on the walls with student answers to these questions. The class textbook is Rosenberg, D. (1998). *World mythology: An anthology of the great myths and epics,* 3rd edition. Lincolnwood, IL: NTC Publishing Group.

TEN STEPS TO MYTHOLOGY MAPPING

Mapping a path to understanding myths

1. Use concept map as planning tool to create lesson/unit/semester plan.
    *   Generate key topics, questions, and concepts to be covered
    *   Provide a visual reference for course of study
2. Define mythology as introductory activity.
    *   Utilize K-W-L strategy to determine knowledge base
    *   Categorize our knowledge: Legend, Hero, and Type of Myth
3. Brainstorm purposes of myths and mythology.
    *   Review types of myths: Etiological, entertaining, historical
4. Categorize purposes generated from brainstorming.
    *   Create initial concept map
5. Jigsaw introductory information for mythology text—*World Mythology.*
    *   Students read assigned topics to gather information on purposes of myths
    *   "Expert teams" discuss information and prepare "Expert findings"
6. Jigsaw groups present.
    *   "Expert teams" prepare presentations of their reading/research
    *   "Experts" present
7. Prepare concept map as course overview from "Expert" information (Weaver's Course Overview Map)
8. Read, discuss, present, and research myths in Greek mythology.
    *   Learn concept mapping software with Computer Information students
    *   Conceptualize a hero
9. For semester review, return to course overview map to locate examples, representations, and selections for recognizing concepts in mythology.
10. Create semester exam with original maps.
    *   Identify three purposes of myths
    *   Select three example myths or selections to illustrate and define concept
    *   Create an original concept map

Weaver's Course Overview Map

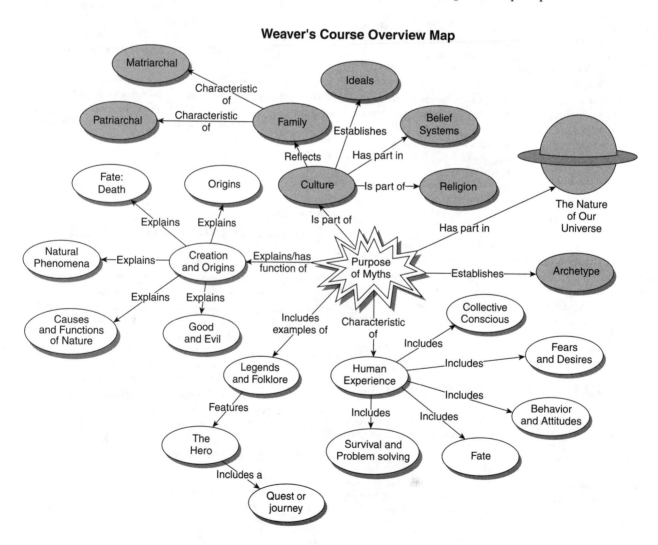

Appendix C

OVERVIEW OF OLD, MIDDLE, AND MODERN ENGLISH

Old English Period (450–1066). The invading German tribes found a Celtic people recently abandoned by withdrawing Roman legions. The language of these sea raiders almost completely replaced the Celtic language but was itself influenced by St. Augustine's conversion of the English to Christianity in 597 and then by successive invasions from Scandinavia. In the course of this six hundred-year history, the language developed characteristic sounds, inflections (a word's change in form to mark distinctions such as gender, number, and tense), vocabulary, and word order.

Sound: The sound system apparently was similar to modern Dutch or German.

Inflection: Nouns, pronouns, articles, adjectives, verbs, and adverbs were inflected for gender, case, and number.

Vocabulary: The word stock was primarily Germanic. Of the few Celtic words that remained, most were place names such as *London* and *Avon*. The tribes brought a few Latin words from the Roman occupation; Christian conversion brought many more. Scandinavian invasions added vocabulary, but most important, changed the third-person plural form of the personal pronoun with the addition of *th*-forms (i.e., "their").

Word order: The extensive use of inflections made word order extremely flexible.

During this period, Latin became the universal language for learned use. Late in the period, Alfred the Great (d. 899) struggled to make English (the vernacular) accepted for religious and governmental purposes.

Middle English Period (1066–1500). With the invasion of the Normans in 1066, English became unacceptable for cultivated purposes, especially governmental administration. Latin retained its preeminent status and French became the vehicle for government, law, poetry, and history. It was the second language, after Latin, in the developing universities. Because almost all writing in English ceased, there was no stabilizing force for the language. Consequently, change accelerated, foreign influences became more potent, and regional differences more pronounced.

Sound: The guttural sounds of German weakened, and vowel distinctions blurred.

Inflection: Inflections lost their distinctness and later disappeared. Many linguists regard the loss of grammatical gender as one of the most important developments in the history of the English language.

Vocabulary: Latin borrowings grew, and thousands of French words were added. French linguistic influence was almost entirely confined to vocabulary.

Word order: With the loss of inflections, sentence word order became more rigid, and auxiliary verbs became more common. Most sentences followed a subject-verb-complement pattern. Relationships were indicated by prepositions and other connecting words.

Chaucer, writing toward the end of this period, worried that with no authoritative standard of English, readers would not be able to understand his book. Its spelling ("myswrite") and pronunciation ("mysmetre") would be unfamiliar in this great "diversite" of language:

And for ther is so gret diversite
In Englissh and in writyng of oure tonge,
So prey I God that non myswrite the,
Ne the mysmetre for defaute of tonge.
And red wherso thow be, or elles songe,
That thow be understonde, God I biseche!
> (*Troilus and Criseyde*, Book 5: 1793-1798)

Chaucer prays that, despite English's diversity, his book will be understood, whether read or heard.

Modern English Period (1500–present). Near the beginning of this period, when the structure of English was changing and writers enjoyed greater grammatical freedom, Shakespeare took advantage of this opportunity for verbal expansion. Modern English has since grown stable in its basic sounds, vocabulary, syntax, and semantics through diverse forces: the development of the printing press, the education of large numbers of people, the spread of English through the expansion of the British Empire, and its present adoption as the linguistic currency of international trade and diplomacy.

Sound: The great vowel shift in the sixteenth and seventeenth centuries changed the pronunciation of many words.

Inflection: Inflections disappeared.

Vocabulary: English freely borrowed words from many languages. One of the most interesting developments was the second person pronoun. *Thou* (nominative), *thee* (objective), and *thy* and *thine* (possessive) gave way to *you* (nominative and objective) and *your* (possessive).

Word order: Sentence word order became more firmly fixed. Present dialectical differences now tend to be in pronunciation or vocabulary.

Many regard American English as a dialect of British English whose sounds and grammar deviate very little from its source and whose primary difference is one of vocabulary. We Americans have put original English words to new uses, formed new compounds, and appropriated the words first of Native Americans and then of immigrant groups.

GRAMMAR IN A NUTSHELL

Diana Purser's (1996) "Grammar in a Nutshell" is a graphic organizer that provides both a visual jigsaw puzzle and a roadmap through the study of grammar. Her chart is color-coded: red for "nouns and noun substitutes"; blue for verbs; green for modifiers; yellow "for prepositions, coordinate and subordinate conjunctions"; and orange "for special cases like interjections" (p. 108). (Teachers can ask students to color the sections themselves.) Purser directs students to cut the chart into sections, place each section in a sealed plastic bag, and label each bag. Then as she presents the grammatical concepts, students paste the pertinent puzzle pieces on a blank chart that she provides. Her scheme allows the teacher to choose the pace and sequence of presentation—for instance, slower and yearlong for seventh grade students and quicker and more concentrated for twelfth grade students. She schedules writing between presentations so that students have "soak time" for the concepts and she and they have a shared vocabulary with which to examine literature and

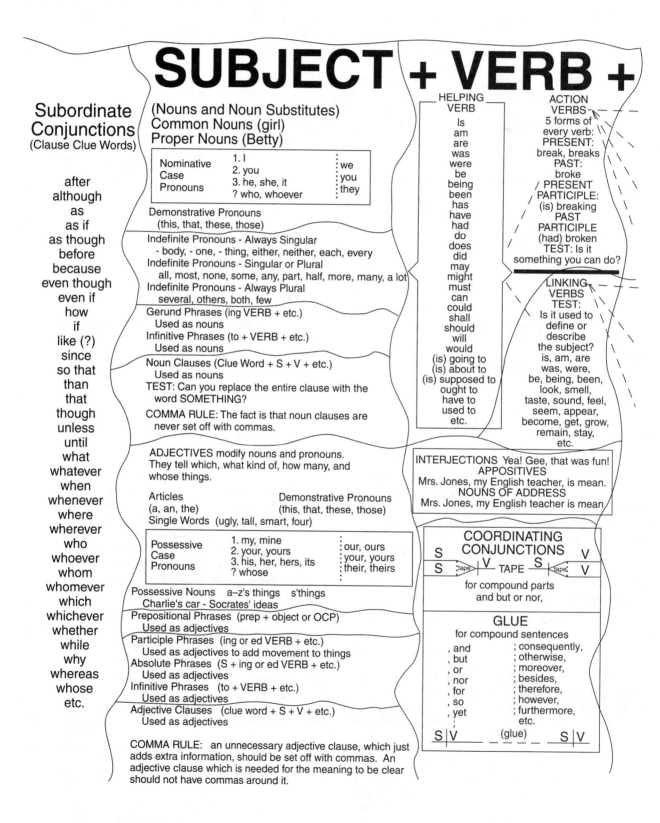

SUBJECT + VERB +

Subordinate Conjunctions
(Clause Clue Words)

after
although
as
as if
as though
before
because
even though
even if
how
if
like (?)
since
so that
than
that
though
unless
until
what
whatever
when
whenever
where
wherever
who
whoever
whom
whomever
which
whichever
whether
while
why
whereas
whose
etc.

(Nouns and Noun Substitutes)
Common Nouns (girl)
Proper Nouns (Betty)

Nominative Case Pronouns	1. I / 2. you / 3. he, she, it / ? who, whoever	we / you / they

Demonstrative Pronouns
(this, that, these, those)

Indefinite Pronouns - Always Singular
- body, - one, - thing, either, neither, each, every
Indefinite Pronouns - Singular or Plural
all, most, none, some, any, part, half, more, many, a lot
Indefinite Pronouns - Always Plural
several, others, both, few

Gerund Phrases (ing VERB + etc.)
Used as nouns
Infinitive Phrases (to + VERB + etc.)
Used as nouns
Noun Clauses (Clue Word + S + V + etc.)
Used as nouns
TEST: Can you replace the entire clause with the word SOMETHING?
COMMA RULE: The fact is that noun clauses are never set off with commas.

ADJECTIVES modify nouns and pronouns. They tell which, what kind of, how many, and whose things.

Articles   Demonstrative Pronouns
(a, an, the)   (this, that, these, those)
Single Words (ugly, tall, smart, four)

Possessive Case Pronouns	1. my, mine / 2. your, yours / 3. his, her, hers, its / ? whose	our, ours / your, yours / their, theirs

Possessive Nouns   a–z's things   s'things
Charlie's car - Socrates' ideas
Prepositional Phrases (prep + object or OCP)
Used as adjectives
Participle Phrases (ing or ed VERB + etc.)
Used as adjectives to add movement to things
Absolute Phrases (S + ing or ed VERB + etc.)
Used as adjectives
Infinitive Phrases (to + VERB + etc.)
Used as adjectives
Adjective Clauses (clue word + S + V + etc.)
Used as adjectives

COMMA RULE: an unnecessary adjective clause, which just adds extra information, should be set off with commas. An adjective clause which is needed for the meaning to be clear should not have commas around it.

HELPING VERB
Is
am
are
was
were
be
being
been
has
have
had
do
does
did
may
might
must
can
could
shall
should
will
would
(is) going to
(is) about to
(is) supposed to
ought to
have to
used to
etc.

ACTION VERBS
5 forms of every verb:
PRESENT: break, breaks
PAST: broke
PRESENT PARTICIPLE: (is) breaking
PAST PARTICIPLE (had) broken
TEST: Is it something you can do?

LINKING VERBS
TEST:
Is it used to define or describe the subject?
is, am, are
was, were,
be, being, been,
look, smell,
taste, sound, feel,
seem, appear,
become, get, grow,
remain, stay,
etc.

INTERJECTIONS Yea! Gee, that was fun!
APPOSITIVES
Mrs. Jones, my English teacher, is mean.
NOUNS OF ADDRESS
Mrs. Jones, my English teacher is mean

COORDINATING CONJUNCTIONS
S   V
S   tape   V   TAPE   S   tape   V
for compound parts
and but or nor,

GLUE
for compound sentences
, and   ; consequently,
, but   ; otherwise,
, or   ; moreover,
, nor   ; besides,
, for   ; therefore,
, so   ; however,
, yet   ; furthermore,
;   etc.
S | V   (glue)   S | V

language together. She believes that "Grammar in a Nutshell" allows students to:

- build upon basic concepts "as they move into more complex structures—without getting lost in the process" (p. 108-109)

- understand the "interrelatedness of the parts of our language" (p. 109)
- experience the cumulative effect of their learning that remains visually before them
- review old learning each time a new concept is introduced
- profit from visual and kinesthetic clues to grammar.

(COMPLEMENT)

No Complement
Intransitive Action Verbs
(I waited.)

Objective Case Pronouns	1. me 2. you 3. him, her, it ? whom, whomever	us you them

Reflective Case Pronouns	1. myself 2. yourself 3. himself, herself, itself	ourselves yourselves themselves

Direct Objects
Transitive Action Verbs
(The car hit Pat!)   TEST: S + Action V + What?

Direct Objects + Object Complements
(Tr. Action Verbs which imply a changing of something)
(We painted our bedroom hot pink.)

Indirect Objects + Direct Objects
(Tr. Action Verbs which imply a "handling over" of something)
(She mailed her sister a present.)
TEST: S + Action V + DIRECT OBJECT + to whom? for whom?

Predicate Nouns
TEST: The subject is A WHAT?
(My dad is a photographer.)
Predicate Pronouns N C P's
("May I speak to Charlie?" "Yes, this is he.")

Predicate Adjectives
TEST: What is the subject like?
(She is very nice and considerate.)
Predicate Possessive Pronouns P C P's
(This book is mine.)

Predicate Adverbs
TEST: WHERE or WHEN is the subject?
(There is my pencil.) (The party is tomorrow.)

ADVERBS modify verbs, adjectives and other adverbs.★

They tell how, when, where, why, and on what condition the events happen.

Single words (quickly, tonight, here)
Negative Adverbs (not, n't, never)
*Intensifiers (very, too, rather, really)

Prepositional Phrases (prep + object or OCP)
Used as adverbs

Infinitive Phrases (to + VERB + etc.)
Used as adverbs

Adverb Clauses (clue words + S + V + etc.)
Used as adverbs

COMMA RULE: When an adverb clause starts the sentence, it should have a comma after it. No commas are usually needed when the clause comes later in the sentence.

Prepositions

about	in front of
above	inside
according to	instead of
across	in spite of
after	into
against	like
ahead of	minus
along	near
alongside	of
along with	off
amid	on
among	onto
around	opposite
as well as	out
at	outside
before	over
behind	past
below	plus
beneath	prior to
beside	since
besides	through
between	throughout
beyond	till
by	to
but (except)	together with
concerning	toward
despite	under
down	underneath
due to	up
during	upon
except	up to
for	until
from	via
in	with
in addition to	within
in between	without
	etc.

Source: © 1987, 1992 by Diana Purser, Nutshell Educational Products, 2925 Cambridge Court, Bartlesville, OK 74006, www.nutshellpuzzle.com. All rights reserved. Reprinted with permission.

FOUR AREAS OF LINGUISTIC STUDY

Historical Linguistics. Some linguists study changes in language that occur over time in order to establish relationships among languages and trace their historical development. To such linguists as Jacob Grimm in the nineteenth century, we owe our early knowledge of the evolution of language. Today the field is so immense that, as linguist Raven I. McDavid, Jr. (1985) acknowledges, even detailed histories of the language are "bound to be overviews" (p. 288).[3]

Descriptive Linguistics. All linguistic study is basically descriptive, but twentieth-century anthropologists such as Edward Sapir and phoneticians such as Henry Higgins of *Pygmalion* fame made the description of written and spoken language more exact. Techniques of transcription developed throughout the twentieth century that allowed the collection of massive amounts of data about many aspects of different speech communities. A systematic investigation was undertaken in 1931 to collect data for a *Linguistic Atlas of the United States and Canada,* for instance, and is not yet finished. Descriptive linguists regard language as an artifact to be collected, explored,

and catalogued. They see language as a matter of culture, habit, and convention, not as a matter of logic and correctness.

Psychological/Sociological Linguistics. A diverse and interdisciplinary group of linguists from various subspecialties in psychology, sociology, and even anthropology study the way in which language works in the lives of individuals and the larger society as an integral part of the individual and of group culture. They study the psychological/sociological mechanisms of language acquisition and linguistic behavior and the impact they have on users. Benjamin Lee Whorf studied the Hopi Indians of Arizona, for instance, and through that study formulated what is for us the most fascinating hypothesis in the field of linguistics: that the structure of one's language influences how one perceives and understands one's world.

Structural Linguistics. Other twentieth-century linguists stressed the structural aspect of language, its systematic form and internal organization. They have worked to describe and penetrate its deep structure. They are interested in the particularity of a language and analyze each on its own terms. The academic study of language structures entered school grammars with Noam Chomsky's (1957) publication of *Syntactic Structures.* His transformational and generative grammar represents a different approach to language rules, not as consciously and systematically developed dogmas, but as patterns emerging unconsciously from the human mind.

---

[3]The field of comparative linguistics originated with eighteenth-century historical dialect studies, but its practitioners separated from historical linguists to compare language systems existing in different cultures at a given point in time.

TIME LINE OF METHODS OF LINGUISTIC ANALYSIS

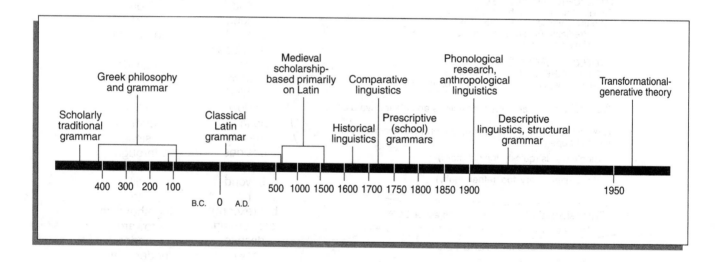

Appendix D

WEB SITES FOR CLASSIC AND CONTEMPORARY SHORT STORIES

General Resources for Full Texts

The Classic Short Stories Website:
http://www.bergtraum.k12.ny.us/cybereng/shorts/
The Short Story Classics: The Best From The Masters Of The Genre
http://www.geocities.com/short_stories_page/index.html

Specific Story/Author Sites

"A Rose for Emily":
William Faulkner on the Web
http://www.mcsr.olemiss.edu/~egjbp/faulkner/faulkner.html

"A Rose for Emily" Resources
http://www.mcsr.olemiss.edu/~egjbp/faulkner/r_ss_roseforemily.html

"The Sky is Gray"
Perspectives in American Literature: A Research and Reference Guide on Ernest Gaines (on the author, his life, his themes)
http://www.csustan.edu/english/reuben/pal/chap10/gaines.html

"I Stand Here Ironing"
Tillie Olsen
http://mockingbird.creighton.edu/NCW/olsen.htm

"Harrison Bergeron"
The Vonnegut Web
http://www.duke.edu/~crh4/vonnegut/vonnegut.html

ERIKSON'S STAGES OF PSYCHOSOCIAL DEVELOPMENT

Age Period	Focal Crisis	Determinants
0–2 years	Trust versus mistrust	If parents meet the preponderance of the infant's needs, the child develops a stronger sense of trust than of mistrust.
2–4 years	Autonomy versus shame or doubt	If parents reward the child's successful actions and do not shame his or her failures (say in bowel or bladder control), the child's sense of autonomy will outweigh the sense of shame and doubt.
4–6 years	Initiative versus guilt	If parents accept the child's curiosity and do not put down the need to know and to question, the child's sense of initiative will outweigh the sense of guilt.
7–12 years	Industry versus inferiority	If the child encounters more success than failure at home and at school, he or she will have a greater sense of industry than of inferiority.
13–18 years	Identity versus role diffusion	If the young person can reconcile diverse roles, abilities, and values and see continuity with past and future, the sense of personal identity will not give way to a sense of role diffusion.
19–35 years	Intimacy versus isolation	With a sufficiently strong sense of personal identity, one can give much of oneself to another person without feeling a loss of identity. The person who cannot do this experiences a sense of loneliness.
35–55 years	Generativity versus stagnation	The individual who has had children or produced some meaningful work invests much in those children and/or work as continuities of personal identity that will persist when the personal identity no longer does. The person who cannot so invest himself or herself experiences a sense of stagnation, of standing still rather than of growing.
55–	Integrity versus despair	The individual who has attained a sense of personal identity, intimacy, and generativity can look back upon life as having been well spent and can accept death without regrets. But the individual who reaches old age without having involved himself or herself in other people or work experiences a sense of despair at a life ill spent.

Kohlberg's Stages of Moral Development

Stages	*Characteristics*
PRECONVENTIONAL LEVEL Good or bad, right or wrong, labels are interpreted in terms of physical power. The basic frame of reference for moral decisions is the self.	1. *Punishment and obedience.* Physical consequences of an action determine if it's good or bad. Avoidance of punishment is valued. 2. *Satisfy one's own needs and sometimes others.* "You scratch my back and I'll scratch yours," instead of loyalty, gratitude, and justice. If fairness and sharing are present, they are viewed in terms of one's personal needs. 3. *"Good boy–nice girl."* Good behavior is that which pleases or helps others and therefore is approved by them. Much conformity to stereotypical images.
CONVENTIONAL LEVEL Maintaining expectations of others is valued regardless of consequences. Loyalty to and support of the established order. The concern with self is incorporated into an awareness of groupness.	4. *Law and order.* Authority, fixed rules, and maintaining the social order are valued. Right behavior is doing one's "duty" and showing respect for authority. 5. *Individual rights.* Utilitarian overtones. Awareness of personal values and openness. Other than that which is constitutionally and democratically agreed upon, right is a matter of personal value and opinion.
POSTCONVENTIONAL LEVEL Individual reaches a personal definition of moral values, principles that are valid and applicable apart from authority. Groups and their laws are important, but principles underlie them.	6. *Universal ethics.* Abstract and ethical principles (Golden Rule) not concrete moral codes like the Ten Commandments. Justice, human rights, respect for the dignity of human beings as individuals are valued.

Loevinger's Stages of Ego Development

Stages	*Character Style*
Impulsive	Fear of retaliation, dependent, aggressive, conceptual confusion
Self-protective	Fear of being caught, manipulative, conceptual cohesion
Conformist	Guilt for rule breaking, superficial niceness, social acceptability, conceptual simplicity
Conscientious	Self-criticism, responsible, self-respect, conceptual complexity
Autonomous	Coping with inner conflict, respect for autonomy, body-psyche integration, increased conceptual complexity
Integrated	Reconciling inner conflict, cherishing of individuality, identity, tolerance of ambiguity

Rabinowitz's Rules of Notice

These rules, or conventions, are governed by culture, genre, and history. Although they are always open to change, they present an illuminating methodology of the way in which writers shape a text and readers read it.

Rules of notice raise the question "What should we notice?" They help readers to establish which characters are important and which are minor; which details of plot are significant and which need only passing attention. Cues can be very simple, such as titles, typography, or paragraphing. They can include more complex ideas such as the extra weighting given to the first or last sentence in a unit. Interruptions and deviations also attract notice. "Different norms characterize different sets of narratives; what stands out as deviant, therefore, depends not only on social context but also on the intertextual grid against which the text is read" (Rabinowitz, 1987, p. 70). In other words, readers will perceive different details as noteworthy if the text is seen as romance rather than mystery.

Rules of signification provoke the question "What is significant about what we notice?" They assist readers in deciding how much and what kind of attention we pay to what we have decided to notice. They help us to establish the source of a particular sentence or idea: author, narrator, or character (reliable or unreliable). They assist us in making ethical judgments about characters or situations, in working out the relationship of the particular fictional world to the real world, in establishing causes and effects. The author makes use of conventional cues to enable us to sort out how to attend to whatever we decide is important.

Rules of configuration play off the first two rules and grind the text more finely: How do its various elements hang together? They are used to help the reader fit the pieces of the text into a whole. These are the conventions that activate expectations—if certain elements appear in a certain arrangement, we expect a certain kind of outcome. Even if these expectations are confounded at the end of the story, they still play a role in how we approach the text. Rabinowitz suggests that "if too many of these activated expectations are ignored, readers may find the results dull or chaotic" (p. 113). Rules of configuration vary according to genre, but Rabinowitz says there are two general "metarules" of configuration: "First it is appropriate to expect that *some*thing will happen. Second, it is appropriate to expect that not *any*thing can happen" (p. 117).

Rules of coherence are applied retrospectively and ask, "Given the completed piece, what can we conclude?" As readers approach the end of the text, they attempt to make sense of it as a whole. "We assume, to begin with, that the work *is* coherent and that apparent flaws in its construction are intentional and meaning bearing" (p. 147). We must come to terms with what has been left out and with what seems to be surplus or excessive, reshaping the story in our minds to make sense of what is given. Rules of coherence also involve the interpretation of patterns—both within the text and in relationship to other texts.

Appendix E

U.S. POET LAUREATES, 1937–2001

From 1937-1986 poets held the post of Poetry Chair or Consultantship in Poetry in the English Language at the Library of Congress. Robert Penn Warren (in his second term) was the first poetry consultant to the Library of Congress who was called Poet Laureate.

- Joseph Auslander, 1937-1941 (*his appointment to the poetry chair had no fixed term*)
- Allen Tate, 1943-1944
- Robert Penn Warren, 1944-1945
- Louise Bogan, 1945-1946
- Karl Shapiro, 1946-1947
- Robert Lowell, 1947-1948
- Leonie Adams, 1948-1949
- Elizabeth Bishop, 1949-1950
- Conrad Aiken, 1950-1952 (*first to serve two terms*)
- William Carlos Williams (*appointed in 1952 but did not serve*)
- Randall Jarrell, 1956-1958
- Robert Frost, 1958-1959
- Richard Eberhart, 1959-1961
- Louis Untermeyer, 1961-1963
- Howard Nemerov, 1963-1964
- Reed Whittemore, 1964-1965
- Stephen Spender, 1965-1966
- James Dickey, 1966-1968
- William Jay Smith, 1968-1970
- William Stafford, 1970-1971
- Josephine Jacobsen, 1971-1973
- Daniel Hoffman, 1973-1974
- Stanley Kunitz, 1974-1976
- Robert Hayden, 1976-1978
- William Meredith, 1978-1980
- Maxine Kumin, 1981-1982
- Anthony Hecht, 1982-1984
- Robert Fitzgerald, 1984-1985 (*appointed and served in a health-limited capacity but did not come to the Library of Congress*)
- Reed Whittemore, 1984-1985 (*interim Consultant in Poetry*)
- Gwendolyn Brooks, 1985-1986
- Robert Penn Warren, 1986-1987 (*first to be designated Poet Laureate Consultant in Poetry*)
- Richard Wilbur, 1987-1988
- Howard Nemerov, 1988-1990
- Mark Strand, 1990-1991
- Joseph Brodsky, 1991-1992
- Mona Van Duyn, 1992-1993
- Rita Dove, 1993-1995
- Robert Hass, 1995-1997
- Robert Pinsky, 1997-2000 (*first to serve three consecutive terms*)
- Rita Dove, Louise Glück, and W. S. Merwin, 1999-2000 (*Special bicentennial consultants*)
- Stanley Kunitz, 2000-2001
- Billy Collins, 2001-2003

BECKY BROWN'S FAVORITE POEMS FOR STUDENT RESPONSES

Poet	*Poem*
Edmund Spenser (1552-1599)	*One day I wrote her name upon the strands*
William Shakespeare (1564-1616)	*Let me not to the marriage of true minds*
	When, in disgrace with fortune and men's eyes
	That time of year thou mayest in me behold
John Donne (1572-1631)	Song: *Go and Catch a Falling Star*
	The Indifferent
	A Valediction: Forbidding Mourning
George Herbert (1593-1633)	*The Pulley*
John Dryden (1631-1700)	*A Song for St. Cecilia's Day*
Alexander Pope (1688-1744)	from *An Essay on Man*
William Blake (1757-1827)	*The Lamb*
	The Tyger
	London
	Infant Sorrow
	The Chimney Sweeper (from *Songs of Innocence*)
	The Chimney Sweeper (from *Songs of Experience*)

William Wordsworth (1770–1850)
The World is Too Much with Us
Anecdote for Fathers
The Tables Turned
London, 1802
Nuns Fret Not at Their Convent's Narrow Room

John Keats (1795–1821)
To Autumn
Bright Star

Elizabeth Barrett Browning (1806–1861)
How do I love thee?

Walt Whitman (1819–1892)
A Noiseless Patient Spider

Matthew Arnold (1828–1888)
Dover Beach

Dante Gabriel Rossetti (1828–1882)
Sudden Light

Emily Dickinson (1830–1886)
There's a Certain Slant of Light,
One Need Not Be a Chamber—To Be Haunted
The Last Night That She Lived

Thomas Hardy (1840–1928)
The Man He Killed

Gerard Manley Hopkins (1844–1889)
Pied Beauty

A. E. Housman (1859–1936)
To an Athlete Dying Young
When I Was One-and-Twenty
Loveliest of Trees

William Butler Yeats (1865–1939)
The Lake Isle of Innisfree
The Magi
When You Are Old
Sailing to Byzantium
Leda and the Swan

Edwin Arlington Robinson (1869–1935)
Richard Cory

Robert Frost (1874–1963)
The Telephone
A Considerable Speck
Mending Wall
The Objection to Being Stepped On
"Out, Out—"
Choose Something Like a Star

Don Marquis (1878–1937)
The Lesson of the Moth

Wallace Stevens (1879–1955)
Thirteen Ways of Looking at a Blackbird
The Snow Man

William Carlos Williams (1883–1963)
Landscape with the Fall of Icarus
The Yachts
Tract

T. S. Eliot (1888–1965)
Journey of the Magi
The Hippopotamus

Camillo Sbarbaro (1888–1967)
Even If You Weren't My Father

Edna St. Vincent Millay (1892–1950)
An Ancient Gesture

Dorothy Parker (1893–1967)
Finis

e. e. cummings (1894–1962)
somewhere i have never traveled, gladly beyond
when faces called flowers float out of the ground
i thank you God for most this amazing
since feeling is first

Langston Hughes (1902–1967)
Theme for English B

Stevie Smith (1902–1971)
Not Waving but Drowning

C. Day Lewis (1904–1972)
Walking Away

Robert Penn Warren (1905–1989)
Original Sin: A Short Story

W. H. Auden (1907–1973)
Their Lonely Betters
Musée des Beaux Arts
Voltaire at Ferney

Theodore Roethke (1908–1963)
The Walking

Elizabeth Bishop (1911–1979)
One Art

Josephine Miles (1911–1985)
Family

John Berryman (1914–1972)
Winter Landscape

William Stafford (1914-1993)	*At Cove on the Crooked River*
Isabella Gardner (1915-1981)	*Collage of Echoes*
Joseph Langland (1917-)	*Hunters in the Snow: Breughel*
Gwendolyn Brooks (1917-2000)	*The Bean Eaters*
Lawrence Ferlinghetti (1919-)	*Dog*
May Swenson (1919-1989)	*Bleeding*
Howard Nemerov (1920-1991)	*Storm Windows*
Richard Wilbur (1921-)	*Advice to a Prophet*
	The Writer
	The Mill
	She
Philip Larkin (1922-1985)	*Aubade*
	Mr. Bleaney
Alan Dugan (1923-)	*Love Song: I and Thou*
Anthony Hecht (1923-)	*More Light! More Light!*
Denise Levertov (1923-1997)	*Life at War*
	The Secret
A. R. Ammons (1926-2001)	*Still*
	Reflective
	Terminus
	Reading
	The Role of Society in the Artist
Robert Bly (1926-)	*Driving to Town Late to Mail a Letter*
Robert Creeley (1926-)	*I Know a Man*
	The Rain
Anne Sexton (1928-1974)	*The Farmer's Wife*
John Wakeman (1928-)	*Love in Brooklyn*
Adrienne Rich (1929-)	*Living in Sin*
Gary Snyder (1930-)	*Milton by Firelight*
Sally Buckner (1931-)	*Aunt Maud*
Linda Pastan (1932-)	*Unveiling*
Sylvia Plath (1932-1963)	*The Colossus*
	Words
John Updike (1932-)	*Mosquito*
	Ex-Basketball Player
	The Great Scarf of Birds
Mark Strand (1934-)	*Eating Poetry*
Lois Holt (1935-)	*Southern Style*
Fred Chappell (1936-)	*Second Wind*
John Haines (1936-)	*Foreboding*
	And When the Green Man Comes
	The Tundra
Marge Piercy (1936-)	*If They Come in the Night*
	A Work of Artifice
	For the Young Who Want To
Ishmael Reed (1938-)	*Beware: Do Not Read This Poem*
Emily Herring Wilson (1939-)	*Up-One*
Martha Collins (1940-)	*The Story We Know*
Billy Collins (1941-)	*Schoolsville*
Paul Simon (1942-)	*Richard Cory*
Sharon Olds (1942-)	*The Race*
Nikki Giovanni (1943-)	*Linkage*
Jim Morrison (1943-1971)	*In Russia, the Czar, each year, granted—* (from *The Lords and New Creatures*)
Kathryn Stripling Byer (1944-)	*Daughter*
Robert Morgan (1944-)	*Catalogue*
Billy Joel (1949-)	*Allentown*
Edward Hirsch (1950-)	*For the Sleepwalkers*
	Execution
Paul Muldoon (1951-)	*Meeting the British*
Kaye Gibbons (1960-)	*Back Roads*

Kate Blackburn[4]	*Memo to the Caretaker*
Marcia Denius	*Family Receipts*
Becky Gould Gibson	*Getting Through*
Marie Howe	*What the Living Do*
Agnes McDonald	*Placing Markers*
Merry McDonnell	*Multiple Listings*

---

[4]Dates cannot be found for the remaining authors.

BROWN'S POETRY RESPONSE ASSIGNMENT, 1991–1992

Poetry is unique among the genres we study. Poems demand more than just reading. They want rereading, being read aloud, being memorized, and being understood when you are in different moods. They want your time and energy. They want to become a part of you. Sound a little eerie? Not really.

You have probably studied poetry before. You have probably taken a poem, answered a few questions about it for homework, talked about it in class for twenty minutes, and considered it "done." Not so. Poetry is not like that. It is alive, fluid, breathing, changing, and evolving even as you read this assignment. Why? Because *we* are alive, fluid, breathing, changing, and evolving.

I will give you, therefore, a collection of poems about every four weeks. The collections will be poems that reflect different time periods from early English literature to the present—perhaps from this week's *New Yorker*. I hope you find that after a while some of these poems stick in your memory, that they are difficult to get rid of, that they stake out a small place for themselves in your imagination. Indeed, I encourage you to memorize a few of these. (I will not test you on that; that is a gift you give yourself.) Read them out loud, read them quickly, read them slowly, and read them when you are in different moods. In other words, give these poems as many chances as possible to claim your attention. Carry them around with you.

Doing the above is the important part of the assignment. But this is a real world we live in, so I must ask you to *do* a couple of things:

1. Get a spiral-ring notebook with about ninety pages in it. Whenever I give you a collection of poems, write the name of each poem at the top of a page, giving each poem one page. Read all the poems *every week* and write no more than two or three sentences about what the poem says to you on the page designated for that poem. At the end of the four-week period, you should have nearly a full page of responses to the poem. The important aspect of this exercise is that you will have read the poem at least four times in four different moods. Notice how your perceptions of the poem change from week to week. I will check these notebooks at least once a quarter. Stay current. The successful completion of this part of the assignment is an *A*.

2. Every week when you do your responses in your notebook, choose one poem and write a longer response. This response should be about one page in length and should be turned in to me on the day I specify for your class period. (I stagger them so that I can respond appropriately.) I will not take these late. Successful completion of this assignment also will result in an *A. Put your response in the box provided for it on the bookshelf. I do not take them up—class time is valuable. You are responsible for leaving them in the box.*

At the end of the year, you will have accumulated all of these poems as part of your knowledge. This assignment should take no more than one to two hours weekly. If I were you, I would set aside a "poetry" evening to do it. Two warnings: Do not get behind on part 1 of the assignment. You do not know when I will ask to see your notebook. Turn your weekly responses in on time.

BROWN'S EXPLANATION OF HER POETRY ASSIGNMENT'S EVOLUTION

This poetry assignment is still evolving. It has gone through revision after revision over the past two decades. It was first developed because my students were passively waiting for me to tell them what poems mean. They waited until they heard that before they ventured interacting with themselves. Besides wanting them to become independent learners, I also wanted them to realize that they could read poetry for themselves. I wanted poetry to be *theirs*. By the regular attention to this assignment, students do become comfortable talking about poetry in their own language; and poetry is not relegated to a month's study in the spring, thereby isolating it and making it somehow mysterious.

I like the current revision of the assignment because students are asked to do a brief biography of one of the six poets and find and respond to five poems by that poet. While I've only done this a few years, I find it is more successful than the old notebook idea. Only a few students kept the notebook current; most simply changed colors of ink and wrote gibberish about the poems on the night before the notebook was to be checked! It was a good idea that didn't really work for many of my students. The newer assignment is better. Students have to read several poems by a poet before they choose five, and their responses to those chosen poems have more depth than if I had chosen them!

In selecting poems each month, I pick poems that I particularly like or that coordinate well with the other literature we are studying. Introducing these old friends to my students and hearing what they have to say about them continues to teach me wonderful new things.

BROWN'S POETRY RESPONSE ASSIGNMENT, 2001–2002

Poetry is unique among the genres we study. Poems demand more than just reading. They want rereading, being read aloud, being memorized, and being understood when you are in different moods. They want your time and energy. They want to become a part of you. Sound a little eerie? Not really.

You have probably studied poetry before. You have probably taken a poem, answered a few questions about it for homework, talked about it in class for twenty minutes, and considered it "done." Not so. Poetry is not like that. It is alive, fluid, breathing, changing, and evolving even as you read this assignment. Why? Because *we* are alive, fluid, breathing, changing, and evolving.

I will give you, therefore, a collection of six poems about every four weeks. The collections will be poems that reflect different time periods from early English literature to the present—perhaps from this week's *New Yorker*. I hope you find that after a while some of these poems become a part of you, that they are difficult to get rid of, that they stake out a small place for themselves in your imagination. I encourage you to memorize a few. (I will not test you on that; that is a gift you give yourself.) Read them out loud, quickly, slowly, and when you are in different moods. In other words, give these poems as many chances as possible to become a part of you.

Doing the above is the important part of the assignment. But this is a real world we live in, so I must ask you to *do* a couple of things:

1. Choose one poem every week and write a response. This response should be about one page in length and should be turned in to me on the day that I specify for your class period. (I stagger them so that I can respond appropriately.) **I will not take these late.** Successful completion of this assignment will result in an "*A.*" *You are responsible for leaving them with me as you leave class on the day they are due. I may not ask for them.*

2. After the second week with these poems, choose one of the poets you would like to get to know better. Do some biographical research on that poet and jot down the pertinent information (you be the judge of what that is—it will vary with the degree of your genuine interest) about him/her. Copy (or make copies) of at least five other poems by this poet and write two or three sentences about why you chose each of them. I may ask that you choose one to present to the class. Turn in the report on the poet, the poems, and your comments on the day specified on your syllabus. These will be graded according to the depth of the comment and care you give the assignment.

At the end of the year, you will have accumulated all of these poems and poets as a part of your knowledge. My goal is to introduce you to some sustaining poetry—sustaining for both your personal and academic life.

BOOKS ON POETRY AND POETRY TEACHING

Alderson, D. (1996). *Talking back to poems: A working guide for the aspiring poet.* Berkeley, CA: Celestial Arts Publishing.

Behn, R., & Twichell, C. (Eds.). (1992). *The practice of poetry: Writing exercises from poets who teach.* New York: HarperCollins.

Bizzaro, P. (1993). *Responding to student poems: Applications of critical theory.* Urbana, IL: NCTE.

Brown, B., & Glass, M. (1991). *Important words: A book for poets and writers.* Portsmouth, NH: Heinemann.

Brown, R., Hoffman, M., Dushner, M., Lopate, P., & Murphy, S. (1972). *The whole word catalogue, vol. 1.* New York: Teachers & Writers Collaborative.

Collum, J., & Noethe, S. (1994). *Poetry everywhere: Teaching poetry writing in school and in the community.* New York: Teachers & Writers Collaborative.

Duke, C., & Jacobsen, S. (Eds.). (1992). *Poets' perspectives: Reading, writing, and teaching poetry.* Portsmouth, NH: Boynton/Cook.

Dunning, S., & Stafford, W. (1992). *Getting the knack: 20 poetry writing exercises.* Urbana, IL: NCTE.

Fagin, L. (1991). *The list poem: A guide to teaching and writing catalog verse.* New York: Teachers & Writers Collaborative.

Grossmann, F. (1991). *Listening to the bells: Learning to read poetry by writing poetry.* Portsmouth, NH: Boynton/Cook.

Heard, G. (1989). *For the good of the earth and sun: Teaching poetry.* Portsmouth, NH: Heinemann.

Hewitt, G. (1998). *Today you are my favorite poet: Writing poems with teenagers.* Portsmouth, NH: Boynton/Cook.

Johnson, D. M. (1990). *Word weaving: A creative approach to teaching and writing poetry.* Urbana, IL: NCTE.

Koch, K. (1973). *Rose, where did you get that red? Teaching great poetry to children.* New York: Random House.

Koch, K., & Farrell, K. (1981). *Sleeping on the wing: An anthology of modern poetry with essays on reading and writing.* New York: Vintage.

Lies, L. B. (1993). *The poet's pen: Writing poetry with middle and high school students.* Englewood, CO: Teacher Ideas Press.

Livingston, M. C. (1984). *Child as poet: Myth or reality?* Boston: Horn Books.

Morice, D. (1995). *The adventures of Dr. Alphabet: 104 unusual ways to write poetry in the classroom and the community.* New York: Teachers & Writers Collaborative.

Moyers, B., & Haba, J. (Eds.). (1995). *The language of life: A festival of poets.* New York: Doubleday.

Nims, J. F. (1974). *Western wind: An introduction to poetry.* New York: Random House.

Padgett, R. (Ed.). (1987). *The teachers' and writers' handbook of poetic forms.* New York: Teachers & Writers Collaborative.

Somers, A. B. (1999). *Teaching poetry in high school.* Urbana, IL: NCTE.

Thomas, L. (Ed.). (1998). *Sing the sun up: Creative writing ideas from African American literature.* New York: Teachers & Writers Collaborative.

Tsujimoto, J. I. (1988). *Teaching poetry writing to adolescents.* Urbana, IL: NCTE.

Wormser, B., & Cappella, D. (2000). *Teaching the art of poetry: The moves.* Mahwah, NJ: Erlbaum.

Zavatsky, B., & Padgett, R. (1977). *The whole word catalogue, vol. 2.* New York: Teachers & Writers Collaborative.

Ziegler, A. (1981, 1984). *The writing workshop, vols. 1 & 2.* New York: Teachers & Writers Collaborative.

Appendix F

The Adventures of Huckleberry Finn, 1982, 1985, 1986, 1987, 1991, 1992, 1994, 1995, 1996

Absalom, Absalom, 2000

The Age of Innocence, 1997

Agnes of God, 2000

Alias Grace, 2000

All My Sons, 1985, 1990

All the King's Men, 2000

All the Pretty Horses, 1996

An American Tragedy, 1982, 1995

America is in the Heart, 1995

Another Country, 1995

Anna Karenina, 1991, 1999

Antigone, 1990, 1994, 1999

Apprenticeship of Duddy Kravitz, 1959

Antony and Cleopatra, 1991

As I Lay Dying, 1989, 1990, 1994, 2001

As You Like It, 1992

The Awakening, 1987, 1988, 1991, 1992, 1995, 1997, 1999

The Bear, 1994

Beloved, 1990, 1999, 2001

Benito Cereno, 1989

Billy Budd, 1981, 1983, 1985, 1999

Bleak House, 1994, 2000

The Birthday Party, 1989, 1997

Brave New World, 1989

Bless Me, Última, 1996, 1997

The Brothers Karamazov, 1990

The Bluest Eye, 1995

Candide, 1996

The Caretaker, 1985

Catch-22, 1982, 1985, 1987, 1989, 1994, 2001

Cat on a Hot Tin Roof, 2000

Cat's Eye, 1994

The Centaur, 1981

Ceremony, 1994, 1997, 1999, 2001

The Color Purple, 1991, 1992, 1994, 1996, 1997

Crime and Punishment, 1985, 1991, 1996, 1999, 2000, 2001

Cry, the Beloved Country, 1985, 1987, 1991, 1995, 1996

The Crucible, 1983, 1987

Daisy Miller, 1997

Dancing at Lughnasa, 2001

David Copperfield, 1983

Death of a Salesman, 1986, 1988, 1994

The Dead, 1997

Delta Wedding, 1997

The Death of Ivan Ilyich, 1986

Desire Under the Elms, 1981

Dinner at the Homesick Restaurant, 1997

The Diviners, 1995

Doctor Faustus, 1986, 1999

A Doll House, 1983, 1987, 1988, 1995

Don Quixote, 1992, 2001

The Dollmaker, 1991

An Enemy of the People, 1987, 1999, 2001

Equus, 1992

Ethan Frome, 1985

Emma, 1996

The Eumenides, 1996

The Fall, 1981

A Farewell to Arms, 1991, 1999

The Father, 2001

Fathers and Sons, 1990

Fifth Business, 2000

Frankenstein, 1989, 2001

A Gathering of Old Men, 2000

Ghosts, 2000

The Glass Menagerie, 1990, 1994, 1997, 1999

Go Tell It on the Mountain, 1988, 1990

The Grapes of Wrath, 1981, 1985, 1987, 1995

Great Expectations, 1988, 1989, 1992, 1996, 2000, 2001

The Great Gatsby, 1982, 1983, 1988, 1991, 1992, 1997, 2000

Gulliver's Travels, 1987, 1989, 2001

The Hairy Ape, 1989

Hamlet, 1988, 1992, 1994, 1997, 1999, 2000

The Handmaid's Tale, 1992

Hard Times, 1987, 1990

Heart of Darkness, 1991, 1994, 1996, 1999, 2000, 2001

Hedda Gabler, 1992, 2000

Henry IV, 1990

The Homecoming, 1990

The House of the Seven Gables, 1989

House Made of Dawn, 1995

The Invisible Man, 1982, 1983, 1985, 1987, 1988, 1989, 1991, 1994, 1995, 1996, 1997, 2001

Jane Eyre, 1988, 1991, 1994, 1995, 1996, 1997, 1999, 2000

Jasmine, 1999

J. B., 1981, 1994

Joe Turners Come and Gone, 2000

Joseph Andrews, 1991

The Joy Luck Club, 1997

Jude the Obscure, 1985, 1987, 1991, 1995

Julius Caesar, 1982, 1997

The Jungle, 1987

King Lear, 1982, 1989, 1990, 1996, 2001

A Lesson Before Dying, 1999

The Little Foxes, 1985, 1990

Light in August, 1981, 1982, 1983, 1985, 1995, 1999

Long Day's Journey into Night, 1990

Lord of the Flies, 1985, 1992

Lord Jim, 1982, 1986, 2000

Love Medicine, 1995

"The Lovesong of J. Alfred Prufrock," 1985

Lysistrata, 1987

Macbeth, 1983, 1999

Madam Bovary, 1985

Main Street, 1987

Major Barbara, 1996
Man and Superman, 1981
Mansfield Park, 1991
Mayor of Casterbridge, 1993, 1999, 2000
M. Butterfly, 1995
Medea, 1982, 1992, 1995, 2001
The Member of the Wedding, 1997
The Merchant of Venice, 1985, 1991, 1995
The Metamorphosis, 1989
A Midsummer Night's Dream, 1991
Middlemarch, 1995
The Mill on the Floss, 1991, 1992
The Misanthrope, 1992
Miss Lonelyhearts, 1989
Moby-Dick, 1989, 1994, 1996, 2001
Moll Flanders, 1986, 1987, 1995
Monkey Bridge, 2000
Mother Courage, 1985, 1987
Mrs. Dalloway, 1994, 1997
Mrs. Warren's Profession, 1987, 1990, 1995
Much Ado About Nothing, 1997
Murder in the Cathedral, 1985, 1995
"My Last Duchess," 1985
Native Son, 1982, 1983, 1985, 1987, 1995, 2001
Native Speaker, 1999
Nineteen Eighty-Four, 1987, 1994
No Exit, 1986
No-No Boy, 1995
Notes from Underground, 1989
Obasan, 1994, 1995
The Odyssey, 1986
Oedipus Rex, 2000
Of Mice and Men, 2001
One Flew Over the Cuckoo's Nest, 2001
One Hundred Years of Solitude, 1989
The Optimist's Daughter, 1994
Oresteia, 1990
Othello, 1985, 1988, 1992, 1995
Our Town, 1986, 1996
Pale Fire, 2001
Pamela, 1986
Paradise Lost, 1985, 1986
A Passage to India, 1988, 1991, 1992
Persuasion, 1990
The Piano Lesson, 1996, 1999
Phaedre, 1992
Pnin, 1997
The Power and the Glory, 1995
Portrait of a Lady, 1992, 1996
Portrait of the Artist as a Young Man, 1981, 1986, 1988, 1996, 1999
Praisesong for the Widow, 1996
Pride and Prejudice, 1983, 1988, 1992, 1997
The Prime of Miss Jean Brodie, 1990
Pygmalion, 1992
A Raisin in the Sun, 1987, 1990, 1991, 1992, 1994, 1996, 2000
The Rape of the Lock, 1981
Redburn, 1987
The Remains of the Day, 2000

Romeo and Juliet, 1990, 1992, 1997
Rosencrantz and Guildenstern Are Dead, 1981, 1994, 2000
Saint Joan, 1995
The Scarlet Letter, 1983, 1988, 1991, 1999
A Separate Peace, 1982
The Shipping News, 1997
Sister Carrie, 1987
Slaughterhouse Five, 1991
Snow Falling on Cedars, 2000
Song of Solomon, 1981, 1988, 1996, 2000
Sons and Lovers, 1990
The Sound and the Fury, 1986, 1997, 2001
The Stone Angel, 1996
The Stranger, 1982, 1986
A Streetcar Named Desire, 1991, 1992, 2001
Sula, 1992, 1997
The Sun Also Rises, 1985, 1991, 1995
A Tale of Two Cities, 1982, 1991
Tartuffe, 1987
The Tempest, 1996
Tess of the D'Urbervilles, 1982, 1991
Their Eyes Were Watching God, 1988, 1990, 1991, 1996
Things Fall Apart, 1991, 1997
Tom Jones, 1990, 2000
To the Lighthouse, 1986, 1988
The Trial, 1989, 2000
Trifles, 2000
Tristram Shandy, 1986
Turn of the Screw, 1992, 1994, 2000
Twelfth Night, 1985, 1994, 1996
Uncle Tom's Cabin, 1987
Victory, 1983
Volpone, 1983
Waiting for Godot, 1985, 1986, 1989, 1994, 2001
The Warden, 1996
Washington Square, 1990
The Waste Land, 1981
Watch on the Rhine, 1987
The Watch That Ends the Night, 1992
Who's Afraid of Virginia Woolf, 1988, 1994, 2000
Wide Sargasso Sea, 1989, 1992
Winter in the Blood, 1995
The Winter's Tale, 1986, 1989
Wise Blood, 1982, 1989, 1995
The Woman Warrior, 1991
Wuthering Heights, 1982, 1983, 1986, 1989, 1990, 1991, 1992, 1996, 1997, 1999, 2001
The Zoo Story, 1982, 2001
Zoot Suit, 1995

AUTHORS LISTED ON AP ENGLISH LITERATURE EXAM 1993

For one year, the prompts for the open-ended questions on the AP English Literature exam included authors rather than titles of specific texts. The following authors were listed on the 1993 exam.

Aristophanes   Jane Austen
Margaret Atwood   Samuel Beckett

Lord Byron	Henry James	Walker Percy	Jonathan Swift
Geoffrey Chaucer	Ben Jonson	Harold Pinter	Anthony Trollope
Charles Dickens	Franz Kafka	Alexander Pope	Mark Twain
T. S. Eliot	Margaret Laurence	Barbara Pym	Voltaire
William Faulkner	Bobbie Ann Mason	William Shakespeare	Evelyn Waugh
Henry Fielding	Moliere	George Bernard Shaw	Oscar Wilde
Zora Neale Hurston	Vladimir Nabokov	Tom Stoppard	
Aldous Huxley	Gloria Naylor		

READER RESPONSE RESOURCES

Author	Publications	Date
Anderson, Philip, and Rubana, Gregory	*Enhancing Aesthetic Reading and Response*	1991
Beach, Richard	*A Teacher's Introduction to Reader-Response Theories*	1993
Berthoff, Ann E.	*The Making of Meaning*	1981
Bleich, David	*Readings and Feelings: An Introduction to Subjective Criticism*	1975
Christenbury, Leila, & Kelly, Patricia	*Questioning: A Path to Critical Thinking*	1983
Clifford, John (Ed.)	*The Experience of Reading: Louise Rosenblatt and Reader-Response Theory*	1990
Cooper, Charles R. (Ed.)	*Researching Response to Literature and the Teaching of Literature*	1985
Corcoran, Bill, & Evans, Emrys (Eds.)	*Readers, Texts, Teachers*	1987
Eco, Umberto	*The Role of the Reader: Explorations in the Semiotics of the Text*	1978
Fish, Stanley E.	*Is There a Text in this Class? The Authority of Interpretive Community*	1980
Holland, Norman	*Five Readers Reading*	1975
Iser, Wolfgang	*The Act of Reading: A Theory of Aesthetic Response*	1978
Karolides, Nicholas (Ed.)	*Reader Response in the Classroom: Evoking and Interpreting Meaning in Literature*	1992
Langer, Judith (Ed.)	*Literature Instruction: A Focus on Student Response*	1992
Langer, Judith	*Envisioning Literature: Literary Understanding and Literature Instruction*	1995
Milner, Joseph, & Milner, Lucy (Eds.)	*Passages to Literature: Essays on Teaching in Australia, Canada, England, the United States, and Wales*	1989
Nelms, Ben F. (Ed.)	*Literature in the Classroom: Readers, Texts, and Contexts*	1988
Probst, Robert E.	*Response and Analysis: Teaching Literature in Junior and Senior High School*	1988
Protherough, Robert	*Developing Response to Fiction*	1983
Purves, Alan C., Rogers, Theresa, & Soter, Anna O.	*How Porcupines Make Love II: Notes on a Response-Centered Curriculum* (2e)	1990
Purves, Alan C., Foshay, Arthur W., & Hansson, Gunnar	*Literature Education in Ten Countries*	1973
Rosenblatt, Louise	*The Reader, the Text, the Poem: The Transactional Theory of the Literary Work*	1978
Rosenblatt, Louise	*Literature as Exploration* (5e)	1995
Scholes, Robert	*Textual Power: Literacy Theory and the Teaching of English*	1985
Tompkins, Jane P. (Ed.)	*Reader-Response Criticism: From Formalism to Post-Structuralism*	1980
Wilhelm, Jeffrey	*"You Gotta BE the Book": Teaching Engaged and Reflective Reading with Adolescents*	1997

FICTION BY WOMEN

Author	Work	Date
Alcott, Louisa May	*Little Women*	1868
Arnow, Harriette	*The Dollmaker*	1954
Atwood, Margaret	*The Handmaid's Tale*	1985
	Wilderness Tips	1991
Austen, Jane	*Pride and Prejudice*	1813
	Persuasion	1818
Austin, Doris	*After the Garden*	1987
Bambara, Toni Cade	*The Salt Eaters*	1980
Bridgers, Sue Ellen	*Home Before Dark*	1976
Brontë, Anne	*Tenant of Wildfell Hall*	1848
Brontë, Charlotte	*Jane Eyre*	1847
Brontë, Emily	*Wuthering Heights*	1847
Buck, Pearl	*The Good Earth*	1931
Burney, Fanny	*Camilla*	1796
Burns, Olive Ann	*Cold Sassy Tree*	1984
Cather, Willa	*My Antonia*	1918
Chopin, Kate	*The Awakening*	1899
Christie, Agatha	*And Then There Were None*	1940
Cisneros, Sandra	*The House on Mango Street*	1983
Collette	*Gigi*	1995
Davis, Rebecca Harding	*Life in the Iron Mills*	1861
Dinesen, Isak	*Seven Gothic Tales*	1934
Eliot, George	*Middlemarch*	1871
Erdrich, Louise	*Love Medicine*	1984
	Tracks	1988
Freeman, Mary Wilkins	"The Revolt of Mother" in *Selected Stories*	1983
Gibbons, Kaye	*Ellen Foster*	1987
Gilman, Charlotte Perkins	*Herland*	1915
Glasgow, Ellen	*Barren Ground*	1925
Golden, Marita	*A Woman's Place*	1986
Gordimer, Nadine	*July's People*	1981
Gordon, Caroline	*The Collected Stories of Caroline Gordon*	1981
Greene, Bette	*The Summer of My German Solider*	1973
Guy, Rosa	*A Measure of Time*	1983
Head, Bessie	*Maru*	1971
Hulme, Keri	*The Bone People*	1983
Hurston, Zora Neale	*Their Eyes Were Watching God*	1937
Jackson, Shirley	*Come Along with Me*	1968
	The Magic of Shirley Jackson	1966
Jewett, Sarah Orne	*The Country of the Pointed Firs and Other Stories*	1896
Kingsolver, Barbara	*Animal Dreams*	1990
	The Bean Trees	1988
Laurence, Margaret	*The Stone Angel*	1964
Lee, Harper	*To Kill a Mockingbird*	1960
LeGuin, Ursula	*The Dispossessed*	1974
L'Engle, Madeleine	*A Ring of Endless Light*	1980
Lessing, Doris	*The Golden Notebook*	1962
Mansfield, Katherine	*The Garden Party and Other Stories*	1922
Marshall, Paule	*Praisesong for the Widow*	1983
Mason, Bobbie Ann	*In Country*	1985
McCullers, Carson	*The Member of the Wedding*	1946
McMillan, Terry	*Disappearing Acts*	1989
	Mama	1987
Miller, Sue	*The Good Mother*	1986
Morrison, Toni	*The Bluest Eye*	1969
Naylor, Gloria	*Mama Day*	1988
Oates, Joyce Carol	*The Wheel of Love*	1970

O'Connor, Flannery	*Everything That Rises Must Converge*	1965
	A Good Man Is Hard to Find	1955
Olsen, Tillie	*Tell Me a Riddle*	1961
Paley, Grace	*Enormous Changes at the Last Minute*	1974
Plath, Sylvia	*The Bell Jar*	1963
Porter, Katherine Anne	*Collected Stories*	1967
Proulx, E. Annie	*The Shipping News*	1993
Rhys, Jean	*Wide Sargasso Sea*	1966
Sanders, Dori	*Clover: A Novel*	1990
Sayers, Dorothy	*Gaudy Night*	1935
Shelley, Mary	*Frankenstein*	1818
Silko, Leslie	*Ceremony*	1977
Smiley, Jane	*A Thousand Acres*	1991
	Moo	1995
Smith, Lee	*Family Linens*	1985
Stead, Christina	*The Man Who Loved Children*	1940
Stewart, Mary	*The Hollow Hills*	1973
Stowe, Harriet Beecher	*Uncle Tom's Cabin*	1852
Tan, Amy	*The Joy Luck Club*	1989
Tyler, Anne	*Dinner at the Homesick Restaurant*	1982
	Breathing Lessons	1988
Walker, Alice	*The Color Purple*	1982
Walker, Margaret	*Jubilee*	1965
Welty, Eudora	*Losing Battles*	1970
	Thirteen Stories	1965
West, Jessamyn	*Friendly Persuasion*	1945
Wharton, Edith	*Ethan Frome*	1911
Woolf, Virginia	*Mrs. Dalloway*	1925

AFRICAN AMERICAN WRITERS

	Writer	Work
1800–1899		
1829	David Walker	*Appeal*
1831	Nat Turner	*The Confessions of Nat Turner*
1845	Frederick Douglass	*Narrative of Frederick Douglass*
1861	Harriet Jacobs	*Incidents in the Life of a Slave Girl*
1900–1929		
1904	W. E. B. DuBois	*The Souls of Black Folk*
1912	James Weldon Johnson	*Autobiography of an Ex-Colored Man*
1923	Jean Toomer	*Cane*
1930s/1949		
1936	Richard Wright	*Uncle Tom's Children*[†]
1937	Zora Neale Hurston	*Their Eyes Were Watching God*
1945	Gwendolyn Brooks	*A Street in Bronzeville*[*]
1947	Countee Cullen	*On These I Stand*[*]
1950s		
1950	William Denby	*Bettlecreek*
1952	Ralph Ellison	*Invisible Man*
1953	Gwendolyn Brooks	*Maud Martha*
1953	James Baldwin	*Go Tell It on the Mountain*
1958	Langston Hughes	*The Langston Hughes Reader*
1959	Paule Marshall	*Brown Girl, Brownstones*

---

[*]Collections of poems

[†]Collections of short stories

1960s

1961	Paule Marshall	*Soul Clap Hands and Sing*[†]
1963	Gordon Parks	*The Learning Tree*
1964	William Melvin Kelly	*Dancers on the Shore*[†]
1966	Margaret Walker	*Jubilee*
1969	James Alan McPherson	*Hue and Cry*[†]
1969	Toni Morrison	*The Bluest Eye*

1970s

1970	Alex Haley and Malcolm X	*The Autobiography of Malcolm X*
1971	Maya Angelou	*I Know Why the Caged Bird Sings*
1972	Toni Cade Bambara	*Gorilla, My Love*[†]
1973	Alice Childress	*A Hero Ain't Nothing but a Sandwich*
1974	Ernest Gaines	*The Autobiography of Miss Jane Pittman*
1974	Albert Murray	*Train Whistle Guitar*
1974	Sharon Bell Mathis	*Listen for the Fig Tree*
1974	Alice Walker	*In Love and Trouble*
1976	Virginia Hamilton	*Arilla Sun Down*
1977	Mildred Taylor	*Roll of Thunder, Hear My Cry*
1977	James Alan McPherson	*Elbow Room*[†]
1977	Toni Morrison	*Song of Solomon*
1978	Ernest Gaines	*In My Father's House*
1979	Rosa Guy	*The Disappearance*

1980s

1980	Anne Moody	*Coming of Age in Mississippi: An Autobiography*
1982	Gloria Naylor	*The Women of Brewster Place: A Novel in Seven Stories*
1982	Alice Walker	*The Color Purple*
1982	Ntozake Shange	*Sassafras, Cypress, and Indigo*
1983	Ernest Gaines	*A Gathering of Old Men*
1983	Paule Marshall	*Praisesong for the Widow*
1984	Andrea Lee	*Sarah Philips*[†]
1984	Virginia Hamilton	*A Little Love*
1984	J. California Cooper	*A Piece of Mine*[†]
1985	Jamaica Kincaid	*Annie John*
1985	Ntozake Shange	*Betsey Brown*
1985	John A. Williams	*The Man Who Cried I Am*
1986	August Wilson	*Fences*

1990s

1990	August Wilson	*Piano Lesson*
1990	Toni Morrison	*Beloved*
1990	Dori Sanders	*Clover: A Novel*
1990	Charles Johnson	*Middle Passage*
1990	Walter Mosley	*Devil in a Blue Dress*
1991	Mary Helen Washington	*Memory of Kin*[†]
1991	J. California Cooper	*Family: A Novel*
1992	Brent Wade	*Company Man: A Novel*
1992	Randall Kenan	*Let the Dead Bury Their Dead and Other Stories*[†]
1992	Walter Dean Myers	*Somewhere in the Darkness*
1993	Gloria Naylor	*Mama Day*
1993	Arthur Ashe	*Days of Grace*
1994	Ernest Gaines	*A Lesson Before Dying*
1994	Alex Pate	*Losing Absalom*
1995	Yvonne Thornton	*The Ditchdigger's Daughters*
1996	Gloria Naylor	*Children of the Night*[†]

2000s

| 2001 | Bertice Berry | *The Haunting of Hip Hop: A Novel* |

---

*Collections of poems

[†]Collections of short stories

NATIVE AMERICAN WRITERS

Allen, Paula Gunn	*Woman Who Owned the Shadows*	1983
Dorris, Michael	*Yellow Raft in Blue Water*	1987
Erdrich, Louise	*Baptism of Desire: Poems*	1989
	Beet Queen	1986
	Bingo Palace	1994
	Jacklight (poetry)	1984
Harjo, Joy	*The Woman Who Fell From the Sky: Poems*	1994
Highwater, Jamake	*Anpao: An American Indian Odyssey*	1977
	Many Smokes, Many Moons	1978
Hogan, Linda	*Mean Spirit*	1990
Lesley, Criag	*River Song*	1990
	Winterkill	1990
Momaday, N. Scott	*The Ancient Child: A Novel*	1989
	House Made of Dawn	1969
Neilhardt, John	*Black Elk Speaks*	1932
Owens, Louis	*Sharpest Sight*	1992
Rain, Mary Summer	*Dreamwalker: The Path of Sacred Power*	1993
	Earthway	1992
	Phoenix Rising: No-Eyes Vision of the Changes to Come	1993
	Spirit Song: An Introduction to No-Eyes	1993
Silko, Leslie Marmon	*Ceremony*	1986
	Storyteller	1981
Wall, Steve, and Arden, Harvey	*Wisdom's Daughters: Conversations with Women Elders of Native America*	1993
Welch, James	*Fools Crow*	1986
	The Indian Lawyer	1990
	Winter in the Blood	1974

HISPANIC WRITERS

Acosta, Oscar	*The Revolt of the Cockroach People*	1973
Allende, Isabel	*The House of the Spirits*	1985
Álvarez, Julia	*How the García Girls Lost Their Accent*	1991
	In the Time of the Butterflies	1994
Anaya, Rudolfo A.	*Bless Me, Última*	1972
Chavez, Denise	*The Last of the Menu Girls*	1986
Cisneros, Sandra	*The House on Mango Street*	1983
	Woman Hollering Creek	1991
Eliade, Mircea	*Two Strange Tales*	1986
Fuentes, Carlos	*Old Gringo*	1985
García, Cristina	*Dreaming in Cuban*	1992
	The Aquero Sisters	1997
García Márquez, Gabriel	*One Hundred Years of Solitude*	1970
	Leaf Storm, and Other Stories	1979
	No One Writes to the Colonel	1968
	Chronicle of a Death Foretold	1983
Islas, Arturo	*The Rain God*	1984
Lopez-Medina, Sylvia	*Cantora*	1992
Paz, Octavio	*Convergences: Essays on Art and Literature*	1987
	The Monkey Grammarian	1981
Rodriguez, Richard	*Hunger of Memory*	1982
Thurston, Lawrence	*Imagining Argentina*	1989
Vargas Llosa, Mario	*The Storyteller*	1989

ASIAN AMERICAN WRITERS

Chin, Frank	*Donald Duk*	1991
Chan, Jeffrey P., Chin, Frank, Inada, Lawson F., and Wong, Shawn, (Eds.)	*The Big Aiiieeeee!: An Anthology of Chinese-American & Japanese-American Literature*	1974
Chang, Jung	*Wild Swans: Three Daughters of China*	1991
Criddle, JoAn D.	*To Destroy Is No Loss: The Odyssey of a Cambodian Family*	1987
Guterson, David	*Snow Falling on Cedars*	1994
Jen, Gish	*Typical American*	1991
Kadohata, Cynthia	*In the Heart of the Valley of Love*	1992
Kingston, Maxine Hong	*Woman Warrior*	1976
Kogawa, Joy	*Obasan*	1981
Lee, Chang-rae	*Native Speaker*	1995
Lee, Gus	*China Boy*	1991
Moore, David L.	*Dark Sky, Dark Land: Stories of the Hmong Boy Scouts, Troop 100*	1989
Ng, Fae Myenne	*Bone*	1993
Okada, John, and Inada, Lawson F.	*No-No Boy*	1976
Salzman, Mark	*The Laughing Sutra*	1991
Schanberg, Sydney	*Death and Life of Dith Pran*	1985
Tan, Amy	*The Joy Luck Club*	1989
	The Kitchen God's Wife	1991
Tyau, Kathleen	*A Little Too Much is Enough*	1996
Watanabe, Sylvia, and Bruchac, Carol (Eds.)	*Home to Stay: Asian American Fiction by Women*	1990
Wong Lee, David	*Pangs of Love*	1991
Yamashita, Karen Tei	*Through the Arc of the Rain Forest*	1990
Yep, Laurence	*Dragonwings*	1997

BENEDICT'S RECOMMENDATIONS: YOUNG ADULT FICTION[5]

Adams, Douglas	*The Hitchhiker's Guide to the Galaxy*	1980 Harmony
Alexander, Lloyd	*Westmark* (one of a series)	1981 Dutton
Anonymous	*Go Ask Alice*	1971 Prentice-Hall
Auel, Jean	*The Clan of the Cave Bear*	1982 Crown
Baldwin, James	*If Beale Street Could Talk*	1974 Dial
Beagle, Peter S.	*The Last Unicorn*	1968 Ballantine
Blos, Joan	*A Gathering of Days*	1979 Scribner
Blume, Judy	*Forever*	1975 Bradbury
Bond, Nancy	*Another Shore*	1988 Macmillan
Bradford, Richard	*Red Sky at Morning*	1968 Lippincott
Bradshaw, Gillian	*Bearkeeper's Daughter*	1987 Houghton Mifflin
	The Beacon at Alexandria	1986 Houghton Mifflin
Brancato, Robin	*Winning*	1976 Bantam
Bridgers, Sue Ellen	*Home Before Dark*	1976 Knopf
	All Together Now	1979 Bantam
	Permanent Connections	1987 Harper & Row
Brooks, Bruce	*The Moves Make the Man*	1984 Harper & Row
Brooks, Terry	*The Wishsong of Shannara* (one of a series)	1985 Ballantine
Burns, Olive Ann	*Cold Sassy Tree*	1984 Ticknor & Fields
Card, Orson Scott	*Ender's Game* (one of a series)	1985 Tor
	Seventh Son (one of a series)	1987 Doherty
Carter, Alden	*Sheila's Dying*	1987 Putnam
	Up Country	1989 Putnam
Childress, Alice	*A Hero Ain't Nothin but a Sandwich*	1973 Coward McCann
	Rainbow Jordan	1981 Coward McCann
Clarke, Arthur C.	*Rendezvous with Rama*	1973 Harcourt Brace Jovanovich

[5]Many titles here were first marketed for an adult audience but are now read more by young adults than adults and so have moved primarily to a young adult list.

Cole, Brock	*Celine*	1989 Farrar, Straus, & Giroux
	The Goats	1987 Farrar, Straus, & Giroux
Conroy, Pat	*The Great Santini*	1976 Houghton Mifflin
	Lords of Discipline	1980 Bantam
	The Prince of Tides	1986 Houghton Mifflin
Cooper, Susan	*The Dark Is Rising* (one of a series)	1973 Atheneum
Cormier, Robert	*After the First Death*	1979 Pantheon
	Beyond the Chocolate War	1985 Knopf
	The Bumblebee Flies Anyway	1983 Pantheon
	The Chocolate War	1974 Pantheon
Crutcher, Chris	*The Crazy Horse Electric Game*	1987 Greenwillow
	Running Loose	1983 Greenwillow
Davis, Jenny	*Sex Education*	1988 Orchard
Deavers, Julie Reece	*Say Goodnight, Gracie*	1988 Harper & Row
Doherty, Berlie	*White Peak Farm*	1990 Orchard
Duncan, Lois	*Killing Mr. Griffin*	1978 Little, Brown
Edgerton, Clyde	*The Floatplane Notebook*	1988 Algonquin
	Raney	1985 Algonquin
Fox, Paula	*The Slave Dancer*	1973 Bradbury
Gaines, Ernest	*A Gathering of Old Men*	1983 Knopf
Garden, Nancy	*Annie on My Mind*	1982 Farrar
Golding, William	*Lord of the Flies*	1955 Coward, McCann, & Geoghegan
Greenberg, Joanne	*I Never Promised You a Rose Garden*	1964 Holt, Rinehart, & Winston
	In This Sign	1970 Holt
Greene, Bette	*Summer of My German Soldier*	1973 Dial
Guest, Judith	*Ordinary People*	1976 Ballantine
Guy, Rosa	*The Disappearance*	1979 Doubleday
	The Friends	1973 Holt
Hadley, Irwin	*Abby, My Love*	1985 Atheneum
Hamilton, Virginia	*Sweet Whispers, Brother Rush*	1982 Philomel
Head, Ann	*Mr. and Mrs. BoJo Jones*	1967 Putnam
Hinton, S. E.	*The Outsiders*	1967 Dell
	Tex	1979 Doubleday
	That Was Then, This Is Now	1971 Dell
Hogan, William	*The Quartzsite Trip*	1980 Avon
Holland, Isabelle	*The Man Without a Face*	1972 Harper
Kerr, M. E.	*Fell*	1987 Harper
	Gentlehands	1978 Harper
	Night Kites	1986 Harper
Kesey, Ken	*One Flew over the Cuckoo's Nest*	1962 Viking
Keyes, Daniel	*Flowers for Algernon*	1966 Harcourt
Klaus, Annette Curtis	*Silver Kiss*	1990 Delacorte
Knowles, John	*A Separate Peace*	1959 Macmillan
Lasky, Kathryn	*Beyond the Divide*	1983 Macmillan
LeGuin, Ursula	*A Wizard of Earthsea* (one of a series)	1968 Parnassus
	Enchantress from the Stars	1970 Atheneum
Lipsyte, Robert	*The Contender*	1967 Harper & Row
	One Fat Summer	1977 Harper & Row
Mahy, Margaret	*The Catalogue of the Universe*	1986 Macmillan
Mathias, Sharon Bell	*Teacup Full of Roses*	1972 Viking
Mazer, Harry	*The Last Mission*	1979 Dell
McCaffrey, Anne	*Dragon Song* (one of a series)	1976 Atheneum
	The Ship Who Sang	1969 Walker
McIntyre, Vonda	*Dreamsnake*	1978 Houghton Mifflin
McKillip, Patricia	*The Forgotten Beasts of Eld*	1974 Atheneum
	The Riddle-Master of Hed (one of a series)	1976 Atheneum
McKinley, Robin	*Beauty*	1978 Harper & Row
	Blue Sword	1982 Greenwillow
	Hero and Crown	1985 Greenwillow
Myers, Walter Dean	*Fallen Angels*	1988 Scholastic
	Hoops	1981 Doubleday

Naylor, Phyllis Reynolds	*The Keeper*	1986 Atheneum
Noonan, Michael	*McKenzie's Boots*	1987 Orchard
O'Brien, Robert	*Z for Zachariah*	1975 Antheneum
Paulsen, Gary	*Hatchet*	1987 Bradbury
Peck, Richard	*Are You in the House Alone?*	1976 Viking
	Remembering the Good Times	1985 Delacorte
Peck, Robert Newton	*A Day No Pigs Would Die*	1973 Knopf
Pierce, Meredith Ann	*The Darkangel* (one of a series)	1982 Little, Brown
Portis, Charles	*True Grit*	1968 Simon & Schuster
Potok, Chaim	*The Chosen*	1967 Ballantine
Rylant, Cynthia	*A Kindness*	1988 Orchard
Salinger, J. D.	*Catcher in the Rye*[6]	1951 Little, Brown
	Franny and Zooey	1961 Bantam
Sleator, William	*House of Stairs*	1974 Dutton
	Interstellar Pig	1984 Dutton
Strasser, Todd	*Friends Till the End*	1981 Dell
Swarthout, Glendon	*Bless the Beasts and Children*	1970 Pocket
Tan, Amy	*The Joy Luck Club*	1989 Putnam
	The Kitchen God's Wife	1991 Putnam
Taylor, Mildred D.	*Let the Circle Be Unbroken*	1981 Dial
	Road to Memphis	1990 Dial
	Roll of Thunder, Hear My Cry	1976 Dial
Tolkien, J. R. R.	*The Hobbit*	1966 Houghton Mifflin
	The Lord of the Rings (trilogy)	1967 Houghton Mifflin
Vinge, Joan D.	*Psion*	1982 Doubleday
Voigt, Cynthia	*Dicey's Song*	1982 Atheneum
	Homecoming	1981 Macmillan
	On Fortune's Wheel	1990 Atheneum
	The Runner	1985 Atheneum
	A Solitary Blue	1983 Atheneum
	Tree by Leaf	1988 Atheneum
Walker, Alice	*The Color Purple*	1983 Harcourt Brace Jovanovich
West, Jessamyn	*Massacre at Fall Creek*	1975 Harcourt Brace Jovanovich
Wharton, Wiliam	*A Midnight Clear*	1982 Knopf
White, Robb	*Deathwatch*	1972 Dell
Zindel, Paul	*My Darling, My Hamburger*	1969 Harper & Row
	The Pigman	1968 Harper

---

[6]Donelson and Nilsen (1980) report that in the early 1980s it was still "the most widely censored book in American schools" (p. 164).

BENEDICT'S RECOMMENDATIONS: MODERN INTERPRETATIONS AND RETELLINGS (REVISIONIST FANTASY AND TWICE-TOLD TALES)

Bradley, Marion Zimmer. *Firebrand.* 1987. (*The Iliad*).

Bradley, Marion Zimmer. *Mist of Avalon.* 1982. (Arthurian legend).

Gardner, John. *Grendel.* 1971. (*Beowulf*).

Lewis, C. S. *Till We Have Faces.* 1956. ("Cupid and Psyche").

McKinley, Robin. *Beauty.* 1978. ("Beauty and the Beast").

McKinley, Robin. *Rose Daughter.* 1997. ("Beauty and the Beast").

Napoli, Donna Jo. *The Magic Circle.* 1993. ("Hansel and Gretel").

Napoli, Donna Jo. *Zel.* 1996. ("Rapunzel").

Stewart, Mary. *The Crystal Cave.* 1984. (Arthurian legend).

Stewart, Mary. *The Hollow Hills.* 1984. (Arthurian legend).

Stewart, Mary. *The Last Enchantment.* 1984. (Arthurian legend).

Sutclif, Rosemary. *The Road to Camlann.* 1994. (Arthurian legend).

Sutclif, Rosemary. *The Sword and the Circle.* 1994. (Arthurian legend).

Sutclif, Rosemary. *Sword at Sunset.* 1987. (Arthurian legend).

White, T. H. *The Once and Future King.* 1958. (Arthurian legend).

Williams, Tad. *Caliban's Hour.* 1994. (*The Tempest*).

WORKS ON CENSORSHIP

American Library Association. (1995). *Hit list: Frequently challenged young adult titles: References to defend them.* Chicago, IL: ALA.

Bracken, Harry M. (1994). *Freedom of speech: Words are not deeds.* Praeger.

Brown, J. (Ed.) (1996). *Preserving intellectual freedom: Fighting censorship in our schools.* Urbana, IL: NCTE.

Burress, L., & Jenkinson, E. B. (1982). *The students' right to know.* Urbana, IL: NCTE.

DelFattore, J. (1992). *What Johnny shouldn't read: Textbook censorship in America.* New Haven, CT: Yale University Press.

Garry, P. M. (1993). *An American paradox: Censorship in a nation of free speech.* Praeger.

Karolides, N., & Burress, L. (Eds.). (1985). *Celebrating censored books!* Racine: Wisconsin Council of Teachers of English.

Moffett, J. (1988). *Storm in the mountains: A case study of censorship, conflict, and consciousness.* Carbondale, IL: Southern Illinois University Press.

National Council of Teachers of English. (1991). *The students' right to read.* Urbana, IL: Author.

People for the American Way. (1994). *Attacks on the freedom to learn: 1993–1994 report.* Washington, DC: Author.[7]

Shugart, D. (1983). *Rationales for commonly challenged/taught books.* Enfield: Connecticut Council of Teachers of English.

Zeisel, W. (1993). *Five hundred years of conflict.* New York: New York Public Library.

---

[7]Published annually.

Appendix G

SMITH'S (2002) GUIDE FOR MAKING MOVIES IN THE CLASSROOM[8]

Camera Tips

Do	*Don't*
Turn the camera slowly, like in slow motion	Move the camera quickly
	Overdo it
Keep the camera very still—don't try to follow action	Let anything not important to your film get in the picture
Draw a story board	Shoot every piece of scenery
When shooting a scene that won't change for a while, switch camera angles	Have bad sound
	Shoot the whole sequence
Make use of camera transition features	
Set up a scene so that it says what you want it to	
Make sure you have plenty of light—avoid backlighting subjects	

Camera Effects

Picture Effects

Negative Art   The color and brightness of the picture is reversed.

Sepia   The picture is sepia-toned.

B&W   The picture is monochrome (black and white).

Solarize   The light intensity is clearer, and the picture looks like an illustration.

Slim   The picture expands vertically.

Stretch   The picture expands horizontally.

Pastel   The contrast of the picture is emphasized, and the picture looks like an animated *cartoon*.

Mosaic   The picture is mosaic.

Digital Effects

Still   You can record a still picture so that it is superimposed on a moving picture.

Flash Motion   You can record still pictures successively at constant intervals.

Luminance Key   You can swap a brighter area in a still picture with a moving picture.

Trail   You can record the picture so that an incidental image like a trail is left.

Slow Shutter   You can slow down the shutter speed. The slow shutter mode is good for recording dark pictures more brightly. However, the picture may be less clear.

Old Movie   You can add an old movie type atmosphere to pictures. Your camcorder automatically sets the wide mode to ON, picture effect to SEPIA, and the appropriate shutter speed.

MEDIA SOURCES

Periodicals

Booklist (22/yr.)
American Library Association
50 E. Huron St.
Chicago, IL. 60611

Media and Methods (5/yr.)
Media and Methods
1429 Walnut St.
Philadelphia, PA 19102

TV Guide (weekly)
1211 Avenue of the Americas
New York, NY 10036

Distributors of Videotapes, Films, and Recorded Books

Ambrose Video Publishing, 28 W. 44th St., New York, NY 10036, (212) 768-9282

Benchmark Media, 569 N. State Rd., Briarcliff Manor, NY 10510, (914) 762-3838

Books on Tape, P.O. Box 7900, Newport Beach, CA 92658-9924, (800) 626-3333

Coronet/MTI Film and Video, 2349 Chafee Dr., St. Louis, MO 63146, (800) 221-1274

Facets Video, 1517 West Fullerton Ave., Chicago, IL 60614, (800) 331-6197

Films for the Humanities, P. O. Box 2053, Princeton, NJ 08543, (800) 257-5126

Lannan Literary Video, c/o Small Press Distribution, 1341 Seventh St., Berkeley, CA 94710, (800) 869-7553

Merit Audio Visual 132 W. 21st St., New York, NY 10011, (800) 753-6488

National Film Board of Canada, 1251 Avenue of the Americas, New York, NY 10020, (514) 283-9000

Pyramid Media, 2801 Colorado Ave., Santa Monica, CA 90404, (800) 421-2304

Recorded Books, 270 Shipjack Rd., Prince Frederick, MD 20678, (800) 638-1304

Wombat Productions, 9 West 57th St., Suite 4190, New York, NY 10019, (212) 230-9543

Zenger Video, 10200 Jefferson Blvd., Culver City, CA 90232-0802, (800) 421-4246

Video Series

The Story of English

Host: Robert MacNeil
9 episodes/60 minutes
Producer: MacNeil-Lehrer-Gannett Productions
Distributor: Public Media Education
4411 N. Ravenswood Ave.
Chicago, IL 60640-5802
(800) 826-3456

---

[8]Adapted from the *Digital Video Camera Recorder Manual* for models DCR-TRV203/TRV210/TRV310/TRV315, ©1999 Sony Corporation. Used with permission.

The American Short Story Video Series
Stories include such American classics as:
  "The Music School," John Updike
  "Almos' a Man," Richard Wright
  "Bernice Bobs Her Hair," F. Scott Fitzgerald
  "Soldier's Home," Ernest Hemingway
  "Paul's Case," Willa Cather
Producer: Learning in Focus, Inc.
Distributor: Coronet/MTI Film & Video
  2349 Chafee Dr.
  St. Louis, MO 63146
  (800) 221-1274

Bill Moyers: A World of Ideas
Host: Bill Moyers
Producer: Public Affairs Television, Inc.

The Power of Myth
Host: Bill Moyers
6 interviews/60 minutes each
Producer: Apostrophe S Productions, Inc.
Distributor: Mystic Fire Video
  P. O. Box 422
  Prince Street Station
  New York, NY 10012
  (212) 941-0999

American Cinema
Five videocassettes of a 1994 documentary shown on PBS.
An additional cassette with three short segments:
  Film Language
  Writing and Thinking about Film
  Classical Hollywood Style Today
Producer: The Annenberg/CPB Collection
Distributor: The Annenberg/CPB Collection
  P. O. Box 2345
  S. Burlington, VT 05407–2345
  (800) LEARNER

Basic Film Terms: A Visual Dictionary
One 14-minute introduction to film language
Distributor: Pyramid Media
  2801 Colorado Avenue
  Santa Monica, CA 90404-1048
  (800) 421-2304

MULTIPLE FILM VERSIONS OF *HAMLET* AND *JANE EYRE*

Hamlet

1948. Dir. Lawrence Olivier. With Lawrence Olivier, Jean Simmons, and Felix Aylmer.

1969. Dir. Tony Richardson. With Nicol Williamson, Gordon Jackson, Anthony Hopkins, and Judy Parfitt.

1980. Dir. Rodney Bennett. With Derek Jacobi, Claire Bloom, and Eric Porter.

1990. Dir. Franco Zeffirelli. With Mel Gibson and Glenn Close.

1997. Dir. Kenneth Branagh. With Kenneth Branagh, Julie Christie, and Kate Winslet.

Jane Eyre

1944. Dir. Orson Welles. With Orson Welles and Joan Fontaine.

1952. Westinghouse Studio, made for TV. With Katherine Bard and Kevin McCarthy.

1971. Dir. Delbert Mann. With George C. Scott, Susannah York, and Jack Hawkins.

1983. Dir. Julian Aymes. With Zelah Clark and Timothy Dalton.

1997. Arts & Entertainment Production. With Samantha Morton and Ciaran Hinds.

TEASLEY AND WILDER'S ONE HUNDRED GREAT FILMS FOR ADOLESCENTS: ANNOTATED FILMOGRAPHY

Ten Best Films About Coming of Age

Alan and Naomi (Sterling Van Wagenen, 1991, PG, 95 min.)
Brighton Beach Memoirs (Gene Saks, 1987, PG-13, 110 min.)
Crooklyn (Spike Lee, 1994, PG-13, 112 min.)
Dark Horse (David Hemmings, 1992, PG, 95 min.)
Empire of the Sun (Steven Spielberg, 1987, PG, 153 min.)
Hope and Glory (Great Britain, John Boorman, 1987, PG-13, 118 min.)
King of the Hill (Steven Soderberg, 1993, PG-13, 102 min.)
The Outside Chance of Maximilian Glick (Canada, Allan A. Goldstein, 1988, G, 92 min.)
This Is My Life (Nora Ephron, 1992, PG, 94 min.)
7 Up (Great Britain, Michael Apted, 1985, NR, 136 min.)

Ten Best Films About Families

Breaking Away (Peter Yates, 1979, PG, 100 min.)
Clara's Heart (Robert Mulligan, 1988, PG-13, 108 min.)
The Great Santini (Lewis John Carlino, 1979, PG, 116 min.)
Rich in Love (Bruce Beresford, 1993, PG-13, 105 min.)
A River Runs Through It (Robert Redford, 1992, PG, 123 min.)
Running on Empty (Sidney Lumet, 1988, PG-13, 116 min.)
Unstrung Heroes (Diane Keaton, 1995, PG, 94 min.)
The War (John Avnet, 1995, PG-13, 126 min.)
What's Eating Gilbert Grape? (Lasse Hallstrom, 1993, PG-13, 118 min.)
A World Apart (Chris Menges, 1988, PG, 135 min.)

Ten Best Films About Belonging

Addams Family Values (Barry Sonnenfeld, PG-13, 94 min.)
Angus (Patrick Read Johnson, 1995, PG-13, 87 min.)
Housekeeping (Bill Forsyth, 1988, PG, 112 min.)
Lucas (David Seltzer, 1986, PG-13, 100 min.)
Mask (Peter Bogdanovich, 1985, PG-13, 120 min.)
My Bodyguard (Tony Bill, 1980, PG, 96 min.)
Powder (Victor Salva, 1995, PG-13, 112 min.)
Rebel Without a Cause (Nicholas Ray, 1955, NR, 111 min.)
School Ties (Robert Mandel, 1992, PG-13, 110 min.)
Welcome Home, Roxy Carmichael (Jim Abrahams, 1990, PG-13, 98 min.)

Ten Best Films About Dreams and Quests

Chariots of Fire (England, Hugh Hudson, 1981, PG, 123 min.)
The Cure (1995, Peter Horton, PG-13, 99 min.)
The Gods Must Be Crazy (Botswana, Jamie Uys, 1981, PG, 108 min.)
Hoop Dreams (Steve James, 1994, PG-13, 176 min.)
Hoosiers (David Anspaugh, 1986, PG, 114 min.)
The Journey of Natty Gann (Jeremy Kagan, 1985, PG, 101 min.)
The Loneliness of the Long-distance Runner, (Great Britain, Tony Richardson, 1962, NR, 104 min.)
Rudy (David Anspaugh, 1993, PG 112 min.)
Stand and Deliver (Ramon Menendez, 1988, PG, 105 min.)
Wild Hearts Can't Be Broken (Steve Miner, 1991, G, 89 min.)

Ten Best Films on Love and Romance

Benny and Joon (Jeremiah S. Chechik, 1993, PG, 98 min.)
Clueless (Amy Heckerling, 1995, PG-13, 97 min.)
Gregory's Girl (Scotland, Bill Forsyth, 1981, NR, 87 min.)
The Man in the Moon (Robert Mulligan, 1991, PG-13, 99 min.)
My American Cousin (Canada, Sandy Wilson, 1985, PG, 94 min.)
My Brilliant Career (Australia, Gillian Armstrong, 1979, G, 102 min.)
A Room with a View (James Ivory, 1986, NR, 117 min.)
Sitting in Limbo (Canada, John N. Smith, 1986, PG, 95 min.)
The Umbrellas of Cherbourg (France, Jacques Demy, 1964, NR, 90 min., in French)
The Year My Voice Broke (Australia, John Duigan, 1987, PG-13, 103 min.)

Ten Best Films for World Literature Courses

Au Revoir les Enfants (France, Louis Malle, 1987, PG, 104 min., in French)
Gallipoli (Australia, Peter Weir, 1981, PG, 111 min.)
Inner Circle (U.S., [filmed in Russia], Andrei Konchalovsky, 1991, PG-13, 122 min., in English)
The Last Emperor (U.S., [filmed in Beijing], Bernardo Bertolucci, 1987, PG-13, 164 min., in English)
My Life as a Dog (Sweden, Lasse Hallstrom, 1987, NR, 101 min., in Swedish)
Musashi Miyamoto (Samurai I) (Japan, Hiroshi Inagaki, 1954, NR, 92 min., in Japanese)
Pathfinder (Norway, Nils Gaup, 1988, NR, 88 min., in Lapp)
The Return of Martin Guerre (France, Daniel Vigne, 1982, NR, 111 min., in French)
Sarafina! (South Africa, Darrell James Roodt, 1992, PG-13, 98 min.)
Sugar Cane Alley (Martinique, Euzhan Palcy, 1983, NR, 100 min., in French)

Ten Best Films for American Literature Courses

The Age of Innocence (Martin Scorsese, 1993, PG, 138 min.)
American Graffiti (George Lucas, 1973, PG, 112 min.)
Citizen Kane (Orson Welles, 1941, NR, 119 min.)
Death of a Salesman (Volker Scholondorff, 1986, NR, 135 min.)

Dr. Strangelove, or How I Learned to Stop Worrying and Love the Bomb (Stanley Kubrick, 1964, NR, 93 min.)
The Grapes of Wrath (John Ford, 1940, NR, 129 min.)
The Little Foxes (William Wyler, 1941, NR, 116 min.)
Malcolm X (Spike Lee, 1992, PG-13, 201 min.)
Roots (Episode I, David Greene, 1977, NR, 99 min.)
1776 (Peter H. Hunt, 1972, G, 141 min.)

Ten Best Films of British Literature

Anne of the Thousand Days (Hal B. Wallis, 1969, PG, 145 min.)
Cromwell (Ken Hughes, 1970, G, 139 min.)
The Dead (John Huston, 1987, PG, 82 min.)
Hamlet (Franco Zeffirelli, 1990, PG, 135 min.)
A Man for All Seasons (Fred Zinneman, 1966, G, 120 min.)
Much Ado About Nothing (Kenneth Branagh, 1993, PG-13, 110 min.)
Sense and Sensibility (Ang Lee, 1995, PG, 136 min.)
Tess (Roman Polanski, 1980, PG, 170 min.)
Tom Jones (Tony Richardson, 1963, NR, 121 min.)
Wuthering Heights (William Wyler, 1939, NR, 104 min.)

Ten Best Films for Genre Study

Westerns
High Noon (Fred Zinneman, 1952, NR, 85 min.)
The Searchers (John Ford, 1956, NR, 119 min.)
Stagecoach (John Ford, 1939, NR, 100 min.)
Detective Films
The Big Sleep (Howard Hawks, 1946, NR, 114 min.)
The Maltese Falcon (John Huston, NR, 101 min.)
Murder, My Sweet (Edward Dmytryk, 1944, NR, 95 min.)
Screwball Comedies
Bringing Up Baby (Howard Hawks, 1938, NR 103 min.)
The Philadelphia Story (George Cukor, 1940, NR, 112 min.)
Gangster Films
Public Enemy (William A. Wellman, 1931, NR, 85 min.)
Scarface (Howard Hawks, 1931, NR, 93 min.)

Ten Best Films for Film Study

American Cinema (The Annenberg/CPB Collection, 1994)
Basic Film Terms: A Visual Dictionary (Sheldon Renan, 1970, NR, 14 min.)
The Battleship Potemkin (Russia, Sergei Eisenstein, 1935, NR, 75 min., silent with English titles)
The Birth of a Nation (D. W. Griffith, 1915, NR, 175 min.)
Cinema Paradiso (Italy, Giuseppe Tornatore, 1989, NR, 123 min., in Italian)
The General (Buster Keaton and Clyde Bruckman, 1927, NR, 78 min.)
The Great Train Robbery (Edwin S. Porter, 1903, NR, 10 min.)
Modern Times (Charlie Chaplin, 1937, NR, 87 min.)
Singin' in the Rain (Gene Kelly and Stanley Donen, 1952, NR, 103 min.)
Visions of Light: The Art of Cinematography (Todd McCarthy, Stuart Samuels, and Arnold Glassman, 1993, NR, 95 min.)

Appendix H

RECOMMENDED WRITING TEXTBOOKS

Atwell, Nancie	*In the Middle: New Understandings About Writing, Reading, and Learning* (2nd ed.)	1998 Boynton/Cook
Ballenger, Bruce, & Lane, Barry	*Discovering the Writer Within*	1989 Writer's Digest Books
Benson, Chris, & Christian, Scott (Eds.)	*Writing to Make a Difference: Classroom Projects for Community Change*	2002 Teachers College Press
Berthoff, Ann	*The Making of Meaning*	1981 Boynton/Cook
Calkins, Lucy	*The Art of Teaching Writing* (2nd ed.)	1994 Heinemann
Elbow, Peter, & Belanoff, P.	*A Community of Writers: A Workshop Course in Writing*	1995 McGraw-Hill
Elbow, Peter	*Writing Without Teachers*	1973 Oxford U. Press
Fletcher, Ralph	*Breathing In; Breathing Out: Keeping a Writer's Notebook*	1996 Heinemann
Foster, David	*A Primer for Writing Teachers: Theories, Theorists, Issues, Problems*	1992 Boynton/Cook
Goldberg, Natalie	*Writing Down the Bones: Freeing the Writer Within*	1986 Shabhala
Graves, Donald	*A Fresh Look at Writing*	1994 Heinemann
Graves, Donald	*Writing: Teachers and Children at Work*	1983 Heinemann
Harris, Muriel	*Teaching One-to-One: The Writing Conference*	1987 NCTE
Kirby, Dan, Liner, Tom, & Vinz, Ruth	*Inside Out: Developmental Strategies for Teaching Writing*	1988 Boynton/Cook
Lamott, Anne	*Bird by Bird: Some Instructions on Writing and Life*	1995 Random House
Moffett, James	*Teaching the Universe of Discourse*	1983 Boynton/Cook
Murray, Donald	*A Writer Teaches Writing*	1985 Houghton Mifflin
Newkirk, Thomas	*Nuts and Bolts: A Practical Guide to Teaching College Composition*	1993 Boynton/Cook
Rief, Linda	*Seeking Diversity: Language Arts with Adolescents*	1992 Heinemann
Romano, Tom	*Clearing the Way: Working with Teenage Writers*	1987 Heinemann
Romano, Tom	*Writing with Passion: Life Stories, Multiple Genres*	1995 Boynton/Cook
Sloan, Glenna Davis	*Child as Critic*	1991 Teachers College Press
Weaver, Constance	*Teaching Grammar in Context*	1996 Boynton/Cook

Appendix I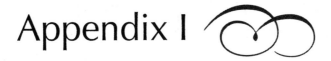

SAT Essay Exam Assessment: Diederich Scale[9]

```
        1—Poor   2—Weak   3—Average   4—Good   5—Excellent
                                    Reader _____
Quality and development of ideas        1      2      3      4      5
Organization, relevance, movement       1      2      3      4      5
                                    _____ × 5 = _____
                                    Subtotal
Style, flavor, individuality            1      2      3      4      5
Wording and phrasing                    1      2      3      4      5
                                    _____ × 3 = _____
                                    Subtotal
Grammar, sentence structure             1      2      3      4      5
Punctuation                             1      2      3      4      5
Spelling                                1      2      3      4      5
Manuscript form, legibility             1      2      3      4      5
                                    _____ × 1 = _____
                                    Subtotal
                                    Total rate: _____ %
```

How to Interpret This Scale

1. This scale weighs content and organization 50%, aspects of style 30%, and mechanics 20%. The multiplication translates the 40 point scale into a 100 point scale.

2. The ratings for each item range from 1 to 5. Regard 1 as the lowest grade, 3 as the average, and 5 as the highest. Use 2 to designate below-average performance but not marked deficiency and use 4 to designate above-average performance but not marked proficiency. *Reading five randomly selected papers from a set before you attempt to grade the set will help you to form a realistic notion of 1, 3, and 5 performance for that particular assignment.*

3. Observing the following guidelines will also help to assure more uniform and consistent grading.

   a. *Quality and development of ideas.* Grant the writer his choice of subject matter. He was, after all, offered choices dictated by the teacher and should *not* be penalized by the value you place on one choice as compared to another. Look at how well he has supported his subject and *his* point of view or attitude toward the subject.

   b. *Organization, relevance, movement.* A 5 paper will begin with a clear indication of its controlling idea, offer convincing relevant support, and come to a close. A 1 paper begins anywhere and goes nowhere. A 3 paper may be skimpily but relevantly developed or fully developed, but including some irrelevant material.

   c. *Style, flavor, individuality.* Guard against the temptation to give a low score for the use of substandard Eng-

lish. Papers containing substandard English are often rich in flavor and individuality. Reserve 5 for the truly arresting paper. A single apt, precise, or arresting phrase can move a paper from a 3 to a 4.

   d. *Wording and phrasing.* Here is the place to give a low score for impoverished vocabulary and a high one for apt and precise diction and clear phrasing.

   e. *Grammar, sentence structure.* Low scores should be given for frequent and varied substandard constructions like errors in agreement between pronoun and antecedent, dangling constructions, subject-verb agreement, etc.

   f. *Punctuation.* Again, frequent *and varied* abuses of standard punctuation marks deserve a low score; occasional varied errors in common punctuation marks a middle score; freedom from common errors a high score. Errors in the use of the comma, the apostrophe and end punctuation should be regarded as more serious than errors in the use of the semicolon, quotation marks (especially double quotes), parentheses, and brackets. Regard the mistaken presence or absence of the apostrophe as a punctuation error, not a spelling error.

   g. *Spelling.* Give a score of 5 if the writer has misspelled no words; a 4 for one spelling error; a 3 for two spelling errors; a 2 for three spelling errors, and a 1 for four or more errors. This is the only place on the scale where you are to assess spelling. Misspelling the same word is only one error.

   h. *Adherence to manuscript form and a clearly readable paper* merits a 5. An unreadable paper without margins and without a proper heading merits a score of 1. Perhaps readers should attempt only a 1, 3, or 5 judgment on this item. Do *not* give a low score for neat cross-outs. (Remember that the students are writing their papers in class and that they have been encouraged not to waste time recopying.)

[9] Reprinted with permission from Dan Kirby and Tom Liner, with Ruth Vinz: *Inside Out: Developmental Strategies for Teaching Writing,* 2nd edition (Boynton/Cook Publishers, Portsmouth, NH, 1988, 1981), pp. 225–226. Diederich Scale adapted from Paul Diederich *Measuring Growth in English.* Copyright © 1974 by the National Council of Teachers of English.

ORAL COMMUNICATIONS ACTIVITIES LOG[10]

STUDENT NAME _____ GRADE _____

TEACHER NAME _____ COURSE NUMBER _____

SCHOOL _____ DATE OF COURSE _____/_____/_____

Communication Forms	Month/Day																			
	1	2	3	4	5	6	7	8	9	10	11	12	13	14	15	16	17	18	19	20
Conversation																				
Interview																				
Formal Discussion																				
Dramatization																				
Oral Interpretation																				
Impromptu																				
Prepared Speech																				
Giving Directions																				
Introductions																				
Introducing A Speaker																				
Acceptance Speech																				
Welcoming Speech																				
Storytelling																				
Informal Discussion																				
Role-Playing																				
Telephone Usage																				

Total number of days in attendance _____

Total number of days with speaking activities _____

Total number of different forms _____

[10]Permission to reprint these next five exercises given by Francis Snow, Winston Salem/Forsyth County Schools.

TWO COMMUNICATION INVENTORIES

Shyness Scale (SS)

Student Name _____ Course No. _____ Grade _____

Teacher Name_____ Date _____

Directions: The following 14 statements refer to talking with other people. If the statement describes you very well, circle "YES." If it somewhat describes you, circle "yes." If you are not sure whether it describes you or not, or if you do not understand the statement, circle, "?". If the statement is a poor description of you, circle "no." If the statement is a very poor description of you, circle "NO." There are no right or wrong answers. Work quickly; record your first impression.

1. I am a shy person.	YES	yes	?	no	NO
2. Other people think I talk a lot.	YES	yes	?	no	NO
3. I am a very talkative person.	YES	yes	?	no	NO
4. Other people think I am shy.	YES	yes	?	no	NO
5. I talk a lot.	YES	yes	?	no	NO
6. I tend to be very quiet in class.	YES	yes	?	no	NO
7. I don't talk much.	YES	yes	?	no	NO
8. I talk more than most people.	YES	yes	?	no	NO
9. I am a quiet person.	YES	yes	?	no	NO
10. I talk more in a small group (3–6 people) than other people do.	YES	yes	?	no	NO
11. Most people talk more than I do.	YES	yes	?	no	NO
12. Other people think I am very quiet.	YES	yes	?	no	NO
13. I talk more in class than most people do.	YES	yes	?	no	NO
14. Most people are more shy than I am.	YES	yes	?	no	NO

Personal Report of Communication Fear (PRCF)

Directions: (Essentially the same directions as above)

1. Talking with someone new scares me.	YES	yes	?	no	NO
2. I look forward to talking in class.	YES	yes	?	no	NO
3. I like standing up and talking to a group of people.	YES	yes	?	no	NO
4. I like to talk when the whole class listens.	YES	yes	?	no	NO
5. Standing up to talk in front of other people scares me.	YES	yes	?	no	NO
6. I like talking to teachers.	YES	yes	?	no	NO
7. I am scared to talk to people.	YES	yes	?	no	NO
8. I like it when it is my turn to talk in class.	YES	yes	?	no	NO
9. I like to talk to new people.	YES	yes	?	no	NO
10. When someone asks me a question, it scares me.	YES	yes	?	no	NO
11. There are a lot of people I am scared to talk to.	YES	yes	?	no	NO
12. I like to talk to people I haven't met before.	YES	yes	?	no	NO
13. I like it when I don't have to talk.	YES	yes	?	no	NO
14. Talking to teachers scares me.	YES	yes	?	no	NO

EVALUATION FORM FOR GROUP DISCUSSION

Teacher Name _____ Course No. _____ Date_____
Group No. _____ Grade _____

Directions: Rate each student on each objective using the following scale:
1 5 unsatisfactory; 2 5 below average; 3 5 average; 4 5 above average; 5 5 excellent.

NAME _____

Objectives: The student	Individual Score	Group Average
1. Displays a knowledge of the difference between discussion and debate		
2. Displays a positive attitude toward group		
3. Makes short, frequent, constructive comments		
4. Displays an ability to evaluate information		
5. Stays on the topic		
6. Facilitates group task and interaction		
7. Solicits contributions from others		
8. Displays an awareness of need for order and group leader		
9. Responds directly to comments and follows up ideas		
10. Displays knowledge of summarizing		
Total		
Student Average Across Objectives		

EXPLANATION OF RATINGS USED FOR THE EVALUATION FORM FOR GROUP DISCUSSION

1. Displays a knowledge of the difference between discussion and debate
   (5) Open-minded; gives and solicits ideas to reach best conclusion
   (4) Has definite ideas but honestly tries to understand others
   (3) Tries to sell his own ideas; reluctant to understand others
   (2) Refuses to listen to ideas other than his own or doesn't initiate his own ideas
   (1) Refuses to actively participate
2. Displays a positive attitude toward group
   (5) Encourages others to comment; seeks information; freely contributes
   (4) Gives lots of information but does nothing to encourage others
   (3) Detrimentally slows down process
   (2) Must be prodded to contribute; or makes only destructive comments
   (1) Refuses to participate
3. Makes short, frequent, constructive comments
   (5) Makes short, frequent, constructive comments
   (4) Frequently gives information but lacks tact dealing with others
   (3) Monopolizes time

(2) Contributes very little and usually only if asked or makes irrelevant comments

(1) Refuses to participate

4. Displays an ability to evaluate information

(5) Interprets, clarifies, restates, and reflects upon ideas and suggestions; offers solutions

(4) Interprets and restates information and recognizes the need for consensus

(3) Asks for relevant information

(2) Sees only one side

(1) Shows no understanding of evaluating information

5. Stays on the topic

(5) Knows purpose and pursues it

(4) Works on topic but gets too involved in some aspects of the topic

(3) Occasionally strays from topic or is occasionally distracted

(2) Frequently strays from topic or is frequently distracted

(1) Is inattentive or tries to distract attention[11]

6. Facilitates group task and interaction

(5) Makes others feel good about group; works well on task; practices summarizing and consensus taking

(4) Makes others feel good; works on task

(3) Either makes others feel good or works well on task

(2) Must be prodded to contribute

(1) Refuses to participate

7. Solicits contributions from others

(5) Actively encourages others to participate, asks questions, responds to others

(4) Asks for comments but fails to respond verbally and nonverbally

(3) Wants others to comment but doesn't know how to get a meaningful response

(2) Excludes one or two members

(1) Refuses to participate

8. Displays an awareness of need for order and group leader

(5) Practices self-control and encourages others to do so *if necessary*

(4) Practices self-control but does not encourage others to do so *when necessary*

(3) Excitable; uncontrollable urge to participate but is unresponsive to others

(2) Ignores leader's attempts to maintain order and organization and shows lack of awareness of group process

(1) Does his own thing; oblivious to group; may be distracting

9. Responds directly to comments and follows up ideas

(5) Responds directly to points; analyzes and discusses specific comments

(4) Recognizes points of agreement as well as disagreement

(3) Student hears only part of what is said; insists on stating his ideas

(2) Jumps around from idea to idea without a sense of group direction

(1) Refuses to actively participate

10. Displays knowledge of summarizing

(5) Helps group by reflecting, summarizing ideas; draws conclusions for group to accept or reject

(4) Restates suggestions after the group has discussed them

(3) Shows understanding of the mood and attitude of the group

(2) Lacks understanding of the group's position

(1) Makes no effort to follow the group's development

---

[11]Tension release in the form of humor is not straying from the topic.

TEACHER'S EVALUATION OF ANNOUNCEMENTS

Name _____

Articulation	precise	clear	careless	inaudible
Volume	regulated	satisfactory	erratic	too high
				too low
Rate	flexible	satisfactory	monotonous	too fast
				too slow
Tone	colorful	average	monotonous	
Juncture	used pauses effectively	used pauses ineffectively	no noticeable use of pauses	
Stress	used emphasis effectively	used emphasis ineffectively	no noticeable use of emphasis	

Content:

1. Organized clearly _____
2. Captured audience attention immediately _____
3. Motivated audience to listen _____
4. Presented complete information _____
5. Presented accurate information _____

Delivery:

6. Looked directly at audience _____
7. Maintained effective posture _____
8. Spoke loudly enough to be heard _____
9. Articulated clearly _____
10. Handled notes well _____

Additional Comments:

Appendix J

DEVELOPING A UNIT:
WILLIAM SHAKESPEARE

The creative teaching activities that follow were developed by able high school teachers in Indiana, Kentucky, Maryland, and North Carolina.

General

Bringing Oprah to the Classroom. Mary Ann Downs asks students to act as characters, hosts, expert guests, and audience members in a talk-show format. Each student takes on a role based on the literary work being studied. One student is the host/hostess. The panel is made up of students playing the roles of the major characters from the work and "expert" guests. Students in the audience must prepare and ask questions of panelists. Themes for each show range from "Was the assassination of Julius Caesar really in the best interest of Rome?" (*Julius Caesar*) to "Who was to blame for the murder of Duncan?" (*Macbeth.*) After reading *Julius Caesar*, for instance, one panel included Calpurnia, Julius Caesar, Portia, Brutus, Cassius, Casca, and a political analyst. (Some characters appeared posthumously.) Audience members stated their names, told what they were doing when Julius Caesar was assassinated, and proceeded with their questions. Panelists had to stay in character and answer the questions based on what they read. Downs reports that the talk-show format serves many purposes. It makes discussion student-centered, assesses the students' understanding of plot and character, and gives students the opportunity to think on their feet.

Shakespeare with Puppets. David Sampson divides students into groups. Each is responsible for condensing a scene to under five minutes. Key scenes and speeches can be abbreviated but not completely cut. Transitional words and phrases can be added but only if necessary. His students create puppets and film their completed work. These puppet shows necessitate a thorough knowledge of the play, critical skills for the editing process, and an understanding of filming techniques. The class produces a video that can be shown to other classes as well.

Julius Caesar

Julius Caesar newspaper. An unnamed teacher asks her sophomores to create a "Julius Caesar newspaper" dated the day of Caesar's assassination. During the course of reading *Julius Caesar*, students write stories relating to the play that correspond to the different sections of a newspaper (editorials, straight news stories, letters to the editor, feature stories on main character, sports stories). Three sample assignments follow.

NEWS STORY: Write a straight news story for a Roman newspaper covering the assassination of Caesar. Be objective (no opinions at all, please) and use third person. Be sure to include who, what, where, why, and how in the article.

LETTER TO THE EDITOR: Write a letter to the editor of a Roman newspaper about an event (from the play, or one you make up). Choose an issue brought up by the event, take a side, and argue for your position. Include a complimentary closing and sign it (you may make up a name if you would like).

FEATURE STORY: Write a feature story about a person or an event (real or made up) from the play. It should have a human interest slant—i.e., it ought to tug at the reader's heart. Human interest stories appeal to the emotions: happy, sad, good, bad, exciting, etc.

Small groups develop layout and pictures for each article. All of the pieces are assembled under a masthead. The paper includes other elements usually found in newspapers such as want ads, personals, advertisements, and advice columns.

Romeo and Juliet

Romeo and Juliet signaled suicide. Nancy Nelson's idea was inspired by a local newspaper article critical of teaching *Romeo and Juliet* because it appeared to glamorize teen suicide. To make students aware of the warning signs of a serious teen problem—suicide—and to provide an interesting composition topic for a classic piece of literature, she developed the following activity.

After reading *Romeo and Juliet*, I hand out a list of common warning signs of suicide. We talk about each and how common suicide is for teens today. Then I give the following assignment: Write a four paragraph composition identifying the suicide warning signs in *Romeo and Juliet*. Begin with a general introduction. In the body discuss Romeo's and Juliet's warning signs in separate paragraphs using quotations for support if desired. End with a concluding paragraph.

Common warning signs taken from several different sources in our school library are listed below.

1. persistent morbid thoughts, dreams, or talk about death or suicide
2. changes in grades, appetite, or sleep patterns
3. threats of suicide, implied or direct
4. isolation, where a formerly active and social person now spends much time alone
5. inability or reluctance to express anger or rage, particularly when you would expect such an expression
6. giving away of valued possessions
7. drug and alcohol addiction or abuse
8. severe guilt and shame
9. helpless or hopeless feelings
10. severe depression or despondence
11. any of these signs following a serious disruption in the family, school, or social group, especially the loss of a significant person, thing, or condition

Characters' values sort. Katherine Greene developed the following value sort for sophomores studying *Romeo and Juliet*. After students write their individual responses, they are primed for lively small group or whole class discussions.

Paris is in love with Juliet	T	F
Friar Laurence suggests a valid, sound plan for Juliet to follow.	T	F
Juliet should follow Friar Laurence's advice.	T	F
Juliet should marry Count Paris.	T	F
Lord Capulet's feelings regarding the marriage of his daughter are noble.	T	F
The nurse meaningfully mourns Juliet's "death."	T	F
Lady and Lord Capulet express genuine remorse at Juliet's "death."	T	F
Friar Laurence's role as a mediator between Juliet, Romeo, and their elders is a good one.	T	F
The apothecary should have sold Romeo the poison.	T	F
Friar John is responsible for the tragedy.	T	F

Macbeth

Macbeth Times. Mary Beth Braker uses a simplified newspaper activity to help students enter *Macbeth* imaginatively. She asks them to assume the roles of reporters traveling with Macduff as he leaves Scotland for England (like the White House reporters who follow the U.S. president on his travels). Write an article for an underground Scottish newspaper opposed to the murderous reign of Macbeth and chronicle the most recent events, including Macduff's flight to England, the police state imposed by the tyrannous Macbeth, the murder of Macduff's family. Come up with a headline and explore the journalistic questions *who, what, where, when, why,* and *how.*

Hamlet

Hamlet questionnaire. Joe Taylor designed an activity to enable students to address many of the universal issues and concerns that will pertain not only to their readings of *Hamlet* but also to the world in which high school students live today. After students complete a true-false questionnaire, the class spends the next twenty minutes discussing the issues that students are reacting to most vigorously.

True or False

1. It is never right to kill another person. _____
2. It is better to suffer whatever life brings than to commit suicide. _____
3. If someone murders your father, you can justify killing that person. _____
4. There are acceptable reasons for lying to your friends. _____
5. Our lives are preordained. _____
6. Leaders usually act in the best interest of their countries. _____
7. People should never compromise their ideals or beliefs. _____
8. No cause, political or otherwise, is worth dying for. _____
9. Sexual passion motivates the behavior of young people more than it does the behavior of their parents' generation. _____
10. It is better to act quickly than to be indecisive. _____
11. At times it is appropriate to sacrifice yourself for a greater good. _____
12. Fathers have a different set of expectations for their sons than they do for their daughters. _____
13. It is unmanly for men to express their emotions in public. _____
14. Parents can be optimistic about the world into which they bring their children. _____

Next Taylor places two of each of the individual statements on the questionnaire into the replica of a human skull. (But alas poor Yorick, a hat or box will work just fine.) One statement is then labeled "pro" while the other copy of the same statement is labeled "con." Students randomly choose the statement they must defend or oppose in class the next day (even though it usually takes two days to complete the point-counterpoint activity). They then prepare a two- to three-minute oral presentation in defense of their position. This presentation will be immediately followed by the student with the opposing point of view. After the pros and cons have been stated, students will take two to three minutes to respond. Students are graded on their oral presentations and their written responses to each statement. This same questionnaire can be used as an effective follow-up to reading *Hamlet.* Taylor then has students discuss whether or not their opinions have changed based upon their actual reading of the play.

Creative Projects for Hamlet. Mary Beth Braker assigns these projects for *Hamlet.* Students choose to complete one.

1. Pretend that you are a character *other than Hamlet* in the play (Gertrude, Ophelia, Polonius, Claudius, Laertes, Horatio, Rosencrantz, Guildenstern, etc.) and tell the basic story of the play from your character's *point of view.* Be sure to develop the plot in detail and pay special attention to the relationships your character has with other characters.
2. Write Ophelia's farewell to Hamlet. The correspondence could be in the form of a poem, song, or letter; but it must be composed from Ophelia's point of view and state of mind and must reflect the complicated relationship between Ophelia and Hamlet.
3. As one of the characters in the play, write a letter to either "Dear Abby" or "Ann Landers" expressing your dilemma and asking for advice *and* write the columnist's imaginary reply to your character.
4. Rewrite the ending of the play. You must include the following characters in the final scene: Gertrude, Claudius, Laertes, Horatio, and Hamlet. The only plot requirement is that *only* Claudius dies in the end. You may write this as a play with dialogue and stage directions or as a narrative account of the play's ending.

FOUR PERSPECTIVES ON LANGUAGE LEARNING

Gere, Fairbanks, Howes, Roop, and Schaafsma (1992) observed teachers and students in middle and high school classrooms and found four distinct perspectives on teaching English based on four quite different views of language. Their description provides a further clarification of the reasons for the diverse instructional choices that today's English teachers make—

goals, strategies, activities, and texts. While most English teachers situate themselves primarily under one perspective, many borrow ideas and methods from all four. We present the premises and practices of each.

Language as Artifact

Language is a cultural artifact to be understood and interpreted in order to open students to the richness of the human experience. Students should read to discover meaning and write to demonstrate their "ability to think clearly and well" (p. 87). Language study concentrates on its formal characteristics and often focuses on the formal rules of grammar or on "key grammatical concepts" (p. 91). Literature study employs the skills of intensive close reading of texts that are privileged by tradition and aesthetics. The text is paramount as an expression of the author's view of the human condition. Analysis is valued more highly than other approaches to literature and language. Evaluation of student knowledge is measured by a common standard.

Language as Development

Language is a tool for cognitive and personal development. Cognitive and developmental psychologists suggest that all students can learn in school if a teacher (1) identifies a student's present developmental stage and proficiencies, (2) develops and sequences appropriate strategies to help the student acquire new skills, and (3) sets realistic goals for the student to meet. Teachers use cognitive structures and models (of their skills and others) to solve reading and writing problems. For instance, they might use prereading strategies to prepare students to comprehend literature and sentence-combining exercises to teach sentence variety and concept development. Texts are usually read to teach reading and writing skills, not to deepen interpretive insight or broaden aesthetic appreciation. Evaluation of measurable skills helps the student and teacher track progress.

Language as Expression

Language provides a crucial means for exploring our own inner worlds and describing what we find there. Teachers center on the individual student and encourage student self-discovery and self-expression. In literature, teachers are interested not in analysis primarily, but in the student's personal response to the text. The writing of professional writers is not prized above student writing. Language study is integrated into reading and writing study; grammar and language rules are invoked not as the subjects of separate study, but as aids to expression. Writing instruction is more personal and expressive with students choosing their topics, experimenting with technique and form, and evaluating their own and their peers' work. Journal writing is common, and like other forms, is ungraded by the teacher. Process is emphasized over product.

Language as Social Construct

Language is a social instrument by which we grow in critical understanding of the self and the world of which it is a part. Students are again at the center of the classroom, but teachers are more concerned with preparing them to be critical and committed "citizens in the political world" (p. 195). Consequently, students are more empowered to design their own learning in nontraditional ways. Teachers, interested in students' becoming more critical of the world around them, encourage a variety of classroom structures, some of which operate outside the walls of schools or the bindings of printed texts. For instance, community-based research projects may be undertaken by students working collaboratively to collect, interpret, and "publish" data. Professionally written texts and student-created texts are used to train students to question and examine their worlds and construct their own interpretations.

Appendix K

NCTE ORGANIZATIONS AND PERIODICALS FOR THE ENGLISH TEACHER

Organizations

National Council of Teachers of English (NCTE)
1111 Kenyon Road
Urbana, Illinois 61801
Phone: 217-328-3870 and 800-369-6283
Fax: 217-328-9645

NCTE Constituent Organizations and Journals (Published quarterly)

Organization	Journal
Conference on College Composition and Communication (CCCC)	College Composition and Communication
Conference on English Education (CEE)	English Education
Conference on English Leadership (CEL)	English Leadership Quarterly

Professional Journals of the NCTE

Title	Intended Readers
English Journal	Teachers of middle, junior, high schools
College English	Teachers of college students
Language Arts	Teachers of elementary schools (K–8)
Teaching English in the Two-Year College	Teachers of two-year college students
Research in the Teaching of English	English teachers at all levels: elementary to university

Professional Conventions

Convention	Dates
NCTE Annual Convention	Time: week preceding Thanksgiving
Conference on College Composition and Communication	Time: usually mid-March

NCTE Series

Series	Content
Theory and Research into Practice (TRIP) (booklets)	This series describes research and then gives examples of practical classroom applications.
Ideas Plus, Books 1–10	This series presents classroom-tested ideas from classroom teachers.

EDUCATIONAL PERIODICALS RECOMMENDED FOR ENGLISH TEACHERS

Educational Leadership
Association for Supervision and Curriculum Development
1703 N. Beauregard St.
Alexandria, VA 22314
(703) 578-9600, (800) 933-2723
8 issues per year/ISSN 0013-1784

Kappan
Phi Delta Kappa
8th and Union
PO Box 789
Bloomington, IN 47402
(812) 339-1156
Monthly, September–June

Contemporary Education
School of Education
Indiana State University
Statesman Towers, Room 1005
Terre Haute, IN 47809
(812) 237-2970
4 issues per year/ISSN 0010-7476

Education Digest
Prakken Publications, Inc.
3979 Varsity Dr.
Ann Arbor, MI 48107
(734) 975-2800
Monthly, Sept.–May/ISSN 0013-127X

Teacher
Editorial Projects in Education
6935 Arlington Rd., Suite 100
Bethesda, MD 20814
(301) 280-3100
9 issues per year/ISSN 1046-6193

The New York Times Book Review
229 West 43rd St.
New York, NY 10036
(212) 556-1234
52 issues per year/ISSN 0028-7806

The ALAN Review
Assembly on Literature for Adolescents, NCTE
1111 W. Kenyon Road
Urbana, IL 61801-1096
(800) 369-6283

Booklist
American Library Association
50 E. Huron St.
Chicago, IL 60611
(312) 944-6780
Semi-monthly/22 issues per year

Horn Book Magazine
The Horn Book, Inc.
56 Roland St.
Boston, MA 02129
(617) 628-0225

Journal of Adolescent and Adult Literacy
International Reading Association
800 Barksdale Rd.
Box 8139
Newark, DE 19714-8139
(302) 731-1600
8 issues per year/ISSN 1081-3004

School Library Journal
R. R. Bowker Company
245 W. 17th St.
New York, NY 10011
(212) 463-6824

Voice of Youth Advocates (VOYA)
Scarecrow Press
4720 Boston Way, Suite A
Lanham, MD 20706
(301) 459-3360
bi-monthly/ISSN 0160-4201

References

Abbot, M. (1990). Idea exchange: To kill a mockingbird. *North Carolina English Teacher, 47*(2), 16-17.

Abrahamson, R. F., & Carter, B. (1987). Of survival, school, wars, and dreams: Nonfiction that belongs in English classes. *English Journal, 76*(2), 104-109.

Abrahamson, R. F., & Carter, B. (1991). Nonfiction: The missing piece in the middle. *English Journal, 80*(1), 52-58.

Abrams, M. H. (1953). *The mirror and the lamp.* New York: Oxford University Press.

Abse, D., & Abse, J. (Eds.). (1986). *Voices in the gallery.* London: Tate Gallery.

Adams, P. (1987). Writing from reading—"Dependent authorship" as a response. In B. Corcoran & E. Evans (Eds.), *Readers, texts, teachers* (pp. 119-152). Upper Montclair, NJ: Boynton/Cook.

Adams, P. (1989). Imaginative investigations: Some nondiscursive ways of writing in response to novels. In J. O. Milner & L. F. M. Milner (Eds.), *Passages to literature: Essays on teaching in Australia, Canada, England, the United States, and Wales* (pp. 53-75). Urbana, IL: NCTE.

Adkison, S., & Tchudi, S. (2001). Reading the data: Making supportable claims for classroom assessment. *English Journal, 91*(1), 43-50.

Adler, M. J., & Van Goren, C. (1972). *How to read a book.* New York: Simon & Shuster.

Agee, J. (1999). "There it was, that one sex scene": English teachers on censorship. *English Journal, 89*(2), 61-69.

Alexander, J. (1988). Oral communication: A survey of teacher's attitudes. *Use of English* (Vol. 39). Edinburgh: Scottish Academic Press.

Allen, J. (1995). *It's never too late: Leading adolescents to lifelong literacy.* Portsmouth, NH: Heinemann.

Allen, W. (1963). *Reading a novel.* London: Phoenix House.

Allen, W. (1980). The Kugelmass episode. In *Side effects.* New York: Random House.

Allen, W. (1991). If the impressionists had been dentists. In *The complete prose of Woody Allen.* New York: Wings Books.

Alvarez, J. (1998). Ten of my writing commandments. *English Journal, 88*(2), 36-41.

Anderson, D. (2001). The writing process rejected. *Quarterly. 23*(2), 30-33.

Anderson, P. M., & Rubano, G. (1991). *Enhancing aesthetic reading and response.* Urbana, IL: NCTE.

Anderson, S. (1964). *Between the Grimms and "The Group."* Princeton, NJ: Educational Testing Service.

Andrasick, K. D. (1990). *Opening texts: Using writing to teach literature.* Portsmouth, NH: Heinemann.

Anthony, R. J., Johnson, T. D., Mickelson, N. I., & Preece, A. (1991). *Evaluating literacy: A perspective for change.* Portsmouth, NH: Heinemann.

Applebee, A. (2000, Winter). Engaging students in meaningful conversation leads to higher achievement. *English Update: A Newsletter from the Center on English Learning & Achievement, 1,* 9.

Applebee, A. N. (1974). *Tradition and reform in the teaching of English: A history.* Urbana, IL: NCTE.

Applebee, A. N. (1977). The elaborative choice. In M. Nystrand (Ed.), *Language as a way of knowing.* Toronto: Ontario Institute for Studies in Education.

Applebee, A. N. (1978). *A survey of teaching conditions in English, 1977.* Urbana, IL: NCTE and ERIC/RCS.

Applebee, A. N. (1981). *Writing in the secondary school: English and the content areas.* Urbana, IL: NCTE.

Applebee, A. N. (1984). *Contexts for learning to write: Studies of secondary school instruction.* Norwood, NJ: Ablex.

Applebee, A. N. (1993). *Literature in the secondary school: Studies of curriculum and instruction in the United States.* Urbana, IL: NCTE.

Applebee, A. N. (1996). *Curriculum as conversation: Transforming traditions of teaching and learning.* Chicago: University of Chicago Press.

Applebee, A. N. (1997). Rethinking curriculum in the English language arts. *English Journal, 86*(5), 25-31.

Appleman, D. (1992). "I understood the grief": Theory-based introduction to *Ordinary People.* In N. J. Karolides (Ed.), *Reader response in the classroom: Evoking and interpreting meaning in literature* (pp. 92-101). New York: Longman.

Appleman, D. (2000). *Critical encounters in high school English: Teaching literary theory to adolescents.* New York: Teachers College Press.

Armstrong, C. (1996). Deborah Tannen comes to class: Implications of gender and conversation in the classroom (one person's opinion). *English Journal, 85*(2), 15-16.

Armstrong, T. (1994). *Multiple intelligences in the classroom.* Alexandria, VA: Association for Supervision and Curriculum Development.

Arnig, G. (1991). *National test: "Nay"; Nationwide assessment system: "Yea."* Princeton, NJ: Educational Testing Service.

Arnold, R. (1987). The hidden life of a drama text. In B. Corcoran & E. Evans (Eds.), *Readers, texts, teachers* (pp. 218-233). Upper Montclair, NJ: Boynton/Cook.

Aronowitz, S. (1977). Mass culture and the eclipse of reason: The implications for pedagogy. *College English, 38*(8), 768-774.

Arrowsmith, W. (1986, Feb. 3). *Liberal education vs. egalitarianism.* The Toqueville Forum, Wake Forest University, Winston-Salem, NC.

Arthur, B. (1973). *Teaching English to speakers of English.* New York: Harcourt Brace Jovanovich.

Athanases, S. Z., Christiano, D., & Lay, E. (1995). Fostering empathy and finding common ground in multiethnic classes. *English Journal, 84*(3), 26-34.

Atwell, N. (1987). *In the middle: Writing, reading, and learning with adolescents.* Upper Montclair, NJ: Boynton/Cook.

Atwell, N. (1996). Cultivating our garden. *Voices from the Middle, 3*(4), 47-51.

Atwell, N. (1998). *In the middle: New understandings about writing, reading, and learning* (2nd ed.). Portsmouth, NH: Boynton/Cook & Heinemann.

Auer, J. (1991). *On teaching speech in elementary and junior high schools.* Bloomington, IN: University of Indiana Press.

Austen, J. (1962). *Northanger Abbey* and *Persuasion.* New York: Everyman.

Axelrod, A. (2000). *The Metropolitan Life Survey of the American Teacher 2000.* New York: Metropolitan Life Insurance Company.

Axline, V. (1964). *Dibs: In search of self.* Boston: Houghton Mifflin.

Baker, H. A. (1980). *The journey back: Issues in black literature and criticism.* Chicago: University of Chicago Press.

Baker, R. (1980). Schlemiel. In *So this is depravity* (pp. 307–309). New York: Congdon & Lattis.

Baker, R. (1981, April 26). The English mafia. *New York Times Magazine,* p. 29.

Barker, A. P. (1989). A gradual approach to feminism in the American-literature classroom. *English Journal, 78*(6), 39–44.

Barlow, C., & Stankwytch, C. (1982). *Guidelines for teaching oral communication: English 9–12.* With S. Dahlen, V. Martin, R. Parker, S. Sink, and F. Snow. Winston-Salem/Forsyth County Schools, Winston-Salem, NC.

Barnes, D. (1992). *From communication to curriculum.* (2nd ed.). Portsmouth, NH: Boynton/Cook.

Barnes, D., Britton, J., & Torbe, M. (1990). *Language, learner, and the school* (4th ed.). Portsmouth, NH: Boynton/Cook.

Barth, J. (1968). Lost in the funhouse. In J. Barth (Ed.), *Lost in the funhouse.* New York: Doubleday.

Barton, G. (1998). Grammar without shame. *The Use of English, 49*(2), 107–118.

Barzun, J. (1983). *A stroll with William James.* Chicago: University of Chicago Press.

Bateson, M. C. (1990). *Composing a life.* New York: Atlantic Monthly Press.

Bayer, A. S. (1990). *Collaborative-apprenticeship learning: Language and thinking across the curriculum, K–12.* Mountain View, CA: Mayfield.

Beach, R., & Marshall, J. (1991). *Teaching literature in the secondary school.* Orlando: Harcourt Brace.

Beals, T. J. (1998). Between teachers and computers: Does text-checking software really improve student writing? *English Journal, 87*(1), 67–72.

Beaven, M. H. (1977). Individualized goal setting, self-evaluation and peer evaluation. In C. R. Cooper & L. Odell (Eds.), *Evaluating writing: Describing, measuring, judging* (pp. 135–156). Urbana, IL: NCTE.

Beck, R. (1988). *Stagecraft.* Lincolnwood, IL: National Textbook Company.

Beers, J. W. (1980). Developmental strategies of spelling competence in primary school children. In E. H. Henderson & J. W. Beers, *Developmental and cognitive aspects of learning to spell* (pp. 36–45). Newark, DE: IRA.

Beers, J. W., & Henderson, E. H. (1977). A study of developing orthographic concepts among first graders. *Research in the Teaching of English, 11*(2), 133–148.

Belanoff, P., & Dickson, M. (1991). *Portfolios: Process and product.* Portsmouth, NH: Boynton/Cook.

Belgard, M. (1987). Idea exchange: What if . . . Huck Finn? *North Carolina English Teacher, 44*(2), 16–17.

Bencich, C. B. (1996). Writing and teaching. *English Journal, 85*(3), 91–93.

Bennett, W. J. (1984). *To reclaim a legacy: A report on the humanities in higher education.* Washington, DC: National Endowment for the Humanities.

Bennett, W. J. (1986). *What works. Research about teaching and learning.* Washington, DC: U.S. Department of Education.

Benseler, D. P., & Shultz, R. (1980). Methodological trends in college foreign language. *Modern Language Journal, 64*(1), 88–96.

Berenson, B. G., & Carkhuff, R. R. (1967). *Beyond counseling and therapy.* New York: Holt, Rinehart, & Winston.

Berliner, D. C., & Biddle, B. J. (1995). *The manufactured crisis: Myths, fraud, and the attack on America's public schools.* Reading, MA: Addison-Wesley.

Berthoff, A. E. (1978). *Forming/thinking/writing.* Upper Montclair, NJ: Boynton/Cook.

Berthoff, A. E. (1981). *The making of meaning: Metaphors, models, and maxims for writing teachers.* Portsmouth, NH: Boynton/Cook.

Bickford, S. (1991). Idea exchange: Huckleberry Finn town meeting. *North Carolina English Teacher, 48*(2), 27–28.

Bigsby, C. W. E. (1980). *The second black renaissance: Essays in black literature.* Westport, CT: Greenwood.

Billings, P. (1992). Only a well-digger's teacher. In C. Duke and S. Jacobsen (Eds.), *Poets' perspectives: Reading, writing, and teaching poetry* (pp. 82–87). Portsmouth, NH: Boynton/Cook.

Birk, L. (1996). What's so bad about the lecture? *Harvard Education Letter, 13*(6), 7–8.

Birkerts, S. (1994). *The Gutenberg elegies.* Winchester, MA: Faber & Faber.

Bissex, G., & Bullock, R. (Eds.). (1987). *Seeing for ourselves: Research by teachers of writing.* Portsmouth, NH: Heinemann.

Bjorklund, A. L. (2000). One more tool for the toolbox. *English Journal, 90*(2), 42–46.

Black, M. (1997). *Using comics to teach English.* Unpublished master's thesis, Wake Forest University, Winston-Salem.

Blair, L. (1991). Developing student voices with multicultural literature. *English Journal, 80*(8), 24–28.

Blanscet, K. (1988). Themes in stories and songs. In F. A. Kaufmann (Ed.), *Ideas plus: A collection of practical teaching ideas, book 6* (pp. 31–33). Urbana, IL: NCTE.

Bleich, D. (1975). *Readings and feelings: An introduction to subjective criticism.* Urbana, IL: NCTE.

Bleich, D. (1978). *Subjective criticism.* Baltimore: Johns Hopkins University Press.

Bleich, D. (1987). Gender interests in reading and language. In E. Flynn & P. Schweickart (Eds.), *Gender and reading: Essays on readers, texts and contexts* (pp. 234–266). Baltimore: Johns Hopkins University Press.

Block, C. C. (1997). *Teaching the language arts.* Boston: Allyn & Bacon.

Bloom, A. (1987). *The closing of the American mind.* New York: Simon & Schuster.

Bloom, B. (1968). Learning for mastery. *Evaluation Comment, 1*(2). Los Angeles: Center for the Study of Evaluation of Instructional Programs.

Bloom, B. S., Englehart, M. D., Furst, E. J., Hill, W. H., & Krathwohl, D. R. (1956). *Taxonomy of educational objectives, handbook 1: Cognitive domain.* New York: McKay.

Bloom, H. (1973). *The anxiety of influence: A theory of poetry.* New York: Oxford University Press.

Bloom, H. (1994). *The western canon: The books and school of the ages.* New York: Harcourt Brace.

Bloomfield, M. W., & Newmark, L. (1963). *A linguistic introduction to the history of English.* New York: Knopf.

Bonnycastle, S. (1996). *In search of authority: An introductory guide to literary theory* (2nd ed.). Peterborough, Ontario: Broadview.

Book, C., & Galvin, K. (1975). *Instruction in and about small group discussion.* Urbana, IL: ERIC/ACS and SCA. ERIC Document Reproduction Service No. ED 113773.

Booksearch. (1988). Magazines in the English classroom. *English Journal, 77*(7), 91–93.

Booksearch. (1989). Using adolescent novels as transitions to literary classics. *English Journal, 78*(3), 82–84.

Booksearch. (1990a). Magazine and newspaper columns for the English classroom. *English Journal, 79*(2), 79–82.

Booksearch. (1990b). Nonfiction: A link to other lives. *English Journal, 79*(1), 91–95.

Booth, W. (1961). *The rhetoric of fiction.* Chicago: University of Chicago Press.

Booth, W. (1979). *Critical understanding: The power and limits of pluralism.* Chicago: University of Chicago Press.

Booth, W. (1988a). *The company we keep: An ethics of fiction.* Berkeley: University of California Press.

Booth, W. (1988b). *The vocation of a teacher: Rhetorical occasions, 1967–1988.* Chicago: University of Chicago Press.

Borich, G. D. (1992). *Effective teaching methods* (2nd ed.). New York: Macmillan.

Bowen, B. (1991). A multi-genre approach to the art of the biographer. *English Journal, 80*(4), 53–54.

Bracey, G. (2002). *The war against America's public schools.* Boston: Allyn & Bacon.

Bradbury, R. (1983). *Dandelion wine.* New York: Knopf.

Braddock, R., Jones, R. L., & Schoen, L. (1963). *Research in written composition.* Urbana, IL: NCTE.

Braun, E., Feaster, S., Toth, M., & Weaver, L. (2001, Nov.). *Mapping your way to understanding.* Presentation at the NCTE fall conference, Baltimore.

Brewbaker, J. M. (1997). On Tuesday morning: The case for standards for the English language arts. *English Journal, 86*(1), 76–82.

Bridgers, S. E. (1997, April). *Story matters in young adult literature.* Presentation at the NCTE spring conference, Charlotte, NC.

Bridgers, S. E. (1999). Notes from a guerrilla. *English Journal, 88*(6), 41–47.

Brinkley, E. (1998). Learning to use grammar with precision through editing conferences. In C. Weaver (Ed.), *Lessons to share on teaching grammar in context* (pp. 120–136). Portsmouth, NH: Boynton/Cook & Heinemann.

Britton, J. (1970). *Language and learning.* Harmondsworth, UK: Penguin.

Britton, J. (1986). Talking to learn. In D. Barnes, J. Britton, & M. Torbe (Eds.), *Language, the learner and the school.* Harmondsworth, UK: Penguin.

Britton, J., Burgess, T., Martin, N., McLeod, A., & Rosen, H. (1975). *The development of writing abilities: 11–18.* London: Macmillan Education.

Britzman, D. P. (1991). *Practice makes practice: A critical study of learning to teach.* Albany: State University of New York Press.

Brock, R., & Mirtz, R. (1994). *Small groups in writing workshops.* Urbana, IL: NCTE.

Bromley, K. (1998). *Language arts: Exploring connections.* Boston: Allyn & Bacon.

Brooke, R., Mirtz, R., & Evans, R. (1994). *Small groups in writing workshops: Invitations to a writer's life.* Urbana, IL: NCTE.

Brooks, C. (1947/1968). *The well-wrought urn: Studies in the structure of poetry.* London: Methuen.

Brooks, P. (1973). Mimesis: Grammar and the echoing voice. *College English, 35*(2), 161–168.

Brown, A. L., & Palincsar, A. S. (1989). Guided, cooperative learning and individual knowledge acquisition. In L. B. Resnick (Ed.), *Knowing, learning, and instruction: Essays in honor of Robert Glaser* (pp. 393–451). Hillsdale, NJ: Erlbaum.

Brown, C. R. V. (1992). Contemporary poetry about painting. *English Journal, 81*(1), 41–45.

Brown, D. E. (1983). Films in the English class. *English Journal, 72*(8), 71–72.

Brown, J., & Stephens, E. (1996). Being proactive, not waiting for the censor. In J. Brown (Ed.), *Preserving intellectual freedom: Fighting censorship in our schools* (pp. 125–132). Urbana, IL: NCTE.

Brown, J. R. (1981). *Discovering Shakespeare.* New York: Columbia University Press.

Bruchac, J. (1987). *Survival this way: Interviews with American Indian poets.* Tucson: Sun Tracks and University of Arizona Press.

Bruffee, K. A. (1984). Collaborative learning and the conversation of mankind. *College English, 46*(7), 635–652.

Bruner, J. (1966). *Toward a theory of instruction.* Cambridge: Belknap Press of Harvard University.

Bruner, J. (1975). From communication to language: A psychological perspective. *Cognition, 3*(3), 255–287.

Bruner, J. (1983). *In search of mind: Essays in autobiography.* New York: Harper & Row.

Bruner, J. (1986). *Actual minds, possible worlds.* Cambridge: Harvard University Press.

Brunwin, B. (1985, July). *Historical writing project.* Presentation at Triad Writing Project, Winston-Salem, NC.

Bryson, B. (1990). *The mother tongue: English and how it got that way.* New York: Avon.

Bryson, B. (1994). *Made in America: An informal history of the English language in the United States.* New York: Morrow.

Buckelew, M. (2000). Teacher to teacher: What works of nonfiction do you recommend for the English classroom? *English Journal 89*(6), 35–36.

Burbach, H., & Figgins, M. (1993). A thematic profile of the images of teachers in film. *Teacher Education Quarterly, 20*(2), 65–75.

Burch, C. B. (1997). Creating a two-tiered portfolio rubric. *English Journal, 86*(1), 55–58.

Burch, C. B. (1999). Inside the portfolio experience. *English Education, 32*(1), 34–47.

Burke, J. (1999). *The English teacher's companion: A complete guide to classroom, curriculum, and the profession.* Portsmouth, NH: Boynton/Cook & Heinemann.

Burmester, D. (1983). Electronic media: Media probes. *English Journal, 72*(4), 95–97.

Burnett, R. E. (1994). Productive and unproductive conflict in collaboration. In L. Flower, D. L. Wallace, L. Norris, & R. E. Burnett (Eds.), *Making thinking visible: Writing, collaborative planning, and classroom inquiry* (pp. 237–242). Urbana, IL: NCTE.

Caccia, P. (1991). Getting grounded: Putting semantics to work in the classroom. *English Journal, 80*(2), 55–59.

Cage, T., & Rosenfeld, L. B. (1989). Ekphrastic poetry in performance: An examination of audience perceptions of the relationship between poetry and painting. *Text and Performance Quarterly, 9*(3), 199-206.

Cain, B. N. (1989). With worldmaking, planning models matter. *English Education, 21*(1), 5-29.

Caine, R., & Caine, G. (1997). *Education on the edge of possibility.* Alexandria, VA: Association for Supervision and Curriculum Development.

Calkins, L. (1994). *The art of teaching writing* (2nd ed.). Portsmouth, NH: Heinemann.

Calkins, L. M. (1983). *Lessons from a child: On the teaching and learning of writing.* Exeter, NH: Heinemann.

Calkins, L. M. (1986). *The art of teaching writing.* Portsmouth, NH: Heinemann.

Calkins, L. M. (1989, Nov.). *Autobiography: The living that surrounds the writing.* Paper presented at the NCTE Annual Convention, Baltimore.

Callies, R. (1998). When grammar matters: Guiding students through revision. In C. Weaver (Ed.), *Lessons to share on teaching grammar in context* (pp. 110-119). Portsmouth, N.H.: Boynton/Cook & Heinemann.

Cameron, R. (1994). Writing to internalize themes in literature. *English Journal, 83*(8), 91-93.

Camp, R. (1990, Spring). Thinking together about portfolios. *Quarterly of the National Writing Project and the Center for the Study of Writing,* pp. 12-13.

Carey-Webb, A. (1991). Auto/biography of the oppressed: The power of testimonial. *English Journal, 80*(4), 44-47.

Carey-Webb, A. (1999). Insights for interns: Sometimes things just don't work out. *English Journal, 88*(6), 19-22.

Carey-Webb, A. (2001). *Literature and lives: A response-based, cultural studies approach to teaching English.* Urbana, IL: NCTE.

Carlson, M. A. Z. (1989). Guidelines for a gender-balanced curriculum in English, grades 7-12. *English Journal, 78*(6), 30-33.

Carney, B. (1996). Process writing and the secondary school reality: A compromise. *English Journal, 85*(6), 28-35.

Carter, B. (1987). *A content analysis of the most frequently circulated information books in three junior high libraries.* Unpublished doctoral dissertation, University of Houston.

Cartwright, C. A., & Cartwright, G. P. (1984). *Developing observation skills* (2nd ed.). New York: McGraw-Hill.

Caswell, E., Villaume, E., Johnson, J., Butler, D., & Barnett, D. (2001, Nov.). *Nonfiction reading strategies for success.* Presentation at NCTE annual conference, Baltimore.

Cazden, C. B. (1972). *Child language and education.* New York: Holt, Rinehart, & Winston.

Cazden, C. B. (1976, Summer). How knowledge about language helps the classroom teacher—or does it: A personal account. *Urban Review, 9,* 74-90.

Cazden, C. B. (1979, Nov.). Keynote speech at the National Council of Teachers of English. Boston.

Cazden, C. B. (1988). *Classroom discourse: The language of teaching and learning.* Portsmouth, NH: Heinemann.

Cazden, C. B., Cordeiro, P. A., & Giacobbe, M. E. (1985). Spontaneous and scientific concepts: Young children's learning of punctuation. In G. Wells & J. Nicholls (Eds.), *Language and learning: An interactional perspective* (pp. 107-124). Philadelphia: Falmer.

CEE Commission on Inservice Education. (1994). Inservice education: Ten principles. *English Education, 26*(2), 125-128.

Chambers, I. (1985). Popular culture, popular knowledge. *One, Two, Three, Four: A Rock and Roll Quarterly,* 1-8.

Cheney, L. V. (1987). *American memory: A report on the humanities in the nation's public schools.* Washington, DC: National Endowment for the Humanities.

Chiseri-Strater, E., & Sunstein, B. (Eds.). (1997). *Field working.* Boston: St. Martins.

Chomsky, C. (1969). *The acquisition of syntax in children from five to ten.* Cambridge: MIT Press.

Chomsky, C. (1972). Write now, read later. In C. Cazden (Ed.), *Language in early childhood education* (pp. 119-126). Washington, DC: National Education Association.

Chomsky, C. (1979). Approaching reading through invented spelling. In L. B. Resnick & P. Weaver (Eds.), *Theory and practice in early reading* (Vol. 2, pp. 43-65). Hillsdale, NJ: Erlbaum.

Chomsky, C. (1984). Finding the best language arts software. *Classroom Computer Learning, 4*(6) 61-63.

Chomsky, N. (1957). *Syntactic structures.* The Hague: Mouton.

Chomsky, N. (1968). *Language and mind.* New York: Harcourt, Brace, World.

Christel, M. T. (1988). Idea exchange: *A Tale of Two Cities:* Journal assignment. *North Carolina English Teacher, 46*(1), 19-20.

Christenbury, L. (1994). *Making the journey: Being and becoming a teacher of English language arts.* Portsmouth, NH: Boynton/Cook.

Christenbury, L. (1996). From the editor. *English Journal, 85*(7), 11-12.

Christenbury, L. (2000). *Making the journey: Being and becoming a teacher of English language arts* (2nd ed.). Portsmouth, NH: Boynton/Cook.

Christenbury, L., & Kelly, P. P. (1983). *Questioning: A path to critical thinking.* Urbana, IL: NCTE.

Christensen, F. (1967). *Notes toward a new rhetoric: Six essays for teachers.* New York: Harper & Row.

Christensen, L. (2000, Nov. 18). *Rethinking our classroom: Creating classrooms for equity and social justice.* Presentation at NCTE annual conference, Milwaukee, WI.

Christensen, L. M. (1990). Teaching Standard English: Whose standard? *English Journal, 79*(2), 36-40.

Christensen, L. M. (2000). Critical literacy: Teaching reading, writing, and outrage. In D. Allender (Ed.), *Trends and issues in secondary English, 2000 edition* (pp. 53-67). Urbana, IL: NCTE.

Christian, D. (1987, Dec.). Vernacular dialects in U.S. schools. (CN 400-86-0019. *ERIC Digest*).

Ciardi, J. (1959). *How does a poem mean?* Cambridge, MA: Houghton Mifflin.

Cintorino, M. A. (1991). Learning to talk, talking to learn. *English Journal, 80*(7), 69-71.

Clark, C., & Elmore, J. (1981). *Teacher planning in the first weeks of school.* (Research Series No. 56). East Lansing, MI: Institute for Research on Teaching, Michigan State University.

Clark, C., & Yinger, R. (1979). *Three studies of teacher planning* (Research Series No. 55). East Lansing, MI: Institute for Research on Teaching, Michigan State University.

Claxton, M. M., & Cooper, C. C. (2000). Teaching tools: American literature and the World Wide Web. *English Journal, 90*(2), 97-103.

Cobb, M. K. (1985). From oral to written: Origins of a black literary tradition. In C. K. Brooks (Ed.), *Tapping potential: English and language arts for the black learner.* Urbana, IL: NCTE.

Cocteau, J. (1969). Le secret professionel. (1926). In V. Erlich (Ed.), *Russian Formalism: History-Doctrine* (3rd ed.). The Hague.

Coen, R. J. (1997). Ad spending tops 175 billion during robust '96. *Advertising Age, 68*(19).

Coffin, E. (1988). Idea exchange: Microdebates of Benjamin Franklin's moral perfection. *North Carolina English Teacher, 45*(2), 7-8.

Cohen, E. G. (1994). Restructuring the classroom: Conditions for productive small groups. *Review of Educational Research, 64*(1), 1-35.

Cole, C. (2001). The dynamics of English classes with gender minorities. In L. P. McCoy (Ed.), *Studies in teaching.* Winston-Salem, NC: Wake Forest University Education Department.

Coles, R. (1989a). *The call of stories: Teaching and the moral imagination.* Boston: Houghton Mifflin.

Coles, R. (1989b, Nov. 17). Keynote address at NCTE National Convention, Baltimore.

Collette, C., & Johnson, R. (1993). *Common ground: Personal writing and public discourse.* New York: Harper Collins.

Collins, A. (1991). The role of computer technology in restructuring schools. *Phi Delta Kappan, 73*(1), 28-36.

Collins, B. (2001). *Sailing alone around the room.* New York: Random House.

Collins, K. M., & Collins, J. (1996). Strategic instruction for struggling writers. *English Journal, 85*(6), 54-61.

Collum, J., & Noethe, S. (1994). *Poetry everywhere: Teaching poetry writing in school and in the community.* New York: Teachers & Writers Collaborative.

Coltelli, L. (1990). *Winged words: American Indian writers speak.* Lincoln: University of Nebraska Press.

Combs, W. E. (1977). Sentence-combining practice: Do gains in judgment of writing "quality" persist? *Journal of Educational Research, 70*(6), 318-321.

Conference on College Composition and Communication. (1974). *Students' right to their own language.* (E. Corbett, Ed.). Urbana, IL: NCTE.

Cooke, M. (1989). The humanities in contemporary life or, the bull that could waltz away. In J. O. Milner & L. F. M. Milner (Eds.), *Passages to literature: Essays on teaching in Australia, Canada, England, the United States, and Wales* (pp. 116-124). Urbana, IL: NCTE.

Coon, L. (1991). Planning a poetry unit: The process is the structure. *English Journal, 80*(3), 28-32.

Cooper, C. R. (Ed.). (1985). *Researching response to literature and the teaching of literature: Points of departure.* Norwood, NJ: Ablex.

Cooper, P., & Davies, C. (1993). The impact of national curriculum assessment arrangements on English teachers' thinking and classroom practice in English secondary schools. *Teaching and Teacher Education, 9*(5-6), 559-570.

Coover, R. (1993, Aug. 29). Hyperfiction: Novels for the computer. *New York Times Book Review,* pp. 8-10.

Corcoran, B. (1987). Teachers creating readers. In B. Corcoran & E. Evans (Eds.), *Readers, texts, teachers* (pp. 41-74). Upper Montclair, NJ: Boynton/Cook.

Cordeiro, P. A., Giacobbe, M. E., & Cazden, C. (1983). Apostrophes, quotation marks, and periods: Learning punctuation in the first grade. *Language Arts, 60*(3), 323-332.

Costanzo, W. V. (1987, Aug.). The English teacher as programmer. *Computers and Composition, 4,* 65-76.

Couch, L. L. (1987). "So much depends" . . . on how you begin: A poetry lesson. *English Journal, 76*(7), 29.

Cox, C. (1987). Film as documentation, social comment, satire, and spoof. *English Journal, 76*(4), 85-87.

Cox, M. (1991). Bards and Beatles: Connecting spontaneity to structure in lesson plans. *English Journal, 80*(3), 33-36.

Crosman, R. (1982). How readers make meaning. *College Literature, 9*(2), 7-15.

Crowe, C. (1999). Young adult literature: Dear teachers: Please help my kids become readers. *English Journal, 89*(1), 139-142.

Cuban, L. (1986). *Teachers and machines: The classroom use of technology since the 1920s.* New York: Teachers College Press.

Culler, J. (1982). *On deconstruction: Theory and criticism after structuralism.* Ithaca, NY: Cornell University Press.

Cussler, E. B. (1987). Vietnam: An oral history. *English Journal, 76*(7), 66-67.

D'Arcy, P. (1977). *Writing across the curriculum: Language for learning.* Exeter, UK: Exeter School of Education.

D'Arcy, P. (1989). *Making sense, shaping meaning.* Portsmouth, NH: Boynton/Cook.

Daiches, D. (1956). *Critical approaches to literature.* New York: Norton.

Daiute, C. (1986). Physical and cognitive factors in revising. *Research in the Teaching of English, 20*(2), 141-159.

Daiute, C., & Dalton, B. (1988). Let's brighten it up a bit: Collaboration and cognition in writing. In B. A. Rafoth & D. L. Rubin (Eds.), *The social construction of written communication* (pp. 249-269). Norwood, NJ: Ablex.

Dale, H. (1994). Collaborative writing interactions in one ninth-grade classroom. *Journal of Educational Research, 87*(6), 334-344.

Dale, H. (1997). *Co-authoring in the classroom.* Urbana, IL: NCTE.

Davis, B. M. (1989). Feminizing the English curriculum: An international perspective. *English Journal, 78*(6), 45-49.

Davis, K., & Hollowell, J. (Eds.). (1977). *Inventing and playing games in the English classroom: A handbook for teachers.* Urbana, IL: NCTE.

Davydov, V. (1995). The influence of L. S. Vygotsky on education theory, research, and practice. *Educational Researcher, 24*(3), 12-21.

De Beauvoir, S. (1949). *The second sex* (H. M. Parshley, Trans.). New York: Bantam.

De Villeas, J., & de Villeas, P. (1978). *Language acquisition.* Cambridge: Harvard University Press.

DeCristofaro, D. S. (2001). Author to author. *Quarterly, 25*(2), 13-17.

Dellinger, D. (1982). *Out of the heart: How to design writing assignments for high school courses.* Berkeley: National Writing Project, University of California.

Delpit, L. (1988). The silenced dialogue: Power and pedagogy in educating other people's children. *Harvard Educational Review, 58*(3), 280-98.

Delpit, L. (1995). *Other people's children: Cultural conflict in the classroom.* New York: New Press.

Denman, C. (1995). Writers, editors, and readers: Authentic assessment in the newspaper class. *English Journal, 84*(8), 55-57.

Desai, L. (1997). Reflections on cultural diversity in literature and in the classroom. In T. Rogers & A. Soter (Eds.), *Reading across cultures: Teaching literature in a diverse society* (pp. 161-177). New York: Teachers College Press.

Dewey, J. (1916/1944). *Democracy and education.* New York: Free Press.

Dewey, J. (1933). *How we think* (Rev. Ed.). Boston: Heath.

Dias, P. (1996). *Reading and responding to poetry: Patterns in the process.* Portsmouth, NH: Boynton/Cook.

Diederich, P. (1974). *Measuring growth in English.* Urbana, IL: NCTE.

Dilg, M. A. (1995). The opening of the American mind: Challenges in the cross-cultural teaching of literature. *English Journal, 84*(3), 18-25.

Dilg, M. A. (1997). Why I am a multiculturalist: The power of stories told and untold. *English Journal, 86*(6), 64-69.

Dill, N. L., & Purves, A. C., with Weiss, J., & Foshavy, A. W. (1967). *The teaching of literature.* Unpublished report of the U.S. National Committee, International Literature Project, Teachers College, Columbia University. Available through NCTE, ERIC, ED-039-399.

Dillard, A. (1995). Introduction. In A. Dillard and C. Conley (Eds.), *Modern American memoirs.* New York: Harper Collins.

Dillard, A. (1988). Introduction. In A. Dillard (Ed.), *The best American essays, 1988* (pp. xiii-xxii). New York: Ticknor & Fields.

Dillon, D., & Hamilton, S. (1985, Nov.). Dimensions of classroom talk. Document drafted at the NCTE International Assembly, Philadelphia.

Dilworth, C., & Wilde, P. (1979). Correspondence: A medium rediscovered. In G. Stanford (Ed.), *Activating the passive student.* Urbana, IL: NCTE.

Disenhaus, N. R. (2000). Teacher to teacher: What works of nonfiction do you recommend for the English classroom? *English Journal 89*(6), 34-35.

Dittmer, A. E. (1991). Letters: The personal touch in writing. *English Journal, 80*(1), 18-24.

Ditzian, M. (1990). Idea exchange: A child custody hearing: *Black Boy. North Carolina English Teacher, 47*(2), 14-15.

Dixon, J. (1967). *Growth through English.* London: Oxford University Press.

Dixon, J. (1984, Nov.). National faculty lecture, East Grand Rapids, MI.

Dixon, J., & Stratta, L. (1986). *Writing narrative and beyond.* Ottawa: Canadian Council of Teachers of English.

Dixon, J., & Stratta, L. (1989). Developing responses to character in literature. In J. O. Milner & L. F. M. Milner (Eds.), *Passages to literature: Essays on teaching in Australia, Canada, England, the United States, and Wales* (pp. 25-38). Urbana, IL: NCTE.

Donahue, D., & McKelvey, T. (2001, Sept. 25). Poetry soothes in world without rhyme, reason. *USA Today,* pp. 13A, 1D.

Donelson, K. L. (1984). Ten teachers and scholars who influenced the secondary English curriculum, 1880-1970. *English Journal, 73*(3), 78-80.

Donelson, K. L. (1997). "Filth" and "pure filth" in our schools—Censorship of classroom books in the last ten years. *English Journal, 86*(2), 21-25.

Donelson, K. L. (2000). Oh, those golden teaching days of yore. *English Journal, 89*(3), 45-48.

Donelson, K. L., & Nilsen, A. P. (1980). *Literature for today's young adults.* Glenview, IL: Scott, Foresman.

Donelson, K., & Nilsen, A. P. (1984). History of English education. *English Journal, 73*(3), 1-12.

Donovan, J. (1985). *Feminist theory: The intellectual traditions of American feminism.* New York: Ungar.

Donovan, J. M. (1990). Resurrect the *dragon grammaticus. English Journal, 79*(1), 62-65.

Donovan, T., & McClelland, B. (Eds.). (1981). *Eight approaches to teaching composition.* Urbana, IL: NCTE.

Dorney, J. M. (1988). The plain English movement. *English Journal, 77*(3), 49-51.

Downie, N. M. (1967). *Fundamentals of measurement: Techniques and practices* (2nd ed.). New York: Oxford University Press.

Downing, F. (1997). Strike a pose. In E. Chiseri-Strater & B. Sunstein (Eds.), *Field working* (pp. 162, 163). Boston: St. Martins.

Doyle, D., & Pimentel, S. (1993). A study in change. *Phi Delta Kappan, 74*(7), 534-539.

Dressel, P. L. (1964). Role of external testing programs in education. *Kansas Studies in Education, 14*(2). Lawrence: University of Kansas.

Dreyfuss, H. (1984). *Symbol sourcebook: An authoritative guide to international graphic symbols.* New York: Van Nostrand Reinhold.

Dudley, M. (1997). The rise and fall of a statewide assessment system. *English Journal, 86*(1), 15-20.

Duke, C. (1974). *Creative dramatics and English teaching.* Urbana, IL: NCTE.

Duke, C. R. (1994). Giving students control over writing assessment. *English Journal, 83*(4), 47-53.

Duke, C. R., & Jacobsen, S. (Eds.). (1992). *Poets' perspectives: Reading, writing, and teaching poetry.* Portsmouth, NH: Boynton/Cook.

Duke, C., & Sanchez, R. (1994). *Writing rubric.* Developed for the Pennsylvania State assessment project.

Dunfey, J. (1989). Integrating computers into the language arts curriculum at Lesley College. In C. Selfe (Ed.), *Computers in English and the language arts: The challenge of teacher education.* Urbana, IL: NCTE.

Durkin, D. (1978-1979). What classroom observations reveal about reading comprehension instruction. *Reading Research Quarterly, 14,*(4) 481-533.

Dyson, A. H., & Freedman, S. W. (1990). *On teaching writing: A review of the literature.* Berkeley, CA: Center for the Study of Writing.

Dyson, E. (1997). *Release 2.0: A design for living in the digital age.* New York: Broadway.

Eagleton, T. (1983). *Literary theory: An introduction.* Minneapolis: University of Minnesota Press.

Earthman, E. A. (1997). The siren song that keeps us coming back: Multicultural resources for teaching classical mythology. *English Journal, 86*(6), 76-81.

Ebel, R. L. (1982). Proposed solutions to two problems of test construction. *Journal of Educational Measurement, 19*(4), 267-78.

Edwards, V. (1997, Nov. 10). Technology counts. *Education Week, 17*(11), 11.

Eisner, E. W. (1990). *The enlightened eye: Qualitative inquiry and the enhancement of educational practices.* Upper Saddle River, NJ: Macmillan/Prentice Hall.

Elbow, P. (1973). *Writing without teachers.* New York: Oxford University Press.

Elbow, P. (1981). *Writing with power.* New York: Oxford University Press.

Elbow, P. (1985). The shifting relationship between speech and writing. *College Composition and Communication, 36*(3), 283–303.

Elbow, P. (1986). *Embracing contraries: Explorations in learning and teaching.* New York: Oxford.

Elbow, P. (1991). Forward. In P. Belanoff & M. Dickson (Eds.), *Portfolios: Process and product.* Portsmouth, NH: Boynton/Cook.

Elbow, P., & Belanoff, P. (1986). Portfolios as a substitute for proficiency examination. *College Composition and Communication, 37*(3), 336–339.

Elifson, J. (1977). Teaching to enhance bidialectalism: Some theoretical and practical considerations. *English Education, 9*(1), 11–21.

Eliot, T. S. (1958). *The complete poems and plays, 1909–1950.* New York: Harcourt, Brace.

Elk Grove High School English Staff. (1979). A glossary of poetic terms. *English Journal, 68*(5), 45–46.

Elley, W. B., Barham, I. H., Lamb, H., & Wyllie, M. (1979). *The role of grammar in a secondary school curriculum.* Wellington: New Zealand Council for Educational Research.

Elliott, C. B. (2000). Helping students weave their way through the World Wide Web. *English Journal, 90*(2), 87–92.

Ellis, W. G. (1987). To tell the truth or at least a little nonfiction. *ALAN Review, 15*(2), 39–40.

Ellmann, M. (1968). *Thinking about women.* New York: Harcourt Brace Jovanovich.

Emig, J. (1971). *The composing processes of twelfth graders.* Urbana, IL: NCTE.

Emig, J. (1977). Writing as a mode of learning. *College Composition and Communication, 28*(2), 122–128.

Emig, J. (1980). Non-magical thinking: Presenting writing developmentally in schools. In H. Fredericksen & J. Dominic (Eds.), *Writing process, development and communication* (Vol. 2 of *Writing: The nature, development and teaching of written communication)* (pp. 21–30). Hillsdale, NJ: Erlbaum.

Epstein, J. (1997). Six types of school-family-community involvement. *Harvard Education Letter, 13*(5), 4.

Ericson, B. O. (1993). Introducing *To Kill a Mockingbird* with collaborative group reading of related young adult novels. In J. F. Kaywell (Ed.), *Adolescent literature as a complement to the classics* (pp. 1–12). Norwood, MA: Christopher-Gordon.

Erikson, E. H. (1963). *Childhood and society* (2nd ed.). New York: Norton.

Erikson, E. H. (1968). *Identity: Youth and crisis.* New York: Norton.

Fader, D., & McNeil, E. B. (1968). *Hooked on books: Program and proof.* New York: Putnam.

Farnan, N. (1993, March). Writers workshop. *Middle School Journal, 24*(3), 61–65.

Farr, J. (1997). New teachers: Becoming a balanced teacher: Idealist goals, realist expectations. *English Journal, 86*(6), 106–109.

Fearn, L., & Farnan, N. (1990). *Writing effectively.* Boston: Allyn & Bacon.

Fehlman, R. H. (1987). Quoting films in English class. *English Journal, 76*(5), 84–87.

Ferguson, C. A. (1977). Baby talk as a simplified register. In C. A. Snow & C. A. Ferguson (Eds.), *Talking to children: Language input and requisition.* Cambridge: Cambridge University Press.

Ferrara, C. L. (1981). The joys of leading a discussion. *English Journal, 70*(2), 68–70.

Fischetti, J. (2001, Sept. 27). *Overcoming the tensions between preparing teachers to use best practices and preparing them to help get school test scores up.* Presentation at the North Carolina Teacher Education Forum. Raleigh.

Fish, S. E. (1980). *Is there a text in this class? The authority of interpretive communities.* Cambridge: Harvard University Press.

Fish, S. E. (1990, July 11). Lecture. North Carolina Governor's School West. Winston-Salem, NC.

Fishkin, S. (1993). *Huck black? Mark Twain and African-American voices.* Oxford: Oxford University Press.

Fitzgerald, J. (1995). English-as-a-second-language reading instruction in the United States: A research review. *Journal of Reading Behavior, 27*(2), 115–152.

Flanders, N. A. (1965). *Teacher influence, pupil attitudes and achievement* (Office of Education, Cooperative Research Monograph No. 12). Washington, DC: U.S. Government Printing Office.

Flynn, E. (1986). Gender and reading. In E. Flynn & P. Schweickart (Eds.), *Gender and reading: Essays on readers, texts and contexts* (pp. 267–288). Baltimore: Johns Hopkins University Press.

Forrestal, P. (1990, Aug.). Presentation at the International Federation of Teachers of English Conference, Auckland, NZ.

Forster, E. M. (1927). *Aspects of the novel.* New York: Harcourt Brace & World.

Foster, D. (1992). *A primer for writing teachers: Theories, theorists, issues, problems* (2nd ed.). Portsmouth, NH: Boynton/Cook & Heinemann.

Foster, D. (2000). *Author unknown: On the trail of anonymous.* New York: Holt.

Fowler, J. W. (1981). *Stages of faith: The psychology of human development and the quest for meaning.* San Francisco: Harper & Row.

Fowler, L. J., & Pesante, L. H. (1989). Engaging students with gaps: The whale and the cigar. *English Journal, 78*(8), 28–34.

Francis, W. N. (1958). *The structure of American English.* New York: Ronald.

Franza, A. (1984). To make you see: The art of film in the English class. *English Journal, 73*(1), 40–41.

Fraser, K. (1997, Oct. 14). As writers despair, book chains can only exult. *New York Times.*

Freire, P. (1970). *Pedagogy of the oppressed* (M. B. Ramos, Trans.). New York: Herder & Herder.

Freire, P., & Shor, I. (1987). *A pedagogy for liberation.* South Hadley, MA: Bergin & Garvey.

Frey (1993). Goals and limits in student performance of Shakespeare. In J. E. Davis & R. E. Salomone (Eds.), *Teaching Shakespeare today: Practical approaches and productive strategies* (pp. 72–78). Urbana, IL: NCTE.

Fries, C. C. (1954). *The structure of English: An introduction to the construction of English sentences.* New York: Harcourt Brace.

Frost, R. (1973). The figure a poem makes. In E. Barry (Ed.), *Robert Frost on writing* (pp. 125-128). New Brunswick, NJ: Rutgers University Press.

Frye, N. (1963). *The developing imagination.* Cambridge: Harvard University Press.

Fuentes, C. (1992, Oct. 8). Columbus Day address. Wake Forest University, Winston-Salem, NC

Fuller, F. (1989). O, reform it altogether. *Virginia English Bulletin, 39*(1), 89-96.

Fulwiler, T. (1987). *Teaching with writing.* Upper Montclair, NJ: Boynton/Cook.

Fulwiler, T., & Young, A. (1982). *Language connections: Writing and reading across the curriculum.* Urbana, IL: NCTE.

Funk, W. (1978). *Word origins and their romantic stories.* New York: Bell.

Gagne, R. M., & Smith, E. C. (1962). A study of the effects of verbalization on problem solving. *Journal of Experimental Psychology, 63*(1), 12-18.

Gallagher, B. (1988). Film study and the teaching of English: Technology and the future of pedagogy. *English Journal, 77*(7), 58-61.

Gallo, D. R. (1989). Who are the most important YA authors? *Alan Review, 16*(1), 18-20.

Gambrell, L., & Bales, R. J. (1986). Mental imagery and the comprehension-monitoring performance of fourth and fifth grade readers. *Reading Research Quarterly, 21*(4), 454-464.

Gardiner, S. (2001, Oct.). Ten minutes a day for silent reading. *Educational Leadership, 59*(2), 33-34.

Gardner, H. (1983). *Frames of mind.* New York: Basic Books.

Gardner, H. (1984). The seven frames of mind. *Psychology Today, 18*(6), 21-26.

Gardner, H. (1991). *The unschooled mind.* New York: Basic Books.

Gasparro, M. & Falletta, B. (1994, April). Creating drama with poetry: Teaching English as a second language through dramatization and improvisation. Retrieved September 29, 2001, from ERIC Clearinghouse on Languages and Linguistics, http://www.cal.org/ericcll/digest/gaspar01.html.

Gates, H. L., Jr. (2002a, Feb. 18 & 25). The fugitive: Searching for the author of an escaped slave's story. *New Yorker,* pp. 104-115.

Gates, H. L., Jr. (2002b, March 4). Dept. of amplification. *New Yorker,* p. 5.

Gay, G. (1988, Aug.). Designing relevant curricula for diverse learners. *Education and Urban Society, 20*(4), 327-340.

Geisler, E. (1987). A Foxfire introduction to *The Grapes of Wrath.* In F. A. Kaufmann (Ed.), *Ideas plus: A collection of practical teaching ideas, book 5* (pp. 40-41). Urbana, IL: NCTE.

Gendernalik, A. L. (1984). I seen it. *English Journal, 73*(8), 42.

Gerbner, G., Gross, L., Morgan, M., & Signorielli, N. (1982). Charting the mainstream: Television's contributions to political orientations. *Journal of Communication, 32*(2), 100-127.

Gere, A. R., Fairbanks, C., Howes, A., Roop, L., & Schaafsma, D. (1992). *Language and reflection: An integrated approach to teaching English.* Upper Saddle River, NJ: Macmillan/Prentice Hall.

Gerlach, J. M., & Monseau, V. R. (1991). *Missing chapters: Ten pioneering women in NCTE and English education.* Urbana, IL: NCTE.

Giacobbe, M. E. (1982, July 6). *Beginning writing.* Presentation to the North Carolina Writing Project, Winston-Salem, NC.

Giacobbe, M. E., & Cazden, C. (1986). *NCTE Research Report.* Spring conference, Boston.

Giles, J. (2000, Nov. 5). Errors and "corrections." *Newsweek,* pp. 68-69.

Gillard, P. (1994). Insight from the inside: A new perspective on family influences over children's television viewing and its implications for teachers. In J. Milner & C. Pope (Eds.), *Global voices: Culture and identity in the teaching of English* (pp. 68-83). Urbana, IL: NCTE.

Gillespie, J. S. (1991). The life of a seventh grader: Writing a memoir. *English Journal, 80*(4), 48-51.

Gilligan, C. (1982). *In a different voice: Psychological theory and women's development.* Cambridge: Harvard University Press.

Gillis, C. (1994). Writing partners: Expanding the audiences for student writing. *English Journal, 83*(3), 64-67.

Giovanni, N. (1994). *Knoxville, Tennessee.* (L. Johnson, Illus.). New York: Scholastic.

Giroux, H. A. (1992). *Border crossings: Cultural workers and the politics of education.* New York: Routledge.

Giroux, H. A., & Simon, R. I. (1988). Schooling, popular culture, and a pedagogy of possibility. *Journal of Education, 170*(1), 9-26.

Glasser, W. (1990). *The quality school.* New York: Harper & Row.

Glatthorn, A. (1975). Teacher as person: The search for the authentic. *English Journal, 64*(9), 37-39.

Glatthorn, A. (1988). What schools should teach in the English language arts. *Educational Leadership, 46*(1), 44-50.

Glazer, N. (1997, June). The hard questions: Unsolved mysteries. *New Republic,* p. 29.

Goebel, B. (1995). Expanding the literary canon and reading the rhetoric of "race." *English Journal, 84*(3), 42-48.

Goldberg, N. (1986). *Writing down the bones.* Boston: Shambhala.

Goldman, R. (1987). Marketing fragrances: Advertising and the production of commodity signs. *Theory, Culture, and Society, 4*(4), 691-725.

Goldstein, R. (1969). *The poetry of rock.* New York: Bantam.

Goldwasser, M. M. (1997). Censorship: It happened to me in southwest Virginia—It could happen to you. *English Journal, 86*(2), 34-42.

Golson, E., & Sagel, E. (2000). The creation project. In S. Gruber (Ed.), *Weaving a virtual web* (pp. 43-56). Urbana, IL: NCTE.

Golub, J. (1994). *Activities for an interactive classroom.* Urbana, IL: NCTE.

Golub, J., & Reid, L. (1989). Activities for an "interactive" classroom. *English Journal, 78*(4), 43-48.

Good, T. L., & Brophy, J. E. (2000). *Looking in classrooms* (8th Ed.). New York: Longman.

Goodlad, J. I. (1984). *A place called school: Prospects for the future.* New York: McGraw-Hill.

Goodman, M. (1980). *Proposal writing to RFP specifications.* National Humanities Faculty, ETE Summer Institute, Vassar College.

Gorrell, N. (1989). Let found poetry help your students find poetry. *English Journal, 78*(2), 30-34.

Gorrell, N. (2000). Teaching empathy through ecphrastic poetry: Entering a curriculum of peace. *English Journal, 89*(5), 32-41.

Goslin, D. A. (1967). *Teachers and testing.* Hartford, CT: Russell Sage Foundation.

Goswami, D. (1989, Fall/Winter). Assessing assessment. *Bread Loaf News,* p. 20.

Goswami, D., & Stillman, P. (Eds.). (1987). *Reclaiming the classroom: Teaching research as an agent for change.* Upper Montclair, NJ: Boynton/Cook.

Gould, C. (1987). Josephine Turck Baker, correct English, and the ancestry of pop grammar. *English Journal, 76*(1), 22-27.

Goulden, N. R. (1998a). Implementing speaking and listening standards: Information for English teachers. *English Journal, 88*(1), 90-96.

Goulden, N. R. (1998b). The roles of national and state standards in implementing speaking, listening, and media literacy. *Communication Education, 47,* 194-208.

Grace, P. (1987). Butterflies. In *Electric city and other stories* (pp. 61-62). Auckland, NZ: Penguin.

Graff, G. (1987). *Professing literature: An institutional history.* Chicago: University of Chicago Press.

Grambs, J. D., & Carr, J. C. (1991). *Modern methods in secondary education* (5th ed.). Fort Worth, TX: Holt, Rinehart, & Winston.

Grasmick, N. S. (2001, Jan. 11). A mistake we can't repeat. *Education Week, 20*(18), 88.

Graves, D. H. (1983a, Oct.). Keynote speaker at southeast regional meeting of NCTE, Charleston, SC.

Graves, D. H. (1983b). *Writing: Teachers and children at work.* Exeter, NH: Heinemann.

Graves, D. H. (1986, Jan. 8). Kids learn to write well if they don't fear errors. *USA Today.*

Graves, D. H. (1991). *The reading/writing teacher's companion: Build a literate classroom.* Portsmouth, NH: Heinemann.

Graves, D. H. (1992). *Helping students learn to read their portfolios.* Portsmouth, NH: Heinemann.

Graves, D. H. (1996). Spot the lifetime writers. *Instructor, 105*(7), 26-27.

Graves, D. H., & Stuart, V. (1985). *Write from the start: Tapping your child's natural writing ability.* New York: New American Library.

Graves, D. H., & Sunstein, B. (1992). *Portfolio portraits.* Portsmouth, NH: Heinemann.

Greenblatt, S. J. (1990). *Learning to curse: Essays in early modern culture.* London: Routledge.

Greene, G. (1999 [originally published 1951]). *The end of the affair.* New York: Penguin.

Greene, M. (1978). *Landscapes of learning.* New York: Teachers College Press.

Greene, M. (1985). Evaluation and dignity. In D. E. Purpel & H. S. Shapiro (Eds.), *Schools and meaning: Essays on the moral nature of schooling.* Lanham, MD: University Press of America.

Greene, M. (1988). *The dialectic of freedom.* New York: Teachers College Press.

Greenlaw, J. C. (2001). *English language arts and reading on the Internet: A resource for K-12 teachers.* Upper Saddle River, NJ: Merrill/Prentice Hall.

Gregory, D. (1998). Letters: Ignoring Canadian literature. *English Journal, 87*(2), 8.

Gribbin, B. (1996). The role of generalization in studying grammar and usage. *English Journal, 85*(7), 55-58.

Griffin, C. W. (1989). Teaching Shakespeare on video. *English Journal, 78*(7), 40-43.

Griffiths, N. (1991, April 2). Lecture. Winston-Salem Forsyth County Schools, Winston-Salem, NC.

Griffiths, N. (2000, March). *Strategies for reading aloud with children.* Presentation at the NCTE spring conference, New York.

Grimes, M. (1991). Finding hooks to catch reluctant readers. *English Journal, 80*(1), 45-47.

Gross, R. (1967, June 11). Speaking of books: Found poetry. *New York Times Book Review,* p. 2.

Grossman, F. (1982). *Getting from here to there: Writing and reading poetry.* Portsmouth, NH: Boynton/Cook.

Grossman, F. (1991). *Listening to the bells: Learning to read poetry by writing poetry.* Portsmouth, NH: Boynton/Cook.

Grossman, P. L. (1990). *The making of a teacher: Teacher knowledge and teacher education.* New York: Teachers College Press.

Guerin, G. R., & Maier, A. S. (1983). *Informal assessment in education.* Palo Alto, CA: Mayfield.

Guerin, W. L., Labor, E. G., Morgan, L., & Willingham, J. R. (1979). *A handbook of critical approaches to literature* (2nd ed.). New York: Harper & Row.

Guilford, D. (1985). Facets: What 1985 classroom teachers should know about women's studies. *English Journal, 74*(3), 24.

Guskey, T. R. (1985). *Implementing mastery learning.* Belmont, CA: Wadsworth.

Haberman, M. (1995). *Star teachers of children in poverty.* West Lafayette, IN: Kappa Delta Pi.

Hahn, J. (1985). Tennis anyone or whose paper is it? *National Writing Project Newsletter,* 5.

Hairston, M. (1981). Not all errors are created equal: Nonacademic readers in the professions respond to lapses in usage. *College English, 43*(8) 794-806.

Hale, S. J. (Ed.). (1856). *The letters of Madame de Sévigné.* New York: Mason Brothers.

Halio, J. L. (1977). Shakespeare's plays as plays. In W. Edens (Ed.), *Teaching Shakespeare.* Princeton, NJ: Princeton University Press.

Halio, J. L. (1988). *Understanding Shakespeare's plays in performance.* Manchester, UK: Manchester University Press.

Hall, D. (1987). *To read literature: Fiction, poetry, drama* (2nd ed.). New York: Holt, Rinehart, & Winston.

Hall, D. (1992). *Their ancient glittering eyes.* New York: Ticknor & Fields.

Hall, D. (1973). *Writing well.* Boston: Little, Brown.

Halpern, M. (1997). A war that never ends. *Atlantic Monthly, 278*(3), 19-22.

Hannafin, M., & Land, S. (1997). The foundations and assumptions of technology-enhanced student-centered learning environments. *Instructional Science, 25*(3), 167-200. Norwell, MA: Kluwer Academic Publishers.

Harmston, D. (1988). Impromptu poetry. In F. A. Kaufmann (Ed.), *Ideas plus: A collection of practical teaching ideas, book 6* (pp. 55-56). Urbana, IL: NCTE.

Harrington-Lueker, D. (1997). Technology works best when it serves clear educational goals. *Harvard Education Letter 13*, 6.

Harris, J. (1991). After Dartmouth: Growth and conflict in English. *College English, 53*(6), 631–646.

Harrison, L. R. (1991). *Speaking and listening are much used but little taught: Incorporating oral language instruction into the high school English curriculum.* Unpublished master's thesis, Wake Forest University, Winston-Salem, NC.

Hartwell, P. (1985). Grammar, grammars and the teaching of grammar. *College English, 47*(4), 105–127.

Hasselriis, P. (1991). From Pearl Harbor to Watergate to Kuwait: Language in thought and action. *English Journal, 80*(2), 18–35.

Hawisher, G., & Selfe, C. (1991). *Evolving perspective on computers and composition studies.* Urbana, IL: NCTE.

Hawkey, K. (1995). Learning from peers: The experience of student teachers in school-based teacher education. *Journal of Teacher Education 46,* 175–183.

Hawkins, S. (1984). Teaching the theatre of imagination: The example of Henry IV. *Shakespeare Quarterly* [Special issue], 517–527.

Hawley, R. A. (1979). Teaching as failing. *Phi Delta Kappan 60*(4), 597–600.

Hayakawa, S. I. (1950). Linguistic science and the teaching of composition. *ETC: A Review of General Semantics, 7*(2), 97–103.

Hayakawa, S. I. (1978). *Language in thought and action* (4th ed.). New York: Harcourt Brace Jovanovich.

Hayakawa, S. K. (1987). Why English should be our official language. *Education Digest, LII*(9), 36–37.

Hayden, C. D. (Ed.). (1992). *Venture into cultures: A resource book of multicultural materials and programs.* Chicago: American Library Association.

Hayes, J. R., & Tierney, R. J. (1982). Developing readers' knowledge through analogy. *Reading Research Quarterly, 17*(2), 256–280.

Hayn, J. S. (1997, March 7). *Another opening, another show: Using reader's theater to enhance composition skills.* Presentation at the annual conference on Writing and Literature, Lawrence, KS.

Heard, G. (1989). *For the good of the earth and sun: Teaching poetry.* Portsmouth, NH: Heinemann.

Heath, S. B. (1987). The literate essay: Using ethnography to explode myths. In J. Langer (Ed.), *Language, literacy, and culture.* Norwood, NJ: Ablex.

Heathcote, D. (1980). *Drama as context.* Upper Montclair, NJ: Boynton/Cook.

Heathcote, D. (1984). *Dorothy Heathcote: Collected writings on drama and education.* (L. Johnson & C. O'Neill, Eds.). London: Hutchinson.

Heilbrun, C. (1979). *Reinventing womanhood.* New York: Norton.

Heilbrun, C. (1988). *Writing a woman's life.* New York: Ballantine.

Heisenberg, W. (1962). *Physics and philosophy.* New York: Harper & Row.

Heller, D. A. (1996). This world of English: Magnetic poetry. *English Journal, 85*(6), 125–126.

Henry, G. (1974). *Teaching reading as concept development: Emphasis on affective thinking.* Newark, DE: International Reading Association.

Henry, G. (1986). What is the nature of English education? *English Education, 18*(1), 4–41.

Herber, H. L. (1970). *Teaching reading in content areas* (2nd ed.). Upper Saddle River, NJ: Prentice Hall.

Herndon, J. (1970). *A survey of modern grammars* (2nd ed.). New York: Holt, Rinehart, & Winston.

Herter, R. J. (1991). Writing portfolios: Alternative to testing. *English Journal, 80*(1), 90–91.

Herz, S. K., with D. R. Gallo. (1996). *From Hinton to Hamlet: Building bridges between young adult literature and the classics.* Westport, CT: Greenwood.

Higgins, J., & Fowinkle, J. (1993). *The adventures of Huckleberry Finn,* prejudice, and adolescent literature. In J. F. Kaywell (Ed.), *Adolescent literature as a complement to the classics* (pp. 37–60). Norwood, MA: Christopher-Gordon.

Higginson, W. J., & Harter, P. (1989). *The haiku handbook: How to write, share, and teach haiku.* New York: Kodansha International.

Hillocks, G., Jr. (1986). *Research on written composition: New directions for teaching.* Urbana, IL: NCTE.

Hillocks, G., Jr. (1987). Synthesis of research on teaching writing. *Educational Leadership, 44*(8), 71–82.

Hillocks, G., Jr. (1995). *Teaching writing as reflective practice.* New York: Teachers College Press.

Hillocks, G., Jr., & Smith, M. (1991). Grammar and usage. In J. Flood, *Handbook of research on teaching the English language arts* (pp. 591–603). New York: Free Press.

Hipple, T. (1989). Have you read . . .? *English Journal, 78*(8), 79.

Hipple, T. (2000). Have you read? *English Journal, 89*(4), 138.

Hipple, T. (2001). Somnolent bulls revisited. *English Journal, 90*(6), 17–18.

Hirsch, E. D., Jr. (1987). *Cultural literacy: What every American needs to know.* New York: Vintage.

Hitchcock, G. (Ed.). (1969). *Losers weepers: Poems found practically everywhere.* San Francisco: Kayak.

Hodges, R. E. (1982). *Improving spelling and vocabulary in the secondary school.* Urbana, IL: NCTE.

Hogarty, K. (1991). Audit them: Biographies, autobiographies, and other nonfiction. *English Journal, 80*(4), 57–60.

Holden, H. (1994). *Turning the page: Reading in the DEM.* Unpublished paper, Western Carolina University.

Holland, N. N. (1968). *The dynamics of literary response.* New Haven: Yale University Press.

Holland, N. N. (1975). *Five readers reading.* New Haven: Yale University Press.

Hollander, J. (1988). Kitty and bug. In *Harp Lake.* New York: Knopf.

Hollman, M. J. (1989). From art to poetry: "Prance as they dance." *English Journal, 78*(3), 24–27.

Holman, C. H. (1980). *A handbook to literature* (4th ed.). Indianapolis: Bobbs-Merrill.

Holt, J. (1967). *How children fail.* New York: Pitman.

Holt, J. (1969). *The under-achieving school.* New York: Pitman.

Honegger, M. (2001). ESL and dialects in the writing classroom. In M. L. Warner (Ed.), *Winning ways of coaching writing: A practical guide to teaching writing* (pp. 87–104). Boston: Allyn & Bacon.

Hook, J. N. (1975). *History of the English language.* New York: Ronald.

Hook, J. N. (1979). *A long way together: A personal view of NCTE's first sixty-seven years.* Urbana, IL: NCTE.

Hooks, B. (1998, February 26). *Confronting the future—race, gender, and class in America.* Presentation at the American Association of Colleges for Teacher Education Annual Conference. New Orleans, LA.

Horn, E. L. (1988). Beware Greeks bearing gifts: Sharing a classic with reluctant twelfth graders. *English Journal, 77*(8), 25-26.

Howe, F. (1982). Feminist scholarship: The extent of the revolution. *Change, 14*(3), 12-20.

Hullet, D. (1991). *NCTE idea exchange.* NCTE annual conference, Seattle.

Hunt, K. (1965). *Grammatical structures written at three grade levels.* Champaign, IL: NCTE.

Hunter, A. D. (1996). A new grammar that has clearly improved writing. *English Journal, 85*(7), 102-107.

Hunter, M. (1976). Teacher competency: Problem, theory, and practice. *Theory into Practice, 15*(2), 162-171.

Hunter, M. (1989). Madeline Hunter in the English classroom. *English Journal, 78*(5), 16-18.

Hutchinson, J., & Suhor, C. (1996). The jazz and poetry connection: A performance guide for teachers and students. *English Journal, 85*(5), 80-85.

Inchautsti, R. (1993). *Spitwad sutras: Classroom teaching as sublime vocation.* Westport, CT: Bergin & Garvey.

Isenberg, J. (1994). *Going by the book: The role of popular classroom chronicles in the professional development of teachers.* Westport, CT: Bergin & Garvey.

Iser, W. (1978). *The act of reading: A theory of aesthetic response.* Baltimore: Johns Hopkins University Press.

Iser, W. (1980). The reading process: A phenomenological approach. In J. P. Thompkins (Ed.), *Reader-response criticism: From formalism to post-structuralism* (pp. 50-69). Baltimore: Johns Hopkins University Press.

Jago, C. (2000). Where life and art intersect. In D. Allender (Ed.), *Trends & issues in secondary English, 2000 edition* (pp. 142-155). Urbana, IL: NCTE.

Jago, C. (2001, Nov.). *Making challenging texts accessible.* Presentation at NCTE annual conference, Baltimore.

James, W. (1907/1981). What pragmatism means. In O. A. Johnson (Ed.), *The individual and the universe: An introduction to philosophy* (pp. 392-399). New York: Holt, Rinehart, & Winston.

Jameson, F. (1983). Postmodernism and the consumer society. In H. Foster (Ed.), *The anti-aesthetic.* Port Townsend, WA: Bay.

Jarrell, R. (1965). *The bat poet.* New York: Macmillan.

Jay, G. S. (1991). The end of "American" literature: Toward a multicultural practice. *College English, 53*(3), 264-281.

Jensen, E. (1987). *Grading the advanced placement examination in English language and composition.* Princeton, NJ: College Board Advanced Placement Program.

Jensen, J. M. (2000). Broad shoulders and big issues: Council leaders tell their stories. *English Journal, 89*(3), 97-103.

Jody, M., & Saccardi, M. (1996). *Computer conversations and books on-line.* Urbana, IL: NCTE.

Johannessen, L. R. (1994). Enhancing response to literature: A matter of changing old habits. *English Journal, 83*(7), 66-70.

Johannessen, L. R., Kahn, E. A., & Walter, C. C. (1982). *Designing and sequencing prewriting activities.* Urbana, IL: NCTE.

Johnson, B. (1980). *The critical difference: Essays in the contemporary rhetoric of reading.* Baltimore: Johns Hopkins University Press.

Johnson, D. (1990). *Telling tales: The pedagogy of promise of African-American literature for youth.* Westpoint, CT: Greenwood.

Johnson, D. (1990, November). *Fostering collaborative learning in the English curriculum.* Presentation at NCTE Convention, Atlanta, GA.

Johnson, D. M. (1990). *Word weaving: A creative approach to teaching and writing poetry.* Urbana, IL: NCTE.

Johnson, D. W., & Johnson, R. T. (1985). The internal dynamics of cooperative learning groups. In R. Slavin, S. Sharan, S. Kagan, R. Hertz-Lazarowitzc, C. Webb, & R. Schuck (Eds.), *Learning to cooperate, cooperating to learn* (pp.103-124). New York: Plenum.

Johnson, J. (1993). The language of teenagers—Slang. *English Journal, 82*(1), 76.

Johnson, L., & O'Neill, C. (1985). *Dorothy Heathcote: Collected writings on education and drama.* London: Hutchinson.

Johnson, N. J. (1997, April 11). *Literature circles in secondary classrooms.* Presentation at NCTE's spring conference, Charlotte, NC.

Johnson, S. (1986). The biography: Teach it from the inside out. *English Journal, 75*(6), 27-29.

John-Steiner, V. (1987). *Notebooks of the mind: Explorations of thinking.* New York: Harper & Row.

Jones, J. (2001). Recomposing the AP English exam. *English Journal, 91*(1), 51-56.

Jones, R. L. (1982, Dec. 27). What's wrong with Black English. *Newsweek,* p. 7.

Judy, S. N., & England, D. A. (1979). An historical primer on the teaching of English. *English Journal, 68*(4), 1-112.

Judy, S. N., & Judy, S. J. (1979). English teachers' literary favorites: The results of a survey. *English Journal, 68*(2), 6-9.

Jung, C. G. (1933). Psychology and literature. In W. S. Dell & C. F. Baynes (Trans.), *Modern man in search of a soul* (pp. 152-172). New York: Harcourt Brace.

Kaestle, C. (1991). *Literacy in the United States.* New Haven, CT: Yale University Press.

Kagan, D. (1992). Professional growth among preservice and beginning teachers. *Review of Education Research, 62*(2), 129-169.

Kahn, E. A. (1984, June). Lecture to the National Humanities Faculty, Summer Institute, Grand Rapids, MI.

Kahn, E. A., Walter, C. C., & Johannessen, L. R. (1984). *Writing about literature.* Urbana, IL: NCTE.

Kearns, E. A. (1997). Words worth 1,000 pictures: Confronting film censorship. *English Journal, 86*(2), 51-54.

Keating, M. (1996). Exploring Charles M. Russell and others through biography. *English Journal, 85*(8), 66-69.

Kehl, D. G., & Livingston, H. (1999). Doublespeak detection for the English classroom. *English Journal, 88*(6), 77-82.

Kell, J. (1995). Teaching ideas: Illustrating imagery. *English Journal, 84*(4), 66-67.

Keller, R. D. (1985). The rhetorical cycle. *Leaflet, 84,* 27-32.

Kellner, D. (1988). Reading images critically: Toward a postmodern pedagogy. *Journal of Education, 170*(3), 31-52.

Kelly, P. P. (1992). Two reader-response classrooms: Using pre-reading activity and readers theatre approaches. In N. J. Karolides (Ed.), *Reader response in the classroom: Evoking and interpreting meaning in literature* (pp. 84-91). New York: Longman.

Kelly, P. P. (1993). Reading from a female perspective: Pairing *A Doll House* with *Permanent Connections*. In J. F. Kaywell (Ed.), *Adolescent literature as a complement to the classics* (pp. 127-142). Norwood, MA: Christopher-Gordon.

Kennedy, X. J. (1966). *An introduction to poetry.* Boston: Little, Brown.

Kennedy, X. J. (1976). *Literature: An introduction to fiction, poetry, and drama.* Boston: Little, Brown.

Kent, R. (1997). *Room 109: The promise of a portfolio classroom.* Portsmouth, NH: Boynton/Cook Publishers.

Kernan, A. (1990). *The death of literature.* New Haven, CT: Yale University Press.

Kidder, T. (1989). *Among schoolchildren.* Boston: Houghton Mifflin.

Kiel, J. (1998). How language is learned: From birth through the elementary years and beyond. In C. Weaver (Ed.), *Lessons to share on teaching grammar in context* (pp. 1-17). Portsmouth, N.H.: Boynton/Cook & Heinemann.

Kimball, S., & Grotewold, S. (1989). The round table: Tell me a story. *English Journal, 78*(7), 76.

Kinneavy, J. (1971). *A theory of discourse.* Upper Saddle River, NJ: Prentice Hall.

Kirby, D., & Kuykendall, C. (1991). *Mind matters: Teaching for thinking.* Portsmouth, NH: Boynton/Cook.

Kirby, D., & Liner, T. (1981). *Inside out: Developmental strategies for teaching writing.* Montclair, NJ: Boynton/Cook.

Kirby, D., Liner, T., & Vinz, R. (1988). *Inside out: Developmental strategies for teaching writing* (2nd ed.). Portsmouth, NH: Heinemann.

Kirschenbaum, H., Napier, R., & Simon, S. B. (1971). *"Wad-ja-get?" The grading game in American education.* New York: Hart.

Kirszner, L. G., & Mandell, S. R. (1986). *The Holt handbook.* New York: Holt, Rinehart, & Winston.

Klem, E., & Moran, C. (1991). Computers and instructional strategies in the teaching of writing. In G. Hawisher & C. Selfe (Eds.), *Evolving perspectives on computers and composition studies.* Urbana, IL: NCTE.

Kliebard, H. M. (1970). The Tyler rationale. *School Review, 78*(2), 259-272.

Kneeshaw, D. (1992). Writing portfolios in secondary schools. In K. Yancey (Ed.), *Portfolios in the writing classroom.* Urbana, IL: NCTE.

Kneeshaw, D. (1992). Portfolios in English classrooms. *English Journal, 81*(6).

Knowles, L. (1983). *Encouraging talk.* New York: Methuen.

Knowles, M. T. (1996). The English teacher's Internet resource guide. *English Journal, 85*(8), 91-94.

Knowles, M. T. (1997). Software: More Internet resources for the English teacher. *English Journal, 86*(2), 90-93.

Kohl, H. (1967). *36 Children.* New York: New American Library.

Kohl, H. (1973). *Reading: How to.* New York: Dutton.

Kohlberg, L. (1984). *The psychology of moral development: The nature and validity of moral stages.* San Francisco: Harper & Row.

Kohn, A. (2002, Feb.). *Raising the scores, ruining the schools: Rethinking tests for teachers and students.* Speech at annual AACTE conference, New York.

Kolln, M. (1981). Closing the books on alchemy. *College Composition and Communication, 32*(2), 139-151.

Kolln, M. (1996). Rhetorical grammar: A modification lesson. *English Journal, 85*(7), 25-31.

Kolodny, A. (1985). The integrity of memory: Creating a new literary history of the United States. *American Literature, 57*(2), 291-307.

Kooy, M., & Chiu, A. (1998). Language, literature, and learning in the ESL classroom. *English Journal, 88*(2), 78-84.

Kooy, M. & Wells, J. (1996). *Reading response logs: Inviting students to explore novels, short stories, plays, poetry, and more.* Portsmouth, NH: Heinemann.

Kopp, S. B. (1973). *If you meet the Buddha on the road, kill him! The pilgrimage of psychotherapy patients.* Ben Lomond, CA: Science and Behavior Books.

Korg, J. (1966). *The force of few words: An introduction to poetry.* New York: Holt, Rinehart, & Winston.

Kozol, J. (1975). The politics of syntax. *English Journal, 64*(9), 22-27.

Kozol, J. (1991). *Savage inequalities: Children in America's schools.* New York: Crown.

Kozol, J. (2002, March). *Education and social justice.* Speech at Wake Forest University, Winston-Salem, NC.

Krashen, S. (1982). *Principles and practices in second language acquisition.* Oxford: Pergamon.

Krest, M. (1987). Time on my hands: Handling the paper load. *English Journal, 76*(8), 37-42.

Krest, M. (1990). Adapting the portfolio to meet student needs. *English Journal, 79*(2), 29-34.

Kretzschman, W. A., Jr. (1985). English in the middle ages: The struggle for acceptability. In S. Greenbaum (Ed.), *The English language today* (pp. 20-29). Oxford: Pergamon.

Krogness, M. M. (1995). *Just teach me, Mrs. K.: Talking, reading, and writing with resistant adolescent learners.* Portsmouth, NH: Heinemann.

Krueger, C. Y. (1988). *Experiences in composition: A comparison of the Foxfire and writing process methods of teaching composition.* Unpublished master's thesis, Wake Forest University, Winston-Salem, NC.

Kutz, E., & Roskelly, H. (1991). *An unquiet pedagogy: Transforming practice in the English classroom.* Portsmouth, NH: Boynton/Cook.

Kystron, V. S. (2001). *The wonderful writing skills unhandbook.* (http://www.wonderfulwritingskillsunhandbook.com)

Labov, W. (1973). The logic of nonstandard English. In J. S. DeStepheno (Ed.), *Language, society and education: A profile of Black English* (pp. 10-44). Worthington, OH: Jones.

Labov, W. (1981). *The study of non-standard English.* Urbana, IL: NCTE.

LaBrant, L. (1934). The changing sentence structure of children. *Elementary English Review, 11*(3), 59-65, 86.

LaBrant, L. (1957). Writing is more than structure. *English Journal, 46*(5), 252-56, 293.

LaBrant, L. (1959). As of now. *English Journal, 48*(5), 295-303.

Lacks, C. (1997). The teacher's nightmare: Getting fired for good teaching. *English Journal, 86*(2), 29-33.

LaConte, R. (1980). A literary heritage paradigm for secondary English. In B. J. Mandel (Ed.), *Three language arts curriculum models.* Urbana, IL: NCTE.

LaFontana, V. R. (1996). Throw away that correcting pen. *English Journal, 85*(6), 71-73.

Laird, C. (1953). *The miracle of language.* Cleveland, OH: World.

Lake, P. (1988). Sexual stereotyping and the English curriculum. *English Journal, 77*(6), 35-38.

Lambert, D. (1976). What is a journal? In K. Macrorie (Ed.), *Writing to be read* (2nd ed.). Rochelle Park, NJ: Hayden.

Lamott, A. (1994). *Bird by bird.* New York: Anchor.

Langer, J. A. (1995). *Envisioning literature: Literary understanding and literature instruction.* New York: Teachers College Press.

Langer, J. A. (1997). Literacy acquisition through literature. *Journal of Adolescent and Adult Literacy, 40*(8), 606-613.

Langer, J. A., & Applebee, A. N. (1987). *How writing shapes thinking: A study of teaching and learning.* Urbana, IL: NCTE.

Langer, S. K. (1958). The cultural importance of the arts. In M. F. Andrews (Ed.), *Aesthetic form and education.* Syracuse, NY: Syracuse University Press.

Larsen, A. (2001, July). *Controlling genre to develop film drama.* Presentation at the North Carolina Governor's School, East, Raleigh.

Larson, C. R. (1978). *American Indian fiction.* Albuquerque: University of New Mexico Press.

Larson, R. L. (1974). Students' rights to their own language. *College Composition and Communication* [Special issue], *25,* 1-32.

Laughlin, R. (1993). How do you pronounce *greasy? English Journal, 82*(1), 77.

Lawrence, B. (1995). Teaching ideas: New looks at old literature. *English Journal, 84*(3), 80-82.

Leggo, C. (1991). The reader as problem-maker: Responding to a poem with questions. *English Journal, 80*(7), 58-60.

Lenneberg, E. H. (1967). *Biological foundations of language.* New York: Wiley.

Lensmire, T. (1994). *When children write: Critical revisions of the writing workshop.* New York: Teachers College Press.

Lerman, L. (1993, Summer). Toward a process for critical response. In *Alternate roots.* Regional Organization of Theatres South.

Lester, J. (1969). *Search for the new land: History of subjective experience.* New York: Dial.

Levine, L. W. (1996). *The opening of the American mind: Canons, culture, and history.* Boston: Little, Brown.

Lewis, C. S. (1961). *An experiment in criticism.* Cambridge: Cambridge University Press.

Lewis, L. J. (1984). Developing critical thinking through media study. *English Journal, 73*(1), 52-53.

Ley, T. C. (1995, Nov. 14). *Fostering productive collaborative transactions with poetry.* Presentation at the First Combined International Reading Association Regional Conference.

Lincoln, K. (1983). *Native American renaissance.* Berkeley: University of California Press.

Lindemann, E. (1982). *A rhetoric for writing* (2nd ed.). New York: Oxford University Press.

Ling, A. (1990). *Between worlds: Women writers of Chinese ancestry.* New York: Pergamon.

Linkin, H. K. (1991). The current canon in British romantics studies. *College English, 53*(5), 548-570.

Lloyd-Jones, R. & Lunsford, A. A. (1989). *The English coalition conference: Democracy through language.* Urbana, IL: NCTE.

Loban, W. (1969). *Teaching literature and language.* New York: Harcourt, Brace, & World.

Lockward, D. (1994). Poets on teaching poetry. *English Journal, 83*(5), 65-70.

Loevinger, J. (1976). *Ego development: Conceptions and theories.* San Francisco: Jossey-Bass.

Loevinger, J. (1987). *Paradigms of personality.* New York: Freeman.

Lott, J. G. (1989). Not teaching poetry. *English Journal, 78*(4), 66-68.

Luce-Kapler, R. (1994). *Never stepping in the same river twice: Teaching and writing in school.* Unpublished master's thesis, University of Alberta, Edmonton.

Luce-Kapler, R. (1996). Narrating the portfolio landscape. *English Journal, 85*(1), 46-49.

Lucking, R., & Stallard, C. (1988). *How computers can help you teach English.* Portland, OR: J. Weston Walch.

Luna, C., & Turner, C. L. (2001). The impact of the MCAS: Teachers talk about high-stakes testing. *English Journal, 91*(1), 79-87.

Lutz, W. (1989). *Doublespeak.* New York: Harper.

Lynch, J. J., & Evans, B. (1963). *High school English textbooks: A critical examination.* Boston: Little, Brown.

Lynn, S. (1990). A passage into critical theory. *College English, 52*(3), 258-271.

Lytle, S. (1982). *Exploring comprehension style: A study of twelfth-grade readers.* Unpublished dissertation, Stanford University.

Macey, D. (2000). *The Penguin dictionary of critical theory.* New York: Penguin.

MacKail, J. W. (1970). *The approach to Shakespeare.* New York: AMS Press.

Mackey, M. (1993). Lost in a book: The invisible problems of a learning reader. *English Journal, 83*(1), 65-68.

MacNeil, R. (1988). Listening to our language. *English Journal, 77*(6), 16-21.

MacNeil, R. (1989). *Wordstruck: A memoir.* New York: Viking.

Macrorie, K. (1970). *Uptaught.* New York: Hayden.

Macrorie, K. (1984). *Searching writing.* Portsmouth, NH: Boynton/Cook.

Madden, F. (1987, Aug.). Desperately seeking literary response. *Computers and Composition, 4,* 17-34.

Madden, F. (1989). Using computers in the literature class. In C. Selfe, D. Rodrigues, & W. Oates (Eds.), *Computers in English and the language arts* (pp. 227-241). Urbana, IL: NCTE.

Maimon, E. P., Nodine, B. F., & O'Connor, F. W. (1989). *Thinking, reasoning, and writing.* White Plains, NY: Longman.

Mallick, D. (1984). *How tall is this ghost, John?* Portsmouth NH.: Boynton Cook.

Marcus, S. (1986). *Analyzing fiction software: Literature and composition data base for PFS: File.* New York: Scholastic.

Marcus, S. (1987). Computers and English: Future tense . . . future perfect. *English Journal, 76*(5), 88-92.

Marcus, S. (1989). Creating writing activities with the word processor. In C. Selfe, D. Rodrigues, & W. Oates (Eds.), *Computers in English and the language arts* (pp. 241-246). Urbana, IL: NCTE.

Marlowe, B. A., & Page, M. L. (1998). *Creating and sustaining the constructivist classroom.* Thousand Oaks, CA: Corwin.

Marr, P. M. (2000). Grouping students at the computer to enhance the study of British literature. *English Journal, 90*(2), 120-125.

Marshall, J. (1991, Dec. 5-6). Presentation at Yale-New Haven Teachers Institute, Conference on School-College Collaboration, New Haven, CT.

Marshall, J. (1999). Closely reading ourselves: Teaching English and the education of teachers. In P. Franklin, D. Laurence, & E. B. Welles (Eds.), *Preparing a nation's teachers: Models for*

English and foreign language programs (pp. 380-389). New York: Modern Language Association of America.

Marshall, J. (2000, Oct.). *Teaching texts in a new century.* Presentation at the meeting of the North Carolina English Teachers Association, Winston-Salem, NC.

Marshall, J. (2001). Language and learning. In J. E. Many (Ed.), *Handbook of instructional practices for literacy teacher-educators: Examples and reflections from the teaching lives of literacy scholars* (pp. 269-276). Mahwah, NJ: Erlbaum.

Martin, J. M. (1991, July). *Poetry in a postmodern world.* Presentation at the North Carolina Governor's School West, Winston-Salem, North Carolina.

Martin, J. R. (1985). *Reclaiming a conversation: The ideal of the educated woman.* New Haven, CT: Yale University Press.

Martin, N. (1983). So all talk is significant. In *Mostly about writing: Selected essays.* Upper Montclair, NJ: Boynton/Cook.

Martinsen, A. (2000). The Tower of Babel and the teaching of grammar: Writing instruction for a new century. *English Journal, 90*(1), 122-126.

Matthews, R., & Chandler, R. (1998). Using reader response to teach *Beloved* in a high school American studies classroom. *English Journal, 88*(2), 85-92.

Mayer, R. (1979). Can advance organizers influence meaningful learning? *Review of Educational Research, 49*(2), 371-383.

Mayer, Sister J. E. (1988). Neighborhoods: Maya Angelou's "Harlem Hopscotch." *English Journal, 77*(5), 86-88.

Mayher, J. S. (1990). *Uncommon sense: Theoretical practice in language education.* Portsmouth, NH: Boynton/Cook.

McAlexander, P., Dobie, A., & Gregg, N. (1992). *Beyond the "SP" Label.* Urbana, IL: NCTE.

McCarthy, D. (1954). Language development in children. In L. Carmichael (Ed.), *Manual of child psychology* (2nd ed., pp. 492-630). New York: Wiley.

McCaslin, N. (1984). *Creative drama in the classroom* (4th ed.). New York: Longman.

McClaskey, J. (1995). Assessing student learning through multiple intelligences. *English Journal, 84*(8), 56-58.

McClaskey, J. (2001). Who's afraid of the big, bad TAAS? Rethinking our response to standardized testing. *English Journal, 91*(1), 88-95.

McCleary, W. (1995). Grammar making a comeback in composition teaching. *Composition Chronicle, 8*(6), 1-4.

McClure, M. F. (1990). Collaborative learning: Teacher's game or students' game? *English Journal, 79*(2), 66-68.

McCollum-Clark, K. (1995). *National Council of Teachers of English, corporate philanthropy, and National Education Standards: Challenging the ideologies of English education reform.* Unpublished dissertation, University of Pennsylvania, Philadelphia.

McCrum, R., Cran, W., & MacNeil, R. (1986). *The story of English.* New York: Viking.

McDavid, R. I., Jr. (1985). A linguist to the lay audience. In S. Greenbaum (Ed.), *The English language today* (pp. 280-292). Oxford: Pergamon.

McEwan, H. (1992). Five metaphors for English. *English Education, 24*(2), 101-128.

McGlynn, P. D. (1969). The chronology of "A Rose for Emily." *Studies in Short Fiction, 6*(4), 461-462.

McGonigal, E. (1988). Correlative thinking: Writing analogies about literature. *English Journal, 71*(1), 66-67.

McGowen, P. (1997, March 7). *Another opening, another show: Using reader's theater to enhance composition skills.* Presentation at the Annual Conference on Writing and Literature, Lawrence, KS.

McGuire, R. L. (1973). *Passionate attention.* New York: Norton.

McKenzie, B. (1978). *Fiction's journey.* New York: Harcourt Brace Jovanovich.

McKeown, M. G., & Beck, I. L. (1999). Getting the discussion started. *Educational Leadership, 57*(3), 25-28.

McLuhan, M. (1957, May). *Explorations number seven.* A broadcast of the Canadian Broadcasting Corporation.

McLuhan, M. (1964). *Understanding media.* New York: Signet.

McNees, C. (1977). Can one teach each student at his own level? In R. B. Shuman (Ed.), *Questions English teachers ask.* Rochelle Park, NJ: Hayden.

Megyeri, K. A. (1996). Reading aloud student writing. *English Journal, 85*(3), 74-76.

Meiers, M. (1990, Aug.). *Assessing development in English.* Presentation at International Federation of Teachers of English Conference, Auckland, NZ.

Mellon, J. (1975). *National assessment of the teaching of English.* Urbana, IL: NCTE.

Mellon, J. C. (1969). *Transformational sentence combining: A method of enhancing the development of syntactic fluency in English compositions* (NCTE Research Report No. 10). Urbana, IL: NCTE.

Mellown, E. (1986). The use of computers in literary studies: An experimental course. *Computer Assisted Composition Journal, 1*(1), 55-61.

Meyer, J., Youga, J., & Flint-Ferguson, J. (1990). Grammar in context: Why and how. *English Journal, 79*(1), 66-70.

Meyer, M. (1990). *The Bedford introduction to literature* (2nd ed.). Boston: St. Martin's.

Meyer, M. (1996). *The Bedford introduction to literature* (4th ed.). Boston: Bedford.

Meyers, G. D. (1993). Three functions of language. *English Journal, 82*(1), 75.

Meyers, J. B. (1993). Where do words come from? *English Journal, 82*(1), 76.

Michael, I., & Swaim, M. (1980). Theoretical bases of communicative approaches to second language teaching and testing. *Applied Linguistics, 1*, 1-47.

Milgram, S., & Shotland, R. L. (1973). *Television and antisocial behavior: Field experiments.* New York: Academic Press.

Mill, J. S. (1859/1989). *On liberty and other writings.* Cambridge: Cambridge University Press.

Miller, S. (1991). Planning for spontaneity: Supporting the language of thinking. *English Journal, 80*(3), 51-56.

Milner, J. O. (1975). Ken Kesey's classroom corrective. *English Journal, 64*(7), 34-37.

Milner, J. O. (1976). Right-left writer: Composition's march to a developmental drummer. *Arizona English Bulletin, 20*(2), 58-62.

Milner, J. O. (1991). Suppositional style and teacher evaluation. *Phi Delta Kappan, 72*(6), 464-467.

Milner, J. O. (1997). Using a flat structure in a hierarchical world. *Clearing House, 70*(3), 129-135.

Milner, J. O., & Elrod, M. M. (1986). Language reception in three modes. *Journal of Genetic Psychology, 147*(1), 123-133.

Milner, J. O., & Milner, L. M. (Eds.). (1989). *Passages to literature: Essays on teaching in Australia, Canada, England, the United States, and Wales.* Urbana, IL: NCTE.

Milner, J. O., & Richman, C. (1983). *Impulsivity and revision skills.* Presentation at National Council of Teachers of English, Columbus, OH.

Milner, L. F. M. (1986). *A study of the impact of instruction in theories of literary criticism on gifted secondary students.* Unpublished master's thesis, Wake Forest University, Winston-Salem, NC.

Mini Digest of Education Statistics. (1997). Washington, D.C.: National Center for Educational Statistics, Department of Education, OERI. NCES97-541.

Mitchell, D. (1994). Teaching ideas: Putting poetry in its place. *English Journal, 83*(5), 78-80.

Mitchell, D. (1995). Teaching ideas: Bringing literary terms to life. *English Journal, 84*(4), 64-68.

Mitchell, D. (1996). Writing to learn across the curriculum and the English teacher. *English Journal, 85*(5), 93-95.

Mitchell, D. (1997). Teaching ideas: Creating thematic units. *English Journal 86*(5), 80-84.

Mitchell, D. (1998). Fifty alternatives to the book report. *English Journal, 87*(1), 92-95.

Moffett, J. (1968). *Teaching the universe of discourse.* Boston: Houghton Mifflin.

Moffett, J. (1981). *Active voice: A program of writing assignments.* Upper Montclair, NJ: Boynton/Cook.

Moffett, J. (1992). *Active voice: A writing program across the curriculum* (2nd ed.). Portsmouth, NH: Boynton/Cook.

Moffett, J., & Wagner, B. J. (1976). *Student-centered language arts and reading, K-13: A handbook for teachers* (2nd ed.). Boston: Houghton Mifflin.

Moffett, J., & Wagner, B. J. (1992). *Student-centered language arts, K-12.* (4th ed.). Portsmouth, NH: Boynton/Cook & Heinemann.

Momaday, N. S. (1966). *House made of dawn.* New York: New American Library.

Mondock, S. (1997). Portfolios—The story behind the story. *English Journal, 86*(1), 59-64.

Monroe, R. (1993). *Writing and thinking with computers.* Urbana, IL: NCTE.

Monseau, V. R., & Knox, W. L. (1984). Looking back to the future through oral history. *English Journal, 73*(3), 49-51.

Montgomery, M. (1962). Robert Frost and his use of barriers: Man vs. nature toward God. In J. M. Cox (Ed.), *Robert Frost: A collection of critical essays* (pp. 138-150). Upper Saddle River, NJ: Prentice Hall.

Montrose, L. (1989). Professing the Renaissance: The poetics and politics of culture. In H. Veeser (Ed.), *The new historicism.* London: Routledge.

Moon, B. (2000). Reading practices/readings. In D. Allender (Ed.), *Trends and issues in secondary English, 2000 edition* (pp. 68-75). Urbana, IL: NCTE.

Moore, L. (1989). One-on-one: Pairing male and female writers. *English Journal, 78*(6), 34-38.

Morine-Dershimer, G. G. (1990). Instructional planning. In J. M. Cooper (Ed.), *Classroom teaching skills* (pp. 18-49). Lexington, MA: Heath.

Morris, B. S. (1989). The television generation: Couch potatoes or informed critics? *English Journal, 78*(8), 35-41.

Morris, C. (2001). Proximity, touch, and participation. In L. P. McCoy (Ed.), *Studies in teaching.* Winston-Salem, NC: Wake Forest University Education Department.

Morrison, T. (1992). *Playing in the dark: Whiteness and the literary imagination.* Cambridge: Harvard University Press.

Morrow, L. (1997). *Literacy development.* Boston: Allyn & Bacon.

Morse, D. (1972). *Grandfather rock.* New York: Delacorte.

Moyers, B. (1997, Nov. 19). *Religion in American life: Reflections from a long-time observer.* Speech at Wake Forest University, Winston-Salem, NC.

Muinzer, L. A. (1960, Nov.). Historical linguistics in the classroom. *Illinois English Bulletin, 48*(2).

Muir, K. (1984). The wrong way and the right. *Shakespeare Quarterly* [Special issue], 642-643.

Mura, D. (1988). Strangers in the village. In R. Simonson & S. Walker (Eds.), *The Graywolf annual five: Multicultural literacy* (pp. 135-153). St. Paul, MN: Graywolf.

Murdick, W. (1996). What English teachers need to know about grammar. *English Journal, 85*(7), 38-45.

Murphy, G. (1968). *The study of literature in high school.* Waltham, MA: Blaisdell.

Murphy, S., & Smith, M. A. (1990). Talking about portfolios. *Quarterly 12*(2), 1-3, 24-27.

Murphy, S., & Smith, M. A. (1992). Looking into portfolios. In *Portfolios in the writing classroom.* Urbana, IL: NCTE.

Murray, D. M. (1968). *A writer teaches writing.* Boston: Houghton Mifflin.

Murray, D. M. (1977). Our students will write—If we let them. *North Carolina English Teacher, 30*(1), 1-5.

Murray, D. M. (1980). Writing as process: How writing finds its own meaning. In T. R. Donovan & B. W. McClelland (Eds.), *Eight approaches to teaching composition* (pp. 3-20). Urbana, IL: NCTE.

Murray, D. M. (1982). *Learning by teaching: Selected articles on writing and teaching.* Upper Montclair, NJ: Boynton/Cook.

Murray, D. M. (1985). *A writer teaches writing* (2nd ed.). Boston: Houghton Mifflin.

Myers, K. L. (1988). Twenty (better) questions. *English Journal, 77*(1), 64-65.

Myers, M. (1980). *A procedure for writing assessment and holistic scoring.* Urbana, IL: NCTE.

Myers, M. (1991, Oct.). *How to measure the mind.* Presentation at the Southeastern Regional National Council of Teachers of English Conference, Asheville, NC.

Nagy, W. E. (1988). *Teaching vocabulary to improve reading comprehension.* Urbana, IL: NCTE.

Nash, R. J., & Shiman, D. A. (1974). The English teacher as questioner. *English Journal, 63*(9), 38-44.

Nathanson, S. (1992). Guidelines for using videotape: A checklist for educators. *English Journal, 81*(3), 88-89.

National Assessment of Educational Progress. (2000). NAEP scoring on eighth-grade information writing. *NAEP Facts, 5*(2), 1-5.

National Board for Professional Teaching Standards. (1994). *What teachers should know and be able to do.* Washington, DC: Author.

National Center for Educational Statistics. (1998, Sept.). *Mini-digest of education statistics 1997.* Washington, DC: U.S. Department of Education.

National Commission on Teaching and America's Future. (1996). *What matters most: Teaching for America's future.* New York: Author.

National Council of Teachers of English. (1991). *The Council Chronicle, 1*(2).

National Council of Teachers of English and International Reading Association. (1996). *Standards for the English language arts.* Urbana, IL, and Newark, DE: Authors.

Neenan, J. (1989). Idea exchange: Journal entries. *North Carolina English Teacher, 47*(1), 7-8, 12.

Neff, J. (1998). From a distance: Teaching writing on interactive television. *Research in the Teaching of English, 33*(2), 136-157.

Nelms, B. F. (1989). EJ survey: What works (ten years later). *English Journal, 78*(5), 81-83.

Nelms, B. F. (1992). Cases: English teachers at work. *English Journal, 83*(3), 43.

Nelms, B. F. (2000). Reconstructing English: From the 1890s to the 1990s and beyond. *English Journal, 89*(3), 49-59.

Nelms, B. F. (Ed.). (1988). *Literature in the classroom: Readers, texts, and contexts.* Urbana, IL: NCTE.

Nelms, B. F., & Nelms, E. D. (Eds.). (1989). Books for teachers: A new magazine for gifted students—and for their teachers. *English Journal, 78*(2), 91-92.

Nelms, E. D. (1988). Two laureates in April: Lyrics of Wordsworth and Ted Hughes. *English Journal, 77*(4), 23-26.

Nelms, E. D. (Ed.). (1990). Instructional materials: Classroom magazines: A timely alternative to textbooks. *English Journal, 79*(3), 77-78.

Nelms, E. D. (Ed.). (1993). The round table: Mini-lessons on language. *English Journal, 82*(1), 75-77.

Nelson, G. L. (1991). Bringing language back to life: Responding to the new illiteracy. *English Journal, 80*(2), 16-20.

Newkirk, T. (Ed.). (1990). *To compose: Teaching writing in high school and college* (2nd ed.). Portsmouth, NH: Heinemann.

Newlin, L. F. (1984). Shakespeare saved from drowning. *Shakespeare Quarterly* [Special issue], 596-601.

Newmann, F., & Wehlage, G. (1995). *Successful school restructuring.* Madison, WI: Center on Organization and Restructuring of Schools.

Nilsen, A. P. (2001). Why keep searching when it's already *their?* Reconsidering *everybody's* pronoun problem. *English Journal, 90*(4), 68-73.

Noden, H., & Moss, B. (1994). Perceiving discussion as Eskimos perceive snow. *Reading Teacher, 47*(6), 504-506.

Noguchi, R. (1991). *Grammar and the teaching of writing.* Urbana, IL: NCTE.

Noll, E. (1994). The ripple effect of censorship: Silencing in the classroom. *English Journal, 83*(8), 59-64.

Norris, K. (1996). *The cloister walk.* New York: Berkley.

Norris, K. (2001). Introduction: Stories around a fire. In K. Norris (Ed.), *The best American essays, 2001* (pp. xiv-xvi). Boston: Houghton Mifflin.

Noskin, D. (1994). The round table: "Can we talk?" *English Journal, 83*(3), 87.

Nystrand, M., & Gamoran, A. (1991). Instructional discourse, student engagement, and literature achievement. *Research in the Teaching of English, 25*(3), 261-290.

Oates, J. C. (2000). Introduction: The art of the (American) essay. In J. C. Oates (Ed.), *The best American essays of the century* (pp. xvii-xxvii). Boston: Houghton Mifflin.

O'Brian, E. J. (1984). Inside Shakespeare: Using performance techniques to achieve traditional goals. *Shakespeare Quarterly* [Special issue], 621-631.

Ochs, J. (2001). The effectiveness of global versus focal questions in secondary English classroom discussions. In L. P. McCoy (Ed.), *Studies in teaching.* Winston-Salem, NC: Wake Forest University Education Department.

O'Fallon, K. (1977). Varieties of voice: A proposal for dealing with dialect differences in the composition classroom. *Kansas Association of Teachers of English, 8*-15.

O'Hare, F. (1973). *Sentence combining: Improving student writing without formal grammar instruction* (NCTE Research Report No. 15). Urbana, IL: NCTE.

O'Hare, F. (1975). *Sentencecraft.* Lexington, MA: Ginn.

Ohmann, R. (1976). *English in America: A radical view of the profession.* New York: Oxford University Press.

O'Keefe, J., & Nadel L. (1990). *Four mat in action.* Barrington, IL: Excel.

Oliver, D. W., & Bane, M. J. (1971). Moral education: Is reasoning enough? In C. M. Beck, B. S. Crittenden, & E. V. Sullivan (Eds.), *Moral education: Interdisciplinary approaches.* New York: Newman.

Olsen, T. (1978). *Silences.* New York: Delacorte.

Olson, L. (2001, Jan. 11). Overboard on testing? *Education Week, 20*(18), 23.

O'Neill, C., & Lambert, A. (1982). *Drama structures: A practical handbook for teachers.* London: Thornes.

Oran, S. M., DeMarrais, K. B., & Lewis, J. B. (2001). Social foundations as a foundation for literacy instruction: An effort in collaboration. In J. E. Many (Ed.), *Handbook of instructional practices for literacy teacher-educators: Examples and reflections from the teaching lives of literacy scholars* (pp. 21-30). Mahwah, NJ: Erlbaum.

Orlich, D. C., Harder, R. J., Callahan, R. C., Kauchak, D. P., Pendergrass, R. A., Keogh, A. J., & Gibson, H. (1990). *Teaching strategies: A guide to better instruction.* Lexington, MA: Heath.

Ornstein, R. (1972). *The psychology of consciousness.* San Francisco: Freeman.

Orser, E. (2001). Teacher response to wrong answers in the English classroom. In L. P. McCoy (Ed.), *Studies in teaching.* Winston-Salem, NC: Wake Forest University Education Department.

Our readers write. (1984). What's an especially good nonfiction book for young readers? *English Journal, 73*(7), 87-88.

Our readers write. (1987). What's a new and interesting way to test students? *English Journal, 76*(1), 71-76.

Owen, F. (1991). Teaching as a composing process. *English Journal, 80*(3), 57-62.

Owen, T. (2000). Learning with technology. *English Journal, 90*(1), 131-137.

Packard, V. (1957). *The hidden persuaders.* New York: McKay.

Palincsar, A. S., & Brown, A. (1984). Reciprocal teaching of comprehension fostering and comprehension monitoring activities. *Cognition and Instruction, 1*(2), 117-125.

Parker, R. P., & Goodkin, V. (1987). *The consequences of writing: Enhancing learning in the disciplines.* Upper Montclair, NJ: Boynton/Cook.

Patterson, N. G. (2000). Hypertext and the changing roles of readers. *English Journal, 90*(2), 74-80.

Paz, O. (1956). *The bow and the lyre.* (R. L. C. Simms, Tran.). Austin: University of Texas Press.

Pearson, M. (1997, June 30). *Critical response process.* Presentation at the North Carolina Governor's School West, Winston-Salem, NC.

Pennac, D. (1994). *Better than life.* Toronto: Coach House.

People for the American Way. (1995, Aug. 26). *Attacks on the freedom to learn, 1994-1995 report.*

Perera, C. (1990). *Divergence and convergence in English: A creative tension?* Paper presented at the International Federation of Teachers of English Fifth International Congress, Auckland, NZ.

Perkins, D. (1995). *Outsmarting IQ: The emerging science of learned intelligence.* New York: Free Press.

Perrin, R. (1991). When junk mail isn't junk. *English Journal, 80*(1), 30-32.

Perrin, R. (1994). The round table: Whose questions? *English Journal, 83*(3), 89.

Perrin, R. (1999). "Barbie doll" and "G. I. Joe": Exploring issues of gender. *English Journal, 88*(3), 83-85.

Perrine, L. (1978). *Story and structure* (5th ed.). New York: Harcourt Brace Jovanovich.

Perrine, L. (1983). *Literature: Structure, sound, and sense* (4th ed.). San Diego: Harcourt Brace Jovanovich.

Peters, R. L., & Hitchcock, G. (Eds.). (1967). *Pioneers of modern poetry.* San Francisco: Kayak.

Peterson, B. (1987). Why they talk that talk: Language in Appalachian studies. *English Journal, 76*(6), 53-55.

Petruzzella, B. A. (1996). Grammar instruction: What teachers say. *English Journal, 85*(7), 68-72.

Phillips, A. (1997). Feeling expressed. *Language Arts, 74*(5), 325-32.

Phillips, L. (1989). First impressions: Introducing Monet to Megadeth. *English Journal, 78*(3), 31-33.

Pichaske, D. R. (Ed.). (1972). *Beowulf to Beatles: Approaches to poetry.* New York: Free Press.

Pope, C. (1998, Jan. 21) *Connecting students by e-mail.* Presentation at the Technology and Teaching Video Conference, University of North Carolina General Administration, Chapel Hill.

Pope, C., & Kutiper, K. L. (Eds.). Instructional materials: Using magazines in the English classroom. *English Journal, 77*(8), 66-68.

Popham, W. J. (1997). The standards movement and the emperor's new clothes. *NAASP Bulletin, 81*(590), 21-25.

Porter, C., & Cleland, J. (1995). *The portfolio as a learning strategy.* Portsmouth, NH: Boynton/Cook.

Portfolio News. (1990). Encinitas, CA: Portfolio Assessment Clearing House.

Postal, P. M. (1968). Epilogue. In R. A. Jacobs & P. S. Rosenbaum (Eds.), *English transformational grammar* (pp. 267-289). Waltham, MA: Blaisdell.

Postman, N. (1979a). *Schools should give children what the media don't.* Times Washington Post News Service.

Postman, N. (1979b). *Teaching as a conserving activity.* New York: Delacorte.

Postman, N. (1985). *Amusing ourselves to death.* New York: Viking.

Postman, N. (1988). *Conscientious objections: Stirring up trouble about language, technology, and education.* New York: Knopf.

Postman, N. (1993). *Technopoly: The surrender of culture to technology.* New York: Knopf.

Postman, N. (1995). *The end of education: Redefining the value of school.* New York: Vintage.

Postman, N., & Weingartner, C. (1966). *Linguistics: A revolution in teaching.* New York: Dell.

Postman, N., & Weingartner, C. (1969). *Teaching as a subversive activity.* New York: Dell.

Pound, E. (1954). A few don'ts. In T. S. Eliot (Ed.). *Literary essays of Ezra Pound* (pp. 3-4). London: Faber & Faber.

Probst, R. (1984). *Adolescent literature: Response and analysis.* Upper Saddle River, NJ: Merrill/Prentice Hall.

Probst, R. (1986a). Three relationships in the teaching of literature. *English Journal, 75*(1), 60-68.

Probst, R. (1986b). Mom, Wolfgang and me: Adolescent literature, critical theory and the English classroom. *English Journal, 75*(6), 33-39.

Probst, R. (1988a). Dialogue with a text. *English Journal, 77*(1), 32-38.

Probst, R. (1988b). *Response and analysis: Teaching literature in junior and senior high school.* Portsmouth, NH: Boynton/Cook.

Probst, R. (1994). Reader-response theory and the English curriculum. *English Journal, 83*(3), 37-44.

Probst, R. (2000, Oct.). *"I'll get along with a little help from my friends": Social and solitary dimensions of literary experience.* Speech presented at the meeting of the North Carolina English Teachers Association, Winston-Salem, NC.

Progoff, I. (1975). *At a journal workshop.* New York: Dialogue House Library.

Protherough, R. (1983). *Developing response to fiction.* Milton Keynes, UK: Open University Press.

Prown, J. D. (1982). Mind in matter: An introduction to material culture theory and method. *Winterthur Portfolio, 17*(1), 1-19.

Purcell-Gates, V. (1991). On the outside looking in: A study of remedial-readers' meaning-making while reading literature. *Journal of Reading Behavior, 23*(2), 235-254.

Purpel, D. E. (1989). *The moral and spiritual crisis in education: A curriculum for justice and compassion in education.* Granby, MA: Bergin & Garvey.

Purser, D. (1996). Grammar in a nutshell. *English Journal, 85*(7), 108-114.

Purves, A. (1971). Evaluation of learning in literature. In B. Bloom, J. T. Hastings, & G. F. Madaus (Eds.), *Handbook on formative and summative evaluation of student learning* (pp. 697-766). New York: McGraw-Hill.

Purves, A. (1981). *Reading and literature: American achievement in international perspective.* Urbana, IL: NCTE.

Purves, A. (1986). Commentary on George Henry's "What is the nature of English education?" *English Education, 18*(1), 42-45.

Purves, A., & Monson, D. (1972). *Experiencing children's literature.* Glenview, IL: Scott Foresman.

Purves, A., Foshay, A. W., & Hanson, G. (1973). *Literature education in ten countries.* New York: Wiley.

Purves, A., Jordan, S., & Peltz, J. (1996). *Using portfolios in the English classroom.* Norwood, MA: Christopher-Gordon.

Purves, A., Quattrini, J., & Sullivan, C. (1995). *Creating the writing portfolio.* Lincolnwood, IL: NTC Publishing.

Purves, A., Rogers, T., & Soter, A. O. (1990). *How porcupines make love II: Teaching a response-centered literature curriculum.* New York: Longman.

Pyles, T., & Algeo, J. (1978). *English: An introduction to the language.* New York: Harcourt Brace Jovanovich.

Pynchon, T. (1973). *Gravity's rainbow.* New York: Viking.

Rabinowitz, P. J. (1987). *Before reading: Narrative conventions and the politics of interpretation.* Ithaca, NY: Cornell University Press.

Rabinowitz, P. J. (1992). Against close reading. In M. Kecht (Ed.), *Pedagogy in politics: Theory and critical teaching* (pp. 230–243). Champaign: University of Illinois Press.

Rabinowitz, P. J., & Smith, M. W. (1998). *Authorizing readers: Resistance and respect in the teaching of literature.* New York: Teachers College Press.

Radway, J. A. (1984). *Reading the romance: Women, patriarchy, and popular literature.* Chapel Hill: University of North Carolina Press.

Radway, J. A. (1987). *A feeling for books: The Book-of-the-Month Club, literary taste, and middle-class desire.* Chapel Hill: University of North Carolina Press.

Raines, P. A. (1996). Writing portfolios: Turning the house into a home. *English Journal, 85*(1), 41–45.

Rakow, S. R. (1991). Young-adult literature for honors students? *English Journal, 80*(1), 48–51.

Randolph, R., Robbins, S., & Gere, A. (1994). Writing across institutional boundaries: A K–12 and university collaboration. *English Journal, 83*(3), 68–74.

Raths, J. (1991, May). Lecture. Presented to the North Carolina model clinical teaching network, Durham, NC.

Ravitch, D., & Finn, C. (1987). *What do our 17-year-olds know? A report on the first national assessment of history and literature.* New York: Harper & Row.

Ray, J. K. (1985). The ethics of feminism in the literature classroom: A delicate balance. *English Journal, 74*(3), 54–59.

Redfern, R. K. (2001). Can the English language take care of itself? A dialogue. *English Journal, 90*(4), 60–66.

Reed, D. W. (1986). *Children's creative spelling.* London: Routledge & Kegan Paul.

Regina, T. E. (1988). Composing skills and television. *English Journal, 77*(7), 50–52.

Reid, L. (1994). A symposium: Cultivating student expertise. *English Journal, 83*(3), 59.

Reid, L. (1999). Professional Links: Shakespeare in Performance. *English Journal, 88*(6), 53–54.

Reising, R. W., & Wolfe, D. (1983). *Writing for learning.* Portland, OR: J. Weston Walch.

Remmick, D. (1997, Oct. 20 & 27). The next magic kingdom: Future perfect. *New Yorker,* pp. 210–224.

Renwick, M. K. (1994). Real research into the real problems of grammar and usage instruction. *English Journal, 83*(6), 29–32.

Resnick, L. B. (1987, Nov.). *National assessment.* Presentation at NCTE annual conference, Pittsburgh, PA.

Resnick, L. B. (Ed.). (1976). *The nature of intelligence.* Hillsdale, NJ: Erlbaum.

Resnick, L. B., & Glaser, R. (1976). Problem solving and intelligence. In L. B. Resnick (Ed.), *The nature of intelligence* (pp. 205–230). Hillsdale, NJ: Erlbaum.

Reyes, M. (1992). Challenging venerable assumptions. *Harvard Educational Review, 62*(4), 427–446.

Rice, M., & Wilson, E. K. (1999). How technology aids constructivism in the social studies classroom. *Social Studies, 90*(1), 28–33.

Richards, I. A. (1938). *Interpretation in teaching.* New York: Harcourt Brace.

Rico, G. L. (1983). *Writing the natural way: Using right-brain techniques to release your expressive powers.* Los Angeles: Tarcher.

Rilke, R. M. (1954). *Letters to a young poet.* (M. D. Herter Norton, Trans.). New York: Norton.

Robbins, S., Brandt, N., Goering, S., Nassif, J., & Wascha, K. (1994). Using portfolio reflections to reform instructional programs and build curriculum. *English Journal, 83*(7), 71–78.

Roberts, P. (1956). *Patterns of English.* New York: Harper & Row.

Robinson, M. (1988). Idea exchange: Another *Heart of Darkness. North Carolina English Teacher, 46*(1), 20.

Roblyer, M. D. (1990). The glitz factor. *Educational Technology, 30*(10), 34–36.

Roblyer, M. D., & Edwards, J. (2000). *Integrating educational technology into teaching* (2nd ed.). Upper Saddle River, NJ: Merrill/Prentice Hall.

Rogers, C. (1957). The necessary and sufficient conditions of therapeutic personality change. *Journal of Consulting Psychology, 21,* 95–103.

Rogers, C. (1961). *On becoming a person.* Boston: Houghton Mifflin.

Rogers, M. L. (1990). Idea exchange: Writing half a note. *North Carolina English Teacher, 48*(1), 12–14.

Romand, E. (1992). Dream teaching. *English Journal, 80*(4), 96.

Romano, T. (1987). *Clearing the way: Working with teenage writers.* Portsmouth, NH: Heinemann.

Romano, T. (1995). *Writing with passion: Life stories, multiple genres.* Portsmouth, NH: Boynton/Cook & Heinemann.

Romano, T. (2000). The living legacy of Donald Murray. *English Journal, 89*(3), 74–79.

Rose, M. (1984). *Writer's block: The cognitive dimension.* Carbondale: Southern Illinois Press.

Rose, M. (1989). *Lives on the boundary: A moving account of the struggles and achievements of America's educationally underprepared.* New York: Penguin.

Rose, P. (1984, March 22). Heroic fantasies, nervous doubts. *New York Times.*

Roseboro, A. J. S. (1994). Student choice/teacher control: *Braided Lives* in the classroom. *English Journal, 83*(2), 14–18.

Rosen, L. M. (1998). Developing correctness in student writing: Alternatives to the error hunt. In C. Weaver (Ed.), *Lessons to share on teaching grammar in context* (pp. 137–154). Portsmouth, N.H.: Boynton/Cook & Heinemann.

Rosenblatt, L. M. (1968). *Literature as exploration* (2nd ed.). New York: Noble & Noble.

Rosenblatt, L. M. (1969). Pattern and process—A polemic. *English Journal, 58*(7), 1005–1012.

Rosenblatt, L. M. (1976). *Literature as exploration* (3rd ed.). New York: Noble & Noble.

Rosenblatt, L. M. (1978). *The reader, the text, the poem: The transactional theory of the literary work.* Carbondale: Southern Illinois University Press.

Rosenblatt, L. M. (1983). *Literature as exploration* (4th ed.). New York: Modern Language Association.

Rosenblatt, L. M. (1985). Language, literature, and values. In S. N. Tchudi (Ed.), *Language, schooling and society.* Upper Montclair, NJ: Boynton/Cook.

Rosenblatt, L. M. (1995). *Literature as exploration* (5th ed.). New York: Noble & Noble.

Roszak, T. (1969). *The making of a counter culture: Reflections on a technocratic society and its youthful opposition.* Garden City, NY: Doubleday.

Rothwell, D. (1992). Periodic phases of group development. In *In mixed company: Small-group communication* (pp. 55-79). New York: Harcourt Brace Jovanovich.

Roundtable. (1989). Involving students in evaluation. *English Journal, 78*(7), 75-77.

Rouse, J. (1989). In the temple art. *English Journal, 78*(7), 87-88.

Rowe, M. B. (1974). Wait-time and rewards as instructional variables—Their influences on language, logic, and fate control: Part one—Wait time. *Journal of Research in Science Teaching, 11*(2), 81-94.

Rudd, R. (1990). Idea submitted to Idea Exchange at NCTE Annual Convention, Atlanta, GA.

Ruggiero, V. R. (1988). *Teaching thinking across the curriculum.* New York: Harper & Row.

Russ, J. (1983). *How to suppress women's writing.* Austin: University of Texas Press.

Ruthven, K. K. (1979). *Critical assumptions.* Cambridge: Cambridge University Press.

Salomon, G., & Leigh, T. (1984). Predispositions about learning from print and television. *Journal of Communication, 34*(2), 119-135.

Samuels, B. G. (1993). The beast within: Using and abusing power in *Lord of the Flies, The Chocolate War,* and other readings. In J. F. Kaywell (Ed.), *Adolescent literature as a complement to the classics* (pp. 195-214). Norwood, MA: Christopher-Gordon.

Sanborn, J. (1986). Grammar: Good wine before its time. *English Journal, 75*(3), 72-80.

Sanders, T. E., & Peek, W. W. (1973). *Literature of the American Indian.* Beverly Hills, CA: Glencoe.

Sato, K. (1995). Resources and reviews: Engaging students in poetry. *English Journal, 84*(7), 89-91.

Sauvé, V. (1996). Working with the cultures of Canada in the ESL classroom: A response to Robert Courchene. *TESL Canada Journal, 13*(2), 17-23.

Schaars, M. J. (1992). Hill-climbing with Thoreau: Creating meaningful carryover. In N. J. Karolides (Ed.), *Reader response in the classroom: Evoking and interpreting meaning in literature* (pp. 144-154). New York: Longman.

Schaffer, J. C. (1989). Improving questions: Is anyone out there listening? *English Journal, 78*(4), 40-42.

Scheffler, I. (1967). *Science and subjectivity.* New York: Bobbs-Merrill.

Schneider, D. (1994). The round table: Journaling—A revolution. *English Journal, 83*(3), 88.

Scholes, R. (1985). *Textual power: Literary theory and the teaching of English.* New Haven, CT: Yale University Press.

Scholes, R. (1998). *The rise and fall of English: Reconstructing English as a discipline.* New Haven, CT: Yale University Press.

Scholes, R. (1999). Mission impossible. *English Journal, 88*(6), 28-35.

Scholes, R., Comley, N. R., & Ulmer, G. L. (1988). *Textbook: An introduction to literary language.* New York: St. Martin's.

Schorer, M. (1948). Technique as discovery. *Hudson Review, 1*(1), 67-87.

Schroeder, F. E. H. (1966). How to teach a research theme in four not-so-easy lessons. *English Journal, 55*(7), 898-902.

Schwartz, E., & Vockell, E. (1988). *The computer in the English curriculum.* Santa Cruz, CA: Mitchell.

Schwartz, H. (1989). Creating writing activities with the word processor. In C. Selfe, D. Rodriques, & W. Oakes (Eds.), *Computers in English and the language arts* (pp. 197-204). Urbana, IL: NCTE.

Schwartz, J. (1991). Let them assess their own learning. *English Journal, 80*(2), 67-73.

Scimone, A. J. (1999). At home with poetry: Constructing poetry anthologies in the high school classroom. *English Journal, 89*(2), 78-82.

Scimone, A. J. (2000). At home with poetry: Constructing poetry anthologies in the high school classroom. In D. Allender (Ed.), *Trends and issues in secondary English, 2000 edition* (pp. 180-186). Urbana, IL: NCTE.

Scott, F. N. (1913). Our problems. *English Journal, 2*(1), 1-10.

Sears, C. (1987). Mood poem. *North Carolina English Teacher, 45*(1), 15-16.

Segel, E. (1986). As the twig is bent . . .: Gender and childhood reading. In E. A. Flynn & P. P. Schweickart (Eds.), *Gender and reading: Essays on readers, texts, and contexts* (pp. 165-186). Baltimore: Johns Hopkins University Press.

Seidman, E. I. (1991). *Interviewing as qualitative research.* New York: Teachers College Press.

Selden, R., & Widdowson, P. (1993). *A reader's guide to contemporary literary theory* (3rd ed.). Lexington: University Press of Kentucky.

Senge, P. (2000). *Schools that learn.* New York: Doubleday.

Shadiow, L. K. (2000). Glimpses of lives close to mine: English teaching at a new century. *English Journal, 89*(3), 68-73.

Shafer, G. (2000). Teacher to teacher: What works of nonfiction do you recommend for the English classroom? *English Journal 89*(6), 33-34.

Shamel, M. T. (1988). Using forms to discover poetry. *North Carolina English Teacher, 20*(2), 1-3.

Shange, N. (1972). *Nappy edges.* New York: St. Martin's.

Shange, N. (1978). *Nappy edges: (love's a lil rough/sometimes).* New York: St. Martin's.

Shannon, E. (2001). Attention deficiency in the writing classroom. In M. L. Warner (Ed.), *Winning ways of coaching writing* (pp. 105-122). Boston: Allyn & Bacon.

Shannon, P. (1991). The struggle for control of literacy lessons. In B. M. Power and R. Hubbard (Eds.), *Literacy in progress.* Portsmouth, NH: Heinemann.

Sharka, J. (2000, Nov.). *Virtual classroom strategies.* Presentation at the NCTE annual meeting, Milwaukee, WI.

Shaughnessy, M. (1977). *Errors and expectations: A guide for the teacher of basic writing.* New York: Oxford University Press.

Shaw, E. (1991). Letters from Vietnam: A film/book combination for a nonfiction course. *English Journal, 80*(1), 25.

Sheingold, K. (1991). Restructuring for learning with technology: The potential for synergy. *Phi Delta Kappan, 73*(1), 17-27.

Shepard, L. (2002, Feb.). *Preparing teachers for classroom assessment.* Speech at annual AACTE conference, New York.

Shepard, R., & Thomas, J. (Eds.). (1986). *Sudden fiction: American short-short stories.* Salt Lake City, UT: Peregrine Smith.

Sherwin, J. (1969). *Four problems in teaching English: A critique of research.* Scranton, PA: International Textbook.

Shor, I. (1972). Questions Marxists ask about literature. *College English, 34*(2), 178-179.

Shor, I. (1987). *Critical teaching and everyday life.* Chicago: University of Chicago Press.

Showalter, E. (1971). Women writers and the double standard. In V. Gornick and B. K. Moran (Eds.), *Woman in sexist society: Studies in power and powerlessness.* New York: Penguin Group.

Shuman, R. B. (1985). English language in the secondary school. In S. Greenbaum (Ed.), *The English language today* (pp. 315-326). Oxford: Pergamon.

Shuman, R. B., & Wolfe, D. (1990). *Teaching English through the arts.* Urbana, IL: NCTE.

Shuy, R. (1982, Nov. 21). *Language and success: Who are the judges?* Presentation at NCTE English conference, Washington, DC.

Silko, L. M., & Wright, J. (1986). *The delicacy and strength of lace.* (Anne Wright, Ed.). St. Paul, MN: Graywolf.

Sizer, T. R. (1984). *Horace's compromise: The dilemma of the American high school.* Boston: Houghton Mifflin.

Skinner, B. F. (1957). *Verbal behavior.* New York: Appleton, Century, Crofts.

Skretta, J. A. (1996). Why debates about teaching grammar and usage 'tweek' me out. *English Journal, 85*(7), 64-67.

Slatin, J. (1992). Reading hypertext: Order and coherence in a new medium. In P. Delaney & G. P. Landow (Eds.), *Hypermedia and literary studies* (pp. 153-69). Cambridge: MIT Press.

Sledd, J. (1996). Grammar for social awareness in times of class warfare. *English Journal, 85*(7), 59-63.

Slifkin, J. M. (1997). New teachers: Mixing memory and desire: Some reflections on student teaching and teacher education. *English Journal, 86*(2), 87-89.

Smagorinsky, P. (1991). *Expressions: Multiple intelligences in the English class.* Urbana, IL: NCTE.

Smagorinsky, P., & Fly, P. K. (1994). A new perspective on why small groups do and don't work. *English Journal, 83*(3), 54-58.

Small, R. C. (1972). Teaching the junior novel. *English Journal, 61*(2), 222-229.

Small, R. C. (1977, Winter). The adolescent novel as a working model. *ALAN Newsletter,* p. 4.

Small, R. C. (1992, Spring). The literary value of the young adult novel. *Journal of Youth Services in Libraries.* pp. 227-285.

Smede, S. D. (1995). Flyfishing, portfolios, and authentic writing. *English Journal, 84*(2), 92-94.

Smith, M. W. (1991). *Understanding unreliable narrators: Reading between the lines in the literature classroom.* Urbana, IL: NCTE.

Smith, M. W. (1995). Adult book-club discussions: Toward an understanding of the culture of practice. In J. Marshall, P. Smagorinsky, and M. Smith (Eds.), *The language of interpretation: Patterns of discourse in discussions of literature* (pp. 100-120). Urbana: NCTE.

Smith, M. W. (2001). Creating a common project in the study of diversity. In J. E. Many (Ed.), *Handbook of instructional practices for literacy teacher-educators: Examples and reflections from the teaching lives of literacy scholars* (pp. 277-282). Mahwah, NJ: Erlbaum.

Smith, J. P. (2002). *Making movies in the classroom.* Columbia, NC: Author.

Smitherman, G. (1989, April 8). *A three part language program.* Presentation at the NCTE regional conference, Charleston, SC.

Smitherman, G. (1990, April 4). *Diversity and pluralism in language.* Speech at Wake Forest University, Winston-Salem, NC.

Sontag, S. (1967). *Against interpretation.* New York: Dell.

Sorenson, M. (1989). Television: Developing the critical viewer and writer. *English Journal, 78*(8), 42-46.

Soven, M. I. (1999). *Teaching writing in middle and secondary schools.* Boston: Allyn & Bacon.

Spencer, P. (1989). YA novels in the AP classroom: Crutcher meets Camus. *English Journal, 78*(7), 44-46.

Spolin, V. (1967). *Improvisation for the theater.* Evanston, IL: Northwestern University Press.

Squire, J. R. (Ed.). (1968). *Response to literature.* Champaign, IL: NCTE.

Squire, J. R., & Applebee, R. K. (1968). *High school English instruction today.* New York: Appleton-Century Crofts.

Stainborn, S. (2001). Photo realism. *Teacher Magazine 13*(2), 23-29.

Stallman, R. W. (1976). Stephen Crane: A reevaluation. In S. Bradley, R. Beatty, E. Long, & D. Pizer, (Eds.), *The Red Badge of Courage: An authoritative text.* New York: Norton.

Steinberg, A. (1997). Making school work more like real work. *Harvard Education Letter, 13*(2).

Stensland, A. L. (1979). *Literature by and about the American Indian: An annotated bibliography* (2nd ed.). Urbana, IL: NCTE.

Stern, D. N. (1977). *The first relationship: Infant and mother.* Cambridge: Harvard University Press.

Sternberg, R. (1997). Technology changes intelligence. *Technos, 16*(2), 12-14.

Stetson, M. (1996). Freedom of voice. *English Journal, 85*(6), 74-78.

Stevenson, J. W. (1972). The illusion of research. *English Journal, 61*(7), 1029-1032.

Stewart, W. A. (1964). *Non-standard speech and the teaching of English.* Washington, DC: Center for Applied Linguistics.

Stock, P. L. (1995). *The dialogic curriculum.* Portsmouth, NH: Heinemann.

Stock, R. (1998). Teaching on-line communication skills: An activity using aspects. *English Journal, 87*(1), 63-66.

Stotsky, S. (1994). Academic guidelines for selecting multiethnic and multicultural literature. *English Journal, 83*(2), 27-34.

Strauss, P. (1993). *Talking poetry: A guide for students, teachers and poets.* Pietermaritzburg, South Africa: University of Natal Press.

Strong, W. (1973). *Sentence combining: A composing book.* New York: Random House.

Strong, W. (1976). Sentence combining: Back to the basics—and beyond. *English Journal, 65*(2), 56, 60-64.

Strong, W. (1981). *Sentence combining and paragraph building.* New York: Random House.

Strong, W. (1986). *Creative approaches to sentence combining.* Urbana, IL: NCTE/ERIC.

Strunk, W., Jr., & White, E. B. (1979). *The elements of style* (3rd ed.). New York: Macmillan.

Stubbs, B. (1995). *Specific strategy instruction to enhance revising and editing skills for the learning disabled.* Unpublished master's thesis, Rowan College of New Jersey.

Styan, J. L. (1965). *The dramatic experience.* London: Cambridge University Press.

Styan, J. L. (1980). Teaching through performance: An interview with J. L. Styan. Conducted by Derek Peat. *Shakespeare Quarterly, 31*(2), 142-152.

Styan, J. L. (1993). Shakespeare off the page. In J. E. Davis & R. E. Salomone (Eds.), *Teaching Shakespeare today: Practical approaches and productive strategies* (pp. 61-71). Urbana, IL: NCTE.

Suhor, C. (1977). In search of articulate conservatism. *English Journal, 66*(5), 81-82.

Suhor, C. (1994). National standards in English: What are they? Where does NCTE stand? *English Journal, 83*(8), 25-27.

Suhor, C. (1997). Censorship—When things get hazy. *English Journal, 86*(2), 26-28.

Suhor, C., & Suhor, B. (1992). *Teaching values in the literature classroom: A debate in print.* Bloomington, IN: NCTE/ERIC.

Summerfield, G. (1982). Literature teaching and some of our responsibilities. In D. Mallick, P. Moss, & I. Hansen (Eds.), *New essays in the teaching of literature.* Norwood: Australian Association for the Teaching of English.

Sunstein, B. (2000). *The portfolio: Inside out.* Presentation at the Inside Out Conference at the University of North Carolina, Charlotte.

Swander, H. (1984). In our time: Such audiences we wish him. *Shakespeare Quarterly* [Special issue], 528-540.

Swartz, L. (1988). *Dramathemes: A practical guide for teaching drama.* Marham, Ontario: Pembroke.

Swartz, S. H. (1989). Setting up sense centers. In F. A. Kaufmann (Ed.), *Ideas plus: A collection of practical teaching ideas, book 7* (pp. 32-33). Urbana, IL: NCTE.

Taba, H. (2001). *Writing generalizations: Thinking skills model.* Raleigh: North Carolina Department of Public Instruction.

Taba, H., Durkin, M. C., Frankel, J. R., & McNaughton, A. H. (1971). *A teacher's handbook to elementary social studies: An inductive approach* (2nd ed.). Reading: Addison Wesley.

Tabbert, R. (1984). Raising the question "Why teach grammar?" *English Journal, 73*(8), 38-42.

Tannen, D. (1984). *Conversational style: Analyzing talk among friends.* Norwood, NJ: Ablex.

Tannen, D. (1990). *You just don't understand: Women and men in conversation.* New York: Ballantine.

Taylor, M. M. (2000). Nancie Atwell's *In the middle* and the ongoing transformation of the writing workshop. *English Journal, 90*(1), 46-52.

Taylor, P. (1970). *How teachers plan their courses.* Slough, UK: National Foundation for Education Research in England and Wales.

Taylor, T. E. (1965). Let's get rid of research papers. *English Journal, 54*(2), 126-127.

Tchudi, S. (2000). English education in the 1970s: An editor's perspective. *English Journal, 89*(3), 33-39.

Tchudi, S. (2001). The grading game. In M. L. Warner (Ed.), *Winning ways of coaching writing* (pp. 176-193). Boston: Allyn & Bacon.

Tchudi, S. N., & Tchudi, S. J. (1991). *The English/language arts handbook.* Portsmouth, NH: Boynton/Cook & Heinemann.

Tchudi, S., & Mitchell, D. (1989). *Explorations in the teaching of English.* New York: Harper & Row.

Tchudi, S., & Thomas, L. (1996). Taking the g-r-r-r out of grammar. *English Journal, 85*(7), 46-54.

Tchudi, S., Estrem, H., & Hanlon, P. (1997). Unsettling drafts. *English Journal, 86*(6), 27-33.

Teasley, A., & Wilder, A. (1996, Oct.). *100 great films for adolescents.* Presentation at North Carolina English Teachers Association Conference, Winston-Salem.

Teasley, A., & Wilder, A. (1997). *Reel conversations: Reading film with young adults.* Portsmouth, NH: Heinemann.

Temple, C., Burris, N., Nathan, R., & Temple, F. (1988). *The beginnings of writing.* Boston: Allyn & Bacon.

Thiesmeyer, E. C., & Thiesmeyer, J. E. (1990). *Editor.* New York: Modern Language Association.

Thoman, E. (1998). Media literacy: A guided tour of selected resources for teaching. *English Journal, 87*(1), 34-37.

Thomas, O. (1965). *Transformational grammar and the teacher of English.* New York: Holt, Rinehart, & Winston.

Thomas, P. L. (2000). Blueprints or houses? Lou LaBrant and the writing debate. *English Journal, 89*(3), 85-89.

Thompson, N. S. (1988). Media and mind: Imaging as an active process. *English Journal, 77*(7), 47-49.

Thompson, N. S. (2000). Sylvia Ashton-Warner: Reclaiming personal meaning in literacy teaching. *English Journal, 89*(3), 90-96.

Tierney, R. (1990, July). *Writing to learn in science.* Lecture at Wake Forest University, Winston-Salem, NC.

Tierney, R., & Clark, C. (1998). Portfolio: Assumptions, tensions, and possibilities. *Reading Research Quarterly, 33*(4), 474-486.

Timpson, W. M., & Tobin, D. N. (1982). *Teaching as performing.* Upper Saddle River, NJ: Prentice Hall.

Tinajero, J. V. (1994). Are we communicating? Effective instruction for students who are acquiring English as a second language. *Reading Teacher, 48*(3), 260-264.

Tobin, K. (1987). The role of wait time in higher cognitive level learning. *Reviews of Educational Research, 57*(1), 51-67.

Tompkins, G. (1996). *Literacy for the twenty-first century.* Upper Saddle River, NJ: Prentice Hall.

Tompkins, G. E. (1990). *Teaching writing: Balancing process and product.* Upper Saddle River, NJ: Merrill/Prentice Hall.

Tompkins, J. (1985). *Sensational designs: The cultural work of American fiction, 1790-1860.* New York: Oxford University Press.

Tompkins, J. (Ed.). (1980). *Reader-response criticism: From formalism to post-structuralism.* Baltimore: Johns Hopkins University Press.

Torsberg, S. (2000, Nov.). *Website collaboration projects.* Presentation at the NCTE annual meeting, Milwaukee, WI.

Trimbur, J. (1985). Collaborative learning and teaching writing. In B. W. McClelland & T. R. Donovan (Eds.), *Perspectives on research and scholarship in composition* (pp. 87-109). New York: Modern Language Association.

Tsujimoto, J. I. (1988). *Teaching poetry writing to adolescents.* Urbana, IL: NCTE.

Turner, D. T., & Stanford, B. D. (1971). *Theory and practice in the teaching of literature by Afro-Americans.* Urbana, IL: NCTE.

Turner, M. (1985). Our readers write: Computer software that works. *English Journal, 88*(2), 88.

Tweeten, J. (1988). Odyssey travelogue. *North Carolina English Teacher, 46*(1), 18.

Twitchell, J. B. (1992). *Carnival culture: The trashing of taste in America.* New York: Columbia University Press.

Tyler, R. W. (1975). Specific approaches to curriculum development. In J. Schaffarzick & D. H. Hampson (Eds.), *Strategies for curriculum development* (pp. 17-33). Berkeley, CA: Mc-Cutchan.

U.S. Census Bureau. (2000). *Statistical abstract of the United States, 2000.* (120th edition). Washington, DC: U.S. Government Printing Office.

U.S. Department of Education. (1998). *Writing framework and specifications for the 1998 National Assessment of Educational Progress.* Washington, DC: Author.

Van den Heuvel, C. (Ed.). (2000). *The haiku anthology: Haiku and senryu in English* (3rd ed.). New York: Norton.

Van Wyhe, T. L. C. (2000). A passion for poetry: Breaking rules and boundaries with online relationships. *English Journal, 90*(2), 60-67.

VanZalingen, C. (1998). Sacred cows make the best hamburger. *English Journal, 87*(3), 12-13.

Vavra, E. (1996). On not teaching grammar. *English Journal, 85*(7), 32-37.

Veidemanis, G. V. (1988). *Tess of the D'Urbervilles:* What the film left out. *English Journal, 77*(7), 53-57.

Velie, A. R. (Ed.). (1979). *American Indian literature: An anthology.* Norman: University of Oklahoma Press.

Viadero, D. (1997, Oct. 15). Few U.S. schools use technology well, two studies report. *Education Week, 17*(8), 6.

Virginia Department of Education. (1994). *Virginia's literacy passport program: The literacy tests.* Richmond: Author.

Vonnegut, Z. (2001). Archetypal criticism in the classroom and student response to literature. In L. P. McCoy (Ed.), *Studies in teaching.* Winston-Salem, NC: Wake Forest University Education Department.

Vygotsky, L. S. (1962). *Thought and language* (E. Hanfmann & G. Vakar, Trans.). Cambridge: MIT Press.

Vygotsky, L. S. (1978). In M. Cole, V. John-Steiner, S. Scribner, & E. Souberman (Eds.), *Mind in society: The development of higher psychological processes.* Cambridge: Harvard University Press.

Wagner, B. J. (1976). *Dorothy Heathcote: Drama as a learning medium.* Washington, DC: National Education Association.

Wahlenmayer, C. W. (1991). Ray Charles has been in my classroom. *English Journal, 80*(4), 55-56.

Walker, A. (1982). *The color purple.* New York: Washington Square Press.

Walker, A. (1983). *In search of our mothers' gardens: Womanist prose.* San Diego: Harcourt Brace Jovanovich.

Walker, M. (1997). Authentic assessment in the literature classroom. *English Journal, 86*(1), 69-73.

Walkington, J. W. (1991). Women and power in Henrik Ibsen and Adrienne Rich. *English Journal, 80*(3), 64-68.

Wall, D. (1971). The state of grammar in the state of Iowa. *English Journal, 60*(8), 1127-1130.

Wallace, M. (1988). Invisibility blues. In R. Simonson & S. Walker (Eds.), *Multi-cultural literacy* (pp. 161-172). St. Paul, MN: Graywolf.

Walton, B. H., & Bork, T. (2001). "Telling stories long into the night": Romantic circles high school project. (Learning with technology). *English Journal, 91*(1), 103-107.

Ward, R. (1997, Nov. 14). Aim higher and make the money go further. *The Times Higher Education Supplement, 1306,* 4-5.

Ward, W. (1930). *Creative dramatics for the upper grades and junior high school.* New York: Appleton.

Warstler, D., (1997, April 11). *Response projects to develop and extend interpretation.* Presentation at NCTE's spring conference, Charlotte, NC.

Washington, M. H. (1991, Spring). Selected bibliography of African-American literature. *Bread Loaf News,* pp. 5-16.

Watson, G. (1986). *The literary critics: A study of English descriptive criticism.* London: Hogarth Press.

Weathers, W. (1980). *An alternate style: Options in composition.* Portsmouth, NH: Boynton/Cook.

Weaver, C. (1996a). *Teaching grammar in context.* Portsmouth, NH: Heinemann.

Weaver, C. (1996b). Teaching grammar in the context of writing. *English Journal, 85*(7), 15-24.

Weaver. C. (1998). Teaching grammar in the context of writing. In C. Weaver (Ed.), *Lessons to share on teaching grammar in context* (pp. 18-38). Portsmouth, NH: Boynton/Cook & Heinemann.

Webb, N. (1982). Student interaction and learning in small groups. *Review of Educational Research, 52*(3), 421-445.

Weiner, L. (1997). Designing lesson plans: What new teachers can learn from Moffet and Wagner. *English Journal, 86*(4), 78-79.

Wendt, M. (1990). *Bio-poem.* Presentation at the University of North Carolina at Greensboro.

West, C. (1982). *Prophesy deliverance! An Afro-American revolutionary Christianity.* Philadelphia: Westminster.

Whetsone, C. (1997, April 11). *Literature circles in one high school classroom.* Presentation at NCTE's spring conference, Charlotte, NC.

Whishaw, I. (1994). Translation project: Breaking the "English only" rule. *English Journal, 83*(5), 28-30.

White, E. (1995). Apologia for the timed impromptu essay test. *College Composition and Communication, 46*(1), pp. 30-45.

Whitworth, R. (1991). A book for all occasions: Activities for teaching general semantics. *English Journal, 80*(2), 50-54.

Wideen, M. F., O'Shea, T., & Pye, Ivy. (1997). High-stakes testing and the teaching of science. *Canadian Journal of Education, 22*(4), 428-444.

Wiersma, W., & Jurs, S. G. (1990). *Educational measurement and testing* (2nd ed.). Boston: Allyn & Bacon.

Wiggins, G. (1989). A true test: Toward a more authentic and equitable assessment. *Phi Delta Kappan, 70*(9), 703-713.

Wiggins, G. (1997). Work standards: Why we need standards for instruction and assessment design. *NASSP Bulletin, 81*(50), 56-64.

Wigginton, E. (1985). *Sometimes a shining moment.* Garden City, NJ: Anchor.

Wilhelm, J. D. (1997). *"You gotta BE the book": Teaching engaged and reflective reading with adolescents.* Urbana, IL: NCTE.

Wilhelm, J. D. (1998, Feb. 2). *Reading between the lines.* Presentation at Wake Forest University, Winston-Salem, NC.

Wilhelm J. D., Baker, T. N., & Dube, J. (2001). *Strategic reading: Guiding students to lifelong literacy, 6-12.* Portsmouth, NH: Boynton/Cook & Heinemann.

Wilkinson, A. (1971). *Foundation of language.* Oxford: Oxford University Press.

Will, G. E. (1978). Winston Churchill: In the region of mass effects. In *The pursuit of happiness and other sobering thoughts* (pp. 31-33). New York: Harper & Row.

Williams, J. (1990). *Style: Toward clarity and grace.* Chicago: University of Chicago Press.

Williams, R. (1980). *Problems in materialism and culture.* London: Verso.

Wilson, M. (2001). The changing discourse of language study. *English Journal, 90*(4), 31–36.

Winterowd, W. R. (1975). *Contemporary rhetoric: A conceptual background with readings.* New York: Harcourt Brace Jovanovich.

Winterowd, W. R. (1981). *The contemporary writer.* New York: Harcourt Brace Jovanovich.

Winterowd, W. R., & Murray, P. Y. (1985). *English: Writing and skills* (Teacher's Ed.). San Diego: Coronado.

Wiske, M., Niguidula, D., & Shepard, J. (1988). *Collaborative research goes to school: Guided inquiry with computers in classrooms.* Washington, DC: Office of Education Research and Improvement.

Wolf, A. (1990). *Something is going to happen: Poetry alive!* Asheville, NC: IAMBIC.

Wolf, K. (1996). Developing an effective teaching portfolio. *Educational Leadership, 53*(6), 34–37.

Wolfe, D., & Antinarella, S. (1997). *Deciding to lead.* Portsmouth, NH: Heinemann.

Wolfram, W. (1983, April). *Standard English: Demythologizing an American myth.* Lecture at Wake Forest University, Winston-Salem, NC.

Wolk, R. A. (1998, Dec. 9). Education's high-stakes gamble. *Education Week on the Web* (http://www.edweek.org/ew/vol-18/15wolk.h18)

Wood, F. (1985). *The asymmetrical brain: Librarians and cowboys.* Presentation at the North Carolina Governor's School West, Winston-Salem.

Woolf, V. (1928/1970). Mr. Bennett and Mrs. Brown. In L. Woolf & V. Woolf (Eds.), *The Hogarth Essays* (pp. 3–29). Freeport, NY: Books for Libraries Press.

Woolf, V. (1929). *A room of one's own.* New York: Harcourt Brace & World.

Wootton, M. (Ed.). (1982). *New directions in drama teaching: Studies in secondary school practice.* London: Heinemann.

Wormser, B., & Cappella, D. (2000). *Teaching the art of poetry: The moves.* Mahwah, NJ: Erlbaum.

Wresch, W. (Ed.). (1991). *The English classroom in the computer age: Thirty lesson plans.* Urbana, IL: NCTE.

Wykoff, G. S., & Shaw, H. (1957). *The Harper handbook of college composition.* New York: Harper.

Wyngaard, S., & Gehrke, R. (1996). Responding to audience. *English Journal, 85*(6), 67–70.

Yagelski, R. P. (1994). Literature and literacy: Rethinking English as a school subject. *English Journal, 83*(3), 30–36.

Young, G. (2001). Speaking my mind: Shame on whom? *English Journal, 90*(4), 20–22.

Young, M. W. (1996). English (as a second) language arts teachers: The key to mainstreamed ESL student success. *English Journal, 85*(8), 17–24.

Zeeman, K. L. (1997). Grappling with Grendel or what we did when the censors came. *English Journal, 86*(2), 46–49.

Zemelman, S., Daniels, H., & Hyde, A. (1993). *Best practice: New standards for teaching and learning in America's schools.* Portsmouth, NH: Heinemann.

Zimpher, N. (1988). A design for the development of teacher leaders. *Journal of Teacher Education, 39*(1), 53.

Zinsser, W. (Ed.). (1987). *Inventing the truth: The art and craft of memoir.* Boston: Houghton Mifflin.

Zitlow, C. (1995). Young adult literature: Did Patty Bergen write this poem? Connecting poetry and young adult literature. *English Journal, 84*(1), 110–113.

Zitlow, C. S. (2001). Professional links: The linguistic nature of language and communication. *English Journal 90*(4), 113–118.

Zollo, C. (1997). Friday night at Iowa 80. In E. Chiseri-Strater & B. Sunstein (Eds.), *Field working* (pp. 22–36). Boston: St. Martins.

Zorn, J. (2001). Diplomas dubiously denied: A taxonomy and commentary. *English Journal, 91*(1), 73–78.

Index